Paris Metro

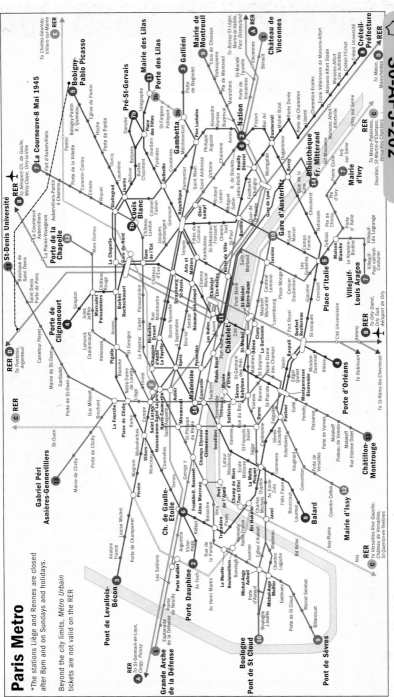

*The stations Liège and Rennes are closed after 8pm and on Sundays, Metro and holidays.

Beyond the city limits, *Métro Urbain* tickets are not valid on the RER

S0-AFJ-202

Paris: Overview and Arrondissements

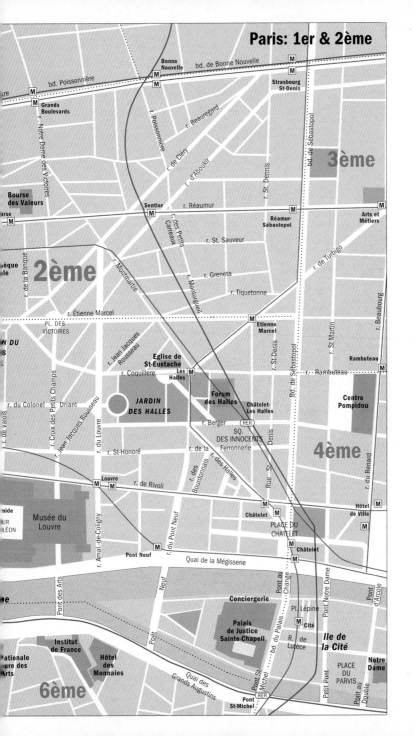

Paris: 1er & 2ème

3ème

2ème

4ème

6ème

Bonne Nouvelle

bd. de Bonne Nouvelle

Strasbourg St-Denis

bd. Poissonnière

Grands Boulevards

r. Notre Dame des Victoires

r. Poissonnière

r. Beauregard

r. de Cléry

r. d'Aboukir

r. St. Denis

bd. de Sébastopol

Bourse des Valeurs

Sentier

r. Réaumur

Réaumur-Sébastopol

Arts et Métiers

r. des Petits Carreaux

r. St. Sauveur

r. de la Banque

r. Montmartre

r. Greneta

r. Montorgueil

r. Tiquetonne

r. de Turbigo

r. Beaubourg

r. Étienne Marcel

PL. DES VICTOIRES

Etienne Marcel

r. St-Martin

r. Jean Jacques Rousseau

Eglise de St-Eustache

r. Coquillere

Les Halles

r. St-Denis

Rambuteau

Bd. de Sébastopol

r. Rambuteau

r. du Colonel   Driant

JARDIN DES HALLES

Forum des Halles

Châtelet-Les Halles

Centre Pompidou

r. de valois

r. Croix des Petits Champs

r. Jean Jacques Rousseau

r. du Louvre

r. Berger

r. St-Honoré

SQ. DES INNOCENTS

Ferronnerie

r. de la

r. des Bourdonnais

r. des Halles

Rue   St   Denis

4ème

r. du Renard

Louvre

r. de Rivoli

Pyramide

SUR NAPOLÉON

Musée du Louvre

r. Amal -de-Coligny

r. du Pont Neuf

Châtelet

Hôtel de Ville

Pont Neuf

Quai de la Mégisserie

PLACE DU CHÂTELET

Châtelet

Pont Neuf

Pont des Arts

Pont au Change

Pont du Palais

Pont Notre Dame

Pont d'Arcole

Institut de France

Hôtel des Monnaies

Conciergerie

Pont St Michel

Palais de Justice Sainte-Chapell

Pl. Lépine

Cité

R.   de Lutèce

Ile de la Cité

ationale ure des Arts

Quai des Grands Augustins

bd. du Palais

Notre Dame

PLACE DU PARVIS

Petit Pont

Pont au Double

Pont St-Michel

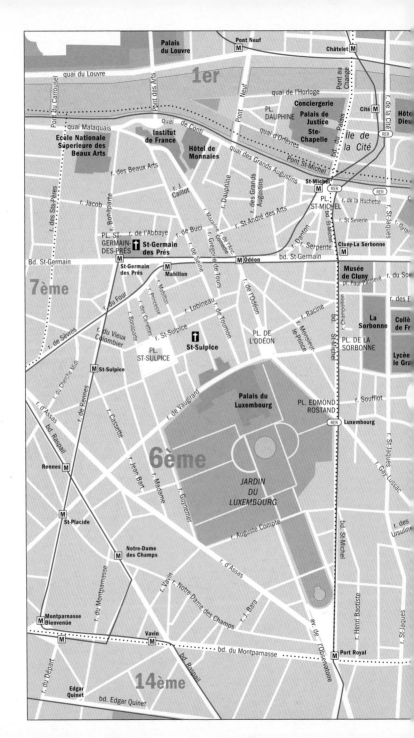

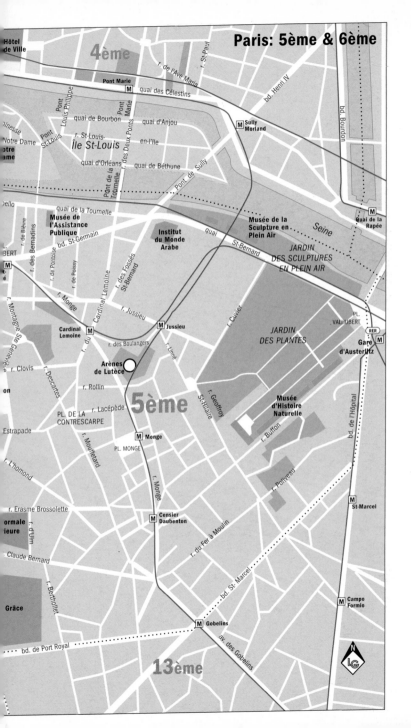

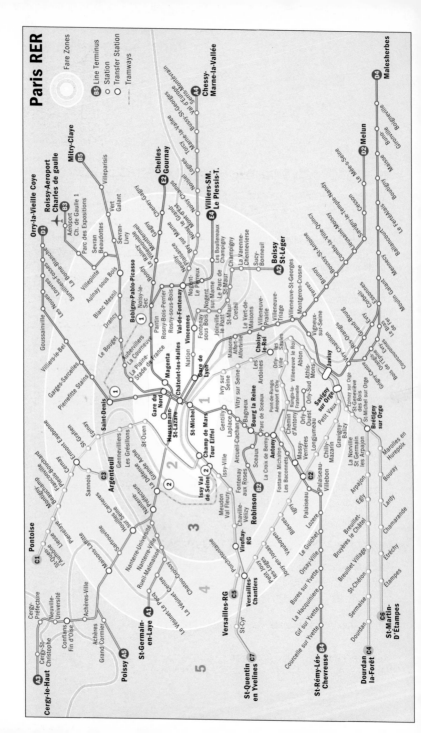

Paris RER

- **B5** Line Terminus
- ○ Station
- ◉ Transfer Station
- ○ Tramways

Fare Zones

LET'S GO

■ THE RESOURCE FOR THE INDEPENDENT TRAVELER

"The guides are aimed not only at young budget travelers but at the indepedent traveler; a sort of streetwise cookbook for traveling alone."

—The New York Times

"Unbeatable; good sight-seeing advice; up-to-date info on restaurants, hotels, and inns; a commitment to money-saving travel; and a wry style that brightens nearly every page."

—The Washington Post

"Lighthearted and sophisticated, informative and fun to read. [Let's Go] helps the novice traveler navigate like a knowledgeable old hand."

—Atlanta Journal-Constitution

"A world-wise traveling companion—always ready with friendly advice and helpful hints, all sprinkled with a bit of wit."

—The Philadelphia Inquirer

■ THE BEST TRAVEL BARGAINS IN YOUR PRICE RANGE

"All the dirt, dirt cheap."

—People

"Anything you need to know about budget traveling is detailed in this book."

—The Chicago Sun-Times

"Let's Go follows the creed that you don't have to toss your life's savings to the wind to travel—unless you want to."

—The Salt Lake Tribune

■ REAL ADVICE FOR REAL EXPERIENCES

"The writers seem to have experienced every rooster-packed bus and lunar-surfaced mattress about which they write."

—The New York Times

"Value-packed, unbeatable, accurate, and comprehensive."

—The Los Angeles Times

"[Let's Go's] devoted updaters really walk the walk (and thumb the ride, and trek the trail). Learn how to fish, haggle, find work—anywhere."

—Food & Wine

LET'S GO PUBLICATIONS

TRAVEL GUIDES

Australia 2005
Austria & Switzerland 12th edition
Brazil 1st edition
Britain & Ireland 2005
California 10th edition
Central America 9th edition
Chile 2nd edition
China 5th edition
Costa Rica 2nd edition
Eastern Europe 2005
Ecuador 1st edition **NEW TITLE**
Egypt 2nd edition
Europe 2005
France 2005
Germany 2005
Greece 2005
Hawaii 3rd edition
India & Nepal 8th edition
Ireland 2005
Israel 4th edition
Italy 2005
Japan 1st edition
Mexico 20th edition
Middle East 4th edition
Peru 1st edition **NEW TITLE**
Puerto Rico 1st edition
South Africa 5th edition
Southeast Asia 9th edition
Spain & Portugal 2005
Thailand 2nd edition
Turkey 5th edition
USA 2005
Vietnam 1st edition **NEW TITLE**
Western Europe 2005

ROADTRIP GUIDE

Roadtripping USA **NEW TITLE**

ADVENTURE GUIDES

Alaska 1st edition
New Zealand **NEW TITLE**
Pacific Northwest **NEW TITLE**
Southwest USA 3rd edition

CITY GUIDES

Amsterdam 3rd edition
Barcelona 3rd edition
Boston 4th edition
London 2005
New York City 2005
Paris 2005
Rome 12th edition
San Francisco 4th edition
Washington, D.C. 13th editio

POCKET CITY GUIDES

Amsterdam
Berlin
Boston
Chicago
London
New York City
Paris
San Francisco
Venice
Washington, D.C.

LET'S GO

FRANCE
2005

ERIN PEARSON EDITOR
PAT GRIFFIN ASSOCIATE EDITOR
ALEX TAN ASSOCIATE EDITOR

RESEARCHER-WRITERS
SARAH CHARLTON
MEHDI EL HAJOUI
SARAH FINE
JOSHUA SAMUELSON
KATIA SAVCHUK
EMILY SIMON

GENEVIEVE CADWALADER MAP EDITOR
ELLA M. STEIM MANAGING EDITOR

ST. MARTIN'S PRESS ✹ NEW YORK

HELPING LET'S GO. If you want to share your discoveries, suggestions, or corrections, please drop us a line. We read every piece of correspondence, whether a postcard, a 10-page email, or a coconut. **Address mail to:**

    Let's Go: France
    67 Mount Auburn Street
    Cambridge, MA 02138
    USA

Visit Let's Go at **http://www.letsgo.com,** or send email to:

    feedback@letsgo.com
    Subject: "Let's Go: France"

In addition to the invaluable travel advice our readers share with us, many are kind enough to offer their services as researchers or editors. Unfortunately, our charter enables us to employ only currently enrolled Harvard students.

Maps by David Lindroth copyright © 2005 by St. Martin's Press.

Distributed outside the USA and Canada by Macmillan, an imprint of Pan Macmillan Ltd.
20 New Wharf Road, London N1 9RR
Basingstoke and Oxford
Associated companies throughout the world
www.panmacmillan.com

ISBN: 0-312-33547-4
EAN: 978-0312-33547-2
First edition
10 9 8 7 6 5 4 3 2 1

Let's Go: France is written by Let's Go Publications, 67 Mount Auburn Street, Cambridge, MA 02138, USA.

Let's Go® and the LG logo are trademarks of Let's Go, Inc.
Printed in the USA.

ABOUT LET'S GO

GUIDES FOR THE INDEPENDENT TRAVELER

At Let's Go, we see every trip as the chance of a lifetime. If your dream is to grab a machete and forge through the jungles of Brazil, we can take you there. If you'd rather bask in the Riviera sun at a beachside cafe, we'll set you a table. We write for readers who know that there's more to travel than sharing double deckers with tourists and who believe that travel can change both themselves and the world—whether they plan to spend six days in London or six months in Latin America. We'll show you just how far your money can go, and prove that the greatest limitation on your adventures is not your wallet, but your imagination. After all, traveling close to the ground lets you interact more directly with the places and people you've gone to see, making for the most authentic experience.

BEYOND THE TOURIST EXPERIENCE

To help you gain a deeper connection with the places you travel, our researchers give you the heads-up on both world-renowned and off-the-beaten-track attractions, sights, and destinations. They engage with the local culture, writing features on regional cuisine, local festivals, and hot political issues. We've also opened our pages to respected writers and scholars to hear their takes on the countries and regions we cover, and asked travelers who have worked, studied, or volunteered abroad to contribute first-person accounts of their experiences. We've also increased our coverage of responsible travel and expanded each guide's Alternatives to Tourism chapter to share more ideas about how to give back to local communities and learn about the places you travel.

FORTY-FIVE YEARS OF WISDOM

Let's Go got its start in 1960, when a group of creative and well-traveled students compiled their experience and advice into a 20-page mimeographed pamphlet, which they gave to travelers on charter flights to Europe. Four and a half decades later, we've expanded to cover six continents and all kinds of travel—while retaining our founders' adventurous attitude toward the world. Our guides are still researched and written entirely by students on shoestring budgets, experienced travelers who know that train strikes, stolen luggage, food poisoning, and marriage proposals are all part of a day's work. This year, we're expanding our coverage of South America and Southeast Asia, with brand-new *Let's Go: Ecuador*, *Let's Go: Peru*, and *Let's Go: Vietnam*. Our adventure guide series is growing, too, with the addition of *Let's Go: Pacific Northwest Adventure* and *Let's Go: New Zealand Adventure*. And we're immensely excited about our new *Let's Go: Roadtripping USA*—two years, eight routes, and sixteen researchers and editors have put together a travel guide like none other.

THE LET'S GO COMMUNITY

More than just a travel guide company, Let's Go is a community. Our small staff comes together because of our shared passion for travel and our desire to help other travelers see the world. We love it when our readers become part of the Let's Go community as well—when you travel, drop us a postcard (67 Mt. Auburn St., Cambridge, MA 02138, USA) or send us an e-mail (feedback@letsgo.com) to tell us about your adventures and discoveries.

For more information, visit us online: www.letsgo.com.

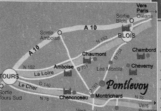

CONTENTS

RESEARCHER-WRITERS

Sarah Charlton *Burgundy, Champagne, Flanders, Pas de Calais*

This intellectual history major dug predictably deep during her travels, fearlessly spending most days up to her elbows in regional "specialties" like *aspic de poulet*. Her research brought a touch of class to the Champagne coverage, a futuristic feature about Segways in Dijon, and dead-on descriptions throughout her Northeast. When asked why she liked France, she responded, "Crêpes and wine. How can you dislike a people that make you feel so good?"

Mehdi El Hajoui *Loire Valley, Provence, Languedoc-Roussillon*

A native French speaker, Mehdi unearthed the local scoop like no other, tenaciously checking facts while keeping a keen eye out for tourist traps. This versatile RW stormed the castles of the Loire Valley and then switched gears to cover nightlife in Montpellier. Even during tiresome travel days, Mehdi never lost sight of what he saw as the key to French *joie de vivre:* "Good food, good wine, and good people."

Sarah Fine *Rhône-Alps, Massif Central, Dordogne*

This Massachusetts trailblazer beefed up coverage in the Alps and the heart of France, from the Italian border to the caves of Sarlat. Her cheerful and professional outlook paid off: anyone wanting to take advantage of the natural beauty of these stunning regions will find the most up-to-date tips. She was no doubt prepared by her prior experience leading a Freshman Outdoor Program, guiding frosh on a wilderness trek before they entered the wild college life.

Joshua Samuelson *Poitou-Charentes, Périgord, Aquitaine, Pays Basque*

A *Let's Go: Italy 2004* vet, Josh handled his route like an old pro despite the inevitable perils of weeks on the road. When he wasn't chowing down on seafood in La Rochelle or catching some rays in Biarritz, Josh updated our coverage of the Southwest with inimitable style. Unfazed by sweltering Aquitaine days and frozen Pyrenees nights, he calmly sipped red wine in Bordeaux at the end of it all. Here's to *you, Let's Go* readers.

Katia Savchuk *Brittany and Normandy*

A thoughtful writer and tireless researcher, Katia went above and beyond the call of duty to bring a personal touch to the overwhelming sights of Normandy. A Social Studies major, she got a slice of all walks of life along the road. From chilling with disillusioned corporate executives in search of themselves to trying (in vain) to win a game of French charades with a Korean backpacker, Katia's sincerity won people over from Rouen to Rennes.

Emily Simon *Côte d'Azur and Corsica*

A varsity sailor, Emily breezed around with style and grace. You would never guess that the same young woman who once fell off a dogsled in the Upper Peninsula of Michigan would blend in so effortlessly at the world's ritziest nightclubs, but then, you've never met this researcher. Emily's ever-present smile helped her deal with every situation she encountered, and *Let's Go* readers reap the benefits: sparkling new coverage in Corsica and the Côte d'Azur.

CONTRIBUTING WRITERS

Amelia Lester
Researcher-Writer, Let's Go: Paris

This stylish Aussie has made a career out of the journalism of the cool, tackling everything from fashion to gossip to the literary avant-garde.

Marc Lizoain
Researcher-Writer, Let's Go: Paris

Marc used his studies in history to bypass travel-writing romance and elaborate prose, instead cutting straight to the heart of the matter—all while being mercilessly funny.

Maude Emerson
Editor, Let's Go: Paris

Matthew Lazen spent two years in Brittany and Alsace on a Chateaubriand Fellowship for dissertation research on regional cultures. He has taught literature, film, and history at Harvard University, and he is currently revising his dissertation on regional cultures in postmodern France for publication.

Charlotte Houghteling has worked on Let's Go's _Middle East_, _Egypt_, and _Israel_ titles. She wrote her senior thesis on the development of department stores during the Second Empire and is in the process of completing her M.Phil at Cambridge on the consumer society of Revolutionary Paris.

Sarah Houghteling was a researcher-writer for _Let's Go: France 1999_. She spent a year teaching at the American School in Paris and is now a graduate student in creative writing at the University of Michigan.

Cat Walleck is an undergraduate at Harvard University, majoring in Romance Language Studies (French, English, and Italian). She plans to travel to the Avignon Theater Festival to conduct thesis research.

ACKNOWLEDGMENTS

LET'S GO

Team France thanks: Our researchers, who kept us entertained and earned major Pat Points along the way; Team Italy and LT for the endless dance party that was Disco Ciao Belle; Genevieve; Vicky; and the Ella-nator, without whose calm expertise and remarkable good humor, we would have been adrift, without a book, and without nearly as many laughs.

Erin thanks: Glorious Team France, for mean-spirited good fun; Pat for coffee; Alex for Vichy-Mint generosity; Alexie and Noga-nator for good talks and musical diversity; LT for general fabulosity; Ella for being, handsdown, the best; Naomi, EB, John, and Ali for the joys of porches; Outback Jack for, well, everything. I'm indebted to Allie and Lau Lau for rationality, to twitchy Faulkner jokes for keeping me smiling, and finally to my parents and grandparents for their endless support.
Pat thanks: Erin, Alex, and Ella—you held this ship together, thanks for being so awesome. Mom and Kerry for everything. Alexie and Nogurt for keeping the tunes pumping, L-Tizz for being from Buffalo, Genevieve and Ariel for sick maps and typesetting. Big up to Hodge, Reg, Matty, Kolin and the whole label.
Alex thanks: Erin, Pat, and Ella: The Triplets of Bellinator; Erin, my vichy is your vichy; Ella, for kindness; Pat, for Burgundy; LT, an all-star; Noga, Alexie, and Joel, for my split-personality; Jenny and Katelyn, for worry-free best-friendship; Lexi and Amy, #s 1 and 2; Seth, for writing songs and making me like cats; Simes, for helping me endure psychbabyness; and Dad and Mom, for being so fun.
Genevieve thanks: The fabulous France bookteam, all the RWs and their outstanding input on maps, and mapland for an entertaining summer and musical education.

Editor
Erin Pearson
Associate Editors
Pat Griffin, Alex Tan
Managing Editor
Ella M. Steim
Map Editor
Genevieve Cadwalader
Typesetter
Ariel Fox

Publishing Director
Emma Nothmann
Editor-in-Chief
Teresa Elsey
Production Manager
Adam R. Perlman
Cartography Manager
Elizabeth Halbert Peterson
Design Manager
Amelia Aos Showalter
Editorial Managers
Briana Cummings, Charlotte Douglas, Ella M. Steim, Joel August Steinhaus, Lauren Truesdell, Christina Zaroulis
Financial Manager
R. Kirkie Maswoswe
Marketing and Publicity Managers
Stef Levner, Leigh Pascavage
Personnel Manager
Jeremy Todd
Low-Season Manager
Clay H. Kaminsky
Production Associate
Victoria Esquivel-Korsiak
IT Director
Matthew DePetro
Web Manager
Rob Dubbin
Associate Web Manager
Patrick Swieskowski
Web Content Manager
Tor Krever
Research and Development Consultant
Jennifer O'Brien
Office Coordinators
Stephanie Brown, Elizabeth Peterson

Director of Advertising Sales
Elizabeth S. Sabin
Senior Advertising Associates
Jesse R. Loffler, Francisco A. Robles, Zoe M. Savitsky
Advertising Graphic Designer
Christa Lee-Chuvala

President
Ryan M. Geraghty
General Manager
Robert B. Rombauer
Assistant General Manager
Anne E. Chisholm

PRICE RANGES >> FRANCE

Our researchers list establishments in order of value, starting with the best; our favorites are denoted by the Let's Go ☑thumbs-up. Since the best value is not always the cheapest price, we have incorporated a system of price ranges for quick reference. Our price ranges are based on a rough expectation of what you will spend. For **accommodations,** we base our price range off the cheapest price for which a single traveler can stay for one night. For **restaurants** and other dining establishments, we estimate the cost of eating there. The table below gives an idea of what one will typically find in France in the corresponding price range. Numbers are assigned based on actual cost, not value or prices relative to those of similar establishments. Thus, a very expensive *crêperie* may still only be marked a ❶.

ACCOMMODATIONS	RANGE	WHAT YOU'RE *LIKELY* TO FIND
❶	under €15	Camping; most dorm rooms, including HI or other hostels or university dorm rooms. Expect bunk beds and a communal bath; you may have to provide or rent towels and sheets.
❷	€16-25	Upper-end hostels or small hotels. You may have a private bathroom, but most likely there will be a sink in your room and communal shower in the hall.
❸	€26-35	A small room with a private bath and some amenities, like a phone and TV. Breakfast may be included in the price of the room. Prices uniformly higher on the Côte d'Azur and in Corsica.
❹	€36-55	You'll have more amenities or be in a more touristed area. You'll usually have TV, A/C, phone, shower, and toilet.
❺	above €55	Large hotels or upscale chains. If it's a ❺ and it doesn't have the perks you want, you've paid too much.

FOOD	RANGE	WHAT YOU'RE *LIKELY* TO FIND
❶	under €7	Street-corner stand fare like sandwiches and crêpes. Also bakery quiches or fast-food. Rarely ever a sit-down meal.
❷	€7-10	Sandwiches, appetizers at a bar, or low-priced entrees. You may have the option to sit down or take out.
❸	€11-15	Mid-priced entrees, possibly coming with a soup or salad, and some *prix fixe menus*. Typically a sit-down meal with a waiter or waitress, but tip is usually *compris* (included).
❹	€16-25	Somewhat fancier, usually because of amazing French sauces. Expect large portions or multiple courses for this price range, or you've paid too much. Again, tip is *compris*.
❺	above €25	*Haute cuisine* and a decent wine list. Slacks and dress shirts may be expected. Don't order PB&J.

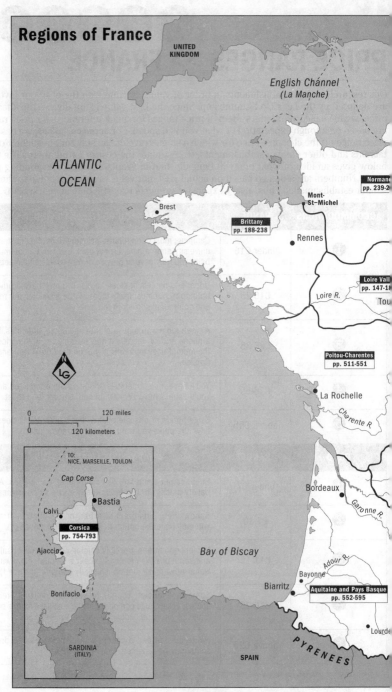

Regions of France

UNITED KINGDOM

English Channel
(La Manche)

ATLANTIC OCEAN

Brest

Brittany
pp. 188-238

Mont-St-Michel

Norman
pp. 239-2

Rennes

Loire Vall
pp. 147-1

Loire R.

Tou

Poitou-Charentes
pp. 511-551

La Rochelle

Charente R.

0   120 miles
0   120 kilometers

Bordeaux

Garonne R.

Adour R.

Bayonne

Biarritz

Aquitaine and Pays Basque
pp. 552-595

Lourde

Bay of Biscay

PYRENEES

SPAIN

TO:
NICE, MARSEILLE, TOULON

Cap Corse

Calvi

Bastia

Corsica
pp. 754-793

Ajaccio

Bonifacio

SARDINIA
(ITALY)

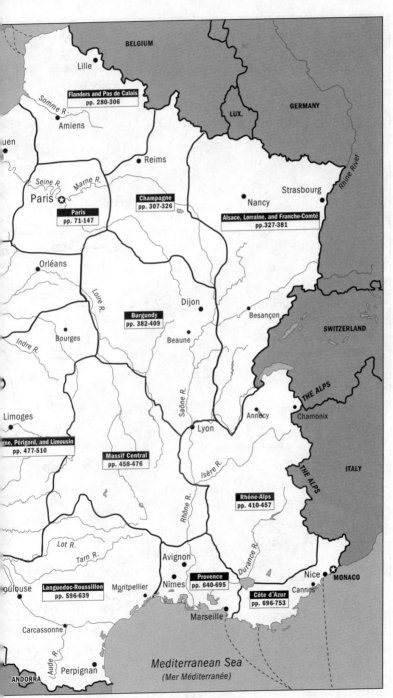

BELGIUM

Lille

Somme R.

Amiens

uen

Reims

Seine R.

Marne R.

Paris

GERMANY

LUX.

Nancy

Strasbourg

Rhine River

Orléans

Loire R.

Dijon

Besançon

SWITZERLAND

Indre R.

Bourges

Beaune

Limoges

Saône R.

Annecy

Chamonix

THE ALPS

Lyon

Isère R.

THE ALPS

ITALY

Rhône R.

Lot R.

Tarn R.

Avignon

Durance R.

Nice

MONACO

oulouse

Montpellier

Nîmes

Cannes

Carcassonne

Aude R.

Perpignan

Marseille

ANDORRA

Mediterranean Sea
(Mer Méditerranée)

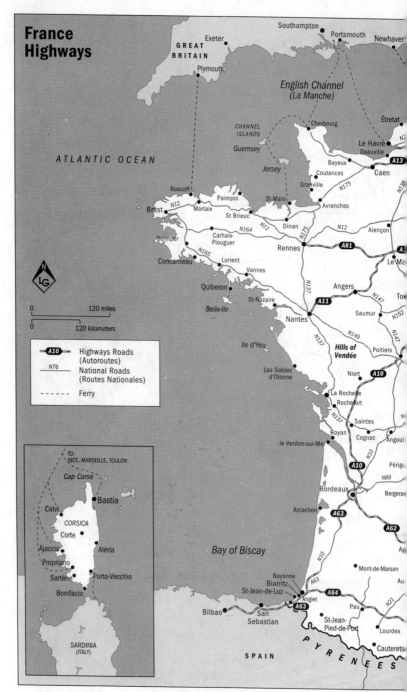

France
Highways

GREAT
BRITAIN

Exeter

Plymouth

Southampton Portsmouth Newhaver

English Channel
(La Manche)

Étretat

CHANNEL
ISLANDS

Cherbourg

Le Havre

Guernsey

Deauville **A13**

ATLANTIC OCEAN

Bayeux

Caen

Jersey

Coutances

Granville

N175

Roscoff

Paimpol

St-Malo

Avranches

Alençon

Brest

Morlaix

N12

Quimper

Carhaix-
Plouguer

N164

N12

St Brieuc

Dinan

N175

N12

Rennes

A81

Le Ma

Concameau

N165

Lorient

Vannes

Angers

N147

To

N137

A11

Saumur

N152

Quiberon

St-Nazaire

N147

St-Nazaire

Nantes

N149

Hills of
Vendée

Poitiers

Belle-Ile

Ile d'Yeu

N137

0   120 miles

0   120 kilometers

A10 Highways Roads
(Autoroutes)

N76 National Roads
(Routes Nationales)

------ Ferry

Les Sables
d'Olonne

Niort **A10**

La Rochelle
Rochefort

N137

Saintes

N

Royan

Cognac Angoul

le Verdon-sur-Mer

A10

Périgu

N89

TO:
NICE, MARSEILLE, TOULON

Cap Corse

Bastia

Bordeaux

Bergerac

Calvi

CORSICA

Corte

Ajaccio

Aléria

Arcachon **A63**

A62

Propriano

Sartène

Porto-Vecchio

Ag

Bonifacio

Mont-de-Marsan

Au

N10

Bay of Biscay

Bayonne
Biarritz
St-Jean-de-Luz

A63

A64

Pau

N21

SARDINIA
(ITALY)

Bilbao

San
Sebastian

Anglet

A63

St-Jean-
Pied-de-Port

Lourdes

SPAIN

P Y R E N E E S

Cauterets

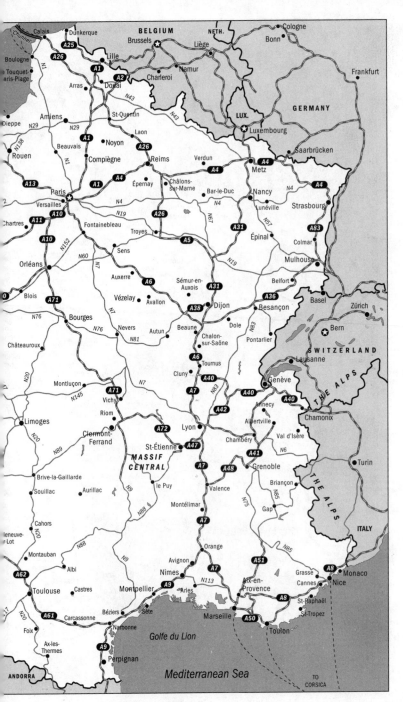

France
Rail Lines

GREAT BRITAIN

Southampton
Exeter
Bournemouth
Portsmouth
Weymouth
Newhaven
Plymouth

Falmouth

ATLANTIC OCEAN

Féca
Cherbourg
Le Havre
Guernsey
Deauville-Trouville
St-Lô
Caen
Li
Coutances
Granville
Foligny
Argentan
Roscoff Lannion Paimpol
St-Malo
Avranches
Brest Morlaix
St-Brieuc
Dol-de-Bretagne
Alençon
Guingamp
Dinan
Lamballe
Carhaix
Loudéac
Rennes
Le Mans
Quimper
Laval
Lorient
Châteaubriant
Auray
Redon
Angers
Quiberon
Vannes
Saumur
Pontchâteau
Ch
Le Croisic
Châtellera
St-Nazaire
Nantes
Poitier
Pornic
Clisson St-Christopher du Bois
Ste-Pazanne
Croix-de-Vie-St-Gilles
La Roche-sur-Yon
Niort
Les Sables d'Olonne
St-Saviol
La Rochelle
Rochefort
Cognac
Saintes
Angoulê
Pointe-de-Grave
Royan
Coutres
Pé
Libourne
Bordeaux
Bergerac
Bui
Arcachon
Villen
Su
Marmande
Morcenx
A
Mont-de-Marsan
Dax
Bayonne
Puyoô
Pau
Biarritz
A
St-Jean-Pied-de-Port
Ta
San Sebastian
Lourdes
Luch

TO MADRID

SPAIN

TO:
NICE, MARSEILLE, TOULON
Centuri
Macinaggio
I'Ile Rousse
Bastia
Calvi
CORSICA
Porto
Ponte-Leccia
Ajaccio
Corte
Propriano
Solenzara
Sartene
Porto-Vecchio
Bonifacio
Santa Theresa

SARDINIA (ITALY)

0 ____ 120 miles
0 ____ 120 kilometers

Rail Line
High Speed Rail Line (TGV)
Ferry

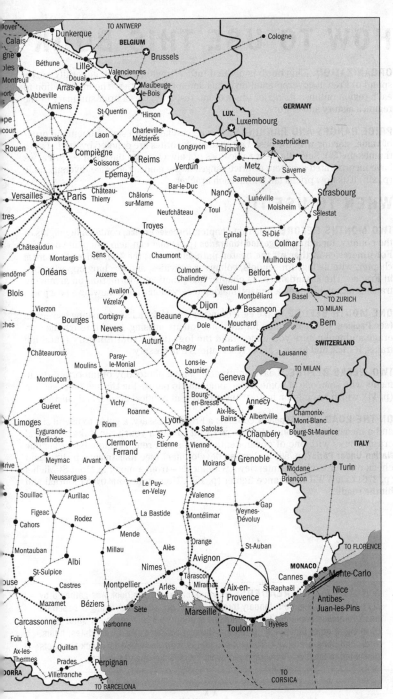

HOW TO USE THIS BOOK

ORGANIZATION. This book is divided into 17 regions, which generally correspond to French governmental divisions and local identities. The introduction to each region outlines its major areas of interest and gives a brief summary of the region's history and culture.

PRICE RANGES AND RANKINGS. Our researchers list establishments in order of value, starting with the best. Our absolute favorites are denoted by the *Let's Go* thumbs-up (🖑). Since the best value does not always mean the cheapest price, we have incorporated a system of price ranges in the guide. The price diversity table (p. xiii) lists how prices fall within each bracket.

WHEN TO USE IT

TWO MONTHS BEFORE. The first chapter, **Discover France,** contains highlights of the country, including **Suggested Itineraries** (p. 4) that can help you plan your trip. For itineraries farther off the beaten path, check out the **Alternatives to Tourism** chapter, with listings for schools, volunteer activities, and teaching opportunities in France. The **Essentials** (p. 7) chapter has practical information on arranging transportation, planning a budget, making reservations, and renewing a passport.

ONE MONTH BEFORE. Take care of insurance. Make a list of packing essentials (see **Packing,** p. 14) and shop for anything you are missing. Read through the coverage and make sure you understand the logistics of your itinerary (catching trains, ferries, and buses). Make reservations if necessary.

TWO WEEKS BEFORE. Leave an itinerary and a photocopy of important documents with someone at home. Take some time to peruse the **Life and Times** section (p. 44), which has info on history, the arts, recent political events, and cuisine.

ON THE ROAD. The **Appendix** contains a French glossary, a guide to useful signs, and a measurement converter. As you wait to catch your train, take a cultural crash course with one of our in-depth articles on French regionalism (see **One Nation Under Paris?,** p. 50) and urban development (see **Haussmania,** p. 109), and check out our exclusive interviews with locals—from a monk in Mont-St-Michel (p. 276) to a WWII Resistance fighter (p. 156). Now, grab your travel journal and hit the road!

DISCOVER
FRANCE

With its lavish châteaux, fields of lavender, medieval streets, and sidewalk cafes, France rightfully conjures any number of postcard-ready scenes. Then there are the pictures that belong in history books or perhaps on canvas at a world-class French museum: revolution, conquest, intrigue, and, well, more revolution. Despite its storied past and undeniable beauty, however, France is a country best encountered not through still images, but firsthand experience. From their pungent cheeses to their elaborate fashions, the French have the original *je ne sais quoi*. It makes their pastries impossibly intricate, their cuisine exquisite, their craftsmanship impeccable, and their wines divine. You might experience it as you watch a fierce, high-stakes game of *pétanque* in a Provençal village or eavesdrop on the low conversation of the elegant Parisians beside you at a bistro; it might come to you in a single impression as you bite into a warm chocolate croissant at dawn after a night of clubbing in Lille or as you haggle for the perfect piece of *batik* in a North African market in Marseille.

And although those postcard images capture many aspects of France's allure, they rarely express the country's remarkable diversity. Centuries-old farms and churches share the landscape with inventive, often stunning, modern architecture; street posters advertise jazz festivals as well as Baroque concerts. Even the countryside ranges from the misty islands off the coast of Brittany to the dazzling turquoise waters of the Riviera to the giant lava needles of the Auvergne. There is something for the most urbane city-phile and for the most adventurous outdoor enthusiast. France will always have the icons that have made it a capital of culture, but those who look deeper are destined for exhilarating surprises as well.

FACTS AND FIGURES

OFFICIAL NAME: République Française

POPULATION: 60,100,000

CAPITAL: Paris

GDP PER CAPITA: US$24,400

PRESIDENT: Jacques Chirac

MAJOR RELIGIONS: 90% Catholic, 3% Muslim, 2% Protestant, 1% Jewish

AVERAGE LIFE EXPECTANCY: 78.9 years

LITERACY RATE: 99% of those over 15

WINE PRODUCED PER YEAR: Equivalent to 1,927 Olympic-size pools

BAGUETTES CONSUMED PER YEAR: Laid end-to-end, they would span the Earth's circumference 1.14 times

ESTIMATED NUMBER OF ROMANTIC ENCOUNTERS PER DAY: 4,959,476 in Paris alone. *Ah, l'amour!*

WHEN TO GO

In July, Paris starts to shrink; in August, it positively shrivels. The city in August is devoid of Parisians, animated only by tourists and the pickpockets who love them. At the same time, the French themselves hop over to the Norman coast, swell the beaches of the western Atlantic coast from La Rochelle down to Biarritz, and move along the shores of rocky Corsica. From June to

September, the Côte d'Azur becomes one long tangle of halter-topped, khaki-shorted Anglophones; a constant, exhausting party. Early summer and autumn are the best times to visit Paris, while winter there can be abominable, presided over by a terrible *grisaille*—chill "grayness." The north and west of France are prone to wet but mild winters and springs, while summers are warm but undependable. The center and east of the country have a more continental climate, with harsh winters and long, dry summers; these are also generally the least crowded and most unspoiled regions. During the winter, the Alps provide some of the best skiing in the world, while the Pyrenees offer a calmer, if less climatically dependable, alternative.

As a general rule, the farther south you travel in the summer, the more crucial hotel reservations become. Reserve a month in advance for the Côte d'Azur, Corsica, Provence, Languedoc, and the Pays Basque.

THINGS TO DO

WHERE ALL THE LIGHTS ARE BRIGHT

While **Paris** (p. 71) is one of the world's great cities, you'll also find plenty to do in France's major regional centers. **Lyon** (p. 410) has had a reputation for staid *bourgeoisie*, but today it provides non-stop action and France's best cuisine. In its 2600-year history, multicultural **Marseille** (p. 640) has never failed to make itself heard. **Nice** (p. 696) is a party town packed with museums, and only a pebble's throw from the rest of the sandy Côte d'Azur. With a hybrid Franco-German culture, **Strasbourg** (p. 344) is the obvious home for the European Parliament. In Brittany, **Rennes** (p. 188) mixes a medieval *vieille ville* (old town) and major museums with frenzied party kids. In the southwest, sophisticated **Montpellier** (p. 630) is the gay capital of France, while rosy **Toulouse** (p. 596) holds Languedoc together with student-filled nightlife and modern art.

ONCE UPON A TIME...

French châteaux range from imposing feudal ruins to the well-preserved country homes of 19th-century industrialists. The greatest variety and concentration is found in the **Loire Valley** (p. 147), where the defensive hilltop fortresses of **Chinon** (p. 169) and **Saumur** (p. 173) contrast with the Renaissance grace of **Chenonceau** (p. 171) and **Chambord** (p. 159). **Ussé** (p. 172) inspired Charles Perrault to pen *Sleeping Beauty*, and **Villandry** (p. 172) has been called "the most beautiful garden of the garden that is France."

The Loire has no monopoly on châteaux, however. You can find a tribute to the great "Sun King" Louis XIV's even greater ego at **Versailles** (p. 139). In Provence, you'll be hard-pressed to decide whether the Palais des Papes in **Avignon** (p. 661) is a castle or a palace, while the craggy ruins of nearby **Les Baux** (p. 681) will take you back to the age of chivalry. Perhaps the most impressive château is the fortress of **Carcassonne** (p. 608), a medieval citadel which still stands guard over the Languedoc. If you prefer smaller, less-touristed castles, head to the **Route Jacques Cœur** near **Bourges** (p. 477).

Paris's **Notre Dame** (p. 107) is the most famous church building in France, but a more exquisite Gothic jewel is the nearby **Sainte-Chapelle** (p. 108). The Gothic style of architecture first reached maturity in the majestic cathedral at **Chartres** (p. 142), while several other medieval masterpieces await at **Strasbourg** (p. 344) and **Reims** (p. 307). A more modern sensibility animates Le Corbusier's post-war masterpiece chapel at **Ronchamp** (p. 368).

AU NATUREL

Everyone's heard about the **Alps,** where some of the best hiking and skiing in the world can be found around **Val d'Isère** (p. 451) and **Chamonix** (p. 442). But the Alps represent just one of France's four major mountain ranges. To the north, you'll find the rolling **Jura** mountains (p. 375) in Franche-Comté, while **Le Mont-Dore** (p. 465), in the **Massif Central,** provides spectacular hiking near extinct volcanoes. To the southwest, you can climb into Spain from the western **Pyrenees** (p. 591). If snow-capped peaks aren't your thing, lowland pleasures can be found exploring the flamingo-filled plains of the **Camargue** (p. 685). For advanced hikers, it's possible to trek the length of rugged **Corsica**'s interior (p. 754), but those less advanced can find great day and overnight hikes everywhere on the island, especially on the **Cap Corse** (p. 784).

LA VIE EN *ROSÉ*

France produces some of the finest wines and inebriants in the world. Start with an aperitif of a champagne cocktail from one of **Reims**'s spectacular *caves* (wine cellars, p. 307). To try a little bit of everything, check out the red wines in **Bordeaux** (p. 552) and **Burgundy** (p. 382), or the whites of Alsace's **Route du Vin** (p. 354) and the **Loire Valley** (p. 147). Top it all off with an after-dinner drink—either **Cognac** in the eponymous town (p. 525) or calvados, made throughout **Normandy** (p. 239).

HERE COMES THE SUN

The Côte d'Azur attracts two types of people—the stars who create its glamor, and the masses who come looking for it. You'll party among the tanned youth of Europe in **Nice** (p. 696) and **Juan-les-Pins** (p. 731). Surfers should head straight for the big rollers of the Atlantic coast in **Anglet** (p. 574). If sun and sand are your only desires, try **Île Rousse** (p. 774) in Corsica or the dune beaches near **Arcachon** (p. 562). Some of France's most beautiful beaches await in foggy Brittany, at **Belle-Île** (p. 230) and **St-Malo** (p. 197). Find solitude on the pristine untouched *plages* of **Île de Ré** and **Île d'Aix** (p. 542).

FINE FRENCH WARES

Those with the most refined taste decorate their homes with Brittany's *faïence,* brightly painted French porcelain, the bubble glass unique to **Biot** (p. 730), and linen from **Alençon** (p. 187), the lace capital

NO MORE CHÂTEAUX! UNIQUE FRENCH EXCURSIONS

1. Maison Satie (p. 452). Wander through a maze of rooms that housed artist Erik Satie. The eccentric mansion includes an indoor rainshower room.

2. Cave Raymond (p. 727) in Antibes lets you pump delicious wine from giant casks with a garden hose—a deal to remember.

3. Dijon by Segway (p. 386). Don't miss the chance to let the city's tourist office lead you through the *vieille ville* on these amazing machines.

4. Monte-Carlo (p. 714). Hop over to this amazingly decadent city for the height of conspicuous consumption.

5. Vichy Thermes (p. 475). Cool your jets in the Massif Central in the luxurious hot springs.

6. Marais Poitevin (p. 543). Canoe through a magical landscape for unique outdoor experiences in Poitou-Charentes.

7. Molinard Parfumerie (p. 740.) Capture your essence as you create your own perfume like an expert at this Grasse factory.

8. Lac D'Annecy (p. 436). Plunge into the cool waters of the lake or down the surrounding Alps on skis or in hang gliders.

9. Musée de la Bande Dessinée (p. 522). This fantastic comic book museum has an out-of-this world take on art.

10. Parc Buttes-Chaumont (p. 123). Chill out on fake cliffs surrounding a lake in this wonderfully unique French park of France. **Strasbourg** (p. 344), the birthplace of the Christmas tree, is a one-stop shopping center for charming Christmas decorations of all kinds. For a sample of the biggest names in France's *haute couture*, visit the high-end boutiques in **Nice** (p. 696). Stop by nearby **Grasse** (p. 739), the capital of the world's perfume industry, where even the most bath-phobic backpacker can smell sweet.

LET'S GO PICKS

■ LET'S GO PICKS: FRANCE

BEST PLACE TO KISS: Dusk on **Pont Neuf** (p. 110), on Paris's Île de la Cité.

BEST MUSES: The gorgeous orchards and harbor of **Collioure** (p. 617) inspired Matisse, Dalí, and Picasso. Van Gogh left his heart and his ear in **Arles** (p. 675), where he painted cafes and starry nights. Check out fruit Cézanne made famous in **Aix-en-Provence** (p. 654).

LONGEST SHOTS: The **bar-o-mètre** in Nice's Tapas la Movida (p. 708); the still-loaded **German artillery** in Longues-sur-Mer (p. 267); your chances at the famous **Monte-Carlo Casino** (p. 719).

BEST PRE-HISTORIC DECOR: Don't miss the awesome cave paintings at Lascaux (p. 499) and Les-Eyzies-de-Tayac (p. 500), the world's oldest art exhibits.

BEST EXCUSE FOR DRINKING WINE: The free *dégustations* don't stop as you stumble merrily along the **Côte d'Or** (p. 393)—and neither should you.

BEST ISLANDS: White homes with blue shutters cover idyllic **Île d'Yeu** (p. 549). Sheep and stone crosses are the main inhabitants of **Île d'Ouessant** (p. 219). Neither island is larger than a Peugeot.

BEST REASONS FOR WORLD PEACE: Normandy's World War II **D-Day Beaches** (p. 263); tiny **Oradour-sur-Glane** (p. 489), untouched since Nazis massacred its entire population; the bones of 130,000 unknown soldiers at the Ossuaire outside **Verdun** (p. 343).

MOST INTRIGUING PALACE: Le Palais Idéal in Hauterives (p. 433), assembled stone by stone over 33 years by the local postman, Ferdinand Cheval.

SCARIEST GARGOYLES: Viollet-le-Duc's *chimera* on the **Cathédrale de Notre-Dame** in Paris (p. 107); Front Nationale leader and defeated presidential candidate **Jean-Marie Le Pen** (p. 47).

SUGGESTED ITINERARIES

The following itineraries are designed to give you the highlights of France's distinct regions, from cosmopolitan hubs to sleepy villages. While these itineraries are intended for those who haven't traveled around France very much, even initiated Francophiles can use them as a template for additional daytrips and excursions. There are many Frances, however, and these are not the only ones; in fact, we've left out more than half the country. For more ideas, see **Other Trips,** below, or the regional chapter introductions.

LA CRÈME DE LA CRÈME (1 MONTH)

To see everything worth seeing in France in only a few weeks is impossible, but you can still try. You'll need at least 4-5 days to see the sights and shops of **Paris** (p. 71)—be sure to make time for a daytrip to **Versailles** (p. 139). **Caen** is a must-see for World War II history buffs, which makes it a worthwhile stop on France's lovely northwest coast (1 day; p. 256). While in the area, travel to the island abbey of **Mont-St-Michel** (1 day; p.

274) and **St-Malo** (1 day; p. 197), popular for its ramparts, beaches, and fantastic seafood. Head down to **Rennes** (2 days; p. 188) for medieval sights and modern nightlife. Next, slip down to the Loire Valley. Visit **Chambord** (1 day; p. 159), which is perhaps as grand as Versailles and has as many chimneys as there are days in a year, and the château at **Amboise** (1 day; p. 162), which was home to four French kings. For a change of pace, soak up the sun in beach-blessed, historical **La Rochelle** (1

LA CRÈME DE LA CRÈME

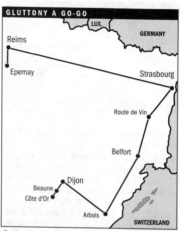

GLUTTONY A GO-GO

day; p. 531) or contemplate some of the world's oldest art exhibits in the 17,000-year-old cave paintings of **Les-Eyzies-de-Tayac** (1 day; p. 495). Test your taste buds in the vineyards of **Bordeaux** (2 days; p. 552) before zipping southward to *basque* on the beach in **Biarritz** (1 day; p. 564). Keep heading east to reach the stunning walls of **Carcassonne** (1 day; p. 608), which guard the town as they have done for centuries. No less formidable are the fortifications of the Palais-des-Papes in festive **Avignon** (1 day; p. 661). Students have been partying in elegant **Aix-en-Provence** (1 day; p. 654) for 600 years, but for non-stop action go to Cannes, one of the more fun, laid-back stops on the Côte d'Azur. Complete your tour of the Riviera in **Nice** (2 days; p. 696), the region's undisputed capital. From there, climb into the Alps to reach dynamic **Grenoble** (2 days; p. 426) and breathtaking **Chamonix** (1 day; p. 442), home to Western Europe's tallest peak, Mt. Blanc. You'll find highs of a very different sort in the town of **Beaune** (1 day; p. 389), home of Burgundy's most precious wines, while to the northeast, international **Strasbourg** (2 days; p. 344) offers a variety of Alsatian wines and an interesting hybrid Franco-German culture. Finally, finish off in style with a tasting at one of the champagne *caves* in **Reims** (1 day; p. 307).

GLUTTONY A GO-GO (2 WEEKS)

This orgy of gastronomic indulgence begins just east of Paris in **Epernay** (1 day; p. 314) the stomping ground of world-famous Dom

Perignon champagne. The bubbly will keep flowing as you roll into charming **Reims** (2 days; p. 307), home to famous vineyards and an iconic 10th-century cathedral. Trade your *brut* for the more brutish pleasures of Bratwurst, beer, and *choucroute garnie* (sauerkraut with meats) in German-influenced **Strasbourg** (2 days; p. 344). Wash it all down with countless wine *dégustations* on the **Route de Vin** (2 days; p. 354) as you sample the Alsatian products of one of the most prolific wine-making regions on the globe. Biting into raspberry-almond tart in **Belfort** (1 day; p. 365) in Franche-Comté will satisfy any sweet tooth, and countless *pâtisseries* make sure you have plenty to choose from. **Arbois** (1 day; p. 375) will show you the spirit of wine country as this proud little village offers free tastings of its rustic *vin jaune*. Back to business in the big city of **Dijon** (2 days; p. 382)—the condiment capital that lays it on thick in affordable gourmet restaurants around town. They've been enjoying local wine in **Beaune** (1 day; p. 389) since Roman times, and they could still give Caesar a run for his money. Go out in a blaze of gourmet glory along the golden hills of the **Côte d'Or** (2 days; p. 393), an El Dorado of viticulture and fine cuisine.

DE-BEACHERY (2 WEEKS)

Visit the Côte d'Azur for beaches and glamor, and tour Provence for spicy cuisine and sun-drenched villages. **Nice** is the unofficial capital of the Côte d'Azur, a nonstop anglophone beach party with more nightlife and budget

DISCOVER

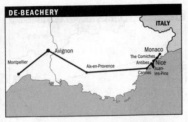

housing than you can shake a glowstick at (2 days; p. 696). Recover at the **Corniches** (2 days; p. 710), breathtaking clifftop villages near Nice that are not to be missed. It doesn't cost anything to look at the micro-state of **Monaco**, which is without doubt the richest place on the Riviera—not an easy title to earn (1 day; p. 714). Twin towns **Antibes** and **Juan-les-Pins** (1 day; p. 731) provide a double dose of beautiful beaches and even more beautiful partygoers. **Cannes,** home to the famous and exclusive film festival, is star-packed year-round, yet has some of the cheapest housing on the coast (1 day; p. 735). **Aix-en-Provence:** Cézanne by day, drunk international students by night (2 days; p. 654). **Avignon,** city of Popes, goes wild for its yearly drama festival (2 days; p. 661). **Montpellier** is a city with intellectual and cultural sophistication and unbeatable gay nightlife (3 days; p. 630).

THE SWORD AND THE CHÂTEAU (10 DAYS)

The Northwest has everything you need to submerge yourself in a medieval reverie: hike in the forests of Arthurian legends and wander in vast castles. Begin at the top with the "Sun King" Louis XIV's mind-boggling property at **Versailles** (1 day; p. 139). From there, check out unbelievable decadence, Renaissance-style, at **Chambord**—a flaunt-it-if-you-got-it hunting getaway built by King François I (½ day; p. 159). To finish the day, hop over to **Blois** to check out another one of France's most famous châteaux (½ day; p. 155). If nobles needed a place to crash, the King's place in **Amboise** could house a modest 4000 friends, with winemaking *caves* built in to ensure refreshments (1 day; p. 162). The bustling, student-filled **Tours** serves as a daytrip hub for the medieval town of **Chinon** and the graceful lines of the river-spanning Renaissance château of **Chenonceau** (2 days; p. 171). Stop and smell the roses at **Villandry** (½ day; p. 172); they are among the 125,000 flowers in the gardens. **Ussé** (½ day; p. 172) inspired *Sleeping Beauty* with all of its fairy-tale beauty. Check out all the student hotspots in the bustling Breton university town of **Rennes** and daytrip to nearby **Brocéliande Forest,** the ancient haunt of Merlin and Guinevere and one of Brittany's most mystical sites (3 days; p. 196).

OTHER TRIPS

France's best hiking and windsurfing are in the rugged sun-blasted island of **Corsica** (p. 754), ringed with beautiful beaches and crumbling Genoese watchtowers. **Burgundy** (p. 382) is known for great wines and sleepy villages, as are the towns around **Bordeaux** (p. 552) to the southwest. Don't forget the exquisite **Dordogne,** a river-cut valley of walnut trees, lazy flowing water, and enough *pâté* for several coronaries (p. 477).

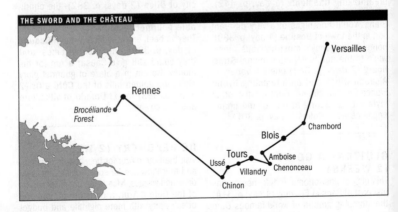

ESSENTIALS

PLANNING YOUR TRIP

ENTRANCE REQUIREMENTS
Passport (p. 8). Required for non-EU citizens, plus UK and Irish citizens.
Visa (p. 10). Required of all other non-EU citizens for stays of over 90 days.
Work Permit (p. 10). Required of all non-EU citizens planning to work in France.

EMBASSIES AND CONSULATES

FRENCH CONSULAR SERVICES ABROAD

All consulates will provide information on obtaining visas or travel to France in general. The hours listed below are for visa concerns unless otherwise stated. Most consulates will receive inquiries by appointment.

Australia: Consulate General, Level 26, St. Martins Tower, 31 Market St., Sydney NSW 2000 (☎02 92 61 57 79; www.consulfrance-sydney.org). Open M-F 9am-1pm.

Canada: Consulat Général de France à Montréal, 1 pl. Ville-Marie, Suite 2601, 26th floor, **Montréal,** QC H3B 4S3 (☎514-878-4385; www.consulfrance-montreal.org). Open M-F 8:30am-noon. Consulat Général de France à Québec, Maison Kent, 25 rue Saint-Louis, **Québec,** QC G1R 3Y8 (☎418-694-2294; www.consulfrance-quebec.org). Open M-F 8:30am-noon. Consulat Général de France à Toronto, 130 Bloor St. West, Suite 400, **Toronto,** ON M5S 1N5 (☎416-925-8041; www.consulfrance-toronto.org). Open M-F 9am-1pm.

Ireland: French Embassy, Consulate Section, 36 Ailesbury Rd., Ballsbridge, Dublin 4 (☎01 277 5000; www.ambafrance.ie). Open M-F 9:30am-12:30pm.

New Zealand: New Zealand Embassy and Consulate, 34-42 Manners St., P.O. Box 11-343, **Wellington** (☎04 384 25 55; fax 04 384 25 77). Open M-F 9am-1pm. French Honorary Consulate in Auckland, P.O. Box 1433, **Auckland** (☎09 379 58 50; www.ambafrance-nz.org).

United Kingdom: Consulate General, P.O. Box 520, 21 Cromwell Rd., London SW7 2EN (☎020 7073 1200; www.ambafrance-uk.org). Open M-W 8:45am-3pm, Th-F 8:45am-noon. Visa service: P.O. Box 57, 6a Cromwell Pl., London SW7 2EW (☎020 7073 1250). Open M-F 8:45-11:30am.

United States: Consulate General, 4101 Reservoir Rd. NW, Washington, D.C. 20007-2185 (☎202-944-6195; www.consulfrance-washington.org). Open M-F 8:45am-12:45pm. Visa service ☎202-944-6200 M-F 2-5pm, answering machine 8:45am-12:45pm; fax 944-6212. Consulates also in Atlanta, Boston, Chicago, Houston, Los Angeles, Miami, New Orleans, New York, and San Francisco. See www.info-france-usa.org/intheus/consulates.asp for more info.

ESSENTIALS

CONSULAR SERVICES IN FRANCE

Travelers visit these embassies only when they encounter trouble and need assistance. The most common concern is a loss of passport or worry about potentially dangerous local conditions. In serious trouble, your home country's embassy or consulate usually can provide legal advice, and may even be able to advance you money in emergency situations. But don't expect them to get you out of every scrape: you must always follow French law in France. In the case of arrest, your consulate can do little more than suggest a lawyer. Dual citizens of France cannot call on the consular services of their second nationality for assistance. Hours vary—call before visiting. Visa services tend to be available only in the morning.

Australia: Australian Embassy and Consulate, 4 rue Jean Rey, 75724 Paris Cédex 15 (☎01 40 59 33 00, after-hours emergency 01 40 59 33 01; www.austgov.fr). Open daily 9:15am-noon and 2-4:30pm.

Canada: Canadian Embassy and Consulate, 35 av. Montaigne, 75008 Paris (☎01 44 43 29 00; after-hours emergency assistance ☎01 44 43 29 00; www.amb-canada.fr). Open daily 9am-noon and 2-5pm. General Delegation of **Quebec**, 66 rue Pergolèse, 75116 Paris (☎01 40 67 85 00; www.mri.gouv.qc.ca/paris).

Ireland: Embassy of Ireland, 12 Avenue Foch, 75116 Paris (☎01 44 17 67 00, emergencies 01 44 17 67 67; www.embassyofirelandparis). Open M-F 9:30am-noon. Also in **Antibes, Cherbourg, Lyon, and Monaco.**

New Zealand: New Zealand Embassy and Consulate, 7ter rue Leonardo de Vinci, 75116 Paris (☎01 45 00 24 11; www.nzembassy.com/france). Open July-Aug. M-Th 9am-1pm and 2-4:30pm, F 9am-2pm; Sept.-June M-Th 9am-1pm and 2-5:30pm, F 9am-1pm, 2pm-4pm.

United Kingdom: British Embassy, Consulate Section, 18bis rue d'Anjou, 75008 Paris (☎01 44 51 31 00; www.amb-grandebretagne.fr). Open M and W-F 9:30am-12:30pm and 2:30-5pm, Tu 9:30am-4:30pm. Also in **Bordeaux, Lille, Lyon,** and **Marseille.**

United States: Consulate General, 2 rue St-Florentin, 75001 Paris (☎01 43 12 22 22 calls and 24 hr. emergency assistance; www.amb-usa.fr). Send mail to 2 rue St-Florentin, 75382 Paris Cédex 08. Open M-F 9am-12:30pm and 1-3pm; notarial services Tu-F 9am-noon only. Tell guard you want American services. Also in **Bordeaux, Lille, Lyon, Marseille, Nice, Rennes, Strasbourg,** and **Toulouse;** visa services Paris only.

TOURIST OFFICES

The **French Government Tourist Office (FGTO),** also known as Maison de la France, runs tourist offices in French cities and offers tourist services to travelers abroad. The FGTO runs the useful website **www.franceguide.com.** *Let's Go* lists the tourist office in every town where one exists.

DOCUMENTS AND FORMALITIES

PASSPORTS

REQUIREMENTS

Citizens of Australia, Canada, Ireland, New Zealand, the UK, and the US need valid passports to enter France and re-enter home countries. France doesn't allow entrance if a passport expires in under three months from the planned departure date; returning home with an expired passport is illegal, and may result in a fine.

NEW PASSPORTS

Citizens of Australia, Canada, Ireland, New Zealand, the UK, and the US can apply for a passport at certain post offices, a passport office, or court of law. Any new passport or renewal applications must be filed well in advance of the departure date, though most passport offices offer rush services for a very steep fee. Even then they can take up to two weeks. Citizens abroad needing passports or renewal should contact their home country's nearest passport office well in advance.

ONE EUROPE. European unity has come a long way since 1958, when the European Economic Community (EEC) was created to promote European solidarity and cooperation. Since then, the EEC has become the European Union (EU), a mighty political, legal, and economic institution. On May 1, 2004, ten South, Central, and Eastern European countries—Cyprus, the Czech Republic, Estonia, Hungary, Latvia, Lithuania, Malta, Poland, Slovak Republic, and Slovenia—were admitted to the EU, joining 15 other member states: Austria, Belgium, Denmark, Finland, France, Germany, Greece, Ireland, Italy, Luxembourg, the Netherlands, Portugal, Spain, Sweden, and the UK.

What does this have to do with the average non-EU tourist? The EU's policy of **freedom of movement** means that border controls between the first 15 member states (minus Ireland and the UK, but plus Norway and Iceland) have been abolished, and visa policies harmonized. While you're still required to carry a passport (or government-issued ID card for EU citizens) when crossing an internal border, once you've been admitted into one country, you're free to travel to other participating states and to transport goods for your own use without custom controls. Britain and Ireland have also formed a **common travel area,** abolishing passport controls between the UK and the Republic of Ireland. The official currency of 12 members of the EU—Austria, Belgium, Finland, France, Germany, Greece, Ireland, Italy, Luxembourg, the Netherlands, Portugal, and Spain—is the **euro.** More countries have joined the EU but will not adopt the euro as official currency until 2006.

PASSPORT MAINTENANCE

Photocopy the page of your passport with your photo, as well as any other important documents. Carry one set of copies apart from the originals, and leave another set at home. Consulates also recommend that you carry an expired passport or an official copy of your birth certificate separate from other documents.

If you lose your passport, immediately notify the local police and the nearest embassy or consulate of your home government. To expedite its replacement, you will need to know all information previously recorded and show ID and proof of citizenship. In some cases, a replacement may take weeks to process and be valid for a limited time. Any visas in the old passport will be irretrievably lost. In an emergency, ask for immediate temporary traveling papers.

VISAS AND WORK PERMITS

VISAS

Citizens of Australia, Canada, Ireland, New Zealand, the UK and the US do not need visas to visit France less than 90 days. Double-check entrance requirements at the nearest embassy or consulate of France (listed under **Embassies and Consulates Abroad,** on p. 7) for up-to-date info before departure.

ESSENTIALS

VISITS OF OVER 90 DAYS. All non-EU citizens need a long-stay visa *(long séjour)* for stays of over 90 days. Visas can be purchased at your local French consulate, and all forms and fees must be presented in person. The visa can take two months to process and cost around €100. US citizens can take advantage of the **Center for International Business and Travel** (**CIBT;** ☎ 800-925-2428), which secures visas for travel to almost all countries for a variable service charge. All foreigners (including EU citizens) who plan to stay over 90 days must apply for a temporary residence permit *(carte de séjour temporaire)* at the prefecture in their town of residence within eight days of their arrival in France.

STUDY AND WORK PERMITS

Admission as a visitor does not include the right to work, which is authorized only by a work permit. Entering France to study requires a special student visa. For more information, see **Alternatives to Tourism** (see p. 60).

IDENTIFICATION

When you travel, always carry at least two forms of identification on your person, including a photo ID; a passport and a driver's license or birth certificate is usually adequate. Never carry all of your IDs together; split them up in case of theft or loss, and keep photocopies of all of them in your luggage and at home.

STUDENT, TEACHER, AND YOUTH IDENTIFICATION

The **International Student Identity Card (ISIC),** the most widely accepted form of student ID, provides discounts on many sights, accommodations, food, and transport; access to a 24hr. emergency helpline, and insurance benefits for US cardholders. Applicants must be full-time secondary or post-secondary school students at least 12 years of age. Because of the proliferation of fake ISICs, some services (particularly airlines) require additional proof of student identity.

The **International Student Exchange Card (ISE)** is a similar identification card available to students, faculty, and youth aged 12 to 26. The card provides discounts, medical benefits, access to a 24hr. emergency helpline, and the ability to purchase student airfares. The card costs US$25; call US ☎ 800-255-8000 for more info, or visit www.isecard.com.

The **International Teacher Identity Card (ITIC)** offers teachers the same insurance coverage as the ISIC and similar but limited discounts. For travelers who are 25 years old or under but are not students, the **International Youth Travel Card (IYTC)** also offers many of the same benefits as the ISIC.

Each of these identity cards costs US$22 or the equivalent. ISIC and ITIC cards are valid through the academic year in which they are issued; IYTC cards are valid for one year from the date of issue. Many student travel agencies (see p. 20) issue the cards; for a list of issuing agencies or more information, see the **International Student Travel Confederation (ISTC)** website (www.istc.org).

CUSTOMS

Upon entering France, you must declare certain items from abroad and pay a duty on the value of those articles if they exceed a pre-established customs allowance. Goods and gifts purchased at **duty-free** shops abroad are not exempt from duty or sales tax; "duty-free" means that you need not pay a tax in the country of purchase. Duty-free allowances were abolished for travel within the EU in 1999, but still exist for those arriving from outside the EU. Upon returning home, you must likewise declare all articles acquired abroad and pay a duty on the value of articles in excess of your home country's allowance. In order to expedite your return, make a list of any valuables brought from home and register them with customs before traveling abroad, and be sure to keep receipts for all goods acquired abroad.

MONEY

CURRENCY AND EXCHANGE

The currency chart below is based on August 2004 exchange rates between local currency and Australian dollars (AUS$), Canadian dollars (CDN$), European Union euros (EUR€), New Zealand dollars (NZ$), British pounds (UK£), and US dollars (US$). Check the currency converter on websites like www.xe.com and www.bloomberg.com or a large newspaper for the latest exchange rates.

EUROS (€)	
AUS$1 = €0.59	€1 = AUS$1.71
CDN$1 = €0.63	€1 = CDN$1.58
NZ$1 = €0.54	€1 = NZ$1.84
UK£1 = €1.49	€1 = UK£0.67
US$1 = €0.83	€1 = US$1.20

As a general rule, it's cheaper to convert money in France than at home. While currency exchange will probably be available in your arrival airport, it's wise to bring enough foreign currency to last for the first 24 to 72 hours of your trip.

When changing money abroad, try to only go to banks or *bureaux de change* that have at most a 5% margin between their buy and sell prices. Since you lose money with every transaction, **convert large sums** (unless the currency is depreciating rapidly), **but no more than you'll need.**

If you use traveler's checks, carry some in small denominations (the equivalent of US$50 or less) for times when you are forced to exchange money at disadvantageous rates, but bring a range of denominations since charges may be per check cashed. Store money in a variety of forms. All travelers should also consider carrying some US dollars (about US$50), which are often preferred by local tellers.

TRAVELER'S CHECKS

Traveler's checks are one of the safest and least troublesome means of carrying funds. American Express and Visa are the most recognized brands. Many banks and agencies sell them for a small commission. Check issuers provide refunds if the checks are lost or stolen, and many provide additional services like toll-free refund hotlines, emergency message services, and stolen credit card assistance. They are readily accepted in France though some establishments only take checks in euros; a passport is often required to cash them. Always carry emergency cash.

American Express: Checks available with commission at select banks, at all AmEx offices, and online (www.americanexpress.com; US residents only). American Express cardholders can also purchase checks by phone (☎800-721-9768). For purchase locations or more information contact AmEx's service centers: in Australia ☎800 68 80 22; in New Zealand 0508 555 358; in the UK 0800 587 6023; in the US and Canada 800-221-7282; elsewhere, call the US collect at 801-964-6665.

Visa: Checks available (generally with commission) at banks worldwide. For the location of the nearest office, call Visa's service centers: in the UK ☎0800 51 58 84; in the US 800-227-6811; elsewhere, call the UK collect at 44 1733 31 89 49. AAA (see p. 27) offers commission-free checks to its members.

Travelex/Thomas Cook: In US and Canada ☎800-287-7362; in the UK call 0800 62 21 01; elsewhere call the UK collect at 44 1733 31 89 50. Issues Visa traveler's checks. 25% commission discount on check purchases for AAA and affiliated auto associations.

CREDIT, DEBIT, AND ATM CARDS

Credit cards often offer superior exchange rates—up to 5% better than the rate used by banks and currency exchange establishments. Credit cards may also offer services such as insurance or emergency help, and are sometimes required to reserve hotels or rental cars. **Mastercard** (EuroCard) and **Visa** (Carte Bleue) are widely accepted; **American Express** cards work at some ATMs and at AmEx offices and major airports. **ATM cards** are widespread in France. Depending on the system that your home bank uses, you can most likely access your personal bank account from abroad, but there is often a limit on the amount you can withdraw per day (often US$500) and a US$1-5 surcharge per withdrawal. **A debit card** can be used wherever its associated credit card company (usually Mastercard or Visa) is accepted, yet the money is withdrawn directly from the holder's checking account. Debit cards often also function as ATM cards and can be used to withdraw cash. The two major international money networks are **Cirrus** (US ☎ 800-424-7787; www.mastercard.com) and **Visa/PLUS** (US ☎ 800-843-7587; www.visa.com).

GETTING MONEY FROM HOME

If you run out of money abroad, the easiest, cheapest solution is to have someone at home deposit cash to the bank account for your credit card or ATM card. Failing that, consider one of the following options. Check the **International Money Transfer Consumer Guide** (http://international-money-transfer-consumer-guide.info).

WIRING MONEY

It is possible to arrange a **bank money transfer,** where a bank at home wires money to a French bank—the cheapest (but slowest) way to transfer cash, often taking several days. Some banks may only release funds in euros, potentially sticking you with a poor exchange rate; inquire about this in advance. Transfer services like **Western Union** are faster, more convenient, and much pricier. Western Union has many locations worldwide. To find one, visit www.westernunion.com, or call in Australia ☎ 800 501 500, in Canada 800-235-0000, in the UK 0800 83 38 33, in the US 800-325-6000, or in France 01 41 33 25 15. Transfer services are also available at **American Express** and **Thomas Cook** (☎ 08 26 82 67 77; www.thomascook.fr) offices.

US STATE DEPARTMENT (US CITIZENS ONLY)

In serious emergencies only, the US State Department will forward money within hours to the nearest consular office, which will then disburse it for a US$30 fee. For this service, contact the Overseas Citizens Service division of the US State Department (☎ 317-472-2328; nights, Su, and holidays 202-647-4000).

STAYING ON BUDGET

To give you a general idea, a bare-bones day in France (camping or sleeping in hostels/guesthouses, buying food at supermarkets) would cost about US$25 (about €20); a slightly more comfortable day (sleeping in hostels/guesthouses and the occasional budget hotel, eating one meal per day at a restaurant, going out at night) would cost US$50 (about €40). Don't forget to factor in emergency reserve funds (at least US$200) when planning how much money you'll need. To save money, eat at supermarkets instead of restaurants, bring a **sleepsack** (see p. 11) to save on sheet charges in hostels, and do your **laundry** in the sink (unless it's explicitly prohibited).

ESSENTIALS

TIPPING AND BARGAINING

By French law, service must be included at all **restaurants, bars,** and **cafes.** Look for *service compris* on the menu. If service isn't included, tip 15-20%. Even when it's included, it is polite to leave a *pourboire* (half a euro to 5% of the bill) at a cafe, restaurant, or bar. Tip your hairdresser well; don't tip taxis more than a euro. People like concierges may expect to be tipped for extra services, never less than €1.50.

You should inquire about discounts and less pricey options, but don't try to bargain at established places like hotels, hostels, restaurants, cafes, museums, nightclubs. Bargaining is acceptable at outdoor markets, but don't expect any deals.

TAXES

The **value-added tax (VAT)** is a general tax on doing business in France; it applies to a wide range of goods (entertainment, food, accommodations) and services. The tax can be up to 19.6% of the price of the good. Some of the VAT can be recovered.

PACKING

Pack lightly: Lay out only what you absolutely need, then take half the clothes and twice the money. The Travelite FAQ (www.travelite.org) is a good resource for tips. The **Universal Packing List** (http://upl.codeq.info) will generate a customized list of suggested items based on trip length, expected climate, planned activities, and other factors. If you plan to hike, also consult **and the Outdoors,** p. 35.

Luggage: If covering most of your itinerary by foot, a sturdy **frame backpack** is unbeatable. (For the basics on buying a pack, see p. 36.) Toting a **suitcase** or **trunk** is fine for living in 1 or 2 cities and exploring from there, but not wise for frequent moves. In addition to your main piece of luggage, a **daypack** (a small backpack or courier bag) is useful.

Clothing: No matter when you're traveling, it's a good idea to bring a warm jacket or wool sweater, a rain jacket (Gore-Tex® is both waterproof and breathable), sturdy shoes or hiking boots, and thick socks. Flip-flops or waterproof sandals are musts for grubby hostel showers. You may also want an outfit for going out, and maybe a nicer pair of shoes. In the summer, wearing shorts will be a surefire signal that you're a tourist.

Sleepsack: Some hostels require that you either provide your own linen or rent sheets from them. Save cash by making your own sleepsack: fold a full-size sheet in half the long way, then sew it closed along the long side and one of the short sides.

Converters and Adapters: In France, electricity is 220 volts AC, enough to fry any 120V North American appliance. 220/240V electrical appliances won't work with a 120V current, either. Americans and Canadians should buy an adapter (which changes the shape of the plug; US$5) and a converter (which changes the voltage; US$20-30). Don't make the mistake of using only an adapter (unless appliance instructions explicitly state otherwise). New Zealanders and Australians (who use 230V at home) won't need a converter, but will need a set of adapters to use anything electrical. For more on all things adaptable, check out http://kropla.com/electric.htm.

Toiletries: Toothbrushes, towels, cold-water soap, talcum powder (to keep feet dry), deodorant, razors, tampons, and condoms are often available, but may be difficult to find; bring extras. **Contact lenses** are likely to be expensive and difficult to find, so bring enough extra pairs and solution for your entire trip. Also bring your glasses and a copy of your prescription in case you need emergency replacements.

First-Aid Kit: For a basic first-aid kit, pack bandages, a pain reliever, antibiotic cream, a thermometer, a Swiss Army knife, tweezers, moleskin, decongestant, motion-sickness remedy, diarrhea or upset-stomach medication (Pepto Bismol or Imodium), an antihistamine, sunscreen, insect repellent, and burn ointment.

Other Useful Items: For safety purposes, you should bring a **money belt** and small **padlock**. Basic **outdoors equipment** (plastic water bottle, compass, waterproof matches, pocketknife, sunglasses, sunscreen, hat) may also prove useful. A needle and thread can repair tears. To do laundry by hand, bring detergent, a small rubber ball to plug the sink, and string for a clothes line. Other things you're liable to forget are an umbrella; sealable **plastic bags** (for damp clothes, soap, food, shampoo, and other spillables); an **alarm clock;** safety pins; rubber bands; a flashlight; earplugs; garbage bags.

SAFETY AND HEALTH

SPECIFIC CONCERNS

DRUGS AND ALCOHOL

Possession of **illegal drugs** (including marijuana) in France can result in a substantial jail sentence or fine. Drug dealers often sell drugs to tourists and then turn them in to authorities for a reward. In France, police may arbitrarily stop and search anyone on the street. **Prescription drugs,** particularly insulin, syringes, or narcotics, should be left in their original, labeled containers and accompanied by their prescriptions and a doctor's statement. In case of arrest, your home country's consulate can suggest attorneys and inform your family and friends but can't get you out of jail. For more info, contact the Office of Overseas Citizens Services (US ☎202-647-5225; after-hours 647-4000; http://travel.state.gov).

The French love alcohol, but they drink carefully. Virtually no one drinks "to get drunk." Drinking on the street is uncouth. Restaurants may serve alcohol to anyone 16 or over. Smoking is banned in public places, but people light up almost anywhere. Some eateries have non-smoking sections, but they're often not respected.

DEMONSTRATIONS AND POLITICAL GATHERINGS

In France, violent civil disorder is not very common. However, in the past, demonstrations by students, labor groups, and other routine protesters have grown into more violent confrontations with the police. Tourists are advised to avoid such demonstrations. The most common form of violence when demonstrations get out of hand is property damage, and tourists are unlikely targets. In general, use common sense in conversation and, as in dealing with any issues of a different culture, be respectful of locals' religious and political perspectives.

TERRORISM

Terrorism has not been as serious a problem in France as in other European countries, but after September 11, 2001, the French government heightened security at public places. Many train stations no longer permit luggage storage, for example. France contains cells of al Qaeda and other terrorist groups. Many cities have recently experienced unrest, but more often because of immigrant conditions than terrorism. Since its colonial period, France has always been an enemy of unstable Algeria and has been a source of sporadic violent outbursts. Also, domestic anti-Semites firebombed several Jewish synagogues in the past few years. The box on **Travel Advisories** lists offices to contact and webpages to visit to get the most up-to-date list of your home country's government's advisories about travel.

TRAVEL ADVISORIES. The following government offices provide travel information and advisories by telephone, by fax, or via the web:

Australian Department of Foreign Affairs and Trade: ☎ 13 00 555135; faxback service 02 6261 1299; www.dfat.gov.au.

Canadian Department of Foreign Affairs and International Trade (DFAIT): In Canada and the US call ☎ 800-267-8376, elsewhere call ☎ 1 613-944-4000; www.dfait-maeci.gc.ca. Call for their free booklet, *Bon Voyage...But.*

New Zealand Ministry of Foreign Affairs: ☎ 04 439 8000, fax 494 8506; www.mft.govt.nz/travel/index.html.

United Kingdom Foreign and Commonwealth Office: ☎ 020 7008 0232, fax 7008 0155; www.fco.gov.uk.

US Department of State: ☎ 202-647-5225, faxback service 202-647-3000; http://travel.state.gov. For *A Safe Trip Abroad,* call ☎ 202-512-1800.

PERSONAL SAFETY

EXPLORING AND TRAVELING

Tourists are the biggest targets for crime in France. When confronted by a suspicious individual, do not respond or make eye contact. Walk quickly away, and keep a solid grip on your belongings. When driving, lock your doors and keep bags away from windows; scooter-borne thieves often snatch purses and bags from cars stopped at lights. In **Paris,** be especially careful on public transportation at rush hour and traveling to and from the airport. Pick-pocketing is common on the Paris metro, especially on line #1 and the RER B line to CDG Airport. As a rule, always be vigilant with your baggage at **airports** and **train stations.** Also be aware at department stores, particularly on the escalators. Only take a **licensed taxi.** Outside Paris, tourist-related crime is most prevalent on the **Côte d'Azur,** in **Marseille,** and in **Montpellier.**

To avoid unwanted attention, try to blend in as much as possible. Familiarize yourself with your surroundings before setting out, and carry yourself with confidence. Check maps in shops and restaurants rather than on the street. If you are traveling alone, be sure someone at home knows your itinerary, and never admit that you're by yourself. When walking at night, stick to busy, well-lit streets and avoid dark alleyways; leave any area that makes you feel uncomfortable. There is no sure-fire way to avoid all the threatening situations, but a good **self-defense course** will give you concrete ways to react to unwanted advances. **Impact, Prepare,** and **Model Mugging** can refer you to local self-defense courses in the US (☎ 800-345-5425). Visit the website at www.impact-safety.org for a list of nearby chapters. Workshops (1½-3hr.) start at US$75; full courses (20-25hr.) run US$350-400. If driving, park in a garage or well traveled area, and use a steering wheel locking device in larger cities. For info on the perils of **hitchhiking,** see p. 27. **Sleeping in your car** is one of the most dangerous (and often illegal) ways to get your rest.

POSSESSIONS AND VALUABLES

Never leave belongings unattended; crime occurs in even the most demure-looking hotel. Bring your own **padlock** for hostel lockers. Be particularly careful on **buses** and **trains;** horror stories abound about determined thieves who wait for travelers to fall asleep. Carry your backpack in front of you. When alone, never stay in an empty train compartment, and use a lock to secure your pack to the luggage rack. Try to sleep on top bunks with your luggage above you (if not in bed with you), and keep important documents and other valuables on your person. **Bring as little with you as possible,** and carry as little cash as possible. Keep your traveler's checks and ATM/credit cards in a **money belt**—not a "fanny pack"—along with your passport and ID cards. **Keep a small cash reserve separate from your primary stash** (about US$50), sewn into or stored in the depths of your pack, along with your traveler's check numbers and important photocopies.

In large cities **con artists** often work in groups and may involve children. Beware of certain classics: sob stories that require money, rolls of bills "found," mustard spilled (or saliva spit) on your shoulder to distract you while they snatch your bag. **Never let your passport and bags out of your sight.** Beware of **pickpockets** in city crowds, especially on public transportation. Be alert in telephone booths: if you must say the calling card number, do so very quietly; if you punch it in, make sure no one can look over your shoulder. For electronics, check whether your homeowner's insurance covers loss, theft, or damage during travel. **Safeware** (☎ US 800-800-1492; www.safeware.com) specializes in covering computers and charges $90 for 90-day comprehensive international travel coverage up to $4000.

PRE-DEPARTURE HEALTH

In your **passport,** write the names of anyone you wish to be contacted in case of medical emergency, and list any allergies or medical conditions. Finding a prescription's foreign equivalents is not always easy or safe; bring a full supply, and carry legible prescriptions. Keep all medication in carry-on bags. Travelers over two years old should ensure that the following **vaccines** are up to date: MMR (for measles, mumps, and rubella); DTaP or Td (for diphtheria, tetanus, and pertussis); IPV (for polio); Hib (for *haemophilus* influenza B); and HepB (for Hepatitis B).

USEFUL ORGANIZATIONS AND PUBLICATIONS

The US **Centers for Disease Control and Prevention** (**CDC;** ☎877-FYI-TRIP; www.cdc.gov/travel) maintains an international travelers' hotline and an informative website. For quick information on health and other travel warnings, call the **Overseas Citizens Services** (☎888-407-4747 M-F 8am-8pm; after-hours 202-647-4000; 317-472-2328 from overseas), or contact a passport agency, embassy, or consulate abroad. For information on medical evacuation services and travel insurance, see the US government's website at http://travel.state.gov/medical.html or the **British Foreign and Commonwealth Office** (www.fco.gov.uk). For general health info, contact the **American Red Cross** (☎800-564-1234; www.redcross.org).

STAYING HEALTHY

ENVIRONMENTAL HAZARDS

Heat exhaustion and dehydration: Heat exhaustion leads to nausea, excessive thirst, headaches, and dizziness. Avoid it by **drinking plenty of fluids,** eating salty foods (e.g. crackers), abstaining from dehydrating beverages (e.g. alcohol and caffeinated beverages), and always wearing sunscreen. Continuous heat stress can eventually lead to heatstroke, characterized by a rising temperature, severe headache, delirium and cessation of sweating. Victims should be cooled off with wet towels and taken to a doctor.

Sunburn: Always remember to wear sunscreen (SPF 30 is good) when spending excessive amounts of time outdoors. Near water, in the desert, or in the snow, you are at a higher risk of getting burned, even through clouds. If sunburned, drink more fluids and apply an aloe-based lotion. Severe sunburns can lead to sun poisoning, causing fever, chills, nausea, and vomiting. Sun poisoning should always be treated by a doctor.

Hypothermia and frostbite: A rapid drop in body temperature is the clearest sign of overexposure to cold. Victims may also shiver, feel exhausted, have poor coordination or slurred speech, hallucinate, or suffer amnesia. *Do not let hypothermia victims fall asleep.* To avoid hypothermia, keep dry, wear layers, and stay out of the wind. When the temperature is below freezing, watch out for frostbite. If skin turns white or blue, waxy, and cold, do not rub the area. Drink warm beverages, stay dry, and slowly warm the area with dry fabric or steady body contact until a doctor can be found.

High Altitude: Allow your body a couple of days to adjust to less oxygen before exerting yourself. Those exploring the Alps and the Pyrenees should note that alcohol is more potent and UV rays are stronger at high elevations.

INSECT-BORNE DISEASES

Many diseases are transmitted by insects like mosquitoes, fleas, ticks, and lice. Be aware of insects in wet or forested areas; wear long pants and sleeves and tuck pants into socks. Use insect repellents like DEET. **Ticks**—responsible for Lyme and other diseases—can be particularly dangerous in rural, forested regions.

Tick-borne encephalitis: A viral infection of the central nervous system transmitted during the summer by tick bites or by consumption of unpasteurized dairy products. The risk of contracting the disease is relatively low, especially if precautions are taken.

Lyme disease: A bacterial infection carried by ticks and marked by a circular bull's-eye rash of 2 in. or more. Later symptoms include fever, headache, fatigue, and aches and pains. Antibiotics are effective if administered early. Left untreated, Lyme can cause problems in joints, the heart, and the nervous system. If you find a tick attached to your skin, grasp the head with tweezers as close to your skin as possible and apply slow, steady traction. Removing a tick within 24 hours greatly reduces the risk of infection. Do not try to remove ticks with petroleum jelly, nail polish remover, or a hot match.

FOOD- AND WATER-BORNE DISEASES

Traveler's diarrhea in France is usually only the body's temporary reaction to bacteria in unfamiliar food ingredients; it tends to last 3-7 days and causes nausea, bloating, and urgency. Try quick-energy, non-sugary foods with protein and carbohydrates. Over-the-counter anti-diarrheals (e.g. Imodium) may counteract symptoms. The most dangerous side effect is dehydration; drink 8 oz. of water with ½ tsp. of sugar or honey and a pinch of salt, and try uncaffeinated soft drinks. If symptoms don't go away after 4-5 days, consult a doctor. Consult a doctor immediately for treatment of diarrhea in children.

OTHER INFECTIOUS DISEASES

Rabies: Transmitted through the saliva of infected animals; fatal if untreated. By the time symptoms (thirst and muscle spasms) appear, the disease is in its terminal stage. If you are bitten, wash the wound thoroughly, seek immediate medical care, and try to have the animal located. Rabies is often transmitted through dogs.

Hepatitis B: A viral infection of the liver transmitted via blood or other bodily fluids. Symptoms, which may not surface until years after infection, include jaundice, loss of appetite, fever, and joint pain. It is transmitted through activities like unprotected sex, injections of illegal drugs, and unprotected health work. A 3-shot vaccination sequence is recommended for health-care workers, sexually-active travelers, and anyone planning to seek medical treatment abroad; it must begin 6 months before traveling

Hepatitis C: Like Hepatitis B, but the mode of transmission differs. IV drug users, hemodialysis patients, and recipients of blood transfusions are at the highest risk, but the disease can also be spread through sexual contact or sharing items like razors and toothbrushes that may have traces of blood on them. Symptoms are rarely exhibited, but if there are any, they can include loss of appetite, abdominal pain, fatigue, nausea, and jaundice. If untreated, Hepatitis C can lead to liver failure.

AIDS and HIV (SIDA in French): This is a major problem in France; Paris has the largest HIV-positive community in Europe. France has only recently lifted immigration bans on HIV-positive individuals. For detailed information on Acquired Immune Deficiency Syndrome (AIDS) in France, call the US Centers for Disease Control's 24hr. hotline at ☎800-342-2437, or contact the Joint United Nations Programme on HIV/AIDS (UNAIDS), 20, av. Appia, CH-1211 Geneva 27, Switzerland (☎22 791 3666; fax 22 791 4187). France's AIDS hotline is ☎01 44 93 16 16. Contact the consulate of France for more information.

Sexually Transmitted Diseases (STDs): Gonorrhea, chlamydia, genital warts, syphilis, herpes, and other STDs are more common than HIV and can cause serious complications. Though condoms may protect you from some STDs, oral or even tactile contact can lead to transmission. If you think you may have an STD, see a doctor immediately.

MEDICAL CARE ON THE ROAD

Medical care in France is as good (and as expensive) as anywhere in the world. All but the smallest towns have a hospital, generally with English-speaking staff, which is listed under the Practical Information in each city listing. Every town has a **24hr. pharmacy** *(pharmacie de garde)*. Pharmacies assume this duty on rotation; check with the police or on pharmacy doors for location.

EU citizens get "reciprocal health benefits" (including immediate urgent care) if they fill out an **E-111** form, available at most post offices, before departure. EU citizens studying in France qualify for long-term care. Other travelers should get adequate medical insurance before leaving. US Medicare doesn't cover foreign travel.

If you need a **doctor** *(un médecin)*, call the local hospital for a list of nearby practitioners or inquire at a pharmacy. If you are receiving reciprocal health care, make sure you call an **honoraires opposables** doctor (linked to the state health care system). Legally, they may not charge more than €17 for a consultation. Doctors registered as **honoraires libres** can charge whatever they like, and their fees will not be reimbursed under reciprocal health care agreements.

If you are concerned about getting medical assistance while traveling, you may wish to employ special support services. The *MedPass* from **GlobalCare, Inc.,** 6875 Shiloh Rd. East, Alpharetta, GA 30005, USA (☎800-860-1111, fax 678-341-1800; www.globalcare.net), provides 24hr. international medical assistance, support, and medical evacuation resources. The **International Association for Medical Assistance to Travelers (IAMAT;** US ☎716-754-4883, Canada 519-836-0102; www.cybermall.co.nz/NZ/IAMAT) has free membership, lists English-speaking doctors worldwide, and offers detailed info on immunization requirements and sanitation.

Those with medical conditions like diabetes, allergies to antibiotics, epilepsy, and heart conditions may want a **Medic Alert** membership (first year US$35, annually thereafter US$20), which includes a stainless steel ID tag and a 24hr. collect-call number. Contact the Medic Alert Foundation, 2323 Colorado Ave, Turlock, CA 95382, USA (☎888-633-4298, outside US 209-668-3333; www.medicalert.org).

WOMEN'S HEALTH

Women traveling in unsanitary conditions are vulnerable to **urinary tract (including bladder and kidney) infections:** if symptoms persist, see a doctor. Over-the-counter remedies like Monostat or Gynelotrimin help **vaginal yeast infections. Tampons, pads,** and **contraceptive devices** are widely available. Recent changes have relaxed restrictions on surgical and pharmaceutical **abortions,** permitting them up to 12 weeks into pregnancy. Contact the French branch of the International Planned Parenthood Federation, the **Mouvement Français pour le Planning Familial (MFPF),** which can supply the names of French hospitals and OB/GYN clinics performing abortions. (☎01 48 07 29 10. €550 if not covered by insurance.) More info about family planning centers can also be obtained through the **International Planned Par-**

TRAGEDY AT CHARLES DE GAULLE

On May 23, 2004, travelers in Roissy-Charles de Gaulle Airport Terminal 2E were startled by an enormous crash. A 40m section of the roof of the departure lounge plunged 20m to the ground, killing four.

The terminal had opened 11 months earlier, and its impressive span of glass and steel over the terminal hall was widely admired. The new construction had cost €750 million (approximately US$920 million) and was the centerpiece of a project to increase the capacity of Roissy-CDG to 50 million passengers annually. Investigators identified flaws in engineering as the cause of the collapse. Construction of the terminal had been delayed by terrorism concerns (definitively ruled out as a cause), and some speculate that the terminal's structural integrity was compromised by a rush to complete it on time. The terminal's architect, Paul Andreu, who was working on the National Theater in Beijing at the time of the collapse, claimed that all the necessary precautions had been taken and was naturally appalled at the tragedy.

Parts of terminal 2E will be closed at least until mid-2005 and maybe longer, depending on investigations into the safety of the rest of the terminal. Officials don't anticipate delays or inconvenience, however, as the rest of the aiport shifts to accommodate the redistributed traffic.

enthood Federation, European Regional Office, Regent's College Inner Circle, Regent's Park, London NW1 4NS, England (☎020 7487 7900).

CONTRACEPTION

Contraception is readily available in most pharmacies and supermarkets. To obtain **condoms** in France, visit a pharmacy and ask for "*une boîte de préservatifs.*"

GETTING TO FRANCE

BY PLANE

AIRFARES

Airfares to France peak between June and September; Christmas and Easter are also expensive. In general, a Saturday night stay results in a cheaper airfare. Midweek (M-Th morning) round-trip flights run US$40-50 cheaper than weekend flights, but they are generally more crowded and less likely to permit frequent-flier upgrades. Not fixing a return date ("open return") or arriving in and departing from different cities ("open-jaw") can be pricier than round-trip flights.

If France is only one stop on a global trip, consider a round-the-world (RTW) ticket, which usually includes at least five stops and is valid for a year; prices range US$3400-5000. Round-trip fares to Paris from the US range from US$300-500 (low season) to US$350-800 (high season); from Australia, between AUS$1600 and AUS$2500; from New Zealand, NZ$5000-9000; from Britain, UK$60-80.

BUDGET AND STUDENT TRAVEL AGENCIES

Travelers holding **ISIC** and **IYTC cards** (see p. 10) qualify for big discounts from student travel agencies.

CTS Travel, 30 Rathbone Pl., London W1T 1GQ, UK (☎0207 209 0630; www.ctstravel.co.uk). A British student travel agent with offices in 39 countries.

STA Travel, 5900 Wilshire Blvd., Suite 900, Los Angeles, CA 90036, USA (24hr. reservations and info ☎800-781-4040; www.sta-travel.com). A student and youth travel organization with over 150 offices worldwide. Ticket booking, travel insurance, railpasses, and more. Walk-in offices are located throughout Australia (☎03 9349 4344), New Zealand (☎09 309 9723), and the UK (☎0870 1 600 599).

Travel CUTS (Canadian Universities Travel Services Limited), 187 College St., **Toronto,** ON M5T 1P7 (☎416-979-2406; www.travelcuts.com). Offices across Canada and US.

usit, 19-21 Aston Quay, Dublin 2 (☎01 602 1777; www.usitworld.com). Ireland's leading budget travel agency has 22 offices in Northern Ireland and the Republic of Ireland.

Wasteels, Skoubogade 6, 1158 Copenhagen K. (☎3314 4633; www.wasteels.com). A huge chain with 180 locations across Europe. Sells Wasteels BIJ tickets discounted 30-45% off regular fare, 2nd-class international point-to-point train tickets with unlimited stopovers for those under 26 (sold only in Europe).

COMMERCIAL AIRLINES

Generally, reservations must be made seven to 21 days ahead of departure, with 7- to 14-day minimum-stay and up to 90-day maximum-stay restrictions. These fares carry hefty cancellation and change penalties (fees rise in summer). Use **Expedia** (www.expedia.com) or **Travelocity** (www.travelocity.com) to get an idea of the lowest published fares. Fares listed are high-season (mid-June to September).

TRAVELING FROM NORTH AMERICA

Round-trip fares to Paris run roughly US $300-700. Standard carriers like **American** (☎800-433-7300; www.aa.com), **United** (☎800-538-2929; www.ual.com), and **Northwest** (☎800-447-4747; www.nwa.com) will probably offer the most convenient flights, but they may not be the cheapest. Check **Lufthansa** (☎800-399-5838; cms.lufthansa.com), **British Airways** (☎800-247-9297; www.britishairways.com), **Air France** (☎800-237-2747; www.airfrance.us), and **Alitalia** (☎800-223-5730; www.alitaliausa.com). You might find an even better deal on one of the following airlines.

Icelandair: (☎800-223-5500; www.icelandair.com). Stopovers in Iceland for no extra cost on most flights. New York to Paris May-Sept. US$500-730; Oct.-May US$390-450.

Finnair: (☎800-950-5000; www.us.finnair.com). Cheap round-trips from San Francisco, New York, and Toronto to Helsinki; connections throughout Europe.

TRAVELING FROM THE UK AND IRELAND

Because of the many carriers flying from the British Isles to the continent, we only include discount airlines or those with cheap specials here. **Cheapflights** (www.cheapflights.co.uk) publishes airfare bargains.

Aer Lingus: (Ireland ☎0818 365 000; www.aerlingus.ie). Return tickets from Dublin, Cork, Galway, Kerry, and Shannon to Paris (from €44).

bmibaby: (UK ☎0870 264 22 29; www.bmibaby.com). Departures from throughout the UK. Service from Manchester to Paris (UK£40).

easyJet: (UK ☎0871 750 01 00; www.easyjet.com). London to Paris and Nice (UK£72-141). Online tickets.

KLM: (UK ☎0870 507 40 74; www.klmuk.com). Cheap return tickets from London and elsewhere to Paris and Amsterdam.

Ryanair: (Ireland ☎0818 303 030, UK 087 246 00 00; www.ryanair.com). From Dublin, London, and Glasgow to destinations in France, Ireland and elsewhere.

TRAVELING FROM AUSTRALIA AND NEW ZEALAND

In addition to the airlines listed below, good deals may be found from **Australian Airlines** (www.australianairlines.com).

Air New Zealand: (New Zealand ☎0800 73 70 00; www.airnz.co.nz). Auckland to London and Frankfurt.

Qantas Air: (Australia ☎13 13 13, New Zealand 0800 808 767; www.qantas.com.au). Flights from Australia and New Zealand to London around AUS$2400.

Singapore Air: (Australia ☎13 10 11, New Zealand 0800 808 909; www.singaporeair.com). From Auckland, Sydney, Melbourne, and Perth to Western Europe.

Thai Airways: (Australia ☎1300 65 19 60, New Zealand 09 377 02 68; www.thaiair.com). Auckland, Sydney, and Melbourne to Amsterdam, Frankfurt, and London.

Cathay Pacific: (France ☎01 41 43 75 75; Australia 1 300 361 060). Reasonable RTW fares and flights to Paris, connecting to Australia via Hong Kong.

AIR COURIER FLIGHTS

If you travel light, consider courier flights. As a courier, you take only a carry-on and allow the airline to use your luggage space to transport cargo. Most flights leave from New York, Los Angeles, San Francisco, or Miami in the US; and from Montreal, Toronto, or Vancouver in Canada. Round-trip courier fares from the US to France can be as low as US$200. Generally, couriers must be over 21 (in some cases, 18). In summer, the most popular destinations usually require an advance reservation of about two weeks. Discounts are common for last-minute flights.

STANDBY FLIGHTS

Traveling standby requires considerable flexibility in arrival and departure dates and cities. Companies dealing in standby flights sell vouchers rather than tickets, along with the promise to get you to your destination (or near your destination) within a certain window of time (typically 1-5 days). You call in before your specific window of time to hear your flight options and the probability that you will be able to board each flight. Carefully read agreements with any company offering standby flights as tricky fine print can leave you in the lurch. To check on a company's service record in the US, call the Better Business Bureau (☎703-276-0100).

TICKET CONSOLIDATORS

Ticket consolidators, or **"bucket shops,"** buy unsold tickets in bulk from commercial airlines and sell them at discounted rates. The best place to look is in the Sunday travel section of any major newspaper (such as the *New York Times*), where many bucket shops place tiny ads. Not all bucket shops are reliable, so insist on a receipt that gives full details of restrictions, refunds, and tickets, and pay by credit card (in spite of the 2-5% fee) so you can stop payment if you never receive your tickets. For more info, see www.travel-library.com/air-travel/consolidators.html.

CHARTER FLIGHTS

Charters are flights a tour operator contracts with an airline to fly extra passengers during peak season. Charter flights fly less frequently, make refunds particularly difficult, and are almost always fully booked, but they can also be cheaper. Discount clubs and fare brokers offer members savings on last-minute charter deals. Study contracts closely. Travelers Advantage, 7 Cambridge Dr., Trumbull, CT 06611, USA (☎877-259-2691; www.travelersadvantage.com; US$90 annual fee includes discounts and cheap flight directories) specializes in European travel.

BY TRAIN, BUS, OR CAR

BY TRAIN. Traversing 27 mi. under the sea, the **Chunnel** is undoubtedly the fastest, most convenient, and least scenic route from England to France. **Eurostar,** Eurostar House, Waterloo Station, London SE1 8SE (UK ☎08705 186 186, Belgium 02

528 28 28, France 08 92 35 35 39; www.eurostar.com) runs frequent trains between London and the continent. 10 to 28 trains per day run to 100 destinations including Paris (4hr., US$75-300, 2nd class), Disneyland Paris, Brussels, and Lille.

BY BUS. Both **Eurolines** and **Eurobus** provide bus-ferry combinations (see p. 23).

BY CAR. Eurotunnel (UK Customer relations, P.O. Box 2000, Folkestone, Kent CT18 8XY; www.eurotunnel.co.uk) shuttles cars and passengers between Kent and Nord-Pas-de-Calais. Return fares for vehicle and all passengers range from UK£283-317 with car. Same-day return costs UK£19-34, five-day return for either a car or a campervan UK£163-197. Book online or via phone. Travelers with cars can also look into sea crossings by ferry (see below).

BY BOAT

The fares below are **one-way** for **adult foot passengers** unless otherwise noted. Though standard return fares are usually just twice the one-way fare, **fixed-period returns** (usually within five days) are almost invariably cheaper. A directory of ferries in this region can be found at www.seaview.co.uk/ferries.html.

Brittany Ferries: (UK ☎08 703 66 53 33, France 08 25 82 88 28; www.brittany-ferries.com). **Plymouth** to **Roscoff, France** (6hr.; in summer 1-3 per day, off-season 1 per week; UK£20-58 or EUR€30-70). **Portsmouth** to **St-Malo** (9hr., 1-2 per day, EUR€60-100) and **Caen, France** (6hr, 1-3 per day, EUR€30-70). **Poole** to **Cherbourg** (4¼hr., 1-2 per day, EUR€30-70). **Cork** to **Roscoff** (14hr., Apr.-Sept. 1 per week, EUR€52-99).

Hoverspeed: (UK ☎08 702 40 80 70, France 0080 012 11 12 11; www.hoverspeed.co.uk.) **Dover** to **Calais** (1 hr., every 1-2hr., UK£15). **Newhaven** to **Dieppe, France** (2¼-4¼hr., 1-3 per day, UK£25).

Irish Ferries: (France ☎01 44 88 54 50, Ireland 1890 31 31 31, UK 08 705 17 17 17; www.irishferries.ie). **Rosslare** to **Cherbourg** and **Roscoff** (18hr., EUR€50-120, students EUR€40-96); and **Pembroke, UK** (3¾hr., UK£20-24, students UK£15-18). **Holyhead, UK** to **Dublin** (2-3hr., £26-30, students £20-23).

P&O Ferries: (UK ☎08 705 20 20 20; www.poferries.com). From **Portsmouth** to **Caen, Cherboug,** and **Le Havre.** From **Dover** to **Calais** (1¼hr., every 30min.-1hr., 30 per day; UK£17).

SeaFrance: (UK ☎08 705 71 17 11, France 08 03 04 40 45; www.seafrance.com). **Dover** to **Calais** (1½hr., 15 per day, UK£18).

GETTING AROUND FRANCE

France is blessed with a well-maintained and exceptionally complete network of roads, and traveling by car, though more expensive, can offer greater freedom and flexibility to explore the countryside than trains. Nevertheless, traveling by train is probably the most comfortable way to travel in France. France's network of high-speed and local trains connects all but the most minor towns.

 TRANSPORTATION LISTINGS: CENTER-OUT. Let's Go employs the "center-out" principle for transportation listings: for each town, we describe only how to reach towns of similar or greater importance. If you're in a big city, information on reaching neighboring small towns will be in the small towns themselves rather than in the big city.

BY PLANE

With most major cities linked by high-speed rail lines, taking a train can be just as fast as flying. The one exception is travel to **Corsica;** frequent air services from Nice, Marseille, and Paris to Ajaccio and Bastia compare competitively to the 10hr. ferry crossing. Expect to pay about US$150 round-trip from **Nice** to Corsica or US$200 from **Paris;** see **Corsica: Intercity Transportation,** p. 756, for details. Check www.ebookers.fr for deals on flying within France and in Europe.

BY TRAIN

Trains in France are generally comfortable, convenient, and reasonably swift, though not always safe (for **safety tips,** see p. 16). For long trips, make sure you are on the correct car, as trains sometimes split at crossroads. Towns listed in parentheses on European train schedules require a train switch at the town listed immediately before the parenthesis. Locate the *guichets* (ticket counters), the *quais* (platforms), and the *voies* (tracks), and you will be ready to roll. Terminals can be divided into *banlieue* (suburb) and the *grandes lignes* (bigger inter-city trains). Yellow *billetteries* (ticket machines) sell tickets for credit cards with PINs.

 VALIDATE = GREAT. Be sure to validate *(composter)* your ticket! Orange validation boxes lie around every station, and you must have it stamped with date and time by the machine before boarding the train.

French trains offer discounts of at least 25% and up to 50% on tickets for travelers under 26 with the **Carte 12-25** (€48, good for 1 year). Once in France, call SNCF at ☎ 08 36 35 35 35 or visit www.sncf.com for **train info** or **tickets.**

RESERVATIONS. While seat reservations are required only for selected trains, you are not guaranteed a seat without one (usually US$3-10). Consider reserving in advance during peak holiday and tourist seasons. Some railpasses require a **supplement** (US$10-50) or special fare for high-speed or high quality trains such as TGVs.

OVERNIGHT TRAINS. On night trains, you won't waste valuable daylight hours traveling and you can avoid the hassle and expense of staying at a hotel. However, the main drawbacks include discomfort, sleepless nights, and the lack of scenery. You can either sleep upright in your seat (for free) or pay for **couchettes** (berths) typically have four to six bunks per compartment (about US$20 per person); **sleepers** (beds) in private sleeping cars offer more privacy and comfort, but are considerably more expensive (US$40-150). If you are using a railpass, inspect train schedules to maximize the use of your pass: an overnight train or boat journey uses up only one of your travel days if it departs after 7pm.

SHOULD YOU BUY A RAILPASS? If you are planning to spend extensive time on trains, a railpass will probably be worth it. But in many cases, especially if you are under 26, point-to-point tickets may be cheaper. Eurail is **valid** in most of Western Europe, including France, though not in the UK. Standard **Eurailpasses,** valid for a given number of consecutive days, are best for those spending extensive time on trains every few days. **Flexipasses,** valid for any 10 or 15 (not necessarily consecutive) days within a two-month period, are more cost-effective for those traveling longer distances less frequently. **Youthpasses** and **Youth Flexipasses** provide parallel second-class perks for those under 26. It is best to purchase a pass before leaving. For prices and more info, contact student travel agencies like STA and Council (p. 20), **Rail Europe** (Canada ☎ 800-361-7245, UK 08 705 848 848, US 877-257-2887; www.raileurope.com), or **DER Travel Services** (☎ 800-782-2424; www.der.com).

BY CAR

Primers on French road signs and the French highway code can be found at www.travlang.com/signs and www.franceguide.com. **The Association for Safe International Travel (ASIRT)**, 11769 Gainsborough Rd., Potomac, MD 20854 (US ☎ 301-98-5252; www.asirt.org), can provide information on French road conditions and safety. Roadway conditions in France can also be obtained at ☎ 01 47 05 90 01.

Tolls in France are high. *Autoroutes* (marked on signs with an A) are tolled express highways. *Routes nationales* (marked with an N) and the smaller, more scenic *routes départementales* (marked with a D) do not have tolls.

RENTING

RENTAL AGENCIES

Local desk numbers are included in town listings; for home-country numbers, call your toll-free directory. To rent a car in France, you must be at least 21 years old, and there are typically extra fees for ages 21-24 (around €21 per day).

Auto Europe: ☎ 888-223-5555; www.autoeurope.com.

Avis: France ☎ 00 34 93 344 3715; www.avis.com.

Budget: international ☎ 800-472-3325; www.budgetrentacar.com.

Europe by Car: US ☎ 800-223-1516; www.europebycar.com.

Europcar: US and Canada ☎ 877-940-6900, France 01 55 66 83 00; www.europcar.com. Rents to ages 21-24 at many sites.

Hertz: US ☎ 800-654-3001, Canada 800-263-0600, UK 08708 415 161, Australia 613 9698 2555, France 33 1 41 919 525; www.hertz.com.

COSTS AND INSURANCE

Expect to pay at least US$200 per week, plus 19.6% tax, for a small car rental. 4WD and air conditioning each generally add US$7 per day. Many packages offer unlimited kilometers, while others allow 250km per day, then approximately US$0.35 per km after that. Cars with **automatic transmission** can cost up to US$150 a day more than stick shift. In many places, automatic transmission is hard to find in the first place—call ahead. Be sure to ask whether the price includes **insurance** against theft and collision and about coverage details. National chains often allow you to pick up in one city and drop off in another, sometimes for extra cost.

ON THE ROAD

It is mandatory for all passengers to wear seatbelts in the front of the car and in the backs—where seatbelts are possible. French police can fine any who do not comply with these laws. Check out **Itinéraire** (www.iti.fr) if you plan to drive in France; enter your start and end points, your desired speed and budget, and you will receive directions as well as estimates of driving time and toll and gas costs. **Gas stations** in most towns won't accept cash after 7pm, but they will take the French *Carte Bleue* (analogous to Visa). Petrol generally costs around €0.85-1.15 per liter. Diesel *(gazole)* fuel tends to be cheaper than unleaded *(essence sans plomb)*.

LAWS. Drivers in France stick to the far right lane, and the lanes further left are used for overtaking other cars. Roads range from very narrow one lane streets to wide highways known as *autoroutes*. The speed limit on tolled *autoroutes* is generally 130kph/81mph, and on non-toll *autoroutes*, it reads

DRIVING PRECAUTIONS. When traveling in the summer, bring substantial amounts of water (suggested 5L of **water** per person per day) for consumption and the radiator. For long distance travel, bring good maps and make sure tires are in good repair. Always carry: a **compass, car manual, spare tire** and **jack, jumper cables, extra oil, flares,** a **torch (flashlight),** and **heavy blankets.** Make sure you know how to **change a tire.** If you are stranded in deserted areas, **stay with your car;** if you wander off, trackers are less likely to find you.

around 110kph/68mph. However, in harsher weather conditions, the speed limit for tolled *autoroutes* is reduced to 110kph/68mph as well. By French law, cars entering a road from the right have the right of way over cars already on the road, even on major thoroughfares, so be prepared for cars to turn into the road ahead without warning. Inverted-triangle road signs with exclamation marks and text *"vous n'avez pas la priorité"* or *"cédez le passage"* indicate that the rule does not apply—a practice that generally holds on major roundabouts. A driver who flashes his highbeams wants to send the message: "I *am* going first," rather than "Go right ahead."

DRIVING PERMITS AND CAR INSURANCE

If you plan to drive a car while in France, you must be over 18 and have an **International Driving Permit (IDP),** though certain countries allow travelers to drive with a valid American or Canadian license for a limited number of months. It may be a good idea to get one anyway, in case you're in a situation (e.g. an accident or stranded in a small town) where the police do not know English; information on the IDP is printed in ten languages, including French. To apply, contact the national or local branch of your home country's automobile association.

BY BICYCLE

Cycling is a great (and often economic) way to see the countryside and reach sites not served by public transportation (see **Car-less and Carefree,** p. 462). Most towns offer bicycle rentals for the half-day or day, and some offer the possibility of longer rentals.

While avid cyclists, the French aren't always as keen on cycling safety. When renting a bike, you may have to insist on being given *un casque* (a helmet) and *un anti-vol* (a lock). Don't be afraid to stand your ground; even if helmets aren't legally required, most bike shops have a few in their back room waiting for "crazy" customers like you.

BY THUMB

Let's Go never recommends hitchhiking as a safe means of transportation, and none of the information presented here is intended to do so.

Let's Go strongly urges you to consider the risks before you choose to hitchhike *(faire l'autostop).* Hitching puts you at risk for theft, assault, sexual harassment, and more. If you're a woman traveling alone, don't hitch, period.

France is the hardest country in Europe in which to get a lift. If you do decide to chance it, remember that hitching (or even standing) on *autoroutes* is illegal and thumbing is tolerated only at rest stops, tollbooths, and highway entrance ramps.

KEEPING IN TOUCH

BY MAIL

SENDING MAIL HOME FROM FRANCE

Airmail is the best way to send mail home from France—write "airmail" and "par avion" on the front. **Surface mail** is by far the cheapest and slowest way to send mail. It takes one to two months to cross the Atlantic and one to three to cross the Pacific—good for heavy items you won't need for a while.

SENDING MAIL TO FRANCE

To ensure timely delivery, mark envelopes "par avion." In addition to the standard postage system whose rates are listed below, Federal Express (Australia ☎ 13 26 10, Canada and US 800-463-3339, Ireland 1800 535 800, New Zealand 0800 733 339, UK 0800 123 800; www.fedex.com) handles express mail services from most countries to France; for example, they can get a letter from New York to Paris in two days for US$50, and from London to Paris in two days for UK£16.

RECEIVING MAIL IN FRANCE

Mail can be sent Poste Restante (General Delivery) to be picked up by the addressee. We list post offices and postal codes and note when a town's Poste Restante code differs from its postal code. To pick up Poste Restante mail, bring a passport, €0.25 for periodicals, and €0.50 for packages. Mail is held for up to 15 days. Offices will not accept courier service deliveries (e.g. Federal Express) or anything requiring a signature for *Poste Restante*. Address letters in this format:

> BONAPARTE, Napoleon
> Poste Restante: [post office address]
> [5-digit postal code] [TOWN]
> FRANCE.
> HOLD.

BY TELEPHONE

TO PLACE INTERNATIONAL CALLS, DIAL:

1. The **international dialing prefix**. To call from **Australia,** dial 0011; **Canada** or the **US,** 011; **France, Ireland, New Zealand, UK,** 00.
2. The **country code** of the country you're calling. To call **Australia,** dial 61; **Canada** or **US,** 1; **Ireland,** 353; **New Zealand,** 64; the **UK,** 44; **France,** 33.
3. If the first digit is a zero (e.g., 020 for London), omit the zero when calling from abroad.
4. The **local number.**

CALLING HOME FROM FRANCE

A **calling card** is probably your cheapest bet, purchased from a service provider back home, though prepaid phone cards purchased in France also work (see below). Before settling on a calling card plan, be sure to research your options in order to pick the one that best fits both your needs and your destination. With calling cards, calls are billed collect or to your account. You can call collect without even possessing a company's card just by calling their access number and following the instructions. To call home with a calling card, contact the operator for your service provider in France by dialing the toll-free access number listed below in the second column.

COMPANY	TO OBTAIN A CARD, DIAL:	TO CALL ABROAD, DIAL:
AT&T (US)	800-364-9292	0 800 99 00 11
Canada Direct	800-561-8868	0 800 99 00 16 or 0 800 99 02 16
MCI (US)	800-777-5000	0 800 99 00 19
Telstra Australia	13 22 00	0 800 99 00 61

CALLING WITHIN FRANCE

Prepaid phone cards (*Télécarte*, available at newspaper kiosks, *tabacs*, etc.), which carry a certain amount of phone time depending on the card's denomination, are required at most French public phones. One kind (with an embedded chip) is inserted into the phone to place calls. Another kind of card comes with a Personal Identification Number (PIN) and a toll-free access number: with these cards, you call the access number and follow the directions on the card. *Télécartes* are available in 50-unit (€7.50) and 120-unit (€15) denominations; 1min. of a local call uses about one unit. Emergency numbers, directory information (☎12), and toll-free numbers (*numéros verts*) beginning with 0800 can be dialed without a card.

If the phone you use does not provide English commands, proceed with caution; French payphones are notoriously unforgiving. *Décrochez* means pick up; *patientez* means wait. Do not dial until you see *numérotez* or *composez*. *Raccrochez* means "hang up." To make another call, press the green button instead of hanging up. Rates tend to be high in the morning, intermediate in the evening, and low on Sundays and late at night.

Most American **cell phones** do not work in France. The international standard for cell phones is **GSM,** a system that began in Europe and has spread to much of the rest of the world. To make and receive calls in France you will need a **GSM-compatible phone** and a **SIM card,** a country-specific, thumbnail-sized chip that gives you a local phone number and plugs you into the network. Many SIM cards are **prepaid,** meaning that they come with calling time included and you don't need to sign up for a monthly service plan. Incoming calls are frequently free. Companies like **Cellular Abroad** (www.cellularabroad.com) rent cell phones that work in a variety of destinations around the world Check with your service provider to see if your phone's band can be switched to 900/1800, which will register your phone with one of the three French servers: **Bouygue** (www.bouygtel.com), **Itineris** (www.ifrance.com/binto/itineris.htm), or **France Télécom** (www.francetelecom.com/fr/). If you plan to stay in France for several months, buy a French cell phone. Incoming calls to cell phones are free (even from abroad), local calls are charged the local rate, and cell phone service is free. Cell phone calls are paid for with a **Mobicarte,** a prepaid card, available in denominations of €15, €25, or €35..

 GSM PHONES. Just having a GSM phone doesn't mean you're necessarily good to go when you travel abroad. The majority of American GSM phones operate on a different **frequency** (1900) than international phones (900/1800) and will not work abroad. Tri-band phones work on all three frequencies (900/1800/1900) and will operate in most of the world. As well, some GSM phones are **SIM-locked** and will only accept SIM cards from a single carrier. You'll need a **SIM-unlocked** phone to use a SIM card from a local carrier when you travel.

TIME DIFFERENCES

France is one hour ahead of **Greenwich Mean Time (GMT)**, 6hr. ahead of New York, 9hr. ahead of San Francisco, 10hr. behind Sydney (AUS) and 12hr. behind Aukland (NZ).

BY EMAIL AND INTERNET

Most major **post offices** and some branches now offer Internet access at special Cyberposte terminals. Rechargeable cards provide 1hr. of access for €7, €4 each subsequent hour. Most large towns in France have at least one **cybercafe;** listings can be found in the **Practical Information** section. Though in some places it's possible to forge a remote link with your home server, in most cases this is a much slower (and thus more expensive) option than taking advantage of free **web-based email accounts** (e.g., www.hotmail.com and www.yahoo.com). Increasingly, travelers find that taking their **laptop computers** on the road with them can be a convenient option for staying connected. Laptop users can call an Internet service provider via a modem using specific long-distance phone cards. They may also find Internet cafes that allow them to connect their laptops to the Internet. I

 TYPE LIKE HOME. Your accent may be flawless and your fanny-pack safely stowed, but your keystroke may still give you away. Tourists are hopelessly conspicuous at Internet cafes—they're the ones struggling with those peskily rearranged French keyboards. What most don't know is that pressing Alt or Ctrl and the left Shift button will often change a PC keyboard to English. If that doesn't work, ask the manager; many can configure keyboards to QWERTY.

ACCOMMODATIONS

HOSTELS

Many hostels are laid out dorm-style, with large single-sex rooms and bunk beds, though private rooms for two to four are becoming more common. They may have kitchens and utensils for your use, bike rentals, storage areas, breakfast and other meals, laundry, and Internet access. There can be drawbacks: some hostels close during certain daytime "lockout" hours, have a curfew, don't accept reservations, impose a maximum stay, or, less frequently, require that you do chores. A dorm bed in a French hostel averages around €8-15, a private room around €12-22.

> **A HOSTELER'S BILL OF RIGHTS.** There are certain standard features that we do not include in our hostel listings. Unless we state otherwise, you can expect that every hostel has no lockout, no curfew, a kitchen, free hot showers, some system of secure luggage storage, and no key deposit.

HOSTELLING INTERNATIONAL

Joining the youth hostel association in your own country (listed below) automatically grants you membership privileges in **Hostelling International (HI),** a federation of national hosteling associations. HI's umbrella organization's web page (www.hihostels.com) can be a great place to begin researching French hostels. Most student travel agencies (see p. 20) sell HI cards, as do all of the national hosteling organizations listed below. Prices listed below are for **one-year memberships** unless otherwise noted.

ESSENTIALS

Australian Youth Hostels Association (AYHA), 422 Kent St., Sydney, NSW 200 (☎02 9261 1111; www.yha.com.au). AUS$52, under 18 AUS$19.

Hostelling International-Canada (HI-C), 205 Catherine St. #400, Ottawa, ON K2P 1C3 (☎613-237-7884; www.hihostels.ca). CDN$35, under 18 free.

An Óige (Irish Youth Hostel Association), 61 Mountjoy St., Dublin 7 (☎830 4555; www.irelandyha.org). €20, under 18 €10.

Hostelling International Northern Ireland (HINI), 22 Donegall Rd., Belfast BT12 5JN (☎02890 31 54 35; www.hini.org.uk). UK£13, under 18 UK£6.

Youth Hostels Association of New Zealand (YHANZ), Level 1, Moorhouse City, 166 Moorhouse Ave., P.O. Box 436, Christchurch (☎0800 278 299 (NZ only) or 03 379 9970; www.yha.org.nz). NZ$40, under 18 free.

Scottish Youth Hostels Association (SYHA), 7 Glebe Cres., Stirling FK8 2JA (☎01786 89 14 00; www.syha.org.uk). UK£6, under 17 £2.50.

Youth Hostels Association (England and Wales), Trevelyan House, Dimple Rd., Matlock, Derbyshire DE4 3YH, UK (☎0870 770 8868; www.yha.org.uk). UK£13.50, under 18 UK£6.75.

Hostelling International-USA, 8401 Colesville Rd., Suite 600, Silver Spring, MD 20910 (☎301-495-1240; www.hiayh.org). US$28, under 18 free.

 BOOKING HOSTELS ONLINE. One of the easiest ways to ensure you've got a bed for the night is by reserving online. Click to the **Hostelworld** booking engine through **www.letsgo.com,** and you'll have access to bargain accommodations from Argentina to Zimbabwe with no added commission.

OTHER TYPES OF ACCOMMODATIONS

YMCAS AND YWCAS

Young Men's Christian Association (YMCA) lodgings are usually cheaper than a hotel but more expensive than a hostel. Many YMCAs accept women and families; some will not lodge those under 18 without parental permission.

World Alliance of YMCAs, 12 Clos Belmont, 1208 Geneva, Switzerland (☎41 22 849 5100; www.ymca.int), has listings of YMCAs worldwide.

HOTELS, GUESTHOUSES, AND PENSIONS

Two or more people traveling together can save money by staying in cheap hotels rather than hostels. All accredited hotels are ranked with between zero and four stars by the French government, according to various factors such as room size, facilities, and plumbing. Prices are generally per room. Expect to pay at least €18 for a single room and €25 for a double. If you want a room with twin beds, ask for *une chambre avec deux lits;* otherwise you may find yourself in *une chambre avec un grand lit.* French hotels must display a list of the prices of rooms, breakfast, and any residency tax on the back of each room's door. It is illegal to charge more than shown. Rooms in cheap hotels normally have no *en suite* facilities—even the sink is in the hall. Occasionally you must pay extra for a hot shower (€2.30-3.80). Some very cheap hotels have no washing facilities at all. Otherwise, rooms can come *avec WC* or *avec cabinet* (with sink and toilet), *avec douche* (with shower), and *avec salle de bain* (with full bathroom).

DE SÉJOUR. Applied to almost all hotel and hostel bills in France, x can be added from April to October, or only from June to September, ding on the city. It ranges from €0.20 to €1 per person per night, and host hotels include it in prices, some hotels and most hostels do not.

d in *Let's Go* are generally small, family-run establishments close to sights of interest. *Let's Go* doesn't list the budget chains like Hôtels Formule 1, Etap Hôtel, and Hôtels Première Classe, which can usually be found on the outskirts of town. These typically charge €27-31 for one- to three-person rooms, have rooms with sink, TV, hall showers, toilets, and telephones.

B&BS AND CHAMBRES D'HÔTE

For a cozy alternative to impersonal hotel rooms, B&Bs and *chambres d'hôte* (private homes with rooms available to travelers) range from the acceptable to the sublime. Rooms in B&Bs generally cost €30-45 per night in France. For more information, check out **InnFinder** (www.inncrawler.com), **InnSite** (www.innsite.com), **BedandBreakfast.com** (www.bedandbreakfast.com), or **Pamela Lanier's Bed & Breakfast Guide Online** (www.lanierbb.com).

 CHAMBRES D'HÔTE. France's *chambres d'hôte*, or bed and breakfasts, give you the chance to stay with local families. Organized through the **Gîtes de France**, *chambres d'hôte*, or *ferme auberges* if they are located on a working farm, provide an unparalleled glimpse into French culture. Many also offer *tables d'hôte*, where guests are served a full French-style dinner with the hosts. Check tourist offices for extensive listings of *chambres d'hôte* in the region.

UNIVERSITY DORMS

Many **colleges and universities** open their residence halls to travelers when school is not in session; some do so even during term-time. Getting a room may take a couple of phone calls and require advanced planning, but rates tend to be low.

HOME EXCHANGES AND HOSPITALITY CLUBS

Home exchange offers various types of homes (houses, apartments, villas, even castles in some cases), plus the opportunity to live like a native and to cut down on accommodation fees. For more information, contact HomeExchange.Com, P.O. Box 787, Hermosa Beach, CA 90254 USA (☎800-877-8723, fax 310-798-3865; www.homeexchange.com),or Intervac International Home Exchange (☎41 07 19 44 47 79; www.intervac.com). **Hospitality clubs** link their members with individuals or families abroad who are willing to host travelers for free or for a small fee to promote cultural exchange and general good karma. In exchange, members usually must be willing to host travelers in their own homes; a small membership fee may also be required. **GlobalFreeloaders.com** (www.globalfreeloaders.com) and **The Hospitality Club** (www.hospitalityclub.org) are good places to start. **Servas** (www.servas.org) is an established, more formal, peace-based organization, and requires a fee and an interview to join. As always, use common sense when planning to stay with or host someone you do not know. Check out **Worldwide Homestay Exchanges** (http://membres.lycos.fr/elcd/) for various listings in France.

LONG-TERM ACCOMMODATIONS

Travelers planning to stay in France for extended periods of time may find it most cost-effective to rent an **apartment**. A basic one-bedroom (or studio) apartment in Paris will run around €1500 per month. Besides the rent itself, prospective tenants usually are also required to front a security deposit (frequently one month's rent). Check out www.psrparis.com or www.france-apartements.com.

CAMPING AND THE OUTDOORS

The French are avid campers, but not in the sense you might be used to. After 3000 years of settled history, there is little wilderness in France. It is illegal to camp in public spaces or light your own fires. Forget those romantic dreams of roughing it and prepare to share organized *campings* (campsites) with hundreds of fellow campers. Sites generally cost around €3. Most campsites have toilets, showers, and electrical outlets, though often at extra expense (€1.50-6). The **Great Outdoor Recreation Pages** (www.gorp.com) provides excellent general information for travelers planning on camping or spending time in the outdoors.

 LEAVE NO TRACE. Let's Go encourages travelers to embrace the "Leave No Trace" ethic, minimizing their impact on natural environments and protecting them for future generations. Trekkers and wilderness enthusiasts should set up camp on durable surfaces, use cookstoves instead of campfires, bury human waste away from water supplies, bag trash and carry it out with them, and respect wildlife and natural objects. For more detailed information, contact the **Leave No Trace Center for Outdoor Ethics**, PO Box 997, Boulder, CO 80306, USA (☎800-332-4100 or 303-442-8222; www.lnt.org).

USEFUL PUBLICATIONS AND RESOURCES

A variety of publishing companies offer hiking guidebooks to meet the educational needs of novice or expert. For information about camping, hiking, and biking, write or call the publishers listed below to receive a free catalog.

Automobile Association, Contact Centre, Carr Ellison House, William Armstrong Drive, Newcastle-upon-Tyne NE4 7YA, UK. (☎0870 600 0371; www.theAA.com). Publishes Caravan and Camping Europe and Britain (both UK£8). **The Caravan Club,** East Grinstead House, East Grinstead, West Sussex, RH19 1UA, UK (☎44 01342 326 944; www.caravanclub.co.uk). For UK£30, members receive travel equipment discounts, maps, and a monthly magazine.

Sierra Club Books, 85 Second St., 2nd fl., San Francisco, CA 94105, USA (☎415-977-5500; www.sierraclub.org). Publishes general resource books on hiking and camping.

The Mountaineers Books, 1001 SW Klickitat Way, Suite 201, Seattle, WA 98134, USA (☎206-223-6303; www.mountaineersbooks.org). Boasts over 600 titles on hiking, biking, mountaineering, natural history, and conservation.

WILDERNESS SAFETY

THE GREAT OUTDOORS

Staying **warm, dry, and well-hydrated** is key to a happy and safe wilderness experience. For any hike, prepare yourself for an emergency by packing a first-aid kit, a reflector, a whistle, high energy food, extra water, raingear, a hat, and mittens. For warmth, wear wool or insulating synthetic materials designed for the outdoors.

ESSENTIALS

Cotton is a bad choice since it dries slowly and doesn't retain heat. Check **weather forecasts** often and pay attention to the skies when hiking, as weather patterns can change suddenly. Always let someone, either a friend, your hostel, a park ranger, or a local hiking organization, know when and where you are going hiking. Know your physical limits and do not attempt a hike beyond your ability. See **Safety and Health,** p. 15, for information on outdoor ailments and medical concerns.

CAMPING AND HIKING EQUIPMENT

WHAT TO BUY

Sleeping Bags: Most sleeping bags are rated by season; "summer" means 30-40°F (around 0°C) at night; "four-season" or "winter" often means below 0°F (-17°C). Bags are made of **down** (warm and light, but expensive and miserable when wet) or of **synthetic** material (heavy, durable, and warm when wet). Prices range US$50-250 for a summer synthetic to US$200-300 for a good down winter bag.

Tents: The best tents are free-standing (with their own frames and suspension systems), set up quickly, and only require staking in high winds. Low-profile dome tents are the best all-around. Worthy 2-person tents start at US$100, 4-person at US$160. Other good accessories are a **battery-operated lantern,** plastic **groundcloth,** and nylon **tarp.**

Backpacks: Internal-frame packs mold well to your back, keep a lower center of gravity, and flex adequately to allow you to hike difficult trails, while **external-frame packs** are more comfortable for long hikes over even terrain, as they carry weight higher and distribute it more evenly. Make sure your pack has a strong, padded hip-belt to transfer weight to your legs. Sturdy backpacks cost anywhere from US$125-420; your pack is an area where it doesn't pay to economize. Either buy a **rain cover** (US$10-20) or store all of your belongings in plastic bags inside your pack.

Boots: Be sure to wear hiking boots with good **ankle support.** They should fit snugly and comfortably over 1-2 pairs of **wool socks** and a pair of thin **liner socks.** Break in boots over several weeks before you go to spare yourself blisters.

Other Necessities: Synthetic layers, like those made of polypropylene or polyester, and a pile jacket will keep you warm even when wet. A **space blanket** (US$5-15) will help you to retain body heat and doubles as a groundcloth. Plastic **water bottles** are vital; look for shatter- and leak-resistant models. Carry **water-purification tablets** for when you can't boil water. You'll need a **camp stove** (the classic Coleman starts at US$50) and a propane-filled **fuel bottle** to operate it. Also bring a **first-aid kit, pocketknife, insect repellent,** and **waterproof matches** or a **lighter.**

WHERE TO BUY IT

A visit to a local camping or outdoors store will give you a good sense of the look and weight of certain items, but the options below offer better prices.

Campmor, 28 Parkway, P.O. Box 700, Upper Saddle River, NJ 07458, USA (US ☎888-226-7667; www.campmor.com).

Discount Camping, 880 Main North Rd., Pooraka, South Australia 5095, Australia (☎08 8262 3399; www.discountcamping.com.au).

Eastern Mountain Sports (EMS), 1 Vose Farm Rd., Peterborough, NH 03458, USA (☎888-463-6367; www.ems.com).

L.L. Bean, Freeport, ME 04033 (US and Canada ☎800-441-5713, UK ☎0800 891 297; www.llbean.com).

Mountain Designs, 51 Bishop St., Kelvin Grove, Queensland 4059, Australia (☎07 3856 2344; www.mountaindesigns.com).

ESSENTIALS

Recreational Equipment, Inc. (REI), Sumner, WA 98352, USA (US and Canada ☎800-426-4840, elsewhere 253-891-2500; www.rei.com).

YHA Adventure Shop, 19 High St., Staines, Middlesex, TW18 4QY, UK (☎1784 458625; www.yhaadventure.com).

CAMPERS AND RVS

Renting an RV costs more than hosteling but less than staying in hotels while renting a car. The convenience of bringing along your bedroom makes RVing an attractive option, especially for older travelers or families with children. **Auto Europe** (UK ☎0800 169 6414, US 888-223-5555; www.autoeurope.com) rents RVs in Paris.

SPECIFIC CONCERNS

SUSTAINABLE TRAVEL

As the number of travelers on the road continues to rise, the detrimental effect they can have on natural environments becomes an increasing concern. With this in mind, *Let's Go* promotes the philosophy of **sustainable travel.** Through a sensitivity to issues of ecology and sustainability, today's travelers can be a powerful force in preserving and restoring the places they visit.

Ecotourism, a rising trend in sustainable travel, focuses on the conservation of natural habitats and using them to build up the economy without exploitation or overdevelopment. Travelers can make a difference by doing advance research and by supporting organizations and establishments that pay attention to their impact on their natural surroundings and strive to be environmentally-friendly.

ESSENTIALS

RESPONSIBLE TRAVEL

The impact of tourism on the destinations you visit should not be underestimated. The choices you make during your trip can have potent effects on local communities—for better or for worse. Travelers who care about the destinations and environments they explore should become aware of the political, social, and cultural implications of the choices they make when they travel.

Community-based tourism aims to channel tourist finances into the local economy by emphasizing tours and cultural programs run by members of the host community and that often benefit disadvantaged groups. An excellent resource for info on community-based travel is *The Good Alternative Travel Guide* (UK£10), a project of **Tourism Concern** (☎020 7133 3330; www.tourismconcern.org.uk).

WOMEN TRAVELERS

Women exploring on their own inevitably face some additional safety concerns, but it's easy to be adventurous without taking undue risks. If you are concerned, consider staying in hostels which offer single rooms that lock from the inside or in religious organizations with rooms for women only. Stick to centrally located accommodations and avoid solitary late-night treks or metro rides.

Wearing a conspicuous **wedding band** sometimes helps to prevent unwanted overtures. Your best answer to verbal harassment is no answer at all; feigning deafness, sitting motionless, and staring straight ahead at nothing in particular will do a world of good that reactions usually don't achieve. The extremely persistent can sometimes be dissuaded by a firm, loud, and very public *"laissez-moi tranquille!"* ("go away!"). Don't hesitate to seek out a police officer or a passerby if you are being harassed. Consider carrying a whistle on your keychain. A self-defense course will both prepare you for a potential attack and raise your level of awareness of your surroundings (see **Self Defense,** p. 17).

GAY, LESBIAN, BISEXUAL, AND TRANSGENDERED TRAVELERS

France is fairly liberal toward gay, lesbian, bisexual, and transgendered (GLBT) travelers, and there are prominent gay and lesbian communities in Paris and in southern towns. There are still things that every traveler should keep in mind. To avoid hassles at airports and border crossings, transgendered travelers should make sure that all of their travel documents consistently report the same gender. Many countries (including the US, the UK, Canada, Ireland, Australia, and New Zealand) will amend the passports of post-operative transsexuals to reflect their true gender, although governments are generally less willing to amend documents for pre-operative transsexuals and other transgendered individuals. **Out and About** (www.planetout.com) offers a biweekly newsletter addressing travel concerns and a comprehensive site addressing gay travel concerns. The online newspaper **365gay.com** also has a travel section (www.365gay.com/travel/travelchannel.htm).

Gay's the Word, 66 Marchmont St., London WC1N 1AB, UK (☎20 7278 7654; www.gaystheword.co.uk). The UK's largest gay and lesbian bookshop. Mail-order service.

Giovanni's Room, 1145 Pine St., Philadelphia, PA 19107, USA (☎215-923-2960; www.queerbooks.com). An international lesbian/feminist and gay bookstore with mail-order service (carries many of the publications listed below).

International Lesbian and Gay Association (ILGA), 81 rue Marché-au-Charbon, B-1000 Brussels, Belgium (☎2 502 2471; www.ilga.org). Provides political information, such as homosexuality laws of individual countries.

FURTHER READING: GLBT TRAVEL.
Spartacus 2003-2004: International Gay Guide. Bruno Gmunder Verlag (US$33).
Ferrari Guides' Gay Travel A to Z, Ferrari Guides' Men's Travel in Your Pocket, Ferrari Guides' Women's Travel in Your Pocket, and *Ferrari Guides' Inn Places.* Ferrari Publications (US$16-20).
The Gay Vacation Guide: The Best Trips and How to Plan Them, Mark Chesnut. Kensington Books (US$15).

TRAVELERS WITH DISABILITIES

Those with disabilities should inform airlines and hotels of their disabilities when making reservations; some time may be needed to prepare special accommodations. Call ahead to restaurants, museums, and other facilities to find out if they are accessible. **Rail** is probably the most convenient form of travel for disabled travelers: many stations have ramps, and some trains have wheelchair lifts, special seating areas, and specially equipped toilets. SNCF offers wheelchair compartments on all TGV services. Ask for the *Guide du voyageur a mobilité réduit* at train stations for more details. Guide dog owners from Britain and Ireland might have trouble getting their dogs past quarantine on their return. Contact the PETS helpline at UK☎087 0241 1710 or www.defra.gov.uk for details. In Paris and other major cities, public transport has seats reserved for disabled passengers. Taxi drivers are obliged to take wheelchair-bound passengers and help them enter and exit the taxi. Hertz, Avis, and National car rental agencies have hand-controlled vehicles at some locations, which must be reserved at least 48hr. in advance.

USEFUL ORGANIZATIONS

Access Abroad, www.umabroad.umn.edu/access. A website devoted to making study abroad available to students with disabilities. The site is maintained by Disability Services Research and Training, University of Minnesota, University Gateway, Suite 180, 200 Oak St. SE, Minneapolis, MN 55455, USA (☎612-626-1333).

Accessible Journeys, 35 West Sellers Ave., Ridley Park, PA 19078, USA (☎800-846-4537; www.disabilitytravel.com). Designs tours for wheelchair users and slow walkers.

Directions Unlimited, 123 Green Ln., Bedford Hills, NY 10507, USA (☎800-533-5343). Books individual vacations for the physically disabled; not an info service.

Flying Wheels, 143 W. Bridge St., PO Box 382, Owatonna, MN 55060, USA (☎507-451-5005; www.flyingheelstravel.com). Specializes in escorted trips to Europe for people with physical disabilities; plans custom accessible trips worldwide.

Society for Accessible Travel & Hospitality (SATH), 347 Fifth Ave., #610, New York, NY 10016, USA (☎212-447-7284; www.sath.org). An advocacy group that publishes free online travel information and the travel magazine *OPEN WORLD* (annual subscription US$13, free for members). Annual membership US$45, students and seniors US$30.

MINORITY TRAVELERS

Like much of Europe, France has experienced a wave of immigration from former colonies in the past few decades. North Africans compose the greatest part of the immigrants, at over a million, followed by West Africans and Vietnamese. Many of the immigrants are uneducated and face discrimination, causing poverty and crime in the predominately immigrant inner cities. In turn, there has been a surge in support for the far-right National Front party and its cry, *"La France pour les français."* Anyone who might be taken for **North African** may encounter verbal abuse and is more likely than other travelers to be stopped and questioned by the police. Racism is especially prevalent in the Southeast. The following organizations can give you advice and help in the event of an encounter with racism.

S.O.S. Racisme, 51 av. de Flandre, 75019 Paris (☎01 40 35 36 55; www.sos-racisme.org). Provides legal services and helps negotiate with police.

MRAP (Mouvement contre le racisme et pour l'amitié entre les peuples), 43 bd. Magenta, 75010 Paris (☎01 53 38 99 99; www.mrap.asso.fr). Handles immigration issues; monitors publications and propaganda for racism.

DIETARY CONCERNS

Those with special dietary requirements may feel left behind in France. **Vegetarians** will find dining out difficult and **vegans** will find it nearly impossible. The travel section of the The Vegetarian Resource Group's website, at www.vrg.org/travel, has comprehensive info to help vegetarians and vegans traveling abroad. For more information, visit your local bookstore or health food store, and consult *The Vegetarian Traveler: Where to Stay if You're Vegetarian, Vegan, Environmentally Sensitive*, by Jed and Susan Civic (Larson Publications; US $16), *Vegetarian France* (US $12; www.vegetarianguides.com), www.vegdining.com, www.happycow.net, and www.vegetariansabroad.com.

Kosher food does exist in France, which has one of Western Europe's largest Jewish populations, but finding it may prove difficult, particularly in rural regions. Travelers who keep kosher should contact synagogues in larger cities for information on kosher restaurants. Your own synagogue or college Hillel should have access to lists of Jewish institutions internationally. Check out http://shamash.org/kosher/ for more information. If you are strict in your observance, you may have to prepare your own food on the road. A good resource is the *Jewish Travel Guide*, edited by Michael Zaidner (Vallentine Mitchell; US$18). Travelers looking for halal restaurants may find www.zabihah.com a useful resource.

OTHER RESOURCES

Let's Go tries to cover all aspects of budget travel, but we can't put *everything* in our guides. Listed below are books and websites that can serve as jumping-off points for your own research.

USEFUL PUBLICATIONS

We like these books and think you might as well.

Fragile Glory: A Portrait of France and the French, Richard Bernstein. Plume, 1991 (US$15). A witty look at France by the former *New York Times* Paris bureau chief.

Portraits of France, Robert Daley. Little, Brown & Co., 1991 (US$23). An engaging, informed collection of essays on France and the French, organized by region.

Culture Shock! France: A Guide To Customs and Etiquette, Sally Adamson Taylor. Graphic Arts Center Publishing Company, 1991 (US$14). Tips and warnings.

Merde! The Real French You Were Never Taught at School, Genevieve, Michael Heath. Fireside, 1998 ($9). Lots of gutter slang and a collection of very dirty things to say.

French or Foe? Getting the Most Out of Visiting, Living and Working in France, Polly Platt. Distribooks Intl., 1998 (US$17). A popular guide to getting by in France.

A Traveller's Wine Guide to France, Christopher Fielden. Interlink Publishing Group, 1999 (US$20). Exactly what it says it is, by a well-known oenophile.

Traveling Solo, Eleanor Berman. Globe Pequot Press, 2003 (US$18).

ESSENTIALS

WORLD WIDE WEB

Listed here are some regional and travel-related sites to start off your surfing; other relevant web sites are listed throughout the book. Because website turnover is high, use search engines (such as www.google.com) to strike out on your own.

 WWW.LETSGO.COM Our freshly redesigned website features extensive content from our guides; community forums where travelers can connect with each other and ask questions or advice—as well as share stories and tips; and expanded resources to help you plan your trip. Visit us soon to browse by destination, find information about ordering our titles, and sign up for our e-newsletter!

Maison de la France: www.francetourism.com, the French government's site for tourists. Tips on everything from accommodations to smoking laws. English version.

Youth Tourism: www.franceguide.com, the official site of the French Government Tourist Office. For youth planning long stays in France. Mostly in English.

France Diplomatie: www.france.diplomatie.fr/ is the site of the Department of Foreign Affairs. Info on visas and current affairs. Mostly in English.

Secretariat for Tourism: www.tourisme.gouv.fr has a number of government documents about French tourism; links to all French tourist authorities. In French.

Tourism in France: www.tourisme.fr has info in French and mildly amusing English.

Nomade: www.nomade.fr is a popular French search engine.

TF1: www.tf1.fr is the home page of France's most popular TV station.

Météo-France: www.meteo.fr has 2-day weather forecasts and maps. In French.

THE ART OF TRAVEL

How to See the World: www.artoftravel.com. A compendium of great travel tips, from cheap flights to self defense to interacting with local culture.

Solo Travelers: www.travelaloneandloveit.com. Also Connecting: Solo Travel Network, 689 Park Rd., Unit 6, Gibsons, BC V0N 1V7, Canada (☎604-886-9099; www.cstn.org; membership US$28-45).

ESSENTIALS

Travel Library: www.travel-library.com. A fantastic set of links for general information and personal travelogues.

Backpacker's Ultimate Guide: www.bugeurope.com. Tips on packing, transportation, and where to go. Also tons of country-specific travel information.

Travel Intelligence: www.travelintelligence.net. A large collection of travel writing by distinguished travel writers.

World Hum: www.worldhum.com. An independently produced collection of "travel dispatches from a shrinking planet."

BootsnAll.com: www.bootsnall.com. Numerous resources for independent travelers, from planning your trip to reporting on it when you get back.

INFORMATION ON FRANCE

CIA World Factbook: www.odci.gov/cia/publications/factbook/index.html. Tons of vital statistics on (your country's) geography, government, economy, and people.

Geographia: www.geographia.com. Highlights, culture, and people of France.

Atevo Travel: www.atevo.com/guides/destinations. Detailed introductions, travel tips, and suggested itineraries.

World Travel Guide: www.travel-guides.com. Helpful practical info.

TravelPage: www.travelpage.com. Links to official tourist office sites in France.

PlanetRider: www.planetrider.com. A subjective list of links to the "best" websites covering the culture and tourist attractions of France.

A-Z of Tourism: www.a-zoftourism.com. Everything from reservations to French driving laws.

ESSENTIALS

LIFE AND TIMES

LAND

France is a 543,965km² hexagonal country: to the southwest, the **Pyrenees mountains** form a frontier with Spain, to the east the snow-capped peaks of the **Alps** and **Jura** separate France from Italy and Switzerland, and just above the Jura, the **Rhine River** marks the divide between France and Germany. France's only artificial border is with Belgium, in the northeast corner of the country. The **English Channel** *(La Manche)* keeps Normandy's chalky cliffs at a 35km distance from England at its narrowest point. The **Atlantic Ocean** laps upon beaches of fine sand in the west and the **Mediterranean** greets the pebbly beaches of the south. The interior of France is primarily characterized by low-lying plains and river valleys, with the exception of the rugged **Massif Central** plateau in the southeast, a landscape of extinct volcanoes, deep gorges, and stalagmites. **Corsica,** France's Mediterranean island territory, is 170km off the French coast. Its 8681km² are mostly mountainous, with craggy rocks and cliffs to the west and a lagoon-spotted east coast loved by hikers from the French mainland. For more information on French national parks, check out www.parcsnationaux-fr.com; for more on French environmental concerns, see the French Institute for the Environment's website: www.ifen.fr.

HISTORY

FROM GAULS TO GOTHS

27,000 years have passed since advanced hominids roamed **Périgord,** but in 1868 the skull of one of these now-famous people was unearthed at Cro-Magnon. Ten thousand years ago, his descendants left their mark on history in the graffiti-filled caves of the **Dordogne Valley,** and by 4500 BC Neolithic peoples were carving huge stone monuments *(menhirs)* at **Carnac.** These mysterious creations were admired by the Celtic **Gauls,** who arrived from the east around 600 BC. Gauls traded and co-existed peacefully with the Greek colonists who settled during the seventh century BC at Massilia (modern day **Marseille**). Rome made **Provence** a province in 125 BC and quickly conquered the rest of the south. Fierce resistance from France's northern Gauls kept the Romans out of their territory until **Julius Caesar**'s victory at Alesia in 52 BC. By the time Rome itself fell in AD 476, Gaul had suffered Germanic invasions for centuries. While many of the Gothic tribes plundered and passed on, the **Franks** eventually dominated Gaul. The Frankish **Clovis** founded the Merovingian dynasty and was baptized a Christian in AD 507. His empire was succeeded by the grander Carolingian dynasty of **Charlemagne.**

FRANCE AND ENGLAND DUKE IT OUT

After the fall of the Carolingian dynasty, the noble-elected **Hugh Capet** quickly consolidated power. His descendant, **Louis VII,** set off 500 years of fighting between France and England by making the fatal error of not signing a prenuptial agreement. When his ex-queen **Eleanor of Aquitaine** married into the English Plantagenêt dynasty in the 12th century, a broad swath of land stretching from the Channel to the Pyrenees became English territory. The plot thickened in the 14th century, when England's **Edward III** tried to claim the throne of France. He landed his troops in Normandy, triggering the **Hundred Years' War** in 1328. The English crowned their own **Henri VI** king of France 90 years later, but salvation for France soon arrived in the form of a 17-year-old peasant girl— **Joan of Arc,** who won a string of victories and turned the tides before being captured and burned at the stake in 1430.

RELIGIOUS DEVOTION AND WAR

The Middle Ages left an impressive legacy of cathedrals, convents, and monasteries, including the haunting isle of **Mont-St-Michel** (p. 274). **Pope Innocent II** proclaimed the first Crusade from **Clermont** (p. 458) to wrest Jerusalem from the Saracens. Dismayed by the Church's growing power, king **Philip IV** arrested **Pope Boniface VIII** at the opening of the 14th century. Old Boniface died after the arrest, and his French successor, **Pope Clement V,** moved the pope's court from Rome to Church-owned **Avignon** (p. 661), where it stayed until 1377.

In the 16th century, religious conflict between **Huguenots** (French Protestants) and **Catholics** instigated the **Wars of Religion.** The fervently Catholic queen **Catherine de Médicis** orchestrated a marriage between her daughter and the Huguenot **Henri de Navarre** in 1572. The seemingly peaceful political move turned out to be a deadly trap. Two thousand Huguenots who came to Paris to celebrate their wedding were slaughtered in the **St-Bartholomew's Day Massacre.** Henri survived, quickly converted to Catholicism, and ascended the throne as the first **Bourbon** monarch. In 1598 he issued the **Edict of Nantes,** granting tolerance for French Protestants.

BOURBON ON THE ROCKS

The French Bourbon monarchy reached the height of its power and extravagance in the 17th century. **Louis XIII**'s capable and ruthless minister, **Cardinal Richelieu,** consolidated political power in the hands of the monarchy. They were succeeded in 1642 by another cardinal-and-king combo, **Cardinal Mazarin** and the five-year-old **Louis XIV.** By 1661, however, the 24-year-old monarch had decided he was ready to rule alone. Not known for his modesty, Louis styled himself as the **Sun King** and took the motto *"l'état, c'est moi"* (I am the state).

Financial problems (and resentment) were brewing, however. When **Louis XVI** inherited the throne in 1774, peasants blamed the soon-to-be-**Old Regime** for their mounting debts. In 1789, Louis XVI called a last-resort meeting of delegates from the three classes of society. The bourgeois-dominated **Third Estate** soon broke away and proclaimed itself the **National Assembly.** In the tennis courts of Versailles they swore the **Tennis Court Oath,** promising to draft a new constitution. The news of these radical political moves spurred on the bourgeois and working-class activists in Paris, who took action against one of its biggest symbols and stormed the **Bastille** on July 14th. With this attack they freed political prisoners and seized arms for themselves. Despite the Revolutionary principles of *liberté, égalité,* and *fraternité* and the Assembly's recently authored **Declaration of the Rights of Man,** events in this unprecedented, volatile political system soon turned ugly. In 1793, after the people had overthrown the monarchy and officially replaced it with the **First Republic,** the radical **Jacobin** faction, led by **Maximilien Robespierre,** took over the Convention and guillotined the King and his Queen, **Marie-Antoinette.** The liberal slaughter of the **Reign of Terror** finally ended when Robespierre met with the guillotine in 1794, at which point power was entrusted to a five-man Directory.

THE LITTLE DICTATOR

After overthrowing the Directory in 1799, the young general **Napoleon Bonaparte** and a handful of supporters established the Consulate. Time slowly revealed that this new government was essentially a dictatorship; Napoleon was dubbed First Consul for life in 1802 and crowned himself **Emperor** in 1804. Domestically, his **Napoleonic Code** centralized government control and streamlined France (and later much of Europe) into a more efficient state, yet it also regressed by re-establishing slavery and limiting the legal rights of women. Napoleon constantly sought more power for his newfound empire. After his army crushed the Austrians, Prussians, and Russians, only Britain was left undefeated, safe in her island refuge after Horatio Nelson's 1807 naval victory at **Trafalgar**. In 1812, during a disastrous campaign to reign in a rebellious tsar, Napoleon's army of 700,000 captured Moscow only to find it deserted, with winter fast approaching. Barely 200,000 of his troops survived the freezing trek home. A war-weary nation turned against Napoleon. In return for abdicating in 1814, he was given the Mediterranean island of **Elba**, and the monarchy was reinstated under **Louis XVIII**, of the Bourbon line. In a final flourish, Napoleon abandoned Elba and landed with a small party at Cannes in 1815. He marched north, once again rallying France behind him as the king fled to England. The ensuing **Hundred Days** rule ended on the field of **Waterloo** in Flanders, where the **Duke of Wellington** triumphed. Napoleon was banished to **St-Helena** in the south Atlantic, where he died in 1821.

SAY YOU WANT A REVOLUTION

The **Bourbon Restoration** was quick to step into the power vacuum left by Napoleon but never regained their old power. When **Charles X** restricted the press and limited the electorate, the people spoke up. Following the **July Revolution of 1830,** Charles, remembering the fate of his brother, abdicated quickly, and a **constitutional monarchy** was created under a new Orléan regime, "bourgeois king" **Louis-Philippe.**

The industrialization of France created a class of urban poor receptive to the new ideas of socialism. They provided the muscle behind the **February Revolution of 1848,** which culminated in the declaration of the **Second Republic** and the adoption of universal male suffrage. The people elected Louis Napoleon, nephew of Napoleon Bonaparte, as their president. Louis Napoleon later seized power in an 1851 coup and declared himself **Emperor Napoleon III.** During his reign, France was economically revived. Civil engineer **Baron Haussmann** revamped Paris to its modern grandeur by sweeping through webs of narrow alleys with broad boulevards.

Across the Rhine, **Bismarck** baited France into declaring war. With German armies advancing, Parisian deputies declared the **Third Republic.** Finally capitulating just as its citizens were reduced to eating rats, France was forced to give up the Alsace-Lorraine territory and pay an exorbitant occupation indemnity. The Parisian mob revolted and declared the **Commune,** which was quickly crushed as over 10,000 *communards* died under the rifles of French troops. The Third Republic was further undermined by the **Dreyfus Affair.** In search of a scapegoat for the leaking of military documents to the rival Germans, Dreyfus, a Jewish captain in the French army, was convicted in 1894 on unfounded treason charges, igniting a decade of heated controversy; Dreyfus was finally pardoned in 1904.

THE TWO GREAT WARS

Germany's 1871 unification changed the balance of power in Europe. France formed the **Triple Entente** with Britain and czarist Russia, while Germany, Italy, and the Austro-Hungarian Empire formed the **Triple Alliance.** When **World War I** erupted in 1914, German armies rapidly advanced on France (again), but a stalemate developed as armies dug trenches along the country's length. France and her allies triumphed in 1918, after US troops arrived. Devastated by four years of fighting and the loss of 1.3 million men, France demanded crippling reparations from Germany.

During the depression of the 1930s, tensions between Fascists and Socialists, bourgeois and workers, left France ill-equipped to deal with the dangers of the massive mobilization of **Adolf Hitler**'s Germany. The German invasion of Poland in 1939 ignited **World War II.** In May 1940, the Germans swept through Belgium and into France, which capitulated in June. The north fell under German occupation, while a puppet state in the south, led by WWI hero **Maréchal Pétain,** ruled from **Vichy** (p. 473). Escaped French forces operated under the command of the French government-in-exile, under **General Charles de Gaulle.** On August 25th, 1944, De Gaulle insisted that French troops lead the **liberation of Paris.**

FOURTH REPUBLIC AND POST-COLONIAL FRANCE

The **Fourth Republic** was proclaimed in 1944 under the leadership of de Gaulle. In the next two years, his vision of a restructured society led to female suffrage and nationalized energy companies. He stepped down in 1946, unable to adapt to the deadlock of democratic politics. The next 14 years saw 25 governments. Meanwhile, between 1945 and 1975, France went through a period called the **Glorious Thirties,** during which the French began to embrace technology as the formerly agriculture-based economy became urbanized and industrialized.

The end of WWII signaled great change in the quickly disintegrating 19th-century **colonial empire.** The 1954 liberation of **Dien Bien Phu** in Vietnam helped to mobilize the colonized peoples of France's other protectorates and colonies. **Morocco** and **Tunisia** gained independence in 1956, followed by **Mali, Senegal,** and the **Ivory Coast** in 1960. But France drew the line when Algerian nationalists moved for independence, and the result was one of the ugliest processes of decolonization in modern history. De Gaulle was voted into power in 1958 to deal with the impending crisis. At a peaceful demonstration in Paris against curfew restrictions in 1961, police opened fire on the largely North African crowd, killing hundreds and dumping their bodies into the Seine. In the next year, with a new **constitution** in hand, France declared itself the **Fifth Republic.** A 1962 referendum from the new government reluctantly granted independence to Algeria, the last existing French colony, which finally ended years of brutal conflict that had begun in 1954.

In **May 1968,** what started as a student protest rapidly became a full-scale revolt as 10 million state workers went on strike in support of social reform. The government responded by deploying tank and commando units into the city. Another revolution was averted only with the Gaullists' return, but the aging General had lost his magic touch, however, and he resigned following a referendum defeat in 1969.

THE 80S, 90S, AND TODAY

By 1981, Socialist **François Mitterrand** took over the presidency and the Socialists gained a majority in the National Assembly. They raised the minimum wage and began widespread nationalization, but the international climate could not support a socialist economy. In the face of the Socialist loss in the 1986 elections, Mitterrand appointed conservative **Jacques Chirac** as Prime Minister.

At the same time, the **far right** began to flourish under the leadership of **Jean-Marie Le Pen.** He formed the **Front National (FN)** on an anti-immigration platform with racist overtones, targeting the new working class from North Africa and other former colonies. In the 1986 parliamentary elections, the FN picked up 10% of the vote by blaming unemployment on immigrants. Meanwhile, in an unprecedented power-sharing relationship known as "cohabitation," Mitterrand withdrew to control foreign affairs, allowing Chirac to assume domestic power. In 1995, Mitterrand chose not to run again, and Chirac was elected president. Denounced around the globe for conducting underground **nuclear weapons tests** in the South Pacific, and facing a 12.2% unemployment rate, Chirac faced a difficult year. In 1998, Chirac was forced to accept **Lionel Jospin,** head of the Socialist majority, as Prime Minister. June 2002 marked the end of cohabitation between president and prime minister, as Chirac appointed conservative **Jean-Pierre Raffarin.**

One of the most important challenges in the 1980s and 1990s has been the question of European integration (see **One Europe,** p. 9). Throughout European economic integration, Franco-German cooperation has played a central role. In early 2003, France and Germany celebrated the anniversary of a postwar friendship treaty. They joined with Russia to voice opposition to the US-led **war with Iraq,** insisting on the use of political and diplomatic means to disarm Iraq, leading to a breach in US-France relations. The friendship between the one-time allies seems to be redeveloping, notably at Evian's June 2003 **G-8 summit.**

The terrorist attacks of September 11 and the war in Iraq have been damaging to France's economy, and in particular the tourism and airline industries. The situation was not helped by the months-long strikes that occurred in protest of Raffarin's proposed state pension reform in spring and summer 2003.

One of the biggest educational and political flashpoints of the last ten years has been the wearing of Muslim headscarves *(hijab)* in public schools; Jacques Chirac approved this law to be put into effect in September 2004. This issue has marked a point of controversy throughout the nation, with some viewing it as the infiltration of far-right discrimination towards Muslim immigrants into educational policy while others maintain that it is meant to maintain the long-standing secular tradition of French public education (see **Headscarf Controversy,** right).

DEMOGRAPHICS

ETHNIC MINORITIES

The influx of immigrants from France's former colonies, particularly the West Indies and Africa, has somewhat offset the country's perpetually low birth rate. Of these, the largest number of minorities trace their roots to Algeria. Historically, France has been fairly welcoming of immigrants, although ethnic minorities still face some hostility. The popularity of far-right nationalist **Jean-Marie Le Pen,** who edged out Socialist **Lionel Jospin** in the 2002 preliminary presidential election, is the most visible sign of negative attitudes toward immigrants. After Le Pen's success in the preliminary, however, voters turned out in droves to assure his sound defeat in the final run-off against Chirac. Jospin's 1998 law on immigration allows foreign scientists and scholars more relaxed conditions of entry into France.

RELIGIOUS MINORITIES

Overwhelmingly Roman Catholic France hasn't always been an accepting environment for religious minorities. An alarming wave of anti-Semitic violence flared up in 2002 in response to intensification of the Israel-Palestine conflict in the Middle

East: synagogues in Marseille, Lyon, and Paris were firebombed, and street fighting broke out as well. Though the plight of the Palestinians triggered this backlash, religious and racial tension also surrounds Muslim citizens in France.

GLBT

Homophobia remains a problem in France, but the number of reported hate crimes based on sexual orientation or gender identity has decreased in recent years. French law prohibits discrimination based on sexual orientation in the workplace, and some French courts have allowed gender reassignment on birth registers. In 1999, France became the first traditionally Catholic country in the world to legally recognize homosexual unions, in the **Pacte Civil de Solidarité,** known by its acronym **PACS,** although gay activists still struggle to attain the same rights to adoption and reproductive technologies that married couples enjoy.

WOMEN

France has progressive legislation criminalizing sexual harassment; nevertheless, women continue to face problems in the workplace and elsewhere. The office of the Prime Minister has set up a watchdog group, *L'Observatoire de la parité entre les femmes and les hommes* to monitor gender equality in the government and in the business world.

CULTURE

FOOD AND DRINK

De Gaulle complained that no nation with 400 types of cheese could ever be united; watch a pack of ravenous French shoppers tearing through a *fromagerie* and you'll agree. Though *le fast-food* has recently invaded France, many people still shop daily for their ingredients, and restaurants follow the traditional order of courses.

MEALS. The French ease into their day with a light breakfast *(le petit déjeuner)*, consisting largely of bread *(le pain)* or sometimes croissants plus an espresso with hot milk *(café au lait)* or a hot chocolate *(le chocolat)*. The largest meal is lunch *(le déjeuner)* between noon and 2pm. Dinner *(le dîner)* begins fairly late. A complete French meal includes an aperitif, an *entrée* (appetizer), a *plat* (main

IN RECENT NEWS

HEADSCARF CONTROVERSY

In February 2004, an overwhelming majority in the French legislature voted to ban "overt religious symbols" in public schools. While the law includes Jewish *yarmulkes* and large Christian crosses, public attention has focused on the *hijab,* or Muslim headscarf. While the issue is not a new one—girls had been expelled for refusing to remove headscarves as early as the late 80s—the new law has ignited controversy, with many arguing that the law specifically discriminates against France's already marginalized Muslim community—the largest in Europe.

The law continues France's fervently maintained tradition of secularism and, according to President Chirac, is designed not only to maintain separation of church and state, but to bring Muslims into mainstream French culture. Opponents counter that driving girls from public schools into religious private schools, where the ban won't apply, will do little to aid cultural integration.

Surveys have shown that a large majority of the French, as well as 40-50% of Muslim women, support the ban. Some officials have suggested compromises like discreet bandanas, but such alternatives haven't satisfied those who claim the law infringes on civil liberties. The ban is set to be re-evaluated in 2005.

Regional Identities in Modern France

Athough the average traveler may catch a glimpse of other corners of France, Paris, that luminous center of the French solar system, can often blind us to the rest of the country. France is one of the most centralized countries in the West, both politically and culturally, and its notorious defense of its language has only reinforced the image of a unified French culture. Yet even before the recent wave of immigration, France has dealt with cultural diversity in its territory. In fact, the French State was unified by annexing several ethnically diverse territories: parts of Catalonia and the Basque Country in the South, the ever volatile island of Corsica in the Mediterranean, the rest of Southern France (which goes by the name of Occitania), the Germanic regions of Alsace and part of Lorraine, Celtic Brittany, and the Flemish northern tip of France. Until this last century, these regions were like foreign countries on French soil.

It was the Revolution that replaced the hodgepodge of these semi-autonomous provinces with *départements*, administrative subdivisions operating under one law for all. Opponents of the Revolution saw the provinces as threats. In 1793, Bertrand Barère famously declared "Federalism and superstition speak Lower Breton; emigration and hatred of the Republic speak German [Alsatian]; the counter-revolution speaks Italian [Corsican]; and fanaticism speaks Basque." The project of unifying French language and culture was never given much support, however, until public schooling became mandatory in the 1880s. In many schools, children caught speaking their local tongues were punished with a *symbole*, usually a dunce cap or scarlet letter. In return, however, schools assigned readings on rural France like the enduring *Le Tour de la France par deux enfants*, a picaresque journey around France by two Alsatian boys (and the inspiration for today's famous nationwide bike race). It was only after WWII that France was fully synchronized by mass media, consumerism, and the decline of traditional peasantry. Travel around France today, and you will see the same stores, television, post offices, and phone booths everywhere, and you will rarely hear a peep of local parlance, which is spoken mostly in the home and by the elderly, when it is still spoken at all.

Yet, local identity has not, for all that, disappeared. Rather, it has made a startling comeback since the 1960s. Most conspicuously, Corsican t rorist attacks (which often involve criminal corr tion as much as autonomist movements) have be making front-page news for years. There are al many quieter manifestations of local ident around France. In 1986, regional governmei were elected for the first time since the Revoluti and regional languages have entered some sch curricula, though not without controver Whereas the French State had once gone so far to prohibit the use of non-French names on bii certificates, ethnic names like Yann (the Bret equivalent of the French Jean or the English Jo have caught on strong. In the 1980s and 199 French television suddenly discovered what otl countries had long known, that local news w extremely popular, a rather belated realization c sidering that the regional newspapers like *Oue France* and *Les Dernières Nouvelles d'Alsa* had long outsold the national press. At the movi every year produces several paeans to commur and rural life, such as the many film adaptations the mid-twentieth century regional novelist Mar Pagnol (*Jean de Florette, My Mother's Castl* And of course, tourists are treated to a parade folkloric festivals, dance, and souvenirs.

Anyone looking for some elusive "authent ity" should be skeptical, however, for local c ture ain't what it used to be. If you get a chan to attend a Breton village festival, the drunk peasant might be a Belgian professor who aba doned his career for the pastoral life. After su radical transformation as France has expe enced, even the most seemingly authen images of regional culture and country life— fact, especially those—are little more th show. This is not to say, however, that all d plays of local difference and identity are me sham. Vestiges of regional culture combine c atively with other cultures these days, as in regionalist rap or world music of the Celtic m stro Alan Stivell or the Southern bands The Fa ulous Troubadours, Massilia Sound System, a Zebda. And of course, as any traveler will see, two places are exactly alike. Local variatic persist, and the French continue to nurture intimate bond to community and place.

Matthew Lazen has taught film, literature, and history at Harvard University. He is currently revising his dissertation on regional cultures in postmodern France for publication.

course), salad, cheese, dessert, fruit, coffee, and a *digéstif* (after-dinner drink). The most common and most popular aperitifs are *kir*, white wine with sweet *cassis* (black currant liqueur), and *pastis*, a potent licorice-flavored liqueur.

MENUS. Most restaurants offer a *menu à prix fixe* (fixed-price meal) that costs less than ordering a la carte. The *menu* may include an appetizer, *plat*, *fromage* (cheese), and dessert. The *formule* is a cheaper, two-course version. Order sparkling water *(eau pétillante* or *eau gazeuse)* or flat mineral water *(eau plate); for a pitcher of tap water, ask for *une carafe d'eau*. Finish the meal with espresso *(un café).* When *boisson comprise* is written on the menu, you are entitled to a free drink (usually wine) with the meal. Vegetarians will probably have the best luck at *crêperies*, ethnic restaurants, and places catering to a younger crowd.

GROCERIES. For an occasional €15 spree you can have a marvelous meal, but it's easy to assemble inexpensive meals yourself with a ration of cheese, *pâté*, wine, and bread. Start with bread from the *boulangerie* (bakery), and then proceed to the *charcuterie* for *pâté*, *saucisson* (hard salami), and *jambon* (ham), or buy a freshly roasted chicken from the *boucherie* (butcher). If you want someone else to do the work, *boulangeries* often sell fresh sandwiches. *Pâtisseries* will sate nearly any sweet tooth with treats ranging from candy to ice cream to pastries.

 THE BEST BAKERS. France is packed with *boulangeries* and *pâtisseries*—so many, in fact, that it's hard to tell the good from the bad. Look for a bakery with a blue sticker featuring a chef's hat, which declares the house a *pâtisserie artisanale*, where master bakers prepare breads on the premises.

CAFES. Cafes on a major boulevard can be more expensive than smaller establishments a few steps down a side-street. Prices in cafes are two-tiered, cheaper at the counter *(comptoir)* than in the seating area *(salle);* outdoor seating *(la terrasse)* may charge even more. Coffee, beer, and (in the south) the anise-flavored *pastis* are the staple cafe drinks, while *citron pressé* (lemonade) and *diabolo menthe* (peppermint soda) are popular non-alcoholic choices. If you order *café*, you'll get espresso; for coffee with milk or cream, ask for a *café au lait* or a *café crème*. *Bière à la pression*, or draft beer, is 660ml of either pale *(blonde)* or dark *(brune)* lager; for something smaller, ask for *une demi* (330ml).

THE ELIXIR OF LIFE

Wine *(le vin)* pervades French culture, and no occasion is complete without a glass or four. Wines vary tremendously, not only according to which of the 60 grape varieties it is made from, but also the climate and soil type in which the grapes were grown. On the Dordogne and Garonne rivers, the famous **Bordeaux** region produces mostly reds, white Pomerol, Médoc and Graves, and sweet white Sauternes. **Burgundy** is especially famous for its reds, from Chablis and the Côte d'Or in the north, to the Beaujolais and Mâconnais in the south. The northeast offers **Alsatian** whites that tend to be dry and fruity, complementing spicy foods. Delicately bouqueted whites predominate in the **Loire Valley.** In Provence, the **Côtes de Provence** around Marseille are recognized for their *rosés*, while the **Côtes du Rhône** produce celebrated reds such as the famous *Châteauneuf du Pape*. Only those grown and produced in **Champagne** can legally bear its name.

Budget travelers need not splurge to drink well; bad wine is virtually unheard of in France. To indulge for absolutely nothing, visit vineyards, like Burgundy and Bordeaux, where wine producers frequently offer free *dégustations* (tastings).

THE GOÛT DE VIN

Thus far on your trip to France you've managed to avoid looking like an amateur by waving vaguely at the wine menu and demanding, "of course... ahem... the most obvious choice for this meal... right... *there.*" But the wine lists along the Route du Vin are more daunting and complex than your average *carte*. It's time to learn if the wine you've been drinking was a *première cuvée* or just has a bouquet of walnuts and dirty old socks:

Gewurztraminer: This dry, aromatic white wine has been called "The Emperor of Alsatian wines." Drink it as an aperitif, with *foie gras*, pungent cheeses, or Indian, Mexican, or Asian cuisine.

Riesling: Considered one of the world's best white wines, Riesling is fruity, dry, and drunk with white meats, sauerkraut, and fish.

Sylvaner: From an Austrian grape, Sylvaner is a light, fruity, slightly sparkling white that goes well with seafood, *charcuterie*, and salads.

Muscat: A sweet and highly fruity white wine, often used as an aperitif.

Pinot family: *Pinot Blanc* is an all-purpose white wine for chicken, fish, and all sorts of appetizers; *Pinot Gris* is a smoky, strong white wine that can often take the place of a red wine in accompanying rich meats, roasts, and game; and *Pinot Noir*, the sole red wine of the Alsatian bunch, tastes of cherries and complements red meats.

CUSTOMS AND ETIQUETTE

In Paris they simply stared when I spoke to them in French; I never did succeed in making those idiots understand their language.
—Mark Twain

BLENDING IN. The more of an effort that you make to blend in, the better your experience in France will be. For dress, what may look perfectly innocuous in Miami will mark you out instantly in Menton. The French are known for their conservative stylishness: go for restrained sneakers or closed-toe shoes, solid-color pants or jeans, and plain t-shirts or button-down shirts, rather than Teva sandals and baggy pants. French people rarely wear shorts, but if you choose to wear them, they definitely shouldn't be too short. For women, skirts or dresses are more appropriate generally. Be sure to dress respectfully in churches.

LES CHIENS. The French *love* their dogs. Don't be surprised to find a pampered pet in your hotel, on your train, or, yes, sitting under the dinner table next to you.

ÉTAGES. The French call the ground floor the *rez-de-chaussée* and start numbering with the first floor above the ground floor *(premier étage)*. The button labeled "R" and not "1" is typically the ground floor. The *sous-sol* is the basement.

HOURS. Most restaurants open at noon for lunch and close in the afternoon before reopening for dinner. Some bistros and cafes remain open during the afternoon. Small businesses, banks, and post offices close daily noon-3pm. Many establishments shut down on Sundays, and most museums are closed on Mondays.

LANGUAGE AND POLITESSE. Even if your French is near-perfect, waiters and salespeople who detect the slightest accent will often immediately respond in English. If your language skills are good, continue to speak in French. More often than not, the waiter or salesperson will respond in French. The French put a premium on polite pleasantries. Always say *"Bonjour Madame/Monsieur"* when you come into a business, restaurant, or hotel, and *"Au Revoir"* when you leave. If you knock into someone on the street, always say *"Pardon."* When meeting someone for the first time, a handshake is appropriate. However, friends and acquaintances greet each other with a kiss on each cheek (the exception is two men).

PUBLIC RESTROOMS. French public toilets are worth the €0.30 they require, as these magic machines are self-cleaning after each use. Toilets in train stations and public gardens are tended by *gardiens* and generally cost €0.40-0.60.

SERVICE. There is no assumption in France that "the customer is always right," and complaining to managers about poor service is rarely worth your while. When engaged in any official process (e.g., opening a bank account, purchasing insurance), don't fret if you get shuffled from one desk to another. Hold your ground, patiently explain your situation, and you will eventually prevail.

TABLE MANNERS. Bread is served with every meal; it is perfectly polite to use a piece to wipe your plate. Etiquette dictates keeping one's hands above the table, not in one's lap, but elbows shouldn't rest on the table. When dining in restaurants, waiters will not bring the check until you ask. Enjoy a leisurely meal, then say, *"L'addition, s'il vous plaît."* And no matter what movies would suggest, waiters should never, ever be addressed as *"garçon,"* but as *"monsieur"* (or *"madame"*).

THE ARTS

ARCHITECTURE

ANCIENT BEGINNINGS. Long before the arrival of the "civilizing" Greeks and Romans, the French were leaving their own impressive marks. The pre-historic murals of **Lascaux** (p. 499) and the huge stones of **Carnac** (p. 232) testify to the engineering and artistic ingenuity of ancient peoples in France. Rome's remnants are most visible in Provence, particularly in the theater at **Orange** (p. 694), and the impressive ruins of the arena and temple at **Nîmes** (p. 688). Nearby are the arches of the **Pont du Gard** aqueduct (p. 693), which served up some 44 million gallons of water to Nîmes's thirsty citizens every day.

MEDIEVAL CATHEDRALS. With round arches and barrel-vaulting, the beauty of the 11th- to 12th-century **Romanesque** school is one of simple grandeur, characterized by churches like the **Basilique St-Sernin** in Toulouse (p. 601) and the **Basilique Ste-Madeleine** at Vézelay (p. 406). The architecture that characterizes the later Middle Ages is known as the **Gothic** style, which uses a system of arches to distributes weight outward. Flying buttresses (the stone supports outside cathedrals) relieve the walls of the roof's weight. As a result, the walls of Gothic churches seem to soar effortlessly skyward, and light streams in through enormous stained glass windows. The cathedrals at **Laon** (p. 291), **Amiens** (p. 299), **Chartres** (p. 142), and **Reims** (p. 307) exemplify the Gothic style.

RENAISSANCE, BAROQUE, AND NEOCLASSICISM. During the Renaissance, François I hired Italian artists to improve his lodge at **Fontainebleau** and commissioned the remarkable **Château de Chambord** (p. 159). French aristocrats soon followed, and lavish châteaux sprang up in the Loire Valley. In the 17th century, **Nicolas Fouquet**, Louis XIV's finance minister, commissioned the splendid Baroque **Château de Vaux-le-Vicomte**. Louis XIV tried to outdo Fouquet with **Versailles** (p. 139), an extravagant palace (and world's largest royal residence) packed with crystal, mirrors, and gold. The end of the 18th century welcomed the columns and clean lines of Neoclassicism, exemplified by **Soufflot**'s grandiose **Église Ste-Geneviève** in Paris—rededicated as the **Panthéon** (p. 115) during the Revolution.

19TH-CENTURY HAUSSMANIA. Today's Paris was remade under the direction of **Baron Georges-Eugène Haussmann** (see **Haussmania,** p. 109). From 1852 to 1870, Haussmann plowed long, straight boulevards through the tangled clutter and narrow alleys of medieval Paris. Not incidentally, the wide avenues also impeded insurrection, finally eliminating the effectiveness of street barricades. Engineering came onto the architectural scene in late 19th century, as **Gustave Eiffel** created the star exhibit of 1889's Universal Exhibition. First decried by Parisians as hideous and unstable, his **Eiffel Tower** (p. 117) is now France's best-loved landmark. The ornate, organic style of **Art Nouveau** developed in the late 19th century, exemplified by the Paris metro, where **Guimard**'s vinelike signs sprout from the pavement.

20TH-CENTURY MODERNISM AND SUBURBAN MISERY. In the interwar period, radical French architects began to incorporate new materials in their designs. A Swiss citizen who lived and built in Paris, Charles-Edouard Jean-neret, known as **Le Corbusier**, was the architectural pioneer in reinforced concrete, as in his mushroom-like chapel at **Ronchamp** (p. 368). In the post-war years, large housing projects or **HLMs** *(habitations à louer modéré)* were originally intended as affordable housing, but have since become synonymous with suburban misery, racism, and the exploitation of the immigrant poor. In the 1980s, Paris became the hub of Mitterand's 15 billion franc endeavor known as the *Grands Projets*, which included the construction of the **Parc de la Villette,** the **Opéra** at the Bastille, and **I. M. Pei**'s glass pyramid at the **Louvre.** Skyscrapers have been exiled to the business suburb of **La Défense,** home to a wide array of sleek modern structures.

FINE ARTS

MEDIEVAL MASTERPIECES. Brilliant stained glass and intricate stone facades like those at **Chartres, Reims,** and **Ste-Chapelle** in Paris, served as large reproductions of the Bible. Monastic industry brought the art of illumination to its height, as monks added ornate illustrations to manuscripts. During the Middle Ages, artisans perfected the skill of weaving. The 11th-century **Bayeux tapestry,** a 70m long narrative of the Battle of Hastings, can still be seen in its original Norman town (p. 260).

THE RENAISSANCE IN FRANCE. Sixteenth-century France imported its styles from the painting, sculpture, and architecture of the **Italian Renaissance.** On the invitation of François I, **Leonardo da Vinci** trekked up from Florence bearing the smiling **Mona Lisa** in tow. Da Vinci's final home can still be seen in **Amboise** (p. 162).

BAROQUE AND ROCOCO. Italy remained the arbiter of France's aesthetic taste in the 17th century, when Louis XIV imported the baubled excesses of the **Baroque** style to his own court at Versailles. The enduring masterpieces of French Baroque, however, remain the more realist paintings of the brothers **Le Nain** and **Georges de La Tour.** Founded in 1648, the **Académie Royale** dictated taste in all matters artistic in annual **salons,** the country's "official" art exhibitions. The early 18th century brought on the even more frilly **Rococo** style. Catering to the tastes of the nobility, **Antoine Watteau** painted the *fêtes* and secret *rendez-vous* of the aristocracy, and **François Boucher** painted landscapes and rosy-cheeked shepherdesses.

NEOCLASSICAL AND ROMANTIC SCHOOLS. The French Revolution inspired painters to create heroic depictions of scenes from their own time. **Jacques-Louis David**'s *Death of Marat* paid gory tribute to the Revolutionary leader, Jean-Paul Marat. Napoleon I's reign saw the emergence of **Neoclassicism** as the emperor tried to model his empire, and his purple capes, on the Roman empire. Painters created large, dramatic pictures, often of the emperor as Romantic hero and god. Later, the paintings of **Eugène Delacroix** were a shock to the salons of the 1820s and 1830s.

His *Liberty Leading the People* displays the extraordinary sense of color and a penchant for melodrama that exemplify **Romanticism**. Both he and **Jean-Auguste-Dominique Ingres** pursued orientalist subjects, as in the latter's *Grande Odalisque*.

REALISM AND IMPRESSIONISM. After the Revolution of 1848, **realists** like **Gustave Courbet** shifted their artistic focus to the "humble" aspects of peasant life. His *Burial at Ornans* caused a scandal when first exhibited because it used the huge canvases associated with history painting to depict a simple village scene. **Edouard Manet** facilitated the transition from earlier Realism to what we now consider **Impressionism** by turning his focus to texture and color. The combination of classical poses and scandalous nudes in *Luncheon on the Grass* shocked his colleagues but held center stage at the Salon des Refusés (the exhibition of works rejected by the official Salon) in 1863. By the late 1860s Manet's new aesthetic had set the stage for **Claude Monet, Camille Pissarro,** and **Pierre-Auguste Renoir,** these artists used colors to depict visual impressions as they appeared to the eye, striving to capture the effects of light. The Impressionist movement went on to inspire **Edgar Dégas**'s ballerinas, **Gustave Caillebotte**'s rainy Paris streets, and **Berthe Morisot**'s tranquil studies of women. Monet's garden at **Giverny** (p. 145), the source of his monumental *Waterlilies* series, remains a popular daytrip from Paris. The influence of Impressionism extended to sculpture, where **Auguste Rodin** captured barely-constrained energy and a range of motion in bronzes like *The Kiss*.

POST-IMPRESSIONISM. **Paul Cézanne** worked in Aix-en-Provence and created still-lifes, portraits, and geometric landscapes (among them his many versions of *Mont Ste-Victoire*) composed of blocks of color. **Georges Seurat** developed **Pointillism,** a style in which thousands of tiny dots of paint merge to form a coherent picture in the viewer's eye. **Paul Gauguin** used large, flat blocks of color with heavily drawn outlines to paint "primitive" scenes from Brittany, Arles, Tahiti, and Martinique. He went to **Arles** (p. 675) to join his friend **Vincent Van Gogh,** a Dutch painter who had moved to France in search of new imagery. Struggling with Pointillism, **Henri Matisse** abandoned the technique and began squeezing paint from the tube directly onto the canvas. This aggressive style earned the name **Fauvism** (from *fauves*, wild animals) and characterizes Matisse's mature works like *The Dance*.

CUBISM AND BEYOND. In the 1910s, former Fauve artist **Georges Braque** and Spanish-born **Pablo Picasso** developed **Cubism,** a technique of using shaded planes to reassemble familiar images and objects into an abstracted form. Picasso went on to become arguably the greatest artist of the 20th century, breaking new artistic ground with his constant innovations in style. The **Musée Picasso** in Paris (p. 126) and the Musée Picasso in Antibes (p. 725) both chronicle his extensive career.

DADAISM, SURREALISM, AND THE SCENE TODAY. The sense of loss and disillusionment after WWI prompted a group of artists to reject the responsible bourgeois culture. The anarchy and nonsense of the **Dada** movement found its best expression in the works of **Marcel Duchamp,** who scrambled artistic conventions by signing a factory-made urinal as if it were a piece of high art *(La Fontaine)*. **Surrealism,** on the other hand, strove to unify fantasy with the everyday world, creating "an absolute reality, a surreality," according to poet and leader of the movement, **André Breton.** The period's exemplary works—the bowler-hatted men of **René Magritte,** the dreamscapes of **Joan Miró,** the patterns of **Max Ernst,** and the melting timepieces of **Salvador Dalí**—arose from time the artists spent in Paris. Modern 20th-century experiments in photography, installation art, and sculpture can be seen in the **Centre Pompidou** and the **Fondation Cartier pour l'Art Contemporain.**

LIFE AND TIMES

LITERATURE AND PHILOSOPHY

MEDIEVAL AND RENAISSANCE LITERATURE. Beginning in the 12th century, **chansons de gestes,** tales of 8th-century crusades and conquests were popular, while medieval aristocrats enjoyed literature extolling knightly honor and courtly love from authors like **Marie de France** and **Chrétien de Troyes.** In the Renaissance, **John Calvin**'s humanist treatises criticized the Catholic Church and opened the road to the ill-fated Protestant Reformation in France. **François Rabelais**'s fantastical satire *Gargantua and Pantagruel* explored the world from giants' points of view, and **Michel de Montaigne**'s *Essais* pushed the boundaries of individual thought and gave birth to that literary form modern students have learned to dread.

RATIONALISM AND THE ENLIGHTENMENT. The **Académie Française** was founded in 1635 to regulate and codify French literature and language. French philosophers reacted to the mushy musings of humanists with **Rationalism,** a school of thought that championed logic and order. In his *Discourse on Method,* **René Descartes** proved his own existence with the famously catchy deduction, "I think, therefore I am." **Molière,** the era's comic relief, used his plays to satirize the social pretensions of his age, his actors initiating the great **Comédie Française.** In the 18th century, the French **Enlightenment** (as with the Enlightenment across Europe) sought to promote reason and tolerance. The ambition of **Denis Diderot**'s *Encylopédie* was no less than to record the entire body of human knowledge. **Voltaire**'s satire *Candide* refuted that this is "the best of all possible worlds." In *Confessions,* **Jean-Jacques Rousseau** suggested we abandon society rather than stay in a corrupt world.

ROMANTICISM AND REALISM. During the 19th century the expressive ideals of **Romanticism,** which first came to prominence in Britain and Germany, found their way to analytically minded France. Such great writers as **Henri Stendhal** and **Honoré de Balzac** 'helped establish the novel as the preeminent literary medium, but **Victor Hugo**'s *The Hunchback of Notre Dame* dominated the Romantic age. In the same period, the young Aurore Dupin left her husband, took the *nom de plume* of **George Sand,** and published passionate novels condemning sexist conventions. The heroine of **Gustave Flaubert**'s *Madame Bovary* (1856) spurned provincial life for romantic, adulterous daydreams in his famous realist novel. Flaubert was prosecuted for immorality in 1857 and only narrowly acquitted. Poet **Charles Baudelaire** was not so lucky; the same tribunal fined him 50 francs. Although he gained a reputation for obscenity during his own lifetime, today his *Fleurs du Mal* (Flowers of Evil) is considered the most influential piece of 19th-century French poetry.

BELLE ÉPOQUE TO WWII. Literary **Symbolism** used new techniques to capture instants of perception. Led by **Stéphane Mallarmé, Paul Verlaine,** and the precocious **Arthur Rimbaud,** the movement was instrumental in the creation of modern poetry. In the early 20th century, **Marcel Proust**'s seven-volumes *Remembrance of Things Past,* about *fin de siècle* high society decadence, inquired into the nature of time, and love. In 1924, **André Breton** abandoned the Dada movement to argue for the artistic supremacy of the subconscious in his *Surrealist Manifesto.* After WWII, **Jean-Paul Sartre**'s theory of **Existentialism** held that life in itself was meaningless, and existence could only take on a purpose when one commits oneself to a cause. Algerian-born **Albert Camus** achieved fame with his debut novel *The Stranger,* in which a dispassionate social misfit is condemned to death for murder.

THE BEST EXPATRIATE LITERATURE

Ernest Hemingway. *A Moveable Feast*. The quintessential tale of a young expat in Paris. F. Scott Fitzgerald and Gertrude Stein make colorful cameo appearances.

George Orwell. *Down and Out in London and Paris*. A writer takes grimy jobs in the dark underbelly of Paris. Beautifully descriptive and funny.

W. Somerset Maugham. *The Moon and Sixpence*. A dull London businessman leaves his family to paint in Paris and Tahiti. Loosely based on the life of Paul Gauguin.

Henry James. *The American*. The New World meets the Old in this classic story of friendship, love, and betrayal in turn of the century Paris.

F. Scott Fitzgerald. *Tender is the Night*. No one captures the 1920s flapper set quite like Fitzgerald—his story of scandal and intrigue on the Riviera is a classic.

Peter Mayle. *A Year in Provence*. A staple of book clubs everywhere, a lighthearted autobiography, travelogue, and culinary guide to life in the rural town of Ménerbes.

Julian Barnes. *Flaubert's Parrot*. An elderly English doctor journeys to France to research Flaubert's life and inspiration for his short story *Un Coeur Simple*.

Adam Gopnik. *Paris to the Moon*. A *New Yorker* journalist settles down in Paris with his family. Small observations on Parisian life, lyrically woven into larger cultural themes.

FEMINISM AND LA PRÉSENCE AFRICAINE. Existentialist and feminist **Simone de Beauvoir** attacked the myth of femininity with *The Second Sex*, inspiring a whole generation of second-wave **feminism** in the 1950s, 1960s, and 1970s. In turn, writers like **Marguerite Duras** *(The Lover)*, **Hélène Cixous** *(The Laugh of the Medusa)*, and **Luce Irigaray** *(This Sex Which Is Not One)* explored gender identity and sparked feminist movements in France and abroad. Throughout the 20th century, France's colonial exploitation has been powerfully condemned by writers from the **Antilles,** the **Maghreb** (Algeria, Tunisia, Morocco), **Haiti, Québec,** and **West Africa.** With the foundation of the **Négritude** movement in the 1920s by intellectuals **Aimé Césaire** (Martinique) and **Léopold Sédar Senghor** (Senegal), francophone literature began to flourish. Maghreb writers in France like **Mehdi Charef** *(Le thé au harem d'Archi Ahmed)* have written provocative novels about *beur* (slang for an Arab resident of France) culture and the difficulties of cultural assimilation.

FILM

BEGINNINGS. Not long after he and his brother Louis presented the world's first paid screening in a Paris cafe in 1895, **Auguste Lumière** remarked, "the cinema is a medium without a future." Luckily, Lumière was a better inventor than he was a visionary. Paris was the Hollywood of early cinema, dominating production and distribution worldwide. Although WWI stunted the growth of French film, the inter-war period yielded a large number of diverse and influential films. **Luis Buñuel** and **Salvador Dalí**'s *Un Chien Andalou* was a surrealist marvel of jarring associations. **Jean Renoir,** son of the Impressionist painter, directed the powerful anti-war film *La Grande Illusion*.

NEW WAVE. In 1956, a star was born when **Jean Vadim** sent **Brigitte Bardot** shimmying naked across the screen in *Et Dieu créa la femme*. In 1959, films like **François Truffaut**'s coming-of-age story *Les 400 Coups* and **Jean-Luc Godard**'s gangster flick *A Bout du souffle* (Breathless), and **Alain Resnais**'s *Hiroshima, Mon Amour* incited the **French New Wave,** a movement interested in the distinction between fiction and documentary and the fragmentation of linear time.

CONTEMPORARY CLASSICS AND CINÉMA BEUR. The 1960s brought international recognition of French talent, including stunning **Catherine Deneuve,** gothic priestess **Isabelle Adjani,** and omnipresent **Gérard Depardieu.** Later, **Edouard Molinaro**'s campy *La Cage aux folles* and **Colline Serraud**'s *Trois hommes et un couffin* (Three Men and a Baby) both inspired American remakes, while **Claude Berri**'s *Jean de Florette* and Polish **Krzysztof Kieslowski**'s *Three Colors* trilogy, *Bleu*, *Blanc*, and *Rouge*, have become instant classics of late 20th-century French cinema. Several recent French films have explored the issue of gay identity and sexual orientation, including Belgian **Alain Berliner**'s transgender tragicomedy *Ma vie en rose*. The charming **Audrey Tautou** has earned international fame for her role in *Le fabuleux destin d'Amélie Poulain*. **Cinéma Beur,** à movement exploring second-generation North Africans coming to terms with life in Parisian housing projects, has produced explosive films like **Mehdi Charef**'s *Le thé au harem d'Archi Ahmed* and **Mathieu Kassovitz**'s *La Haine*.

MUSIC

The history of music in France begins with the Gregorian chants of 12th-century monks and progresses through the ballads of medieval troubadours, the Renaissance masses of **Josquin des Prez,** the lavish Baroque Versailles court operas of **Jean-Baptise Lully.** During **Robespierre**'s terrifying reign, the people rallied to the strains of **revolutionary music,** such as **Rouget de Lisle**'s *War Song of the Army of the Rhine*. It was so adored by volunteers from Marseille that it was dubbed **La Marseillaise** and became the national anthem in 1795.

Paris became the center of influence for 19th-century European music. **Grand opera** merged with the simpler **opéra comique** to produce the Romantic **lyric opera,** an amalgam of soaring arias, exoticism, and tragic death best exemplified by **Georges Bizet**'s *Carmen*. Paris served as the musical center for foreign Romantic composers as well, including **Frédéric Chopin, Franz Liszt,** and **Félix Mendelssohn.**

Music at the turn of the 20th century began a new period of intense, often abstract invention. **Claude Débussy,** an Impressionist composer, used tone color and nontraditional scales. **Erik Satie** composed in an anti-sentimental spirit. **Ravel**'s Basque origins surfaced in the Spanish rhythms of his most famous work, *Boléro*. The music of **Igor Stravinsky,** whose *Rite of Spring* caused a riot at its 1913 premiere at the Théâtre des Champs-Élysées, was violently dissonant and rhythmic.

JAZZ AND CABARET. The French have been particularly receptive to jazz over the years. Jazz crooner **Josephine Baker** left the US for Paris in 1925, finding France more accepting than her segregated home. **Cabaret,** which grew in popularity in the 1930s, was made famous by the iconic voice of Edith Piaf in ballads like *"La Vie en Rose."* The pair of violinist **Stéphane Grapelli** and Belgian-Romany guitarist **Django Reinhardt** innovated swing. After WWII, a stream of American musicians came to Paris, including a young **Miles Davis,** who took the stage at a 1949 festival.

THE NEXT BIG THINGS. In the late 1950s and 1960s, a unique French take on American rock emerged; the movement was termed, in a stroke of onomatopoetic genius, **yé-yé.** Teen idol **Johnny Hallyday** took the limelight, and youth-oriented **Salut les Copains** was the moment's rage. Contemporary musical taste is divided between the music played on the radio and the various forms of electronica that dominate dance clubs. Radio pop music includes solo artists like French singers **Isabelle Boulay** and **Lara Fabien.** France's hip-hop and rap scene includes artists like **MC Solaar** and **Rohff,** but American rappers still dominate many radio playlists. World music also rules the airwaves, incorporating artists from North Africa (including raï musicians **Cheb Khaled, Cheb Mami,** and **Faudel**), the Middle East (**Natacha Atlas**), Latin America (**Manu Chao** and **Yuri Buenaventura**), and the West Indies (with the sounds of **reggae** and **zouk**).

SPORTS AND RECREATION

FOOTBALL

The French take *le football* very seriously. Their national team, *Les Bleus*, emerged from a half-century of mediocrity to capture the 1998 **World Cup,** igniting celebrations from the Champs-Élysées to the Pyrenees. The charismatic star of the team, **Zinedine Zidane,** has become a national hero. The son of an Algerian immigrant, "Zizou" has helped unite a country divided by tension over immigration.

CYCLING

Cycling is another national obsession. France annually hosts the only cycling event anyone can name: the grueling 3-week, 3500km **Tour de France,** which celebrated its 100 year anniversary in 2003. Competitors from the host country haven't had much recent success in the competition: American **Lance Armstrong** has triumphed over the field to capture a record-setting six straight championships.

OTHER ACTIVITIES

For those who prefer a bit less exertion, **pétanque,** once dominated by old men, has been gaining popularity among all ages. The basic premise of *pétanque*, like bocce or bowls, is to throw a large metal ball as close as possible to a small metal ball. **Alpine** and **cross-country skiing** are also popular in France, thanks to the country's several mountainous escapes. Despite the objections of French traditionalists, other sports are also gaining a foothold in France, particularly **rugby** and **golf.**

HOLIDAYS AND FESTIVALS

The most important national holiday is **Bastille Day,** July 14, the anniversary of the storming of the Bastille in 1789. The event is celebrated with a solemn military march up the Champs-Élysées followed by dancing, drinking, and fireworks all over the country. When Bastille Day falls on a Tuesday or Thursday, the French often also take off the Monday or Friday, a crafty practice known as *faire le pont* (making the bridge). The dates listed below are for 2005. For more information on specific events, check out www.franceguide.com, under "Art de vivre."

DATE	NATIONAL HOLIDAY
January 1	Le Jour de l'An (also called la St-Sylvestre): New Year's Day
March 28	Le lundi de Pâques: Easter Monday
May 1	La Fête du Travail: Labor Day
May 8	Fête de la Victoire 1945: Celebrates the end of World War II in Europe
May 5	L'Ascension: Ascension Day
May 15	Le Lundi de Pentecôte: Whit Monday
July 14	La Fête Nationale: Bastille Day
August 15	L'Assomption: Feast of the Assumption
November 1	La Toussaint: All Saints' Day
November 11	L'Armistice 1918: Armistice Day
December 25	Noël: Christmas

LIFE AND TIMES

ALTERNATIVES TO TOURISM

A PHILOSOPHY FOR TRAVELERS

One of the largest countries in Europe, France hosts around 77 million trips each year. Despite the allure of beaches and château gardens, or of cafes and wine-tasting festivals, tourism has impacted French communities and natural life heavily.

Let's Go believes that the connection between travelers and their destinations is an important one. We've watched the growth of the 'ignorant tourist' stereotype with dismay, knowing that many travelers care passionately about the communities and environments they explore—but also knowing that even conscientious tourists can inadvertently damage natural wonders and harm cultural environments. With this "Alternatives to Tourism" chapter, *Let's Go* hopes to promote a better understanding of France and to enhance your experience there.

There are several different options for those who seek to participate in alternatives to tourism. Opportunities for **volunteering** abound, both with local and international organizations. **Studying** can also be instructive, either in the form of direct enrollment in a university or in an independent research project. **Working** is both a way to immerse yourself in the local culture and a means to finance your travels. To get more ideas for various educational activities, contact the Specialty Travel Index (US ☎ 800-442-4922, elsewhere 415-459-4900; www.specialtytravel.com).

As a **volunteer** in France, you can participate in projects all the way from Paris to Nice, either on a short-term basis or as the main component of your trip. Later in this section, we recommend organizations that can help you find the opportunities that best suit your interests, whether you're looking to pitch in for a day or a year. **Studying** at a college or language program is another option. Beyond having some of the oldest universities in Europe, France hosts world-renowned fine arts and culinary schools. Many travelers also structure their trips by the **work** that they can do along the way—either odd jobs as they go, or full-time stints in cities where they plan to stay for some time. Both short-term and long-term jobs in France require a work permit, which is discussed further in the upcoming sections.

 Start your search at ☒ **www.beyondtourism.com,** Let's Go's brand-new searchable database of Alternatives to Tourism, where you can find exciting feature articles and helpful program listings divided by country, continent, and program type.

VOLUNTEERING

Volunteering can be one of the most fulfilling experiences you have in life, especially if you combine it with the thrill of traveling in a new place. Though France is considered wealthy in worldwide terms, there is no shortage of aid organizations to benefit the very real issues the country does face. Short-term volunteering stints can be found in virtually every city. Most people who volunteer in France do so on a short-term basis, at organizations that make use of drop-in or once-a-week volunteers. More intensive volunteer services may charge a participation fee. These costs can be surprisingly hefty (although frequently covering airfare and most living expenses). Most people choose to go through a parent organization that takes care of logistical details and provides a group environment and support system.

Care France, CAP 19, 13 rue de Georges Auric, 75019 Paris (☎01 53 19 89 89; www.carefrance.org). An international organization providing volunteer opportunities in 6000 locations throughout France, from combatting AIDS to promoting education.

Centre National du Volontariat, 127 rue Falguière, 75015 Paris (☎01 40 61 01 61; www.globenet.org/CNV). 70 offices in France help people find the volunteer associations in which they would be the most helpful.

International Volunteer Program, 678 13th St., Suite 100, Oakland, CA 94612 (☎510-433-0414; www.ivpsf.org). 6-week programs in France ranging from hospital service to elderly assistance. Fee of US$1800 includes in-country transportation, room, and meals. Intermediate knowledge of French required.

COMMUNITY AND DEVELOPMENT

Community-based projects involve close work with disadvantaged populations of France. Programs range from working with the elderly to prison reform. Due to the one-on-one nature of these projects, knowledge of French is often necessary, but these are among the most rewarding of all volunteer experiences.

Action Contre la Faim, 4 rue Niepce, 75014 Paris (☎01 43 35 88 88; www.acf-fr.org). An international organization combating hunger. Volunteers help organize and carrying out the Race Against Hunger, a running competition to raise money for the cause.

Fédération Familles de France, 28 pl. St-Georges, 75009 Paris (☎01 44 53 45 90, www.familles-de-france.org). Volunteers help the organization in supporting families in need by offering grants and providing assistance with education and resumes.

Fondation Claude Pompidou, 42 rue du Louvre, 75001 Paris (☎01 40 13 75 00; www.fondationclaudepompidou.asso.fr). Aids the sick, elderly, and disabled withhome-care and companionship. Volunteers are generally expected to commit to 1 yr.

GENEPI, 4/14 rue Ferrus, 75014 Paris (☎01 45 88 37 00; www.genepi.asso.fr). Promotes the social rehabilitation of those in prison in France by creating relationships between students and prisoners. Student volunteers. Offices throughout France.

Secours Catholique: Delegation de Paris, 13 rue St Ambroise, 75011 Paris (☎01 48 07 58 21; www.quiaccueillequi.org). Works to support the poor, the unemployed, children with social problems, foreigners, and other marginalized groups.

Secours Populaire Français, 9/11 rue Froissart, 75140 Paris (☎01 44 78 21 00; www.secourspopulaire.asso.fr). Provides food and clothing to poor children and families. Arranges sports and social activities, all done with a commitment to human rights.

Simon Wiesenthal Center, 64 av. Marceau, 75008 Paris (☎01 47 23 76 37; www.wiesenthal.org). Fights anti-Semitism and Holocaust denial throughout Europe. Small, variable donation required for membership.

Médicins Sans Frontières (Doctors without Borders), 8 rue Saint Sabin, 75011 Paris (☎01 40 21 29 29; www.msf.fr). Coordinates volunteers ages 18+ to provide healthcare for immigrants and asylum seekers. Interview required.

ENVIRONMENTAL PROTECTION

France enacted new, stiff pollution controls to protect the coastal areas of the Mediterranean after oil spills in 1999 and 2002. Individual volunteers continue to aid the environment where the government cannot.

Mission Environnement Mer et Littoral (☎04 97 13 44 02; www.nice-coteazur.org/ francais/tourisme/environnement). Preserves natural habitats in the midst of a growing industrial environment. Programs offered throughout the year.

Concordia International Volunteer Programs, Heversham House, 20-22 Boundary Rd., Hove BN34ET, England (☎44 1273 422 218). Free volunteer activities (food and lodging provided) throughout France. Ages 18-30. Also archaeological restoration projects.

Jeunesse et Reconstruction, 8 et 10 rue de Trevise, 75009 Paris (☎01 47 70 15 88; www.volontariat.org). Database of volunteer opportunities for young people in preservation and historical reconstruction. Open June-Sept. M-Sa 9:30am-1pm and 2-6pm.

Organisation Mondiale de Protection de la Nature (www.wwf.fr). Offers various opportunities for environmental activism around France and the EU. €30 membership fee.

Council on International Educational Exchange, 7 Custom House St., 3rd fl., Portland, ME 04101, USA (☎207-553-7600; www.ciee.org). Large database of short-term volunteer opportunities in France, from agriculture to festivals.

HISTORICAL RESTORATION

The preservation and reconstruction of French landmarks is an ongoing concern. Volunteers looking for a more labor-intensive experience can find groups assisting this process—a great opportunity to experience France's architectural history.

APARE, 25 bd. Paul Pons, 84800 L'Isle sur la Sorgue (☎04 90 85 51 15; www.apare-gec.org). Arranges short-term historical restoration projects in Provence for young people from France and abroad. (See **A Different Path,** p. 69.)

Archaeological Institute of America, 656 Beacon St., Boston, MA 02215, USA (☎617-353-9361; www.archaeological.org). *Archaeological Fieldwork Opportunities Bulletin,* on the website, lists field sites in Europe (including France) at which you can volunteer.

Association CHAM, 5 et 7 rue Guilleminot, 75014 Paris (☎01 43 35 15 51; www.cham.asso.fr). Organizes groups to restore medieval French landmarks. Open M-F 8:30am-12:30pm and 1:30-6pm, Sa 9am-12:30pm and 1:30-4pm.

Club du Vieux Manoir, Ancienne Abbaye du Moncel, 60700 Pontpoint (☎03 44 72 33 98; cvmclubduvieuxmanoir.free.fr). Year-long and summer work restoring castles and churches. €14 membership/insurance fee; €16 per day, including food and tent.

GEC, 41 cours Jean Jaurès, 84000 Avignon (☎04 90 85 51 15; www.apare-gec.org). Opportunities including long-term projects in historical and environmental preservation for professionals and young volunteers from France and abroad.

REMPART, 1 rue des Guillemites, 75004 Paris (☎01 42 71 96 55; www.rempart.com), Offers summer and year-long programs for the restoration of monuments. Anyone 13 or over is eligible. Membership fee €17; most projects charge €6-8 per day.

La Sabranenque, rue de la Tour de l'Oume, 30290 Saint Victor la Coste France (☎04 66 50 05 05; www.sabranenque.com). Restoration of Mediterranean architecture. Programs from June-Sept.

STUDYING

Study-abroad programs range from basic language and culture courses to college-level classes, often for credit. Research as much as you can before making your decision—determine costs and duration, as well as what kind of students participate in the program and what sort of accommodations are provided.

In programs that have large groups of students who speak the same language, there is a trade-off. You may feel more comfortable in the community, but you will not have the same opportunity to practice a foreign language or to befriend other international students. For accommodations, dorm life provides a better opportunity to mingle with fellow students, but there is less of a chance to experience the local scene. If you live with a family, there is a potential to build lifelong friendships and to truly experience day-to-day life, but conditions can vary greatly.

As a student at a French university, you will receive a student card *(carte d'étudiant)* upon presentation of a residency permit and a receipt for your university fees. The **Centre Régional des Oeuvres Universitaires et Scolaires (CROUS)** offers several student benefits and discounts, including cheap meals. Most university-level study-abroad programs are conducted in French, although many programs offer classes in English and lower-level language courses. Those relatively fluent in French may find it cheaper to enroll directly in a French university. You can search www.studyabroad.com for various semester-abroad programs.

VISA INFORMATION. Those hoping to study abroad in France must apply for a special student visa from the French consulate. There is a **short-stay** visa for stays up to 90 days, as well as two **long-stay** visas: one for three to six months, and a one-year visa for programs over six months. Prospective students must fill out two applications for the appropriate visa, and provide a passport and two extra passport photos. Additionally, the student must give proof of enrollment or admission in a French learning institute, a financial guarantee with a monthly allowance of US $600 per month during the intended stay, and proof of medical insurance. Finally, there is a visa fee which can be paid during the time of application. When in France, students with long-stay visas must obtain a **carte de séjour** (a student residency card) from the local "Prefecture de Police."

ALTERNATIVES TO TOURISM

AMERICAN PROGRAMS

Institute for American Universities, P.O. Box 592, Evanston, IL 60204 (☎800-221-2051; www.iaufrance.org). University-affiliated programs in various regions of France.

European Institute for International Education, The Eur-Am Center, 32500 Telegraph Rd., Suite 209, Bingham Farms, MI 48025 (☎248-988-9341; www.euramcenter.com). Created to encourage a stronger relationship between US and Europe. Provides both educational and private sector opportunities for people of all ages.

Cultural Experiences Abroad, France, (☎800-266-4441; www.gowithcea.com). Programs in Aix-en-Provence, Grenoble, Dijon, and Paris. Students can take classes in both French and English. Affiliated with several schools in the US.

American Institute for Foreign Study, College Division, River Plaza, 9 West Broad St., Stamford, CT 06902, USA (☎800-727-2437, ext. 5163; www.aifsabroad.com). Organizes programs for high school and college study in Cannes, Grenoble, and Paris.

Council on International Educational Exchange (CIEE), 7 Custom House St., 3rd fl., Portland, ME 01401, USA (☎800-407-8839; www.ciee.org/study). Sponsors work, volunteer, academic, and internship programs in Paris and Rennes.

International Association for the Exchange of Students for Technical Experience (IAESTE), 10400 Little Patuxent Pkwy. Suite 250, Columbia, MD 21044, USA (☎410-997-2200; www.aipt.org). Offers 8- to 12-week programs in France for college students who have completed 2 years of technical study. US$25 application fee.

School for International Training, College Semester Abroad, Admissions, Kipling Rd., P.O. Box 676, Brattleboro, VT 05302, USA (☎800-257-7751 or 802-257-7751; www.sit.edu). Semester- and year-long programs in France run US$10,600-13,700. Also runs the **Experiment in International Living** (☎800-345-2929; www.usexperiment.org), 3- to 5-week summer programs that offer high-school students homestays, community service, language training in France (US$1900-5000).

FRENCH PROGRAMS

French universities are far cheaper than their American equivalents; however, it can be hard to receive academic credit at home for a non-approved program. Expect to pay at least €500 per month in living expenses. EU citizens studying in France can take advantage of the three- to twelve-month **SOCRATES** program (www.socrates-france.org), which offers grants to support inter-European educational exchanges. For info on programs of study, requirements, and grants or scholarships, visit www.egide.asso.fr.

French universities are segmented into three degree levels. Programs at the first level (except the **Grandes Écoles,** below) are two or three years long and generally focus on science, medicine, and the liberal arts. They must admit anyone holding a *baccalauréat* (French graduation certificate) or recognized equivalent to their first year of courses (British A levels or two years of college in the US). French competency or other testing may be required for non-native speakers. The more selective and more demanding **Grandes Écoles** cover specializations from physics to photography to veterinary medicine. These have notoriously difficult entrance examinations which require a year of preparatory schooling.

Agence EduFrance (www.edufrance.fr), is a one-stop resource for North Americans thinking about studying for a degree in France. Info on courses, costs, and grant opportunities. Housing options available in both universities as well as with French families.

American University of Paris, 31 av. Bosquet, 75343 Paris Cédex 07 (☎01 40 62 06 00; www.aup.fr), offers US-accredited degrees and summer programs in English at its Paris campus. Intensive French language courses offered. Tuition US$9620 per semester, not including living expenses.

Université Paris-Sorbonne, 1 rue Victor Cousin, 75005 Paris Cédex 05 (☎01 40 46 22 11; www.paris4.sorbonne.fr), the grandfather of French universities, was founded in 1253 and is still going strong. Inscription into degree courses costs about €400 per year. Also offers 3- to 9-month-long programs for American students.

LANGUAGE SCHOOLS

Language schools can be independently run international or local organizations or divisions of foreign universities. They rarely offer college credit but are a good alternative to university study for a deeper focus on the language or a less rigorous course load. These programs are also good for younger high school students who might not feel comfortable with older students in a university program.

Alliance Française, École Internationale de Langue et de Civilisation Française, 101 bd. Raspail, 75270 Paris Cédex 06 (☎01 42 84 90 00; www.alliancefr.org). Instruction at all levels, with courses in legal and business French. Courses are 1-4 months in length, costing €267 for 16 2hr. sessions and €534 for 16 4hr. sessions.

Institut de Langue Française, 3 av. Bertie-Albrecht, 75008 Paris (☎01 45 63 24 00; www.inst-langue-fr.com). M: Charles de Gaulle-Étoile. Language, civilization, and literature courses. Offers programs of varying lengths, including anywhere from 4-week to year. 6-20hr. per week, starting at €185.

World Link Education: Study French and Experience France, Storgaten 24, 302 43 Halmstad, Sweden (☎46 35 106680). French language and culture classes in different cities around the country. Tuition fees vary with accommodations and duration of study.

Eurocentres, 101 N. Union St. Suite 300, Alexandria, VA 22314, USA (☎703-684-1494; www.eurocentres.com) or in Europe, Head Office, Seestr. 247, CH-8038 Zurich, Switzerland (☎+41 1 485 50 40; fax 481 61 24). Language programs for beginning to advanced students with homestays in France.

Language Immersion Institute, 75 South Manheim Blvd., SUNY-New Paltz, New Paltz, NY 12561, USA (☎845-257-3500; www.newpaltz.edu/lii). 2-week summer and some overseas courses in French for students and professionals. 2-week course US$1000.

CULINARY AND ART SCHOOLS

One final—and pricier—study-abroad option for students and amateurs of all ages is enrollment in a French culinary institute or art school. Many programs allow budding chefs and closet Van Goghs to participate in semester- or year-long programs, or in some cases individual class sessions. For smaller, more intimate courses based in farms and homes, amateur cooks should check out www.cookingschools.com, which lists private schools and gastronomy tours in France.

Grande École des Arts Culinaires et de l'Hôtellerie de Lyon (Lyon Culinary Arts and Hotel Management School), Château de Vivier–BP25, 69131 Lyon-Ecully Cédex (☎04 72 18 02 20; www.each-lyon.com). Premier school affiliated with Paul Bocuse, located in France's capital city of *haute cuisine*. 8- and 16-week summer courses in French and English for amateurs (€4200-7000). Offers individual day courses ranging €62-76 (reserve in advance to dchabert@each-lyon.com).

Cordon Bleu Paris Culinary Arts Institute, 8 rue Léon Delhomme, 75015 Paris (☎01 53 68 22 50; www.cordonbleu.edu). M: Porte de la Chapelle. The *crème de la crème* of French cooking schools. The *Grand Diplôme* Program is the basic curriculum.

Pont Aven School of Art, 5 pl. Paul Gauguin, 29930 Pont-Aven (☎02 98 09 10 45; www.pontavensa.org). English-speaking school in Brittany offers studio art courses and art history, and French language. 4- and 6-week sessions €3700-4750.

Lacoste School of Art, P.O. Box 3146, Savannah, GA 31401, USA (☎912-525-5803; www.scad.edu/lacoste). In the Provençal town of Lacoste, this school is administered by the Savannah College of Art and Design. Summer and fall courses in architecture, painting, and historical preservation. Tuition, minimum of two courses €4230 for undergraduates; program fee (room and board, weekend excursions, admissions) €3350.

Painting School of Montmiral, rue de la Porte Neuve, 81140 Castelnau de Montmiral (☎ 05 63 33 13 11; www.painting-school.com). 2-week classes at student to professional levels in English or French. With accommodations and half-board €1680.

WORKING

As with volunteering, work opportunities tend to fall into two categories. Some travelers want long-term jobs that allow them to get to know another part of the world as a member of the community, while other travelers seek out short-term jobs to finance the next leg of their travels.

The French unemployment rate remains stubbornly at 10%, and unqualified foreigners are unlikely to meet with much sympathy from French employers. **Non-EU citizens** will find it near-impossible to get a work permit without a firm job offer. In order to hire a non-EU foreigner in France, the employer must prove that the hiree can perform a task which cannot be performed by a French person. On the bright side, many employers look favorably on English-language skills; if you're bilingual, your chances

VISA INFORMATION. EU citizens have the right to work and study in France without a visa, but they are required to have a **residency permit** (*carte de séjour*). By law, all EU citizens must be given equality of opportunity when applying to jobs not directly related to national security. In addition, **non-EU citizens** wishing to **work** in France must have a firm offer of employment authorization from the French Ministry of Labor before applying for a **long-stay visa** (US$101) through a French consulate. International students looking for part-time work (up to 20hr. per week) can apply for a provisional work authorization upon completing their first academic year in a French university. For **au pairs, scientific researchers,** and **teaching assistants,** special rules apply; check with your local consulate.

of obtaining employment can be greater. For US college students, recent graduates, and young adults, the simplest way to get legal permission to work abroad is through **Council Exchanges Work Abroad Programs.** Fees range from US$300 to US$475. Council Exchanges can help you obtain a three- to six-month work permit/visa and also provides assistance with finding jobs and housing.

LONG-TERM WORK

If you're planning on spending a substantial amount of time (more than three months) working in France, search for a job well in advance. International placement agencies are often the easiest way to find employment abroad, especially for teaching English. **Internships**—a good option for college students—are a good way to segue into working abroad. Although they are often unpaid or poorly paid, many say the experience is well worth it. Be wary of companies that claim the ability to get you a job abroad for a fee—often the same listings are available online or in newspapers, or are even out-of-date. Reputable organizations include:

French-American Chamber of Commerce (FACC), International Career Development Programs, 1350 Avenue of the Americas, 6th fl., New York, NY 10019 (☎212-765-4460; www.faccnyc.org) has work programs, internships, and teaching opportunities.

International Association for the Exchange of Students for Technical Experience (IAESTE), 10400 Little Patuxent Pkwy., Suite 250, Columbia, MD 21044, USA (☎410-997-2200; www.aipt.org). 8- to 12-week programs in France for college students who have completed 2 years of technical study.

TEACHING ENGLISH

Teaching jobs abroad are rarely well-paid, with the exception of some elite private American schools. Volunteering as a teacher in lieu of getting paid is also a popular option; even in those cases, teachers often get some sort of a daily stipend to help with living expenses. In almost all cases, you must have at least a bachelor's degree to be a full-fledged teacher, although college undergraduates can often get summer positions teaching or tutoring. The **Fulbright Teaching Assistantship and French Teaching Assistantship** program, offered through the French Ministry of Education, is the best option for students and recent grads.

Many schools require teachers to have a **Teaching English as a Foreign Language (TEFL)** certificate. Not having this certification does not necessarily exclude you from finding a teaching job, but certified teachers often find higher-paying jobs. Native English speakers working in private schools are

LET'S GO

ALTERNATIVES TO TOURISM

most often hired for English-immersion classrooms where no French is spoken. Those volunteering or teaching in poorer public schools are more likely to be working in both English and French. Placement agencies or university fellowship programs are the best resources for finding teaching jobs. Alternatively, you can contact schools directly or just try your luck once you get there. If you are going to try the latter, the best time to look is several weeks before the start of the school year.

International Schools Services (ISS), 15 Roszel Rd., Box 5910, Princeton, NJ 08543-5910, USA (☎609-452-0990; www.iss.edu). Hires teachers for more than 200 overseas schools including France; candidates should have experience teaching or with international affairs. 2-year commitment expected.

Fulbright English Teaching Assistantship, US Student Programs Division, Institute of International Education, 809 United Nations Plaza, New York, NY 10017-3580, USA (☎212-883-8200; www.iie.org). Sends college graduates to teach in France. Sponsors international relations, civil service, and human rights training initiatives.

French Ministry of Education Teaching Assistantship in France, Cultural Service of the French Embassy, 972 Fifth Ave., New York, NY 10021, USA (☎212-439-1407; www.frenchculture.org/education). Program for US citizens sends 1500 college students and recent grads to teach English part-time in France.

AU PAIR WORK

Au pairs are typically women (although sometimes men), aged 18-27, who work as live-in nannies, caring for children and doing light housework in foreign countries in exchange for room, board, and a small spending allowance or stipend. Most former au pairs speak favorably of their experience. One perk of the job is that it allows you to really get to know the country without the high expenses of traveling. Drawbacks, however, often include long hours of constantly being on duty and somewhat mediocre pay. In France, au pair jobs can pay around €75 per week. Much of the au pair experience really does depend on the family with whom you're placed. The agencies below are a good starting point.

L'Accueil Familial des Jeunes Étrangers, 23 rue du Cherche-Midi, 75006 Paris (☎01 42 22 50 34; accueil@afje-paris.org/fr/accuieller.php). Arranges summer and 18-month au pair jobs (€25 fee) and similar jobs for non-students which require 30hr. of work per week in exchange for room, board, employment benefits, and a metro pass.

Au Pair Homestay, World Learning, Inc., 1015 15th St. NW, Suite 750, Washington, DC 20005, USA (☎800-287-2477; fax 202-408-5397).

Au Pair in Europe, P.O. Box 68056, Blakely Postal Outlet, Hamilton, Ontario, Canada L8M 3M7 (☎905-545-6305; www.princeent.com).

Childcare International, Ltd., Trafalgar House, Grenville Pl., London NW7 3SA (☎44 020 8906-3116; www.childint.co.uk).

InterExchange, 161 Sixth Ave., New York, NY 10013, USA (☎212-924-0446; www.inter-exchange.org).

SHORT-TERM WORK

Traveling for long periods of time can get expensive. Therefore, many travelers try their hand at odd jobs for a few weeks at a time to help finance another month or two of touring around.

Farm work is one possibility; the autumn *vendanges* (grape harvests) provide plentiful opportunities for backbreaking work for a small allowance and cheap wine. Check out **WWOOF** (World-Wide Opportunities on Organic Farms; WWOOF International, P.O. Box 2675, Lewes BN7 1RB, UK; www.phdcc.com/wwoof), which maintains a list of farms seeking temporary workers in exchange for room and board. **Appellation Contrôlée,** Ulgersmaweg 26c, 9731 BT, Groningen, Holland, offers grape-and other fruit-picking programs in France for a placement fee of €99, or €245 with transportation (☎050 549 2434; www.apcon.nl).

Another popular option is to work at a hostel in exchange for free or discounted room and/or board. Most often, these short-term jobs are found by word of mouth. Youth centers *(centres de jeunesse)* often have job listings—check out our practical information sections in larger cities. Due to the high turnover in the tourism industry, many places are eager for help, even if it is only temporary.

The Information Center, 65 quai d'Orsay, 75007 Paris (☎01 45 56 09 50). Garden level at the American Church. A clearinghouse of info and referrals, providing immediate service to the English speaking people of Paris. The Center maintains a comprehensive database of resources available to those in need of information regarding legal matters, medical resources, housing, language courses, and more. Open Tu-Th 1:15-4pm.

Agence Nationale Pour l'Emploi (ANPE), 4 impasse d'Antin, Paris (☎01 43 59 62 63; www.anpe.fr). ANPE has lots of specific information on employment opportunities in France. Interested parties should bring a work permit and *carte de séjour.* Open M-W and F 9am-5pm, Th 9am-noon.

Centre d'Information et de Documentation Jeunesse (CIDJ), 101 quai Branly, 75740 Paris (☎01 44 49 12 00; www.cidj.asso.fr). CIDJ is an invaluable state-run youth center that provides info on such work-related topics as education, resumes, employment, and careers, both in Paris and throughout France. English spoken. Jobs are posted on the bulletin boards outside. Open M-F 10am-6pm, Sa 9:30am-1pm.

Cultural Restoration in the Côte d'Azur

The summer before my junior year of high school, I went to France for the month of August to work with L'Association pour la Participation et l'Action Régionale (Association for Participation and Regional Action). Established in 1979, this group is an educational youth organization based in Avignon and certified by the French Ministry for Youth and Sport and the Ministry for Regional Development and the Environment. The group organizes young volunteers from around the world to come to Southern France (Provence Alpes-Côte d'Azur region and the Mediterranean) and work on the restoration and management of 25-30 sites. Projects last from three weeks to six months and are highly subsidized: a three-week trip costs €200-300 on average and includes food, housing, training, materials, weekend trips, and transportation around France. APARE focuses on areas of architectural heritage and also on maintaining the natural environments in which they are found.

My *chantier*, or worksite, was in St-Tropez, perched on the Mediterranean among 100-year-old stone ruins, snobby cafes, and beautiful people. We lived in the Citadel, camping underneath tents and on army cots, living out of backpacks. I was the only American volunteer among a group of 12 other European teenagers, the majority of whom were French but who also included Danish, German, Swiss, and Dutch participants. For the teenage group, we had two friendly group leaders: Ouialda, originally from Algeria, was our main supervisor and took care of us at the campsite, and Phillip, a skilled artisan who helped us with our on-site work. On an average day, we woke up at 7am to clean up and eat breakfast by 8am, when everyone (except two people who stayed behind on the clean-up/cooking shift for the day) headed off to the site—a 17th-century arms battery called Point-Sur-Capon on the coast. As the scorching sun lifted over the rocky hillside, we trudged uphill about 500m with our pick-axes, hoes, rakes, and cement shovels.

There were two areas to the site: below, an old stone building where arms had been stored; a little farther up the craggy hillside was a semi-circular stone arc about 20m long where canons were once perched. We spent most of the first week clearing away the undergrowth in the area. Along both sites, we removed a few trees and used machetes to clean out the underbrush. When we had finished, we could not only see the amazing stone work on the site but also, suddenly, the Mediterranean's deep blue water, dotted with sailboats and pleasure-cruisers. The second week focused on the lower site, where we attempted to clean up the building by restoring some of the stones in the walls and raking out the interior. We made our own cement with lime and sand from the beach below and filled in the dilapidated walls. After that, we moved up to the top for the third week and rebuilt the wall with stones found along the area, making it as even as possible. We ate lunch at the site, usually French bread with cheese and meat, and then we finished up work around 1:30 or 2pm to avoid the afternoon heat. Afternoons were spent drinking beer in the cafes, playing on the stone beaches of St. Tropez, or sleeping under the pine canopies of the Citadel accompanied by a few dozen peacocks.

This was no vacation tripping through hostels and looking at museums. I got to experience so much of southern French life in three weeks, very cheaply, as well as being immersed into its cultural history. Every weekend we took long trips to visit other *chantiers*, where we stayed up all night in centuries-old castles draining liters of wine from the next-door vineyard. We daytripped into little villages dotting Provence, visiting leather fairs and wine festivals where the only other people there were locals. We drove to a monastery where we bought bottles of lavender sugar and rose petal-lilac jam and swam in a frozen waterfall three miles off the road.

This is the perfect trip for the enthusiastic Francophile because you not only experience the ancient castles, the fragrant hillsides, the incredible food, and the warm people, but because you are helping to maintain and rebuild some of France's most majestic spots as well.

For more info on L'Association pour la Participation et l'Action Régionale, see listing for APARE on page p. 62.

***Cat Walleck** is an undergraduate at Harvard University, majoring in Romance Language Studies (French, Spanish, and Italian). She plans to travel to the Avignon Theater Festival to conduct thesis research.*

European Employment Services (EURES; ☎ 08 00 90 97 00) facilitates employment between EU countries. For EU citizens only.

FOR FURTHER READING ON ALTERNATIVES TO TOURISM.

How to Get a Job in Europe, by Sanborn and Matherly. Surrey Books, 1999 (US$22).

How to Live Your Dream of Volunteering Overseas, by Collins, DeZerega, and Heckscher. Penguin Books, 2002 (US$17).

International Directory of Voluntary Work, by Whetter and Pybus. Peterson's Guides and Vacation Work, 2000 (US$16).

International Jobs, by Kocher and Segal. Perseus Books, 1999 (US$18).

Overseas Summer Jobs 2002, by Collier and Woodworth. Peterson's Guides and Vacation Work, 2002 (US$18).

Work Abroad: The Complete Guide to Finding a Job Overseas, by Hubbs, Griffith, and Nolting. Transitions Abroad Publishing, 2000 ($16).

Work Your Way Around the World, by Susan Griffith. Worldview Publishing Services, 2001 (US$18).

Invest Yourself: The Catalogue of Volunteer Opportunities, published by the Commission on Voluntary Service and Action (☎ 718-638-8487).

PARIS

Paris has been a center of culture, trade, and conflict for centuries. In the midst of it all, it became a symbol of romance, revolution, heroism, and hedonism. From tangled medieval alleys to broad 19th-century boulevards, from Notre Dame's gargoyles to the futuristic motions of the Parc de la Villette, from the masterpieces of the Louvre to the installations of avant-garde galleries, Paris presents itself as both a harbor of tradition and a hotbed of innovation. The city seems, miraculously, to foster simultaneously a spirit of revolution and a reverence for history, devoting as much energy to preserving conventions as to shattering them.

HIGHLIGHTS OF PARIS

FROM THE TOP, Paris looks even more beautiful. Share the view with gargoyles at **Notre Dame** (p. 107); ascend the **Arc de Triomphe** (p. 118) to see both Champs-Élysées glamor and the modern architecture of La Défense; or, if the **Eiffel Tower** (p. 117) is just too last-century, try the hot-air balloon at the **Parc André-Citroën** (p. 122).

RELISH world-class art at major museums like the **Louvre** (p. 125), **Musée d'Orsay** (p. 126), **Centre Pompidou** (p. 126). See sculpture and paintings in centuries-old mansions and elegant gardens at the **Musée Rodin** (p. 126) and **Musée Picasso** (p. 126). Finally, walk among the waterlilies that inspired Monet at his house in **Giverny** (p. 145).

REVOLUTIONARY NIGHTLIFE. Storm the **Bastille** district (p. 134)—once home to the legendary prison, now a center of Parisian partying. Enjoy a beer on the Left Bank next to a real guillotine, then bounce downstairs to frolic in the 18th-century prison (p. 133).

◼ INTERCITY TRANSPORTATION

THE AIRPORTS

ROISSY-CHARLES DE GAULLE

Transatlantic flights use Charles de Gaulle (☎01 48 62 22 80; www.adp.fr). The airport includes a 24hr. English-speaking info center.

Trains: RER. To **Paris** from Roissy-CDG, take the free shuttle bus *(navette)* from Terminal 1. (every 6-10min.) From there, the RER B (one of the Parisian commuter rail lines) runs to central Paris. To transfer to the metro, get off at Gare du Nord, Châtelet-Les-Halles, or St-Michel. To **Roissy-CDG** from Paris, take the RER B to Roissy, which is the end of the line. 30-35min.; RER every 15min. 5am-midnight; €7.75, children €5.50.

Buses: Roissybus (☎01 49 25 61 87) runs between 9 rue Scribe, near M: Opéra, and terminals 1, 2, and 9. Tickets can be purchased on the bus (45min.; to airport every 15min. 5:45am-11pm, from airport every 15min. 6am-11pm; €8.10). **Air France Buses** (recorded info in English ☎08 92 35 08 20) run to 2 sections of the city. Stops at or between terminals 2A and 2F and at Terminal 1 on the Departures level. Buy tickets on board. Line # 2 runs to: the **Arc de Triomphe** (M: Charles de Gaulle-Etoile) at 1 av. Carnot and **place de la Porte de Maillot/Palais des Congrès** (M: Porte de Maillot) on bd. Gouvion St-Cyr (both 35min.; every 15min. 5:45am-11pm; €10, children €5, round-trip €17; 15% group discount). Line # 4 runs to: **rue du Commandant**

Île-de-France

Mouchette opposite the Hôtel Méridien (M: Montparnasse-Bienvenüe) and **Gare de Lyon** (M: Gare de Lyon) at 20bis bd. Diderot (both every 30min. 7am-9:30pm; €11.50, children €5.75, round-trip €19.55; 15% group discounts).

ORLY

Charters and many continental flights use Orly, located 18km south of the city. Info in English 6am-11:45pm (☎01 49 75 15 15).

Trains: RER. From Orly Sud Gate G or Gate I, Platform 1, or Orly Ouest Level G, Gate F, take the **Orly-Rail** shuttle bus (every 15min. 6am-11pm; €5.15, children €3.55) to the Pont de Rungis/Aéroport d'Orly train stop, where you can board the RER C2 for a number of destinations in **Paris.** (Call RATP ☎08 36 68 41 14 for info in English. 35min., every 15min. 6am-11pm, €5.35.) The **Jetbus** (every 15min. 6:20am-10:50pm, €5.15) provides a quick connection between Orly Sud, gate H, platform 2, or Orly Ouest Level 0, Gate C, and **M: Villejuif-Louis Aragon** on Line 7 of the metro.

Bus: RATP Orlybus (☎08 36 68 77 14) runs to metro and RER stop **Denfert-Rochereau,** 14ème, from Orly Sud (30min.; every 10-15min. 6am-11:30pm from Orly to Denfert-Rochereau, 5:35am-11pm from Denfert-Rochereau to Orly; €5.70). You can also board the Orlybus at Dareau-St-Jacques, Glacière-Tolbiac, and Porte de Gentilly. **Air France Buses** run between Orly and **Gare Montparnasse,** near Hôtel Méridien, 6ème (M: Montparnasse-

Bienvenüe), and the **Invalides** Air France agency, pl. des Invalides (30min.; every 15min. 6am-11:30pm; €7.50, round-trip €12.75). **Air France** shuttles stop at Orly Ouest and Orly Sud's departures levels.

Orlyval: RATP also runs **Orlyval** (☎01 69 93 53 00), a combination of metro, RER, and VAL rail shuttles, and probably your fastest option. The VAL shuttle goes from Antony (a stop on the RER Line B) to Orly Ouest and Sud. You can either get a ticket just for the VAL (€7), or a combination VAL-RER ticket (€8.80 and up). Buy tickets at any RATP booth in the city, or from the Orlyval agencies at Orly Ouest, Orly Sud, and Antony. **To Orly:** Be careful when taking the RER B from Paris to Orly, because it splits into 2 lines right before the Antony stop. Get on the train that says "St-Rémy-Les-Chevreuse" or just look for the track that has a lit-up sign saying "Antony-Orly." (35min. from Châtelet; every 10min. M-Sa 6am-10:30pm, Su and holidays 7am-11pm.) **From Orly:** Trains arrive at Orly Ouest 2min. after reaching Orly Sud (32min. to Châtelet; every 10min. M-Sa 6am-10:30pm, Su 7am-11pm).

BEAUVAIS

Ryanair, easyJet, and other intercontinental airlines often fly to **Aéroport Beauvais.** Buses run between the airport and bd. Pershing in the 17ème, near the hotel Concorde Lafayette (M: Porte Maillot). Tickets are €10 and can be purchased in the arrivals lounge of the airport or on the bus. Call ☎03 44 11 46 86 or consult www.aeroportbeauvais.com for bus schedules and other information.

BY TRAIN

If you're traveling between Paris and another European city, trains can be a scenic and convenient option. The prices below are the undiscounted fares for one-way, second-class tickets unless otherwise noted. Timetables and prices vary greatly according to the time of day, day of the week, and season; for the most current listings, consult the SNCF website at www.sncf.fr.

Gare du Nord: to northern France, Britain, Belgium, the Netherlands, Scandinavia, Eastern Europe, and northern Germany (Cologne, Hamburg). To: **Brussels** (1½hr., €68); **Amsterdam** (4-5hr., €90); **London** (by the Eurostar Chunnel; 3hr., up to €300).

Gare de l'Est: to eastern France (Champagne, Alsace, Lorraine, Strasbourg), Luxembourg, parts of Switzerland (Basel, Zürich, Lucerne), southern Germany (Frankfurt, Munich), Austria, Hungary, and Prague. To: **Luxembourg** (4-5hr., €45); **Munich** (9hr., €154); **Prague** (15hr., €152); **Vienna** (15hr., €154); **Zürich** (7hr., €73).

Gare de Lyon: to southern and southeastern France (Lyon, Provence, Riviera), parts of Switzerland (Geneva, Lausanne, Berne), Italy, and Greece. To: **Geneva** (4hr., €97); **Florence** (13hr., €120); **Rome** (15hr., €176).

Gare d'Austerlitz: to the Loire Valley, southwestern France (Bordeaux, Pyrenees), Spain, and Portugal. (TGV to southwestern France leaves from Gare Montparnasse.) To: **Barcelona** (12hr., €140) and **Madrid** (12-13hr., €102).

Gare St-Lazare: to Normandy.

Gare Montparnasse: to Brittany and southwestern France on the TGV.

BY BUS

International buses arrive in Paris at **Gare Routière Internationale du Paris-Gallieni** (M: Gallieni), just outside Paris at 28 av. du Général de Gaulle, Bagnolet 93170. **Eurolines** (☎01 49 72 57 80, €0.34 per min.; www.eurolines.fr) sells tickets to most destinations in France and neighboring countries.

Paris Overview

1 Cimetière Montmartre
2 Basilique du Sacré-Coeur
3 Parc de la Villette
4 Parc des Buttes-Chaumont
5 Jardins du Trocadéro
6 Palais de Chaillot
7 Cimetière de Passy
8 American Embassy
9 British Embassy
10 Petit Palais
11 Grand Palais
12 Arc de Triomphe
13 Madeleine
14 Gare St-Lazare
15 Parc Monceau
16 Palais de la Découverte
17 Opéra Garnier
18 Galeries Lafayette
19 Au Printemps
20 Gare du Nord
21 Gare de l'Est
22 Opéra Bastille
23 Palais Omnisports de Paris-Bercy
24 Ministère des Finances
25 Gare de Lyon
26 Parc Montsouris
27 Cité Universitaire
28 Cimetière Montparnasse
29 Gare Montparnasse

30 Bureau des Objets Trouvés (Lost and Found)
31 Louvre
32 Palais Royale
33 Forum des Halles
34 Musée de l'Orangerie
35 Central Post Office
36 Bourse
37 Bibliothèque Nationale
38 Ecole des Arts et Métiers
39 Archives Nationales
40 Musée Carnavalet
41 Musée Picasso
42 Centre George Pompidou
43 place des Vosges
44 Musée Victor Hugo
45 Notre Dame
46 Mémorial de la Déportation
47 Université de Paris (Sorbonne)

48 Ecole Normal Supérieure
49 Musée de Cluny
50 Museum Nationale d'Histoire Naturelle
51 Panthéon
52 Eglise St-Etienne du Mont
53 La Mosquée
54 Jardin des Plantes
55 Jardins du Luxembourg
56 Eglise St-Sulpice
57 Théâtre Nationale de l'Odéon
58 Eiffel Tower
59 Champs de Mars

60 Ecole Militaire
61 UNESCO
62 Hôtel des Invalides
63 Assemblée Nationale
64 Musée d'Orsay
65 Cimetière de l'Est de Pere Lachaise

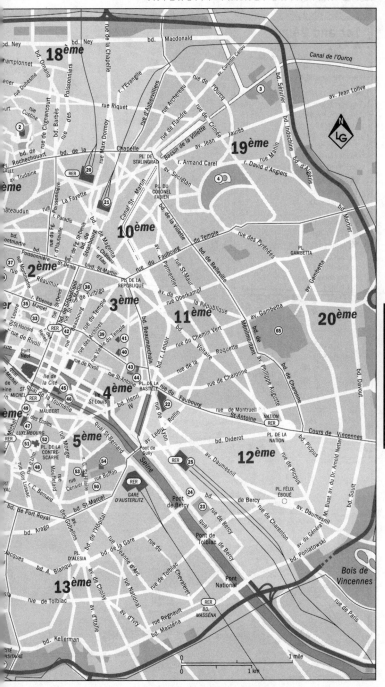

PARIS

1er and 2ème

ACCOMMODATIONS

Centre International de Paris, **15**   D4
Hôtel Montpensier, **14**   C4
Hôtel Tiquetonne, **9**   F3

FOOD

Au Père Fouettard, **12**   F4
Babylone Bis, **8**   F3
Le Fumoir, **18**   E5
Lamen Kintaro, **3**   C3
Les Noces de Jeannette, **2**   C2
Papou Lounge, **10**   E3
La Victoire Suprême du Coeur, **16**   E4

SHOPPING

Espace Kiliwatch, **7**   E3
Samaritaine, **19**   E5
Le Shop, **5**   E3
W. H. Smith, **13**   A4
Zadig & Voltaire, **11**   E3

NIGHTLIFE

Banana Café, **17**   F4
Le Café Noir, **6**   E3
Le Champmeslé, **4**   C3
Rex Club, **1**   E1

Map labels:

9ème

RICHELIE

r. Chaussée d'Antin

Chaussée d'Antin La Fayette M

bd. Haussmann

r. Marivaux
r. de Gramont
r. de Choiseul

Opéra

bd. des Italiens

r. Auber

r. Scribe

RER AUBER

bd. des Capucines

M OPÉRA
RER

r. de la Michodière

r. du Quatre

QUATRE SEPTEMBRE

r. Daunou

bd. de la Madeleine

r. des Capucines

r. de la Paix

r. des Petit Champs

av. de l'Opéra

La Colonne
PL. VENDÔME

PL. DU MARCHÉ ST-HONORÉ

r. de la Sourdière

M PYRAMIDES

Fontai
de Molle

8ème

r. St-Honoré

r. Royale

Musée Bouilhet Christofle

r. du Marché St-Honoré

r. de Castiglione

r. du Mont Thabor

r. du 29 Juillet

r. St-Honoré

r. St-Roch

r. des Pyramides

1er

r. Boissy d'Anglas

M CONCORDE M

r. de Rivoli

M TUILERIES

PL. AN
MA

PAL

PL. DE LA CONCORDE

Galerie Nationale du Jeu de Paume

JARDIN DES TUILERIES

Musée de l'Orangerie

Pont de la Concorde

quai des Tuileries

Seine River

Pont Passerelle Solférino

qua

Pont Royal

Pont Carro

MUSÉE D'ORSAY
RER

Musée d'Orsay

7ème

0   200 yards
0   200 meters

PARIS

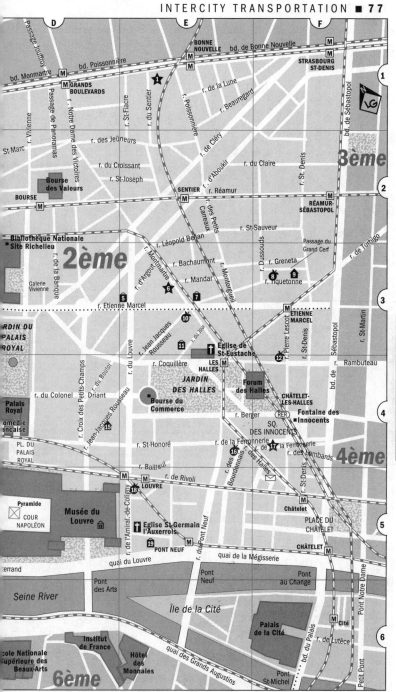

PARIS

3ème and 4ème

ACCOMMODATIONS	
Le Fauconnier, **32**	D5
Le Fourcy, **30**	D5
Grand Hôtel Jeannne d'Arc, **27**	E4
Hôtel du Marais, **2**	C2
Hôtel Picard, **1**	C4
Hôtel Rivoli, **29**	D2
Hôtel du Séjour, **6**	C4
Maubuisson, **31**	C5
FOOD	
L'As du Falafel, **20**	C4
B Tea's, **9**	C3
Chez Janou, **13**	E4
Au Petit Fer à Cheval, **19**	C4
Pain, Vin, Fromage, **10**	B3
Piccolo Teatro, **24**	C4
★ **NIGHTLIFE**	
3W Kafé, **23**	C4
Amnésia Café, **17**	C4
L'Apparement Café, **7**	D3
Les Bains, **3**	A3
La Belle Hortense, **22**	C4
Chez Richard, **16**	C4
Le Dépôt, **4**	A3
Les Étages, **18**	C4
Villa Keops, **5**	A3
■ **SHOPPING**	
Alternatives, **25**	D4
Bernie X, **28**	D4
Culotte, **26**	D4
Free "P" Star, **14**	E4
Monic, **21**	C4
Les Mots à la Bouche, **15**	C4

PL. DE LA BASTILLE

Colonne de Juillet

D4
D3

Musée Carnavalet, **12**
Musée Picasso, **8**

bd. Bourdon

BASTILLE

r. de la Bastille

BASTILLE

BASTILLE

r. St-Antoine

r. Castex

r. de la Cerisaie

r. de l'Arsenal

r. de Mornay

quai Henri IV

Mémorial du Martyr Juif Inconnu

Roger Verlomme

PL. DES VOSGES

r. de Birague

r. de Turenne

r. du Petit Musc

bd. Henri IV

r. de Sully

r. de Sully

Seine

Hôtel de Lamoignon

r. Necker

Hôtel de Ville

r. de Jarente

r. d'Ormesson

r. de Beautreillis

4ème

17 r. Beautreillis

r. des Lions St-Paul

r. de Morland

bd. Morland

Pavillon de l'Arsenal

Carnavalet

r. Payée

r. de Sévigné

r. de Sicile

PL. DU MARCHÉ STE-CATHERINE

ST-PAUL

r. Charles v

r. St-Paul

St-Paul-St-Louis

SULLY MORLAND

r. Mahler

r. Charlemagne

Village St-Paul

Pont de Sully

Institut du Monde Arabe

r. des Rosiers

r. des Écouffes

F. Duval

r. du Roi de Sicile

r. du Trésor

r. du Fauconnier

r. de l'Ave Maria

quai des Célestins

Voie G. Pompidou

quai d'Anjou

r. St-Louis en l'île

Église St-Louis en l'île

Pont de Béthune

r. Vieille du Temple

r. Cloche-Perce

La Maison Européenne de la Photographie

r. du Figuier

r. du Prévôt

r. de Fourcy

Hôtel de Sens

Pont Marie

r. des Deux Ponts

ÎLE ST. LOUIS

quai de Bourbon

quai de Béthune

Pont de la Tournelle

quai de la Tournelle

des Blancs-Manteaux

r. du Bourg-Tibourg

Hôtel de Beauvais

r. Geoffroy l'Asnier

PONT MARIE

quai de l'Hôtel de Ville

Voie G. Pompidou

PL. BAUDOYER

r. des Barres

r. St-Louis-Philippe

r. François Miron

quai de l'Hôtel de Ville

PONT MARIE

Pont Louis Philippe

Pont St-Louis

quai d'Orléans

r. Ste-Croix de la Bretonnerie

r. de Moussy

des Mauvais Garçons

Église St-Gervais -St-Protais

PL. ST. GERVAIS

Hôtel de Ville

Pont de la Tournelle

Pont Marie

r. du Platre

r. des Archives

r. de la Verrerie

r. du Temple

HÔTEL DE VILLE

Hôtel de Ville

PL. DE L'HÔTEL DE VILLE

Pont d'Arcole

ÎLE DE LA CITÉ

Notre Dame

Cloître Notre Dame

quai de Montebello

r. St-Merri

r. du Renard

Beaub

PL. IGOR STRAVINSKY

av. Victoria

Pont Notre Dame

Pont d'Arcole

r. de la Cité

r. St-Jacques

Place E. Michelet

r. des Lombards

r. St-Martin

r. St-Bon

r. de la Coutellerie

quai de Gesvres

r. Pernelle

Tour St-Jacques

CHÂTELET

Central Nightbus Hub

PL. DU CHÂTELET

quai de Gesvres

Pont au Change

Pont Notre Dame

CITÉ

cité

r. de Lutèce

bd. du Palais

r. du Palais

ST-MICHEL (RER)

PARIS

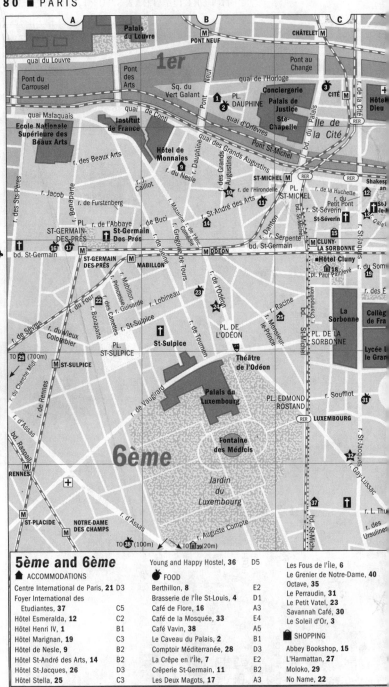

5ème and 6ème

▲ ACCOMMODATIONS

Centre International de Paris, 21	D3
Foyer International des Etudiantes, 37	C5
Hôtel Esmeralda, 12	C2
Hôtel Henri IV, 1	B1
Hôtel Marignan, 19	C3
Hôtel de Nesle, 9	B2
Hôtel St-André des Arts, 14	B2
Hôtel St-Jacques, 26	D3
Hôtel Stella, 25	C3

Young and Happy Hostel, 36 — D5

🍴 FOOD

Berthillon, 8	E2
Brasserie de l'Île St-Louis, 4	D1
Café de Flore, 16	A3
Café de la Mosquée, 33	E4
Café Vavin, 38	A5
Le Caveau du Palais, 2	B1
Comptoir Méditerranée, 28	D3
La Crêpe en l'Île, 7	E2
Crêperie St-Germain, 11	B2
Les Deux Magots, 17	A3

Les Fous de l'Île, 6	
Le Grenier de Notre-Dame, 40	
Octave, 35	
Le Perraudin, 31	
Le Petit Vatel, 23	
Savannah Café, 30	
Le Soleil d'Or, 3	

🛍 SHOPPING

Abbey Bookshop, 15	
L'Harmattan, 27	
Moloko, 29	
No Name, 22	

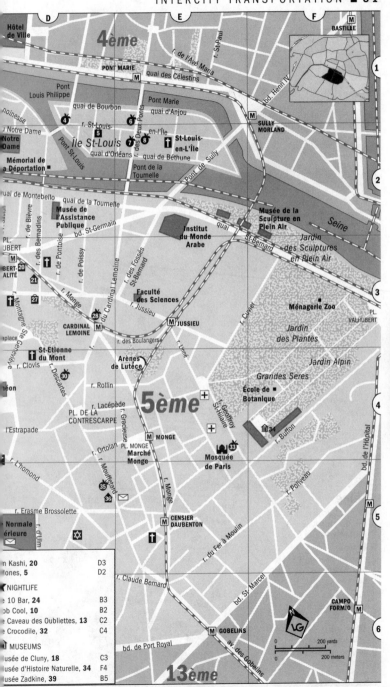

16ème

Musée Guimet
Palais Galliera
Palais de Tokyo
Musée d'Art Moderne
TROCADÉRO
av. du Président D'IÉNA
PL. Wilson
IÉNA
Palais de Chaillot
PL. DE VARSOVIE
Pont de d'Iéna
Seine
av. de New York
quai Branly

8ème

av. George V
av. Montaigne
r. Jean Goujon
r. François
cours Albert 1er
PL. DE L'ALMA
ALMA MARCEAU
Pont de l'Alma
PONT DE L'ALMA (RER)
PL. DE LA RÉSISTANCE
quai d'Orsay
The American Church in Paris
r. de l'Université
r. Jean Nicot
r. Malar
r. de la Comète
av. Franco-Russe
r. E. Valentin
r. de Monttessuy
r. de Rapp
r. Dupont des Loges
r. St-Dominique
r. Amélie
Tour Eiffel
av. Élie de Reclus
av. du Général Camou
r. Sédillot
r. de l'Exposition
r. de Grenelle
LA TOUR MAUBOUR
RER CHAMP DE MARS / TOUR EIFFEL
av. Gustave Eiffel
J. Bouvard
av. de la Bourdonnais
r. Augereau
r. du Champ de Mars
r. Cler
av. Charles Floquet
av. Émile Deschanel
PL. JACQUES RUEFF
av. de la Motte-Picquet
r. Jean Ray
PARC DU CHAMPS DE MARS
av. Charles Risler
ECOLE MILITAIRE M
PL. DE L'ECOLE MILITAIRE
JAF L'IN
r. de la Fédération
av. de Suffren
Mur de la Paix
Statue de Maréchal Joffre
av. E. Acollas
Ecole Militaire
av. Duq
BIR HAKEIM M
bd. de Grenelle
r. Desaix
COUR D'HONNEUR
PL. DE FONTENOY
av. de Ségur
av. de Saxe
LA MOTTE-PICQUET GRENELLE M
U.N.E.S.C.O.
PL. CAMBRONNE M CAMBRONNE
bd. Garibaldi
r. Frémicourt
r. Pérignon
M SÉGUR
15ème
r. Cambronne
av. de Suffren
r. François Bonvin
r. Jean Daudin
SÈVRES LECOURBE M
Rousain

7ème

🏠 **ACCOMMODATIONS**

Hôtel Eiffel Rive Gauche, **5**	B3
Hôtel Montebello, **9**	E5

🍎 **FOOD**

L'Auberge Bressane, **6**	C4
Café des Lettres, **3**	F3

🛍 **SHOPPING**

Ciné-Images, **8**	D5
Florent Monestier, **4**	C3
Moloko, **10**	E6

⭐ **NIGHTLIFE**

Le Club des Poètes, **2**	D3

🏛 **MUSEUMS**

Musée d'Orsay, **1**	F3
Musée Rodin, **7**	D4

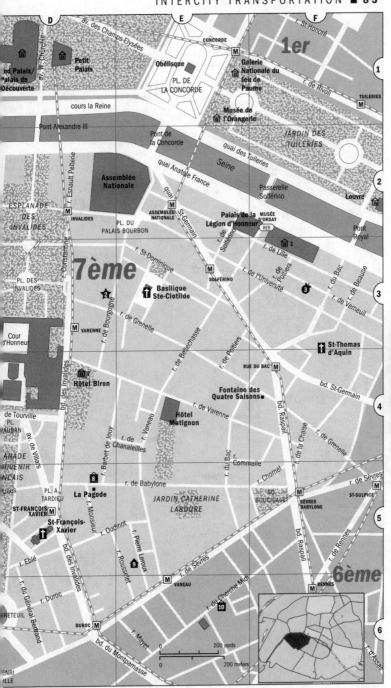

PARIS

8ème

■ ACCOMMODATIONS

Hôtel Europe-Liège, **3** — F1
Union Chrétienne des Jeunes
Filles, **1** — E1

● FOOD

Objectifs Crêpes, **2** — C3
Toi, **8** — E1

■ SHOPPING

Sephora, **4** — B3

★ NIGHTLIFE

buddha-bar, **9** — E4
House of Live, **7** — B3
Latina Café, **5** — B3
Le Queen, **6** — B3

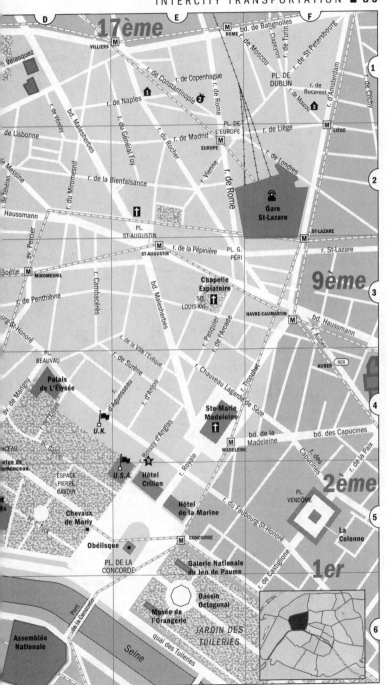

PARIS

18ème

9ème

17ème

r. du Faubourg Poissonnière

PL DU CHATEAU ROUGE

r. Myrha

r. de la Goutte

BARBÈS ROCHECHOUART

bd. de Magenta

bd. Barbès

r. Christiani

r. de Sofia

Belhomme

r. du Delta

r. de Dunkerque

r. de Rochechouart

r. Pétrelle

r. Feutrier

r. de Clignancourt

r. Muller

r. A del Sarte

r. Cazotte

r. Nodier

r. P. Picard

r. d'Orsel

r. Gérando

r. Turgot

r. Ramey

r. du Baigneur

r. Custine

r. Ferme

r. Lamarck

Basilique du Sacré-Coeur

r. de la Bonne

r. Ronsard

r. Sevestre

r. Briquet

ANVERS

r. de Steinkerque

Mont Cenis

r. Lamarck

Cimetière St-Vincent

r. St-Vincent

r. Lamarck np

r. Paul Féval

Lapin Agile

Clos Montmartre

PL DU TERTRE

r. St-Rustique

r. Poulbo

r. A. Barsacq

r. Gabrielle

r. Foyatier

PL ST-PIERRE

bd. de Rochechouart

r. d'Orsel

B. de Saron

r. Cretet

r. Say

r. des Saules

r. des

r. du Calvaire

r. Berthe

r. des trois Frères

r. de Laveuville

r. Y. Le Tac

r. des Martyrs

r. André Gill

r. Violet-le-Duc

r. Victor M

Moulin Radet

av. Junot

Moulin de la Galette

PL. EMILE GOUDEAU

r. Burq

r. Durantin

ABBESSES

av. Antoine Plemonnes

r. Houdon

r. Germain Pilon

av. Frochot

PL PIGALLE

r. Victor M

r. Lamarck

Sq. Caulaincourt

r. Caulaincourt

r. de l'Abreuvoir

LAMARCK CAULAINCOURT

r. de Curat

r. Tholoze

r. des Abbesses

r. Véron

r. Lepic

PIGALLE

PL PIGALLE

r. J.-Baptiste pigalle

r. Duperr

r. Frochot

r. Forest

r. Cavallotti

r. Joseph de Maistre

r. Tourlaque

Cimetière de Montmartre

r. Joseph de Maistre

r. Damrémont

r. Coustou

r. Puget

r. Fontaine

r. Mansart

Hôtel Renan-Scheffer

r. Chaptal

r. Blanche

r. de Douai

r. de Calais

r. Ballu

r. Duperr

r. Doual

Bal du Moulin Rouge

PL. BLANCHE

BLANCHE

r. Bruxelles

bd. de Clichy

av. Rachel

r. Forest

bd. de Clichy

PL. DE CLICHY

av. de Clichy

r. d'Amsterdam

r. de Parme

r. de Bucharest

r. Cardinal Mercier

r. Moncey

r. de Vintimille

r. A. MAX

PL. DE CLICHY

PARIS

9ème and 18ème

▲ ACCOMMODATIONS	
Hôtel Caulaincourt, 1	C1
Hôtel Chopin, 14	D6
Perfect Hôtel, 10	D4
Woodstock Hostel, 11	E4
Village Hostel, 7	E2

● FOOD	
Anarkali Sarangui, 9	C4
Comme Par Hasard, 13	C4
Djerba Cacher Chez Guichi, 2	F2
Restaurant Américain	
Chez Haynes, 12	D4
Refuge des Fondues, 6	D2
Le Soleil Gourmand, 4	C2

◆ SHOPPING	
Spree, 5	D2

★ NIGHTLIFE	
Bus Palladium, 8	C3
Chez Camille, 3	C2

PARIS

✦ ORIENTATION

The **Seine River** flows from east to west through the heart of Paris. Two islands in the Seine, **Île de la Cité** and neighboring **Île St-Louis**, are situated in the geographical center of the city. The Seine splits Paris into two sections: the **Rive Gauche** (Left Bank) to the south of the river and the **Rive Droite** (Right Bank) to the north. Modern Paris is divided into **20 arrondissements** (districts) that spiral clockwise outward from the center of the city. Each *arrondissement* is referred to by its number (e.g. the Third, the Sixteenth). In French, "Third" is said *troisième* (TWAZ-yem) and abbreviated "3ème"; "Sixteenth" is said *seizième* (SEZ-yem) and abbreviated "16ème." The same goes for every *arrondissement* except the First, which is said *premier* (PREM-yay) and abbreviated 1er.

⌷ LOCAL TRANSPORTATION

The **RATP (Régie Autonome des Transports Parisiens)** coordinates a network of subways, buses, and commuter trains in and around Paris. For info, contact **La Maison de la RATP**, right across the street from M: Gare de Lyon (190 rue de Bercy) or the **Bureau de Tourisme RATP**, pl. de la Madeleine, 8ème (☎01 40 06 71 45; M: Madeleine; open daily 8:30am-6pm). The RATP also has a helpful English website for visitors (www.ratp.fr/ParisVisite/Eng/index.htm) with extensive information on fares, routes, passes, and services for disabled visitors.

FARES AND PASSES

Individual tickets for the RATP cost €1.30 each and €9.60 for a *carnet* of 10. Each metro ride requires one ticket. The bus takes at least one, sometimes more, depending on connections you make and the time of day. If you're staying in Paris for several days or weeks, a **Carte Orange** can be very economical. Bring an ID photo (taken by machines in most major stations for €3.81) to the ticket counter and ask for a weekly *carte orange hebdomadaire* (€14.50) or the equally swank monthly *carte orange mensuelle* (€48.60). These cards have specific start and end dates (the weekly pass runs M-Su; the monthly starts at the beginning of the month). Prices quoted here are for passes in Zones 1 and 2 (the metro and RER in Paris) and work on all metro, bus, and RER modes of transport. If you're only in town for a day or two, a cheap option is the **Carte Mobilis** (☎08 91 36 20 20; €5.20 for a one-day pass in Zones 1 and 2, available in metro stations), which provides unlimited metro, bus, and RER transportation within Paris.

Paris Visite tickets are valid for unlimited travel on bus, metro, and RER, as well as discounts on sightseeing trips, museum admission, and shopping at stores like Galeries Lafayette, though the discounts do not necessarily outweigh the extra cost. (Available at the airport, metro, and RER stations. One-day pass €8.35, 2 days €13.70, 3 days €18.25, 5 days €26.65.)

METRO

Metro stations are marked with an "M" or with fancy *"Métropolitain"* lettering designed by Art Nouveau legend Hector Guimard. The first trains start running around 5:30am and the last ones leave the end-of-the-line stations (the *portes de Paris*) for the center of the city at about 12:15am. Connections to other lines are indicated by orange *correspondance* signs, exits by blue *sortie* signs. Transfers are free if made within a station; it is not always possible to reverse direction on the same line without exiting the station. **Hold on to your ticket** until you pass the point marked **Limite de Validité des Billets** on the way to the exit. Do not count on buying a metro ticket late at night; some ticket windows close by 10pm. The following stations can be dangerous at night: Barbès-Rochechouart, Pigalle, Anvers, Châtelet-Les-Halles, Gare du Nord, Gare de l'Est. If concerned, take a taxi or Noctambus.

RER

The RER *(Réseau Express Régional)* is the RATP's commuter rail. It passes through central Paris. Within the city, the RER travels much faster than the metro. There are five RER lines, marked A-E, with different branches designated by a number, like the C5 line to Versailles-Rive Gauche. Like the metro, the RER runs from about 5:15am to midnight.

BUS

Although slower and often more costly than the metro, buses can serve as cheap sightseeing tours and helpful introductions to the city's layout. The RATP's *Grand Plan de Paris* includes a map of the bus lines (free at metro stations). The free bus map *Autobus Paris-Plan du Réseau* is available at the tourist office and at metro information booths. Bus tickets are identical to those used on the metro, and can be purchased either in metro stations or on the bus from the driver. *Cartes oranges* and other transport passes *(Paris Visite, Mobilis)* are equally valid in buses and subways (see **Metro**). When you wish to leave the bus, press the red button to illuminate the *arrêt demandé* sign.

NIGHT BUSES. Most buses run daily 6:30am-8:30pm; those marked **Autobus de nuit** continue until 1am. Those named **Noctambus** run all night. Night buses (€2.50) run from the Châtelet stop to the *portes* (end-of-the-line stations) of the city (daily every hr. on the half-hour 1:30-5:30am). Buses also run from the suburbs to Châtelet (every hr. on the hr. 1-6am). Noctambuses I through M, R, and S run along the Left Bank to the southern suburbs. Buses A through H, P, T, and V run on the Right Bank heading north. Look for bus stops marked with a bug-eyed moon sign.

TOUR BUSES. Balabus (☎01 44 68 43 35) stops at virtually every major sight in Paris (Bastille, St-Michel, Louvre, Musée d'Orsay, Concorde, Champs-Élysées, Charles de Gaulle-Etoile; whole loop 1¼ hours). The circuit requires three standard bus tickets and starts at the Grande Arche de La Défense or Gare de Lyon.

TAXIS

Taxis take three passengers; a fourth costs €2.60. Companies include: **Alpha Taxis** (☎01 45 85 85 85), **Taxis Bleus** (☎01 49 36 10 10), and **Taxis G7** (☎01 47 39 47 39).

BIKE RENTAL

Paris à velo, c'est sympa!, 22 rue Alphonse Baudin, 11*ème* (☎01 48 87 60 01; www.paris-velosympa.com). M: St-Richard Lenoir. Half-day (9am-2pm or 2-7pm) €9.50; 9am-7pm €12.50; 24hr. rental €16; credit card deposit. Open daily 9am-1pm and 2-6pm.

Paris-Vélo, 2 rue de Fer-à-Moulin, 5*ème* (☎01 43 37 59 22). M: Censier-Daubenton. Bike rental €14 per day. Open M-Sa 10am-7pm, Su 10am-2pm and 5-7pm.

▓ PRACTICAL INFORMATION

TOURIST AND FINANCIAL SERVICES

Tourist Offices:

Bureau Tour Eiffel, Champs de Mars, 7*ème* (☎08 92 68 31 12). M: Champs de Mars. Open daily May-Sept. 11am-6:40pm.

PARIS

Bureau Gare de Lyon, 12ème (☎01 43 43 33 24). M: Gare de Lyon. Open M-Sa 8am-6pm.

Montmartre Tourist Office, 21, pl. du Tertre, 18ème (☎01 42 62 21 21). M: Anvers. Open daily 10am-7pm.

Tours:

Bateaux-Mouches (☎01 42 25 96 10, info 01 40 76 99 99; www.bateaux-mouches.fr). M: Alma-Marceau. 70min. tours in English. Departures every 30min. 10:15am-10:40pm (no boats 1-2pm) from the Right Bank pier near Pont d'Alma.

Mike's Bullfrog Bike Tours (☎01 56 58 10 54; www.mikesbiketours.com). New Segway tours. Tours meet by the south leg (Pilier Sud) of the Eiffel Tower. Every F 10pm from pl. d'Italie, return 12:30am). Tickets €30, students €28.

Consulates and Embassies: See **Essentials,** p. 8.

Currency Exchange:

American Express, 11 rue Scribe, 9ème (☎01 47 77 79 28). M: Opéra or Auber. Open M-Sa 9am-6:30pm; exchange counters also open Su 10am-5pm.

Thomas Cook, 26 av. de l'Opéra, 1er (☎01 53 29 40 00; fax 01 47 03 32 13). M: Georges V. Open M-Sa 9am-10:55pm, Su 8am-6pm.

Work Opportunities: See **Alternatives to Tourism,** p. 65.

LOCAL SERVICES

GLBT Organizations:

ACT-UP Paris, 45 rue de Sedene, 11ème (☎01 48 06 13 89). M: Bréguet-Sabin.

Boobs Bourg, 26 rue de Montmorency, 3ème (☎01 42 72 80 86). Sign up at this bar to join a Paris-wide lesbian email list with information on lectures and social events.

Centre Gai et Lesbien, 3 rue Keller, 11ème (☎01 43 57 21 47; fax 01 43 57 27 93). M: Ledru-Rollin or Bastille. Open M-F 4-8pm.

Ecoute Gaie (☎01 44 93 01 02). Crisis hotline. Open M-Tu and F evenings; if no one answers, a message will give the hours for the next 2 weeks.

Dry Cleaning:

Arc en Ciel, 62 rue Arbre Sec, 1er (☎01 42 41 39 39). M: Louvre. Open M-F 8am-1:15pm and 2:30-7pm, Sa 8:30am-1:15pm.

Buci Pressing, 7 rue Ancienne Comédie, 6ème (☎01 43 29 49 92). M: Odéon. Open M-Sa 8am-7pm. MC for over €13.

Pressing de Seine, 67 rue de Seine, 6ème (☎01 43 25 74 94). M: Odéon. Open M-Sa 8am-7pm; hours vary in Aug. MC/V

Pressing Villiers, 93 rue de Rocher, 8ème (☎01 45 22 75 48). M: Villiers. Open M-F 8am-7:30pm. MC/V.

EMERGENCY AND COMMUNICATIONS

Crisis Lines

Poison: (☎01 40 05 48 48). In French, but some English assistance is available.

Rape: SOS Viol (☎08 00 05 95 95). Open M-F 10am-7pm.

SOS Help! (☎01 46 21 46 46). An anonymous, confidential hotline for English speakers in crisis. Open daily (including holidays) 3-11pm.

SOS Homophobie (☎01 48 06 42 41). Hotline for victims of homophobia. Open M-F 8-10pm.

Pharmacies

Pharmacie Les Champs, in the Galerie des Champs, 84 av. des Champs-Élysées, 8ème (☎ 01 45 62 02 41). M: George V. Open 24hr.

British and American Pharmacy, 1 rue Auber, 9ème (☎01 42 65 88 29 or 01 47 42 49 40). M: Auber or Opéra. Open daily 8am-8:30pm.

Hospital/Medical Services:

American Hospital of Paris, 63 bd. Hugo, Neuilly (☎01 46 41 25 25). M: Port Maillot, then bus #82 to the end of the line.

Hertford British Hospital (Hôpital Franco-Britannique de Paris), 3 rue Barbès, in Levallois-Perret (☎01 46 39 22 22). M: Anatole France. Some English speakers, but don't count on finding one.

Centre Médicale Europe, 44 rue d'Amsterdam, 9ème (☎01 42 81 93 33). M: St-Lazare. Open M-F 8am-7pm, Sa 8am-6pm.

SOS Dentaire, 87 bd. Port-Royal (☎01 40 21 82 88). RER: Port-Royal. Open daily 9am-6pm and 8:30-11:45pm. No walk-ins.

SOS Médecins (☎01 48 07 77 77). Makes house calls.

Internet Access:

easyInternetCafé, 31 bd. de Sébastopol, 1er (☎ 01 40 41 09 10). M: Les Halles. €3 per hr. Open daily 7:30am-midnight.

Akyrion Net Center, 19 rue Charlemagne, 4ème (☎01 40 27 92 07). €2.80 per hr. Open M-Th 11am-10:30pm, F-Sa 11am-11pm, Su 2-9:30pm.

Cyber Cube, 5 rue Mignon, 6ème (☎01 53 10 30 50). M: St-Michel or Odéon. €0.15 per min., €30 for 5hr., €40 for 10hr. Open M-Sa 10am-10pm.

Post Office:

Federal Express (☎01 40 06 90 16). Call M-F before 5pm for pick-up. Drop-off at 63 bd. Haussmann, 8ème. Open M-Sa 9am-7pm, drop-off by 4:45pm.

Poste du Louvre, 52 rue du Louvre, 1er (postal info ☎01 40 28 20 40). M: Louvre. Open daily 24hr.

Postal Code: 750xx, where "xx" is the *arrondissement* number (75007 in the 7ème, 75017 in the 17ème).

◪ ACCOMMODATIONS

Accommodations in Paris are expensive. At the absolute minimum, expect to pay €20 for a dorm-style bed in a hostel and €25 for a single room in a hotel. Groups of two or more may find it more economical to stay in a hotel than a hostel, since hotels charge by the room and not by the body. The area around rue Montorgeuil in the *2ème* is excellent for budget accommodations in the heart of they city. On the Left Bank, there is a wealth of inexpensive hotels in the 5ème and 6ème *arrondissements*, many with a great deal of old-fashioned character. If a central location is not your top priority, you may have luck with the hotels around the train stations in the 10ème. Hostels are scattered throughout the city; some of the best are in the 15ème. Only six are official **Hostelling International (HI)**; most are privately run organizations, usually with services comparable to those at HI. For any hotel or hostel in Paris, reserve well in advance—from one week to one month.

ÎLE DE LA CITÉ

▧ **Hôtel Henri IV,** 25 pl. Dauphine (☎01 43 54 44 53). M: Pont Neuf. Henri IV is one of Paris's best located and least expensive hotels. Named in honor of Henri IV's printing presses, which once occupied the 400-year-old building. Big windows, charming views of the tree-lined pl. Dauphine, and mismatched furnishings. Breakfast included. Showers €2.50. Reserve 1 month in advance, earlier in the summer. Singles €25; doubles €32, with shower and toilet €55; triples €43, with shower €69; quads €49. ❶

FIRST AND SECOND ARRONDISSEMENTS

▧ **Hôtel Tiquetonne,** 6 rue Tiquetonne, 2ème (☎01 42 36 94 58; fax 01 42 36 02 94). M: Etienne-Marcel. Walk against traffic on rue de Turbigo; turn left on rue Tiquetonne. Near Marché Montorgueil, the rowdy English bars near Etienne-Marcel, and rue St-Denis's sex shops—what more could you ask for? Elevator. Breakfast €5. Hall showers €5. Reserve 2 weeks in advance. Closed Aug. and 1 week at Christmas. Singles €28, with toilet €38; doubles with shower and toilet €46. AmEx/MC/V. ❸

BY PRICE

UNDER €15 (❶)	
▨ Hôtel Henri IV (91)	Île de la Cité

€16-25 (❷)	
▨ Aloha Hostel (97)	15ème
Aub. de Jeun. "Le D'Artagnan" (98)	20ème
▨ Aub. de Jeun. "Jules Ferry" (96)	11ème
Ctr. Int'l CISP "Kellerman" (97)	13ème
▨ Ctr. Int'l (BVJ) Paris Louvre (92)	1er
▨ FIAP Jean-Monnet (96)	14ème
Foyer Int'l des Etudiantes (94)	5ème
Hôtel du Marais (93)	3ème
Hôtel Palace (95)	10ème
Maison Internationale (96)	11ème
Ouest Hôtel (97)	14ème
▨ Three Ducks Hostel (97)	5ème
Union Chrétienne de Jne. Filles (95)	8ème
Union Chrétienne de Jne. Gens (95)	9ème
Village Hostel (98)	18ème
Woodstock Hostel (95)	9ème
▨ Young and Happy Hostel (93)	5ème

€26-35 (❸)	
▨ Cambrai Hôtel (95)	10ème
Ctr. Int'l (BVJ) Quartier Latin (94)	5ème
Hôtel de l'Aveyron (96)	12ème
▨ Hôtel Caulaincourt (97)	18ème
Hôtel Esmeralda (94)	5ème
▨ Hôtel des Jeunes (MIJE) (92)	4ème

Hôtel de Milan (96)	10ème
Hôtel Montebello (95)	7ème
Hôtel Picard (93)	3ème
Hôtel Printemps (97)	15ème
Hôtel de Reims (96)	12ème
Hôtel Rivoli (93)	4ème
▨ Hôtel du Séjour (92)	3ème
▨ Hôtel Tiquetonne (91)	2ème
▨ Perfect Hôtel (95)	9ème

€36-55 (❹)	
Eden Hôtel (98)	20ème
▨ Hôtel de Blois (97)	14ème
▨ Hôtel Eiffel Rive Gauche (94)	7ème
Hôtel Marignan (94)	5ème
▨ Hôtel de Nesle (93)	6ème
▨ Hôtel St-Jacques (94)	5ème
Hôtel Stella (94)	6ème
Rhin et Danube (98)	19ème

€55+ (❺)	
Grand Hôtel Jeanne d'Arc (93)	4ème
▨ Hôtel Beaumarchais (96)	11ème
Hôtel Boileau (97)	16ème
▨ Hôtel Chopin (95)	9ème
Hôtel Europe-Liège (95)	8ème
Hôtel Montpensier (92)	1er
▨ Hôtel St-André des Arts (94)	6ème

▨ **Centre International de Paris (BVJ): Paris Louvre,** 20 rue Jean-Jacques Rousseau, 1er (☎01 53 00 90 90). M: Louvre or Palais-Royal. From M: Louvre, take rue du Louvre away from the river, turn left on rue St-Honoré and right on rue Jean-Jacques Rousseau. Draws an international crowd. Courtyard with brass lanterns and *brasserie* chairs. Bright, dorm-style rooms with 2-10 beds. English spoken. Internet €1 per 10min. Breakfast and showers included. Lockers €2. 24hr. reception. Weekend reservations up to 1 week in advance; reserve by phone only. Rooms held for only 5-10min. after your expected check-in time; call if you'll be late. Dorms €25; doubles €28. ❷

Hôtel Montpensier, 12 rue de Richelieu, 1er (☎01 42 96 28 50; fax 01 42 86 02 70). M: Palais-Royal. Walk around the left side of the Palais-Royal to rue de Richelieu. Clean rooms, lofty ceilings, bright decor. English-speaking staff. Small elevator. TV in rooms with shower or bath. Internet access €1 per 4min. Breakfast €7. Shower €4. Reserve 2 months in advance in high season. Singles and doubles with toilet €57, with toilet and shower €78, with toilet, bath, and sink €92. Extra bed €12. AmEx/MC/V. ❺

THIRD AND FOURTH ARRONDISSEMENTS

▨ **Hôtel du Séjour,** 36 rue du Grenier St-Lazare, 3ème (☎/fax 01 48 87 40 36). From M: Etienne-Marcel, follow traffic on rue Etienne-Marcel, which becomes rue du Grenier St-Lazare. 1 block from Les Halles and the Centre Pompidou. 20 clean, bright rooms and a warm welcome. Showers €4. Reception 7am-10:30pm. Reserve in advance. Singles €33; doubles €45, with bath €55, 3rd person €23. ❸

▨ **Hôtel des Jeunes (MIJE),** 4ème (☎01 42 74 23 45; www.mije.com). Books beds in Le Fourcy, Le Fauconnier, and Maubuisson (see below), 3 small hostels on cobblestoned streets in beautiful old Marais residences. English spoken. Internet €0.15 per min.

Breakfast, in-room shower, and sheets included. Public phones and free lockers (with a €1 deposit). Ages 18-30 only. 7-day max. stay. Reception 7am-1am. Lockout noon-3pm. Curfew 1am. Quiet after 10pm. Arrive before noon the 1st day of reservation (call in advance if you'll be late). Groups of 10+ may reserve a year in advance. Individuals should reserve 1 month in advance and buy MIJE membership (€2.50). 5+ bed dorms €27-28; singles €42; doubles €32; triples €28; quads €27. ❸

Le Fourcy, 6 rue de Fourcy. M: St-Paul or Pont Marie. From M: St-Paul, walk opposite the traffic on rue François-Miron and turn left on rue de Fourcy. Large courtyard ideal for meeting travelers or for open-air picnicking. Light sleepers should avoid rooms on the social courtyard.

Le Fauconnier, 11 rue du Fauconnier. M: St-Paul or Pont Marie. From M: St-Paul, take rue du Pre-vôt, turn left on rue Charlemagne, and turn right on rue du Fauconnier. Ivy-covered, sun-drenched building steps away from the Seine and Île St-Louis.

Maubuisson, 12 rue des Barres. M: Hôtel-de-Ville or Pont Marie. From M: Pont Marie, walk opposite traffic on rue de l'Hôtel-de-Ville and turn right on rue des Barres. A half-timbered former convent on a silent street by the St-Gervais monastery. Quieter atmosphere. Elevator.

Hôtel Picard, 26 rue de Picardie, 3*ème* (☎01 48 87 53 82). M: République. Follow bd. du Temple and turn right on rue Charlot. Take the 1st right on rue de Franche Comté, which becomes rue de Picardie. Superb location; helpful staff. TVs in rooms with showers. Breakfast €4.50. Hall showers €3. Reserve 2 weeks ahead Apr.-Sept. Wheelchair-accessible. Singles €33, with shower €41, with shower and toilet €51; doubles €40-43, with shower €52, with bath €63; triples €59-82. Extra person €63. 5% discount with *Let's Go*. MC/V. ❸

Grand Hôtel Jeanne d'Arc, 3 rue de Jarente, 4*ème* (☎01 48 87 62 11; www.hotel-jeannedarc.com). From M: St-Paul, walk against traffic on rue de Rivoli and turn left on rue de Sévigné, then right on rue de Jarente. Bright, clean hotel on a quiet side-street. Recently renovated rooms with bath and TV. Breakfast €6. Reserve 2-3 months in advance. Wheelchair-accessible rooms available. Singles €57-70; doubles €80-95; triples €112; quads €140. MC/V. ❺

Hôtel du Marais, 16 rue de Beauce, 3*ème* (☎01 42 72 30 26; hotelmarais@voila.fr). M: Temple or Filles-de-Calvaire. From M: Temple, follow rue du Temple south; take a left on rue de Bretagne and a right on rue de Beauce. Dirt cheap without the dirt. This small hotel offers very simple but spotless rooms in a great location near an open-air market. Ideal for students. Take the small stairs above the cafe owned by the same friendly man. 3rd floor showers €3. Curfew 2am. Singles with sink €25; doubles €38. ❷

Hôtel Rivoli, 44 rue de Rivoli/2 rue des Mauvais Garçons, 4*ème* (☎01 42 72 08 41). M: Hôtel-de-Ville. Walk against traffic on rue de Rivoli. Basic rooms, but great location. Curfew 2am. Reserve 6 weeks in advance. Singles €29, with shower €37; doubles €40, with shower €45, with bath and toilet €50; triples €60. Extra bed €10. ❸

FIFTH AND SIXTH ARRONDISSEMENTS

▨ **Young and Happy (Y&H) Hostel,** 80 rue Mouffetard, 5*ème* (☎01 45 35 09 53; www.youngandhappy.fr). M: Monge. Cross rue Gracieuse and take rue Ortolan to rue Mouffetard. A funky, lively hostel located on rue Mouffetard. The laid-back staff, clean rooms, and commission-free currency exchange make this a perfect place for 20-somethings to crash for a few weeks. English spoken. Kitchen. Internet €1 per 10min. Breakfast included. Sheets €2.50, towels €1. Laundry nearby. Lockout 11am-4pm. Curfew 2am. Dorms from €20; doubles from €23 per person; Jan.-Mar. €2 less per night. ❷

▨ **Hôtel de Nesle,** 7 rue du Nesle, 6*ème* (☎01 43 54 62 41). M: Odéon. Walk up rue de l'Ancienne Comédie, take a right onto rue Dauphine and then take a left on rue du Nesle. Friendly and sparkling. Each room represents a particular time period or locale. The lobby's ceiling is made of bouquets of dried flowers. Garden with duck pond. Laundry room. Reserve by telephone; confirm 2 days in advance with arrival time. Singles €50-69; doubles €69-99. Extra bed €12. AmEx/MC/V. ❹

▨ **Hôtel St-André des Arts,** 66 rue St-André-des-Arts, 6ème (☎01 43 26 96 16; hsaintand@minitel.net). M: Odéon. Take rue de l'Ancienne Comédie, then turn right on rue St-André-des-Arts. Stone walls and exposed beams give a country inn feeling. New bathrooms, free breakfast, and friendly owner. Reservations recommended. Singles €64; doubles €82; triples €100; quads €110. MC/V. ❺

▨ **Hôtel St-Jacques,** 35 rue des Écoles, 5ème (☎01 44 07 45 45; hotelstjacques@wanadoo.fr). M: Maubert-Mutualité. Turn left on rue des Carmes, then left on rue des Écoles. Cary Grant filmed *Charade* here. Rooms with balcony, renovated bath, and TV. Chandeliers and walls decorated with *trompe-l'œil* designs give it a regal feel. English spoken. Internet access. Breakfast €7. Singles €49, with toilet and shower €75; doubles with toilet and shower €85, some with baths €112. AmEx/MC/V. ❹

Hôtel Marignan, 13 rue du Sommerard, 5ème (☎01 43 54 63 81). From M: Maubert-Mutualité, turn left on rue des Carmes, then right on rue du Sommerard. Clean, freshly decorated, amenable rooms that can sleep up to 5. English-speaking owner welcomes backpackers and families. Free laundry and kitchen access. TV (upon request). Internet access. Breakfast included. Hall showers open until 11pm. Reserve 2 months in advance with credit card or check deposit. Singles €47; doubles €60, with bath €82; triples €90/€110; quads €100/€130. 15% discount from mid-Sept. to Mar. AmEx/MC/V for 5 nights or longer. ❹

Hôtel Stella, 41 rue Monsieur-le-Prince, 6ème (☎01 40 51 00 25; http://site.voila.fr/hotel_stella). M: Odéon. Walk against traffic on bd. St-Germain and make a left on rue Monsieur-le-Prince. Takes the exposed beam look to a whole new level with centuries-old woodwork. Gigantic triples have pianos. All rooms have bath. Reserve in advance with deposit. Singles €45; doubles €55; triples €75; quads €85. ❹

Centre International de Paris (BVJ): Paris Quartier Latin, 44 rue des Bernardins, 5ème (☎01 43 29 34 80; fax 01 53 00 90 91). M: Maubert-Mutualité. Walk with traffic on bd. St-Germain and turn right on rue des Bernardins. Boisterous, 97-bed generic hostel with a large cafeteria. English spoken. Microwave, TV, and message service. Internet €1 per 10min. Breakfast included. In-room showers. Lockers €2. 24hr. reception. Reserve at least 1 week in advance or arrive at 9am to check for availability. 5- and 6-person dorms €26; singles €35; doubles €56; triples €84. ❸

Foyer International des Etudiantes, 93 bd. St-Michel, 5ème (☎01 43 54 49 63). RER: Luxembourg. Across from the Jardin du Luxembourg. Library, laundry facilities, and TV lounge. Kitchenettes, showers, and toilets on hallways. Rooms are elegant (if faintly musty), some with balcony. Breakfast included in summer. 3 night min. Reserve in writing as early as Jan. for summer months; €35 deposit. July-Sept. foyer is co-ed and open 24hr. Oct.-June foyer is women only, and rooms are available for rent by the month (inquire at desk for prices). Singles €27.50; 2-bed dorms €20 per person. ❷

Hôtel Esmeralda, 4 rue St-Julien-le-Pauvre, 6ème (☎01 43 54 19 20; fax 01 40 51 00 68). M: St-Michel. Walk along the Seine on quai St-Michel toward Notre Dame, then turn right at Parc Viviani. Antique wallpaper, ceiling beams, and red velvet. Great location near a small park, within sight of the Seine and earshot of Notre Dame's bells. Breakfast €6. Singles €35, with bath €65; doubles €90; triples €110; quads €120. ❸

SEVENTH AND EIGHTH ARRONDISSEMENTS

▨ **Hôtel Eiffel Rive Gauche,** 6 rue du Gros Caillou, 7ème (☎01 45 51 24 56; www.hotel-eiffel.com). M: École Militaire. Walk up av. de la Bourdonnais, turn right on rue de la Grenelle, then left on Gros-Caillou. On a quiet street. Bright courtyard and cheerful staff. A favorite of Anglophones. Rooms have cable TV, phone, Internet jack, and bath; some have Eiffel Tower views. Breakfast buffet €9. Safe €3. Singles €69-89; doubles €76-80; triples €96. Double bed must be requested upon booking. Extra bed €14. MC/V. ❹

Hôtel Montebello, 18 rue Pierre Leroux, 7ème (☎01 47 34 41 18; hmonte-bello@aol.com). M: Vaneau. A bit far from the sights of the 7ème, but unbeatable rates for this upscale area. Clean, cheery rooms with full bath. Reserve at least 2 weeks in advance. Breakfast 7:30-9:30am, €4. Singles €30; doubles €37-47. ●

Union Chrétienne de Jeunes Filles (UCJF/YWCA), 22 rue Naples, 8ème (☎01 53 04 37 47; fax 01 53 04 37 54). M: Europe. Take rue de Constantinople and turn left onto rue de Naples. Also at 168 rue Blomet, 15ème (☎01 56 56 63 00; fax 01 56 56 63 12). M: Convention. For **women only;** men should contact the YMCA Foyer **Union Chrétienne de Jeunes Gens,** 14 rue de Trévise, 9ème (☎01 47 70 90 94). The UCJF has spacious (if a bit worn) rooms. Fireplace, TV, books, and family-style dining room. Free Internet access. June-Aug. 3-day min. stay; Sept.-May longer stays for women ages 18-26. Kitchen, laundry. Breakfast included, dinner €7. Reception M-F 8am-12:25am, Sa 8:30am-12:25pm, Su 9am-12:25pm and 1:30pm-12:30am. Guests permitted until 10pm; men not allowed in bedrooms. Curfew 12:30am (ask for key). Singles €27, €162 per week, €511-527 per month; doubles or dorms €24/€130/€416-466 per person. €5 YWCA membership fee or €15 (for stays of 1+ month). ●

Hôtel Europe-Liège, 8 rue de Moscou, 8ème (☎01 42 94 01 51; fax 01 43 87 42 18). M: Liège. Walk down rue d'Amsterdam and turn left on rue de Moscou. Cheerful, quiet, and reasonably priced (for the 8ème). Sparkling clean rooms and a lovely interior court-yard. Many restaurants nearby. All rooms have TV, hair dryer, phone, and shower or bath. Breakfast €7. Reserve 15 days in advance. 2 wheelchair-accessible rooms on the ground floor. Singles €68; doubles €84. AmEx/MC/V. ●

NINTH AND TENTH ARRONDISSEMENTS

▨ **Hôtel Chopin,** 10 bd. Montmartre, or 46, passage Jouffroy, 9ème (☎01 47 70 58 10; fax 01 42 47 00 70). M: Grands Boulevards. Walk west on bd. Montmartre and make a right into passage Jouffroy. Rooms are new, very clean, and tastefully decorated. TVs, phones, and fans by request. Breakfast €7. Singles with shower €57, with full bath €64-72; doubles with bath €73-84; triples with bath €97. AmEx/MC/V. ●

▨ **Perfect Hôtel,** 39 rue Rodier, 9ème (☎01 42 81 18 86 or 01 42 81 26 19; perfectho-tel@hotmail.com). M: Anvers. From the metro, walk against traffic on pl. Anvers, turn right on av. Trudaine and left on rue Rodier. Lives up to its name with hotel-quality rooms at hostel prices. Some with balcony; upper floors have a beautiful view. Phones, communal refrigerator and kitchen access, free coffee, beer vending machine (€1.50). English-speaking staff. Breakfast free for Let's Go users. Singles €30, with bath €50; doubles €36/€50; triples €53/€65. MC/V. ●

▨ **Cambrai Hôtel,** 129bis bd. de Magenta, 10ème (☎01 48 78 32 13; www.hotel-camb-rai.com). M: Gare du Nord. Follow traffic on rue de Dunkerque to pl. de Roubaix and turn right on bd. de Magenta. Close to the Gare du Nord. Bright rooms with high ceilings and TV. Breakfast €5.50. Showers €3. Singles €30, with toilet €35, with shower €41, with full bath €48; doubles with shower €46, with bath €54, with twin beds and bath €60; triples €80; quad €90; quint €110 (wheelchair-accessible). AmEx/MC/V. ●

Hôtel Palace, 9 rue Bouchardon, 9ème (☎01 42 06 59 32; hotel.palace@club-inter-net.fr). M: Strasbourg-St-Denis. Walk against traffic on bd. St-Denis until the small arch; follow rue René Boulanger on the left, then turn left on rue Bouchardon. Clean, centrally located hotel with the rates of a hostel. Laundromat and supermarket nearby. Breakfast €3.50. Shower €3.50. Reserve 2 weeks ahead. Singles €19-21, with shower €31; dou-bles €26/€36; triples €48; quads €58; quints €69. AmEx/MC/V. ●

Woodstock Hostel, 48 rue Rodier, 9ème (☎01 48 78 87 76; www.woodstock.fr). Across from the Perfect Hôtel (see directions p. 95). With incense, reggae music, tie-dyed par-aphernalia, and a Beatles-decorated VW Bug hanging from the ceiling. Nicest rooms are off the courtyard. Communal kitchen and safe deposit box. English spoken. Internet €1 per 10min. Breakfast included. Sheets €2.50, towels €1. Showers on every floor are free (and clean). Max. stay 1 week. Lockout 11am-4pm. Curfew 2am. Call ahead to reserve a room. 4- to 8-person dorms €21; doubles €24; max. 8 people per room. ❷

Hôtel de Milan, 17 rue de St-Quentin, 10ème (☎01 40 37 88 50; fax 01 46 07 89 48). M: Gare du Nord. Follow rue de St-Quentin from outside Gare du Nord; the hotel is on the right-hand corner of the 3rd block. Well suited for access to the nearby *gares* and the concierge is extremely friendly. Breakfast €4. Hall showers €4. Singles €27-30; doubles €34-41, with full bath €47-52, with twin beds and full bath €59; triples with full bath €69. Extra person €17. MC/V. ❸

ELEVENTH AND TWELFTH ARRONDISSEMENTS

▓ **Auberge de Jeunesse "Jules Ferry" (HI),** 8 bd. Jules Ferry, 11ème (☎01 43 57 55 60; auberge@easynet.fr). M: République. Walk east on rue du Faubourg du Temple; turn right on the far side of bd. Jules Ferry. Wonderful location in front of a park and next to pl. de la République. Modern, clean rooms. Party atmosphere. Internet access in lobby €0.15 per min. Breakfast and showers included. Lockers €1.55. Laundry €3.50 wash, €1.60 dry. 1 week max. stay. 24hr. reception and dining room. Lockout 10:30am-2pm. No reservations; arrive by 8am. If there are no vacancies, staff will try to book you in one of the nearby hostels. 4- to 6-bed dorms €19.50; doubles €40. MC/V. ❷

▓ **Hôtel Beaumarchais,** 3 rue Oberkampf, 11ème (☎01 53 36 86 86; www.hotelbeau-marchais.com). M: Oberkampf. Exit on rue de Malte and turn right on rue Oberkampf. Newly renovated, with colorful, modern furniture, clean baths, and cable TV. Spacious rooms decorated in the style of a different artist, like Kandinsky or Gaudi. Elevator. A/C. Breakfast buffet €10. Reserve 2 weeks in advance. Singles €75-90; doubles €110; suites €150. Baby beds €16. No extra adult-sized beds. AmEx/MC/V. ❺

Hôtel de l'Aveyron, 5 rue d'Austerlitz, 12ème (☎01 43 07 86 86; fax 01 43 07 85 20). M: Gare de Lyon. Walk away from the train station on rue de Bercy and take a right on rue d'Austerlitz. On a quiet street, with clean, unpretentious rooms. Downstairs lounge and bar with TV. Helpful, English-speaking staff. Breakfast €5. Reserve 2 months in advance. Singles €32; doubles €42, with shower €55. MC/V. ❸

Hôtel de Reims, 26 rue Hector Malot, 12ème (☎01 43 07 46 18; fax 01 43 07 56 62). M: Gare de Lyon. Take bd. Diderot away from the tall buildings and turn left onto rue Hector Malot. Near Opéra Bastille and the Gare de Lyon. Breakfast €4. Reserve by phone 1 week in advance and confirm by fax. Singles €30, with shower €40, with shower and toilet €43; doubles €36/€42/€45; triples with shower €48. MC/V. ❸

Maison Internationale des Jeunes pour la Culture et pour la Paix, 4 rue Titon, 11ème (☎01 43 71 99 21). M: Faidherbe-Chaligny. Walk along rue de Montreuil and turn left on rue Titon. Spare, clean rooms with 2-8 cot-like beds. Guests without children must be age 18-30. Internet access with *Télécarte*. Breakfast and showers included. Sheets €2.30. 5 night max. stay. Reception 8am-2pm. Lockout 10am-5pm. Curfew 2am. Reserve 2 weeks in advance, sooner for large groups. €20 per night. ❷

THIRTEENTH AND FOURTEENTH ARRONDISSEMENTS

▓ **FIAP Jean-Monnet,** 30 rue Cabanis, 14ème (☎01 43 13 17 00, reservations 01 43 13 17 17; www.fiap.asso.fr). M: Glacière. From the metro, walk straight down bd. Auguste-Blanqui, turn left on rue de la Santé, then right on rue Cabanis. High-end, pre-fab feel. Spotless rooms with phone and bath. Game room, TV rooms, 2 restaurants, outdoor terrace, and disco. Wheelchair-accessible. Breakfast included; add €1.60 for buffet. 3-month max. stay. Check-in after 2:30pm. Check-out 9am. Curfew 2am. Reserve 2-4 weeks in advance. Specify if you want a dorm bed or you will get a single. Apr.-July. singles €51.30; doubles €33; quads €29.90; 6-bed rooms €23.10. Aug.-Mar. €50.20/€32.40/€29.40/€22.70. €15 deposit per person per night. MC/V. ❷

Hôtel de Blois, 5 rue des Plantes, 14ème (☎01 45 40 99 48; fax 01 45 40 45 62). M: Mouton-Duvernet. Turn left on rue Mouton-Duvernet, then left on rue des Plantes. One of the best deals in Paris. Glossy wallpaper and velvet chairs. TV, phones, hair dryers, and big clean baths. Laundromat and pool nearby. Breakfast €6. Free hall showers. Reserve at least 10 days ahead. Singles €41, with shower €44, with shower and toilet €47, with bath and toilet €53; doubles €44/€46/€53/€58; triples €64. AmEx/MC/V. ❹

Ouest Hôtel, 27 rue de Gergovie, 14ème (☎01 45 42 64 99; fax 01 45 42 46 65). M: Pernety. Walk against traffic on rue Raymond Losserand and turn right on rue de Gergovie. Modest furnishings, outstanding rates, and helpful staff. Small library. Breakfast €5. Hall shower €5 (sometimes long waits). Singles with small bed €22, with larger bed €28; 1-bed doubles €28, with shower €37; 2-bed doubles €34/€39. MC/V. ❷

Centre International du Séjour de Paris: CISP "Kellerman," 17 bd. Kellerman, 13ème (☎01 44 16 37 38; www.cisp.asso.fr). M: Porte d'Italie. Cross the street and turn right onto bd. Kellerman. Resembles a retro spaceship on stilts but is surprisingly modern inside. Adequate, clean rooms. TV room, meeting rooms, Internet access and cafeteria (open daily noon-1:30pm and 6:30-9:30pm). Wheelchair-accessible. Breakfast included (7-9am). Free showers on floors with dorms. Reception 6:30am-1:30am. Reserve 2-3 weeks in advance. 8-bed dorms €16; 2- to 4-bed dorms €20; singles with shower and toilet €30; doubles with shower and toilet €24. AmEx/MC/V. ❷

FIFTEENTH AND SIXTEENTH ARRONDISSEMENTS

Three Ducks Hostel, 6 pl. Etienne Pernet, 15ème (☎01 48 42 04 05; www.3ducks.fr). M: Félix Faure. Walk against traffic on the left side of the church; hostel is on the left. With palm trees in the courtyard and bizarre beach-style shower shacks, this hostel is aimed at anglo fun-seekers. In-house bar. Kitchen, lockers, and 2- to 8-bed dorm rooms. Laundry and groceries nearby. Internet access in lobby. Shower and breakfast included. Sheets €2.29, towels €0.76. 1 week max. stay. Reception 8am-2am. Lockout daily 11am-5pm. Curfew 2am. Reserve with credit card a week ahead. Mar.-Oct. dorms €22; doubles €50. Special low-season rates Nov.-Feb. MC/V. ❷

Aloha Hostel, 1 rue Borromée, 15ème (☎01 42 73 03 03; www.friends@aloha.fr). M: Volontaires. Walk against traffic on rue de Vaugirard then turn right on rue Borromée. More tranquil than the Three Ducks (see above), but still lively. Music and drinks in the cafe. Breakfast included. Safety deposit boxes. Sheets €3, towels €3—but you get to keep them. Reception 8am-2am. Lockout 11am-5pm. Curfew 2am. Reserve 1 week ahead. Apr. to mid-Sept. dorms €22; doubles €25. Mid-Sept. to Apr. €18/€22. ❷

Hôtel Boileau, 81 rue Boileau, 16ème (☎01 42 88 83 74; www.hotel-boileau.com). M: Exelmans. Walk down bd. Exelmans away from its curving corner and turn right on rue Boileau. Features marble busts, Tuscan tiling, Oriental rugs, and a sunny breakfast room complete with fishtank. Spotless rooms with cable TV and telephone. Internet access. Breakfast €8. Singles €69; doubles €79-81; triples €112. AmEx/MC/V. ❺

Hôtel Printemps, 31 rue du Commerce, 15ème (☎01 45 79 83 36; hotel.printemps.15e@wanadoo.fr). M: La Motte-Picquet-Grenelle. Pleasant, clean, and cheap. In a busy neighborhood, surrounded by shops and budget restaurants. Breakfast €4. Hall showers €3. Reserve ahead if possible. Singles and doubles with sink €34, with shower €40, with shower and toilet €43; twin with bath and toilet €47. MC/V. ❸

OUTER ARRONDISSEMENTS

Hôtel Caulaincourt, 2 sq. Caulaincourt, 18ème (☎01 46 06 46 06; bienvenue@caulaincourt.com). M: Lamarck-Caulaincourt. Walk up the stairs to rue Caulaincourt and proceed to your right, between no. 63 and 65. Located in a quiet area of picturesque Montmartre. Once used as artists' studios, the large, simple rooms have views of Montmartre and the Paris skyline. Rooms with TV and phone. Breakfast €5.50. Reserve up to 1 month in advance. Singles €35, with shower €45, with shower and toilet €55, with bath and toilet €65; doubles €48-74; triples with shower €66-82. MC/V. ❸

Eden Hôtel, 7 rue Jean-Baptiste Dumay, 20ème (☎01 46 36 64 22; fax 01 46 36 01 11). M: Pyrénées. Turn right from the metro; off rue de Belleville. An oasis of hospitality. Clean rooms with TV and toilets. Breakfast €4.50. Bath or shower €4. Reserve rooms by fax 1 week in advance. Singles €38, with shower €51; doubles €56, with shower €51-54, with bath €54. Extra bed €10. MC/V. ❹

Rhin et Danube, 3 pl. Rhin et Danube, 19ème (☎01 42 45 10 13; fax 01 42 06 88 82). M: Danube; or bus #75 from M: Châtelet. (30min.) Just steps from the metro. Spacious suites are not fancy but have kitchen, fridge, dishes, coffeemaker, hair dryer, shower, toilet, direct phone, and satellite TV. Many look onto a quaint *place*. Singles €46; doubles €61; triples €73; quads €83; quints €92. MC/V. ❹

Village Hostel, 20 rue d'Orsel, 18ème (☎01 42 64 22 02). M: Anvers. Go uphill on rue Steinkerque and turn right on rue d'Orsel. Amid the Sacré-Coeur tourist traffic, but clean and cheap. Doubles and 3- to 5-bed dorms, some in view of Sacré-Coeur, some off a patio, and some facing the noisy street (be sure to specify). Kitchen, beer dispenser, TV, stereo, telephones, and Internet access in the lounge. Toilet and shower in every room. Breakfast included. Sheets €2.50, towels €1. 7-day max. stay. Lockout 11am-4pm. Curfew 2am. Reservation online. For same-day phone reservations, call at 8am. 4-bed dorms €23; doubles €50; triples €81. ❷

Auberge de Jeunesse "Le D'Artagnan" (HI), 80 rue Vitruve, 20ème (☎01 40 32 34 56; www.hostels-in.com). M: Porte de Bagnolet or Porte de Montreuil. From Porte de Bagnolet, walk south on bd. Davout and make a right on rue Vitruve. An enormous backpacker's colony. Neon lights and funky decorations welcome boisterous young people as well as older single travelers and families. Restaurant, bar (happy hour 8-9pm; open 9pm-2am), and a small cinema (free films nightly 6pm). Breakfast (served 7am-11am) and sheets included. Lockers €2-4 per day. Laundry €3 per wash, €1 per dry. 6 night max. stay. Reception 8am-1am. Lockout noon-3pm. Reservations by fax or email a must. 2-, 3-, 4-, and 8-bed dorms €22 per person; children under 10 €11. ❷

▣ FOOD

Don't approach dining in Paris with the assumption that chic equals *cher*. It's worth it to splurge on a world-class meal in the capital of cuisine, but there are a wealth of ways to eat well on a budget. Though it can be difficult to find inexpensive options in the 1er, 7ème, 8ème, and 16ème, the 13ème, 17ème, and 19ème abound in excellent budget choices, particularly in ethnic restaurants. The upper Marais, in the 3ème, is characterized by international eateries and quiet bistros along **rue St-Martin,** while the lower Marais, in the 4ème, is all about dressing up and being seen. Also home to a significant Jewish population, the Marais offers cheap falafel and kosher deli-fare around **rue des Rosiers, rue de Vertbois,** and **rue Volta** to the north. In the Latin Quarter, head to the area around the **Pantheon** for sidewalk bistros, the streets around **place St-Michel** for tiny, bustling restaurants, **rue St-André-des-Arts** for *crêperies* and *panini* vendors, **St-Germain-des-Prés** for pricey but historic literary cafes, and **rue de Buci** for Greek fare. In the 14ème, **rue du Montparnasse,** which intersects with the boulevard, teems with authentic Breton *crêperies,* **rue Daguerre** is a haven of vegetarian-friendly restaurants, and couscous restaurants line **avenue du Maine.**

BY TYPE

AFRICAN

Babylone Bis (101)	2ème ❹
Café Flèche d'Or (106)	20ème ❸
🏠 Café de la Mosquée (101)	5ème ❸
Djerba Cacher Chez Guichi (106)	18ème ❷

AMERICAN

🏠 Restaurant Américain Chez Haynes (103)	
	9ème ❸

BASQUE

🏠 Le Caveau du Palais (99)	Île de la Cité ❹

BISTRO

Au Père Fouettard (101)	1er ❸
Le Bistro de Théo (105)	17ème ❸
🏠 Cantine d'Antoine et Lili (103)	10ème ❶
🏠 Chez Paul (104)	11ème ❸
Le Dix Vins (105)	15ème ❹
Les Fous de l'Île (100)	Île St-Louis ❸
🏠 Les Noces de Jeannette (100)	2ème ❹
Le Perraudin (102)	5ème ❷
Le Petit Vatel (102)	6ème ❷

CLASSIC CAFE

B Tea's (101)	3ème ❷
Café Vavin (102)	6ème ❸
Café de Flore (102)	6ème ❸
Les Deux Magots (102)	6ème ❸

CRÊPERIE/ICE CREAM

Le Crêpe en l'Île (100)	Île St-Louis ❶
Berthillon (100)	Île St-Louis ❶
Octave (102)	5ème ❶
Crêperie Saint Germain (102)	6ème ❹
Objectifs Crêpes (103)	8ème ❷

INDIAN

Anarkali Sarangui (103)	9ème ❷

IRISH

🏠 The James Joyce Pub (105)	17ème ❸

JAPANESE

Lamen Kintaro (101)	2ème ❷

MIDDLE EASTERN

🏠 L'As du Falafel (101)	4ème ❶
Byblos Café (105)	16ème ❸

PROVENÇALE

Comptoir Méditerranée (102)	5ème ❶
Savannah Café (102)	5ème ❸

PROVENÇALE

Aux Arts et Sciences Réunis (106)	19ème ❹
🏠 Le Soleil Gourmand (105)	8ème ❸

SANDWICHERIE

Comme Par Hasard (103)	9ème ❶

SCANDINAVIAN

🏠 Café des Lettres (103)	7ème ❹

SOUTHEAST ASIAN

Lao Siam (106)	19ème ❷
🏠 Thai Phetburi (104)	15ème ❷
🏠 Tricotin (104)	13ème ❶

TRADITIONAL AND MODERN FRENCH

L'Amuse Bouche (104)	14ème ❺
Au Bon Café (103)	10ème ❷
Au Petit Fer à Cheval (101)	4ème ❸
L'Auberge Bressane (103)	7ème ❺
🏠 Aux Artistes (105)	15ème ❷
Brasserie de l'Île St-Louis (100)	Île-St Louis ❷
🏠 Chez Papa (104)	14ème ❷
L'Ebauchoir (104)	12ème ❹
Musée du Vin Restaurant (105)	16ème ❺
🏠 Pain, Vin, Fromage (101)	4ème ❸
🏠 Papou Lounge (100)	1er ❷
Refuge des Fondues (105)	18ème ❸
Le Soleil d'Or (100)	Île de la Cité ❶
Le Temps des Cerises (104)	13ème ❸
🏠 Toi (103)	8ème ❹

TRENDY/INTELLIGENTSIA

Café de l'Industrie (104)	11ème ❷
🏠 Chez Janou (101)	3ème ❸
🏠 Le Fumoir (100)	1er ❹

VEGETARIAN AND VEGAN

Le Grenier de Notre-Dame (102)	5ème ❷
Piccolo Teatro (101)	4ème ❷
La Victoire Suprême du Coeur (100)	1er ❷

PARIS

SEINE ISLANDS

🏠 **Le Caveau du Palais,** 19 pl. Dauphine, Île de la Cité (☎01 43 26 04 28). M: Cité. Chic, intimate local favorite that serves hearty fare from an old-fashioned brick oven. Basque dishes with steak (€19-25) and fish (€18-25). Prices are high, but so is the level of ambience. Open daily noon-3pm and 7-10:30pm. Reservations encouraged. MC/V. ❹

Berthillon, 31 rue St-Louis-en-l'Île (☎43 54 31 61). M: Cité or Pont Marie. Commonly regarded as the best ice cream and sorbet in Paris. Choose from dozens of flavors, ranging from passion fruit to gingerbread to the house speciality *nougat miel* (honey nougat). Look for stores nearby that sell Berthillon indulgences; they usually offer a wider selection of flavors and they're open in Aug., when the main outfit is closed. 1 scoop €2; 2 scoops €3; 3 scoops €4. Open Sept.-July 14. Closed 2 weeks in Feb. and Apr. Takeout W-Su 10am-8pm; eat-in W-F 1-8pm, Sa-Su 2pm-midnight. ❶

Le Soleil d'Or, 15 bd. du Palais, Île de la Cité (☎01 43 54 22 22). M: Cité. Don't be frightened by the posh, faux-velvet chairs: this classy-looking *brasserie* is a real bargain. Eclectic menu offers delicious crêpes (€4.50), milkshakes (€5.50), and Su brunch (€10). Pizza and sandwiches from €4.50. Open daily 9am-10pm. MC/V. ❶

La Crêpe en l'Île, 13 rue des Deux Ponts, Île St-Louis (☎01 43 26 28 68). M: Pont Marie. Choose from among 20 crêpes, including the indulgent "La Super" (chocolate, ice cream, whipped cream, and nuts). "La Provençale" (ratatouille, egg, and roasted pepper) is a meal in itself. Crêpes from €2.50 to €7.20. 3-course *menu* €8.80. Open daily high season 11:30am-midnight; low season 11:30am-11pm. ❶

Brasserie de l'Île St-Louis, 55 quai de Bourbon, Île St-Louis (☎01 43 54 02 59). M: Pont Marie. Cross the Pont Marie and turn right on rue St-Louis-en-l'Île; continue to the end of the island. This old-fashioned *brasserie* is known for its delectable Alsatian specialities like *choucroute garnie* (sausages and pork on sauerkraut, €16.50). Omelettes and other typical cafe fare €8-11. Outdoor seating with a view of the Pantheon through the rooftops. Open M-Tu and F-Su noon-1am, Th 5pm-1am. AmEx/MC/V. ❷

Les Fous de l'Île, 33 rue des Deux Ponts, Île St-Louis (☎01 43 25 76 67). M: Pont Marie. A mellow bistro for the neighborhood crowd. Displays local art and has evening concerts (jazz, Brazilian, traditional French) every Tu-W except in Aug. Appetizers €3-7. *Plats* €10.50-14. €13 lunch *menu* is delicious. Healthy brunch €16, with all the trimmings €23. Open Tu-F noon-11pm, Sa 3-11pm, Su noon-7pm. MC/V. ❸

FIRST AND SECOND ARRONDISSEMENTS

🍽 **Les Noces de Jeannette,** 14 rue Favart, and 9 rue d'Amboise, 2ème (☎01 42 96 36 89). M: Richelieu-Drouot. Exit onto bd. des Italiens, turn left, and go left onto rue Favart. Named after a 19th-century *opéra comique* playing across the street when the restaurant opened. Elegant restaurant will impress your date. *Menu du Bistro* €27.50. Free *kir* with meal. Open daily noon-1:30pm and 7-9:30pm. Reservations recommended. ❹

🍽 **Papou Lounge,** 74 rue Jean-Jacques Rousseau, 1er (☎01 44 76 00 03). M: Les Halles. Take the rue Rambuteau Exit, walk toward Église St-Eustache, turn left onto rue Coquillère, then right on rue Jean-Jacques Rousseau. Delicious cuisine is flavorful (rump-steak €13) and inventive (tuna tartare with strawberries €13.50). World music, tile floors, and photos of tribal warriors contribute to the atmosphere. Lunch special €10. Open daily 10am-2am, food served noon-4:30pm and 7pm-midnight. MC/V. ❷

🍽 **Le Fumoir,** 6 rue de l'Amiral Coligny, 1er (☎01 42 92 05 05). M: Louvre. As you cross rue de Rivoli on rue du Louvre, it becomes rue de l'Amiral Coligny. Decidedly un-touristy types sip drinks in deep leather sofas. Part bar, part tea house in feel. 1 of the best brunches in Paris (€20) Su noon-3pm. Open daily 11am-2am. AmEx/MC/V. ❹

La Victoire Suprême du Coeur, 41 rue des Bourdonnais, 1er (☎01 40 41 93 95). M: Châtelet. From the rue des Halles Exit, follow traffic to a left turn on rue des Bourdonnais. Vegetarian and vegan options like *escalope de seitan à la sauce champignon* (seitan in mushroom sauce; €8.50). Walls decked with photos of the owners' Yul Brynner-esque guru up to his elbows in dough. 2-course lunch *menu* (€10.80). Open M-F 11:45am-3pm and 6:40-10pm, Sa noon-3pm and 6:40-10pm. MC/V. ❷

Babylone Bis, 34 rue Tiquetonne, 2ème (☎01 42 33 48 35). M: Etienne-Marcel. Walk against traffic on rue de Turbigo and turn left onto rue Tiquetonne. Antillean and African cuisine. With zebra skin on the walls, banana leaves on the ceiling, and loud *zouk* music, this place gets wild. Don't miss the *poulet braisé* (lime-marinated chicken; €14). Cocktails €8-13. Dinner served all night. Open daily 8pm-8am. MC/V. ❹

Lamen Kintaro, 24 rue St-Augustin, 2ème (☎01 47 42 13 14). M: Opéra. Walk down av. de l'Opéra and turn left on rue St-Augustin. Delicious and popular Japanese restaurant. With no sushi in sight, Kintaro offers great noodle bowls (€7.80) and an array of *menus* (€8-13). Sapporo €4.30. Open M-Sa 11:30am-10pm. MC/V. ❷

Au Père Fouettard, 9 rue Pierre Lescot, 2ème (☎01 42 33 74 17; www.paris-zoom.com). M: Les Halles. No inventive combinations, just high-quality bistro fare. Sit out on the terrace and be entertained by the friendly (and sometimes crazy) waiters. Appetizers €8-10, salads €11-13, *plats* €12-20. Open daily 8am-2am. ❸

THIRD AND FOURTH ARRONDISSEMENTS

▨ **Pain, Vin, Fromage,** 3 rue Geoffrey L'Angevin, 4ème (☎01 42 74 07 52). On a side-street near the Centre Pompidou. Serves France's three basic food groups in original combinations. Fondues (€14) and salads (€7.50-9) are accompanied by a winning wine list. Open M-Sa 7-11pm. ❸

▨ **L'As du Falafel,** 34 rue des Rosiers, 4ème (☎01 48 87 63 60). M: St-Paul. This kosher falafel stand and restaurant displays pictures of Lenny Kravitz, who called it "the best falafel in the world, particularly the special eggplant falafel with hot sauce." Go his way. Falafel special €6. Open M-F and Su 11:30am-midnight. MC/V. ❶

▨ **Chez Janou,** 2 rue Roger Verlomme, 3ème (☎01 42 72 28 41). From M: Chemin-Vert, take rue St-Gilles and turn left almost immediately on rue des Tournelles. On the corner of rue Roger Verlomme. No menus; the dishes are listed on blackboards throughout the restaurant. *Plat du jour* €12. Delicious *ratatouille* €8.50. Open daily noon-3pm and 8pm-midnight. Reservations strongly recommended. ❸

Au Petit Fer à Cheval, 30 rue Vieille-du-Temple, 4ème (☎01 42 72 47 47). M: Hôtel-de-Ville or St-Paul. From M: St-Paul, go with the traffic on rue de Rivoli and turn right; the restaurant will be on your right. An oasis of *chèvre, kir,* and *Gauloises,* graced by a crowd of low-key sophisticates. Excellent *filet mignon de veau* (veal; €16) and salads (€6-10). If outdoor seating is full, try **Les Philosophes** or **La Chaise au Plafond**—owned by the same man. Open daily 9am-2am; food served noon-1:15am. MC/V. ❸

Piccolo Teatro, 6 rue des Ecouffes, 4ème (☎01 42 72 17 79). M: St-Paul. Walk with the traffic down rue de Rivoli and turn right on rue des Ecouffes. A romantic vegetarian hide-out draped in red velvet. Weekday lunch *menus* €8.90, €10.50, and €14.70. *Entrées* €3.80-7.50. *Plats* €8.10-11.70. Open daily noon-3pm and 7-11pm. AmEx/MC/V. ❷

B Tea's, 78 rue Vieille-du-Temple, 4ème (☎01 42 74 34 65). M: Hôtel-de-Ville. From rue de Rivoli, turn left on rue Vieille-du-Temple. This friendly *pâtisserie*/lunch cafe with a bright Mediterranean ambience serves enormous salads (€9.80) and delicious *tartines* (€8.90). Lunch *menu* €8.60. Su brunch €19.50. Large selection of coffee from 4 continents (€2). Open Tu-Th and Su 11am-6pm, F-Sa 11am-8pm. MC/V. ❷

FIFTH AND SIXTH ARRONDISSEMENTS

▨ **Café de la Mosquée,** 39 rue Geoffrey St-Hilaire, 5ème (☎01 43 31 38 20). M: Censier-Daubenton. In the Mosquée de Paris. With fountains, marble floors, and an exquisite multi-level terrace, this cafe deserves a visit whether a trip to the Mosquée is on your itinerary or not. Savor Persian mint tea (€2.50) and *maghrebain* pastries (€2) under the shade of fig and olive trees. Restaurant serves couscous (€9-25). Tea room open daily 9am-11:30pm; restaurant daily noon-3pm and 7:30-10:30pm. ❸

Le Petit Vatel, 5 rue Lobineau, 6ème (☎01 43 54 28 49). M: Mabillon. Follow traffic on bd. St-Germain, turn right on rue de Seine, and then take the second right onto rue Lobineau. French-Mediterranean specialties like *catalan pamboli* (bread with puréed tomatoes, ham, and cheese), all €10, in a rare 100% non-smoking environment. Lunch *menu* €11. Vegetarian options. Open Tu-Sa noon-2:30pm and 7-10:30pm. ❷

Savannah Café, 27 rue Descartes, 5ème (☎01 43 29 45 77). M: Cardinal Lemoine. Follow rue du Cardinal Lemoine uphill, turn right on rue Clovis, and walk 1 block. Decorated with eclectic knick-knacks, this cheerful restaurant serves Lebanese food, including eggplant caviar, taboule, and an extensive pasta selection (€12.50). Appetizers €7-12.50. *Menu* €23. Open M-Sa 7-11pm. MC/V. ❸

Comptoir Méditerranée, 42 rue du Cardinal Lemoine, 5ème (☎01 43 25 29 08). Run by the same welcoming owner as Savannah Café. Tastes from Lebanon and elsewhere in a fresh array of ingredients. Select from 20 hot and cold dishes to make your own plate (€6). Sandwich or thyme pizza €3.50. Open M-Sa 11am-10pm. ❶

Octave, 138 rue Mouffetard, 5ème (01 45 35 20 56). M: Censier-Daubenton. If heaven ever froze over, it would be served in a cone at Octave. With no preservatives or artificial coloring, all you taste in each scoop is fresh melon, rich chocolate, or soothing cinnamon. One scoop €2, two scoops €3.50. Open M 2-7:30pm, Tu-Su 10am-11:30pm. ❶

Crêperie Saint Germain, 33 rue St-André-des-Arts, 6ème (☎01 43 54 24 41). M: St-Michel. Cross pl. St-Michel and walk down rue St-André-des-Arts. Serves filling wheat-flour *crêpes noirs,* like the "Chihuahua" (chicken, peppers, tomato, onion, banana; €8.60). Sweet dessert crêpes (€2.80-7.60). €8.50 *menu* (M-F noon-3pm) includes 2 crêpes and *cidre.* Open daily noon-midnight. AmEx/MC/V. ❶

Café Vavin, 18 rue Vavin, 6ème (☎01 43 26 67 47). The elusive creature: a cafe with personality, location, and delicious food. Funky tiling on the walls. Excellent smoked duck salad (€7.65), chicken with bearnaise sauce (€11.30). Espresso €2.30. Open M-F 7am-midnight, Sa 7am-6pm. MC/V. ❷

Le Grenier de Notre-Dame, 18 rue de la Bucherie, 5ème (☎01 43 29 98 29; www.grenierdenotredame.com). M: St-Michel. Walk along quai St-Michel to quai de Montebello; turn right on rue Lagrange and left on rue de la Bucherie. Macrobiotic, vegetarian, and vegan specialties with a French spin. 3-course *formule zen* (€12.50) might help you reach Nirvana. Salads €10-11. Open M-Th noon-2:30pm and 7:30-11pm, F-Sa noon-2:30pm and 7:30-11:30pm, Su noon-3pm and 7:30-11:30pm. MC/V. ❷

Le Perraudin, 157 rue St-Jacques, 5ème (☎01 46 33 15 75). M: Cluny-La Sorbonne. Walk down bd. St-Michel, turn left on rue Soufflot, then right on rue St-Jacques; the restaurant is on the corner. Serves Parisian favorites like *confit de canard* and *boeuf bourguignon* to a boisterous crowd, mostly students and locals. *Plat du jour* €9-12. Lunch *menu* €18. *Menu gastronomique* €28. Open M-F noon-2:30pm and 7-11pm. ❸

Café de Flore, 172 bd. St-Germain, 6ème (☎01 45 48 55 26). M: St-Germain-des-Prés. Walk against traffic on bd. St-Germain. Sartre wrote *Being and Nothingness* here; Apollinaire, Camus, Artaud, Picasso, Breton, and Thurber sipped brew, and in the contemporary feud between Café de Flore and Les Deux Magots, Flore reportedly snags more local intellectuals—possibly by offering a well-respected literary prize. Espresso €4. *Salade Flore* €12.50. Open daily 7:30am-1:30am. AmEx/MC/V. ❸

Les Deux Magots, 6 pl. St-Germain-des-Prés, 6ème (☎01 45 48 55 25). M: St-Germain-des-Prés. Just down the street from the Église St-Germain-des-Prés. The cloistered area behind the high hedges has been home to literati (from Mallarmé to Hemingway) since 1885, but is now favored mostly by tourists. The cafe is named for 2 Chinese porcelain figures, not for fly larvae. Sandwiches €6.50-8, pastries from €6.70. Coffee €4, hot chocolate €6. Breakfast *menu* €15. Open daily 7:30am-1:30am. AmEx/V. ❸

SEVENTH AND EIGHTH ARRONDISSEMENTS

▨ **Toi,** 27 rue de Colisée, 8ème (☎01 42 56 56 58). M: Franklin D. Roosevelt. Walk toward the Arc on the Champs-Elysée and take the 1st street on the right. Toi might almost be too cool for school, were the food not fresh and original enough to speak for itself. M*ikado* of grilled prawns with shrimp tempura (€17). *Crème brûlée* with rose water syrup (€10). Open M-Sa noon-2am, except Sa lunch. ❹

▨ **Café des Lettres,** 53 rue de Verneuil, 7ème (☎01 42 22 52 17). Exit M: Solférino onto pl. J. Blainville and take rue de Villersexel; turn right onto rue de l'Université, left on rue de Poitiers, and right on rue de Verneuil. Scandinavian cafe, located in the same sunny courtyard as the Maison des Écrivains, with fresh, healthy fare. Smoked salmon and *blindis* (€16) and other Danish seafood dishes (€12-20). Su Scandinavian-style brunch buffet (€26); reservations recommended. Open M noon-3pm, Tu-F noon-11pm, Sa noon-7pm. ❹

Objectifs Crêpes, 10 rue de Constantinople, 8ème (☎01 40 08 00 17). M: Europe. Walk up rue de Rome and turn left on rue de Constantinople. Intimate, rustic *crêperie*. Choose your own ingredients (*galettes* €7.30-9.60, crêpes €3.20-7.20) or try a house specialty (Democritus has minced beef, ratatouille, and egg). *Cidres* €2.50-9. Lunch *menu* €14. Takeout cheaper. Open M-F noon-2pm and 7-10:30pm, Sa 7-10:30pm. ❷

L'Auberge Bressane, 16 av. de la Motte Picquet, 7ème (☎01 47 05 98 37). M: École Militaire or Tour Mauberg. A small, luxuriously decorated restaurant full of regular patrons. Butter-soft artichoke hearts in a light vinaigrette €9, famous *poulet à la crème et aux morilles* (chicken in creamy mushroom sauce) €19. Order one of the famous house soufflés (Grand Marnier or chocolate) at the start of your meal to ensure a fine finale. 3-course lunch *menu* M-F €15-24, dinner *menu* (with wine) €25. Open daily noon-2:30pm and 8-10:30pm, closed Sa during lunch. Reservations are a must. ❺

NINTH AND TENTH ARRONDISSEMENTS

▨ **Restaurant Américain Chez Haynes,** 3 rue Clauzel, 9ème (☎01 48 78 40 63). M: St-Georges. Head uphill on rue Notre Dame de Lorette and turn right on rue Henri Monnier, then right on rue Clauzel to the end of the block. The 1st African American-owned restaurant in Paris (opened in 1949) and a former hangout of Louis Armstrong, James Baldwin, and Richard Wright. Haynes is famous for its "Original American Soul Food" and cornbread with meat sauce. Ma Sutton's fried chicken with honey €14. Sister Lena's BBQ spare ribs €14. Vocal jazz concerts F nights; funk and groove Sa nights (€6 cover). Open Tu-Sa 7pm-12:30am. AmEx/MC/V. ❸

▨ **Cantine d'Antoine et Lili,** 95 quai de Valmy, 10ème (☎01 40 37 34 86). M: Gare de l'Est. Go down rue Faubourg St-Martin and make a left on rue Récollets; Cantine is on the corner of quai de Valmy. This canal-side cafe-bistro is one-third of the Antoine and Lili operation, which also includes a neighboring furniture store and a clothing boutique. Friendly staff, vibrant decor, and tasty, light fare. Salads €6.50. Quiche €7.50. Takeout €0.50 less. Open M-Tu and Su 11am-8pm, W-Sa 11am-1am. AmEx/MC/V. ❶

Comme Par Hasard, 48 rue Notre-Dame-de-Lorette, 9ème (☎01 42 80 45 09). M: St-Georges. Who knew a sandwich joint could be hip? Delicious sandwiches beyond the standard *jambon beurre*. Sit outside, or stay inside and chat with the hip owners. €6 *menu* is a great value. Open 10am-8pm. ❶

Anarkali Sarangui, 4 pl. Gustave Toudouze, 9ème (☎01 48 78 39 84). M: St-Georges. Walk uphill on rue Notre Dame de Lorette and turn right on rue Henri Monnier. North Indian restaurant with outdoor seating. Tandoori and curries €7.50-12.50. Open M 7-11:30pm, Tu-Su noon-2:30pm and 7-11:30pm. MC/V. ❷

Au Bon Café, 2 bd. St-Martin, 10ème (☎01 42 00 21 45). M: République. Just to the right of pl. de la République if you exit the station facing the statue. A nice alternative to the McDonald's and pizza. Try a crisp salad with ingredients like scallops, grapefruit, pear, avocado, and tomato. Salads €9-10. Quiche €6-8. AmEx/MC/V. ❷

ELEVENTH AND TWELFTH ARRONDISSEMENTS

▧ **Chez Paul,** 13 rue de Charonne, 11ème (☎01 47 00 34 57). M: Bastille. Go east on rue du Faubourg St-Antoine and turn left on rue de Charonne. Classic bistro feel downstairs; cozy, romantic atmosphere upstairs. Regulars go for the house speciality *steak tartare* (€13.50), while the very brave can give in to St. Antoine's Temptation (€16), a dish of pig ear, foot, tail, and groin. Open daily noon-2:30pm and 7pm-2am; food served until 12:30am. Reservations are a must during peak hours. AmEx/MC/V. ❸

L'Ebauchoir, 45 rue de Citeaux, 12ème (☎01 43 42 49 31). M: Faidherbe-Chaligny. Walk down rue du Faubourg St-Antoine, turn left on rue de Citeaux. Feels like a funky, dressed-up diner. €13 lunch *menu*, all-day *menu* €25. *Plats* from €12. Open M-Th noon-2:30pm and 8-10:30pm, F-Sa noon-2:30pm and 8-11pm. MC/V. ❹

Café de l'Industrie, 16 rue St-Sabin, 11ème (☎01 47 00 13 53). M: Breguet-Sabin. Happening cafe frequented by happening 20-somethings. Decorated with palm trees and framed by huge windows. €9 lunch *menu*. Coffee €2, *vin chaud* €4. Salads €7.50-8. Popular brunch Sa-Su €18. Open M-F and Su 10am-2am; lunch noon-2pm. ❷

THIRTEENTH AND FOURTEENTH ARRONDISSEMENTS

▧ **Chez Papa** 6 rue Gassendi, 14ème (☎01 43 22 41 19). M: Denfert-Rochereau. Walk down Froidevaux along the cemetery; the restaurant will be on the left at the intersection with rue Gassendi. Feast on the massive *salade boyarde,* with lettuce, potatoes, cantal, and *bleu de brebis* (€7.05)—eggs and ham for just €0.75 more. Hearty *menu* (€9.15) served M-F until 4pm. Also in the 8ème (29 rue de l'Arcade; ☎01 42 65 43 68), 10ème (206 rue Lafayette; ☎01 42 09 53 87), and 15ème (101 rue de la Croix Nivert; ☎01 48 28 31 88). Open daily 11am-1am. AmEx/MC/V. ❷

▧ **Tricotin,** 15 av. de Choisy, 13ème (☎01 45 84 74 44). M: Porte de Choisy. 6 chefs prepare delicious food from Cambodia, Thailand, and Vietnam, served in 2 giant, cafeteria-style rooms. Try the famed Cambodian fried rice with beef (€6.80) or any of the *vapeur* foods (steamed shrimp ravioli, €3.40). Open daily 9:30am-11:30pm. MC/V. ❶

L'Amuse Bouche, 188 rue du Château, 14ème (☎01 43 35 31 61). M: Alésia. Take av. du Maine to rue du Château. Traditional French cuisine prepared to perfection. The €29 dinner *menu* offers, among other things, *escargots* with mushrooms and lamb fondant with couscous, plus 1 of the delightful desserts. Open Tu-Sa noon-2pm and 7:30-10:15pm. Reservations recommended. MC/V. ❺

Le Temps des Cerises, 18 rue de la Butte-aux-Cailles, 13ème (☎01 45 89 69 48). M: Place d'Italie. Take rue Bobillot and turn right on rue de la Butte-aux-Cailles. A local restaurant cooperative, Le Temps has been in shared ownership between all its workers, from cook to bartender, since 1976. Classic French dishes. Try the *Assiette Grècque,* piled-high with cold cuts (€12). Lunch *menu* €10, anytime *menus* €13.50 and €22. Open M-F 11:45am-2:15pm and 7:30-11:45pm, Sa 7:30-11:45pm. AmEx/MC/V. ❸

FIFTEENTH AND SIXTEENTH ARRONDISSEMENTS

▧ **Thai Phetburi,** 31 bd. de Grenelle, 15ème (☎01 40 58 14 88; www.phetburi-paris.com). M: Bir-Hakeim. Head away from the river on bd. de Grenelle; the restaurant is on your left. Award-winning food, friendly service, and low prices, just minutes from the Eiffel Tower. The *tom yam koung* (shrimp soup flavored with lemongrass; €7) and the *lab kai* (chicken in Thai grass; €8.80) are both favorites. Vegetarian options available. Open M-Sa noon-2:30pm and 7-10:30pm. AmEx/MC/V. ❷

▓ **Aux Artistes,** 63 rue Falguière, 15ème (☎01 43 22 05 39). M: Pasteur. Take Pasteur away from rails and turn left on rue Falguière. Lively cafe draws a mix of professionals, students, and artists. Modigliani was supposedly a regular. Lunch *menu* €9.20, dinner *menu* €12.50. Open M-F noon-2:30pm and 7:30pm-midnight, Sa 7:30pm-midnight. ❷

Le Dix Vins, 57 rue Falguière, 15ème (☎01 43 20 91 77). M: Pasteur. Follow Pasteur away from the rails and make a left onto rue Falguière. The pun in this outstanding bistro's name fits—both the meals and the wines are divine. The *menu,* while not exactly cheap (€18.50), offers diners a classic meal with a *nouvelle cuisine* twist. Open M-F noon-2:30pm and 7:30-11pm. MC/V. ❹

Byblos Café, 6 rue Guichard, 16ème (☎01 42 30 99 99). M: La Muette. Walk down rue Passy 1 block and turn left on rue Guichard. Airy, modern Lebanese restaurant. Cold *mezzes* (think Middle Eastern *tapas*) that are good for pita-dipping: taboule, moutabal, moussaka, and a variety of hummus dishes, all €5.80-8. Ideal for large groups, with various meal combinations starting at €38 for 2. Takeout 15-20% less. Vegetarian options. Open daily 11am-3pm and 5-11pm. AmEx/MC/V. ❸

Musée du Vin Restaurant, rue des Eaux, or 5-7, pl. Charles Dickens, 16ème M: Passy. Go down the stairs, turn right on Square Alboni, and then turn right on rue des Eaux. Enjoy a lunch *menu* (€45-55) with specialized wines for each plate you choose. French delicacies like smoked cheeses and *foie gras* are served beneath the gaze of wine-making wax monks. Open Tu-Su noon-3pm. MC/V. ❺

SEVENTEENTH AND EIGHTEENTH ARRONDISSEMENTS

▓ **Le Soleil Gourmand,** 10 rue Ravignan, 18ème (☎01 42 51 00 50). M: Abbesses. Facing the church in Place des Abbesses, go right on rue des Abbesses, then right (uphill) on rue Ravignan. Local favorite with funky artistic flair. Refreshing, light Provençal fare. Try the specialty *bricks* (grilled stuffed filo dough; €11) and fresh cakes (€4.50-7). Vegetarian options include the *assiette sud* (€12), with plenty of grilled and marinated vegetables. Open daily 12:30-2:30pm and 7:30-11pm. Evening reservations a must. ❸

▓ **The James Joyce Pub,** 71 bd. Gouvion St-Cyr, 17ème (☎01 44 09 70 32; www.kittyosheas.com). M: Porte Maillot (exit at Palais de Congrès). Take bd. Gouvion St-Cyr past Palais de Congrès. Upstairs is a friendly restaurant with stained-glass windows depicting scenes from Joyce's novels. Spectacular Su brunch (noon-3pm) is a full Irish fry: eggs, bacon, sausage, puddings, beans, chips, and coffee (€16). Downstairs, the pub pulls pints of what Joyce called "Ghinis." An informal tourist office for anglophone expats. Traditional Irish meals from €10. Pub open M-Th 9pm-1:30am, F-Su 10am-2am; restaurant M-Sa noon-3pm and 7:30-10:30pm, Su noon-5pm. AmEx/MC/V. ❸

Le Bistrot de Théo, 90 rue des Dames, 17ème (☎01 43 87 08 08). M: Villiers. From rue de Lévis, turn right on rue des Dames. This classy bistro serves cuisine as quirky as its minimalist decor. Try the roast duck and prunes garnished with apple and mango chutney (€13.50) or the veal with honey and fig (€13). Lunch *menu* €12.20, dinner *menu* €22.50 or €27. Open M-Sa noon-2:30pm and 7:30-11:30pm. AmEx/MC/V. ❸

Refuge des Fondues, 17 rue des Trois Frères, 18ème (☎01 42 55 22 65). M: Abbesses. Walk down rue Yvonne le Tac and go left on rue des Trois Frères. Only 2 main dishes: *fondue bourguignonne* (meat) and *fondue savoyarde* (cheese). Wine (2 choices: red or white) is served in baby bottles with rubber nipples. Forget your Freudian hang-ups and join the party at the 2 long tables. *Menu* €15. Open daily 6:30pm-2am (no seating after 12:30am); closed Aug. Reserve a table or show up early. ❸

Djerba Cacher Chez Guichi, 76 rue Myrha, 18ème (☎01 42 23 77 99). M: Barbès-Rochechouart. Walk up bd. Barbès and turn right onto rue Myrha. Guichi's owners opened this watering hole to provide cheap North African fare to local merchants. Parisians come from all over the city to sample the *brochette foie gras* (€10). Sandwiches €4-7.50. *Plats* €7-11.50. Open M-Th and Su noon-4pm and 7-11pm, F noon-4pm. ❷

NINETEENTH AND TWENTIETH ARRONDISSEMENTS

Lao Siam, 49 rue de Belleville, 19ème (☎01 40 40 09 68). M: Belleville. With a wall full of articles touting the Thai and Chinese cuisine served up at this local favorite, it's no surprise that every bite is worth writing about. Try the dried calamari salad (€8.40) or the Royal Curry Chicken (€8.40). Finish it off with kumquats (€2.80), and you won't mind coming so far out of the way. Open daily noon-3pm and 6:30-11:30pm. MC/V. ❷

Café Flèche d'Or, 102 rue de Bagnolet, 20ème (☎01 43 72 04 23). M: Alexandre Dumas. Follow rue de Bagnolet until it crosses rue des Pyrénées; the cafe is on the right. Near Porte de la Réunion at Père Lachaise. In an old train station, this bar/cafe/performance space serves North African, French, Caribbean, and South American cuisine with nightly music. Political cafe 1st Sa morning of every month; political debates every other Su morning. Dinner *menus* €12-15. Su brunch *menu* €11. Bar-cafe open daily 10am-2am; dinner 8pm-1am. MC/V over €15.25. ❸

Aux Arts et Sciences Réunis, 161 av. Jean-Jaurès, 19ème (☎01 42 40 53 18). M: Ourcq. A short stroll away after a day at La Villette. Serving up hearty southwestern French meals family-style, Aux Arts brings in a local crowd. *Plats* like salmon with hollandaise sauce €13-22. French piano music Sa during dinner. Open M-Sa 7:30am-10:30pm. Food served noon-2:30pm and 7:30-10:30pm. MC/V. ❹

SALONS DE THÉ

Parisian *salons de thé* (tea rooms) fall into three categories: stately salons piled high with macaroons, Seattle-inspired joints for pseudo-intellectuals, and cafes that simply want to signal they also serve tea.

Ladurée, 16 rue Royale, 8ème (☎01 42 60 21 79). M: Concorde. Ever wondered what it would be like to dine inside a Fabergé egg? The Rococo decor of this classic tea salon attracts the well-groomed shoppers who frequent the boutiques in the area. Famous for the mini macaroons stacked in the window (€3, in 9 different varieties). Specialty tea *Ladurée mélange* €6.50. House-branded champagne €5.50 a glass. Su brunch €29. Open daily 8:30am-7pm; lunch served until 3pm. AmEx/MC/V. Also at 75 av. des Champs-Élysées, 8ème (☎01 40 75 08 75). M: FDR.

Mariage Frères, 30 rue du Bourg-Tibourg, 4ème (☎01 42 72 28 11). M: Hôtel-de-Ville. Started by 2 brothers who found British tea shoddy, this salon offers 500 varieties of tea (€7-15) and an in-house book detailing the history and uses of each variety. Classic French institution. Tea *menu* includes sandwich, pastry, and tea (€25). Classic brunch *menu* is excellent (brioche, eggs, tea, cakes; €25), as is the decadent Snob Salad (€21) which comes piled high with *foie gras* and smoked salmon. Open daily 10:30am-7:30pm; lunch M-Sa noon-3pm; afternoon tea 3-6:30pm; Su brunch 12:30-6:30pm. Reserve for brunch. AmEx/MC/V. Also at 13 rue des Grands Augustins, 6ème (☎01 40 51 82 50) and at 260 rue du Faubourg St-Honoré, 8ème (☎01 46 22 18 54).

MARKETS

Marché Monge, 5ème. M: Monge. In pl. Monge at the metro exit. A bustling, friendly, and easy-to-navigate market. You'll find everything from cheese to shoes to jewelry and flowers in these stalls. Look for the very popular prepared foods (perfect for a lunch picnic at the Arènes de Lutèce). Open W, F, and Su 8am-1:30pm.

Marché rue Montorgueil, 2ème. M: Etienne-Marcel. Walk along rue Etienne Marcel away from the river. rue Montorgueil is the 2nd street on your right. A center of food commerce and gastronomy since the 13th century, this marble market is comprised of wine, cheese, meat, and produce shops. Open Tu-Su 8am-7:30pm.

Marché Mouffetard, 5ème. M: Monge. Walk through pl. Monge and follow rue Ortolan to rue Mouffetard. Cheese, meat, fish, produce, and housewares. The bakeries here are some of the best of all Paris's markets, and don't miss the ice cream at Octave near the far end of the market. Open Tu-Su 8am-1:30pm.

Marché Président-Wilson, on av. Président-Wilson between rue Debrousse and pl. d'Iéna, 16ème. M: Iéna or Alma-Marceau. The smart alternative to the 16ème's exorbitantly priced restaurants. Agricultural and dairy products, meat, fish, exotic breads, rich pastries and ready-to-eat Chinese and Middle Eastern fare. Flower stalls, clothing, table linens, and other household goods. Open W and Sa 7am-2:30pm.

SPECIALTY SHOPS

Barthélémy, 51 rue Grenelle, 7ème (☎01 45 48 56 75). M: Rue du Bac. A cluttered, old-fashioned store-front; inside, the finest *fromagerie* in Paris. President Chirac has been known to stop in. Open Tu-F 7:30am-7:30pm.

Julien, 75 rue St-Honoré, 1er (☎01 42 36 24 83). The best of everything: breads, sandwiches, pastries, cakes. For an indulgent breakfast, try the *pain au chocolat* (a flaky, buttery chocolate croissant) or the very different but equally delicious *pain chocolat* (a small loaf of bread with chocolat chips). Long lines at lunch.

Gérard Mulot, 76 rue de Seine, 6ème (☎01 43 26 85 11). M: Odéon or St-Sulpice. Outrageous selection of painstakingly crafted pastries, from flan to marzipan with virtually any kind of fruit. The *macaron* is heaven on earth (€4.50). Tarts from €2.50, eclairs €2, *mousse chocolat noisettes* €6.10. Open Tu and Th-Su 7am-8pm.

L'Epicerie, 51 rue St-Louis-en-l'Île, Île St-Louis (☎01 43 25 20 14). A condiment mecca. Homemade jams, sweets, mustards, olive oil, vinegar, and even flavored sugar are found inside this shop. Pear and honey or pistachio and almond jams €7.

Tang Frères, 48 av. d'Ivry, 13ème (☎01 45 70 80 00). M: Porte d'Ivry. Look for no. 44 and go down a few steps, or look for no. 48 and follow the sign through a parking lot. Also at 174 rue de Choisy, M: Place d'Italie. Huge shopping center in the heart of Chinatown, with grocery store, flower store, bakery, *charcuterie*, and porcelain shop. Rice, spices, teas, soups, and noodles in bulk. Exotic fruits (*durian* €5 per kg), cheap Asian beers (€1.19), rice wines, and sake. Open Tu-F 9am-7:30pm, Sa-Su 8:30am-7:30pm.

Nicolas, 142 rue de Rivoli, 1er (☎01 42 33 58 45). Locations throughout Paris. English-speaking staff will help you pick the perfect Burgundy. They'll even pack it up in a sturdy travel box with handles. Most branches open M-F 10am-8pm. AmEx/MC/V.

◉ SIGHTS

ÎLE DE LA CITÉ

NOTRE DAME

Once the site of a Roman temple to Jupiter, the ground upon which Notre Dame stands housed three churches before Maurice de Sully, the bishop of Paris under King Philip II, began construction of the Catholic cathedral in 1163. He wanted an edifice filled with air and light, in a style that would later be dubbed **Gothic.** He died before his plan was completed, and later generations reworked the cathedral into today's masterpiece, which was finally finished in 1361. Royals used Notre Dame for weddings, most notably that of **Henri of Navarre** to Marguerite de Valois.

In addition to its royal functions, the cathedral was also the setting of **Joan of Arc's** trial for heresy in 1455. During the Revolution, secularists renamed the cathedral Le Temple de la Raison (The Temple of Reason) and defaced its Gothic arches with Neoclassical plaster facades. Re-consecrated after the Revolution, the church was the site of **Napoleon's** papal coronation in 1804, but the building fell into disrepair and was used to shelter livestock before **Victor Hugo's** 1831 novel *The Hunchback of Notre Dame* revived the cathedral's popularity and inspired Napoleon III and Haussmann to invest time and money in its restoration. Modifications by Eugène Viollet-le-Duc invigorated the cathedral and once again made Notre Dame a valued symbol of civic unity: in 1870 and again in 1940 thousands of Parisians attended masses to pray for deliverance from the invading Germans. On August 26, 1944, **Charles de Gaulle** braved Nazi sniper fire to give thanks here for the imminent liberation of Paris. All these upheavals (not to mention hordes of tourists) seem to have left the cathedral unscarred.

EXTERIOR. Notre Dame is in the throes of a massive cleaning project, though its newly glittering **West Facade** is now scaffolding-free. The oldest work is above the **Porte de Ste-Anne** (right), dating from 1165 to 1175. Not content with decapitating Louis XVI, the Revolutionaries attacked the Kings of Judah above the doors. The heads are now exhibited in the Musée de Cluny (p. 114).

TOWERS. The soot-smeared towers of Notre Dame were an imposing shadow on the Paris skyline for years, but two years of sandblasting have brightened the exterior, revealing the rose windows and rows of saints. The claustrophobia-inducing staircase emerges onto a spectacular perch, where rows of gargoyles survey the city. In the south tower, a tiny door opens onto the 13-ton bell that even Quasimodo couldn't ring: it requires the force of eight people to move.

INTERIOR. From the inside, the cathedral seems to be constructed of soaring, weightless walls, thanks to the exterior flying buttresses that create room for delicate stained-glass walls by supporting the vaulted ceiling from outside. The transept's **rose windows,** nearly 85% 13th-century glass, are the most spectacular feature. The **treasury,** south of the choir, contains an assortment of gilded artifacts. The famous Crown of Thorns, which is supposed to have been worn by Christ, was moved to Notre Dame at the end of the 18th century. The relic is presented only on Fridays (5-6pm) during Lent. Far below the cathedral towers, the **Crypte Archéologique,** pl. du Parvis du Notre Dame, houses artifacts unearthed in the construction of a parking garage. (*M: Cité.* ☎ *01 53 10 07 02, crypt 01 55 42 50 10. Cathedral open M-F 8am-6:45pm and Sa-Su 8am-7:45pm. Towers open July-Aug. 9am-7:30pm; Apr.-June and Sept. 9:30am-7:30pm; Jan.-Mar. and Oct.-Dec. 10am-5:30pm. €6, ages 18-25 €4.10. Free tours begin at the booth to the right as you enter. In English W-Th noon, Sa 2:30pm; in French M-F noon, Sa 2:30pm. Treasury open M-Sa 9:30am-12:30pm and 1:30-5:30pm, Su 1:30-5:30pm; last ticket at 5pm. €2.50, students and ages 12-17 €2, 6-12 €1, under 6 free. Mass M-F 8, 9am, noon, 6:15pm; Sa 8, 8:45, 10, 11:30am, 12:45, 6:30pm; Vespers sung 5:30pm in the choir. Before Vespers, free organ recital starting at 4:30pm. High Mass with Gregorian chant is celebrated Su 10am, with music at 11:30am, 12:45, 6:30pm. Crypt open daily 10am-5:30pm; last ticket sold 30min. before closing. €3.90, over 60 €2.80, under 27 €2.20, under 13 free.*)

PALAIS DE LA CITÉ

STE-CHAPELLE. Ste-Chapelle remains the foremost example of Flamboyant Gothic architecture and medieval stained glass. The chapel was constructed in 1241 to house King Louis IX's most precious possession: the Crown of Thorns from Christ's Passion (now in Notre Dame). The simpler Lower Chapel has portraits of saints beneath the blue vaulted ceiling, but the real star is the breathtaking Upper Chapel. On sunny days, light pours through its walls of stained glass, illuminating frescoes of

How Paris Cleaned Up Its Act

ke a clock, twelve straight boulevards radiate
twards from the pl. Charles de Gaulle. A view
rough the arc at the foot of the Louvre aligns
th the Obelisk in the pl. de la Concorde, the Arc
Triomphe, and the modern arch at La Défense.
fe-lined streets and wide tree-lined boulevards
em as organic to Paris as the murky snaking of
e Seine. Yet none of this is an accident. And,
spite our modern notions that Paris is a city to
hich pleasure—be it amorous, gastronomic,
tistic, or commercial—comes naturally, the
y's charm is as calculated as the strategic
plication of paint to a courtesan's lips, and the
y wasn't always so beautiful.

Social commentator Maxime Du Camp
served in the mid-19th century: "Paris, as we
it in the period following the Revolution of
48, was uninhabitable. Its population…was suf-
ating in the narrow, tangled, putrid alleyways in
ich it was forcibly confined." Sewers were not
ed until 1848, and waste and trash rotted in the
ine. Streets followed a maddening 12th-century
sign; in some *quartiers*, winding thoroughfares
re no wider than 3.5m. Toadstool-like rocks
ed the streets allowing pedestrians to jump to
fety as carriages sped by. In the hands of the
ine prefect, Baron Georges-Eugène Haussmann,
reaucrat and social architect under Emperor
uis Napoleon, the city's medieval layout was
molished and replaced with a new urban vision
ided by the second emperor's technological,
itary, and political agenda.

Haussmann replaced the tangle of medieval
eets with his sewers, trains, and *grand boule-
rds*. The prefect's vision bisected Paris along
o central, perpendicular axes: the rue de Rivoli
d the bd. de Sébastopol (which extended
ross the Seine to the bd. St-Michel). Hauss-
nn, proclaiming the necessity of unifying Paris
d promoting trade among the different
rondissements, saw the old streets as anti-
ated impediments to modern commercial and
litical progress. His wide boulevards swept
ough whole neighborhoods of cramped row

houses and little passageways; incidentally, he
displaced 350,000 of Paris' poorest residents.

The widespread rage at Haussmann's plans
reinforced the emperor's desire to use the city's
layout to reinforce his authority. The old, narrow
streets has been ideal for civilian insurrection in
preceding revolutions; rebels built barricades
across street entrances and blocked off whole
areas of the city from the government's military.
Haussmann believed that creating *grands boulevards* and carefully mapping the city could bring
to an end the use of barricades, and more importantly, prevent future uprisings. However, he was
gravely mistaken. During the 1871 revolt of the
Paris Commune, which saw the deposition of
Louis Napoleon and the rise of the Third Republic, the *grands boulevards* proved ideal for the
construction of higher and stronger barricades.

Despite the underlying political agenda of
Haussmannization, many of the prefect's changes
were for the better. Haussmann transformed the
open-air dump and grave (for the offal of local
butchers and the bodies of prisoners) at Mont-
fauçon with the whimsical waterfalls, cliffs, and
grottoes of the Parc des Buttes-Chaumont. Paris
became eminently navigable, and to this day a
glance down one of Paris's many grands boulevards will offer the *flâneur* (wanderer) an unexpected lesson in the layout of the city. Stroll
down the bd. Haussmann, the street bearing its
architect's name. En route to the ornate Opéra
Garnier, one glimpses the Church of the
Madeleine and the Gare St-Lazare; Haussmann's
layout silently links these monuments to religion,
art, and industry. The facades of the *grands
magasins* (department stores) Printemps and
Galeries Lafayette, respectively resemble a temple and a theater, again suggesting something of
the religious and the panoptic in the art of strolling and shopping along Paris's grand streets.

It is hard to imagine the city of Paris as a
sewer-less, alley-ridden metropolis; but it is perhaps all the more beautiful today if we do so.

Charlotte Houghteling has worked on Let's Go's Middle East, Egypt, and Israel titles. She wrote her senior thesis on the development of department stores during the Second Empire and is in the process of completing her M.Phil. at Cambridge on the consumer society of Revolutionary Paris.

Sara Houghteling was a Researcher-Writer for Let's Go: France 1999 and has taught at the American School in Paris. She is now a graduate student in creative writing at the University of Michigan.

saints and martyrs. Read from bottom to top, left to right, the 1136 windows narrate the Bible from Genesis to the Apocalypse. *(4 bd. du Palais. M: Cité. Within Palais de la Cité.* ☎ *01 53 73 78 50; www.monum.fr. Open daily Apr.-Sept. 9:30am-6pm; last admission 30min. before closing. Occasional candlelit classical music concerts (€16-30) held in the Upper Chapel mid-Mar. to Oct. Check FNAC (www.fnac.fr) or the booth to the left of the ticket-taker for details. €6.10, seniors and ages 18-25 €4.10, under 18 free. Twin ticket with Conciergerie €9, seniors and ages 18-25 €6, under 18 free.)*

CONCIERGERIE. Glowering over the Seine, this dark monument to the Revolution is a good example of secular medieval architecture. Originally an administrative building, then a royal prison, it was taken over by the Revolutionary Tribunal after 1793. Three thousand people were sentenced to death here between 1792 and 1794, among them Marie-Antoinette, Robespierre, and 21 Girondins. Today, the rows of cells display replicate prisoners and prison conditions. Plaques explain how the rich and famous could buy themselves private rooms with tables for writing while the poor slept on straw in pestilential cells. *(1 quai de l'Horloge, entrance on bd. du Palais, to the right of Palais de Justice. M: Cité.* ☎ *01 53 73 78 50; www.monum.fr. Open daily Apr.-Sept. 9:30am-6pm; Oct.-Mar. 10am-5pm; last ticket 30min. before closing. Includes tour in French, 11am and 3pm. For English tours, call in advance. €6.10, students €4.10.)*

PALAIS DE JUSTICE. Built after the great fire of 1776, the Palais is home to the district courts of France. Stone steps at the main entrance lead to three doorways marked *Liberté, Egalité,* and *Fraternité.* All trials are open to the public: choose a door and make your way through the green gates that stand beyond *Egalité.* Climb the stairs to the second floor and go immediately left (look for "Cour d'Appel" signs) and guards will let you into a viewing gallery. *(4 bd. du Palais; use the entrance for Ste-Chapelle. M: Cité.* ☎ *01 44 32 51 51. Courtrooms open M-F 9am-noon and 1:30-6pm. Free.)*

MÉMORIAL DE LA DÉPORTATION

This haunting memorial commemorates the 200,000 French victims of Nazi concentration camps. Inside, the focal point is a tunnel lined with 200,000 quartz pebbles, reflecting the Jewish custom of placing stones on graves of the deceased. Look for the numerous references to triangles, the mark of the deported, in the memorial's design. *(M: Cité. At the very tip of the island on pl. de l'Île de France, a 5min. walk from the back of the cathedral, and down a narrow flight of steps. Open daily Apr.-Sept. 10am-noon and 1-7pm; Oct.-Mar. 10am-noon and 1-5pm. Free.)*

PONT NEUF

Leave Île de la Cité by Pont Neuf (New Bridge), the oldest bridge in Paris, located just behind pl. Dauphine. Before the Champs-Élysées, it was Paris's most popular thoroughfare; now it's Paris's most popular make-out spot.

ÎLE ST-LOUIS

QUAI DE BOURBON. Sculptor **Camille Claudel** lived and worked at **no. 19** from 1899 until her brother, the poet Paul Claudel, had her committed to an asylum in 1913. Claudel was driven mad by the rejection of her mentor and lover, sculptor Auguste Rodin. Claudel's most striking work is displayed in the Musée Rodin (p. 126). At the intersection of the quai and rue des Deux Ponts sits the cafe **Au Franc-Pinot,** whose wrought-iron facade is almost as old as the island itself. Closed in 1716 when authorities discovered a stash of anti-government tracts, the cafe-cabaret reemerged as a center for treason during the Revolution: Cécile Renault, daughter of the proprietor, mounted an unsuccessful attempt on Robespierre's life in 1794 and was guillotined. Today the Pinot houses a mediocre jazz club.

ÉGLISE ST-LOUIS-EN-L'ILE. Louis Le Vau's 17th-century Rococo interior is lit by a striking number of windows. The third chapel has a splendid gilded wood relief, *The Death of the Virgin. (19bis rue St-Louis-en-l'Île. ☎01 46 34 11 60. Open Tu-Su 9am-noon and 3-7pm. Check with FNAC (www.fnac.com) or call the church for concert details; concert ticket prices vary, around €20 general admission and €15 for students.)*

FIRST ARRONDISSEMENT

JARDIN DES TUILERIES. Sweeping down from the Louvre to pl. de la Concorde, the Jardin des Tuileries celebrates the victory of geometry over nature. Missing the public promenades of her native Italy, Catherine de Médicis had the gardens built in 1564. In 1649, André Le Nôtre (gardener for Louis XIV and designer of the gardens at Versailles) imposed straight lines and sculpted greenery on the grounds. The elevated terrace by the Seine offers remarkable views of the **Arc de Triomphe du Carrousel** and the glass pyramid of the Louvre's Cour Napoléon. Sculptures by Rodin and others stand amid the garden's cafes and courts. In the summer, the rue de Rivoli terrace becomes an amusement park with children's rides, food stands, and a huge ferris wheel. The **Galerie National du Jeu de Paume** and the **Musée de l'Orangerie** flank the pathway at the Concorde end of the Tuileries. *(☎01 40 20 90 43. Open daily Apr.-Sept. 7am-9pm; Oct.-Mar. 7:30am-7:30pm. English tours from the Arc de Triomphe du Carrousel. Free. Amusement park open late June to mid-Aug. Rides €2-15.)*

PLACE VENDÔME. Stately pl. Vendôme, three blocks north of the Tuileries, was begun in 1687 by Louis XIV. Designed by Jules Hardouin-Mansart, the square was built to house embassies, but bankers created lavish private homes behind the elegant facades. Today, the smell of money is still in the air: bankers, perfumers, and jewelers, including Cartier (at no. 7), line the square.

PALAIS-ROYAL. One block north of the Louvre along rue St-Honoré lies the once regal and racy Palais-Royal, constructed in the 17th century as Richelieu's Palais Cardinal. After the Cardinal's death in 1642, Anne d'Autriche moved in with her son, young Louis XIV. In 1781, a broke Duc d'Orléans rented out the buildings around the palace's garden to boutiques, restaurants, theaters, wax museums, and gambling joints. In the central courtyard, the controversial **colonnes de Buren**, a set of black-and-white-striped pillars, were installed by artist Daniel Buren in 1986. *(Palace closed to the public. Fountain open daily June-Aug. 7am-11pm; Apr.-May 7am-10:15pm; Sept. 7am-9:30pm; Oct.-Mar. 7am-8:30pm. Free.)*

ÉGLISE DE ST-EUSTACHE. There is a reason why Richelieu, Molière, and Madame de Pompadour were all baptized in the Église de St-Eustache, why Louis XIV received communion in its sanctuary, and why Mozart chose to have his mother's funeral here: it is magnificent. Eustache was a Roman general who adopted Christianity upon seeing the sign of a cross between the antlers of a deer. Construction began in 1532 and wasn't completed until the mid-1700s. The chapels contain paintings by Rubens, as well as the British artist Raymond Mason's bizarre relief *Departure of the Fruits and Vegetables from the Heart of Paris*, commemorating the closing of the market at Les Halles. *(M: Les Halles. Above rue Rambuteau. ☎01 42 36 31 05. Open M-F 9am-7:30pm, Su 9:15am-7:30pm. High mass with choir and organ Su 11am and 6pm. Free organ recital Su 5:30-6pm. Hours and masses vary in Aug.; call in advance.)*

LES HALLES. A sprawling market since 1135, Les Halles received a much-needed face-lift in the 1850s with the construction of large iron and glass pavilions. In 1970, when authorities moved the old market to a suburb, planners destroyed the pavilions to build a transfer-point between the metro and the new commuter rail and a subterranean shopping mall, the **Forum des Halles,** with over 200 boutiques and three movie theaters. The metro station Les Halles exits directly into the underground mall. The escalators lead up to the striking gardens. Beware of pickpockets.

SECOND ARRONDISSEMENT

GALERIES AND PASSAGES. Paris's *passages* (and *galeries*, their posh siblings) might be considered the world's first shopping malls. In the early 19th century, speculators built shopping arcades in alleys all over central Paris. They designed panes of glass, held in place by lightweight iron rods, to attract window shoppers. Most have disappeared with urban development, but the 20 or so that remain have been restored and are perfect for a rainy-day stroll. Today, they house upscale clothing boutiques, cafes, and gift shops (look for the several that sell antique postcards).

BIBLIOTHÈQUE NATIONALE: SITE RICHELIEU. Site Richelieu was the main branch of the **Bibliothèque Nationale de France** (National Library) until 1998, when most of the collection was moved to the new Site Miterrand in the the 13*ème* arrondissement (p. 121). Richelieu still holds collections of stamps, money, photography, medals, maps, and manuscripts. Scholars must pass through a strict screening process to gain access to the main reading room. For viewing by the general public, the **Galerie Mazarin** and **Galerie Mansart** host excellent temporary exhibits of items from the collection. Upstairs, the **Cabinet des Médailles** displays coins, medallions, and *objets d'art* confiscated from the French Revolution. (*58 rue de Richelieu. M: Bourse. Just north of the Galeries Vivienne and Colbert, across rue Vivienne. Info line ☎01 53 79 59 59, galleries 01 47 03 81 10, cabinet 01 47 03 83 30; www.bnf.fr. Library open M-Sa 9am-7pm. Books available only to researchers who prove they need access with a letter of introduction from their university, research advisor, or editor. Tours of the former reading room (through a window) 1st Tu of the month 2:30pm in English and French; €7; ☎01 53 79 86 87. Galleries open Sa 10am-7pm, Su noon-7pm. Admission €5, students €4. Cabinet des Médailles open M-F 1-6pm, Sa 1-5pm. Free.*)

RUE SAINT-DENIS. In the mid-1970s, Paris's prostitutes demonstrated in churches and public squares, demanding unionization and protection under the law. They marched down rue St-Denis, the central artery of the city's prostitution district. Their campaign was successful and prostitution is now legal in France, though far less common than in The Netherlands. You might think otherwise along rue St-Denis, an enclave of debauchery, sex shops, and sketchy clubs in the otherwise G-rated 2*ème*.

THIRD ARRONDISSEMENT

RUE VIEILLE-DU-TEMPLE. Rue Vieille-du-Temple is lined with stately residences, including the 18th-century **Hôtel de la Tour du Pin** (no. 75) and **Hôtel de Rohan** (no. 87)—built for Armand-Gaston de Rohan, Bishop of Strasbourg and alleged lovechild of Louis XIV. Frequent temporary exhibits allow access to the original interior. Now a part of the National Archives, the Hôtel de Rohan also boasts a grand courtyard and rose garden. At the corner of rue des Francs-Bourgeois and rue Vieille-du-Temple are the Gothic turrets of the **Hôtel Hérouët**, built in 1528. (*M: Hôtel-de-Ville or St-Paul. ☎01 40 27 63 94 for info on guided tours of Hôtel de Rohan.*)

ARCHIVES NATIONALES. The most famous documents of the National Archives are on display in the **Musée de l'Histoire de France,** usually housed in the plush 18th-century Hôtel de Soubise. The Treaty of Westphalia, the Edict of Nantes, the Declaration of the Rights of Man, Marie-Antoinette's last letter, Louis XVI's diary, letters between Benjamin Franklin and George Washington, and Napoleon's will are all preserved here. Until June 2005, the Hôtel de Soubise is closed except to groups. Temporary exhibits of museum collections will be on display at the Hôtel de Rohan. Call ahead for upcoming exhibits. *(60 rue des Francs-Bourgeois. M: Rambuteau. ☎01 40 27 62 18.)*

MÉMORIAL DU MARTYR JUIF INCONNU. The Memorial to the Unknown Jewish Martyr is the result of a 1956 committee that included de Gaulle, Churchill, and Ben-Gurion; it commemorates European Jews who died at the hands of the Nazis and their French collaborators. *(37 rue de Turenne. M: St-Paul. ☎01 42 77 44 72, fax 01 48 87 12 50. Open M-W 1-5:30pm, Th 2-8pm.)*

FOURTH ARRONDISSEMENT

RUE DES ROSIERS. At the heart of the Jewish community of the Marais, rue des Rosiers is packed with kosher shops and falafel counters. When Philippe-Auguste expelled the Jewish population from the city limits in the 13th century, many families moved to here, just outside the walls. Since then, the quarter has become home to the influx of Russian Jews in the 19th century and North African Sephardim fleeing Algeria in the 1960s. During WWII, many who had fled to France to escape the pogroms of Eastern Europe were murdered by the Nazis. Assisted by French police, Nazi soldiers hauled families to the Vélodrome d'Hiver, an indoor cycling stadium, where they awaited deportation to concentration camps. Today, the Jewish community thrives, with two synagogues, at 25 rue des Rosiers and 10 rue Pavée, both designed by Art Nouveau master Hector Guimard. *(M: St-Paul.)*

RUE VIEILLE-DU-TEMPLE AND RUE STE-CROIX DE LA BRETTONERIE. The epicenter of Paris's thriving gay community, the intersection of rue Vieille-du-Temple and rue Ste-Croix de la Brettonerie boasts stylish men and beautiful boys in tight pants. Chic women wander through trendy boutiques while intellectuals of all orientations sip merlot at **La Belle Hortense,** a bookish oasis in this on-the-move and in-the-scene enclave. *(M: St-Paul or Hôtel-de-Ville.)*

HÔTEL DE VILLE. Paris's grandiose city hall dominates a large square filled with fountains and Belle Époque lampposts. The present edifice is a 19th-century replica of the original medieval structure, a meeting hall for the cartel that controlled traffic on the Seine. Municipal executions took place on pl. Hôtel-de-Ville: in 1610, Henri IV's assassin Ravaillac was drawn and quartered here. On May 24, 1871, the *communards* doused the building with petrol and set it on fire. The blaze, which lasted eight days, spared only the frame. The square occasionally hosts concerts and TV specials. *(29 rue de Rivoli. M: Hôtel-de-Ville. ☎01 42 76 43 43. Open M-F 9am-6:30pm when there is an exhibit; until 6pm otherwise. Group tours available with advance reservations.)*

TOUR ST-JACQUES. The Tour St-Jacques, standing in the center of its own park, is the only remnant of the 16th-century Flamboyant Gothic Église St-Jacques-la-Boucherie. The 52m tower's meteorological station and the statue of Pascal at its base commemorate Pascal's experiments on the weight of air, performed here in 1648. *(39-41 rue de Rivoli. M: Hôtel-de-Ville. 2 blocks west of the Hôtel-de-Ville.)*

HÔTEL DE SENS. The Hôtel de Sens is one of the city's few surviving examples of medieval residential architecture. Built in 1474 for Tristan de Salazar, the Archbishop of Sens, its military features reflect the violence of the times. The turrets were designed to guard the streets outside; the square tower served as a dungeon. An enormous Gothic arch entrance is carved with chutes for pouring boiling water on invaders. The Hôtel de Sens is the former residence of Queen Margot, Henri IV's first wife. In 1606, the 55-year-old queen drove up to her courtyard to find her two lovers-of-the-month arguing. One opened the lady's carriage door, and the other shot him dead. Unfazed, the queen ordered the perpetrator's execution. The Hôtel houses

ily Chronicle

IN-RECENT NEWS

BEACH BUMMING

n 2001, the inauguration of the super-fast TGV line to the Mediterranean brought Paris closer to the beach. In 2002, Mayor Bertrand Delanoë did even better: he came up with Paris Plage, an annual event that turns the banks of the Seine into a sunsplashed summer paradise.

From mid-July to mid-August, kilometers of quaiside are covered with sand and planted with palm trees. In 2004, the artificial beach was 3.5km long and 1800m² in area. The beaches are free and open to all, and Parisians come in droves to sunbathe by the Seine. The city provides hammocks, deckchairs, and beach umbrellas, and ice-cream carts are everywhere.

The festival was such a success in its first two years that in 2004 a 20m swimming pool was thrown into the mix, perhaps to make up for the polluted and unswimmable Seine. The pool held morning aquagym classes for adults and afternoon free-swims for kids. Add to that a paddling pool, changing rooms, and a humified solarium, and Paris felt about as posh as St-Tropez. With other facilities including volleyball courts and trampolines, Paris Plage leaves little to complain about but—unlike its Côte d'Azur counterparts—much to the imagination: the city discourages nude sunbathing. Parisians can still get a tan in the heart of the city—just not a seamless one.

the **Bibliothèque Forney.** *(1 rue du Figuier. M: Pont Marie. Courtyard open to the public. Library open Tu-F 1:30-8:30pm, Sa 10am-8:30pm; closed early to mid-July.)*

ÉGLISE ST-PAUL-ST-LOUIS. The large dome of the 17th-century Église St-Paul-St-Louis is visible from quite a distance. Paintings inside the dome depict four French kings: Clovis, Charlemagne, Robert the Pious, and St-Louis. Before being destroyed during the Revolution, the embalmed hearts of Louis XIII and Louis XIV were kept in vermeil boxes guarded by gilded silver angels. The holy-water vessels were gifts from Victor Hugo. *(99 rue St-Antoine. M: St-Paul. ☎01 49 24 11 43. Open M-Sa 8am-9pm, Su 9am-8:30pm. Free tours every 2nd Su of the month 3pm. Mass M 7pm; Tu, W, F 9am and 7pm; Th 9am, 7, 10pm; Sa 9am and 6pm; Su 9:30, 11:15am, 7pm.)*

PLACE DES VOSGES. The magnificent pl. des Vosges, at the end of rue des Francs-Bourgeois, is Paris's oldest public square and one of its most charming spots. Kings built several mansions on this site, including the Palais de Tournelles, which Catherine de Médicis ordered destroyed after her husband Henri II died there in a jousting tournament in 1563. Henri IV subsequently ordered it rebuilt. Each of the 36 buildings lining the square has arcades on street level, two stories of pink brick, and a slate-covered roof. Molière, Racine, and Voltaire filled the grand parlors with their *bon mots*, and Mozart played a concert here at the age of seven. During the Revolution, however, the 1639 Louis XIII statue in the center of the park was destroyed (the statue there now is a copy), and the park was renamed pl. des Vosges after the first department in France to pay its taxes. **Victor Hugo** lived at no. 6, which is now a museum of his life and work. *(M: Chemin Vert or St-Paul.)*

HÔTEL DE SULLY. Built in 1624, the Hôtel de Sully was eventually acquired by the Duc de Sully, the minister under Henri IV. The small inner courtyard of the hotel offers fatigued tourists several stone benches and an elegant formal garden. The Hôtel occasionally hosts small exhibits. *(62 rue St-Antoine. M: St-Paul. Info Centre ☎01 44 61 20 00. Open M-Th 9am-12:45pm and 2-6pm, F 9am-12:45pm and 2-5pm.)*

FIFTH ARRONDISSEMENT

PLACE ST-MICHEL. The busiest spot in the Latin Quarter, pl. St-Michel is where the Paris Commune in 1871 and the student uprising of 1968 took off. The majestic 1860 fountain features the archangel St-Michel slaying a dragon and a WWII memorial commemorating the citizens who fell here defending their *quartier* in August 1944. Nearby **Église St-Séverin** is decorated with spiraling columns and modern stained glass. Follow rue de la Harpe away from the *place* and turn left on rue St-Séverin. **Église St-Julien-le-Pauvre,** across bd. St-Jacques from St-Séverin, is one of the oldest churches in Paris, dating to 1170. The **Musée de Cluny,** at the intersection of bd. St-Germain and bd. St-Michel, houses an extraordinary collection of medieval art, tapestries, and illuminated manuscripts (see p. 127). A major tourist and student thoroughfare, **boulevard St-Michel** (or *boul' Mich'*) doesn't have a lot of flavor these days—for that, visitors should check out the many traditional bistros on nearby rue Soufflot and rue des Fossés St-Jacques.

LA SORBONNE. Founded in 1253 by Robert de Sorbon as a dormitory for 16 poor theology students, the Sorbonne is one of Europe's oldest universities. Soon after its founding, it became the administrative base for the University of Paris and the site of France's first printing house in 1469. As it grew in power and size, the Sorbonne often defied the French throne, even siding with England during the Hundred Years' War. Visitors can stroll through the **Chapelle de la Sorbonne** (entrance off of the pl. de la Sorbonne), which houses temporary exhibits on the arts and letters. The **place de la Sorbonne** is sprinkled with an assortment of cafes, bookstores, and—during term-time—students. *(45-7 rue des Écoles. M: Cluny-La Sorbonne or RER: Luxembourg.)*

COLLÈGE DE FRANCE. Created by François I in 1530 to contest the University's authority, the prestigious Collège de France stands just behind the Sorbonne. The humanist motto "Doce Omnia" (Teach Everything) is emblazoned in mosaics in the interior courtyard. Courses at the Collège—given in the past by such luminaries as Henri Bergson, Pierre Boulez, Paul Valéry, and Milan Kundera—are free and open to all. *(11 pl. Marcelin-Berthelot. M: Maubert-Mutualité. Walk against traffic on bd. St-Germain, turn left on rue Thenard; the entrance is at the end of the road, across rue des Écoles and up the steps. ☎01 44 27 12 11; www.college-de-france.fr. Courses Sept.-May. Closed Aug.)*

THE PANTHÉON. The Panthéon is one of Paris's most beautiful buildings. Louis XV, ascribing his recovery from a grave illness to the powers of Ste-Geneviève, vowed to build a memorial to the saint and entrusted its design to architect Jacques-Germain Soufflot in 1755, laying the first stone himself in 1764. The Revolution converted the church into a mausoleum of heroes in 1791. Some of France's most distinguished citizens are now buried in the Pathéon, including Marie and Pierre Curie, Jean Jaurès, Louis Braille, Voltaire, Jean-Jacques Rousseau, Emile Zola, and Victor Hugo. The Panthéon's other main attraction is **Foucault's Pendulum.** The plane of oscillation of the pendulum stays fixed as the Earth rotates around it. The pendulum's rotation confirmed the rotation of the Earth for nonbelievers like Louis Napoleon III. *(Pl. du Panthéon. M: Cardinal Lemoine. From rue Cardinal Lemoine, turn right on rue Clovis; walk around to the front of the building to enter. ☎01 44 32 18 00. Open daily 10am-6:30pm; last admission 5:45pm. Guided tours in French leave from inside the main door daily at 2:30 and 4pm. €7, students €4.50, under 18 free. Free 1st Su of the month Oct.-Mar.)*

PLACE DE LA CONTRESCARPE. South on rue Descartes, past the prestigious Lycée Henri IV, is pl. de la Contrescarpe, the geographical center of the 5ème. Lovely outdoor restaurants and cafes cluster around a fountain. From here, it's only a 5min. walk to St-Germain, the Panthéon, or the Jardin des Plantes.

RUE MOUFFETARD. Rue Mouffetard, south of pl. de la Contrescarpe, hosts one of Paris's liveliest street market and a friendly mix of Parisians and visitors. Poet Paul Verlaine died at 39 rue Descartes in 1844. Hemingway lived down the Mouff' at 74 rue du Cardinal Lemoine. The winding stretch up rue Mouffetard, past pl. de la Contrescarpe, and onto rue Descartes and rue de la Montagne Ste-Geneviève is the perfect Latin Quarter stroll. *(M: Cardinal Lemoine, Place Monge, or Censier Daubenton.)*

PARIS

JARDIN DES PLANTES. The Jardin des Plantes has 45,000m² of carefully tended flowers and lush greenery. Opened in 1640 by Louis XIII's doctor, the gardens originally grew medicinal plants to promote His Majesty's health. The **École de Botanique** is a landscaped garden tended by students, horticulturists, and amateur botanists. The **Roserie** contains roses from all over the world (full bloom in mid-June). The gardens also include the tremendous **Musée d'Histoire Naturelle** and the **Ménagerie Zoo,** with 240 mammals, 500 birds, and 130 reptiles. During the siege of Paris in 1871, starving Parisians martyred some of the elephants for the cause. *(M: Gare d'Austerlitz, Jussieu, or Censier-Daubenton. ☎01 40 79 37 94. Jardin des Plantes, École de Botanique, Jardin Alpin, and Roserie open daily summer 7:30am-8pm, winter 7:30am-5:30pm. Free. Menagerie Zoo, 3 quai St-Bernard and 57 rue Cuvier. Open daily Apr.-Sept. 10am-6pm; Oct.-Mar. 10am-5:30pm; last entrance 30min. before closing. €4.60, students €3.05.)*

MOSQUÉE DE PARIS. The Institut Musulman houses the beautiful Persian gardens, elaborate minaret, and shady porticoes of the Mosquée de Paris, constructed in 1920 by French architects to honor the role played by the countries of North Africa in WWI. The cedar doors open onto an oasis of blue and white, with fountains and carpeted prayer rooms (visible from the courtyard but closed to the public). Frenzied tourists can relax in the steam baths at the exquisite *hammam* or sip mint tea at the soothing cafe. *(Behind the Jardin des Plantes at pl. du Puits de l'Ermite. M: Censier Daubenton. Walk down rue Daubenton; the mosque is at the end of the street on the left. ☎01 48 35 78 17. Open daily 10am-noon and 2-5:30pm, June-Aug. until 6:30pm. Guided tour €3, students €2. Hammam open for men Tu 2-9pm, Su 10am-9pm; women M, W-Th, and Sa 10am-9pm, F 2-9pm; €15. Massage €10 for 10min., €30 per 30min; bikini wax €11. MC/V.)*

SHAKESPEARE & CO. BOOKSTORE. A legend among Parisian Anglophones, this shop seeks to reproduce the atmosphere of Sylvia Beach's establishment of the same name at 12 rue de l'Odéon, a gathering place for expatriates in the 20s. The original shop closed in 1941, and George Whitman, alleged grandson of Walt, opened his rag-tag replica in 1951. Frequented by Allen Ginsberg and Lawrence Ferlinghetti, Shakespeare hosts poetry readings, Sunday evening tea parties, a literary festival, and other events. *(37 rue de la Bucherie. M: St-Michel. Open daily noon-midnight.)*

INSTITUT DU MONDE ARABE. The Institut du Monde Arabe (IMA) is one of the Paris's most striking buildings. Facing the Seine, the IMA was built with the lines of a ship to represent those on which Algerian, Moroccan, and Tunisian immigrants sailed to France. The southern face is comprised of 240 Arabesque portals that open and close, powered by light-sensitive cells that determine how much light is needed to illuminate the interior of the building without damaging the art. Inside, the spacious museum exhibits 3rd- to 18th-century Arab art. Other facilities include an extensive **public library** and an auditorium that shows Arabic movies from September through June. *(1 rue des Fossés St-Bernard. M: Jussieu. Walk down rue Jussieu away from the Jardin des Plantes and take the first right on rue des Fossés St-Bernard. ☎01 40 51 38 38; www.imarabe.org. Museum open Tu-Su 10am-6pm. €4, students €3, under 12 free. Library open Tu-Sa 1-8pm, July-Aug. until 6pm. Free. Cinema €4, students €3.)*

SIXTH ARRONDISSEMENT

JARDIN DU LUXEMBOURG. Parisians flock to these formal gardens to sunbathe and read. A residential area in Roman Paris, the site of a medieval monastery, and later the home of 17th-century French royalty, the gardens were liberated during the Revolution and are now free to all. *(M: Odéon or RER: Luxembourg. Open daily dawn-dusk. The main entrance is on bd. St-Michel. Guided tours in French Apr.-Oct. 1st W of every month at 9:30am; depart from pl. André Honorat behind the observatory.)*

PARIS

PALAIS DU LUXEMBOURG. The Palais du Luxembourg, located within the park and now home to the French Senate, was built in 1615 at Marie de Médicis's request. Homesick for her native Florence, she tried to recreate its architecture and gardens in her new home in Paris. In 1630, during a titanic power play between Marie and her erstwhile ally Cardinal Richelieu, Marie threw such a legendary tantrum that her son, Louis XIII, kicked her off the royal council and exiled her to Cologne. During WWII, the palace was used by the Nazis as the headquarters of the *Luftwaffe.* *(www.monum.fr. Infrequent tours May-Sept. Call ☎01 44 54 19 49 to reserve a spot.)*

ÉGLISE ST-SULPICE. The balconied, neoclassical facade of the huge Église St-Sulpice dominates the enormous square of the same name. Designed by Servadoni in 1733, the church remains unfinished. St-Sulpice's claims to fame are a set of fierce, gestural Delacroix frescoes in the first chapel on the right, Jean-Baptiste Pigalle's *Virgin and Child* in a rear chapel, and an enormous organ. *(M: St-Sulpice or Mabillon. From M: Mabillon, walk down rue du Four and make a left on rue Mabillon. Rue Mabillon intersects rue St-Sulpice at the entrance to the church. 2 blocks west of the theater. ☎01 46 33 21 78 or 01 42 34 59 60. Open daily 7:30am-7:30pm. Guided tour in French daily 3pm.)*

BOULEVARD ST-GERMAIN. Most famous as the ex-literati hangout of existentialists (who frequented the Café de Flore) and surrealists (who preferred Les Deux Magots) bd. St-Germain is stuck somewhere between nostalgia for its intellectual cafe-culture past and an unabashed delight with all things fashionable and cutting edge. The boulevard and its many side-streets have become a serious shopping neighborhood in recent years, filled with high-end designer boutiques.

ÉGLISE DE ST-GERMAIN-DES-PRÉS. The Église de St-Germain-des-Prés is the oldest standing church in Paris, completed in 558 and decorated only by pink and white hollyhocks growing outside. King Childebert I commissioned a church on this site to hold relics he had looted from the Holy Land. Completely redone in the 19th century, the magnificent interior is painted in shades of maroon, deep green, and gold with enough grandeur to counteract the modest exterior; especially striking are the royal blue and gold starred ceiling, frescoes depicting the life of Jesus, and decorative mosaics along the archways. The information window at the church's entrance has a schedule of the church's frequent concerts. *(3 pl. St-Germain-des-Prés. M: St-Germain-des-Prés. Walk into pl. St-Germain-des-Prés to enter the church from the front. ☎01 55 42 81 33. Open daily 8am-8pm. Info office open M 2:30-6:45pm, Tu-Sa 10:30am-noon and 2:30-6:45pm. Mass in Spanish Su 5pm. Free maps at the entrance to the church.)*

ODÉON. The **Cour du Commerce St-André** is one of the most picturesque walking areas in the 6*ème*, with cobblestoned streets, centuries-old cafes (including **Le Procope**), and outdoor seating. Beyond the arch stands the **Relais Odéon**, a Belle Époque bistro whose stylishly painted exterior is a fine example of Art Nouveau. The **Carrefour d'Odéon,** just to the south of bd. St-Germain-des-Prés, is a favorite Parisian hangout filled with sidewalk bistros and cafes.

PONT DES ARTS. The wooden footbridge across from the Institut, at the very heart of France's prestigious Academy of Arts and Letters, is the best bridge in Paris. It is celebrated for its delicate ironwork and is perfect for a picnic dinner, a view of the sunset, and a little romancing.

SEVENTH ARRONDISSEMENT

EIFFEL TOWER. Gustave Eiffel wrote of his tower: "France is the only country in the world with a 300m flagpole." Designed in 1889 as the tallest structure in the world, the Eiffel Tower was conceived as a monument to engineering, intended to surpass the Egyptian pyramids in size and notoriety. Critics dubbed it a "metal asparagus" and a "Parisian Tower of Babel." Writer Guy de Maupassant ate lunch every day at its ground-floor restaurant—the only place in Paris, he claimed, from which he couldn't see the offensive thing. Nonetheless, when it was inaugurated in March 1889 as the centerpiece of the *Exposition Universelle* (World's Fair), the Eiffel Tower immediately earned the Parisians' love; nearly two million people ascended during the event alone. Some still criticize its glut of tourists and trinkets, but don't believe the anti-hype. The tower is a wonder of design and engineering, and is surprisingly beautiful up close. *(M: Bir-Hakeim or Trocadéro. ☎ 01 44 11 23 23; www.tour eiffel.fr. Open daily mid-June to Aug. 9am-midnight; Sept. to mid-June 9:30am-11pm (stairs 9:30am-6pm). Elevator to 1st floor €4, under 12 €2.20; 2nd €7.30/€4; 3rd (top) €10.40/ €5.70. Stairs to 1st and 2nd €3.50. Under 3 free. Last access to top 30min. before closing.)*

CHAMPS DE MARS. The Champs de Mars, a tree-lined expanse stretching from the École Militaire to the Eiffel Tower, is named, appropriately enough, after the god of war. Close to the 7ème's monuments and museums, the field was a drill ground for the École Militaire in the days of Napoleon. Today, the flower-strewn lawns are filled with tourists and children and a monument to international peace.

INVALIDES. The gold-leaf dome of the Hôtel des Invalides shines at the other end of the grassy **Esplanade des Invalides** from the gilded lampposts of **Pont Alexandre III**. The Invalides museum complex houses the **Musée de l'Armée, Musée des Plans-Reliefs, Musée de l'Ordre de la Libération,** and **Napoleon's tomb,** in the **Église St-Louis.** Enter from either pl. des Invalides or pl. Vauban and av. de Tourville. *(127 rue de Grenelle. M: Invalides. Enter from either pl. des Invalides or pl. Vauban and av. de Tourville.)*

QUAI VOLTAIRE. The quai Voltaire boasts an artistic heritage more distinguished than any other block in the city. Voltaire spent his last days at no. 27. No. 19 was home to Baudelaire while he wrote *Les Fleurs du Mal* (Flowers of Evil) from 1856 to 1858, Richard Wagner as he composed *Die Meistersinger* between 1861 and 1862, and to Oscar Wilde while he was in exile. Eugène Delacroix lived at no. 13, followed by Jean-Baptiste-Camille Corot. Jean-Auguste-Dominique Ingres died at no. 11 in 1867. The Russian ballet dancer Rudolf Nureyev lived at no. 23 from 1981 until his death in 1993. *(Along the Seine between Pont Royal and Pont du Carrousel. M: rue du Bac. Walk up rue du Bac to the river.)*

EIGHTH ARRONDISSEMENT

ARC DE TRIOMPHE. The arch is situated at the top of a hill with a view down the Champs-Élysées to the Tuileries. In 1758, architect Charles François Ribart envisaged the spot as the perfect setting for a monument to France's military prowess—in the form of a huge, bejeweled elephant. Fortunately for France, construction of the monument was not actually undertaken until 1806, when Napoleon imagined a more decorous monolith with which to welcome his troops home. After the Prussians marched through in 1871, the mortified Parisians purified the ground with fire. On July 14, 1919, the Arc provided the backdrop for an Allied victory parade headed by Maréchal Foch. During WWII, Frenchmen were reduced to tears as the Nazis goose-stepped through their beloved monument. After the German occupation, a sympathetic Allied army made sure that a French general would be the first to drive under the arch. Inside the Arc, visitors can climb up to the **terrasse** observation deck to catch a brilliant view of the "Historic Axis" from the Arc de Triomphe du Carrousel and the Louvre Pyramid at one end to the Grande Arche de la Défense at the other. *(M: Charles de Gaulle-Etoile. ☎ 01 44 09 89 84. Open daily Apr.-Sept. 10am-11pm; Oct.-Mar. 10am-10:30pm; last entry 30min. before closing. €7, ages 18-25 €4.50, under 17 free. Expect lines even on weekdays, although you can escape the crowds if you go before noon. You will kill yourself trying to dodge the 10 "lane" merry-go-round of cars (and face a hefty fine), so use the pedestrian underpass on the right side of the Champs-Élysées facing the Arc. Buy your ticket in the pedestrian underpass before going up to the ground level. AmEx/MC/V for charges over €14.)*

AVENUE DES CHAMPS-ÉLYSÉES. The Champs-Élysées, one of the 12 avenues radiating from pl. Charles de Gaulle-Etoile, is a legendary center of chic. The Second Empire saw the height of the Champs, when elegant mansions and splashy cafes sprang up along the avenue. In recent years, it has been thoroughly commercialized and its glamor has faded. The shops along the avenue range from designer boutiques to the low-budget Monoprix; overpriced cafes compete with fast-food outlets for the patronage of swarms of tourists. From a distance, however, the tree-lined Champs-Élysées remains a magnificent vista of pomp and glory.

GRAND AND PETIT PALAIS. At the foot of the Champs-Élysées, the Grand and Petit Palais face one another on av. Winston Churchill. Built for the 1900 World's Fair, they exemplify Art Nouveau architecture. The Petit Palais houses an eclectic mix of artwork; the Grand Palais has been turned into a space for temporary exhibits on art, architecture, and French history. The Grand Palais also houses the **Palais de la Découverte,** a childen's science museum (see p. 128). The Palais is most beautiful at night, when its statues are backlit and the glass dome glows from within.

PLACE DE LA CONCORDE. Paris's largest and most infamous public square is the eastern terminus of the Champs-Élysées. If you stand between the Champs-Élysées and the Tuileries Gardens, the *place* affords a fine view of the gold-domed Invalides, the columns of the Assemblée Nationale (across the river) and the Madeleine. In the center of the *place* is the monumental **Obélisque de Luxor,** a gift from the Viceroy of Egypt to Charles X in 1829. Constructed between 1757 and 1777 by Louis XV, the *place* soon became an epicenter of public grievance against the monarchy. It eventually became pl. de la Révolution, the site of the guillotine that severed 1343 aristocratic heads. In 1793, Louis XVI was beheaded by guillotine on a site near where the statue representing the city of Brest now stands. After the Reign of Terror, the square was optimistically renamed pl. de la Concorde, though the noise of the cars zooming through this busy intersection today hardly makes for a harmonious visit.

MADELEINE. Mirrored by the Assemblée Nationale across the Seine, the Madeleine was begun in 1764 by Louis XV and modeled after a Greek temple. Construction was halted during the Revolution, but was completed in 1842. The structure is distinguished by four ceiling domes that light the interior, 52 exterior Corinthian columns, and a curious altarpiece. A sculpture of the ascension of Mary Magdalene, the church's namesake, adorns the altar. A flower market thrives alongside the church. *(M: Madeleine.* ☎ *01 44 51 69 00. Open daily 7:30am-7pm. Regular organ and chamber concerts; contact the church for a schedule and Virgin or FNAC for tickets.)*

PARC MONCEAU. The signs say *Pelouse interdite* (keep off the lawn), but, on a sunny day, no one's listening. This expansive urban oasis, guarded by gold-tipped, wrought-iron gates, borders the elegant bd. de Courcelles. A number of architectural oddities—covered bridge, Dutch windmills, Roman ruins, and roller rink— make this a kids' romping ground as well as formal garden. *(M: Monceau or Courcelles. Open daily Apr.-Oct. 7am-10pm; Nov.-Mar. 7am-8pm; last entrance 15min. before closing.)*

CATHÉDRALE ALEXANDRE-NEVSKI. The onion-domed Cathédrale Alexandre-Nevski, also known as the Église Russe, is Paris's primary Russian Orthodox church and unofficial Russian cultural center. The spectacular and recently restored domes were intricately painted by artists from St. Petersburg in gold, deep reds, blues, and greens. *(12 rue Daru. M: Ternes.* ☎ *01 42 27 37 34. Open Tu, F, Su 3-5pm. Services in French and Russian Sa 6-8 pm, Su 10am.)*

NINTH ARRONDISSEMENT

OPÉRA GARNIER. The exterior of the Opéra Garnier—with its newly restored multi-colored marble facade, sculpted golden goddesses, and ornate columns and friezes—is one of Paris's most impressive sights. Designed by Charles Garnier under Napoleon III, the Opéra is perhaps most famous as the home of the fictional Phantom. *(M: Opéra. General info and reservations ☎08 36 69 78 68, tour info 01 40 01 22 63; www.opera-de-paris.fr. Concert hall and museum open daily mid-July to Aug. 10am-6pm, last entry 5:30pm; Sept. to mid-July 10am-5pm, last entry 4:30pm. Concert hall closed during rehearsals; call ahead. Admission €6; ages 10-16, students, and over 60 €3. English tours daily at noon and 2pm. €10; ages 10-16, students, and over 60 €8; under 10 €4.)*

PIGALLE. Farther north, at the border of the 18ème, the salacious, voracious, and generally naughty area of Pigalle stretches along bd. de Clichy from pl. Pigalle to pl. Blanche. The area is home to famous cabarets (Folies Bergère, Moulin Rouge, Folies Pigalle) and well-endowed newcomers like Le Coq Hardy and Dirty Dick. The areas north of bd. Clichy and south of pl. Blanche are comparatively calm, but visitors traveling alone should exercise caution. *(M: Pigalle.)*

TENTH ARRONDISSEMENT

CANAL ST-MARTIN. The most pleasant area of the 10ème is unquestionably the tree-lined Canal St-Martin. Measuring 4.5km, the canal runs from rue du Faubourg du Temple to the Bassin de la Villette. In recent years, the city has made efforts to improve water quality in the canal and clean up its banks, and the result has been a local renaissance. Children line up along the banks to watch the several working locks lift barges and boats. On Sundays an antique market takes place along the quai de Valmy and the streets along the canal close to traffic, making room for bikes and rollerblades. *(M: République or Goncourt will take you to the more beautiful end of the canal.)*

ELEVENTH ARRONDISSEMENT

THE BASTILLE PRISON. The Bastille Prison is the most visited sight in Paris that doesn't actually exist. A Parisian mob stormed this symbol of the monarchy's tyranny on July 14, 1789, sparking the French Revolution. Two days later, the National Assembly ordered the prison demolished. Today, pl. de la Bastille is a busy intersection, but the ground plan of the fortress is still visible as a line of paving-stones in the *place*, beneath which some of the cellars are said to survive. *(M: Bastille.)*

TWELFTH ARRONDISSEMENT

OPÉRA BASTILLE. One of Mitterrand's *Grands Projets*, the Opéra opened in 1989 to loud protests over its unattractive design. The "People's Opera" has been described as a huge toilet because of its resemblance to the coin-operated *pissoirs* on the streets of Paris. The opera has not struck a completely sour note, though, as it has helped renew local interest in the arts. The guided tour (expensive but extremely interesting) offers a behind-the-scenes view of the largest theater in the world. The immense auditorium seats 2703 people, but 95% of the building is taken up by exact replicas of the stage for rehearsals and workshops. *(130 rue de Lyon. M: Bastille. Look for the word Billeterie on the building. ☎01 40 01 19 70; www.opera-de-paris.fr. 1hr. tour almost every day, usually at 1 or 5pm; call ahead. Tours are in French, but groups of 10 or more can arrange for English. Admission €10, over 60 €8, students and under 26 €5.)*

VIADUC DES ARTS AND PROMENADE PLANTÉE. The *ateliers* in the **Viaduc des Arts** produce everything from *haute couture* fabric to hand-painted porcelain. Restorers of all types fill the arches of the old railway viaduct; they can make an oil painting, 12th-century book, or childhood dollhouse look as good as new. Interspersed among the stores are gallery spaces that are rented by new artists each month. High above the avenue, on the "roof" of the viaduct, runs the rose-filled

Promenade Plantée, Paris's skinniest park. *(9-129 av. Daumesnil. M: Bastille. Entrances to the Promenade at Ledru Rollin, Hector Malot, and bd. Diderot. Open M-F 8am, Sa-Su 9am; closing hours vary, around 5:30pm in winter and 9:30pm in summer.)*

THIRTEENTH ARRONDISSEMENT

QUARTIER DE LA BUTTE-AUX-CAILLES. Historically a working-class neighborhood, the old-fashioned Butte-aux-Cailles *quartier* has a long-standing tradition of defiance. The area was one of the first to fight during the Revolution of 1848, and 120 years later it was the unofficial headquarters of the student activists behind the 1968 riots in Paris. Funky new restaurants and bars have cropped up amongst the old standards. The nascent gentrification of the entire *arrondissement* has attracted trend-setters and artists to the area, but this process is still slow-moving. *(M: Corvisart. Exit onto bd. Blanqui and turn onto rue Barrault, which will meet rue de la Butte-aux-Cailles.)*

CHINATOWN. Paris's Chinatown, in the area bounded by rue de Tolbiac, bd. Masséna, av. de Choisy, and av. d'Ivry, is home to large Chinese, Vietnamese, and Cambodian communities and a host of Asian restaurants and markets. Shop windows on av. de Choisy and av. d'Ivry are filled with beautiful embroidered dresses, elegant chopstick sets, ceramic Buddhas, and *à la vapeur* (steamed) specialties.

BIBLIOTHÈQUE NATIONALE DE FRANCE: SITE FRANÇOIS MITTERRAND. This library is the last and most expensive of Mitterrand's *Grands Projets*. The Site Mitterand was built to accommodate the ever-increasing number of books housed in the old Bibliothèque Nationale in the *2ème*—since 1642, every book published in France has been required to enter the national archives at the library. The four L-shaped towers of Dominique Perrault's stunning, controversial design are meant to look like open books from above. Inside, the ultra-modern building features grand reading rooms and multiple galleries. *(Quai François Mauriac. M: Quai de la Gare or Bibliothèque François Mitterrand. ☎01 53 79 59 79; www.bnf.fr. Open Tu-Sa 10am-8pm, Su noon-7pm; closed 1st-3rd Su of Sept. and the 2nd half of Aug. Open to those over the age of 16. €3. Annual membership €30. MC/V.)*

FOURTEENTH ARRONDISSEMENT

BOULEVARD MONTPARNASSE. In the early 20th century, avant-garde artists like Modigliani, Chagall, and Léger moved to Montparnasse, many of them fleeing Montmartre's rising rents. Exiles Lenin and Trotsky talked strategy over cognac in cafes like **Le Dôme, Le Sélect,** and **La Coupole.** Between the World Wars, Montparnasse attracted American expatriates like Calder, Hemingway, and Henry Miller. Now heavily commercialized, Montparnasse is crowded with chain restaurants and tourists. Classics still hold their own, however (the best is the pricey **La Coupole**), providing a wonderful place to sip coffee, read Apollinaire, and sigh longingly.

CATACOMBS. A series of tunnels 20m below ground and 1.7km in length, the Catacombs were originally excavated to provide stone for building the city. By the 1770s, much of the Left Bank was in danger of caving in and digging promptly stopped. The former quarry was converted into a mass grave to relieve Paris's overcrowded cemeteries. During WWII, the Resistance set up headquarters there. The tunnels are laid out like an underground city, with street names on walls lined with whimsically arranged femurs and craniums. The catacombs are not recommended for the faint of heart or leg: there are 83 steep steps to climb on the way out. *(1 pl. Denfert-Rochereau. M: Denfert-Rochereau. Take Exit pl. Denfert-Rochereau, cross av. du Général Leclerc. ☎01 43 22 47 63; www.paris-france.org/musees. Open Tu 10am-4pm, W-Su 10am-4pm. €5, seniors €3.30, ages 14-26 €2.50, under 14 free. Tour lasts 45min. Exits at 36 rue Remy Dumoncel, 2 blocks to the right at av. du Général Leclerc is M: Mouton Duvernet.)*

FIFTEENTH ARRONDISSEMENT

LE PARC ANDRÉ CITROËN. The futuristic Parc André Citroën was created by landscapers Alain Provost and Gilles Clément in the 1970s. Rides in the hot-air balloon that launches from the central garden offer spectacular aerial views of the park and the city. Located alongside the Seine, the six gardens contain a variety of fountains, two glass greenhouses, and a wild garden whose plant life changes from one year to the next. In the summer months, the grass is crowded with sunbathers and picnickers of all ages. *(2 rue de la Montagne de la Fage. M: Javel-André Citroën or Balard. ☎01 44 26 20 00. Open M-F 7:30am-9:30pm, Sa-Su 9am-9:30pm. Balloon rides €12, ages 12-17 €10, ages 3-11 €6, under 3 free.)*

SIXTEENTH ARRONDISSEMENT

PLACE D'IÉNA. The pl. d'Iéna positions you next to the rotunda of the **Conseil Economique** and in front of popular museums, including the Palladian facade of the **Musée Guimet,** home to an outstanding collection of Asian art. It is a 5min. walk west to the Trocadéro and 5min. east to the museums of the **Palais de Tokyo.** *(M: Iéna.)*

PLACE DU TROCADÉRO. In the 1820s, the Duc d'Angoulême built a memorial to his victory in Spain at Trocadéro. Jacques Carlu's modern design for the **Palais de Chaillot,** created for the 1937 World's Fair, features two white stone wings cradling an austere, Art Deco courtyard that extends from the *place* over spectacular cannon-shaped fountains. The terrace attracts tourists, vendors, and skateboarders and offers brilliant panoramic views of the Eiffel Tower and Champs de Mars, particularly at night. Be aware of pickpockets and traffic as you gaze upward.

PASSY AND AUTEUIL. Located southwest of Trocadéro, **Passy** and **Auteuil,** famous for their avant-garde architecture, once attracted such visitors as Molière, Racine, and Proust. Now, the ex-hamlets are a pricey shopping district, best known as the site where *Last Tango in Paris* was filmed. The intersection of rue Passy, rue Mozart, and avenue Paul Doumer, near M: La Muette, is the glitziest.

SEVENTEENTH ARRONDISSEMENT

VILLAGE BATIGNOLLES. The Village Batignolles, in the eastern half of the 17*ème*, is an old-fashioned, working-class neighborhood. It centers around rue des Batignolles, stretching from bd. des Batignolles at the southern end to **place du Dr. Félix Lobligeois,** where a cluster of hip cafes overlook the greenery-filled town square. Just north of the *place* are the craggy waterfalls and duck ponds of the English-style park, **square des Batignolles.** To the west rue des Dames is lined with restaurants and cafes rue de Lévis with shops (M: Villiers). On the other side of rue des Batignolles, at rue Lemercier between rue Clairaut and rue des Moines (M: Brochant), is a daily covered market filled with meats, cheeses, flowers, produce, and old women who have shopped here since WWII. **La Cité des Fleurs,** 59-61 rue de la Jonquière (at the intersection with rue des Epinettes), is a row of exquisite private homes and gardens. Designed in 1847, this prototypical condominium complex required each owner to plant at least three trees in his garden.

EIGHTEENTH ARRONDISSEMENT

MOUNTING MONTMARTRE. One does not merely visit Montmartre; one climbs it. The standard approach is from the south, via M: Anvers or M: Abbesses, although other directions provide interesting, less crowded climbs. From M: Anvers, walk up rue Steinkerque to the ornate switchbacked stairway. The longer climb from M: Abbesses passes by more worthwhile cafes and shops. For children, the infirm, and the lazy, the glass-covered **funiculaire** from the base of rue Tardieu offers a painless ascent (from M: Anvers, walk up rue Steinkerque and take a left on rue Tardieu). *(Funicular runs every 2min. Accepts normal metro tickets. Open daily 6am-12:30am.)*

BASILIQUE DU SACRÉ-COEUR. In 1873, in yet another episode of strife between the supporters and detractors of the 1789 Revolution, the reactionary Assemblée Nationale selected the birthplace of the Paris Commune as the location for Sacré-Coeur, "in witness of repentance and as a symbol of hope." Needless to say, the government was not repenting for the massacre of 25,000 citizens in the suppression of the Commune, but for the fact that the Commune, and indeed the French Revolution, had occured in the first place. After a massive fund-raising effort, the basilica was completed in 1914 and consecrated in 1919. The basilica's onion domes, arches, and white color set it apart from the smoky grunge of most of Paris's buildings.

RUES DES ABBESSES AND LEPIC. Great restaurants, trendy cafes, and *boulangeries* crowd the corner of Montmartre around rue des Abbesses and rue Lepic. The hit film *Amélie* (2002) was filmed here, and fans have been making pilgrimages since. Predictably, longtime residents are complaining about the "Amélie Poulainization" of their neighborhood, but, truth be told, the damage isn't conspicuous. Tall iron gates hide the beautiful gardens of 18th-century townhouses. Walking down rue Lepic will take you past the **Moulin Radet,** one of the last windmills on Montmartre, and the site of the **Moulin de la Galette,** immortalized by Auguste Renoir. Even farther down is one of Vincent Van Gogh's former homes at 54 rue Lepic.

BAL DU MOULIN ROUGE. Along bd. de Clichy and bd. de Rochechouart are many Belle Époque cabarets and nightclubs, including the notorious Bal du Moulin Rouge. At the turn of the century, Paris's bourgeoisie came to the Moulin Rouge to play at being bohemian. After WWI, pl. Pigalle became a world-renowned red-light district. Today, the crowd consists of tourists out for an evening of sequins, tassels, and skin. The revues are still risqué, but the price of admission is prohibitively expensive (show and dinner €135). Be risky yourself and buy a ticket for a spot at the bar (€70), including two drinks but no guarantee that you'll have a place to sit. *(82 bd. de Clichy. M: Blanche. ☎01 53 09 82 82; www.moulin-rouge.com. Shows 7, 9, 11pm.)*

NINETEENTH ARRONDISSEMENT

PARC DES BUTTES-CHAUMONT. Parc des Buttes-Chaumont is a mix of manmade topography and transplanted vegetation, commissioned by Napoleon III out of a longing for London's Hyde Park, where he spent much of his time in exile. Since the 13th century, the *quartier* had been host to a *gibbet* (an iron cage filled with the rotting corpses of criminals), a dumping-ground for dead horses, and a gypsum quarry (the source of plaster of Paris). Making a park out of the existing mess took four years and 1000 workers. Designer Adolphe Alphand had the quarried remains built up to create enormous fake cliffs surrounding a lake. Today's visitors walk the winding paths and enjoy a great view of the *quartier* from the cave-filled cliffs topped with a Roman temple. *(M: Buttes-Chaumont or Botzaris. Open daily 7am-10:30pm.)*

PARC DE LA VILLETTE. La Villette is the product of a successful urban renewal project. Once a meat-packing district, the area became outmoded after the advent of refrigerated trucks. A decision was made to replace the neighborhood slaughterhouses with a neighborhood park, and *voilà:* what President Mitterrand inaugurated in 1985 as "the place of intelligent leisure." Parc de la Villette separates the Cité des Sciences from the Cité de la Musique and is dominated by the steel and glass **Grande Halle,** which features frequent plays, concerts, and films. The park has funny-shaped red buildings called *folies.* Every July and August, La Villette hosts a free open-air **film festival.** The **Zénith** concert hall hosts major rock bands, and the **Trabendo** jazz and modern music club holds a very popular annual jazz festival. *(M: Porte de Pantin. General info, including Grande Halle ☎01 40 03 75 03. Promenade des Jardins open 24hr. Free.)*

TWENTIETH ARRONDISSEMENT

CIMETIÈRE PÈRE LACHAISE. With its winding paths and elaborate sarcophagi, Cimetière du Père Lachaise has become the final resting place of French and foreign giants. Balzac, Colette, Jacques Louis David, Delacroix, La Fontaine, Haussmann, Molière, and Proust are buried here, as are Chopin, Jim Morrison, Gertrude Stein, and Oscar Wilde. With so many tourists, however, they're hardly resting in peace. Many of the tombs remind visitors of the dead's worldly accomplishments: the tomb of French Romantic painter **Géricault** wears a reproduction of his *Raft of the Medusa*; on **Chopin's** tomb sits the muse Calliope. The most visited grave is that of **Jim Morrison,** the former lead singer of The Doors. In summer, dozens of people bring flowers, joints, beer, poetry, and Doors paraphernalia to his tomb each day. Perhaps the most moving sites in Père Lachaise are those that mark collective deaths. The **Mur des Fédérés** (Wall of the Federals), where 147 members of the Paris Commune were lined up and shot, has become a site of pilgrimage for left-wing sympathizers. Near the wall, a number of moving monuments commemorate the Resistance fighters of WWII and Nazi concentration camp victims. *(16 rue du Repos. M: Père Lachaise. ☎01 55 25 82 10. Open Mar.-Oct. M-F 8am-6pm, Sa 8:30am-6pm, Su and holidays 9am-6pm; Nov.-Feb. M-F 8am-5:30pm, Sa 8:30am-5:30pm, Su and holidays 9am-5:30pm. Last entrance 15min. before closing. Free. Free maps at the Bureau de Conservation near Porte Gambetta; ask at guard booths by main entrances. 2hr. guided tour in English June-Sept. Sa 3pm; in French Sa 2:30pm, occasionally Tu 2:30pm and Su 3pm as well as numerous theme tours. €6, students €3. Tours meet at the bd. de Ménilmontant entrance; call ☎01 40 71 75 60 for info.)*

PERIMETER SIGHTS

BOIS DE BOULOGNE. A former royal hunting ground, the Bois de Boulogne is over 2000 acres of green canopy where Parisians walk, jog, bike, boat, and picnic among man-made lakes and waterfalls. The Bois has served many functions, from aristocratic playground to supplier of firewood during the Revolution. More recently, the Bois by night has become a bazaar of sex and drugs, complete with transvestite prostitutes and violent crime, and is best avoided after dark. *(M: Porte Maillot, Sablons, Pont de Neuilly, Porte Dauphine, or Porte d'Auteuil. Open 24hr.)*

BOIS DE VINCENNES. The largest expanse of greenery in Paris, the Bois de Vincennes's bikepaths, horsetrails, zoo, and Buddhist temple offer an escape from the city. Its large fortress, the **Château de Vincennes,** was the favored court of French kings as early as the 13th century and has been called "the Versailles of the Middle Ages." The flat terrain is given definition by two irregularly shaped lakes and numerous thematic gardens. *(M: Château de Vincennes or Porte Dorée. To best enjoy the park, rent a bike from the van near the château in the Esplanade St-Louis, or at the late on av. Daumsnil; both open Sa-Su and holidays 9am-7pm. About €4 per hr.)*

LA DÉFENSE. Just outside Paris's most exclusive suburbs lies a gleaming space crammed with eye-popping contemporary architecture, office buildings, sculptures by Miró and Calder, and one very geometric arch. A white 35-story building in the shape of a hollow cube, this **Grande Arche de la Défense** completes the axis from the Arc de Triomphe du Carrousel in front of the Louvre, down the Champs-Élysées, and through the Arc de Triomphe. The roof of this unconventional office space covers one hectare—Notre Dame could nestle in its hollow core. *(M or RER: La Défense. The RER is faster; the metro is cheaper. Note: an RER ticket may get you through the turnstile at the Paris station, but it won't get you out without a fine at La Défense.)*

🏛 MUSEUMS

Listed below are some of Paris's best museums. The **Carte Musées et Monuments,** valid for admission at 70 museums in the area, is economical if you visit three or more museums per day; it also allows you to move to the front of most lines. It's sold at major museums and metro stations (1-day pass €15, 3 days €30, 5 days €45). Most museums are closed on Mondays, while the Louvre, Centre Pompidou, and Musée Rodin are closed on Tuesdays.

MAJOR MUSEUMS

MUSÉE DU LOUVRE. Construction of the Louvre began in 1190. Under King Philippe-Auguste, the structure was a fortress attached to the city walls, designed to defend Paris while he was away on a crusade. In the 14th century, Charles V built a second city wall beyond what is now the Jardin des Tuileries (p. 111), rendering the Louvre's defensive function obsolete. Not one to let a good castle go to waste, Charles converted the fortress into a residential château. In 1528, François I returned to the Louvre, razing Charles's château and commissioning a Renaissance-style palace from architect Pierre Lescot. Henri IV was responsible for the next stage of renovation—his Grand Design planned to extend the Louvre to the Tuileries with the two large wings you see today. He only built a fraction of the project before his death in 1610. Louis XIV moved into the Louvre in 1650 and hired a trio of architects—Le Vau, Le Brun, and Perrault—to transform it into the grandest palace in Europe, but later abandoned it in favor of Versailles.

In 1725, after years of relative abandonment, the Academy of Painting inaugurated annual salons in the halls to show the work of its members. In 1793, the exhibit was made permanent and the Musée du Louvre was born. Napoleon filled it with plundered art, most of which later had to be returned. He happily continued Henri IV's Grand Design, extending the Louvre's two wings to the Tuileries palace and remodeling the facades of the older buildings. Mitterrand's *Grands Projets* campaign transformed the Louvre into an accessible, well-organized museum. Architect I. M. Pei moved the museum's entrance to the center of the Cour Napoléon, on an underground level below his controversial glass pyramid.

Renaissance works in the collection include Leonardo da Vinci's *Mona Lisa (La Joconde)* and canvases by Raphaël and Titian, while among the French paintings are David's *Oath of the Horatii*, Ingres's sensual *Odalisque*, Géricault's gruesome *Raft of the Medusa*, and Delacroix's patriotic *Liberty Leading the People*. Sculptures include Michelangelo's *Slaves*, as well as an incredible collection of antiquities; be sure to see the *Venus de Milo* and the *Winged Victory of Samothrace*. Visitors can either enter through the pyramid or directly from the metro into the new Carrousel du Louvre mall—follow the signs. If you have a *Carte Musée et Monuments*, you can enter from the Richelieu entrance, in the passage connecting the Cour Napoléon to the rue de Rivoli. Otherwise, you can buy full-price tickets from machines underneath the pyramid; reduced-rate tickets must be bought from ticket offices. The Louvre is less crowded on weekday afternoons and on Monday and Wednesday evenings. The museum is enormous—you'll only be able to cover a fraction of it in any one visit. Pick up an updated map at the info desk below the pyramid. *(1er. M: Palais-Royal/Musée du Louvre.* ☎*01 40 20 51 51; www.louvre.fr. Open M and W 9am-9:45pm, Th-Su 9am-6pm; last entry 45min. before closing, but people are asked to leave 15-30min. before closing. Admission M and W-Sa 9am-3pm €8.50, M and W-Sa 3pm-close and Su €6; under 18 and 1st Su of the month free. Prices include both the permanent and most temporary collections. Temporary exhibits in the Cour Napoléon open at 9am. English tours M and W-Sa at 11am, 2, 3:45pm; €3; sign up at the information desk. Bookstore and cafes open same hours as the museum on M and W; Th-Su close at 7pm.)*

MUSÉE D'ORSAY. If only the *Académiciens* who turned the Impressionists away from the Louvre could see the Musée d'Orsay. Every day, the museum hosts hundreds of visitors, all of whom come to see these famous rejects. The collection, installed in a former railway station, includes painting, sculpture, decorative arts, and photography from 1848 until WWI.

The best plan of attack for the museum is to visit the ground floor first, then the top floor, and then the mezzanine. The central atrium is dedicated to sculpture and highlights the likes of Jean-Baptiste Carpeaux. Galleries around the atrium display 19th-century works of the Neoclassical, Romantic, Barbizon, and Realist schools; important canvases include Manet's *Olympia*, Ingres's *La Source*, Delacroix's *The Lion Chase*, and Courbet's *Burial at Ornans*. The top floor is dedicated to the Impressionists, with works by virtually all the movers and shakers of the school of light; of particular note are Monet's *Gare St-Lazare* and Manet's *Luncheon on the Grass*. The Post-Impressionist collection includes Van Gogh's *Portrait of the Artist* (1889) and still-lifes and landscapes by Cézanne. The small mezzanine is dedicated to Rodin and his *Gate of Hell*. The museum is least crowded on Sunday mornings and Thursday evenings. *(62 rue de Lille, 7ème. M: Solférino. Or, RER: Musée d'Orsay. ☎01 40 49 48 14; www.musee-orsay.fr. Open Tu-W and F-Sa 10am-6pm, Th 10am-9:45pm; June 20-Sept. 20 Su 9am-6pm; last ticket sales 45min. before closing. Bookstore open Tu-W and F-Su 9am-6:30pm, Th 9am-9:30pm. English tours 1½hr. Tu-Sa 11:30am, 2:30pm; €5.50. Wheelchair-accessible. €7, ages 18-25 and Su €5, under 18 and 1st Su of month free. AmEx/MC/V.)*

CENTRE POMPIDOU. The Centre Pompidou is considered alternately an innovation and an eyesore. The design, pioneered by architects Richard Rogers, Gianfranco Franchini, and Renzo Piano, features color-coded electrical tubes (yellow), water pipes (green), and ventilation ducts (blue) along the exterior of the building. The center sees more than 20,000 visitors per day, and more visitors per year than the Louvre. The **Musée National d'Art Moderne,** the Pompidou's main attraction, boasts an awesome collection of 20th-century art, from the Fauvists and Cubists to Pop and Conceptual Art. *(Pl. Georges-Pompidou rue Beaubourg, 4ème. M: Rambuteau or Hôtel-de-Ville, RER: Châtelet-Les-Halles. ☎01 44 78 12 33, wheelchair info 01 44 78 49 54; www.centrepompidou.fr. Centre open M and W-Su 11am-10pm; museum open M and W-Su 11am-9pm, last ticket sales 8pm; library open M and W-F noon-10pm, Sa-Su 11am-10pm. Library and Forum free. Audioguides €5. Museum admission prices vary: permanent collection €7, students €5, under 18 and 1st Su of month free; current exhibition €9, students €7, under 13 free.)*

MUSÉE RODIN. Many Parisians say the Musée Rodin is one of the best museums in Paris, and they're right. Located in the elegant 18th-century Hôtel Biron, where Auguste Rodin lived and worked at the end of his life, the museum displays many of his better-known sculptures, like *The Hand of God* and *The Kiss*. The museum also boasts several sculptures by Camille Claudel, Rodin's muse, collaborator, and lover. The star of the collection, *The Thinker*, is tucked in among the rose bushes and fountains of the expansive garden. *(77 rue de Varenne, 7ème. M: Varenne. ☎01 44 18 61 10; www.musee-rodin.fr. Open Apr.-Sept. Tu-Su 9:30am-5:45pm; Oct.-Mar. 9:30am-4:45pm; last admission 30min. before closing. €5; seniors, ages 18-25, and Su €3. Park open Apr.-Sept. Tu-Su 9:30am-6:45pm; Oct.-Mar. 9:30am-5pm; €1. Audiotour €4. Temporary exhibits housed in the chapel to your right as you enter. Persons who are blind or vision-impaired may obtain advance permission to touch the sculptures. Ground floor and gardens wheelchair-accessible. Cafe open Apr.-Oct. Tu-Sa 10am-5:45pm; Nov.-Jan. 10am-5:30pm. MC/V.)*

MUSÉE PICASSO. When Picasso died in 1973, his family paid the French inheritance tax in artwork. The French government put this collection, which includes work from his Cubist, Surrealist, and Neoclassical years, on display in 1985 in the 17th-century Hôtel Salé. Arranged chronologically, each room situates his art within the context of his life, including his many mistresses and his reactions to the World Wars. *Two Women Running on the Beach* and *Woman Reading* are among the highlights. *(5 rue de Thorigny, 3ème. M: Chemin Vert. ☎ 01 42 71 63 15 or 01 42 71 70 84. Open Apr.-Sept. M and W-Su 9:30am-6pm; Oct.-Mar. 9:30am-5:30pm; last entrance 45min. before closing. Admission €5.50, Su and ages 18-25 €4, under 18 free.)*

MUSÉE DE CLUNY. The **Hôtel de Cluny** houses the **Musée National du Moyen Âge,** one of the world's finest museums of medieval art. The collection includes stained glass from Ste-Chapelle, the exquisite 14th-century **Gold Rose,** and the series of allegorical tapestries ▓**La Dame et la Licorne** (The Lady and the Unicorn), made famous by George Sand, who discovered them hanging in the Château Broussac in Chantelle, south of Paris. The Hôtel itself is a 14th-century manor built on first-century Roman ruins. *(6 pl. Paul Painlevé, 5ème. M: Cluny-La Sorbonne. ☎ 01 53 73 78 00. Open M and W-Sa 9:15am-5:45pm; last ticket sold 5:15pm. €7; students, under 25, over 60, and Su €5.50; under 18 free. Garden open 9am-dusk; free. Call ☎ 01 53 73 78 16 for info on weekly concerts.)*

EXPLORA SCIENCE MUSEUM. Dedicated to bringing science to young people, the Explora Science Museum is the star attraction of La Villette, in the complex's Cité des Sciences et de l'Industrie. The museum also features a **planetarium** (Floor 2), the **Cinéma Louis Lumière** with 3D movies, a modest **aquarium** (Floor S2), and **Médiathèque,** a multimedia scientific and technical library. Although programs are in French, the interactive exhibits are just as fun for English speakers. Ground-floor *vestiaire* rents strollers and wheelchairs. *(19ème. M: Porte de la Villette. ☎ 01 40 05 70 00; www.cite-sciences.fr. Museum open Tu-Sa 10am-6pm, Su 10am-7pm. €7.50, under 25 or those accompanying children €5.50, under 7 free. Planetarium €3, under 7 free. Médiathèque open Tu noon-7:45pm, W-Su noon-6:45pm; last admission M-Sa 5:30pm, Su 6pm. Free)*

OTHER MUSEUMS

FONDATION CARTIER POUR L'ART CONTEMPORAINE. The Fondation Cartier looks like an avant-garde indoor forest, with a stunning glass facade surrounding the grounds' natural greenery. The gallery hosts exhibits of contemporary art, from Andy Warhol to African sculpture, getting attention in 2004 for *Pain Couture,* a show of Jean-Paul Gaultier designs rendered in rolls and baguettes. *(261 bd. Raspail, 14ème. M: Raspail or Denfert-Rochereau. ☎ 01 42 18 56 51; www.fondation.cartier.fr. Open Tu-Su noon-8pm. €6, students and seniors €4.50, under 10 free. Soirées Nomades performance art Th 8:30pm, check website. Reserve ahead ☎ 01 42 18 56 72.)*

MUSÉE CARNAVALET. Housed in Madame de Sévigné's 16th-century mansion, this museum traces Paris's history with exhibits from prehistory and the Roman conquest to 18th-century extravagance and Revolution, 19th-century Haussmanization, and Mitterrand's *Grands Projets. (23 rue de Sévigné, 3ème. M: Chemin Vert. Take rue St-Gilles (it turns into rue de Parc Royal), and turn left on rue de Sévigné. ☎ 01 44 59 58 58; www.paris.fr/musees/musee_carnavalet. Open Tu-Su 10am-5:40pm; last entrance 5:15pm. Free. Special exhibits €5.50, students and elderly €4, ages 13-18 €2.50, under 12 free.)*

MAISON DE BALZAC. In this three-story hillside *maison,* home of Honoré de Balzac from 1840-47, visitors can see the desk where the author reportedly wrote and edited for 17 hours each day. The picturesque garden is filled with aromatic lilies and violets in the summertime. *(47 rue Raynouard, 16ème. M: Passy. From the exit of the metro, walk up the hill and turn left onto rue Raynouard. ☎ 01 55 74 41 80. Open Tu-Su 10am-6pm, last entrance 5:40pm. Admission to permanent collection free.)*

PALAIS DE TOKYO. Part of the magnificent Palais houses the **Musée d'Art Moderne de la Ville de Paris,** one of the world's foremost collections of 20th-century art, including Matisse's *La Danse Inachevée* and Dufy's electric epic, *La Fée Electricité.* The Museum is closed for renovations until early 2005. On the other side of the Palais, the **site création contemporaine** displays several exciting, controversial exhibits a year. The large, warehouse-like space of the *site* accommodates massive abstract sculpture, video displays, and multimedia installations. *(13 av. du Président Wilson, 16ème. M: Iéna. Follow av. du Président Wilson with the Seine on your right. ☎01 47 23 54 01; www.palaisdetokyo.com. Musée d'Art Moderne open Tu-F 10am-5:30pm, Sa-Su 10am-6:45pm. Site création open Tu-Su noon-midnight. Wheelchair-accessible. Permanent exhibits free. Special exhibit admission varies, usually €5, students €2.20-3, art students free.)*

MUSÉE JACQUEMART-ANDRÉ. The fantastic 19th-century home of Nélie Jacquemart and her husband contains a world-class collection of Renaissance art, including *Madonna and Child* by Botticelli and *St-George and the Dragon* by Ucello. *(158 bd. Haussmann, 8ème. M: Miromesnil. ☎01 45 62 11 59. Open daily 10am-6pm; last entrance 5:30pm. €8.50, students and 7-17 €6.50, under 7 free. English audioguides included.)*

MUSÉE ZADKINE. In the house and studio where he worked, the Zadkine Museum highlights the work of Russian sculptor Ossip Zadkine (1890-1967). In addition to its regular collection and sculpture garden, the museum features temporary exhibits by contemporary artists. *(100bis rue d'Assas, 6ème. M: Vavin. Just south of the Jardin du Luxembourg. Cross bd. Raspail on bd. Montparnasse and turn left on rue de la Grande Chaumière; then right on rue Notre Dame des Champs, left on rue Joseph Bara, and a final left on rue d'Assas. ☎01 43 26 91 90. Open Tu-Su 10am-5:30pm. €4, seniors and students €2.50.)*

PALAIS DE LA DÉCOUVERTE. Kids tear around the Palais's interactive science exhibits, following comets' celestial trajectories and making faces at very large bugs. The **planetarium** has four shows per day. *(In the Grand Palais, entrance on av. Franklin D. Roosevelt, 8ème. M: Franklin D. Roosevelt or Champs-Élysées-Clemenceau. ☎01 56 43 20 20, planetarium 01 40 74 81 73; www.palais-decouverte.fr. Open Tu-Sa 9:30am-6pm, Su 10am-7pm. €6.50, students, seniors and under 18 €4, under 5 free. Family entrance €13 for 2 adults and 2 children over 5. Planetarium entrance €3.50. AmEx/MC/V.)*

MUSÉE MARMOTTAN MONET. Owing to generous donations by Monet's family, the Empire-style house has been transformed into a shrine to Impressionism. The top floor is dedicated to paintings by Berthe Morisot, the First Lady of Impressionism, but most visitors come for the Monet's famed water lilies in the basement. *(2 rue Louis Boilly, 16ème. M: La Muette. Follow Chaussée de la Muette, which becomes av. Ranelagh, through the Jardin du Ranelagh park. ☎01 44 96 50 33; www.marmottan.com. Open Tu-Su 10am-6pm. Wheelchair-accessible. Admission €6.50, students €4, under 8 free.)*

MUSÉE D'ART ET D'HISTOIRE DU JUDAÏSME. Housed in the grand **Hôtel de St-Aignan**, once a tenement populated by Jews fleeing Eastern Europe, this museum displays a history of Jews in Europe, France, and North Africa. The collection includes an ornate 15th-century Italian ark, letters written to wrongly accused French general Dreyfus, a small collection of Chagall and Modigliani paintings, and modern art collections looted from Jewish homes by the Nazis. *(71 rue de Temple, 3ème. M: Rambuteau. ☎01 53 01 86 60; www.mahj.org. Open M-F 11am-6pm, Su 10am-6pm; last entrance at 5:15pm. Includes an excellent English audioguide. Wheelchair-accessible. €6.10, students and ages 18-26 €3.80, under 18 free.)*

MUSÉE D'HISTOIRE NATURELLE. The Jardin des Plantes features three museums. The modern **Grande Galerie de l'Evolution** explores evolution and the environment. Next door, the **Musée de Minéralogie** displays fantastic stones and mineral formations. The **Gallery of Comparative Anatomy and Paleontology** is filled with a ghastly collection of fibias, rib-cages, vertebrae, and fossils. *(57 rue Cuvier, in the Jardin des Plantes, 5ème. M: Gare d'Austerlitz. ☎01 40 79 30 00; www.mnhn.fr. Grande Galerie de l'Evolution open M and W-Su 10am-6pm, Tu 10am-10pm. €6.50, students €5. Musée de Minéralogie open M and W-Su 10am-6pm. €5, students €3.50. Galeries d'Anatomie Comparée et de Paléontologie open M and W-Su 10am-5pm, Apr.-Oct. Sa-Su until 6pm. €5, students €3.50.)*

MUSÉE DE L'ÉROTISME. The Erotic Museum has everything from bronze statues in missionary position to Japanimation sex cartoons. The museum is designed to celebrate representations of sex across all mediums and cultures, not to make you hot under the collar—those looking for less edifying titillation will be better served by the sex shop next door. (*72 bd. de Clichy, 18ème. M: Blanche.* ☎ *01 42 58 28 73; www.musee-erotisme.com. Open daily 10am-2am. €7, students and groups €5.*)

GALLERIES

Paris has dozens of galleries displaying the work of both established and up-and-coming international artists. The highest concentrations of hip contemporary art galleries are in the **Marais** (along rue de Perche, rue Debellyme, rue Vieille-du-Temple, rue Quincampoix, rue des Coutures St-Gervais, rue de Poitou, and rue Beaubourg) and in the *6ème*'s **St-Germain-des-Prés** area. The area around the **Champs-Élysées** is loaded with Old Masters. Galleries near M: Franklin D. Roosevelt on the Champs-Élysées, av. Matignon, rue du Faubourg St-Honoré, and rue de Miromesnil focus on Impressionism and post-Impressionism. The *13ème* also has a coterie of new galleries along **rue Louise-Weiss** (M: Chevarelet) and **rue Duchefdelaville**. The *Portes Ouvertes* festival (May-June; check *Pariscope* for information) allows visitors to witness artists in action in their studios. Almost all galleries close on Mondays, in August, and at lunchtime.

Galerie Thullier, 13 rue de Thorigny, 3*ème* (☎ 01 42 77 33 24; www.galeriethuillier.com). M: St-Sébastien-Froissart, behind the Picasso Museum. Featuring over 1500 pieces of art each year at 21 annual expositions across 2 sizeable shopfronts, this is among the city's most active galleries. Exhibition (and free refreshments) Tu evening from 7pm. Open Tu-Sa noon-7pm.

Fondation Taylor, 1 rue la Bruyère, 9*ème* (☎ 01 48 74 85 24). M: St-Georges. Take rue Notre Dame de Lorette away from pl. St-Georges and turn left onto rue la Bruyère. Run as a not-for-profit art space. Gives annual prizes in painting, sculpture, and engraving. Year-round exhibits ranging from figurative to non-objective work. Open Tu-Sa 1-7pm.

Galerie Patrice Trigano, 4bis rue des Beaux-Arts, 6*ème* (☎ 01 46 34 15 01). Just down the street from the École des Beaux-Arts, Trigano is one of the most stellar spaces in the 6*ème*. Excellent contemporary sculpture, painting, and mixed media in several rooms (don't forget to check out the basement). Ask to see the small sculpture garden in the back. Open Tu-Sa 10am-1pm and 2:30-6:30pm.

Fait & Cause, 58 rue Quincampoix, 3*ème* (☎ 01 42 74 26 36). M: Rambuteau or Etienne-Marcel. Aims at spreading humanist and humanitarian consciousness, mostly through documentary photography. Exhibits draw large crowds, and past artists have included Jacob Riis, Jane Evelyn Atwood, and Robert Doisneau. Open Tu-Sa 1-6:30pm.

Espace d'Art Yvonamor Palix, 13 rue Keller, 11*ème* (☎ 01 48 06 36 70; yapalix@aol.com). M: Ledru-Rollin. Walk up av. Ledru-Rollin, turn left on rue de Charonne and right on rue Keller. Small gallery displays contemporary Abstract painting. Exhibits change monthly. Open Tu-F 2-5pm and Sa 2-7pm.

🎭 ENTERTAINMENT

FREE CONCERTS

For concert listings, check the free magazine *Paris Selection*, available at tourist offices throughout the city. Free concerts are often held in churches and parks, especially during summer festivals, and are extremely popular, so plan to arrive at the host venue early. The **American Church in Paris**, in the 7*ème*, **Église St-Germain-des-Prés**, in the 6*ème*, and **Église St-Merri**, in the 4*ème* host frequent free concerts. Concerts take place W-Su in the **Jardin du Luxembourg**'s band shell, 6ème (☎01 42 34 20 23); show up early if you don't want to stand. Occasional free concerts are held in the **Musée d'Orsay,** 1 rue Bellechasse, 7ème (☎01 40 49 49 66; M: Solférino).

OPERA AND BALLET

Opéra de la Bastille, pl. de la Bastille, 12ème (☎08 92 69 78 68; www.opera-de-paris.fr). M: Bastille. Opera and ballet with a modern spin. Call, write, or stop by for the season's brochure; 2005 season includes operas The Magic Flute and Tristan and Isolde, ballets Cinderella and Romeo and Juliet. Tickets can be purchased by Internet, mail, fax, phone (M-Sa 9am-7pm), or in person (M-Sa 11am-6:30pm). Rush tickets for students under 25 and over 65 15min. before show. For wheelchair access, call 2 weeks ahead (☎01 40 01 18 08). Tickets €60-105. MC/V.

Opéra Garnier, pl. de l'Opéra, 9ème (☎ 08 92 89 90 90; www.opera-de-paris.fr). M: Opéra. Symphonies, chamber music, and ballet. Box office open M-Sa 11am-6pm. Last-minute discount tickets 1hr. before shows. For wheelchair access call 2 weeks ahead (☎01 40 01 18 08). Tickets €19-64. AmEx/MC/V.

Opéra Comique, 5 rue Favart, 2ème (☎01 42 44 45 46; www.opera-comique.com). M: Richelieu-Drouot. Operas on a lighter scale. The 2004-2005 season will proceed despite major renovations in the building. Box office open M-Sa 11am-7pm. Tickets €29-112. Student rush tickets available 15min. before show.

CABARET

Au Lapin Agile, 22 rue des Saules, 18ème (☎01 46 06 85 87). M: Lamarck-Coulaincourt. Turn right on rue Lamarck, then right again up rue des Saules. Picasso, Verlaine, Renoir, and Apollinaire hung out here during Montmartre's heyday; now a mainly tourist audience crowds in for comical poems and songs. It came to be known as le lapin à Gill (Gill's Rabbit) in 1875, when the artist André Gill painted a rabbit on the facade; the name eventually morphed into Au lapin agile. Shows Tu-Su at 9pm-2am. Admission and 1st drink €25, M-F and Su students €18. Subsequent drinks €6-7.

THEATER

Much of Parisian theater is highly accessible for non-French speakers, thanks in part to its dependence on the classics and its love of a grand spectacle. Most theaters have shows Sept.-June Tu-Su. Pariscope (€0.40 at any newsstand) and l'Officiel des Spectacles (€0.35) provide listings and information on one of the best ways to see theater in Paris—half-price previews.

La Comédie Française, 2 rue de Richelieu, 1er (☎01 44 58 15 15; www.comedie-francaise.fr). M: Palais-Royal. Founded by Molière, now the granddaddy of all French theaters. Expect wildly gesticulated slapstick farce; you don't need to speak French to understand the jokes. Performances take place in the 896-seat Salle Richelieu. Box office open daily 11am-6pm. Tickets €10-35. Rush tickets (€5-6) available 1hr. before show. For wheelchair access, reserve in advance (tickets €11). AmEx/MC/V.

Bouffes du Nord, 37bis bd. de la Chapelle, 10ème (☎01 46 07 34 50; www.bouffes-dunord.com). M: La Chapelle. An experimental theater that produces cutting-edge performances and concerts, and occasional productions in English. Closed Aug. Box office open M-Sa 11am-6pm. Concerts €18.50, under 26 and over 60 €12; plays €14-24.50. Wheelchair-accessible, but call in advance.

Odéon Théâtre de l'Europe, 1 pl. Odéon, 6ème (☎01 44 85 40 00; www.theatre-odeon.fr). M: Odéon. Programs range from classics to avant-garde, but the Odéon specializes in foreign plays in their original language. 1042 seats. The 2005 season includes Ibsen's Hedda Gabler and James Dillon's Philomela. Box office open daily

11am-7pm. Tickets €5-28 for most shows; under 27 rush tickets (€7.50) available 1½hr. before performance; cheaper rates Th and Su; call ahead. Affiliated **Petit Odéon** has 82 seats. Tickets €10. Call ahead for wheelchair access. MC/V.

La Cartoucherie, rte. du Champ de manoeuvre, 12ème. M: Château de Vincennes; free shuttle departs from station every 15min. beginning 1hr. before performance. In a 19th-century factory. Cutting-edge, socially conscious theater since 1970. Most shows €18-25. For more information, check www.la-tempete.fr/theatre/cartoucherie.html or *Pariscope.*

JAZZ

🎵 **Au Duc des Lombards,** 42 rue des Lombards, 1er (☎01 42 33 22 88; www.jazzvalley.com/duc). M: Châtelet. From rue des Halles, walk down rue de la Ferronerie and turn right on rue St-Denis, then right on rue des Lombards. Murals of Ellington and Coltrane cover the exterior. Still the best in French jazz, with occasional American soloists. Three sets each night—lower cover for just the last set. Cover €12-25, music students €8-19. Drinks €5-9. Music 9:00pm-1:30am. Open M-Sa 8pm-2am. MC/V.

🎵 **Le Baiser Salé,** 58 rue des Lombards, 1er (☎01 42 33 37 71). M: Châtelet. From rue des Halles, walk down rue de la Ferronerie and make a right on rue St-Denis and another right on rue des Lombards. Cuban, African, and Antillean music featured together with modern jazz and funk in a welcoming, mellow space. Concerts start at 10pm, music until 3am (typically 3 sets). Cover €13-18, depending on performers; mainly new talent. Free M jam sessions at 9:30pm with 1 drink min. Beer €4.80, cocktails €9. Happy hour 5-7:15pm. Open daily 5pm-6am. AmEx/MC/V.

Aux Trois Mailletz, 56 rue Galande, 5ème (☎01 43 54 00 79; before 5pm 01 43 25 96 86). M: St-Michel. Walk along the Seine on the quai St-Michel, make a right on rue du Petit Pont and a left on rue Galande. World music and jazz vocals in basement cafe; well-dressed students and 40-somethings upstairs. Club admission on weekends €13-19; bar free. Grog €9, cocktails €12.50. Bar open daily 5pm-dawn; *cave* 10pm-dawn.

New Morning, 7-9 rue des Petites-Ecuries, 10ème (☎01 45 23 51 41; www.newmorning.com). M: Château d'Eau. This 400-seat former printing plant now plays host to some of the biggest American headliners in the city. The venue's best acoustics are in the lower front section or near the wings of the stage. Tickets can be purchased from the box office, any branch of FNAC, or the Virgin Megastore; average €16-20. Drinks €6-10. Open Sept.-July from 8pm, though exact times vary; concerts begin at 9:30pm. MC/V.

CINEMA

Every night, Parisians crowd the city's cafes after a night at the movies, continuing Paris's century-long love affair with the cinema. You'll find scores of cinemas throughout the city, particularly in the Latin Quarter and on the Champs-Élysées. The two big theater chains—**Gaumont** and **UGC**—have *cartes privilèges* discounts for five visits or more and student discounts for shows before 7pm, Sunday through Thursday. Several summer film festivals offer discounted tickets and outdoor screenings. Check the *Pariscope* or *L'Officiel des Spectacles* (€0.40 and €0.35, available at any newsstand) for weekly film schedules, prices, and reviews.

Cinémathèque Française, pl. du Trocadéro, 16ème (☎01 45 53 21 86, recorded info 01 47 04 24 24 lists all shows; www.cinemathequefrancaise.com). M: Trocadéro. At the Musée du Cinéma in the Palais de Chaillot; enter through the Jardins du Trocadéro. Also 42 bd. Bonne Nouvelle, 10eme. M: Bonne Nouvelle. A must for film buffs. 2-3 classics or soon-to-be classics per day. Foreign films usually in original language. €5, students €4, discounted 10-ticket packages available. Open W-Su 5-9:45pm.

Accattone, 20 rue Cujas. 5ème (☎01 46 33 86 86). M: Luxembourg. Carefully selected classics from art-house maestros. All films in original language. €6.50, students €5.50.

Musée du Louvre, 1er (☎01 40 20 53 17, schedules and reservations 01 40 20 52 99; www.louvre.fr). M: Louvre. Art films, films on art, silent movies. Free. Open Sept.-June.

Les Trois Luxembourg, 67 rue Monsieur-le-Prince, 6ème (☎01 46 33 97 77). M: Cluny. Turn left on bd. St-Michel, right on rue Racine, and left on rue M-le-Prince. Good independent, classic, and foreign films (all in original language) €6.70, students €5.30.

La Pagode, 57bis rue de Babylone, 7ème (☎01 45 55 48 48). M: St-François-Xavier. A pseudo-Japanese pagoda built in 1895 and reopened as a cinema in 2000, La Pagode screens independent and classic French films and the occasional American new release. Tickets €7.30; over 60, under 21, students, and M and W €5.80. MC/V.

▣ NIGHTLIFE

Bars in Paris are either chic nighttime cafes or more laid-back neighborhood spots that often double as anglo havens. In the 5ème and 6ème, bars draw French and foreign students, while the Bastille and Marais teem with Paris's young and hip, gay and straight. Clubbing in Paris is less about hip DJs and cutting-edge beats, and more about dressing up, getting in, and being seen. Tune in to *Radio FG* (98.2 FM) or *Radio Nova* (101.5 FM) to find out about upcoming events.

FIRST AND SECOND ARRONDISSEMENTS

▣ **Le Champmeslé,** 4 rue Chabanais, 2ème (☎01 42 96 85 20). M: Pyramides or Quatre Septembre. Walk down av. de l'Opéra and make a right on rue des Petits Champs and another right onto rue Chabanais. This welcoming lesbian bar is Paris's oldest and most famous. Mixed crowd in the front; women-only in back. Beer €4. Cocktails (€8) garnished with a glow stick. Popular cabaret show Th 10pm (1st drink €8). No cover. Open M-Th 2pm-2am, F-Sa 2pm-2am. MC/V.

Banana Café, 13-15 rue de la Ferronerie, 1er (☎01 42 33 35 31). M: Châtelet. Take rue Pierre Lescot to rue de la Ferronerie. The most popular gay bar in the 1er draws an extremely mixed group; head downstairs for a more exclusively male crowd. Legendary theme nights. "Go-Go Boys" W-Sa midnight-dawn. 2-for-1 drinks during happy hour (6-9pm), cocktails excluded. Beer M-F €6, Sa-Su €7. Open daily 4pm-dawn. AmEx/MC/V.

Le Café Noir, 65 rue Montmartre, 2ème (☎01 40 39 07 36). M: Sentier. Walk down rue Réaumur and make a left onto rue Montmartre. Plastic creatures hanging from the ceiling, crazy tiling on the floor, and bartenders leaping onto the bar to perform comedy. A true mix of locals and Anglophones: patrons gladly overcome language barriers to meet one another. Beer €2.50-3. Open M-F 8am-2am, Sa 2pm-2am. AmEx/MC/V.

DANCE CLUBS

Rex Club, 5 bd. Poissonnière, 2ème (☎01 42 36 10 96). M: Bonne-Nouvelle. Non-selective club with the most selective of DJ line-ups. Young clubbers dance to cutting-edge techno, jungle, and house fusion on one of the best sound systems in Paris. Large dance floor and lots of seats. Shots €5. Cover €11-13. Open Th-Sa 11:30pm-6am.

THIRD AND FOURTH ARRONDISSEMENTS

▣ **L'Apparemment Café,** 18 rue des Coutures St-Gervais, 3ème (☎01 48 87 12 22). M: Chemin Vert. Beautiful wood lounge hosts a chill, young crowd. Come to chat or to play ping pong or Scrabble in the game room. Late-night meals €10-13, served until closing. Cocktails €7. Open M-F noon-2am, Sa 4pm-2am, Su 12:30pm-midnight. MC/V.

▣ **Chez Richard,** 37 rue Vieille-du-Temple, 4ème (☎01 42 74 31 65). M: Hôtel-de-Ville. Inside a courtyard off rue Vieille-du-Temple. Slowly spinning ceiling fan and shadow-casting palm leaves are reminiscent of *Casablanca*. Suave bartenders and mellow beats. Happy hour 6-8pm, cocktails €5. Open daily 6pm-2am. AmEx/MC/V.

▨ **Amnésia Café,** 42 rue Vieille-du-Temple, 4ème (☎01 42 72 16 94). M: Hôtel-de-Ville. A largely gay crowd comes to lounge on plush sofas in classy wood-paneled interior. 1st floor cafe, 2nd floor bar/club. One of the top see-and-be-seen spots in the Marais, especially on Sa nights. Espresso €2, *kir* €4. Open daily 10:30am-2am. MC/V.

Les Étages, 35 rue Vieille-du-Temple, 4ème (☎01 42 78 72 00). M: St-Paul. Set in an 18th-century hotel-turned-bar. 3 floors populated by dressed-down, nonthreatening 20-somethings. Limited selection of €4 cocktails during happy hour (3:30-9pm) come with a side of nuts and olives. Open daily 3:30pm-2am. MC/V.

Villa Keops, 58 bd. Sébastopol, 3ème (☎01 40 27 99 92). M: Etienne-Marcel. Walk east on rue Etienne Marcel; Villa Keops is on the corner with bd. Sébastopol. Stylish, candlelit couch bar where the boy-toy waiters are as beautiful as the designer drinks. Divine "Rose du Nile" €8.50, caramelized vodka €7.50. Happy hour 7-9pm. Open M-Th noon-2am, F-Sa noon-4am, Su 4pm-3am. AmEx/MC/V.

3W Kafé, 8 rue des Ecouffes, 4ème (☎01 48 87 39 26). M: St-Paul. Walk with traffic along rue de Rivoli and turn right onto rue des Ecouffes. The Marais's hippest lesbian bar recently got a face-lift and a new name—3W stands for "women with women." Sleek interior, smooth beats. Men welcome accompanied by women. Downstairs club with DJ F-Sa. Beer €5-6. Happy hour 6-8pm. Open daily 6pm-2am. MC/V.

La Belle Hortense, 31 rue Vieille-du-Temple, 4ème (☎01 48 04 71 60). M: St-Paul. Walk with traffic along rue de Rivoli and turn right onto rue Vieille-du-Temple. An intellectual break from the hyper-chic scene along the rest of the *rue*. Walls and walls of books and mellow music to go with your merlot. Frequent exhibits, readings, and discussions in the small leather-couch-filled back room advertised on the front window. Wine from €3 per glass, €20-36 a bottle. Coffee €1.30-2. Open daily 5pm-2am. MC/V.

DANCE CLUBS

Les Bains, 7 rue du Bourg l'Abbé, 3ème (☎01 48 87 01 80). From M: Etienne-Marcel or Réaumur-Sébastopol, take rue Etienne Marcel east, turn left on bd. Sébastopol, and take the next right. Look for the long line of people. Selective, super-crowded, and expensive. It used to be a public bath. Models on the floor; mirrored bar upstairs. New management promises a friendlier door policy and occasional student nights. Funky house and garage grunge; W hip-hop. Drinks €5-13. Cover (includes 1st drink) M-Th and Su €13, F-Sa €16. Open daily 11pm-5am. AmEx/MC/V.

Le Dépôt, 10 rue aux Ours, 3ème (☎01 44 54 96 96; www.ledepot.com). M: Etienne-Marcel. Take rue Etienne Marcel east; it becomes rue aux Ours. Pleasure complex for gay men. Dance to everything from disco to techno but don't waste time on small talk; find the night's boy toy in the designated "cruising" area while watching porn on mounted TVs and take him to a room in the downstairs labyrinth. Women welcome after 11pm upstairs. The post-Su-brunch Gay Tea Dance is especially popular. Cover (includes 1st drink) M-Th €8, F €12, Sa €14, Su €12. Open daily 2pm-8am. V.

FIFTH AND SIXTH ARRONDISSEMENTS

▨ **Le 10 Bar,** 10 rue de l'Odéon, 6ème (☎01 43 26 66 83). M: Odéon. Walk against traffic on bd. St-Germain and make a left on rue de l'Odéon. Le 10 Bar is a classic student hangout, where Parisian students indulge in philosophical and political discussion. After several glasses of their famous sangria (€3), you might feel inspired to join in. Jukebox plays everything from Edith Piaf to Aretha Franklin. Open daily 5:30pm-2am.

▨ **Le Caveau des Oubliettes,** 52 rue Galande, 5ème (☎01 46 34 23 09). M: St-Michel. Leave pl. St-Michel on quai de Montebello, turn right on rue Petit Pont, then left on rue Galande. 3 mellow scenes in 1: upstairs bar La Guillotine has sod carpeting and a real guillotine; below is an outstanding jazz club; beneath the club, you can romp through the narrow *caveau des oubliettes* (cave of the forgotten ones), where criminals were locked up and forgotten. Free jam session M-Th and Su 10:30pm-1:30am; F-Sa concerts €7.50. Beer €4, rum cocktail €4. Happy hour daily 5-9pm. Open daily 5pm-2am.

■ **Bob Cool,** 15 rue des Grands Augustins, 6ème (☎01 46 33 33 77). M: Odéon. Walk up rue de l'Ancienne Comédie, turn right on rue St-André-des-Arts and left on to the small rue des Grands Augustins. Bob Cool has a friendly vibe and a reputation as one of the best bars in the city. Mezcal €8.50, wine €4. Open daily 5pm-2am.

Le Crocodile, 6 rue Royer-Collard, 6ème (☎01 43 54 32 37). M: Cluny-La Sorbonne. Walk 7 blocks up bd. St-Michel and turn left onto rue Royer Collard. A lively crowd of local 20-somethings packs into this unassuming bar in the heart of the 6ème. 238 tasty, potent cocktails (€8, before midnight M-Th €6). Open M-Sa 10:30pm-4am.

SEVENTH AND EIGHTH ARRONDISSEMENTS

■ **Le Club des Poètes,** 30 rue de Bourgogne, 7ème (☎01 47 05 06 03; www.poesie.net). M: Varenne. Walk up bd. des Invalides with the Invalides behind you and to your left. Go right on rue de Grenelle and left on rue de Bourgogne. Since 1961, Jean-Pierre Rosnay has been making "poetry contagious and inevitable." A restaurant by day, Le Club des Poètes transforms nightly at 10pm when readers recite Baudelaire, Rimbaud, and others. If you arrive after 10pm, wait for a break in the performance to enter. Drinks €9, for students €5-7. Open M-Sa noon-2:30pm and 8pm-1am; food until 10pm. AmEx/MC/V.

■ **buddha-bar,** 8 rue Boissy d'Anglas, 8ème (☎01 53 05 90 00). M: Madeleine or Concorde. If you're going to break the bank, this is the place to do it. A giant Buddha watches over the beautiful (and often famous) people eating on the ground floor; the upstairs has a more relaxed atmosphere. Mixed drinks and martinis €12, "experiment" cocktails with flavors like anise and cucumber €13. Weekday lunch *menu* €32 includes wine and coffee. Open M-F noon-3pm and daily 6pm-2am.

House of Live, 124 rue La Boétie, 8ème (☎01 42 25 18 06) M: Franklin D. Roosevelt. Walk toward the Arc on the Champs; rue La Boétie will be the 2nd street on your right. Welcome to middle America on the Champs Élysées. Live music most nights, usually free. Snack bar has good ol' Yankee fare: hamburgers from €11, brownies €5.10, cheese nachos €7.90. Cocktails €6.80, beer €6. Open daily 9am-5am. AmEx/MC/V.

DANCE CLUBS

■ **Latina Café,** 114 av. des Champs-Élysées, 8ème (☎01 42 89 98 89). M: George V. 1 of the largest nightclub crowds on the Champs. Basement club, 1st floor cafe, 2nd floor restaurant. Energetic world music mix, including salsa, Cuban, and hip-hop. Drinks €10-12. Th-M women free, men pay €7 cover which includes a drink. F-Sa €16 cover includes first 2 drinks. Cafe open daily 7:30pm-2am, club open daily 10pm-5am.

Le Queen, 102 av. des Champs-Élysées, 8ème (☎01 53 89 08 90). M: George V. Where drag queens, superstars, moguls, and go-go boys get down to a 10,000-gigawatt sound system. One of the cheapest and most accessible gay clubs in town. Women welcome if accompanied by men. M disco, Th-Sa house, Su 80s. All drinks €10. Cover M-Th and Su €14, F-Sa €20, includes 1 drink. Open daily midnight-dawn. AmEx/MC/V.

NINTH TO THIRTEENTH ARRONDISSEMENTS

■ **Boteco,** 131 rue Oberkampf, 11ème (☎01 43 57 15 47). M: Parmentier. Popular Brazilian bar-restaurant. Jungle decor and avant-garde art. Flip-up benches transform the small space into a spontaneous late-night dance floor. Delicious Boteco (€6.50) has the traditional Brazilian rum *cachaça*, pineapple juice, and vanilla extract. 3-course lunch *menu* €10. Beer €3.10. Happy hour 6-9pm (cocktails €4). Open daily 9am-2am.

▓ **Le Bar Sans Nom,** 49 rue de Lappe, 11ème (☎01 48 05 59 36). M: Bastille. Take rue de la Roquette and make a right on rue de Lappe. Dim, seductive lounge famous for creative cocktails (some *flambé*), posted on oversized wooden menus. Older, calmer crowd. Don't leave Paris without trying their mojito (€8.50). Free tarot-card reading Tu 7-9pm. Beer €5-6.20, shots €6.20, cocktails €8.50. Open M-Sa 7pm-2am. MC/V.

La Folie en Tête, 33 rue de la Butte-aux-Cailles, 13ème (☎01 45 80 65 99). M: Corvisart. World music and exotic instruments line the walls of this beaten-up, wood-fronted hole in the wall. Crowded concerts on Sa nights (€8); no concerts July-Aug. Beer €2.40, *Ti* punch €4.50. Happy hour 6-8pm, *kir* €1.50. Open M-Sa 6pm-2am. MC/V.

DANCE CLUBS

▓ **Barrio Latino,** 46/48 rue du Faubourg St-Antoine, 12ème (☎01 55 78 84 75). M: Bastille. No wallflowers on this hot Latin dance floor, and not an empty barstool on weekends. Sneakers and jeans will get you in, but the clientele prefers to salsa in style. Strawberry margarita €10.50. Su brunch is an institution among stylish locals (noon-4pm, €26). Open daily noon-2am; DJ arrives at 10pm. AmEx/MC/V.

▓ **Batofar,** facing 11 quai François-Mauriac, 13ème (☎01 56 29 10 33). M: Quai-de-la-Gare. Facing the river, walk right along the quai—Batofar has the red lights. This barge/bar/club has made it big with the electronic music crowd but maintains a friendly vibe. "Electronic brunch" Su afternoon. Cover €6.50-9.50, usually includes 1st drink. Open Tu-Th 9pm-3am, F-Sa until 4am; hours change for special film and DJ events. MC/V.

Bus Palladium, 6 rue Fontaine, 9ème (☎01 53 21 07 33). From M: Pigalle, walk down rue Jean-Baptiste Pigalle, turn right on rue Fontaine, and look for the blue and silver facade. Getting past the bouncers can be tough—look hot. A trendy, beautiful crowd rocks this rock and roll club, which sports vintage posters and faded gilt decor. Drinks €13. Cover €16, Tu free cover and drinks for ladies. Open Tu-Sa 11pm-6am. AmEx/V.

Wax, 15 rue Daval, 11ème (☎01 48 05 88 33; www.le-wax.com). M: Bastille. Head north on bd. Richard Lenoir. Go right on rue Daval. Always free, always fun. In a concrete bunker, with retro couches. Tu-Th groove, F-Sa house. Cocktails €9, beer €4.50. Open M-Su 6pm-2am; closed Su in summer months. AmEx/MC/V.

FOURTEENTH TO TWENTIETH ARRONDISSEMENTS

▓ **L'Entrepôt,** 7-9 rue Francis de Pressensé, 14ème (☎01 45 40 07 50, film schedule 08 36 68 05 87, restaurant reservations 01 45 40 07 50; www.lentrepot.fr). From M: Pernety, turn right down rue Raymond Losserand and turn right on rue Francis de Pressensé. Savvy establishment offers a quadruple combo: a 3-screen cinema, a restaurant, an art gallery, and a trendy bar that features live jazz, latin, and world music. Poetry readings (Tu 7pm) and jazz (Th 7pm). 2 screenings and discussion cafes per month Sa 2pm. Concerts F-Sa; usually around €5. Beer €3. Su brunch 11:30am-4:30pm (€15). Open M-Sa 9am-midnight, Su 11:30am-midnight; food noon-3pm and 7:30-11:30pm.

Chez Camille, 8 rue Ravignan, 18ème (☎01 46 06 05 78). M: Abbesses. From the metro, walk down rue de la Vieuville and turn left on rue Drevet, then left on rue Gabrielle, which becomes rue Ravignan. Small, bright yellow bar on the slopes of Montmartre with a terrace looking down to the Invalides dome. Cheap coffee (€1.20). Beer €2.50-3.30, cocktails €6.50. Open M 11am-2pm, Tu-Sa 9am-2am, Su 9am-8pm.

L'Endroit, 67 pl. du Dr. Félix Lobligeois, 17ème (☎01 42 29 50 00). M: Rome. Follow rue Boursault to rue Legendre, and make a right. Hip, young 17ème-ers come for the snazzy bar and idyllic location in the tree-lined *place*. Try the mysterious and fruity "Bitch." Beer €4.50-5.10, wine €3.50-4, cocktails €6. Open daily noon-2am. MC/V.

Café Flèche d'Or, 102bis rue de Bagnolet, 20ème (☎01 43 72 04 23). Live music nightly, from reggae to hip-hop to Celtic rock. North African, French, Caribbean, and South American food. Beer €4-5, cocktails €4-7. Cover €5-6, free with dinner. Open daily 10am-2am. MC/V.

⌐ SHOPPING

Shopping in Paris is as diverse as the city itself, from the wild club wear near rue Etienne-Marcel to the unique boutiques of the Marais to the upscale designer shops of St-Germain-des-Prés. The great *soldes* (sales) of the year begin after New Year's and at the very end of June, with the best prices at the beginning of February and the end of July. If at any time of year you see the word *braderie* (clearance sale) in a store window, enter without hesitation.

CLOTHING

▨ **Le Shop,** 3 rue d'Argout, 2ème (☎01 40 28 95 94). M: Etienne-Marcel. Whatever you buy here, you'll be the only one with it back home. 2 levels, 1200m² of sleek club wear. Shirts and pants start at around €50. Open M 1-7pm, Tu-Sa 11am-7pm. AmEx/MC/V.

▨ **Espace Kiliwatch,** 64 rue Tiquetonne, 2ème (☎01 42 21 17 37). M: Etienne-Marcel. Walk against traffic on rue de Turbigo and go left on rue Tiquetonne. One of the most popular, fun shops in Paris. Pre-owned *(fripe)* shirts from €19, pants from €30. New and pricier clothes, books, furnishings, and other funky stuff also for sale. MC/V.

▨ **Culotte,** 7 rue Malher, 4ème (☎01 42 71 58 89). M: St-Paul. The deconstructed is *de rigeur* at this cutting-edge, Japanese-inspired boutique. Designs range from ripped printed tees to 40s-style dresses, all handmade and reasonably priced. Bold vintage jewelry, especially of the mod and 80s variety. Most items under €100. Open Tu-Sa 12:30-7pm, Su 2-7pm. AmEx/MC/V.

▨ **Spree,** 16 rue de Lavieuville, 18ème (☎01 42 23 41 40). M: Abbesses. Carries some of the most original women's wear in Paris. Don't miss the baskets of patterned underwear and socks. Skirts around €70, screen-printed t-shirts €30. Open Tu-Sa 11am-7pm.

Alternatives, 18 rue de Roi de Sicile, 4ème (☎01 42 78 31 50). M: St-Paul. Upscale second-hand shop sells an eclectic collection of quality clothes, including many designers at reasonable (if not exactly cheap) prices. Most items over €100. Prada bags €80, Charles Jourdan heels €100. Open Tu-Sa 11am-1pm and 2:30-7pm. MC/V.

Zadig & Voltaire, 15 rue du Jour, 1er (☎01 42 21 88 70). M: Etienne-Marcel. 6 other locations in the city. Funky, sleek, and expensive women's designs. A big selection of handbags. Opening hours vary by branch. Main branch open M 1-7:30pm, Tu-Sa 10:30am-7:30pm. AmEx/MC/V.

Moloko, 53 rue du Cherche-Midi, 6ème (☎01 45 48 46 79). M: Sèvres-Babylone, St-Sulpice, or Rennes. Simple, Asian-inspired women's clothing with surprising colors, shapes, and closures. Dresses from €120. Branches in the 4ème and Forum des Halles. Open Tu-Sa 11am-1pm and 2-7pm; closed Aug. MC/V.

Doria Salambo, 38 rue de la Roquette, 11ème (☎01 46 34 28 76). M: Bastille. Downtown-inspired print sun-dresses (€60), sharply cut denim with zipper details (from €35), and brightly colored blazers (€70). Open M 3-8pm, Tu-Sa 11am-8pm. MC/V.

Free 'P' Star, 8 rue Ste-Croix-de-la-Bretonnerie, 4ème (☎ 01 42 76 03 72). M: Hôtel-de-Ville. Enter as Plain Jane, leave as a star. Choose a sexy sailor top (€20) from a range of naughty nautical apparel, add a velvet blazer (€50), and finish off with hot pants, available for long-limbed boys and girls alike (€20). Open M-Sa 2-11pm, Su 2-10pm.

Bernie X, 12 rue de Sévigné, 4ème (☎01 44 59 35 88). M: St-Paul. Pieces with old-fashioned glamor. Centerpiece candles, lacy 50s-style underwear, and wispy dresses. Bags €100-160. Open M 2-7:30pm, Tu-Sa noon-7:30pm, Su 3-7:30pm. MC/V.

Stone Company, 6 rue Bréguet, 12ème (☎01 47 00 56 81). M: Bastille. Swiss-owned and operated but specializing in Italian menswear. Shoes (€180), shirts (€60), and leather jackets (up to €2500) by Alkis, Portland, and others. No wardrobe is complete without a cheetah-print belt (€78). Open M 1-8pm, Tu-Su 10am-noon and 1-8pm. MC/V.

SHOES AND ACCESSORIES

■ **Sephora,** 70-72 av. des Champs-Élysées, 8ème (☎01 53 93 22 50). M: Charles de Gaulle-Etoile. The fairest cosmetics store of them all: an enormous array of beauty products to color your world. Frequent makeover promotions by prestige cosmetics companies on the premises. Prices run the gamut from reasonable to absurd. Open daily 10am-midnight. AmEx/MC/V.

■ **Om Kashi,** 7 rue de la Montagne Ste-Geneviève, 5ème (☎01 46 33 46 07). M: Maubert-Mutualité. Imported boxes of henna, 300 kinds of incense, and shelves of clothing and jewelry mix with 18th-century furniture. Also carries unusual scarves and fabrics. Open M 2-7pm, Tu-Sa 10am-7pm.

Pylones, 57 rue St-Louis-en-l'Île (☎01 46 34 05 02). M: Pont Marie. Housewares and accessories range from vaguely useful (psychedelic patterned toaster, €44) to delightfully absurd (a roomy, kettle-shaped "tea bag" with shoulder strap, €27.50). Open daily 10:30am-7:30pm. AmEx/MC/V. Also at 13 rue Ste-Croix de la Brettonerie, 4ème.

Monic, 5 rue des Francs-Bourgeois, 4ème (☎01 42 72 39 15). M: Chemin Vert or St-Paul. Silver, gold, precious and semi-precious stone jewelry (€1-300; most under €50). Open M and Su 2:30-7pm, Tu-Sa 10am-7pm. AmEx/MC/V. Also at 14 rue de l'Ancienne-Comédie, 6ème (☎01 43 25 36 61). M: Odéon.

Florent Monestier, 47bis av. Bosquet, 7ème (☎01 45 55 03 01). M: École Militaire. Traditional wood-carved children's toys and retro household goods. Quintessentially Parisian gifts for anyone fed up with tacky souvenirs. Open M-Sa 10:30am-7pm.

No Name, 8 rue des Canettes, 6ème (☎01 44 41 66 46). M: St-Sulpice. Sneakers in every color, fabric, and shade of glitter possible. Sandals €53-61, sneakers €60-90. Open M-Tu 10am-1pm and 2-7:30pm, W-Sa 10am-7:30pm. AmEx/MC/V.

BOOKS AND MUSIC

■ **Abbey Bookshop,** 29 rue de la Parchiminerie, 5ème (☎01 46 33 16 24). M: St-Michel or Cluny. Overflows with new and used English-language titles and Canadian pride, furnished by its friendly expat owner. Good selection of travel and scholarly titles. Takes special orders. Open M-Sa 10am-7pm.

■ **L'Harmattan,** 16 and 21bis rue des Écoles, 5ème (☎01 46 34 13 71; www.editions-harmattan.fr). M: Cluny-La Sorbonne. Walk with traffic down bd. St-Germain, turn right on rue St-Jacques, and a left onto rue des Écoles. Over 90,000 titles of francophone literature from Africa, the Indian Ocean, Antilles, the Middle East, Asia, and Latin America. Great place for classic novels. Open M-Sa 10am-12:30pm and 1:30-7pm. MC/V.

■ **Les Mots à la Bouche,** 6 rue Ste-Croix de la Bretonnerie, 4ème (☎01 42 78 88 30; www.motsbouche.com). M: Hôtel-de-Ville. Walk with traffic along rue du Temple, turn right on rue Ste-Croix de la Bretonnerie. 2-level bookstore offering queer literature, magazines, and art. Don't miss the video collection (titles somewhere between art and porn, from €15) in the corner of the bottom level. Open M-Sa 11am-11pm, Su 2-8pm. MC/V.

■ **Ciné-Images,** 68 rue de Babylone, 7ème (☎01 47 05 60 25; www.cine-images.com). M: St-François Xavier. A cinephile's paradise. Original movie posters from the beginning of film to the late 1970s. Prices from €23 to €15,250, but it's worth a browse even if you can't afford a thing. The kind, English-speaking owner also does restorations and mounting (entoilage) for around €100. Open Tu-F 10am-1pm and 2-7pm, Sa 2-7pm.

W.H. Smith, 248 rue de Rivoli, 1er (☎01 44 77 88 99; www.whsmith.fr). M: Concorde. Large general selection includes many scholarly works in English. A solid array of magazines and tourist guidebooks. Su *New York Times* available M after 2pm. Open M-Sa 9am-7:30pm, Su 1-7:30pm. AmEx/MC/V.

FNAC, the big Kahuna of music chains in Paris, has 10 locations throughout the city. Champs-Élysées (74 av. des Champs-Élysées; ☎01 53 53 64 64), Bastille (4 pl. de la Bastille; ☎01 43 42 04 04), Italiens (24 bd. des Italiens; ☎01 48 01 02 03), and Etoile (26-30 av. des Ternes; ☎01 44 09 18 00) are the largest, with a comprehensive selection of music, stereo equipment, and, in some cases, books. Tickets to nearly any concert and many theater shows can be purchased at the FNAC ticket desk. For info (in French), visit the website at www.fnac.com. All branches open at 10am and most close at 7:30 or 8pm. The Champs-Élysées and Italiens branches close at midnight. MC/V.

DEPARTMENT STORES

Galeries Lafayette, 40 bd. Haussmann, 9ème (☎01 42 82 34 56). M: Chaussée d'Antin. Chaotic (the equivalent of Paris's entire population visits here each month), but carries it all, including mini-boutiques of Kookaï, agnès b., French Connection, and Cacharel. The astounding food annex on the first floor, Lafayette Gourmet, has everything from a sushi counter to a mini-*boulangerie*. Haussmann open M-W and F-Sa 9:30am-7:30pm, Th 9:30am-9pm; Montparnasse open M-Sa 9:45am-7:30pm. AmEx/MC/V. Also at 22 rue du Départ, 14ème (☎01 45 38 52 87), M: Montparnasse.

Samaritaine, 67 rue de Rivoli, on the quai du Louvre, 1er (☎01 40 41 20 20). M: Pont Neuf, Châtelet-Les Halles, or Louvre-Rivoli. 4 historic Art Deco buildings between rue de Rivoli and the Seine, connected by tunnels and bridges. Not as chic as Galeries Lafayette, as it dares to sell souvenirs (gasp!) and merchandise at down-to-earth prices (the horror!), but a calmer shopping experience. The rooftop observation deck provides one of the best views of the city; take the elevator to the 9th floor and climb the short spiral staircase. Some hotels offer 10% discount coupons for use in the store. Open M-W and F-Sa 9:30am-7pm, Th 9:30am-10pm. AmEx/MC/V.

FLEA MARKETS

PUCES DE ST-OUEN. The granddaddy of all flea markets, the Puces de St-Ouen is an overwhelming smorgasbord of stuff. It opens early and shuts down late, and serious hunters should allow themselves the better part of a day to cover significant ground. In general, merchandise is either dirt-cheap and shoddy or expensive and antique, but those with patience might find incredible deals in the mix. Located on rue des Rosiers and rue Jules Vallès, the market is officially divided into 15 sub-markets, each theoretically specializing in a certain type of item. Don't try to follow a set path; your best bet is to get lost and then keep browsing. *(Located just north of the 18ème. www.parispuces.com. M: Porte-de-Clignancourt. Open M and Sa-Su 7am-7:30pm, although most stalls open between 9-10am; most vendors open only between 9am-6pm on M; many of the official stalls close early, but renegade vendors may open at 5am and stay open until 9pm.)*

❀ FESTIVALS

Paris has a festival (or 20) for every season; check with the Paris tourist offices (see p. 89), or consult listings in *Pariscope* and *Time Out*. These are only some of the best—all are guaranteed to keep you fat, happy, or drunk (or all three).

■ **Bastille Day (Fête Nationale),** July 14. Paris begins celebrating France's independence day the night of the 13th, when *Bals Pompiers* (Firemen's Balls) take place inside Parisian firestations, with music and cheap alcohol (€5). Call ☎01 47 54 68 22 for info. July 14 begins with a parade on the Champs-Élysées (10:30am, be there by 8am) and ends with fireworks at 10:30-11pm, best seen from any bridge or the Champs de Mars.

■ **Jazz à la Villette,** early Sept.(☎01 40 03 75 75 or 01 44 84 44 84; www.villette.com). M: Porte de Pantin. A week-long celebration of jazz from big bands to new international talents at the Parc de la Villette. Past performers include Herbie Hancock, Ravi Coltrane, Taj Mahal, and B. B. King. Marching bands every day. An enormous picnic closes the festival. Concerts €18, under 26 €15.

Course des Serveuses and Garçons de Café, mid-June (☎01 42 96 60 75). Thought service was slow by necessity? During the annual Waiters' Race, over 500 tuxedo-clad waiters and waitresses sprint 8km through the streets of Paris carrying a full bottle and glass on a tray. Starts and finishes at Hôtel-de-Ville, 4*ème*.

Fête de la Musique, June 21 (☎01 40 03 94 70). Also called "Faites de la Musique" (Make Music), this nation-wide festival is certainly at its biggest and best in the capital, where every *place* and *palais* hosts a different musical act, from big-name rock bands to little-known world musicians. It gives everyone the chance to make as much racket as possible, as Paris's usual noise laws don't apply for the duration of the festival.

◪ DAYTRIPS FROM PARIS

VERSAILLES

By sheer force of ego, the Sun King converted a simple hunting lodge into the world's most famous palaces. The sprawling château and gardens testify to the absolute power of Louis XIV, who lived, entertained, and governed here on the grandest of scales. A century later, the extravagant court of Louis XVI and Marie-Antoinette gave the unhappy citizenry a lightning rod for their resentment.

A child during an aristocratic insurgency, Louis XIV is said to have entered his father's bedchamber one night only to find (and frighten away) an assassin. Still fearing conspiracy when he became king, Louis chose to move the center of royal power out of Paris and away from potential aristocratic insubordination. In 1661, the Sun King renovated his small hunting lodge in Versailles. Naturally, the nobility followed him there, but on Louis's terms.

No one knows just how much it cost to build Versailles; Louis XIV burned the accounts to keep the price a mystery. At the same time, life there was less luxurious than one might imagine: courtiers wore rented swords and urinated behind statues; wine froze in the drafty dining rooms; dressmakers invented the color *puce* (literally, flea) to camouflage the insects crawling on noblewomen.

Louis XIV was succeeded by his great-grandson Louis XV in 1722. His most memorable act was to commission the Opéra, in the North Wing, for the marriage of Marie-Antoinette and the future Louis XVI. The newlyweds inherited the throne and Versailles when Louis XV died of smallpox in 1774. On October 5, 1789, 15,000 Parisian fishwives and National Guardsmen marched out to the palace and hauled the royal family back to Paris, where they were guillotined in 1793.

In the 19th century, King Louis-Philippe established a museum to preserve the château, against the wishes of many French, who wanted to see Versailles demolished like the Bastille had been. In 1871, the château took the limelight again, when Wilhelm of Prussia became Kaiser Wilhelm I of Germany in the Hall of Mirrors. On June 28, 1919, at the end of WWI, France forced Germany to sign the ruinous Treaty of Versailles in the same room.

🔁 🔁 TRANSPORTATION AND PRACTICAL INFORMATION

RER trains beginning with "V" run from M: Invalides or any stop on **RER Line C5** to the Versailles Rive Gauche station (30-40min., departs every 15min, €5.20 round-trip). Buy your RER ticket before going through the turnstile to the platform; although a metro ticket will get you through these turnstiles, it will not get you through RER turnstiles at Versailles and could get you fined. From the RER station, turn right down av. de Général de Gaulle, walk 200m, and turn left at the first big intersection on av. de Paris; the entrance to the château is straight ahead.

To get to the **Office de Tourisme de Versailles**, 2bis av. de Paris (☎01 39 24 88 88), from the RER Versailles train station, follow directions to the château; the office will be on your left on av. de Paris before you reach the château court-yard. The tourist office is a great place to get a patient explanation of your options in Versailles before reaching the tourist mayhem in the palace. The office sells tickets for château events like the Fêtes de Nuit, and provides bro-chures on accommodations, restaurants, and events in town. Open daily sum-mer 9am-7pm; winter 9am-6pm.

While there are a number of tourist dining options along the walk from the train station to the palace, your best warm-weather bet is to bring a picnic (and a blan-ket) to enjoy in the gardens after you tour the palace. There are also moderately priced snack bars in various corners of the gardens.

👁 SIGHTS

Arrive early in the morning to avoid the crowds, which are worse on Sundays from May to September and in late June. Pick up a map at an entrance or the info desk in the center of the courtyard. There are half a dozen entrances. Most visitors enter at **Entrance A,** on the right-hand side in the north wing, or **Entrance C,** in the archway to the left, where you can pick up audioguides. **Entrance B** is for groups; **Entrance D** is where tours with a live guide begin; and **Entrance H** is for those in wheelchairs. For more info, contact ☎01 30 83 76 79 or www.chateauversailles.fr.

SELF-GUIDED TOUR. With a general admission ticket, begin at Entrance A and start your visit in the **Musée de l'Histoire de France,** created in 1837 by Louis-Phil-ippe to celebrate his country's glory. The 21 rooms, arranged in chronological order, lay out a helpful historical context for the château. Up the staircase to the right is the dual-level **royal chapel** where the king heard mass. Back toward the staircase and to the left is a series of gilded drawing rooms in the **State Apart-ments** that are dedicated to Hercules, Mars, and the ever-present Apollo (rather unoriginally, the Sun King had a particular affinity for the sun god). The ornate **Salon d'Apollo** was Louis XIV's throne room. Framed by the War and Peace Draw-ing Rooms is the **Hall of Mirrors** (under renovation until 2007, only portions are open to visitors), originally a terrace until Mansart added a series of mirrored panels and windows to double the light in the room and reflect the gardens out-side. These mirrors were the largest that 17th-century technology could pro-duce and therefore an unthinkable extravagance. The **Queen's Bedchamber,** where royal births were public events, is now furnished as it was on October 6, 1789, when Marie-Antoinette left the palace for the last time. A version of David's painting of Napoleon's self-coronation dominates the **Salle du Sacré** (also known as the Coronation Room). The **Hall of Battles,** installed by Louis-Philippe, is a monument to 14 centuries of France's military. *(Open Apr.-Oct. Tu-Su 9am-6:30pm; Nov.-Mar. 9am-5:30pm; last admission 30min. before closing. Admission to palace and self-guided tour, Entrance A: €7.50, over 60 and after 3:30pm €5.30, under 18 free.)*

OTHER TOURS. Audioguides are available at Entrance C. At Entrance D, you can choose between four excellent tours of different parts of the château. The best is the 1½hr. tour of the Louis XV apartments and the Opéra. Other tours include the King's Rooms *(Chambres du Roi)* and the more comprehensive full-day "A Day at Versailles." *(Tours require a supplement in addition to general admission (see above). 1hr. audioguided tour €4, under 7 free. 1hr. tour of Chambres du Roi €4, under 18 €2.70. 1½hr. tour of the apartments of Louis XV and the Opéra €6, ages 7-17 €4.20. Full-day tour "A Day at Versailles" consists of 2 1½hr. segments: 1 in the morning, 1 in the afternoon; €20. Sign-language tours available; make reservations with the Bureau d'Action Culturelle ☎01 30 83 77 88.)*

GARDENS. Numerous artists, including Le Brun, Mansart, and Coysevox, created statues and fountains for Versailles's gardens, but master gardener Le Nôtre provided the overall plan. Louis XIV wrote the first guide to the gardens, entitled the *Manner of Presenting the Gardens at Versailles*, and they remain a spectacular testament to Louis XIV's attempt to master nature. The Sun King even exercised control over his visitors' vision: the cross-shaped canal is wider on the westernmost end, creating a perspective-defying illusion when viewed from the terrace.

Though the château offers a decent 2hr. **Discovering Groves Tour** of the gardens, the best way to visit the park is during the spectacular summer festival, **Les Grandes Eaux Musicales,** when the fountains are turned on and chamber music groups perform among the groves. Any self-guided tour of the gardens must begin, as the Sun King commanded, on the terrace. Start by heading down the left-hand aisle from the terrace and working your way to the right. To the left of the terrace, the Parterre Sud graces the area in front of Mansart's **Orangerie,** once home to 2000 orange trees. In the center of the terrace lie the fountains of the Parterre d'Eau, while down the steps, the **Bassin de Latone** features Latona, the mother of Diana and Apollo, shielding her children as Jupiter turns villains into frogs.

Past the Bassin de Latone and to the left is one of the Versailles Gardens' undisputed gems: the fragrant, flower-lined sanctuary of the **Jardin du Roi**, accessible only from the easternmost side facing the **Bassin du Miroir.** Near the south gate of the grove is the magnificent **Bassin de Bacchus,** one of four seasonal fountains depicting the Greek god of wine reclining on a bunch of grapes. Working your way toward the center of the garden brings you to the exquisite **Bosquet de la Colonnade,** where the king used to take light meals amid 32 violet and blue marble columns. The north gate to the Colonnade exits onto the 330m long **Tapis Vert** (Green Carpet), the central mall linking the château to the garden's conspicuously central fountain, the **Bassin d'Apollon,** whose charioted Apollo rises out of the water to enlighten the world.

On the north side of the garden is the incredible **Bosquet de l'Encelade.** When the fountains are turned on, a 25m high jet bursts from Titan's enormous mouth, which is plated with shimmering gold and half buried under rocks. Flora reclines on a bed of flowers in the **Bassin de Flore,** while a gilded Ceres luxuriates in sheaves of wheat in the **Bassin de Cérès.** The Parterre Nord, full of flowers, lawns, and trees, overlooks some of the garden's most spectacular fountains. The Allée d'Eau, a fountain-lined walkway, provides the best view of the **Bassin des Nymphes de Diane.** The path slopes toward the sculpted **Bassin du Dragon,** where a beast slain by Apollo spurts water 27m into the air. Next to the Bassin du Dragon, 99 jets of water issue from seahorns encircling Neptune in the **Bassin de Neptune,** the gardens' largest fountain.

Beyond Le Nôtre's classical gardens stretch wilder woods, meadows, and farmland perfect for a picnic away from the manicured perfection of Versailles. Stroll along the **Grand Canal,** a rectangular pond beyond the Bassin d'Apollon that measures an impressive 1535m long. To explore destinations farther afield around Versailles, rent a **bike** or a **boat,** or go for a **horse-drawn carriage** ride. *(Open daily sunrise-sunset. Apr.-Oct. M-F €3, under 18 and after 6pm free. Fountains turned on for special displays, like the Grandes Eaux Musicales, Apr.-Oct. Sa-Su 11am-noon and 3:30-5:30pm, €6. Most convenient place for bike rentals is across from the base of the canal. 2 other locations: to the north of* *the Parterre Nord by the Grille de la Reine and by the Trianons at Porte St-Antoine. ☎ 01 39 66 97 66. Open Feb.-Nov. M-F 1pm-closing and Sa-Su 10am-closing. 30min. €3.30, 1hr. €5. Rent boats for 4 at the boathouse to the right side of the base of the canal. ☎ 01 39 66 97 66. Open Tu-F noon-5:30pm, Sa-Su 11am-6pm. 30min. €8, 1hr. €11. €7.70 deposit. Horse-drawn carriages run Tu-Su, departing from near the main terrace. ☎ 01 30 97 04 40.)*

TRIANONS AND MARBLE-ANTOINETTE'S HAMLET. The Trianons and Hameau provide a racier counterpoint to the château: here kings trysted with lovers and Marie-Antoinette lived like the peasant she wasn't. On the right down the wooded path from the château is the **Petit Trianon,** built between 1762 and 1768 for Louis XV and his mistress Madame de Pompadour. Marie-Antoinette took control of the Petit Trianon in 1774, and it soon earned the nickname "Little Vienna." Exit the Petit Trianon, turn left, and follow the marked path to the **Temple of Love,** a domed rotunda surrounded by swans where Marie-Antoinette held intimate nighttime parties. The Queen was at her happiest and most ludicrous at the **Hameau,** her own pseudo-peasant "hamlet" down the path. Inspired by Rousseau's theories on the goodness of nature, she commissioned Richard Mique to build a compound of 12 buildings (including a mill, dairy, and gardener's house, all surrounding an artificial lake) where she could live a country life. At the center is the **Queen's Cottage,** which contained ornate furniture, marble fireplaces, and walk-in closets for linens, silverware, and wayward footmen.

The single-story, stone-and-pink-marble **Grand Trianon** was intended as a château-away-from-château for Louis XIV. Here the king could be reached only by boat along the Grand Canal. The palace consists of two wings joined together by a porch. Formal gardens are located behind the colonnaded porch. The mini-château was stripped of its furniture during the Revolution but was later restored and inhabited by Napoleon and his second wife. (*Reachable by 15min. walk or shuttle. Shuttle trams from the palace to the Trianons and the Hameau leave from behind the palace facing the canals; head right. Round-trip €5, ages 3-12 €3. Open Nov.-Mar. Tu-Sa noon-5:30pm; Apr.-Oct. noon-6:30pm; last entrance 30min. before closing. €5, after 3:30pm €3, under 18 free.*)

CHARTRES

If not for a piece of fabric, Chartres might be a sleepy hamlet. But because of a sacred relic—the cloth that the Virgin Mary supposedly wore when she gave birth to Jesus—Chartres became a major medieval pilgrimage center. The spectacular cathedral that towers above the rooftops is not the only reason to take the train ride here: the *vieille ville* is also a masterpiece of medieval architecture.

◪ ◪ TRANSPORTATION AND PRACTICAL INFORMATION

Chartres is accessible by frequent **SNCF trains** from Gare Montparnasse on the Nogent-le-Rotrou line. At least one train per hour during the summer; call ahead for winter schedule. (50-75min.; round-trip €23.60, under 26 and groups of 2-4 €17.80, over 60 €17.60.) To reach the cathedral from the train station, walk straight along rue Jehan de Beauce to pl. de Châtelet and turn left into the *place*, right onto rue Ste-Même, and left onto rue Jean Moulin.

The **tourist office,** (☎ 02 37 18 26 26; www.chartres-tourisme.com), located in front of the cathedral's main entrance at pl. de la Cathédrale, helps find accommodations (€2 surcharge) and supplies visitors with a helpful map that includes a walking tour and a list of restaurants, hotels, and sights. (Open Apr.-Sept. M-Sa 9am-7pm, Su and holidays 9:30am-5:30pm; Oct.-Mar. M-Sa 10am-6pm, Su and holidays 10am-1pm and 2:30-4:30pm. Closed Jan. 1, Nov. 1 and 11, and Dec. 25.) Visitors can also buy the *Chartres Pass* (€13), which includes free or reduced admission to sights—worthwhile if you are staying overnight. For those with difficulty walking or who want a relaxed tour, the **petit train Chart'train** runs late March to early November with 35min. narrated tours (in French) of the old city. (☎02 37 21 87 60. Tours begin in front of the tourist office every hr. starting at 10:30am. €5.50, under 12 €3.) English-language walking tours (1½hr.) depart from the tourist office every Saturday in summer at 4:15pm (€5, under 14 €3.50).

🍴 FOOD

Located on a medieval stone landing along the town's beautiful stream, **Le Moulin de Poneau ❹**, 21/23 rue de la Tannerie, serves classic French fare that is worth every penny. Three-course weekday lunch *menu* (€20) includes wine and coffee. (☎02 37 35 30 05. Open M-F noon-2pm and 7:30-9pm, Sa 7:30-9pm, and Su noon-2pm. Reservations recommended.) **Crousty Poulets ❶**, 26 rue Saint Même, just before the cathedral, is a tiny *sandwicherie* on the ground floor and a cozy restaurant upstairs. This local favorite serves sandwiches (€3.70-5.20) like the *crousty chêvre* (goat cheese, emmenthal, and tomatoes) and *crousty poulet* (whole chicken) for €12. (☎02 37 21 29 56. Open M-Sa 11am-3pm and 6-9pm.)

👁 SIGHTS

THE CATHEDRAL

Chartres's cathedral is the best-preserved medieval church in Europe, having miraculously escaped major damage during the French Revolution and WWII. A patchwork masterpiece of Romanesque and Gothic design, the cathedral was constructed by generations of masons, architects, and artisans. On clear days, its towers are visible from the top of the Eiffel Tower, 88km away. Approaching from the pl. de la Cathedrale, you can see the discrepancy between the two towers: the one on the left, finished in 1513, is Flamboyant Gothic; the one on the right, built just before an 1194 fire, is Romanesque and octagonal (the tallest of its kind still standing). The 12th-century statues of the Portale Royale present an assembly of Old Testament figures. (☎02 37 21 75 02; www.cathedrale-chartres.com. Open daily Easter-Oct. 8am-8pm; Nov.-Easter 8:30am-7pm. No casual visits during mass. Mass M-F 11:45am and 6:15pm, Sa 11:45am and 6pm, Su 9:15 (Latin), 11am, 6pm (in the crypt).)

TOURS. The only English-language tours of the cathedral are given by Malcolm Miller, an authority on Gothic architecture who has been leading visitors through the church for the past 40 years. His presentations on the cathedral's history and symbolism are intelligent, witty, and enjoyable for all ages. If you can, take both his morning and afternoon tour—no two are alike. (English audioguides available at the gift shop (€3, €4, or €6, depending on tour) require an ID deposit. 1¼hr. English tours of the cathedral by Malcolm Miller begin outside gift shop in the cathedral. Easter to early Nov. M-Sa noon and 2:45pm; call ☎02 37 28 15 58 for tour availability during winter. €8, students €5.)

SANCTA CAMISIA. The year after he became emperor in AD 875, Charlemagne's grandson, Charles the Bald, donated to Chartres the Sancta Camisia, the cloth believed to have been worn by the Virgin Mary when she gave birth to Christ. The emperor's bequest required a new cathedral to accommodate the growing number of pilgrims. Thousands journeyed to the church on their knees in hope that the sacred relic would heal them and answer their prayers. The powers of the relic were confirmed in AD 911 when the cloth supposedly saved the city from invading Goths and Vikings. Today, it is preserved behind glass in the back of the church on the left.

STAINED GLASS. At a time when books were rare and the vast majority of people illiterate, the cathedral served as a multimedia teaching tool. Most of the 172 stained-glass windows date from the 12th century and were preserved through both World Wars by heroic town authorities, who dismantled over 2000m² of glass and stored the windows pane by pane in Dordogne. The famous **Blue Virgin, Tree of Jesse,** and **Passion and Resurrection of Christ** windows are among the surviving originals, many of which feature a stunning color known as "Chartres blue." The medieval merchants who paid for the windows are represented in the lower panels. Binoculars are useful for viewing high windows. Stories read from bottom to top, left to right.

LABYRINTH. The winding labyrinth carved into the floor in the rear of the nave was designed in the 13th century as a substitute for a journey to the Holy Land. Pilgrims followed symbolic voyage on their hands and knees.

TOUR JEHAN-DE-BEAUCE. The adventurous, the athletic, and the non-claustrophobic can climb the narrow staircase to the cathedral's north tower, Tour Jehan-de-Beauce (named after its architect), for a stellar view of the cathedral roof, the flying buttresses, and the city below. *(Open May-Aug. M-Sa 9:30am-noon and 2-5:30pm, Su 2-5:30pm; Sept.-Apr. M-Sa 9:30am-noon and 2-4:30pm, Su 2-4:30pm; closed Jan. 1 and 5 and Dec. 25. €4, ages 18-25 €2.50, under 18 free.)*

CRYPT. Visitors may enter the 110m long subterranean crypt only as part of a guided tour. Parts of the crypt, including a well down which Vikings tossed the bodies of their victims during raids, date back to the 9th century. *(Tours (in French) leave from La Crypte, the store opposite the cathedral's south entrance. ☎02 37 21 75 02. Tours 30min. Apr.-Oct. M-Sa 11am, 2:15, 3:30, 4:30pm; Nov.-Mar. 11am and 4:15pm; additional 5:15pm tour June 22-Sept. 21. €2.60, students €1.80, under 7 free.)*

OTHER SIGHTS

MUSÉE DES BEAUX-ARTS. The Musée des Beaux-Arts is housed in the former Bishop's Palace, which is itself an impressive sight. Built principally in the 17th and 18th centuries, the palace houses a wildly eclectic collection of painting, sculpture, and furniture, including works by Vlaminck, Navarre, and Soutine. A harpsichord collection dating back to the 17th century Oceanic art collection are also on display. *(29 rue du Cloître Notre-Dame, next to the cathedral. ☎02 37 36 41 39. Open May-Oct. M and W-Sa 10am-noon and 2-6pm, Su 2-6pm; Nov.-Apr. M and W-Sa 10am-noon and 2-5pm, Su 2-5pm; closed Jan. 1, May 1 and 8, Nov. 1 and 11, and Dec. 25. €3.80, students and over 60 €2.60, under 12 free.)*

OTHER MUSEUMS. Chartres has a number of small museums that cater to specific interests. The small **Centre International du Vitrail,** 5 rue du Cardinal Pie (facing the cathedral), housed in a 13th-century barn, hosts two temporary exhibitions on stained glass per year. *(☎02 37 36 15 34; www.centre-vitrail.org. Open M-F 9:30am-12:30pm and 1:30-6pm, Sa-Su 10am-12:30pm and 2:30-6pm. €4, students €3.)* The **Maison Picassiette,** 22 rue du Repos, is an extraordinary house covered entirely in mosaic tiles. *(☎02 37 34 10 78. Open Apr.-Oct. M and W-Sa 10am-noon and 2-6pm, Tu and Su 2-6pm. €3, students €1.50; combination ticket with the Musée des Beaux-Arts €6, students €3.)* The **Maison de l'Archéologie,** 16 rue St-Pierre, has a fascinating collection of archaeological finds relating to the history of the town. *(☎02 37 30 99 38. Open W-Su 2-5pm; closed Dec. 21-Jan. 3. €1.50, under 16 free.)*

MONUMENT TO JEAN MOULIN. A monument to WWII Resistance hero Jean Moulin, on rue Jean Moulin off bd. de la Résistance, consists of a giant stone hand gripping the hilt of a broken sword. Moulin, who was Prefect of Chartres before the war, attempted suicide rather than sign a Nazi document accusing French troops of atrocities. Tortured and killed by the Gestapo in 1943, he was eventually buried in the Panthéon. The monument is plotted on the tourist office's walking tour.

GIVERNY

Drawn to the verdant hills, haystacks, and lily pads of this stretch of the Epte River, French painter Claude Monet and his eight children settled in Giverny in 1883. By 1887, John Singer Sargent, Paul Cézanne, and Mary Cassatt had placed their easels beside Monet's and turned the village into a major artists' colony. Today, the town remains as it was back then (the cobblestoned street that was the setting for Monet's *Wedding March* is instantly recognizable), save for the tourists, who come in droves.

⊫ TRANSPORTATION

The **SNCF trains** run regularly from Paris's Gare St-Lazare to Vernon, the station nearest Giverny (round-trip €22, ages 18-25 €16.80). The fastest way from Vernon to Giverny is by **bus** (☎ 02 32 71 06 39). Four buses per day leave for Giverny just a few minutes after the train arrives in Vernon, so hurry over. Three buses per day go from Giverny to Vernon; look for the schedule inside the information office in the train station (10min., Tu-Su, €1.50 each way). You can rent a **bike** from many of the restaurants opposite the Vernon station for €12 per day, plus ID deposit. The 6km pedestrian and cyclist path from the Vernon station to Giverny is unmarked: it begins as the dirt road that intersects rue de la Ravine above the highway (free map at Vernon tourist office). **Taxis** (☎ 06 08 63 04 85) run from the train station for a flat rate (M-F €10, Sa-Su and holidays €13).

◎ SIGHTS

Monet's beautiful house and gardens are maintained by the **Fondation Claude Monet,** 84 rue Claude Monet. From April to July, the gardens overflow with wild roses, hollyhocks, poppies, and the scent of honeysuckle. The water lilies, Japanese bridge, and weeping willows of the Orientalist Water Gardens look like they've stepped straight out of Monet's canvas. The only way to avoid the crowds is to go early in the morning and, if possible, early in the season. Inside, big windows, solid furniture, and pale blue walls complement his collection of 18th- and 19th-century Japanese prints. (☎ 02 32 51 28 21; www.fondation-monet.com. Open Apr.-Oct. Tu-Su 9:30am-6:30pm. €5.50, students and ages 12-18 €4, ages 7-12 €3. Gardens €4.) Nearby, the incongruously modern but respectfully hidden **Musée d'Art Américain,** 99 rue Claude Monet, houses a large number of works by American expatriates to France (and specifically Giverny), including Theodore Butler and John Leslie Breck, who came to Giverny to learn the Impressionist style. (☎ 02 32 51 94 65; www.maag.org. Open Apr.-Oct. Tu-Su 9:30am-6:30pm. Audioguides €1. €5.50; students, seniors, and teachers €4; 12-18 years €3; 1st Su of each month free.)

DISNEYLAND RESORT PARIS

It's a small, small world, and Disney is hell-bent on making it even smaller. When EuroDisney opened on April 12, 1992, Mickey Mouse, Cinderella, and Snow White were met by the jeers of French intellectuals and the popular press, who called the Disney theme park a "cultural Chernobyl." Resistance seems to have subsided since Walt and Co. renamed it Disneyland Paris and started serving wine. Despite its small size, this Disney park is the most technologically advanced yet, and the special effects on some rides will blow you away.

PARIS

⌐ TRANSPORTATION

Take **RER A4** from either M: Gare de Lyon or Châtelet-Les Halles (dir: Marne-la-Vallée) to the last stop, M: Marne-la-Vallée-Chessy. Before boarding the train, check the boards hanging above the platform to make sure there's a light next to the Marne-la-Vallée stop and not the Boissy-Saint-Leger stop (40min., every 30min., round-trip €11). The last train to Paris leaves Disney at 12:22am, but the metro closes at midnight, so you'll have to catch an earlier train to make it to the metro in time. **TGV** service from Charles de Gaulle airport reaches the park in a mere 15min., making Disneyland Paris easily accessible for travelers with Eurail passes. Disneyland Paris **buses** make the rounds between both Orly and CDG and the bus station near the Marne-la-Vallée RER. (40min.; departs every 45-60min. F 8:30am-7:30pm, Sa 8:30am-10pm, Su 8:30am-9:30pm; round-trip €14, ages 3-11 €11.50.) By **car,** take the A4 highway from Paris and get off at Exit 14, marked "Val d'Europe, Parc Disneyland" about 30min. from the city. Parking €8 per day.

⃗ PRACTICAL INFORMATION

Everything in Disneyland Paris is in English and French. The detailed guide called the *Park Guide Book* (free at Disney City Hall to the left of the entrance) has a map and information on everything from restaurants and attractions to bathrooms and first aid. The *Guests' Special Services Guide* has info on wheelchair accessibility. For more info on Disneyland Paris, call ☎ 01 60 30 60 81 (from the US) or 01 60 30 63 53 from all other countries, or visit their website at www.disneylandparis.com.

Disneyland Paris issues **passeports,** valid for 1 day and available at the ground floor of the Disneyland Hotel. *Passeports* are also sold at Paris tourist office kiosks, FNAC, Virgin Megastores, or at any major station on RER line A. These options beat buying tickets at the park, as lines can be very long. A one-day *passeport* allows entry to either Disneyland Park or Walt Disney Studios. For an extra €10, you can visit both theme parks. (Nov.-Jan. €38, ages 3-11 €29; Jan.-Apr. €29/€25; Apr.-Oct. €40/€30. 2- and 3-day *passeports* also available.) ◪**Fastpasses** allow guests to make reservations to ride attractions, shaving 45min. off the wait to ride a roller coaster. Inquire at the Fastpass counters outside of each attraction.

The parks are open daily July-August 9am-11pm; September-June Monday-Friday 10am-8pm and Saturday-Sunday 10am-10pm. Hours are subject to change, especially during winter; call ahead for details.

◉ SIGHTS

Divided into five areas, each filled to bursting with families, **Disneyland Park** centers around "Main Street, U.S.A." Each day at either 4 or 7pm the Princess Parade—a **parade** of Disney characters marching to a loud fanfare of Disney tunes—takes place on Main Street. At 10:30pm each evening, the street is home to the Fantillusion Parade, a display of pyrotechnic lighting and lasers featuring Disney characters. Finally, at 11:15pm, Disney caps off the night with Tinker Bell's **fireworks.** Main Street, Frontierland, Adventureland, Fantasyland, and Discoveryland circle around the park's central plaza—a flowery garden in front of **Sleeping Beauty Castle.** The park's main draws are its 41 rides and attractions, like **Pinocchio's Fantastic Journey, Indiana Jones and the Temple of Peril: Backwards!,** and ◪**Space Mountain.** More technical than Disneyland Park, **Walt Disney Studios** features motor stunt shows (daily 10:30am, 12:15, 3:15pm) and an Armageddon special effects exhibit. The **Rock 'N' Roll Roller Coaster with Aerosmith** is a thrilling indoor coaster with loud music and strobe lights. Each day at 10:30, 11:30am, 12:30, 2:30, 3:15, and 4:15pm, children can enjoy an Animagique show with Mickey, Donald, and the rest of the gang. Daily cinema **parades** at 3:30pm.

LOIRE VALLEY
(VAL DE LOIRE)

The Loire Valley, in the heart of France, is primarily known for its châteaux. The country owes much to the history of these edifices, some of which date back to the ninth century, when France was splintered by Viking invasions. Local communities, under the leadership of feudal lords, erected fortresses to protect landholdings from invaders. Later, the region became a focal point of the incessant Anglo-French wars. At Chinon in 1429, Joan of Arc persuaded the Dauphin to give her an army to liberate Orléans. During the Renaissance, many castles were converted into comfortable palaces, framed by spectacular gardens and heaped with artistic masterpieces. Today, the rolling hills of the lovely "Garden of France" are perfect for an afternoon bike ride, while its fertile soil grows some of the nation's best wines. Owing to its central location and proximity to Paris, the valley now draws travelers from all corners of the world.

Visitors could spend weeks wandering through the vast salons and manicured gardens of the region's many castles. Gems include elegant Chenonceau (p. 171), which gracefully spans a river, and the medieval fortress Loches (p. 171), perched on top of a cliff. The cities of the Loire are convenient bases for exploring the region's châteaux, but they also are exciting destinations in and of themselves. Fun, affordable Tours (p. 164) offers the lively nightlife you would expect from a town with 30,000 students, while Amboise (p. 162) features Leonardo da Vinci's final residence and bizarre troglodyte dwellings.

HIGHLIGHTS OF THE LOIRE VALLEY

MELDED STAINED GLASS glows in an underground chapel from the 13th century at the **Musée du Gemmail** (p. 168).

EXPERIENCE François I's hunting shack at **Chambord** (p. 159), complete with a passable 440 rooms and 365 chimneys.

FACE YOUR DOOM at the world-renowned Apocalyptic Tapestry in **Angers** (p. 178), in which Saint John battles evil and a seven-headed Satan gobbles down babies.

☐ TRANSPORTATION

An ambitious itinerary in the Loire Valley can only be realized with a **car,** and three châteaux a day is a good limit. **Trains** often have inconvenient schedules and don't reach many châteaux. Tours is the region's best rail hub, with connections to 12 châteaux, while the smaller city of Blois is also a convenient base from which to explore the area. A group of four renting a car can generally undercut **tour bus** prices, but **biking** is probably the most popular way to see most of the region. Distances between châteaux and hostels tend to be short, and many small, flat roads cut through fields of poppies and grain. Most stations distribute the useful booklet *Châteaux pour Train et Vélo*, which details train schedules, distances, and information on bike and car rentals. The Michelin map of the region and tourist biking guides will steer drivers away from truck-laden highways and onto delightful

Loire Valley

LOIRE VALLEY

Château

Rennes
Vitré
Laval
Mayenne
Alençon
Le Mans
Nogent-le-Rotrou
Chartres
Châteaudun
Étampes
Fontainebleau
Maleherbes
Nemours
Montargis
Gien
Briare
Argent
Sancerre
Bourges
TO LYON (300km)
TO PARIS (120km)

Germigny-des-Prés
St-Benoît
Sully
Orléans
Châteauneuf-sur-Loire
Meung-sur-Loire
Beaugency
Chambord
Beauregard
Cheverny
Valençay
Selles-sur-Cher
Lucay-le-Mâle
Vierzon
Romorantin-Lanthenay
Issoudun
Châteauroux
Nohant
la Châtre

Blois
Chaumont-sur-Loire
Montrichard
Amboise
Chenonceau
Loches
Châtillon-sur-Indre
le Blanc

Tours
Saché
Ste-Maure-de-Touraine
Descartes
Châtellerault
TO TOULOUSE (410km)

Villandry
Langeais
Azay-le-Rideau
Chinon
Richelieu
Poitiers

Usé
Fontevraud-l'Abbaye
Loudun
Parthenay

Saumur
Montsoreau
Doué
Bressuire

Angers
Brissac-Quincé
Cholet

la Flèche
Baugé

Château-du-Loir
Bessé-sur-Braye
Vendôme

Château-Gontier
Châteaubriant

Nantes
la Roche-sur-Yon

0   10 miles
0   10 kilometers

N
LG

country roads. Nature buffs should ask at tourist offices for the excellent free bilingual booklet *Loisirs and Randonnées of the Val de Loire*, which has info on **hiking, biking, canoeing, horseback riding, rock climbing,** and **parachuting.**

ORLÉANS

With its winding streets, crowded bistros, and numerous historical sights, Orléans (pop. 113,000) is busy but not overwhelming. The people of Orléans, eager to share their local history, welcome visitors to the city and a *vieille ville* laden with beautifully preserved Renaissance architecture. A lovely mixture of both past and present, Orléans maintains a powerful presence among neighboring cities.

▐ TRANSPORTATION

Trains: A train shuttles passengers between the two stations every 30min. The tramway also runs between the stations every 6min.

    Gare d'Orléans: on pl. Albert I (☎02 38 79 91 00), in the center of town and in a better location for tourists. Info office open M-Sa 9am-7:30pm. Ticket booths open daily 5:30am-8:30pm To: **Blois** (30min., more than 15 per day 6:30am-9pm, €8.60); **Nantes** (2½hr., M-F 3 per day 6:45am-5:30pm, €32.10); **Paris** (1¼hr., approx. every 15min. 5am-10:15pm, €15); **Tours** (1hr., every 30min. 6:30am-11:45pm, €15).

    Gare Les-Aubrais, rue Pierre Semard (☎02 38 79 91 00), a 30min. walk 2.5km north of the town center. A train shuttles new arrivals from quai 2 to Gare d'Orléans (€1.20; free with a train ticket to Orléans).

Buses: 2 rue Marcel Proust (☎02 38 53 94 75), connects to the Gare d'Orléans. Info desk open M-Tu and Th 10am-1pm and 4-6:45pm, W and F 10am-1pm and 3-6:45pm, Sa 10am-1pm. **Les Rapides du Val de Loire** (☎02 38 53 94 75; www.rvl-info.com) runs to **Sully** via **Germigny** and **St-Benoit-sur-Loire** (1¼hr.; M-Sa 5 per day 6:40am-6:25pm, Su 5:30pm; € 7.60). **Transbeauce** (☎02 37 18 59 00) runs to **Chartres** (1¼hr; M-F 4-5 per day 7am-6:50pm, Sa 7am-6:55pm, Su 5:25pm and 8:30pm; €11.10, under 20 €5.50). Tickets sold on bus.

Public Transportation: SEMTAO, 2 rue de la Hallebarde (toll free ☎08 00 01 20 00), under pl. Jeanne d'Arc shopping mall. Info desk open M-F 6:45am-7:15pm, Sa 8:15am-6:15pm. €1.20 (good for 1hr.), *carnet* of 10 €11, day pass €2.90.

Taxis: Taxi Radio d'Orléans (☎02 38 53 11 11), toward the exit of the train station. €7 to hostel from train station. 24hr.

Car Rental: Ecoto, 19 av. Paris (☎02 38 77 92 92). From €29 per day. Open daily 8am-noon and 2-6pm.

Scooter and Bike Rental: CAD, 95 faubourg Bannier (☎02 38 81 23 00). Scooters €25 per day. Bikes €10 per day. Open M-Sa 9am-noon and 2-7pm. **Jerry Bike,** 1 rue de Bourgogne (☎02 38 54 38 16). Bikes €10-13.

▐ ▐ ORIENTATION AND PRACTICAL INFORMATION

Most places of interest in Orléans are on the north bank of the Loire, a 5min. walk south of the train station. To get to the city center from the station, walk straight onto **rue de la République,** which leads to **place du Martroi,** a large intersection marked by an impressive statue of Joan of Arc on horseback. Here, **rue de la République** becomes **rue Royale** and runs to the river, intersecting with **rue de Bourgogne** and **rue Jeanne d'Arc,** mainly pedestrian streets lined with most of the city's sights, restaurants, shops, and bars. To reach the tourist office, take the rue d'Escures from pl. du Martroi until you arrive on the pl. de l'Etape.

Orléans

🏠 ACCOMMODATIONS
Auberge de Jeunesse (HI), **11**
Hôtel de l'Abeille, **2**
Hôtel Charles Sanglier, **4**

🍴 FOOD
Les Alpages/
Aux Antilles, **9**
L'Arrosoir, **7**
Mijana, **10**
Les Musardises, **1**

⭐ NIGHTLIFE
Bowling, **12**
Cabaret Restaurant
L'Insolite, **13**

Le Datcha, **8**
Entr-acte, **3**
Havana Café, **6**
Paxton's Head, **5**

La Loire

Tourist Office: 2 pl. de l'Etape (☎02 38 24 05 05; infos@tourisme.com). Maps (€0.50) and an excellent walking tour guide of the *vieille ville*. Free tour book containing info and maps of all tourist sites. Call office for info regarding tours. Open Tu 10am-1pm and 2-6pm, W-Sa 9:30am-1pm and 2-6pm.

Budget Travel: Thomas Cook Voyages (formerly Havas Voyages), 38 Rue Jeanne d'Arc (☎02 38 42 11 80). Open M-Sa 9:30am-1pm and 2-6:30pm. AmEx/MC/V.

Banks: Banks are on rue de la République and pl. du Martroi. For the best currency exchange, head to the post office (see listing).

English-Language Bookstore: Librairie Paes, 184 rue de Bourgogne (☎02 38 54 04 50). Also carries books in Italian, German, Russian, Portuguese, and Spanish. Open Tu-Sa 10am-12:30pm and 1:30-7pm.

Youth Information: Centre Régional d'Information Jeunesse (CRIJ), 5 bd. de Verdun (☎02 38 78 91 78; fax 02 38 78 91 71). Provides info on sporting events, jobs, volunteer opportunities, and travel. Also helps choose courses at the Université d'Orléans. Open M and Th 1-6pm, W noon-6pm, Tu and F 10am-1pm and 2-6pm, Sa 2-6pm.

Laundromat: 26 rue du Poirier. Open daily 7am-11pm. **Laverie Bourgogne,** 176 rue de Bourgogne. Open daily 7am-7pm.

Police: 63 rue du fauborg St-Jean (☎ 02 38 24 30 00).

Crisis Lines: Battered women (☎08 00 05 95 95); battered men (☎01 40 24 05 05).

24hr. Pharmacy: 7-9pm, call ☎ 15. After 9pm, call police with ID card and prescription.

Hospital: Centre Hospitalier Régional, 1 rue Porte Madeleine (☎02 38 51 44 44).

Internet Access: Odysseüs Cyber Café, 32 rue du Colombier (☎02 38 77 98 48; odysseus2@wanadoo.fr). 7 PCs with ADSL Internet. €1.50 per 15min., €4.50 per hr. Open M-Tu 11am-9pm, W 11am-1am, Th and Sa 11am-1am.

Post Office: pl. du Général de Gaulle (☎02 38 77 35 35). Currency exchange services open M-F 8:15am-7pm, Sa 8:15am-12:15pm.

Postal Code: 45000.

▐ ACCOMMODATIONS

Cheap hotels are hard to find, and many accommodations close in August. Geranium-decorated balconies adorn seven delightful rooms at ▨**Hôtel Charles Sanglier ❸,** 8 rue Charles Sanglier, which boasts friendly service and a central location. (☎02 38 53 38 50; fax 02 38 81 24 07. Breakfast €4.50. Parking available. 1- to 2-person rooms with bath and cable TV €35-39. Extra bed €7.60.) One block from the station, ▨**Hôtel de L'Abeille ❹,** 64 rue Alsace Lorraine, celebrated its 100th anniversary last year and has been owned by the same family since 1919. Thirty-one luxurious rooms feature antique furniture and (non-functional) fireplaces. (☎02 38 53 54 87; www.hoteldelabeille.com. Breakfast in bed €7.50. Singles with toilet €35, with shower €42-47; doubles with shower €42-59; triples €59; quads €65.) Take rue de Bourgogne, and make a right on bd. de la Motte Sanguin to reach the **Auberge de Jeunesse (HI) ❶,** 1 bd. de la Motte Sanguin. The former 19th-century school now keeps 2-person rooms with private showers. Spotless hallway bathrooms are cleaned daily. Kitchen facilities, a TV room, foosball, ping-pong tables, phone, and laundry are all on-site. (☎02 38 53 60 06; asse.crjs@libertysurf.fr. Breakfast €3.50. Parking available. Reception M-F 8am-7pm, Sa-Su 9-11am and 5-7pm. Book ahead in summer. Dorms €8.80.)

▐ FOOD

In late summer and autumn, locals feast on fresh *gibier* (game) hunted in the nearby forests. One can enjoy specialty sausages like the *andouillettes de Jargeau* and *saumon de Loire* (salmon), fresh from the river. Orléans's most important culinary contributions are its tangy wine vinegars, which many local *brasseries* serve on salads and in marinades. The local cheeses are frinault cendré, a savory relative of camembert, and a mild chèvre. Wash it all down with Gris Meunier or Auvergnat wines, or nearby Olivet's pear and cherry brandies.

Les Halles Châtelet, place du Châtelet, is attached to Galeries Lafayette, a large department store. (Open Tu-Sa 7am-7pm, Su 7am-1pm.) The extensive **Carrefour supermarket,** which occupies the back of the mall at place Jeanne d'Arc (open M-Sa 8:30am-9pm), is conveniently close to the *centre ville*. Just three blocks from the hostel is a **Marchéplus supermarket,** on the corner of rue de la Manufacture and bd. Alexandre Martin. (Open M-Sa 7am-9pm, Su 9am-1pm.)

Brasseries and bars around Les Halles Châtelet and rue de Bourgogne are your best bet for good, cheap food. Sandwich-frites and Turkish shawarma are the best bargain (€4-5). Chinese, Indian, and Middle Eastern restaurants lie between rue de la Fauconneries and rue de l'Université, including ▨**Mijana ❸,** 175 rue de Bourgogne, where a charming Lebanese couple prepares gourmet Lebanese cuisine

THE BIG SPLURGE

AROUND THE LOIRE IN 80 MINUTES

t takes a lot of time and patience o see all the châteaux in the Loire Valley, but it is certainly possible—and even enjoyable—for hose up to the challenge. Some determined château-crawlers will spend hours traveling by bike or car, but more intrepid souls cut he work out of touring by throwng all caution to the wind and visting the châteaux via hot air balloon. From the air, all parts of he château estates can be fully appreciated, from the exquisite patterns of the gardens to the buildings' turrets and facades.

Total excursion time is 3½hr., and actual flight time approximates 1hr. You can either choose to take off in the early morning, a few minutes before sunrise, or in the evening, right before the sun sets. Champagne toasts are graciously offered prior to departure, making for a once-in-a-lifetime experience.

While hot air balloons offer an indisputable source of romance, even they may be too tame for the most adventurous travelers. Many companies also book helicopter tours of the valley or offer opportunities to sky dive onto the lawns of Chambord or Cheverny.

(To visit by hot air balloon, contact France Montgolfieres, 24 rue Nationale, 41400 Montrichard. ☎02 54 32 20 48. €250, ages 6-2 €145. For helicopters, contact et Systems, Aérodrome d'Amboise, 37150 Dierre. ☎02 47 30 20 21; www.jet-systems.fr.)

with pride. Vegetarian options are also available. (☎02 38 62 02 02; www.mijanaresto.com. Appetizers €6.50-8, *plats* from €11, *menus* €13.50-24. Open M 7-11pm, Tu-Sa noon-2pm and 7-11pm. AmEx/MC/V.) A good place for breakfast, **Les Musardises ❸**, 38 rue de la République, is a classic *salon de thé* that specializes in truffles and regional specialities like *Macarons d'Orléans* and *Chocolat Cyrano*. (☎02 38 53 30 98. Cakes €4-6, chocolate €5.80 per 100g, tea €3. Open M-F 8am-7:15pm. MC/V.) **L'Arrosoir ("L'Arroz") ❸**, 224 rue de Bourgogne, serves salads (€7) as well as classic bistro fare (€17-21.50). Hip crowds congregate here during the evenings, so stick around for a lively bar scene with a DJ on Saturdays. (☎02 38 81 01 08. Open Tu-Sa 11:30am-3pm, and 6pm-2am.) **Les Alpages/Aux Antilles ❷**, 182 rue de Bourgogne, serves traditional French cuisine (Oct.-May) but starting mid-May turns into a Creole bar-restaurant until mid-September. The decor reflects the Carribbean bent. (☎02 38 54 12 34. Open M-Sa 7:30pm-late. In summer, appetizers €5-6, *plats* €11-16, *menus* €22, desserts €4-5.50; in winter, salads €7.50, *plats* €9-11, *menus* €15-21, fondue for 2 people €12-14, dessert €5.20.)

🄶 SIGHTS

Most of Orléans's highlights are near pl. Ste-Croix, including the Église St-Paterne, remarkable for stained-glass artwork from the 11th century to modern times. In 1429, Joan of Arc, having liberated Orléans from a seven-month siege, marched triumphantly down nearby rue de Bourgogne, the city's oldest street.

CATHÉDRALE STE-CROIX. With towering Gothic buttresses and dramatic interior arches, the cathedral is Orléans's crown jewel. Its spire rises over 106m and can be seen from anywhere in town. Originally erected in the 13th century, the cathedral was rebuilt in large part under the reigns of Henry IV and Louis XIII. Vivid 19th-century stained-glass windows depict Joan of Arc's life story. Mass is celebrated every Sunday at 10:30am. *(Pl. Ste-Croix. Open daily June-Aug. 9:15am-7pm; Sept. 9:15am-5:45pm; Jan.-May and Oct.-Dec. 9:15am-noon and 2:15-5:45pm. Free.)*

PARC FLORAL DE LA SOURCE. Originally created to host the International Flower Show of 1967, this massive park contains rare flowers, aviaries, a petting zoo, and a butterfly reserve featuring 40 exotic species. The beautiful grounds draw both the young and old with picnic areas and playgrounds. For an extra fee, take the *petit train* and travel around the park. *(By car, take RN-20, dir: Vierzon-Bourges and exit at St-Cyr-En-Val. By tramway, take dir: Orléans-La*

Source and exit at the Université-Parc Floral stop. From the train, take a right, cross the tracks, and proceed down the path that leads to the park entrance. ☎02 38 49 30 00. Open Apr.-Oct. 9am-6pm; Nov.-Mar. 2-5pm. €3.80, students €2.10, under 18 free. Butterfly reserve €2.50. Bike rentals €10.70 per day.)

MUSÉE DES BEAUX ARTS. This fine collection includes Italian, Flemish, and French painting and sculpture from the 15th to the 20th centuries. Despite a particularly strong collection of 17th- and 18th-century art, the museum regularly hosts modern and archaeological exhibits as well. See Velazquez's world famous *Apostle of St. Thomas*, as well as paintings by artists like Van Dyck, Boucher, Delacroix, and Gauguin. *(1 rue Fernand Rabier, to the right as you exit the cathedral. ☎02 38 79 21 83; musee-ba@ville-orleans.fr. Open Su 2-6:30pm, Tu-Sa 9:30am-noon and 1:30-6pm, W until 8pm. €3, students €1.50, under 16 free.)*

HÔTEL GROSLOT D'ORLÉANS. Built in 1550 by bailiff Jacques Groslot, this beautiful Renaissance mansion was the king's local residence for two centuries and Orléans's city hall until the 19th century. In 1560, François II died here amid scandal, and his bedroom is now a popular site for many of Orléans's weddings and receptions. Royal portaits and 16th-century tapestries evoke the atmosphere of centuries past. Behind the building, a peaceful 19th-century garden, home to a Renaissance chapel, provides respite from the busy city. *(Pl. de l'Etape, to the left of the Musée des Beaux Arts. Walk up the stairs to entrance. ☎02 38 79 22 30. Open July-Sept. M-F and Su 9am-7pm, Sa 5pm-8pm; Oct.-June M-F and Su 10am-noon and 2-6pm. Free tours available through tourist office. Garden open daily Apr.-Sept. 7:30am-8pm; Oct.-Mar. 8am-5:30pm.)*

MAISON DE JEANNE D'ARC. This museum reconstructs the original house where the ill-fated saint stayed during her sojourn in Orléans. Models of the city in 1429 and an automated narration in multiple languages depict the events surrounding the seven-month siege of Orléans. The **Centre Jeanne d'Arc**, at 24 rue Jeanne d'Arc, has a library with over 16,000 documents related to the city's heroine. *(3 pl. Charles de Gaulle. ☎02 38 52 99 89. Open May-Oct. Tu-Su 10am-noon and 1:30-6pm; Nov.-Apr. 1:30-6pm. €2; students, groups over 10, under 16 €1.)*

OTHER SIGHTS. Popular with local schoolchildren as well as with nature enthusiasts, the curious **Musée des Sciences Naturelles** makes natural history fun. In this taxidermy heaven, wild animals are displayed in front of artwork that evokes their natural environment. Don't miss the human skulls in the Cabinet des Curiosités. *(6 rue Marcel Proust. ☎02 38 54 61 05. Open daily 2-6pm. €3.10, students €1.50, under 16 and school groups free.)* Orléanais are quite proud of the two-room **Musée Historique et Archéologique de l'Orléannais,** housed in the courtyard of the **Hôtel Cabu**, which displays the treasure of Neuvy-en-Sullias, a remarkable set of Gallo-Roman bronze statues from the Orléans region. *(Sq. Abbé Desnoyers. ☎02 38 79 25 60. Open July-Aug. M-Sa 9:30am-1:30pm and 2-6:30pm, Su 2-6:30pm; Oct.-Apr. W 1:30-6:30pm and Su 2-5:45pm; May-June and Sept. Tu-Sa 1:30-6pm, Su 2-6:30pm. €3, students €1.50, under 16 free. Admission to Musée Historique included with admission to Musée des Beaux Arts. Tours by reservation; €3.80 per person or €5 for tours in languages other than French.)*

🎵 🌿 ENTERTAINMENT AND FESTIVALS

Some locals head for the nightlife of Paris, but the bars along rue de Bourgogne and the new movie theater complex near Les Halles-Châtelet keep the homefront happy. Leather couches and live jazz music (Th nights) give **Paxton's Head,** 264 rue de Bourgogne, its classy feel. The British pub welcomes a mixed crowd of older students and vibrant young professionals. (☎02 38 81 23 29. Beer €7, whiskey €5. Open daily 3pm-3am.) For a great night with a younger crowd, head to **Havana Café,** 28 pl. du Châtelet. (☎02 38 52 16 00. Open daily 10pm-3am.) Get into the act with Thursday night karaoke at **Entr-acte,** 81 bd. Alexandre. (☎02 38 62 71 37. Open daily until 11pm.) Facing L'Arrosoir at 203 rue de Bourgogne, **Le Datcha** is the new hip nightspot. This self-described "Slavic bar" specializes in vodka and other Russian drinks. (Closes at 2am, sometimes later.) **Bowling,** 2 rue Moreau, proves the universal appeal of smoke, beer, bowling, and billiards. Take the tramway to Victor Hugo, then take bus #1 to the Moreau stop. Families gather here in the afternoon, but the bar's extensive list of international beers and whiskeys attracts a a young crowd during the evening. (☎02 38 66 31 55. Beer €2-6, bowling €6.60 per game. Student discounts available. 18+, unless accompanied by an adult. Open M-Th 2pm-1am, F 2pm-2am, Sa 2pm-3am, Su 2pm-midnight.) **Cabaret Restaurant l'Insolite,** 14 rue du Coq St-Marceau, serves dinner with a cabaret show. Reservations must be made in advance. (☎02 38 51 14 15; www.l-insolite.com. Show and dinner combo €41-47. Dinner 8:30pm, show begins at 10:30pm. Open F and Sa.)

The city comes alive with parades, music, and food for the **Fête de Jeanne d'Arc** (May 7-8) in commemoration of the heroine's miraculous victory over the British. During the last two weeks of June, Orléans hosts **Jazz d'Orléans,** a festival held in its gardens with musicians from around the world. (www.orleans.fr/orleansjazz. Tickets €10-20, under 26 €10; some concerts free.) In the last week of September, once every two years (including 2005), the **Fête de Loire** comes to Orléans with theatrical events, fireworks, and nautical displays on the banks of the Loire (☎02 38 79 24 05), while on weekends in November and December, the **Semaines Musicales Internationales d'Orléans (SMIO)** brings the Orchestre National de France to town.

▶ DAYTRIPS FROM ORLÉANS

GERMIGNY, ST-BENOÎT, AND SULLY. A day's drive eastward along the Loire reveals these three small towns, each dating from a different era of the Middle Ages. About 30km southeast of Orléans lies the Carolingian church of **Germigny-des-Près.** Though heavily restored, it remains the oldest church in France. The monks offer a 45min. tour of the church for groups. (☎02 38 58 27 97. Open daily Apr.-Sept. 8:30am-7pm; Oct.-Mar. 8:30am-6pm. Free. Call ahead to arrange a tour; €46 per group.)

The prize of **St-Benoît-sur-Loire,** 35km southeast of Orléans, is an exquisite 11th-and 12th-century Romanesque basilica. Originally part of the Abbaye de Fleury, the basilica is all that remains of the entire monastery, with a Romanesque mosaic floor and 75 arched pillars supporting a barrel vault. The church rings twice daily with chanted services. The monks offer a tour of the monastery in French (€3) or other languages (€4, by reservation only), at 10am and 1pm. (☎02 38 35 72 43. Masses M-Sa 6am, noon, 9pm; Su 11am. Church open daily 6am-10pm.)

Described by Voltaire as "the most likeable of castles," the white-turreted château fortress **Sully-sur-Loire** offered a pleasant hideout to the exiled phiiosopher, as well as to Charles VII, Joan of Arc, and Louis XIV. Don't miss an exceptional set of tapestries embedded with the Créquy coat of arms, depicting the Hellenic legend of Psyche. Walk all the way up to the chamber of guards for a beautiful view of the Loire. Throughout the year, special themed tours are given in French. (☎02 38 36 36 86; chateau.sully@cg45.fr. Open Apr.-Sept. M and W-Su 10am-6pm; Feb.-Mar. and Oct.-Dec. 10am-noon and 2-5pm; open Tu in July-Aug. French tours daily June-Sept., English tours mid-July to mid-Aug. M 1:30pm. €5.00, students and children 7-15 €3.50; tours are free.) The 17th-century garden adjacent to the château offers a lovely respite from the summer crowds. (Open daily 8am-sunset.) In June, the grounds stage a famous music festival with classical musicians from around the world. (Call tourist office. For reservations call toll-free ☎0800-452-818.)

BLOIS

Watch your French: Blois (pop. 50,000) is a far cry from blah. Not only was it once home to François I and Louis XIII, but it is also where Joan of Arc first raised the army that would later liberate Orléans. Today the town stands as a testament to centuries of French architecture, from its slate roofs and brick chimneys to the narrow cobblestone lanes that evoke the simple beauty of a Vermeer village. Blois is also a good base for visits to Chambord and Cheverny, arguably the most famous châteaux in the Loire Valley; each is a short bike or bus trip away.

◧ TRANSPORTATION

Trains: pl. de la Gare (☎08 92 35 35 35). Open M-Sa 5:30am-8:20pm, Su 7:15am-10pm. To: **Amboise** (20min., 15 per day, €5.40); **Angers** via **Tours** (3hr., 5 per day, €18.40); **Orléans** (30min., 14 per day 6am-11pm, €8.40); **Paris** via **Orléans** (1¾hr., 8 per day 6am-9pm, €20); **Tours** (1hr., 13 per day 7am-11pm, €8.20). Check with the SNCF for current train schedules.

Buses: Point Bus, 2 pl. Victor Hugo (☎02 54 78 15 66). Open M 1:30-6pm, Tu-F 8:30am-noon and 1:30-5:30pm, Sa 9am-noon. **Transports Loir-et-Cher** (TLC; ☎02 54 58 55 44) sends a bus to nearby **Chambord** and **Cheverny** (mid-May to Aug. 2 per day; 9:10am, returning 1pm, and 1:25pm, returning 6pm; €10, under 12 or over 65 with ID €8; reduced entry to châteaux with bus ticket). Tickets purchased onboard. Schedules available at the train station or by calling TLC. Buses also to **Vendôme.**

Taxis: Taxis Radio, pl. de la Gare (☎02 54 78 07 65). €10 to hostel near Blois. 24hr.

Bike Rental: Amster Cycles, 7 rue du Dr. Desfray (☎02 54 56 07 73; www.amstercycles.com), 1 block from train station. €13 per day, tandem bikes €35. Open M-Sa 9:15am-1pm and 2-6:30pm, Su 10am-1:30pm and 3-6:15pm. MC/V.

◪ ◲ ORIENTATION AND PRACTICAL INFORMATION

The château and town center are 5min. from the train station, left down **avenue Jean Laigret.** Between the château and **rue Denis Papin** is a bustling pedestrian quarter. When in doubt, descend, as all roads lead down to the city center.

LOIRE VALLEY

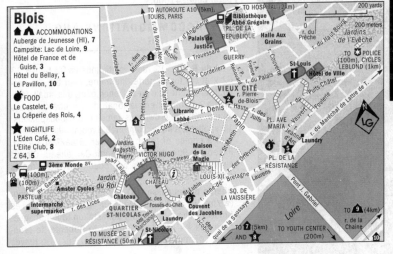

Blois

▲ ♠ ACCOMMODATIONS
Auberge de Jeunesse (HI), **7**
Campsite: Lac de Loire, **9**
Hôtel de France et de Guise, **3**
Hôtel du Bellay, **1**
Le Pavillon, **10**

◖ FOOD
Le Castelet, **6**
La Crêperie des Rois, **4**

★ NIGHTLIFE
L'Eden Café, **2**
L'Elite Club, **8**
Z 64, **5**

THE LOCAL STORY

INTERVIEW WITH A RÉSISTANT

An imposing man in his mid-70s, Raymond Casas is the heart and soul of Blois's Musée de la Résistance. Speaking in a clear and assured voice, the former Résistant continues to give fascinating tours of the museum he helped found.

LG: How did you come to join the Resistance?

A: I was 14, and my father had left for the French Army. A few days before the Nazis took Paris, he told the family to leave Blois. We arrived in Bordeaux on June 17, 1940—the day and place General de Gaulle had left for London. On June 18th, I heard de Gaulle's call to resist on the radio. I returned to Blois and joined up.

LG: Tell me more about your activities during the war.

A: Many of our actions involved sabotage. It was a bit chaotic at first. We set a lot of German barracks and facilities on fire, without orders coming from above. In 1943, we were able to free 183 prisoners from the Blois prison without murdering a single German soldier. We lost a lot of people—over 20 of my friends died between the beginning of the Resistance and May 10, 1945.

LG: What inspired the museum?

A: For over 50 years, other former *Résistants* and myself had been asked to speak in schools and other places. We see the museum as a permanent testimony to younger generations—we are old, and will not always be there to tell them the story.

Tourist Office: pl. du château (☎02 54 90 41 41; www.loiredeschateaux.com). Offers free maps of the city and of Loire Valley (prices vary), complete info on châteaux, tickets for bus circuits, **currency exchange** with a €5 fee, and an accommodations service €2.30. Open May-Sept. Tu-Sa 9am-7pm, Su-M and holidays 10am-7pm; Oct.-Apr. M 10am-12:30pm and 2-6pm, Tu-Sa 9am-12:30pm and 2-6pm, Su 9:30am-12:30pm.

English-Language Bookstore: Librairie Labbé, 9 rue Porte Chartraine. Open M 2-7:15pm, Tu-F 9:30am-7:15pm, Sa 9am-7:15pm.

Youth Center: Bureau d'Information Jeunesse de Loir-et-Cher, 7 av. Wilson (☎02 54 78 54 87). Brochures, job info, and help planning travel and booking inexpensive tickets. Open M-F 9am-12:30pm and 2-6:30pm, Sa 9am-12:30pm and 2-5pm.

Laundromat: Laverie, 6 rue St-Lubin, pl. Louis XIIn. Open daily 7am-9pm. Wash €4, dry €2. **Laverie du Mail,** 1 rue Jeanne d'Arc. Open daily 7am-9pm. Wash €4, dry €1 per 5min.

Police: 42 quai St-Jean (☎02 54 55 17 99).

Hospital: Centre Hospitalier de Blois, mail Pierre Charlot (☎02 54 55 66 33).

Library and Internet Access: Bibliothèque Abbé Grégoire, pl. Jean Jaurès (☎02 54 56 27 52). Reservations necessary. Limit 1hr. €0.20 per 5min., €2.40 per hr. Open Tu-W and F-Sa 2-8pm. **3ème Monde,** 39 av. Jean Laigret (☎02 54 74 38 22). €4 per hr. Open M-Sa 8am-10pm, Su 2-8pm.

Post Office: 2 rue Gallois (☎02 54 57 17 17). **Currency exchange.** Open M-F 8am-7pm, Sa 8am-12:30pm.

Postal Code: 41000.

ACCOMMODATIONS AND CAMPING

Hôtel du Bellay, 12 rue des Minimes (☎02 54 78 23 62.), at the top of porte Chartraine, near the city center. Named after the great French poet, this small, family-run establishment is located in a charming old house. Amicable owner is familiar with backpackers. 12 spotless, simple, comfortable rooms, the cheapest with a choice of toilet or shower. Breakfast €4.50. Reception 9am-1pm and 5-8pm. Call ahead. Closed early to late Jan. Singles and doubles €24-30; triples €58; quads €60. MC/V. ❷

Auberge de Jeunesse (HI), 18 rue de l'Hôtel Pasquier (☎/fax 02 54 78 27 21), 5km west of Blois in Les Grouets. Take bus #2 from train station to République. Take bus #4 (dir: Les Grouets) to Auberge de Jeunesse. (45min., 2 per hr. 7am-7pm). Bus also leaves from the SNCF train station at 7:45pm. Single-sex dorms far from town. Excellent kitchen facilities and hot showers in outdoor bathroom. Breakfast (€3.30) 8am. Sheets €2.80. Reception 6:45-10am and 6-10:30pm. Lockout 10am-6pm. Curfew 10:30pm. Open Mar. to mid-Nov. Bunks €10.60, with HI membership €7.60. ❶

Le Pavillon, 2 av. Wilson (☎02 54 74 23 27; fax 02 54 74 03 36), overlooking the Loire. 20min. walk from the train station, or take the local bus (line 3A) from the station. Bright, fairly comfortable, simply furnished rooms, half of which overlook the Loire and the château from across the Pont Gabriel. TVs and phones in some rooms. Breakfast €6.50. Singles and doubles €20-40; 1 quad €50. Extra bed €10. MC/V. ❷

Hôtel de France et de Guise, 3 rue Gallois (☎02 54 78 00 53; fax 02 54 78 29 45). In an ideal location next to the château, this hotel offers 50 elegantly decorated rooms that recall the days of the 19th century. Reproductions of impressionist works by Cézanne, Van Gogh, Renoir, and Degas hang on the walls. All rooms with toilet, TV, telephone, and shower or sink. Breakfast €6, in bed €7. Singles €39-44; doubles €44-56; triples €56-72. Extra bed €3. MC/V. ❹

Camping: Lac de Loire (☎02 54 78 82 05; fax 02 54 78 62 03). From the station or city center, take bus #S7 to Lac de Loire (20min., July and Aug. 3 per day, €1). 2-star site with 220 spots, swimming pool, mini-golf, and tennis courts. Reception open daily 8am-9pm. Open June to mid-Sept. Tent and 2 person €8, €3 per extra person, €1.50 per child. Electricity €10. Hot showers free. MC/V. ❶

◩ FOOD

Locals have been perfecting *le chocolat blésois* ever since Catherine de Medici brought her own pastry-makers from Italy. Sumptuous *pavés du roi* (chocolate-almond cookies) and *malices du loup* (orange peels in chocolate) peer invitingly from *pâtisseries* along **rue Denis Papin.** Traditional, homey restaurants line **rue St-Lubin** and **place Poids du Roi,** and inexpensive Chinese and Greek restaurants surround the **place de la Résistance.** Bakeries and fruit stands dot the central pedestrian area. An **Intermarché supermarket** is at 16 av. Gambetta (open M-Sa 9am-7pm) and at **Utile/Près d'ici,** 6 rue Drussy (open M-Sa 9am-8pm, Su 8:30am-1:30pm). **Place Louis XII** bustles with an open-air **market** (Sa morning). *Crêperies* are found on almost every block, but ◩**La Crêperie des Rois** ❷, 3 rue Denis Papin, has the widest selection. Try the "Texas" (meat, egg, tomatoes, potatoes), the more exotic "Martinique" (pineapple, ham, cheese, egg), and other specialty crêpes (€6-8). An outdoor terrace in summer provides nice seating. (☎02 54 90 01 90. Crêpes €4-8, dessert crêpes €2-6, *cidre* €2 per glass. MC/V.) ◩**Le Castelet** ❸, 40 rue St-Lubin, offers gourmet French fare at affordable prices (*menus* €14-24). Regional specialties and local wines (€1.50-3 per glass) are served in the lovely, rustic interior or on the outdoor terrace in the evening. (☎02 54 74 66 09. Appetizers from €5, salads €3-5, *plats* €10-12. Open July-Aug. M-Tu and Th-Sa noon-2pm and 7-10pm, W and Su 7-10pm; Sept.-June M-Tu and Th-Sa noon-2pm and 7-10pm. MC/V.)

◉ SIGHTS

CHÂTEAU DE BLOIS. Brilliant gold trimming and carved pillars give this château more than just a touch of elegance. Home to Louis XII and François I, Blois's château was as influential in the 15th and early 16th centuries as Versailles was in later years. The motto of François I (1494-1547), *Nutrisco et extingo* (I feed on fire and I extinguish it), explains the abundance of carved and painted fire-breathing salamanders. Blois was meticulously restored by 19th-century architect Félix Duban. It now houses three museums: the recently renovated **Musée des Beaux-Arts**, featuring a 16th- to 19th-century portrait gallery and a wrought-iron works collection; the **Musée d'Archéologie,** with a fascinating display of locally excavated glass and ceramics; and the **Musée Lapidaire,** exhibiting impressively sculpted pieces from nearby 17th-century châteaux. (☎02 54 90 33 33. Open daily Apr.-Sept. 9am-6pm; Jan.-Mar. and Oct.-Dec. 9am-12:30pm and 2-5:30pm. Historical tours in French May-Sept. depart from courtyard; free with admission; call ahead to request English. 25min. tours of the city by carriage depart from the entrance to the château €5. Admission €6.50, students under 25 and under 17 €4.50. Light show (son-et-lumière) mid-Apr. to late Sept. daily 10pm; €9.50, students €6. English show on W. Combined tickets for the château and light show or for the château and Maison de la Magie €11.50, students €8, and children €5. Ticket for all three attractions €15, students and children €11. MC/V.)

VIEILLE VILLE. The most enjoyable attractions in Blois might be its hilly streets and ancient staircases. Bars and bakeries on **rue St-Lubin** and **rue des Trois Marchands** tempt those en route to the 12th-century Abbaye St-Laumer, now the **Église St-Nicolas.** (Open daily 9am-6:30pm.) East of **rue Denis Papin** lie the most beautiful streets of all, which narrow gradually into intimate alleys and courtyards. Five hundred years of expansions to **Cathédrale St-Louis,** one of Blois's architectural jewels, endowed it with a beautiful mix of styles. (Open daily 7:30am-6pm; crypt open June-Aug.) In splendor and historical appeal, St-Nicolas and St-Louis give the château a run for its money. The view of the Loire from the ◾**Jardin de l'Evêché,** behind the cathedral, is utterly spectacular. At sunset, cross the Loire and turn right onto **quai Villebois Mareuil** to see the château rising above the roofs of the town.

OTHER SIGHTS. The ◾**Musée de la Résistance, de la Déportation et de la Libération** is a powerful memorial to French Holocaust victims and Resistance fighters from Blois. The museum is staffed by an 80-year-old veteran of WWII, the best of all tour guides. (1 pl. de la Grève. ☎02 54 56 07 02. Open M-F 9am-noon and 2-6pm, Sa 2-6pm. €3, students and children €1.) The **Maison de la Magie,** next to the château, entertains with films and displays, but the Hallucinoscope, a large optical illusion device, is the most popular attraction. (1 pl. du Château. ☎02 54 55 26 26; www.maisondelamagie.fr. Open July-Aug. 10am-12:30pm and 2-6:30pm; Apr.-June and Sept.-Nov. Tu-Su 10am-12:30pm and 2-6pm. 1½hr. live shows 2-3 times per day. €7.50, ages 6-17 €5, under 6 free.)

🎵 🎭 ENTERTAINMENT AND NIGHTLIFE

Blois appears tame—and then the sun goes down. Around midnight, neon signs beckon party-goers to ◾**Z 64,** 6 rue Maréchal de Lattre de Tassigny, the hip combination discotheque, lounge bar, and karaoke joint near the town center. (☎02 54 74 27 76. Cocktails €5-8. Open Tu-Su 8:30pm-4am.) Near the *place,* **L'Eden Café,** 15 rue Haute, serves 30 international beers (€4-6) and a selection of cocktails (€6) in a bar that resembles a medieval chapel. (☎02 54 78 36 32. Open daily 6pm-3am.) At **L'Elite Club,** 19 rue des Ponts Chartrains, locals gather to rock the night away with house music. (☎02 54 78 17 73. Open Th-Sa 11pm-5am.)

From October through April, the city hosts world-class jazz and classical musicians, dancers, and actors in the **Halle Aux Grains,** 1 pl. de la République. Schedules are available by phone. (☎02 54 90 44 00. Tu-F 1:30-6:30pm, Sa 2-5pm. Tickets €19-23; students €16-21.) **Le Soleil a Rendez-Vous avec la Lune** has recently been replaced by **Tous sur le Pont.** Now in its second year, this musical festival rocks the town for the first two weeks in July. (☎02 54 58 84 56. Daily 9am-7pm. Most concerts free.)

DAYTRIPS FROM BLOIS

TLC buses, outside the Blois train station, runs a châteaux circuit to Chambord and Cheverny, 2hr. at each. For those who prefer to go at their own pace, the châteaux are within easy **biking** distance over beautiful terrain. From Blois, it's 10km to **Cheverny** and 6km to **Beauregard,** and the châteaux and towns are well-marked along the roads. Cyclists are advised to stay off the major French highways. The **tourist office** branch at the Châteaux de Blois has maps of safe, efficient routes. The **Regional Tourism Committee** (☎ 02 54 78 62 52) offers one-week cycling packages.

CHAMBORD

Take the TLC bus from the SNCF station in Blois (45min., 9:10am and 1:20pm, €10) or enjoy the 1hr. bike ride. To bike or drive, cross the Loire in central Blois and ride 1km down av. Wilson. At the roundabout, take rte. D956 south for 2-3km followed by a left onto D33. Château: ☎ 02 54 50 40 00. Open daily Apr.-Sept. 9am-6:15pm; Oct.-Mar. 9am-5:15pm. Last entry 30min. before closing. €7, ages 18-25 €4.50, under 18 free.

Built by François I between 1519 and 1545 for his hunting trips and impressive fêtes, Chambord is the largest and most extravagant of the Loire châteaux. A testament to the monarchy's desire to flaunt their power before visiting dignitaries, the castle could accommodate the entire royal court—up to 10,000 people. With 440 rooms, 365 chimneys, and 83 staircases, the castle is a realization of François's interest in a multitude of architectural styles. The Greek cross-floor design used for the keep was formerly reserved for sacred buildings, but François co-opted it for his mansion. In the center of the castle, he built a spectacular double-helix staircase whose design is attributed to Leonardo da Vinci, and the ornamentation of the château marks the first influence of the Italian Renaissance in French architecture. François stamped Chambord with 200 of his trademark stone salamanders, commissioned 14 4m tall tapestries of his hunting conquests, and splayed his initials across the large stone chimneys on the rooftop terrace. After all this, François graced Chambord with his presence for 77 days.

In the 17th century, a new wing was built for Louis XIV. Busts of Molière and Sully adorn the antechamber to his room. The rooms are labeled in English, but more detailed explanations of the architecture are available through rented headsets (€4) in English, German, Spanish, Italian, or French.

An **ATM** stands next to the snack shops and restaurants outside the tourist office. To explore the surrounding forests, **boat** and **bike rentals** are available through **Alizés** from a little shelter at the foot of the château. (☎ 02 54 33 37 54. 2-person boats €11 per hr., electric boats €6.50, children €5.50 for 55min. Golf carts €8 per hr. Bikes €5.50 per hr., €10 per half-day, €13 per day. Call ahead to have your bike brought to the SNCF station in Blois at 8am and to return it there 7-8pm. Open daily June-Sept. 10am-8pm; Oct. and Mar.-Apr. 11am-6:30pm.) Campers can trek to **Camping Huisseau-sur-Cosson ❶,** 6 rue de Châtillon, about 5km southwest of Chambord on D33. (☎ 02 54 20 35 26. Open May-Sept. 9am-8pm. €3 per tent; €3.50 per person, under 7 €2. Electricity €2.50. Shower included.) Or try **Camping des Châteaux ❶,** between Chambord and Cheverny in Bracieux. (☎ 02 54 46 41 84; fax 02 54 46 09 15. Open daily late Mar. to mid-Oct. 8:30am-noon and 3-7:30pm. €4.50 per adult, €1.50 per child, €5 per tent. Electricity €2. Shower included.)

CHEVERNY

To bike or drive to the château, take D956 or D765 south for 45min. Château: ☎ 02 54 79 96 29. Open July-Aug. daily 9:15am-6:45pm; Apr.-June and early Sept. 9:15am-6:15pm; Oct. and Mar. 9:30am-noon and 2:15-5:30pm; Nov.-Feb. 9:30am-noon and 2:15-5pm. €6.10, students €4.10, ages 7-14 €3. Guided tours available upon request. MC/V. The same bus that leaves from the SNCF station to Chambord also goes to Cheverny after a 2hr. stop at the 1st château. Luxurious (but expensive) 4-star Camping Les Saules, located 2km away on the road to Contres. Swimming pool, bike rental on-site. 18-hole golf course nearby. Online reservations possible. (☎02 54 79 90 01; www.camping-cheverny.com. Open Apr.-Sept. 8:30am-8:30pm. €4.50 per person, ages 3-11 €2; €17-21.10 per spot.)

Since its completion in 1634, Cheverny has been privately owned by the Hurault family, whose members have served as financiers and officers to the kings of France. The family's wealth is reflected in the impeccably maintained grounds and luxuriously restored decor of the château, which remains inhabited by the marquis, his wife, and his three children. In 1922, Cheverny became one of the first privately owned castles to open its doors to visitors. Although much smaller than other châteaux, its magnificent furnishings capture the feel of a wealthy 17th-century home. Murals, armor, and elegant tapestries cover every inch of the walls in the luxurious *Chambre du Roi*. In the dining room, a series of paintings by Jean Monier recreate the story of *Don Quixote*. Works by the great renaissance painter Titian can also be found inside the castle. Fans of Hergé's **Tintin** books may recognize Cheverny's Renaissance facade as the inspiration for the design of Captain Haddock's mansion, *Moulinsart*. A gallery of Hergé's art and comics is adjacent to the grounds. A permanent exhibition can be visited, but expect to fork out an extra €4.50. Cheverny sheltered the **Mona Lisa** in its Orangerie during WWII. The kennels are home to nearly 90 mixed English-Poitevin hounds still used in hunting expeditions. (Oct.-Mar. Tu and Sa.) The **souper des chiens** offers a bizarre opportunity to see these hounds gulp down their dinner in less than 60 seconds. (M, Su, and W-F 5pm.) Next to the kennels, in the **trophy room,** thousands of antlers poke out of the ceiling and surround a striking stained-glass window depicting a hunt.

BEAUREGARD

A 30min. bike ride from Blois. Off D956, en route to Cheverny. Ask at bike rental for more detailed directions. A taxi from Blois costs €14. Château: ☎02 54 70 36 74 or 02 54 70 40 05. Open July-Aug. daily 9:30am-6:30pm; Apr.-June and Sept. daily 9:30am-noon and 2-6:30pm; Oct.-Jan. M-Tu and Th-Su 9:30am-noon and 2-5pm; early Feb. to Mar. daily 9:30am-noon and 2-5pm. €6.50, students and ages 7-18 €4.50, under 8 free. Gardens alone €4.50.

Before François I unleashed his fantasies on Chambord, he designed Beauregard as a hunting lodge for his uncle René. Though the château later became the property of nobles and congressmen, Beauregard, 6km south of Blois, remains cozier than its flashy cousin. Paul Ardier, treasurer to Louis XIII, commissioned Jean Monier to paint what became the world's largest portrait gallery. Today this collection of over 300 wall-to-wall, unframed paintings is a *Who's Who* of European powers, from Philippe de Valois (1378) and all of the Valois monarchs through Louis XIII (1638), as well as the faces of Elizabeth I, Thomas More, and Columbus. The 5616 hand-painted Delft tiles that cover the floor portray Louis XIII's army marching to war, and are currently undergoing a 20-year restoration project. Outside the château, the ruins of a 14th-century chapel invite a walk into the woods. Tours are available in French and English; times vary depending on season and availability of guides; call ahead. English guide sheets are always available.

⬛ VALENÇAY

Trains run from rue de la Gare to Salbris, which connects to Orléans (2hr.; M-Sa 8 per day, 3 on Su; €15) and Paris via Orléans (3hr.; M-Sa 8 per day, 3 on Su; €25.60). Buses run to Valençay from the train station in Blois (1½hr., 3 per day 7:40am-5:15pm, €8). To get there from the pl. de la Halle bus stop, walk down rue de l'Auditoire and turn right on pl. Talleyrand.

Château: ☎02 54 00 10 66; www.chateau-valencay.com. Open daily July-Aug. 9:30am-7:30pm; Apr.-June and Sept.-Oct. 9:30am-6pm; closed Nov.-Mar. Free shows in French feature actors (daily July-Aug. 11am-5:30pm. No pictures inside the château). €8.50, students 18-25 €6. The tourist office is on av. de la Résistance. (☎02 54 00 04 42. Open daily July-Aug. 10:30am-12:30pm and 2:30-6:30pm. For low season, call the tourist office for hours.)

Though farther out than most Loire Valley châteaux, popular Valençay, built in 1540, is a unique mix of interesting history and luxurious furnishings, modeled after the imposing style of Chambord (see p. 159). The original owner, Jacques d'Etampes, wanted to inspire awe in those who visited the buildings and grounds. After the Revolution, the estate was sold to Napoleon, and its vast woodlands, vineyards, and fields, became a prized feather in the emperor's cap.

Like Chambord, but unlike many other Loire châteaux, Valençay was decorated almost entirely in the Imperial style that developed during the reign of Napoleon I. The château's 19th-century owner, Charles-Maurice Talleyrand-Périgord, began his career under Louis XVI, but survived the Revolution and was made Minister of Foreign Affairs by Napoleon. The Emperor bought the château for Talleyrand to augment the empire's popularity by entertaining important guests here. After Napoleon deposed King Ferdinand VII of Spain in 1808, he sent the Spanish royal family to Talleyrand at Valençay. The Spanish princes and their ladies-in-waiting remained here until Ferdinand was reinstated as monarch. Ferdinand's room, with its elegant frescoes and Louis XVI furniture, is perhaps the most beautiful in the château. The exquisite interior contains a number of remarkable items from the early 19th century, including the table used for the Congress of Vienna. The *grande galerie* filled with portraits of Talleyrand and his family, is a must-see.

Admission to the château includes an audioguided tour in English, free of charge, and visits to the wine cellars, underground kitchens, and an animal park. Children will delight in the oversized maze in the château grounds. The labyrinth also has educational value: to decipher the code that will open the exit doors, one must resolve puzzles about Napoleon's life.

CHAUMONT

Chaumont is easily accessible by a 1hr. bike ride or 20min. car ride from Blois (16km along N152 in the direction of Tours, follow the sign that directs you across the bridge to Chaumont). Buses also run from Blois to Onzain (15min. walk to the castle). The tourist office, 24 rue Maréchal Leclerc, right across the bridge from N152, rents bikes for €2 per hr.; €5 per half-day; €10 per day, €8 for children. Château: ☎02 54 51 26 26. Open daily Jan. to mid-Mar. and Nov.-Dec. 10am-4:30pm; mid-Mar. to Oct. 9:30am-6pm. €6.10, students €4.10.

Chaumont, which occupies a strategic position overlooking the Loire, was originally built in the 10th century by the Comte de Blois to protect his territories from his rival, the Comte d'Anjou. The present castle, which was rebuilt in the following decade, reflects the stylistic transition between the late middle ages and the Renaissance. It also reflects renovations made by subsequent owners, including Marie-Charlotte Say, the daughter of a wealthy sugar trader, who acquired the château at age seventeen. Following Henri II's death in 1559, his widow Catherine took revenge against Diane de Poitiers, the King's mistress, forcing her to move from Chenonceau to Chaumont. While Chaumont is not the most lavish of the Loire châteaux, it is one of the most creatively decorated, with giant fake flowers hanging from staircases and sprawling across tables. The grounds and gardens of Chaumont are spectacular, and are perhaps more of an attraction that the château itself. The courtyard of the château offers an expansive view of the Loire valley. The château also hosts an international garden festival with a different theme every year, from May to mid-October. (☎02 54 20 99 22. Admission to gardens €8, students €6.50, children €3.20. Festival runs daily 9:30am-dusk.)

AMBOISE

One of the oldest cities in the Loire Valley, Amboise (pop. 12,000) was home to the first *Tourangeaux* (people from Tours) in 100 BC. Over 1000 years later, Charles VIII, Louis XI, Louis XII, Catherine de Medici, and François I enjoyed the peaceful countryside and extraordinary panorama of the river valley from the hillside château. Amboise's most famous former resident may be Leonardo da Vinci; the great inventor spent his last years in the town, where he died on May 2, 1519. Life-size versions of da Vinci's unrealized projects stand in the park at Clos Lucé. While citizens of Amboise enjoy their place in history, their great local vineyards, and a lovely old quarter, they doggedly retain a healthy appreciation for the country life.

TRANSPORTATION. Trains run from bd. Gambetta to: Blois (20min., 20 per day, €5.40); Orléans (1hr., 18 per day, €12.20); Paris (2¼hr., 7 per day, €23.40); Tours (20min., about 11 per day, €4.30). Buy tickets at the ticket office. (☎02 47 23 18 23. Open M-Sa 5:40am-9:30pm, Su 7:15am-9:30pm.) **Fil Vert buses** leave the tourist office for Chenonceau and Chambord (30min., 1 departure per day 10:52 am, round-trip €2.10) and Tours (35min., 3 per day 6:45-9am, €2.10). **Taxis,** 12 quai du Général de Gaulle, are easier to find by calling ☎02 47 57 01 54. To rent a **car,** walk to Avis, 12 quai du Général de Gaulle, across the way from the tourist office (☎02 47 23 21 11; MC/V) or Garage Jourdain, 105 av. de Tours. (☎02 47 57 01 54; MC/V.) To rent **bikes,** head to Loca Cycles, 3 Jean-Jacques Rousseau, right off quai du Général de Gaulle when walking toward the château. (☎02 47 57 00 28. €14 per day. Passport deposit. Open M-Su 9am-12:30pm and 2-7pm.)

ORIENTATION AND PRACTICAL INFORMATION. To reach the **tourist office,** take a left from the station and follow rue Jules-Ferry, crossing both bridges past the residential Île d'Or. The office is 30m to the right of the bridge, on quai du Général de Gaulle (15 minutes). The office posts a list of hotels with vacancies each night, and tourists can call the accommodations hotline for the same information (☎02 47 23 27 42). Hotel reservations can be made for a flat €2.50 fee. Themed tours available during the summer. Call the tourist office to reserve. (☎02 47 57 09 28; www.amboise-valdeloire.com. Open July-Aug. M-Sa 9am-8pm, Su 10am-6pm; Apr.-June and Sept. M-Sa 9:30am-1pm and 2-6:30pm, Su 10am-1pm and 3-6:30pm; Oct.-Mar. M-Sa 9:30am-12:30pm and 2-6:30pm, Su 10am-1pm. Schedules change all the time, so make sure to call ahead for the most up-to-date information. Tours daily, €6.) The quai du Général de Gaulle is full of **banks** and **ATMs.** The most central **laundromat** is LavCentre, 5 allée du Sergent Turpin, across the street from the tourist office. (Open daily 7am-8pm. Last wash at 7pm.) The **gendarmerie** are at 1 bd. A. France (☎02 47 30 63 70), and the **hospital** is on rue des Ursulines (☎02 47 23 33 33). **Cyber Café,** 119 rue Nationale, provides **Internet** access. (Open Su 3-10pm, M 3-10pm, Tu-Th 10am-10pm, F-Sa 10am-midnight.) The **post office** sits at 20 quai du Général de Gaulle, three blocks down the street to the left as you face the tourist office. **Currency exchange** available at good rates. (Open M-Sa 8am-12:30pm and 2-6pm.) **Postal Code:** 37400.

ACCOMMODATIONS AND FOOD. The **Hôtel Belle-Vue** ❹, 12 quai Charles Guinot, at the end of the two bridges from the train station to the château, offers some of Amboise's nicest rooms, furnished in a charming country style. A flowered terrace overlooking the Loire helps this three-star hotel live up to its name, though only about one-third of the rooms offer a view. (☎02 47 30 40 40; fax 02 47 30 51 23. Breakfast €7. Singles with bath €43; doubles €48; triples €58, quads €67. MC/V.) The best inexpensive accommodations are at the **Centre International de Séjour Charles Péguy (HI)** ❶, Île d'Or. Follow rue Jules-Ferry from the station and head downhill to the right after the first bridge (10 minutes). The 25-room youth hostel is niched at the very edge of the tiny island. Guests are housed in 1- to 4-bed dorm rooms; ask for a room with a view of the Loire and the château, preferably on the third floor. Individual travelers must call a few weeks in advance in peak season, since the hostel receives a number of large groups. TV room, game room and dining room are reserved for groups. (☎ 02 47 30 60 90; www.ucrif.asso.fr. Breakfast €2.70. Sheets €3.30. Free parking. Reception M-F 3-8pm. Dorms €8.80.) Two-star **Hôtel Le Français ❸**, 6 rue Voltaire, has clean, sleekly furnished and fairly large rooms in a calm setting just three blocks from the château. Reservations are recommended 3-4 weeks in advance in July-August. (☎ 02 47 57 11 38; fax 02 47 57 71 42. Breakfast €5.80. Singles and doubles with shower and TV €35-45; triples €55; quads €58. MC/V.) Located inside a beautiful, tree-filled park, **■Île d'Or camping ❶** offers such clean, well-maintained facilities it feels like an outdoor hotel. The riverside campsite offers a swimming pool (€2), mini-golf (€2.40), and a restaurant, all in the midst of a peaceful view of the Loire and very quiet setting. Large sites and clean bathrooms are also available. (☎ 02 47 23 47 23. Reception 8-12:15pm and 3:30-7pm. Open early Apr. to Oct. €2.30 per person, children under 12 €1.60. €3.10 per site. Electricity €1.90. Shower €1.30. MC/V.)

The rue Victor Hugo and rue Nationale, both at the base of the château, are lined with *brasseries* and bakeries. For a cheap picnic with a great view of the Loire, climb uphill to **ATAC supermarket**, pl. de la Croix Bernard, at rue Grégoire de Tours. (Open M-F 8:30am-12:30pm and 2:30-7:30pm, Sa 8:30am-7:30pm, Su 9:30am-12:30pm.) There's also a **Marché Plus**, 5 quai du Général de Gaulle. (Open M-Sa 7am-9pm, Su 9am-1pm.) A local **Marché** takes place twice a week along the banks of the Loire. It's one of the very first markets in the region, with a large selection of fruits, vegetables, and other products of the area. (F and Su morning, more info at tourist office.) Try the local favorite **■Le Blason ❸**, 11 pl. Richelieu, for great regional cuisine, including delicious *foie gras* and delicate *soufflé glacé* topped with Grand Marnier. (☎ 02 47 23 22 41. Lunch *menu* €11.50. Dinner *menu* €14.50-25. *Entrées* €13-20. MC/V.) Even the highest tolerances will be tested by the enormous cocktails at trendy **Le Shaker**, 1 rue de l'Entrepont, on Île d'Or. A young, rowdy crowd from nearby campsites and hostels gathers there in the evenings, amidst sumptuous views of the Loire and the château. (Cocktails €5-9. Beers €3-6. Open Su-Th 6pm-2am, F-Sa 6pm-3am. AmEx/MC/V.)

⬛ SIGHTS. Six French kings have held court in Amboise, considered by many to be one of the most beautiful French châteaux. Its battlements at one time held as many as 4000 people. In 1560, a failed Protestant conspiracy against the influential arch-Catholic de Guise family led to grisly murder. Some of the rebelling Huguenots were thrown into the Loire in sacks, while others were killed on the château balcony, now described by smiling tour guides as the "Balcony of the Hanging People." Most of the château was destroyed during the French Revolution, and its stones were sold on the market. The **Logis de Roi**, the main part of the château, remains decorated to fit the 15th- and 16th-century royalty who once inhabited it. Intricately carved Gothic chairs stand over 6 ft. high in order to prevent surprise attacks from behind. In contrast, the 2nd floor is furnished with 19th-century pieces that recall the period during which the château was inhabited by Louis Philippe. Finish your visit atop the "Tour Cavalière," and enjoy an outstanding 360° view. The jewel of the grounds is the **Chapelle St-Hubert**, outside the château, the final resting place of Leonardo da Vinci. Amboise is also home to one of the very first Renaissance gardens in France, before French gardens became popular in the 17th century. In summer, people flock to the "Court of King François" **light show** *(son-et-lumière)* staged by 450 Amboise residents and resurrecting everyone from

LOIRE VALLEY

gallant knights to court jester. (☎02 47 57 00 98. Open daily July-Aug. 9am-7pm; Sept.-Oct. 9am-6pm; Nov.-Jan. 9am-noon and 2-5pm; Mar. 9am-noon and 1:30-5:30pm; Apr.-June 9am-6:30pm. Free tour. €7.50, students €6.50, ages 7-14 €4.20. Light show W and Sa June-July 10:30pm, Aug. 10pm. €12, children €6.)

Built right into the walls of the château, the **Caveau des vignerons**, pl. du Château, offers free tastings of locally made wine, goat cheese, *foie gras*, and preserved meats. All products sold at affordable prices, by a very friendly staff. (☎02 47 57 23 69. Open daily Apr.-Nov. 10am-7pm.) From the château, follow the cliffs along narrow and sinuous rue Victor Hugo beside the centuries-old **maisons troglodytiques**, houses built in hollowed-out cliffs still inhabited today. Four hundred meters away rests ◪**Clos Lucé**, by far Amboise's most interesting attraction. This Renaissance manor and its Italian-style gardens were given to Leonardo da Vinci by his biggest patron, François I, who often visited da Vinci using an underground tunnel that connects Clos Lucé to the château. Da Vinci's bedroom, library, drawing room, and chapel are inside, but the main attraction is the underground level, which contains a collection of 40 machines built from da Vinci's visionary designs. Opened from April to November, the park is home to 12 giant machines and 32 translucent canvases reproducing da Vinci's paintings. (☎02 47 57 62 88; fax 02 47 30 54 28. Open daily July-Aug. 9am-8pm; Apr.-June and Sept.-Oct. 9am-7pm; Feb.-Mar. and Nov.-Dec. 9am-6pm; Jan. 10am-5pm. €11, students €9. MC/V.)

TOURS

The city of Tours was born amidst the chaos of the Hundred Years' War (1337-1453) when three small towns joined together in an attempt at self-preservation. Tours went on to become the heart of the French kingdom in the 15th and 16th centuries. Once Balzac's home and now home to 30,000 students, this dynamic city blends history with modernity. By day, joggers fill paths along the banks of the Loire, but by sunset, as illuminated bridges glow above the river, bar-hoppers take over the cafe-lined boulevards, and young people gather around the lively place Plumereau ("place Plum" to locals). Only an hour from Paris by TGV, and conveniently located on the banks of the Loire, Tours is also a perfect base for travelers hoping to visit several of the valley's châteaux.

▐ TRANSPORTATION

Trains: pl. du Général Leclerc. Info office open M-F 6am-10pm, Sa-Su 7:15am-10pm. Many destinations require a change at **St-Pierre-des-Corps**, 5min. outside Tours. To: **Bordeaux** (2½hr., 9 TGV per day, €36.70); **Paris** (2¼hr., 14 per day, €27; TGV via St-Pierre 1hr., 18 per day, €35-45); **Poitiers** (45min., 6 per day, €13.10; TGV via St-Pierre 13 per day, €16).

Public Transportation: Fil Bleu, 5 rue de la Dolve (☎02 47 66 70 70). Office open M-Sa 7am-7pm. Tickets €1.10, weekly pass €10.90. Buses run 6am-8:30pm; map available from the Fil Bleu office near the train station.

Taxis: Taxis-Radio, 13 rue de Nantes (☎02 47 20 30 40), at the train station. 24hr.

Car Rental: The tourist office has a list of companies. **Avis** (☎02 47 20 53 27), in the train station. AmEx/DC/MC/V. **Europcar**, 7 rue B. Palissy (☎02 47 64 47 76).

Bike Rental: Amster Cycles, 5 rue du Rempart (☎02 47 61 22 23; www.amstercycles.com). €14 per day, €54 per week. Can drop bikes at different locations along the Loire. Motorcycle rentals. Passport or credit card deposit. Open M-Sa 9am-12:30pm and 1-7pm, Su 9am-12:30pm and 6-7pm. MC/V.

LOIRE VALLEY

Tours

ACCOMMODATIONS
Camping St-Avertin, 13
Foyer des Jeunes Travailleurs, 11
Hôtel des Châteaux de la Loire, 10
Hôtel Foch, 5
Hôtel Regina, 6

FOOD
La Bigouden, 3
Boccaccio, 9
La Souris Gourmande, 7

NIGHTLIFE
Le Café, 1
GI Club, 8
Juanita Banana, 4
Le Petit Faucheux, 2
Le Pym's, 12

TO & LAC DE LA BERGEONNERIE (1km)
TO (5km)
TO (300m)

300 yards
300 meters

pont Wilson
pont Neuf
pont Napoléon

La Loire

quai - d'Orléans
quai du Pont Neuf

r. du Petit Cupidon
r. Traversière
r. du Petit Pré
r. des Ursulines
r. du Général Mеur
r. Albert Thomas
r. des Maures
Cathédrale St-Gatien
r. Jules Simon
Musée des Beaux-Arts
PL. SICARD
r. Lavoisier
r. Bernard Palissy
Château de Tours
r. de la Barre
r. Colbert
Library
r. Voltaire
Musée du Compagnonnage
St-Julien
Berthelot
Lambert
Théâtre Municipal
Nouvel Olympia
La Boîte à Livres de L'Étranger
r. de Lucé
r. des Halles
r. Nationale
r. Émile Zola
Église Réformée
r. de Buffon
Chapelle des Minimes
r. des Minimes
r. Chaptal
Centre de Congrès Vinci
Europcar
bd. Heurteloup
PL. DU GAL. LECLERC
r. du Rempart
r. Édouard Vaillant
Amster Cycles
Avis Car Rental
rue de Nantes
r. B. Pascal
ATAC Supermarket
Hôtel de Ville
PL. JEAN JAURÈS
Monoprix
r. Gambetta
r. Étienne Pallu
r. de la Préfecture
Marceau
r. Georges Sand
av. de Grammont
r. de la Dolve
r. Béranger
bd. de la Grandière
r. de Clocheville
r. des Déportés
Nouvelle Basilique St-Martin
r. Richelieu
r. Néricault Destouches
Balzac's Birthplace
r. Marceau
r. du Maréchal DE LA RESISTANCE
r. des Fusillés
r. du Commerce
Jardin École Régionale des Beaux-Arts
ANATOLE FRANCE
University Humanities Building
r. des Tanneurs
r. des Cerisiers
Musée du Gemmail
r. Bretonneau
Langry
r. du Mûrier
PLUMEREAU
r. du Petit Soleil
r. de la Monnaie
Cyber Café
r. de Châteauneuf
Tour de l'Horloge
r. de la Rôtisserie
r. du Change
Tour de Charlemagne
r. Descartes
r. Rapin
r. Léonard de Vinci
r. Rabelais
r. Chanoineau
r. de la Grosse Tour
r. du Grand Marché
pl. du Grand Marché
PL. DES HALLES
Market
PL. ROUGET DE L'ISLE
PL. DE LA VICTOIRE
Laundry
r. de la Victoire
r. du Petit St-Martin
PL. DE LA GRANDE
r. Henri Barbusse
r. Chartentier
r. Proudhon
av. de Ballan
r. de Courteille
r. Alleron
r. P.-L. Courier
r. Constantine
r. des Maréchal Foch
r. P.-L. Courier
r. Victor Hugo
r. de Bordeaux
rue Gilles de la Vendée
r. Charles Gilles
r. Michelet

> **CHÂTEAU HOPPING.** Few châteaux are accessible by public transportation, but travelers have other options. Renting a car provides the most freedom, but at an often prohibitive price. The cheapest way is by **bike.** With several drop-off locations along the Loire, **Amster Cycles** (☎02 47 61 22 23; www.amstercycles.com) offers convenience and competitive prices (€13 per day), though it's hard to cover much more than two châteaux per day. For those in a hurry, plush minibuses depart from Tours everyday at 9am and visit four to five châteaux (€40-45). Companies include: **Aliénor** (☎06 1085 35 39); **Saint-Eloi Excursions** (☎02 47 37 08 04); **Touraine Evasion** (☎06 07 39 13 31); **Acco-Dispo Excursions** (☎02 47 57 67 13); **Quart de Tours** (☎06 30 65 52 01).

⚘ ❼ ORIENTATION AND PRACTICAL INFORMATION

Place Jean Jaurès is the vertex of four boulevards and the center of the town. The busy **rue Nationale**, once part of the main road between Paris and Spain, runs north to the Loire, while **avenue de Grammont** reaches toward the Cher River to the south. **Boulevard Béranger** and **boulevard Heurteloup** run west and east, respectively, from pl. Jean Jaurès. The pedestrian *vieille ville*, the lively **place Plumereau**, and most historic sites are northwest of pl. Jean Jaurès toward the Loire.

Tourist Office: 78-82 rue Bernard Palissy (☎02 47 70 37 37; www.ligeris.com). Free maps, accommodations booking, and reservations for châteaux tours. 2hr. walking tours daily mid-July to mid-Aug. at 10am (€5.50, ages 6-12 €4.50). Call in advance for English tours. 1½hr. night walking tour (July-Aug. every F 9:30pm; €8.50, children €6.50). The *Carte Multi-Visites* (€7.70) provides access to 6 museums and a city tour. Open mid-Apr. to mid-Oct. M-Sa 8:30am-7pm, Su 10am-12:30pm and 2:30-5pm; mid-Oct. to mid-Apr. M-Sa 9am-12:30pm and 1:30-6pm, Su 10am-1pm.

Bank: Banque de France, 2 rue Chanoineau (☎02 47 60 24 00), off bd. Heurteloup.

English-Language Bookstore: La Boîte à Livres de l'Etranger, 2 rue du Commerce (☎02 47 05 67 29; fax 02 47 66 64 24). Wide selection in many languages. Open M 2-7pm, Tu-Sa 9:30am-7pm. MC/V.

Laundromat: Cyber-Laverie, 16bis pl. de la Victoire. M-F Internet €1.50 per 15min., €3 per hr. Open M-Sa 10am-7:30pm, Su 11am-7:30pm. **Lavo 2000,** 17 rue Bretonneau (☎02 47 73 14 69). Open daily 7am-8:30pm.

CROUS (☎02 47 60 42 42) provides info on discount meals and long-term housing.

Police: 70-72 rue de Marceau (☎02 47 33 80 69).

Hospital: Hôpital Bretonneau, 2 bd. Tonnellé (☎02 47 47 47 47).

Internet Access: Cyber Gate, 11 rue de Prés. Merville (☎02 47 05 95 94). 28 PC computers with cable/ADSL connection. €1 per 20min.; €5 for 1hr., a sandwich, and a drink. Open M 1-10pm, Tu-Sa 11am-midnight, Su 2-10pm.

Post Office: 1 bd. Béranger (☎02 47 60 34 20). **Currency exchange** at competitive rates. Open M-F 8am-7pm, Sa 8am-noon. Branch office on 92 rue Colbert.

Postal Code: 37000.

⌂ ⌂ ACCOMMODATIONS AND CAMPING

In peak season, call a week or two in advance.

■ **Hôtel Regina,** 2 rue Pimbert (☎02 47 05 25 36; fax 02 47 66 08 72), offers a handful of rooms in a charming private house. Hosts make guests feel like family. They might even throw in a free knitting lesson. Near river, good restaurants, and city center. Clean hallway showers. TV lounge. Free parking for bikes. Breakfast €4.30. Reception closed noon-2pm and after 1am. Singles and doubles €20-24; triples €23-36. MC/V. ❷

▓ **Hôtel Foch,** 20 rue du Maréchal Foch (☎02 47 05 70 59; hotel-foch.tours@wanadoo.fr), just off pl. Plumereau. Modest facade hides a warm hotel, offering large rooms in an unbeatable location. The owner, a Classics professor, is extremely knowledgeable about Tours and the Loire region. All but one room have showers. Continental breakfast €5. Garage €5 for cars, free for bikes. Reservations up to a week in advance during peak time. Singles €26-34; doubles €31-46; triples €39-45; quads €51-58. MC/V. ❸

Foyer des Jeunes Travailleurs, 16 rue Bernard Palissy (☎02 47 60 51 51; fjt.tours@wanadoo.fr). Centrally located hostel offers long-term housing for workers. Draws a crowd of backpackers in the summer, but tourists are not allowed to stay outside of peak season. Very basic furnishings. Kitchen on every floor, free Internet access. Breakfast €1.90, other meals €7. One-time €4 restaurant membership. Reception open M-F 8am-6:30pm. Singles with shower €17; doubles with bath €13. MC/V. ❶

Hôtel des Châteaux de la Loire, 12 rue Gambetta (☎02 47 05 10 05; hoteldeschateaux.tours@wanadoo.fr). 30-room "logis de France" hotel earns its 2 stars, providing elegant wooden furnishings at reasonable prices. All rooms come with a shower or bath, toilet, and cable TV. Breakfast €6.30. Parking €5.50. Open mid-Mar. to mid-Dec. Singles €38-46; doubles €38-53; triples, quads, and quints available. MC/V/AmEx/D. ❹

Camping: Camping St-Avertin, 63 rue de Rochepinard in St-Avertin (☎02 47 27 27 60), 5km outside of Tours, accessible by bus #5. Ask for stop near campsite and follow signs. Tennis, volleyball, pool, kayaking nearby. Reception 8am-noon and 3-8pm. Open Apr. to mid-Oct. 10pm curfew. Reserve 1-2 months ahead in summer. €3.15 per person, €2.10 per child under 7, €5 per site, €1.30 per car. Electricity €2.50-4. MC/V. ❶

▶ FOOD

Rue Colbert and **place Plumereau** have dozens of pleasant outdoor options, including many *crêperies* with *menus* under €12. Bistros and pubs crowd around **place Jean Jaurès.** Be sure to try the melt-in-your-mouth macaroons *à l'ancienne* and anything *aux pruneaux* (with prunes). Connoisseurs sip the light, fruity whites of Vouvray, Monmousseau, and Montlouis. The **indoor market,** pl. des Halles, expands outdoors Wednesday and Saturday mornings (M-Su 6am-1:30pm). **Marché Gourmand** at pl. de la Résistance (1st and 3rd F of each month 4-10pm) sells only the choicest gourmet products. A **Marché Traditionnel** (in front of the Tourist office, Tu) sells fresh fruits and vegetables. There is an **ATAC** supermarket, 5 pl. du Maréchal Leclerc, near the station (open M-Sa 7:30am-8pm) and a **Monoprix** in Galeries Lafayette on the corner of rue Etienne Pallu and rue Nationale, just north of pl. Jean Jaurès (open M-Sa 9am-7:30pm). Cheese lovers converge at the unique ▓**La Souris Gourmande** ❷, 100 rue Colbert, where the delicious selection of cheese dishes is almost overshadowed by the astonishing, bovine-obsessed decor. (☎02 47 47 04 80. Fondue €12-14. Open Tu-Sa noon-2pm and 7-10:30pm.) ▓**La Bigouden** ❷, 3 rue du Grand Marché, stands out among the many *crêperies* nearby pl. Plumereau. The popular restaurant spices up classic dishes into pairings like camembert and jam. (☎02 47 64 21 91. *Plats* from €7. Desserts €5-8. Open M-Tu and Th-Su noon-2pm and 7-11pm. MC/V.) Locals know to come to the pizzeria **Boccacio** ❸, 9 rue Gambetta, for its fresh ingredients, wood-oven pizzas, and tempting tiramasu. (☎02 47 05 45 22. Lunch *menus* €12. Open M-Th noon-2pm and 7:30-9:30pm, F-Sa noon-2pm and 7:30-10pm. Closed Tu and Su nights. MC/V.)

◉ SIGHTS

Those in search of peace and quiet find it at the beautiful **Lac de la Bergeonnerie** (also called Lac de Tours), a 10min. ride away (bus #1) on the banks of the Cher.

▧ MUSÉE DU GEMMAIL. Located in a beautiful courtyard, the one-of-a-kind **Musée du Gemmail** is dedicated to an art form that originated in Tours in the 1950s. Brightly colored glass is melded together to form mosaic works and interpretations of classic paintings, including da Vinci's *Mona Lisa*. *(7 rue du Murier. Off rue Bretonneau, near pl. Plumereau. ☎ 02 47 61 01 19. Open Apr.-Nov. Tu-Su 10am-noon and 2-6:30pm. €4.70, students €3.10, under 10 €1.60.)*

▧ CATHÉDRALE ST-GATIEN. Although the interior demonstrates high Gothic architecture at its purest, the wildly intricate facade of this cathedral combines several centuries of architectural caprice. First erected in the fourth century, St-Gatien was rebuilt in *Angevine* style in the 12th century. Since then the religious edifice has witnessed many transformations: solid Romanesque columns were embellished with delicate Gothic micro-carvings in the Middle Ages, and two spires were added to the cathedral in classic Renaissance style. The cathedral also has a dazzling display of 13th- to 20th-century stained-glass windows. *(Rue Jules Simon. ☎ 02 47 70 21 00. Cathedral open daily 9am-7pm. Free. Cloister open Easter-Sept. 9:30am-12:30pm and 2-6pm; Oct.-Mar. W-Su 9:30am-12:30pm and 2-5pm. €2.50, free for children. Mass every day 7pm. and Su 10am and 6:30pm.)*

TOURS OF BASILIQUE ST-MARTIN. The Tour de l'Horloge and Tour de Charlemagne, flanking rue des Halles, reveal the incredible proportions of the 12th-century Basilique St-Martin. The two towers were once part of a fifth-century Romanesque church that was pillaged by the Huguenots in 1562 and eventually turned into a stable. St-Martin, the city's first bishop, now sleeps undisturbed in the Nouvelle Basilique St-Martin, a *fin-de-siècle* church. *(Rue Descartes. ☎ 02 47 05 63 87. Open daily Feb.-Nov. 8am-6:45pm. Mass daily 11am.)*

MUSÉE DE COMPAGNONNAGE. Tours once served as the center for every type of apprenticeship, and this museum, founded in 1910, exhibits products from these **compagnons** (companions), members of artisans' guilds, that date back to the Middle Ages. While the exhibits may be difficult to follow for those who do not speak French, the intricate handiwork is easy for anyone to appreciate. Amid the curios is an impressively detailed model cathedral and a miniature spiral staircase carved in wood. *(8 rue Nationale, next to Église Saint-Julien. ☎ 02 47 61 07 93. Open daily mid-June to mid-Sept. 9am-12:30pm and 2-6pm; mid-Sept. to mid-June M and W-Su 9am-noon and 2-6pm. €4, students and seniors €2.50, under 12 free.)*

MUSÉE DES BEAUX-ARTS. A succession of stunning salons, the Musée des Beaux-Arts is located within a beautiful historical mansion. The upper floors house mostly 17th- and 18th-century French paintings, but works by Monet, Delacroix, and Rodin add variety. The *primitif* collection downstairs includes two wood-carved paintings by Andrea Mantegna. The Lebanese cedar outside was planted during Napoleon's reign and occupies the entire courtyard. *(18 pl. François Sicard, next to the cathedral. ☎ 02 47 05 68 73. Open M and W-Su 9am-12:45pm and 2-6pm. €4, students €2. Gardens open in summer daily 7am-8:30pm; low season 7am-6pm.)*

🎵 🎎 ENTERTAINMENT AND FESTIVALS

Place Plumereau is *the* place to be, where cheerful students sip drinks and chat at cafes and bars. Three clubs on the square fit snugly together, and the **rue du Commerce,** off pl. Plumereau, also hosts a large number of bars. **Le Pym's,** 170 av. de Grammont, is the most popular nightclub in Tours, where two lively dance floors are hopping almost every night of the week. (Cover €11. Open Tu-Su.) The **GI Club,** 13 rue Lavoisier, spins house, disco, and techno every night of the week. (☎ 02 47 66 29 96. Open nightly 11pm-5am.) Those in search of a quieter night can head to **Le Petit Faucheux,** 23 rue des Cerisiers, for some soul-soothing jazz. (☎ 02 47 38 29 34.

Live combos play weekly; call ahead for a schedule. Cover €7-14, students €10.) **Juanita Banana,** 13 rue du Change, keeps its customers coming back with its spicy food and even spicier salsa music. Cocktails €5. (Open until midnight, 2am on weekends. MC/V.) The hip crowd cools its heels with cocktails (€6) at the trendy **Le Café,** 39 rue Bretonneau. Monthly concerts. (☎02 47 61 37 83. Happy hour daily 6:30-8:30pm. Open daily noon-2am.)

Late in May, the **Florilège vocal** welcomes choirs from all over the world (ask tourist office for more info). Early July brings the **Fêtes Musicales en Touraine,** a 10-day celebration of classical and church music, now in its 40th year. (☎02 47 21 65 08. €12-23 per night.) Tours hosts the annual **Jazz en Touraine** festival at the end of September, and the **Acteurs-Acteurs** festival of film and theater in June. Formerly the Théâtre Louis Jouvet, **Olympia,** 7 rue de Lucé (☎02 47 64 50 50), and the **Théâtre Municipal,** 34 rue de la Scellerie (☎02 47 60 20 00), have productions year-round.

▶ DAYTRIP FROM TOURS

CHINON
Trains and SNCF buses run from the station (☎02 47 93 11 04) via St-Pierre-des-Corps to Saumur (1½hr., 2 per day, €10.80) and Tours (45min.; 9 per day M-Sa, 5 on Su; €7.40). A train runs from Saumur to Port Boulet (10 min., 6 per day, €3.20), from which a bus continues on to Chinon (15min., 6 per day, €2.40). Check the ticket office (Open M-Sa 6am-12:30pm and 1-7:40pm, Su 2:30-8pm).

Perched between the banks of the Vienne River and the majestic, crumbling château where Richard the Lionheart drew his last breath, Chinon (pop. 9000) was one of the most important cities in France under the reign of Henry II, King of England and Anjou. Chinon is also remembered as the hometown of the great Renaissance writer Francois Rabelais—many streets, hotels, and restaurants in the *vieille ville* are named after his famous characters. Though townspeople remain proud of their rich historic and literary heritage, Chinon today is more defined by its vineyards, which produce both red and white wine, as well as the distinctive *confiture de vin de Chinon,* a delicious wine jam.

For a charming stroll, take the less-traveled impasse du Roberdeau past the ivy-covered ramparts to reach the august rubble of Chinon's 10th-century **château.** The interior displays a few medieval tapestries and fragments of Gallo-Roman art. The grounds are spread between three main fortresses, all of which are connected by secret underground tunnels. The 14th-century **Tour Marie-Javelle** has withstood the Hundred Years' War, the Wars of Religion, and the French Revolution without a blemish, probably thanks to a popular legend that anyone who captured the bell tower would die a horrible death. Its bell has struck every half-hour since 1399. The **Joan of Arc Museum** that occupies the three-story tower is dedicated to the young warrior, who stopped by Chinon to talk with the Dauphin in 1429. Presentations about Joan's military travels are given in English and French. (☎02 47 93 13 45. Open daily Apr.-Sept. 9am-7pm; Oct.-Mar. 9:30am-5pm. Free tours are available in French, English, or German. €6, students €4.60, ages 7-18 €3.20.)

Wine tastings can be enjoyed at **Caves Plouzeau,** 94 rue Haute St-Maurice, in the heart of the *vieille ville.* M. Plouzeau's son, Marc, conducts free tours in a cave beneath the château. (☎02 47 93 16 34; www.plouzeau.com. Open Apr.-Oct. Tu-Sa 11am-1pm and 3-7pm.) The **Caves Painctes de Chinon,** rue Voltaire, is an extensive network of underground tunnels and cellars running deep beneath Chinon's castle. A guild of Rabelais admirers holds chapter meetings there four times a year. (☎02 47 93 30 44; fax 02 47 93 36 36. Open July to mid-Sept. Tours at 11am, 3, 4:30, and 6pm. €3, includes wine *dégustation.*) The small ▧**Maison de la Rivière,** 12 quai Pasteur, devoted to local river culture, has everything from aquariums to workshops that explore traditional boat-building and river wildlife. (☎ 02 47 93 21 34, 02 47 95 93 15 to reserve a boat excursion. Open July-Aug. Tu-F 10am-12:30pm and 2-6:30pm, Sa-Su 3-6:30pm; Apr.-Sept. Tu-F 10am-12:30pm and 2-5:30pm, Sa-Su 2-5:30pm. Guided tours in French €4. Boat excursion €4-6. 1 hr. boat tour €8. €3, under 12 €2.) **Maison de la Devinière,** located 5km from Chinon in Seuilly, is Rabelais's birthplace. The 15th-century house is now a museum dedicated to the great humanist writer. (☎ 02 47 95 91 18. Open daily Apr.-Sept. 9:30am-7pm; Jan.-Mar. and Oct.-Dec. 9:30am-12:30pm and 2-5pm. €4.50, students €3.)

Every third Sunday in August, all of Chinon turns out for **Marché à l'Ancienne,** featuring regional foods like *fouaces* (a pastry popular in medieval times) and a parade of citizens costumed in 19th-century *chinonais* garb. The **Avoine Zone Blues,** now in its fifth year, brings jazz groups from France and other countries for a weekend of classic and contemporary music in the beginning of July. (Info ☎ 02 47 98 11 15. Tickets €15-30, some concerts free.) Since 1994, **Festival Rock** has hosted rock, punk, and metal bands during the last weekend in June. (Info ☎ 02 47 93 10 48. All concerts free.) **Cinéma Le Rabelais,** 7bis rue J. J. Rousseau, plays French films and American blockbusters nightly. (☎ 08 92 68 47 07. Tickets €6.50.)

There is a **Shopi supermarket** at 22 pl. de l'Hôtel de Ville (open M-Sa 9am-1pm and 2:30-7pm) and an **open-air market** every Thursday and Saturday on pl. Jeanne d'Arc and every Sunday on pl. du Général de Gaulle. Stroll along **rue Voltaire** and **place de l'Hôtel de Ville** to find the best cheap meals in town. For regional cuisine, try **La Bonne France ❸,** 4 pl. de la Victoire. Tucked into a 15th-century house, this quiet spot offers tasty regional *menus* (€14). Try the trout with red Chinon sauce and roasted duck leg. (☎ 02 47 98 01 34. Appetizers €5; *menus* €9, €14, or €22. MC/V.)

To get to the **tourist office,** pl. d'Hofheim, from the station, take a left and walk beside the river along quai Jeanne d'Arc toward the *centre ville* for 20 min., then turn right at Café de la Paix (facing the Rabelais statue) to pl. de l'Hôtel de Ville. Turn right onto the little road at the back of the square. (☎ 02 47 93 17 85; fax 02 47 93 93 05. Walking tours with various themes, including Joan of Arc in Chinon. €4.70, students €2.40. Night tours available July-Aug. Tu and Sa. 9:30pm. Accommodations booking €2.50. Mini-train tour daily July-Aug. 6 times per day; Easter-June and Sept. on weekends. €4, students €3. Office open daily May-Sept. 10am-7pm; Oct.-Apr. M-Sa 10am-noon and 2-6pm.) **Bike rentals** are available at the Hôtel Agnès Sorel, 4 quai Pasteur, at the end of the quai Jeanne d'Arc. (☎ 02 47 93 04 37; www.agnes-sorel.com. €8 per half-day, €14 per day.) Amster Cycles, at 12 place Jeanne d'Arc, offers several pick-up and drop-off locations alongside the Loire River. (☎ 02 47 93 36 92; www.amstercycles.com. €13.50 per day, tandems €35.)

CHÂTEAUX NEAR TOURS

Dozens of beautiful châteaux lie within 60km of Tours; *Let's Go* covers the most popular sites, but it's worthwhile to visit the smaller châteaux. Driving is a convenient, though generally expensive way to travel. Biking between châteaux is extremely popular and beautiful, although frequent minibuses depart from Tours every day. **Valleybus** (www.touring-france.com) offers English-language excursions (from €25) of one or two châteaux, museums, and lunch. 🔳**Alienor** (06 10 85 35 39) offers similar services for €16-46, and is staffed by a very friendly English-speaking tour guide. For other tour companies, contact **Saint-Eloi Excursions** (☎ 02 47 37 08 04), **Touraine Evasion** (☎ 06 07 39 13 31), **Acco-Dispo Excursions** (☎ 02 47 57 67 13), or **Quart de Tours** (☎ 06 30 65 52 01). All tours have English-speaking guides. Most châteaux have free tours as well as performances and special events during the summer. Light shows *(son-et-lumière)* are a fun alternative to day visits. Wine cellars often offer free *dégustations*. Vouvray's 30 cellars, 9km east of Tours on the N152, specialize in sweet white wine. (☎ 02 47 52 75 03. Open daily 9am-noon and 2-7pm.) By bus, take #61 from pl. Jean Jaurès to les Patis. (20min., M-Sa 14 per day, €3.) In Montlouis, across the river to the south, 10 caves pour wonderful dry whites. Trains run from Tours. (20min., M-Sa 3 per day, €2.40.)

CHENONCEAU

Trains run to Chenonceau from Tours (30min., 8 per day 9am-9pm, €5.10). The station is right in front of the château. Fil Vert buses leave for Chenonceau from Amboise (20min., 2 per day, round-trip €1.05) and Tours (1¼hr., 2 per day, €2.10). Château: ☎02 47 23 90 07. Open daily mid-Mar. to mid-Sept. 9am-7pm. Call for low-season hours. €10 for audio visit in 12 languages with your own i-pod. July-Aug. light show at 10pm. €8, students €6.50. Entry to Château des Dames wax museum €1.50 extra.

Perhaps the most elegant château in France, Chenonceau arches gracefully over the Cher River. Take the less-traveled pedestrian walk for a view of the 16th-century farm, the flower garden, and a small pond protected by a black swan.

The *château des dames* (castle of the ladies) owes its beauty to centuries of female designers. True to contemporary tastes, royal tax collector Thomas Bohier originally commissioned the Venetian-inspired château. While he fought in the Italian Wars (1513-21), his wife Catherine oversaw its practical design, which features Italian staircases and four rooms branching from a central chamber. In 1547, Henri II gave the château to his mistress, Diane de Poitiers, who added symmetrical gardens and constructed an arched bridge over the Cher so she could hunt in the nearby forest. Later, Henri's widow, Catherine de Médici, forced Diane to give up the castle. She designed her own gardens and the spectacular two-story gallery atop the bridge built by Diane as a way to assert her domination over the king's mistress. Perhaps the most amazing part of the castle, the 60m long gallery, is lit by 18 windows (9 on each side) overlooking the Cher. The *cabinet d'estampes*, filled with drawings of Chenonceau's history, is well worth exploring. Chenonceau's kitchens are stocked with all the trappings of a 15th-century kitchen. **La Cave Cellar,** on the château grounds, offers wine tastings for €1.50 (open 10:30am-7pm).

LOCHES

Trains and buses travel from Tours's train station to Loches (50min., 13 per day, €7). The tourist office is in a pavilion near the station on pl. de la Marne. ☎02 47 91 82 82; logisroy-alloches@cg37.fr. Open daily Apr.-Sept. 9am-7pm; Jan.-Mar. and Oct.-Dec. 9:30am-5pm. Hours change frequently; check in advance. Château: ☎02 47 59 01 32; fax 02 47 59 17 45. Open daily Apr.-Sept. 9am-7pm; Oct.-Mar. 9:30am-5pm. Donjon or Royal Lodge €5, students €3.50; both sights €7, students €4.50. Light show mid-July to mid-Aug. W and F-Sa at 10 or 10:30pm; call for specific dates and times. €11, ages 6-12 €6.

Originally built around 1250 on the site of a 4th-century fortress, as a solitary tower on a cliff, Loches's walled fortifications frame the town with an extravagant royal residence at one end and an 11th-century Romanesque Tower at the other. Anne de Bretagne made further additions to the medieval fortress, including a stone chapel in Flamboyant Gothic style, around 1500. Louis XI converted the 11th-century keep and watchtowers to the north into a state prison. The "Louis XI" Cage, an intricate, solitary confinement cell, once held da Vinci's protector, Ludovico Sforza, who decorated the walls with frescoes that are still clear today. Additional curiosities include a torture chamber, underground galleries, and a replica of the suspension cages used to hold revolutionary prisoners. Take the spiral staircase all the way up to the gun tower, and enjoy a panoramic view of the medieval village and its surroundings. The **Logis Royal,** or Royal Lodge, pays tribute to the famous ladies who once held court here. In the early Renaissance mansion, Agnès Sorel, lover of Charles VII, became the first woman to hold the official title of Mistress of the King of France; she was entombed here following her early death at age 28. In the state room, Joan of Arc, on the heels of her 1429 victory over the

LOIRE VALLEY

English at Orléans, told the indifferent Dauphin that she had cleared the way for him to travel to Reims to be crowned king. A beautiful triptych on canvas (1485) decorates Anne de Bretagne's room. The **Collegiate Saint-Ours**, a wonderfully preserved 10th-century church, can be visited on the way back to the train station. City tours are available in French or English by reservation (€5.60). In the summer, there is the **Loches-en-Jazz** music festival (check info with tourist office).

■ VILLANDRY

Trains leave from the station in Tours to Savonnières (10 min., 3 per day, €2.60). Many tour agencies run a bus to Villandry and Ussé (see p. 172 for info). From Tours, cyclists can travel 15km west along D16, a narrow road that winds past Villandry to Ussé; drivers should take D7. Château: ☎02 47 50 02 09. Open daily July-Aug. 9am-6pm; mid-Feb. to June and Sept. to mid-Nov. 9:30am-5pm. Gardens open daily May-Sept. 9am-7:30pm; Oct.-Apr. 9am-7pm. Château and gardens €7.50, students €5. Gardens only €5, students €4. Free tours are available in French. The tourist office, across D7 from the château, has maps and train schedules. ☎02 47 50 12 66. Open daily 9:30am-12:30pm and 2-6pm.

Villandry lives up to its claim of being *"le plus beau des jardins du jardin de la France"* (the most beautiful gardens in France). With 125,000 flowers and 85,000 vegetables all weeded by hand, it is among the largest. Built on the banks of the Cher by Jean le Breton, minister to François I, the château was purchased in 1906 by Dr. Joachim Carvallo, great-grandfather to the present owner. He renovated the decaying structure and reconstructed the gardens, which had been redone in the English style. Today, the formal French gardens are Villandry's main attraction; their symmetry and intricately planned color design make them incredibly beautiful, especially when viewed from above. The middle terrace level is the most artistic. In the "gardens of love," above the kitchen garden, each of the four squares of flowers is an allegory for a different type of love: tender, passionate, fickle, and tragic. The upper level is lined with lime groves, swan pools, and waterfalls, which provide irrigation for the rest of the garden. Inside the château, the medieval Moorish ceiling is tiled with 3000 gold-leafed wooden pieces. If you can't afford the extra buck for the castle, enjoy an overall view from the belvedere above.

USSÉ

Ussé is easily reached by château minibus tour. Service Touristique runs buses from the Tours train station to the château for €18 (☎02 47 05 46 09). Château: ☎02 47 95 54 05. Open daily Apr.-Sept. 9am-6:30pm; Oct.-Nov. 15 and Feb. 15-Mar. 1 daily 10am-noon and 2-5:30pm. Tours 1½hr. Adults €10, ages 8-16 €3.

Though no king ever laid his head on the fancy four-poster bed of Ussé's *chambre du roi*, its fairy-tale spires inspired one 17th-century visitor: Charles Perrault, who penned the tale of Sleeping Beauty during his stay here in 1697. The mansion, located by the Indres river, is now billed as the *"château de la belle au bois dormant"* (Sleeping Beauty's Castle), complete with costumed mannequins that illustrate the story's unfolding—watch out for the Beauty's fancy lace underwear. The rest of the 15th- to 16th-century château can be seen during a 50min. English tour. While waiting, explore Le Nôtre's fabulous gardens, the follow-up to his work at Versailles. You can also check out the Gothic chapel, wine caves, and stables. A small door leads from the moat to the prison, a single tiny room deep within the walls; graffiti scratched by former prisoners looks suspiciously well-preserved. Ussé remains the property of the Count of Blacas, whose numerous descendants occupy a large portion of the château.

AZAY-LE-RIDEAU

Trains run from Tours to the town of Azay-le-Rideau (25min., 8 per day 5:30am-7:28pm, €4.40). Turn right from the station and head left on D57. Buses run from Tours train station to the tourist office (45min., daily 3 per day 6:40am-5:50pm, pay on bus). Château: ☎02 47

*45 42 04. Open daily July-Aug. 9:30am-7pm; Apr.-June and Sept.-Oct. 9:30am-6pm; Nov.-
Mar. 9:30am-12:30pm and 2-5:30pm. Last entrance 45min. before closing. Light show daily
July 10:30pm, Aug. 10pm; May-June F-Sa 10:30pm, Sept. 9:30pm. €9, with daytime visit
€12, 18-25 €7, under age 18 €5. €6.10, ages 18-25 €4.10, under 18 free. The tourist office
is at 4 rue du château. ☎02 47 45 44 40; www.ot-paysazaylerideau.fr. Open May-June and
Sept., M-Sa 9am-1pm and 2-6pm, Su 10am-1pm and 2-5pm; Oct.-Mar. M-Sa 9am-1pm and
2-6pm; July-Aug. M-Sa 9am-7pm, Su 10am-6pm. Picturesque* **Camping Parc de Sabot** ❶ *is
across from the château. (☎02 47 45 42 72. Open Easter-Oct. Showers available. €9.60 for
2 people with a tent, €3 each additional person, children €1.30. Electricity €2.)*

Surrounded by acres of breeze-ruffled trees and grass atop an island in the Indre,
the flamboyant château at Azay-le-Rideau stands on the ruins of an earlier fortress.
The village acquired the nickname "Azay-le-Brûlé" (Azay the Burned) in 1418 after
Charles VII razed the village in revenge against a Burgundian guard who had
refused to let him in. Today it still contains some houses that date back to the 15th
century. The corrupt financier Gilles Berthelot bought the land just before the battle of Marignan in 1515, and he set about designing a new castle three years later.
Though smaller than François I's Chambord, the château was intended to rival its
contemporary in beauty; the Berthelots succeeded so thoroughly that François
seized the château before its third wing was completed. Before entering the château, take a stroll in the park and listen to Renaissance music. The salamanders
without crowns on the exterior walls mark the castle as a non-royal residence
built under François. Azay's flamboyant style is apparent in the furniture and the
ornate Italian second-floor staircase, the latter carved with the faces of 10 Valois
kings and queens, lit by open, glassless windows. Portraits of the royal family and
other members of the 16th- and 17th-century French aristocracy adorn the walls.
The Gothic influence appears in the *grande salle* (grand drawing room), where
the walls and tapestries from the 1500s are remarkably preserved.

SAUMUR

Saumur (pop. 30,000) is best known for its wine, dark mushroom caves, and long
equestrian tradition. For the past two centuries, the city's commerce has been shaped
by an abundance of *tuffeau*, the stone used to build the châteaux of the Loire. The
huge caves left by the mined stone have created a prime environment for mushroom
farms; Saumur supplies at least 80% of all French *champignons de Paris* (button
mushrooms). The region's clay-like soil also puts the wines of Saumur in high demand.

⌐ TRANSPORTATION

The **train station** is 10min. from pl. Bilange, on av. David d'Angers. To get there by
bus, take bus A from pl. Bilange (dir: St-Lambert or Chemin Vert). The ticket office
is open daily until 7:30pm. **SNCF trains** and **buses** run to Angers (30min., 15 per
day, €6.80); Nantes (1hr., 9 per day, €16.60); Paris (1½hr., 12 per day, €40-50);
Poitiers (2½hr., 8 per day, €15.80); and Tours (45min., 21 per day, €9). **Autocars
Val de Loire** and **Anjou Bus**, pl. St-Nicolas (☎02 41 40 25 00 or 02 41 81 49 49), run
from pl. St-Nicolas or from the parking lot next to the train station to Angers
(1½hr., 6 per day, €5.50) and Fontrevaud (30min., 3 per day, €2.30). Local Bus
Saumur, 19 rue F. Roosevelt, run Monday to Saturday 7am-7:30pm. (☎02 41 51 11
87. Office open M 2-6pm, Tu-F 9am-12:15pm and 2-6pm, Sa 9am-noon. Tickets
€1.20.) **Car rental** is available at Europcar, 40 av. du Général de Gaulle (☎02 41 67
30 89; open M-F 8am-noon and 2-6pm, Sa 8am-noon), and Hertz, 80 av. du
Général de Gaulle (☎02 41 67 20 06; open M-F 8am-noon and 2-6:30pm, Sa 8am-
noon and 2-5:30pm). Find **bike rentals** at Amster Cycles, 25 rue Paul Bert. (02 41
53 01 01; www.amstercycles.com. €13.50 per day, tandems €35.)

✈ 🛈 ORIENTATION AND PRACTICAL INFORMATION

Many of the sights are outside of the center of town, best accessed either by bus or bike. At the **tourist office,** pl. de la Bilange, on the left bank of the Loire, multilingual staff book accommodations for €0.75, as well as boat tours on the Loire. (☎02 41 40 20 60; fax 02 41 40 20 69. Open mid-May to Sept. M-Sa 9:15am-7pm, Su 10:30am-5:30pm; Oct. to mid-May M-Sa 9:15am-12:30pm and 2-6pm, Su 10am-noon.) **Laundromats** are located at 12 rue du Maréchal Leclerc (open daily 7am-9:30pm) and 16 rue Beaurepaire (open daily 7:30am-9:30pm, summer until 10pm). The **police** are at 415 rue du Chemin Vert (☎02 41 83 24 00), and the **Centre Hospitalier** (☎02 41 53 30 30) is on rue de Fontevraud. **Internet** access is available at Online Station, 70 quai Maynaud. (€2 per hr. Open M-Sa 11am-11pm, Su 2-10pm.) The **post office,** pl. Dupetit Thouars, also offers **currency exchange.** (☎02 41 40 22 08. Open 8am-6:30pm, Sa 8am-noon.) **Postal Code:** 49400.

🏠 🏕 ACCOMMODATIONS AND CAMPING

Find rustic charm at 🏠**Le Volney** ❸, 1 rue Volney, the best deal in town. Cheerful owners let comfortable rooms within walking distance of the *centre ville.* (☎02 41 51 25 41; www.levolney.com. Breakfast €5.50. Singles and doubles with TV, telephone, and toilet €28, with shower €36-48 Sept-June. 10% off breakfast with *Let's Go* guide. AmEx/MC/V.) **Hôtel de la Bascule** ❹, 1 pl. Kléber, near Église St-Nicolas on quai Carnot, offers sunny bedrooms with spotless bathrooms, TV, and showers; some have excellent river views. (☎02 41 50 13 65. Breakfast €6. Singles and doubles €38-42; 1 large room for 2-4 people €40. Extra bed €7. MC/V.) At the **Centre International de Séjour** ❶, rue de Verden, on Île d'Offard between train station and tourist office, helpful staff provide small but adequate rooms for a young crowd. (☎02 41 40 30 00; www.cvtloisirs.com. Ask reception for free tickets to Gratien and Meyer and many other caves. Breakfast included. Reception daily July-Aug. 8am-9pm; Sept. and June 8:30am-12:30pm and 2-6pm; Mar.-May and Oct. 9am-noon and 2-7pm. Closed mid-Nov. to Feb. Reservations recommended. 2- to 8-bed dorms €14.50; 2- to 4-bed dorms with shower €22 for first person, €9 each additional person. 10% off for stays over 5 nights. MC/V.) Standing at the tip of the Île d'Offard, four-star 🏕**Camping de l'Île d'Offard** ❶ offers an unbeatable view of the Loire, as well as pool, laundry, tennis, a snack shop, minigolf, and TV. (☎02 41 40 30 00; www.cvtloisirs.com. Lunch and dinner €4-7. Ask reception for free tickets to Gratien and Meyer and many other caves. Reception daily July-Aug. 8am-9pm; Sept. and June 8:30am-12:30pm and 2-6pm; Mar.-May and Oct. 9am-noon and 2-7pm. June-Aug. 2 people with car €14.50, €4 for each additional person, €2 per child. Tent rental €32 per day. Electricity €3. MC/V.)

🍴 FOOD

Saumur is renowned for its sparkling *crémant de Loire* wine and, of course, its mushrooms. Stock up at the indoor **market** in **Les Halles** at the far end of pl. St-Pierre (Tu-F 8am-12:30pm and 3-7:30pm, Sa 7am-1pm and 3-7:30pm, Su 9am-12:30pm), or try its outdoor equivalents on av. du Général de Gaulle (Th morning) and pl. St-Pierre (Sa morning). The **ATAC supermarket,** 6 rue Roosevelt, sits inside the shopping center across from the Printemps department store with a back entrance on rue St-Nicolas. (☎02 41 83 54 54. Open M-F 9am-1pm and 2:15-7:30pm, Sa 9am-7:30pm, Su 9am-12:30pm.) An assortment of cheap restaurants are sprinkled along rue St-Nicolas. Enjoy delicious regional cuisine in the intimate dining room of 🍴**Le Pullman** ❸, 52 rue d'Orléans, charmingly deco-

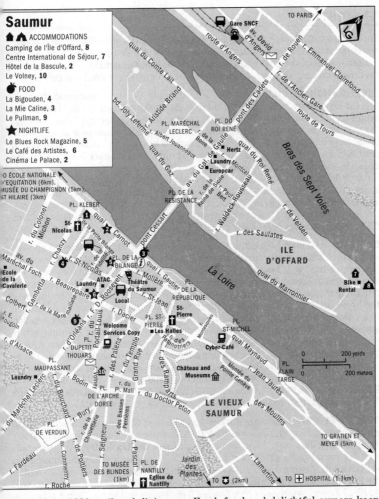

Saumur

🏠 🏠 ACCOMMODATIONS
Camping de l'Île d'Offard, **8**
Centre International de Séjour, **7**
Hôtel de la Bascule, **2**
Le Volney, **10**

🍴 FOOD
La Bigouden, **4**
La Mie Caline, **3**
Le Pullman, **9**

⭐ NIGHTLIFE
Le Blues Rock Magazine, **5**
Le Café des Artistes, **6**
Cinéma Le Palace, **2**

rated like a 1920s railroad dining car. Fresh food and delightful owners keep customers coming back for another ride. (☎ 02 41 51 31 79. *Plats* €11-15, *menus* €12.50 and €25. Garden dining available in summer. Open M and Th-Su. MC/V.) At **La Bigouden ❷**, 67 rue St-Nicolas, you can savor sweet crêpes with romantic names like *Belle Angèle* (Beautiful Angel; sautéed apples, corinthian grapes, and honey) or *Nid de Coucou* (Cuckoo's Nest, whipped cream, maple syrup, walnuts). Over 35 lunch crêpes (€5-9) and a large selection of salads (€5.50-8.50) make this place a great lunch option. (☎ 02 41 67 12 59. Open daily July-Aug. noon-2pm; Sept.-June M and Th-Su noon-2pm.) Grab a sandwich, dessert, and drink combo for a mere €3 at the centrally located **La Mie Caline ❶**, 25 pl. de Bilange. A light breakfast is available for €1. (☎ 02 41 50 98 66. Open daily 5am-8pm. MC/V.) **Place St-Pierre** and its offshoots have several great options for light food and drinks.

⊙ SIGHTS

Three 12th- to 15th-century churches brighten Saumur's main district, and a very pretty **Jardin des Plantes** is tucked between rue Docteur Peton and rue Marceau, on the other side of the château. The picturesque **Pont Cessart** has a fantastic view over the Loire, and the promenades along the river make for lovely sunset strolls.

ÉCOLE NATIONALE D'EQUITATION. In 1763, Louis XV chose Saumur as the location for his cavalry training camp, thereby establishing this town as France's top center for horsemanship. The town has continued the spectacular Cadre Noir tradition in this civilian national riding school, whose students compete at an international level and often go on to train equestrians around the country. The palatial premises, located 15min. from the center of town, contain over 50km of training grounds, 400 fine purebreds, and the world's best veterinarians. Tours pass through the facilities and explain the rigorous demands of equestrianism; morning visits, your visit will include a 30min. viewing of daily training. (☎02 41 53 50 60; www.cadrenoir.fr. Take bus B (dir: St Hilaire) to Alouette, and then follow signs. No sidewalk; exercise caution. Visitors only allowed on grounds by tour. Tours Apr.-Sept. Tu-F 9:30-11am and 2pm. €5-7, children €3-4. View daily training routines €12 and shows throughout the year. Call for info.)

CHÂTEAU. Saumur's 14th-century château is best known for its cameo appearance in the famous medieval manuscript *Les très riches heures du duc de Berry.* For two centuries, it housed a prestigious Huguenot academy before being pillaged and abandoned. It was eventually converted into a prison by Napoleon. The intriguing **Musée du Cheval** celebrates everything equine, tracing the evolution of the horse and displaying a vast collection of international riding gear. Guided tours, available in French or English, lead visitors through the **Musée des Arts Décorations,** where there are exhibits on medieval and Renaissance painting, sculpture, and tapestries, and brightly decorated *faïence* (pottery). The south wing of the château, now closed, is undergoing a major restoration that is expected to be completed in 2007; a double spiral staircase, a rare architectural structure for its time, has been discovered during the process. (☎02 41 40 24 40. Open daily June-Aug. 9:30am-6pm; July and Aug. W and Sa also 8:30-10:30pm; Apr.-May and Sept. 10am-1pm and 2-5:30pm. 40min. English and German tours. €6, students €4, gardens only €2.)

GRATIEN ET MEYER. Saumur's wines have been in high demand since the 12th century, when Plantagenêt kings took their favorite casks with them to England. Many wine cellars offer tours and tastings. **Caves Gratien & Meyer,** an especially well-known vineyard, offers 30min. tours (€2.50) of their cellars and museum as well as a wine-tasting session of award-winning vintages. Over four million bottles are kept in a maze of galleries dating from the Middle Ages. (Rte. de Montsoreau. ☎02 41 83 13 32; www.gratienmeyer.com. Take bus D (dir: Dampierres) from pl. Bilange to Beaulieu. Open daily Apr.-Nov. 9am-6:30pm; mid-Nov. to Mar. M-F 10am-noon and 2-5:30pm, Sa-Su 10am-noon and 3-4:30pm (Jan.-Feb. only). Groups of 10 or more may also reserve a visit.)

MUSÉE DU CHAMPIGNON. In dark caves carved out of *tuffeau* stone, this museum explores the massive mushroom industry of the Saumur region. A variety of mushroom species grow in its dank interior, from classic white-button mushrooms (*champignon de Paris*) to velvet shank, filling the air with rich aromas. In October, the mushroom festival takes place on the grounds of the museum. The rest of the caves are an actual production site, and tours trace their history in France. The grill outside serves gourmet hors d'œuvres (€4.60-7.10) noon-3pm. Take an extra layer, as the caves are fairly cold. (Rte. de Gennes, Ste-Hilaire-St-Florent. ☎02 41 50 31 55; www.musee-du-champignon.com. Take bus B (dir: Ste-Hilaire) to Pompiers. Follow signs for 2km to museum. Open daily Feb. to mid-Nov. 10am-7pm. €7, students €5.50.)

MUSÉE DES BLINDES. Commonly known as "the tank museum," this interesting collection of over 800 tanks follows the evolution of warfare in the 20th century. Keep an eye out for the camouflaged Tiger I, a monstrous German cruiser, and the Leclerc, France's first tank. Another exhibit shows the role of tanks during the two World Wars. *(1043 rte. de Fontevraud. ☎02 41 83 69 99; www.musee-des-blindes.asso.fr. Take bus C (dir: Chemin Vert) to Fricotelle; walk 1km down rue du Tunnel. 90min group visits. Open daily May-Sept. 9:30am-6:30pm; Oct.-Apr. 10am-5pm. €5.50, children €3.)*

♫ ❀ ENTERTAINMENT AND FESTIVALS

The **Théâtre de Saumur** (☎02 41 83 30 83), next to the tourist office, hosts everything from *galas de danse* to jazz concerts in its 19th-century hall. (Schedules are irregular, check with the tourist office.) Dance the night away to live music at the small but friendly ⬛**Le Blues Rock Magazine,** 7 rue de la Petite Bilange. Since 1994, the club throws themed evenings which draw energetic young crowds. (☎02 41 50 41 69. Drinks €3-6. Open daily May-Sept. 11pm-4am; Oct.-Apr. Tu-Sa 11pm-4am. MC/V.) Shoot some darts at **Le Café des Artistes,** 4 rue Beaurepaire, a large bar in the *centre ville.* The exotic "beer cocktails" (€3-4), including the *Singapour* (Malibu, cherry, pineapple, and, of course, beer), are worth a try. (☎02 41 51 21 72. M and Sa 10:30am-2am, Tu-F 8:30am-2am. MC/V.) Late-night crowds gather in pl. St-Pierre beside the illuminated cathedral and in the **Irish pubs** at pl. de la République. Saumur residents line up around the block to catch the latest flic at **Cinéma Le Palace,** 13 quai Carnot. (☎08 92 68 00 73. Tickets €7.20, afternoons €5.80.)

During the first week of July, the three-day **Estivales de Saumur** brings vendors, outdoor dining, music, and free food to rue St-Nicolas around a specific theme. In past years, the festival has featured themes like "South America" and "Asia." In the third week of September, the Cadre Noir show off their horsemanship with competitions and shows at **La Grande Semaine de Saumur.** The **International Festival of Military Music** occurs in late June every other year; the next one occurs in 2005. Alternating years, also in late June, bring the **Festival des Géants,** a march of oversized puppets. In late July, the **Carousel** draws large crowds. After 2hr. of equestrian performances, the elite Cadre Noir enter the stage for a demonstration of equestrian *dressage.* The spectacle no longer includes the motorcycle show or tank parade that made it popular in the past. (Info and reservations ☎02 41 40 20 66. Tickets €26-32.) Saumur also hosts dozens of free equestrian events annually.

▶ DAYTRIP FROM SAUMUR

FONTEVRAUD-L'ABBAYE

The #16 bus makes the 14km trip from the Saumur train station. (25min., 3-5 per day, €2.20.) The tourist office dispenses free maps of the town. (☎02 41 51 79 45. Open Easter-Sept. M-Sa 9:30am-12:30pm and 2-6:30pm. Tours of Fontevraud July-Aug. F at 3pm, €4.) One stop before Fontevraud, in Montsoreau, are curious troglodyte cliff dwellings and a château. Call the tourist office in Montsoreau (☎02 41 51 70 22) for info.

The ⬛**Abbaye de Fontevraud,** the largest monastic complex in Europe, has awed visitors for nine centuries. The founder of this now-defunct community, Robert d'Arbrissel, settled in the forest of Fontevraud in 1101. To increase the humility of his monks, he placed a woman at the head of the order. Of its 32 abbesses, about half were of royal blood; under their rule, the abbey became a place of refuge for women of all classes—from prostitutes to princesses escaping unhappy marriages. Following the Revolution, the abbey became a prison, and remained so from 1804 until 1963. The 12th-century church also serves as a Plantagenêt necropolis; Eleanor of Aquitaine, who lived out her days here after being repudiated by her second husband, Henry II, now lies next to him alongside their son Richard the Lionheart. The abbey's chapter house is painted with scenes depicting Christ's last hours. Over time, part of the fresco's chronology has been disrupted by intruding nuns, as seven abbesses have had themselves added to the wall paintings, depicting themselves as witnesses to the trials of Jesus. Don't miss the 12th-century Romanesque kitchens and the ceiling model's fascinating architecture. An English booklet and signs help visitors along, but 1hr. tours give the best sense of the abbey's history. Themed visits put a different spin on life in the abbey, but are only available in French. (☎02 41 51 71 41; www.abbaye-fontevraud.com. Abbey open daily June-Sept. 9am-6:30pm, Oct.-May 10am-5:30pm. €6.10, €4.10 students (prices slightly higher in peak season). Themed tours free with price of admission. Theatrical tours of the abbey nightly in Aug. at 9:30pm.)

ANGERS

■**Angers** (pop. 151,000) is a modern, sophisticated city with illustrious royal roots. From behind the imposing walls of their fortress, the medieval dukes of Anjou ruled over the surrounding territory and a smallish island across the Channel called Britain. Angers's 13th-century château and cathedral and its world-famous apocalyptic tapestry are majestic reminders of the city's past. Today, the town bustles with shops, museums, and excellent restaurants.

▐ TRANSPORTATION

Trains run from rue de la Gare to Le Mans (40-50 min., about 15 per day, €12.80); Nantes (1hr., about 15 per day, €13.50); Orléans (3-4hr., 8 per day, €24.60), change at St-Pierre des Corps; Paris (1-2hr., 15 per day, €42.20-53.80); Poitiers (2-2½hr., 6 per day, €25.10), change at St-Pierre or Tours; and Tours (1hr., 10 per day, €14). The info desk is open Monday through Saturday 7:30am-9pm and Sunday 7:30am-10pm. **Buses** (☎02 41 88 59 25) leave from pl. de la République for Rennes (3hr., 2 per day, €15.90) and Saumur (1½hr., 4 per day, €7.60). Check the ticket office (open M-Sa 6:30am-7pm). COTRA buses provide local service from pl. Kennedy or pl. Ralliement 6am-8pm. (☎02 41 33 64 64. Tickets €1.10.) **Angers Taxi-Anjou Taxi** (☎02 41 85 65 00) is available 24hr. To rent **cars,** head to Avis (☎02 41 88 20 24; open M-F 7:30am-7pm, Sa 8am-noon and 2-6pm), Europcar (☎02 41 87 87 10; open M-F 7:30am-7pm, Sa 8am-noon and 2-6pm), or Hertz (☎02 41 88 15 16; open M-F 8am-noon and 2-7pm, Sa 8am-noon and 2-6pm), all in the train station. **Bike rentals** are at the tourist office (€8 per half-day, €11 per day).

▐▐ ORIENTATION AND PRACTICAL INFORMATION

Most of the restaurants and nightlife in Angers are in the pedestrian-only streets radiating outward from pl. du Ralliement. To reach the château (when coming from the train station), walk straight onto rue de la Gare, then turn right at pl. de la Visitation, onto rue Targot. At the traffic light, turn left onto bd. du Roi-René. The **tourist office** at pl. Kennedy organizes trips to châteaux, reserves rooms (€2), **exchanges currency** (€4), and provides free maps. (☎02 41 23 50 00; www.angers-tourisme.com. Open May-Sept. M-Sa 9am-7pm, Su 10am-6pm; Oct.-Apr. M 2-6pm, Tu-Sa 9am-6pm, Su 10am-1pm.) The **Centre d'Information Jeunesse,** 5 allée du Haras, offers info on employment, lodging, and discounts. (☎02 41 87 74 47. Open M-F 1-3:30pm, Sa 10am-noon.) A **FNAC** is located at 23 rue Lenepveu. (Open M-Sa 10am-7pm. MC/V.) **Laundromats** are at pl. de la Visitation

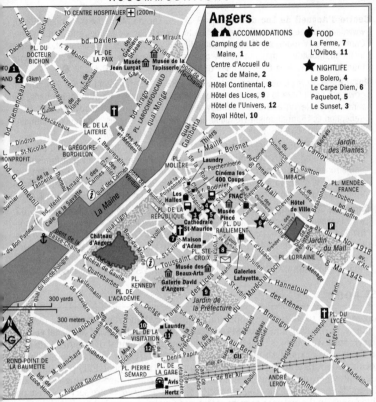

Angers

🏠🏠 ACCOMMODATIONS

Camping du Lac de Maine, **1**
Centre d'Accueil du Lac de Maine, **2**
Hôtel Continental, **8**
Hôtel des Lices, **9**
Hôtel de l'Univers, **12**
Royal Hôtel **10**

🍴 FOOD

La Ferme, **7**
L'Ovibos, **11**

⭐ NIGHTLIFE

Le Bolero, **4**
Le Carpe Diem, **6**
Paquebot, **5**
Le Sunset, **3**

(☎02 41 86 11 20; open M-Th 7:30-11:30am and 2:30-7pm) and 15 rue Plantagenêt. (Open daily 8am-9pm.) The **gendarmerie** are at 33 rue Nid de Pie (☎02 41 22 94 00), and the **Centre Hospitalier** is at 4 rue Larrey (☎02 41 35 36 37). Access **Internet** at Cyber Espace, 25 Rue de la Roë. (☎02 41 24 92 71. €1 per 15min. €3 per hr. Open M-Th 9am-10pm, F-Sa 9am-midnight, Su 2-8pm.) The **post office**, 1 rue Roosevelt, just off Corneille near rue Voltaire, also provides currency exchange. (☎02 41 20 81 81. Open M-F 9am-6:30pm, Sa 9am-12:30pm.) **Postal Code:** 49100.

🏠🏨 ACCOMMODATIONS AND CAMPING

Hôtel Continental, 12 rue Louis de Romain (☎02 41 86 94 94; www.hotellecontinental.com). Right in the center of town, on pl. du Ralliement. The 25 newly renovated rooms include double beds, cable, phone, Internet (modem provided, €6 per day), and sleek furnishings. Buffet breakfast €6.50. Singles and doubles with toilet and shower or bath €42-56; triples €64; quads €72. Extra bed €8. AmEx/DC/MC/V. ❹

Hôtel de l'Univers, 2 pl. de la Gare (☎02 41 88 43 58; www.citotel.com/hotels/univ_fr). 5-10min. from downtown. Kind staff welcomes visitors to 45 rooms that are slightly bare but have comfortable beds, telephones, and cable TV. Internet. Breakfast €5.80. Dinner served in room €9. Hall shower €4. Singles and doubles with sink €26, with shower €35, with toilet and shower €47-52; quads €63. MC/V.❸

Centre d'Accueil du Lac de Maine, 49 av. du Lac de Maine (☎02 41 22 32 10; www.lacdemaine.fr). Take bus #6 or 16 to Accueil Lac de Maine, and follow signs. Comfortable TV room, bar, billiards, pinball, and video games. Free Internet. Breakfast included. Individuals may not reserve a room over 3 weeks in advance or stay for more than 10 days. Singles €29; doubles €38; quads €64. AmEx/DC/MC/V. ❸

Royal Hôtel, 8bis pl. de la Visitation (☎02 41 88 30 25; fax 02 41 81 05 75), straight down rue de la Gare to the corner of rue d'Iena. Spacious rooms with double beds, big windows, cable TV, and clean hallway showers. Free Internet in lobby. Breakfast €5. Reception 6:45am-midnight (reduced hr. on weekend). Singles and doubles with sink €28, with bath €38-46; triples €52; quads €60. AmEx/DC/MC/V. ❸

Hôtel des Lices, 25 rue des Lices (☎/fax 02 41 87 44 10), near the château and center. 2 charming sisters keep bright rooms with double beds and elegant furnishings. Some rooms overlook the castle or the beautiful *jardin de la Préfecture.* Don't fret over the name—it refers to jousting. Breakfast €4.30. Reception M-F 7am-9pm, Sa-Su 5-9pm. Singles and doubles with bath €34; triples and quads with shower €44. V. ❸

Camping: ☒**Camping du Lac de Maine** (☎02 41 73 05 03; www.lacdemaine.fr), near the Centre d'Accueil, rte. des Pruniers. Take bus #6 to Camping du Lac de Maine. 4-star campsite with unparalleled facilities. Mobile-home and bungalow rentals from €149 a week. (€299 July-Aug.) Open late Mar. to mid-Oct. Reception 8am-7pm in high season. 2 people with tent and car €14, low season €10. Additional person €2 (€1.30 for children). Electricity €3. Free hot showers. MC/V. ❶

◖ FOOD

Angers caters to its student population with everything from crêpes and pizza to Chinese, particularly along **rue St-Laud, rue St-Aubin,** and **boulevard Maréchal Foch.** A **grocery store** with an excellent bakery resides in the basement of Galeries Lafayette on the corner of rue d'Alsace and pl. du Ralliement. (Open M-Sa 9:30am-7:30pm.) Locals and tourists alike pack into ☒**La Ferme ❸,** 2 pl. Freppel. Fill up on delicious regional wines, meats, and cheeses in this family-run, award-winning restaurant. Classic French dishes, like *coq au vin* or *magret de canard,* are served at reasonable prices. In the summer months, enjoy a view of the cathedral from the pleasant terrace. (☎02 41 87 09 90. Wine by the glass €2, appetizers €7, *plats* €9-12, dinner *menus* €15 to €30. Reservations recommended on weekends. Open M-Tu noon-2pm and 7-10pm, Th-Sa noon-2pm and 7-10pm, Su noon-2pm. AmEx/MC/V.) **L'Ovibos ❸,** 3 rue d'Anjou, grills up a variety of steaks and meats that complement their many salads. Salads and *menus* are named after US locales, so pick a region and dig in. The *formule Miami* (€9), which includes an entree plus an appetizer or a dessert, is a deal. (☎02 41 87 48 90. Open daily noon-2pm and 7-11pm. Salads €5-7, meat dishes €8-13, *menus* €9-15. MC/V.)

◉ SIGHTS

The city pass, which includes admission to over 10 sites and some guided visits, is available from the tourist office (€14 for a one-day pass, €21 for two days, €26 for three days). Angers is famous for its exquisite tapestries, which hang in many of the city's main sights. The town is situated near several beautiful parks, including the **Jardin du Mail,** a landscaped garden with terrific promenades, and the **Jardin des Plantes,** a beautiful, botanical wonder with provocative sculptures and a large, tranquil pond. (Jardin des Plantes open daily until 8:30pm.)

CHÂTEAU D'ANGERS. Angers's château can best be described as two castles in one. Bristling with 17 towers and protected by a 900m long, 15m high wall, the medieval fortress, erected over Gallo-Roman ruins in the 13th century, does its job well. Behind the thick wall lies a more pleasant residence: the palace of the Duke d'Anjou. The Renaissance mansion, in Flamboyant Gothic style, stands inside a beautiful inner courtyard, also built in the 14th and 15th centuries. During the Wars of Religion, Henri III ordered the château's demolition; fortunately, his subjects only managed to lower the towers by one story. Today it is a well-preserved monument, where enjoyable promenades in a French-syle garden have replaced a more utilitarian moat. Climb atop the field gate terrace for a view of the entire castle and the city of Angers below. Among the furnishings in the interior, the most notable is the ■**Tapisserie de l'Apocalypse.** Commissioned by Louis I and completed in 1382 its 74 scenes depict the life of Saint John in his battle against evil, subtly weaving in references to the war between France (conveniently represented by John) and Britain (appearing as—who else?—the evil aggressor). *(2 promenade du Bout du Monde, on pl. Kennedy. ☎02 41 86 81 94. Open daily May-Aug. 9:30am-6:30pm; Sept.-Apr. 10am-5:30pm. Last entrance 45min. prior to closing. French tours leave from the chapel 5 times daily, English tours daily 1-3 times daily. €6.10, students €4.10, under 18 free.)*

■ **MUSÉE JEAN LURÇAT.** While France's oldest hospital (12th-century) once stood on its grounds, the Musée Lurçat is now home to Angers's second woven masterpiece. The 80m long **Chant du Monde** (Song of the World), is a symbolic journey through human destiny inspired by the Apocalypse Tapestry. The nearby **Musée de la Tapisserie Contemporaire** has a permanent collection of textiles and tapestry. Jean Lurçat and Grau-Garriga are given special attention, but many other cloth sculptors have their works on display. The monographic tapestries, including Thomas Gleb's *Spark of Life*, should not be missed. *(4 bd. Arago. ☎02 41 24 18 45. Open daily mid-June to mid-Sept. 10am-7pm; late Sept.-early June Tu-Su 10am-noon and 2-6pm. €4 for each museum, ages 18-25 €3, under 18 free.)*

MUSÉE COINTREAU. This factory that has been making Cointreau, a liqueur native to Angers, since 1849. The testing showroom is dedicated to cocktail-making, with a barman present. Free ■**tasting** follows afterwards. *(Bd. des Bretonnières, St-Barthélemy-d'Anjou. Take bus #7, which passes by the train station to Cointreau. ☎02 41 31 50 50; www.cointreau.com. Tours Nov.-Apr. M-Sa 3pm and Su 3, 4:30pm; May-June and Sept.-Oct. M-Sa 10:30am, 3pm, Su 10:30am, 3, and 4:30pm; daily July-Aug. 10:30am, 2:30, 3:30, 4:30pm. €5.50, under 18 €2.60.)*

GALERIE DAVID D'ANGERS. This beautifully restored 11th-century Toussaint Abbey, now with a soaring glass roof, holds a vast collection of David d'Angers's 19th-century sculptures. One of the most renowned artists of his time, d'Angers produced 30 full-size figures and over 100 busts, many of which are kept in this museum. His subjects are both literary and historical characters, including the artist's personal friends Victor Hugo and Balzac, as well as Goethe and Lafayette. *(37bis rue Toussaint. ☎02 41 87 21 03. Open daily mid-June to mid-Sept. 10am-7pm; late Sept.-early June Tu-Su 10am-noon and 2-6pm. €4, students €2, under 18 free.)*

CATHÉDRALE ST-MAURICE. The 12th-century building is a hodgepodge of historical periods—a Norman porch, a 13th-century chancel intersecting a 4th-century Gallo-Roman wall, and some of the oldest stained-glass windows in France, dating back to the 12th century. The single nave of the church is classic Angevin Plantagenêt style with heavily decorated vaults. Like everything in Angers, the church is adorned with a rotating exhibit of beautiful, rare tapestries. Linger long enough and the lovely local nuns might offer a free tour. *(Pl. Chappoulie. ☎02 41 87 58 45. Open daily Apr.-Nov. 8:30am-7pm; Dec.-Mar. 8:30am-5:30pm. Mass daily 9:30am and 7pm)*

MUSÉE DE BEAUX-ARTS. The museum features 15th- to 20th-century art and displays on the history of Angers. *(14 rue du Musée. ☎02 41 05 38 00. Open daily June-Oct. 10am-7pm, F until 9pm; Oct.-June Tu-Su 1-6pm; first F of the month 1-8pm. €4, students €3.)*

OTHER SIGHTS. The **Musée Pincé,** housed in a 15th-century Renaissance mansion, displays a small, unique collection of art from ancient Japan, China, Egypt, and the Roman Empire. From Japanese engravings to miniature statues of horses, these tiny works are all impressively crafted. *(32bis rue Lenepveu. ☎02 41 88 94 27. Open Tu-Su mid-June to mid-Sept.9:30am-6:30pm; Oct.-early June 10am-noon and 2-6pm. Adults €2, under 18 €1.)* In the heart of the *vieille ville,* a few blocks from the château, **place du Ralliement** is home to numerous stores and cafes as well as a magnificent **theater,** which was rebuilt in the 19th century and decorated by local painter Lenepveu. The *vieille ville* derives its name from the 16th-century stone houses here, among which stands **La Maison d'Adam,** a timber-framed house—Angers's oldest—with wooden carvings. On its bottom floor, the **Maison des Artisans** sells hand-crafted objects from the region; the upper floors remain inhabited. *(On the corner of pl. Ste-Croix and rue Montault, just behind the cathedral.)*

🎵 🎋 ENTERTAINMENT AND FESTIVALS

The discos have been exiled to the suburbs, but cafes along **rue St-Laud** are always packed, and bars on student-dominated **rue Bressigny** get down before the sun does. **Le Carpe Diem,** 15 rue St-Maurille, a small bar in the tradition of the Parisian *cafés-philo,* schedules weekly philosophical discussions. Concerts are Fridays 7:30pm. (☎02 41 87 50 47. Open M-Sa noon-1am. Irregular hours. Concert tickets €5.) Try the local beer in the laid-back **Paquebot,** 45 rue St-Laud. **La Soute,** the hip bar/club underneath (open 9pm-2am) hosts a lively crowd of students. (☎02 41 81 06 20. Beer €2-4. Wine €2, cocktails €6. Open M-F 11:30am-2:30am, Sa 3pm-2:30am.) **Le Sunset,** 44 rue St-Laud, caters to a feisty crowd and serves Le Sun, its own tropical punch. (☎02 41 87 85 58. Beer €2-5, cocktails €5-6. Open M-F noon-2am, Sa 2pm-2am. MC/V.) Music echoes through the streets from **Le Bolero,** 38 rue St-Laud. (☎02 41 88 61 19. Cocktails €8.) **Cinéma Les 400 Coups,** 12 rue Claveau, shows international films and Cannes Film Festival selections with French subtitles. (☎08 36 68 00 72. Tickets €6.70, 11am matinee €4.50.)

From mid-June to mid-July, Angers attracts renowned French comedy and dramatic troupes to the château for the **Festival d'Anjou,** one of the largest theater festivals in France. (Info office at 1 rue des Arènes. ☎02 41 88 14 14; www.festivaldanjou.com. €27-30 per show, students €14.) In July and August, **Angers l'Eté** brings music artists from Spain to Cape Verde, as well as prestigious jazz bands. Most concerts take place in the fabulous *cloître* Toussaint. (Tickets on sale at tourist office, pl. Kennedy. €8, students €6.50.)

LE MANS

Le Mans (pop. 146,000) is a melange of contrasts, a mix of post-war concrete structures, 12th-century churches, ancient Roman walls, and a world-famous 24hr. car race. Although it may not be the most beautiful city in the Loire Valley, the former Communist bastion has possibly the best-preserved *vieille ville* in France. Most travelers will want to make Le Mans a daytrip, but for racing fans, the city is certainly worth a night's stay.

🚆 TRANSPORTATION

Trains leave from bd. de la Gare to: Nantes (1hr.; 7 per day, also 17 TGV; €22.50); Paris (1-3hr., over 10 per day, €31.10); Rennes (1hr.; 7 per day, also 10 TGV; €20.60); Tours (1hr., over 10 per day, €12.40). Ticket windows open M-F

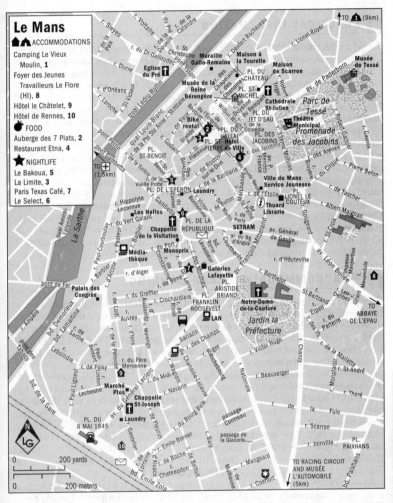

Le Mans

⌂⌂ ACCOMMODATIONS

Camping Le Vieux
  Moulin, **1**
Foyer des Jeunes
  Travailleurs Le Flore
  (HI), **8**
Hôtel le Châtelet, **9**
Hôtel de Rennes, **10**

🍴 **FOOD**

Auberge des 7 Plats, **2**
Restaurant Etna, **4**

★ **NIGHTLIFE**

Le Bakoua, **5**
La Limite, **3**
Paris Texas Café, **7**
Le Select, **6**

(map labels)
TO ▲ (9km)
r. Steves
r. Voltaire
r. du Dr-Douillet
r. de la Calandre
r. St-Christophe
r. St-Galloudec
Lionel-Royer
r. Denfert-Rochereau
Muraille
Gallo-Romaine
Maison à
la Tourelle
Musée
de Tessé
r. de Paderborn
r. de la Paix
r. Ducre
Eglise
du Pré
PL. DU
CHÂTEAU
Maison
de Scarron
r. d'Orléans
Musée de la
Reine
Bérengère
des
Chapalan
PL. ST-
MICHEL
Cathédrale
St-Julien
av. de Paderborn
Parc de
Tessé
quai Ledru-Rollin
r. Laroche
Wilbur-Wright
PL. DU
Doyenne
Robert
Triger
Théâtre
Municipal
Promenade
des Jacobins
quai Louis-Blanc
Bike
rental
PL. DU
HALLAI
JET-D'EAU
PL. DES
COMEDIE
r. Cauvin
pont Perrin
pont Gambetta
TO ✚
(1,5km)
PL.
ST-BENOIT
PIERRE de Ville
des Jacobins
PL. DES
JACOBINS
des Arènes
r. Pierre Belon
Vieille Porte
PL. DE L'EPERON
Laundry
Ville du Mans
Service Jeunesse
r. de Tascher
r. Albert-Maignan
Les Halles
du Vert Galant
PL. DE LA
RÉPUBLIQUE
SETRAM
r. de
Paris
Thuard
Librairie
LIONEL LE
COUTEUX
Chappelle
de la Visitation
av. Général
de Gaulle
av. Léon Bollée
Média-
thèque
Monoprix
Berthelot
r. d'Hauteville
impasse
Maurepuis
Palais des
Congrès
Galeries
Lafayette
PL.
ARISTIDE
BRIAND
St-Bertrand
TO 8
pont de Fer
FRANKLIN
ROOSEVELT
LAN
Notre-Dame-
de-la-Couture
Jardin la
Préfecture
TO
ABBAYE
DE L'EPAU
La Sarthe
Sarrazin
Victor Hugo
r. de la Mariette
r. St-André
Marché
Plus
Chappelle
St-Joseph
r. Beauverger
r. Thoré
N
LG
Laundry
PL. DU
8 MAI 1945
passage
Contreau
r. Scarron
r. Joinville
PL.
PAIXHANS
200 yards
200 meters
passage
de la Glacerie
bd. Emile Zola
TO RACING CIRCUIT
AND MUSÉE
L'AUTOMOBILE
(5km)

5:15am-10:15pm, Sa 6am-10:50pm, Su 6:40am-10:30pm. There are also **buses** run by **SNCF** (☎02 43 25 30 12) from the station to Saumur (1½hr.; 2 per day M-Sa, 1 on Su at 9pm; €13.20). Use **SETRAM buses**, 65 av. Gal. de Gaulle to get around the city during the day. (☎02 43 24 76 76. Buses run 5:30am to 8 or 9pm. Info office open M-F 7am-7pm, Sa 8:30am-6:30pm. Ticket €1, *carnet* of 10 €7.80; sold on bus or in office. MC/V.) The city's **Hi'bus** lines take over until midnight or 1am. For **taxis,** call Radio Taxi, 2 av. du Général Leclerc, (☎02 43 24 92 92). There are **car rental** offices at the train station, including Avis (☎02 43 24 30 50; open M-F 7:30am-7pm, Sa 9am-noon and 2-6pm; AmEx/DC/MC/V) and National Car Rental (☎02 43 24 03 34; from €75 per day; open M-F 8am-noon and 2-6:30pm, Sa 8:30am-noon and 2-5pm; AmEx/MC/V). Rent two wheels with Top Team **bike rentals**, 9 pl. St-Pierre. (☎02 43 24 88 32. From €15 per day. ID deposit. Open Tu-Sa 10:30am-7pm. MC/V.)

⚡ PRACTICAL INFORMATION

To get to the **tourist office,** rue de l'Étoile, in the 17th-century Hôtel des Ursulines. From the train station, walk down av. du Général Leclerc, then keep going on av. François Mitterand. Staff distributes maps (€3.20) and info booklets. English tours are only available by reservation. (☎02 43 28 17 22; www.ville-lemans.fr. Open June-Aug. M-Sa 9am-6pm, Su 10am-12:30pm and 2:30-5pm; Sept.-May M-F 9am-6pm, Sa 9am-noon and 2-6pm, Su 10am-noon.) Other services include: **English-language books** at cosmopolitan Thuard Librairie, 24 rue de l'Étoile (☎02 43 82 22 22; open M-Sa 8:30am-7:30pm; DC/MC/V); **youth information** at Ville du Mans Service Jeunesse, 13 rue de l'Etoile (☎02 43 47 38 95; student discounts, sports trips, and info on jobs and housing; open M, W, F 10am-noon and 1:30-6pm, Tu and Th 1:30-6pm, Sa 2-6pm); **laundry** at Lav'Ideal, 4 pl. l'Eperon (☎02 43 24 53 99; open daily 7am-9pm); **police** at 6 rue Coeffort (☎02 43 61 68 00); a **hospital** at Centre Hospitalier, 194 av. Rubillard (☎02 43 43 43 43); **Internet** access at LAN Station, 41 rue Nationale (☎02 43 27 94 56; €2 per hr.; open M-Sa noon-midnight, Su 2-11pm) and Cyber@Net, 27 av. du Général Leclerc (☎02 43 21 45 48; €4 per hr.; open M-Sa 10am-midnight, Su 2pm-midnight); and a **post office** at 13 pl. de la République (☎02 43 21 75 00; **currency exchange;** open M-F 8am-7pm, Sa 9am-noon; branch office: 1 pl. du 8 Mai 1945, right by the train station). **Postal Code:** 72000.

⚡ ACCOMMODATIONS AND CAMPING

Plenty of hotels line up on av. de la Gare, but the best deals are on the small streets within walking distance of the station. The city also lacks the charming, affordable *auberges* found elsewhere. **Hôtel de Rennes ❸,** 43 bd. de la Gare, right across from the train station, offers spacious, modern rooms, some with TV. (☎02 43 24 86 40. Breakfast €6. Singles with shower €36; doubles with shower and toilet €42; triples €45.) The worn exterior of **Hôtel le Châtelet ❷,** 15 rue du Père Mersenne, keeps nine basic rooms with a hallway shower. (☎02 43 43 92 36. Breakfast €4. Weekend stays require advance notice. Singles with bunks €23; doubles €37; triples €45.) Close to the city center, **Foyer des Jeunes Travailleurs Le Flore (HI) ❶,** 23 rue Maupertuis, serves as a dorm for local students, the town's youth info center, and a hostel, with small triples and large, basic singles. (☎02 43 81 27 55. Wheelchair-accessible. Free Internet. Self-serve restaurant €5-6 per meal. Breakfast included M-Sa. Sheets €2.90. 3-night max. stay, extended once upon request. Bunks €12, €9 when kitchens close. HI members only.) Take the train from Le Mans (8min., 4 per day, €2.50) to **Camping Le Vieux Moulin ❶,** 9km away in Neuville-sur-Sarthe. The two-star riverside site has bikes (€6.10 per day), laundry, a pool, and tennis courts. (☎02 43 25 31 82; fax 02 43 25 38 11. Open July-early Sept. Call ahead for exact dates. €10.70 for 2 people, €3.10 per extra person. Electricity €3.10. MC/V.)

⚡ FOOD

Renowned for its poultry, Le Mans's regional cuisine commonly includes *pintade* (guinea fowl) and *canard* (duck). The succulent *marmite sarthoise*, a warm casserole of rabbit, chicken, ham, carrots, cabbage, and mushrooms bubbling in a bath of Jasnière wine, is an omnivore's dream. Find the best *menus* in the *brasseries* lining **place de la République.** Pleasant, affordable restaurants settle along Grande Rue or behind pl. de l'Eperon in the *vieille ville.* The **indoor market** sells portable goodies in **Les Halles,** pl. du Marché, while an **outdoor market** occupies pl. des Jacobins. (Open W and Su 7am-12:30pm.) There is a **Monoprix supermarket** at 30 pl. de la République (open M-Sa 9am-8pm) and a mid-sized **Marché Plus** at 68 av. du Gal. Leclerc (open M-Sa 7am-9pm and Su 9am-1pm). The nine appetizers, seven *plats*, and ten desserts of extremely popular ■ **Auberge des 7 Plats ❸**, 79 Grande Rue, are rearranged into copious combinations on the €14.50/ €16.40 a la carte *menus*. Traditional French cuisine is served amid a rustic dining room. The bottom-level dining room boasts an amazing vault carved into medieval stone. Free *calvados* with your coffee. (☎ 02 43 24 57 77. *Formules* €11.50 and €14.50. Open Tu-Sa noon-1:30pm and 7-10:30pm. MC/V.) With delicious Italian fare, **Restaurant Etna ❸**, 37 rue des Ponts Neufs, a peaceful haven on a busy street, evokes fantasies of southern Italy in both food and decor. The restaurant is divided into two distinct dining rooms: The front room offers pizzas (€7-9) to a busy crowd, and the second room, around a beautiful atrium, is much quieter and serves gourmet Italian cuisine at reasonable prices (pasta €10-13, fish €19). Try the *tagliatelle* with sausage and gorgonzola cheese, or the delicious pasta mix. (☎ 02 43 24 18 28. Open M 7-10:30pm, Tu-Sa noon-2pm and 7-10:30pm. MC/V.)

⊚ SIGHTS

Le Mans holds a remarkable set of churches, including the Maison-Dieu founded by Henry Plantagenêt, and Notre Dame de la Couture, a Romanesque church near the train station. The *billet couple* includes visits to two of the following: Musée de Tessé, Musée Vert, or Musée de la Reine-Bérengère. €5.20, students €2.60.

■ **CATHÉDRALE ST-JULIEN.** Built between the 11th and 15th centuries, Le Mans's cathedral reflects both Romanesque and Gothic styles. After a fire destroyed the town in 1134, the cathedral was repaired using Gothic styles. The great chancel was added in the 13th century, doubling the size of the cathedral and necessitating the tangle of flying buttresses around the exterior. The organ was built in the 16th century, while many of the stained-glass windows date back to the early Middle Ages. *(Pl. des Jacobins. Open daily July to mid-Sept. 8am-7pm; mid-Sept. to June 8am-6pm. Tours given by tourist office M 3pm, W 10am, Su 3pm. €3.)*

VIEILLE VILLE. Rising up behind thick Roman walls and the river Sarthe, Le Mans's *vieille ville* is considered one of the most picturesque in France. The winding streets and alleys, in which *Cyrano de Bergerac* was filmed, are lined with 15th- to 17th-century houses. Tours depart from the cathedral fountain. *(2hr. Daily 3pm. €5.50, students €3. French only.)* At the heart of the *vieille ville*, inside a charming 15th-century residence, the **Musée de la Reine Bérengère** displays artifacts from Le Mans's past. Don't miss the well-preserved 18th-century *métier à tisser* in the attic or, on the way out, the 16th-century carvings of the Virgin Mary and Gabriel on the facade. *(9 rue Reine-Bérengère. Open Tu-Su May-Sept. 10am-12:30pm and 2-6:30pm; Oct.-Apr. 2-6pm. €2.80, students €1.40, free for children. Su half-price.)*

MURAILLE GALLO-ROMAINE. The stocky 4th-century walls hugging the city's southwestern edge helped make the town of Vindunum a strong base for the protection of the *Civitas* territory in ancient Roman times. Punctuated by three arched gates and 11 massive towers, the 1.25km long *muraille* is the longest and perhaps best preserved in all of France. Steep staircases along the ramparts allow people to leave the modern town and break into the *vieille ville*.

RACING CIRCUIT AND MUSÉE AUTOMOBILE. The 4km stretch of racetrack south of the city is a must-see for car enthusiasts. Since 1923 the circuit has hosted the annual **24 Heures du Mans,** a grueling test of endurance that attracts crowds each June. *(Tickets ☎ 02 43 40 24 75 or 02 43 40 24 77. Free to enter and walk around track.)* The massive **Musée Automobile de la Sarthe** traces the evolution of motor vehicles in racing with high-tech and vintage models. Over 140 vehicles are displayed in the

LOIRE VALLEY

THE BIG SPLURGE

TRAVELERS, START YOUR ENGINES!

One of Europe's legendary race tracks, Le Mans is home to the most prestigious endurance race in the world. It is also where you oo can drive a CLIO V6 (250 CV) on the world-famous Bugatti Circuit. For €648, you can have a lesson on the techniques of driving followed by a series of laps 30min.) in the company of a professional instructor. Insurance, clothing, and a personalized debriefing are all included in this package. Best of all, drivers receive a special certificate upon completion of their sessions— a souvenir certain to impress friends at home.

Those feeling more adventurous (and even less frugal) can opt for a more extreme package which, after a €1500 deposit, puts drivers in command of a Formula car. If that kind of power is oo intimidating (or the price tag oo distressing), don't despair: hriftier automobile fans can still eel the rush of racing around the rack, albeit at slightly lower speeds, by renting their own car and driving on the Le Mans track for a fee (between €50 and €60 per lap).

(For up-to-date info and prices, contact A.C.O. (Automobile Club de 'Ouest), École de Pilotage Auto, Circuit des "24 Heures," 72019 Le Mans. ☎02 43 40 24 30, fax 02 43 40 24 35. Reservations necessary.)

futuristic building. *(From bd. Levasseur, take bus #6 to Raineries, the end of the line. Walk down rue de Laigne, following signs to the track. ☎02 43 72 72 24. Open daily June-Sept. 10am-7pm; Oct.-May 10am-6pm; Jan.-Feb. Sa-Su 10am-6pm. €6, students and ages 12-18 €5.)*

MUSÉE AND PARC DE TESSÉ. Housed in the former 19th-century bishop's palace, the museum's fabulous collection celebrates over 600 years of art. The modern, heavily restored interior displays 14th-to 19th-century painting (including some works by Le Sueur), temporary exhibits of firearms (2004-2006) and freemason art, and even an Egyptian collection of artifacts and sarcophagi dating from around 1230 BC. The museum's jewel is the *émail Plantagenet*, a unique 12th-century piece kept under thick protective glass. In the depths of the museum lies the ■**Egyptian collection's reproduction of the underground tomb of Nofetari,** one of the wives of Pharaoh Ramses II, decorated with hieroglyphics and full of dark recesses. *(Guided tours July and Aug. Th 5pm. €6.)*

After a visit to the museum, catch some rays in the beautiful **Parc de Tessé** with its acres of grass. Though frequented by families and students in the afternoon, the park becomes more dangerous after night falls. *(2 av. de Paderborn, a 15min. walk from pl. de la République. Take bus #3 (dir: Bellevue) from rue Gastelier by the station or from av. du Général de Gaulle to Musée, or bus #9 (dir: Villaret) from av. du Général de Gaulle. ☎02 43 47 38 51. Open July-Aug. Tu-Su 10am-12:30pm and 2-6:30pm; Sept.-June Tu-Sa 9am-noon and 2-6pm, Su 10am-noon and 2-6pm. €4, students up to 18 free, half-price Su.)*

🎵 🌺 ENTERTAINMENT AND FESTIVALS

Le Mans packs most of its nocturnal revelry in the narrow side-streets off **place de la République.** The young, funky scene is down **rue du Dr. Leroy,** where bars resonate with techno or rock. A few blocks away, the **rue des Ponts Neuf** has its own share of bars decorated with everything from model cars to artistic film projections. **Paris Texas Café,** 21 rue du Dr. Leroy, is a cavernous pub with saloon-like decor that caters to a younger crowd. *(☎02 43 23 71 00. Beer €4-6. Open daily 11am-2am.)* Caribbean-themed ■**Le Bakoua,** 5 rue de la Vieille Porte, off pl. de l'Eperon, keeps summer alive year-round with its calypso music and rum-based tropical drinks, though its fun setting may be the product of its "mysterious punch." *(☎02 43 23 30 70. Open daily 6pm-2am. MC/V.)* Several discotheques sit right in town, including **Le Select,** 44 pl. de la République, with wild strobe lights and good beats. *(☎02 43 28 87 41. Cover €10,* includes 1 drink. Open Th-Su 11pm-5am.) Gay-friendly **La Limite,** 7 rue St-Honoré, has a mixed crowd, depending on the night and type of music. (☎02 43 24 85 54. Cover F €6.50, Sa €10. Open Th-Su 11:30pm-4am.)

Cannes festival winners, independent films, and lesser-known international productions are featured nightly at the *vieille ville's* artsy **Ciné-Poche,** 97 Grande Rue. (☎02 43 24 73 85. €6.50, children under 13 €3.50.) For the entire month of April, the city hosts contemporary jazz artists for the **Le Mans Jazz Festival.** (Info and tickets at 9 rue des Frères Greban, ☎02 43 23 78 99.) Throughout July and August, **Les Soirs d'Eté** features around 50 free theater, comedy, and music performances on Thursdays and Fridays. Pick up a L'Eté au Mans schedule, or the *à l'Affiche* supplement from the tourist office. Late in June, parades and circus performances take over the streets in **Le Mans fait son Cirque.**

⚑ DAYTRIP FROM LE MANS

ALENÇON

Trains run from the station on rue Denis Papin to Le Mans (30min., 5 per day, €8.10) Bus TIS (☎02 43 39 97 30) travels to the Le Mans bus station (1½hr., 2 per day, €7.70). For taxis, call Radio Taxis (☎02 33 28 05 06). The most convenient car rental agency is Europcar, 3 rue Demées, 1 block from the station down av. Wilson and the 1st street to the left. (☎02 33 28 91 11. Open M, F 8:30am-noon and 2-6:30pm; Tu-Th 8am-noon and 2-6pm; Sa 9am-1pm. AmEx/DC/MC/V.)

A small town on the southern border of Normandy, Alençon (pop. 30,000) had humble Gallo-Roman roots but gained international renown in the 1650s for its lacemaking industry, which employed close to 8000 residents. The influence of the industry is present today in every window and shop along Alençon's wide avenues, and fine examples of lace craftsmanship are displayed in two museums.

The ▓**Musée de la Dentelle,** 33 rue du Pont Neuf, introduces visitors to the history of Alençon lace. An enthusiastic curator has magnifying glasses which reveal the efforts of hundreds of laborers over many years. (☎02 33 26 27 26. Open M-Sa 10am-noon and 2-6pm. €3.10, under 18 €1.80.)

Alençon's gorgeous architecture includes the beautiful 16th-century Église Notre-Dame, the towering Château des Ducs, and the elegant homes that pepper the *centre ville.* The massive stone walls of the **Église Notre-Dame** dominate the surrounding buildings. With stained-glass windows and flamboyant lace-like carvings, the church is a wonder of architectural diversity. (Pl. de la Magdeleine. Open 9:30am-noon and 2-5:30pm. Free.)

Ring the bell and enter the ▓**birthplace of Saint Theresa,** 50 rue St-Blaise. A friendly nun will give you a tour of the house, which was built the same year Theresa was sanctified. The site has remained largely untouched since then. Pictures of the young Thérèse Martin adorn the walls of the house, and much of the furnishing is original. A lovingly preserved Neoclassical chapel is home to Theresa since 1925. (Open daily June-Sept. 9am-noon and 2-6pm; Oct.-Dec. and Feb.-May M and W-Su 9:30am-noon and 2:30-5pm. Free. Mass daily, schedules vary.)

Housed in the 15th-century Maison d'Ozé, the **tourist office** in pl. de la Magdeleine provides free accommodations booking and an English walking guide of the city. A gallery next door contains exhibits on the history and architecture of Alençon. (☎02 33 80 66 33; www.paysdalencontourisme.com. Open July-Aug. M-Sa 9:30am-7pm, Su 10am-12:30pm and 3-5:30pm; Sept.-June M-Sa 9:30am-noon and 2-6:30pm. City tours of Alençon and the Musée des Beaux-Arts June-Sept. €4.)

LOIRE VALLEY

BRITTANY
(BRETAGNE)

 Brittany's millennia-old Celtic heritage has withstood Paris's many efforts to Frenchify the province and to this day defines the region's identity. The traditional costume of Breton women—a black dress and an elaborate white lace *coiffe* (headdress), which varies with sub-region—still appears in folk festivals and some markets. Black and white Breton flags dot flower gardens and street signs bear names in Brezhoneg, the lilting dialect spoken energetically at pubs in the western part of the province, especially in the fiercely Breton haven Quimper (p. 222).

Despite a history of invasions and heavy tourism, Brittany has managed to maintain its natural splendor and vibrant cultural life. Mysterious Neolithic *menhirs* have stood watch over fields and dense forests for thousands of years. Misty islands off the coast remain relatively untouristed, catering more to sheep than backpackers. The woodland streams of Pont-Aven (p. 227) inspired Paul Gauguin and other 19th-century artists to found a new school of painting. Brittany offers far more than striking landscapes and rich traditions, however—no one could accuse the rowdy nightlife of its university towns of living in the past. In the summer, locals enjoy the beaches and watersports in towns like St-Malo (p. 197) and Quiberon (p. 228). Such coastal resorts all but close down in the low season, but the churches, beaches, and cliffs become more eerily romantic.

HIGHLIGHTS OF BRITTANY

WATCH craftsmen hand-paint world-renowned faïencerie, or earthenware, just as they have for 300 years in **Quimper** (p. 222).

ENJOY beautiful waterfront spots without Côte D'Azur prices. The dramatic tides of the **St-Malo beaches** (p. 197) let you walk hundreds of meters offshore to some of the town's hidden treasures.

MIX UP A COCKTAIL of old and new in **Rennes** (p. 194), a lively university town where you can party 'til dawn in centuries-old buildings and even a former prison.

RENNES

It would be easy to compare Rennes (pop. 206,000) to Paris, but such comparisons wouldn't do it proper justice. The cultural capital of Brittany, Rennes has many faces. A cobblestoned *vieille ville*, filled with charmingly imperfect half-timbered houses, gives way to wide *places* with majestic buildings and designer shops. A university town filled to the brim with colorful nightspots, Rennes also has a well-earned reputation as the party mecca of northwest France. Rennes may not be Paris, but then again, you may not care.

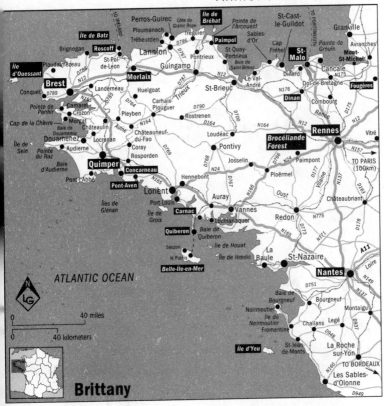

Brittany

TRANSPORTATION

Trains: pl. de la Gare (☎02 99 29 11 92). Info and ticket office open M-Sa 8:45am-7:45pm, Su 12:10-7:30pm. To: **Brest** (2-2½hr., at least 1 per hr., €27.60); **Caen** (3hr., 8 per day, €28); **Nantes** (1¼-2hr., 7 per day, €29.20); **Paris** (2hr., 1 per hr., €47.50); **St-Malo** (1hr., 15 per day, €11.50); **Tours** (2½-3hr., every 2-3hr., €30.50) via **Le Mans.**

Buses: 16 pl. de la Gare (☎02 99 30 87 80), to the right when you come out of the train station's north entrance. **Cars 35** (☎02 99 30 87 80) services **Dinan** (1¼hr.; M-Sa 5-6 per day, Su 3 per day; €8.70); **Fougères** (1hr.; M-F 9 per day, Sa 4 per day, Su 2 per day; €8.50); **Paimpont,** site of **Brocéliande Forest** (1¼hr.; M-F 6 per day, Sa 3 per day; €2.80); **St-Malo** (2hr.; M-F 3 per day, Sa-Su 1 per day; €10). **Cariane Atlantique** (☎02 40 20 46 99, in Nantes 08 25 08 71 56) goes to **Nantes** (2hr., 1-2 per day, €15.70). **Anjou Bus** (☎02 99 30 87 80) goes to **Angers** (2½-3hr.; 3-4 per day; €15.90, express €19.80). **Les Courriers Bretons** (☎02 99 19 70 80) serves **Mont-St-Michel** (1½hr.; M-Sa 5 per day, Su 3 per day; €11.20).

Public Transportation: Star, 12 rue du Pré Botté (☎02 99 79 37 37; www.star.fr). Office open M-Sa 7am-7pm. **Buses** M-Sa 5:15am-12:30am, Su 7:25am-12:30am. Buy tickets on bus, from bus office, or at newsstands. A **metro** line runs through the heart of Rennes and accepts the same ticket. Dir: Kennedy runs from train station to pl. de la République; dir: Poterie the other way (€1.10, *carnet* of 10 €8.40, 1-day pass €3).

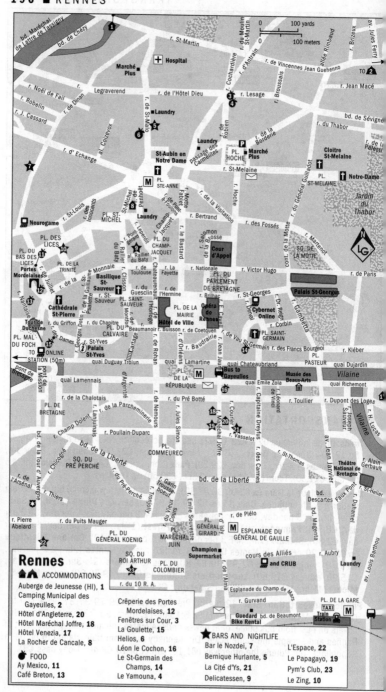

Rennes

🏠 ACCOMMODATIONS

Auberge de Jeunesse (HI), 1
Camping Municipal des Gayeulles, 2
Hôtel d'Angleterre, 20
Hôtel Maréchal Joffre, 18
Hôtel Venezia, 17
La Rocher de Cancale, 8

🍴 FOOD

Ay Mexico, 11
Café Breton, 13
Crêperie des Portes Mordelaises, 12
Fenêtres sur Cour, 3
La Goulette, 15
Helios, 6
Léon le Cochon, 16
Le St-Germain des Champs, 14
Le Yamouna, 4

★ BARS AND NIGHTLIFE

Bar le Nozdei, 7
Bernique Hurlante, 5
La Cité d'Ys, 21
Delicatessen, 9
L'Espace, 22
Le Papagayo, 19
Pym's Club, 23
Le Zing, 10

Taxis: 4 rue Georges Dottin (☎02 99 30 79 79). Stand at train station. 24hr.

Bike Rental: Guedard, 13 bd. Beaumont (☎02 99 30 43 78). €12.50 per day. Open M 2-7pm, Tu-Th 9am-12:30pm and 2-7pm, F 10am-7pm, Sa 9am-6:30pm. MC/V.

■ ■ ORIENTATION AND PRACTICAL INFORMATION

The Vilaine River separates the station in the south from most of the city's historic sights in the north. **Avenue Jean Janvier,** at the north exit of the station, runs through the town center; to reach the old city, take it across the river and turn left. **Place Ste-Anne** is home to some unsavory characters, so be wary at night.

Tourist Office: 11 rue St-Yves (☎02 99 67 11 11; infos@tourisme-rennes.com). From the station, take av. Jean Janvier to quai Chateaubriand. Turn left and walk along the river and through pl. de la République. Turn right on rue George Dottin, then right again on rue St-Yves. The office is on the right, just past the church on the corner. Free maps, directions, and lists of hotels, restaurants, and shops. Accommodations service (€1, €2 for the *département,* €3 for the region). Call in advance for tours of the Parliament, the *vieille ville,* the Jardin du Thabor, or themed visits of historical houses (daily July-Aug.; Sept.-June 1-3 times per week; €6.10, students €3.05, under 7 free). Open Apr.-Sept. M-Sa 9am-7pm, Su 11am-6pm; Oct.-Mar. M-Sa 9am-6pm, Su 11am-6pm.

Hiking and Biking Information: France Randonnée, 4 rue Ronsard (☎02 99 26 13 50; fax 02 99 26 13 54). Info on **GR trails.** Open M-F 10am-6pm, Sa 10am-1pm.

Consulate: US, 30 quai Duguay-Trouin (☎02 23 44 09 60; fax 02 99 35 00 92).

English-Language Bookstore: Comédie des Langues, 25 rue de St-Malo (☎02 99 36 72 95; www.comediedeslangues.fr). Carries books in a variety of foreign languages; features a well-chosen selection of English fiction. Open M-Sa 9:30am-7pm.

Youth Center: Centre Régional Information Jeunesse Bretagne (CRIJB), Maison du Champ de Mars, 6 cours des Alliés (☎02 99 31 47 48; www.crij-bretagne.com), has info on summer jobs. Internet €3 for a yearly membership, then €1 per hr. Open Tu-F 10am-6pm, Sa 2-6pm, but hours change frequently.

Laundromat: 23 rue de Penhoet (open daily 7am-8pm), 48 rue de St-Malo, by the hostel (open M-Tu and Th-Sa 9am-noon and 2-7pm, W 2-7pm), and 59 rue Jean-Marie Duhamel (open daily 7am-10pm).

Police: 22 bd. de la Tour d'Auvergne (☎02 99 65 00 22).

Hospital: The most central of Rennes's hospitals is **Hôpital Pontchaillou,** past rue St-Malo at 2 rue Henri le Guilloux (☎02 99 28 42 91).

Internet Access: At the **CRIJB** (see above). **Neurogame,** 2 rue de Dinan (☎02 99 65 53 85; www.neurogame.com). €3 per hr.; min. €1. Open M 2pm-1am, Tu-Th noon-1am, F noon-3am, Sa noon-5am, Su 2-10pm. **Online Station,** 5 quai d'Ille et Rance (☎02 99 14 23 93). €2 per hr. Open M-Sa noon-midnight, Su 2-11pm. **Cybernet Online,** 22 rue St-Georges (☎02 99 36 37 41; www.cybernetonline.com). €0.80 per 5min., €2.50 per 30min, €4 per hr. Open M 2-10pm, Tu-F 10:30am-8pm. Closed most of Aug.

Post Office: 27 bd. du Colombier (☎02 99 01 22 11), 1 block left of the train station exit, offers **currency exchange** with 1.5% commission. Branch office, pl. de la République (☎02 99 78 43 35). From the station, walk up av. Jean Janvier and turn left onto the quai 3 blocks over. Another branch at pl. Hoche (☎02 23 20 02 05). All locations have Cyberposte, fax, photocopies, and **Western Union.** First 2 locations open M-F 8am-7pm, Sa 8am-noon; third branch open M-F 8:45am-12:15pm and 1:45-6:15pm, Sa 8:45am-noon.

Postal Code: 35000.

ACCOMMODATIONS AND CAMPING

Reserve ahead, especially for the first week of July, during the Tombées de la Nuit festival. Several moderately priced hotels are between quai Richemont and the train station. Unfortunately, most budget hotels are not central.

■ **Le Rocher de Cancale,** 10 rue St-Michel (☎02 99 79 20 83). This half-timbered building houses charming, stylish rooms with bath on a bar-packed street in the heart of the old quarter. Restaurant downstairs serves traditional cuisine (*menus* €13-23). Breakfast €5.50. Reception closed Sa-Su. Reservations recommended, especially July-Aug. Singles and doubles €37; triples €46. MC/V. ❹

Auberge de Jeunesse (HI), 10-12 canal St-Martin (☎02 99 33 22 33; rennes@fuaj.org). From the station, take the metro (dir: Kennedy) to Ste-Anne. Walk past the church onto rue de St-Malo. Continue over the bridge; hostel is on the right. Simple beds on clean, color-coded floors, some with views of the adjacent canal. Kitchen, common room with TV and pool table, cafeteria, and Internet with *télécarte*. Discount on bus to Mont-St-Michel and St-Malo. Breakfast included. Shower and sink in all rooms; lockers in most. Bottom sheet, pillowcase, and blanket provided; top sheet €2.80. Laundry. Wheelchair-accessible. Lockout 10am-3:30pm. Reception daily 7am-11pm. Night guard lets you in after 11pm. Doubles, triples, and quads €13.55 per person. AmEx/MC/V. ❶

Hôtel Maréchal Joffre, 6 rue Maréchal Joffre (☎02 99 79 37 74; fax 02 99 78 38 51). Small, cheerful, and quiet rooms over an Asian lunch counter on a busy street. No front door lock. Breakfast €5. 24hr. reception. Closed Christmas to New Year's Day and 15 days in the summer. Singles €20.50, with shower and toilet €31.50; doubles €22.50, with shower €29-33, with shower and toilet €34.50, with bath and toilet €36; triples with shower and TV €37.50, with shower, toilet, and TV €41.50. MC/V. ❷

Hôtel Venezia, 27 rue Dupont des Loges (☎02 99 30 36 56; hotel.venezia@wanadoo.fr). On an island in the Vilaine River. Tranquil, spacious, and elegantly decorated rooms with comfortable beds and spectacular views of the canal. Breakfast €5. Reception 7am-11pm. Reservations recommended. Singles €28, with bath and TV €33; doubles €35-43. Extra bed €10. AmEx/MC/V. ❸

Hôtel d'Angleterre, 19 rue Maréchal Joffre. (☎02 99 79 38 61; fax 02 99 79 43 85). Between the station and the center of town. Rooms with street or courtyard views. Most rooms have TV. Breakfast €5. Reception M-Sa 7am-10:30pm, Su 7am-noon and 6-10:30pm. Singles €23-25, with shower €32, with shower and toilet €36-38, with bath and toilet €38; doubles with shower €34, with shower and toilet €38-44, with bath and toilet €40-46; triples with shower and toilet €48, with bath and toilet €50. MC/V. ❷

Camping: Municipal des Gayeulles, in Parc des Gayeulles (☎02 99 36 91 22). Take bus #3 (dir: St-Laurent) from pl. du Colombier (left of the train station) or pl. de la République to Piscine/Gayeulles (M-Sa every 10min., Su every 40min.; last bus midnight). Follow the path around the swimming pool on the right until reaching a paved road. Turn left; follow signs to campsite, deep within the Parc des Gayeulles. Tranquil site has 128 spots separated by bushes, with 50 more added on an open field in the high season. Laundry and safes available. Internet €1 per 30min. Reception daily mid-June to mid-Sept. 7:30am-1pm and 2-8pm; mid-Sept. to Oct. and Apr. to mid-June 9am-12:30pm and 4:30-8pm; Nov.-Mar. 8-9am and 6-8pm. Mid-June to mid-Sept. gates closed 11pm-7am; mid. Sept. to mid-June 10pm-7am. €3.10 per person, €1.50 per child under 10; tents €2.40-5.40; caravans €6.90; €1.50 per car. Electricity €2.70. Prices vary by season. Nov.-Mar. 20% discount on stays of 8 or more days. AmEx/MC/V. ❶

FOOD

Rennes boasts an astounding quantity of ethnic restaurants. Cajun, African, Afghani, Greek, and Indian restaurants sit cheek by jowl on **rue St-Malo**, while *crêperies* and pizzerias cluster on rue St-George. Inside the *vieille ville* there are more traditional *brasseries* and cheap kebab stands, though in general, the best food is on the outskirts of the city center. A huge **market** livens pl. des Lices. (Sa 7am-1pm.) Local **supermarkets** include **Champion**, underground in a mall on rue d'Isly near the train station (open M-Sa 9am-8pm), and **Marché Plus** at 10 pl. Hoche (open M-Sa 7am-9pm, Su 9am-noon; closed Su July to mid-Aug.); there's another in the apartment complex at 43 rue de St-Malo, near the hostel. (Open M-Sa 9am-9pm, Su 9am-noon.)

Café Breton, 14 rue Nantaise (☎02 99 30 74 95). As its name implies, this excellent restaurant features an ever-changing menu of the freshest Breton cuisine in a colorful ambience of bright walls, giant sardine labels, and bunches of fresh flowers. *Plats* €7.30; salads €5-7.30; desserts €3.50-4. Open M noon-3:30pm, Tu-F noon-3pm and 7-11pm, Sa noon-3:30pm. Reservations highly recommended. ❷

Le St-Germain des Champs (Restaurant Végétarien-Biologique), 12 rue du Vau St-Germain (☎02 99 79 25 52). This restaurant's chef-owners happily welcome guests to their popular organic and vegetarian kitchen and dining room accented with bamboo, cloth lanterns, and nature photos. Sandwiches with salad €5, €4.50 to go; *menus* €12-18. Open Tu-Sa noon-2:30pm and F-Sa 7-9:30pm. Closed Aug. MC/V. ❸

Léon le Cochon, 1 rue Maréchal Joffre (☎02 99 79 37 54). Enticing local dishes and chili-pepper decorations fuse modern and traditional at this elegant restaurant. A pig motif emerges in paintings, a giant statue, and much of the menu, although plenty of other options exist. *Plats* €11-14, *menu* €11.50. Open July-Aug. M-F noon-2:30pm and 8-11pm, Sa until 11:30pm; Sept.-June open Su and dinner starts at 7:30pm. MC/V. ❸

Le Yamouna, 16 rue de Robien (☎02 99 63 40 95), close to pl. Hoche. Rennes's best Indian restaurant has a traditional menu of well-prepared and filling dishes, with a variety of vegetarian options. Lunch *menu* €8.50, dinner *menu* €17, vegetarian *menu* €14. Open M-Sa noon-2pm and 7-10pm, Su 7-10pm. MC/V. ❹

Créperie des Portes Mordelaises, 6 rue des Portes Mordelaises (☎02 99 30 57 40). Below the old city walls, this small, simple, and authentic *crêperie* is one of the best in the city, as long lines of students attest. *Galettes* and crêpes €3-7. Salads €2-7.50. Open daily 11:45am-2pm and 6:45-11pm. MC/V. ❶

Ay Mexico, 7 rue de Juillet (☎02 99 31 67 02). Don't be shocked if someone whips out a guitar and bursts into song at this rowdy Mexican hotspot, where controlled chaos feels more like a family reunion than a restaurant. Delicious standard fare (€11-13) served with style. Lunch *menu* €8. Open M and Sa 7pm-midnight, Tu-F noon-2pm and 7pm-midnight. Reservations recommended. AmEx/MC/V. ❸

Fenêtres sur Cour, 18 rue de Robien (☎02 99 36 13 26; fax 02 23 20 17 96). A charming brick-walled restaurant near the hostel, with homey knick-knacks, a flower-garnished courtyard, and jazz music. Artfully prepared traditional bistro dishes. *Plat du jour* €7.50, *menus* €9-20. Open Tu-Sa noon-2pm and 7-10:30pm. MC/V. ❸

Helios, 5 rue de St-Malo (☎02 99 79 61 49). An award-winning chef cooks up huge portions of traditional Greek cuisine, served among authentic vases and paintings, as well as huge murals of Greek buildings. The €16 *menu* is especially designed to allow sampling of a variety of dishes; the patient staff carefully explains each one. *Menus* €9.45-21. *Plats* €10-16. Open Tu-Sa 11am-2pm and 7pm-midnight. AmEx/MC/V. ❸

BRITTANY

La Goulette, 3 rue des Dames (☎ 02 99 31 57 23), features a tempting menu of Mediterranean specialties, including paella (€12) and all manner of couscous (€9-12.50). Open M-Th 7pm-midnight, F-Sa 7pm-1am. MC/V. ❸

👁 SIGHTS

Rennes's beautiful *vieille ville* resembles a quintessential medieval village. Half-timbered buildings, now filled with bars, pubs, and modern storefronts, pepper the old city, on **rue St-Georges** and in **place Ste-Anne** and **place St-Michel.** For a tour of the old buildings, turn left from the tourist office onto rue St-Yves, then right onto rue Georges Dottin, passing the buildings on rue du Chapitre. Pass the old buildings on **rue de la Psalette,** which becomes **rue St-Guillaume.** Turn left onto rue de la Monnaie, which becomes rue de la Cathédrale, to visit the Cathédrale St-Pierre.

MUSÉE DES BEAUX-ARTS. This worthwhile museum features a small but lively and highly eclectic collection. A few works by Picasso and Gauguin, although many of the most interesting pieces are anonymous. Pictorialism (Feb.-Mar.) and the work of Francis Pellerin (Oct.-Dec.) are among temporary exhibits planned for 2005. *(20 quai Emile Zola. ☎ 02 99 28 55 85; fax 02 99 28 55 99. Open M and W-Su 10am-noon and 2-6pm. Wheelchair-accessible. €4, students €2, under 18 free.)*

JARDIN DU THABOR. Some of the most beautiful gardens in France, these lush grounds contain shaped hedges, flower designs, sculptures, fountains, a carousel, a massive bird cage, and the "caves of hell." The rose garden alone holds 1700 varieties of the *fleur d'amour.* Concerts are often held here, and a small gallery on the north side exhibits local artwork. *(Open daily June-Sept. 7:30am-8:30pm.)*

PARC DES GAYEULLES. The park is a 15min. bus ride from the center of Rennes (see **Accommodations** for directions to the campground and bus info). Gayeulles's forests are interspersed with an indoor pool, several lakes (with paddle-boats in the summer), sports fields, tennis courts, mini-golf, and a campground. Many walking paths and bike paths cut through the park. (Cyclists should check the maps posted in the park to be sure they're cycling legally.) The park is also home to a working farm and animal reserve. The farm, an instructional facility where local youngsters are taught about gardening, milking cows, and feeding horses, is open to children staying at the campground when accompanied by a parent. *(☎ 02 99 36 71 73. Open July-Aug. M-F 9am-5:30pm; Sept.-June Tu and Th-F 4:30-6pm, W-Sa 9am-5:30pm. Free.)*

OTHER SIGHTS. Cathédrale St-Pierre was founded in 1787 on a site previously occupied by a pagan temple, a Roman church, and a Gothic cathedral. The 5th chapel houses the cathedral's treasure: a delicately carved, glass-encased 16th-century altarpiece that traces the life of the Virgin Mary. The cathedral itself is somewhat unusual, with a ceiling of painted panels, a facade with shutters and stained glass, and a modern, mint-green altar. *(Open daily 9:30am-noon and 3-6pm. Closed to visitors during high mass Su 10:30-11:30am, July-Aug. also M and Su afternoon.)* Across the street, tucked in an alleyway bearing the same name, the unassuming **Portes Mordelaises,** once the entrance to the city, is the last vestige of the medieval city walls, along with the crumbling **Tour de Duchesne,** which stands flush with an apartment building. The best view is from pl. Maréchal Foch; take rue de la Monnaie from the Portes.

🍷 NIGHTLIFE

After the sun sets (as late as 10:30pm in the summer), the city's population seems to double, and the revelers don't disappear until dawn. Much of the action centers around pl. Ste-Anne, pl. St-Michel, **place des Lices,** and the radiating streets, but don't stop there—hot nightspots pervade the city, including a few great bars and discotheques to the south of the Vilaine.

BARS

▧ **Le Zing,** 5 pl. des Lices (☎ 02 99 79 64 60). 2 floors, 4 bars, and 8 unusually configured rooms fill with the young and the beautiful, who appear even more alluring under the flattering amber lights. DJ spins on the 1st floor W-Sa. Beer €3 before midnight, €3.50 after. Cocktails €8-9. Open from 3pm; filled from around midnight until the crowd heads for the discos at 2am. AmEx/MC/V.

Bernique Hurlante, 40 rue de St-Malo (☎ 02 99 38 70 09), welcomes a diverse crowd in an intimate, funky space with modern art pieces and walls encrusted with shells and glass mosaics. Beer €2.20; punch €2.50. Open daily 4pm-1am.

Le Papagayo, 10 rue Maréchal Joffre (☎ 02 99 79 65 13). An unassuming *tapas* bar by day, this tropical spot becomes a party after dark—especially on beach and disco nights (twice a month) and tequila nights in Aug. (tequila €1.50), when salsa music blares. Sangria €3. Open M-Sa 7:30am-1am. MC/V.

Bar le Nozdei, 39 rue de Dinan (☎ 02 99 30 61 64), is a little out of the way but serves relatively cheap drinks in an intimate atmosphere and hosts live music 2 Tu per month, except in the summer. The basset hound that appears on the sign has a very friendly living counterpart who is a fixture at the bar. Beer €2.30, house punch €3.50. Open M-Sa 11am-1am. AmEx/MC/V.

La Cité d'Ys, 31 rue Vasselot (☎ 02 99 78 24 84), is so staunchly Breton that regulars won't even speak French. 2 floors, adorned with Celtic knots and crosses, are linked by a twisting spiral staircase. Fabulous variety of live traditional music twice a month. Coreff €2.40. Open M-Sa 11:30am-1am. Closed first 3 weeks in Aug.

CLUBS

▧ **Délicatessen,** 7 allée Rallier du Baty (☎ 02 99 78 23 41), one of Rennes's hottest clubs, around the corner from pl. St-Michel in a former prison, has swapped jailhouse rock for dance cages and electronic beats. Drinks Tu-Th €5-7, after 2am €9-10; F-Sa €9-10. Cover Tu-Th €10 after 1:30am; F-Sa €8, after 1:30am €14. Obligatory coatcheck €2, €5 for big bags. Open Tu-Sa midnight-5am.

Pym's Club, 27 pl. du Colombier (☎ 02 99 67 30 00). Look for the signs for Colombier, not Colombes, from pl. Maréchal Juin. Walk up the stairs to the platform. The club is located below a cinema. The poshest of Rennes's discotheques; Pym's 3 rooms and techno, house, and 80s hits draw a young crowd hellbent on having a raucous good time. One room, Le Salon, is exclusively for those 28 and under. Pym's is in an otherwise dark area, so it's wise to travel in a group. Cover F-Sa €13. Open M-Th and Su 11pm-4am, F-Sa 11pm-5am.

L'Espace, 45 bd. de la Tour d'Auvergne (☎ 02 99 30 21 95; fax 02 99 30 99 21). From 2am on, a young and lively crowd fills the stage, cage, and dance floor of L'Espace, gyrating under video screens, strobe lights, and disco balls to thumping house music spun by a DJ. As with Pym's, L'Espace is located amid darkened storefronts on a poorly lit street; travel in a group for safety. Cover €10, includes 1 drink. For students W-F €7; Th before 1am free; Sa before 2am €8, after 2am €10. Long drinks half-price Th before 1am. Open W midnight-4am, Th 10pm-4am, F-Sa 11pm-5am. AmEx/MC/V.

♫ ▧ ENTERTAINMENT AND FESTIVALS

Consult the tourist office for a guide listing theater, dance, and classical music performances. For information on **Orchestre de Bretagne** concerts call ☎ 02 99 27 52 75.

The best-known of Rennes's summer festivals, **Les Tombées de la Nuit,** is a weeklong riot of music, theater, mime, and dance (complete with a 14hr. traditional Breton dancefest) in early July (www.tdn.rennes.fr). The Rencontres **Transmusicales** in early December fills the city with local artists and international bands (www.lestrans.com). March brings the **Festival Les Mythos,** a celebration of *contes* (tales), the spoken word, and oral tradition. April features the **Festival du Cinéma.** The tourist office has more information on all of the above.

◪ DAYTRIPS FROM RENNES

BROCÉLIANDE FOREST

TIV buses depart from Rennes (☎02 99 07 84 23; 1hr.; M-F 6 per day, Sa 3 per day; €2.80) and stop in the village of Paimpont, in the middle of the forest. From the bus stop, walk back 200m in the direction from which the bus came. Before the road crosses the water, turn left at the sign for the "Syndicat d'Initiative." Proceed toward the old abbey ahead, now a Presbyterian church and town hall. The tourist office next to the abbey has info on bike and car routes, local accommodations, and the forest's legends, as well as maps of the area. (☎02 99 07 84 23. Basic map free; hiking routes €4; complete road map recommended for serious hikers €8. 4hr. tours in French M, F, and Su 2pm; Tu-Th and Sa 10am-12:30pm and 2-6:30pm. €8-10 per person; reserve a spot by phone. July-Aug. guided car tours to major forest sites. Open Feb.-Dec. M-F 10am-noon and 2-5pm, Sa-Su until 6pm.) Rent bikes at Le Bar Brecilien, 1 rue Général Charles de Gaulle, beside the tourist office. Their selection is small, and the bikes a little worn, but they can handle the paved roads and flat terrain of Brocéliande. (☎02 99 07 81 13. €3 per hr., €9 per half-day, €14 per day. Open daily July-Aug. 8am-8pm; Sept.-June closed M.)

Brocéliande, 1hr. from Rennes, is enshrouded in legend deeply tied to King Arthur and his knights. A 75km road through the forest passes **Merlin's Tomb, the Fountain of Youth, the Valley of No Return,** and the field where Lancelot confessed his forbidden love for Guinevere and stole the kiss that would ruin Camelot. Many of the forest's supposedly Arthurian structures are probably the remnants of stone-age megaliths (à la Stonehenge) dating from 3000 to 2000 BC; the stones are so worn that many of the sites don't amount to much. Fenced in and heavily touristed by myth-seekers, the forest's attractions have more fanciful than literal appeal. But away from the main roads, magic emanates from the misty woodlands and moors, where some trees have lived 6000 years.

Those in a hurry should try the 9km route (2-3hr. round-trip by bike) to Merlin's Tomb and the Fountain of Youth, north of Paimpont. The former is all that remains of a Neolithic vaulted passageway built between 3000 and 2500 BC, allegedly the site where Merlin was burned; the incongruously puny "tomb" is upstaged by the often-amusing wish-notes and tokens visitors leave for the wizard. Even more anticlimactic is the **Fountain of Youth,** a small, unromantic pool of still water. Drinking from the fountain between the setting moon and the rising sun after a long walk in bare feet is supposed to restore youth, but imbibing the rancid liquid seems more likely to shorten life. The spot may have gotten its name from an ancient ritual in which a priest washed and registered newborns at the site on the night of summer solstice; babies that couldn't make it were registered the next year, officially making them a year younger.

Those with an entire day to spend can continue to the alluring **Valley of No Return,** supposedly a magical prison for untrue lovers created by the fairy Morgane after she was betrayed. Lesser-known treasures lie in the small paths that veer off the pavement toward sun-splattered clearings or vast lakes. One such sanctuary is the Pas du Houx, the forest's largest lake, which lies between Paimpont and Merlin's Tomb. A Norman-style manor, complete with grazing cows, overlooks the water.

FOUGÈRES

TIV buses (☎02 99 99 77 46) run from Rennes (1¼hr.; M-F 10 per day, Sa 4 per day, Su 2 per day; €8.50). Get off at Fougères Jean Jaurès for the historical center of the city; there's also a stop at the château. The main bus terminal (☎02 99 99 08 77) is at pl. de la Répub-

BRITTANY

lique. From Fougères Jean Jaurès, walk downhill on bd. Jean Jaurès for 7min. until you reach the fountain in the center of the traffic circle. The terminal is on the left side of the fountain. (Office open M-Sa 9:30am-noon and 2-7pm.) Les Courriers Bretons (☎02 99 19 70 70) run from St-Malo (2¼hr., 2 per day, €12.50) via Pontorson (1hr., 2 per day, €7). To get to the tourist office, 2 rue Nationale, walk uphill on bd. Jean Jaurès; at the traffic circle, continue straight uphill to the end of rue de Paris; pl. Aristide Briand will be on the right. Walk to the end of the place and turn left at the Marché Plus; the tourist office is ahead to the left of the Théâtre. (☎02 99 94 12 20; www.ot-fougeres.fr. Open July-Aug. M-Sa 9am-7pm, Su 10am-noon and 2-4pm; Sept.-June M 2-6pm, Tu-Sa 9:30am-12:30pm and 2-6pm, Su 1:30-5:30pm; Oct.-Easter closed Su.) To reach the château from pl. Aristide Briand, turn left onto rue Porte Roger (near the tourist office) and head to the right of the fountain onto rue de la Pinterie, the main artery of the medieval city. Proceed downhill until the château appears ahead. Go right into the castle, or make a detour into the garden immediately to the left.

Atop a hill overlooking the pristine Nançon Valley, picturesque Fougères has been a center for feudal lords and a haven for artists. Today, it is a modern town with a perfectly preserved historic center and a breathtaking château.

Fougères's awesome ▇**château,** pl. Pierre Symon, sits on a promontory flanked by rock walls and the Nançon River. Its construction began around AD 1000 as part of a plan to reinforce the entire Breton duchy. The château fell into disrepair centuries later, but a number of architectural ingenuities remain standing. The behemoth **Tour Mélusine,** built by the Lusignans of Poitou to honor their half-human, half-snake ancestor, stands 30m high, with 3m thick walls and a dungeon to boot—peek through the trap door to check it out. (☎02 99 99 79 59; www.ot-fougeres.fr. Open daily mid-June to mid-Sept. 9am-7pm; mid- to late Sept. and Apr. to mid-June 9:30am-noon and 2-6pm; Feb.-Mar. and Nov.-Dec. 10am-noon and 2-5pm. French tours July-Aug., on the hr., 9am-noon and 2-6pm. English tours leave 5min. later. Entrance €4.60, students €3.55, ages 10-16 €2.05, under 10 free. Low-season prices lower.) Look for signs to the **Jardin Public,** which has panoramic views of the château and surrounding countryside. The **Musée Emmanuel de la Villéon,** 51 rue Nationale, features over 100 works and a few worthwhile gems by one of the last Impressionists. (☎02 99 99 19 98. Open daily mid-June to mid-Sept. 10:30am-12:30pm and 2-6pm; mid-Sept. to mid-June W-Su 10am-noon and 2-5pm. Free.) In summer the tourist office offers **Promenades Nocturnes,** historical tours of the city and château by night. (Mid-July to mid-Aug. Th-Sa at 8:45pm. €4, students €2. Departs from the tourist office.)

ST-MALO

Scenic St-Malo (pop. 50,600) combines all the best qualities of France's northern cities. It has the most beautiful beaches outside of the Côte d'Azur, without the Côte d'Azur's pretension, as well as a charming walled *vieille ville* with countless *crêperies*, art galleries, boutiques, and cafes. Though 80 percent of the town was destroyed in 1944, careful reconstruction (some buildings were reassembled stone by stone) makes it nearly impossible to distinguish the old from the new.

▐ TRANSPORTATION

Trains: square Sean Coquelin (☎02 99 36 70 11). Info office open daily 9am-7pm. Trains run, all via **Dol,** to: **Caen** (3½hr., 3 per day, €24.30); **Dinan** (1hr., 4 per day, €7.60); **Paris** (5hr., 10 per day, €63.50); **Pontorson** (45min., 3 per day, €6.80); **Rennes** (1hr., 7-15 per day, €11).

Buses: At esplanade St-Vincent. Offices beside tourist office, pick-up across the street. **Tourisme Verney** (☎02 99 40 83 33) runs to: **Cancale** (30min., 4 per day, €3.40); **Dinard** (30min., 11 per day, €3.40); **Rennes** (1¾hr.; M-F 5 per day, Su 1 per day;

€9.90). Purchase tickets on the bus. Office open M-F 9am-noon and 2-5pm. **Courriers Bretons** (☎02 99 19 70 80; www.lescourriersbretons.fr) goes to: **Cancale** (45min., 4 per day, €3.80) and **Mont-St-Michel** (1½hr.; M-Sa 4 per day, Su 1 per day; €9.20). Buses also stop at the hostel. Office open July-Aug. M-F 8:30am-6pm; Sept.-June 8:30am-12:15pm and 2-6:15pm.

Ferries: Gare Maritime de la Bourse. Brittany Ferries (☎02 99 40 64 41; www.brittanyferries.com) serves **Portsmouth** (9hr., 1-2 per day, €60-100). See **Getting There: By Boat**, p. 23, for details. **Condor Ferries** (☎08 25 16 03 00; www.condorferries.com) travels to **Jersey** (70min.) and **Guernsey** (2hr.; 1-2 daily in high season, fewer in low season; €50, ages 4-15 €30). **Emeraude Jersey Ferries** (☎08 25 16 51 80; www.emeraude.co.uk) runs to **Jersey** (70min.; 1-3 per day; €50, ages 15-23 €43, ages 4-14 €30).

Public Transportation: St-Malo Bus (☎02 99 56 06 06), in the bus office pavilion. Buses run daily July-Aug. 7am-midnight; Sept.-June 7am-8pm. The tourist office and the hostel have free copies of the master map and schedule. Tickets €1.10 (valid 1hr.), *carnet* of 10 €8.15, 24hr. pass €3.60. Office open July-Aug. M-Sa 8:15am-12:15pm and 1:45-6:10pm. Sept.-June closed Sa afternoon.

Taxis: Allo Taxi Malouins (☎02 99 81 30 30) or **Taxi Daniel** (☎06 60 21 59 95). Stands at St-Vincent and the train station.

Bike Rental: Les Vélos Bleus, 19 rue Alphonse Thébault (☎02 99 40 31 63; www.velos-bleus.fr), by the train station, also has mountain bikes. €9-12 per ½-day, €12-15 per day, €40-60 per week. €100 or passport deposit. Open daily Mar.-Oct. 9am-noon and 2-6pm.

Windsurfer Rental: Surf School St-Malo, 2 av. de la Hoguette (☎02 99 40 07 47; www.surfschool.asso.fr). Along Grande Plage, about 1km away from the walled city (look for the sign). Rental €25 per first hr., €17 each additional hr., €42.40 per ½-day, €37 additional ½-day. Lessons €35 per hr. Open daily 9am-noon and 1:30-6pm.

■✦ 🛈 ORIENTATION AND PRACTICAL INFORMATION

The small walled neighborhood (*intra-muros*) is the northernmost point of the city and the heart of the shopping and restaurant district. The train station is closer to the uninteresting town center. The area from four blocks to the west of the train station down to the old city is prime beach territory.

Tourist Office: esplanade St-Vincent (☎02 99 56 64 48; www.saint-malo-tourisme.com), near entrance to the old city. From train station, cross bd. de la République and follow av. Louis Martin to esplanade St-Vincent. (10min.) Or, take bus #1, 2, 3, 4, or 6 (every 20min.) from bd. de la République to St-Vincent. From *gare maritime*, turn left onto quai St-Louis. Free map (or detailed map €1.50), city guide with walking tours, tide timetables, and list of accommodations. Open July-Aug. M-Sa 9am-7:30pm, Su 10am-6pm; Apr.-May, June, and Sept. M-Sa 9am-12:30pm and 1:30-7:30pm, Su 10am-12:30pm and 2:30-6pm; Oct.-Mar. M-Sa 9am-12:30pm and 1:30-6pm.

Tours: Couriers Bretons (see **Transportation,** p. 197) runs tours in summer to Fréhel (5hr., M and F €19) or Dinan (8hr., Th, €24); Île de Bréhat (10hr., W, €36); and Mont-St-Michel (half-day W and Th 1:45-6:15pm, €22; full-day Tu and Sa 9:30am-6:15pm, €25; ages 4-11 free).

Bank: Exchange currency at **Banque de France,** rue d'Asfeld at the southeast corner of the walled city. Exchange desk open M-F 9am-noon.

Laundromat: 27 bd. de la Tour d'Auvergne. Open daily 7am-9pm.

Police: 3 pl. des Frères Lamennais (☎02 99 20 69 00).

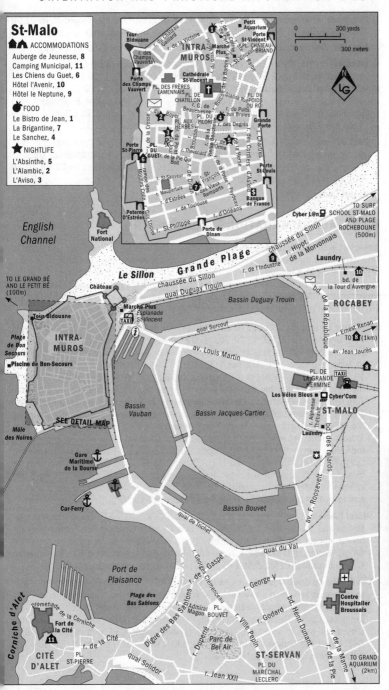

St-Malo

🏠 ACCOMMODATIONS

Auberge de Jeunesse, **8**
Camping Municipal, **11**
Les Chiens du Guet, **6**
Hôtel l'Avenir, **10**
Hôtel le Neptune, **9**

🍴 FOOD

Le Bistro de Jean, **1**
La Brigantine, **7**
Le Sanchez, **4**

★ NIGHTLIFE

L'Absinthe, **5**
L'Alambic, **2**
L'Aviso, **3**

Pharmacy: Pharmacie de la Cathédrale, 4 rue du Pourpris by the cathedral. (☎02 99 40 93 41. Open M 2-7:30pm, Tu-Sa 9am-12:30pm and 2-7:30pm.)

Hospital: Centre Hospitalier Broussais, 1 rue de la Marne (☎02 99 21 21 21).

Internet Access: Cyber L@n, 68 chausseé du Sillon (☎02 99 56 07 78; cyberlanst-malo@wanadoo.fr). €2.50 per 30min., €4 per hr. Open M-Sa noon-1am and Su 3pm-1am. **Cyber'Com,** 26bis bd. des Talards (☎02 99 56 05 83; fax 02 23 18 01 97), 2 blocks left of the train station and across the street. €3.80 per hr. Half-price for the unemployed. Open M 2-6pm, Tu-W and F 9am-noon and 2-6pm, Th 1-8pm, Sa 9am-noon and 2-5:30pm. Also at **L'Alambic** (see **Entertainment,** p. 203).

Post Office: 1 bd. de la Tour d'Auvergne (☎02 99 20 51 70), at the intersection with bd. de la République. **Currency exchange,** Cyberposte, fax, and photocopies. Open M-F 8am-7pm, Sa 8am-noon. Branch office, pl. des Frères Lamennais (☎02 99 40 89 90). Open M-F 8:45am-12:15pm and 1:30-5:45pm, Sa 8:45am-noon.

Postal Code: 35400.

⌂ 🏕 ACCOMMODATIONS AND CAMPING

Reserve up to six months in advance to stay in the *vieille ville* in July and August. The extremely popular hostel doesn't take phone reservations; book by fax or letter—and well in advance—to stay there in summer. Aside from camping and the hostel, the best budget options are far and away Hôtel l'Avenir and Hôtel le Neptune; beware of similarly outfitted options next to the train station, which run €10-15 higher and offer nothing extra other than emptier pockets.

🏠 **Auberge de Jeunesse/Centre de Rencontres Internationales (HI),** 37 av. du Révérend Père Umbricht (☎02 99 40 29 80; fax 02 99 40 29 02; www.centrevarangot.com). From the train station, take bus #5 (dir: Paramé or Davier) or bus #1 (dir: Rothéneuf) to Auberge de Jeunesse (last bus 7:30pm). Or, bus #1 (July-late Aug., 1 per hr. 8am-11:30pm) from St-Vincent or the tourist office. By foot, follow bd. de la République to the right from the station; turn right onto av. Ernest Renan, then left onto av. de Moka. Turn right on av. Pasteur, which becomes av. du Rév. Père Umbricht; keep right at the "Auberge de Jeunesse" sign (30min.) Enormous establishment in pretty stone building 3 blocks from beach. Clean, bright 2- to 6-person rooms with new furniture, sinks, bathrooms. Tennis, volleyball, and basketball courts. Common room with TV. Kitchen with individual refrigerators (€1.50). Wheelchair-accessible. M-F meals €6.40. Laundry. Luggage storage €2. Reception M-F 8:30am-10pm, Sa-Su 8:45am-10pm. May be closed at lunch; code for late entry. 4- to 6-person rooms with sink €13.20; 2- to 3-person rooms with shower and toilet €16; 2- to 5-person rooms with bunk beds, shower, and toilet €14.20; singles €6 extra. Prices lower Oct.-Apr. ❶

Hôtel l'Avenir, 31bd. de la Tour d'Auvergne (☎02 99 56 13 33). 5min. from the train station and 10min. from the walled city. Small hotel lets simple but adequate rooms over a modest bar. Some second-story rooms over street may lack privacy. Breakfast €4.50. Reception M-W and F 7:30am-8pm, Th and Sa 7am-8pm, Su 7am-1pm. Singles €21, with shower €25; doubles €22/€27; quad with shower and toilet €45. ❷

Les Chiens du Guet, 4 pl. du Guet (☎02 99 40 87 29; fax 02 99 56 08 75). Any closer to the beach and you'd be swimming in your sleep. Overlooking the plage de Bon Secours, this charming hotel features bright rooms and the lowest prices *intra-muros*. Breakfast €5.50. Reception 8am-midnight. Reserve 1-2 weeks in advance June-Aug. Closed mid-Nov. to Jan. Sept.-June doubles with shower €36, with shower and toilet €42; triples with shower and toilet €52.50; quads with shower and toilet €63. July-Aug. prices slightly higher. AmEx/MC/V. ❹

Hôtel le Neptune, 21 rue de l'Industrie (☎02 99 56 82 15), on an empty street 5min. from both station and *intra-muros*, 1 block from the beach. Unremarkable hotel, recently renovated, above a bar with a foosball and pool table. Breakfast €5.50. Reception M-Sa 9:30am-1pm and 4:30-10pm. Singles and doubles with shower €28, with shower and toilet €33-38, with bath €33-42. Extra bed €8. MC/V. ❸

Camping: Camping Municipal La Cité d'Alet, at the western tip of St-Servan (☎02 99 81 60 91; www.ville-saint-malo.fr/campings). Buses #1 and 6 to Alet about twice per day (or, take a bus to St-Servan and head northwest to Alet). From bus stop, head uphill and left at the ruined Cathédrale St-Pierre onto allée Gaston Buy; campground is 50m away. 350 spots in a quiet, scenic location by the beach. Reception daily July-Aug. 8am-9pm; Sept.-June M-F 9am-12:30pm and 3-6pm, Sa-Su 8:30am-6:30pm. Gates closed 10pm-7am; after 8pm see the night guard in the office across from mini-golf course. 2 people and tent €11.10, 2 people and caravan with electricity €14.80. Each additional adult €5.20, under 10 free. ❶

⚡ FOOD

Skip the generic, overpriced restaurants huddled just within the *intra-muros*. **Outdoor markets** (8am-12:30pm) are on pl. Bouvet in St-Servan, at the Marché aux Légumes (Tu and F) and on pl. du Prieuré in Paramé (W and Sa). There is a **Marché Plus supermarket** underground, 9 rue St-Vincent, near the entrance to the city walls at Porte St-Vincent (open M-Sa 7am-9pm and Su 9am-1pm), and a **Champion** supermarket on av. Pasteur near the hostel. (Open M-F 8:30am-1pm and 3-7:30pm, Sa 8:30am-7:30pm, Su 9:30am-noon. Longer hours July-Aug.)

Sweet-toothed travelers will want to swing by ◤**Le Sanchez ❶**, 9 rue de la Vie-ille Boucherie at pl. du Pilori, where exotic flavors of delicious homemade *gelato* are heaped with goodies like huge chocolate chunks and served in tall cones. (☎02 99 56 67 17. 1 scoop €1.80, 2 scoops €2.60; truly decadent "Super Sanchez" a bargain at €4.50. Open daily about 11am-11pm. Sept. to mid-Nov. closed W. Closed mid-Nov. to Jan.) For an inexpensive meal, dine in the classy country interior of **La Brigantine ❷**, 13 rue de Dinan, where the savory *galettes* (€2-7) are stuffed to bursting and the sweet crêpes (€1.50-6) show off in-house recipes. (☎02 99 56 82 82. Salads €2.30-6.50. *Prix-fixe menu* €9.55. Open M and Th-F 11am-3pm and 6:30-8pm, Sa-Su noon-11pm. Hours may vary. MC/V.) The freshest market fare is given the traditional French bistro treatment at **Le Bistro de Jean ❹**, 6 rue de la Corne de Cerf, close to the Porte St-Vincent, where the menu changes daily and there's always something interesting. (☎/fax 02 99 40 98 68. Starters €7.50-9.50; *plats* €14-28; desserts €6. Wine €2.50-4.10. Open for lunch and dinner M-Sa; closed W and Sa afternoons.)

◉ SIGHTS

It's hard to go wrong with the beaches in St-Malo. On the western side of the *intra-muros*, best accessed by stairwells that lead down from the walls, the **plage de Bon-Secours** is secluded (by St-Malo standards, at least) and features the curious **Piscine de Bon-Secours,** three cement walls that hold in a pool's worth of warm salt water even when the tide recedes. To the east is the larger **Grande Plage,** edged by a double row of dry, gnarled tree trunks that appear to be walking two-by-two into the sea. Farther up the coast is the couple-filled **plage Rochebonne.**

The best view of St-Malo is from its **ramparts.** From the northern side of the city, the sea is speckled with a series of small islands. The three largest, Fort National, Le Grand Bé, and Le Petit Bé, can only be reached during a narrow time window at low tide over a pebbly path strewn with stranded mollusks. **Fort National** (look for

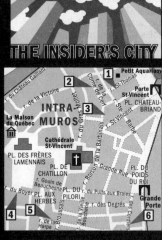

ST-MALO'S ART ATELIERS

The alleys of St-Malo's walled city hide an assortment of *ateliers* (art studios) open to the public.

1 **Les Naufrages du Temps,** 12 rue St-Thomas, showcases both traditional and contemporary African art.

2 **Denise and Andre Aleth Masson,** 14 rue de la Corne de Cerf, use mixed media—including wood, paint, and pacifiers—in sculptures and paintings.

3 At **Atelier Patrick Vaillant,** 3 rue de la Corne de Cerf, the artist ties painted canvas fragments on a base of metal rods to make an image.

4 Peasants, roosters, and flowers bring Breton legends to life on tiles at the **Galerie Gwen & Dodik,** 10 rue du Boyer.

5 **Galerie Sklerijenn,** 3 rue de la Harpe, has shown art and jewelry for more than a decade.

6 **The Galerie Ombre et Lumière,** 9 rue des Cordiers, explores light and shadow in eight yearly exhibitions.

the French flag) was built in 1689 by the military's master architect, Vauban, to protect St-Malo from the English. He must have done his job well, as the fort has never been successfully taken by sea. German forces based on land, however, imprisoned 380 men here during World War II. It's not really worth paying for a tour of the empty, stony fortresses, except for the fabulous view of the bay and the city from the top. (☎02 99 85 34 33; fax 02 99 85 34 33. Open daily June-Sept. Hours depend on the tides; call the tourist office for a schedule. Tours in French at low tide (1-2 per day); written explanations in English, German, Spanish, and Italian. €4, ages 6-15 €2.) The other two islands, west of the Fort and near the Piscine de Bon-Secours, are worth a visit for their strange rocky seclusion. **Le Grand Bé** ("Bé means "tomb" in Breton) holds the grave of native son **Chateaubriand** (1768-1848), who asked to be buried amid the wind and waves that inspired his books. Those who prefer their excursions dry should heed the posted warnings not to set out for any of the islands if the tide is within 10m of the causeway.

The **Grand Aquarium,** av. du Général Patton, (not to be confused with the smaller aquarium *intra-muros*), is sure to please the young—in years or at heart—with a well-organized, interactive aquatic display that includes an outdoor tide pool, a *Finding Nemo* tank, and a talking octopus robot. The unusual Nautibus takes visitors underwater, and the giant wraparound CineMerScope brings sharks closer than you may want them. Take bus #5 (dir: Moinerie or Grassinais) from the station, the tourist office, or the hostel; in summer a special A-line goes straight there from the tourist office. (☎02 99 21 19 00; www.aquarium-st-malo.com. Open daily mid-July to mid-Aug. 9:30am-10pm; early July and late Aug. 9:30am-8pm; Apr.-June and Sept. 10am-7pm; Oct.-Mar. 10am-6pm. Closed Nov. 15-19 and 22-26, Jan. 5-23. Last entry 1hr. before closing. €13, ages 4-14 €9.50, under 4 free.)

St-Malo native and explorer of Canada Jacques Cartier is buried in the 12th-century **Cathédrale St-Vincent,** which has been carefully restored following heavy damage in WWII. Purists may disdain them, but the distinctively modern 20th-century altar and iridescent stained glass have an undeniably psychedelic allure. (Open June-Aug. M-Sa 9:45am-7pm, Su 9:30am-6pm; Sept.-May closed noon-2pm. Mass Sa 6:30pm; Su 10, 11:30am, 6pm.) During July and August, the cathedral presents a series of classical and choral music concerts through the Festival de Musique Sacrée. (☎02 99 56 05 38, reservations 06 08 31 99 93.)

🎴 🌿 ENTERTAINMENT AND FESTIVALS

Keep a lookout at bars for *L'Omnibus*, a small brochure that lists a diverse mix of cheap contemporary concerts in town. **◼L'Absinthe**, 1 rue de l'Orme, attracts a wildly varied clientele in an equally varied interior, where multi-hued lamps and an oversized clock give the aura of a Magritte painting. (☎02 99 40 85 40. Frozen margaritas €3.50. Aperitifs €2.20. Open daily 3pm-2am; in winter noon-1am. Closed Su in low season. MC/V.) **L'Alambic**, 8 rue du Boyer, looks like a brewery with its brass lamps, stone walls, and timbered ceilings, and draws a young crowd every night. Internet available for €1 per 10min. (☎02 99 40 86 41. Beer €2.30-3.20. Liquor €5.50-7. Open daily around 11am-2am.) **L'Aviso**, 12 rue du Point du Jour, sells 300 types of beer (starting at €2.60) and 12 whiskeys in a hip version of the neighborhood corner bar. Soccer matches are televised on a huge screen during the season. (☎02 99 40 99 08; fax 02 99 56 31 14. Open daily July-Aug. 5pm-2:45am, Sept.-June closes at 1:45am.)

St-Malo draws big crowds to its many festivals. Writers pour in from around the world and book fairs abound at the end of May for **Etonnants Voyageurs**, the pre-eminent international literary festival in France. (☎02 99 31 05 74; etonnants.voyageurs@wanadoo.fr.) The **Festival des Folklores du Monde** attracts international folk musicians and dancers the first week of July (☎02 99 40 42 50). The **Route du Rock** draws 20 bands to the city during the second weekend of August (☎02 99 54 01 11; www.laroutedurock.com). The **Quai des Bulles,** held the last weekend in October, lets you meet the creators of your favorite comic strips (☎02 99 40 39 63; www.quaidesbulles.com). The recently inaugurated **Festival des Films de l'Eté** screens 20 films, many of them French. (Late June; check www.festivaldesfilms-delete.com for more information.)

DINAN

Dinan (pop. 10,000) leads multiple lives. Its *vieille ville*, imposingly lodged 66m above the river Rance, has all the charms of a well-preserved Breton medieval town, with cobblestoned streets, traditional artisans, and *crêperies*. But breach the ramparts, and you'll either find yourself in a lush river valley or a lively commercial center, depending on your location. Together, these different faces make up one of Brittany's more appealing destinations.

🚌 TRANSPORTATION

Trains: pl. du 11 Novembre 1918 (☎02 96 39 00 78). Office open M-Th 6am-7pm, F-Sa 7:10am-7pm, Su 9am-8pm. To: **Morlaix** (1½hr., 2-3 per day, €17.90) via **St-Brieuc; Paris** (3hr., 8 per day, €53.50); **Rennes** (1hr., 8 per day, €11.60); **St-Malo** (1hr., 7 per day, €7.60) via **Dol.**

Buses: CAT/TV buses (☎02 96 39 21 05) leave from the train station and pl. Duclos. Office open M-F 8am-noon and 2-6pm. To **St-Malo** (50min.; M-Sa 5 per day, Su 3 per day; €5.70). **TAE buses/Cars 35** (☎02 99 26 16 00), leave from the station to **Dinard** (30min., 7 per day, €1.80) and **Rennes** (70min., 7 per day, €8.80).

Taxis: (☎02 98 39 06 00).

Bike Rental: Cycles Scardin, 30 rue Carnot (☎02 96 39 21 94). Bikes €12.20 per half-day, €15 per day, €90 per week. €100 deposit. Open Tu-Sa 9am-noon and 2-7pm. MC/V.

Canoe and Kayak Rental: Club Canoë Kayak, 18 rue du Quai Talard, off rue Petit Fort at the Port de Dinan (☎/fax 02 96 39 01 50). Canoes €12 per hour, €20 per half-day, €30 per day. Kayaks €8/€15/€21. Passport deposit. Swimming ability required. Open daily July-Aug. 10am-noon and 2-5:30pm; open Sa-Su in June.

✈ 🛈 ORIENTATION AND PRACTICAL INFORMATION

Below the Jerzual Gate, rue du Petit Fort leads downhill from the walled city to the valley. To get to the **tourist office**, 9 rue du Château, from the station, bear left across pl. du 11 Novembre 1918 onto rue Carnot, then right onto rue Thiers, which brings you to pl. Duclos. Turn left to go inside the old city walls and bear right onto rue du Marchix, which becomes rue de la Ferronnerie. Pass parking lots on pl. du Champ and pl. Duguesclin to the left; the tourist office is ahead on right. Multilingual team provides a free walking-tour city map, an excellent historical guide with circuits in the city and region (€2), a "Keys to the City" pass (€6.10, €13.50 for families) in July and August that gives access to four of Dinan's major sights, a reservations service (€2), and walking tours of the ramparts and the *intra-muros*. (☎ 02 96 87 69 76; www.dinan-tourisme.com. Open mid-June to mid-Sept. M-Sa 9am-7pm, Su 10am-12:30pm and 2:30-6pm; mid-Sept. to mid-June M-Sa 9am-12:30pm and 2-6pm. Tours in French daily July-Aug. 3pm; Tu, Th, Sa in English 2:30pm. Tours in French Apr.-June and Sept. Sa at 3pm. €5, children €2.50.)

Other services include: a **laundromat**, 19 rue de Brest, off rue Thiers on rue des Rouairies, which becomes rue de Brest (open M 2-7pm, Tu and Th 8:30am-noon and 2-7pm, W and F-Sa 8:30am-7pm); **police**, 16bis pl. du Guesclin (☎ 02 96 87 65 87), near the château; a **hospital**, rue Chateaubriand (☎ 02 96 85 72 85), in Léhon; **Internet** at Aerospace Cybercafé, 9 rue de la Chaux, off rue de l'Horloge. (☎ 02 96 87 14 85; arospace@wanadoo.fr. €1.50 per 15min. Open Tu-Sa 10am-12:30pm and 2-7pm.) The **post office**, 7 pl. Duclos, has **currency exchange**, a Cyberposte, and fax. (☎ 02 96 85 83 50. Open M-F 8am-6:30pm, Sa 9am-12:30pm.) **Postal Code:** 22100.

🏠 🏕 ACCOMMODATIONS AND CAMPING

The best place to **camp** is at the hostel in a shaded field behind the main building (€5.30). The tourist office lists other more urban sites.

▩ **Auberge de Jeunesse "Moulin du Méen" (HI)** (☎ 02 96 39 10 83; dinan@fuaj.org), slightly outside town in Vallée de la Fontaine-des-Eaux. Turn left from train station, left across tracks, then right; follow tracks and signs downhill for 1km. Turn right and continue through wooded lanes (be careful—no sidewalk) for 0.5km until you reach the hostel on the right. (30min.) Housed in a beautiful old mill 2km from the town center, this hostel offers clean, pretty 2- to 8-bed rooms. Features summer photo workshops (€36.60 per week), and equestrian and athletic activities. Guests can bake their own bread once monthly in outdoor oven. Volleyball courts. Kitchen access. Breakfast €3.30, lunch or dinner €8.60. Sheets €2.80. Laundry. Reception July-Aug. 8am-noon and 5-9pm; Sept.-June 9am-noon and 5-8pm; code for late entry. Closed Jan. Beds €9.30. MC/V. HI members only. ❶

Hôtel du Théâtre, 2 rue Ste-Claire (☎ 02 96 39 06 91), above a quiet bar, has bright well-priced rooms, some with large windows, in the heart of the *vieille ville*. The owner, proudly Breton, has adorned the building's stone facade with regional flags. Cheaper top-floor rooms are a bit cramped. Breakfast €4 or €5.50. Reception daily 8am-8pm. One single with sink €15; double with sink €21.50-22.50; singles or doubles with shower and toilet €27.50; triples with shower and toilet €36.50. ❷

Hôtel de la Gare, pl. de la Gare (☎ 02 96 39 04 57; fax 02 96 39 02 29), across from the station, 10min. from the old quarter. Friendly owners rent bright, clean, comfortable rooms, some with TV, over a corner bar. Breakfast €4.60. Shower €1.60. Reception M-Sa 7am-8pm, Su 5-8pm. Singles €22; doubles €24-26, with shower €28, with toilet €45; triples or quads with shower €37-45. Extra bed €4.60. MC/V. ❷

Hôtel de la Tour de l'Horloge, 5 rue de la Chaux (☎02 96 39 96 92; hiliotel@wana-doo.fr). Spacious and colorful rooms in the shadow of the Tour de l'Horloge, all with bath and toilet. Breakfast €6. Reserve at least one week in advance. Doubles with either large bed or 2 single beds €43-66; quads €77. Extra bed €12. AmEx/MC/V. ❹

🍴 FOOD

Simple bars and *brasseries* line the streets linking rue de la Ferronnerie with pl. des Merciers, especially on narrow **rue de la Cordonnerie**. A **Monoprix supermarket** is at 7 pl. du Marchix. (Open M-Sa 9am-7:30pm.) There is also a **Marché Plus**, 28 pl. Duclos, near the post office. (☎02 96 87 50 51. Open M-Sa 7am-9pm, Su 9am-1pm.) Put together a picnic of fruit and *gavottes*, the town's specialty crêpes, at the outdoor **market** on pl. du Champ and pl. du Guesclin in the *vieille ville*. (Open Th 8am-noon.) Small restaurants cluster in the cobbled streets outside the ramparts and along the port. Within the walls of the old town, you'll need to beat the *crêperies* off with a stick.

Framed by pink flowers and yellow awnings, the **Crêperie des Artisans ❶**, 6 rue Petit Fort, on a charming street leading to the river, serves a varied menu of *galettes* (€1.60-6) and crêpes (€1.30-5). Communal wooden tables, dark stone walls, and hanging garlic bunches create a rustic atmosphere. (☎02 96 39 44 10. Open Apr.-Sept. Tu-Su noon-2:30pm and 7-10pm. Hours may vary.) Right around the corner from the Tour de l'Horloge, **Taj Mahal ❸**, 9 rue Ste-Claire, serves authentic Indian delights, including *naan* (€2-3.50) and plenty of vegetarian options. Fixed *menus* (€9-20) are tasty, filling, and come with exotic desserts. (☎02 96 85 45 30. Starters €4-6, *plats* €8-12. Open daily for lunch and dinner. MC/V.)

👁 SIGHTS

Spanning nearly 3km, the town's **ramparts** are the longest and oldest in Brittany and a sight unto themselves. **Rue du Petit Fort** hosts an array of local art galleries selling, among other things, unique samples of sculpture and medieval clothing.

The 🏛**Maison d'Artiste de la Grande Vigne**, 103 rue du Quai, past the port, is the former home of painter Yvonne Jean-Haffen (1895-1993), who moved here in 1937. Reaching it entails a long but pleasant walk from the town through the Jerzual Gate, down the steep rue du Petit Fort, and left along the rue du Quai, which takes you down into the city's picturesque valley. Visitors are free to wander through the rooms, all designed by the artist, whose murals and paintings adorn the walls; a faux fur bedspread on the top floor is a somewhat incongruous detail. Leave by the back door to descend through a flower-garnished hillside garden. (☎02 96 87 90 80 or 02 96 39 22 43. Open daily July-Aug. 10am-6:30pm; mid-May to June and Sept. 2-6:30pm. Last entry at 6pm. €2.60, students and ages 12-18 €1.65.)

On the ramparts, the 13th-century **Porte du Guichet** marks the entrance to the **Château de Dinan**, which has served alternately as a military stronghold, residence, and prison. Today its former keep in the **Tour de la Duchesse Anne** houses a small museum of local art and history. A great view of the town greets those who make it up the 150 steps of the 34m tower. Included in the ticket is the 15th-century **Tour de Coëtquen,** next to the keep. Along with the occasional temporary exhibit, its dank, drafty basement possesses a fine collection of funerary ornaments and medieval sculptures. (☎02 96 39 45 20. Open daily June-Sept. 10am-6:30pm, last entrance 6pm; Oct.-Dec. and Feb.-May 1:30-5:30pm. €4, ages 12-18 €1.55.) The **Jardins "des Petits Diables" du Val Cocherel,** on the ramparts behind the château and the tourist office, begins hilly and

BRITTANY

densely wooded, but gives way to huge bird cages, a rose garden, a checker-board for life-sized chessmen, a small zoo, and a children's library. (Garden open daily 8am-7:30pm. Nov.-Mar. closed Su mornings. Library open daily 10am-noon and 1:30-6:30pm. Free.)

The **Basilique St-Sauveur** was built by a local man grateful to have been spared in the Crusades. The Romanesque facade, including the lion and bull above the doorway and four statues in side arches, dates to AD 1120. Within are 12 painted and gilded wooden altars and screens made by local craftsmen, as well as the heart of the unfortunate Bertrand du Guesclin, perhaps the only Frenchman to have five tombs for various body parts. Begun in the 15th century, the **Église St-Malo,** on Grande Rue, contains a remarkable 19th-century English organ with blue and gold pipes and a massive Baroque altar. (Mass M-Th 8am, F 10am, Sa 7pm, Su 10:30am.)

The summit of the 30m 15th-century **Tour de l'Horloge,** on rue de l'Horloge, commands a brilliant view of Dinan's jumbled streets and the Rance Valley. Pass through the stone rooms that once held council meetings and town archives. (☎ 02 96 87 02 26. Open daily July-Aug. 10am-6:30pm; Apr.-June and Sept. 2-6pm. €2.60, ages 12-17 and students €1.65, under 12 free. Explanations available in English.)

⚏ ✿ NIGHTLIFE AND FESTIVALS

L'Absinthe, 15 pl. St-Sauveur, near the basilica, feels like an old-fashioned speak-easy, except for the sunny, inviting porch on its doorstep. Soft jazz and tables painted to resemble French posters add a touch of sophistication. (☎ 02 96 87 39 28. Beer €2.20-3.70. Aperitifs €2-3.30. Open daily Apr.-Sept. 9am-10pm; Sept.-Apr. M 5-10pm, Tu-Sa 9am-10pm.)

Every two years (next in 2006), Dinan hosts the two-day **Fête des Remparts** during the second half of July, when the whole town dons medieval garb for jousting tournaments, markets, and merrymaking. (☎ 02 96 87 94 94; http://perso.wanadoo.fr/fete-remparts.dinan. Daily 10am-9pm. All-day access to 4 sites €10, under 10 and those in medieval garb free; tournaments €10, ages 5-9 €6.)

PAIMPOL

Anchored on the border of the Côte de Granite Rose and the Côte de Goëlo, Paimpol (PAM-pol; pop. 8200) is a pleasant little fishing village. While its traditional ties are to rod and reel, a string of snazzy bars, restaurants, and yachts around the port brings a lively modern flair. Paimpol itself has few sights, but it provides easy access to surrounding islands, cliffs, beaches, hiking trails, nautical activities, and the picturesque ruins of the Abbaye de Beauport.

⌫ TRANSPORTATION

Trains run to Pontrieux (16min., 5 per day, €2.80). At Guingamp (☎ 02 96 20 81 22), there are connections to Morlaix (1¼hr., 4 per day, €10). Station is located at av. du Général de Gaulle. (Office open M-F 6:40-7:10am and 8am-7pm, Sa 7:30am-7pm, Su and holidays 8:45am-7pm.) **CAT buses** (☎ 02 96 22 67 72) run from the train station to Pointe de l'Arcouest (12min.; M-Sa 7 per day, Su 5 per day; €1.80.) The same bus system runs throughout the Côtes d'Armor and to the campground. Buy tickets on the bus. **Bikes** can be rented at Cycles du Vieux Clocher, pl. de Verdun. (☎ 02 96 20 83 58. €6 per half-day, €11 per day. Open M-Sa 8:30am-12:30pm and 2-7:30pm, Su 8am-noon. MC/V.)

PRACTICAL INFORMATION

To reach the port and the **tourist office** on pl. de la République, turn right onto av. du Général de Gaulle and follow it to the roundabout, then bear left. The tourist office will be on the left, opposite the Marché Plus; the port will be to the right. The jolly staff provides a map of the hiking trails leading from Paimpol to the Pointe de l'Arcouest and organizes tours of the city and region. (☎02 96 20 83 16; www.paimpol-goelo.com. Open mid-June to mid-Sept. M-Sa 9:30am-7:30pm, Su 10am-6pm; mid-Sept. to mid-June M-Sa 9:30am-12:30pm and 1:30-6:30pm. Tours mostly May-Sept. €5, under 12 free. Reservations required.) Other services include: **currency exchange** at the Société Générale, 6 pl. de la République (☎02 96 20 80 05; open Tu-F 8:30am-12:15pm and 1:30-5:15pm, Sa 8:30am-12:45pm); **police** at rue Raymond Pellier (☎02 96 20 80 17); a **hospital** at chemin de Malabry (☎02 96 55 60 00), off the right side of the port; and **Internet** at L'Esp@ce M.S.P., rond point du Goelo, at the roundabout by the train station and tourist office (☎02 96 20 47 29; msp-paimpol@wanadoo.fr. €0.75 per min.; open M 2:15-7pm, Tu-Sa 9:30am-12:30pm and 2:15-7pm), or at Cybercommune, Centre Dunant, near the church. (☎02 96 20 74 74; http://cybercommune.paimpol-goelo.com. €0.09 per min., €5 per hr. Open M 2:30-7pm, Tu-Sa 9:30am-12:30pm and 2:30-7pm.) Do **laundry** or rent sheets at Au Lavoir Pampolais, 23 rue du 18 Juin, near the station. (☎02 96 20 96 41. Open daily 8am-8pm. Alterations and sheet rental Tu-Sa 9:30am-noon and 2:30-6pm. Also near the port on rue de Labenne. Open daily 7am-10pm.) The **post office,** 10 av. du Général de Gaulle, also has **currency exchange.** (☎02 96 20 82 40. Open M and W-F 8am-noon and 1:30-5:30pm, Tu 8am-12:30pm and 1:30-5:30pm, Sa 8am-12:30pm.) **Postal Code:** 22500.

ACCOMMODATIONS AND CAMPING

Relatively identical options crowd the port area. The cheapest stay in the center of town is **Hôtel Berthelot ❸,** 1 rue du Port. From the tourist office, walk straight toward the port and turn left after three blocks onto rue du Port. A giant blue "H" on a pink facade marks the hotel's entrance on the right. An exceedingly cheerful staff oversees two floors of large, comfy rooms with lots of light. Noise from the bar across the street travels to some rooms at night. (☎02 96 20 88 66. Breakfast €4.50. Singles and doubles €27, with shower €38, with bath and toilet €39, with shower, toilet, and TV €41; quads with sink €35. MC/V.) **Le Terre-Neuvas ❸,** 16 quai Duguay-Trouin, on the waterfront, over the restaurant of the same name (see **Food,** p. 208), has small, welcoming rooms, some with harbor views and all with TV and phone. (☎02 96 55 14 14; fax 02 96 20 47 66. Breakfast €5. Call ahead in summer. Rooms for 1-2 people with bath €31, with harbor view €37; rooms for 2-3 people €39/€45. Extra bed €12. MC/V.) **Hôtel Le Goëlo ❹,** quai Duguay-Trouin, has the nicest rooms, all modern and well-furnished, with TV and bath, some overlooking the port. From the tourist office, walk toward the water and take the first right; the hotel is just ahead. (☎02 96 20 82 74; www.hotel-legoelo.com. Wheelchair-accessible. Reserve in advance in the summer. Breakfast €5. Singles and doubles €43-55; quads €70. Prices higher July-Aug. MC/V.) The **Auberge de Jeunesse (HI) ❶,** Château de Kéraoul (☎02 96 20 83 60), 20min. uphill on the western edge of town, will reopen in 2005 after massive renovations.

The popular seaside **Camping Municipal de Cruckin ❶,** off the plage de Cruckin, is by the Abbaye de Beauport. From the station, turn right onto av. du Général de Gaulle and take the third exit at the roundabout onto rue du Général Leclerc. Follow the street as it twists through four name changes and take rue de Cruckin from rue de Beauport. The entrance is 150m down the hill on the right (25 minutes). Sparse rows of hedges separate 154 flat grass plots. (☎ 02 96 20 78 47 or 02 96 55 11 83. Wheelchair-accessible. Showers included. Laundry available. Open Apr.-Sept. Reception M-Sa 8am-noon and 4:30-8pm; Su 9-11am and 6:30-7:30pm. Gates closed 10pm-7am. One person and tent €7.60; 2-3 people and tent €12.40. Extra adult €2.90, child under 7 €1.50. Electricity €2.40-2.90. Prices slightly lower Apr.-June and Sept. MC/V.)

◨ FOOD

Picnic supplies are at both the Tuesday morning **market** at pl. des Halles and the **Marché Plus supermarket,** 11 rue St-Vincent, located directly across from the tourist office. (Open M-Sa 7am-9pm, Su 9am-1pm; July-Aug. also open Su 5-8pm.)

Those who don't like seafood may be at a loss for sit-down fare in Paimpol. Instead of the overpriced options by the port, try **La Braise ❸,** 20 rue des 8 Patriotes, with its homey kitchen feel and high-quality grilled seafood and meat dishes (€8.60-12.65), including Breton duck. (☎ 02 96 55 11 41. *Menus* €16 and €22. Salads €5-9. Open daily 11:30am-2pm and 6:30-10pm, closed W afternoon. MC/V.) Portside **Le Terre-Neuvas ❷,** quai Duguay-Trouin, serves elegant food at backpacker prices. The specialties of the house are *moules frites* (fried mussels, €8; with appetizer and dessert €13). In July and August, five *grandes assiettes gourmandes* are served with grilled and seasoned bread, the catch of the day, salad, vegetables, and a side dish for only €11-15. (☎ 02 96 55 14 14. Fixed *menus* €14.50-29. Open daily July-Aug. noon-2pm and 7-10pm; Sept.-June closed M. MC/V.)

◉ SIGHTS

Hidden from the road by vegetation, the ruins of the ◪**Abbaye de Beauport,** chemin de l'Abbaye, look dreamily out to sea. Built in 1202, the abbey, east of Paimpol, was revamped for its 800th anniversary. The now-roofless church sprouts flowers from its flying buttresses and birds flutter where rafters once were. The crumbling building, overgrown with greenery and bordered by a meadow of poppies and butterflies, gives the sense of an undiscovered ruin. The book-guided self-tour (in French, English, or German) gives a complete account of the abbey's history and its many sections, from the intact cellars to the picturesque garden. To get there, follow directions to the campground, but continue past rue de Cruckin to the next major left turn; the abbey is at the end of the lane. (☎ 02 96 55 18 58; www.abbaye-beauport.com. Open daily mid-June to mid-Sept. 10am-7pm; mid-Sept. to mid-June 10am-noon and 2-5pm. Last entry 30min. before closing. English tours daily July-Aug. 11am; 3-4 tours in French per day. Audioguides available in French, English, German, and Italian. July-Aug. €5, students and seniors €4.50, ages 11-18 €3.50, ages 5-10 €2.50. Prices reduced in low season.)

◧ ✿ NIGHTLIFE AND FESTIVALS

Pick up *La Presse d'Armor,* a local weekly publication with a news summary and schedule of events (€1), at newsstands.

The port, overrun by private yachts, is boxed in by bars and restaurants, but the side-streets that trickle away from the waterfront have the real gems. As the sun sets, crowds head across the port to bars along quai de Kernoa. Just around the corner from Hôtel Berthelot, **Le Corto Maltese,** 11 rue du Quai, earns its popularity among locals with its loud mix of classic rock, laid-back atmosphere, interesting selection of Dutch and Irish beers on tap, and two time-worn pinball machines in the back. (☎ 02 96 22 05 76. Beer under €3. Irish coffee €5.50. Open daily 5pm-2am.) Decked out in primary colors, popular **Le Cargo,** 15 rue des 8 Patriotes, lines its walls with nautical artifacts and its chairs with talkative locals. (☎ 02 96 20 72 46. Beer €2.20-3.50. Aperitifs €2.20-5. Open July-Aug. Tu-Su 2:30pm-2am. Closed Su in low season. MC/V.) The heavy oak door of **Le Pub,** 3 rue Islandais, can't contain the revelry into the early hours. Irish folk music spices up the atmosphere every Thursday at 10pm; at midnight, people put on their dancing shoes as the bar turns into a discotheque. (☎ 02 96 20 82 31. Beer €3.10-4. Cocktails €7-9. Drinks go up in price after 2am. Cover for dancing €8, includes a drink. Non-alcoholic drinks half price for designated drivers. Open daily June-Sept. 7pm-3am; Oct.-May Th-Sa 7pm-3am, Su 10pm-3am.) For a true Breton dockside atmosphere, the **Tavarn An Tri Martolod** (Tavern of the Three Sailors), 10 quai de Kernoa, can't be topped. Breton song lyrics, fishnets, and the scrawls of patrons coat the yellow walls and ceilings. (☎ 02 96 20 75 15 or 06 03 35 19 65. Beer or cider €2. Open daily 5pm-2am.)

Every two years in early August (next in 2005), the **Fête du Chant de Marin** draws sailor-musicians from around the world for three days of dancing, boating, and general merriment (☎ 02 96 55 12 77; paimpol.fcm@wanadoo.fr).

▶ DAYTRIP FROM PAIMPOL

POINTE DE L'ARCOUEST AND ÎLE DE BRÉHAT

To reach the point, take a CAT bus (☎ 02 96 22 67 72) from Paimpol (12min.; M-Sa 7 per day, Su 5 per day, last bus from the Pointe 5:20pm; €1.80). Drivers can follow the clearly marked GR34 from the Paimpol port. Les Vedettes de Bréhat (☎ 02 96 55 79 50; www.vedettesdebrehat.com) sends boats from the point to the island (10min.; 8-17 per day; round-trip €7.50, ages 4-11 €6.50, passenger with bike €15.50). 45min. tours of the island €12, ages 4-11 €9. Tickets available at a booth on the Pointe or at the Paimpol tourist office.

Six kilometers north of Paimpol, the peninsula ends in a tumble of pink granite called the **Pointe de l'Arcouest.** The surrounding blue-green waters provide some of France's best sea kayaking; the Centre Nautique de Loguivy-de-la-Mer, just outside the Pointe on GR34, rents kayaks and catamarans. (☎ 02 96 20 94 58; www.voile-kayak-mer.com. Kayak rental with a guide €30 per half-day, €49 per day. Catamarans €40 per hr. Open M-Sa 9am-noon and 2-5pm.) On an island two kilometers across the water lies a mesh of rocky beaches, small tracts of farmland, flower-draped cottages, and fields of elbow-high grasses. Only 3.5km in length, the idyllic **Île de Bréhat** (pop. 410 in winter, 5000 in summer) is divided in the center by a small bridge. The rugged northern half is known for its lighthouse, while the southern half contains the *bourg* (town center) and the port. The Île de Bréhat is actually the largest landmass in an archipelago of 96 islets, some of them so minute that they essentially amount to single rocks. To get a good view of the island group, take the first boat of the day, then head north to avoid the crowds. For a few extra euros, take a 45min. circuit of the island from the sea to appreciate its cliff-strewn beauty before setting a foot on shore. The best way to tackle the island is by foot; paths to major sights are clearly marked. Even a short visit will take at least 2hr., so coordinate ferry and bus schedules appropriately.

Follow signs from the *bourg* to the tiny, white **Chapelle St-Michel,** on a hilltop on the west side of the island; the rock-speckled seascape that opens from the chapel is paralleled only by the view from the ■**Phare du Paon,** the lighthouse at the island's northern tip. Overlooking open blue waters, it blends smoothly into the reddish cliffs, which themselves resemble carved sculptures. According to a legend, when unwed women throw a pebble between the two parts of the rock, the number of bounces reveals the years separating them from marriage. The lighthouse is a 40-50min. walk from the center of town; make sure to allow at least 3hr. on the island in order to visit it.

A 15min. walk from the port is the *bourg*. Here, you can find restaurants, a **post office** that offers **currency exchange** and fax (☎ 02 96 20 00 71; open July-Aug. 9am-noon and 2-5pm, Sa 9am-noon; shorter hours in low season), and a **8 à Huit supermarket.** (Open M-Sa 9am-12:30pm and 4-7pm, Su 10am-1pm.) The île's restaurants serve similar, overpriced dishes in comparable settings; better bets are picnicking (come prepared) or a lunch counter. Of the latter, **La Bernique Affamée ❶,** in the square, has a good selection of cheap, fresh sandwiches (€3.50-4.50), served hot or cold on half-baguettes. (Crêpes €1.50-2. Open Tu-Su €10am-6pm. MC/V.)

To reach the **tourist office,** follow the main road toward the *bourg*, passing the 8 à Huit. When you reach the main square, the building, labeled "Syndicat d'Initiative," will be on your right. The office dispenses info about camping and a guide to the island (€2), although the *Vedettes de Bréhat* brochure offers an equivalent map for free. (☎ 02 96 20 04 15; Syndicatinitiative.Brehat@wanadoo.fr. Open daily July-Aug. 10am-1pm and 2-5:30pm; Sept.-June M and Th 10am-12:30pm and 2-4:30pm, Sa 10am-12:30pm.) **Bike rental** is available at the port: turn right, and look for the sign "Vélos a Louer." (€10 per half-day, €13 per day; children €7/€10. Open daily 9am-7pm. MC/V from May-Sept.) Although biking is a good way to cover ground on the island, some paths take quick ups and downs, and thick packs of pedestrians may block wheeled vehicles during the high season.

MORLAIX

Morlaix (pop. 17,000) traces its origins back to Gallo-Roman times, when Armorican Celts built a fort here called "Mons Relaxus" (Mount of Rest). Ironically, the town did not see much rest during its tumultuous history: it was continually invaded during the Middle Ages by the Duchy of Brittany as well as the French and British crowns. The city got its modern name after British invaders successfully captured the port, and the town's angry citizens surprised them in their drunken excess with cries of *"S'ils te mordent, mords-les!"* ("If they bite you, bite them back!"). History looms large over Morlaix in the form of an impressive two-tier viaduct above the city, but the fast-paced town refuses to live in its shadow. Although small and pleasantly untouristed, Morlaix has the distinctive feel of a big city, with busy cafes and *crêperies*, active commerce, and lively squares.

▐ TRANSPORTATION

Train Station: rue Armand Rousseau (☎ 08 36 35 35 35). Info office open M 5am-7:20pm, Tu-F 8:50am-7:20pm, Sa 8:50am-6:20pm, Su 1-8:25pm. To: **Brest** (45min.; 8-10 per day; €8.60, TGV €10.30); **Paimpol** (1¼hr., 5 per day, €13.70); **Quimper** via **Landerneau** or **Brest** (2hr., 5-7 per day, €15.50); **Roscoff** (30min., 2 per day, €4.70).

Buses: SNCF also leaves from the train station for **Roscoff** (30-45min., 4 per day, €4.70). **CAT** (☎ 02 98 72 01 41) runs to: **Quimper** (2hr., 3-5 per week, €10); **Roscoff** (30-45min.; M-Sa 3-4 per day, Su 1 per day; €7.20). Buses also run from the Morlaisiennes stop, in front of the Monoprix on rue d'Aiguillon, or at the station.

Public Transportation: TIM, 15 pl. Cornic (☎ 02 98 88 82 82). Tickets €0.90, *carnet* of 10 €8.40. Buses run 7:30am-7pm.

Taxis: Radio Taxis (☎ 02 98 88 08 32) are usually at pl. des Otages and the station.

✦ ❼ ORIENTATION AND PRACTICAL INFORMATION

All roads run downhill from the station to the city center. The most direct route is to go down **rue Courte,** also known as the Cent Marches, which is actually a long, steep stairwell. From the station, walk straight on **rue Gambetta** for 100m and turn left onto the stairs. For a slightly more roundabout path that avoids the steps, continue down rue Gambetta and turn left on steep rue Longue. Both paths lead directly to the central **place Emile Souvestre**. From here, a right on rue du Mur will take you to pl. Allende and a right on rue d'Aiguillon leads to **place des Jacobins.**

Tourist Office: pl. des Otages (☎02 98 62 14 94; officetourisme.morlaix@wanadoo.fr). From pl. Emile Souvestre, turn left and continue to pl. des Otages. Tourist office is the free-standing brown building across the *place*, in front of the viaduct. Pick up maps, info on lodging, and a complete city guide. Tours of the city in French July-Aug. Th 2:30pm. Open July-Aug. M-Sa 10am-12:30pm and 1:30-7pm, Su 10:30am-12:30pm; Sept.-June M-Sa 10am-noon and 2-6pm.

Laundromat: 4 rue de Lavoirs (open daily 8am-8pm) or 28 pl. Charles de Gaulle (open daily 8am-8:30pm).

Police: 17 pl. Charles de Gaulle (☎02 98 88 17 17).

Pharmacy: Pharmacie Centrale, 9 rue Carnot (☎02 98 88 10 71). Open M 2-7pm, Tu-Sa 9am-12:15pm and 2-7pm.

Hospital: Hôpital Général, 15 rue Kersaint Gilly (☎02 98 62 61 60).

Internet Access: Free for patrons at **Café de l'Aurore** (see **Entertainment,** p. 212). **Cyber @rena,** 16 rue Basse (☎02 98 88 15 83), past pl. Allende. €4.50 per hr. Open M-Th 11am-midnight, F-Sa 11am-1am, Su 2pm-1am. **Le Millenium Café,** 9 rue Gambetta (☎02 98 63 99 78; www.lemillenium.fr.fm), just off pl. Emile Souvestre, bottom of rue Courte. €2.25 per 30min., €3.80 per hr. Open Tu-F 8am-8pm, Sa 1pm-1am.

Post Office: 15 rue de Brest (☎02 98 88 93 22), off pl. Emile Souvestre. **Currency exchange,** Cyberposte, fax, and photocopies. Open M and W-F 8:30am-6pm, Tu 9am-6pm, Sa 8:30am-noon.

Postal Code: 29600.

▐ ▓ ACCOMMODATIONS AND CAMPING

Morlaix no longer has a hostel, and budget options are in short supply. Ask the tourist office about local *gîtes d'étape* (€8-14) or *chambres d'hôte* (€15-30).

Hôtel Le Roy d'Ys, 8 pl. des Jacobins (☎02 98 63 30 55). Near the town center. Follow directions to pl. Emile Souvestre; head straight on rue Carnot, which is to the right; follow to the end and turn right on rue au Fils to pl. des Jacobins. Brightly decorated, spacious rooms fitted with stained glass, above a bar frequented by locals; some rooms with TV and/or a view of the *place*. Breakfast €4.60. Reception Tu-Su 8am-midnight. Doubles or triples with sink €23, with shower and/or toilet €30.60. MC/V. ❷

Hôtel de la Gare, 25 pl. St-Martin (☎02 98 88 03 29 or 06 83 46 42 93; fax 02 98 63 97 80), on rue Gambetta south of the train station, across the street from the top of rue Courte. In a quiet location above a *brasserie*, with quick access to the center of town via the Cent Marches. This hotel has large, clean rooms with yellow walls, lots of light, and spare but pretty furniture. All rooms with shower, TV, and phone. Breakfast €6. Reception daily 7:30am-10pm. Mar.-Sept. singles €35, with toilet €38; doubles €38/€42. Extra bed €9. Prices reduced in low season. MC/V. ❸

Camping: Camping à la Ferme, in Croas-Men (☎/fax 02 98 79 11 50; croas-men@wanadoo.fr), is worth the 7km walk. From the center of town, follow signs first to Plouigneau, then to Garlan. Campsite past Garlan on the left. The owners, third-generation farmers, want campers to love the farm as much as they do. They offer breakfast in the 1840s farmhouse, a petting farm, tractor rides for kids, and fresh yogurt and cider for a modest price. Reception 8am-10pm; gates open 24hr. Open Apr.-Oct. €4 per site, €2.80 per person, children under 7 €2.30, pets €0.80. Electricity €2.80. ❶

◖ FOOD

An all-day food and crafts **market** stretches from pl. des Otages to pl. Allende (Sa). A **Marché Plus supermarket** is at 22 rue de Paris. (☎02 98 63 39 25. Open M-Sa 7am-9pm, Su 9am-noon.) With its Breton tablecloths and congenial proprietors, comforting **Ar Bilig ❶**, 6 rue au Fil, in an alley off pl. des Jacobins, stands out in a city stuffed to the gills with indistinguishable *crêperies*. A friendly couple prepares a generous *menu* of a *galette* and two dessert crêpes for €8.50. (☎02 98 88 50 51. Open daily July-Aug. 11:30am-3pm and 6:30-10pm, closed Su for lunch; Sept.-June Tu-Sa 11:30am-2pm and 6:30-9pm. AmEx/MC/V.) At **La Marée Bleue ❹**, 3 rampe St-Melaine, just off pl. des Otages near the tourist office, an attentive waitstaff serves the swankiest meals in town, featuring a delectable variety of fresh fish and meat *plats* from €10-19. (☎02 98 63 24 21. *Menus* €14, €19, €28, and €36. Open Tu-Sa noon-2pm and 7-10pm, Su 7-10pm. MC/V.)

◐ ♫ SIGHTS AND ENTERTAINMENT

The **Circuit des Venelles,** an organized walking tour through medieval Morlaix, is the best way to see the city's ancient sights. The steep *venelles* (alleys) were the city's main thoroughfares in medieval times and still lead past all of Morlaix's main attractions, including churches and impressive views. The tourist office has a map of the circuit, as well as info about summer theatrical tours of the *venelles*, in which costumed actors provide lively guided visits. (☎02 98 99 09 94. Tours early July to early Aug. Tu at 8:30pm. €5, children €3.50.)

The **viaduct,** 58m high and 285m long, is Morlaix's most visible sight. Though the airy walkway is now closed to the public, sightseers can still get a good view of near-vertical Morlaix from its gates. **La Maison de la Duchesse Anne,** across pl. Allende at 33 rue du Mur, commemorates the Queen's 1505 visit to the city. Originally the private home of aristocrats, the building is a prime example of a *morlaisienne maison à pondalez*, or lantern house. The oak staircase, which showcases the family's patron saints, is supported by an intricately carved 30 ft. column formed from a single tree trunk. (☎02 98 88 23 26. Open July-Aug. M-Sa 11am-6:30pm; May-June 11am-6pm; Sept. 11am-5pm. €1.60, ages 12-16 and students €0.80, under 12 free.)

After the sun goes down, things heat up with drinks and occasional live concerts at the inviting **Café de L'Aurore,** 17 rue Traverse, on the other side of the square. A mostly young crowd of locals crowds the red folding chairs on the sidewalk until late at night. Free Internet access for customers. (☎02 98 88 03 05; www.aurore-cafe.com. Beer €2. Cocktails €4.50-6. Open July-Aug. M-Sa 8am-1am, Su 3pm-1am. June and Sept. closed Su. MC/V.) **Ty Coz** (Old House), 10 venelle au Beurre, overlooking the pl. Allende, seems straight out of an Arthurian legend; there's Breton music, Breton beer, and thick cross-sections of trees for tables. The porch overlooking the *place* is perfect for a late afternoon drink in the sun. (☎02 98 88 07 65. Coreff beer €2. Open M-W and F-Sa 11am-1am, Su 6pm-1am. Closed Sept.)

ROSCOFF

With a bevy of seafood restaurants, a variety of watersports, and several beaches, Roscoff (pop. 3700) is a city of the sea. While there's not too much to see, Roscoff's nautical activities, stunning church tower, and proximity to Île de Batz make it worth a stop.

▐ ♫ TRANSPORTATION AND PRACTICAL INFORMATION. SNCF trains and buses (☎02 98 69 70 20) go from the station to Morlaix (30-45min., 7-11 per day, €4.80) with connections to Brest and Paris. The train station provides free long-

term parking. **CAT buses** (☎ 02 98 44 46 73) go to Morlaix (30-45min., M-Sa 6-7 per day, €4.60) and Quimper (2¼hr.; M-Sa 2 per day, Su 1 per day; €15.30). **Brittany Ferries** (☎ 02 98 29 28 00; www.brittany-ferries.fr) sends **ferries** to Plymouth, England, and Cork, Ireland. **Irish Ferries** (☎ 02 98 61 17 17; shamrock@wanadoo.fr) serves Rosslare, Ireland. Both offer Eurail discounts of up to 50% and sail from the Pointe de Bloscon. To reach Roscoff's town center and the Vieux Port, where ferries to the Île leave, turn right from the bus station onto rue Ropartz (unmarked) and follow the bus signs to the *centre ville* (turn right on rue Brizeux and then bear left).

The **tourist office,** 46 rue Gambetta, set back from the port, has transportation schedules, walking tours, maps, info on *chambres d'hôte,* a shiny visitor's guide, and Internet access with a *télécarte.* (☎ 02 98 61 12 13; www.roscoff-tourisme.com. Open July-Aug. M-Sa 9am-12:30pm and 1:30-7pm, Su 10am-12:30pm; Sept.-June M-Sa 9am-noon and 2-6pm.) There is a **laundromat** in Roscoff at 23 rue Jules Ferry. (Open daily 9am-8pm.) **Internet** is accessible at the tourist office (see above); Hôtel des Arcades, 15 rue Amiral Réveillère (☎ 02 98 69 70 45); and Hôtel Talabardon, 27 pl. Lacaze Duthiers (☎ 02 98 61 24 95). The **post office,** 19 rue Gambetta, offers **currency exchange,** fax, and photocopies. (☎ 02 98 69 71 28. Open July-Aug. M-F 9am-12:30pm and 1:30-5:30pm, Sa 9am-12:15pm; Sept.-June M-F 9am-noon and 2-5:30pm, Sa 9am-12:15pm.) **Postal Code:** 29680.

⌐◱ ACCOMMODATIONS AND FOOD. Roscoff has few budget hotels. The **Hôtel d'Angleterre ❸,** 28 rue Albert de Mun, is in an old mansion that retains original Breton furniture and stained-glass windows in the restaurant downstairs. An adjacent sunroom with wicker chairs looks onto the enormous backyard garden; a TV room and charming sitting room with chessboards are also below. (☎ 02 98 69 70 42; fax 02 98 69 75 16. Breakfast €6. *Demi-pension* available. Reception 7:30am-11pm. Open Easter-Sept. Singles and doubles €31, with toilet €38, with bath or shower €51. Extra bed €15. Apr.-May and Sept.-Oct. prices €3-5 lower. MC/V.)

Roscoff's only camping option is **Le Camping de Perharidy "Aux 4 Saisons" ❶,** near the allée des Chênes Verts, 2km from the train station. From the station, turn left on rue Ropartz, right on rue des Capucins, right again on rue Laënnec, and right a third time on rue de la Baie. Turn left at the coast, following route du Laber until the Jardin Louis Kerdilés; turn right, and the campsite will be on your left. Two hundred spots by the beach include access to a volleyball court, hot showers, and laundry. (☎ 02 98 69 70 86 or 06 07 41 28 53 in low season; campingaux4saisons@wanadoo.fr. Reception M-Sa 9am-noon and 2-6pm, although someone's usually around. Reserve in advance. Open Apr. to mid-Oct. €2.70 per adult, under 7 €1.45; €2.45 per tent; €4.40 per caravan; €0.80 per motorcycle. Electricity €1.60-3.20.)

Restaurants serving seafood *menus* (€12.20-15.30) line the port. There is a **market** (W 9am-1pm) on quai Auxerre, and a **Casino supermarket** off rue du Pontigou, on the right side; from the port, follow rue Albert de Mun, which becomes rue Laënnec and then rue du Pontigou. (Open M-Th 9am-12:30pm and 2:30-7:15pm, F-Sa 9am-7:15pm, Su 9am-noon.) One of Roscoff's more distinctive *crêperies,* **Ti Saozon ❶,** 30 rue Gambetta, just past the tourist office, feels like a traditional Breton home. (☎ 02 98 69 70 89. Open M-Sa for dinner, usually around 6:30pm.) **Le Surcouf ❸,** 14 rue Amiral Réveillère, dishes up fresh fish from €12 (*plat du jour* €7.50) in a simple interior with crisp white tablecloths and a huge lobster tank. (☎ 02 98 69 71 89; www.jalima.fr. *Menus* €10-15. Open daily July-Aug. 11:30am-2pm and 6:30-9:30pm; Sept.-June closed Tu-W. Closed Jan. 4 to Feb. 12. MC/V.)

◎ SIGHTS. The most popular sight in Roscoff is **Le Jardin Exotique,** which features over 3000 species of tropical flora and a panoramic view of the bay of Morlaix. From the tourist office, walk to the dock and turn right. Follow quai d'Auxerre, bear right on rue Jeanne d'Arc, then right again on rue Plymouth; when it ends, turn right on Voie de Port en Eau Profonde. The garden is on the left. (☎ 02 98 61 29 19; www.jardinexotiqueroscoff.com. Open daily June-Sept. 10am-7pm; Apr.-May and Oct. 10:30am-12:30pm and 2-6pm; Mar. and Nov. 2-5pm.) The 16th-century **Église Notre-Dame de Croaz-Batz** is reminiscent of an overgrown sand castle with turreted spires, a massive golden choir, and a Renaissance-style two-tiered belfry. Sculpted ships adorn the exterior, symbolizing Roscoff's maritime prosperity. (Open daily 10am-12:30pm and 2-6pm. Tours Su at noon and F night.) On the far right side of the port is the **Pointe St-Barbe**, a tall rock outcropping wrapped in spiraling stone steps and crowned with a white chapel, which provides a soaring vista of the coast, the port, and Île de Batz. Take a walking tour (6-12km, 1½-3hr.) around the environs of Roscoff from the free *Circuits Pedestre* brochure.

ÎLE DE BATZ

Fifteen minutes off the coast of Roscoff sits Île de Batz (pop. 596), a tiny, wind-battered sanctuary only 3.5km long and 1.5km wide. Thanks to unusual meteorological phenomena, Batz experiences quite temperate weather. Even when clouds build over Roscoff, the skies over the island stay deep blue and cloud-free. With acres of small farms and unspoiled coastline, and without many conveniences, Batz is little known even within France and manages to be a true haven.

⌨ TRANSPORTATION AND PRACTICAL INFORMATION. Three associated ferry companies—**Armein** (☎ 02 98 61 77 75), **Armor Excursions** (☎ 02 98 61 79 66), and **CFTM** (☎ 02 98 61 78 87)—connect Roscoff and Batz in 10-15min. Boats leave from Roscoff's port during high tide and from the long walkway extending into the harbor at low tide. (Late June to early Sept. every 30min., last boat from island at 7:30pm; mid-Sept. to late June 8-9 per day. Round-trip €6.50, ages 4-11 €3.50, under 4 free.) Circle the island before landing for a few more euros. (Tours July-Aug. Tu-Th at 11am, Su at 3pm. €9, ages 4-11 €5.)

The island's tiny **tourist office** is in the town hall *(mairie)*. Turn left out of the port and follow signs. The small staff hands out an equally small guide; a more detailed map, labeled with establishments, is available for €1. Also ask for brochures for two 2hr. walking tours. (☎ 02 98 61 75 70; iledebatz.com. Open Sept.-June M-F 9am-noon and 2-5pm, Sa 10am-noon, though hours sometimes fluctuate.) There are a number of **bike rental** places in convenient locations on the island, including Vélos le Saoût, to the right of the hotel at the ferry dock. Maps and guided tours are also available. Look for the sign "Location de Vélos." (☎ 02 98 61 77 65. Bikes €3 per hr., €7 per half-day, €9 per day, €65 per 5 days. 10% discount if paid by traveler's check. Hours depend on ferry schedules, but generally 9am-8pm.) The Île de Batz **post office**, with **currency exchange** and fax, is up the hill in the center of town, downhill from the 8 à Huit; look for the signs. (☎ 02 98 61 76 46. Open M-F 9:30am-noon and 1:30-4:30pm, Sa 9:30am-noon.) **Postal Code:** 29253.

⌨ ACCOMMODATIONS AND FOOD. Backpackers enjoy the **Auberge de Jeunesse Marine ❶**. Be sure to call ahead, especially in summer, as the 48 beds fill up quickly. To reach the hostel from the port, take the road that goes sharply uphill immediately to the left of the hotel. Signs clearly mark the path to the hostel (5 minutes). Perched on a hill, the newly renovated, five-building hostel has amazing views of the water and access to a private beach. (☎ 02 98 61 77 69; brest.aj.cis@wanadoo.fr. Breakfast €3.30. *Demi-pension* €19.30. Sheets €3.80. Reception 6:30-8:45pm, although someone may be around during the day. Open Apr.-Oct. Beds €9, bunk cots in big tent €7.50, camping €7.50.) The *chambres d'hôte* **Ty Va Zadou ❸**, which overlooks the port, is more expensive but a good value. From the ferry, head left toward town. The stone house with light blue shutters is at the top of a hill on the right fork just before the church. A pleasant proprietress oversees four carefully color-coordinated guest rooms. All rooms come with bath and toilet. (☎ 02 98 61 76 91. Breakfast included. Laundry available. Open Mar. to mid-Nov. Reception 9am-10pm. Reserve at least a month in advance June-Aug. Singles €35; doubles €55; 2-room family suite €65-75.) The grassy, wind-scoured **Terrain d'Hébergement de Plein Air ❶**, on the beach near the lighthouse, is the only legal campground on the island, but only allows tents. (☎ 02 98 61 75 70. Open mid-June to mid-Sept. Reception 11am-noon and 6-8:30pm. €2.50 per person, €1 per child, €1.50 per tent.)

A **8 à Huit supermarket,** home to Batz's sole **ATM** machine, is located at the island's highest point. From the port, bear left, continue past the church, and turn right at the sign indicating the store. (☎ 02 98 61 78 79; fax 02 98 61 74 44. Open July-Aug. M-Sa 9am-1pm and 2:30-8pm, Su 9am-12:30pm; Sept.-June Tu-Sa 9am-12:30pm and 2:30-7:30pm, Su 10am-12:30pm.)

◼◼ **SIGHTS AND HIKING.** The best way to see the Île de Batz is to take the *sentier côtier,* 14km of easy-to-follow **trails** that line the coast. They run past the rugged *côte sauvage* on the west side of the island, along small, sandy beaches, over massive rocks, and beside inland lakes. The 4hr. hike is not difficult. Find the trails from any point on the island by heading toward water or by following signs from the port. The tourist office also has maps for easy 2hr. hikes covering either side of the island. Some areas of the trails are private property, but many still use them.

Slightly west of the town center, climb the 198 steps of the **lighthouse** *(phare),* which is built almost entirely out of granite from the island, for a great view of the island and Roscoff. (☎ 02 98 61 75 70; fax 02 98 61 75 85. Open daily July-Aug. 1-5:30pm; June and early to mid-Sept. M-Tu and Th-Su 2-5pm. €1.70, children €1.) At the southeast tip of the island rests the tranquil **Jardin Georges Delaselle,** which features exotic plants from every continent and good views of Roscoff and the coast of Batz. (☎ 02 98 61 75 65. Open daily July-Aug. 1-6pm; Apr.-June and Sept. M and W-Su 2-6pm; Oct. Sa-Su 2-6pm. 1hr. guided visits Su 3pm. €4, students and seniors €3.50, ages 10-16 €2, under 10 free; guided visits €5.) Slightly inland, just before the garden, stand the ruins of the 12th-century **Chapelle Ste-Anne,** originally the site of a monastery founded in AD 530 and destroyed by Vikings in AD 878. During the **Fête de Ste-Anne,** the year's largest celebration (held the last Saturday in July), everyone on the island comes out to light a massive bonfire on the dunes.

BREST

Brest (pop. 149,000) became a somber wasteland in 1944 when Allied bombers drove out the occupying German flotilla. Despite efforts to rebuild, the city still feels somewhat large and impersonal. Although it is known as one of Brittany's drearier locales, signs of life have begun to emerge. Brest features a number of pleasant cafes, an impressive town hall, a buzzing commercial district, and a summer concert series, as well as one of the largest aquariums around. It is also the ideal jumping-off point for nearby gem Île d'Ouessant.

◼ **TRANSPORTATION**

Trains: pl. du 19*ème* Régiment d'Infanterie (☎ 02 98 31 51 72). Info office open M-Sa 8am-7:30pm, Su 10am-6:30pm. To: **Morlaix** (€8.80, TGV €10.50); **Nantes** (€36.70); **Paris** (€63.73); **Quimper** (30min., 5 per day, €13.70); **Rennes** (1½hr., 15 per day, €29.30).

Buses: Buses leave from next to the train station (☎02 98 44 46 73). Open July-Aug. M-F 7am-12pm and 1-7pm, Sa 8:45am-1:15pm and 4:30-7pm, Su 1-2:15pm and 5:15-7pm; Sept.-June M-F 7am-12:30pm and 1-7pm, Sa 8:45am-1:15pm and 2:30-7pm, Su 6-7pm. Buses run to: **Crozon** and **Camaret** (1½hr.; M-Sa 2 per day, Su 1 per day; €9.30/€9.50); **Quimper** (1¼hr.; M-Sa 4 per day, Su 1 per day; €13.70); **Roscoff** (30-45min., 7-11 per day, €9.40).

Ferries: For ferry lines serving Brest, see **Île d'Ouessant** (p. 219).

Public Transportation: Bibus, 33 av. Georges Clemenceau (☎02 98 80 30 30; www.bibus.fr). Buses run daily 6am-9pm with erratic service on a specially designated route until about 11pm, F-Sa until midnight. Service is infrequent, particularly in the summer months, so plan ahead. Ask at the tourist office or the Bibus *point d'accueil* near the Hôtel de Ville (M-F 8:15am-6:15pm, Sa 9am-5pm) for a bus map and schedule. Buy tickets on the bus and *carnets* at the *point d'accueil:* €1.05, *carnet* of 10 €8.35; day pass €3, 1-week student pass €8.45.

Taxis: Allô Taxis, 234 rue Jean Jaurès (☎02 98 42 11 11), or **Radio Taxi Brestois** (☎02 98 80 43 43).

■✚ 🖪 ORIENTATION AND PRACTICAL INFORMATION

To the right of the train station, av. Georges Clemenceau leads to the central **place de la Liberté,** the main terminal for the city's internal bus system. **Rue Jean Jaurès,** north of the *place*, is prime shopping territory, but be careful at night. **Rue de Siam,** south of the *place* and overlooking the water, is the most vibrant street in the city. A handful of good restaurants and bars cluster at **Port du Commerce,** where ferries leave for nearby isles.

The **tourist office,** 8 av. Georges Clemenceau, on pl. de la Liberté near the Hôtel de Ville, provides free maps, a reservations service, tickets for the ferry to Île d'Ouessant, and info on restaurants, sights, and tours. (☎02 98 44 24 96; office.de.tourisme.brest@wanadoo.fr. Open mid-June to mid-Sept. M-Sa 9:30am-7pm, Su 10am-noon; mid-Sept. to mid-June M-Sa 9:30am-12:30pm and 2-6pm.) The **Bureau Information Jeunesse Brest,** 4 rue Augustin Morvan, off pl. de la Liberté, has free **Internet** access and info on jobs. (☎02 98 43 01 08; bij.brest@wanadoo.fr. Open July-Aug. M-Tu and Th-F 1:30-4:30pm, W 9:30am-noon and 1:30-4:30pm; Sept.-June M-Tu and Th-F 1:30-6pm, W 9:30am-noon and 1:30-6pm, Sa 9:30am-noon and 1:30-5pm. Closed Aug. 2-14.) Other services include: a **laundromat** at Point Blue, 7 rue de Siam (open daily 8am-9:30pm), at 9 pl. de la Liberté (open daily 7am-8:30pm), and at 33 rue Monge (open daily 7am-10:30pm); **police** at 15 rue Colbert (☎02 98 43 77 77), a **hospital** at rue de la Cavale Blanche (☎02 98 22 33 33); **Internet** access free at BIJB (see above), or at @cces.cibles, 31 av. Clemenceau (☎02 98 46 76 10; €2.50 per hr. 10% discount for students; open M-Sa 11am-1am, Su 2-11pm); **English-language bookstore** at Dialogues, 37 rue Louis Pasteur. (☎02 98 44 88 68; www.librairiedialogues.fr. Open M-Sa 9:30am-7:30pm.) The **post office,** rue de Siam, on pl. Général Leclerc, has **currency exchange,** a Cyberposte, fax, and photocopier. (☎02 98 33 73 07. Open M-F 8am-7pm, Sa 8am-noon.) **Postal Code:** 29285.

🏠 🎪 ACCOMMODATIONS AND CAMPING

Reserve two to three weeks ahead in July and August.

🛏 **Auberge de Jeunesse (HI),** 5 rue de Kerbriant (☎02 98 41 90 41; brest.a.cis@wanadoo.fr), about 4km from the train station, near Océanopolis and next to the artificial beach in Le Moulin Blanc. Take bus #7 to its terminus at Port de Plaisance (M-Sa 6:45am-7:30pm, Su 2-5:45pm). With your back to the stop, go left toward beach. Turn left on rue Moulin Blanc. Follow signs to hostel: look for "*ostaleri ar yaouankiz.*" This site looks like an IKEA ad set in the tropics. Ping pong, foosball, piano, pool, and TV room. Kitchen, luggage storage, bicycle garage, laundry available. All rooms have 4 beds. Breakfast included. Dinner €8. Sheets €3.80. Reception July-Aug. M-F 5-midnight, Sa-Su 6-midnight; June and Sept. closes at 11pm; Oct.-Apr. at 10pm. Lockout 10am-5pm. Curfew July-Aug. midnight; Sept.-June 11pm; code for late entry. Beds €12.70. HI members only. MC/V. ❶

Hôtel Astoria, 9 rue Traverse (☎02 98 80 19 10). Central, quiet, and spotless, this hotel boasts modern rooms with TV and classy accents like paper lanterns or armchairs. Helpful staff. Breakfast €6. Showers €4. Reception M-Sa 7am-11pm, Su 7am-noon. Call ahead, especially July-Aug. Singles and doubles €26, with shower and toilet €41-46, with bath and toilet €49-51; triples with shower and toilet €51. AmEx/MC/V. ❸

Kelig Hôtel, 12 rue de Lyon (☎02 98 80 47 21; lucas.pascale@wanadoo.fr). Spacious rooms with TV, dark wooden wardrobes, and extraordinarily comfortable beds, run by amiable owners. Showers may be a bit grimy. Located just 5min. from rue de Siam and the train station. Breakfast €6-7. Laundry available. Reception M-F 7am-9:30pm, Sa 8am-12:30pm and 5-9:30pm, Su 8am-12:30pm. Singles with shower €24, with shower and toilet €30-36, with bath and toilet €37; doubles €27/€34-40/€40-44; triple with shower and toilet €44, with bath €47. AmEx/MC/V. ❷

Camping: Camping du Goulet (☎/fax 02 98 45 86 84), 7km from downtown in Ste-Anne du Portzic; take bus #14 (dir: Plouzané) to Le Cosquer. (15min.) At night take bus B, route A (dir: Plouzané). Follow signs 100m down side road to this large, often-crowded 2-star site (on left). 100 spots divided by thick, tall hedges. Clean facilities, lots of greenery, basic mini-market, hot showers, and laundry. Reception daily July-Aug. 8:30am-noon and 2-8pm; Sept.-June 9:30am-noon and 2:30-7pm. €3.50 per person, under 7 €2; €4 per tent; €1.30 per car, €1.10 per motorcycle. Electricity €2.50. ❶

◘ FOOD

Markets are held every day in various locations, including the traditional and organic market on **rue du Moulin à Poudre** (Tu 4-8pm and Sa 9am-1pm) and the enormous market in the area around St-Louis (Su 9am-1pm), and a slightly pricey **indoor market** at Les Halles St-Louis, one block from rue de Siam. (Daily 7am-1pm and 4-7:30pm.) Bakeries, *pâtisseries*, and lunch counters can be found on and around rue de Siam; more filling meals are at the end of the street, near the port. A **Marché Plus supermarket** is just off rue de Siam at 59 rue Louis Pasteur (☎02 98 43 51 51. Open M-Sa 7am-9pm, Su 9am-1pm), and a **Monoprix** at 46 rue de Siam has food on the bottom floor (open M-Sa 8am-8pm).

Couples frequent intimate **Le Mont Liban ❸**, 8 pl. de la Liberté, to chat over catchy Arabic music and sample *mezzes* (€38.80-46.80), an assortment of 15 different Middle-Eastern delicacies. (☎02 98 80 12 76. *Menus* €7.50-13.70. Open M-F noon-2pm and 7:30-10pm, Sa noon-2pm. MC/V.) **Amour de Pommes de Terre ❸**, 23 rue des Halles St-Louis, just behind the indoor market, is an inventive, albeit slightly pricey, spuds-only establishment. Oddly, there are almost no vegetarian options. (☎02 98 43 48 51; fax 02 98 43 61 88. *Plats* €11.80-23.50. Open M noon-2pm and 7:30-10:30pm, Tu-F noon-2pm and 7:30-11pm, Sa noon-2:30pm and 7pm-midnight, Su noon-2:30pm and 7:30-10:30pm. MC/V.) At the end of rue de Siam near the port, **Brasserie de Siam ❸**, 12 rue de Siam, serves up a variety of seafood dishes and *brasserie* standards in a sleek, modern setting where the bold and calculated use of color might have come from one of Keith Haring's milder dreams. The day's catch is cooked up for €8-15. (☎02 98 46 05 52; www.labrasseriedesiam-brest@wanadoo.fr. Open daily noon-midnight. MC/V.)

BRITTANY

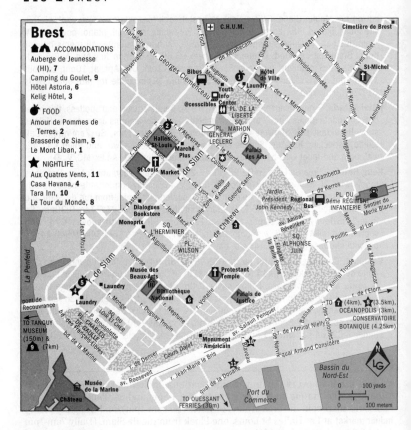

Brest

🏠🏠 **ACCOMMODATIONS**
Auberge de Jeunesse
  (HI), 7
Camping du Goulet, 9
Hôtel Astoria, 6
Kelig Hôtel, 3

🍴 **FOOD**
Amour de Pommes de
  Terres, 2
Brasserie de Siam, 5
Le Mont Liban, 1

⭐ **NIGHTLIFE**
Aux Quatres Vents, 11
Casa Havana, 4
Tara Inn, 10
Le Tour du Monde, 8

🔆 SIGHTS

Brest's **château** was the only major building to survive the bombings of World War II. In its over 1700 strife-laden years, the world's oldest active military institution—formerly a residence, fortress, and prison—has withstood Roman, Breton, English, French, and German attacks. You can only enter the château through the **Musée de la Marine,** which occupies most of the sprawling fortress. The museum itself is somewhat dull and occurs rather spontaneously at points throughout the château, featuring small exhibits on points of nautical interest. A stroll through the château, however, provides great views of the water. A thorough pamphlet is available in English. (☎02 98 22 12 39; www.musee-marine.fr. Open daily Apr. to mid-Sept. 10am-6:30pm; mid-Sept. to Mar. M and W-Su 10am-noon and 2-6pm. Closed mid-Dec. to Jan.; last entrance 1hr. before closing. Tours daily July-Aug. 2:30 and 4pm, M-F also at 11am; €6.10, students €4.60, under 18 free. Entrance €4.60, students €3, ages 6-18 €2.30, under 6 free.) The rose-colored **Monument Américain,** on rue de Denver, overlooks the Port du Commerce, a reminder of the Americans' landing in 1917. Locals joke that you need a passport to visit this American-built monument, guarded by American officers on American-owned soil.

Massive **Océanopolis,** port de Plaisance, spotlights Brittany's marine life (much of it in tidal tanks) as well as the Iroise Sea (which surrounds the Île d'Ouessant). A polar pavilion with a 3D theater that opens onto the penguin playland, and a tropical area, complete with a coral reef, are some of the highlights here. Océanopolis is huge and can have massive lines; don't expect to spend less than a day. To get there, take bus #7 (dir: Port de Plaisance) from the Liberty Terminal (M-Sa every 30min. until 7:30pm) to Océanopolis. (Aquarium ☎ 02 98 34 40 40; www.oceanopolis.com. Open daily Apr.-Aug. 9am-6pm; Sept.-Mar. Tu-Sa 10am-5pm, Su 10am-6pm. Closed for 2 weeks in January. €14.50, ages 4-17 €10, under 4 free.) The beautiful **Conservatoire Botanique de Brest,** 5min. away, stretches through 3km of exotic plant life, bamboo groves, and trickling brooks.

🎵 NIGHTLIFE

Nightlife centers around the Port de Commerce, the **pont de Recouvrance** at the end of rue de Siam, and the streets near pl. de la Liberté. You may want to avoid the neighborhoods on the other side of pl. de la Liberté after dark. On Thursdays, the popular **Jeudis du Port** concerts dominate the streets of the Port with the sounds of Breton music, rock, and jazz. (Port du Commerce. Open mid-July to late Aug. Th 7:30pm-midnight. Free.) The sea-themed **Le Tour du Monde,** port du Moulin Blanc, near the aquarium and hostel, is owned by a famous navigator and draws crowds with cheap beer, mussels (€8.50-9.40), and second-story port views. (☎ 02 98 41 93 65. Beer around €2. Open daily 11am-1am.) The young, fresh crowd in **Casa Havana,** 2 rue de Siam, munches *tapas* and other Mediterranean treats (€2.50-3.40) amid tropical plants, bright red walls, and Latin music. Unusual list of cocktails, including the "Hemingway Special" (rum, lime, grapefruit, cherry liqueur; €5.50). Free salsa lessons Mondays 8:30-10:30pm. (☎ 02 98 80 42 87. Cocktails €4.80-5.50, beer €2.50. Restaurant open M-Sa noon-2pm; *tapas* served all day except Su. Bar open 11am-1am. AmEx/MC/V.) Locals pack nearby **Aux Quatres Vents,** 18 quai de la Douane, an intimate boatside bar with inexpensive drinks and tables covered with real maps. (☎ 02 98 44 42 84. Beer €2-3. Aperitifs €2-2.50. Open M-F 9am-1am, Sa 10am-1am, Su 2pm-1am. MC/V.) The aggressively Celtic-themed **Tara Inn,** 1 rue Blaveau, near the Port du Commerce, attracts live traditional Irish music every Tu night at 10pm, and the last Su afternoon of the month. Features an unusually large selection of beer on tap. (☎ 02 98 80 36 07. Beer €2-3, *kir* €2. Open M-F 11am-1am, Sa-Su 3pm-1am. MC/V.)

ÎLE D'OUESSANT

The westernmost point in France, windswept Ouessant (*Enez Eussa* in Breton; pop. 951) is a peaceful oasis for hikers, bikers, and naturalists, an hour's boat ride from the nearest point on the mainland. Ouessant's mysterious jagged rock formations rise up from rugged grounds, covered in wildflowers and grazing sheep.

🚢 TRANSPORTATION. Two **ferry** companies offer service to Ouessant. Buy tickets at the port or at the Brest tourist office; reserve in advance in summer. If traveling from Brest, the best and easiest route is to use **Penn Ar Bed,** which sails year-round between Ouessant and Brest via Le Conquet and Molène (2½ hours). It also serves the islands of Molène and Sein. (☎ 02 98 80 80 80; www.pennarbed.fr. Mid-July to Aug. 1-3 per day; Sept.-June 1-2 per day. Brest-Ouessant round-trip €30, students €27, ages 4-16 €18; Le Conquet-Ouessant €25.90, students €22, children €15.50. Reservations required.) **Finist'mer** runs "fast ferries" from Ouessant to Camaret (1hr.) and Ouessant to Le Conquet in 30min. (☎ 02 98 89 16 61; www.finist-mer.fr. Camaret 1 per day. Le Conquet 1 per day. Round-trip

BRITTANY

SHEEP JUST WANNA HAVE FUN

On Île d'Ouessant, the sheep are the life of the party. In accordance with an ancient custom, the fuzzy animals have free rein on the island during the winter months, roaming about unattached and mating naturally. On the first Wednesday of February, owners come to collect their animals, which have been previously marked with a distinguishing cut or piercing on the ear. The process of rounding up the sheep is a large, festive event known as La Foire au Mouton (Sheep Fair). Volunteers chase the sheep into one of two pens, located in the north and south points of the island (the benevolent chasers expect a "donation" from owners afterwards for their goodwill).

The process is accompanied by a large celebration involving drinks, cakes, and merrymaking. Many visitors take a trip out to the island especially for the occasion, and the *fête*, well attended by members of the press, is also televised. The custom itself is a practical matter: families with only one sheep do not have to concern themselves with breeding, as reproduction occurs naturally in the wild. The sheep remain captive from the Wednesday of the festivities to September 29, when they are again let loose to play the field on the island's grassy terrain.

Le Conquet-Ouessant late July to late Aug. €31, students and over 60 €26, ages 4-16 €18; prices €4-7 lower in low season. Bikes €11.) To get to Le Conquet, take the **Cars de St-Mathieu bus** (☎02 98 89 12 02) from Brest (40min., €4.30), though it ranges from difficult to impossible to coordinate the bus schedule with Finist'mer departures. It's a better idea to use Penn Ar Bed from Brest.

Boats dock at Port du Stiff, 3.5km from Lampaul, the main town on the Île d'Ouessant. **Ouessant Voyages buses** (☎06 07 90 07 43) await the boats' arrival at the port and take you into town in a few air-conditioned minutes (€1.50), stopping at the central church. Get off the boat early to grab a seat, and be punctual meeting the return bus. On foot it's a 45min. stroll to town. The bus company also offers a guided visit of the island that stops for promenades (€12, including return ticket).

Biking is the best way to get around on the island, as distances between landmarks are long and the roads are well paved. Four companies rent **bikes** for identical prices at the port and in Lampaul. (€10 per day, €11 for a beach bike, €14 for a mountain bike; €7/€8/€10 per half-day, €37/€39/€50 per week. Most accept MC/V and offer a €2 per bike discount with a coupon from the tourist office.)

■ ▮ ORIENTATION AND PRACTICAL INFORMATION. Lampaul's **tourist office,** near the church in the town center, sells a pedestrian guide (€2.30) with four routes that cover the entire coastline in 1½-3hr. hikes. Bike paths are marked on a separate map since cycling is forbidden on the foot paths. (☎02 98 48 85 83; www.ot-ouessant.fr. Office open July-Aug. M-Sa 9am-6pm, Su 10am-noon; Sept.-June 10am-noon and 1:30-6pm, Su 10am-noon.) **Police** (☎02 98 48 81 61) only operate on the island July-Aug. The **post office** is to the left of the church and 30m downhill, across from the 8 à Huit; it has **currency exchange** and a fax. (☎02 98 48 81 77. Open mid-June to mid-Sept. M-F 9am-noon and 2-5pm, Sa 9am-noon; mid-Sept. to mid-June M-F 9:30am-noon and 2-5pm, Sa 9am-noon.) **Postal Code:** 29242.

▮ ▮ ACCOMMODATIONS AND CAMPING. Tiny Lampaul is home to all the island's food and practically all the lodgings. Reserve ahead in the summer. The cheerful and spotless **Auberge de Jeunesse d'Ouessant ❶** is 5min. from the tourist office and the center of Lampaul. Take the stairs to the right of the SPAR supermarket across from the church and turn right on the first road (not at the top of the stairs). Follow it as it bears left; the hostel is ahead on the right. There are 48 beds in sunny, clean 2- to 6-person rooms with speckled walls, a communal kitchen, and a dining area with ocean views. (☎02 98 48 94 53 or 06 81 23 72 95; ajouessant@club-internet.fr. Breakfast included. Sheets €3.37-3.69. Reception closed midday. Dorms €13.68, students and under 26 €11.78. *Demi-pension* €23.58/€20.91, full-*pension* €33.62/€30.14. Singles €25.) The lovely **Le Roc'h Ar Mor ⑤** has spacious blue and yellow bedrooms and bathrooms in a prime seaside location with a grassy courtyard, just beyond the center of Lampaul. An appealing seafood restaurant is downstairs (*menus* €15, €17, €46). Room prices vary depending on view; all have bath, telephone, and cable TV. (☎02 98 48 80 19; www.rocharmor.com. Wheelchair-accessible. Breakfast €8.50, children €5.80. Singles and doubles €52.50-82.50; triples €63-82.50; quads €77. Extra bed €10. Discounts Oct.-Dec. MC/V.) **Le Fromveur ❹** has simpler rooms with plain pastel decor and TV in the dead center of Lampaul, over a popular restaurant (*menus* €13-26) that serves up local catches. (☎02 98 48 81 30; fax 02 98 48 85 97. Breakfast €5.50. 24hr. reception. Closed mid-Nov. to late Dec. and early Jan. to early Feb. *Demi-pension* €48. Singles and doubles with TV and bath €41; triples and quads €70. MC/V.) The **Centre d'Etude du Milieu Ouessantin ❶,** an environmental studies and ornithological center, doubles as a hostel. From Lampaul's tourist office, bear right onto the road just past the supermarket and follow the signs for the Musée des Phares. It is the last major building before you reach the lighthouse, down a path on the left—it's unmarked but its modern architecture makes it unmistakable (30minutes). The rooms and facilities are much less spiffy than those at the *Auberge*, but it's a sunny facility, just down the road from the Créac'h Lighthouse and the spectacular coast. (☎02 98 48 82 65; cemouessant@wanadoo.fr. Sheets €3.10. Reception M-F 8am-noon and 1:30-5pm. Reservations are required and should be made early, especially for late July and Aug. 4- to 5-person dorms €11 per person, students €8.40, under 15 €8.50. Price drops on a sliding scale, €0.50 per night, for 2nd to 6th nights.) **Camping Municipal ❶,** located just 2km from the port along the main road, is on the left about 300m before the church in Lampaul. The quiet site is divided from the softly rolling hills of the surrounding countryside by a low stone wall. The bus from the port stops here; ask the driver. (☎02 98 48 84 65; low season 02 98 48 80 06. Laundry €4.70. Showers €1.60. BBQ rental €3. Reception daily July-Aug. 7am-11pm; call ahead in the low season. Night guard 11pm-7am. Open Apr.-Sept. €2.65 per person, under 7 €1.30; €2.65 per tent, bed in communal tent €3.25.)

❏ FOOD. A **SPAR supermarket** is next door to the tourist office (open M-Sa 8:30am-7:30pm, Su 9am-12:30pm) and a **8 à Huit** supermarket lies just downhill (open Tu 8:30am-12:30pm, W-Sa 8:30am-7:30pm, Su 9:30am-12:30pm); they have the island's only **ATMs.** There is also a small market, **Le Marché des Iles,** on the road to the *bourg*, 50m before the campground. (☎02 98 48 88 08. Open M-Sa 8:30am-7:30pm, Su 8:30am-12:30pm.) For a wallet-friendly sit-down meal, try **Crêperie Ti A Dreuz ❶,** which serves filling *galettes* and crêpes (€1.60-6.50) in two sunny, homey rooms that look out on a garden. (☎02 98 48 83 01. Tea €1.60. Open daily noon-2pm and 7-9pm. MC/V.) **Ty Korn ❸,** across from the church in Lampaul, offers a variety of marine delights in a second-floor room. (☎/fax 02 98 48 87 33. *Menus* for €20 and €28. Fish and meat *plats* €12-18. Open Tu-Sa noon-1:30pm and 7-9:30pm, Su noon-1:30pm. MC/V.)

◪ SIGHTS. Biking is forbidden on footpaths and, for safety reasons, along the coast. There are bike trails, however, and the island's roads, well-paved and almost devoid of cars, are ideal for biking and lead to all the major sights. The tourist office's booklet of coastline paths (€2.30) is helpful and includes details of all of the ruins and rocks along each route. A free basic map is also available. The

BRITTANY

terrain is relatively flat, and if you lose your way it is always easy to mark your position by the large lighthouses. If you only have time to choose one path, take the 12km northwest trail to the ⬛**Pointe de Pern,** where breathtaking rock formations rise from the ocean, the westernmost point in continental Europe. Ouessant's two museums lie on this trail. A joint ticket for the two is available for €6.30, ages 8-14 €4. The **Ecomusée and Maison du Niou,** 1km northwest of Lampaul, is a worthwhile museum about the island's culture and history, including a display of traditional local women's clothing. The highlight is a traditional *ouessantine* home, lived in until 1962. The compact cottage has no interior walls, as furniture is used to divide rooms, and was constructed out of wood rejected by shipbuilders, painted white and blue to hide imperfections. (☎ 02 98 48 86 37. Open daily Jan. to early Mar. and May-Oct. 1:30-5pm; early Mar. to Apr. 1:30-5:30pm; Nov. to mid-Dec. 1:30-4pm. €3.20, ages 8-14 €2.) The **Musée des Phares et Balises,** in the striped du Créac'h, once Europe's most powerful lighthouse, explores the history of lighthouses and maritime signaling. The area around the museum is made of layered rocks perfect for climbing and sitting. (☎ 02 98 48 80 70. Open daily Apr.-Sept. 10:30am-6:30pm; Jan., Mar., and Oct. 1:30-5:30pm; Nov. to mid-Dec. 1:30-5pm; Feb. 10:30am-6pm. Last entry 30min. before closing. €4, ages 8-14 €2.50, under 8 free.)

In late August, Ouessant hosts the **Salon International du Livre Insulaire,** four days of literary conferences, exhibits, and meetings with writers. (Info ☎ 02 98 90 33 32; www.perso.club-internet.fr/jacbayle/livres/salon.html.)

QUIMPER

Its central waterway criss-crossed by flower-lined pedestrian footbridges, Quimper (kem-PAIR; pop. 63,000) has a quaint charm and fierce pride in both its deep-rooted Breton heritage (one local school teaches exclusively in Breton) and its *faïencerie* (stoneware), still hand-painted just as it was 300 years ago.

▀ TRANSPORTATION

Trains: av. de la Gare. Open M-Sa 8:15am-7pm. To: **Brest** (1½hr., 4 per day, €13.70); **Nantes** (2¾hr., 4 per day, €28.20); **Paris** (4¾hr., 8 TGV per day, €64.90); **Quiberon** via **Auray** (1hr., €16.50); **Rennes** (2¼hr.; 10 per day, 4 TGV; €29.20).

Buses: next to the train station (☎ 02 98 90 88 89). To: **Brest** (1¼hr.; M-Sa 5-8 per day, 2 on Su; €13.30); **Pointe du Raz** (1½hr.; M-Sa 3-4 per day, 2 on Su; €8.85); **Pont-Aven** (1¼hr.; M-Sa 6 per day, 2 on Su; €6.40); **Roscoff** (2hr., July-Aug. 1 per day, €25.40).

Public Transportation: QUB (Quartabus), 2 quai Odet (☎ 02 98 95 26 27), by pl. de la Résistance. Buses run 6am-7:30pm. Tickets €1; day pass €3; *carnet* of 10 €8.40. Bus #1 serves the hostel and campground. The office has schedules and a map of the bus lines. Open July-Aug. M-Sa 9am-noon and 2-6pm; Sept.-June 8am-12:15pm and 1:30-6:30pm.

Taxis: Radio-Taxi Quimperois (☎ 02 98 90 21 21), in front of the train station.

Car Rental: Avis (☎ 02 98 90 31 34), next to the train station. Open M-F 8am-noon and 2-7pm, Sa 8am-noon and 1-6pm, Su 2-6pm. **Hertz** (☎ 02 98 53 12 34, reservations 08 25 86 18 61), 19 av. de la Gare, across the street from the train station. Open M-F 8am-noon and 2-7pm, Sa 8am-noon and 2-6pm.

Bike Rental: MBK s.a. Lennez, 13 rue Aristide Briand (☎ 02 98 90 14 81; fax 02 98 53 11 68), off av. de la Gare. Bikes €8 per half-day, €14 per day. Passport or check deposit. Open Tu-F 9am-noon and 2-7pm, Sa 9am-noon and 2-6:30pm. AmEx/MC/V. **Torch'VTT,** 58 rue de la Providence (☎ 02 98 53 84 41). €15 per day. €500 or passport deposit. Open Tu-Sa 9:30am-12:30pm and 2:30-7pm. MC/V.

✈ 🏠 ORIENTATION AND PRACTICAL INFORMATION

In the heart of the Cornouaille region, Quimper is separated from the sea to its south and west by rich farmland. To reach the center of town from the train station, go right onto av. de la Gare, which becomes bd. Dupleix. Keeping the river on your right, follow it to pl. de la Résistance. The tourist office will be on your left; the *vieille ville* will be across the river to your right (10 minutes).

Tourist Office: 7 rue de la Déesse, at pl. de la Résistance (☎02 98 53 04 05; www.quimper-tourisme.com). Free map; more detailed map €1. Tours of city in English (1½hr., July-Aug. Tu and F 10:30am; call to reserve). Office open July-Aug. M-Sa 9am-7pm, Su 10am-1pm and 3-5:45pm; mid-Mar. to June and Sept. M-Sa 9:30am-12:30pm and 1:30-6:30pm; June and 1st half of Sept. Su 10am-12:45pm; Oct. to mid-Mar. M-Sa 9am-12:30pm and 1:30-6pm.

Bookstore: Librairie de Mousterlin, 19 rue de Frout (☎02 98 64 37 94), has a large collection of English books, mostly classics. Open July-Aug. M-Sa 10am-7pm; Sept.-June opens at 3pm.

Youth Center: Bureau Information Jeunesse Quimper, pl. Louis Armand (☎02 98 64 42 15; bij.quimper@wanadoo.fr), next to the train station, has free **Internet access.** Open M and F 1:30-5:30pm, Tu-Th 10am-noon and 1:30-5:30pm, Sa 10am-4pm.

Laundromats: Point Laverie, 47 rue de Pont l'Abbé, about 5min. from the hostel. Open daily 8am-10pm. **Laverie de la Gare,** 2 av. de la Gare. Open daily 8am-8pm. **Lavomatique,** 9 rue de Locronan. Open daily 7am-9pm.

Police: 3 rue Theodore Le Hars (☎02 98 90 15 41).

Hospital: Hôpital de Cornouaille, 14bis av. Yves-Thépot (☎02 98 52 60 60).

Internet Access: Free at **BIJQ** (see above). **C.com,** 9 quai du Port au Vin, across from les Halles (☎02 98 95 81 62). €1.50 for 15min., €3 for 30min., €4.50 per hr. Open M-Sa 8am-7pm. **CyberCopy,** 3 bd. Amiral de Kerguelen (☎02 98 64 33 99; fax 02 98 64 25 15), on the way to the train station from town. €2 for 30min., €3.50 per hr. Open M 1-7pm, Tu-F 9am-7pm, Sa 9am-3pm. **L'Astrolabe,** 6 pl. de Locronan, past pl. St-Mathieu (☎02 98 53 71 25; http://pro.wanadoo.fr/astrolabe/). €3 for 30min., €5 per hr. Open M-F 9:30am-noon and 1:30-6pm.

Post Office: 37 bd. A. de Kerguelen (☎02 98 64 28 28). **Currency exchange,** Cyberposte, fax, and photocopies. Open M-F 8am-6:30pm, Sa 8am-noon. Branches on chemin des Justices, 2min. from hostel, and on rue Châpeau Rouge.

Postal Code: 29000.

🏠 🏕 ACCOMMODATIONS AND CAMPING

Ask at the tourist office about *chambres d'hôte.* For July and August, it's a good idea to make reservations in writing as early as possible.

Centre Hébergement de Quimper (HI), 6 av. des Oiseaux (☎02 98 64 97 97; quimper@fuaj.org). Cross the river from pl. de la Résistance and go left on quai de l'Odet. Turn right onto rue de pont l'Abbé and continue through the large roundabout; the hostel will be on your left. (20-25min.) Or, take bus #1 from pl. de la Résistance (dir: Kermoysan) to Chaptal (last bus 7:30pm). Facilities are clean, communal, and conducive to conversation, albeit at the expense of privacy. Common room with TV, foosball, and games. Bike garage and kitchen. Breakfast €3.30. Sleepsack €2.80,

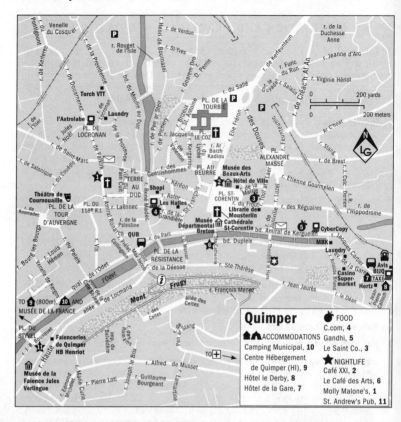

Quimper

ACCOMMODATIONS
Camping Municipal, 10
Centre Hébergement
de Quimper (HI), 9
Hôtel le Derby, 8
Hôtel de la Gare, 7

FOOD
C.com, 4
Gandhi, 5
Le Saint Co., 3

NIGHTLIFE
Café XXI, 2
Le Café des Arts, 6
Molly Malone's, 1
St. Andrew's Pub, 11

sheets €3.10. Reception daily 8-11am and 5-9pm; call if arriving later. Lockout 11am-5pm; code for late entry. Open Apr.-Sept. Bunks in 8- to 14-bed dorms €8.90; 2 singles available for €11. HI members only. ❶

Hôtel le Derby, 13 av. de la Gare (☎02 98 52 06 91; fax 02 98 53 39 04). Cheerful rooms, somewhat small, are modern, pristine, and tastefully decorated, with bath and TV, over a bar that screens horse races. Breakfast €5.60. Reception M 7am-8pm, Tu-Sa 7am-11pm, Su 7am-9:30pm. Singles €25; doubles €35. Extra bed €4. May-Sept. prices increase €3. MC/V. ❷

Hôtel de la Gare, 17 av. de la Gare (☎02 98 90 00 81; hoteldelagarequimper@free.fr), across from the station. Modern, freshly redone rooms face the inner courtyard and parking lot, away from street traffic. All rooms are well equipped, with bath, phone, kitchenette, and TV with foreign channels. Breakfast €5.50. Reception daily 7:30am-10:30pm. *Demi-pension* €60-63. Singles €40-50; doubles €46-56. MC/V. ❹

Camping: Camping Municipal, av. des Oiseaux (☎/fax 02 98 55 61 09 or 02 98 98 89 24 outside of office hours; expo@mairie-quimper.fr), next to the hostel. A forested area with shady trees and small wooden fences, not entirely removed from city life—the town center is 15min. away. Open all year. Reception June-Sept. M 1-7pm; Tu and Th 8-11am and 3-8pm, W 9am-noon, F 9-11am and 3-8pm, Sa 8am-noon and

3-8pm, Su 9-11am; shorter hours in low season.
€3.06 per person, under 7 €1.55; €1.55 per car;
€0.70 per tent; €1.30 per caravan. Electricity €2.70.
❶

FOOD

The lively covered **market** at **Les Halles,** off rue
Kéréon on rue St-François, has bargains on produce, seafood, meats, and cheeses (as well as fabulous crêpes), but the earlier you get there the better.
(Apr.-Oct. M 7am-8pm, Tu-Th 5:30am-8pm, F-Sa
5am-8pm, Su 7:30am-1pm; Nov.-Mar. opens 30min.
later.) An **open market** is held twice per week, outside Les Halles (W and Sa 7am-6pm) and in pl. des
Ursulines (Sa 6am-1:30pm). A **Casino supermarket** is
at 41 av. de la Gare. (Open M-Sa 8:30am-7:30pm, Su
9:30am-1pm and 5-7:30pm.) There is a **Shopi** grocery
downstairs at 20 rue Astor. (Open M-Sa 8:30am-
7:30pm, Su 9:30am-12:30pm.) Near the hostel,
there's a **Proxi** on quai de l'Odet. (Open M-Sa 7:30am-
8pm, Su 8:30am-12:30pm.)

Hidden among the booths inside Les Halles, **Krampouz Mad ❶,** booth #10, offers delicious crêpes at
even more delicious prices (see **Mad for Crêpes,**
right) On a quiet street just around the corner from
the cathedral, the sleek modern bistro **Le Saint Co.
❸,** 20 rue Frout, offers a tasty variety of steak *plats,*
as well as creative and filling salads and mussels.
(☎02 98 95 11 47; lesaint-co@wanadoo.fr. Steak
€12-16.50, salads €3-14, mussels €7-8. *Menus* €12-
25. Open M-Th noon-2pm and 7-10:30pm, F-Sa noon-
2pm and 7-11pm. Kitchen closes at 9pm. MC/V.)
Quimper also has a surprising number of quality
ethnic restaurants. One of the best is **Gandhi ❷,** 13
bd. de Kerguélen, near the train station. Despite its
slightly tacky homage to its namesake, Gandhi still
serves up delicious authentic cuisine, including
ample vegetarian entrees. (☎02 98 64 29 50. *Plats*
€7.70-13, *menus* €10-18. Open daily noon-2pm and
7-10:30pm. MC/V.) Bunches of fresh flowers and
pastel furniture fill the three sun-lit floors of **C.com
❶,** 9 quai du Port au Vin, across from Les Halles.
The popular cafe serves its young, urban clientele
appetizing salads (€6-9) and sandwiches (€2.40), as
well as delicious muffins (€1.80). Internet available. (☎02 98 95 81 62; Open M-Sa 8am-7pm.)

SIGHTS

The *Passeport culturel* gets you into four sites from
a list of six, including the Musée des Beaux-Arts,
Musée Départemental Breton, Faïenceries de

THE HIDDEN DEAL

MAD FOR CRÊPES

A gradually lengthening line is the
sole give-away to Quimper's best-
kept culinary secret. Outwardly
unremarkable **Krampouz Mad ❶,**
a cramped booth wedged amid
grocery and cheese vendors in the
covered market at les Halles, is
home to the best crêpes in
Quimper and the best prices practically anywhere. Catherine
Quéau, a bespectacled, gray-
haired Breton lady, works long
hours behind the counter, artfully
spreading homemade batter on a
sizzling pan with a flat comb.
While most other over-the-counter
establishments fry crêpes in
advance, at Krampouz Mad they
are cooked to order, producing
crêpes that are at once soft and
crispy, not to mention exceptionally fresh. She fills mealtime
crêpes with various combinations
of cheese, ham, tomatoes, and
other staples. A *complet* (egg,
ham, and cheese) is a supreme
bargain at €2.30 (it runs at least
€2 higher everywhere else). Her
true specialty is dessert crêpes
which she coats with unusual
combinations of sweet ingredients like apples and chocolate
(€1.85) or white chocolate and
almond (€1.50). The vendor is
generous with fillings, and the
great taste that results has gained
Booth #10 high esteem among
locals who sing its praises, while
in line for another crêpe.

*(Booth #10 in les Halles, off
of rue Kéréon on rue St-François.
☎02 98 95 03 24. Open Tu-Sa
6am-7pm.)*

Quimper HB-Henriot, Centre d'Art Contemporain, Musée de la Faïence, and the tourist office city tour (available at the tourist office or at the sites; €11.50).

⊠Faïenceries de Quimper HB-Henriot, rue Haute, is the production site for Quimper's world-renowned earthenware. Guides take visitors through the studios, where potters and painters design each piece by hand. The artists have undergone two years of specialized, on-site training and can paint an average plate in 15min. An adjoining boutique sells pricey but beautiful samples fresh from the workshops. (☎ 08 00 62 65 10; www.hb-henriot.com. Open July-Aug. M-Sa 9-11:15am and 1:30-4:45pm; rest of the year closed Sa. Tours every 30-60min. Boutique open M-Sa 9:30am-7pm. English text available with French tour. €3, ages 7-17 €1.50, under 7 free.) The magnificent dual spires of the **Cathédrale St-Corentin,** built between the 13th and 15th centuries, mark the entrance to the old quarter from quai St-Corentin. The cathedral hides several unusual features, including a beautiful pink ceiling with yellow ribs. Quimper's patron is one of dozens of Breton saints not officially recognized by the Church. (Open May-Oct. M-Sa 9:30am-noon and 1:30-6:30pm, Su 1:30-6:30pm; Nov.-Apr. M-Sa 9am-noon and 1:30-6pm, Su 1:30-6pm. Mass held Sa 6:30pm, Su 8:45, 10am, and 6:30pm. Detailed explanation in English €1. Guided visits every 30min. on demand.) **Mont Frugy,** next to the tourist office, offers an amazing view of the cathedral spires and some relief from the bustle of the city center. It's an easy hike, with numerous wooded walking trails. The **Musée des Beaux-Arts,** 40 pl. St-Corentin, across from the cathedral, has a fascinating exhibit on poet and artist Max Jacob, a Quimper native killed in the Holocaust. It includes portraits by several of his friends, including Picasso. The first room on the left holds a dozen paintings that render Breton folklore with surprising vitality. Each year, the museum hosts three large temporary exhibits. (☎ 02 98 95 45 20; musee-beauxarts.quimper.fr. Open daily July-Aug. 10am-7pm; Apr.-June M and W-Su 10am-noon and 2-6pm; Nov.-Mar. M and W-Sa 10am-noon and 2-6pm, Su 2-6pm. Tours daily July-Aug.; €5.60 including entry, ages 13-26 €4; call for info. Wheelchair-accessible. €4, ages 13-26 and over 60 €2.50, under 12 free.)

The **Musée Départemental Breton,** 1 rue du Roi Gradlon, through the cathedral garden, offers unusually stylish exhibits on local history, archaeology, and ethnography, including an elaborate display of traditional Breton clothing and innovative temporary exhibits. (☎ 02 98 95 21 60; www.cg29.fr/culture/mdb.htm. Open daily June-Sept. 9am-6pm; Oct.-May Tu-Sa 9am-noon and 2-5pm, Su 2-5pm. Tours in French, at least 1 per day; call for details and reservations; €1.50. €3.80; students €2.50; under 18, Su, Jan.-May, and Oct.-Dec. free.)

NIGHTLIFE AND FESTIVALS

The best Irish pub in Brittany may well be cavernous **⊠Molly Malone's,** pl. St-Mathieu, on rue Falkirk. One end of its long bar twists into a swirl; the other terminates in a large, dimly lit room filled with friendly chatter, Irish music, and shelves of erratically piled old books. (☎ 02 98 53 40 42. Beamish stout €3.10, pint €5.40. Jazz on Sunday afternoons Oct.-Mar. Open daily 11am-1am. AmEx/MC/V.) Quimper has no shortage of typically large European cafes, some around the cathedral, but the best is **Le Café des Arts,** 4 rue Ste-Catherine, down the street from the tourist office, which occupies nearly an entire block of its own and exudes a local vibe. For some mind-teasing, attend the *café philo,* a philosophical discussion held the first Friday of every month at 7pm. (☎ 02 98 90 32 06. Beer €1.60. Inventive cocktails €3.50-5.90. Open M-F 11am-1am, Sa-Su 3:30pm-1am. MC/V.) A metallic bar, curving walls, and boxy chairs create a modern feel in glittering **Café XXI,** 38 pl. St-Corentin, across from the cathedral and next to the Musée des Beaux-Arts. This popular daytime people-watching venue doubles as a glam nightspot, serving its "XXI" specialty (white rum, curaçao, pineapple juice, and fresh citrus juice; €5.40) to a sophisticated clientele. (☎02 98 95 92 34. Wine €3. Open daily July-Aug. 8:30am-1am; *brasserie* noon-3pm; Sept.-June Tu-Sa 8:45am-10pm. MC/V.) **St. Andrew's Pub,** 11 pl. du Styvel, is just across the river from rue de Pont l'Abbé. Its breezy, riverside terrace and classy interior are the perfect setting for a relaxed drink. (☎02 98 53 34 49. Drinks €2-4. Open daily 11am-1am. AmEx/MC/V.)

Catch some Breton culture at the **Festival de Cornouaille,** Quimper's annual summer gala. The festival is held every year in the attractive cathedral gardens, right next to the Odet, which fill with Breton dancers in traditional costume, accompanied by lively music from the *biniou* (bagpipes) and the reed instrument *bombarde,* similar to an oboe. (Held in late July, schedule and prices vary; see tourist office or www.festival-cornouaille.com for details.) Quimper holds its increasingly popular **Semaines Musicales** during early to mid-August every year. Various quality orchestras and choirs perform nightly in the Théâtre Municipal and the cathedral (info ☎02 98 95 32 43; www.semaines-musicales-quimper.org).

▶ DAYTRIP FROM QUIMPER

PONT-AVEN

Pont-Aven is connected by Caoudal buses (☎02 98 56 96 72) to Quimper (1¼hr.; 3 per day; €6.40, round-trip €10) and nearby towns (line 14A).

The first to paint Pont-Aven (pop. 3000) was Paul Gauguin (1848-1903), who, fed up with mainstream Impressionism, came here in 1886 and inspired a movement that emphasized pure color, absence of perspective, and simplified figures. Pont-Aven's pride and joy are the museums and studios celebrating its art—it is likely that Pont-Aven has more art galleries per capita than anywhere else in the world. Almost as prevalent are the shops selling the town's famous *galettes* (butter cookies), whose production is the town's economic lifeblood; most stores offer free samples. Pont-Aven's true beauty, however, is natural. The tourist office provides maps detailing a number of short hikes through acres of surrounding woodland, many of which pass through places where artists once congregated. From the town center, you can follow the **Promenade Xavier Graal,** a series of bridges that hover over the swift, salmon-filled Aven River as it makes its way to the **Chaos de Pont-Aven,** a set of flat rocks around which the river swirls. A path through the tranquil **Bois d'Amour** (Lovers' Wood) meanders along the river in the shade of gnarled tree trunks. The most enticing part of the walk runs closest to town, along the river. Above the woods, amid thriving farmland and avenues lined with oaks and beeches, is the **Chapelle de Trémalo.** The 16th-century Gothic church, itself quite simple, is an isolated retreat and houses the 17th-century wooden painted crucifix that inspired Gauguin's *Le Christ Jaune.*

After seeing the environs, view the paintings they inspired: the **Musée de Pont-Aven,** pl. de l'Hôtel de Ville, up the street to the left when facing the tourist office, showcases the works of Gauguin, Sérusier, and other adherents of the Pont-Aven school, along with photographs from the period. A film in French shown every 30min. is a well-made introduction to the movement. (☎02 98 06 14 43; musee.pont-aven@wanadoo.fr. Open daily July-Aug. 10am-7pm; Apr.-June and Sept.-Oct. 10am-12:30pm and 2-6:30pm; Feb.-Mar. and Nov.-Dec. 10am-12:30pm and 2-6pm. €4, students and ages 13-20 €2.50, under 12 free.)

The **tourist office,** 5 pl. de l'Hôtel de Ville, is a block from the bus stop on pl. Gauguin. Turn away from the river and walk toward the square and the museum beyond; the office is on the right side of the street. The staff distributes a handbook detailing art in the area, sells a walking-tour guide (€0.50), and organizes tours, in French, of the town and museum (town €4, museum €5.50 including entry; both €6). The office can also provide information on the **Fleurs d'Ajonc Folk Festival,** on the first Sunday of August. (☎ 02 98 06 04 70, for info on the folk festival call 02 98 06 12 33; www.pontaven.com. Open July-Aug. M-Sa 9:30am-7:30pm, Su 10am-1pm and 3-6:30pm; Apr.-June and Sept. M-Sa 9:30am-12:30pm and 2-6:30pm, Su 10am-1pm; Oct.-Mar. M-Sa 10am-12:30pm and 2-6pm. Tours daily June-Sept. 11am and 4:30pm, except W morning July-Aug.)

QUIBERON

Though it lacks a wealth of museums, monuments, and history, the small peninsula of Quiberon (pop. 4500) has more than its fair share of summer sunshine. Join the sun-worshipping crowds on the popular Grande Plage at the southern tip, or visit the spectacular smaller beaches on the eastern side of the peninsula, which are prime spots for surfing, kayaking, and sailing. Stunning Belle-Île is only a 45min. ferry ride away, and the countryside surrounding Quiberon offers many opportunities for excursions.

▐ TRANSPORTATION

Most of the year, the train to Quiberon stops at Auray (☎ 02 97 24 44 50). A special train connects Auray and Quiberon (45min., July-Aug. 10 per day, €2.80). Trains run through Auray on the way to Brest, Paris, and Quimper (call ☎ 08 36 35 35 35 for schedules). Quiberon train station open July-Aug. M-Sa 8:45am-6:50pm, Su 8:45am-7:50pm; daily Sept.-June 9:15am-12:15pm and 2:14-5:30pm. **TIM buses** (☎ 02 97 21 28 29) run from Auray (1hr., €6), Carnac (30min., €3.40), and Vannes (2hr., €8), stopping at Quiberon's port and train station. All buses July-Aug. 1 per day; Sept.-June M-Sa 7-9 per day. Explore the Côte Sauvage on **bikes,** tandems, or scooters from Cyclomar, 47 pl. Hoche (☎ 02 97 50 26 00), which also has an annex at the train station. (Bikes €7 per half-day, €9 per day, €38.50 per week. Scooters €25.50 per half-day, €37.50 per day. Mopeds €15 per half-day, €24 per day. Insurance for both scooters and mopeds €5.50 per day. 10% off with *Let's Go,* ISIC card, or note from the youth hostel. Credit card, personal ID, or passport deposit. Open daily July-Aug. 7:30am-10pm; Oct.-June and Sept. 8:30am-7pm. Annex open daily July-Aug. 8:30am-8pm. MC/V.) For a **taxi,** call ☎ 06 07 09 01 27.

▐ PRACTICAL INFORMATION

To find the **tourist office,** 14 rue de Verdun, turn left from the train station and walk down rue de la Gare, then right down rue de Verdun (5 minutes). The staff distributes a comprehensive city guide and a detailed handbook (€2) with six walking tours. (☎ 02 97 50 07 84; www.quiberon.com. Open July-Aug. M-Sa 9am-1:30pm and 2-7pm, Su 10am-1pm and 2-5pm; Nov. and Feb.-June M-Sa 9am-12:30pm and 2-6pm; Dec.-Jan. M-Sa 9am-12:30pm and 2-5pm. Hours change frequently.) Other services include: a **laundromat** on rue de Port-Maria, near the beach (open daily 9:15am-8pm); **police** (☎ 02 97 30 24 00) at 7 rue de Verdun; a **hospital** at the Centre Hospitalier du Pratel in Auray (☎ 02 97 29 20 20; open Sept.-June until 8pm); **emergency services** at the Centre Hospitalier Bretagne Atlantique, bd. Maurice Guillaudot in Vannes (☎ 02 97 01 41 41). **Internet** is available (for a pretty penny) at Rhumerie Le Nelson, a bar at 20 pl. Hoche, near the beach. (☎ 02 97 50 31 37; fax 02 97 30 37 51. €1 to connect, €0.20 per min. Open July-Aug. M-Sa noon-2am, Su 3pm-2am; Sept.-June opens F-Sa at 3pm. Closed Jan.) The **post office,** pl. de la Duchesse

Anne, has **currency exchange,** Cyberposte, fax, and photocopies. (☎02 97 50 11 92. Open July-Aug. M-F 9am-12:30pm and 2-5pm, Sa 9am-noon; Sept.-June M-F 9am-noon and 2-5pm, Sa 9am-noon.) **Postal Code:** 56170.

ACCOMMODATIONS AND CAMPING

The central **Hôtel de l'Océan ❸,** 7 quai de l'Océan, offers well-furnished rooms, some facing the harbor, with colorful bedspreads and lots of storage space. An enormous, sunny salon with wicker chairs and views of the quai makes a lovely place to people-watch. (☎02 97 50 07 58; hoteldelocean@wanadoo.fr. Breakfast €6.50. Reception 8am-9pm. Singles and doubles €34-42, with shower €46-50, with toilet €51-60. Extra bed €12. MC/V.) Quiberon is generally expensive, but the **Auberge de Jeunesse (HI) "Les Filets Bleus" ❶,** 45 rue du Roch-Priol, in a quiet, residential neighborhood, is affordable and close to both the town center and beach. From the station, turn left and take rue de la Gare toward the beach and the church. Turn left onto rue de Port-Haliguen, then right onto bd. Anatole France, and left onto rue du Roch-Priol (12 minutes). Three somewhat cramped and less-than-spotless 8-bed rooms open onto a covered outdoor eating area. Camping and spots in a communal tent are also available. (☎02 97 50 15 54. Kitchen. Breakfast €3.30. Sheets €2.80. Reception daily 9am-noon and 5-10pm. July-Aug. reserve in advance. Open Apr.-Sept. Bunks €7.70. On-site communal tent €6. 2-person tents €6.80. Camping €5.30 per person, €1.40 per tent. HI members only.) The vine-draped **Hôtel Men-Er-Vro ❹,** 22 rue de Port-Haliguen, 10min. from the beach and 5min. from the town center, lets cozy rooms above a *crêperie*. Though somewhat small, the rooms are comfortable, bright, and individually decorated; all come with TV, phone, and clean modern bathrooms. (☎02 97 50 16 08; fax 02 97 29 50 75. Breakfast €7. Reception daily 8am-4pm and 6-11pm. Reservations essential June-Sept. Singles €39; doubles €53.50-62.50; triples and quads €68; all prices €4-9 lower in the low season. MC/V.)

The Quiberon Peninsula has nearly a dozen campsites; the tourist office provides information on all of them. One of the best is well-tended ▨**Camping Bois d'Amour ❶,** rue St-Clément, just off plage du Goviro. The site has slick, spacious grounds, a heated pool, a bar, a small restaurant, a TV room, and laundry. The staff organizes sports during the day and nightly events like karaoke. (☎02 97 50 13 52 or 04 42 20 47 25; fax 02 97 50 42 67. Reception daily 9am-noon and 2-7pm. €4.50-9 per person, under 10 €3.50-4.50; tent or caravan with car €8-16.50. Electricity €4.50. Prices vary by season.)

FOOD

Quiberon's menus feature seafood and the lollipop-topped, caramel-like *niniche* candy, available from beachside vendors. For **groceries,** there's an extra-large **Marché Plus,** 2 rue de Verdun (☎02 97 50 11 03; open July-Aug. M-Sa 7am-9pm, Su 9am-8pm; Sept.-June closes at noon Su), which has a wide variety of inexpensive pre-packaged sandwiches and salads, or **Casino,** close to the hostel at 66 rue de Port Haliguen. (☎02 97 29 50 60. Open M-Sa 8:30am-8pm, Su 9am-12:30pm.) Produce **markets** appear on pl. du Varquez, behind the *mairie* (Sa 6:30am-1pm), and Port Haliguen (mid-June to mid-Sept. W 6:30am-1pm).

Set in an alley just off the street, charming **Au SaFran ❹,** 20 rue Verdun, near the tourist office, finds creative ways to spice up traditional meat and seafood dishes. (☎02 97 50 18 64. *Menus* €15, €21, €22.50, €28. Open July-Aug. M-Sa noon-2pm and 7-10pm, Su noon-2pm; Sept.-June closed M. Reserve ahead on the weekend. MC/V.) For a taste of the sea, try **La Criée ❹,** 11 quai de l'Océan. Catches are displayed on ice in an attached *poissonerie;* if these fish were any fresher they'd be flopping. The *plateau gargantua*, an awesome array of oysters, crab, and other sea-creatures (€49.50), is perfect for large groups. More modest fish dishes run €17-21. (☎02 97 30 53 09. Open Tu-Sa from 12:15pm for lunch and from 7:15pm for dinner, Su lunch only. MC/V.) Down the quai toward the Grande Plage, **L'Elfenn ❸**, 1 rue de Kervozès, provides a less expensive alternative in a comfortable atmosphere with great views of the port. (☎02 97 30 40 43. Generous *menus* €14.50-18, fish €8-13, *plat du jour* €9, mussels €6-8. Open Tu-Su noon-7pm. MC/V.)

🎵 🎎 ENTERTAINMENT AND FESTIVALS

The beaches don't empty until it's too dark to see the volleyball. Close to midnight, an energetic crowd heads to the tropical **Hacienda Café**, 4 rue du Phare, off pl. Hoche. Young teenage *Quiberonnais* drink flaming cocktails and dance until the wee hours. Black lights illuminate fluorescent murals that cover every surface, including the bar. Order a pitcher of frozen margarita and a glass of punch before 1am and get a free t-shirt. (☎02 97 30 51 76. Rum vanilla or beer €2.50. Cocktails €3.50-6.50. 1-drink min. Open M-Th, Su 10pm-4am, F-Sa 10pm-5am.) To escape the teenybopper crowd, try the nightclub **Le Surtoit**, 29 rue Port Maria, where the clientele tends to be older, probably because they're the only ones who can afford the €5 beer, €8 liquor, and €10 cocktails. (Open daily 11:30pm-5am.) In early to mid-April, the **Semaine Océane** takes the town by storm with dance, music, and plays.

🏖 BEACHES

The aptly named Côte Sauvage stretches a wild, windy 10km along the western edge of Quiberon. Though views from the road are amazing, drivers must take to the foot paths to fully enjoy the boulder-strewn beaches and eroded archways. Heed the signs marked *Baignades Interdites* (Swimming Forbidden); many have drowned in these tempting waters. Green flags mean safe supervised swimming; orange means dangerous but usually supervised swimming; and red means swimming prohibited. On the tourist-office map, a red cross indicates a supervised beach. SOS posts with flotation devices dot the coastline.

Grande Plage, the most popular beach, is coated with sun-worshipping tourists and carefree teenagers when the weather is good, while the small, rocky **Plage du Goviro** appeals to those who prefer solitude. To reach it from the port, follow bd. Chanard to the left as it becomes bd. de la Mer and then bd. du Goviro. The east side of the peninsula is dotted with beaches perfect for sunbathing.

🗺 DAYTRIPS FROM QUIBERON

BELLE-ÎLE-EN-MER

Boats dock on the northern coast at Le Palais, the island's largest town. SMN, in Port Maria, Quiberon, serves Belle-Île (45min.) from the gare maritime, quai de Houat. (☎08 20 05 60 00, for foreigners 02 97 35 02 00; www.smn-navigation.fr. 5-13 per day; round-trip €23, under 25 €13.90, seniors €15.70. Bikes €13.10, cars €105-200. Baggage €2.20 per item.) Taol Mor Buses run from Le Palais to Belle-Île's other main towns: Bangor (33min., 7 per day); Locmaria (30min., 5 per day); Sauzon (15-25min., 10 per day). Tickets are available on the bus or at Point Taol Mor, quai Bonelle in Le Palais. (☎02 97 31 32 32. Single ticket €2.50, ages 4-12 €1.60; 2-day pass €10.) Cars Verts, at the gare maritime in Quiberon, runs 1-day bus tours of the island and recommends taking the 9:30am ferry to the island. (☎02 97 50 11 60. €11.50, under 25 €6, over 60 €10.50.) Rent bikes and mountain bikes at Cyclotour, quai Bonelle, near the tourist office. (☎02 97 31 80 68. Bikes €8 per half-day, €10 per day. Passport, ID, or check deposit. Open daily July-

Aug. 8:30am-7pm; Sept.-June M-Sa 9am-12:30pm and 2-7pm.) Bike trails are well marked, although bicycles share the road with cars and coastal paths are reserved for pedestrians. The most spectacular area, the Côte Sauvage, is also accessible by boat. See Quiberon Beaches, p. 230, for safety info).

The coast of Belle-Île (pop. 4800), an island known as *Le Bien-Nommé* (The Well-Named), is even more breathtaking than that of the neighboring peninsula. Through the course of history, Belle-Île's high cliffs, crashing seas, and heathered fields have sheltered *menhir*-carvers, monks, pirates, and German POWs. Belle-Île, 20km long and about 50km in circumference, is large enough to make bike rental or shuttle use necessary.

The massive **Citadelle Vauban**, built in 1549 by Henri II to protect monks from pirates, grew to an impressive network of snaking passageways between 30 ft. walls. Today, they protect a grass-roofed museum that traces the island's history, with displays on famous visitors like Sarah Bernhardt, Monet, and 400 German WWI POWs. It takes about 2hr. to thoroughly explore the sprawling fortress, which provides great views of the water. (☎ 02 97 31 84 17; fax 02 97 31 45 83. Open daily July-Aug. 9am-7pm; Apr.-June and Sept.-Oct. 9:30am-6pm; Nov.-Mar. 9:30am-noon and 2-5pm. €6.10, ages 7-16 €3.05, under 7 free.)

Belle-Île's natural treasures lie scattered along the coastline. The **plage de Donnant,** on the western coast, with its expansive dunes and mysterious stone boundary, is the widest and most popular beach. Equally gorgeous are the pristine **plage Port-Maria**, on the eastern shore, and the powder-white **plage Grands Sables,** the longest beach on the island, southeast of Le Palais. To see the more rugged side of the island's coastline, head 6km northwest from Le Palais to postcard-like **Sauzon.** Crisp white houses with multicolored shutters line the port, facing mossy rock cliffs on the other side. Massive rock formations rise over the thunderous **Grotte de l'Apothicairerie,** southwest of **Pointe des Poulains** on the northern tip of the island. While access to the grotto was recently restricted for safety reasons, the site still offers a spectacular panorama of the Côte Sauvage. Monet was inspired by another coastal wonder—the ▨**Aiguilles de Port Coton,** a small colony of needle-like rocks shooting up through electric-green water. The **Port Coton** owes its name to its bursting sea foam, whipped by the winds to resemble cotton.

From late July to mid-August, **Lyrique-en-Mer** brings Mozart concerts and several operas to the island. (☎ 02 97 31 59 59; tickets@belli-ile.net.) The Palais **tourist office,** quai Bonnelle, is on the dock's left end. The energetic staff distributes thorough guides to the island, a French hiking and biking brochure with plans, and a map (€8) that is helpful for exploring the island on foot or bike. They also have info on sailing, sea kayaking, and many other island activities. (☎ 02 97 31 81 93; www.belle-ile.com. Open July-Aug. M-Sa 8:45am-7:30pm; Apr.-June and Sept. M-Sa 9am-12:30pm and 2-6pm, Su 10am-12:30pm; Oct.-Mar. M-Sa 9am-12:30pm and 2-6pm.)

CARNAC

TIM buses (☎ 02 97 21 28 29) go to Quiberon (30min.; July-Aug. 1 per day, Sept.-June 7 per day; €6.30). There are 2 bus stops corresponding to Carnac's 2 tourist offices: Carnac-Ville, close to the town center, and Carnac-Plage, near the main tourist office and the beach. Tatoovu, a local shuttle, connects them. (June-Sept. M-Sa 9:15am-1pm and 2:30-8pm, Su 9:15am-1pm. Tickets €1.10, carnet of 10 €10. Buy tickets on bus. Tourist office has schedules.) In the summer months, when bus service is minimal, it's more convenient to take the train from Quiberon to the Plouharnel-Carnac station and take the TIM bus to town from there. (Trains July-Aug. 10 per day, Sept.-June 6 per day; €2.80, round-trip €5.)

The series of ancient megaliths in Carnac (pop. 4500) is collectively the oldest prehistoric site in Europe. Built from 4500 to 2500 BC, Carnac's 3000 *menhirs* stretch along the horizon for 4km, steadily increasing in height as they extend westward.

The 800,000 visitors who trample the grounds annually have destroyed vegetation and contributed to erosion; as a result, a massive restoration program is underway, and public access to the monuments is restricted. The closest *menhirs* to town are the **Alignements du Ménec**, the largest of their kind in the world. More than 1000 *menhirs*, some over 4m tall, stretch 2km along the horizon, unromantically bordered by a highway. The somewhat more dynamic **Alignements de Kermario,** which holds Carnac's best *menhir* specimens among its 1029 stones, stands adjacent to the **Géant du Manio** (a big rock) and the **Quadrilatère** (rocks in a square). Call the **Maison des Mégalithes,** rte. des Alignements, across from the Alignements du Ménec, to reserve a spot on one of the guided tours—the only way to get beyond the barriers. To get there from the Carnac-Ville tourist office, take a right onto rue St-Cornély, another right on rue de Courdiec, then turn left onto rte. des Alignements (7 minutes). Be careful, as there is no sidewalk at some points. (☎02 97 52 89 99; alignements.carnac@monuments-France-fr. Open daily July-Aug. 9am-8pm; May-June 9am-7pm; Sept.-Apr. 10am-5:15pm. 1hr. tours July-Aug. at 1, 3, and 4:30pm in French and at 11:30am in English. Longer visits and workshops for children also available. €4, ages 12-25 €3, under 12 free.) The Maison also has info about restoration and a 50min. film about the monuments.

Behind the tourist office in the town center, the **Musée de Préhistoire,** 10 pl. de la Chapelle, provides good background information for a visit to the megaliths with rich exhibits on cultural evolution from the Paleolithic Age to the Roman period, including replicas of Megalithic art and even a vertebra of a man killed 6600 years ago. (☎02 97 52 22 04; www.museedecarnac.com. Open June-Sept. M-F 10am-6pm, Sa-Su 10am-noon and 2-6:30pm; Oct.-May M and W-Su 10am-noon and 2-5pm. €5, students €2.50, under 18 free. Combined admission with tour of alignments or Table des Marchands in Locmariaquer available.) To get to Carnac's **beaches** from the tourist office in the historic center, take av. de la Poste, which becomes av. de l'Atlantique, following signs to *plages*.

NANTES

The gory history of Nantes (pop. 270,000) would spice up even the dullest textbook. In 1440, the infamous pirate Bluebeard (the Maréchal de Retz) was brought to trial here and burned at the stake for his grisly crimes. The city's brushes with brutality continued between the 16th and 18th centuries, when Nantes established itself as a nexus of the slave trade, which made it France's largest port. During the Revolution, putting the efficiency of the guillotine to shame, bloodthirsty and impatient *Nantais* resorted to mass drownings in the Loire. Bearing no resemblance to its violent past, modern Nantes, less intimate than its northern neighbors, successfully blends a high-tech industry and professional population with a large university crowd. Down the street from the modern train station, towering buildings, an expansive shopping district, cafes, and 15th- to 16th-century wood-paneled houses line winding cobblestone streets. Street musicians perform on summer nights in the central squares and lively pedestrian streets.

▌ TRANSPORTATION

Flights: The airport is 10km south of Nantes (☎02 40 84 80 00; www.nantes.aeroport.fr). **Air Inter** (☎02 51 88 31 08) flies daily to **Lyon, Marseille, Nice,** and **Paris. Air France** (☎08 20 82 08 20) sends at least 6 flights per week to **London.** A **Tan Air shuttle** (☎02 40 29 39 39) runs to the airport from pl. du Commerce and the south side of the train station (25min.; 1 per hr. 5:30am-9pm; tickets €6, *carnet* of 4 €16.) Schedule available at the info desk outside the train station or at the tourist office.

Nantes

⌂▲ ACCOMMODATIONS
Auberge de Jeunesse (HI), **5**
Camping du Petit Port, **1**
Foyer des Jeunes Travailleurs, **14**
Hôtel Renova, **10**
Hôtel St-Daniel, **11**
Hôtel du Tourisme, **6**

🍴 FOOD
La Cigale, **12**
Le Clin d'Oeil, **9**
L'Ile Verte, **4**
Midi-Pile, **13**

★ NIGHTLIFE
Le John McByrne, **7**
Le Loft, **8**
La Maison, **3**
Le Temps d'Aimer, **15**

Jardin des Plantes

TO **5** (500m)

GARE SNCF
Gare d'Orléans (North Building)
Gare d'Orléans (South Building)
Europcar
TAXI
Canal Saint-Félix
quai Ferdinand
av. Carnot

r. Stanislas Baudry
r. Elie Delaunays
Musée des Beaux-Arts
r. Jules Dupré
Chapelle de l'Immaculée
r. de Richebourg
cours John Kennedy
PL. DE LA DUCHESSE ANNE
DUCHESSE ANNE
r. Malherbe

r. Gambetta
r. Maréchal Joffre
r. Lebrun
r. Sully
Chapelle de l'Oratoire
r. Henri IV
cours St-Pierre
PL. MARÉCHAL FOCH
Cathédrale St-Pierre
PL. ST-PIERRE
impasse St-Laurent
r. Mathelin Rodier
Château des Ducs de Bretagne
allée Baco

r. de Strasbourg
cours St-André
r. Tournefort
PL. DU ROI ALBERT
r. du Roi Albert
r. du Refuge
r. des Cordeliers
r. Notre Dame
PL. ROGER SALENGRO
r. d'Alger
r. LeClerc
r. de Strasbourg
r. du Château
r. de l'Emery
r. du Bouffay
Cybercity
NEPTUNE

r. de Verdun
Cyberkebab
PL. DU PILORI
r. des Chapeliers
r. des Petites Écuries
BOUFFAY
Pont Mallard
PL. DU BOUFFAY
Tramway

r. Maurice Duval
r. de Garde Dieu
r. Maréchal
r. Fénélon
SPAR Supermarket
r. des Halles
Ste-Croix
SPAR Supermarket

Hôtel de Ville
r. de l'Hôtel de Ville
r. du Moulin
r. des Carmes
r. de la Paix
r. de la Marne

r. St-Léonard
Laundry
Cartiane Atlantique Buses
Le Frutier
Librairie
PL. DU COMMERCE
L. Durance

r. de l'Écluse
cours des 50 Otages
allée de la Maison Rouge
cours Olivier de Clisson
ALEXIS RICORDEAU
Cartiane Atlantique

50 OTAGES
TO △ (2km)
allée Duquesne
allée d'Orléans
allée de la Clavrerie
TAN
GARE CENTRALE (BUS-TRAM HUB)
COMMERCE
COMMERCE
r. du Couëdic
PL. DU COMMERCE

r. Sarrazin
r. Jeanne d'Arc
r. le Nôtre
TO RTC
PL. ST-SIMILIEN
ST-SIMILIEN
r. Léopold Cassegrain
r. de l'Abreuvoir
PL. DU CIRQUE
r. de l'Échafaud
Cyberpiment
PL. BRETAGNE
Tour Bretagne
r. Mercœur
r. du Pont Sauvetout
Monoprix
St-Nicolas
PL. ROYALE
PL. FOURNIER

r. Jean Jaurès
r. Herriot
r. du Calvaire
PL. DE LA DÉFENSE PASSIVE
PL. DES VOLONTAIRES
r. de Feltre
r. du Puits
r. des Gorges
r. de l'Arche
r. Guépin
r. Paré
r. de la Fosse
r. Contrescarpe
Passage Pommeraye
Passage du Commerce
r. d'Argentré

TO ⚓ (50m)
LAUNDRY (50m) AND ⚓ (1km)
r. du Guesclin
TO LOIRE RIVER (500m) AND MUSÉE JULES VERNE (1km)
r. Franklin Roosevelt
r. Cassard
Gaston Veil

Galeries Lafayette
AND CRU
Change Graslin
PL. GRASLIN
Théâtre Graslin
Corneille
Molière
r. Scribe
r. Crébillon
r. Boileau
r. Santeuil
r. Suffren
r. Jean Jacques Rousseau
r. du Chapeau Rouge
PL. DELORME
r. Copernic
r. Voltaire
r. Racine
Apollo Theater

BRITTANY

Tram

0   100 meters
0   110 yards

Trains: The train station has 2 entrances: North, at 27 bd. de Stalingrad, and South, rue de Loumel, across the tracks. Info and tickets at northern entrance. To: **Angers** (40min.; every 30min. 5am-11pm; €12.10, TGV €13.80); **Bordeaux** (4hr., 5 per day, €38.30); **La Rochelle** (2hr., 6 per day, €21.60); **Paris** (2-4hr., 1 per hr., €49.10); **Rennes** (2hr.; M-F 6-8 per day, Sa 1 per day, Su 2 per day; €19.20); **Saumur** (70min., 1 per hr., €17.10). Ticket counters open M-F 4:30am-11:30pm, Sa 5:30am-11:45pm, Su 6am-11:20pm. Luggage check at north side of station. (Open 6:15am-11pm. Backpack €3.50, larger luggage €6-8. 72hr. limit.)

Buses: Cariane Atlantique (☎08 25 08 71 56) goes to **Rennes** (line #10; 2hr.; July-Aug. M-Sa 1 per day, Sept.-June 2 per day; €23). Info office, 5 allée Duquesne, has schedules. (Open M-F 9:15am-noon and 2:15-6:15pm.) Depart station's south entrance and the parking lot on allée Baco, by the Hôtel de Dieu. MC/V.

Public Transportation: TAN, 4/6 allée Brancas (☎08 01 44 44 44), opposite pl. du Commerce. Runs buses and 3 tram lines daily, some until 1am. Ticket €1.20, day pass €3.30, *carnet* of 10 €9.90, weekend pass €4.30. Office open M-Sa 7:15am-7pm.

Taxis: Allô Radio-Taxis Nantes Atlantique at train station (☎02 40 69 22 22). 24hr.

Car Rental: A row of rental agencies sits to the left of the south exit of the train station. Among them is **Budget** (02 40 20 25 70). Open M-F 8am-noon and 2-6pm, Sa 8am-12:30pm and 2:30-6pm. AmEx/MC/V. **Europcar** is across the street (☎02 40 47 19 38). Open M-F 7:45am-10:15pm, Sa 8:30am-12:30pm and 2-6pm, Su 10:30am-12:30pm and 5:30-8:30pm. AmEx/MC/V.

Bike Rental: The tourist office provides rental information. In the summer, bike rental is available at major parking lots in the city as part of the Ville à Vélo program. Pick-up locations include pl. Graslin, pl. Bretagne, the north train station, and Camping du Petit Port. Pl. du Commerce location open year-round. (☎02 51 84 94 51. €1.50 per hr., €5 for half-day, €8 per day. Open daily 8am-8pm.)

Canoe Rental: Contre Courant (☎02 40 14 31 24), on the Île de Versailles. Take tram line #2 (dir: Orvault Grand Val) to St-Mihiel. Cross the bridge to the island. €5 per hr., €15 per day. 2hr. free with Nantes City Card. Open Apr.-Sept. Tu-F 2-7:45pm, Sa-Su 10am-7:45pm. Oct.-Mar. by reservation.

■ ? ORIENTATION AND PRACTICAL INFORMATION

Nantes's tangle of neighborhoods, hills, and pedestrian streets spreads along the north bank of the Loire. Shadowed by a modest skyscraper, the **Tour de Bretagne**, the city's axes run east-west along **cours John Kennedy,** which becomes **cours Franklin D. Roosevelt** and later **quai de la Fosse,** and north-south along **cours des 50 Otages.** The pedestrian district between the château and the **place du Commerce** is the liveliest part of town, as well as the hub for local transportation.

Tourist Office: 3 cours Olivier de Clisson (☎02 40 20 60 00; www.nantes-tourisme.com). Excellent maps and free walking tour guides in French and English. Tours of the city in French cover a variety of topics, from history to parks. Tours €6, students €3; call for a schedule. Office open M-W and F-Sa 10am-6pm, Th 10:30am-6pm. Branch at 2 pl. St-Pierre. Open M-W and F-Su 10am-1pm and 2-6pm, Th opens at 10:30am.

Budget Travel: Voyage au Fil (☎02 51 72 94 60), at CRIJ (see below). Ground and air tickets. Matches travelers with drivers. Books nature and adventure trips. Open July-Aug. Tu-W and F 10am-12:30pm and 2-6pm; Th and Sa 2-6pm; Sept.-June closes at 6:30pm. AmEx/MC/V.

Currency Exchange: Good rates at **Change Graslin,** 17 rue Rousseau (☎02 40 69 24 64), in pl. Graslin right next to La Cigale. Open M-F 9am-noon and 2-5:45pm, Sa 10am-noon and 2-4:45pm.

English-Language Bookstore: Librairie L. Durance, 4 allée d'Orléans (☎02 40 48 68 79). Take a right off cours des 50 Otages. (Open M 2-7pm, Tu-Sa 9:30am-7pm. MC/V.)

Youth Information: Centre Régional d'Information Jeunesse (CRIJ), 28 rue du Calvaire (☎02 51 72 94 50; crij.pdl@wanadoo.fr), will soon move into the Tour de Bretagne. Info on youth discounts, housing, and volunteer and employment opportunities. Free **Internet** access (30min. limit). Open July-Aug. Tu-W and F 10am-6pm, Th 2-6pm; Sept.-June closes at 6:30pm.

Laundromat: 7 rue de l'Hôtel de Ville (open daily 7am-8:30pm); others at 11 rue Chaussée de la Madeleine (open M 2:30-8pm, Tu-F 11am-8pm, Sa 1-7pm) and 10 quai de Versailles, which also has Internet with a *télécarte* (open daily 8am-10pm).

Police: 6 pl. Waldeck-Rousseau (☎02 40 37 21 21).

Youth Hotline: École Parents Educateurs Loire Atlantique, 21 allée Baco (☎02 40 47 71 28). Support hotline for ages 12-25. Free, anonymous counseling. Drop in or call.

Hospital: Centre Hospitalier Universitaire, 1 pl. Alexis-Ricordeau (☎02 40 08 33 33; www.chu-nantes.fr). Women's emergencies ☎02 40 73 57 32.

Internet Access: Cybercity, 14 rue de Strasbourg (☎02 40 89 57 92). €3 per hr. Open daily 10am-1am. **Cyberkebab,** 30 rue de Verdun (☎02 40 47 09 21), also sells falafel and kebabs. €3 per hr., €3.30 per kebab. Student discounts. Open daily 10am-2am. **Cyberpl@net,** 18 rue de l'Arche Sèche, near the Tour de Bretagne (☎02 51 82 47 97; www.cyberplanet.fr). €1 for 20min., €3 per hr. Open M-Sa 10am-2am, Su 2-10pm.

Post Office: 2 rue du Président Edouard Herriot (☎02 51 10 57 25), at pl. de Bretagne near Tour Bretagne. From pl. du Cirque, take elevator in the Tour de Bretagne to pl. Bretagne. **Currency exchange** M-Sa 9:30am-5pm. Cyberposte, fax, photocopies, and **Western Union.** Open M-F 8:30am-6:45pm, Sa 8:30am-12:30pm. Branch at 3/5 rue du Moulin (☎02 40 35 09 40) has currency exchange, photocopies, and Western Union. Open M 2-6:30pm, Tu-F 9:30am-6:30pm, Sa 9:30am-5pm.

Postal Code: 44038.

▛▜ ACCOMMODATIONS AND CAMPING

Nantes has plenty of good budget hotels and student dorm space in summer. The hotels across from the station are overpriced and in an uninteresting, slightly seedy neighborhood.

▨ **Hôtel St-Daniel,** 4 rue du Bouffay (☎02 40 47 41 25; hotel.st.daniel@wanadoo.fr), off pl. du Bouffay, in the heart of the pedestrian district. Clean, calm, and well-appointed rooms with firm beds and highly modern bathrooms, some overlooking a church garden. The main greeter is friendly giant Thrace, a black dog of epic proportions. Breakfast €4. Reception 7:30am-10pm, closed Su 2-7pm. Singles and doubles with bath €29, with bath €32; triples and quads with shower and toilet €42. AmEx/MC/V. ❸

Hôtel Renova, 11 rue Beauregard (☎02 40 47 57 03; fax 02 51 82 06 39), off cours des 50 Otages. Chunky candles and loud modern art greet guests at this centrally located hotel. Upstairs, spacious but somewhat bare rooms come with bathrooms and satellite TV. Breakfast €3. Reception 7am-10pm. Reserve one week ahead. Singles with shower €30; double with shower €34, with bath €40. Extra bed €10. AmEx/MC/V. ❸

Hôtel du Tourisme, 5 allée Duquesne, centrally located on the cours des 50 Otages (☎02 40 47 90 26; fax 02 40 35 57 25). Comfortable rooms, nice bathrooms, TV, and phone. For quality star-gazing, request the small single with a skylight. Breakfast €4.80. Free bike storage. Nightly parking €2. Reception 7am-10pm (call if arriving later). Reserve ahead. Singles and doubles with shower €28, with shower and toilet €31-36.50; triples and quads with shower and toilet €45. Extra bed €8.50. AmEx/MC/V. ❷

Auberge de Jeunesse (HI), 2 pl. de la Manu (☎02 40 29 29 20; fax 02 51 12 48 42). From the north exit of the station, go right down bd. de Stalingrad, and left at rue de Manille. The hostel is on the left. (5min.) Located in a former tobacco manufacturing plant, the hostel has an institutional feel. Clean bathrooms and sterile 3- to 5-bed rooms. About 15min. walk from town. Communal kitchen. TV room with ping pong and foosball. Good breakfast included. Baggage storage (except at arrival) €1.50. Sheets €2.80. Reception 8am-noon and 5-11pm. Lockout 10am-3pm. Closed last 2 weeks of the year. €12.30 per bed. MC/V. HI members only. ❶

Foyer des Jeunes Travailleurs Beaulieu (HI), 9 bd. Vincent Gâche (☎02 40 12 24 00; fax 02 51 82 00 05). Only takes short-term guests June-Aug. Rooms for ages 16-30 for stays of 1 month to 1 year Sept.-May. From the north exit of the station, take tram #1 (dir: François Mittérand) to pl. du Commerce and switch to line 2 (dir: Trocadie), to Vincent Gâche. Bd. Vincent Gâche is ahead on the left. Feels more like a mini-hotel than a hostel. Modern 1- to 3-person rooms with bath. Communal kitchen. Breakfast included. Cafeteria buffet (price varies). Laundry. Sheets €3. Reception daily 8am-9pm. Beds €18.45, non-members €22.70. Singles €22.60/€23.30. Rooms and studio apartments with *demi-pension* for €385-€454 per month. AmEx/MC/V. HI members only. ❶

Camping: Camping du Petit Port, 21 bd. du Petit Port (☎02 40 74 47 94; www.nge-nantes.fr). From pl. du Commerce, take tram #2 (dir: Orvault Grand Val) to Morrhonnière (10min.) Shady, well-tended 4-star site with plenty of outdoor activities and group events during the summer. Laundry, showers, snackbar, and minigolf. 3-person canoe rental €10 per hr. Reception daily mid-June to mid-Sept. 8am-7:30pm; mid-Sept. to mid-June 9am-7pm. Reserve in writing or arrive early in summer. €2.85 per person, €4.10 per tent, €5.85 per car and tent, €7.80 per caravan. Electricity €2.80. MC/V. ❶

🞄 FOOD

Local specialties include *fruits de mer au beurre blanc* (seafood with butter sauce), *canard nantais* (duck prepared with grapes), and Muscadet and Gros Plant white wines. *Le Petit Beurre* cookies and *muscadines* (chocolates filled with grapes and Muscadet wine) are both local inventions. The alleys radiating from **place du Pilori** are full of eateries. The *crêperies* behind **place du Bouffay** are also especially good. The biggest **market** in Nantes is the **Marché de Talensac,** along rue de Bel-Air near pl. St-Similien behind the post office. (Open Tu-Su 8am-noon.) Pl. du Bouffay hosts a smaller market (W-Su 8am-noon, Tu organic market) while another stretches down pl. de la Petite Hollande, opposite pl. du Commerce. (Su 8am-1pm.) The best selection of fresh fruit in town, though a bit pricey, is at **Le Fruitier des Carmes,** 17 rue des Carmes. Pint-sized baskets of berries (€3-5.50) and mini-cheeses are convenient for snacking. (☎02 40 12 08 09. Open M-Sa 8am-8pm.) **Monoprix supermarket,** 2 rue de Calvaire, is off cours des 50 Otages, down from the Galeries Lafayette. (Open M-Sa 9am-9pm.) There are small **SPAR** supermarkets at 5 pl. du Bouffay (open M-F 9am-1pm and 2:30-8:30pm, Sa 9am-8pm, Su 9am-1pm) and at 31 rue de Strasbourg (open M-F 9am-1pm and 1:30-9pm, Sa 9am-1pm and 6-9pm, Su 9:30am-1:30pm and 6-9pm).

🞄**Midi-Pile,** 11 chausée de la Madeleine, feels more like a country kitchen than a popular lunch counter in a major city. The generously stuffed *paninis* and remarkably underpriced sandwiches make this a can't miss lunch stop. (☎02 40 48 46 37. Salads €1.40-3.80, sandwiches €3.40-3.80. Open M-F 11am-3pm.) 🞄**La Cigale** ❸, 4 pl. Graslin, is one of the most beautiful bistros in France. Fashioned in 1895 by *nantais* ceramist Emile Libaudière, the vast rooms are filled floor to ceiling with painted tiles, huge mirrors, and wall sculptures. Although some may visit to take pictures of the architecture (the site is a classified historical monument), the food, especially the *soupe de poisson*, deserves equal acclaim. Diners hand-pick their dinner from a large display of fresh seafood. (☎02 51 84 94 94; www.lacigale.com. *Menus* €11.90, €22.90; *plats* €11.90-18.90; desserts €7; breakfast €9. Fabulous brunch Sa and Su 10am-4pm €20. Open daily 7:30am-12:30am. MC/V.) **L'Ile Verte ❷,** 3 rue Foucault, serves vegetarian, organic salads, and tarts in a bright, garden-like atmosphere in a quiet alley. Although the fare is unique and made from the freshest market produce, dishes may be a bit bland for some. (☎02 40 48 01 26. Salads €4.20-8.80, *plats* €8.80, desserts €1.60-5.10. *Plats* available to go. Open M-Tu and Th-Sa 11:30am-2:30pm. Tea room open 2:30-6:30pm. Closed Aug.) A life-sized robot, funky artwork (some furry), and lots of color spice up **Le Clin d'Oeil ❸,** 15 rue Beauregard, which serves traditional cuisine infused with modern flavor. (☎02 40 47 72 37. *Menus* €13.90-18.50, *plats* €12.50-13.90, desserts €5.45. Open July-Aug. M-Sa 7:30-11pm; Sept.-June M noon-2pm, Tu-Sa noon-2pm and 7:30-11pm. AmEx/MC/V.)

🔘 SIGHTS

Ask the tourist office about the **Nantes City Card,** a pass covering admission to the château, the Musée des Beaux-Arts, the Musée d'Histoire Naturelle, and the Musée Jules Verne. The pass also includes free access to trams and buses and a tour guided by the tourist office. For a complete list of the many venues covered, look for a key symbol next to listings in the tourist guide. The pass is also available at some hotels, campsites, and the youth hostel. (€14 for 24hr. access., €24 for 48hr., €30 for 72hr., under 12 free). Walk around the city to experience Nantes's elaborate 19th-century facades fashioned with wrought-iron balconies. Make sure to see the **Passage Pommeraye,** an unusual 19th-century shopping arcade off pl. du Commerce built on three levels around a monumental staircase.

CHÂTEAU DES DUCS DE BRETAGNE. Designed as a fortress by François II as part of the duchy of Brittany's struggle for independence, this château has seen as much history as any in the Loire. Its imposing walls once held Gilles de Retz, the original Bluebeard, who was convicted of sorcery in 1440 for sacrificing hundreds of children in gruesome rituals. In 1598, Henri IV composed the famous Edict of Nantes here in an effort to soothe religious tensions. Although most of the structure is closed off until Fall 2006 due to renovations, tourists can still pass over the drawbridge to admire the architecture from the vast inner courtyard and visit art exhibits housed in the temporary **Musée du Château des Ducs de Bretagne,** 4 pl. Marc-Elder. The promenades around the moat are perfect for a picnic or an afternoon in the grass with a good book. *(☎02 40 41 56 56; fax 02 40 48 62 81; musee.chateau@mairie-nantes.fr. Courtyard open daily 10am-6pm. Free. Tours in French daily July-Aug. every 30min. 3-6pm provide details on history and architecture, and include visits to select rooms in the castle. Free. Museum open daily July-Aug. 10am-6pm; Sept.-June closed Tu. €3, students €1.60, under 18 free. Free after 4:30pm.)*

CATHÉDRALE ST-PIERRE. Gothic vaults soar 38m in this remarkably bright cathedral, which holds the body of King François II. His early 16th-century tomb is a sculpted masterpiece, with a statue at each corner representing Temperance, Justice, Strength, and Prudence. Built in stages from 1434 to 1891, St-Pierre has survived Revolutionary pillagers, WWII bombs, and a 1972 fire. A complete restoration of the interior has masterfully undone the ravages of time—though it could not salvage the stained glass that shattered during WWII. Only one piece remains, the largest in France, 25m above François's tomb. *(Open daily 10am-7pm.)*

MUSÉE DES BEAUX-ARTS. The museum's collection of fine art by French masters is more decorative than definitive, but the real reason to visit is to check out the often daring temporary exhibits of contemporary French art on the ground floor. *(10 rue Georges Clemenceau. ☎02 51 17 45 00. Take bus #11, dir: Jules Verne, or #12,*

BRITTANY

dir. Colonière, to Trébuchet. Open M and W, and F-Su 10am-6pm, Th until 8pm. €3.10, students €1.60; under 18, first Su of the month, and Th 6-8pm free. Call or consult the museum's pamphlet for its atypically wide range of engaging tours.)

MUSÉE JULES VERNE. The guided tour through the exhibits may be a little much for the science fiction novice, but a pamphlet available in English provides all the info necessary to wander the museum alone. Beautiful first editions of such novels as *Around the World in Eighty Days*, playbills, paraphernalia from Verne's life, and amazingly detailed sketches illustrating his ideas are all proudly displayed. Paintings and posters depict the bustling 19th-century Nantes that inspired the great author. *(3 rue de l'Hermitage. Take bus #81, dir. Indre, from pl. du Commerce to Salonges. At the fork, bear right; the museum is at the top of hill on the left. ☎02 40 69 72 52; fax 02 40 73 28 18. Open M and W-Sa 10am-noon and 2-5pm, Su 2-5pm. Free tours in French July-Aug. 3:30pm. Entrance €1.50, students €0.75.)*

🎵 🎭 ENTERTAINMENT AND NIGHTLIFE

A lot of nightlife is listed in the weekly *Nantes Poche* (€0.50 at the tourist office or any *tabac*). The tourist office has many useful free pamphlets listing the city's rich array of concerts and cultural events, including *Sucré/Salé*, *Vivre l'Été*, and *Arc*. **The Katorza**, 3 rue Corneille (☎08 36 68 05 98), projects international films in their original language (€6, students €5). The **Apollo Theatre**, 21-22 rue Racine (☎08 36 68 71 14), shows movies nightly for €2, with occasional English selections. Nearby **rue Scribe** is full of late-night bars and cafes. A favorite of the funky, **quartier St-Croix**, near pl. du Bouffay, has about three bars per block and as many cafes. More discotheques await the adventurous traveler farther from the *vieille ville*.

■ **Le Loft,** 9 rue Franklin, sports a posh lounge with a vast bar. A chic, comfortable place to relax with friends and a cocktail during the week. An eclectic mix of dance music really gets the place banging on weekends. DJ every night from 11pm, except W. Mixed drinks €7. Open Tu-Sa 9:30am-4am.

La Maison, 4 rue Lebrun (☎02 40 37 04 12), off rue Maréchal Joffre on the other side of town, makes for a silly, carefree time in a beach party atmosphere filled primarily with young people. Drinks from €4. Open daily 3pm-2am. MC/V.

Le John McByrne, 21 rue des Petites Ecuries (☎02 40 89 64 46), is a popular Irish pub with a Christmas-y facade and a fittingly jolly crowd lounging on its large terrace. Located in the heart of town, the bar is packed on weekends, so gear up for an energetic night out. Live Irish music every Su at 9pm. Beer €3-5. Irish coffee €6.10. Open M-Sa 2pm-2am, Su 4pm-2am. MC/V.

Le Temps d'Aimer, 14 rue Alexandre Fourny (☎02 40 89 48 60), is Nantes's favorite gay disco with a variety of party music. From pl. de la République on Île de Nantes, follow rue Victor Hugo to rue Fourny on the left. Or take tram #2 from pl. du Commerce to Wattignies. Walk up the street toward pl. du Commerce and take a left on rue de la Porte Gelée. Continue straight to reach the club. Cocktails €5-8. Cover M-Th €5, F-Su €13. Open daily midnight-7am.

🎊 FESTIVALS

Eastern Orthodox chanters, blues rockers from Mali, and masqueraders from Trinidad and Tobago all converge to perform at the international **Festival d'Eté** in early July. Up-and-coming international filmmakers walk the red carpet at the **Festival des Trois Continents** (info ☎02 40 69 74 14) in late November and early December.

NORMANDY
(NORMANDIE)

Normandy's tumultuous life story begins in AD 911, when Rollo, the leader of a band of Vikings who had settled around Rouen, accepted the title Duke of Normandy. Norman power grew dramatically over the centuries, most notably during the successful 1066 invasion of England, celebrated in a magnificent tapestry that still hangs in Bayeux (p. 260). The tables turned when Normandy was occupied temporarily in 1346 by English King Edward III. The English didn't attempt another invasion until June 6, 1944, when they returned with North American allies to wrest Normandy from the Germans.

Today, Normandy's agricultural towns and villages bear vestiges of the past—from half-timbered houses unchanged since the Middle Ages to municipal buildings still bearing scars from wartime assaults. Its strong ties to the past don't keep it from moving forward, however, as the buzzing shops of Rouen and the lively bars of Caen will attest. This region is also a place of great natural beauty, with stunning coastal rock formations and rolling countryside.

HIGHLIGHTS OF NORMANDY

VISIT the haunting **D-Day beaches** (p. 263), where the Allies landed in 1944, after getting some perspective at the **Caen Memorial** (p. 259), Normandy's best WWII museum.

SAINT MICHEL MAY HAVE SLAIN A DRAGON, but you'll only have to conquer hordes of tourists to appreciate the magnificent abbey of **Mont-St-Michel** (p. 274).

ART AND HISTORY come to life in the famous **Bayeux Tapestry** (p. 260), commemorating the last time England was successfully invaded—in 1066.

ROUEN

However sharply Flaubert's famously discontented housewife may have criticized Rouen in *Madame Bovary*, the author's hometown (pop. 106,000) is no petty provincial hamlet. A city of clanging bells and narrow alleys, Rouen will go down in history as the site where Joan of Arc was burned at the stake in 1431. Cathedrals and museums may be the primary attractions, but Rouen's vibrant urban energy sets it apart from its neighbors. Medieval edifices house world-class designer boutiques and a hip, young population has inherited the *vieille ville*—Madame B. would be jealous.

TRANSPORTATION

Trains: rue Jeanne d'Arc, on pl. Bernard Tissot (☎02 35 52 16 71). Info office open M-Sa 7:45am-7pm. To: **Caen** (2hr., 7 per day, €19.40); **Le Havre** (1hr., 15 per day, €17.40); **Lille** (3hr., 3 per day, €27); **Paris** (1½hr., every hr., €17.40). 25% student discount on fares. Daytime luggage storage.

Buses: SATAR and CNA, both at 9 rue Jeanne d'Arc (☎08 25 07 60 27), in front of the Théâtre des Arts. Info office open M-F 8am-6:30pm. Most buses depart from quai du Havre or quai de la Bourse. To **Le Havre** (2½hr., 7 per day, €12.35) and various small towns in the **Seine Valley.**

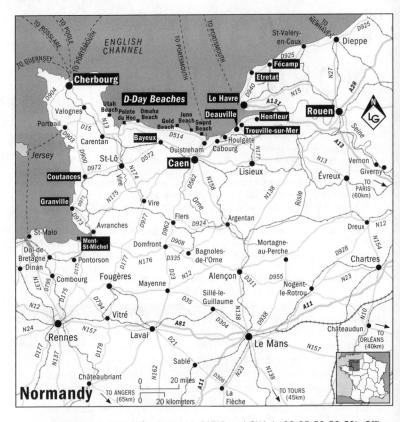

ENGLISH CHANNEL

TO ROSSLARE
TO POOLE
TO GUERNSEY
TO PORTSMOUTH
TO PORTSMOUTH
TO PORTSMOUTH
TO NEWHAVEN

St-Valery-en-Caux
D925
Dieppe

Cherbourg
D940
Fécamp
Etretat
D925
N27
A28

D-Day Beaches
Le Havre
A131
N15
Rouen

Valognes
Utah Beach
Pointe du Hoc
Omaha Beach
Juno Beach
Gold Beach
Sword Beach
Deauville
Honfleur
N

Portbail
D904
D15
N13
Bayeux
D514
Trouville-sur-Mer
Seine

Jersey
Carentan
D903
Ouistreham
Houlgate
Cabourg
A13

St-Lô
D900
D972
D572
Caen
D562
Lisieux
N177
Vernon
Giverny
N13

Coutances
Vire
N174
D158
Risle
Évreux
TO PARIS (60km)

Granville
D973
Avranches
D977
Flers
D924
Argentan
Mortagne-au-Perche
Dreux
N12
N154

St-Malo
Mont-St-Michel
Domfront
D908
Bagnoles-de-l'Orne
D928
Chartres

Dol-de-Bretagne
Pontorson
D177
N176
D335
D23
N12
Alençon
D311
D955
Nogent-le-Rotrou
N23

Dinan
Combourg
D175
Fougères
Mayenne
Sillé-le-Guillaume
N138
D938
A11

Vitré
D794
A81
D304
Châteaudun
TO ORLÉANS (40km)

Rennes
Laval
D21
Le Mans
N157
N10

N24
N157
Sablé
N162
A11
D306
La Flèche

Normandy
Châteaubriant
TO ANGERS (65km)
0   20 miles
0   20 kilometers
N23
N138
TO TOURS (45km)

Public Transportation: Métrobus, with SATAR and CNA (☎02 35 52 52 52). Office open M-Sa 7am-7pm. Most buses run 6am-8pm, some night lines until midnight. Subway 5am-11pm. 1hr. ticket €1.30, *carnet* of 10 €10. Day pass €3.50, 2-day pass €5.

Taxis: 67 rue Jean Lecanuet (☎02 35 88 50 50). Stands at the train and bus stations, as well as the Palais de Justice on rue Jeanne d'Arc. 24hr.

Car Rental: AVIS, at the train station (☎02 35 88 60 94). Open M-F 8:15am-12:15pm and 2-6:30pm, Sa 8:15-noon and 2-5:30pm.

Bike Rentals: Rouen Cycles, 45 rue St-Eloi (☎02 35 71 34 30), between the pl. du Vieux Marché and the Seine. Bike rental €20 per day, €30 per weekend, €50 per week. Reserve a week in advance. Open Tu-Sa 9am-noon and 2-7pm.

✦ ⊉ ORIENTATION AND PRACTICAL INFORMATION

To get to the city center from the station, exit straight out and follow **rue Jeanne d'Arc** several blocks. A left on cobblestoned **rue du Gros Horloge** leads to **place de la Cathédrale** and the tourist office; a right leads to **place du Vieux Marché.** Farther along, almost to the Seine, the regional and local bus station is on the right.

Tourist Office: 25 pl. de la Cathédrale (☎02 32 08 32 40; www.rouentourisme.com). In the oldest Renaissance building in Rouen. Free English map. **Currency exchange,** commission-free for AmEx Traveler's Cheques. The French-language *Le Viking* shows travelers all the local favorites. Open May-Sept. M-Sa 9am-7pm, Su 9:30am-12:30pm and 2-6pm; Oct.-Apr. M-Sa 9am-6pm, Su 10am-1pm.

Bank: Crédit Lyonnais, 48 rue Jeanne d'Arc (☎08 20 82 43 00). Open M 10am-12:30pm and 1:45-5pm, Tu-F 9am-12:30pm and 1:45-5:45pm, Sa 9am-12:30pm and 1:45-4pm. Branch at 25 rue de la République (☎02 35 07 88 41). There are **ATMs** throughout Rouen, including one across the street from the train station.

Work Opportunities: Centre Régional Information Jeunesse (CRIJ), 84 rue Beauvoisine (☎02 32 10 49 49; www.crij-haute-normandie.org), helps find work—primarily as youth group leaders or at hotels—and has info on activities. Free Internet (30min. limit). Open M-F 10am-6pm. Closed 1st M of every month.

English-Language Bookstore: ABC Bookshop, 11 rue des Faulx (☎02 35 71 08 67), behind Église St-Ouen. Ads for au pairs and tutors for hire. Open Jan.-June and Aug.-Dec. Tu-Sa 10am-6pm; July Tu-Sa 10am-3pm. Closed late July to mid-Aug. MC/V.

Laundromat: 87 rue Beauvoisine. Open daily 7am-8pm. Also at rue Cauchoise near pl. du Vieux Marché. Open daily 7am-9pm. Another at 41 rue de la République. Open daily 7am-8pm. Alterations available at 55 rue d'Amiens. Open daily 7:30am-9:30pm.

Police: 7-9 rue Brisout de Barneville (☎02 32 81 25 00).

Pharmacy: Grande Pharmacie du Centre, 29 pl. de la Cathédrale (☎02 35 71 33 17). Open M 10am-7:30pm, Tu-F 9am-7:30pm, Sa 9am-7pm. Branches throughout the city.

Hospital: 1 rue de Germont (☎02 32 88 89 90), near pl. St-Vivien.

Internet Access: Free at **CRIJ** (see **Work Opportunities**). **Cyber@Net,** 47 pl. du Vieux Marché (☎02 35 07 73 02). €4 per hr. Open daily 10am-11pm. **Place Net,** 37 rue de la République (☎02 32 76 02 22; www.place-net.fr), near the Église St-Maclou. €4 per hr. Open M-F 10am-midnight, Sa 10am-8pm, Su 2pm-midnight.

Post Office: 45bis rue Jeanne d'Arc (☎02 35 15 66 73). **Currency exchange** up to US $100. Open M-F 9:30am-6:30pm, Sa 9am-noon. Branch at 112 rue Jeanne d'Arc (☎02 32 10 55 60), left of the train station. Open M-F 8am-7pm, Sa 8:30am-noon.

Postal Code: 76000.

ACCOMMODATIONS AND CAMPING

If in town for the weekend, inquire at the tourist office about the *Bon Week-end en villes* deal for two nights at the price of one at participating hotels.

Hôtel Solférino, 51 rue Jean Lecanuet (☎/fax 02 35 71 10 07). Located between the train station and the center of town. Spare and sometimes noisy rooms, most with TV, feature comfortable beds and pastel walls. Breakfast €5. Reserve in advance. Singles €25, with shower €28; doubles €28/€32. MC/V. ❷

Hôtel des Arcades, 52 rue de Carmes (☎02 35 70 10 30; www.hotel-des-arcades.fr). Sunny, clean rooms with wood trim, in the center of town. Breakfast €6.50. Reception M-Sa 7am-8pm, Su 7am-noon. Singles €29, with shower €39.50; doubles €30/€41; triples €53. AmEx/MC/V. ❸

Hôtel le Morand, 1 rue Morand (☎02 35 71 46 07; www.hotels-rouen.com). Near the Musée des Beaux-Arts. Sizeable beds with colorful trimmings and an old-fashioned salon. Breakfast €6. 24hr. parking €7. Reception daily 7am-1:30pm and 4:30-10pm. Singles €31.40, with bath €40.40; doubles €47.80; triples €60.20. MC/V. ❸

NORMANDY

Rouen

🏠 ACCOMMODATIONS
Camping Municipal de Déville, **6**
Hôtel des Arcades, **16**
Hôtel Beauséjour, **1**
Hôtel de la Cathédrale, **17**
Hôtel le Morand, **7**
Hôtel Solférino, **5**

🍴 FOOD
La Couronne, **14**
Estival Eric, **8**
Marianne, **15**
Le P'tit Zinc, **11**
Restaurant Punjab, **10**

⭐ NIGHTLIFE
Emporium Galorium, **2**
L'Euro, **13**
Murphy's Irish Pub, **12**
Le Nash, **9**
Pub Yesterday, **4**

Hôtel Beauséjour, 9 rue Pouchet (☎02 35 71 93 47; www.hotel-beausejour76.com), turn right from the station. 2-star establishment rents cheery rooms overlooking a small street or pretty courtyard. Nearly all with TV. Access to hotel bar and sitting room. Breakfast €5. Reception 6am-11pm. Singles €24, with shower €36; doubles with shower €36, with bath €43; triples €49; quads €63; MC/V. ❸

Hôtel de la Cathédrale, 12 rue St-Romain (☎02 35 71 57 95; www.hotel-de-la-cathedrale.fr). Tidy rooms with doll-sized furnishings. Prime spot by the Cathédrale and Église St-Maclou. Features a bar, elevator, Internet, parking, and tea room (11am-8pm). Buffet breakfast €7.50. Singles with shower €49; doubles with shower €59. MC/V. ❹

Camping: Camping Municipal de Déville, rue Jules Ferry in Déville-les-Rouen (☎02 35 74 07 59), 4km from Rouen. Take the metro from train station (dir: Technopole or Georges Braque) to Théâtre des Arts. Transfer to Metrobus line TEOR (T2; dir: Mairie). Get off at Mairie de Deville-les-Rouen. Take route de Dieppe 1 block. Turn left on rue Jules Ferry. More gravel than greenery, but space is never a problem. Potable water. Reception open June-Sept. M-F 8am-1pm and 2-8pm, Sa-Su 9am-noon and 2-8pm; Oct.-May M-F 9:30-11am and 4:30-6pm, Sa-Su 9:30-11am and 3-5pm. Gates close 10pm. Open Apr.-Oct. for tents, year-round for caravans. €4.20 per person, €1.55 per tent, €2.80 per caravan. Electricity €0.90. Showers free. ❶

☕ FOOD

Outdoor cafes and *brasseries* crowd around **place du Vieux Marché,** which hosts a **market** with flowers, fish, fruit, and cheese (Tu-Sa and Su 6am-noon). There are also eateries near the **Gros Horloge** and the **Cathédrale de Notre Dame.** For self-serve options, try the **Monoprix supermarket** at rue du Gros Horloge (open M-Sa 8:30am-9pm), **Marché U** on pl. du Vieux Marché (open M-Sa 8:30am-8:30pm), or **Marché Plus,** 11 pl. du Général de Gaulle. (Open M-Sa 7am-9pm.) Those with full wallets indulge at ◼**La Couronne** ❺, 31 pl. du Vieux Marché, housed in the oldest *auberge* in France. Built in 1345, the cozy restaurant has been frequented by figures like Sophia Loren and Salvador Dalí. (☎02 35 71 40 90; fax 02 35 71 05 78. *Prix fixe menus* €28-45. Individual entrees €28-58. Open daily noon-2pm and 7-10pm. AmEx/MC/V.) **Marianne** ❷, 6 rue Massacre, is ideal for afternoon tea or a wholesome lunch. Musically inclined customers can play the piano upstairs. They serve an extensive selection of teas (€2.50) and generous salads (€7.10) in the shadow of the Gros Horloge. (☎02 35 89 33 36; fax 02 35 71 61 75. Open M-Sa 9am-7pm. AmEx/MC/V.) **Le P'tit Zinc** ❸, 20 pl. du Vieux Marché, offers seating both outdoors and in a homey, plant-filled interior. Meals are chosen from the chalkboard menus brought to each table. (☎02 35 89 39 69. Appetizers €12-16. Lunch €14-20. Dessert €6.90. Wine €4. Open M-F noon-3pm and 8-10pm, Sa noon-3pm. MC/V.) **Restaurant Punjab** ❸, 3 rue des Bons Enfants, is just off rue Jeanne d'Arc. Lantern-lit and infused with exotic beats, this restaurant highlights Indian spices at their artistic best. A number of vegetarian options are available, in addition to a full bar and wine list. (☎02 35 88 63 48. Dinner from €9. Lunch *menus* €8-10, dinner *menus* €16-21. Open daily 11:30am-3pm and 7-11:30pm. MC/V.) **Estival Eric** ❶, 23 allée Delacroix, sits between the Musée des Beaux-Arts and the Palais de Justice. Popular with locals looking for a quick lunch, this eatery features 32 types of fresh bread, artful pastries, and sandwiches. (☎02 35 98 28 58. Baguettes €0.94. Pastries around €1.50. Sandwiches €2.50. Open M-Sa 7am-7pm. MC/V.)

◎ SIGHTS

Sights in Rouen fall into two basic categories: museums and churches. A veritable treasure trove for art and history enthusiasts, the town's attractions still manage to charm the more casual observer.

■ **CATHÉDRALE DE NOTRE-DAME.** This undeniably impressive cathedral incorporates nearly every intermediate style of Gothic architecture. It gained artistic fame when Monet chose to use it for his celebrated studies of light. Of the stained-glass windows that survived the bombings of World War II, the portrayal of St-Julien in the ambulatory is the most elaborate. To the left of the cathedral stands the 12th-century **Tour St-Romanus,** and to the right is the 17th-century **Tour de Beurre** (Tower of Butter), which was funded by cholesterol-loving parishioners who preferred to pay a dispensation than going without butter during Lent. The cathedral's central spire is the tallest in France (151m), and has been rebuilt numerous times following damage by fire, lightning, and a tornado. The cathedral is illuminated nightly in summer to striking effect. (*Pl. de la Cathédrale. Open M 2-7pm, Tu-Sa 7:45am-7pm, Su 8am-6pm. Mass held Su 8:30 and noon; Tu-Sa 8 and 10am. Tours in French daily June-Sept. 3pm; Oct.-May Sa-Su 3pm. Tours in English available through the tourist office. Free.*)

MUSÉE FLAUBERT ET D'HISTOIRE DE LA MÉDECINE. Cute but hardly cuddly, this museum packs in a formidable amount of paraphernalia loosely related to Gustave Flaubert (who was raised on the premises) and the history of medicine. A must for Flaubert obsessives, but more notable for its collection of oddities, including Napoleon's death mask, several calcified fetuses, and plaster moldings of the heads of executed criminals. (*51 rue de Lecat, next to the Préfecture. Follow rue de Crosne from pl. du Vieux Marché. ☎ 02 35 15 59 95; fax 02 32 08 04 96. Open Tu 10am-6pm, W-Sa 10am-noon and 2-6pm. Free English brochure. €2.20, ages 18-25 €1.50, under 18 free.*)

MUSÉE DES BEAUX ARTS. Rouen's gem, second only to its bigger counterparts in Paris, houses a reservoir of Impressionist art and 16th- and 17th-century religious works. Caravaggio's *Flagellation of Christ* and Monet's stunning depiction of the Notre Dame Cathedral stand alongside a few Cubist and Abstractionist pieces. Special exhibits rotate periodically. (*26bis rue Jean Lecanuet, down rue Jeanne d'Arc from train station. ☎ 02 35 71 28 40. Open M and W-Su 10am-6pm. Some exhibits closed 1-2pm. Admission €3, ages 18-25 and groups €2, under 18 free. Special exhibits cost more.*)

ABBATIALE ST-OUEN. Although not as architecturally rich as Notre Dame, this cathedral is still impressive, if only because of its neck-straining size. Once part of an 8th-century Benedictine abbey (the monks' dormitory and one gallery of the cloister are all that remains), it has undergone many renovations, including the addition of a 19th-century facade. The beautiful **Jardins de l'Hôtel de Ville,** behind St-Ouen, are popular with Rouen's youth. (*Next to the Hôtel de Ville, at pl. du Général de Gaulle. Open mid-Mar. to Oct. Open Tu-Sa 10am-12:15pm and 2-6pm, Su at 9am; Nov to mid-Dec. and mid-Jan. to mid-Mar. Tu and Sa-Su 10am-noon and 2-5pm.*)

ÉGLISE ST-MACLOU. During the French Revolution, this striking Gothic cathedral housed an arms factory. Look for *les enfants pisseurs,* two urinating cherubs, in the left corner of the facade. Beyond the church to the left, a poorly marked passage at 186 rue de Martainville leads to the **Aître St-Maclou.** This cloister served as the church's cemetery during the Middle Ages, beginning in 1348, when the Black Death claimed more than one-third of the population. Bones were stored on the upper floor of the galleries—hence the grisly 15th-century frieze of skulls and bones that decorates the beams of the inner courtyard. The *Rouennais* once entombed a live black cat inside the walls to exorcise spirits. The shriveled feline remains suspended behind a glass panel to the right of the courtyard entrance. The building now houses the regional fine arts school. (*Église at 3 rue de Général Sarrail. Open to tourists M-Sa 10am-noon and 2-6pm, Su 3-5:30pm. Closes daily Oct.-Mar. 5:30pm. Concerts July and Aug. Tickets available 30min. before concert at the church. For more info, pick up a brochure at the church or call ☎ 02 35 70 84 90. Admission €8, students €5. Aître at Pl. Barthélémy, behind the Église St-Maclou. Courtyard open daily 8am-8pm. Free.*)

TOUR JEANNE D'ARC. Each floor of this tower, the last abode of Joan of Arc before she burned at the stake, has a minor attraction. The best is a scale model of what Rouen might have looked like in Joan's time, reconstructed using old documents and inventories. The dizzying spiral staircase may leave you feeling a bit winded unless you're looking for the extra exercise. *(To the left of the station on rue du Donjon. Entrance on rue Bouvreuil due to renovations. Open M-Sa 10am-12:30pm and 2-6pm, Su 2-6:30pm. Oct.-June closes M-Sa at 5pm, Su at 5:30pm. €1.50, students and under 18 free.)*

OTHER SIGHTS. Built into a bridge across rue du Gros Horloge, the ornately gilded **Gros Horloge** (Great Clock) rings to its own schedule. The 16th-century device marks the days with a rotating disk depicting Greco-Roman divinities; the ball at the top tracks the phases of the moon. When renovations of the belfry are completed in July 2005, visitors will be able to climb it for a view of the clockwork. Under the courtyard of the war-marked Palais de Justice—where visitors can sit in on public trials—stands the **Monument Juif** (Jewish Monument), uncovered in the 1970s. The walls are covered with Hebrew writing which may date as far back as AD 1100 and is the oldest Jewish building ever discovered in France. *(Closed indefinitely for renovations and as a precaution against terrorism at the time of writing.)*

▣ NIGHTLIFE

Rouen has more options for the civilized pubber than for the would-be clubber. One of the better bars is red-walled, zebra-pillowed **Le Nash,** 97 rue Ecuyère, with its wide-ranging DJ selections (F and Sa nights) and a porch that encourages open-air interaction. (☎02 35 98 25 24. Beer €3. Cocktails €5. Open M-Sa 11am-2am.) The hip **L'Euro,** on the pl. du Vieux Marché, welcomes a well-dressed crowd in a large outdoor area or in the multi-leveled interior. The decor varies from purple walls and leopard-print pillows to a psychedelic tearoom. (☎02 35 07 55 66. Beer and wine €4. Cocktails €8.50. Open daily 10am-2am. MC/V.) Live music (twice weekly) and a regular Gothic night easily make the cavern-like **Emporium Galorium,** 151 rue Beauvoisine, the loudest and most raucous of Rouen's weekend bar scenes. (☎02 35 71 76 95. Beer €2.80. Cocktails €5.50. Open M-Sa 8pm-2am.) For a hoppin', but not very Irish, drinking scene, check out **Murphy's Irish Pub,** 12 pl. du Vieux Marché, where a buzzing, mixed crowd spills onto the sidewalk. (☎02 35 71 17 33. Beer €3.50. Cocktails €7. Open daily 10am-2am. MC/V.) More typically Irish is the out-of-the-way **Pub Yesterday,** 3 rue Moulinet, parallel to rue Jeanne d'Arc near the train station. Dimly lit, with old-fashioned bikes and a piano hanging from the ceiling, this spot is a laid-back, friendly place to have a conversation over Guinness (€3) at the bar. (☎02 35 70 43 98. Whiskey €5. Open M-Sa 5pm-2am.)

▣ DAYTRIP FROM ROUEN

SEINE VALLEY. The lazy Seine trails natural and historical gems behind it as it flows to the sea. You can theme-trek along it on an Impressionist route, an Emma Bovary route, a route of major castles and mansions, or the best known of all, the Route des Abbayes. The first you'll encounter out of Rouen is the **Abbaye St-Georges de Boscherville,** in the town of St-Martin-de-Boscherville. This Benedictine abbey was constructed in the 12th century on a site where five religious buildings had been built successively since 50 BC. (☎02 35 32 10 82; fax 02 35 34 97 54. Open daily Apr.-Oct. 9am-6:30pm; Nov.-Mar. 2-5pm. Gardens €4.50, €3.10 for students, under 18 free. Church free.) The star of the bunch is the **Abbaye de Jumièges,** founded by St-Philibert in 654. A legend since Merovingian times, the abbey became a stone quarry during the Revolution but was bought and restored by the state in 1947. Now the complex is a splendid ruin, set in lush grounds that

NORMANDY

incorporate a 17th-century French garden. Art exhibits, plays, and nocturnal visits add to the site's allure. (☎02 35 37 24 02. Open daily July-Aug. 9:30am-6:30pm; mid-Apr. to mid-June M-F 9:30am-1pm and 2:30-6:30pm, Sa-Su 9:30am-6:30pm; mid-Sept. to mid-Apr. 9:30am-1pm and 2:30-5:30pm. Tours available in French every hr. Admission €4.60, students €3.10, under 18 free.) The **Parc Naturel Régional de Brotonne** sprawls across the Seine midway to Le Havre; get in some green time on this network of trails (inquire at the Rouen tourist office). The town of **Caudebec-en-Caux,** accessible by bus from Rouen or Le Havre, makes an excellent base from which to explore the park. A bit farther on toward the sea, the town of **Villequiers,** the site of the tragic drowning of Victor Hugo's daughter Léopoldine, now houses the **Musée Victor Hugo,** rue Ernest Binet. (☎02 35 56 78 31. Open M and W-Sa 10am-12:30pm and 2-6pm, Su 2-6pm. €3, students and under 18 free.) The museum's collection of Hugo memorabilia makes it a good place to stop if you're in the area, but not an essential one. Cap off your tour of the valley with a peek at the enormous **Pont de Normandie,** the stark, futuristic bridge over the Seine just above Le Havre.

The best way to explore the valley is by **car.** If you go by **bus,** allow a whole day for exploration. Bus schedules change frequently and are sometimes inconvenient, as buses are often slightly off schedule. Pick up a schedule at the Metrobus station or call the **CNA buses** directly. (☎08 25 07 60 27.) Line #30A runs from Rouen's bus station to several of the abbeys, stopping in some seasons at Jumièges (45 min., €5.00). Change buses at Caudebec-en-Caux to reach Villequiers and the Musée Victor Hugo. Biking is feasible as well, though distances are great. For any trip into the valley, the Rouen tourist office is the best place to start.

LE HAVRE

Founded in 1517 by François I, Le Havre (pop. 190,000) may be the largest transatlantic port in France, but it has little else to recommend it. In the 1930s, Jean-Paul Sartre served as a teaching assistant in Le Havre, which he renamed Bouville (Mudtown) in his first novel, *La Nausée* (Nausea). Le Havre's solution to the devastation of WWII was to call in architect Auguste Perret, who spewed reinforced concrete everywhere, compounding the unsightliness of the already utilitarian harbor. The town is trying desperately to improve its image with a good museum and tree-lined boulevards, but it is still best as a stopover.

▮ TRANSPORTATION

Trains: Cours de la République (☎08 36 35 35, 36 35 within France). Info office open M-Sa 9:30am-6:15pm. To: **Fécamp** via **Breauté** (1hr., 9 per day, €6.70); **Paris** (2hr., 8 per day, €25.20); **Rouen** (50min., 13 per day, €11.80).

Buses: rue Charles Laffitte (☎02 35 22 34 00). Connected to the train station (exit from the platforms to your left). Info office open M-Sa 7am-7pm. **CNA** runs to **Rouen** (3hr.; M-Sa 9 per day, 2 on Su; €13.25). **Bus Verts** (☎08 01 21 42 14) goes to **Caen** (3hr., 5 per day, €17) and **Honfleur** (30min., 5 per day, €6.80). See p. 256 for Caen-Le Havre express info. **Autocars Gris** (☎02 35 28 19 88) runs to **Fécamp** via Etretat (1½hr.; 8 per day; €7.40, 50% reduction on same-day return at certain hours).

Ferries: P&O European Ferries, Terminal de la Citadelle (☎08 03 01 30 13 or 08 25 01 30 13 for info, 02 35 19 78 78 for tickets; www.poferries.com), near av. Lucien Corbeaux. For **Portsmouth** (see **Getting There: By Boat,** p. 23, for details). Ticket and info office open M-F 8:30am-7pm, Sa 9am-5pm; terminal closes at 11pm.

Taxis: Radio-Taxis wait at the train station and near the gardens by the Hôtel de Ville (☎02 35 25 81 81). Serve destinations outside of Le Havre. 24hr.

✳ 🔋 ORIENTATION AND PRACTICAL INFORMATION

Be cautious when alone at night, especially around the train station and harbor.

Tourist Office: 186 bd. Clemenceau (☎02 32 74 04 04; www.lehavretourisme.com). Exit left from the station. Take a right on bd. de Strasbourg; it becomes av. Foch and eventually hits the beach; here turn left on bd. Clemenceau. (20min.) From the ferry, walk left down quai de Southampton, then right up bd. Clemenceau. Info on nautical activities, hotels, and restaurants; monthly calendar of events; small guide to regional cultural life (*Bazart*); free map. Open May-Sept. M-Sa 9am-7pm, Su 10am-12:30pm and 2:30-6pm; Oct.-Apr. M-Sa 9am-6:30pm, Su 10am-1pm.

ATMS: located throughout the city center. Many at the far end of bd. de Strasbourg, near the Hôtel de Ville. One 2 blocks to the right of the station on cours de la République.

Laundromat: 54 rue Edouard Lang. Open daily 7am-8pm.

Police: 16 rue de la Victoire (☎02 32 74 37 00).

Pharmacy: Pharmacie de la Gare, 35 cours de la République (☎02 35 25 18 74). From the train station, across the street and to the right. Open M-F 9am-12:30pm and 2:30-9pm, Sa 9am-12:30pm.

Hospital: 55bis rue Gustave Flaubert (☎02 32 73 32 32).

Internet Access: Cybermetro, 19-21 cours de la République (☎02 35 25 40 34), across from the train station. €2.50 for 30min., €4 per hr. Cheaper 11:30am-1:30pm and after 9pm. Open daily 9am-midnight. There is access at the **library,** 17 rue Jules Lecesne (☎02 32 74 07 40), by appointment, but you can use a computer if others don't show up. €5 per year. Open July-Aug. Tu-W and F-Sa 10am-5pm, Th 2-6pm; Sept.-June Tu-W and F-Sa 10am-6pm, Th 2-6pm.

Post Office: 62 rue Jules Siegfried (☎02 32 92 59 00). Cyberposte (€7 per hour). Fax machine. Open M-F 8:30am-6:30pm, Sa 8:30am-noon.

Postal Code: 76600.

▐ ACCOMMODATIONS

One-star hotels, offering mostly singles, line the cours de la République by the train station. Affordable two-star establishments can be found on bd. de Strasbourg. For a more upscale feel, try **Hôtel Celtic ❹,** 106 rue Voltaire. From the station, follow bd. de Strasbourg to the Hôtel de Ville, and turn left down rue de Paris. The rooms are reasonably priced, all with shower, TV, and double bed, and most with toilet. (☎02 35 42 39 77. Internet €0.10 per min. Breakfast €5.30. Reception 8am-11pm. Singles €30-44; doubles €32-48. Extra bed €12. AmEx/MC/V.) **Hôtel le Monaco ❸,** 16 rue de Paris, near the ferry terminal, has spacious rooms, all with TV, and a classy decor, all above a popular *brasserie* that serves three-course *menus* for €21-33. (☎02 35 42 21 01. Restaurant open daily 7am-1am. Breakfast €4.60. Reception 6:30am-11pm. Singles €28.30, with shower €31.30, with bath €33.55; doubles €33.55/€35.10/€41.20; triples €38.20-41.30; quads €54.90. AmEx/MC/V.) A reasonable bet by the train station is **Hôtel Britania ❸,** 5 cours de la République, 10min. from the city center. It's not in a great part of town, but its rooms are adequate, with shower and TV, and some with small concrete balconies. (☎02 35 25 42 51; fax 02 35 53 21 75. Breakfast €5. Reception 6am-8pm, check at the bar next door if no one is there. Singles €26, with toilet €30, with bath €32; doubles €29/€33/€35; triples €35, with toilet €38. MC/V.)

NORMANDY

🍴 FOOD

For grocery needs, **Super U**, 5 rue Abbaye Perier, is almost a full turn around the block behind the tourist office (open M-Sa 8:30am-8:30pm), a **Marché Plus** is near the Volcan at 156-158 rue de Paris (open M-Sa 7am-9pm, Su 8:30am-12:30pm), and **Shop Express,** 150 bd. de Strasbourg, is fairly close to the train station. (Open daily 8am-2am.) The freshest food is at the morning **market** at pl. Thiers, by the Hôtel de Ville (M, W, F 8am-noon), or the all-day market on cours République (Tu, Th, Sa, until 4pm). A list of markets is available from the tourist office. Restaurants crowd rue Victor Hugo and the pl. de l'Hôtel de Ville, while the streets between rue de Paris and **quai Lamblardie** host a range of local favorites. Swing into the **Côté Jardin ❷,** 9 pl. de l'Hôtel de la Ville, next to the gardens in the center of town. The attentive waitstaff serves designer salads (€8.60), pastries (€2.80-4.60), and a *plat du jour* (€8), in addition to a full slate of coffee (€2.50), beer, and wine (€2.20). (☎02 35 43 43 04. Open M 11:30am-2:30pm, Tu-Sa 11:30am-6:30pm. Service begins at noon. MC/V.) For a break from French fare, a good choice is **Le Mandarin ❹,** 22 rue de Paris, by the ferry terminal. If you manage to narrow down the extensive selection, you're sure to get a well-prepared, reasonably priced Asian dish. (☎02 35 42 28 81. Open Tu-Su noon-2:30pm and 7-11pm. Entrees €5-10. Fixed *menus* €11-18. MC/V.) Out-of-the-way **La Taverne Paillette ❸,** 22 rue Georges Braque, has a wide assortment of fresh fish entrees (€12-17), the standard *carte* of hot and cold entrees (€11-15), a *prix fixe menu* (€25.50), a lunchtime express *menu* (€16), and a large wine selection (€13 for a half-bottle). Take av. Foch toward the beach, turn right on the unmarked street just before sq. St-Roch, and continue to the end. (☎02 35 41 31 50; fax 02 35 42 50 46. Open daily noon-midnight.)

👁 🎵 SIGHTS AND ENTERTAINMENT

The **Musée Malraux,** 2 bd. Clémenceau, displays a small but worthwhile collection of pre-Impressionist works, as well as paintings by Monet, Dufy, and a host of local artists. The second floor features numerous works by Eugene Boudin, who seems to have painted every cow in Normandy. Exhibits rotate every three months. (☎02 35 19 62 62. Open M and W-F 11am-6pm, Sa-Su 11am-7pm. €5, €3.80 for students, under 18 free.) The quiet shade of the sq. St-Roch, off av. Foch, provides a refreshing contrast to the overall griminess of the town, as do the wooden walkways and sparkling fountains on **place de l'Hôtel de Ville.** Smaller gardens with benches and tidy flowerbeds are in the pl. Léon Meyer, by the post office.

Visible from most of town, the **Église St-Joseph** is another testament to Perret's love affair with concrete. If the church, which looks like an Erector Set version of a rocket ship, doesn't disillusion you about French architecture, the city center will with its Maison de la Culture du Havre, popularly known as **Le Volcan.** Despite the building's resemblance to a decapitated toilet, it is a state-of-the-art venue for renowned orchestras and plays, as well as a cinema that screens new releases and classics. (☎02 35 19 10 10, tickets 02 35 19 10 20; www.levolcan.com. Info and ticket office open Tu and Th-F 4-7pm, W and Sa 1:30-7pm. Closed July 20-Aug.)

If in search of a DJ, try **Le Plazza,** 159 bd. de Strasbourg, near the station. The unassuming exterior hides a hip decor and the latest selection of lounge, house, and other club favorites. (☎02 35 43 04 28; www.leplazza.com. Beer €3; cocktails €6. Open Tu-Sa 9pm-2am.) **Havana Café,** 173 rue Victor Hugo (several blocks off of rue de Paris), exudes a Cuban vibe, and features jungle murals, €6 cocktails, and Thursday night karaoke. (☎02 35 42 35 77. Open Tu-Sa 6pm-2am. MC/V.) Sip beer or wine (€2.50) to the smooth sound of jazz at **Le Saxo Café,** 20 rue Edouard Larne, near the Hôtel de Ville, which holds concerts every Friday night. The two-floor bar features Oriental decor, a pool table, a chessboard, a stocked bookcase, and four live-in dogs. (☎ 02 35 21 80 10. Open M-Th 8:30am-8pm, F 8:30am-2am, Sa 10:30am-2am, Su 3-7:30pm. AmEx/MC/V.)

HIGH NORMANDY COAST

ETRETAT

Northeast of Le Havre is Etretat (pop. 1640). The former fishing village has captivated artists, writers, and tourists since the 19th century. When you reach the water (take rue Monge from the tourist office and bus station), it's easy to see why. Soaring chalk cliffs and panoramic seascapes make this one of the most breathtaking spots along the Channel coast. Guy de Maupassant likened the arching western cliff, the **Falaise d'Aval,** to an elephant dipping its trunk into the sea. Perched atop the eastern cliff, the **Falaise d'Amont,** is the tiny **Chapelle Notre Dame de la Garde,** constructed by the Jesuits in 1854 out of materials brought to the site by sailors. (Not open to visitors.) Behind it is the tiny **Musée Nungesser et Coli** and a wishbone-shaped monument, both dedicated to the first aviators to attempt a transatlantic flight, who were lost off the coast of Etretat in 1927. (☎ 02 35 27 07 47. Open late June to late Aug. M and W-Su 10:30am-noon and 2:30-5:30; Apr. to late June and late Aug. to mid-Sept. Sa-Su only. €0.95, children €0.60.) Dip your toes in refreshingly icy Atlantic waters; at low tide, 18th-century oysterbeds are visible at the edge of the beach. Crooked streets, strewn with eateries and small shops, wind from the main avenue, Georges V, to the beach. Hidden just outside the town center at 15 rue de Maupassant is **Le Clos Arsène Lupin,** the former home of crime novelist Maurice Leblanc, who created Arsène Lupin, the original "gentleman burglar." Visitors solve a murder mystery during an interactive 45min. tour of the antique home. (☎ 02 35 10 59 53; fax 02 35 28 47 60. Open daily Apr.-Sept. 10am-6pm; Oct.-Mar. F-Su 11am-6pm. Tour available in French or English. €6, ages 6-16 €3.50.)

The **tourist office,** pl. Maurice Guillard, behind the bus stop, provides free maps, bike rental information (1 hr. €4, half-day €10, full-day €16), and a tour. (☎ 02 35 27 05 21; www.etretat.net. Open daily mid-June to mid-Sept. 9:30am-7:30pm; mid-Sept. to mid-June 10am-noon and 2-6pm.) **Les Autos Cars Gris** (☎ 02 35 27 04 25) runs **buses** to Fécamp (35min., 9 per day, €4.50) and Le Havre (1hr., 7 per day, €6.10). **Taxis** wait at the bus stop (☎ 06 12 16 48 27). There's an **ATM** at 3 bd. Président René Coty, not far from the water.

There are plenty of hotels, but no truly budget ones: the closer to the beachfront, the higher the rates. Reservations are crucial in summer. **Hôtel l'Angleterre ❹,** 35 av. Georges V, a brick building with white balconies, and **Hôtel de la Poste ❸,** 6 av. Georges V, atop a bar, are not cheap, but they're some of the best options. Both feature immaculate rooms with bath and TV. (Angleterre ☎ 02 35 28 84 97. La Poste ☎ 02 35 27 01 34; fax 02 35 27 76 28. Shared reception 8am-8pm at la Poste. Buffet breakfast €7. Angleterre doubles €42, with bath €46; triples €42/€56; quads €62. La Poste singles €32; doubles €42; triples €52; quads €62. Lower prices Sept.-Easter. MC/V.) Closer to the beach, **Hôtel des Falaises ❸,** 1 bd. Président René Coty, lets rooms with a classy, family feel. (☎ 02 35 27 02 77. Breakfast €6. All-day parking M-F €4.50, Sa-Su €7.50. Reception 8am-9pm. Singles €24-38, with shower €28-43; doubles €28-38/€34-43. Prices vary by season. AmEx/MC/V.) The small **town campsite ❶,** in a quiet, green spot 10min. from the tourist office down rue Guy de Maupassant, is dirt-cheap with spotless bathrooms. Some buses from Le Havre and Etretat stop opposite the site: look for **Camping le Grandval ❶.** (☎ 02 35 27 07 67. Reception daily 9am-noon and 2-7pm. Gates closed 10pm-7:30am. Open Apr.-Sept. €2.70 per adult, €1.60 per child, €2.70 per tent, €3.20 per caravan. Electricity €3.50-4.20. Showers Free. Laundry available. MC/V.)

NORMANDY

HOLY SPIRITS

The story of Fécamp's history begins in 16th-century Venice and ends mostly in the United States and Canada. This is the story of *bénédictine*, the town's famous home-brewed libation.

During the Renaissance, a monk by the name of Dom Bernardo Vincelli moved to Fécamp, bringing with him Asian spices and the determination to create a great medical elixir. His mysterious concoction quickly became a favorite indulgence of François I, but the recipe was later lost during the French Revolution. It wasn't until 1888 that a local wine merchant, the felicitously named Alexandre Le Grand, rediscovered the recipe while leafing through books in an old Benedictine library his grandfather had bought. Le Grand built an ornate palace to distill the spirit, which he named named after the monastical order that invented it.

The amber-colored liqueur is still manufactured at the site using the ancient recipe and traditonal techniques—a process that lasts two years. Though the procedure is a well-kept secret, we know it involves a 17hr. infusion of the plants, four distillations, and aging in oak barrels.

Today 96% of the brew is exported. More than half goes to the United States and Canada, with Asia second at 23%. *Bénédictine* put Fécamp on the map; Fécamp sends *bénédictine* around the globe.

FÉCAMP

Without the natural beauty of Etretat or the charm of Honfleur, Fécamp (pop. 22,000), makes a pleasant daytrip from Le Havre or Rouen. It found fame as a pilgrimage site in the 6th century, when some drops of *précieux-sang* (Christ's blood) allegedly washed ashore in a fig-tree trunk. The holy plasma is still kept at the **Église Abbatiale de la Trinité,** pl. des Ducs Richard, on rue des Forts, which was restored in 1001 after Vikings destroyed the AD 665 original. Most visitors now come for a less sacrosanct liquid—*bénédictine*. Originally a monastic healing elixir, the drink is now made in the magnificent **Palais Bénédictine,** 110 rue Alexandre Le Grand, which remains the town's greatest draw. The museum has a great collection of medieval and Renaissance artifacts and contemporary art, and provides a tour of the distillery, as well as a free shot of the famous liqueur. (☎02 35 10 26 10; www.benedictine.fr. Open daily Apr.-Jun. and Sept. 10am-noon and 2-5:30pm; July-Aug. 10am-6pm; Oct.-Dec. and Feb.-Mar. 10:30-11:45am and 2-5pm. Last admission 1hr. before closing. €5.20, under 18 €2.60.)

Fécamp's pricey lodgings don't come cheaper than **Hôtel Vent d'Ouest ❹,** 3 av. Gambetta, opposite the bus stop, up the steps from the train station. Each of the spotless rooms in this maritime-themed hotel comes with bath, TV, and phone. (☎02 35 28 04 04; www.hotelventdouest.fr. Breakfast €5. Reception 7am-11pm. May-Sept. singles €36; doubles €43; triples €50; quads €57; Oct.-Apr. singles €30; doubles €36; triples €42; quads €48. AmEx/MC/V.) The expansive grounds of **⛺Camping Municipal de Reneville ❶,** chemin de Nesmond, afford spectacular views of the ocean. From the train station or bus stop, turn right on av. Gambetta, which becomes quai Bérigny. Turn left onto rue du Président Coty, right on rue Caron, left on steep rue d'Yport, and right on chemin de Nesmond. (☎02 35 28 20 97; camping-de-reneville@tiscali.fr. Office open 8:30am-1pm and 2-7:30pm. Gates closed 10pm-7am. Tent with 1-2 people €8.50, caravan €10.50, €3 per additional person. Electricity €3. Showers free. Laundry available.)

There is a **Marché-Plus supermarket** at 83-85 quai Bérigny. (Open M-Sa 7am-9pm, Su 9am-1pm.) Nearly identical seafood restaurants cluster around **place Nicolas Selle,** at the end of quai Bérigny. With its sheer burgundy drapes and glassware, **L'Escalier ❸,** 101 quai Bérigny, offers *prix fixe menus* (€11-23), *à la carte* delicacies (€10-16), and a large wine list. (☎02 35 28 26 79. Open daily noon-2:30pm and 7-10pm. MC/V.) A more low-key option is **Waff...Burger ❶,** 10 pl. Nicolas Selle, which makes cheap, fresh sandwiches (€2.50-3.50) half a baguette in length. (☎02 35 10 50 95. Burgers €1.85-3.65. Salads €2.50-5. Open M-F 10:30am-1pm and 6-11pm, Sa-Su 10:30am-11pm. Stays open longer if people are there. MC/V.)

To reach Fécamp's **tourist office,** 113 rue Alexandre Le Grand, from the main bus stop, turn right on av. Gambetta. Gambetta, which becomes quai Bérigny. Turn left on rue du Domaine, then right again on rue Le Grand. The staff books rooms (€1.60) and dispenses maps and nautical info. (☎02 35 28 51 01; www.fecamptourisme.com. Open daily July-Aug. 9am-6:30pm; Apr.-June M-F 9am-6pm, Sa-Su 10am-6:30pm; Jan.-Mar. and Sept.-Dec. M-F 9am-6pm, Sa 9:30am-12:30pm and 2-6pm, Su 9:30am-12:30pm.) Fécamp is accessible by **train** from Bréauté-Beuzeville with connections to: Le Havre (45min., 5 per day, €6.90); Paris (2½hr., 6 per day, €25); Rouen (1¼hr., 6 per day, €11.30). The station is at pl. de la République. (☎02 35 28 24 82. Office open M-F 9:15-11:50am and 1:40-6pm, Sa 10:15-11:50am and 1:40-6pm, Su 10:10am-12:20pm and 3:10-7:10pm.) Get there by **bus** on **Les Autos Cars Gris,** 55-57 chemin du Nid de Verdier, pl. St-Etienne. (☎02 35 27 04 25. Open M-Tu and Th-F 8:30-11:30am and 1:30-5:45pm, W 8:30-11:30am and 1:30-4:30pm, Sa 8am-2pm.) The stop is across from the church on av. Gambetta. Buses run from Le Havre ("rapidbus" 45min., 4 per day; regular bus 1¼hr., 17 per day; €7.30; buy tickets on board). There is a **taxi** stand (☎02 35 28 17 50) on pl. St-Etienne at the top of av. Gambetta. There is an **ATM** at 27 quai Bérigny, by the train and bus stations.

CÔTE FLEURIE

Both resort towns and thalassotherapy centers (seaside health spas), the smaller villages along the northeastern coast of Lower Normandy, known as the Côte Fleurie, have been retreats for Paris's elite since the mid-19th century. Today they cater to an international crowd, which means that they won't turn up their noses at your French, but they might take exception to your attire. Some of the smaller beach towns between Le Havre and Caen aren't always exciting enough to justify the cost; hotels and hostels in either city make good budget bases. Bus Verts provides regular connections between coastal towns, Caen, and Bayeux. Travelers doing a lot of touring will find *Carte Liberté* bus passes very useful (see p. 256).

HONFLEUR

With its brightly colored houses, bobbing boats, and cramped streets, Honfleur (pop. 6000) can't help but seem like the brainchild of Disney animators. Miraculously unharmed by World War II, it stands out among the well-preserved towns in northwestern France for its culture and architecture. The beautiful wilds around the town have attracted a close-knit community of artists; in good weather, many set up their easels on the cobblestoned streets. Large numbers of middle-aged tourists flock to Honfleur in the sunny months to peruse the many local art galleries, sample regional apple liqueurs, and mill around the waterfront Vieux Bassin.

▐▓ TRANSPORTATION AND PRACTICAL INFORMATION. Bus Verts (☎08 10 21 42 14), located at the end of quai Lepaulmier, near Bassin de l'Est, goes to Caen (2hr., 15 per day, €11.05) and Le Havre (30min., 7 per day, €6.80) by lines #20 and 50. For a **taxi,** call ☎06 08 60 17 98.

To get to the **tourist office,** quai Lepaulmier, go right out of the bus station and follow rue des Vases by the Avant Port. A sign hangs outside the office, which is in the stone section of the library. The *Guide Pratique* has a good map that lays out four walking tours (2.5-7km) in the town and its forests, and lists all of the town's businesses, restaurants, and hotels. (☎02 31 89 23 30; fax 02 31 89 31 82. Open July-Aug. M-Sa 10am-7pm, Su 10am-5pm; Easter-June and Sept. M-Sa 10am-12:30pm and 2-6:30pm, Su 10am-5pm; Oct.-Easter M-Sa 10am-12:30pm and 2-6pm.)

ACCOMMODATIONS AND FOOD. The hotels have more stars than most constellations. **Les Cascades ❹,** 17 pl. Thiers, on cours des Fossés, offers comparatively inexpensive rooms in an ideal location next to the port. From the tourist office, cross the street at the roundabout; cours des Fossés is on the left. Huge window-boxes adorn the airy rooms, some with skylights and half-timbered walls. Guests are required to eat dinner every night in the seafood restaurant below, where entrees go for €7-14 and *prix fixe menus* run €13-29. (☎02 31 89 05 83. Breakfast €5.50. Open Feb.-Nov. M and W-Su 8am-10pm, Tu 2-7pm. Rooms for 1-2 people €32-53, all with bath. AmEx/DC/MC/V.) The seaside **Camping du Phare ❶,** 300m from the town center at the end of bd. Charles V, is near the beach, minutes from the town center. From the tourist office, cross the street at the roundabout, turn left onto cours des Fossés, right on quai St-Etienne, and then left after passing the Vieux Bassin. Follow quai de la Quarantaine until it forks; the right fork is rue Haute, which ends at the campsite. Arrive early in summer to get a shady spot on one of the grass plots. (☎02 31 89 10 26. Reception July-Aug. 8:15am-10pm; low season hours vary. Gates closed 10pm-7am. July-Aug. €5.30 per person, Apr.-June and Sept.-Oct. €5 per person, €5.50 per tent and car. Electricity €4-5.80. Shower €1.20. Laundry available.)

The town's central streets, especially rue de la Ville, are filled with merchants selling the regional specialties of **cider** and **calvados,** both distilled from apples. Bottles are generally reasonably priced, and many vendors offer free samples. Many relatively pricey and indistinguishable restaurants and *brasseries* along the Ste-Catherine side of the Vieux Bassin provide a taste of local seafood (most *menus* range €13-25). Less expensive food is available from lunch counters on the quai Ste-Catherine and on streets off the main pedestrian thoroughfare. There is a **Champion supermarket** on pl. Sorel. (Open July-Aug. M-F 8:30am-1pm and 2:30-7:30pm, Sa 8:30am-7:30pm, Su 9am-1pm; Sept.-June closes at 12:30pm instead of 1pm.) A **market** takes place in pl. Ste-Catherine, in front of the church (Sa 10am-1pm), while pl. St-Léonard has an organic **Marché Bio** (W 10am-1pm). One hundred occasionally bizarre and universally delicious flavors of ice cream make **Pom'Cannelle ❶,** 60 quai Ste-Catherine, worth the price. From fig to tiramisu, you'll swear you're eating the real thing. (☎02 31 89 55 25. 1 scoop €2, 2 scoops €3.80. Open M-Th and Su 9am-7pm, F-Sa 9am-11pm. Hours vary with demand. MC/V.) One of the port's most affordable options is **Le Clipper ❸,** 42 quai Ste-Catherine, which serves dessert and dinner crêpes (€2.80-11), fondue (€12.50-18), and seafood under umbrellas at the water's edge. (☎02 31 89 96 50; www.honfleurrestaurant.com. *Prix fixe menus* €11-15. Wine €3-5. Open June-Apr. M-Th and Su noon-8:30pm, F-Sa noon-11pm. Closed Tu-W Sept.-Apr. MC/V.) The textiles on the wall correspond to the exotic blends of coffee (€1.50-4.30) at the pleasantly secluded **Espace Cafe ❶,** 3 allée des Fontaines St-Léonard, by the tourist office. Flavored teas (€3) and sandwiches (€3) are also served. Featured musicians play jazz and original compositions every Saturday night from 9:30pm to midnight. (☎02 31 89 18 19. Open M and Su 1-7pm, Tu-Sa 8am-7pm. Open daily July-Aug. MC/V.)

◙ SIGHTS. Honfleur's side-streets hide architectural delights, small antique shops, specialized boutiques, and countless art studios. The *Pass Musées* gives access to Honfleur's four museums and belltower. (€9, students and children €6, under 10 free.) Worth the trip to Honfleur alone is the **Maisons Satie,** 67 bd. Charles V, the birthplace and now museum of composer, musician, artist, and author Erik Satie, whom you may not have heard of before but won't soon forget. Breathtaking, fanciful, and psychedelic, this maze of rooms is a jaunt through the mind of the artist. Expect indoor rainshowers, flying pears, and a *laboratoire des émotions* (laboratory of emotions), all to a soundtrack of Satie's original compositions. (☎ 02 31 89 11 11; fax 02 31 89 09 09. Open M and W-Su May-Sept. 10am-7pm; Oct.-Dec. and mid-Feb. to Apr. M and W-Su 11am-6pm. €5.10, students and seniors €3.60, under 10 free. Audio tour in French and English takes about 1hr.)

Part of the ramparts that once surrounded the village, the **Porte de Caen** at the end of quai Ste-Catherine is the only remaining gate through which the king rode into the fortified town. A block away from the Bassin is the 15th-century **Église Ste-Catherine,** the largest wooden church in France, built by pious sailors after an earlier stone edifice burned down in 1450. Conceived as a temporary structure, the church, which looks like a cross between an overturned boat and a half-timbered barn, has the architectural quirk of a second nave, built to accommodate a growing population. (Open daily July-Aug. 8am-8pm; Sept.-June 8:30am-noon and 2-6pm.) The wooden **belltower** across the street, built at the same time as the church, exhibits religious art. (Included with Musée Eugène Boudin.) Named after Honfleur's most famous artist, the **Musée Eugène Boudin,** pl. Erik Satie, off rue de l'Homme de Bois, has a small but diverse collection of pre-Impressionist work, as well as pieces by 20th-century artists who were born or worked in Honfleur. The top floor affords a nice view of the Pont de Normandie. (☎ 02 31 89 54 00; fax 02 31 89 54 06. Museum and belltower open mid-Mar. to Sept. M and W-Su 10am-noon and 2-6pm; Oct. to mid-Mar. M and W-F 2:30-5pm, Sa-Su 10am-noon and 2:30-5pm. €5.10, students and children €3.60, under 10 free. Prices lower in low season.)

The **Musée d'Ethnographie et d'Art Populaire,** rue de la Prison off quai St-Etienne, recreates the lives of the town's past inhabitants in nine rooms arranged with furniture, clothing, and household objects typical of 18th- and 19th-century Normandy. Highlights include a dark 16th-century prison and a wooden *promeneuse*, used to teach babies to walk. The nearby **Musée de la Marine,** in the former Église St-Etienne, Honfleur's oldest church, a tiny museum that recounts Honfleur's affair with the sea, is mostly for lovers of maritime history or ships in bottles. (☎ 02 31 89 14 12. Both open Apr.-Sept. Tu-Su 10am-noon and 2-6:30pm; mid-Feb. to Mar. and Oct. to mid-Nov. Tu-F 2:30-5:30pm, Sa-Su 10am-noon and 2:30-5:30pm. Last admission 30min. before closing. €3 for each, €4.20 combined; students and children €1.80/€2.60.) Rose-strung walkways, swingsets, a wading pool, and a waterfall make the **public gardens** on bd. Charles V, beside the port, the perfect spot for a picnic. From the lookout atop **Mont-Joli,** Honfleur

A CHEESY PROCESS

In an effort to get to the bottom of the Norman cheese phenomenon, Let's Go spoke with Céline Gere of the Fromagerie Graindorge, a traditional cheese manufacturer in Livarot in operation since 1910.

LG: Tell me about the *Fromagerie.*
A: It is the oldest traditional *fromagerie* in the region and has existed for three generations.
LG: What exactly makes your enterprise traditional?
A: We're traditional in the sense that, even though machines make the cheese today, all the steps in the chain are the same ones carried out before by people. We are also the last to *lier* the cheese by hand [winding a piece of reed around the circumference of the cheese to preserve its form].
LG: Does cheese have a special meaning for the region?
A: Without a doubt, cheese has become a symbol of Normandy. When you go to Normandy, you speak of D-Day Beaches, but you also speak of cheese.
LG: How long is production?
A: Once the milk arrives, we wait 12 hours and then spend a day making the cheese. For two or three days it is tasted, salted, cleaned. Then, after four to six weeks of aging, it is *lié*, packaged, and shipped.
LG: Is there an aspect of pride in the production of these cheeses?
A: It's the reason that we are so rigorous in the way we produce our cheeses. It's part of the pride of the region.

appears as a toy city complete with the space-age Pont de Normandie. To get to the lookout, follow rue du Puits from pl. Ste-Catherine to the steep, winding rampe du Mont-Joli (about 1.5km).

DEAUVILLE AND TROUVILLE

Deauville and Trouville, with their twin boardwalks, beaches, and casinos, meet at the Pont de Belges, a small bridge across the river Touques. The meandering, narrow streets of Trouville (pop. 5500) contrast with the geometric, fountain-speckled boulevards of stylish Deauville (pop. 4518), but little else is different. The playground of the nouveau riche, these seaside resorts offer travelers long stretches of fine sand, sparkling casinos, and a sore wallet.

⧉ TRANSPORTATION. Trains go to Caen (1hr., 7-8 per day, €10.70); Paris (2hr., 5-6 per day, €24.60); Rouen (2½-3hr., 3 per day, €17.70). **Bus Verts** (☎ 08 01 21 42 14) goes to Caen (1½hr., €8.50); Le Havre (1hr., €9.60) via Honfleur (20min., €3.40). Train and bus stations are located in Deauville, just after the Pont de Belges. **Voyages Fournier** (☎ 02 31 88 16 73), pl. du Maréchal Foch in Trouville, runs **shuttles** between the two towns (€1.70) and arranges daytrips, including D-Day beaches, the Seine Valley abbeys, and a night visit to Mont-St-Michel. **The Bac de Deauville/Trouville,** quai Albert 1er, by the casino in Trouville, runs **ferries** across the canal when the tide is high enough. (See brochure or board by the door for hours, which vary with the tide. €0.90.) For a **taxi,** call ☎ 02 31 88 35 33 or 02 31 87 15 15.

⧉ ⧉ ORIENTATION AND PRACTICAL INFORMATION. To get to **Trouville** from the train station, turn right and cross Pont des Belges onto bd. Fernand Moureaux. Bus Verts stops directly in Trouville, a block away from the same boulevard. Turn left from the train station or right from the bus stop to get to the **tourist office,** 32 quai Fernand Moureaux. Staff distributes vacation guides with listings of Trouville's hotels and restaurants; also available are two walking tours and a town map. (☎ 02 31 14 60 70; www.trouvillesurmer.org. Open July-Aug. M-Sa 9:30am-7pm, Su 10am-4pm; Apr.-June and Sept.-Oct. M-Sa 9:30am-noon and 2-6:30pm, Su 10am-1pm; Nov.-Mar. M-Sa 9:30am-noon and 1:30-6pm, Su 10am-1pm.)

To get to **Deauville,** turn left from the station. At the second roundabout take a right onto rue Désiré le Hoc and follow it through pl. Morny to the **tourist office** on pl. de la Mairie. The office provides a practical guide and free map, as well as info on festivals, horse races, and polo games. (☎ 02 31 14 40 00; www.deauville.org. Open July to early Sept. M-Sa 9am-7pm, Su 10am-1pm and 3-6pm; mid-Sept. to Apr. M-Sa 9am-12:30pm and 2-6:30pm, Su 10am-1pm and 2-5pm; May-June M-Sa 9am-12:30pm and 2-6:30pm, Su 10am-1pm and 2-5pm.) Rent **bikes** at La Deauvillaise, 11 quai de la Marine, near the train station. (☎ 02 31 88 56 33. €4.50 per hr., €14 per day, €40 per week. Scooters and 2-9 person vehicles also available. Open daily July-Aug. 9am-6:30pm; Sept.-June Tu-Su 9:30am-12:30pm and 2-6pm.) Use the **Internet** at Cyber Galerie, 6 rue Thiers, also by the train station. (☎ 02 31 14 04 61. €1 for 10min., €0.10 each additional min. Open M-F 9am-1pm and 2-6pm, Sa 2-6pm.)

⧉ ⧉ ACCOMMODATIONS AND FOOD. You'll have to stay in Trouville if you want to sleep without pawning your pack. Even then, rooms don't let for much less than €35. At **Hôtel les Sablettes ❸,** 13-15 rue Paul Besson, left off av. Victor Hugo after turning onto it from bd. Fernand Moureaux, or one block to the right on bd. Moureaux from the bus stop, an accommodating couple rents peaceful, immaculate rooms with TV, phone, and modern bathrooms. (☎ 02 31 88 10 66; www.trouville-hotel.com. Breakfast €6. Closed Jan. Singles €32; singles and doubles with shower €42-55, with bath €60; triples with shower €67. €4-5 less in the low season. MC/V.) Equally close to the beach and the boulevard, **Au Ch'ti- mi ❸**, 28 rue Victor Hugo, has well-decorated rooms over a little bar, each with a shower. (☎02 31 88 49 22. Breakfast €6. Reception at bar 7:30am-7pm. Doubles with shower €38; triple with bath €53.50.) **Camping Le Chant des Oiseaux ❶**, 11 rte. d'Honfleur, is a well-maintained site 2km from town on cliffs overlooking the sea. From bd. Fernand Moureaux, follow rue Victor Hugo through many name changes until it becomes rue du Général Leclerc, past the Musée Montebello. When the road forks, go right, up the steep incline, and past the giant crucifix. When this route merges with the main road, continue for 5min. and the site will be on the left. (☎02 31 88 06 42; fax 02 31 98 16 09. Open Apr.-Nov. Reception July-Aug. 8am-10pm; in low season, someone is almost always in the office or nearby. Gate closed 10:30pm-7am. €6 per person, ages 2-7 €3, €6 per tent, €3 per car. Electricity €6-8. July-Aug. shower €0.50. Laundry available.)

In Trouville, the **Monoprix supermarket** is at 166 bd. Fernand Moureaux, on the corner of rue Victor Hugo. (Open July-Aug. M-Sa 9am-8pm, Su 9:30am-1pm; daily Sept.-June 9am-12:30pm and 2-7:30pm.) A **market** on pl. Maréchal Foch features produce, cheese, and olives, as well as clothing and accessories. (W and Su 8am-1:30pm.) A **fish market** borders the waterfront on bd. Moureaux (daily 8:30am-12:30pm and 3:30-7pm). Many of the beachfront restaurants face the setting sun; locals flock to these terraces to dine in the last light of day. Reasonably priced pizzerias, *crêperies*, and seafood restaurants, most featuring Norman mussels and *prix fixe menus* between €13 and €35, line the pedestrian **rue des Bains** and **boulevard Fernand Moureaux**. For filling portions of delicious seafood in a more laid-back atmosphere, come to **Cocotte Café ❸**, 58 rue des Bains in Trouville, where the staff is hospitable and the prices reasonable. (☎02 31 88 89 69; www.cocotte-cafe.com. Fixed *menus* €13-17. Dessert €6. Open daily July-Aug. 12:15-2:30pm and 7:15-9:30pm. Sept.-June closed M-Tu. MC/V.) One of the best options may be the traditional **Tivoli Bistro ❹**, 27 rue Charles Mozin in Trouville. (☎/fax 02 31 98 43 44. *Menus* €14-24, *plat du jour* €12, other entrees €11-22. Wine €4. Open Tu and F-Su 12:15-2pm and 7:15-10pm, W 12:15-2pm. MC/V.) In Deauville, **Mamy Crêpes ❶**, 57 rue Désiré le Hoc, just before the tourist office, serves cheap, delicious sandwiches, including a few vegetarian options (€3-4), dessert crêpes (€1.30-3.70), and flan. (☎02 31 14 96 44. Open daily 9am-11pm. MC/V.)

🎭 SIGHTS AND ENTERTAINMENT. Boardwalk promenades are the pride of each town. A beachside stroll in Trouville affords a view of the spectacular houses that inspired realist novelist Gustave Flaubert, as well as volleyball courts and a children's area filled with inflated playhouses. In Deauville, you're more likely to see parasols than beachpails, and planks are lined with names of movie stars. The **Natur'Aquarium de Trouville**, 17 rue de Paris on the boardwalk, will delight the prepubescent set with its small but diverse collection of everything from sharks to tarantulas. (☎02 31 88 46 04; www.natur-aquarium.com. Open daily July-Aug. 10am-7:30pm; Sept.-Oct. and Easter-June 10am-noon and 2-7pm; Nov.-Easter 2-6:30pm. €7, students and seniors €6, ages 6-14 €4.50, ages 3-5 €3.50. MC/V.)

The **Casino Barrière de Trouville,** pl. du Maréchal Foch, has an adjoining nightclub and cinema (☎02 31 87 75 00; open M-Th and Su 10am-2am, F 10am-3am, Sa 10am-4am) and is more laid-back than the stately **Casino Barrière de Deauville.** (☎02 31 14 31 14. Open M-Th 11am-2am, F 11am-3am, Sa 11am-4am, Su 10am-3am.) The cafe and wine bar **La Maison,** 66 rue des Bains in Trouville, off bd. Fernand Moureaux, provides a relaxed yet sophisticated evening. Grass mats and wrought-iron furniture give a Spanish flavor to the terrace; a bookcase and old-fashioned posters create a homey feel inside. (☎02 31 81 43 10. Open M and F-Su 11am-2am.)

NORMANDY

Residents of Deauville satisfy their love of the equestrian at two hippodromes: **Clairefontaine,** dedicated to racing (☎02 31 14 69 00; www.hippodrome-deauville-clairefontaine.com; races held July-Aug.; €3), and **La Touques,** which hosts polo games. (☎02 31 14 20 00; www.france-galop.com. Games held July-Aug., Oct., and Dec.-Jan. €3 per week, €4 on Su, half-price for students and seniors, under 18 free.) Deauville also hosts several festivals, including **Swing'In Deauville** (3rd week of July), which draws big-names in jazz, and the **American Film Festival** (September). **Café Trouville,** a series of cafe-side concerts (July-Aug. 4-5 per week), can be enjoyed from the terrace of a cafe or from the sidewalk for free.

CAEN

At the end of World War II, three quarters of Caen (pop. 113,000) had been destroyed and two thirds of its citizens were left homeless. The city has been skillfully restored to its pre-war beauty and is now part historical monument, part sizzling university town. It makes an ideal base from which to explore the D-Day beaches but, packed with lively bars and outdoor *brasseries*, is also decidedly younger in tenor than many of its neighbors along the Côte Fleurie.

▐ TRANSPORTATION

Trains: pl. de la Gare. Info office open M-Sa 9am-6pm. To: **Cherbourg** (1½hr.; 24 per day, 12 on Su; €16.60); **Paris** (2¼hr., 12 per day, €26.20); **Rennes** (3hr., 2 per day, €27.30); **Rouen** (2hr., 5 per day, €19.40); **Tours** (3½hr., 2 per day, €28.40).

Buses: Bus Verts, (☎08 10 21 42 14), to the left of the train station and at pl. Courtonne in the *centre ville,* covers the region. Office open M-F 7:30am-7pm, Sa 8:30am-7pm, Su 9am-2:30pm. See p. 263 for D-Day beaches coverage. To **Bayeux** (1hr.; M-Sa 4 per day; €5.95, students €4.90) and **Le Havre** (2-3hr.; M-Sa 5 per day, Su 4 per day; €17, students €14). Also **Caen-Le Havre** express (1½hr., 2 per day, €19) stops in **Honfleur** (1hr., 2 per day, €12.35). Full-day *Carte Liberté* (€17.50, 3 days €27, 7 days €43) accepted on local bus Twisto. Schedules change slightly July-Aug.

Ferries: Brittany Ferries go to **Portsmouth, England,** from Ouistreham, 13km north of Caen. See **Getting There: By Boat, p. 23.** Bus Verts #1 links Ouistreham to Caen's center and train station (40min.; 24 per day; €3.40, students €2.80).

Public Transportation: Twisto, 15 rue de Geôle (☎02 31 15 55 55), at Château, pl. St-Pierre. Kiosk at Théâtre (at square where bd. Maréchal Leclerc terminates). Automatic dispensers at most stops. Tickets €1.05, *carnet* of 10 €9; day pass €2.80. Open M-F 7:15am-6:45pm, Sa 10am-4:45pm. Hours vary seasonally.

Taxis: Abbeilles Taxis Caen, 19 pl. de la Gare (☎02 31 52 17 89) or **Radio Taxi** (☎02 31 94 15 15). Both 24hr. Late-night taxi kiosk at bd. Maréchal Leclerc near rue St-Jean (10pm-3am).

■✦ ▐ ORIENTATION AND PRACTICAL INFORMATION

Caen's train station and youth hostel are located quite far from the town center; it's most convenient to take the bus. The two lines of the city's tram system, A and B, leave from the train station and cut through the city center; take either line to stop St-Pierre (5 minutes). From the station, **avenue du 6 Juin** and **rue St-Jean** run parallel to each other toward the city center and to the lively commercial districts between **rue St-Pierre** and **rue de l'Oratoire.**

Tourist Office: pl. St-Pierre (☎02 31 27 14 14; www.caen.fr/tourisme), on rue St-Jean by the Église St-Pierre. Hotel booking and free maps. *Le Mois à Caen* lists concerts and events. City tours July-Sept. (in French; 1hr., €5). Theatrical performances at night in

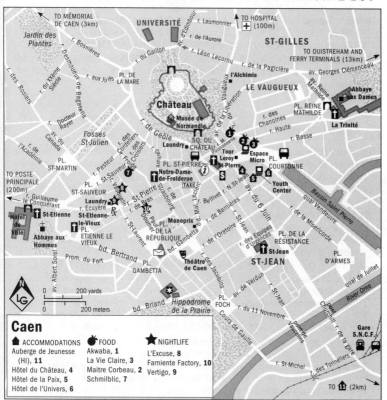

Caen

🏠 ACCOMMODATIONS
Auberge de Jeunesse
(HI), **11**
Hôtel du Château, **4**
Hôtel de la Paix, **5**
Hôtel de l'Univers, **6**

🍎 FOOD
Akwaba, **1**
La Vie Claire, **3**
Maitre Corbeau, **2**
Schmilblic, **7**

⭐ NIGHTLIFE
L'Excuse, **8**
Farniente Factory, **10**
Vertigo, **9**

French mid-July to Aug. (2hr.; €8.50-13, students and children over 10 €6.50-8.50, under 10 free; reservations required). Office open July-Aug. M-Sa 9am-7pm, Su 10am-1pm and 2-5pm; June and Sept. M-Sa 9:30am-6:30pm, Su 10am-1pm.

Currency Exchange: at the post office and most banks. **Crédit Agricole** has a branch on bd. Maréchal Leclerc, at the intersection with rue St-Jean. Open M-F 9:15am-12:15pm and 1:45-6pm, Sa 9:15am-12:15pm and 1:45-5pm.

Youth Center: Centre Régional d'Information Jeunesse (CRIJ), 16 rue Neuve-St-Jean (☎02 31 27 80 80; ij@srij-bn.org), off av. du 6 Juin next to the Hôtel de la Paix. EU information booth and info on events, jobs, lodging, and work opportunities. Free Internet (for research only). Open M 1-6pm, Tu-Th 10am-6pm, F 10am-5pm.

Laundromat: rue de Geôle (☎06 60 55 75 60). Open daily 7am-9pm. Also 16 rue Ecuyère (☎06 80 96 08 26). Ironing M-Sa for €1.50 per piece or €10.50 per hr. Open daily 7am-8pm.

Police: rue Thiboud de la Fresnaye (☎02 31 29 22 22). Kiosk near the tourist office on rue Maréchal Leclerc.

Pharmacy: Pharmacie Danjou Rousselot, 5 pl. Malherbe (☎02 31 30 78 00), at the intersection of rue Ecuyère and rue St-Pierre. Open M 9am-7:30pm, Tu-F 8:30am-7:30pm, Sa 9am-7:30pm.

Hospital: Centre Hospitalier Universitaire, av. Côte de Nacre (☎02 31 06 31 06).

Internet Access: Free at **CRIJ** (see **Youth Center**). **Espace Micro,** 1 rue Basse (☎02 31 53 68 68; fax 02 31 94 08 00). 30 computers. Rents DVDs and videos, some English. €3.80 per hr., lower rate for longer sessions. Open M-Th 10am-11pm, F-Su 10am-1pm.

Post Office: pl. Gambetta (☎02 31 39 35 78). From pl. St-Pierre, take rue St-Pierre and turn left on rue St-Laurent; post office will be at the bottom of the street on your left. **Currency exchange.** Open M-F 8am-7pm, Sa 8:30am-12:30pm.

Postal Code: 14016.

◤ ACCOMMODATIONS

Hôtel de l'Univers, 12 quai Vendeuvre, (☎02 31 85 46 14). From the station, follow av. du 6 Juin to its end and turn right, or take tram A or B. A well-maintained, typical 2-star hotel, a stone's throw from the château. TV, telephone, shower. Breakfast €6. Reception 7:30am-10pm. Single with shower €33; double with shower €36, with toilet €42-44; single or double with bath €50. AmEx/MC/V. ❸

Hôtel de la Paix, 14 rue Neuve-St-Jean (☎02 31 86 18 99; fax 02 31 38 20 74), off av. du 6 Juin, in a great spot. Rooms decorated in vibrant colors, some with flower-adorned balconies, have clean, modern bathrooms, firm beds, and TV. Breakfast €5. 24hr. reception. Singles €26, with shower €29, with toilet €32; doubles €29/€35/€37; triples €37/€43/€45; quads with shower €53. Extra bed €5. AmEx/MC/V. ❸

Hôtel du Château, 5 av. du 6 Juin (☎02 31 86 15 37; www.hotel-chateau-caen.com). Exceptionally large, bright rooms with TV, tasteful furniture, and flawlessly clean bathrooms, on a pedestrian street near the château. All rooms include toilet. Breakfast €6. 24hr. reception. Singles with shower €45, with bath €55; doubles €55/€65; triples with shower €60; quads €65. Extra bed €10. Prices lower Oct.-Easter. AmEx/MC/V. ❹

Auberge de Jeunesse (HI), Foyer Robert Reme, 68bis rue Eustache-Restout (☎02 31 52 19 96; fax 02 31 84 29 49). Turn right from the station, then left on rue de Falaise. The bus stop is on the right. Take bus #5 (dir: Fleury Cimitière) to Lycée Fresnel. From the town center, take line B (dir: Grâce de Dieu) to Rostand Fresnel. Clean 4-person, single-sex dorms with shower, stove, and locker, but hostel is far from the center of town (3km). Breakfast €2. Sheets €2.50. Laundry available. Reception 5-9:30pm. Hostel open June-Sept. Beds €10. HI members only. ❶

◖ FOOD

Brasseries vie with Chinese eateries and African restaurants in the **quartier Vaugueux** near the château and between the Église St-Pierre and the Église St-Jean. Large **markets** are held at pl. St-Sauveur (F 7:30am-1:30pm) and quai Vendeuvre (Su 7:30am-2:30pm). Smaller markets are on Grâce de Dieu and rue de Bayeux (Tu 8am-1:30pm), bd. Leroy (W 8am-1:30pm and Sa 7:30am-1:30pm), and La Guérnière and Le Chemin Vert (Th 8am-1:30pm). A produce stand appears daily at pl. Courtonne, at the end of rue Basse. There's a **Monoprix supermarket** at 45 bd. Maréchal Leclerc (open M-Th and Sa 9am-8:30pm, F 9am-9pm), and a **8 à huit** on av. Charles de Foucauld near the hostel. (Open M-Sa 8:30am-12:30pm and 2:30-7:30pm.)

Herds of people wait for a table at the door of cow-themed ◪**Maître Corbeau** ❸, 8 rue Buquet, where every dish on the menu includes cheese. Locals feast on *fondue normande* (made with camembert, calvados, and *crème fraîche*; €12.20 per person) amid giant sunflowers and bovine paraphernalia. Reserve up to a week in advance. (☎02 31 93 93 00. *Prix fixe menus* €9.60-19.50. Entrees €6.50-12. Open M and Sa 7-10:30pm, Tu-F noon-1:30pm and 7-10:30pm. Closed last week in Aug. and 1st week in Sept. MC/V.) The gigantic, made-to-order sandwiches (€2.40-4.50) at **Schmilblic** ❶, 53 rue Froide, off rue St-Pierre, are incredibly popular with the starving college students. (Dessert crêpes €0.90-2.30. Open M-W 10:30am-8pm, Th-F 10:30am-9:30pm.) For a healthy sit-down lunch, try **La Vie Claire ❷**, 3-5 rue Basse, behind an organic food store, where seasonal vegetarian fare is filling and fresh. (☎02 31 93 66 72. Entrees €6.50-8. Dessert €5. Tea €2.50-4. Open Tu-Sa noon-2:30pm for meals, 11am-5pm for beverages. Store open Tu-Sa 9am-7pm. MC/V.) **Akwaba ❸**, 3bis rue de Vaugueux, is an African restaurant, decorated with tapestries. In a hip section of town, away from traffic and to the left of the château, the restaurant serves spiced chicken and lamb dishes along with delicious sweet potatoes. (☎02 31 93 90 80. Appetizers €3-6. Entrees €8.70-13.80. Open July-Sept. M-Sa noon-2pm and 7pm-midnight; Oct.-June M-Sa 7pm-midnight. MC/V.)

🔆 SIGHTS

Some of Caen's sights are discounted with the purchase of a full-price ticket to other sights or museums in the area. The tourist office has details.

▓ MÉMORIAL DE CAEN. Hands-down the best of Normandy's WWII museums, the Mémorial de Caen is a powerful, creative exploration of the "failure of peace" between the world wars and the modern prospects for global peace. The extremely engaging exhibit unfolds through an artful blend of vintage footage, high-tech audio-visuals, old letters, and even paintings. Especially absorbing are personal accounts from the front and presentations on lesser-known facts, like the solace soldiers sought in art and culture. Allow at least two hours to explore the museum. *(Take bus #2 to Mémorial. ☎02 31 06 06 44; www.memorial-caen.fr. Open daily mid-July to late Aug. 9am-8pm; early Feb. to mid July and late Aug. to Oct. 9am-7pm; mid-Jan. to early Feb. and Nov.-Dec. 9am-6pm. Closed first 2 weeks in Jan. Last entry 1¼hr. before closing. €16.50-17; students, seniors, and ages 10-18 €14-16; prices depend on season.)*

ABBEYS AND CHURCHES. Caen, the seat of William the Conqueror's duchy, owes its first-class Romanesque architecture chiefly to William's guilty conscience: William married his distant cousin Mathilda despite the pope's explicit interdiction. To get back on the road to Heaven, the two built several ecclesiastical structures, most notably Caen's twin abbeys. Begun in 1066, the **Abbaye-aux-Hommes,** off rue Guillaume le Conquérant, has functioned as a boys' school, a shelter for 10,000 of the town's inhabitants during WWII, and is now the Hôtel de Ville. *(☎02 31 30 42 81; fax 02 31 86 02 38. Open to tourists only during 1½hr. tours daily at 9:30, 11am, 2:30pm; meet in lobby. €2, students and seniors €1, under 18 free.)* The adjacent **Église St-Etienne,** whose 11th-century facade and nave are the oldest parts of the complex, contains an imposing organ and William's tomb—now home only to the monarch's right femur following pillaging during the Wars of Religion. *(Open daily 8:15am-noon and 2-7:30pm.)* Across the street from the abbey's gardens sit the remains of the Église St-Etienne-le-Vieux, a standing tribute to the destructive force of the bombings. The smaller Église de la Trinité of the Abbaye-aux-Dames, off rue des Chanoines, houses Mathilda's tomb. *(☎02 31 06 98 98. Church open M-Sa 8am-5:30pm, Su 9:30am-12:30pm. Free 1hr. tours in French M-Sa at 2:30 and 4pm.)*

CHÂTEAU. Between the abbeys sprawl the ruins of William's enormous **château,** begun in 1060. The fortress, besieged several times during the Hundred Years' War and served as military barracks in WWII, now affords a pleasant pre-sunset stroll. *(☎02 31 27 14 14. Open daily May-Sept. 6am-1am; Oct.-Apr. 6am-7:30pm. Free. July-Aug. tours in French 11am, in English 3pm. Info office on the left just after passing through red gates. Open Tu-Sa 10am-1pm and 2-5:30pm.)* The small **Jardin des Simples** holds a collection of plants cultivated in the Middle Ages. *(Same hours as the château.)*

OTHER SIGHTS. The **Musée de Normandie** takes on the broad task of tracing the cultural evolution of people living on Norman soil from the beginning of civilization to the present. (☎ 02 31 30 47 60; www.ville-caen.fr/mdn. Open M and W-Su 9:30am-6pm. €1.60, students €0.75, under 18 and every Su free.) The sheltered **Jardin des Plantes,** 5 pl. Blot, features wooden arches and its own doves. Turn left on rue Bosnières from rue de Geôle. (☎ 02 31 30 48 40. Open daily June-Aug. 8am-sunset; Sept.-May 8am-5:30pm. Greenhouse open daily 2-5pm.)

🎵 ENTERTAINMENT

Well-attended bars and clubs populate **rue de Bras, rue des Croisiers, quai Vendeuvre,** and **rue St-Pierre.** University students wait for the night to heat up while downing cheap drinks at **Vertigo,** 14 rue Ecuyère, just past the intersection with rue St-Pierre. In front, it's standing room only at peak hours. (☎ 02 31 85 43 12. Cocktails €3, beer €1.60-2.50. Happy hour 7-9pm. Open M-Sa 10-1am. MC/V.) Glance at the funky modern artwork on your way to the dance floor at **L'Excuse,** 20 rue Vauquelin, where they work it to everything from house to old French classics. (☎ 02 31 38 80 89. Beer and liquor €4. Cocktails €6. Cover €6 on the weekend, includes €4.50 toward a drink. Open June-Aug. Tu-Sa 11pm-4am. Doors close 2am. MC/V.) Velvety jazz fills the air at **L'Alchimie,** 12 rue du Vaugueux, where red barstools and black leather loveseats make for a classy evening. (☎ 02 31 93 20 30. Beer €3-4.50, cocktails €6-9. Open Tu-Th 6pm-2am, F-Sa 6pm-4am and Su 6pm-1am. AmEx/MC/V.) The young and glamorous grind to hip-hop, reggae, and club hits at **Farniente Factory,** 13 rue Paul Doumer, an ultra-modern bar and lounge that screams "underground chic." (☎ 02 31 86 30 00. DJ every night. Beer €3-4.50. Cocktails €6. Cover €3. Open W-Sa 7pm-2am. AmEx/MC/V.)

Caen hosts a popular festival of Latin music and dance, **Cap Latino,** during the first weekend of June. It takes place inside the walls of the château and tends to bring down the house.

BAYEUX

Bayeux (pop. 15,000), unharmed by Nazi occupation and Allied liberation, retains its original architecture and resplendent cathedral. The town's pleasant pedestrian byways and old-world atmosphere cater to a middle-aged crowd, but its lively hostel is full of backpackers. Bayeux's real jewel is its 900-year-old tapestry, which narrates William the Conqueror's victory over England in 1066. The village also makes a beautiful base for D-Day Beach exploration.

⌷ TRANSPORTATION

Trains: pl. de la Gare (☎02 31 92 80 50). Ticket counters open M-F 6am-8pm, Sa-Su 8am-8pm. To: **Caen** (20min., 15 per day, €5.70); **Cherbourg** (1hr., 12 per day, €13.30); **Paris** (2½hr., 12 per day, €28.80).

Buses: Bus Verts, pl. de la Gare (☎02 31 92 02 92). Open M-F 9:15am-noon and 1:30-6pm. Buses head west to small towns and east to **Caen** (1hr., M-Sa 2-3 per day, €5.60). See p. 263 for coverage of the D-Day beaches. Buy tickets from the driver or at the office. **Bybus,** pl. de la Gare (☎02 31 92 02 92) runs in town about 9am-6pm. 9-11:30am €0.85; 2-4pm €0.65.

Taxis: Taxis du Bessin (☎02 31 92 92 40).

Bike Rental: Available at the hostel. €10 per day with a €20 deposit.

🛈 PRACTICAL INFORMATION

Tourist Office: Pont St-Jean (☎02 31 51 28 28; www.bayeux-tourism.com). At the station, turn left onto bd. Sadi-Carnot. Go right at the roundabout. Continue up rue Larcher; turn right on rue St-Martin. The office is at the edge of the pedestrian zone. Regional guide, info on D-Day tours, Internet access (cards €5 for 30min., €15 for 3hr.), guided walking tour of the old city, and accommodation booking in Calvados (€2). Open June-Aug. M-Sa 9am-7pm, Su 9am-1pm and 2-6pm; daily Apr.-May and Sept.-Oct. 9:30am-12:30pm and 2-6pm; Nov.-Mar. M-Sa 9:30am-12:30pm and 2-5:30pm.

Laundromat: 10 rue Maréchal Foch. Open daily 7am-9pm.

Police: pl. Liberté (☎02 31 92 02 42).

Hospital: 13 rue de Nesmond (☎02 31 51 51 51), next to the tapestry center.

Post Office: 14 rue Larcher (☎02 31 51 24 90). **Currency exchange,** fax, photocopies, and Cyberposte. Open M-F 8:15am-6:30pm, Sa 8:15am-noon.

Postal Code: 14400.

🏠 🏠 ACCOMMODATIONS AND CAMPING

Demand for lodging often outstrips supply, especially in the summer months. Plan with military precision to get a room around June 6, the anniversary of D-Day.

🏠 **The Family Home/Auberge de Jeunesse (HI),** 39 rue Général de Dais (☎02 31 92 15 22; www.fuaj.org), in the center of town. Homey 1- to 7-person rooms branch off a courtyard with a giant chessboard. Laundry, kitchen, TV, and dining room make meeting other guests a cinch. Breakfast included; fantastic home-cooked dinner at 7:30pm every night (€10). Reception inconsistent and staff may be difficult to find, but someone is usually around during the day. Guests may be displaced after 1 night in summer. Shower and toilet in hall. Beds €18, without HI membership €20; single room €30. Help clean the kitchen and they promise lunch and a free bed for the night. ❷

Le Maupassant, 19 rue St-Martin (☎02 31 92 28 53; fax 02 31 92 35 40). Simple, clean rooms with yellow walls over a *brasserie* (salads €7-9, sandwiches €3-5) on a pedestrian-heavy street in the town center. Breakfast €5.80. Reception at bar 7:45am-11:30pm. Singles €29; doubles with shower €40; quads with bath €69. Some rooms come with toilet or TV. Extra bed €10. MC/V.❸

Camping: Camping Municipal, bd. d'Eindhoven (☎/fax 02 31 92 08 43), within easy reach of the town center and N13. Take rue Genas Duhomme to the right off rue St-Martin. Continue straight on av. de la Vallée des Prés. The campground is on your right, near a Champion supermarket. (10min.) Well-kept site but not much green space, next

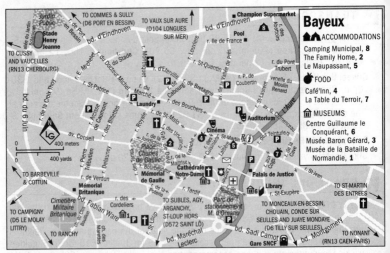

Bayeux

🏠▲▲ **ACCOMMODATIONS**

Camping Municipal, **8**
The Family Home, **2**
Le Maupassant, **5**

🍴 **FOOD**

Café'Inn, **4**
La Table du Terroir, **7**

🏛 **MUSEUMS**

Centre Guillaume le
 Conquérant, **6**
Musée Baron Gérard, **3**
Musée de la Bataille de
 Normandie, **1**

to the town swimming pool. Laundry, great showers. Open May-Sept. Gates close 10pm-7am. Office open July-Aug. 7am-9pm; May-June and Sept. M-Sa 8-10am and 5-7pm, Su 8-10am and 5-8pm. €3 per person, children under 7 €1.60, €3.70 per car or tent. Electricity €3. Showers included. 10% reduction on stays of 5 days or more. ●

🍴 FOOD

There are **markets** on pl. St-Patrice (Sa) and rue St-Jean (W), both from 7am-1pm. The area around the tourist office has small grocery stores and there is a **Champion supermarket** on bd. d'Eindhoven, near the campground. Most of the town's eateries populate rue St-Martin, rue St-Jean, and their side-streets.

Some of the heartiest meals in the city are at **La Table du Terroir ❹**, 42 rue St-Jean, in two adjacent locations down the street from the tourist office. At the livelier site, in an alley off of the main street, the jovial chef/owner and his family serve local meat dishes and delicious desserts at communal wooden tables. (☎/fax 02 31 92 05 53. *Menus* €16, €20, and €26. Entrees €11-20. Open July-Aug. M-Sa noon-2pm and 7-10pm; closes at 9pm the rest of the year. MC/V.) Up the street from the tourist office, **Café'Inn ❶**, 67 rue St-Martin, has shelves lined with flavored teas and natural jams and serves reasonably priced salads (€5-6.30), sandwiches (€3), and omelettes (around €4). The freshly made fare makes a delicious, light option for lunch. (☎02 31 21 11 37. Lunch *menu* €8.40, homemade pastries €2-4.50. Flavored tea €2.85. Open M-Sa 9am-7pm. MC/V.)

🔵 SIGHTS

🖼**TAPISSERIE DE BAYEUX.** The exquisite tapestry, most remarkable for its strikingly modern, film-like narrative technique, illustrates in 58 vibrant frames the events leading up to the Battle of Hastings. In 1066, Guillaume le Bâtard (William the Bastard) earned himself a more sociable nickname by crossing the Channel with a large cavalry to defeat his cousin Harold, who, according to the Norman version of the tale, had stolen the English throne from William. After a grueling 14hr. battle in which Harold was dramatically killed by an archer, William triumphed in this last successful invasion of England, earning the monicker *le Conquérant* (the Conqueror). A mere 50cm wide but 70m long, the tapestry, now over 900 years old, hangs in all its glory at the **Centre Guillaume le Conquérant**, rue de Nesmond. Take particular note of the soldiers flailing in quicksand at Mont-St-Michel (frames 16-17), Halley's Comet (32-33), and poor Harold with the fatal arrow in his eye (57). An edifying exhibit, including an annotated reprint of the tapestry, precedes the viewing of the masterpiece itself, providing historical background and an explanation of one of the great pieces of world art. A well-paced audio tour, included in the entry ticket, is available in 11 languages. (☎02 31 51 25 50; fax 02 31 51 25 59. Open daily May-Aug. 9am-7pm; mid-Mar. to Apr. and Sept.-Oct. 9am-6:30pm; Nov. to mid-Mar. 9:30am-12:30pm and 2-6pm. Last entrance 45min. before closing. €7.40, students €3, seniors €6, under 10 free; includes Musée Baron Gérard.)

CATHÉDRALE NOTRE-DAME. Nearby is the original home of the tapestry, the **Cathédrale Notre-Dame,** consecrated in 1077. Above the transept are Gothic arches with dizzyingly intricate carvings, while the 11th-century crypt beneath displays chipping 15th-century frescoes. To the left of the entrance is the *salle capitulaire,* which contains France's only *chemin de Jerusalem,* a tile labyrinth on the floor that retraces Jesus's *via crucis,* the route he followed to Calvary. (☎02 31 92 14 21. Open daily July-Sept. 8:30am-7pm; Oct.-June 8:30am-6pm. Tours of the old city, including access to the cathedral's chapter house and treasury, daily June-Aug. 11am, 2pm, 4pm. English tours start at the Centre Guillaume le Conquérant, rue de Nesmond. €4, under 15 free.)

MUSÉE BARON GÉRARD. Relocated to the Hôtel du Doyen, rue Lambert-Leforestier, until renovations are complete in 2007, the **Musée Baron Gérard** currently exhibits a modest collection of porcelain, 16th- and 17th-century paintings, and the delicate lace that is characteristic of Bayeux. (☎02 31 92 14 21; fax 02 31 21 91 84. Open daily July-Aug. 10am-12:30pm and 2-7pm; Sept.-June closes at 6pm. €2.60, students €1.50, seniors €2, under 10 free. Free entry with tapestry ticket.)

LOCAL D-DAY SIGHTS. The events of the D-Day landing and the subsequent 76-day battle are recounted in the **Musée de la Bataille de Normandie,** bd. Fabian Ware, through photos, weapons, and innumerable uniform-clad mannequins. The exhibit is a little sterile, but there are interesting newspaper clippings. Do not attempt to cover the entire exhibit—there's just too much small type. (☎02 31 51 46 90; www.mairie-bayeux.fr. Open daily May to mid-Sept. 9:30am-6:30pm, last entrance 5:30pm; mid-Sept. to Apr. 10am-12:30pm and 2-6pm, last entrances noon and 5pm. Closed last 2 weeks in Jan. 30min. film in English approx. every 2hr. €5.50, seniors and military €4.50, students €2.60, under 10 free.) Rows of closely packed tombstones fringed by flowers in the **British Cemetery** across the street provide a more moving wartime record.

D-DAY BEACHES

By 1944, German forces along the northern coasts of France had been waiting four years for an Allied invasion. Normandy was less prepared for a full-scale invasion than heavily fortified Calais, but German General Erwin Rommel's troops still made it a treacherous landing zone. Preparations for the attack began in 1943, when Allied leaders decided that the only way to defeat Hitler was to recapture his "Fortress Europe" from the sea. Allied counterintelligence flooded the radio waves with false plans and inflated dummy tanks near Norway to keep secret "Operation Overlord," the planned landing on the coast between the Cotentin Peninsula and the Orne. In the pre-dawn hours of **June 6, 1944,** 16,000 British and US paratroopers tumbled from the sky; a few hours later, 135,000 troops and 20,000 vehicles landed on the beaches code-named Utah and Omaha (American), Gold and Sword (British), and Juno (Canadian). The losses incurred during the D-Day

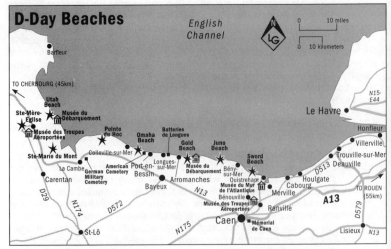

D-Day Beaches

English Channel

0   10 miles
0   10 kilometers

Barfleur

TO CHERBOURG (45km)

Utah Beach
Ste-Mère-Église
Musée du Débarquement
Musée des Troupes Aéroportées
Pointe du Hoc
Omaha Beach
Batteries de Longues
Gold Beach
Juno Beach
Ste-Marie du Mont
Colleville-sur-Mer
Longues-sur-Mer
Musée du Débarquement
Sword Beach
Villerville
Trouville-sur-Mer
Le Havre
Honfleur
La Cambe
American Cemetery
Port-en-Bessin
Bény-sur-Mer
Ouistreham
Deauville
German Military Cemetery
Carentan
Arromanches
Bayeux
Ouistreham
Musée du Mur de l'Atlantique
Cabourg
Houlgate
Merville
Bénouville
Musée des Troupes Aéroportées
Ranville
Caen
Mémorial de Caen
St-Lô
Lisieux
TO ROUEN (55km)

N15-E44
D513
A13
N13
N175
N174
D29
D572
D579
N13

landings were devastating on both sides but were a crucial precursor to later Allied successes. The Battle of Normandy raged for two and a half months, finally ending on August 21. Three days later, Free French forces liberated Paris. Less than a year later, Allied forces took Berlin, and Germany surrendered.

The **Voie de la Liberté** (Liberty Road) follows the US army's advance from Utah Beach to Bastogne in Belgium. For a complete description of the sites and museums that commemorate the battle, pick up *The D-Day Landings and the Battle of Normandy*, a brochure available from most tourist offices in the area. Every year on June 6, veterans return to pay their respects at memorial services.

⌐ TRANSPORTATION

Though many of the D-Day Beaches are not far apart, it is no easy task to get from one to another without a car. Even with a car, it would be difficult to see all the sites in a single day. For a one-day tour of the beaches, the best idea is to focus on either Utah or Omaha Beach and fan out from there. **Bus Verts** (☎ 08 10 21 42 14; operators available M-Sa 7am-8pm) is by far the best way to see the most in one day without a car. Line #70 (M-Sa 5 per day, 3 on Su) runs from Bayeux to Pointe du Hoc and the American Cemetery. Line #75 goes to Arromanches and Ouistreham (3 per day).

Normandy Sightseeing Tours, formerly **Bus Fly,** rue des Cuisiniers in Bayeux, runs private half-day and full-day guided tours with fluent English-speaking guides. Tours are also given in German, Spanish, Italian, Japanese, Chinese, and Russian. (☎ 02 31 22 00 08 or 02 31 51 70 52; www.normandywebguide.com. 4hr. tour €35, students €30; 8hr. tour €70. Pick-up 8:30am and 1:30pm from your hotel or hostel. Reservations required.) **Victory Tours** leads tours in English from behind the Bayeux tourist office. (☎ 02 31 51 98 14; www.lignerolles.homestead.com. 4hr. tour 12:30pm, €31. 8hr. tour 9:15am, €54. Reservations required.) **Overlordtour** offers half- and full-day guided tours in French and English, as well as personalized itineraries. Anecdotes, historical photos, and a Mercedes minibus add color to the visit. (☎ 06 70 21 43 42; www.overlordtour.com. Half-day tour at 8:30am and 1:30pm, €40. Full-day tour 8:30am, €75. Tours leave from Bayeux.) **Normandy Tours**, 26 pl. de la Gare, based in Bayeux's Hôtel de la Gare, across from the train

NORMANDY

station, runs 4-5hr. tours of four major sites with less commentary, in English and French. (☎ 02 31 92 10 70. Tour at 8:30am and 1pm. €35, students €31.) All three companies include admission to the museum in Arromanches.

D-DAY BEACHES BY BUS. D-Day beaches aren't easy to visit without a car. Fortunately, **Bus Verts**'s special summer **D-Day line,** which leaves from Caen and Bayeux, is a practical and inexpensive way to see the beaches. Buses leave Caen at 9:20am and head to Arromanches, site of **Gold Beach,** where the British built Port Winston while under fire. Today it's a beautiful family beach, but the relics of the port still remain an impressive, broken semi-circle. After a 3hr. stay in Arromanches, the bus takes off for a 30min. stop at **Longues-sur-Mer,** where German bunkers remain in the earth, surrounded by miles of scenic pastures. The bus continues to the **American Cemetery** (1hr.), where a panoramic view frames a manicured landscape of white crosses, perhaps the day's most moving experience. The final stop is **Pointe du Hoc** (1hr.), where the pockmarked terrain and barbed-wired cliffs make one imagine what it must have been like for the American Rangers who scaled the cliff sixty years ago. Besides a similar **Omaha Beach line,** two additional circuits run from Bayeux to cover **Utah** and **Sword Beaches.** You'll return to your starting point just past 5pm, fatigued, but fulfilled. (☎ 08 10 21 42 14; www.busverts14.fr. All buses leave between 9:20 and 9:40am. Caen line runs daily June to mid Sept. From Bayeux, buses go to Omaha Tu, Th, Sa; to Utah M, W, F; to Sword W and F-Sa. €14.)

◉ SIGHTS NEAR BAYEUX

Local tourist offices have a list of D-Day sights that offer discounted admission.

▨ **AMERICAN CEMETERY.** On a cliff overlooking Omaha Beach in Colleville-sur-Mer, 9387 American graves stretch across a 172-acre, pristine coastal reserve. Piercingly red rosebushes are scattered between endless rows of white crosses and Stars of David, among them the graves of a father and son and 38 pairs of brothers. A simple marble chapel and a 7m bronze statue, *The Spirit of American Youth Rising from the Waves,* face the soldiers' graves. The Garden of the Missing, behind the memorial, lists the names of 1557 individuals whose remains were never recovered. Embedded in the lawn opposite the information office lies a time capsule containing news reports of the June 6 landings labeled "to Be Opened June 6, 2044." Holding only a fraction of those who died here, a walk through the neat rows of white headstones on the edge of the sea is one of the most moving reminders of the sacrifices of June 6. (☎ 02 31 51 62 00; www.abmc.gov. Open daily 9am-5pm. The American staff at the office can help locate specific graves.)

▨ **UTAH BEACH.** The Americans first landed on Norman soil at **Utah Beach,** near Ste-Marie du Mont, where they spearheaded the western flank of the invasion. Utah was one of the most successful operations of the day. All objectives were completed on schedule, with fewer casualties than expected, a feat honored by the **American Commemorative Monument** (at the termination of Highway N-13D, about 3km east of Ste-Mairie du Mont) and the **Musée du Débarquement,** whose films and models show how 836,000 soldiers and 220,000 vehicles came ashore. (☎ 02 33 71 53 35. Open daily May-Sept. 9:30am-7pm; Apr. and Oct. 10am-12:30pm and 2-6pm; Nov.-Mar. weekends and public holidays 10am-12:30pm and 2-5:30pm. €4.50, ages 6-16 €2.)

▨ **POINTE DU HOC.** The most difficult landing was that of the Ranger Force—the 2nd and 5th Ranger Battalions at Pointe du Hoc. Not only did it stand above 30m cliffs that had to be scaled with ropes and hooks, it was also the most

THE LOCAL STORY

ROBERT HALLIDAY, D-DAY VETERAN

Mr. Halliday served as a parachutist in the 12th Yorks Battalion, 6th British Airborne Division, nicknamed the Red Berets. His division was one of the first to arrive in Normandy on the early morning of June 6, 1944.

LG: How often do you come back to the battle site?

A: We [the Red Berets] come over every year. We gradually get fewer and fewer, because the men are now in their eighties. It gets sadder every year.

LG: What was your experience at Normandy?

A: The American aircraft we jumped out of was hit, and as soon as we left, the plane crashed. The outcome of the crew we don't know; that sort of thing happened all the time.

LG: How do the tributes to the D-Day vets personally affect you?

A: The nicest thing was someone who spoke to me the year before last. He was French. He had our insignias on his jacket, and he showed me an original photo of the beaches he had given his son.

LG: Do you think films teach real lessons about WWII?

A: Hollywood films today fabricate stories about D-Day, with big handsome guys doing impossible things. It was blokes like us, who had next to nothing, on a few shillings a week, all volunteers. I was 17 when I joined the army.

heavily fortified of all the coastline strongholds. Nevertheless, 225 specially trained US Rangers climbed the bluff under a rain of gunfire and grenades. The 150 men who made it to the top neutralized a key German position and single-handedly defended it for two days. In all, only 90 survived. German losses were even heavier: only 40 prisoners were left among the 2000 stationed there. The Pointe is considered to be a military cemetery because so many fallen soldiers remain there, crushed beneath collapsed sections of the 5m thick concrete bunkers. Dozens of unfilled bomb craters from the initial strike are still visible amid both collapsed and surviving bunkers, many of which can be climbed through. A stone monument stands on the cliff's edge against a backdrop of barbwire and blue water. (☎02 31 51 62 00; www.abmc.gov. Info office open daily 10am-1pm and 2-6pm. Grounds open daily 9am-5pm.)

OMAHA BEACH. Often referred to as "bloody Omaha," this is perhaps the most famous of the beaches. Nothing went right here on D-Day: Allied intelligence failed to detect the presence of an additional German division, and the aerial and naval bombardment of the beach and fortifications was delayed due to poor visibility. The beach was protected by three veteran battalions instead of the single motley division that the Americans had expected; it was covered with mine-topped jack-and-pole devices called "Rommel's asparagus," and it ended in concrete walls, anti-tank ditches, minefields, and barbed wire. The first waves of troops to hit the shores suffered casualties of nearly 100%. Of the 32 amphibious tanks that were initially launched, only one made it ashore. Approximately 2000 men were killed in the landing areas—1000 died at Omaha in 24 hours. Today, save for hordes of tourists, the beach remains basically unchanged and uncommercialized. After a heavy rain, pieces of 60-year-old German barbed wire can still be found peeking out of the sand near the grass at the back of the beach.

GOLD BEACH. At Arromanches, a small town at the center of Gold Beach, the British built **Port Winston**, the floating harbor that was to supply the Allied forces until Cherbourg was liberated months later. They used retired ships and 600,000 tons of concrete they had towed across the Channel to build the port. Sixty years later, the hulking ruins of a port built in six days and designed to last only 18 months remain in a broken semicircle just off the coast. The **Musée du Débarquement**, pl. du 6 Juin on the beach, uses models and newsreel footage to show how the port was assembled under fire. (☎02 31 22 34 31;

www.normandy1944.com. Open daily May-Aug. 9am-7pm; Sept. 9am-6pm; Apr. 9am-12:30pm and 1:30-6pm; Oct. and Mar. 9:30am-12:30pm and 1:30-5:30pm; Nov.-Dec. and Feb. 10am-12:30pm and 1:30-5pm. Open Su 10am, except June-Aug. Closed late Dec. to late Jan. Last entry 30min. before closing. €6, students and children €4.)

BATTERIES DE LONGUES. Amid golden wheat fields and green meadows, the Batteries de Longues in tiny Longues-sur-Mer, 6km west of Arromanches, are an ominous reminder of the German presence. Visitors can climb through four bunkers, which were constructed in 1944 but still hold their original artillery. One contains the only cannon in the region still loaded with its original ammunition. The D-Day naval bombardment destroyed the town 1km inland, but left the bunkers mostly intact. On June 7, German troops stationed here surrendered to British troops almost instantaneously. *(☎ 02 31 06 06 45; www.memorial-caen.fr. Open daily June-Aug. 10am-7pm; Sept.-May 10am-6pm. Tours in French and English through the Caen Memorial daily June-Mar. 10am-6pm; Apr.-May Su and W-Sa only. €5.50, €5 with ticket stub from almost any other area museum.)*

OTHER SIGHTS. Not far from Omaha Beach, in La Cambe, is the **German Military Cemetery.** It contains the often overlooked graves of 21,300 German casualties of World War II, marked by embedded plaques designed to blend into the setting and crosses arranged symbolically in groups of five. Also on-site are a Peace Garden of maple trees and a collage of quotes and photos. *(☎ 02 31 22 70 76. Open daily Apr.-Oct. 8am-7pm; Nov.-Mar. 8am-5:30pm.)* The **Arromanches 360° Cinéma** shows a well-made 18min. film, *Le Prix de la Liberté* (The Price of Freedom), on its nine-part circular screen. The movie combines battle footage with peaceful images of modern Normandy. To reach the cinema from the museum, turn left on rue de la Batterie and follow the steps to the top of the cliff. *(☎ 02 31 22 30 30; www.arromanches360.com. Open daily June-Aug. 9:40am-6:40pm; mid- to late May and early Sept. 10:10am-6:10pm; mid-Sept. to Oct. 10:10am-5:40pm; Mar. to mid-May and Nov. 10:10am-5:10pm; Dec. and Feb. 10:10am-4:40pm. Closed Jan. Movies at 10 and 40min. past the hour. €4; students, seniors and 10-18 €3.50; under 10 free.)* Nearby **Ste-Mère-Église,** on the road to a German depot in Carentan and to the strategic German-held port of Cherbourg, was one of the most important targets of the invasion. Many paratroopers were misdropped, falling directly into the town. Visible targets for German artillery and encumbered by heavy equipment, 16% were killed before they hit the ground. Even so, a badly outnumbered group of them broke through heavy German defenses after six hours of fighting. *(☎ 02 33 21 00 33; www.sainte-mere-eglise.info.)* The parachute-shaped **Musée des Troupes Aéroportées,** 14 rue Eisenhower, houses one of the planes that dropped them. *(☎ 02 33 41 41 35; www.airborne-museum.org. Open daily Apr.-Sept. 9am-6:45pm; Feb.-Mar. and Oct.-Nov. 9:30am-noon and 2-6pm; closed Dec.-Jan. €5, ages 6-14 €2.)* Ste-Mère-Église is accessible by STN **bus** *(☎ 02 33 77 44 88)* from Carentan *(15min.; 1 per day 12:50pm, return 6:35pm; €2.90).* Call the Carentan **tourist office** *(☎ 02 33 42 74 01)* for more info. To get to Carentan, take the train from Bayeux *(30min., 10 per day, €6.70).* Utah Beach and the Musée du Débarquement are only accessible by car from Ste-Mère-Église.

◎ SIGHTS NEAR CAEN

These eastern beaches were the landing sites for the Canadian and British armies. German defenders fired on them from expensive stone vacation houses along the beach. The beaches have changed considerably since 1944. The bunkers of Juno, Sword, and Gold Beaches have been replaced by resorts, and the somber taboos against recreation that characterize the American sites are not maintained here.

JUNO BEACH. The Canadians fought at Juno Beach. The last Canadian amphibious attack, in Sicily in 1942, had resulted in 75% casualties and ultimate failure. Bent on revenge at Juno, the Canadian soldiers pushed their attacks through without air or naval support, despite terrible losses. Opened in June 2003, the **Centre Juno Beach,** voie des Français Libres, is devoted to the story of Canadian soldiers during the war, as well as some exhibits on present-day Canada. (☎ *02 31 37 32 17; www.junobeach.org. Open daily Apr.-Sept. 9am-7pm; Oct.-Mar. 10am-1pm and 2-6pm; closed Jan. €6.50, students €5, under 8 free.)* The **Canadian Cemetery,** with just over 2000 tombs, is located at Bény-sur-Mer-Reviers; take Bus Verts #4 from Caen. The British anchored the easternmost flank of the invasion with their landing at **Sword Beach.** This enormously successful mission was accomplished with the help of the quirky "Hobart's Funnies," tanks outlandishly fitted with bridge-building, mine-sweeping, and ditch-digging apparati.

BENOUVILLE. It was here that British paratroopers captured Pegasus Bridge within 10min. of landing and held it until Scottish reinforcements arrived. The **Musée des Troupes Aéroportées Britanniques,** also known as the **Mémorial Pégasus,** av. du Major Howard, at the Pegasus Bridge between Benouville and Ranville, recounts the operations of the British Parachute Brigades, the first of the Allies to arrive in Normandy on the night of June 5, 1944. Take Bus Verts #1 from Caen to Mairie in Benouville. Continue down the road, take a right at the roundabout, and cross the bridge. (☎ *02 31 78 19 44; www.normandy1944.com. Open daily May-Sept. 9:30am-6:30pm; Oct.-Nov. and Feb.-Apr. 10am-1pm and 2-5pm. Closed last 2 weeks of Dec. €5, students and children €3.50.)* One of the largest of the 16 British cemeteries is 1.5km away in Ranville. The only French troops involved in the D-Day landings came ashore at Ouistreham, at the mouth of the Orne River. Life on the other side is memorialized in **Le Grand Bunker: Musée du Mur de l'Atlantique,** av. du 6 Juin, where five levels of weaponry and mannequins recreate history based on the recollections of British Lieutenant Bob Orrell, who captured the tower on June 9, 1944. (☎ *02 31 97 28 69; bunkermusée@aol.com. €6, children 6-12 €4. Open daily Feb. to mid-Nov. 10am-6pm; Apr.-Sept. 9am-7pm.)* The **Musée n°4 Commando,** pl. Alfred Thomas, across from the casino, tells the tale of the landings at Sword Beach through scale models, photographs of destroyed buildings, and sample weapons and uniforms. (☎ *02 31 96 63 10. Open daily Mar.-Oct. 10:30am-6pm. €4, students and children €2.30, under 10 free.)* The museums and the Ouistreham **tourist office** lie in a row: take Bus Verts #1 from Caen and get off at Centre in Ouistreham; turn right down rue Général Leclerc, turn left on av. de la Mer and follow it to the beach. The tourist office will be directly ahead, Musée n°4 Commando is on the left, and the Grand Bunker will be down av. du 6 Juin to the right.

CHERBOURG

Strategically located at the tip of the Cotentin peninsula, Cherbourg (pop. 44,000) was the Allies's "Gateway to France," their major supply port following the D-Day offensive of 1944. Today the town's numerous ferry lines shuttle tourists from France to England and Ireland. With its ethnic eateries, well-stocked bookstores, and unusual boutiques, Cherbourg, while short on noteworthy sights, has a vibrant undercurrent and plenty to keep one busy between ports.

☞ TRANSPORTATION. Ferries leave from the *gare maritime,* northeast of the town center, along bd. Maritime (open daily 5:30am-11:30pm). **Irish Ferries** goes to Rosslare about every other day (☎ 02 33 23 44 44; www.irishferries.com). **P&O European Ferries** goes to Portsmouth (☎ 08 25 12 01 56; www.POferries.com) and **Brittany Ferries** (☎ 08 25 82 88 28; www.brittanyferries.com) to Poole (see **Getting There:**

By Boat, p. 23). It is essential to both reserve ahead and check the most up-to-date ferry schedules. **Trains** run to Bayeux (1hr., 10 per day, €13.30) and Rennes (3½hr., 3 per day, €28.80) via Lison; Caen (1½hr., 13 per day, €16.60); Paris (3hr., 7 per day, €36.60); Rouen (4½hr., 4 per day, €30.90). To reach the train station (☎08 92 35 35 35; open daily 5:30am-7:30pm), take bd. Felix Amiot, go left at the round-about onto av. Aristide Briand, which becomes av. Carnot. Turn right at the end of the canal onto av. Millet; the station will be ahead on the left (25 minutes). **STN** (☎02 33 88 51 00; fax 02 33 43 28 43) sends **buses** around the region; the bus station is across the street from the train station. (Open M-F 9am-noon and 2-6pm.) **Zephir** circles within the city and has a stop in front of the STN office. The hostel rents **bikes** in the summer, and **taxis** (☎02 33 53 36 38) wait at the train station and at the top of quai Alexandre III by the tourist office and the bridge.

⚑ PRACTICAL INFORMATION. To get to the **tourist office,** 2 quai Alexandre III, and the center of town, turn right from the terminal onto bd. Felix Amiot. At the roundabout, go straight and continue around the bend to the left. Turn right over the first bridge; the tourist office is on the left (20 minutes). The staff hands out a thorough city guide and a regional events calendar and leads hikes and bus tours in summer; reservations are required. (☎02 33 93 52 02; www.ot-cherbourg-coten-tin.fr. Open July-Aug. M-Sa 9am-6:30pm, Su 10am-12:30pm; June M-Sa 9am-12:30pm and 2-6:30pm; Sept.-May M-Sa 9am-12:30pm and 2-6pm.) An annex is open at the *gare maritime.* (☎02 33 44 39 92. Open daily June-July 7am-noon and 2-8pm; Sept.-May closes at 6pm.) **Currency exchange** is available at the ferry terminal or at banks around **place Gréville.** Other services include: a **laundromat** at 62 rue au Blé (open daily 7am-8pm), a **pharmacy,** Pharmacie Goffin, at 1 pl. du Général de Gaulle, off of rue Maréchal Foch (☎02 33 20 41 29; open daily 9am-12:30pm and 2-7:30pm); **Internet** access at the Forum Espace Culture, pl. Centrale, a large music and bookstore off rue au Blé (☎02 33 78 19 30; open M 2-7pm, Tu-Sa 10am-7pm; €1.50 per 10min., €2.35 per 30min.), and at Archesys, 16 rue de l'Union, by the hostel. (☎02 33 53 04 93. Open Tu-F 11:30am-10pm, Sa 11:30am-midnight, Su 2-10pm. €0.05 per min., €5 per hr.) A **post office** is at 1 rue de l'Ancien Quai, at pl. Divette. (☎02 33 08 87 01. Open M-F 8am-7pm, Sa 8:30am-noon.) Branch offices are at 2 av. Carnot (☎02 33 10 00 30) near the ferry terminal and at 4 rue de Commerce. (☎02 33 10 12 50. Open M-F 9:30am-noon and 1:30-6pm, Sa 10am-4pm.) **Postal Code:** 50100.

⚏ ACCOMMODATIONS AND FOOD. The tourist office has lists of *chambres d'hôte* (around €23) and campsites. The cheapest option is the ▧**Auberge de Jeunesse (HI) ❷,** 57 rue de l'Abbaye, with some of the best facilities you'll find in a hostel in Normandy. From the tourist office, turn left onto quai de Caligny, then left on rue de Port, which becomes rue Tour Carrée and rue de la Paix. Bear left on rue de l'Union, which feeds into rue de l'Abbey (10 minutes). From the station, take bus #3 or 5 to Arsenal (last bus around 7:30pm); the hostel is across the street from the bus stop. Across town from the train station, it may not be the best option for those planning an in-and-out stay. The hostel has 100 beds in spotless, modern two- to five-person rooms, each with a sink, shower, and lockers (bring your own lock). A kitchen, bar, TV, foosball table, and pool table are also on the premises. A bit institutional, the hostel is not the most conducive to meeting people. (☎02 33 78 15 15; cherbourg@fuaj.org. Internet with a France Télécom phone card. Breakfast included. Bike rental available, approx. €8 per half-day, €12.50 per day. Reception 9am-noon and 6-11pm. Lockout 1-6pm; guests can enter after 1pm if they've already checked in. Bunks €16.05, for 2 nights €29.30; €18.95/€35.10 for non-HI members.) The amiable staff at **Hôtel de la Gare ❷,** 10 pl. Jean-Jaurès, lets large, well-tended rooms painted in bright hues, making this the perfect stopover for an early morning train. Most rooms have TV. (☎02 33 43 06 81; fax 02 33 43 12 20. Breakfast €5.50-6.50. Reception 7am-10pm. Singles and doubles €23-25, with shower €32-36, with shower and toilet €37-40; triples and quads €54-63. MC/V.)

There is a huge **market** on pl. du Théâtre (Tu and Sa 8am-1pm, Th until 6pm), a **Carrefour supermarket,** quai de l'Entrepôt, next to the station (open M-Sa 8:30am-9pm), and a **Proxi,** 15-17 rue de l'Union, near the hostel. (Open M-Sa 8:30am-1pm and 2:30-7:45pm, Su 9am-12:45pm and 5-7:45pm.)

Bars and inexpensive ethnic restaurants line **rue de la Paix,** between the hostel and pl. de la République, where kebabs go for €2.50-6.50 and are typically garnished with fries. **Crêperie Ty-Billic ❷,** 73 rue au Blé, is a tourist-free haven with floor-to-ceiling windows, earthenware dishes, and elegant decor. Two *galettes,* two crêpes, and one cider run €10-13.50. (☎02 33 01 11 90. Open Tu-Sa 11am-2pm and 7-11pm. Dessert €2.50-5.40. MC/V.) For a more upscale meal in a secluded stone courtyard, **L'Antidote ❸,** 41 rue au Blé, serves delicious meat and fish entrees (€10-15), exquisite desserts (€5), and a wide selection of wines. Reserve ahead on weekends. (☎02 33 78 01 28. Open Sept.-June Tu-Sa 10am-2:30pm and 6pm-1am; July-Aug. Tu-Sa 10am-1am. Hours may vary. Kitchen closes at 11pm. MC/V.)

🄖🄙 **SIGHTS AND ENTERTAINMENT.** Cherbourg's newest attraction is **La Cité de la Mer.** At the Gare Maritime Transatlantique, across the bridge from the tourist office, the vast complex is dedicated to the underwater exploits of men and animals. Six thousand creatures swim in the site's cylindrical aquarium, the tallest in Europe, but the highlight of the visit is a full audioguided walking tour (in French or English) of Le Redoutable, the world's largest nuclear submarine open to the public (ages 6 and over only). Convenient to the ferry terminal and equipped with a post office, tourist office, restaurant, and bar, La Cité de la Mer may be the most interesting way to pass an afternoon in Cherbourg. (☎08 25 00 25 50; www.citedelamer.com. Open June-Aug. 9:30am-7pm; Sept.-May 10am-6pm. Last entry 1hr. before closing. Closed Jan. and Mon. from mid-Nov. to mid-Dec. May-Sept. €13, ages 6-17 €9.50; Oct.-Apr. €11.50/€8.50; year-round under 6 free. Student discount.)

Founded by Mathilde, granddaughter of William the Conqueror and daughter of England's King Henry I, the semi-ruined stone skeleton of the 12th-century **Abbaye du Vœu** and its gardens lie at the western edge of town, on your right 5min. past the hostel on rue de l'Abbaye. (☎02 33 87 89 19. The city provides guided tours of the abbey July-Aug. Su 2:30pm. Gardens open daily. Free.) With intricate latticework, pillars painted in wallpaper-like patterns, and dark, angular windows, the **Basilique de la Trinité,** 8 pl. Napoléon, off quai de Caligny, blends centuries of architectural styles. Sixteenth-century carvings above the nave include a grotesque skeleton on the left, who reminds that "death comes for us all." (☎02 33 53 10 63. Open daily 8:30am-7pm.)

The streets around **place Central** are filled with bars and late-night eateries, while **rue de la Paix** has more underground venues, including poolhouses and a discotheque. Multilingual crowds congregate nightly under rotating art exhibits and insect-shaped metal lanterns at laid-back **Art's Café,** 69 rue au Blé. (☎02 33 53 55 11. Concerts F-Sa, live DJ other nights. Beer €2, mixed drinks €4.20. Open July-Aug. M-Sa 2pm-2am; Sept.-June 11am-1am. AmEx/MC/V.) **Le Solier,** 52 Grande Rue, caters to a jovial older crowd of locals and plays a good mix of Celtic music and blues in a pub-like atmosphere. (☎02 33 94 76 63; www.multimedia.com/lesolier. Beer €1.15-2.70. Liquor €3.40-5. Open M-Sa June-Sept. 6pm-2am; Oct.-May 6pm-1am. AmEx/MC/V.) The second week of October, Cherbourg hosts the 21st annual **Festival des Cinémas d'Irlande et de Grande Bretagne** (☎02 33 93 38 94), celebrating films from across the Channel.

GRANVILLE

In 1439, the expatriate Lord Jean d'Argouges sold his great-grandmother's dowry, the rocky peninsula of Granville, to the English. It quickly became a fortified city, from which the English spent 30 years trying to take Mont-St-Michel. The exceptional seaside charms of Granville (pop. 13,700) include a beautiful beach, a walled-in, elevated *haute ville*, and a lively cultural scene. It is a popular base for trips to Mont-St-Michel and the Chausey Islands, but its distance from Paris keeps it less crowded and less expensive than might be expected.

⌨ TRANSPORTATION AND PRACTICAL INFORMATION

The **train station**, pl. Pierre Sémard, off av. Maréchal Leclerc, has service to: Bayeux *(*2hr., 2 per day, €16) via Coutances; Cherbourg (3hr., 2 per day, €20) via Coutances and Lison; Paris (3hr., 5 per day, €34). The info office is open M-Sa 9:10am-noon and 2-6:30pm, Su 10:10am-noon and 1:45-7:30pm.

SNCF buses go to Coutances (30min., 3 per day, €7). **Hugo Express** (☎02 33 61 08 88), at the *gare maritime*, sails to Guernesey (2hr.; 3 per week; €25, ages 17-25 €20, ages 4-16 €15) and Jersey (1¼hr.; 7-13 per week; €25/€20/€15). Ask about family rates. **Compagnie Corsaire** also sails to the Chauseys. Schedules change frequently. (☎08 25 16 80 50; www.compagniecorsaire.com. Trip takes 50min. Ferries daily. Round-trip €16.14, ages 3-14 €9.74.)

To reach the city center from the train station, follow av. Maréchal Leclerc, which becomes rue Couraye. The easiest access to the *haute ville* is the stairwell in front of the casino. The **tourist office**, 4 cours Jonville, is around the corner on your right as soon as you reach the main *place*. They offer tours of the city, a helpful city guide with map, and the *Calendrier des manifestations*, a list of summer events in town. (☎02 33 91 30 03; www.ville-granville.fr. Office open July-Aug. M-Sa 9am-1pm and 2-7pm, Su 10am-1pm; Sept.-June M-F 9am-noon and 2-6pm, Sa 9am-12:30pm and 2-6pm. Tours in French July-Aug. Tu and F-Sa at 3pm, €2.) Access the **Internet** at the post office or at the back of the bar La Citrouille, 8 rue St-Sauveur. (☎02 33 51 35 51. €1 per 15min., €3 per hr. Open daily July-Aug. 9am-2am; Sept.-June M 5pm-1am, Tu-Sa 9am-1am.) Other services include: **ATMs** on av. Maréchal Leclerc, a **laundromat**, 10 rue St-Sauvier (open daily 7am-9pm), **police** at rue du Port (☎02 33 91 27 50), a **hospital** at rue des Menneries (☎02 33 91 50 00), and a **pharmacy**, Pharmacie Centrale, at 47 rue le Campion, across from the tourist office. (Open M-F 9am-12:30pm and 2-7:30pm, Sa 9am-1pm and 2-7pm). The **post office**, 8 cours Jonville, has **currency exchange**, fax, photocopying, and a Cyberposte. (☎02 33 91 12 30. Open M-F 8:30am-12:30pm and 1:30-6:30pm, Sa 8:30am-noon.) **Postal Code:** 50400.

⌂ ACCOMMODATIONS

Hotels and the hostel are packed in summer. To reach ▓**Hôtel le Michelet ❷**, 5 rue Jules Michelet, from the tourist office, head straight across pl. de Gaulle onto rue Paul Poirier. When rue Paul Poirier ends, take a right onto rue Georges Clemenceau (becomes av. de la Libération), then a sharp left up the hill onto rue Jules Michelet. The comfortable, modern rooms, some with balcony and bathroom big enough to hold another bed, are in a calm location near the beach. (☎02 33 50 06 55; fax 02 33 50 12 25. Breakfast €5. Reception 7am-10pm. Doubles €22-23; with toilet €29-30; with shower, toilet, and TV €35-39; with bath, toilet, and TV €44-48. Extra bed €9. Showers €2.50 if in room. AmEx/MC/V.) To get to the **Auberge de Jeunesse (HI) ❷**, bd. des Amiraux Granvillais, from the train station, turn right onto av. Maréchal Leclerc and follow it downhill. Just before the town center, turn left

N O R M A N D Y

onto rue St-Sauveur; head right when the road forks and look for "Centre Nautisme" signs straight ahead. To get to reception, follow sign that says *accueil visiteurs*. Part of a huge sailing center, it runs week-long camps July-August. Dorms are comfortable and newly redone. There is also sailing (€23 per hour), kayaking (single €10, double €15), and parasailing for €15. (☎ 02 33 91 22 62; fax 02 33 50 51 99. Breakfast €2.75, for non-HI members €3.60. Meals €9/€11. Sheets €3.80/€4. Office open 9am-noon and 2-6pm. Code for late entry. Closed last 2 weeks of December. Singles €18.50/€21; 2-bed dorms €14.50/€16.80 per person; 4-bed dorms €10.50/€12.50 per person. AmEx/MC/V.) Run by accommodating owners, **Hôtel Terminus ❷**, 5 pl. Pierre Sémard, right across from the train station, features neatly furnished rooms with bright wallpaper and carpets and a huge aquarium downstairs. All rooms have toilet and TV. (☎ 02 33 50 02 05. Breakfast €4.50. Reception 8am-10:30pm. Reserve ahead. Singles €20, with shower €26; doubles €26, with shower €32, with bath €33; triples €34-41; quads €39-46. MC/V.) **Hôtel de la Gare ❷**, 135 rue Couraye, just as close to the train station as Hotel Terminus, has adequate rooms over a *brasserie*. (☎ 02 33 50 00 05; fax 02 33 51 96 06. Breakfast €4.50. May-Sept. singles €23; singles and doubles with shower €27, with bath €31-38; triples €47. Prices slightly lower Jan.-Apr. Extra bed €8. MC/V.)

🖸 FOOD

There are **markets** on cours Jonville (Sa 9am-3pm) and on pl. du 11 Novembre 1918 (W 8am-1pm). For **groceries**, head to **Marché Plus**, 107 rue de Couraye. (Open M-Sa 7am-9pm, Su 9am-1pm.) Skip the pricey restaurants in town for one of the small *crêperies* of the *haute ville* near the Église de Notre-Dame.

Try the savory *galettes* (€3.85-7.70), dessert crêpes (€1.70-6.80), and meat dishes (€10.50-11) at 🖾**La Gourmandise ❷**, 37 rue St-Jean, amid the stone walls and cobblestoned streets of the *haute ville*. (☎ 02 33 50 65 16. Open M-Sa noon-3pm and 7-11pm. Open Su in July and August. AmEx/MC/V.) The wonderful Turkish cuisine, authentic decor, and cozy pillow-covered window seats at **La Porte de Byzance ❷**, 2 av. de la Libération, set it apart from the other *salons de thé*. (☎ 02 33 51 49 22. *Prix fixe menus* €9-11, starters €4, *plats* €8-9. Open daily noon-3pm and 6pm-midnight. Hours may vary. MC/V.) Near the hostel, **Monte Pego ❷**, 13 rue St-Sauveur, serves sizeable and delicious Italian dishes for €6.80-13.50. Freshly prepared pizzas slide out of a brick oven that stands amid packed tables. (☎ 02 33 90 74 44. Open daily July-Aug. noon-2pm and 7-10pm; Sept.-June closed M and Su. Wine €13.50 a bottle. MC/V.) Kebab and ice cream stands cluster near the beach.

👁 🎭 SIGHTS AND ENTERTAINMENT

Granville's old English walled city, known as the *haute ville*, is its most charming attraction. It stretches from the casino to the somber Église Notre-Dame du Cap-Lihou, pl. du Parvis Notre Dame (where classical concerts are held on summer weekends). A walk around the outer walls of the *haute ville* affords an incredible view of the surrounding shoreline. Stretching northward from the *vieille ville* is Granville's most popular beach. It features a stone swimming pool that gets replenished by the tide, but you'll also find quiet stretches of sand past the port on the opposite side of the point. Anchored at the edge of the *haute ville* at the pl. de l'Isthme, above a vista of sea, sky, and rooftops, is the **Musée Richard Anacréon**, the area's only 20th-century art museum. Featuring artists like Picasso and Dufy, exhibits focus on the first half of the century, and on Fauvism in particular. Intriguing temporary exhibits supplement the permanent collection during the summer. (☎ 02 33 51 02 94; fax 02 33 51 98 52. Open July-Sept. M and W-Su 11am-6pm; Oct.-June W-Su 2-6pm. €2.50, students and children €1.30, permanent collection Oct.-June €1.60/€1.)

NORMANDY

A coastal path leads from the beach promenade to the stairs below the clifftop **Musée Christian Dior,** in the childhood home of Granville's most famous son. This year, the fashion demigod's best creations are on display in honor of the label's 100th anniversary. The museum also provides a sniff of Dior's earliest perfumes and screens runway footage of the label's latest fashions. The villa's gardens are restored to resemble those designed from 1905 to 1930 by Dior and his mother. A spectacular ocean view opens from the rose-threaded white terrace. (☎02 33 61 48 21; museechristiandior@wanadoo.fr. Open mid-May to late Sept. 10am-12:30pm and 2-6:30pm. Gardens 9am-8pm. €5, students and over 60 €4, under 12 free.)

From May to September, boats leave daily for the **Chausey Islands,** a sparsely inhabited archipelago of 52-365 islets, depending on the tide (for ferry info, see **Practical Information**). Visitors revel in the idyllic natural beauty of the site.

Nightlife is limited and pleasantly low-key. The best bet in town is the laidback ▓**La Citrouille,** 8 rue St-Sauveur, which features occasional live concerts in the evenings and plays good music otherwise. Funky artwork, cheap drinks, and cheap Internet access make this a good place to chill. (☎02 33 51 35 51. Beer €1.10-3.20. Liquor €2. Wine €1.50. Open daily July-Aug. 9am-2am; Sept.-June M 5pm-1am, Tu-Sa 9am-1am. MC/V.) Relaxed mid-summer crowds come straight from the beach to the **Bar les Amiraux,** bd. des Amiraux, across from the hostel, where barrel-bottomed tables fill cave-like alcoves and music carries to a large outdoor area. (☎02 33 50 12 83. Cocktails €5.80-7.25. Aperitifs €2-5.95. Liquor €5. Open M-Sa 1pm-1am, Su 3pm-1am. Closes at 2am July-Aug.)

Granville hosts **Carnaval** every year on the Sunday before Mardi Gras and the **Grand Pardon de la Mer,** a maritime festival, at the end of July. Famous writers come down for the **Journées des Livres,** a book fair held in the first week of August. In keeping with its large number of antique shops, Granville hosts a **Salon des Antiquitaires** in mid-August.

▐ DAYTRIP FROM GRANVILLE

COUTANCES

SNCF runs buses to Granville (30min., 3 per day, €7). To reach the cathedral from the bus station, walk straight ahead to the roundabout and turn right onto rue de la Croute, then turn at the first left onto rue de la Mission. Take the second right onto rue Maréchal Foch, then take the first left.

Miraculously unscathed by World War II, the 13th-century **cathedral** of Coutances (pop. 11,000) is second in beauty perhaps only to Chartres. Flanked by the churches of St-Pierre and St-Nicolas, the cathedral forms the centerpoint of the town's three-spired skyline, visible for miles. The cathedral's impressive lantern-tower, a three-tiered structure that catapults upward from the choir loft, fills the interior with light. During the French Revolution, the majestic building was delegated the less-than-glamorous function of theater/grain store, but has since regained its ecclesiastical status. Tours organized by the tourist office guide visitors through its illuminated galleries. (Open daily 8am-7pm. Tours in late May, June, and Sept. in French M-F and Su 2:30pm; July-Aug. 3 per day in French M-F 10:30am, 2:30, 4pm (except Sa and Su morning); in English Tu and Th 2pm. Mass Sa 6:30pm, Su 11am. Tours €5.50, ages 10-18 and students €4.50.)

The ingeniously designed flowerbeds and lacquered lawns of the peaceful, pleasant **Jardin des Plantes,** near the tourist office, are among the oldest in France. The garden features intricate arrangements, including the figures of the Chinese zodiac, a spiraling hedge you can walk through, and creatively illuminated grounds on summer nights. (Open daily July-Aug. 9am-11:30pm; Apr.-June and Sept. 9am-8pm; Oct.-Mar. 9am-5pm.)

NORMANDY

To reach the **tourist office,** pl. Georges Leclerc, from the front of the cathedral, go straight, then take the first left. The well-organized bureau has info on concerts, outdoor activities, and regional sites. (☎02 33 19 08 10; tourisme-coutances@wanadoo.fr. Open July-Aug. M-W and F 10am-12:30pm and 2-6:30pm, Th 10am-6:30pm, Sa 10am-12:30pm and 2-6pm, Su 10am-1pm; June and Sept. M-W and F 10am-12:30pm and 2-6pm, Th 10am-6pm, Sa 10am-12:30pm and 2-5pm; Oct.-May closes Su at 5pm.) For a **taxi** call ☎02 33 45 01 45 or 02 33 07 11 11.

Vendors selling fruits and vegetables set up at the pl. du Général de Gaulle, near the steps to the cathedral (Th 6am-5pm, Sa 7am-1pm). In a colorful space suffused with soft jazz melodies, **Le Râtelier ❶,** 3bis rue Georges Clémenceau, near the tourist office, serves *galettes* (€2.30-9) and dessert crêpes (€2.30-8) on plates depicting life in the French countryside. (☎02 33 45 56 52. Open Tu-Sa 11:45am-2pm and 6:30-11pm. Fixed *menus* €7.50-16.20. Tea €1.70. MC/V.) For provisions, there's a **Marché Plus** at 21-23 rue Tancrède. (Open M-Sa 7am-9pm, Su 9am-1pm.)

There are many treasures to be found within 4-5km of town; the brochure *Monuments et Lieux de Visite* (available in English at the tourist office) covers a number of châteaux, manors, museums, and abbeys a quick drive away. The ruins of **Château de Gratot** are surrounded by a moat and encompass four towers steeped in local legends. (☎02 33 45 18 49. Sept.-May call ☎02 31 57 18 30. Open daily 10am-7pm. €3, ages 10-18 €1.50.)

On the week of Ascension Thursday (Apr. 30-May 7, 2005, Coutances celebrates the 24th annual **Jazz sous les Pommiers,** a week of more than 30 free concerts in the streets and bars. (☎02 33 76 78 61; www.jazzsouslespommiers.com.)

MONT-ST-MICHEL

Visitors are stunned when they round the last bend in the road and Mont-St-Michel (pop. 42) appears on the horizon. It's little wonder that pilgrims in the Middle Ages considered the pyramidal complex an image of paradise on earth and that the English expended such effort trying to capture it. While Brittany and Normandy both understandably claim the Mont, it officially belongs to the latter as a result of an ancient decision to employ the river as a natural divider. A trip into the abbey, with or without a tour, is an indispensable part of the experience, but no less enthralling are the views of soaring spires, stunning marshland, and sheep-dotted fields from the crags and coils around the Mont's outer walls.

▐▀ TRANSPORTATION

Trains: In Pontorson (☎02 33 60 00 35). Open M-Sa 9:15-11:45am and 2:45-7pm, Su 1:30-7pm. To: **Dinan** (1hr., 2-3 per day, €7.40); **Granville** (1hr.; M-F 3 per day, Sa-Su 2 per day; €8.20) via **Folligny; Paris** (3½hr., 3 per day, €39.60 plus TGV supplement) via **Caen; St-Malo** (90min., 2-3 per day, €6.80) via **Dol.**

Buses: Les Courriers Bretons, 104 rue Couesnon (☎02 99 19 70 70) in Pontorson. Buses leave Mont-St-Michel from its entrance at Porte de l'Avancée, and leave Pontorson from outside the train station and the Courriers Bretons office. Buy tickets on board; €1.70. Mont and Pontorson buses run M-Sa about 12 per day, 6 on Su. Last bus back from the Mont 8pm. The same company also runs to **Rennes** (1½hr.; June-Sept. M-Sa 5 per day, Su 3 per day; Sept.-June M-Sa 6 per day, 1 on Su; €11) and **St-Malo** (1½hr.; July-Aug. 3-4 per day, Sept.-June 1-2 per day; €9). Office open July-Aug. M-F 10am-noon and 4-7pm.

Bike Rental: Couesnon Motoculture, 1bis rue du Couesnon (☎02 33 60 11 40), in Pontorson. €7 per half-day, €12 per day, €23 for 2 days, €32 for 3 days. Passport deposit. Open Tu-Sa 8:30am-noon and 2-6:30pm. AmEx/MC/V.

■ ⁊ ORIENTATION AND PRACTICAL INFORMATION

Mont-St-Michel is on the border between Brittany and Normandy. **Pontorson,** 9km due south down D976, has the closest train station, supermarket, and affordable hotels. The tourist office on the Mont is just inside the Porte de l'Avancée, the only entrance. **Grande Rue** is the town's main thoroughfare. There's no public transportation off the Mont late at night. Biking from Pontorson takes about 1hr. on terrain that is relatively flat but not always bike-friendly. The path next to the Couesnon River may be the best route.

Tourist Office at Mont-St-Michel: (☎02 33 60 14 30) Helpful but busy multilingual staff has info on sites and lodging. A free *horaire des marées* (tidetable) will inform you whether your view will be of ocean or sandy marsh. Hours vary in low season. Open July-Aug. M-Sa 9am-7pm, Su 9am-1pm and 2-7pm; Apr.-June and Sept. M-Sa 9am-12:30pm and 2-6:30pm, Su 9am-noon and 2-6pm; Nov.-Feb. and Mar.-Oct. M-Sa 9am-noon and 2-6pm, Su 10am-noon and 2-5pm.

Tourist Office in Pontorson: pl. de l'Église (☎02 33 60 20 65; mont.st.michel.pontorson@wanadoo.fr), has maps and info on walking tours, accommodations, and the Mont. Internet access €4.50 per 30min., €8 per hr. Open July-Aug. M-F 9am-noon and 2-6pm, Sa 10am-noon and 3-6pm, Su 10am-noon. Sept.-June closed Su.

Laundromat: on the rue St-Michel next to the Champion supermarket (see **Food**). From the train station, take a right on rue Dr. Bailleul, following the road as it becomes bd. Général de Gaulle. At the roundabout, take the road to your right (the D976) to Mont-St-Michel, and the laundromat will be just ahead on the right. Open daily 7am-9pm.

Police: entrance just to the left of the Porte de l'Avancée before you enter (☎02 33 60 14 42). Open daily 11am-1pm and 5:30-7:30pm. Also at chausée de Ville Chérel in Pontorson (☎02 33 60 00 17).

Hospital: Emergency services are at 59 rue de la Liberté in Avranches (☎02 33 89 40 00). A small clinic on the Mont, across from the post office.

Internet Access: At the Pontorson tourist office (see above). Also on the Mont on the 2nd floor of Hôtel de la Croix-Blanche, Grand Rue. (☎02 33 60 14 04). One unit per min. with a *Télécarte.*

Post Office: Grande Rue (☎02 33 89 65 00), about 100m to the right of Porte de l'Avancée. **Currency exchange** at tolerable rates. Open July-Aug. M-Sa 9:30am-5:30pm, Su 9am-noon and 1:15-5:30pm; June M-F 9am-5:30pm, Sa 9am-4pm; mid-Mar. to May M-F 9am-noon and 2-5pm, Sa 9am-noon; Jan. to mid-Mar. M-F 9am-noon and 1:30-4:30pm, Sa 9am-noon. In Pontorson, the main branch at 16 rue St-Michel, across from the tourist office, has **currency exchange** and fax. (☎02 33 89 17 71. Open M-F 8:30am-noon and 2-5:30pm, Sa 8:30am-noon.)

Postal Code: 50170.

⁊ ACCOMMODATIONS

Forget about staying on the Mont unless St. Michel himself is bankrolling your visit. More affordable lodging is available in Pontorson, or some choose to day-trip to the Mont from St-Malo. There are also a number of campsites and *chambres d'hôte* in the vicinity (the tourist office in Pontorson or on the Mont can point you in the right direction). Reserve ahead; prices climb faster than the spring tide.

NORMANDY

FRÈRE TOBIE, BROTHER OF JERUSALEM

Frère Tobie, age 26, is a native Breton and monk at Mont-St-Michel. He is a young man who wears a monk's full-length dark blue robe and sandals. Attached to his belt, with his prayer beads, is a mobile phone.

LG: What is it like to live here?

A: Life on the Mont is entirely different than elsewhere, because this is not just a monastery but also a tourist site, a place of pilgrimage, and an ancient monument. Life varies each day, but for us essentially this is a place of sanctuary, although almost three million people visit each year. Living in the midst of the sea, we have to pay attention to the tides, because they dictate when we can venture off the island. At night and in the early morning the Mont is completely deserted. When you look out on the bay, with 500km of sand, it is a great desert.

LG: What is the monastic community like here?

A: We have two communities who live in parallel and have liturgies together. We have four monks and seven nuns. We hope to become more numerous over time, with more brothers and sisters from other communities. The community is here indefinitely; our superior can send us elsewhere, because we pledged obedience.

LG: What is a normal day for you?

A: Our day begins at 6am. At 6:30 we have 30min. of silent

Centre Duguesclin (HI), rue du Général Patton, Pontorson (☎/fax 02 33 60 18 65; aj@ville-pontorson.fr). At the station, turn right on the main road, then left on rue Couesnon. Take the 3rd right on rue St-Michel. Cut diagonally across the square from the tourist office, following signs to the church. Bear left in front of the church on rue Hédou. At the end, turn right on rue Général Patton. (10min.) Clean, bare 2-, 4-, and 6-person single-sex dorms in a stone house with communal lounge, kitchen, and dining area. Breakfast €3.20. Sheets €2.70. Reception July-Aug. 8am-9pm; Sept.-June 8am-noon and 5-9pm. Lockout Sept.-June noon-5pm. Closed mid-Oct. to Easter. Call at least 1 week ahead, 1 month in the summer. Dorms €8.50 for members, €9.50 for non-members. ❶

Hôtel le Grillon, 37 rue du Couesnon, on the right after rue St-Michel, Pontorson (☎02 33 60 17 80). Pleasant owners rent 5 quiet, small, and very clean rooms behind a cheery *crêperie*. All with shower and some with skylights. Breakfast €5. Reception M-W and F-Su 7am-10pm; closed W afternoon. Reserve 1 week ahead July-Aug. Doubles €29, with toilet €32. Extra bed €5. MC/V. ❸

Hôtel du Guesclin, Grande Rue, Mont-St-Michel (☎02 33 60 14 10) halfway up the Grande Rue on the right side. 10 comfortable rooms, some with chandeliers and an ocean view, are one of the best bets for staying on the Mont itself. Half-board available at the restaurant downstairs. Breakfast €8. Reception 9am-9pm. Open Apr.-Nov. Doubles with bath, TV, and telephone €55-70, with bath €60-80; triples with bath €75-90; quads with bath €80-90. Extra bed €10. MC/V. ❺

Hôtel de l'Arrivée, 14 rue du Dr. Tizon, Pontorson (☎/fax 02 33 60 01 57), over a bar across the street from the station, on the other side of the Courriers Bretons office. With modern rooms and light wooden floors, this hotel offers low prices, access to the bus and train stations, and a quiet night's rest. Some of the rooms can get chilly at night. Breakfast €5.50. Reception 8am-10pm (except M Sept.-June). Singles and doubles €15.40-19.90, with shower €24.90-26.90, with shower and toilet €35; triples with shower €40; quads with shower and toilet €65. Extra bed €5. MC/V. ❷

Hôtel de France et Vauban, 50 bd. Clemenceau, Pontorson (☎02 33 60 03 84; www.hotel-france-vauban.com), across from the station on the left. Pleasant bedrooms (all with shower or bath and most with TV and phone) have full-length mirrors and big bathrooms; some rooms have added perks like luxurious sofas or terraces. Breakfast €7. Reception 8am-11pm, in the Restaurant l'Orson Bridge Café. Reserve ahead in summer. Doubles €30, with toilet €45-49;

triples €30, with toilet €65-72; quads with toilet €75. Mention *Let's Go* for a 10% discount during the low season. MC/V. ❸

▓ CAMPING

Camping Haliotis at Pontorson, chemin des Soupirs and rue du Général Patton (☎02 33 68 11 59; www.camping-haliotis-mont-saint-michel.com). Past the hostel on rue du Général Patton, a clearly marked path on the left leads to the site. Amid horses and haystacks, this 3-star site is like a mini resort, with a heated pool, jacuzzi, tennis courts, soccer field, gameroom, bar, and playground. Also included are spacious central bathrooms and free Internet. 25min. bike ride from the Mont on a path along the adjacent Couesnon River (on-site rental €5 per half-day, €9 per day). Open Apr.-Sept. Reception 7:30am-10pm. €4.20-4.50 per person, €1.95-2.50 per child; €3.50-4.50 per tent and car, €3.80-5 per caravan and car. Electricity €2.50-3. Wheelchair-accessible. MC/V. ❶

Camping du Mont-St-Michel, 1.75km from the Mont at the junction of D275 and N776 (☎02 33 60 22 10; www.le-mont-saint-michel.com). Get off at "La Caserne," the stop before the Mont on the Courriers Bretons line from Pontorson. Like a small town, with 350 spots and many dependent businesses. Bike rental and mini-golf. Laundry. Internet at the adjoining Hotel Motel Vert. (€5 per 30min., €8 per hr.) 24hr. reception. Mid-May to Sept. €6.10 per site, €3.90 per adult, €2.20 per child; early Feb.-Apr. and mid-Sept. to Oct. €4.90 per site, €3.20 per adult, under 10 €1.75. Shower included. ❶

Camping St-Michel, 35 rte. du Mont-St-Michel (☎02 33 70 96 90), is by the bay in Courtils, 9km from the Mont (9km). This 3-star site was named the most garden-like campsite in the *département.* Flowers surround the heated swimming pool, common room, small store, breakfast room, and a snack bar July-Aug. They rent bikes (€4.50 per half-day, €8 per day). Open mid-Mar. to mid-Oct. June-Aug. $4.80 per person, €1.80 per child under 7, €4.40 per car and tent. Extra tent €1.60. Electricity €2.50. Prices slightly reduced in low season. ❶

▐ FOOD

If you dare invest in more than a postcard on the Mont, look for local specialties like *agneau du pré salé* (lamb raised on the surrounding salt marshes) and *omelette poulard* (a fluffy soufflé-like dish; about €10-14). **Chapeau Rouge** ❸, Grande Rue, serves these delicacies at lower prices than most, in a homey wood-

prayer, and then *laudes,* the first services of the day. After breakfast we have a reading from the Bible. At noon we have daily mass—in the abbey in summer and the crypt in winter. We eat lunch in silence. In the afternoon we work. At 6:30pm, we have the adoration of the sacrament for an hour and Vespers, in which the public can participate. Later we eat dinner, also in silence, and then *complies,* our final service.

LG: What kind of work do you do?

A: Our vocation is being monks in the town, among people. Here at Mont-St-Michel, we divide our daily tasks; we have one brother who cooks, one who cleans and gardens, our superior who coordinates masses. I am the webmaster, so I develop Internet sites.

LG: Why did you pick monastic life?

A: The monastic life is chosen in response to a call from God. This is our answer. This call from God isn't an apparition, but a verification of spirituality. In the community, we have many possible routes: one brother converted after spending 20 years as a Communist. There are also those from Christian families who joined after finishing high school.

LG: What do you think of tourists?

A: For us, it's not difficult, because we need to interact with people. When they arrive at the top of the Mont, they are out of breath. Tired, they might be more able to receive the Mont's message. We have a mission here, and it allows this place to touch the hearts of those who come.

furnished dining room with stone walls. (☎ 02 33 60 14 29. Appetizers €6-8, *plats* €8-14, 3-course *menus* €12 and €13.50. Open daily 11:30am-2:30pm and 7-9pm. Sometimes closed at night. MC/V.) Find refuge from the tourist-trampled streets at **La Sirène ❶**, Grande Rue, past the post office, which serves fresh salads (€3-8) and bursting crêpes (€2-7.40) at comparatively cheap prices. (☎ 02 33 60 08 60. Open daily 9am-10pm. AmEx/MC/V.) For a splurge, get your eggs from **La Mère Poulard ❹**, Grande Rue, Mont-St-Michel, just on your left as you walk through the gates. The exorbitant prices (*menus* €15-65), are partly for the experience of watching cooks in traditional garb craft omelettes in copper pots over a wood fire. (☎ 02 33 89 68 68; www.mere-poulard.com. Open 11:30am-10:30pm. AmEx/MC/V.)

If you plan to picnic, arrive prepared, as there are no grocery stores within the walls. Pontorson has a **market** (W morning) on rue Couesnon and at pl. de la Mairie and a **Champion supermarket**, 2 rte. du Mont-St-Michel, just outside Pontorson. (☎ 02 33 60 37 38. Open July-Aug. M-Sa 9am-7:30pm, Su 9am-noon; Sept.-June M-Sa 9am-12:30pm and 2:30-7:30pm.) Pontorson's dining options are slim to say the least, but welcoming **Le Grillon ❶**, 37 rue Couesnon, serves well-prepared dinner and dessert crêpes (€1.70-6.40), salads (€2.50-6), and multi-course fixed *menus* (€8 and €14.50) at remarkably low prices. (☎ 02 33 60 17 80. Open M-W and F-Su noon-2pm and 7-10pm. MC/V.)

⬛ SIGHTS

Mont-St-Michel's **Grande Rue** is jam-packed with restaurants, souvenir shops, and tourists who love them. For more detailed information on Mont architecture, pick up one of the many guidebooks (€5-40), although brochures and tours are offered for free within the abbey walls. None of the "museums" on Grande Rue are worth the money or time. During the bi-monthly spring tides, the *mascaret* (initial wave) rushes in at 2m per second, flooding the beaches along the causeway. To see this event, you must be within the abbey two hours ahead of time. Grande Rue has countless little stairwells jutting off of it, some claustrophobically narrow or alarmingly vertiginous. The Chemin des Ramparts takes the curious on a circuit almost all the way around the base of the abbey's walls, where tiny windows set deep in stone peek out on the bay.

> **!** When the waters recede, it may be tempting to explore the sandy marsh around Mont-St-Michel, but pockets of quicksand and powerful, fast-moving tides (about 1m per second) that also happen to be the highest in France make this a dangerous venture. At a place where the sea is said to rush in at the "speed of a galloping horse," it's best to stay off the sand.

HISTORY. Legend holds that the Baie de St-Michel was created by a giant tidal wave that formed three islands: Tombelaine, Mont Dol, and Mont Tomba (meaning "mound" or "tomb"). So appealing was Tomba, the last island, that heaven wanted a piece of it. In AD 708, the Archangel Michael supposedly appeared to St-Aubert, Bishop of Avranches, and asked him to build a place of worship on the barren island. The story goes that it was not until Michael put a flaming finger through Aubert's head that the bishop heeded his vision. Four crypts were built, one in each cardinal direction, to support the base of a church on Tomba's 80m high point. These became the monastery's very first chapels, beginning with Notre-Dame-sous-Terre, which was completed in the 10th century and still stands below the nave of the existing abbey church. The Mont soon became as important a place for French pilgrims to visit as Rome and Jerusalem.

NORMANDY

In the 14th and 15th centuries, Mont-St-Michel was fortified against a 30-year English attack with ramparts designed by Abbot Jolivet. The Benedictines continued their work of copying and illuminating the *Manuscrits du Mont-St-Michel*, the remains of which are now on display in nearby Avranches. In 1789, the Revolutionary government turned the island into a prison, first jailing 600 monks, followed by Robespierre and 14,000 others who ranged from statesmen to common thieves. Closed as a prison in 1863, in 1874 Mont-St-Michel was classified as a national monument. In 1897, the church was topped with a neo-Gothic spire identical to the one atop Ste-Chapelle in Paris, and a copper and gold leaf statue of St. Michel. Around that time a new dike made the island a peninsula, facilitating tourist access. Today the abbey is again home to a small community of monks—no longer Benedictines, but the *moines* (monks) and *moniales* (nuns) of the Brothers and Sisters of Jerusalem.

ABBEY AND CRYPTS. The twisting road and ramparts end at the abbey entrance, but the steps continue to the **west terrace**—the entrance to the **abbey church,** a prime lookout point on the glassy waters of the bay, and the departure point for five free 1hr. English tours daily in summer. (Nine tours daily in French.) Mass is held daily at 12:15pm (entry to the abbey church for the service only free noon-12:15pm). The abbey, built over 1000 years ago, represents an ingenious compromise between the topographic constraints and the requirements of monastic life. The **church,** the most ornate portion of the abbey, spans an impressive 80m in length, thanks to ingenious planning over 1000 years ago. The interior's hodgepodge of architectural styles is the result of reconstruction following the collapse of half of the nave in 1103 and the Romanesque choir in 1421, as well as 13 separate fires over the past 1000 years. The adjacent **cloister,** framed by a unique arrangement of small columns in double rows, is the center of **La Merveille** (the Marvel): the 13th-century Gothic monastery so dubbed because of its record building time of 16 years. Beneath the church and the cloister are the Mont's frigid **crypts,** which can only be seen on 2hr. tours. The descent passes through the **refectory,** where the monks took their meals in silence as St. Benedict's rules were read. The **Chapelle St-Etienne,** below, was the chapel of the dead. Prisoners held on the Mont during the Revolution walked for hours on a giant wheel installed in the former monks' ossuary, their labor powering an elaborate pulley system that hoisted up supplies. Directly under the choir is the **Crypte des gros piliers,** whose pillars, 6m in circumference, were described by Victor Hugo as a forest of palm trees. The narrow abbey gardens, clinging to the side of the rock, surround the compound's exit. (☎02 33 89 80 00; www.monum.fr. Open May-Aug. 9am-7pm; Sept.-Apr. 9:30am-6pm. Last entrance 1hr. before closing. Closed Jan. 1, May 1, Nov. 1 and 11, and Dec. 25. €8, ages 18-25 €5; Oct.-Mar. first Su of the month free. A 2-3hr. conference tour with a guide (only in French) leaves once a day at 2pm (July-Aug. 4 times per day) and costs €4, ages 12-25 €3. Audio tour €4.50, or €5.50 for 2 sets of headphones.)

SPECTACLES. At night, the lit Mont is best seen either from the causeway entrance or from across the bay in Avranches. (Illumination every day at nightfall in the summertime.) At night, a separate entrance opens into the abbey, from which there is an unforgettable view of the pitch-black skies above the bay. However, be aware there is no public transportation off the Mont at night. (Mid-July to Aug. only. Call ahead to reserve. M-Sa 9pm-12:30am, last entrance 11:30pm. There is a musical performance in the gardens at night. Admission same as above.) The **St-Michel d'Automne** festival, held on the Sunday before Michaelmas (September 18 in 2005), is a religious folk festival featuring costumed men and women parading through the streets.

FLANDERS AND
PAS DE CALAIS

Every day, thousands of tourists pass through the channel ports of the Côte d'Opale on their way to Britain, yet few manage more than a quick glimpse at the surrounding regions, leaving Flanders, Picardy, and the coastal Pas de Calais as the final frontiers of unadulterated France.

When fleeing the ferry ports, don't overlook the area's hidden gems. The windmills and gabled homes of once-Flemish Flanders possess gingerbread charm. Chalk cliffs loom along the Brit-accented coast, and cows and sheep graze near collapsed war bunkers. In Picardy, seas of wheat extend in all directions, interrupted in spring and summer by red poppies. Lille (p. 280), a large, lively, but untouristed metropolis, has a strong Flemish flavor and a world-class art collection. Smaller, more picturesque towns include Amiens (p. 299), known for its enormous Gothic cathedral—the largest in France—and floating gardens.

Even after five decades of peace, the memory of two World Wars is never far from the minds northern France. German-built observation towers still peer over dunes and scores of tombstones attest to the terrible tolls exacted at Arras, Cambrai, and the Somme. Today, this testifies to the resilience of this front line region.

HIGHLIGHTS OF FLANDERS AND PAS DE CALAIS

TAKE A CULTURAL DIP at Lille's amazing modern art museum **La Piscine** (p. 285)—a public pool that has been transformed into a sleek exhibition space.

EXPLORE the moving **Caverne des Dragons** (p. 293), underground tunnels where both French and German soldiers slept peacefully between WWI battles.

STROLL through Amiens's cobblestoned **Quartier St-Leu** (p. 303), known to some as the "Little Venice of the North," where canals converge at flower-filled squares.

FLANDERS

LILLE

Once the feared industrial behemoth of the north, Lille has been transformed into a delightful metropolis, its stylish modern architecture melding with the older cobblestoned cityscape. With its Flemish facades crowding broad avenues and picturesque *places*, Lille (pop. 214,000), the hometown of Charles de Gaulle, is one of the most foreign-feeling cities in France. With 100,000 students in the area and 25% of the population under 25, Lille has the best nightlife in the north.

▤ TRANSPORTATION

Flights: Aéroport de Lille-Lesquin (☎03 20 49 68 68). Cariane Nord **Allo Navette shuttles** leave from rue le Corbusier at Gare Lille Europe (☎03 20 90 79 79, 5-6 per day according to flight times, €4.60). Manual luggage storage available.

Trains: Lille has 2 stations:

Gare Lille Flandres, pl. de la Gare, is more central and connects to more of the surrounding area. **Currency exchange** open M-Sa 8am-8pm, Su 10am-6pm. Info desk open M-Sa 9am-7pm. Ticket office open M-Sa 5:45am-10pm, Su 7:30am-10pm. Manual luggage storage available. To: **Arras** (40min., 18 per day, €8.80); **Brussels, Belgium** via **Gant** (1½hr., 20 per day, €21); **Paris** (1hr., 21 per day, €34.50).

Gare Lille Europe, av. le Corbusier. M: Gare Lille Europe. Info office open daily 5:30am-10:45pm. Station open daily 5:30am-12:15am. **Eurostar** (☎08 92 35 35 39) runs to **London** (10 per day, €35-187.50) and **Brussels** (€22.40). **TGVs** run to the south of France and **Paris** (1hr., 4 per day, €46.90).

Buses: Eurolines, office at 23 Parvis St-Maurice (☎03 20 78 18 88), buses from Gare Lille Europe to **London** (round-trip €52), **Brussels** (round-trip €18), **Amsterdam** (round-trip €45), and other European cities. Office open mid-June to mid-Sept. M-Sa 9:30am-12:30pm and 1-7pm, Sa 1-7pm; mid-Sept. to mid-June M-F 9:30am-12:30pm and 1:30-6pm, Sa 1-6pm. MC/V.

Public Transportation: The **Transpole** central **bus terminal** is next to the train station. **Metro (M)** and **trams** serve the town and periphery daily 5:12am-12:12am. Tickets €1.15, *carnet* of 10 €10, day-pass €3.40. Info at the tourist office or below Gare Flandres (☎08 20 42 40 40). Kiosks open M-F 7am-7pm, Sa 9am-1pm and 2-5pm.

Taxis: Taxi Union (☎03 20 06 06 06) or **Taxi Gare** (☎03 20 06 64 00). Both 24hr.

Bike Rental: Peugeot Cycles, 64 rue Léon Gambetta (☎03 20 54 83 39). €7 per day. €160 deposit. Open Tu-Sa 9am-12:30pm and 2-7pm. MC/V.

◪◪ ORIENTATION AND PRACTICAL INFORMATION

Lille is easy to navigate but use a map when tackling Vieux Lille. The newer part of town, with wide boulevards and 19th-century buildings, culminates in the **Marché de Wazemmes.** The city's largest shopping district is in the primarily pedestrian district off **place du Théâtre.** Lille is a big city, and can be unsafe. Be cautious outside the pedestrian city center, especially near the train station, the Marché de Wazemmes, the side-streets between the Gare Lille Flandres and bd. Carnot, rue Molinel, and east of the city.

Tourist Office: pl. Rihour (☎03 20 21 94 21; lilletourism.com), located inside the Palais Rihour. M: Rihour. From Gare Lille Flandres, go straight on rue Faidherbe for 2 blocks. Turn left through pl. du Théâtre and pl. de Gaulle. Beyond pl. de Gaulle, office is in the palace behind the war monument. Various city tours, in French and English, from €6 to €9. **Currency exchange,** though the post office has a better rate. The **Lille Metropole City Pass** (€20) gives 1 day of unlimited transportation in Lille, as well as admission to museums and monuments, a panoramic tour, and discounts (2-day pass €30, 3-day pass €45). Office open M-Sa 9:30am-6:30pm, Su 10am-noon and 2-5pm.

Budget Travel: Wasteels, 25 pl. des Reignaux (☎03 20 06 87 25). Open M-Th 9am-noon and 2-6pm, F 9am-1pm and 2-6pm, Sa 9am-noon.

English-Language Bookstore: V.O., 36 rue de Tournai (☎03 20 14 33 96; lalibrairie.vo@wanadoo.fr). Open Tu-Sa noon-8pm.

Youth Information: Centre Régional Information Jeunesse (CRIJ), 2 rue Nicolas Leblanc (☎03 20 12 87 30), has info on work and long-term lodging, plus Internet (€1.80 per hr). Open Tu and Th 1-8pm, W 10am-6pm, F 1-6pm. **CROUS,** 74 rue de Cambrai (☎03 20 88 66 33). Extremely helpful staff dedicated to helping students find lodging, jobs, and study opportunities. Open M-Th 10am-noon and 1-4:30pm, F closes at 4pm.

Laundromat: 57 rue du Molinel. Open daily 7am-6:30pm. Also **Lavarama,** 2 rue Ovigneuz. Open daily 7am-8pm.

Police: pl. Salengro (☎03 20 49 56 66), in the Hôtel de Ville.

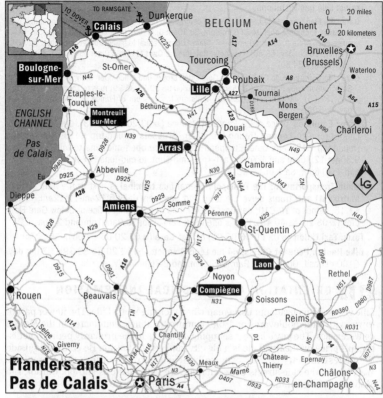

Flanders and Pas de Calais

24hr. Pharmacy: For the **pharmacie de garde**, call ☎03 20 16 96 96.

Hospital: 2 av. Oscar Lambret (☎03 20 44 59 62). M: CHR-Oscar Lambret.

Internet Access: Apart from the inexpensive **CRIJ** (see **Youth Information**), there's also **NetK,** 13 rue de la Clef (☎03 20 55 13 42). €2-4 per hr. Open M-Sa 10am-11pm, Su 3-9pm. **Agence France Télécom,** pl. Général de Gaulle (☎03 20 57 40 00), facing the Vieille Bourse. €0.15 per min., students half-price. Open M 2-7pm, Tu-Sa 9am-7pm.

Post Office: 8 pl. de la République (☎03 28 36 10 20). M: République. **Currency exchange,** good rates. Open M-F 9am-noon and 1:45pm-5pm, Sa 9am-noon. Branches: on bd. Carnot, near pl. du Théâtre. Open M-F 8am-6:30pm and Sa 8am-noon. On the corner of rue Nationale and rue J. Roisin. Open M 10am-6:30pm, Tu-F 9am-6:30pm, Sa 10am-12:45pm and 1:45-4pm. On 125 rue Gambetta. Open M-F 9:30am-12:30pm and 1:45-6:15pm, Sa 10am-4pm.

Postal Code: 59000.

ACCOMMODATIONS AND CAMPING

One- and two-star hotels in the €22-35 range cluster around **Gare Lille Flandres;** more expensive accommodations dot **place du Théâtre** and **place de Gaulle.** Many of Lille's budget options can be ill-maintained and unpleasant—you may want to spring for one of the pricier options listed below.

Auberge de Jeunesse (HI), 12 rue Malpart (☎ 03 20 57 08 94; lille@fuaj.org). M: Mairie de Lille. Friendly reception, international atmosphere, and spacious quarters. Some rooms have showers, others have co-ed hall bathrooms. Bar open 7:30pm-1am. Breakfast included. Kitchen. Luggage storage €2 per day. Sheets €2.80. Laundry. Reception daily 7-11am and 3pm-1am. Check-out 10am. Lockout 10am-3pm. Curfew 1am. Open late Jan. to mid-Dec. 3- to 6-bed dorms €13.45 per person, €2.90 extra per night for non-members; deposit of €10 required for key. MC/V. ●

Hotel de Londres, 16 pl. de la Gare (☎ 03 20 12 09 10). One of the pricier options conveniently near the train station, this hotel boasts small but homey rooms with spotless carpets and lovely bathrooms. Some rooms overlook the pretty but noisy pl. de la Gare, others have a less picturesque view of the quiet back alley. Breakfast €6.10. 24hr. reception. Ring bell downstairs if front door is closed. Singles with shower €46, with toilet €51-55; double with shower and toilet €65. MC/V. ❸

Hôtel de France, 10 rue de Béthune (☎ 03 20 57 14 78; fax 03 20 57 06 01). The least expensive option in the ritzy pedestrian district, Hôtel de France offers newly renovated rooms or older and cheaper rooms. Breakfast €4.50. Reception daily 7am-11pm. Singles €29.45, with shower €35.45-38.45; doubles €33.90/€38.90-60.90; triples with shower €47.25-65.35. Extra bed €4.60. AmEx/D/MC/V. ❸

Le Grand Hôtel, 51 rue Faidherbe (☎ 03 20 06 31 57; www.legrandhotel.com). Between Gare Lille Flandres and pl. du Théâtre. Large, luxurious rooms with full bath, TV, and tasteful decor. Reception daily 7am-11pm. Closed most of Aug. Singles €62; doubles €68-70; triples €78. AmEx/MC/V. ❺

Hôtel Coq Hardi, 34 pl. de la Gare (☎ 03 20 06 05 89; fax 03 20 74 11 95). M: Gare Lille Flandres. The cheapest rooms are clean if a bit worn; the larger €35 rooms are a better value. Linoleum floors and particle-board furniture mean rooms are always clean, if not exactly cozy. Convenient location. Breakfast €4. Reception daily 7am-11pm. Singles €22, with shower €33; doubles €27/€35-40. Extra person €8. MC/V. ❷

Camping: Camping Les Ramiers, 1 chemin des Ramiers (☎ 03 20 23 13 42), in Bondues. Take either bus #35 (dir: Halluin Colbras) or #36 (dir: Comines Mairie) to Bondues Centre, then follow rue Césair Loridan (1km, 25min.). Fences and gardens divide private sites. Reception daily July-Aug. 9am-9pm; Sept.-May 9am-4:30pm. Open mid-Apr. to Oct. €2.60 per site, €1.70 per person, €0.80 per car. Electricity €2.50-4. ●

⬛ FOOD

Lille is known for *maroilles* cheese, *genièvre* (juniper berry liqueur), and—this being Flanders—mussels. Find the cheese in any local market or *épicerie* around the central *places*, the liqueur in a *brasserie* on rue Gambetta, and the mussels, well, everywhere. The highest-value food is south of bd. de la Liberté, near rue Solférino, rue Masséna, and the Halles Centrales. Bustling, crowded **rue Léon Gambetta** boasts a slew of cheap kebab joints, and leads to the enormous Marché de Wazemmes, pl. de la Nouvelle Aventure. **Markets** are open (open M-Th 7am-1pm, F-Sa 7am-8pm, Su 7am-3pm) at Marché de Wazemmes. (Open Su, Tu, and Th 7am-3pm.) **EuraLille,** the shopping center next to the Eurostar station, has an enormous **Carrefour supermarket.** (☎ 03 20 15 56 00. Open M-Sa 9am-10pm.) There is a **Monoprix** in the Centre Commerciale, off rue les Tanneurs. (Open M-Sa 8:30am-8:30pm.)

⬛ **Le Maharajah,** 4 rue du Sec Arembault (☎ 03 20 57 67 77), in the pedestrian district. Scrumptious Indian food in an ornate, nuanced dining area. Vegetarian plates €12-12.50. Open M-Th noon-1:30pm and 7-10pm, F-Sa until 10:30pm. AmEx/MC/V. ❸

⬛ **La Cane à Sucre,** 68 bd. Victor Hugo (☎ 03 20 52 29 00), on the corner of rue Jeanne d'Arc. Vibrant Afro-Caribbean specialties, from *volaille* in coconut sauce (€9) and *poulet à la mangue* (mango chicken, €10) to banana *flambée* for dessert (€4). Open M-Sa 11:30am-2:30pm and 7pm-2am. MC/V. ❷

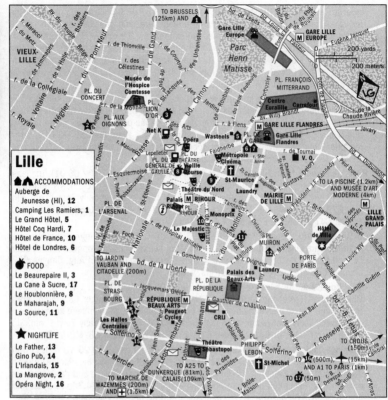

Lille

🏠🏠 **ACCOMMODATIONS**
Auberge de
   Jeunesse (HI), 12
Camping Les Ramiers, 1
Le Grand Hôtel, 5
Hôtel Coq Hardi, 7
Hôtel de France, 10
Hôtel de Londres, 6

🍴 **FOOD**
Le Beaurepaire II, 3
La Cane à Sucre, 17
Le Houblonnière, 8
Le Maharajah, 9
La Source, 11

⭐ **NIGHTLIFE**
Le Father, 13
Gino Pub, 14
L'Irlandais, 15
La Mangrove, 2
Opéra Night, 16

La Source, 13 rue du Plat (☎03 20 57 53 07). Downstairs a friendly natural food store carries vegetarian specialty, upstairs a charming restaurant serves vegetarian and other organic *menus* (€7.50-11). Store open M-Sa 7am-10pm, F until 11pm; restaurant open M-Th and Sa noon-2pm, F also 7-11pm. MC/V. ❷

Le Houblonnière, 42 pl. du Général de Gaulle (☎03 20 74 54 34). With primo terrace space, this eatery's regional specialties include *moules marinière* (€12) and *Le Welsh,* a cheddar fondue cooked with beer (€10). Be adventurous and order the *andouillettes au Cambrai* (€10), intense sausages in sauce made from the local Cambrai cheese. Open daily noon-3pm and 7-10:30pm, F-Sa until 11pm. AmEx/MC/V. ❸

Le Beaurepaire II, 6 pl. Lion d'Or (☎03 20 74 20 36). This cozy brick and wood *crêpe-rie*, nestled in a lively pedestrian area, makes for a superb meal. Filling *galettes* (€2.40-8.50), crêpes (€2.20-5.80), and meal-sized salads (€4-5.80) hit the spot. Open M-Sa noon-2pm and 7:30-11pm. MC/V over €10. ❶

🅖 SIGHTS

🖼**PALAIS DES BEAUX-ARTS.** In a 19th-century mansion surrounded by the lovely gardens of the pl. de la République is the second-largest art collection in France, including an encyclopedic display of 15th- to 20th-century French and Flemish masters. The hallway of Impressionists is particularly dazzling. Guides to each room in English, French, and German. *(Pl. de la République. M: République. ☎03 20 06 78 00; fax 03 20 06 78 15. Open M 2-6pm, Tu and Th and Sa-Su 10am-6pm, F 10am-7pm. Schedule of tours, in French, at the museum. Most tours €7.70. Audioguides in English €4.50. Admission €4.60, students €3.)*

■ **LA PISCINE.** The creative exhibits at this fantastic new museum are both unexpected and exhilarating. The heart of the museum is a glittering renovated indoor pool flanked by 19th- and 20th-century statues and bright former shower-rooms of paintings. As water trickles and lights dance across the ceiling, look through the fabulous portico framing the far end of the pool. *(23 rue de L'Espérance. Take M: Gare Jean Lebas and follow large av. Jean Lebas straight ahead; take a right on rue des Champs, then a left on rue de l'Esperance. The museum is on the right. ☎03 20 69 23 60. Open Tu-Th 11am-6pm, F 11am-8pm, Sa-Su 1-6pm. €3, students €2.)*

MUSÉE D'ART MODERNE. Fascinating for fans of Cubism and postmodernism, this museum displays works by masters like Braque, Picasso, and Miró. Temporary exhibits are quite impressive. *(1 allée du Musée, in Villeneuve d'Ascq. M: Pont de-Bois, then bus #41, dir: Villeneuve d'Ascq, to Parc Urbain-Musée. ☎03 20 19 68 68. Open M and W-Su 10am-6pm. Tours in French Su 11am, €2.50. Admission €3.70, under 25 €1.50, under 12 and first Su of every month 10am-2pm free.)*

VIEILLE BOURSE. The old stock exchange, built between 1652 and 1653, epitomizes the Flemish Renaissance. Encircled by garland-like moldings, it resembles a huge wedding cake. Every day but Sunday it is filled with chess players and booksellers. *(Pl. du Général. de Gaulle. Markets open Tu-Su 9:30am-7:30pm.)*

OTHER SIGHTS. The **Citadel** on the city's north side was redesigned in the 17th century by military genius Vauban using over three million blocks, and is still used by the French military today. *(Open with tour in French. Reserve through the tourist office. Times vary.)* The **Jardin Vauban,** an English garden designed in 1865, has fields for Frisbee-playing, a carousel, and carnival games.

■ ❀ NIGHTLIFE AND FESTIVALS

Lille is a huge party town, liveliest during the school year. Around les Halles Centrales, college students pack the pubs on **rue Solférino** and **rue Masséna.** Across town, the *vieille ville* offers a more sophisticated, though touristed, scene.

■ **L'Irlandais,** 160-162 rue Solférino (☎03 20 57 04 74). Fairly typical Irish setting, but separates itself from the pack with its friendly crowd. Don't be shy: grab a young lad or lass by the arm and join in the jig. Beer €2.50. Open daily 6pm-2am. MC/V.

Gino Pub, 21 rue Masséna (☎03 20 54 45 55), is a rowdy place with a college clientele. Enjoy pool and cheap €1.50 beer. Open M-Sa noon-2am, Su 5pm-2am. MC/V.

Opéra Night, 84 rue de Trevise (☎03 20 88 37 25). This favorite among clubbers blasts "house-happy techno" to a 20- to 30-something clientele. Theme nights from "student dance party" to "gay tea dance." On a deserted street; be cautious. Cover €10, includes 1 drink. Open Th-Sa from 9pm to dawn. MC/V.

La Mangrove, 36 rue d'Angleterre (☎03 20 51 88 89). This *rhumerie* offers a lively dance floor, salsa nights, DJs Th-Sa from 10pm, and a friendly welcome. Beer from €2.40. Open M-Th 5pm-3am, F-Sa 3pm-3am, Su 6pm-3am. MC/V after €10.

Le Father, 19 rue Masséna (☎06 12 70 00 27), is a romantic place with dim lights, wood decor, and a dance floor downstairs. Beer €2-4, cocktails €6. Open Tu-Th 8pm-3am, F-Sa 8pm-dawn. MC/V.

START: Musée de l'Hospice Comtesse
FINISH: Marché de Wazemmes
DISTANCE: 5km/3 mi.
DURATION: 2-3hr.
WHEN TO GO: Start in the early afternoon.

1 MUSÉE DE L'HOSPICE COMTESSE. This dark and atmospheric museum is less visited than most, but the former hospital and orphanage houses an intriguing collection of statues and period rooms. (32 rue de la Monnaie. Open M 2-6pm, W-Su 10am-12:30pm and 2-6pm. €2.30, students €1.50, under 12 free.)

2 LE BEAUREPAIRE. Take a quick crêpe or *galette* break at this tiny *cave*-like eatery, nestled snuggly in the middle of the cobblestone maze of old Lille. (6 pl. Lion d'Or. Open M-Sa noon-2pm and 7:30-11pm.)

3 RUE DE LA CLEF. This quintessential *vieille ville* street is a charming cobbled walk filled with offbeat boutiques and tiny cafes for shoppers and people-watchers.

4 PLACE DU THÉÂTRE. The theater is at the center of it all, flanked by dazzling Flemish facades and numerous restaurants, cafes, pubs, and shops. Take a moment to walk through impossibly ornate **Vieille Bourse,** a former stock exchange, and check if there's anything you like to see at the **Théâtre du Nord.**

5 RUE DE BÉTHUNE. Pass by the elaborate pl. Rihour, and then move down along the bro prettiness of this bustling counterpart to the quiet rue de la Clef. The most popular boutiques, c emas, and terraced restaurants crowd this lively center. If the crêpes didn't fill you up earli stop at **Le Maharajah,** just above rue Béthune, at 4 rue du Sec Arembault. (Open M-Th noo 1:30pm and 7-10pm, F-Sa until 10:30pm.)

6 MUSÉE DES BEAUX-ARTS. One of the most extensive collections in France, this grand a well-designed museum houses a host of 15th- to 20th-century masters under its vaulted ceilin See what this month's featured temporary exhibit is, but don't miss Monet's *Parliament de Lo dres* in the Impressionist wing. (Pl. de la République. Open M 2-6pm, Tu, Th and Sa-Su 10a 6pm, F 10am-7pm. Most tours €7.70. Audioguides in English €4.50. €4.60, students €3.)

7 RUE LÉON GAMBETTA. The more modern section of town begins with this broad avenue a its many restaurants, cafes, and *boulangeries.* Stop at one of the many *pâtisseries* for a quick cream break.

8 MARCHÉ DE WAZEMMES. The tour ends with local produce and *charcuterie* indoors and swirling flea market crowding the outdoor *place.* Spend an hour looking through the endless ro of clothing, regional products, and everything else under the sun, then buy some fresh peach or plums to munch on during the walk back uptown.

Many neighborhood and one-time festivals and events come to cosmopolitan Lille; the tourist office provides a detailed guide. Every year, the **Marché aux Fleurs** carpets the center of town at the end of April, while the huge flea market **La Braderie** sets up shop in the city's central squares on the first weekend of September. For a dose of culture, **Théatre du Nord,** on pl. Général de Gaulle, performs September to June. (☎ 03 20 14 24 24; www.theatredunord.fr. Schedule available at tourist office; prices vary, most student tickets €8.50.) Or visit the **Orchestre Nationale de Lille,** 30 pl. Mendes France. (☎ 03 20 12 82 40; www.onlille.com. Tickets €25, students €9.) The **Opera de Lille,** 2 rue des Bons-Enfants, hosts concerts and musicals each year. (☎ 03 28 38 40 50. Tickets €8 and up.) The tourist office has information on **film festivals,** held at **Le Métropole,** rue des Ponts de Comines (☎ 08 92 68 00 73), and the **Majestic,** 54 rue de Béthune (☎ 03 28 52 40 40; €5.80 student tickets).

ARRAS

The official symbol of Arras (pop. 80,000) may be the noble lion, but for centuries it hasn't been able to escape the "Arras"/"A *rats*" connection that has been made by friends and enemies alike. Its dignified gabled townhouses and Flemish arcades have the regal feel of the king of the jungle, but there's definitely a hint of the small survivor in its battle-plagued history. Go for the well-preserved war monuments, but also enjoy the small-town bustle and gingerbread appeal.

⛃ TRANSPORTATION AND PRACTICAL INFORMATION. Trains (info desk open M-F 6am-8:30pm, Sa 7:30am-7:30pm, Su 8:30am-8:30pm) go from pl. Maréchal Foch to: Amiens (1hr., 12 per day, €9.80); Lille (45min., 20 per day, €8.80); Lyon (3hr., 2 per day, €72.60); Paris (50min., 12 per day, €27.80). The new **ARTIS bus station** is to the right of the train station (open M-F 7:30am-12:30pm and 1:30-6:30pm, Sa 9am-1pm). **Local transportation** is operated by **STCRA** (☎ 03 21 58 08 58; tickets €1.10). **Taxis** wait at the train station. (☎ 03 21 23 69 69. 24hr.) Avis **car rental** is near the train station on 4 rue Gambetta. (☎ 03 21 51 69 03. Open M-F 8:30am-noon and 2-6pm, Sa 9am-noon and 4-6pm. AmEx/D/MC/V.)

To get to the **tourist office,** pl. des Héros, from the station, walk across pl. Maréchal Foch onto rue Gambetta. Continue for five blocks, then turn right on rue Desiré Delansorne. The tourist office is across pl. des Héros in the Hôtel de Ville. The bilingual staff offers a free map and a book of local walking trails. The office leads many tours—call ahead for themes and prices. (☎ 03 21 51 26 95; www.ot-arras.fr. Open May-Sept. M-Sa 9am-6:30pm, Su 10am-1pm and 2:30-6:30pm; Oct.-Apr. M-Sa 9am-noon and 2-6pm, Su 10am-12:30pm and 3-6:30pm.) The town's other main square, **Grand'Place,** is on the opposite side of pl. des Héros, just 1min. away. Crédit Agricole, 9 Grand'Place, has the best rates of **currency exchange,** 24hr. exchange machines, and **ATMs.** (☎ 03 21 50 41 80. Open M 2-6pm, Tu-W 8:45pm-12:30pm and 2-6pm, Th-F 8:45-11:30am and 2-6pm, Sa 8:45am-12:45pm.) Free **Internet** and information on lodging, jobs, and study opportunities are at the **Centre d'Information Jeunesse,** 17 bd. de Strasbourg. (☎ 03 21 23 35 64. Open M-Th 1:30-6pm, F 1:30-5pm; some mornings 10am-noon.) Other services include: **laundromat** Superlav, 17 pl. d'Ipswich, next to the Église St-Jean-Baptiste between the two squares (open daily 7am-8pm); **police** in the Hôtel de Ville (☎ 03 21 23 70 70 or 03 21 50 51 60 after 6pm); a **hospital,** 57 av. Winston Churchill (☎ 03 21 24 40 00); and a **post office,** 13 rue Gambetta, which **exchanges currency.** (☎ 03 21 22 94 94. Open M-F 8am-7pm, Sa 8am-12:30pm.) **Postal Code:** 62000.

⛃ ACCOMMODATIONS AND FOOD. Cheerful **Le Passe Temps ❷,** 1 pl. Maréchal Foch, across from the station, rents spacious though somewhat unfinished rooms above a friendly cafe/bar, with a hall shower available. (☎ 03 21 50 04

04. Breakfast €6.10. Reception Tu-Sa 7am-11pm. Singles €24, with private shower €32; doubles €26/€35. MC/V.) The **Auberge de Jeunesse (HI) ❶**, 59 Grand'Place, is a busy, average hostel with tiny 3- to 10-bed rooms in the middle of the Grand'Place action. (☎03 21 22 70 02; fax 03 21 07 46 15. Breakfast €3.30. Kitchen. Safes €0.15. Sheets €2.80. Reception daily 7:30am-noon and 5-11pm. Curfew 11pm. June-Aug. reserve ahead. Open Feb.-Nov. Bunks €8.90. Non-HI members €2.90 extra. MC/V.) A few doors down, the **Hostel les Trois Luppars ❹**, 47 Grand'Place, is in the oldest house in Arras. Large, sparkling white stucco rooms overlook a charming courtyard. All rooms have bath, TV, and safe. (☎03 21 60 02 03; fax 03 21 24 24 80. Breakfast €7. Sauna €5 for 30min. Reception daily 6:30am-9pm. Singles €44-60; doubles €55-65; triples €65-70; quads €75. AmEx/MC/V.) In the shadow of the massive town hall belfry, **Hotel du Beffroi ❸**, 28 pl. de la Vacquerie, does not have the most creative name, but its sizeable rooms and quiet, central location don't disappoint. (☎03 21 23 13 78; fax 03 21 23 03 08. Breakfast €6. Hall showers. Reception daily 7am-10pm. Singles €30, with private shower €40; doubles €34/€45. AmEx/DC/MC/V.) The local **campsite ❶**, 138 rue du Temple, is basically a parking lot with a few grassy plots. From the station, turn left onto rue du Docteur Brassart, then left on av. du Maréchal Leclerc. Cross the bridge; after 10min., rue du Temple will be on the left. (☎03 21 71 55 06. Reception daily 8:30am-noon and 5-10pm. Open Apr.-Sept. €2.30 per person, €1.40 per child; €1.30 per car; €1.40 per tent. Electricity €2.30.)

There is a huge **Monoprix supermarket** across from the post office at 28 rue Gambetta (open M-Sa 8:30am-8pm), an open-air **market** in **place des Héros** (open W and Sa 8am-1pm), and bakeries and specialty shops in the pedestrian shopping area between the post office and the Hôtel de Ville. Inexpensive cafes skirt pl. des Héros and the pedestrian area, elegant restaurants ornament the Grand'Place, and cheap *friteries* line the alley between the *places*. The tasty, inexpensive ▨**La Cave de l'Ecu ❷**, 54 Grand'Place, serves huge salads (€7.50-12.80), filling crêpes and *galettes* (€3-9.50), and free-range chicken (€9-13.50) in a beautiful brick cellar. (☎03 21 50 00 39. Open daily noon-2:30pm and 7-10pm. MC/V.) For a hearty bit of local finery, pull up a chair at **La Clef des Sens ❹**, 60-62 pl. des Héros. *Menus* range from two courses (€20) to four at €31. (☎03 21 51 00 50. Open Tu-Su noon-3pm and 7-11pm. MC/V.) The mouthwatering aroma of "Les Best Ribs in Town" wafts all the way across the *place* from **Le Saint-Germain ❷**, 14 Grand'Place, where France and America shake greasy hands. Gorge on a plateful of ribs (€11, take-out €9) or the all-you-can-eat *mousse au chocolat* (€6) or *crème caramel*. (☎03 21 51 45 45. Open daily noon-2:30pm and 7-10pm. AmEx/MC/V.)

◪ **SIGHTS.** Arras's two great squares are framed by rows of nearly identical houses. Amid shops, bars, and cafes, the ornate **Hôtel de Ville** is a faithful copy of the 15th-century original that reigned over pl. des Héros until its destruction in WWI. The best view of Arras is from its 75m **belfry.** (Open M-Sa 10-11:45am and 2-5:45pm, Su 10am-12:15pm and 2-6:15pm. €2.40, students €1.60.) Beneath the town hall, eerie labyrinthine tunnels, named **Les Boves,** were bored into the soft chalk in the 10th century and used at various times as chalk mines, wine cellars, and headquarters for the British army during WWI. The tourist office leads fascinating bilingual tours. (☎03 21 51 26 95. €4.40, children and students €2.40.) A few blocks behind the Hôtel de Ville stands the **Abbaye St-Vaast,** built in 667 on the hill where St-Vaast used to pray. Its traditional Gothic floor plan includes massive Corinthian columns. (Open daily Mar.-Nov. 2:15-6:30pm; Dec.-Feb. 2:15-6pm.) Inside the abbey, the **Musée des Beaux-Arts** displays some dull artifacts and paintings, and a surprisingly extensive sculpture collection. Look for (or away from) a gruesome skeletal sculpture of Guillaume Lefrançois and his worm-infested entrails. (☎03 21 71 26 43. Open M, W, and F-Su 9:30am-noon and 2-5:30pm; Th 9:30am-5:30pm. €4, students €2, first Su of each month free.) On the outskirts of the *vieille ville*, a number of military monuments and memorials dot the area around the **Citadel,** another Vauban masterpiece. Still used as a military training site, the citadel is accessible only by tour on Sundays. (Map at the tourist office; tours late June to mid-Sept. 3:30pm. €4.60, students and children €3.)

🎵🎭 **ENTERTAINMENT AND NIGHTLIFE.** Young blood courses into bars and cafes on pl. des Héros, Grand'Place, and the surrounding pedestrian roads. 🏠**The Ould Shebeen,** 6 rue Faidherbe, is an authentic Irish pub with a lively atmosphere and raucous, bilingual "Quiz Nights" every Thursday. (☎03 21 71 87 97. Guinness from €3.70. Open M 8pm-1am, Tu-Sa 4pm-1am, Su 6pm-midnight. MC/V.) **Le Couleur Café,** 35 pl. des Héros, draws the college set with tropical decor and a DJ playing house. (☎03 21 71 08 70. Beer from €2.10. Open M-Th 2pm-1am, F-Sa 11am-2am, Su 4pm-midnight. AmEx/MC/V.) **Dan Foley's Irish Pub,** 7 pl. des Héros, fills with youngsters for karaoke Tuesdays. (☎03 21 71 46 08. Beer from €2.20. Open M-Th 11am-1am, F 11am-2am, Sa 2pm-2am, Su 2pm-1am. AmEx/MC/V.)

Cosmopolitan **Noroit,** 6-9 rue des Capucins, hosts foreign films, concerts, and plays each month. (☎03 21 71 30 12. Office open M-F 8:30am-noon and 1:30-5:30pm. Closed mid-July to Aug.) Nope, you didn't take the wrong train to the shores of the Riviera; that's just **Arras on the Beach.** The last two weeks in July the town dumps a few tons of sand in Grand'Place; wild beach parties and volleyball tournaments ensue, with sports events planned every weekend.

MEMORIALS NEAR ARRAS

VIMY MEMORIAL

The Vimy Memorial is just 3km from the town of Vimy, about 15min. by car from the town of Arras. Catch a taxi in Arras (€18-25). A bus goes from Arras to the Vert Tilleul stop in Thelus (€1.60), but from the walk along the highway to Vimy is a dangerous 50min.

A gift of land from the French to the Canadian government, the Vimy Memorial, 12km northeast of Arras along N17, honors the more than 66,000 Canadian soldiers who were killed during WWI and commemorates the Canadians' impressive success in overtaking the strategic Vimy Ridge in April 1917, after numerous other forces had failed to dislodge the Germans. The two pylons of the monument are covered with the names of 11,000 soldiers thought to have been killed in the battle. Sculpted figures surround the edifice: the most poignant is a woman, *Canada Weeping for Her Children*, carved from a single 30 ton limestone block. Due to long-overdue restoration, the Canadian government is closing the monument to the public for at least two years; the reopening is projected for 2006. The monument will be covered in wooden scaffolding, though the rest of the memorials, including the nearby museum of remembrance and the trenches, will remain open.

The surrounding park, criss-crossed by German and Canadian trenches, is morbidly beautiful; hills and craters carved out by shells and mines are now covered in grass and sheep. Explore the trenches, but stay on the marked paths, as there are still active mines in the fenced-off areas. To the shock of the curators, an enormous mine was only recently discovered under the women's washroom in the visitor's center of the park, though it has since been diffused.

An underground tour of the crumbling tunnels starts at the kiosk near the trenches. Little details suggest the realities of life on the front lines: the registration room, the commander's desk, a maple leaf chiseled in the wall by an anonymous soldier, and a protruding shell that didn't make it all the way into the tunnels. A small museum near the monument recounts the battle and Canada's place in the war. (Monument ☎03 21 50 68 68, museum 03 21 58 19 34, tunnels 03

21 48 98 97. Memorial open daily sunrise to sunset. Museum open daily in summer 10am-6pm; in winter 10am-5pm. Tours May-Nov. 10am-6pm every 30min. in English and French; last tour leaves at 5:15pm; free.)

BATTLE OF THE SOMME MEMORIALS

Memorials are scattered along the Somme region; most are accessible only by car or by tour. Salient Tours offers two excellent minibus tours of the scattered memorials. (☎06 86 05 61 30; www.salienttours.com. Tours Tu-Su, depart from the Albert train station. 4hr. tours leave at 10am, €29; 2½hr. tours, 3pm, €22.) Trains go from Arras to the Albert train station (25min.; M-Sa 8 trains per day, Su fewer; €6.60). If you choose to go by car, pick up the useful brochure The Visitors' Guide to the Battlefields of the Somme, *available at tourist offices throughout the département. The tourist office in Albert, pl. d'Arres, has more detailed transportation information. (Open M-F 9am-12:30pm and 1:30-6:30pm, Sa 9am-noon and 2-6:30pm, Su 10am-12:30pm.)*

When the French concentrated their forces to try to halt the German advance, they left British and Commonwealth forces on the northern front, along the Somme *département*, to the northeast of the tiny town of Albert. Sustaining heavy casualties at Verdun, where they were holding the German advance, the French asked their allies to cause a northern diversion at the Somme to spread out the German forces. The Battle of the Somme, designed for just this purpose, began on July 1, 1916, and was one of the least successful battles of the war. Anticipating such an attack, the entrenched German command had substantially fortified its position. The battle, anticipated by the Allies to be a great success, quickly turned into a rout, and the lines barely moved during six months of heavy Allied losses, until Germany voluntarily left the region for strategic reasons. All in all, over one million men were mobilized along the front, and 330,000 casualties were sustained—58,000 on the first day alone. Memorials all along the Somme commemorate various engagements along the line; most take the form of cemeteries or monuments to whole battalions that lost their lives in the misguided attacks of 1916, though some commemorate the more successful repulsion that finally came in 1918.

Just outside Beaumont-Hamel, the ◙**Newfoundland Park** and its enormous hilltop caribou statue commemorates the loss of nearly an entire regiment of troops from the British colony of Newfoundland (which became part of Canada in 1949). The Allied plan was to bombard the Germans for seven days with artillery, then explode a 17.5 ton underground mine to divert attention, and send thousands of troops out of the trenches in a "surprise" attack. Ordered to walk calmly across 500m of barbed wire, the Newfoundland regiment found the bombardment to have failed completely, for the Germans had hidden safely in fortified underground bunkers; nearly 700 Allies died in the first 30 min. of the attack, lost largely in the first ten yards from the trenches to only five or six German machine gunners. Only 78 men survived. The current park is maintained by the Canadian government, which offers free tours of the trench-marked land (in English and French).

The brand-new **Thiepval Visitor Center,** complete with gift shop, offers a great introduction to the multiple stages of the battle with a small museum, film, and narrative display leading to the monument outside. (☎03 22 74 60 47. Open 10am-5pm daily; closed mid-Dec. to mid-Jan.)

The stoic 45m high **Franco-British War Memorial,** dedicated to the dead or missing from the Battle of the Somme, just outside Thiepval, is the largest British war memorial in the world, and bears the names of over 73,000 soldiers who were lost on the front from 1915 to 1918, and who have no known grave. (Sunrise to sunset.)

Completed in 1921, the ◙**Ulster Memorial Tower,** just outside Thiepval, commemorates the 36th Division troops from Northern Ireland, the only soldiers successful in taking their objectives on July 1 before being subjected to the full force of a German counterattack, losing 5500 troops. The tower itself is a replica of Helen's Tower, a landmark in Clandeboye, Ireland, that stood where the soldiers trained before the war. (Open Mar.-Nov. Tu-Su 10am-3pm.)

LAON

In its glitzier days Laon (pronounced "Laahn;" pop. 28,000) was the capital of the mighty Carolingian Empire, presiding from its hilltop throne over the surrounding farmland. While residences in the fortified *haute ville* were once limited to kings and nobles, a millennium later there's still no royalty to be found on the hilltop cityscape, and many of the traces of the city's ancient grandeur have disappeared. The birthplace of both Charlemagne's mother and the great folk hero Roland, Laon offers a few charming streets and some interesting but slowly decaying architecture, though there's nothing here to merit more than a couple days' exploration.

🖪🖪 TRANSPORTATION AND PRACTICAL INFORMATION. Laon's *haute ville* is built around one main street named rue du Cloître by the cathedral and rue de Bourg by the Hôtel de Ville. **Trains** leave pl. des Droits de l'Homme (☎03 23 79 10 79). Check the ticket office (open M-F 4:55am-9pm, Sa 6am-8pm, Su 6:45am-9pm). Trains run to: Amiens (1½hr., 7 per day, €14.30); Paris (1¼hr., 12 per day, €18); and Reims (50min., 9 per day, €7.90). **SNCF buses** leave from the same station. Call a **taxi** at ☎03 23 79 00 79. The fully automated rollercoaster-style **POMA car** runs every 2-6min. from the station to the *haute ville* and tourist office, providing breathtaking views of the *basse ville* from above. (☎03 23 79 07 59. Open M-Sa 7am-8pm; Sept.-June closed Su. Round-trip, usable for 1 day only, €1.)

Exit straight from the POMA station in the *haute ville*, cross the parking lot, and turn left across pl. du Général Leclerc onto rue Sérurier. Follow it to the cathedral; the **tourist office** occupies the squat 12th-century stone structure on the right (this unlikely building was France's first hospital). The path on foot from the base is straightforward but is at least a 30-40min. hike and quite steep. From the train station, walk toward the hill, past the rotary, onto av. Carnot, and up the endless steps. At the top, circumvent the POMA tracks, and take the pedestrian path to your left that heads uphill and to the right. Head toward the cathedral tower. At the English-speaking tourist office, ask for a free map and *Le Bon P'Laon*, a free practical guide (in French) that also gets various discounts around town. They give tours of the medieval city, underground citadel, and cathedral in French, with a free cellphone audiotour available in English. (☎03 23 20 28 62; www.ville-laon.fr. Cathedral tours daily July-Aug. 3pm; Sept.-Oct. and Apr.-June weekends only. City tours daily July-Aug. 4:30pm; Sept.-Oct. and Apr.-June weekends only. Tours €3, students €2.50, under 12 free. Audioguide €5.44. Office open daily July-Aug. 9:30am-12:30pm and 2-6pm; Sept.-June M-Sa 9:30am-12:30pm and 2-6pm, Su 1-6pm.) Other services include: banks with **ATMs** and **currency exchange** around the train station in the *basse ville* and pl. du Général. Leclerc on the hilltop; a **laundromat** (☎06 24 56 82 61) on bd. Pierre Brossolette in the *basse ville*, right of the train station (open daily 8am-7pm) and in the *haute ville* and the brand-new Lavomatique at 2 pl. Saint Julien (open daily 7am-10pm; wash €4 for 8kg, dry €1); **police** at 30 av. de Charles de Gaulle (☎03 23 22 53 53; call here for the **pharmacie de garde**); a **hospital,** 33 rue Marcellin-Berthelot (☎03 23 24 33 33); and free **Internet** at the Centre Information Jeunesse, 56 bd. Gras Brancourt, in the *basse ville*, which also provides information on lodging, work, and study opportunities. (☎03 23 23 70 09. Open M-F 9am-1pm and 1:30-5:30pm.) In the *haute ville*, get **Internet** at brand-new Cyber'bar, 44 rue Saint-Jean. (☎03 23 26 07 32. €3 per hr. Open Tu-W 2-10pm, Th-Sa 2pm-midnight, Su 2-8pm.) There is a **post office** next to the station on pl. des

Droits de l'Homme with **currency exchange**. (☎03 23 21 55 78. Open M-F 8am-7pm, Sa 8am-noon.) A branch office is located at 6 rue du Bourg in the *haute ville*. (☎03 23 28 61 20. Open M-F 8am-6pm, Sa 8am-noon.) **Postal Code:** 02000.

☎ ☞ ACCOMMODATIONS AND CAMPING. Popular with backpackers, the ▓**Hôtel Welcome ②**, 2 av. Carnot, is just two blocks from the train station, in the *basse ville*, and lets bright-blue, newly renovated rooms at bargain prices. Colorful wall hangings add a touch of sophistication. (☎03 23 23 06 11; hotel-welcome.laon@wanadoo.fr. All showerless rooms have hall shower access. Breakfast €4. Washing machine and microwave access. 24hr. reception. Singles €23, with shower €25; doubles €27/€29; triples without shower €32; quads without shower €38. MC/V.) Château-like **Les Chevaliers ③**, 3-5 rue Sérurier, rents old-fashioned rooms, with quilt bedcovers and a stone arch in the stair, all just a block from the cathedral. (☎03 23 27 17 50; fax 03 23 79 12 07. Breakfast included. Reception 6am-8pm. Singles €28, with shower €35-40; doubles with shower €48-55; triples with shower €55-70; quads with shower €70. Extra bed €10.70. MC/V.) **Hôtel de la Paix ②**, 52 rue Saint Jean, is in the *haute ville*. Dark, winding stairs above a bar lead to surprisingly clean, somewhat worn rooms with uneven floors, all with toilets off the hallway. (☎/fax 03 23 79 06 34. Hall showers available. Reception 7am-10pm. Reserve ahead; there are only a few rooms. Singles €24.50, with shower €30; doubles €26/€36; triples without shower €32.50. MC/V.) Swanky three-star **Hôtel de la Bannière de France ④**, 11 rue Franklin Roosevelt, offers rooms that range from big to large to humongous. With all the fixings (TV, bath), high-ceilinged rooms decorated with style, and a fancy restaurant downstairs, this is the *haute ville*'s classy splurge. (☎03 23 23 21 44; www.hoteldelabanneredefrance.com. Breakfast €7. Reception daily 6:30am-11pm. Front door locks at 11pm; leave a passport for a key to stay out later. Singles €39-54.50; doubles €53-64; triples €75; quads €79; quints €87. AmEx/MC/V.) Rural **Camping Municipale ①**, allée de la Chênaie, about 3km from the train station, is mostly full of caravans but has some private areas for tents. (☎03 23 20 25 56. Reception daily 7am-10pm. Open May-Sept. €3.10 per person, €2.10 per site, €1.70 per car. Electricity €2.70.)

☐ FOOD. Buy your **groceries** at the tiny **Point Coop**, 11 rue du Bourg. (☎03 23 23 05 84. Open M 2:30-6:45, Tu-Sa 9am-12:30 and 2:30-6:45pm. MC/V.) A larger **SPAR** can be found in the *basse ville* at 13 av. Carnot, just by Hotel Welcome. (☎03 23 23 18 97. Open M 2-8pm, Tu-Sa 8am-8pm, Su 9am-1pm. MC/V.) Local **markets** set up Thursday in pl. Victor Hugo and Wednesday in pl. de l'Hôtel de Ville. Full of bakeries, restaurants, and sandwich shops, **rue Châtelaine** and **rue du Bourg**, both leading from pl. du Général Leclerc, are the only places in the *haute ville* to find food. ▓**La Bonne Heure ②**, 52 rue Châtelaine, is the best find in Laon; you'll even forgive the overly enthusiastic regional decor. The friendly owner cooks with local ingredients and has invented a crust for his specialty *tourtinette* (€6.50-7), a pizza-like food topped with ingredients like leeks, ham, smoked trout, lemon, tomatoes, mozzarella, and *escargot*. Be sure to try the *montagne couronnée* (€4), a chocolate-covered wafer filled with berries and dessert cheese; it honors Laon's nickname, "the crowned mountain." (☎03 23 20 57 09. Open Tu-Su 9am-9pm, most food only served noon-2pm and 7-9pm. MC/V.) Nestled in the center of town, **La Crêperie Le St-Jean ①**, 23 rue St-Jean, serves tasty and inexpensive *galettes* (€2-8) and crêpes (€1.90-4.80) in a *brasserie* setting. (☎03 23 23 05 53. Open M-Th 11am-2:30pm and 5:30-11pm, F-Sa closes at midnight. MC/V.) **Les Chenizelles ③**, 1 rue du Bourg, is a hearty *brasserie* on pl. du Général Leclerc with a snazzy, see-it-all terrace and a solid regional menu. Three-course *menus* are €13.50. (☎03 23 23 02 34. Open Tu-F 9am-1am, Sa 10am-1am, Su 10am-6pm. MC/V.) For something on the gourmet side, **Restaurant de la Bannière de la France ④**, 11 rue Franklin Roosevelt, offers a pretty meal with a somewhat hefty dessert bill. Specialties include *foie gras* and egg casserole with shrimp and mushrooms. (☎ 03 23 23 21 44. *Menus* €16.50-€38. Open daily noon-2pm and 7-9:30pm. MC/V.)

◪ SIGHTS. A maze of narrow, twisting alleys and medieval walls surrounds Laon's main attraction, the **Cathédrale de Notre-Dame,** one of the earliest and finest examples of Gothic architecture in France. The striking white interior contrasts with a simple, sumptuous rose window. According to one amusing legend, the Virgin Mary herself showed up here in the 13th century to thank "Jo the Juggler" for a particularly impressive exhibition of in-church flame-juggling. (☎ 03 23 25 14 18. Open daily 9am-6:30pm. 45min. light show July-Aug. Sa 10:30pm. Tours available through the tourist office.) The **ramparts** encircling the *haute ville* offer a panoramic view of the *basse ville* and the surrounding countryside, and their far southwestern tip (20min. from pl. du Général Leclerc), near the **Abbaye St-Vincent,** is home to a fascinating old *Mormot* gun station and a series of trails that wind down to the lower village. Nearby is the crumbling, cool **Église St-Martin,** at the end of rue St-Martin, a worthy walk-by for its aged facade. Behind a lush courtyard at 32 rue Georges Ermant are the tiny **Musée de Laon** and the 13th-century **Chapelle des Templiers.** The tiny chapel's claim to fame, the carved 14th-century corpse of one Guillaume de Harcigny, physician to Charles VI, is delightfully accessible and untouristed. The museum's fairly ho-hum collection of 15th- to 19th-century paintings and Greek and Egyptian antiquities are entertaining but don't merit a detour. (☎ 03 23 20 19 87. Both open June-Sept. Tu-Su 11am-6pm; Oct.-May Tu-Su 2-6pm. Museum €3.20, students €2.50.)

◪ ◪ NIGHTLIFE AND FESTIVALS. At night, a somewhat sedate pub scene emerges in the *haute ville* on pl. du Général Leclerc and rue St-Jean. Black-lit **Outline Café,** 30 rue St Jean (☎ 03 23 29 00 65), fills up on weekend nights, when its leopard-print seats are crammed with guests who come for the nightclub ambience. Lively **Le Gibus,** 14 pl. St-Julien, offers concerts and Thursday night DJs. (☎ 03 23 20 45 47. Beer from €2.50. Open during the school year daily 3pm-1am; during school vacation M-Sa 10am-1am, Su 8pm-1am. Closes M at 8pm. MC/V.) In the *basse ville,* seedy pubs flank the train station.

The **Festival de Laon** presents mainly modern classical music. (☎ 03 23 20 87 50. Oct. to early Nov. Tickets €16-28; students and over 65 €10-28. Tickets at tourist office June-Sept. and over the phone in Sept.) Free **summer concerts** of all kinds invade the pl. de l'Hôtel de Ville June-Aug. On the third weekend of May, **Les Euromédiévals** brings jousts, falconry, street performers, and medieval food to the cathedral area. (☎ 03 23 22 30 30. Free.) The **Festival International du Cinéma Jeune Public,** the first week of April, is an international film and animation festival aimed at kids. (In the Maison des Arts et Loisirs. ☎ 03 23 79 39 37.) In June, **Jazzitudes** hits a number of venues in Laon. (Tickets €4-18.)

◪ DAYTRIPS FROM LAON. South of Laon and reachable by car, the scenic **Chemin des Dames**—named for Louis XIV's daughters Adelaïde and Victoire (les Dames de France), for whose enjoyment the road was paved with cobblestones in the 18th century. Of great military importance since Roman times, the route follows a 200m high ridge whose value as a natural barrier was first noticed by Caesar when he conquered Northern Gaul in 57 BC. The Chemin was the scene of Napoleon's last battle before Waterloo and later the site of a crucial German-held strategic depot during WWI. The route is peppered with monuments to this turbulent history, including the **◪Caverne des Dragons** (Dragon Lair), a former quarry used by the Germans as a barracks, hospital, and chapel during WWI. At the height of the war, both Germans and French used the dark, dreary tunnels as sleeping quarters, but refused to fight each other except when they emerged into the light. The caverns have now been converted into a museum, with walls of windows and soft lighting. Particularly moving are the sculptures and graffiti on display, produced by soldiers during the fighting. (☎ 03 23 25 14 18. Open daily July-Aug. 10am-7pm; Feb.-June and Sept.-Dec. 10am-6pm. Admission only with tours. €5, students €2.50. Reservations strongly recommended. 1½hr. tours in French every 30min.; last tour leaves 1½ hr. before closing.) On request, the tourist office will run 3hr. guided tours by minibus of both sites, at a flat rate of €50 for up to 30 people.

CHANNEL PORTS (CÔTE D'OPALE)

They're big, they're bad, they're ugly. The sprawling ports that greet travelers from Britain and beyond were fought over for centuries, though this might baffle modern visitors confronted with the soggy weather, kitschy boutiques, and cafes promising genuine steak and kidney pie, which altogether suggest the ports combine the worst of both sides of the water. Lively beaches spruce up a bustling coastal atmosphere, making summertime along the Channel merit a few days exploration. Outside prime Coppertone season, however, don't go out of the way to get here.

BOATS TO BRITAIN. Both towns offer frequent service to the UK; Calais is by far more heavily trafficked (though not necessarily the better visit). **Eurostar trains** zip under the tunnel from London and Ashford, stopping outside Calais on their way to Lille, Brussels, and Paris. **Le Shuttle** carries cars between Ashford and Calais. **Ferries** from Calais cross to Dover, while Boulogne services Dunkerque and Ramsgate. For details on operators, schedules, and fares, see **Getting There: By Boat** (p. 23) and **Getting There: By Channel Tunnel** (p. 22).

BOULOGNE-SUR-MER

With a refreshing sea breeze and bright floral displays, Boulogne (pop. 46,000) is by far the most attractive of the channel ports. The busy harbor is the heart of town, the *vieille ville* a charming surprise, and the aquarium an entertaining diversion. Without sun-kissed beach weather, though, Boulogne is less of a treat.

TRANSPORTATION. Trains leave Gare Boulogne-Ville, bd. Voltaire, to: Calais (30min., 13 per day, €6.50); Lille (2½hr., 11 per day, €18.20); Paris (2-3hr., 11 per day, €28.10). Office open M-Sa 8:15am-7pm; ticket office M-Th 4:15am-10:10pm, Tu-Sa 5:15am-7:30pm, Su 6:15am-8:45pm. **BCD buses** leave pl. Dalton for Calais (30min., 4 per day, €6.40) and Dunkerque (1¼hr., 4 per day, €10.50). **TCRB**, with a station at 14 rue de la Lampe (☎ 03 21 83 51 51), sends **local bus #10** from the train station and pl. de France to the *haute ville* (€1); most go through pl. de France. (prices €0.70-1.15). **Taxis** (☎ 03 21 91 25 00 or 06 80 95 14 78) wait at the station.

ORIENTATION AND PRACTICAL INFORMATION. The river Liane separates the ferry terminal from everything else. To reach the central **place de France** from Gare Boulogne-Ville, turn right on bd. Voltaire, then left onto rue Danou before the bridge. Follow rue Danou to the *place*. The tourist office is on quai Gambetta, past pl. de France and the roundabout. On the other side of pl. de France, **Pont Marguet** and a right on Quai Thurot leads to the **ferry port.** The streets between **place Frédéric Sauvage** and **place Dalton** form the town center, while the *vieille ville* is at the top of the hill, up rue de La Lampe and the Grand Rue.

The English-speaking **tourist office,** 24 quai Gambetta, has bus info, reservations service, and a free map. (☎03 21 10 88 10; www.tourisme-boulognesurmer.com. Port tours in French Sa 10am, check office for dates; €5.50, students €4, under 12 free. Open July-Aug. M-Sa 9am-7pm, Su 10am-1pm and 3-6pm; Sept.-June M-Sa 9:15am-12:30pm and 1:30-6:15pm, Su 10am-1pm and 3-6pm.) Crédit Agricole, 26 rue Nationale, has a 24hr. **currency exchange** machine, plus an **ATM** (☎08 10 81 06 96. Open Tu and W 8:45am-12:15pm and 1:30-5:30pm, Th 9:15am-12:15pm and 1:30-4:15pm, F 8:45am-12:15pm and 1:30-6:45, Su 8:45am-12:15pm and 1:30-5pm). Other services include: **laundromats** at 62 rue de Lille in the *haute ville* (☎03 21 80 55 15; open daily 7am-8pm; wash 5kg for €3.60) and 6 pl. Navarin (open daily 8am-8pm); **Internet** at Sirius, 23 rue des Religeuses Anglaises (☎03 21 30 03 47), just off central Rue Faidherbe and at the Youth Hostel (see **Accommodations**); **police** at 9 rue Perrochel (☎03 21 99 48 48; call for the **pharmacie de garde**); a **hospital** on allée Jacques Monod (☎03 21 99 33 33); and a **post office** on pl. Frédéric Sauvage. (☎03 21 99 09 03. Open M-F 8am-6:30pm, Sa 8am-12:30pm.) **Postal Code:** 62200.

⚑ ACCOMMODATIONS. Many hotels in the €17-25 price range are near the ferry terminal; the tourist office has a list. The ⬛**Hôtel Au Sleeping ❷,** 18 rue. Daunou, above a *brasserie* and minutes from the train station and the supermarket, has spotless, newly renovated, lovingly decorated rooms, with shower, TV, and coffee-maker. (☎03 21 80 62 79; fax 03 21 80 63 97. Breakfast €5. Reception daily 7am-10pm. Reserve ahead June-Aug. Singles €30; doubles €34-43. Sept.-June prices about €3 lower. MC/V.) The **Auberge de Jeunesse (HI) ❶,** 56 pl. Rouget de Lisle, across from the train station, feels like a pine cabin and gets crowded during the summer. Pricey two- to four-bed rooms, each with lockless bathroom, are a mixed blessing. The lively bar is packed with backpackers. (☎03 21 99 15 30; fax 03 21 80 45 62. Internet €2 per 40min. Breakfast included. Late-night snack until 1am. Sheets included. Reception M-F 8am-midnight, Sa-Su 8-11am and 5-11pm; 24hr. code access. Check-in 5pm. Checkout 11am. Wheelchair-accessible. 2- to 4-bed dorms €15.50, €5 extra per person to ensure a private room. Non-members €2.90 extra per night for first 6 nights. MC/V.) The central **Hôtel de Londres ❹,** 22 pl. de France, behind the post office, is pricey but looks rather luxurious, with polished hardwood floors and all the amenities, though mattresses are slightly aged. (☎03 21 31 35 63; fax 03 21 83 50 07. Breakfast €5.40. Reception 6:30am-8pm. Doubles €38.50-45.50; family quads with 2 rooms €59.50. Extra bed €7.60. MC/V.)

⬛⬛ FOOD AND ENTERTAINMENT. Scads of restaurants, cafes, and bakeries cluster in the center of town. an excellent **market** is on pl. Dalton. (Open W and Sa 6am-1pm.) **Daily fish markets** surface along pl. Gambetta. A **Champion supermarket,** rue Daunou near bd. de la Liane, in the Centre Commercial de la Liane mall, is up the road from the hostel. (Open M-Sa 8:30am-8pm.) **Rue de Lille,** with its cobbled *haute ville* charm, is the finest place to dine, though the ambience is costly. **Le Restaurant de la Haute Ville ❸,** 60 rue de Lille, serves a three-course *menu végétarien* (€12) and tasty mussel soup (€8) in a timbered, flower-strewn courtyard. (☎03 21 80 54 10. Open July-Aug. Tu-Su 11:30am-10pm, closed M night; daily Sept.-June non-stop noon-10pm, closed M and Su night after 2pm. Closed first 2 weeks of January. MC/V.) Grab a delicious, cheaper bite down the road at **La Scala ❶,** 16 pl. Général de Bouillon, an Italian eatery with a basic €4.30 pizza and pricier pastas. (☎03 21 80 49 49. Open daily noon-2pm and 6-10pm. MC/V.) **Le Doyen ❸,** 11 rue du Doyen, offers seafood-based regional dishes in a cozy, candlelit dining room. (☎03 21 30 13 08. Open M-Sa noon-2:30pm and 7-9:30pm. MC/V.)

Neon-lit bars fill the pedestrian *centre ville,* particularly **place Dalton** or its offshoot **rue du Doyen,** which fits an American, an Irish, an African, and a Cuban pub along its 35m length. For cheap drinks in the *haute-ville*, head to the busy **Wool-**

Pack'Inn, 14 pl. de la Résistance, where a tiny bar serves clientele on comfy low stools and classic and alternative rock are spun by a DJ at the back. (☎03 21 31 62 20. Open Tu-Su 4pm-2am, closes at 1am Sept.-June.)

◨ **SIGHTS.** Boulogne capitalizes on its main source of commerce and nutrition at the huge aquarium ◨**Le Grand Nausicaä,** bd. Ste-Beuve. (☎03 21 30 99 99; www.nausicaa.fr. Audioguides in English, French, and German €3. Open daily July-Aug. 9:30am-8pm; Sept.-June 9:30am-6:30pm. €12.50, students €9.50, ages 5-16 €9.) Next door is the **beach,** where Le Yacht Club Boulonnaise, 234 bd. Ste-Beuve, rents **windsurfers** and **catamarans.** (☎03 21 31 80 67. Windsurfers €9 per hr., €15 for 1hr. lesson. Catamarans €21/€23. Open July-Aug. M-F 10am-5pm, Sa-Su 1-5pm; daily Sept.-Oct. and Mar.-June 10am-noon and 2-5pm.)

Boulogne's *vieille ville* was built by the Romans. Its ramparts, now grassy and tree-covered, have exhilarating views. A block over, on rue de Lille, the domed 19th-century **Basilique de Notre-Dame** sits above a 12th-century crypt. If the church seems oddly shaped, that's because it is: designed by a passionate amateur of architecture, Father Haffreingue built this church after the old one was destroyed following the revolution. (☎03 21 99 75 98. Basilica open daily Apr.-Aug. 9am-noon and 2-6pm; Sept.-Mar. 10am-noon and 2-5pm. Free. Crypt and Treasure House open Tu-Sa 2-5pm, Su 2:30-5:30pm. €2, children €1.)

CALAIS

With neon *centre ville* leading out to the crowded beach, Calais (pop. 80,000) contents itself with being brash and lively. This English-accented swath of shoreline (the Chunnel is right next door) is an interesting, if loud, port city. Outside the summer months, though, Calais loses much of its charm.

◨◨ **TRANSPORTATION AND PRACTICAL INFORMATION.** Free buses connect the ferry terminal, pl. d'Armes, and station (every 30min. 4:45am-9:15pm). Avoid the area around the harbor at night. **Eurostar** stops outside town at the new Gare Calais-Fréthun, but most **SNCF trains** stop in town at the Gare Calais-Ville, bd. Jacquard. Ticket office open M 9am-7pm, Tu-Sa 9am-7:30pm. They go to Boulogne (45min., 11 per day, €6.70); Dunkerque (1hr., 2 per day, €13.60); Lille (1¼hr., 16 per day, €14.30); Paris (3¼hr., 6 per day, €36.30). **BCD buses** (☎03 21 83 51 51) stop at the station en route to Boulogne (30min.; Su-F 5 per day, Sa 2 per day; €6.40) and Dunkerque (40min.; M-F 6 per day, Sa 3 per day; €7). **OpaleBus,** 68 bd. Lafayette, operates **local buses.** (☎03 21 19 72 72. Info office open M-F 9am-noon and 1:30-6:30pm, Sa 9am-noon. Line #3 (dir: Blériot/VVF) runs from the station to the beach, hostel, and campground M-Sa 7:15am-7:20pm, Su 10:30am-7:15pm; €0.90.) For a **taxi,** call ☎03 21 97 13 14.

The **tourist office,** 12 bd. Clemenceau, is near the station; cross the street, turn left, cross the bridge onto bd. Clemenceau, and it's on the right. The English-speaking staff offers free maps and accommodations booking. (☎03 21 96 62 40; www.ot-calais.fr. Open Easter-Aug. M-Sa 9am-7pm, Su 10am-1pm; Sept.-Easter M-Sa 9am-1pm and 2-6:30pm.) **Exchange currency** at the ferry or Hovercraft terminals (both 24hr.), or more cheaply at the post office or **banks** (clustered along rue Royale). Other services include: **police** on pl. de Lorraine (☎03 21 19 13 17; call here for the **pharmacie de garde,** or look in the tourist office window); a **hospital,** at 11 quai du Commerce (☎03 21 46 33 33); **laundromat** Lavorama, 48 pl. d'Armes (open daily 7am-9pm; wash 5kg for €2.60); **Internet** at Médiathèque Louis Aragon, rue du Pont Lottin (☎03 21 19 01 40; €1 per hr.), or at the Hôtel Royal's cafe, 48 rue Royale. (☎03 21 97 20 45. €3 per hr. Open daily 11am-10pm.) The **post office** is on pl.

d'Alsace. (☎ 03 21 85 52 85; open M-F 8:30am-12:30pm and 1:30-6pm, Sa 8:30-noon.); there's a branch on pl. du Rheims, off pl. d'Armes. (Open M-F 8:30am-6pm, Sa 9am-5pm.) **Postal Code:** 62100.

▐▐ ACCOMMODATIONS AND FOOD. The few budget hotels fill quickly in the summer; call 10-14 days in advance. Better than any hotel is the modern, recently renovated █**Centre Européen de Séjour/Auberge de Jeunesse (HI) ❶**, av. Maréchal de Lattre de Tassigny, one block from the beach. From the station, turn left and follow the main road through various name changes past pl. d'Armes. From the ferry, take a shuttle bus to pl. d'Armes. Cross the bridge and take a left at the roundabout onto bd. de Gaulle, then go right on tiny rue Alice Marie; the white hostel is the third building on the left. Or take bus #3 to Pluviose. A fabulous location is complemented by sparkling new doubles and singles that share a bathroom with one neighboring room. Pool table, bar, library, and an attentive staff. Internet runs on France Télécom cards, available at reception. (☎ 03 21 34 70 20; www.auberge-jeunesse-calais.com. Breakfast and sheets included. Cafeteria open M-F 7-9am, noon-1pm, and 5-7pm; Sa 7-9am and noon-1pm. 24hr. reception. Check-out 11am. Wheelchair-accessible. Bunks €15.20 first night, €13.20 every extra night; singles €20/€17.50. Non-members €1.52 extra per night. MC/V.) █**Hotel Pacific ❸**, 40 rue du Duc de Guise, is a top-notch family-run establishment, with large bathrooms and homey rooms, all with shower or bath and toilet. (☎ 03 21 34 50 24; www.cofrase.com/hotel/pacific. High-quality breakfast well worth €6. Reception 7:30am-11pm. Reserve up to a month ahead in summer. Singles €30-37; doubles €37-43; triples €46; family-style quads with bunk beds €56. AmEx/D/MC/V.) The budget option **Hôtel Tudor ❸**, 6 rue Marie Tudor, off rue Duc de Guise, has medium-sized rooms with large TVs, comfortable furnishings, and shower. (☎ 03 21 96 08 15. Reservations suggested. Singles with shower €25; doubles €30-35; triples €40. MC/V.) **Camping Municipal de Calais ❶**, av. Raymond Poincoiré, has small sites with little privacy, packed with RVs, but hey, it's on the beach. (☎ 03 21 34 73 25. Reception daily July-Aug. 7:45am-12:15pm and 2:45-7:15pm; Sept.-June M-F 8am-noon and 2-5pm, Sa 9am-noon, Su 10am-noon. 1 person €3.24, children €2.68; €2.27 per site. Reservations necessary up to 6 months ahead of time. Electricity €1.85.)

Calais cuisine is understandably seafood-centric; English-style fried fish is a local favorite. Any bakery will have the *gâteau Calais*, with a crumbly cookie base and *crème de café* smothered in icing. Morning **markets** are held on pl. Crèvecoeur (Th and Sa) and pl. d'Armes (W and Sa). Otherwise, look for bakeries on **boulevard Gambetta, boulevard Jacquard,** and **rue des Thermes,** or hit the **Match** supermarkets at 50 pl. d'Armes (open M-Sa 9am-7:30pm; July-Aug. Su 9-11:30am). To eat out, the hostel and campsite cafeterias are inexpensive options, while restaurants and *brasseries* line **rue Royale** and bd. Jacquard. Ice-cream stands line the shore. █**Histoire Ancienne ❸**, 20 rue Royale, is the nicest dining option for miles. A deep, tiled dining room is pretty and welcoming, while the tasty regional dishes such as grilled salmon and a *toques d'Opale menu* (€22), are prepared with great care. (☎ 03 21 34 11 20; fax 03 21 96 19 58. Open M-Sa noon-2pm and 7-10pm. Closed for 3 weeks in July-Aug. MC/V.) A fine, value-packed option is the cheery brick **Tonnerre de Brest ❶**, 16 pl. d'Armes. A massive, mouthwatering selection of crêpes and *galettes* ranges from €2.20-8.50. (☎ 03 21 96 95 35. Open M-Tu and Th-Su 11:30am-2pm and 6-10:30pm. MC/V.)

◨ ▐ SIGHTS AND NIGHTLIFE. Your first steps in Calais should be directed to the fantastic sandy **beach;** follow rue Royale to rue de Mer until the end, then walk along the shore away from the harbor. The off-shore sights are less impressive, except for Rodin's evocative sculpture, **The Burghers of Calais,** by the station, framed by the dazzling flowered lawn of the Hôtel de Ville. The statue depicts six leading burghers who, during the Hundred Years' War, surrendered the keys to Calais and offered their lives to England's King Edward III in exchange for those of the starving townspeople. Edward's French wife Philippa pleaded for mercy, and they were spared. The best view in town is from atop **Le Phare de Calais,** pl. Henri Barbuisse, the 58m lighthouse with a draining 271-step climb. On a good day, the cliffs of Dover are visible from the top. You can also rent **bikes** here, €5 for a half-day. (☎ 03 21 34 33 34. €2.50, ages 5-15 €1.50. Open June-Sept. M-F 2-6:30pm, Sa-Su 10am-noon and 2-6:30pm; Oct.-May W 2-5:30pm, Sa-Su 10am-noon and 2-5:30pm.) The noticeably dank **Musée de la Deuxième Guerre Mondiale,** in the slightly seedy Parc St-Pierre, is an old German WWI naval bunker that has been converted into a photographic retelling of the war's history. (☎ 03 21 34 21 57. Open daily May-Aug. 10am-6pm; Apr. and Sept. 11am-5:30pm; Oct. to mid-Nov. Su-M and W-Sa noon-5pm; mid-Feb. to Mar. M and W-Su 11am-5pm. Free audioguide in English, French, and German. €6, students €5.)

Come nightfall, a lively bit of pub life picks up all along rue Royale, especially where it meets rue R. Poincaré. **Le Coco Mambo,** 26 rue de la Mer, is a Cuban-flavored bar with a small terrace and a cozy back corner. (☎ 03 21 97 02 68. Beer from €2.70. Open daily July-Aug. 2pm-2am; Sept.-June Su-Th 2pm-1am. MC/V.)

MONTREUIL-SUR-MER

Though its name is misleading (not a drop of salt water has been seen here since the 13th century, when the ocean began to recede considerably), tiny Montreuil (pop. 2400) could hardly be more idyllic if it actually were on the ocean. Its unmanicured *vieille ville* and the rough, peaceful hills beyond have a simple, authentic appeal, in part because the tourist hordes have not yet discovered them. Montreuil was the setting for a large section of Victor Hugo's *Les Misérables.*

🖅🔀 TRANSPORTATION AND PRACTICAL INFORMATION. The **train station** is just outside the walls of the citadel. (☎ 03 21 06 05 09. Office open M-F 5am-7:30pm, Sa-Su 9am-8pm.) **Trains** go to: Arras (1½hr.; 6 per day, more on Sa-Su; €12.10); Boulogne (40min., 6 per day, €6.30); Calais (1hr., 6 per day, €11.30); Lille (2hr.; 5 per day, Sa-Su 6; €16.20). Rent a **bike** at ETS Vignaux, 73 rue Pierre Ledent. (☎ 03 21 06 00 29. €13 per day, €100 deposit. Open Tu-Sa 9am-noon and 2-7pm. MC/V.)

To reach the **tourist office,** 21 rue Carnot, climb the stairs across from the station, turn right on av. du 11 Novembre, then right at the sign for "Auberge de Jeunesse." Follow rue des Bouchers to its end, then take a left on the footpath at the shrine of Notre-Dame; the office is straight ahead. The English-speaking staff distributes a map and bilingual brochures. (☎ 03 21 06 04 27; www.tourisme-montreuillous.com. Open Apr.-Oct. M-Sa 10am-6pm, Su 10am-12:30pm and 3-5pm; Nov.-Mar. closed Su 3-5pm.) Other services include: **currency exchange** and an **ATM** at BNP, 70 rue Pierre Ledent, off pl. Darnétal (☎ 08 20 35 63 28; open Tu-W 8:30am-noon and 1:30-5:30pm, Th 8:30am-noon, F 1:30-5:30pm, Sa 8:45am-12:30pm); **police** at pl. Gambetta (☎ 03 21 81 08 48; call here for the **pharmacie de garde**); a **hospital** in Rang du Fliers (☎ 03 21 89 45 45); **Internet** at Télé Bureau Services, 64 Grand'rue, near the train tracks (☎ 03 21 90 06 00; €2.50 for 30min., €4 per hr; open M-F 7:30am-7pm, Sa 7:30am-noon); and a **post office** on pl. Gambetta. (☎ 03 21 06 70 00. Open M-F 8:30am-noon and 1:30-5pm, Sa 8:30-noon.) **Postal Code:** 62170.

🖅🖰 ACCOMMODATIONS AND FOOD. The excellent ▧**Renards ❸,** 4 av. du 11 Novembre, rents huge, old-fashioned *chambres d'hôte* at the top of the stairs from the train station, with fireplaces, old furniture, and a charming back garden. (☎ 03 21 86 85 72. Breakfast included. Singles with sink and shared bath €30, with private bath €35; doubles €35/€40. Extra bed €12.50.) The **Auberge de Jeunesse "La**

Hulotte" (HI) ❶, inside the citadel on rue Carnot, is under construction, but still offers 12 beds with summer-camp-style accommodations and sweeping views. (☎ 03 21 06 10 83. Kitchen. Closed during all performances of *Les Misérables* in the citadel. Reception daily 2-6pm. Open Mar. to mid-Oct. Bunks €7.) The **Hôtel le Vauban ❹**, 32 pl. de Gaulle, has sun-drenched yellow and blue rooms with TV and mini-bar in a pink building on the central *place*. (☎ 03 21 06 04 95; fax 03 31 06 04 00. Breakfast €6. Reception 8am-8pm. Standard singles €32, bigger and with shower €40; doubles €32/€47; triples with shower €55; quads with shower €62. AmEx/MC/V.) The beautiful, forested **campground ❶**, 744 rte. d'Etaples, is on the banks of the river, and near a pool, restaurant, and tennis courts. (☎ 03 21 06 07 28. Reception daily 9am-12:30pm and 4-7:30pm. 1 or 2 people with car or tent €9.90, extra person €2.90. Electricity €3.30.)

Many restaurants and a **Shopi** (open Tu-Sa 8:30am-8pm, Su 9am-12:45pm) are located at **place de Gaulle**; bakeries are on the adjacent streets. ▧**La Crêperie Mon-treuil ❶**, 3 rue du Clape en Bas, serves velvety crêpes (€1.50-8) in a jovial atmo-sphere and closes off its tiny cobbled street for free rock, jazz, and blues shows. (Shows July-Aug. Th 9:30pm, Su 5pm. Open daily July to Aug. 4pm-midnight.) If you like *coq*, you'll love **Le Cocquempot ❹**, 2 pl. de la Poissonnerie, off pl. Darnétal, in a grand, old house with a classy, elegant dining room. The famous chicken dish *coq du Cocquempot à la Bière* (beer-battered chicken) is part of the €21.50 *menu*. (☎ 03 21 81 05 61. *Menus* €15-36.50. Open July-Aug. M-W and F-Su noon-1:30pm and 7-8:30pm; Sept.-June closed W. MC/V.) Less ritzy, but equally tasty, is **La Taverne de l'Ecu de France ❷**, 5 porte de France, offering everything from sand-wiches (€4-5) to a €14 regional specialty *menu*. (☎ 03 21 06 01 89. Open daily July-Aug. noon-2:30pm and 7-9:30pm; Sept.-June closed Tu-W. MC/V.)

▣▤ **SIGHTS AND ENTERTAINMENT.** The 3km long **ramparts** look over for-ested valleys and ancient ruins. The crumbling 16th-century **citadel** in the *haute ville* occupies the site of the old royal castle. (Open July-Aug. M and W-Su 10am-noon and 2-6pm; Sept.-June 10am-noon and 2-5pm. €2.50, children €1.30.) Pretty tumbledown cottages line the **rue du Clape en Bas** and the **Cavée St-Firmin**; the latter has actually been featured in several films, including the first version of *Les Mis-érables*. Club Canoë Kayak, 4 rue Moulin des Orphelins, across the canal from the train station, runs **canoe** and **kayak excursions** on the river Canche. (☎ 03 21 06 20 16. Open M-Sa 9am-noon and 2-5pm. Sessions from €10, different difficulty levels available. Call ahead for reservations.) What nightlife there is can be found on **rue d'Herambault** and the streets around **place de Gaulle**. In late July and early August, the citadel stages an impressive light show *(son-et-lumière)* version of *Les Mis-érables* with 250-300 actors, featuring dance, song, and pyrotechnics. (Contact tourist office for info. €14, children €9.50.) A theater festival, **Les Malins Plaisirs**, comes to town every summer. (Call ☎ 03 21 98 12 26 or visit the tourist office for more info. €14-18, under 25 €9-14.) August 15 brings the **Day of the Street Painters**, an exuberant, artsy celebration in the town's winding *haute ville*.

PAS DE CALAIS

AMIENS

Home to France's largest Gothic cathedral, Amiens (pop. 136,000) doesn't boast unique features, but offers everything you expect in a French city and does it a lit-tle better than everyone else. The beautifully maintained *vieille ville* is home to cobblestoned streets and energetic all-hours terrace crowds. A lively student cen-ter with peppy nightlife, it also boasts a canal-lined pedestrian *quartier* known as

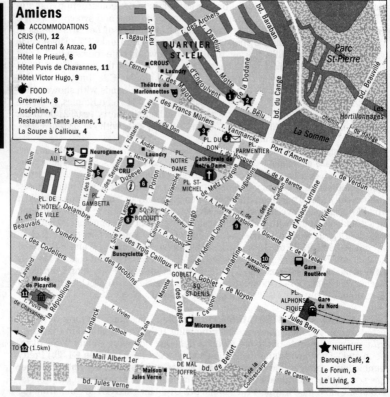

Amiens

⌂ ACCOMMODATIONS
CRJS (HI), **12**
Hôtel Central & Anzac, **10**
Hôtel le Prieuré, **6**
Hôtel Puvis de Chavannes, **11**
Hôtel Victor Hugo, **9**

♥ FOOD
Greenwish, **8**
Joséphine, **7**
Restaurant Tante Jeanne, **1**
La Soupe à Callioux, **4**

★ NIGHTLIFE
Baroque Café, **2**
Le Forum, **5**
Le Living, **3**

"Little Venice." The buildings of the cityscape itself are broken up by colorful and impeccably manicured greenery—gardens may be a pastime elsewhere, but in Amiens their creativity, color, and precise maintenance makes them spectacular.

▗ TRANSPORTATION

Trains: Gare du Nord, pl. Alphonse Fiquet. To: **Boulogne-sur-Mer** (1¼hr., 13 per day, €16.20); **Calais** (2hr., 10 per day, €19.50); **Lille** (1¼hr., 14 per day, €16.60); **Paris** (1¼hr., 20 per day, €17); **Rouen** (1½hr., 3 per day, €29.60). Office open M-F 5am-9:20pm, Sa 5:15am-8:30pm, Su 6am-10:30pm. Info office open M-Sa 9am-6pm.

Buses: ☎03 22 92 27 03. Depart from under the shopping center to the right of the station for **Beauvais** (1-1½hr., 5 per day, €7) and other regional destinations.

Public Transportation: SEMTA, 10 pl. Alphonse Fiquet (☎03 22 71 40 00). Office open M-F 6:45am-7:15pm, Sa 7:45am-5:15pm. Buses run 6am-9pm. Tickets €1.10. All buses stop at the train station; buy tickets onboard or at the office.

Taxis: ☎03 22 91 30 03 or 03 22 71 40 00. 24hr.

Car Rental: Hertz, Camon Zone d'Activity la Blanche Tache (☎03 22 91 26 24), 5km from Amiens. Open M-F 8am-noon and 2-6:30pm, Sa 9am-noon and 4-6pm. MC/V.

Bike Rental: Buscyclette, rue des Corps Nuds Sans Teste (☎03 22 72 55 13). €1 per hr., €3.30 per half-day, €5 per day; €100 deposit. Open M-Sa 8am-noon and 2-7pm.

🔒 PRACTICAL INFORMATION

Tourist Office: 6bis rue Dusevel (☎03 22 71 60 50; www.amiens.com/tourisme). The energetic, English-speaking staff organizes tours, takes care of hotel reservations (€3 in person), and has an excellent free town map. Open Apr.-Sept. M-Sa 9:30am-7pm, Su 10am-noon and 2-5pm; Oct.-Mar. M-Sa closes at 6pm. Cathedral tours daily 11am and 4:30pm; city tours daily 2:30pm. Call ahead for a bilingual guide. €5.50, students €4, under 12 €3. Special themed tours available throughout the year.

Currency Exchange: Banks with **ATMs** and **currency exchange** cluster around the station, around the cathedral, and all over the pedestrian district.

Youth Center: **CROUS,** 25 rue St-Leu (☎03 22 71 24 00; www.crous-amiens.fr), offers info and assistance on lodging, work, and study opportunities in the area, and a helpful practical guide to life in Amiens. Open M-F 8:30am-5pm. Closed 2 weeks in Aug.

Laundromats: Net Express, 10 rue André. (☎03 22 72 33 33). Open daily 8am-7pm. 7kg €3. Also at **Laverie Des Majots** 13 rue des Majots (open daily 8am-8:40pm) and 165 av. du Général Foy, near the hostel. Open daily 8am-7pm.

Police: 2 rue des Chaudronniers (☎03 22 22 25 50).

24hr. Pharmacy: for the **pharmacie de garde,** call ☎03 22 44 72 60 or check the tourist office window.

Hospital: Hôpital Nord, pl. Victor Pauchet (☎03 22 66 80 00); take bus #10 (dir: Collège César Frank).

Internet Access: Surf for free at the **Centre d'Information Jeunesse,** 4 rue Henri IV (www.jeunes-en-picardie.org), near the cathedral. Open Tu-F 1-7pm, Sa 1-6pm. **Neuro-games,** 17 rue Vergeaux (☎03 22 72 68 79). €3.50 per hr., €5 per 2hr. Open M-Sa 10am-midnight, Su 2-8pm. **Micro Game,** 29 rue des Otages (☎03 22 80 16 53). €3.50 per hr. Open M-Sa 10am-8pm. Also available at **Hotel Spatial.**

Post Office: 7 rue des Vergeaux (☎03 22 44 60 00). Open M-F 8am-7pm, Sa 8am-12:30pm. Branch offices located at 37 pl. Alphonse Fiquet (open M-F 8am-7pm, Sa 8am-noon), and at 6 pl. Parmentier (open M-F 10am-12:30pm and 2:30-6pm, Sa 8am-1pm).

Postal Code: 80000.

🔒 ACCOMMODATIONS

Hotels with €25-30 rooms cluster around the train station; options in the center of town tend to be pricier.

🏨 **CRJS (HI),** 24 sq. des 4 Chênes (☎03 22 33 27 30; www.osam.asso.fr). The 35min. walk is tiring; instead, take a bus to Foy (2-3 per hr., fewer on weekends), then walk 75m to the giant square just ahead. The hostel itself is safe, but be careful in the area at night. Spotless new complex offers modern, attractive rooms with 1-4 beds, private bathrooms, and a supermarket outside the door. The staff organizes activities and offers meals. Breakfast €3.05. Other meals €6.10. Laundry. 24hr. reception. 2- to 4-bed rooms €13; singles €15. Non-members €2 extra per night. MC/V. ❶

🏨 **Hôtel Victor Hugo,** 2 rue Lefèvre l'Oratoire (☎03 22 91 57 91; fax 03 22 92 74 02). The spacious rooms at this great bargain are beautifully maintained, and features sparkling bathrooms and homestyle decor; all have bath and TV. Quiet, central location and a friendly owner. Breakfast €5. 24hr. reception. Reserve well in advance. Singles and doubles €38-43; triples and quads €44-53. Extra bed €10. MC/V. ❸

Hôtel Puvis de Chavannes, 6 rue Puvis de Chavannes (☎03 22 91 82 96; fax 03 22 72 95 35), on a quiet street 5min. from the pedestrian district. Rooms are small and hallways are winding, but reception is friendly and prices are low. Breakfast €4.12. Shower €1.52. Reception M-Sa 7:30am-8pm, Su 7:30-11am and 8-9:30pm. Singles and doubles €22-26, with private shower €33; triples with shower €42. Extra bed €9. MC/V. ❷

Hôtel le Prieuré, 17 rue Porion (☎03 22 71 16 71), combines old-fashioned luxury and modern amenities. Classy rooms overlook a quiet courtyard in the cathedral's shadow; prices are still a bit high. Breakfast €6. Reception M-Sa 7pm-9pm, Su 7am-6pm. Singles €34-55 (most €49); doubles €52-68 (most €52); triples €60. MC/V. ❹

Hotel Central and Anzac, 17 rue Alexandre Fatton (☎03 22 91 34 08; hotel-central2@wanadoo.fr). Named after the WWI soldiers of New Zealand and Australia, rooms here are minimal but pleasant, with bright windows and comfy beds. 24hr. reception; call if arriving outside 6:30am-11pm. Singles €27, with shower €32, with toilet and shower or bath €37-40; doubles €31/€36/€44; triples €39/€44/€52. AmEx. ❸

🔾 FOOD

The place to be for a good meal and the best views in town, **quai Bélu** (in the St-Leu quarter of Little Venice) is tightly packed with canal-front cafes and restaurants. Cheaper grub and kebab stands cluster around the station and between the river and the cathedral; *brasseries* surround the ancient **Forum** in the pedestrian district. A **Match supermarket** is in the mall, right of the station (open M-Sa 9am-8pm); another faces the hostel on sq. des 4 Chênes. (Open M-Sa 8:30am-7:30pm.) Amiens's main **market** in pl. Parmentier sells vegetables from the *hortillonages* on Saturday (see **Sights,** p. 302). Smaller markets are on pl. Beffroi. (Open W and Sa.)

Enjoy a great meal at 🖾 **La Soupe à Callioux** ❷, 12 Rue des Bondes, on the beautiful pl. de Don. (☎03 22 91 92 70. *Suggestions du jour* €6.10-13, *Salade spéciale* €8.60. Open daily June-Aug. noon-2pm and 7-10pm. Sept.-May closed M. AmEx/MC/V.) Waterfront 🖾**Restaurant Tante Jeanne** ❶, 1 rue de la Dodane, serves regional specialties just like auntie used to make. (☎03 22 72 30 30; www.restaurant-tantejeanne.com. *Galette chèvrette* €6.50. Open daily noon-2pm and 7-10:30pm.MC/V.) **Joséphine** ❸, 20 rue Sire Firmin Leroux, is a homestyle treat with great local fare.(☎03 22 91 47 38. *Menus* €12-33. Open daily noon-2pm, M and W-Sa also 7-10pm. MC/V.) **Greenwish** ❷, 18 rue Sire Firmin Leroux, is a vegetarian eatery that boasts a huge array of sandwiches (€2-4.50) and salads. (☎03 22 80 19 69. Open M-F 9am-5pm. MC/V.)

🗗 SIGHTS

🖾**CATHÉDRALE DE NOTRE-DAME.** The largest Gothic cathedral in France was built for the less than space-intensive task of holding John the Baptist's head, brought home from the unsuccessful Fourth Crusade. The small, mournful Weeping Angel in the ambulatory behind the choir, with its right hand resting on a skull, its left on an hourglass, was made famous during WWI when Allied troops mailed home thousands of postcards of it. The front portals are lit up nightly mid-June to mid-September to display their dazzling original colors, as in a painting—this is one light show (*son-et-lumière*) not to be missed. An English version of the text plays shortly after the French version. (☎03 22 71 60 56. *Open daily Easter-Oct. 8:30am-6:45pm; Nov.-Feb. 8:30am-noon and 2-5pm; Mar. until 6pm. Nightly illuminations June 10:45pm; July 10:30pm; Aug. 10pm; Sept. 9:45pm; Dec.-Jan. 8pm. Free. French tours daily mid-June to mid-Sept. 11am and 4:30pm; mid-Sept. to mid-June Su 3pm. Tours €5. Audioguides €4, 2 or more €3 each.)*

■ **QUARTIER ST-LEU.** Just north of the cathedral, criss-crossed by branches of the Somme, is the oldest, most attractive part of Amiens. Its narrow, cobbled streets and flower-strewn squares are built along a system of waterways and canals; locals call it "Little Venice of the North." Nearby are the **hortillonages**, market gardens that spread into the marshland. Walk along the towpath starting from **Parc St-Pierre,** or tour the waterways on a traditional *barque à cornets. (Tours ☎03 22 92 12 18. Boat tours in French leave from 54 bd. Beauvillé daily Apr.-Oct. 2-6pm. €5, ages 11-16 €4, ages 3-10 €2.40. MC/V.)* There are a daily antique market and countless small art studios on passage Bélu.

MUSÉE DE PICARDIE. This museum houses a distinguished collection of mostly French paintings and sculptures, as well as a significant collection of Louis XIV and Louis XV furniture. The sparkling white marble of the 19th-century figures is particularly dazzling, as are the Picasso and Balthus works on the second floor. *(48 rue de la République. ☎03 22 97 14 00. Ask for guides and brochures in English. Open Tu-Su 10am-12:30pm and 2-6pm, summer hours change with temporary exhibitions. Wheelchair-accessible. €4, students and ages 6-18 €2.50. Special group rates.)*

MAISON JULES VERNE. One would expect a little more pizzazz from this understated homage to a writer of such a fantastic imagination. The *20,000 Leagues Under the Sea* author wrote most of his illustrious work in the study of this unassuming *maison.* The ground floor might thrill obsessed fans, but the models and posters on display do little to evoke the man's famed art. *(2 rue Charles Dubois. ☎03 22 45 37 84; www.jules-verne.net. Open Apr.-Sept. Tu-F 10am-noon and 2-6pm, Sa-Su 2-6pm; Oct.-Mar. closed mornings. Tours in French or English leave every hour. Last tour 1hr. before closing. €3, students €1.50.)*

🎵 🍸 ENTERTAINMENT AND NIGHTLIFE

Pierre Choderlos de Laclos, author of *Les Liaisons Dangereuses*, was born in Amiens. More dangerous liaisons can be made in the city's canal-crossed older neighborhood. The cobbled **place du Don** and **rue Belu,** in the Quartier St-Leu, teem with everyone from French students to older tourists. Kitschy **Le Living,** 3 rue des Bondes, just off pl. du Don, is packed with a fun-loving, young clientele. (☎03 22 92 50 30. Happy hour 6-8pm with beer €2.50. Open daily 4pm-3am. AmEx/MC/V.) Dark, sexy bar and dance hall **Baroque Café,** 7 quai Bélu, is filled with a sleek, seductive crowd and boasts a great view of the river Somme from its terrace. (☎03 22 92 55 56. Cocktails €5.30. Open Su-M 3pm-1am, Tu-Sa 3pm-3am. MC/V.) **Le Forum,** espace piéton Gambetta, on the Forum in the pedestrian district, is a mellow pubbing alternative packed from the early afternoon onwards. (☎03 22 92 44 45. Beer from €2.70. Open Su 2pm-1am, M-Sa 7:30am-1am. MC/V.)

The adorable **Théâtre de Marionnettes,** 31 rue Edouard David, off rue Vanmarcke, stages elaborate shows in the "Chés Cabotans d'Amiens" theater, with various exhibitions of the stringed puppets during the day. (☎03 22 22 30 90. Check www.ches-cabotans-damiens.com for schedules, exhibition times, and prices.)

The November **Festival du Jazz** brings noted musicians from all over the world. On the third weekend in June, the **Fête dans la Ville** fills the streets with concerts, street festivals, jugglers, and circus performers. It's no Cannes—and this isn't the Riviera—but an international jury and an engaging slate of dramas and documentaries comes out for the November **Festival International du Film.**

COMPIÈGNE

Royalty dating back to Merovingian times fled to the cool woodlands and delicate beauty of this hamlet on the forested southern border of Picardy. The grand Château de Compiègne has played summer home to loads of Louis's, Napoleon I, and

Napoleon III. Today, Compiègne (pop. 40,000) is a picturesque retreat favored by Parisians, its royal pedigree shamelessly apparent in its ornate central square and acres of imperial gardens.

⌨ ⚡ TRANSPORTATION AND PRACTICAL INFORMATION

Trains leave from pl. de la Gare (☎03 44 83 89 65), across the river from the town center, to Paris (45-60min., 27 per day, €11.60) and Lille (2-3hr., 8 per day, €24.70). Buy tickets at the station (ticket windows open M-Sa 4:45am-9:10pm, Su 6:25am-10:10pm). **Regional buses** run from the station to area towns daily. **Local TUC buses** run throughout town daily 6am-8pm, some until 10pm. (☎03 44 83 36 26. Schedules and maps at the tourist office. €0.80 per ride; buy tickets on board.) **Taxis** can be reached at ☎03 44 83 24 24. The local **bike rental** company has no storefront, but delivers free to hotels and sets up on the carrefour Royal weekend afternoons in the summer. (☎06 07 54 99 26. €9-15 per day, depending on type; €150 deposit.)

The **tourist office** is in the Hôtel de Ville. Cross the station parking lot, turn right, cross the bridge, and follow rue Solférino to pl. de l'Hôtel de Ville (5 minutes). A helpful staff provides info on hiking trails in the Compiègne forest (in French). Themed tours (€5), including one on local favorite Joan of Arc, are offered most Sundays from May to October, and leave at 3:30pm; call ahead for the theme. (☎03 44 40 01 00; otsi@mairie-compiegne.fr. Open Easter-Oct. M-Sa 9:15am-12:15pm and 1:45-6:15pm, Su 10am-1pm and 2:30-5pm; Nov.-Dec. closed Su; Oct.-Easter closed M and Su morning.) Other services include: banks with **ATMs** and **currency exchange** along rue Solférino and around the Hôtel de Ville; a **laundromat** at Lav'Club, 15 rue de Paris (open daily 7am-10pm; €3.50 for 6kg), and at Le Lavoire, 29 rue du Pont a Bateaux (open daily 7:30am-9pm; wash €3.20 for 6kg); **police** at 2 av. Thiers (☎03 44 40 00 45; call for the **pharmacie de garde**, or check the tourist office window); a **hospital**, 3-8 av. Henri Adnot (☎03 44 23 60 00); **Internet** access at l'Evasion, 5 rue St Martin, on a pedestrian street by the Hôtel de Ville (☎03 44 40 21 34; open M-Sa 10am-midnight), and at Internet Call Back, 27 rue d'Austerlitz (€3 per hr; open M-Sa 9am-9pm.); **post office** at 42 rue de Paris (☎03 44 36 31 80; open M-F 8:30am-6:30pm, Sa 8:30am-12:30pm); branch at pl. du Marché aux Herbe (☎03 44 40 21 50; open Tu and Th-F 10am-12:30pm and 1:30-6pm, W 9:30am-6pm, Sa 9am-12:30pm and 2-5pm). **Postal Code**: 60200.

⌂ ▢ ACCOMMODATIONS AND FOOD

There is no hostel in Compiègne. Hotels cluster around the train station; just across the river is a slew of more expensive establishments. The rooms in convenient, enormous **Hôtel de Flandre ❸**, 16 quai de la République, off pl. de la Gare, are spacious, comfortable, and TV-equipped, and some come with little balconies overlooking the river. (☎03 44 83 24 06 or 03 44 83 24 40; fax 03 44 90 02 75. Breakfast €7. Reception daily 7am-12:30am. Singles €27, with shower or bath €42-45; doubles €30/€51-54. DC/MC/V.) Above a Chinese restaurant and next to a laundromat, it doesn't get much more convenient for the budget traveler than **Hôtel St-Antoine ❷**, 17-19 rue de Paris, 3-5min. from the Hôtel de Ville. Rooms feature an unspectacular all-beige decor and are a bit worn, but are clean and cheap. (☎03 44 23 22 27. Reception daily 7am-10pm. Hall toilets. No shower available for showerless rooms. Singles €15.50, with shower €19, with shower and TV €24; doubles €22/€25/€30. MC/V.) The **Hôtel Sunset ❷**, 4 rue Solférino, over the bridge from the train station, and 2min. from the Hôtel de Ville, rents clean but small rooms with TV and bath, in the center of town at a fantastic price. (☎03 44 20 47 47. Breakfast €5. Reception M-Sa 6pm-9pm, otherwise go next door to Opticien KRYS. Singles €25; doubles and triples €30-34. MC/V.)

Food, like everything else in Compiègne, is concentrated heavily around **place de l'Hôtel de Ville** and along both sides of the river Oise near the train station. Restaurants also cluster in the pedestrian district between **rue Solférino** and **place du Marché aux Herbes.** For the do-it-yourself type, there's a **Monoprix supermarket** at 33 rue Solférino. (☎03 44 40 04 52. Open M-Sa 8:30pm-8pm, F until 8:30pm. MC/V above €15.) At tasty little crêperie **La Friandine,** 22 rue Jean Legendre, get the usual assortment of salads (€3.50-15) and *galettes* (€3.50-15), as well as a fantastic selection of stuffed baked potatoes (€12), which come with enormous fresh salads. (☎03 44 40 04 06. Open daily noon-2pm and 7-10:30pm, later F and Sa nights. AmEx/D/MC/V.) At **La Rotisserie du Chat qui Tourne ❸**, 17 rue Eugène Floquet, attached to the Hôtel de France, traditional *onglet de veau au bleu* (veal in bluecheese sauce) shares menu space with a series of vegetarian specialties, from roasted vegetable dishes to parmesan zucchini with pasta. (☎03 44 40 02 74. 2-course *menus* from €13, 3-course €20, with wine and a 4th course €32. Open Sept.-June M and W-Sa noon-2pm and 6-9:30pm, Tu and Su noon-2pm. AmEx/MC/V.) Non-vegetarians, put those pointy teeth to work at **Bistrot du Boucher ❷,** 39 rue Vivenel. €12.80 *plats* include veal, steak, duck, and poultry. (☎03 44 36 43 60. Open daily noon-2pm and 7-10:30pm. 4-course *menus* with wine €24. MC/V.)

🄖 SIGHTS

CHÂTEAU DE COMPIÈGNE. The most famous landmark in town, this palace, reconstructed by the monarchy in the 18th century, became a favorite retreat of Napoleon I and especially of Napoleon III. While this place has nothing on Versaille, a tour of the *grands appartements* brings you to the sumptuously restored living quarters of various rulers. Even the cattle-herding tactics of the guides can't obscure some incredible sights. Look for the marble table upon which a sulking, punished young noble carved his initials in 1868, and the leopard-carpeted *salle* in which Napoleon first met his second wife. In addition to the preserved gilded chambers and halls, the large complex houses a fascinating **Musée de la Voiture,** which showcases classic cars, bicycles, and motorcycles. *(Pl. du Général de Gaulle. ☎03 44 48 47 02; chateau.compiegne@culture.gouv.fr. Open M and W-Su 10am-6pm, last admission 5:15pm. 1hr. tours in French, leave every 20-30min.; call ahead for English. Wheelchair-accessible. Château alone €4.50, with Musée de la Voiture €5.50; students and 18-25 €3/€4; 1st Su of each month and under 18 free.)*

PARC DU CHÂTEAU. Behind the palace and, mercifully, too vast to be crowded by tourists, this massive park includes miles of breathtaking royal gardens designed by Berthault under Napoleon. With tree-lined paths, floral *jardins*, wide-open spaces, and shady nooks, the only downside to this park is a giddy overload of space. *(Entrance to the right of the château. Open daily 8am-7pm.)*

HARAS NATIONAL. This national stable along rue de la Procession houses over 50 stallions in what was once the palace stables, befitting a town that was once a famous hunting retreat. Open to visitors free of charge, except during the parts of the summer when the stallions are, ahem, doing their work... *(1 bd. Victor Hugo. ☎03 44 38 54 66; www.haras-nationaux.fr. Accessible only by tour. Tours in French leave from the château every Th, 1st Sa of each month at 10am. €5, under 15 €2.50.)*

OTHER SIGHTS. The squint-inducing but delightful **Musée de la Figurine,** 28 pl. de l'Hôtel de Ville, next to the tourist office, displays over 5000 historic and military figurines from its unique collection. Hand-painted battalions of ½ in. soldiers shine with detail, while 8 in. giants sport tailored cloaks and hats. *(☎03 44 40 72 55. Open Mar.-Oct. Tu-Sa 9am-noon and 2-6pm, Su 2-6pm; Nov.-Feb. closes at 5pm. Wheelchair-accessi-*

ble. €2, ages 18-25 €1, under 18 free; 1st Su of each month free.) The 13th-century **Église St-Jacques,** pl. St-Jacques, is where Joan of Arc prayed on the morning she was captured in 1430.

♫ ⊠ ENTERTAINMENT AND FESTIVALS

The **Théâtre Impérial,** 3 rue Othenin, provides opera, ballet, and drama for the sophisticated masses. Originally planned to have an 1871 debut, the grand building, with its amazing acoustics, was finally finished... in late 1991. (☎08 25 00 06 74; www.theatre-imperial.com. Info office and on-site ticket sales open Sept.-June M-F 8:30am-12:30pm and 2-6pm, Sa 9am-noon and 2-5pm; July-Aug. closed Sa-Su; also open 1½hr. before every show. MC/V.) In mid-May, the **Concours Complet International** takes place in the Hippodrome above the Parc du Château. This equestrian competition, one of the biggest in the world, is free to watch and reaffirms the charming horsiness of the town. Also in mid-May, the annual **Foire aux Vins** brings free wine tastings and exhibits to the pl. St-Jacques. (Call ☎03 44 86 69 45 for details.) Around Easter (May 5-6 in 2005) an international exhibit of amazingly detailed decorated Easter eggs, the **Salon des Œufs Décorés,** hits the Salle Tainturier, rue de Clamart. (€6, under 12 free.) At night, bars and pubs liven up the pedestrian district and the streets around pl. de l'Hôtel de Ville.

⬢ HIKING

The misty trails of the **Forêt de Compiègne** provide a maze of peaceful hikes and winding bike routes, all eventually leading back to the château. Ask at the tourist office for a detailed map of these well-marked paths. Many lengths and levels of difficulty are available; the most rewarding route, a 12km stroll through the center of the forest, culminates in the dazzling **Château de Pierrefonds,** in a tiny village of the same name. Bought by Napoleon I and marvelously restored by Viollet-le-Duc under Napoleon III, the medieval-style château is a breathtaking reminder that, even in the 19th century, "authentic restoration" was a popular and successful endeavor. Walk the ramparts, view the gallery, and visit the cavernous knight's hall. (☎03 44 42 72 72; www.monum.fr. Château open daily mid-May to mid-Sept. 9:30am-6pm; end of Sept. M-Sa 9:30am-12:30pm and 2-6pm, Su 9:30am-6pm; Oct.-Mar. M-Sa 9:30am-12:30pm and 2-5:30pm, Su 9:30am-5:30pm; Apr. to mid-May M-Sa 9:30am-12:30pm and 2-6pm, Su 9:30am-5:30pm. Last admission 45min. before closing. €6, students 18-25 €4, under 18 free.)

Another route passes by the **Wagon de l'Armistice,** with a museum that recounts the famous history of the railway car in which the German army conceded defeat in WWI and the French were forced by Hitler to do likewise in 1940. (☎03 44 85 14 18. Museum open daily Apr. to mid-Oct. 9am-12:30pm and 2-6pm; mid-Oct. to Mar. 9am-noon and 2-5:30pm. €3, ages 7-14 €1.50, under 7 free.)

CHAMPAGNE

Brothers, brothers, come quickly! I am drinking stars!
—Dom Pérignon

Synonymous with both sophisticated celebration and Dionysian revelry, there is something undeniably seductive about the fizzy pop of a champagne cork. While champagne is limited to special occasions in most of the world, in Champagne itself the treasured elixir flows unceasingly, bringing glamor and good times to one of France's wealthiest wine-growing regions throughout the year.

According to European law, the word "champagne" may only be applied to wines made from grapes from this region and produced according to a rigorous, time-honored method. It involves the blending of three varieties of grapes (*pinot noir*, *pinot meunier*, and chardonnay), two stages of fermentation, and frequent realignment of the bottles by *remueurs* (highly trained bottle-turners) to facilitate removal of sediment. So fiercely guarded is the name that when Yves Saint-Laurent brought out a new perfume called "Champagne," the powerful *maisons* sued to force him to change it—and won. Though at first Dom Pérignon had to convince his compatriots to try the sweet nectar, few modern-day visitors need extra incentive to come to the region to see (and taste) the *méthode champénoise* at the region's numerous *caves* (wine cellars)—at their best in the glitzy towns of Reims (p. 307) and Epernay (p. 314). Even regional specialties tend to center around a champagne base; try *volaille au champagne* (poultry in a champagne-based sauce) or *civet d'oie* (goose stew).

The grape-fed high life may buoy the whole region economically, but smaller towns both near and far from the vines have their own distinct characters. Come to Champagne for the giddy luxury of its namesake beverage and the surprisingly boisterous *joie de vivre* of its signature towns, but don't miss out on the region's rich history: the inspiring grandeur of the Cathédral de Notre-Dame in Reims, traditional site of French coronations since its construction in 1311; the ramparts in hilltop Langres (p. 323); and the half-timbered houses and crooked streets of beautifully preserved Troyes (p. 318).

HIGHLIGHTS OF CHAMPAGNE

MAKE THE MOST of your toast at Epernay's **Moët & Chandon** (p. 316), producers of the legendary Dom Pérignon.

BE SURE TO BE THIRSTY when you visit **Champagne Pommery** (p. 312), home of the 75,000L wine cask that was a show-stopper at the 1904 World's Fair.

CHECK OUT kingly fashion at the former archbishop's residence **Palais du Tau** (p. 307), which features some of Charles X's 50 ft. robes.

REIMS

The Mecca of the glitzy Champagne region, Reims (pronounced "rahnce"; pop. 187,000) brings a sparkling touch to everyday city life. Synonymous with celebration, it's fitting that Reims is where both princes and victors of war were transformed into kings: the ornately carved Gothic cathedral has been home to the coronations of 26 monarchs. Today, everything touched by this glamorous and

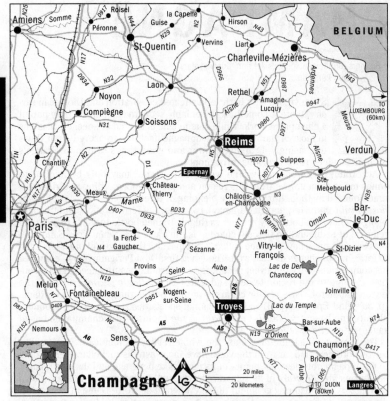

Champagne

stylish city turns to bubbly gold, from the decadent underground *caves* of its signature *champagneries*, to the lively terraces that populate the spectacular streets to all hours of the morning.

TRANSPORTATION

Trains: bd. Joffre (☎03 26 88 11 65). Info office open M-F 9am-7pm, Sa 9:30am-6pm. To: **Epernay** (20min., 11 per day, €4.80); **Laon** (1hr., 7 per day, €7.90); **Paris** (1½hr., 11 per day, €20.90). SNCF boutique with information and reservations at pl. Myron T. Herrick. (Open M-Sa 10am-7pm. AmEx/DC/MC/V.)

Public Transportation: Transport Urbains de Reims (TUR) buses stop in front of the train station. Info office at 6 rue Chanzy (☎03 26 88 25 38). Open M-F 7:30am-7:30pm, Sa 10am-7pm. €0.90 per ticket, *carnet* of 10 €6.50, day pass €2.40; buy from driver. All bus lines run 6:35am-9:45pm; 5 lines run until midnight. Regional **buses** leave from the bus station to Troyes and Châlons-en-Champagne. Schedules at the tourist office.

Taxis: ☎03 26 47 05 05 or 03 26 02 15 02. Both 24hr.

Car Rental: Avis, cour de la Gare (☎03 26 47 10 08). Open M-F 8am-noon and 2-7pm, Sa 8am-noon and 2-6pm. **Budget,** 47 av. Nationale (☎03 26 77 66 66). Open M-F 8am-noon and 2-7pm, Sa closes at 5pm. **Europcar,** 76 bd. Lundy (☎03 26 88 38 38). **Hertz,** 26 bd Joffre (☎03 26 47 98 78). All accept MC/V. Avis also accepts AmEx.

Bike Rental: Centre International de Séjour, chaussée Bocquaine (☎03 26 40 52 60). Half-day €10, full day €15, weekend €25. €77 or passport deposit. MC/V.

⏸ PRACTICAL INFORMATION

Tourist Office: 2 rue Guillaume de Machault (☎03 26 77 45 00; www.tourisme.fr/reims), in a pint-sized ruin beside the cathedral. Free map with sights and caves, loads of free brochures (in French, English, Spanish, and German), and free same-night accommodations service (with deposit). **Currency exchange** on Su. Ask for the student guide Le Monocle (only in French). Tours of the town with audioguides in 6 languages (€7.65). Office open mid-Apr. to mid-Oct. M-Sa 9am-7pm, Su 11am-6pm; mid-Oct. to mid-Apr. M-Sa 10am-5pm, Su 11am-5pm. Walking tours of Reims in French July-Aug. Tu and Sa 2:30pm. Tour of Basilique St-Rémi in French July-Aug. Th 2:30pm. Tour of cathedral daily July-Aug. (except Su morning) 10:30am and 4:30pm in French, 2:30pm in English. Easter-June cathedral tours in French Sa-Su 2:30pm. Tours €5.50, students and over 60 €3.15, under 12 free.

Budget Travel: Wasteels, 26 rue Libergier (☎03 26 79 88 03). ISICs and cheap flights. Open M-F 9am-6pm, Sa 10-6pm.

Banks: Banks with **ATMs** and **currency exchange** around pl. Drouet d'Erlon and cathedral.

English-Language Bookstore: Bookshop, 23 rue du Clou dans le Fer (☎03 26 84 99 80). Open Tu-Sa 10am-noon and 2-7pm. MC/V.

Youth Centers: Centre Régional Information Jeunesse, 41 rue Talleyrand (☎03 26 79 84 79; fax 03 26 79 84 72). Info on jobs and local events. Free Internet: 30min. limit; no email checking, but policy is loosely enforced. Message board with job offers for seasonal work, including camp counselor positions and field work during the harvest. Contact ANPE Saisonnière (☎03 26 77 62 98) for more info about harvest work. Open M-Tu 2-6pm, W-Th 10am-12:30pm and 2-6pm, F 10am-12:30pm and 2-5pm. **CROUS,** 34 bd. Henri Vanier (☎03 26 50 59 00). Comprehensive info and assistance for students seeking lodging, work, or study opportunities in the area. Generally open M-F 10am-noon and 2-6pm; services for foreign students during school year only 1:30-4pm.

Laundry: Lavomatique, 49 rue Gambetta. Open daily 7am-9:30pm. **Laverie Chanzy,** 50 rue Chanzy (☎06 64 36 42 27). Open daily 7am-9:30pm.

Police: 40 bd. Louis Roederer (☎03 26 61 44 00), by the train station.

Hospital: 47 rue Cognac Jay (☎03 26 78 78 78).

Internet Access: Free **Internet** at **CRIJ** (see **Youth Centers**). **Clique & Croque,** 27 rue de Vesle (☎03 26 86 93 92), set back from the street in a plaza. 1st hr. €4.30, €3.80 thereafter. Open M-Sa 10:30am-12:30am, Su 2-9pm. **Ze Cyber,** 31 pl. d'Erlon (☎03 26 02 45 13). 1st hr. €4.50, €4 thereafter. Open M-Th 10am-12:30am, F-Sa 10am-1:30am, Su 2-8pm. Also available at **Centre International de Sejour** (see **Accommodations**).

Post Office: pl. Boulingrin (☎03 26 50 58 01), near Porte Mars. Better **currency exchange** rates than the banks. Open M-F 8am-7pm, Sa 8am-noon. Central branch, 2 rue Cérès (☎03 26 77 64 80), on pl. Royale. Open M-F 8:30am-6pm, Sa 8:30am-noon. Also at 8-10 pl. Drouet d'Erlon (☎03 26 09 60 67). Open M noon-7pm, Tu-F 10am-7pm, Sa 10am-5pm. Another branch at 9 pl. Stalingrad (☎03 26 86 69 30), close to the hostel. Open M-F 9am-noon and 2:15-6pm, Su 8:30am-noon.

Postal Code: 51100.

⏸ ACCOMMODATIONS

Semi-inexpensive hotels cluster west of pl. Drouet d'Erlon, in the region above the cathedral, and near the *mairie*. Reims is a popular destination; call ahead.

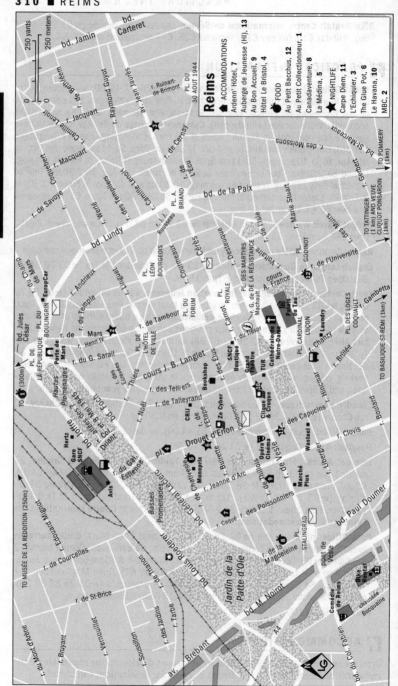

CHAMPAGNE

Reims

■ ACCOMMODATIONS
Ardenn' Hôtel, 7
Auberge de Jeunesse (HI), 13
Au Bon Accueil, 9
Hôtel Le Bristol, 4

● FOOD
Au Petit Bacchus, 12
Au Petit Collectionneur, 1
Canadaventure, 8
La Médina, 5

★ NIGHTLIFE
Carpe Diem, 11
L'Echiquier, 3
The Glue Pot, 6
Le Havana, 10
MBC, 2

■ **Centre International de Séjour/Auberge de Jeunesse (HI),** chaussée Bocquaine (☎03 26 40 52 60; fax 03 26 47 35 70), next to La Comédie-Espace André Malraux. Top-notch hostel living, newly revamped and accordingly spiffy. Recall with nostalgia the classic hostel days of ratty housing and squalid communal living, then thank your lucky stars this is nothing like it. Clean, comfortable new rooms. Friendly staff houses a mix of backpackers and noisy school groups. Breakfast €4.20. Meals by reservation €6.90-11.80. Kitchen. Laundry. 24hr. reception, but front doors locked 10pm-7am. 4- to 5-bed rooms with hall shower €11 per person. Singles €18, with shower €28; doubles €24/€32; triples with shower €39. Non-members €3 one-time fee. AmEx/MC/V. ❶

Au Bon Accueil, 31 rue de Thillois (☎03 26 88 55 74; fax 03 26 05 12 38), off pl. Drouet d'Erlon. A comfortable choice, with some of the most inexplicably inexpensive rooms this side of the hostel. Unspectacular, but on par with hotels at least €10 more expensive. Call well ahead. Breakfast €4.50. Hall shower €1.50. 24hr. reception. Singles €22, with shower €27; doubles with shower €30-39; triples with shower or bath €44-48. Extra person €7.50, extra bed €15. MC/V. ❷

Hôtel Le Bristol, 76 pl. Drouet d'Erlon (☎03 26 40 52 25; www.bristol-reims.com). Definitely not an option for the currency-challenged traveler. From the elegant, chandeliered lobby to the impressively high-ceilinged rooms decorated with Louis XI- to Louis XV-style furniture, Le Bristol offers comfort and beauty and far outshines other options. All rooms with shower or bath, toilet, and TV. Breakfast €7. Reception daily 7am-midnight. Singles €50-54; doubles €55-78; triples €64-74. AmEx/MC/V. ❺

Ardenn' Hôtel, 8 rue Caqué (☎03 26 47 42 38; www.ardennhotel.fr), near pl. Drouet d'Erlon and the train station. A step up from super-economical, a step down from super-decadent—for the indecisive splurger. 14 chandeliered, velvety rooms, priced accordingly. All rooms with shower and TV, all but the cheapest with toilet. Breakfast €5.50. Reception M-Sa 24hr., Su after 6pm. Singles €31-41; doubles €47-49; triples and quads €59. Extra bed €6. AmEx/D/MC/V. ❸

◘ FOOD

The heart of Reims's street life, **place Drouet d'Erlon** is also its stomach; bakeries and sandwich shops compete for space with cheap cafes and classier restaurants. Kebab stands line rue de Vesle. A **Monoprix supermarket** is at 21 rue Chativesle, in espace d'Erlon. (Open M-Sa 9am-8pm. MC/V.) A smaller **Marché Plus** is at 33 rue de Vesle. (Open M-Sa 7am-9pm, Su 9am-1pm. MC/V.) The main **market** is on pl. du Boulingrin near Porte Mars. (Open Sa 6am-1pm.)

■ **Au Petit Collectionneur,** 123 av. de Laon (☎03 26 83 99 74). A taste of Brittany in this Champagne hotspot. *Galettes* and crêpes (€3-9.50) are seriously stacked with marvelous tasties; salads and meals available as well. Don't leave without downing a few mugs of *cidre bretonne* (from €2.50). Open Tu-Sa noon-2pm and 7-10pm. MC/V. ❷

■ **Au Petit Bacchus,** 11 rue de l'Université (☎03 26 47 10 05). Named after the god of champagne and all things scandalous, this beautifully appointed restaurant offers a mouth-watering array of sumptuous meals for the gourmet palate. *Menus* from €18. Open M-Sa noon-2pm and 7:15-10pm. MC/V. ❹

Canadaventure, 24bis rue de la Magdaleine (☎03 26 77 97 86). Drop your French pretenses and dine with kitschy Canada, but no laughing, eh? Canada weeps for this stereotyped cabin-style restaurant, which features teepee-covered menus and an extensive selection of bison and salmon fare. The 2-course *formules de saumon* come in every shape and variety (€14.30), while the Canadian beer is more straightforward (from €4.30). Open W-Th and Su noon-2pm and 7:30-10pm, F-Sa until 11pm. MC/V. ❸

La Médina, 13 rue de Chativesle (☎03 26 88 43 34). Serves North African food to Moroccan music, with a pleasant candlelit atmosphere on the side. Couscous with meat €12-17.50, *menus* from €12.50. Open Tu-Su noon-2pm and 7-10pm; closed Aug. for annual vacations. MC/V above €15.30. ❸

THE KINGMAKER

Reims doesn't feel that far from Paris today, but in horse-and-carriage days it was at least a week's travel along unpaved roads, plagued by bandits and mud. So why did French kings make this treacherous trip to be crowned?

The story goes back to Clovis, the first Catholic French king, who was crowned in Reims in 496. An enormous crowd gathered to watch the ritual, in which the king's forehead was to be annointed with oil while he bathed in baptismal waters. Legend has it that the church was so full that the assistant with the necessary bottle of oil was unable to make his way to the altar. It being winter, the half-naked Clovis began to freeze, and everyone grew impatient (and cold). The despairing bishop prayed for assistance. In response, God sent a dove bearing a bottle of heavenly oil. The ceremony was salvaged, Clovis was baptized, and a Catholic France was born.

Subsequent French kings went to Reims seeking annointment by that same bottle. By the time Joan of Arc dragged a reluctant Charles VII there in 1429, the oil had dried up to a thick, rather vile paste, which had to be mashed with fresh oil to produce a substance that was at least usable. Today, the even-less-fresh oil sits in the museum next door to the cathedral, waiting patiently for the next king of France—if he can get it out of the jar.

◉ SIGHTS

The most popular sights near the center of town are all easily reached by foot. Farther out, the champagne *caves*—the biggest draw along with the cathedral—vary in their distance from downtown, and some are best reached by bus. Many champagne firms give tours (all available in English), though many require reservations at least one day in advance. Consult the tourist office for info on bus lines and which *maisons* are available without reservation. It may not be cheaper to buy champagne directly from the firms; ask the advice of wine shops near the cathedral, where there are sales on local brands, and check the prices at the Monoprix (see **Food**). The big names tend to begin at around €20, but lesser-known *maisons'* bottles start at €9.50, half the price for champagne outside of France.

▧ **CHAMPAGNE CAVES.** Excluding a trip to Epernay (p. 314), this is the best opportunity you'll ever have to swim in bubbly decadence. Four hundred kilometers of *crayères* (Roman chalk quarries) and 200km of more modern French-built *caves* shelter the bottled treasures. The cellars are generally kept at 10°C; bring a sweater. The most elegant and impressive tour is at the massive **Champagne Pommery.** Madame Pommery took over her husband's business and became one of France's foremost vintners; her wealth allowed her to bring art into the workplace, lining the *cave* with exquisite carvings by Gustave Navlet. The firm owns the largest *tonneau* (vat) in the world, carved by Emile Galle and sent to the 1904 World's Fair in St. Louis as a 75,000L gesture of goodwill. *(5 pl. du Général Gouraud. ☎ 03 26 61 62 55. Open Apr. to mid-Nov. 9:30am-7pm, mid-Nov. to Mar. 9:30am-6pm. Tours by reservation only, in French, English and German. Admission €7, students €3.50, children free.)* **Veuve Cliquot Ponsardin** is slightly less elegant, but with a free tour and tasting, who can complain? Tours pass by a small sample vineyard, wind through cellars made from ancient chalk mines, and offer a tasting. *(1 pl. des Droits de L'Homme. ☎ 03 26 89 53 90. Tours M-Sa 10am-6pm; Nov.-Mar. closed Sa. Free.)* The *caves* are the star of **Taittinger**'s tour; see the underground remains of the otherwise destroyed Abbaye St-Nicaise as well as ancient Roman chalk mines, all while getting some of the most detailed explanations around of the champagne-making process. See the largest champagne bottle in the world and watch the *dégorgement* (on certain days), the process by which sediment is removed from the bottles. *(9 pl. St-Nicaise. ☎ 03 26 85 84 33. Open daily mid-Mar. to mid-Nov. 9:30am-1pm and 2-*

5:30pm; 20min.; last tour 1hr. before closing. Mid-Nov to mid-Mar. closed weekends. No reservation necessary. Tours include a winding 100-step staircase and are conducted entirely on foot. Admission €7. AmEx/MC/V.)

PALAIS DU TAU. Connected to the cathedral (see below), this former archbishop's residence got its name from its original floor plan, which resembled a "T." Don't miss its dazzling collection, including reliquaries that date back to Charlemagne; the show-stoppers are the sumptuous 50 ft. robes of Charles X and massive statues rescued from crumbling portions of the old cathedral face. The gargoyles full of metal, placed throughout the museum, were salvaged after a fire melted the copper roof. *(2 pl. du Cardinal Luçon. ☎03 26 47 81 79. Open May-Aug. Tu-Su 9:30am-6:30pm; Sept.-Apr. Tu-Su 9:30am-12:30pm and 2-5:30pm. Tours in English and French €7.50, ages 18-25 €5, under 18 free. Admission €6.10/ €4.10/free.)*

CATHÉDRALE DE NOTRE-DAME. Too lazy to quarry his own stone, the bishop who had this colossal kingly Gothic creation built cannibalized the protective walls of the surrounding city for building materials; in fear of attack the people appealed to the king, who famously declared "God will be the guard." Reims's cathedrals have always witnessed the crowning of French kings: 26 sovereigns were crowned on this spot, beginning famously with Clovis (see **The Kingmaker,** opposite page). The carved opulence of the front facade and exterior of the current church, begun in 1211, boasts 2307 statues worthy of such royalty. More recently, the current building witnessed the reconciliation between President de Gaulle and German Chancellor Adenauer in 1962. While WWI bombing destroyed most of the original stained glass, they were replaced by spectacular sea-blue windows by Marc Chagall. *(☎03 26 77 45 25. Open daily 7:30am-7:30pm. Tours in French and English. Tourist office also gives tours. €6, ages 12-25 and seniors €3.50.)*

MUSÉE DE LA REDDITION. Germany signed its surrender to the Allies on May 7, 1945, in a schoolroom across the railroad tracks—now the small but fascinating Musée de la Reddition. A short film (in French and English) and several galleries of photos and time lines lead to the preserved room, which contains the thirteen chairs in which the British, French, American, Soviet, and German heads of state sat. Nothing here is sleek or showy, but as a potent historical time capsule, the place itself is powerful. *(12 rue Franklin Roosevelt, just north of the train station. ☎03 26 47 84 19. Open M and W-Su 10am-noon and 2-6pm, Tu 2-6pm. €1.60, children and students free.)*

OTHER SIGHTS. Near the Taittinger *caves,* the **Basilique St-Rémi** rises from a bed of lavender at the other end of town from the cathedral. This Romanesque church with Gothic tinges was built around the tomb of St-Rémi, the bishop who baptized Clovis. Almost entirely destroyed during WWI, it has returned to its former glory, just as ornately decorated in the interior. *(Pl. St-Rémi. Open daily 9am-sunset, no later than 7pm. Light show (son-et-lumière) July-Sept. Sa 9:30pm.)* Next door, the **Musée-Abbaye St-Rémi** shelters an extensive collection of religious art, military uniforms, and artifacts from the Merovingian and Carolingian eras. Look for the Enamels of St-Timothy, a series of engraved tiles depicting life under oppressive Roman rule. *(53 rue Simon. ☎03 26 85 23 36. Open M-F 2-6:30pm, Sa-Su 2-7pm. €1.60, first Su of every month free.)* The largest arch in the Roman empire still rises over the modern pl. de la République, though it was badly damaged by WWI fighting. The **Porte Mars** is decorated with reliefs of Romulus and Remus, who gave the city its name.

BUBBLY FOR THE ROAD. When purchasing a souvenir bottle of champagne, don't assume that prices at the *maisons* themselves are the best. Check the local wine shops and supermarkets. You'll often discover the very same bottles that were featured in a *dégustation* for a few euros less than at the *caves.*

CHAMPAGNE

🎵 🌿 ENTERTAINMENT AND FESTIVALS

At night, people concentrate in the cafes and bars of **place Drouet d'Erlon.** ◾**The Glue Pot,** 49 pl. d'Erlon, is a popular English-style pub with food at all hours and a big-screen TV featuring all sports, all the time. (☎03 26 47 36 46. Beer from €2.70. Open daily 10am-3am, though hours vary according to crowds. MC/V above €12.) Hidden off rue de Vesle, tropical-style **Le Havana,** 27 rue de Vesle, is the most diverse watering hole in town; live Afro-Cuban music fills the bar every other Friday. (Happy hour daily 6-7pm with 2 beers for €2.50, 2 glasses of champagne for €6, or 2 cups of punch for €2. Open Tu-F 11am-12:30am, Sa 11:30am-1:30am. MC/V.) **Carpe Diem,** 6 rue des Capucins, is a mellow gay bar with three small rooms that fill up on weekends. (☎03 26 02 00 41. Beer €2.50-3.30. Cocktails €3.90-4.60. Open M-Th 9pm-12:30am, F-Sa 9pm-1:30am, Su 4-11pm. MC/V.) The bar-club **Le Mâle à Bar Café (MBC),** 12 rue de Mars, is another popular choice with its Indian decor and "kitschy Frenchy" music. (☎03 26 09 75 69. Cocktails €4-7. Open M-Th and Su 4pm-12:30am, F-Sa 4pm-1:30am. MC/V.) The enormous club **L'Echiquier,** 10 av. Jean Jaurès, is just outside the pedestrian district—walk in a group. Three tiers of top-40, techno, and rock make for a flashy, pheromone-filled evening with a generally young crowd. (☎03 26 89 12 38. Cover €9 for men, €6 for women; includes 1 drink. Open Th-Sa 10pm-5am. MC/V.)

Like any self-respecting champagne-drenched municipality, Reims offers a host of cultural activities for the cosmopolitan set. Follow the sidewalk of playwrights to the **Comédie de Reims,** 3 chaussée Bocquaine, a regional acting school and theater that stages a host of performances and workshops. (☎03 26 48 49 00. Open Sept.-June M-F noon-7pm, Sa 1-7pm. Tickets to featured productions €8-15, students €5-8. Prices for other events vary.) **Cinéma Opéra,** 3 rue Théodore Dubois, shows a range of films. (☎03 26 47 29 36. Tickets €5.50-7.20. Student discounts with ID during select shows. Ticket office open daily 1:30-10pm.) The **Grand Théâtre de Reims,** 13 rue Chanzy, hosts operas and ballets. (☎03 26 50 03 92. Open Oct.-June Tu-Sa 2:30-6:30pm.) Throughout the year, less traditional **Le Manège de Reims,** 2 bd. du Général Leclerc, presents dance shows, performance art, and music on its stage, with *les dimanches des curiosités* (Sundays of curiosities) providing special themed performances most Sundays. (☎03 26 47 30 40. Open year-round. Box office open Tu-Sa 1-7pm. Tickets €5-18.) During the summer, Reims hosts the fantastic ◾**Flâneries Musicales d'Eté,** with more than 100 free concerts in 60 days. World-famous musicians share the bill with smaller acts, and many of the performances are free. (Late June to early Aug. Call ☎03 26 77 45 00 or stop by the tourist office for more info.) In the fall, **Octob'Rock** brings rap and reggae sounds to venues all over the city (☎03 26 84 86 37; many performances free). The **Reims Jazz Festival** (info ☎03 26 47 00 10) is held this year from the 10th to 18th of November, and brings music to the beautifully manicured lawns of the Pommery champagne firm.

EPERNAY

Epernay (pop. 30,000) is every rugged backpacker's secret dream town. Undeniably ritzy and sparklingly seductive, this mascot for Champagne's wealthiest grape-growing regions plays landlord to the world's most distinguished champagne producers. The *maisons* of Moët & Chandon, Perrier-Jouet, and Mercier all inhabit the palatial mansions along av. de Champagne and keep their 700 million treasured bottles in the 100km of tunnels underneath. Tour a cave, raise a glass, and taste the stars. At the heart of the *Route Touristique du Champagne,* Epernay is also an excellent base for exploring the countryside, including hikes through vineyards, châteaux, and mountains.

▐ TRANSPORTATION

Epernay loses no time introducing you to its main attraction; entering by train from the east, the colorful tiled roofs and blue enameled signs of the de Castellane *maison de champagne* dominate av. de Champagne. The train station is two blocks from the central pl. de la République. **Trains** leave from Cour de la Gare. (☎08 91 67 68 69. Open M 9am-7pm, Tu-F 9:15am-6pm, Sa 8:30am-6pm. Ticket office open daily 6am-8pm.) Trains run to: Paris (1¼hr., 18 per day, €18.10); Reims (25min., 16 per day, €4.80); and Strasbourg (3hr., 3 per day, €39.40). **STDM buses** (☎03 26 65 17 07) serve Paris, Reims, and small towns in Champagne; ask at tourist office for a schedule and map. **Local buses** are run by **Sparnabus,** 30 pl. des Arcades. (☎03 26 55 55 50. Tickets €1, *carnet* of 10 €7.30. Open M 2-6pm, Tu-F 9am-noon and 2-6pm, Sa 9am-noon.) Rent **bikes** at Remi Royer, 10 pl. Hugues Plomb. (☎03 26 55 29 61. €11 per half-day, €17 per day, €77 per week. Open Tu-Sa 9am-noon and 2-7pm. MC/V.)

▐ PRACTICAL INFORMATION

To get to the **tourist office,** 7 av. de Champagne, from the station, walk straight ahead through pl. Mendès France, pass a fountain, walk one block up rue Gambetta or rue J. Moët to **place de la République,** and turn left onto av. de Champagne (5 minutes). The welcoming, English-speaking staff provides free maps, a list of hotels, info on Epernay's *caves,* and suggestions for *routes champenoises,* all available in English. They also publish a free monthly list of local events and festivities, in French. (☎03 26 53 33 00; www.epernay.fr. Open Easter to mid-Oct. M-Sa 9:30am-12:30pm and 1:30-7pm, Su 11am-4pm; mid-Oct. to Easter M-Sa 9:30am-12:30pm and 1:30-5:30pm.) "Bacchus," the *petit train,* feels particularly tacky in a city of such sophistication. The 1hr. tour takes visitors through the cityscape often ignored by those who come only for the bubbly. (☎03 26 59 58 70. French, English, and German audio; Danish in writing. May-Oct. Tu-Su 7 per day. Leaves from av. de la Champagne. €4.60, under 16 €2.80.) Banks with **ATM** and **currency exchange** cluster on pl. de la République and pl. Hugues Plomb, including a Banque de France on pl. de la République. (Open M-F 8:45am-noon and 1:45-4pm; no bills larger than US$50.) Other services include: a **laundromat,** 8 av. Jean Jaurès (☎03 26 54 96 15; open daily 7am-8pm); **police,** 7 rue Jean Chandon-Moët (☎03 26 56 96 60, call here for the **pharmacie de garde**); and a **hospital,** 137 rue de l'Hôpital (☎03 26 58 70 70). Access the **Internet** at Cyberm@nia, 11 pl. des Arcades (€2 per hr.; open M-Sa 2pm-midnight, Su 2-8pm), or Le Babylone, 25 rue Gambetta. (☎03 26 55 96 44. €4 per hr., pay by the min. Open Tu-Sa noon-8pm). The **post office,** pl. Hugues Plomb, has **currency exchange.** (☎03 26 53 31 60. Open M-F 8am-7pm, Sa 8am-noon.) **Postal Code:** 51200.

▐ ▐ ACCOMMODATIONS AND CAMPING

Epernay caters to the champagne set, so budget hotels are rare. ▧**Hôtel St-Pierre ❷,** 14 av. Paul-Chandon, past the covered market and pl. d'Europe, is the best bet. Homey floral wallpaper and three floors of spacious, antique-furnished rooms. (☎03 26 54 40 80; fax 03 26 57 88 68. Breakfast €5. Hall toilets for some rooms. Reception daily 7am-10pm. Singles and doubles €23, with shower €26-40. Extra bed €5. MC/V.) A stone's throw from the station, on the popular pl. Mendès France, **Hôtel de la Cloche ❸** is a pricier, more convenient option. Clean, comfortable rooms all come with bath and TV. (☎03 26 55 15 15; hotel-de-la-cloche.c.prin@wanadoo.fr. Breakfast €6. Reception daily 7am-midnight. Singles and doubles with shower or bath €39-47. Extra bed €8. AmEx/MC/V.) The two-star **Kyriad ❹**, 3bis rue de Lorraine, offers tastefully decorated rooms with bath and TV, though not at a bargain price. (☎03 26 54 17 39; kyriad.epernay@wanadoo.fr. Breakfast €6.50. Reception M-Sa 7am-10pm; Su opens at 8am. Singles and doubles €54. Extra bed €15.) There is a **campground ❶** about 2km from the station (dir: Reims) at allée de Cumières, on the banks of the Marne. (☎03 26 55 32 14. Open mid-Apr. to early Sept. Reception daily June-Sept. 7am-10pm; Apr.-May 8am-9pm. €3.10 per person, €1.50 per child, €2.50 per tent, €1.50 per car. Electricity €3.10.)

🚹 FOOD

The pedestrian district around **place des Arcades** and **place Hugues Plomb** is dotted with delis and bakeries. There are Italian, Moroccan, Asian, and Turkish eateries on **rue Gambetta** and a **Marché Plus supermarket** at 13 pl. Hugues Plomb. (☎03 26 51 89 89. Open M-Sa 7am-9pm, Su 9am-1pm. MC/V above €7.) Halle St-Thibault hosts a **market**. (Open W-Sa 8am-noon.)

For the most delicious ending to a perfect day of *dégustations* and decadence, head to ▨**Au Bacchus Gourmet ❹**, 21 rue Gambetta (see **Au Bacchus Gourmet,** opposite page). The hearty, *brasserie*-style meals are quite tasty at **Le Central ❶**, 15 pl. de la République, a convivial local eatery that also serves crêpes (€3-5.80), *galettes* (€5.10-9), and filling sandwiches for €6-9. (☎03 26 59 19 93. Open M-Tu and Th-Su noon-midnight, food service noon-2pm and 7-11pm; closed Tu afternoons. 4-course *menu* €10. MC/V.) **La Cave à Champagne ❸**, 16 rue Gambetta, has composed a menu that incorporates the local product into a wide array of dishes. From *foie gras à la champagne* to oysters in Champagne sauce, every meal is a bubbly delight—though the wine and champagne menu is dauntingly extensive. (☎03 26 55 50 70. 3-course *menu* €15, other *menus* up to €35. Open M-Tu and Th-Su noon-2pm and 7:30-10pm; July-Aug. closed W; Sept.-June closed W night. MC/V.)

🔀 MAISONS DE CHAMPAGNE

The name says it all: ▨**avenue de Champagne** is a long, broad strip of palatial *maisons de champagne* pouring out bubbly to hordes of middle-aged visitors from around the world. The tours below are all offered in French or English; no reservations are required. All include a *petite dégustation* (ages 16+), and offer more extensive (and expensive) tastings as well. Take note: without springing for a tour, the only thing visitors get to see at the *maisons* is a liquor-lined boutique. *Caves* are maintained between 10 and 12°C; bring a sweater. Each firm's tour may give more or less the same explanations, but everything from the dress of the guides to the design of the lobby reflects the status and character of the producer.

For a cheap but authentic alternative to the big *maisons*, ask the tourist office about *l'esprit de champagne*, a free presentation and sampling given by several smaller companies in the tourist office. (June to mid-Oct. F-Sa; July-Aug. also Th. 10:30am-noon and 3-6pm. Obtain tickets in advance.) One of the younger *maisons* that participates, **Esterlin**, 25 av. de Champagne, also offers a free tasting and a 10min. video history of the product at its mansion. (☎03 26 59 71 52. Open daily 10am-12:15pm and 1:45-5pm. No reservations necessary.)

▨**MOËT & CHANDON.** The granddaddy of them all, Moët & Chandon, the producer of legendary champagne Dom Pérignon, has been "turning nature into art" since 1743. The mansion is full of as much old-money elegance as one would expect, from elegant carvings lining the inside of ancient caves to the stately mansion rooms decorated for no other than Napoleon I himself. The 50min. tour, on foot, details the basic steps in champagne production and gives a detailed history of champagne, highlighting at every turn the superior standards of M&C. The *caves* feel authentic, and the 5min. film is a pompous and thoroughly amusing bit of highbrow commerce. *(20 av. de Champagne. ☎ 03 26 51 20 20; www.moet.com. Open daily early Mar. to early Nov. 9:30-11:30am and 2-4:30pm; early Nov. to Apr. M-F only. Tour with one glass €7.50, two glasses (a rosé and brut vintage) €16, three glasses (non-vintage) €20; ages 12-16 €4.50, under 12 free. AmEx/MC/V.)*

■ **MERCIER.** Slightly less famous but equally swanky, Mercier, 10min. from Moët, is in the middle of a vineyard. The self-proclaimed "most popular champagne in France" certainly knows how to market itself. The 30min. tour, in roller-coaster style cars, includes all the same information on production, but it also tells the fascinating history of the eccentric Mercier himself and his wildly successful advertising schemes of the 19th-century. Maker of France's first advertising film, he also sent a blimp-sized cask of champagne to the 1889 World's Fair in Paris which, according to the tour, "competed only with the Eiffel Tower for the title of most impressive sight." *(70 av. de Champagne. ☎ 03 26 51 22 22; www.champagne-merc-ier.fr. Open daily late Mar. to mid-Nov. 9:30-11:30am and 2-4:30pm; mid-Nov. to mid-Dec. and early Jan. to mid-Mar. M and Th-Su only. €6.50, ages 12-16 €3, under 12 free. MC/V.)*

OTHER MAISONS. Across the street from Mercier is **De Castellane,** 57 rue de Verdun. A less romantic tour than those of M&C and Mercier, this one gets into the nitty-gritty of champagne production. Visitors during the week can observe factory workers unloading, corking, and labeling. Watching the *dégorgement* (sediment-removal process) is a treat. *(☎ 03 26 51 19 11. Open Mar. Sa-Su 10am-noon and 2-6pm, daily Apr. to late Dec. 10am-noon and 2-6pm, last tours 11:15am and 5:15pm. Full cave tour with tasting €6.50, tower and museum with tasting €4. MC/V.)* **Demoiselle Vranken,** 42 av. de Champagne, is a relatively new arrival. The young, hip staff leads tours small, casual tours. (☎ 03 26 59 50 50; www.vranken.net. Open M-Sa 10am-6pm; Oct.-Apr. closed Sa. Tour with tasting €3.50, under 15 free.)*

ENTERTAINMENT

The city's limited selection of watering holes tend to fill up at night. Try pl. de la République, **place Mendès France,** or pl. Hugues Plomb for lively bars and pubs. **Le Progrès,** 5 pl. de la République, draws a mix of 20-somethings and their elders for languorous champagne-sipping on a packed terrace. (☎ 03 26 55 22 72. Glasses of champagne from €3.90. Food served Tu-Su 6am-midnight, F-Sa until

THE BIG SPLURGE

AU BACCHUS GOURMET

Before you leave the gilded walks of Champagne and re-enter the world of the penny-pinching traveler, indulge your last-minute high-culture cravings with a meal at classy **Au Bacchus Gourmet ❺**. Its atmospheric seating area, white stone walls, and low-hanging, wrought-iron chandelier give it a cozy bistro feel, while head chef Jean-Paul Fernandès keeps the menu fresh and exciting with near-monthly updates on old favorites.

With a slew of awards to back up his title as *le meilleur saucier de France* (the best sauce-maker in France), Fernandès is famous for his unique and delicious culinary pairings, like the *homard au pamplemousse* (lobster with grapefruit). One particularly fine option is the veal *plat* featuring warm *foie gras*, asparagus, and various *legumes* (€23.50). The real deal, though, is the full three-course *menu* (€25), an ever-changing line-up of the chef's most recent all-star dishes. With that last glass of *demi-sec* and your dessert of pineapple roasted in butter and exotic *pequillo* pepper jam (€10.50), you can know that, for one day in the heart of Champagne, you sipped some of the high life and ate like a king.

(21 rue Gambetta. ☎ 03 26 5? 11 44; www.aubacchusgour met.com. Open W-Su noon-2pm and 7:30-10pm. Reservations suggested. MC/V.)

1am. MC/V.) **Le Chris's Bar,** 38 rue Sézanne, is a bar/club that sometimes features live music and always gives a friendly welcome. (☎03 26 54 38 47. Cocktails €5. Open M-Sa 3pm-4am. MC/V.)

The **Musiques d'Eté,** a series of free concerts ranging from jazz to classical to modern pop-rock, are held from the end of June to late August. (Free. For a guide of locations and times, check with the tourist office.) There is also occasional rock and world music at pl. Mendès France.

TROYES

Troyes (pop. 60,000), with its numerous pedestrian-only walkways, carefully manicured central parks, and abundant broad plazas, is a stylish city that prides itself on living the good life. Cheap and delicious local cuisine combined with massive volumes of bubbly make this city a gastronomic delight, while the infectious energy of the natives gives it a unique spark. But while Troyes can definitely party, it's no intellectual slum, either: it was here that Chrétien de Troyes wrote *Parsifal,* Jewish scholar Rashi translated the Bible and the Talmud, and a local shoemaker's son became Pope Urbain IV. Today the city is well known for its refreshing combination of well-preserved *vieille ville* beauty and lively urban atmosphere, all along main roads that cleverly form the shape of a *bouchon de Champagne* (a champagne cork).

▐ TRANSPORTATION

Trains: av. Maréchal Joffre (☎08 36 35 35 35; www.voyages-sncf.com for info and reservations). Open M-Sa 4:30am-9pm, Su 6am-9:30pm, help desk open M-Sa 9-11:45am and 2:15-6:30pm. To **Mulhouse** (3hr., 5 per day, €24), **Lyon** (6-8hr., €39.80), and **Paris** (1½hr., 14 per day, €19.80). Train lines marked "bus" are serviced by buses. ATM and lockers available. MC/V.

Buses: Go left after exiting the train station and enter the door just around the corner labeled *"gare routière."* **SDTM TransChampagne** (☎03 26 65 17 07) runs to **Reims** (2hr., 2 per day, €20). **Les Rapides de Bourgogne** (☎03 86 94 95 00) runs to **Auxerre** (2½hr., M-Th 1 per day, €15).

Public Transportation: TCAT (☎03 25 70 49 00; www.tcat.fr), in front of **Les Halles** market. Open M-Sa 8am-12:45pm and 1:30-7pm. Extensive and frequent service (every 12-23min.) Tickets €1.10, 3 for €3, pack of 65 for €10. MC/V.

Taxis: Taxis Troyens (☎03 25 78 30 30), across the street from the bus and train stations, on the curb in front of the Grand Hôtel. Base charge €2.40; before 7pm €1.50 per km, after 7pm €1.80 per km. Service M-Th, Su 4am-midnight, F-Sa 24hr.

Car Rental: Ada, 2 rue Voltaire (☎03 25 73 41 68), just south of the train station. **Budget,** 10 rue Voltaire (☎03 25 73 27 37). Open daily 8am-noon and 2-6:30pm.

▐ ▐ ORIENTATION AND PRACTICAL INFORMATION

Troyes's train station is just three blocks from the edge of the *vieille ville.* The main tourist office is one block from the train station exit, on the right at the corner of bd. Carnot; a branch office is near the town center on rue Mignard. (City website: www.ville-troyes.fr)

Tourist Office: 16 bd. Carnot (☎03 25 82 62 70; www.tourisme-troyes.com), around the corner from the train station, and rue Mignard off rue Champeaux (☎03 25 73 36 88), facing the St-Jean church. Free city map, €0.50 English brochure. Free accommodations service. Bd. Carnot branch open M-Sa 9am-12:30pm and 2-6:30pm. Rue Mig-

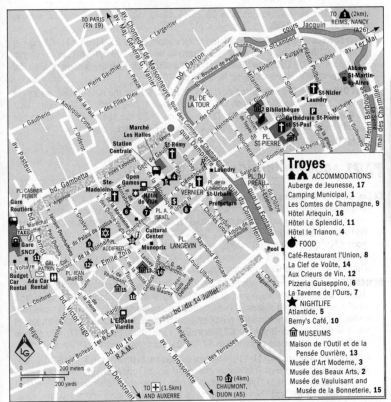

Troyes

▲▲ ACCOMMODATIONS
Auberge de Jeunesse, **17**
Camping Municipal, **1**
Les Comtes de Champagne, **9**
Hôtel Arlequin, **16**
Hôtel Le Splendid, **11**
Hôtel le Trianon, **4**

♦ FOOD
Café-Restaurant l'Union, **8**
La Clef de Voûte, **14**
Aux Crieurs de Vin, **12**
Pizzeria Guiseppino, **6**
La Taverne de l'Ours, **7**

★ NIGHTLIFE
Atlantide, **5**
Berny's Café, **10**

🏛 MUSEUMS
Maison de l'Outil et de la
   Pensée Ouvrière, **13**
Musée d'Art Moderne, **3**
Musée des Beaux Arts, **2**
Musée de Vauluisant and
   Musée de la Bonneterie, **15**

nard branch open mid-Sept. to June M-Sa 9am-12:30pm and 2-6:30pm, Su 10am-noon and 2-5pm; July to mid-Sept. M-Sa 9am-8:30pm (early Sept. 7:30pm) and Su 10am-6:30pm (early Sept. 5pm). Themed, guided tours from the Mignard office; check weekly listing (French only Sept.-June, English July to mid-Sept.; €5.50, students €2.75). The *Pass'Troyes* (€12) is the best value in town, including tastings of 2 champagnes at **Aux Crieurs de Vin**, an audio or personal tour, and admission to major sights. **Pharmacie de garde** posted in the window of the rue Mignard office. **Currency exchange** available at the rue Mignard office when banks are closed. AmEx/MC/V.

Currency Exchange: Banks with **ATMs** and **currency exchange** populate the whole city, although the exchange rate is better at the **post office. Société Générale,** 11 pl. Maréchal Foch (☎03 25 43 57 00; fax 03 25 43 57 57), has **currency exchange** for a hefty commission. Open M-F 8:30am-12:20pm and 1:30-6pm, Sa 8:30am-12:45pm.

Cultural Center: Maison du Boulanger, 16 rue Champeaux (☎03 25 43 55 00), around the corner from the rue Mignard tourist office. Tickets and administration around the corner at 42 Paillot de Montabert. Info on festivals, exhibits, and concerts. Open M-F 9am-noon and 2-6pm, Sa 10am-noon and 2-5pm.

Laundromat: Laverie Automatique, 9 rue Clemenceau (☎03 25 73 93 46). Wash €3.90 for 7kg, €0.40 per min. for a dryer. Open daily 7:30am-8pm. **Laverie St-Nizier,** 107 rue Rév. Père Lafra (☎03 25 80 66 37), past the Cathédrale. Open 24hr.

Police: 28 rue Claude Huez (☎03 25 45 17 95).

Hospital: 101 av. Anatole France (☎03 25 49 49 49). For emergency medical service, call ☎03 25 71 99 00.

Internet Access: Open Games, 24 rue Claude Huez (☎03 25 41 58 71). €1.50 per 30min., €2.80 per hr. Open daily M 2-10pm, Tu-Th 11am-10pm, F-Sa 11am-midnight, Su 2-8pm. MC/V. **L'Espace Viardin,** 10 rue Viardin. €2.50 per hr., a *carte* of 10hr. for €18. Open M-Sa 10am-midnight, Su 2-10pm. MC/V.

Post Office: 2 pl. Général Patton (☎03 25 42 32 32). From the train station, walk right onto bd. Carnot for a block. Open M-F 9am-noon and 1:30-6:30pm, Sa 9am-noon. MC/ V. **Currency exchange** available. Branch office at 38 rue Louis Ulbach, where rue Claude Huez meets rue de la République. Open Tu-F noon-6pm and Sa 9am-noon.

Postal Code: 10000.

🏠🏕 ACCOMMODATIONS AND CAMPING

🏨 **Les Comtes de Champagne,** 56 rue de la Monnaie (☎03 25 73 11 70; www.comtesde-champagne.com). 16th-century mansion features sparkling wood floors, large windows, and a central courtyard. All rooms include TV, toilet, telephone. Breakfast €5. Reception 7am-10pm. Reserve well ahead. Singles start at €28; doubles from €32; triples from €50; quads from €55; some large rooms fit 5 or 6. More expensive rooms are available, well worth the price (singles up to €55, others up to €75). Extra bed €5. Optional kitchenette €8 (available only in select rooms). DC/MC/V. ❷

🏨 **Hôtel Arlequin,** 50 rue Turenne (☎03 25 83 12 70; www.hotelarlequin.com). Though a 10min. walk from the main part of town, this aptly named establishment is worth a detour into *quartier* Vauluisant. Tastefully decorated rooms with large windows and high ceilings make this a welcoming home-away-from-home. Unbeatable multi-room suites for 3 or more guests. Breakfast €7. Reception 7am-10pm. Doubles €37, with shower €50; triples with shower or bath €56-64; quads and quints €64-72. MC/V. ❸

Auberge de Jeunesse, 10430 chemin Ste-Scholastique (☎03 25 82 00 65; www.fuaj.org/aj/troyes). This sunny converted abbey, open all year and clean as a whistle, holds 105 beds. The only catch is that it lies about 5km from the center of town. Take the #8 local bus line from town to the Liberté stop and follow the signs. Reception 8am-11pm. 5- and 6-person dorms with shower, €9. ❶

Hôtel le Trianon, 2 rue Pithou (☎03 25 73 18 52). Small but neat rooms up several flights of stairs. Convenient, central location, right next to *Les Halles* outdoor market and above a *tabac*. Breakfast €4.50. Reception 6:30am-8pm. Twin bed €19, full bed €25, with shower €34; 2 beds €30. Extra bed €4.60. MC/V. ❷

Hôtel Le Splendid, 44 bd. Carnot, across from the post office (☎03 25 73 08 52; fax 03 25 73 41 04). Le Splendid's main appeal comes from its convenience, located just moments from the train station. The rooms, however, are somewhat small and dimly lit, while bd. Carnot can be noisy, and bathrooms are often just plastic wall partitions with folding doors. Most rooms have TV and toilet. Breakfast €5.80. 24hr. reception: ring buzzer and wait. Singles from €22, with shower €37; doubles with shower €42-50. Extra bed €8. MC/V. ❷

Camping: Camping Municipal, 7 rue Salengro (☎03 25 81 02 64), on N60 2km from town. Take bus #1 (dir: Pont Ste-Marie) to this friendly 3-star site. Includes the creature comforts of showers, toilets, TV, and laundry. Open Apr. to mid-Oct. €4 per person, €5.50 per tent or car. ❶

🍴 FOOD

The **quartier St-Jean,** which encompasses the area of **rue Champeaux** south to **rue Emile Zola,** is the best place to find a scenic, hip, and savory meal. Cafes, restaurants, *brasseries,* and inexpensive *crêperies* line these pedestrian streets just west of pl. Alexandre Israël, which also form the center of Troyenne evening life. On another side of the *vieille ville*, is the smaller, charming *quartier* Vauluisant, boasts its own pedestrian avenue of gastronomic delights: **rue Général Saussier.** Reasonably priced kebab places (€5-6) also dot the less attractive **rue de la Cité.**

Les Halles, an English-style market on the corner of rue de la République and rue Général de Gaulle, offers a fresh selection of produce, meats, and baked goods from the Aube region, plus a lively outdoor flea market during the summer. Try the intense *andouillette de Troyes*, a popular tripe sausage, or the creamy and rich *fromage de Troyes*. (Open M-Th 8am-12:45pm and 3:30-7pm, F-Sa 7am-7pm, Su 9am-12:30pm. Many stalls take MC/V.) Grab groceries at the **Monoprix supermarket,** upstairs at 71 rue Emile Zola (☎03 25 73 10 78; open M-Sa 8:30am-8pm), and make it a spectacular park picnic in pl. de la Libération at the end of rue Emile Zola.

▨ **La Clef de Voûte,** 33-35 rue Général Saussier (☎03 25 73 72 07). Cheese lovers will delight in this restaurant's *fromage*, with an extensive selection of regional and exotic fondues (€10-15). The lactose intolerant can order *Andouillette AAAAA*, the local sausage with a seal of approval from the *Association Amicale des Amateurs d'Andouillettes Authentiques*. Open Tu-F noon-2pm and 7:30-10pm, Sa until 11pm. MC/V. ❸

La Taverne de l'Ours, 2 rue Champeaux (☎03 25 73 22 18). Located right off pl. Alexandre Israël, this popular restaurant's terrace is a great place to see and be seen. Their *assiettes,* from *assiette de Troyes* to *assiettes Anglaise* run €9.80-12, and their generous salads are €15. Open daily noon-2:30pm and 7-11pm. MC/V. ❸

Aux Crieurs de Vin, 4-6 pl. Jean Jaurès (☎03 25 40 01 01). Part restaurant, part wine cellar, it seems this simple eatery offers 10 times as many wine selections as meal choices. A friendly, knowledgeable staff helps diners choose the perfect vintage. A meal and glass of wine run €13. 2 glasses of champagne free with the purchase of the *Pass'Troyes* (see **Tourist Office**). Open Tu-Sa noon-2pm and 8-10:30pm; bar 11am-midnight; cave M 3-7pm, Tu-Sa 10am-10pm. MC/V. ❷

Café-Restaurant l'Union, 34 rue Champeaux (☎03 25 40 35 76). This recently established hotspot serves traditional Italian favorites to local folk on its private terrace. Pizza €8. Open noon-2pm and 7-11pm; bar 11am-3am. MC/V. ❷

Pizzeria Guiseppino, 26 rue Paillot de Montabert (☎03 25 73 92 44). Authentic, affordable Italian food served with amazing rapidity, either on a patio or inside. Pastas (€6.50-9) come with a delightful bowl of freshly grated parmesan cheese, to be applied as liberally as you please, while thin-crust pizzas (€6.60-8) taste like the best of Rome. Open daily noon-2pm and 7:30-11pm, F Sa closes at 11:30pm. ❷

⊙ ◪ SIGHTS AND OUTDOOR ACTIVITIES

CATHÉDRALE ST-PIERRE ET ST-PAUL. The sheer size of this enormous Gothic cathedral is only slightly less stunning than its spectacularly intricate stained-glass designs. A long history of fires and other disasters has claimed much of the original architecture, making the surviving windows all the more remarkable. Ranging in age from a youthful 100 to an ancient 700 years, the breathtaking stained glass dominate a cavernous, but otherwise minimalist, interior. Today art exhibits share the space with daily masses. (☎03 25 76 98 18. Pl. St-Pierre, down rue Clemenceau past the town hall. Enter via the small entrance to the right of the main doors. Open daily 10am-noon and 2-5pm, except M morning. Free.)

MUSÉE D'ART MODERNE. This attractive, well-designed museum is Troyes's cultural centerpiece, featuring over 2000 works of French art from the period 1850-1950, including pieces by Dégas, Rodin, Picasso, and Seurat. Housed in a former bishop's palace, the building and its grounds are almost as much of an attraction as the art itself. The garden contains a diverse collection of statuary, masks, and paintings from Africa and Oceania, works which often inspired, or were inspired by, their European counterparts. *(Pl. St-Pierre; directions as above.* ☎ *03 25 76 95 02.* €6, under 25 €0.80; free W. Open Tu-Su 11am-6pm.)*

MAISON DE L'OUTIL ET DE LA PENSÉE OUVRIÈRE. This unique collection of over 8000 tools from the 18th and 19th centuries, housed in a delightful 16th-century Renaissance-style mansion, is the largest such display in the world. Elaborately arranged in fascinating if bizarre artistic configurations, tools for working with wood, iron, leather, and stone never looked so exciting. *(7 rue de la Trinité.* ☎ *03 25 73 28 26; www.maison-de-l-outil.com. Guided tours €1. Open M 1-6pm, Su and Tu-Sa and holidays 10am-6pm. €6.50, children 12-17 €5, families €16. MC/V.)*

ÉGLISE ST-MADELEINE. An ornate, colorful 12th-century structure, this church boasts impossibly intricate stained glass almost as old as those of the Cathédrale. The real sight to see, though, is the impossibly detailed, Flamboyant Gothic carved stone *jubé* (gallery), which sits directly in the middle of the church and divides the nave from the choir. The panels are well labeled in English, German, and French, dispensing fascinating bits of trivia. *(Just off the ruelle des Chats.* ☎ *03 25 73 82 90. Open M 2-5pm, Tu-Sa 10am-noon and 2-5pm.)*

BASILIQUE ST-URBAIN. At night the basilica's spear-like spires are illuminated against the dark sky, but its flying buttresses are best seen in daylight. The Gothic structure was commissioned when Jacques Pantaléon became Pope Urbain IV; it rests upon the site of his father's cobbler shop. The choir and transept remain from the original 13th-century design; the basilica was thoroughly changed as late as the 15th century. *(Walk down rue Clemenceau from the Hôtel de Ville.* ☎ *03 25 73 37 13. Open daily 10am-noon and 2-5pm; closed F and M morning.)*

OTHER SIGHTS. The museum route brings travelers from modern art back through the Renaissance and well into the Stone Age. The city's second largest museum, **Musée des Beaux Arts,** offers a trove of 15th- to 19th-century paintings, regional archaeology exhibits, and some interesting attempts at taxidermy. *(*☎*03 25 76 21 68; museum@ville-troyes.fr. Open M and W-Su 10am-noon and 2-6pm. €6, not including Musée d'Art Moderne €4.60, students or under 25 €0.80; W free.)* More provincial and less organized, the **Musée Vauluisant** (which also houses the textile-centric **Musée de la Bonneterie**) displays a collection of medieval sculptures from the Troyes school, a 19th century textile artisan's workshop. *(4 rue de Vauluisant.* ☎ *03 25 73 05 85. Open June-Sept. 10am-1pm and 2pm-6pm, Oct.-May 10-12pm and 2-8pm.)*

EXCURSIONS. Over 12,500 acres of freshwater lakes dot the region around Troyes. The sunny waters of Lake Orient welcome sunbathers, swimmers, and windsurfers. The wilder Lake Temple is reserved for fishing and bird-watching, while Lake Amance roars with speedboats and waterskiers. The **Comité Départemental du Tourisme de l'Aube,** 34 quai Dampierre, provides free brochures of many local and regional outdoor activities, as well as campsites and cheap summer-camp-style lodgings in the area. *(*☎*03 25 42 60 00; fax 03 25 42 50 88. Open M-F 8:45am-noon and 1:30-6pm.)* The tourist office has bus schedules for the Troyes-Grands Lacs routes. In July and August, the **Courriers de l'Aube** takes travelers to Lake Orient three times daily. *(*☎*03 25 71 28 40. One-way €5.)* There is also a scenic 42km bikes-only path between Troyes and Port Dienville, on Lake Amance. In Dienville there is camping available at **Camping du Tertre.** *(*☎*03 25 92 26 50.)*

🎵 🎭 ENTERTAINMENT AND NIGHTLIFE

The size of Troyes's population may be dwarfed by Paris or even Bordeaux, but even the most jaded locals admit that it's a city *"qui bouge bien"* (that moves well). The most concentrated, and the most touristed, swath of local nightlife can be found amid the cafes and taverns of **rue Champeaux** and **rue Molé** off pl. Alexander Israël. Friendly, unassuming **Berny's Café,** 43 rule Molé, with a gay pride flag prominently displayed inside, is the central hang-out spot for Troyes's gay and lesbian population, though much of the clientele at this cafe/pub is straight. Relaxed during the day, the cafe picks up at night as the whole *quartier* St-Jean comes alive. (☎ 06 22 63 06 62. Open daily 10am-midnight, F, Sa closes 1:30am.) Movie theaters, arcades, and pool halls abut chic boutiques on **rue Emile Zola.** Less consistent and consequently less populated entertainment spots can be found all along the small streets **rue de la République** and **rue Raymod Poincaré.**

The hottest nightclub in Troyes changes nightly, but **Atlantide,** 19 rue Claude Huez, is never a bad bet. The crowd is predominantly gay on Sundays and may seem exclusively young on some nights. Locals of all ages, however, agree that it is a consistently good time. (☎ 03 25 73 85 76; www.club-atlantide.com. Open Su and Th-Sa nights.) Check out the ubiquitous posters advertising all of Troyes's clubs to get an idea of upcoming events and info, or inquire at the tourist office.

Lest it become known solely for the art of imbibing bubbly, Troyes hosts a number of festivals and special events. Summer welcomes the extensive **Ville en Musique,** a series of performances that runs the gamut from modern French rock to classical organ tunes. (Call ☎ 03 25 43 55 00 or stop by the Cultural Center for more info. Runs mid-June to Aug.) **Le Chemin des Bâtisseurs de Cathédrales,** a free sound-and-light spectacle, is held in the Cathedral of St-Rémy on Friday and Saturday nights at 10pm, from the last weekend in June to the end of the summer.

LANGRES

Founded 2000 years ago by the Romans as a strategic hilltop stronghold, sleepy little out-of-the-way Langres (pop. 10,000) still offers an unmatched panoramic view of the surrounding French countryside. Peaceful and gorgeous, it is consistently selected as one of the fifty most beautiful towns in France. While only its triumphal Gallo-Roman outer gate remains from the original 1st-century city walls, fortifications from its economic revival during the Renaissance prove just as stunning a sight as the older stonework. Birthplace of famed Enlightenment thinker Denis Diderot, who compiled and interpreted the known world in the first-ever encyclopedia, today the largely unchanged Langres still gives a sense of the 18th-century world he inhabited. With its ancient (and beautifully restored) limestone ramparts, winding stone-paved streets, compact *centre ville*, and ubiquitous cafes, Langres is the perfect town to relax even the most bustle-weary travelers.

⌸ TRANSPORTATION. Langres sits 3km away—and 0.5km up—from its train station. (☎ 03 25 87 75 04. Open M 5:25-11:30am and 1:45-7:20pm, Tu-Sa 8:30-11am and 1:45-6:30pm, Su 2:40-9pm. Luggage storage available. AmEx/MC/V.) **Trains** roll from the station to: Paris (3hr., 9 per day, €31.10); Reims (2½hr., 5 per day, €25.10); Troyes (1¼hr., 12 per day, €16.40); and to the hub of Culmont-Chalindrey (10min., 6 per day, €2.20). The long walk uphill from the station quickly becomes a painful, gruelling march. Local **buses** run sporadically between the stop across from the train station and the town center (M-Sa; 1 ticket €0.85, *carnet* of 10 €5.55). Schedules of departure times and stops are posted at the train station, all bus stops, and the tourist office. The impatient can call a **taxi** (☎ 03 25 87 47 31; €9 from the station to pl. Bel'Air). Those interested in exploring the countryside, or visiting one of the many tourist-friendly farms in the surrounding area can rent **bikes** from Diderot Cycles et Loisirs, 67 rue Diderot. (☎ 03 25 87 06 98; cycles.diderot@wanadoo.fr. Open Tu-Sa 9am-noon and 2-6pm. €9 per half-day, €13 per day, €22 for the weekend; €200 deposit. MC/V.)

CHAMPAGNE

7 PRACTICAL INFORMATION. The **tourist office,** located in sq. Olivier Halle, is just across from the pl. Bel'Air bus stop, and east along rue Diderot from the statue of Diderot. The friendly staff provides a free and very useful regional guide (available in English), and accommodation booking for €1. Value tickets (€5, students €3.50, under 12 free) provide access to all the major local sights. The office also provides audioguides for €5 in English, German, Dutch, and Italian. (☎03 25 87 67 67; www.tourisme-langres.com. Open May-Sept. M-Sa 9am-noon and 1:30-6:30pm, Su 10am-12:30pm and 2-6pm; Apr. and Oct. M-Sa 9am-noon and 1:30-6pm; Nov.-Mar. M-Sa 9am-noon and 1:30-5:30pm.) You can also rumble along the ramparts for an hour on the shameful *train touristique.* (Leaves from the tourist office. Tickets €5, children 4-12 €3.50. July-Aug. 7 per day 10am-6pm; May-June and Sept. W and Sa-Su afternoons 3 per day.) **Banks** with **ATMs** dot the city and line rue Diderot. The **pharmacie de garde** is listed in every pharmacy's window. There is a **laundromat** at pl. de l'Hôtel de Ville, also at the Foyer des Jeunes for €3.40 for wash and dry. **Internet** is available at Europa, on the corner of bd. de Tassigny and rue Diderot (open M-F noon-midnight, Sa-Su 9am-2am; €1.50 per 30min.), and at the post office (purchase a card, €4.60 per hour). The **police** are at the Hôtel de Ville on rue Charles Beligne (☎03 25 87 00 40). Medical care is available at the **Centre Hospitalier,** 10 rue de la Charité (☎03 25 87 88 88). On Mondays, the only **currency exchange** option is at the **post office,** 1 rue Général Leclerc. (☎03 25 84 33 30. Open M-F 8am-noon and 1:30-6pm, Sa 8am-noon.) **Postal Code:** 52200.

7 7 ACCOMMODATIONS AND CAMPING. Though the architecture and minimalist furnishings seem Soviet-inspired, the **Foyer des Jeunes Travailleurs (HI) ❶,** pl. des États-Unis, offers compact rooms at bargain prices, with the bonus of a cheap cafeteria next door. Ask for a north-facing room, which feature an outstanding view of the surrounding valley that helps to wipe away memories of the dim, institutional hallways. From the tourist office, walk through the 17th-century gateway, then left around the corner. Cross the street to the hostel, marked "Auberge de Jeunesse." (☎03 25 87 09 69; courrier@fljt.asso.fr. Sheets €3. Reception M-F 9am-12pm and 2-6:30pm, Sa 10:30am-noon, Su by reservation. Call ahead. Singles €12.30; doubles €16.40. Singles by the month €230, some with mini-fridge. Discount after 4 nights.) When the Foyer is full, try the **Hôtel de la Poste ❷,** 8-10 pl. Ziegler, directly south of pl. Diderot, a great value with friendly management and a central location. All rooms with sink and TV; ask for one across from the sunny balcony. (☎03 25 87 10 51; hoteldelaposte-langres@wanadoo.fr. Breakfast €5. Reception open M-Sa 7am-10pm, Su 5pm-10pm. Singles and doubles start at €17, with shower €27; triples with shower €44. Attached restaurant serves somewhat pricey regional cuisine in a warm setting. *Menus* start at €15. MC/V.) **Auberge Jeanne d'Arc ❸,** 24-26 rue Gambetta, on pl. Jenson across from Église St-Martin, has more pricey and cramped rooms than other hotels in town, but rooms are clean and come with TV. (☎03 25 86 87 88. Breakfast €6.50. Reception daily 7am-11pm. Singles and doubles with shower and toilet €28-55. Extra person €4.60. MC/V.) **Camping Navarre ❶** occupies prime hilltop space right next to the 16th-century Tour de Navarre at the edge of the old town, with fabulous views over the ramparts. (☎03 25 87 37 92; fax 03 25 90 24 53. Open mid-Mar. to Oct. Reception July-Aug. 6-8am and 4-10:30pm; Sept.-June 6-8am and 4-8pm. Gates closed 10pm-6:30am. €1.70, under 7 €1, €3.50 with tent or car. Electricity €2.75.)

🗂 FOOD. From fresh *foie gras* to the soft orange-cased *fromage de Langres* to the local sweet currant aperitif *rubis de groseilles,* Langrois's *spécialités de terroir* are still made the old-fashioned way: on the *local* farm. Many of these farms provide *dégustation* tours; the regional guide available at the tourist office provides contact info, but all are reachable only by car. About 10km away in Pouilly-en-Bassigny, **L'Escargot-ière des Sources** shows visitors the origins of last night's *escargot* platter. A guided tour of this snail farm, complete with tasting, costs €2.50. (☎03 25 84 29 70. Open June-Sept. Tu-W 2-6pm; M, Th-F with advanced booking. Closed Aug.) For those who wish to remain within the city walls, the **market** at pl. Jenson is open Friday mornings, and cafes on the sidestreets near pl. Diderot offer hearty plates of *fromage de Langres*. Restaurants, like everything else in town, cluster along **rue Diderot.** Lively and friendly ▓**Café de Foy ❷**, pl. Diderot, is a bargain for fresh local specials. Although the salad with walnuts and warm *fromage de Langres* (€6.90) is the most popular dish, the *formule rapide* (€11.90), with appetizer and dessert, comes in a close second. A *petite restauration* of *croque monsiuer* is only €3.35. (☎03 25 87 09 86. Open June-Aug. M-Th and Su 7am-midnight, F-Sa 7am-1:30am. AmEx/MC/V.) Unique and popular Tex-Mex grill/*crêperie* **Bananas ❸**, 52 rue Diderot, whips up both Mexican-inspired and classic French crêpes for bargain-basement prices. Try the classic egg and ham (€5.50) or the spicy "Western." (☎03 25 87 42 96. Open M-Sa noon-2:30pm and 7:30-10pm. MC/V.) The **cafeteria** next to the Foyer is cheap but surprisingly tasty. (Breakfast 8:30-9am €2.50. Lunch daily 11:45am-1:30pm, dinner 7-8:30pm.) There isn't much nightlife in Langres: local pub **Irish Corner ❷**, 22-25 Rue Diderot, is also the only place in town to get late-night grub. For a full meal, the pizza of the day (€7) is a great bargain, while during happy hour (check hours inside) all rejoice in 50dl beers for the price of 25dl. (☎03 25 87 03 56, open noon-12:30am M-Sa,. F and Sa closes at 1:30am.) Cheap, generic goods are available at **Coccinelle,** rue Diderot before pl. du Theatre. (Open M-Sa 9am-12:15pm and 2-7pm.)

◑ ▓ SIGHTS AND FESTIVALS. The ramparts have been the soul of Langres for over 2000 years; a tour of these walls and the stunning views they provide should be visitors' top priority. A good starting point is the squat **Tour de Navarre,** on the southeast corner. Erected in 1521 by François I, this outpost defended the city with 7m thick walls and a spiral ramp for moving artillery. (Open daily July-Aug. 10am-12:30pm and 2-6:30pm; May-June and Sept. Sa-Su 2:30-6pm. €2.50, under 18 €1.50.) Moving clockwise, the first-century AD **Porte Gallo-Romane,** toward the center of the south wall, is the oldest of the seven gates that allow entrance into the fortifications. Farther to the west stands the 16th-century gunnery **Tour du Petit Sault,** whose open-air terrace offers one of

IT HAD TO BE *BRUT*

When it comes time to order authentic champagne, the dizzying array of options and guidelines can intimidate all but the most seasoned connoisseur. These tips will help you join elite drinkers with confidence.

1. What goes what, now? *Brut* is an aperitif, while vintage *brut* goes with meat and mild cheese. For fish or shellfish, chardonnay is the way to go, while dessert calls for *rosé* or the sweeter *demi-sec.*

2. Only the best. *Tête de Cuvée* is the top brand of a *maison. Grand Cru* comes from only the highest quality grapes. *Premier Cru* is a step below that, while *Cru* is the bottom of the barrel. *Millésime* is a vintage bottle, the only one with a date on it.

3. Before you drink. When recently poured, champagne produces a string of bubbles that shoot straight up from the bottom of the glass. The smaller the bubbles, the more delicate the champagne. Grasp only the stem of the flute to avoid warming the liquid.

4. Smell that? Sniff the champagne once and then swish it around. When you smell it again, the odor will reveal hints of coffee, brioche, lemon, and spice.

5. No gulping! Sip the liquid delicately, rolling it around the tongue to reveal different tastes. Pay attention to indicators of quality, including persistence of the flavor (longer-lasting is better). Savor—then rinse and repeat often—you'll pay double for far lowlier champagne back home.

the best panoramic views of the surrounding countryside. (Open July-Aug. M-Tu and Th-F 2:30-6pm; May-June and Sept. Sa-Su 2:30-6pm.) On the north wall, a lonely, immobile train car commemorates the **Old Cog Railway,** the original link between the town and the valley below. **Place de la Crémaillère,** overlooks farmland and the **Réservoir de la Liez,** which offers camping, along with free swimming (complete with lifeguards in the summer) and hiking (check at the tourist office for info on sailing, waterskiing, and windsurfing). Past the **Table d'Orientation,** a fun 19th-century panel noting visible landmarks as well as far-flung destinations like Moscow and Constantinople, lies the zippy glass-and-steel **Panoramics,** the 20th century's answer to the cog railway, which whisks down the ramparts to the parking lot and road below free of charge.

Moving in from the ramparts, the highest view in town is from the south tower of the 12th-century **Cathédrale St-Mammès,** which dominates the center of town. An impressive combination of Burgundian-Romanesque and Gothic styles, the cathedral's interior is defined by its ornate 13th-century cloister and the various *objets d'art* on display in the treasury. (Cathedral open daily 8am-7pm, Nov.-Apr. closes at 5pm. Treasury open July-Aug. Su and Tu-Sa; May-Sept. open Su and holidays. Tours in French July-Aug. Su and Tu-Sa 2:30, 3:30, 4:30, and 5:30pm, Sept.-June Su only. Cathedral free, treasury €2.50, under 12 €1.50.) Also in the center of town at pl. du Centenaire, the large and polished **Musée d'Art et d'Histoire** exhibits impressive artifacts from Egypt, Rome, and Langrois prehistory. Eighteenth- and 19th-century paintings by LeBrun and Poussin are also on display. (☎03 25 87 08 05. Open Apr.-Oct. M and W-Su 10am-noon and 2-6pm; Nov.-Mar. 10am-noon and 2-5pm. English audioguides available. Wheelchair access and tours for the blind available. €3.30, students €1.75, under 18 free.)

Summer in Langres brings a number of festivals and events, mostly geared toward tourists. During **L'Estival des Hallebardiers,** held at 9:15pm every Friday and Saturday in August, locals in full Renaissance costume, along with active spectators, recreate the night watchman's patrol from more turbulent times. Those whose French is up to par can grab their capes and gallivant about town banishing the bandits and spooks of yore; otherwise, chortle over the entire proceedings along the sidelines. The festivities end with music and drink at a Renaissance tavern. (Info ☎03 25 90 77 40. €12 to participate, students €9. Begins at the cathedral cloister.) The first Saturday in June, the **Fête du Pétard** celebrates the defense of Langres in 1591 against attackers from Lorraine who unsuccessfully tried to destroy the city gates with a *pétard* (bomb). Dancers, fire eaters, and jugglers mark the three-century-old tradition. (For info, call ☎03 25 90 77 40.)

ALSACE, LORRAINE, AND FRANCHE-COMTÉ

 An unfortunate history seems the only common thread linking the wildly distinct regions of Alsace, Lorraine, and Franche-Comté together. Bordering Belgium, Switzerland, and most importantly Germany, these largely rural regions formed an eastern frontier that was the top prize in numerous Franco-German wars. Today, this battle-ridden history has given way to a more tranquil state of affairs, where cosmopolitan cities with Germanic influences possess a unique international feel.

German-influenced Alsace and Lorraine are less similar than their hyphenated twinship leads most to believe. To the east, the cities of Alsace cluster on the west side of the Rhine, against the border of their once-fatherland. German influence pervades daily life, from the architecture of half-timbered houses, to the twang of the residents, to the cuisine in the restaurants.

Lorraine unfolds to the west amid wheat fields and gently undulating plains; her elegant, well-planned cities feature broad, tree-lined boulevards and stately Baroque architecture. The cities feel distinctly ill at ease with their war-torn past, which has left farmland in cities like Verdun useless for generations. In Nancy, the region's cultural capital, turn-of-the-century artists created the anti-German Nancy School of Art Nouveau, whose works decorate the streets.

Populated by cheerful farmers, and dotted by vineyards that produce the regional drink *vin jaune* (yellow wine), Franche-Comté makes a great base for hiking in the summer, and for some of France's finest cross-country skiing in the winter.

HIGHLIGHTS OF ALSACE, LORRAINE, AND FRANCHE-COMTÉ

VISIT Ronchamp for a quiet moment at the **Chapelle de Notre-Dame-du-Haut** (p. 368), a touching WWII memorial chapel and architectural marvel by Le Corbusier.

STOP on the Route du Vin to take in the rustic beauty (and intoxicating delights) of **Kaysersberg** (p. 355).

ADMIRE Art Nouveau at its serpentine best at the **Musée de l'École de Nancy** (p. 333), where paintings, sculptures, and whole rooms have been transformed into secret gardens of flowing, organic lines.

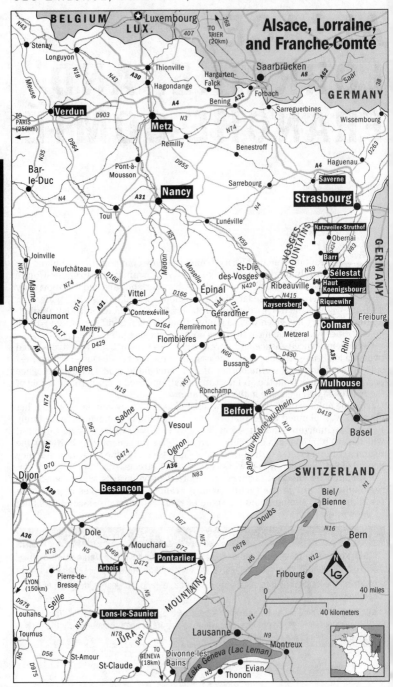

Alsace, Lorraine, and Franche-Comté

LORRAINE

NANCY

Nancy (pop. 100,000) is an intriguing mix of the classically beautiful and the innovatively fresh. During its first flourish, the city was home to the good Duke Stanislas, whose passion for urban planning transformed the city into a model of 18th-century classicism, including broad plazas, wrought-iron grillwork, and cascading fountains. Tired of the relentless order and controlled beauty around them, at the turn of the 20th century Nanciens created the lyrical Nancy School of Art Nouveau, which uses inspiration from nature to craft striking art that melds with the natural landscape. Today, the outgoing locals possess a refreshing nighttime joie de vivre, but it is still the pervasive beauty of the cityscape that makes Nancy a solid step above ordinary.

⌐ TRANSPORTATION

Flights: Aéroport de Metz-Nancy Lorraine, rte. de Vigny (☎03 87 56 70 00). Flights leave for **Alger, Clermont-Ferrand, Lyon, Marseille, Nice, Paris,** and **Toulouse.** Luggage storage available. Shuttles run to the train station (☎03 87 50 02 02; 35-40min.; 7 per day; €7, students €5.20).

Trains: 3 pl. Thiers (☎03 83 22 12 46). Ticket office open M-F 5:40am-9pm, Sa and Su 6:30am-9pm. To: **Metz** (40min., 24 per day, €8.50); **Paris** (3hr., 14 per day, €40); **Strasbourg** (1hr., 17 per day, €19.10). Luggage storage available. **SNCF Boutique** with info and reservations at 18 pl. St-Epvre. Open M 12:30-6pm, Tu-F 9:30am-1pm and 2-6pm. AmEx/MC/V.

Buses: Rapides de Lorraine Buses, 52 bd. d'Austrasie (☎03 83 36 41 14), leave from in front of the train station. Open M-Sa 7am-7:30pm.

Public Transportation: STAN. Bus maps at tourist office or **Agence STAN,** 3 rue du Dr. Schmitt (☎03 83 30 08 08; www.reseau-stan.com). Open M-Sa 7am-7:30pm. Most buses stop at Point Central on rue St-Georges. Tickets €1.15, *carnet* of 10 €8.20; buy onboard or at the station. Buses 5:30am-8pm, some to midnight. MC/V at the office.

Taxis: Taxi Nancy, 2 bd. Joffre (☎03 83 37 65 37).

Car Rental: Avis, 21 pl. des Vosges (☎03 83 36 72 97), Open M-F 8am-noon, 2-6pm, Sa 8:30am-noon and 3-6pm. MC/V. **Loca Vu,** 32 rue des Fabriques (☎03 83 35 15 05). Open daily 8am-noon and 2-7pm. MC/V.

Bike Rental: Cyclotop in the train station near the baggage deposit (☎03 83 22 11 63). €3 per hr., €5 per half-day, €7 per day. Motorbikes €6 per hr., tandems €9 per day. €61 deposit for bike or tandem, €99 for motorbike. ID required. Open M-Sa 9:45am-12:30pm, 1:30-6pm. **Michenon,** 91 rue des 4 Églises (☎03 83 17 59 59). Bikes €22 per day. €160 deposit. Open Tu-Sa 9am-noon and 2-7pm. MC/V.

✴🛈 ORIENTATION AND PRACTICAL INFORMATION

The heart of the city is **place Stanislas,** which is under construction until April 2005. To find the tourist office, head left from the station toward pl. Thiers, until you reach rue Raymond Poincaré (not rue Henri Poincaré). Follow rue Raymond Poincaré to the right (away from the station), through a stone archway, and continue straight to pl. Stanislas and the tourist office (10 minutes).

Tourist Office: pl. Stanislas (☎03 83 35 22 41; www.ot-nancy.fr). Ask for a map, a bus map, and the helpful *Le Fil d'Ariane,* a free French student guide. **Currency exchange** only when banks are closed. Same-day hotel reservation service, only with partner

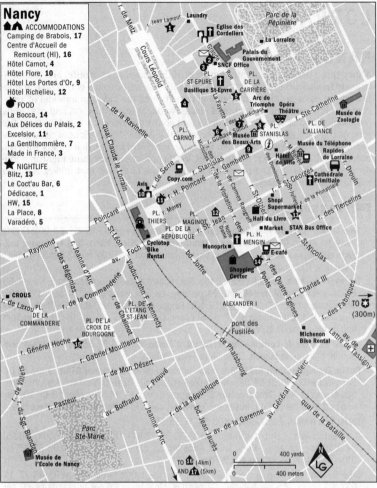

Nancy

🏠⛺ ACCOMMODATIONS
Camping de Brabois, 17
Centre d'Accueil de
    Remicourt (HI), 16
Hôtel Carnot, 4
Hôtel Flore, 10
Hôtel Les Portes d'Or, 9
Hôtel Richelieu, 12

🍴 FOOD
La Bocca, 14
Aux Délices du Palais, 2
Excelsior, 11
La Gentilhommière, 7
Made in France, 3

⭐ NIGHTLIFE
Blitz, 13
Le Coct'au Bar, 6
Dédicace, 1
HW, 15
La Place, 8
Varadéro, 5

hotels, €2 plus partial deposit. English spoken. Sells *Le Pass Nancy* (€13) which
includes a guided tour, entry to most museums, bike rental, and a movie ticket. (☎08
92 68 25 11, then code 023100). Open Apr.-Oct. M-Sa 9am-7pm, Su 10am-5pm;
Nov.-Mar. M-Sa 9am-6pm, Su 10am-1pm.

City Tours: Tourist office leads a few different themed tours of the city, from 1-2hr. July-
Aug. Sa 2:30pm, Su 10:30am; Sept.-Oct. and Mar.-June call tourist office for hours.
€6, students €4, under 6 free. English tours only available for groups by reservation.
Audioguide tours (in English, German, and Japanese) €5. Minibus tour of significant Art
Nouveau sites, in French only, July-Aug. Sa 2:30 and 4pm. €7, children under 16 €4.
Ask about a self-guided walking tour of Art Nouveau buildings in Nancy. *Petit train* offers
the usual plastic-car daily May-Sept. Departs from Porte d'Héré, near pl. Stanislas, 10am-
6pm. (☎03 89 73 74 24; www.petit-train.com. Tours available in English, French, German, Spanish, Italian, Dutch, and Danish. €5.50, €4 children under 16.)

Currency Exchange: Banks with **ATMs** and currency exchange are along rue Stanislas.

English-Language Bookstore: Hall du Livre, 38 rue St-Dizier (☎03 83 35 53 01), has an English book section. Open M-Sa 9am-8pm, Su 11am-7pm. MC/V.

Laundromat: Self Lav-o-matic, 107 rue Gabriel Mouilleron. Open daily 8am-8pm. **Le Bateau Lavoir,** 125 rue St-Dizier (☎03 83 35 47 47). Open daily 7:45am-9:30pm. **Laverie GTI,** 5 rond-point M. Simon. Open daily 7am-9pm, 5kg €2.40.

Police: 38 bd. Lobau (☎03 83 17 27 37), near the intersection with rue Charles III. Call police for the **pharmacie de garde.**

Hospital: CHRU Nancy, 29 av. du Maréchal de Lattre de Tassigny (☎03 83 85 85 85).

Internet Access: Copy.com, 3-5 rue Guerrier de Dumast (☎03 83 22 90 41). €2 for 30min., €2 per hr. Open M-Th 9am-8pm, F 9am-1pm and 3-9pm, Sa 10am-9pm, Su 3-8pm. **E-café,** 11 rue des 4 Églises (☎03 83 35 47 34). €5.40 per hr., students €4.80. Open M 11am-9pm, Tu-Sa 9am-9pm, Su 2-8pm.

Post Office: 10 rue St-Dizier (☎03 83 39 75 20). Open M-F 8am-6:30pm and Sa 8am-noon. Branches: 66 rue St-Dizier (☎03 83 17 39 11). Open M-F 8am-6:30pm, Sa 8am-noon. 75 Grande Rue; open M 12:30-6pm, Tu-F 9:30am-1pm and 2-6pm, Sa 10am-4pm.

Postal Code: 54000.

ACCOMMODATIONS AND CAMPING

CROUS, 75 rue de Laxou, helps students find summer accommodations in university dorms and is a resource for work and study opportunities. Call **Foreign Student Services** at ☎03 83 91 88 26. (Open M-F 9am-5pm. English generally spoken.) There are several nice budget hotels all around the train station, especially on rue Jeanne d'Arc, all about a 10min. walk from pl. Stanislas. The hostel is lovely but far away, and, with bus costs and wasted time factored in, it may not be the best value.

Hôtel Flore, 8 rue Raymond Poincaré (☎03 83 37 63 28; fax 03 83 90 20 94). Jovial owners let bright but well-worn rooms near the station. Some tiny, all with bath and TV. Road below is noisy until midnight. Bar downstairs attracts young people. Breakfast €4.20. Reception M-Sa 7:30am-2am, Su 11am-11pm. Reserve ahead June-Sept. Singles €26.50-32; doubles €37-40; triples €43. MC/V. ❷

Centre d'Accueil de Remicourt (HI), 149 rue de Vandoeuvre (☎03 83 27 73 67; fax 03 83 41 41 35), in Villers-lès-Nancy. From the station, take bus #122 to St-Fiacre. (Dir: Villiers Clairlieu. 2 per hr., last bus 8pm. St-Fiacre is not always a stop—check with the driver.) Turn right on rue de la Grange des Moines, which turns into rue de Vandoeuvre. Hilltop views and the château location compensate for an institutional interior, but transport can be tricky. Breakfast and sheets included. Reception daily 8am-9pm. 4- and 5-bed dorms €16.50; singles €16.50; small doubles with sink €31. MC/V. ❶

Hôtel Les Portes d'Or, 21 rue Stanislas (☎03 83 35 42 34). A small, family-run place just a block from the golden gates of pl. Stanislas. An attractive lobby leads to blue velvet stairs and comfortable, well-decorated rooms, all with bath and TV and worth the price. Breakfast €6. Reception daily 6:30am-10:30pm. Reserve ahead. Singles €45-50; doubles €50-60; triple with bath €70. Extra bed €15. MC/V. ❹

Hôtel Richelieu, 5 rue Gilbert (☎03 83 32 03 03; fax 03 83 30 21 34). A great value just off rue St-Jean, a quiet little street in the heart of the *centre ville*. Hand-decorated rooms with light wood floors, TV, mini-bar, spacious shower or bath, and toilet—take a moment and a few extra euros to live it up in the sauna (30min., €6). All-day breakfast €6. Reception daily 8am-10pm. Singles €40; doubles €45; triples €52. MC/V. ❸

Hôtel Carnot, 2-4 cours Léopold (☎03 83 36 59 58; fax 03 83 37 00 19). Convenient, with a view of peaceful pl. Carnot or a nice courtyard; top floor rooms have a great view of the cathedral. Some rooms are small, with a worn-out 70s look, while others are bright and modern. Breakfast €5. Reception M-Sa 7am-10pm, Su 9am-noon and 5:30-10pm. Singles and doubles with shower €28, with bath €31; doubles with shower and toilet €43, with bath and toilet €50; triples with shower €50. Extra bed €10. MC/V. ●

Camping: Camping de Brabois, av. Paul Muller (☎03 83 27 18 28), near the Centre d'Accueil. Take bus #125 or 122 to Camping (dir: Villiers Clairlieu). Showers, ball courts, and grocery store make this more resort than campground. Reception June-Aug. 7:30am-10pm; Apr.-May and Sept.-Oct. 8am-9pm. Open Apr. to mid-Oct. July-Aug. 2 people with tent €11.20, extra adult €3.60, child €2.10. Apr.-June and Sept.-Oct. 2 people with tent €9.60. Extra adult €3.60, children 2-7 free. Electricity €3.30. ●

▢ FOOD

Nancy's signature *bergamote* is a bitter hard candy flavored by the orange spice used in Earl Grey tea; all of the *pâtisseries* off pl. Stanislas sell these overpriced suckers. Otherwise, Nancy's regional cuisine, including *quiche Lorraine*, contributes generously to the love handles of the world. The covered **marché central** is off rue St-Dizier in pl. Henri Mengin (open Tu-Th 7am-6pm, F-Sa 7am-6:30pm), a **Shopi supermarket** is at 26 rue St-Georges (☎03 83 35 08 35; open M-F 9am-8pm, Sa 9am-7:30pm; MC/V), and a larger **Monoprix** is in the Centre Commercial St-Sebastian off pl. Henri Mengin. (☎03 83 17 78 71. Open M-Sa 8:30am-8:30pm. MC/V.) Restaurants spill from **rue des Maréchaux** onto pl. Lafayette and up Grande Rue to pl. St-Epvre. For afternoon snacks, there are crêpe stands behind pl. Stanislas on the **Terrace de la Pépinière** and cheap kebab joints along **rue Stanislas** and its surroundings.

Reserve ahead or come early to ▨**Aux Délices du Palais ●**, 69 Grande Rue, a hip sandwich and *tartine* joint, where locals swivel on cowprint stools and munch on meat- or veggie-packed monsters with regional nicknames, including the overweight, beefy "Yankee." (☎03 83 30 44 19. Sandwiches €4.50-6. Open Tu-Sa noon-1:45pm and 7-9:30pm.) One of the classier eateries on restaurant row, **La Gentilhommière ●**, 29 rue des Maréchaux, offers scrumptious regional specialties with a twist, including *magret de canard* with seasonal fruits or *filet de saumon* in wine sauce and truffles, each €13. (☎03 83 32 26 44. Open M-F noon-2pm and 7-10pm, Sa 7:30-10pm. Reservations suggested in summer. MC/V.) ▨**La Bocca ●**, 33 rue des Ponts, is a date-worthy Italian restaurant with heart-shaped velvet chairs and zebra-print lamp shades. Drinks (€6.50) are pink, deliciously sweet, and alcoholic. (☎03 83 32 74 47. 3-course *menu* €15.50, lunch *menu* €10, pastas and meal salads €7.50-12.50. Open M and W-F 11:30am-2:30pm and 7-11pm, Tu 11:30am-2:30pm, Sa 11:30am-2:30pm and 7pm-midnight. MC/V.) For huge sandwiches, try **Made in France ●**, 1 rue St-Epvre, a take-out-only hole-in-the-wall that prides itself on its fresh bread and vegetables. (☎03 83 37 33 36. Sandwiches with three toppings €2.30-5.10. Fruit milkshakes €2.80. Open M-Sa 11:30am-9pm. MC/V.) **Excelsior ●**, 50 rue Henri Poincaré, is an Art Nouveau-style *brasserie* that specializes in *choucroute aux trois poissons* in Champagne (€17.50) and other *nancienne* cuisine. (☎03 83 35 24 57; www.brasserie-excelsior.com. Open for drinks daily 8am-midnight, restaurant service noon-3pm and 7pm-midnight. AmEx/MC/V.)

◉ SIGHTS

▨ **PLACE STANISLAS.** The city's cultural center and the most impressive sight in Nancy, its three neoclassical pavilions were commissioned in 1737 by Stanislas Lesczynski, the former king of Poland and then-duke of Lorraine, to honor his nephew, Louis XV. The finely molded *Portes d'Or* (Golden Gates) dazzle during the day, but the nightly light shows *(son-et-lumière;* July-Aug. 10pm) are spectacular. Unfortunately, the entire place is under renovation until April 2005, just in time for the 250th anniversary celebrations in July. From pl. Stanislas, pass through the five-arch **Arc de Triomphe** to the tree-lined **place de la Carrière,** a former jousting ground refurbished by Stanislas with Baroque architecture, classical angel sculptures, and wrought-iron ornaments.

▧ MUSÉE DE L'ÉCOLE DE NANCY. If nature could craft its own art, it would look something like the Nancy School works that populate this tremendous museum. Rejecting the straight-laced straight lines of all art and architecture that came before, the artists of the Nancy School of Art Nouveau used inspiration from organic forms to create truly original works that seem to meld into the natural landscape. The museum is housed in the former home of a Nancy School collector, and a trip through its lushly decorated rooms feels like a step into the wilderness: the delicate beauty of Emile Gallé's butterflied glassworks seems plucked from a nymph-filled forest. No visit is complete without a walk through the tremendous gardens. Ask to borrow the detailed English guide at the front desk. *(36-38 rue du Sergent Blandan. Take bus #122 or 123, dir: Vandoeuvre Cheminots, to Sédillot or Paul-Painlevé. ☎ 03 83 40 14 86; www.ecole-de-nancy.com. Open W-Su 10:30am-6pm. Tours in French F-Su 3pm, €6.10. €4.60, students €2.30, under 12 free. An €8 pass buys entry to Nancy's museums. First Su of each month 10am-1:30pm free, W students free. MC/V over €15.)*

PARC DE LA PÉPINIÈRE. This park is one of the most popular and relaxing places in the city. Expanses of rigorously controlled flowers and trees give way to a sprawling zoo and an outdoor cafe. The aromatic **Roseraie** displays vibrant flowers from around the world. Be sure not to miss Rodin's famous (and controversial) sculpture of **Claude Gallée (le Lorraine),** which features Apollo and galloping horses. To the shock of its commissioners, Gallée himself looks less inspirational than he does confused, awkward, and distorted. The statue is located directly north of the main entrance. *(Just north of pl. de la Carrière, near pl. Stanislas. Open daily June-Aug. 6:30am-10:30pm; Apr.-May and Sept.-Oct. 6:30am-9pm; Nov.-Mar. 6:30am-8pm. Free.)*

MUSÉE DES BEAUX-ARTS. In a stately Baroque building (whose entrance was designed in 1755 for Stanislas himself), a collection of paintings and sculptures spans the centuries from 1380 to the present. It includes gems by Rubens, Delacroix, Monet, Modigliani, Rodin, and Picasso, and a fantastic exhibit of Art Nouveau Daum glasswork, all presented in a bright and colorful exhibition space. *(3 pl. Stanislas. ☎ 03 83 85 30 72. Open M and W-Su 10am-6pm. Tours in French €1.60. €4.60, students and children €2.30. First Su of each month 10:30am-1:30pm free, W students free.)*

OTHER SIGHTS. Unusual for a French city, the churches here are neither the oldest nor the most interesting monuments. The 19th-century **Basilique St-Epvre** is known for its brilliant windows from around the world. It hosts free evening concerts of classical and organ music. *(Off Grande Rue at pl. St-Epvre. Open daily 8am-7pm.)* Notable for its ornate 18th-century painted dome is the **Cathédrale Primitiale,** though the rest of the interior (excluding a few happy cherubs) is classically plain. *(Rue St-Georges, just past rue Montesquieu. Open daily 8am-7pm.)* Undergoing extensive renovations until June 2005, the new **Musée Zoologique** promises to be spectacular. During renovations, the enjoyable reef-replicas that fill the aquariums on the first floor are still open to the public. *(34 rue Ste-Catherine. ☎ 03 83 32 99 97; www.man.uhp-nancy.fr. Open Apr.-Aug. 10am-noon and 2-6pm; Sept.-Mar. M-Sa 2-6pm, Su 10am-noon and 2-6pm. During renovations, €3, students and under 16 free. Normal fees €4.55, students €3.05, under 16 €0.75.)* The innovative little **Musée du Téléphone,** on a quiet street off pl. Stanislas, traces the history of man's quest to reach out, from telegraph stations to today's

NOUVEAU ART, OLD POLITICS

While much of what is *"nouveau"* in Art Nouveau is the artists' rejection of classical themes, which they found stagnant and repetitive, the Nancy School used organic imagery with a much more significant agenda in mind.

It is no coincidence that the Nancy School flourished from 1880 to 1910, when anti-German sentiment ran highest in eastern France; after the 1870 annexation of northern Lorraine by Germany, artists in Nancy sought a way of innovating a regional style to represent a free and French Lorraine. As imposing Greco-Roman styles were still very much the mode in Germany, the Nancy School's embrace of nature represented a fervent rejection of the traditions that gave birth to such a civilization.

In particular, Nancy School artists settled on use of the thistle, the flower of Lorraine, as the dominant motif for their staunchly anti-German work. Its prickly defensive thorns and ability to grow in difficult conditions made it a "warrior" plant, seen as an appropriate representative of the spirit of the maligned people of Lorraine. In the Musée de l'École de Nancy, a dark wooden desk by Emile Gallée bears the mark of a thistle, along with writing declaring it representative of Lorraine on this side of the Rhine." The art changes; the politics remain the same.

cordless wonders. Two floors of exhibits are hands-on. Surf the Internet for €3 per hr. *(11 rue Maurice Barrès. ☎ 03 83 86 50 00; www.maison-communication.asso.fr. Open Tu-F 10am-7pm, Sa 2pm-7pm, 1st Su of every month 2-6pm. €3, students €1.50.)*

🎵 📷 ENTERTAINMENT AND NIGHTLIFE

Soak up the evening beauty of the illuminated **place Stanislas** from one of its ritzy cafes, or grab a cheaper drink on **rue Stanislas** or **Grande Rue.** Check www.nancybynight.com or www.yellow-night.com for updates on bars, clubs, concerts, and theater events. ◼**Blitz,** 76 rue St-Julien, is smoky coolness at its best. Red-velvet everything is peppered with Chinese prints and vintage knick-knacks. (☎03 83 32 77 20. Shots €2, beer €2, absinthe €4, cocktails €2.50. Open June-Aug. Tu-Sa 11am-2am, Su 2pm-2am. MC/V.) Trendy 20-somethings also head to ◼**Varadéro,** 27 Grande Rue, a Cuban-style bar with a live DJ and a revolutionary flavor. Excellent mojitos (€4.50) and tasty mixed drinks make this the perfect social hotspot. (☎03 83 36 61 98. Shots €1.50, cocktails €4.50. Open Tu-Sa 8pm-2am. MC/V.) **Dédicace,** 9 rue Jean Lamour, is a fun-filled, slightly over-the-top gay bar, with regular drag shows and racy theme nights. Come on Tuesday to play *poste-éclair,* a mature version of spin-the-bottle. Outside of theme nights, the bar is much quieter. (☎03 83 36 95 52. Beer €2.50, cocktails €3-7. Open M-Sa 6pm-2am, Su 4pm-2am. MC/V.) Lesbians and their talkative friends of all orientations flock to chill and friendly feeling **Le Coct'au Bar,** 4 rue Gustave Simon, a gay bar that offers *bonbon*-accompanied cocktails and charming service. (☎03 83 32 02 81. Beer from €2.80, cocktails €3-6. Open Tu-Th 11am-midnight, F-Sa 11am-2am. MC/V.) Popular with everyone in Nancy is the techno/house mix and sleek, chic, *magnifique* setting of gay-friendly ◼**La Place,** 7 pl. Stanislas. (☎03 83 35 62 63. Discotheque open W-Su 10pm-5am.) At **HW,** 1 rue du Général Hoche, young crowds dance to techno under the lofty ceilings and chandeliers of a converted warehouse. Be cautious; the walk is dark and deserted at night. (Beer €3. Open M-F 10pm-4am, Sa-Su midnight-6am.)

For two weeks in October, at the **Jazz-Pulsations** festival in **Parc de la Pépinière,** well-known international musicians set feet a-tapping from dusk until dawn. (104 Grande Rue. ☎ 03 83 35 40 86; www.nancyjazzpulsations.com. Tickets €5-66, discounts for students. Prices higher at the door.) In summer, nightly concerts emanate from the Roseraie. A free light show *(son-et-lumière)*, held north of pl. Stansilas, details Nancy's history. (Daily July-Aug. 10pm.) In 2005, **Opéra de Nancy et de Lorraine,** pl. Stanislas, will present *Madame Butterfly*, *The Barber of Seville*, *Un Giorno di Regno*, and *Avis de Tempête* on various dates from December to July. (☎03 83 85 33 11. Open Oct.-June M-Sa 8am-noon and 1-5pm. Tickets available Tu-Sa 1-7pm; tickets €6.10-48.80, students 20% off and €7.60 for all tickets remaining 15min. before show.) Ballets and symphonies will also occur throughout the year. (☎03 83 32 31 25. Ticket office open M-F 1-7pm. Tickets €13.70-20.60, students 20% off and €4.60 rush.) The **Festival International de Chant Choral** brings 2000 singers from around the world. (Office at 150 rue Jeanne d'Arc. ☎03 83 27 56 56. Next concert mid-May 2005. Free.)

July 10-11, 2005, pl. Stanislas is commemorating its **250th anniversary** with an enormous celebration in the newly renovated plaza. Though the events have not as of yet been planned, they are projected to include concerts, guided tours, and general entertainment—all free of charge, in and around the plaza. A full program will be available from the tourist office in early June 2005.

METZ

Metz's calm, honey-colored *vieille ville*, carefully maintained parks, and meandering riverside esplanades belie its turbulent and emotional history. One of the few cities in Lorraine ceded to the Germans following the Franco-Prussian war in 1870, much of the architecture of Metz (pronounced "mess;" pop. 275,000) reflects the culture wars that ensued. While much of the city's traditional yellow-stone monuments are in such quintessential French styles as Louis XIV, the massive neo-Roman Germanic train station—though still in a Metzian yellow stone—was designed by German occupiers to be able to ship 25,000 troops into France per day, and was used against the city's former fatherland at the outbreak of the Great War. Now thoroughly French again, modern Metz is a peaceful stroller's heaven, with fountains, cobblestones, canals, and a fabulous cathedral. The Esplanade, an impressive walkway packed with tourists and locals, extends to the river Moselle, one of the two rivers that has made Metz rich from trade through the centuries. Home to a recently founded university, the refreshingly calm city also knows how to kick up its heels at night.

▐ TRANSPORTATION

Trains: pl. du Général de Gaulle (☎08 36 35 35 35). Office open Sept. to mid-June M-F 8:30am-7pm, Sa 8:30am-6pm; mid-June to Aug. M-F 8:30am-7:30pm, Sa 8:30am-6pm. Ticket window open daily 5:30am-10:30pm. Luggage storage €4.50 per bag per day. To: **Luxembourg** (45min., every hr., €11.40); **Lyon** (5hr., 4 per day, €48); **Nancy** (40min., 15 per day, €8.50); **Paris** (4hr., 8 per day, €41.10); **Strasbourg** (1½hr., 12 per day, €19.80).

Buses: Les Rapides de Lorraine, 2 rue de Nonnetiers (☎03 87 75 26 62, schedules 03 87 36 23 34). Take the underpass to the right of the station, below the tracks, then go left. Ticket window open M-Th 8am-noon and 2-5pm, F until 4pm. To **Verdun** (1hr., 2-3 per day, €6.20) and smaller towns. **Eurolines** travels all over Europe.

Public Transportation: TCRM, pl. de la République (☎03 87 76 31 11; www.republicain-lorrain.fr). Office open July-Aug. M-F 9am-6:30pm; Sept.-June M-F 7:30am-6:30pm, Sa 8:30am-5:30pm. Most lines run M-F 5:30am-8pm, Sa-Su less often. Line #11 runs 10pm-midnight. Tickets €0.90, *carnet* of 6 €4, day pass €3.

Taxis: (☎03 87 56 91 92), at the train station.

Car Rental: Avis (☎03 87 50 60 30), at the train station. Open M-F 8am-12:15pm, 1:30-7pm, and 8-9:30pm; Su 4:30-8:30pm. AmEx/MC/V. **Europcar, Budget, National,** and **Hertz** are also at the station.

Bike Rental: Vélocation (☎03 87 62 61 79), at the train station. €3 per half-day, €5 per day, €12 per week. €50 deposit. Open M-F 6am-8pm.

■✴ 🛈 ORIENTATION AND PRACTICAL INFORMATION

The honey-colored *vieille ville* is mostly off-limits to cars. The cathedral dominates the **place d'Armes;** the tourist office is across the street, in the Hôtel de Ville. From the station, it's about a 20min. walk: take a right, then a left onto rue des Augustins, which becomes rue de la Fontaine, pl. du Quarteau, and pl. St-Louis. At pl. St-Simplice, turn left onto rue de la Tête d'Or, then right onto rue Fabet. Minibus lines A and B go to pl. d'Armes from a stop to the right of the train station (every 8min. 7:30am-8pm).

Tourist Office: 2 pl. d'Armes (☎03 87 55 53 76; www.tourisme.mairie-metz.fr). English-speaking provides hotel reservations (€1.50, only in partner hotels) and maps. Arranges special weekends in Metz with hotel, dinner, and a guided visit; €74 per person, 2 person min. **Internet** with *télécarte* €0.12-0.18 per 3min. **Currency exchange.** Open July-Aug. M-Sa 9am-8:30pm, Su 10am-5pm; Mar.-June and Sept.-Oct. M-Sa 9am-7pm, Su 10am-5pm; Nov.-Feb. M-Sa 9am-6:30pm, Su 10am-5pm.

Tours: City tours by the tourist office M-Sa 3pm in French. €7, under 10 €3.50. English, German, Italian, Dutch, or Spanish audioguides €7. Themed tours, night tours, and other special events; check tourist office for info. Enjoyable 45min. tour by *petit train* takes visitors through city and remote gardens. (☎03 87 73 03 08. Departs from the cathedral; 10:30, 11:30 and 1-6pm on the hr. €5.50, €3.50 children.)

Budget Travel: Agence Wasteels, 3 rue d'Austrasie (☎03 87 50 54 46). Student rates and passes. Open M-Th 9am-noon and 2-6pm, F 9am-noon and 2-7pm, Sa 9am-noon.

Youth Center: Centre Régional d'Information Jeunesse, 1 rue de Coëtlosquet (☎03 87 69 04 50). Info on hiking, religious organizations, concerts, travel, lodging, study, and work opportunities. Open M-Th 9am-5pm, F 10am-5pm.

Laundromat: 23 rue Taison. Open daily 7am-8pm. Also at 22 rue du Pont-des-Morts (☎03 87 63 49 57). Open daily 7am-8pm. €3.50 per 8kg.

Police: 45 rue Belle Isle (☎03 87 53 69 31), near pl. de Pontiffroy.

Hospital: Centre Hospitalier Regional Metz-Thionville, 1 pl. Phillipe de Vigneulles (☎03 87 55 31 31), near pl. Maud Huy.

Internet Access: Espace Multimédia, 2 rue du Four du Cloître (☎03 87 36 56 56). Free. Reservations required. Open M 1-6pm, Tu-Sa 9am-6pm. **Boutique des Services,** 9 rue des Clercs (☎03 87 75 97 13). €0.05 per min., €9 for 3hr. Open M 2-7pm, Tu-Sa 10am-7pm.

Post Office: 9 rue Gambetta (☎03 87 56 74 30). **Currency exchange.** Open M-F 8am-7pm and Sa 8:30am-12:30pm. Branch at Centre Commercial (☎03 87 37 99 00). Open M-F 9am-7pm, Sa 9am-noon and 1:30-5pm; limited Sa afternoons. Another at 3 rue de la Pierre Hardie (☎ 03 87 37 75 74). Open M-F 9am-7pm, Sa 9am-5pm. Also at 39 pl. St-Louis (☎03 87 18 47 74). Open M 2-6pm, Tu-F 9am-6pm, Sa 9am-noon.

Postal Code: 57000.

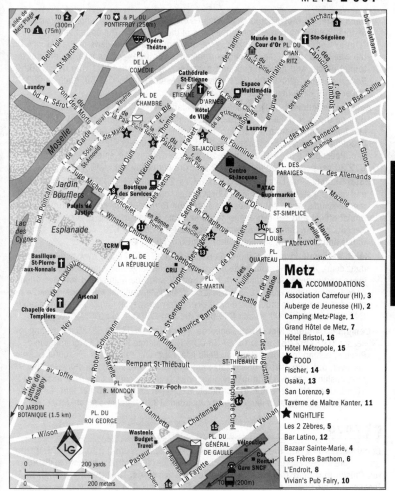

Metz

⌂⌂ ACCOMMODATIONS

Association Carrefour (HI), **3**
Auberge de Jeunesse (HI), **2**
Camping Metz-Plage, **1**
Grand Hôtel de Metz, **7**
Hôtel Bristol, **16**
Hôtel Métropole, **15**

♦ FOOD

Fischer, **14**
Osaka, **13**
San Lorenzo, **9**
Taverne de Maître Kanter, **11**

★ NIGHTLIFE

Les 2 Zèbres, **5**
Bar Latino, **12**
Bazaar Sainte-Marie, **4**
Les Frères Barthom, **6**
L'Endroit, **8**
Vivian's Pub Fairy, **10**

⌂⌂ ACCOMMODATIONS AND CAMPING

Relatively inexpensive (but generally high-quality) hotels cluster around the train station. Pricier accommodations are in the pedestrian district.

Association Carrefour/Auberge de Jeunesse (HI), 6 rue Marchant (☎03 87 75 07 26; www.carrefour-metz.asso.fr). Take minibus A or B from the station to pl. d'Armes (every 15min. 7:30am-7pm, €0.60), head right along rue En Fournirue, and left on rue Taison, which becomes rue Marchant. Clean rooms and a friendly atmosphere, but question-able room security. Singles and doubles are a bargain. Breakfast included. Laundry €3. Sheets €4.25. Reception 24hr. 3- and 4-bed dorms €12.30 per person; singles and doubles €14.10. Non-members €2.90 extra per night for first 6 nights. MC/V. ❶

Grand Hôtel de Metz, 3 rue des Clercs (☎ 03 87 36 16 33; www.hotel-metz.com), a restored 18th-century mansion in the heart of the *vieille ville*. The operative word here is "grand," with comfortable lounges, gorgeous rooms, and fine views of the old city. On the weekends, book 24hr. ahead and mention *Bon week-end en ville*, an offer of the tourist office, and get 2 nights and breakfasts for the price of 1. Breakfast €6.50. Reception daily 7am-11pm. Reservations suggested. Singles €52-59; doubles €59-90 (most €70). Extra bed €6.10. AmEx/MC/V. ❹

Auberge de Jeunesse (HI), 1 allée de Metz Plage (☎ 03 87 30 44 02; fax 03 87 33 19 80), on the river. Take bus #3 (dir: Metz-Nord; last bus 8:30pm) or #11 (dir: St-Eloy; last bus midnight) from the station to Pontiffroy. Friendly staff tends cozy rooms on a beautiful river. Free bike loans. Breakfast included. Sheets €2.90. Free luggage storage. Reception daily 8-10am and 5-10pm. Reservations suggested. 2- to 6-bed dorms €12.30 per person. Non-members €2.90 extra per night. AmEx/MC/V ❶

Hôtel Bristol, 7 rue Lafayette (☎ 03 87 66 74 22; fax 03 87 50 67 89). Small, clean, and near the station, this is Metz's best budget option, with an odd retro 70s look. On the weekends, book 24hr. ahead and mention *Bon week-end en ville,* an offer of the tourist office, and get two nights and breakfasts for the price of 1. Breakfast €5.50. Reception 24hr. Singles €26, with shower €28-41; doubles €29, with shower €41-54; triples and quads with shower €49-54. AmEx/D/MC/V. ❸

Hôtel Métropole, 5 pl. du Général de Gaulle (☎ 03 87 66 26 22; www.hotelmetropole-metz.com). This lovely stationside behemoth features large and sunny rooms, and great views and service. All rooms with bath and TV and free high-speed Internet. Higher priced rooms come with A/C. Breakfast €6. 24hr reception. On weekends, book 24 hr. ahead of time and mention the *Bon week-end en ville* special. Singles €39-54; doubles €43-58; triples €56-62; quads €60-66. Extra bed €6.80. AmEx/DC/MC/V. ❹

Camping: Camping Metz-Plage, allée de Metz-Plage (☎ 03 87 68 26 48, during low season 03 87 62 26 36; fax 03 87 38 03 89), bordering the river. Enter from rue de la Piscine, behind the hospital on rue Belle Isle. Caravans everywhere. Beautiful views of the river, but little privacy on the large grassy plot. Showers, grocery store, laundry, TV room, fishing, and a giant public pool just next door. Reception daily 7am-noon and 2-10pm. Open May-Sept. €2.40 per adult, €1.20 per child, €2.40 per tent, €4.40-per car, €5.70-11.50 per trailer. Electricity included. 10% off in low season. MC/V. ❶

▣ FOOD

Local *pâtissiers* pop the region's yellow *mirabelles* (plums) into everything from tarts to preserves. Bakeries and other cheap eateries cluster in the **pedestrian district** on **rue Coislin** and near the hostel on **rue du Pont-des-Morts.** Restaurants line **place St-Jacques** and **rue Dupont des Loges.** The **Centre St-Jacques,** off pl. St-Jacques, has specialty stores, cheap eateries, and an **ATAC supermarket** in the basement. (☎ 03 87 74 02 90. Open M-Sa 8:30am-7:30pm. MC/V.) The biggest **markets** are near the cathedral and pl. St-Jacques. (Open Oct. to mid-Apr. Th and Sa 7am-1pm.) Kebab stands occupy every corner of pl. St-Jacques and dot many of the surrounding streets. Locals love the German flavor of the **Taverne de Maître Kanter ❸**, 38 rue des Clercs. The €15.20 *formule taverne* incorporates specialties *tarte flambée* (or *Flammeküche*) and *choucroute brasserie*. Shellfish are a particular specialty: pick your lobster out of the giant waterfall tank in the front. (☎ 03 87 75 01 18. *Tartes* a la carte €7-8, *choucroute* €9-18.50. Open daily noon-midnight. AmEx/MC/V.) A scrumptious selection of large, inexpensive sandwiches and a drool-worthy choice of baked goods reflect the devotion of **Fischer ❶**, 6 rue François de Curel, to *l'art du pain*. (☎ 03 87 36 85 97; www.fischer.lu. Sandwiches €3.10-3.55, salads €4.10-5.40. Open M-F 7am-7pm, Sa 7am-6pm.) At **San Lorenzo ❷**, 8 rue Dupont des Loges, sample the taste of *Italia* as rendered by *les Français*. Locals pack down heaping pasta dishes (€7-13) and tasty pizzas (€7-12), but maintain their patriotism with a bottle of local wine. (☎ 03 87 76 15 53. Meal-sized *salade Italienne* €9.50. Open daily 11:45am-2pm and 6:45pm-midnight. MC/V.) Unlike Italian food, good Japanese food isn't exactly a thriving nationwide phenomenon in France, so the spectacular sushi at **Osaka ❸**, 32bis rue Dupont des Loges, is a welcome treat. (☎ 03 87 36 68 90. Sushi *menu* €15, teriyaki dishes €10-13. Open daily noon-2:30pm and 7-10:45pm. MC/V.)

🔆 SIGHTS

▓ CATHÉDRALE ST-ETIENNE. This 13th-century golden cathedral, known to locals as the "lantern of God," stands at 42m tall and is the third-tallest in France. It has the world's largest collection of stained glass, with over 6500m² of glass ranging from the 13th to 20th centuries. Don't miss Chagall's dazzling ultra-modern window in the western transept and the brilliantly illuminated glass of Chapelle de St-Sacrement near the welcome desk. Be sure to stop by after dark to see the glowing stained-glass windows. The climbable Mutte Tower features 300 vertigo-inducing stairs, where the intense claustrophobia is relieved only by a look out the windows and the subsequently fear of falling to certain doom. The view at the top is worth it, but the fearful (or out of shape) shouldn't even consider the precarious climb. *(Pl. d'Armes. ☎ 03 87 75 54 61. Open M-Sa 8am-7pm, Su 1-7pm. Desk open M-Sa 10am-1pm and 2-6pm, Su 2-6pm. Tours in French 10:30am and 3pm. €4, with visit to crypt €5. Crypt and treasury open M-Sa 10am-noon, 2-6pm, Su 2-6pm. €1 each. Tours of the Mutte Tower at 2, 4:30, 5:30pm; €7.)*

▓ ESPLANADE AND GARDENS. At the other end of rue des Clercs from pl. d'Armes, the Esplanade, a vast formal garden overlooking the Moselle Valley, is possibly Metz's best feature. The western end finishes in spectacular waterfall fountains, the 20th-century **fontain de l'esplanade,** which also overlook the lake. The tourist office has a map of trails in the garden, which are also marked on-site. Down the steps from the Esplanade, paths circle the shady **Lac aux Cygnes.** Paddle or pedal your way across this forest-surrounded oasis with rentals from La Flotille. *(1 quai des Régates. ☎ 03 87 36 86 71. Paddleboats €9.40 for 30min., motorboats €15 for 30min.)* In summer, the spectacularly illuminated fountains spurt in tune to music for *Les Eaux Musicales du Lac aux Cygnes. (Late June to early Sept. F-Su at nightfall. Free.)* Swans preen at the **Jardin Botanique,** a botanist's heaven packed with flower beds and tagged trees. In the center, a greenhouse nurtures ferns. *(☎ 03 87 55 54 00. Garden open 8am to sunset; greenhouse open Apr.-Sept. M-F 9am-6:45pm, Sa-Su 9-11:30am and 2-6:45pm; Oct.-Mar. M-F 9am-4:45pm, Sa-Su 9-11:30am and 2-4:45pm.)*

OTHER SIGHTS. The **Basilique St-Pierre-aux-Nonnains** is the oldest church in France, erected by the Romans in AD 380 to accommodate large baths and a sports arena. It became a chapel in the seventh century. Be impressed by the history of this sight, as little except for old and very bricky walls are left to physically indicate its age. It's now an exhibition space for modern art. *(☎ 03 87 39 92 00. Open May-Sept. Tu-Su 2-6:30pm; Oct.-Apr. Sa-Su 2-6pm.)* Built over a swamp, the **Place de la Comédie** served a less-than-comedic function during the Revolution: its main attraction was the guillotine, where 63 men were beheaded. The 1751 **Opéra-Théâtre** here is the oldest functioning theater in France. *(4-5 pl. de la Comédie. ☎ 03 87 55 51 43. For tickets, call the Bureau de Location ☎ 03 87 75 40 50. Ticket office open M-F 9am-12:30pm and 2-5pm. Tickets €9.20-46.20, students €4.60-12.30. MC/V.)* Along with an assortment of Gallo-Roman remnants, the **Musée de la Cour d'Or** is a reconstruction of Roman baths, dimly lit and atmospheric. Upstairs, the **Musée des Beaux-Arts** highlights local works from the 17th to 19th centuries. *(2 rue du Haut-Poirier, in the Cour d'Or. ☎ 03 87 68 25 00. Open M and W-F 9am-5pm, Sa-Su 10am-5pm. Audioguide in 5 languages €2.30. €4.60, under 25 €2.30, under 12 free, everyone free 1st Su of every month.)*

♫ ENTERTAINMENT

During the first half of 2005, the **Opéra-Théâtre** will feature the opera *Death in Venice*, the ballet *Four Days in Paris*, the drama *Driving Miss Daisy*, and a number of other notable works (see **Sights: Place de la Comédie**, for ticket info). **Arsenal,** av. Ney, is a beautiful modern concert hall and exhibition space that hosts a wide range of performances. (☎03 87 39 92 00, reservations 03 87 74 16 16; www.mairie-metz.fr/arsenal. Open Tu-Sa 1-6pm, Su 2-6pm. MC/V.) For bargain shoppers, Metz's twice-monthly **marché aux puces** (flea market) is France's second-largest outside Paris. (Ask tourist office for a brochure or call ☎03 87 55 66 00; www.fim-metz.com. Open Sa 6am-noon, Su 7am-6pm.)

Metz en Fête incorporates free outdoor classical concerts, theater, jazz and blues recitals, and organ music in the cathedral, beginning in July. (Info from the tourist office or www.mairie-metz.fr.) These *soirées* culminate in the **Grandes Fêtes de la Mirabelle** at the end of August, a festival held in honor of the plum that includes conversion of the Grand Corso de la Mirabelle into a huge street party. In the month leading up to Christmas, Metz hosts a particularly elaborate **Marché de Noël,** with over 100 special events held in pl. St-Louis and pl. du Général de Gaulle.

♫ NIGHTLIFE

Metz has an amazing set of bars and some good clubs. At night, students pack the bars and cafes at **place St-Jacques. Place St-Louis** is another hotspot.

▨ **Le Bazaar Sainte-Marie (BSM),** 2bis-4 rue Ste-Marie (☎03 87 21 05 93). A quirky place full of color and the sort of furniture one might find, well, at a bazaar. Perfect for laid-back types with a yen for some atmosphere. Weekends a DJ plays house, groove, and funk. Beer from €2.90. Open M-Th 10am-2am, F-Sa 10am-3am. AmEx/MC/V.

▨ **Les Frères Berthom,** 24 rue du Palais (☎03 87 75 25 52; www.lesfreresberthom.com), on the corner of rue du Palais and en Nexirue. Popular and loud chain pub is silly and fun; it has an interior of fake wooden roofs, stone walls, and trees. Immensely popular with the local student crowd, it's still a good bet during school vacations. International beer list, as well as beer made by monks (€3.80-5). Open M and Su 3pm-midnight, Tu-Th 11:30am-1am, F 11:30am-2am, Sa 3pm-1am. AmEx/MC/V.

Vivian's Pub Fairy, 15 pl. St-Louis (☎03 87 18 95 01). Decorated à la Knights of the Round Table—if they had a castle cluttered with kitschy medieval knick-knacks—and French Celtic music. Beer on tap €4.60-5. Open M 5pm-midnight, Tu-Th 5pm-1am, F-Sa 5pm-3am; Tu-Sa also open noon-2pm. MC/V.

Les 2 Zèbres, 4 pl. St-Jacques (☎03 87 35 06 46). A chic young crowd fills this hotspot's see-and-be-seen terrace and cozy cellar bar area. Pop a Zima with the yuppies. Open M-Th and Su 8am-2am, F-Sa until 3am. MC/V.

Bar Latino, 22 rue Dupont des Loges (☎03 87 75 72 57). Christening itself *la temple de la salsa*, this Latin club is one hot tamale. Come late to drink, listen to hot Latin music, and dance. Salsa classes M and F. Beer from €2.50. 1 drink min. Open M-Th and Su 6pm-2am, F-Sa 6pm-3am; Tu-Sa also open noon-2pm.

L'Endroit, 20 rue aux Ours (☎03 87 35 95 64). New gay and lesbian club. L'Endroit promises a glamorous night of dancing, with weekly and special themes to liven things up. Regular themes include "glam" and "kitschissime." Open F-Sa 11pm-5am. MC/V.

VERDUN

The specter of war haunts the city of Verdun (pop. 20,000), which in WWI was the last eastern stronghold to prevent a German advance on Paris. In 1914, the French resolved "on ne passe pas"—that the Germans would go no further; the Germans resolved to take the city (and beyond) at any cost. Four years of trench warfare along lines that budged only a few feet with each costly assault shattered the lives of an entire generation. In the 1916 Battle of Verdun, one of WWI's most horrific conflicts, each side lost nearly 400,000 men. Though Verdun today winds prettily around a yacht-filled river, surrounded by calm terraces, eerie reminders of the events of almost a century ago remain. 15,000 marble crosses stand in the National Cemetery, the Trench of Bayonets, where almost all of France's 137th Regiment were buried alive, and then there is the Ossuary, where the bones of 130,000 unknown soldiers rest—visible—beneath a touching memorial to peace. In 1987, the UN christened Verdun "World Capital of Peace, Freedom, and Human Rights." After viewing the memorials here, it will be only too easy to understand why.

TRANSPORTATION

Trains leave from pl. Maurice Genovoix (☎03 2984 83 92) to Metz (1½hr., 5 per day, €11.60) and Paris (1½hr., 4 per day, €30.30). Check the ticket booth. (Open M 4:45am-7pm, Tu-F 5:45am-7pm, Sa 9:45am-12:15pm and 2:15-7pm, Su 12:30-7:30pm.) Regional **buses** run by Les Rapides de la Meuxe (☎03 29 86 02 71) depart from the parking lot at the end of rue du 8 Mai, to Metz (2hr., 4-9 per day, €10.50-16). **Rent cars** from AS Location, 22 rue Louis Maury. (☎03 29 86 58 58. Open M-F 9am-noon and 2-7pm. MC/V.) **Bike rental** is available at Flavenot Damien, 1 rond-point des Etats-Unis. (☎03 29 86 12 43. €17.80 per day; passport deposit. Open Tu-Sa 9am-noon and 2-7pm. MC/V.)

ORIENTATION AND PRACTICAL INFORMATION

The **tourist office** is just across a bridge from downtown; to reach it from the station, head to the *rond-point* straight ahead, then take av. Garibaldi (on the left) until it curves to the right and becomes rue Frères Boulhaut. Continue to the Porte Chaussée, turn left and cross the bridge. To reach downtown, do not cross the river, but continue straight past Porte Chaussée to the quai de Londres. English-speaking staff offer a free map of the city center, info on the memorials, **currency exchange** (worse rates than the post office), and daily 4hr. tours (May-Sept. 2pm; €25.50, under 16 €16.50; sells out: email or call ahead) in French on battlefields and monuments. (☎03 29 86 14 18; fax 03 29 84 22 42. Open May-Sept. M-Sa 8:30am-6:30pm, Su 9:30am-5pm; Apr. M-Sa 9am-noon and 2-6pm, Su 9:30am-5pm; Mar. and Oct.-Nov. M-Sa 9am-noon and 2-6pm, Su 10am-1pm; Dec.-Feb. M-Sa 9am-noon and 2-5pm, Su 10am-1pm.) **Laundromats** are located at 56 rue Raymond Poincaré (open daily 6:30am-9:30pm) and at pl. Chevert (☎03 29 84 69 48; open daily 7am-8pm). The **police** are at 2 rue Chaussée (☎03 29 86 00 17), and the **hospital** at 2 rue d'Antohouard (☎03 29 83 84 85). **Internet** is available at Cyberom@nia, 5 quai de Londres. (☎03 29 83 72 11. €1 for 10min., €3 per hr. Open M-Tu and Th 10am-noon and 3-11pm, W and F noon-11pm and Su 3-8pm. The **post office,** on av. de la Victoire, offers currency exchange. (☎03 29 83 45 55. Open M-F 8am-7pm, Sa 8am-noon.) **Postal Code:** 55100.

ACCOMMODATIONS AND CAMPING

■ **Auberge de Jeunesse (HI),** pl. Monseigneur Ginisty (☎03 29 86 28 28; fax 03 29 86 28 82), in the Centre Mondial de la Paix beside the cathedral. From the station, head right on rue Louis Maury to rue de la Belle Vierge. (15min.) Simple, renovated rooms in a converted seminary. Great views, a valuable collection of stained glass, and an amazing chapel-like restaurant. The 2-story 10-bunk room is gorgeous, with large windows that lend a ski-lodge feel. Kitchen. Breakfast €3.40. Sheets €2.80. Reception M-F 8am-noon and 5-11pm, Sa-Su 8-10am and 5-9pm. Bunks €9.50, ages 4-10 €4.20. Non-members €3.90 extra per night for first 6 nights. MC/V. ❶

■ **Le Montaulbain,** 4 rue de la Vieille Prison (☎03 29 86 00 47; fax 03 29 84 75 70), near pl. Maréchal Foch in the heart of the *vieille ville*. Large, colorful rooms on a quiet side-street, all with shower in small bathrooms. Breakfast €5.50. Reception daily 7:30am-10pm. Reservations recommended July-Aug. Singles and doubles €32-40; triples €45; quads €48. MC/V. ❷

Hôtel Les Colombes, 9 av. Garibaldi (☎03 29 86 05 46), around the corner from the station. Clean, cheery rooms with TV, some family-size, and all with shower or bath. Friendly reception and convenient location. Closed mid-Dec. to mid-Jan. Breakfast €5.40. Reception daily 7am-8pm. Singles and doubles €34-40; triples and quads €41-60; "honeymoon suite" €60. MC/V. ❸

Hôtel de la Cloche d'Or, 10 pl. St-Paul (☎03 29 86 03 60; fax 03 29 83 73 96). A nicer and pricier option next to the Port de St-Paul, adjoined to a little restaurant. Antique-furnished rooms with squeaky clean bathrooms. All rooms with shower or bath, TV, and toilet. Call ahead in the summer. Breakfast €6. Reception daily 7am-10pm. Singles and doubles €40-42. Extra bed €10. MC/V. ❹

Camping: Camping Les Breuils, allée des Breuils (☎03 29 86 15 31; www.camping-les-breuils.com), past the Citadelle Souterraine on av. du 5ème RAP, 1km from town. Take a right onto av. Général Boichut and then the first left. Caravans abound at this site, but tall bushes offer some privacy. Bar, grocery store, laundry, showers, and pool. Reception daily 7:30am-noon and 2-10pm. Open Apr.-Sept. July-Aug. €4.20 per person, €4.20 per site; Apr.-May and Sept. €3.80/€3.80. Electricity €3.50. MC/V. ❶

FOOD

Verdun's contribution to confection is the *dragée*, almonds coated with sugar and honey. First engineered by an apothecary in the 13th century to ward off sterility, they are today, appropriately enough, served at weddings and baptisms. The main **covered market** is on rue de Rû. (Open F 7:30am-12:30pm.) Stock up at the **Match supermarket** in front of the station on rond-point des Etats-Unis. (Open M-Sa 8:30am-7:30pm. MC/V.) Restaurants and cafes are in the pedestrian area along **rue Chaussée** and **rue des Rouyers** and by the canal along **quai de Londres.** ■**Pile ou Face** ❶, 54 rue des Royeurs, serves delicious, elaborate, massive crêpes (€2.50-7.50) and *galettes* (€3.10-9.50) on the terrace or in the bustling dining room. (☎03 29 84 20 70. F nights "all you can eat" €14.40. Open daily noon-10pm. MC/V.)

Throngs of locals pack **Le Boucher du Quai** ❷, 19 quai de Londres, a self-proclaimed "meat specialist" that also offers delicious and creative chicken *plats* (€12), as well as cheaper *sandwiches* (€2.90-4.40) and pasta (€6.20-8.60). Try the *steak frites* and salad for €9 and up. (☎03 29 86 72 01. Open daily 11am-11pm. MC/V.) Ritzy three-star **Restaurant du Coq Hardi** ❹, av. de la Victoire, has mastered *cuisse de lapin* (rabbit thigh; €23) and *quiche Lorraine* for two (€45). On the somewhat cheaper terrace, full *plats* cost €10. (☎03 29 86 36 36. Open daily 12:15-2pm and 7-9:15pm. Reservations suggested for inside seating. MC/V.)

🎯 🎵 SIGHTS AND ENTERTAINMENT

The centerpiece of Verdun's pedestrian district is stunning **Le Monument à la Victoire;** the illuminated, fountained av. de la Victoire blazes a path to its base. The monument stands on an old chapel, the remains of the **Église de la Madeleine,** bombed beyond repair in 1916. Inside the chapel, three volumes record the names of soldiers who fought here. (☎03 29 84 37 97. Open daily June 9:30am-12:30pm and 2-6pm; July-Aug. 9:30am-6:30pm; Sept.-Oct. and Apr.-May 9:30am-noon and 2-5:30pm. Free.) The massive **Citadelle Souterraine,** down rue de Rû on av. de la 5ème RAP, is a reconstructed look at trench warfare. The fortress sheltered groups of 10,000 front-bound soldiers in its 4km of underground galleries. The official *petit train* tour (the only means of entering) plays out a bit like Mr. Toad's Antarctic Ride for the lightly clothed. Realistic talking holograms depict the underground lives of hungry soldiers and nervous generals. (Also available in German, Italian, Dutch, and Spanish. Open daily July-Aug. 9am-6:30pm; Apr.-June and Sept. 9am-6pm; Oct.-Nov. 9am-noon and 2-6pm; Dec. 10am-noon and 2-5pm. 30min. tours in French or English every 5min. Wheelchair-accessible. €6, ages 5-15 €2.50. MC/V over €15.40.)

Verdun's older, pre-war constructions include the oft-bombed 10th- to 12th-century **Cathédrale Notre-Dame,** rue de la Belle Vierge, which retains a fine set of post-WWI stained-glass windows. *Les Heures Musicales,* a series of choir and organ concerts, fills the cathedral in summer. (Times vary. Call tourist office for details. Cathedral open daily Apr.-Sept. 8am-7pm; Feb.-Mar. and Oct.-Nov. 8am-6:30pm; Dec.-Jan. 8am-6pm. Free to €12.) Built in 1200, the **Porte Chaussée,** quai de Londres, has served as a prison, a guard tower, and an exit for WWI troops. At the other end of rue Frères Boulhaut, a copy of Rodin's **La Défense** guards the Porte de St-Paul. The Netherlands created the replica for the town just after the conclusion of the Battle of Verdun. For the battle-weary, **Parc Municipal Japiot,** across from the tourist office, rolls out its green carpet along the shady banks of the Meuse. (Open daily Apr.-Sept. 8:30am-8pm; Mar. and Oct. 9am-6pm; Nov.-Feb. 9am-5pm.)

Le Son et Lumière de la Bataille de Verdun recreates the battle, using over 300 actors and 1000 projectors, for a hushed and appreciative crowd. (Info ☎03 29 84 50 00. June-July F-Sa night. Ticket office open M-F 8:30am-noon, 1:30-6pm. €18, ages 12-18 €9, under 12 free.) The sounds of **L'Eté Musicale** waft up the river from quai de Londres Saturday nights all summer. (Free concerts. All types of music.) Stick around the quai de Londres and neighboring **rue Chaussée** for the best nightlife. The pubs around the river fill up most evenings, beginning fairly early. **L'Estaminet,** 45 rue des Rouyers, provides a bit of German *bierstub* in the heart of the district, playing jazz and blues some nights. (☎03 29 86 07 86. German beer from €1.70, others from €2.30. Open M-F 2pm-3am; Sa 2pm-3am. MC/V.) Verdun's only discotheque, **La Bidule,** on the corner of rue Gros Degrès and rue du Rû, fills with mixed beats and a mixed crowd. (☎03 29 86 02 86. Cocktails €7-8. €7 cover includes one drink. Open Th-Sa 11pm-4am.)

MEMORIALS NEAR VERDUN

Many sites 5-8km east of Verdun commemorate the battle of 1916. The 4hr. tourist office tour (p. 341) visits all of the memorials mentioned below, describing each in rapid, non-stop French. Spending more time on the 25km circuit requires a car.

After Alsace and parts of Lorraine were annexed by Germany in 1871, Verdun was thrust within 40km of the German border. France decided to build 38 new forts to protect Verdun and the surrounding area. Right before the war began, however, the French abandoned their fortifications in favor of more offensive-minded tactics. The fortifications became the target of German General von Falk-enhayn's 1916 offensive. Following the French demilitarization, the strongest fort fell first: the immense concrete **Fort de Douaumont**, covering 3km of passageways. The fortress was captured in February 1916, much to the surprise of the French, who shelled it for the next eight months in an attempt to dislodge the German garrison. In October 1916, a fire broke out after heavy shelling, and the Germans fled; a detachment of French-led Moroccan troops retook the fort. The assault of this strategically useless building caused over 100,000 French deaths; a sealed gallery entombs 679 German soldiers that were killed when a flamethrower set fire to a pile of grenades. (☎ 03 29 84 41 91. Open daily Apr.-Aug. 9am-6:30pm; Feb.-Mar. and Sept.-Nov. 10am-1pm, 2-6pm; Dec. 10am-1pm, 2-5pm. €3.40, under 16 €1.50. Info brochures available in French, English, and German.)

The central and most powerful monument is the austere **Ossuaire de Douaumont,** a vast crypt. The 46m granite tower resembles a cross welded to an artillery shell. Funded by an international contingent of war participants, the small windows of the vault at the base reveal the remains of 130,000 unknown soldiers of all nation-alities. Another 15,000 are buried in the military cemetery next door. Christian graves are marked by white crosses; Muslim gravestones point toward Mecca. A small monument to Jewish volunteers, partially destroyed by the Nazis during WWII, is 300m from the building. (Open daily May-Aug. 9am-6:30pm; Sept. 9am-noon and 2-6pm; Mar. and Oct. 9am-noon and 2-5:30pm; Apr. 9am-6pm; Nov. 9am-noon and 2-5pm; closed Dec. and Jan. Brochures available in English. Historical film, with English and German subtitles, contains a few graphic scenes. Ossuary free. Film and tower €3.80, children €2.50.) Nearby, the **Tranchée des Baïonettes** holds the bodies of a detachment of France's 137th infantry regiment who were buried alive while taking cover from heavy enemy fire. The only sign of the men was the points of their bayonets protruding from the ground.

Fort de Vaux, the smallest of the fortifications, surrendered in June 1916 after seven days and nights of murderous hand-to-hand combat. In the dark, the French defenders, who had nothing to drink but their own urine, fended off attacks with gas, grenades, and flamethrowers. Numerous appeals for reinforcements were made to the Verdun garrison, to no avail; inside the fort stands the statue of a carrier pigeon named Valiant, who carried out the last plea. The Germans were so impressed with the resistance they awarded the French commander a saber of honor after taking the fort. (Info in English available. Open daily Apr.-Aug. 9am-6:30pm; Sept. to Nov. 10am-noon, 1-6pm; Dec. and Feb.-March 10am-noon and 1-5pm. €3.30, under 15 €1.30.)

The little town of Fleury at the epicenter of the battle changed hands 16 times during the war. The fighting left it empty and the surrounding farmland unusable for generations. The former railway station is now the **Musée de Fleury,** built by vet-erans to honor dead comrades. (Open daily Apr. to mid-Sept. 9am-6pm; Feb.-Mar. and mid-Sept. to Dec. 9am-noon and 2-6pm. €5, under 16 €2.50.)

ALSACE

STRASBOURG

Perched on the edge of Alsace, just a few kilometers from the German border, Strasbourg (pop. 450,000) is a French city with a truly international character. The prize of centuries of Franco-German border wars, Strasbourg has been annexed so many times that even the residents seem unsure of their current nationality—on the island-city of the *vieille ville,* you're as likely to see *winstubs* as *pâtisseries,* or to hear German rather than French. It's no mistake that the EU placed one of its two administrative headquarters here: with such energetic and multinational city life, the *über-mélange* of Strasbourg feels distinctly like the future of a more cosmopolitan European community.

⌐ TRANSPORTATION

Flights: Strasbourg-Entzheim International Airport, rte. de Strasbourg (☎03 88 64 67 67; www.strasbourg.aeroport.fr), is 15km from Strasbourg. **Air France,** 7 rue du Marché (☎03 88 15 19 59 or 08 20 82 08 20), and other carriers fly to **London, Lyon,** and **Paris.** Shuttle **buses** (☎03 88 77 70 70) run by **Allô CTS** go from the airport to the Strasbourg tram stop Baggarsee, 15min. by tram from the *centre ville* (12min., 3-4 per hr., one-way €4.90). Luggage storage available.

Trains: pl. de la Gare. Ticket office open M 5am-9:10pm, Tu-F 5:30am-9:10pm, Sa 5:30am-8:55pm, Su 5:55am-9:10pm. To: **Frankfurt, Germany** (3hr., 18 per day, €47.20); **Luxembourg** (2½hr., 14 per day, €28); **Paris** (4hr., 16 per day, €42.80); **Zurich, Switzerland** (3hr., 3-4 per day, €36). SNCF **buses** run to many surrounding towns from the station; check station or tourist office for schedules. Luggage storage 7:45am-8:45pm (€4.50 per bag per 24hr.).

Public Transportation: Compagnie des Transports Strasbourgeois (CTS), 14 rue de la Gare aux Marchandises (☎03 88 77 70 11, bus and tram info 03 88 77 70 70). Open M-F 7:30am-6:30pm, Sa 9am-5pm. 4 brand-new tram lines (4:30am-midnight). Tickets €1.20, *carnet* of 5 €4.70, day pass €3; tickets available at *tabacs.*

Taxis: Taxi 13, pl. de la République (☎03 88 36 13 13). 24hr. Also gives 1hr. city tours in French, English, and German (1-4 people €32) and service to the Route du Vin. **France Taxi** ☎03 88 22 19 19. 24hr.

Car Rental: Europcar, 16 pl. de la Gare (☎03 88 15 55 66). From €74.80 per day, €84.50 on weekends. 21+. Open M-F 8am-noon and 2-7pm, Sa 8am-noon and 2-5pm. AmEx/DC/MC/V. **Hertz,** Strasbourg-Entzheim International Airport (☎03 88 64 69 50).

Bike Rental: Vélocation, 4 rue du Maire-Kuss (☎03 88 23 56 75), near the train station. Branch at 10 rue des Bouchers (☎03 88 24 05 61), near the cathedral. Bikes €4 per half-day, €7 per day. €100 deposit with check and photocopy of ID card. Open M-F 6am-7:30pm, Sa-Su 9:30am-noon and 2-7pm. MC/V.

✦ ⓘ ORIENTATION AND PRACTICAL INFORMATION

The *vieille ville* is an eye-shaped island in the center of the city, bounded to the north by a large canal and to the south by the river Ill. To get there from the train station, follow rue du Maire-Kuss across pont Kuss and make a quick right and then left onto **Grande Rue,** which becomes rue Gutenberg. Turn right at **place Gutenberg,** then left to head down rue Mercière toward the cathedral. A right turn after the bridge from the station, at quai Turkheim, leads to **La Petite France,** a neighborhood of old Alsatian houses, restaurants, and narrow canals.

Tourist Office: 17 pl. de la Cathédrale (☎03 88 52 28 28; www.ot-strasbourg.fr), near cathedral. Branches at pl. de la Gare (☎03 88 32 51 49) and pont de l'Europe (☎03 88 61 39 23). Hotel reservations €2 plus deposit. Mediocre free map (better map €1). Open daily 9am-7pm. Pl. de la Gare branch Open Su 9am-12:30pm and 1:45-7pm. MC/V. Bas-Rhine **ADT** at 9 rue du Dome (☎03 88 15 45 88; www.tourisme67.com), has info on the Route du Vin. Open M-F 9:30am-noon and 1:30-6pm.

Tours: Tourist office organizes tours of the *vieille ville* and the cathedral in French or German. Daily July-Aug. 10:30am, Sa also 3pm; May-June and Sept.-Oct. Tu-W and F-Sa 3pm; Dec. 3pm, Sa also 4:30pm. €6.80, students and ages 12-18 €3.40. English audioguides same prices. MC/V. A **minitram** (☎03 88 77 70 03; www.cts.strasbourg.com) gives a 50min. tour of downtown. Every 30min. from pl. du Château. May to mid-Sept. 9:30am-7pm; mid-Sept. to mid-Oct. 9:30am-5pm; Jan.-Apr. 10am-5pm. Tours every hr. mid-Oct. to Nov. 10am-5pm. €4.80 adults, €2.40 ages 4-12.

Budget Travel: Voyages Wasteels, 13 pl. de la Gare (☎08 25 88 70 59). Open M-F 9am-noon and 2-6pm.

Consulates: US, 15 av. d'Alsace (☎03 88 35 31 04, cultural services 03 88 35 38 20; fax 03 88 24 06 95), next to pont John F. Kennedy. Open M-F 9am-noon and 2-5pm.

Currency Exchange: 24hr. automatic currency exchange at **Crédit Commerciale de France,** 11 pl. Gutenberg (☎03 88 37 82 00), at rue des Serruriers.

English-Language Bookstore: Librairie Bookworm, 3 rue de Pâques (☎03 88 32 26 99), off rue du faubourg de Saverne. Open Tu-F 9:30am-6:30pm, Sa 10am-6pm.

Youth Centers: CROUS, 1 quai du Maire-Dietrich (☎03 88 21 28 00; www.crous-strasbourg.fr). Resource center for employment, lodging, and study opportunities. Office open M-F 9am-noon and 1:30-4pm (July-Aug. opens at 10am). Meal tickets for ISIC holders M-F 9am-1pm; during school vacations M-F 10am-noon. €2.40 per meal. **Centre d'Information Jeunesse (CIJA),** 7 rue des Ecrivains (☎03 88 37 33 33; www.cija.org), has info about jobs and lodging plus one computer for Internet access. Open M-Th 10am-noon and 1-6pm, F 10am-noon and 1-5pm.

Laundromat: Augre, 35 rue du faubourg de Saverne (☎03 88 22 92 37). 8kg wash €3.50, 20min. dry €2.50. **Wash'n Dry,** 13 rue des Veaux. 8kg wash €30, 30min. dry €2. Open daily 7am-9pm.

Police: 11 rue de la Nuée Bleue (☎03 88 15 37 37).

24hr. Pharmacy: Association SOS Pharmacie, 10 rue Leicester (☎03 88 41 11 34).

Hospital: Hôpital Civil de Strasbourg, 1 pl. de l'Hôpital (☎03 88 11 67 68), south of the *vieille ville* across the canal.

Internet Access: Ultim@, 31 rue du Fossé (☎03 88 22 94 52). €3 per hr. Open M-Sa 10am-8pm. **M@d Net,** 21 rue de la Krutenau (☎03 88 36 10 00). €2 per hr. Open M-Sa 1pm-8pm, Su 2-8pm. MC/V. Also at the **Centre d'Information Jeunesse, Hôtel le Grillon** (€1 per 15min.), and **Centre International d'Accueil** (see **Accommodations,** p. 346) for €2.55 per 15min.

Post Office: 5 av. de la Marseillaise (☎03 88 52 31 00). Open M-F 8am-5:30pm, Sa 8:30-11:30am. Branches at cathedral (open M-F 8am-6:30pm, Sa 9am-5pm), 1 rue de la Fonderie (open M-F 8am-6:30pm, Sa 8:30am-noon), and 1 pl. de la Gare, which has best **currency exchange** and **ATM** (open M-F 8:30am-6:30pm, Sa 8:30am-noon).

Postal Code: 67000.

⚑ ACCOMMODATIONS AND CAMPING

There are inexpensive high-quality hotels all over the city, especially around the train station. Wherever you stay, make reservations early—especially in summer.

▨ **Centre International d'Accueil de Strasbourg (CIARUS),** 7 rue Finkmatt (☎03 88 15 27 88; www.ciarus.com), 15min. from the train station. This bright, 290-bed hostel boasts friendly service and a charming foyer. Best of all, rooms come with bath. Cable TV room, ping pong, cafeteria, laundry. "Disco" and "make-your-own-crêpes" nights. Internet. (€2.55 per 15min.) Breakfast included. Free luggage storage. Towels €1.50-2.50. Reception 7am-10pm. Check-in 3:30pm; call ahead if arriving earlier. Check-out 9am. Reservations suggested. 6- to 8-bed dorms €16; 3- to 4-bed dorms €19.50; 2-bed rooms €22. Singles €39. Family rooms €16 per person. MC/V. ❷

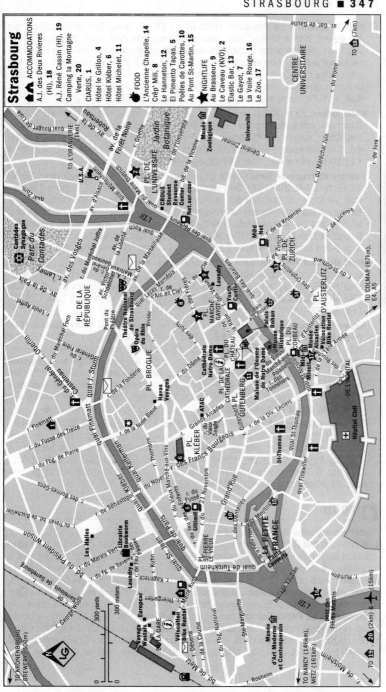

Strasbourg

ACCOMMODATIONS
A.J. des Deux Rivieres
(HI), **18**
A.J. Réné Cassin (HI), **19**
Camping la Montagne
Verte, **20**
CIARUS, **1**
Hôtel le Grillon, **4**
Hôtel Kléber, **6**
Hôtel Michelet, **11**

FOOD
L'Ancienne Chapelle, **14**
Crép' Mili, **8**
Le Hanneton, **12**
El Pimento Tapas, **5**
Poêles de Carottes, **10**
Au Pont St-Martin, **15**

NIGHTLIFE
Au Brasseur, **9**
Le Caveau (KVO), **2**
Elastic Bar, **13**
Le Gayot, **7**
La Voile Rouge, **16**
Le Zoo, **17**

ALSACE, LORRAINE, AND FRANCHE-COMTÉ

Hôtel le Grillon, 2 rue Thiergarten (☎03 88 32 71 88; www.grillon.com), 1 block from the station. With a youthful staff, down comforters, and dark wood, this ski-lodge-like hotel has real character. Sparkling hallway bathrooms make the cheapest rooms the best deal around. Internet cafe (€1 per 15min.) and hip bar where guests get a free drink with a *Let's Go* guide. TV in some rooms. Breakfast €7.50. Reception 24hr. Reservations suggested. Singles €30, with shower €40-55; doubles €37/€47-62; triples €48/€58-73; quads with shower €69-84. Extra bed €10.50. DC/MC/V. ❸

Hôtel Kléber, 29 pl. Kléber (☎03 88 32 09 53; www.hotel-kleber.com), in the heart of downtown, just steps from the tram line that runs to the station and to the airport shuttles. Classy rooms, all with shower and TV, some with mini-bar or balconies. Breakfast €6. 24hr. reception. Singles €33, with toilet €40.50-59; doubles €37, with toilet €47.50-68; triples with toilet €68-75. AmEx/MC/V. ❹

Auberge de Jeunesse René Cassin (HI), 9 rue de l'Auberge de Jeunesse (☎03 88 30 26 46; fax 03 88 30 35 16), 2km from the station. Take bus #2 (dir: Campus d'Illkirch) from the station to stop Auberge de Jeunesse. The quiet setting by the canal is beautiful, though the hotel has dim hallways and an institutional feel. TV room, video games, kitchen, and bar with concerts. Breakfast included, other meals €5-8.40. Sheets €2. Reception 7am-12:30pm, 1:30-7:30pm, and 8:30-11pm. Curfew 1am. Open Feb.-Dec. 3- to 6-bed dorms €15; singles €32; doubles €44. MC/V. HI members only. ❶

Hôtel Michelet, 48 rue du Vieux Marché aux Poissons (☎03 88 32 47 38). Stellar location near the cathedral. Dim hallways lead to carefully decorated but small rooms. Breakfast €5. Reception 7:30am-8pm; other hours call ahead. Singles €23, with bath €38.50; doubles €35/€45.50; triples €45.50/€52.50; quads with bath €59.50. Extra bed €6. MC/V. ❷

Auberge de Jeunesse des Deux Rivieres, Centre International de Rencontres (HI), (☎03 88 45 54 20; fax 03 88 45 54 21), on rue des Cavaliers. 7km from station, but less than 1km from Germany. Take bus #2 (dir: Pond du Rhin) to Parc du Rhin. (50min.) Go left off the stop to rue des Cavaliers, to the end. At night the streets are deserted; be careful. Good facilities overlooking the Rhine, with an unwalkable 50min. trip to the *centre ville.* Internet €3.50 per hr. Breakfast and sheets included. Reception daily 7am-12:30pm, 1:30-7:30pm, and 8:30pm-7am. Reserve ahead. 3- to 5-bed dorms with bath €17. Non-members €2.90 extra up to first 6 nights. MC/V. ❶

Camping: Camping la Montagne Verte, 2 rue Robert Ferrer (☎03 88 30 25 46; fax 03 88 27 10 15), 100m from the René Cassin hostel. Spacious, shady riverside campsite, though there isn't much privacy. Tennis courts, basketball, laundry, and a bar. Reception July-Aug. 7am-12:30pm, 1:30-7:30pm and 8:30-10:30pm; Apr.-June, Sept.-Oct., and Dec. 8:30am-noon and 3-8pm. Car curfew 10pm. €4.50 per site; €3.35 per person, €1.60 per child under 10. Electricity €3.50. MC/V. ❶

🍴 FOOD

Local restaurants are known for *choucroute garnie* (sauerkraut with meats), but you also can find delicious sausages at stands throughout the city. Other specialties include the ubiquitous *tarte flambée* (much like a thin pizza) and a truckload of local wines from the Route du Vin. The streets around the cathedral are filled with reasonable restaurants. A little farther away, off pl. Gutenberg, pretty cafes line **rue du Vieux Seigle** and **rue du Vieux Marché aux Grains.** Smaller restaurants in less touristy packages can be found on and around **rue de la Krutenau.** In **La Petite France,** you'll find small **winstubs** (VIN-shtoob)—classic (and somewhat pricey) Alsatian taverns with a distinctly German flavor and characterized by timber exteriors and checkered tablecloths. Cheap kebab and sandwich joints cluster thickly around the train station and on **Grand'Rue.** Mar-

kets are held at bd. de la Marne (open Tu and Sa 7am-1pm), pl. de Bordeaux (open Tu and Sa 7am-1pm) and pl. de la Gare (open M and Th 10am-6pm). Several **supermarkets** are also scattered around the *vieille ville*, including **ATAC,** 47 rue des Grandes Arcades, off pl. Kléber. (☎ 03 88 32 51 53. Open M, Sa 8:30am-8:30pm, Tu-F 8:30am-8pm. MC/V.)

▧ **Crêp' Mili,** 3 rue du Ciel (☎ 03 88 36 56 88), on a quiet side-street off rue des Frères. Fabulous crêpes (€2.60-5.90) and *galettes* (€3.50-9) served in a stone dining area. Outdoor seating is available, but this is one atmospheric cellar not to be missed. Open daily 11:30am-2pm and 6:30-11:30pm. MC/V. ❶

▧ **El Pimento,** 52 rue du Jeu des Enfants (☎ 03 88 21 94 52), by pl. Homme de fer. This low-lit chili-themed *tapas* joint serves up cheap food with great vibes. Fills up for dinner, and a lively social scene. Creative *ensalada de pimientos* (€3), a salad of roasted peppers and olive oil, is a treat, while traditional Latin favorites like *chorizo* sausage (€3) or *arroz a la Espanola* (Spanish rice, €2.30) are delicious options. Most *tapas* €2.30-4.60. Open M-Sa noon-2pm and 6:30pm-midnight. AmEx/MC/V. ❷

▧ **L'Ancienne Chapelle,** 2b pl. des Orphelins (☎ 03 88 35 35 37). While the meals at this homestyle restaurant may be out of a budget traveler's range, the heavenly desserts are only a slight splurge. The hot *Dome Chocolate* (€6) explodes with molten chocolate in a crispy cake crust, while the *nougat glacée* (creamy nougat ice cream, €6.50) is a rich taste of heaven. Open Tu-Sa noon-2pm and 7-10:30pm. MC/V. ❹

Le Hanneton (Chez Denis), 5 rue Ste-Madeleine (☎ 03 88 36 93 76; fax 03 88 36 93 83). Pieffel Denis, the attentive host and chef at this relatively untouristed *winstub,* prepares Alsatian favorites for a seemingly endless group of friends and fans. Traditional favorite *choucroute à l'alsacienne* (€14) is a heaping pile of sauerkraut with five meaty toppings; the roasted potatoes that come as a side dish or au gratin with muenster cheese (€10.40) are fantastic. *Tarte flambée* €6.50-7. Open noon-2pm and 7-11pm; closed M and Tu lunch. MC/V. ❸

Au Pont St-Martin, 15 rue des Moulins (☎ 03 88 32 45 13). At Au Pont St-Martin, you can peer at canals over huge servings of seafood, salad (€7.20), and sauerkraut (€11.50). This popular, consummately German *winstub* in La Petite France is featured on postcards of the area. Midweek lunch *menu* €9.20, evening *menus* €15.90, beer €2.60. Open daily for food service noon-3pm and 7-10pm, for drinks June-Aug. 11:30am-10:30pm; Sept.-May 11:30am-4pm and 6:30-10:30pm. AmEx/MC/V. ❸

THE LOCAL STORY

ALSATIAN IDENTITY

On old-world Alsatian streets cluttered with costumed boutique owners and *kugelhopf* molds, it's easy to imagine you've wandered into Epcot Center's World Showcase rather than a real town surrounded by fields of trailing vines.

Despite all these cheerful signs of a distinct Alsatian tradition, regional identity has historically been much more complex and far less cheerful. Writer Tom Ungerer described 20th-century Alsace as a public toilet: always occupied. The lives of the oldest Alsatian grandfathers tell national history on a personal level: they were born German citizens before WWI, grew up French, became German during the Occupation and will die French. In WWI, Alsatians were coerced into the Kaiser's army to fight former compatriots; in WWII they were again forced to fight for Germany, calling themselves the *malgré nous* (despite ourselves).

Older Alsatians still speak Alsatian, a Low German dialect, and refer to the rest of France as *la France Intérieure.* Many of their middle-aged children can understand the dialect, but the Alsatian language is being lost on the youngest generation, although it is taught as a second language. Even the Alsatian accent—a Germanic twang lamented by generations of uncomprehending outsiders—is losing its edge. The battle over Alsace is still raging, but the struggle has become purely cultural.

Poêles de Carottes, 2 pl. des Meuniers (☎03 88 32 33 23; poelesdecarottes@netcourrier.com). This adorably small, canary-yellow restaurant is a well-priced vegetarian option in the heart of La Petite France. Lunch *menu* €9.50, hearty salads €8.50-10.50, vegetable *gratins* €8.50-10.80, pizza €6.30-10.50. Elaborate cocktails €4.75-7.75. Open M-Sa noon-2pm and 7-10:30pm. MC/V. ❷

👁 SIGHTS

▓CATHÉDRALE DE STRASBOURG. In Strasbourg, nothing is nearly as impressive, culturally defining, or, well, *tall* as the majestic cathedral. Towering 142m into the sky, Victor Hugo's favorite "prodigy of the gigantic and the delicate" took 260 years to build (it was completed in 1439). German literary giant Goethe scaled its 332 steps regularly to cure his fear of heights. The cathedral's central spire, the **Pilier des Anges,** which is indefinitely under restorative scaffolding, depicts the Last Judgment. In the southern transept, the massive **Horloge Astronomique** is a testament to the wizardry of 16th-century Swiss clockmakers. At 12:30pm, tiny apostles march out of the face, and a rooster greets St. Peter. According to legend, the tiny automata in an organ chest in the nave once ranted at the minister, much to the amusement of medieval parishioners. (☎03 88 24 43 34. Cathedral open M-Sa 7-11:40am and 12:40-7pm, Su 12:45-6pm. Tours July-Aug. M-F 10:30am, 2, 3pm; Sa 10:30am and 2pm; Su 2 and 3pm; €3. Horloge tickets (€0.80) at the postcard stand inside the cathedral 9-11:30am, at the south entrance 11:30am-12:25pm. July-Aug. arrive 30min. early. Tickets limited to 350 during renovations to the central choir. Choral rehearsals and Gregorian chants Su. Tower open for climbing Apr.-Oct. M-F 9am-5:30pm, Sa-Su 10am-5:30pm; Nov.-Mar. M-F 9am-4:30pm, Sa-Su 10am-4:30pm. €3, children 5-18 and students €1.50.)

▓LA PETITE FRANCE. This lovely old tanners' district, tucked away in the southwest corner of the city center, is characterized by slender, steep-roofed houses with carved wooden facades in pastel colors, all surrounded by waterways. Locals flock to this pretty and relaxed neighborhood, chatting in sidewalk cafes to the sound of accordion music and the gurgle of the river. A host of restaurants and *winstubs* also make this the perfect quiet dining spot.

PALAIS ROHAN. This magnificent 18th-century building houses three small museums. The **Musée des Arts Décoratifs,** once a residence for cardinals, was looted during the Revolution, then refurbished for Napoleon in 1805. The majority of your visit will probably be spent whistling appreciatively at the beautifully restored rooms with gold-encrusted ceilings and immense expanses of marble, including the bedroom of the Emperor himself. Ask to borrow an informative English guidebook. The unusually appealing and comprehensive **Musée Archéologique** illustrates the history of Alsace from 600,000 BC to AD 800 (written guide in English, free audioguide in French). Upstairs, the **Musée des Beaux Arts** displays a solid collection of art from the 14th to the 19th centuries, including works by Giotto, Botticelli, Raphaël, Rubens, Van Dyck, El Greco, and Goya. (2 pl. du Château. ☎03 88 52 50 00. Open M and W-Su 10am-6pm. Each museum €4, students €2.50. Free 1st Su of the month. 1-day pass for every museum in Strasbourg €6, students €3. Other combos available.)

MUSÉE D'ART MODERNE ET CONTEMPORAIN. Opened in 1998, Adrien Fainsilber's steel and glass behemoth holds a small but impressive collection of late 19th- and 20th-century painting, including Impressionist, Abstract, Surrealist, and Cubist works. Monet, Gauguin, Picasso, Dufy, Kandinsky, and Ernst are featured, though most of the space is devoted to extensive temporary exhibits. (1 pl. Hans Jean Arp. ☎03 88 23 31 31; www.musees-strasbourg.com. Open Tu noon-10pm, W-Su 11am-7pm. Brochure available in English. €5, students €2.50, under 18 free. Free 1st Su of the month.)

L'ORANGERIE. Strasbourg's largest, most spectacular park, L'Orangerie was designed by the famed Le Nôtre in 1692 after he cut his teeth on Versailles. It has room for picnics, ponds and waterfalls to be explored by rowboat, a stork-filled mini-farm, a zoo, go-carts, and Le Nôtre's original concrete-lined skateboard park. The vastness of this park makes it seem about as touristed as Pluto. The **Pavillon Joséphine** holds free concerts on summer evenings. *(Take bus #6 (dir: Place des Sports) from pl. des Halles to L'Orangerie. Concerts M-Tu and Th-Su 8:30pm.)*

OTHER SIGHTS. The **Palais de l'Europe** houses the Council of Europe and the governing bodies of the European Union, the European Parliament, in spectacular modern architecture in a little plaza off av. de l'Europe at the northwest edge of L'Orangerie. Due to the events of September 11, 2001, however, the buildings are closed to the public. The **Musée Alsacien**, inside a quintessentially Alsatian half-timbered house, showcases everyday life in Alsace since the Middle Ages. Successfully avoiding the pitfalls of other such museums (namely boredom), this museum feels like an enjoyable trip into a fully preserved folk house. *(23-25 quai Saint-Nicolas. ☎03 88 52 50 01. Open M and W-Su 10am-6pm. Free 1st Su of the month.)* The 14th- to 16th-century mansion housing the **Maison de l'Oeuvre Notre-Dame,** however, is dim and stale-smelling; its main attractions are the glowing rooms of 12th- to 14th-century stained glass, just beyond the rooms full of old rocks. *(3 pl. du Château. ☎03 88 52 50 00. Open Tu-Su 10am-6pm. €4; students, seniors, and large families €2 per person, under 18 free. Audioguides in French, German, and English. Free 1st Su of the month.)* The **Kronenbourg brewery** gives visitors a taste of Germany in France, with tours in French, English, or German; get a look at the different stages of brewing and a tasting session. *(68 rte. d'Oberhausbergen. ☎03 88 27 41 59; siege.visites@kronenbourg-fr.com. Take tram to Ducs d'Alsace. By reservation only. Variable hours M-F, May-Sept. and Dec. also Sa. €3, ages 12-18 €2, under 12 free.)* **Heineken** offers free tours of its brewery in French, English, and German, but only for groups and by advance reservation. *(4 rue St-Charles, Schiltigheim. ☎03 88 19 57 55. Call to schedule M-F 8am-noon and 1:30-4:30pm.)*

◼ NIGHTLIFE

Bars are everywhere. **Place Kléber** attracts a student crowd, while **Rue des Frères** and the tiny **place du Marché Gayot** wake up with a mixed crowd after 10pm. The area between **place d'Austerlitz** and **place de Zurich**, across the canal from the *vieille ville*, is lively to the wee hours. Numerous bars and cafes cluster there, particularly around the tiny **place des Orphelins**. It is best to travel in a group.

◼ **Le Gayot,** 18 rue des Frères (☎03 88 36 31 88). The squished terrace of this friendly bar opens onto lively pl. Marché Gayot and draws a young crowd during the school year, when students frequently play jazz piano. Live music Sept.-June Th. Beer €3.10. Open daily June-Aug. 11am-1am; Sept.-May 11am-midnight. MC/V.

◼ **Le Zoo,** 6 rue des Bouchers (☎03 88 24 55 33; lezoobar@libertysurf.fr). Bouncing tunes and a super-hot, mostly male clientele make this the best gay bar in town. Kitschy decor and a friendly welcome leave little room for improvement. W nights the packed bar's patrons send each other flirtatious letters through the "post." Beer €2.20, mixed drinks €6. Open daily 6pm-2am; gets going after 11pm. AmEx/MC/V.

◼ **Elastic Bar,** 27 rue des Orphelins (☎03 88 36 11 10). One of the most energetic scenes in the city. Students and regulars fill an interior that took grunge to heart, with graffiti, winding steel staircases, and metal stickers plastered over the walls. Friendly and laid-back, with reggae in the background, it is packed year-round. Beer from €2.80. Open M-Th 5pm-3am, F 5pm-4am, Sa 6pm-4am, Su 6pm-3am. MC/V.

ALSACE, LORRAINE, AND FRANCHE-COMTÉ

Au Brasseur, 22 rue des Veaux (☎03 88 36 12 13; www.au-brasseur-strasbourg). Au Brasseur is a microbrewery that serves 4 different home brews (€4.30 per glass; cheaper beer available at €2) and good food (*tarte flambée* €4.80-8), all in a dark red and wood interior. Happy hour daily 5-7pm. Open daily 11:30am-1am, service ends at 12:30am; students play piano in the *cave* Th-Sa at 9:30pm. MC/V.

Le Caveau (KVO), 1 pl. de l'Université (☎03 88 15 73 70). One of the best-known night clubs in Strasbourg, especially for its student-heavy crowd, Le Caveau is located directly underneath the Strasbourg University restaurant and goes especially wild for any old holiday that comes along. Quiet during school vacations, however. Beer €4. Cover charges vary with the frequent parties. Open nightly 10pm-4am.

Péniche La Voile Rouge, quai Mathis (☎03 88 36 22 90), one of the few gay-friendly nightclubs in Strasbourg, has outfitted a large barge with a lounge and dance floor, where house tunes keep the crowd going all night long. Not busy until late. Beer €5, *soda* €6, liquor €8. Open F-Sa and holidays 11pm-4am.

🎵 🌸 ENTERTAINMENT AND FESTIVALS

The **Orchestre Philharmonique de Strasbourg** performs at the Palais de la Musique et des Congrès, behind pl. de Bordeaux. (Tickets ☎03 88 15 09 09, info 03 88 15 09 00. Oct.-June. Student tickets half-price or less. MC/V.) The **Théâtre National de Strasbourg,** 1 av. de la Marseillaise, performs Sept.-May. (☎03 88 24 88 24; www.tns.fr. €16-23, students €11.70-16. Th shows €8. MC/V.) The **Opéra du Rhin,** 19 pl. Broglie, features opera and ballet in its 19th-century hall. (☎03 88 75 48 00. Tickets €11.60-55, students under 26 half-price; rush tickets from €16, students from €12. MC/V.)

Summer in Strasbourg is all about the **place de la Cathédrale,** which becomes a stage every afternoon and evening for all manner of performers, mostly a troupe of musicians, flame-eaters, acrobats, and mimes. The cathedral hosts indoor organ concerts throughout the summer. (Free concerts June-Sept. Su 5:30pm. Organ recitals W 8:30pm. €11, students €5.50.) Also on summer nights, pl. du Château hosts the **Nuits de Strass,** a funny and free projection show with accompanying music; **water-jousters** match weapons on the River Ill outside the Palais Rohan.

One of Strasbourg's most popular festivals is the annual June **Festival de Musique de Strasbourg,** a two-week extravaganza that attracts some of Europe's best classical musicians. The **Festival de Jazz,** spanning the first two weeks of July, draws giants of the jazz world. (Tickets €15, students €11.50, under 5 €5.50.) For info on these festivals, contact the helpful Wolf Musique, 24 rue de la Mésange (☎03 88 32 43 10). L'Orangerie park hosts free concerts in the lavish Pavillion Joséphine. (June-Aug. M-Tu and Th-Su 8:30pm.) **Musica,** a contemporary music festival held annually from mid-September to early October in Strasbourg, includes an array of popular concerts, operas, and films. (☎03 88 23 47 23; www.festival-musica.org.)

SAVERNE

The third-century Roman travel guide *Itinerarium Antonin* recommended Saverne (pop. 12,700) as a "good place to rest." This 21st-century guidebook agrees. Punctuated by canals, the city unfolds from the elegant Neoclassical Chateau de Rohan along a wide cobblestoned pedestrian street brimming with animated conversation at all hours. According to legend, an appreciative *licorne* (unicorn) rendered Saverne's Roman baths magical with his touch; the pretty, fountain-happy passages of the *vieille ville* are still brimming with his watery vitality. Party animals may be disappointed here, but others who stay within the cobbled town center will be dazzled by the beautiful gardens and canals.

⚡🔊 ORIENTATION AND PRACTICAL INFORMATION. Trains leave from pl. de la Gare. (☎08 92 35 35 35. Ticket office open M-F 6:30am-7:30pm, Sa 8:30am-6pm, Su 10:15am-8:30pm.) Trains run to: Metz (1hr., 3 per day, €15.20); Nancy (1hr., 8-9 per day, €14.10); Paris (4-6hr., 6 per day, €42); Strasbourg (30min., 29 per day, €7.10). Ask at the ticket window for free luggage storage. **SNCF buses** run from the station to nearby Hugueneau (€6.80). Rent **bikes** at Ohl Sarl, 10 rue St-Nicolas. (☎03 88 91 17 13. Open Tu-F 9:30am-noon and 2-7pm, Sa 9:30am-noon and 2-5:30pm. Half-day €11.50, full day €14.50. ID deposit. AmEx/MC/V.) To get to the **tourist office,** 37 Grande Rue, from the train station, cross the square and bear right (diagonally) onto rue de la Gare. Cross the Zorn River and take a left onto Grande Rue. A helpful, English-speaking staff dispenses maps, and info on sights, accommodations, and hiking. (☎03 88 91 80 47; info@ot-saverne.fr. Open M-Sa 9:30am-noon and 2-6pm; May-Sept. also Su 10am-noon and 2-5pm.) Other services include: **banks** with **ATMs** and **currency exchange** along Grande Rue; a **Société Générale** on pl. de Gaulle (☎03 88 71 57 00; open Tu-F 8:45am-noon and 1:30-6pm, Sa 8:15am-noon); a **Wash'n'Dry** at 7 rue des Clés (open daily 7am-9pm; €4 for 8kg.); **police** at 29a rue St-Nicolas, off the end of Grande Rue (☎03 88 91 19 12; call here for the **pharmacie de garde**); **Hôpital Ste-Catherine** at 19 côte de Saverne, east of the town center, near the forest (☎03 88 71 67 67); **Internet** at Fight Club, 3 rue des Murs, just off rue Poincaré (☎03 88 03 14 47; €2.50 per hr.; open M-F 8am-10pm, Sa 10am-1am), or at Cappadoce, 5 rue des Clés (☎03 88 71 06 91; open daily 10am-1:30am; €2 for 30min., €3 per hr.); and a **post office** at 2 pl. de la Gare. (☎03 88 71 56 40; open M-F 8am-noon and 1:30-6pm, Sa 8am-noon.) **Postal Code:** 67700.

🔊🗒 ACCOMMODATIONS AND FOOD. The 🏠**Auberge de Jeunesse ❶** occupies a stellar location on the fourth floor of the Château des Rohan, right in the center of town. Colorful rooms, unbelievable views, and super friendly staff make it feel more like a tiny hotel. (☎03 88 91 14 84; fax 03 88 71 15 97; aj.saverne@wanadoo.fr. Internet access. Breakfast €3.30. Sheets €2.80. Reception 8-10am and 5-10pm; ask for a key and code if you plan to be out late. Lockout 10am-5pm. Reserve during summer. 8-bed dorms €8.90 per person; €2.90 extra for non-members the first 6 nights. Closed Dec. 24 to Jan. MC/V.) **Hôtel National ❸,** 2 Grande Rue, is located just a 5min. walk from the station and a 2min. walk from the center of town. Rooms are clean and spacious, if not elegant, and come fully loaded with TV, toilet, and shower/bath. Some rooms have stone balconies overlooking the canals or the Roseraie. (☎03 88 91 14 54; fax 03 88 71 19 50. Breakfast €6. Reception daily 6:30am-midnight. Singles €40-45; doubles €45-49; triples €56-59. MC/V.) **Camping de Saverne ❶,** 40 rue du Père Libermann, is near tennis courts, pools, rock climbing sites, and trails to the Vosges. (☎03 88 91 35 65. Reception Apr.-Sept. 8am-noon, 4-7pm. Tax and insurance €0.30 extra. €10.60 per tent or caravan with 2 people, €2.90 with car; €3 per additional person, children €1.30. Electricity €2.35. MC/V.)

Most food options can be found along **Grande Rue.** This includes kebab stands and a **Coop supermarket,** 118 Grande Rue. (Open M-F 8am-12:15pm and 3-7pm, Sa 8am-12:15pm and 2:30-5pm. MC/V.) Look for the **market** at pl. de Gaulle. (Th mornings, with a smaller version Tu and Sa.) 🏠**Haushalter ❶,** 66-68 Grande Rue, is a charming *salon de thé* that provides a bit of the great Saverne atmosphere, with outdoor seating to enjoy good weather. Come for the quiche (€2.30), *tarte à l'oignon,* pizza (€3), and great views of the *place.* (☎03 88 91 13 30. Open M-F 7am-7pm, Sa 7am-6pm, Su 7am-12:30pm and 1:30-6pm; July-Aug. Su no break for lunch. More extensive *plats* available €7-10. MC/V.) **S'zawermer Stuebel ❷,** 4 rue des Frères, serves filling pasta (€6.90-7.40), pizzas (€6-9.20), and *Rapzepfles* (potatoes with flour, €7.80-13.20) on a shady terrace or in a converted wine cellar. (☎03 88 71 29 95. Open daily 11:30am-2pm and 6:30-10pm. MC/V.)

◙ ◪ SIGHTS AND ENTERTAINMENT. Site of the famous Affair of the Necklace, the **Château des Rohan** spreads its elegant Neoclassical arms along pl. de Gaulle in the center of town. Less scandalously, the château contains a dry archaeological museum and the **Musée de Louise Weiss,** a tribute to the local feminist, journalist, and Resistance fighter. (Both open mid-June to mid-Sept. M and W-Sa 10am-noon and 2-6pm, Su 2-5:30pm; Jan. to mid-June and mid-Sept. to Dec. M and W-Su 2-5pm; €2.55, students €1.75.) The "City of Roses," Saverne's pride and joy is its **Roseraie,** a botanical garden along the banks of the Zorn, just off rte. de Paris. Though pretty, the hundreds of rose varieties are hardly gripping; more exciting are their intriguing names, from "Superstar" to "Miss France." In 1993, the garden christened a new rose variety—appropriately tall and prickly—the "Louise Weiss." The best time to visit is the **Fêtes des Roses,** an enormous rose-themed celebration during the third weekend in June. The first weekend in August sees the **Cours de Greffe,** a contest for the most exquisite hybrid rose, while the size-matters **Cours de Taille** competition takes up the first Saturday in March. (☎03 88 71 21 33; www.roseraie-saverne.fr. Open June-Sept. 10am-noon and 2-7pm. €2.50, under 6 free.)

On Friday and Saturday nights from mid-July to August, the Château de Haut-Barr opens up for the **Saga du Haut-Barr,** which features humorous theatrical performances exclusively in French continuously through the evening. (€13, €10 students, €7 ages 5-13, including shuttle from the tourist office. €25-37.50 with a meal included, reserve at the ticket office in the tourist office.) Try some *Bière de la Licorne* (unicorn beer), produced in Saverne and available at most pubs lining the mellow pub scene along Grande Rue.

◪ HIKES. One of Saverne's greatest assets is an endless network of forested **hiking** and **biking** trails. Club Vosgien maintains phenomenal trails and runs hikes in the area; ask the tourist office for info. Bikers can pick up the free brochure *Cyclo Tourisme* (available in English), which includes a map and suggested routes, from the tourist office. Some trails are best left to experts, but many are quite welcoming to all levels. The 100min. moderate hike through shaded woods to the lovely 12th-century mountaintop castle **Le Haut Barr** is particularly scenic—pick up a map at the tourist office and follow rue du Haut Barr (D17) southwest from the starting point at the central canal off the Grande Rue. Nearby is the **Tour du Télégraphe Chappe,** the first telegraph tower along the Paris-Strasbourg line. (☎03 88 52 98 99. Open June to mid-Sept. Tu-Su noon-6pm. €1.50, children €1.20.)

ROUTE DU VIN (WINE ROUTE)

The vineyards of Alsace flourish in a 150km corridor along the foothills of the Vosges from Strasbourg to Mulhouse—a region known as the Route du Vin. The Romans were the first to ferment Alsatian grapes, and today Alsatians sell over 150 million bottles yearly. Hordes of wine-loving and largely middle-aged tourists are drawn to the medieval villages along the route by picture-book houses and wineries giving free *dégustations.* Spread out over nearly 60 wine-producing towns, though, tourists still leave room for an authentic Alsatian experience.

Consider staying in **Colmar** (p. 358) or **Sélestat** (p. 356), larger towns that anchor the southern Route, and daytripping to the smaller (and pricier) towns. Buses run frequently from Colmar to surrounding towns, but smaller northern towns are a little more difficult to get to. **Car rental** from Strasbourg or Colmar smooths out transportation problems, but would drain any wallet. **Biking,** especially from Colmar, is only for those with the stamina to gut out lengthy journeys, but trails and turn-offs are well marked. **Trains** connect Sélestat, Molsheim, Barr, Colmar, and Mulhouse. Country roads have minimal sidewalks for walking. The best source of info on regional *caves* is the **Centre d'Information du Vin d'Alsace,** 12 av. de la Foire aux Vins, at the Maison du Vin d'Alsace in Colmar. (☎ 03 89 20 16 20; fax 03 89 20 16 30. Open M-F 9am-noon and 2-5pm.) Tourist offices in Strasbourg (p. 344) or along the Route dispense helpful advice, including the *Alsace Wine Route* brochure.

▩ KAYSERSBERG

If you only have time for one town on the Route, make it Kaysersberg (pop. 2720). The exceptionally charming and relatively untouristed town bursts with flowers during the summer, while bright facades and mountain views are enjoyable year-round. Its name, from the Latin *Cœsaris Mons* (Caesar's Mountain), dates to Roman times, when it commanded one of the most important passes between Gaul and the Rhine Valley. The ruined castle on the hill above town, which used to guard the pass, is now privately owned and not open to visitors, but you should still make the hour-long trek to the top for a peek. The pastel green **Musée Albert Schweitzer,** 126 rue du Général de Gaulle, contains memorabilia retracing the life and works of the Nobel-Peace-Prize-winning doctor. (☎ 03 89 47 36 55. Open daily Apr.-Nov. 11 9am-noon and 2-6pm. €2 adults, €1 children.) The glassblowing studio **Verrerie d'Art de Kaysersberg,** 30 rue du Général de Gaulle, offers free viewings of its workshops. (☎ 03 89 47 14 97. Workshop open Tu-Sa 10am-12:15pm and 2-5:45pm, Su 2-5:45pm. Brochures in English €3, students €2.) Christmas brings Kaysersberg's greatest *fête,* **Préludes de Noël,** with painting exhibitions and concerts from 11am-8pm for four weekends leading up to the big day.

The **tourist office,** 39 rue du Général de Gaulle, is in the Hôtel de Ville; cross the bridge behind the bus stop and walk straight to a square with a fountain. (☎ 03 89 78 22 78; www.kaysersberg.com. Open mid-June to mid-Sept. M-Sa 9am-12:30pm and 2-6:30pm, Su 10am-1pm; mid-Sept. to mid-June M-Sa 9am-noon and 2:30-5:30pm. Guided tours in French given July-Aug. M-Sa at 2:30pm, Th also 8:30pm. Brochures in English, French, and German. €4.50, under 16 free.) There is no train station, but **buses** run to Colmar (20min., 1 per hr. M-Sa 6:30am-7pm, €2.80).

RIQUEWIHR

One of the most visited villages along the Route and the headquarters of a number of Alsace's biggest wine-shipping firms, the 16th-century walled hamlet of Riquewihr (pop. 1288) maintains a beautiful, accessible *vieille ville.* On the flip side, it's accessible to a distracting number of tourists in summer. The beautiful **Tour des Voleurs** (Tower of Thieves) has an eerily enthralling torture chamber. (Open daily Apr.-Nov. 10:15am-12:30pm and 2-6:30pm. Free audioguides available in English, French, and German. €2, under 10 free.) Less ghastly, and less enjoyable, is the 13th-century **Tour du Dolder,** rue du Général de Gaulle, once a sentinel post, now a museum of local heritage. (Open daily July-Aug. 10:15am-12:30pm and 2-6:30pm; Apr.-June and Sept.-Oct. Sa-Su only. €1.50, under 10 free. Light show *(son-et-lumière)* June-Sept. F at 10pm.; €2, under 10 free.) Riquewihr celebrates a number of alcohol-related holidays. In nearby **Ribeauvillé** the **Foire aux Vins** takes place in the end of July; on the first Sunday of September, music accompanies the clink of glasses during the **Minstrel's Festival,** with free *cave* tours and tastings.

The **tourist office,** 2 rue de la Première Armée, has free maps (most available in English and German) and walking tours in French. (☎ 03 89 49 08 40; www.ribeauville-riquewihr.com. Tours July-Aug. M and W-Su 5pm. Open May-Oct. M-Sa 9:30am-noon and 2-6pm, Su 10am-noon and 2-5pm; Nov.-Apr. M-Sa 9am-noon and 2-6pm.) Pitch a tent at the small four-star **Camping Intercommunal ❶,** 1.5km from the town center. (☎ 03 89 47 90 08 or 03 89 47 90 15. Reception July-Aug. 8:30-noon and 1-9pm; Apr.-June and Sept.-Dec. 8:30am-noon and 3:30-7pm. Open Apr.-Dec. €3.80, children €1.70, animals €1.20, €4 per site. Electricity €4.10.)

BARR

Of the Route du Vin towns, Barr (pop. 6000), on the slopes of Mont Ste-Odile, seems most tied to its grapes: 2min. from the town center, you can sip a glass of white wine while you stroll between the rows of vines that created it. To reach the lovely *vieille ville* from the train station, turn right on rue de la Gare and left on av. des Vosges. Follow this past the roundabout, bearing left, avoiding what becomes rue de l'Hôpital de la Gare, and continuing for several blocks to rue St-Marc. Take a right here, walk two blocks, and turn right onto rue des Bouchers. From the pl. de l'Hôtel de Ville, a right on rue du Dr. Sultzer leads to several *caves*. To the left is the massive, austere **Église Protestante,** starting point for the **sentier viticole** (vineyard trail). The highlight of any trip to Barr, this path winds 2km through bright fields of glistening grapes during the summer, walkable alone or in a tourist office tour. (Tours in French July-Aug. Th at 4pm. Free, with complimentary tastings.) The local *vigniers* pull out their best bottles for the **Foire aux Vins** in the second week of July, and the first weekend in October brings music, markets, and, of course, more wine for the **Fête des Vendanges.**

Trains to Barr run from Sélestat (25min., 9 per day, €3) and Strasbourg (50min., 10 per day, €6.80). The **tourist office,** with an English guide to Barr, is at pl. de l'Hôtel de Ville. (☎03 88 08 66 65; www.pays-de-barr.com. Open Sept.-June M-Sa 9am-noon and 2-6pm; July-Aug. M-Sa 9am-12:30pm and 2-6:30pm, Su 10am-noon and 2-6pm.) Sleep by a tiny vineyard just outside the *centre ville* at two-star **Camping St-Martin ❶,** rue d'Ile. (☎03 88 08 00 45. Reception 9-11am and 5-8pm. Tent €1.80, adult €3.20, child €1.60, car €1.80. Electricity €3.)

SÉLESTAT

Halfway between Colmar and Strasbourg, Sélestat (pop. 17,200) lacks the crowds of its fellow stops on the Route du Vin while still packing in all of the appeal. Once part of the Holy Roman Empire and a center of Renaissance humanism, Sélestat today is a laid-back Alsatian hamlet with a couple of small but delightful museums and an enjoyable terrace nightlife. Light on the "authenticity" of other towns, but heavy on the beautiful views, Sélestat is a haven of good vines and good vibes.

⊟⊠ TRANSPORTATION AND PRACTICAL INFORMATION. From pl. de la Gare, **trains** run to Colmar (15min., 20 per day, €3.80) and Strasbourg (30min., 20 per day, €6.80). **Buses** run from the station to a number of surrounding towns (the tourist office provides a guide of bus companies and schedules).

The **tourist office,** 10 bd. Général Leclerc, in the Commanderie St-Jean, is north of the town center, 10min. from the train station. Go straight on av. de la Gare through pl. Général de Gaulle, to av. de la Liberté. Turn left onto bd. du Maréchal Foch, which becomes bd. du Général Leclerc after pl. Schaal. The efficient staff doles out expert advice and trilingual guides, as well as a free map (more detailed map €1). Also sells the *Pass Passion* (€3), which gives guest discounts at most major sites, and **rents bikes.** (☎03 88 58 87 20; www.selestat-tourisme.com. Bikes €5.50 for 2hr., €8 per half-day, €12.50 per day, €55 per week. €150 deposit. Open July-Aug. M-F 9:30am-12:30pm and 1:30-6:45pm, Sa 9am-12:30pm and 2-5pm, Su 11am-3pm; Sept.-June M-F 9am-noon and 2-5:45pm, Sa 9am-noon and 2-5pm; later hours during festivals. MC/V.) **Banks** with **ATMs** and **currency exchange** line av. de la Gare and cluster thickly in the *vieille ville* along rue des Chevaliers. Access the **Internet** in a hip bar setting at 🖥**Bazook'Kafé,** 3 rue Ste-Foy, where flat-screen monitors and wireless keyboards lend a sleek, high-tech feel. (☎03 90 57 20 66. www.bazook.net. Open M-Sa 8am-1:30am, Su 2pm-1:30am. Under 16 not admitted. €1.50 per 30min.) Other services include: **police** at bd. du Général Leclerc (☎03 88 58 45 50; call here for the **pharmacie de garde**); a **hospital** at 23 av. Pasteur (☎03 88

ALSACE, LORRAINE, AND FRANCHE-COMTÉ

57 55 55), behind the train station; and a **post office,** complete with **ATM,** at 5 rue de la Poste, near the Hôtel de Ville. (☎03 88 58 80 10. Open M-F 8am-noon and 1:30-6pm, Sa 8am-noon.) **Postal Code:** 67600.

⌂⌂ ACCOMMODATIONS AND FOOD. The **Hôtel de l'Ill ❷,** 13 rue des Bateliers, is on a peaceful residential street in the *vieille ville.* From the train station, take av. de la Gare, turn right on av. de Gaulle, which becomes av. de la Liberté, rue du 4ème Zouaves, and rue du Président Poincaré. Make a left onto rue de l'Hôpital and follow it to pl. du Marché aux Choux. Rue des Bateliers is on the right. The hotel packs 15 rooms with character onto three floors presided over by a purring tabby cat. All rooms have bath and TV. (☎03 88 92 91 09. Breakfast €5. Reception daily 7am-3pm and 6:30-11pm. Strict check-out time of 10am. Singles €30; doubles €40; triples with bath €50. MC/V.) The bright, simple rooms at **Auberge des Alliés ❸,** 39 rue des Chevaliers, have the best location, above a bustling restaurant in the *vieille ville.* (☎03 88 92 09 34. Breakfast €7. *Menu du jour* at the restaurant €14. Reception 7am-9am. Reservations suggested. All rooms with bath and TV. Singles €43-48; doubles €50-58; triples €61; quads €65. AmEx/MC/V.) Small, shaded **Camping Les Cigognes ❶,** rue de la Première D.F.L., is outside the ramparts on the southern edge of the *vieille ville,* near tennis courts, parks, and a lake. Located between low-rise buildings, this site has a distinctly suburban feel. (Mid-June to Aug. ☎03 88 92 03 98, Sept. to mid-June 03 88 58 87 20. Reception daily July-Aug. 8-11am and 2-9pm; Apr.-June and Sept. 9-11am and 3-7pm. Open Apr.-Sept. July-Aug. €9.70 per spot, €3.25 each additional adult, under 10 €2.60; Apr.-June and Sept. €8.10/€1.60/€1.30.)

Cobbled streets and culinary treats, from *boulangeries* and grocery stores to fine sit-down meals, define the lovely **rue des Chevaliers.** A **market** fills the town center with breads, meats, and produce (Tu 8am-noon); another for regional specialties fills sq. Albert Ehm (Sa mornings). A casual local favorite, with cheap outdoor dining and a dazzling selection of pastries and ice cream flavors, is **⚑JP Kamm ❶,** 15 rue des Clefs. (☎03 88 92 85 25. Pizza €3.40, quiche €3.40, ice cream from €1.20. Open Tu-F 8am-7pm, Sa 8am-6pm, Su 8am-1:30pm. MC/V after €8.) If you're willing to spend a bit more, **⚑A L'Improviste ❸,** 13 bd. du Général de Leclerc, lives up to its fusion-inspired name. This sexy little out-of-the-way eatery offers a deluxe dining area and shockingly untouristed interior. From the *salade d'avocat au poulet* (avocado and chicken salad; €6) to the *magret du canard au ananas* (pineapple duck breast; €14), each dish is a creative culinary delight. (☎03 88 82 81 81. Open W-Sa 9am-3pm and 6pm-midnight.) **Au Bon Pichet ❸,** 10 pl. du Marché aux Choux, serves up hearty Alsatian fare in a cheerful interior. (☎03 88 82 96 65. Salad from €7.50, *magret du canard* €15.50. Open daily noon-2pm and 7-10pm, closed Su afternoon and M night. AmEx/MC/V.)

◐ ❀ SIGHTS AND FESTIVALS. According to legend, Sélestat was founded by a giant. His thigh bone (a mere mammoth tusk, some claim) graces Sélestat's impressive **⚑Bibliothèque Humaniste,** 1 rue de la Bibliothèque, an austere collection of beautiful books from Sélestat's 15th-century humanistic boom. Its collection, which is presented in a single room, spans 13th-century students' diligently annotated translations of Ovid to the 16th-century *Cosmographie Introductio,* the first book to mention America by name. (☎03 88 58 07 20. Open M and W-F 9am-noon and 2-6pm, Sa 9am-noon; July-Aug. also Sa-Su 2-5pm. €3.60, students and seniors €2. Audioguide €1.55, available in English.) The **FRAC** modern art gallery, 1 espace Gibert Estève, just south of the city centre at quai de l'Ill and rte. de Marckolsheim, has free exhibits within its massive, glass and intriguing artist-created gardens. (☎03 88 58 87 55; www.culture-alsace.org. Open W-Su 2-6pm. Free.)

The **Église St-Georges,** rue de l'Église at the north end of the *vieille ville,* houses Max Ingrand's startlingly modern 1960s stained glass—a stark contrast to the stunning saint-centric 14th-century pieces in the choir. St-Georges's 60m tower, built during the 13th and 14th centuries, marks where Charlemagne spent Christmas in AD 775. Surrounded by ivy-covered homes, the austere 12th-century **Église Ste-Foy** at pl. Marché aux Poissons was constructed by Benedictine monks but taken over by Jesuits. Hints of the imperial Hohenstaufen family (look for their insignia, a grimacing lion) contrast with striking Roman mosaics of the Ganges and Euphrates Rivers. (Brochures in French, English, and German.) The **Maison de Pain,** rue du Sel, appropriately located in the former seat of the breadmakers' guild, provides a drool-inducing history of breadmaking from 12,500 BC to the present. Friendly head baker █François Baltanas answers all questions about his art and the French passion for bread. (✆ 03 88 58 45 90; www.maisondupain-d-alsace.com. Open Jan.-June and Sept.-Nov. Tu-F 10am-noon and 2-6pm, Sa-Su 10am-1pm and 2-5pm; July-Aug. Tu-Su 10am-12:30pm and 1:30-6pm, Sa-Su closes 5pm; daily Dec. 10am-7pm. €4.60, students €2.30, 12-16 €1.53, under 12 free. MC/V.)

Bars and pubs, like everything else in the *vieille ville,* cluster along **rue des Chevaliers.** For a livelier time, visit the *winstubs* of **rue du Président Poincaré,** along the old town's southern wall. Sélestat's major festival is the **Corso Fleuri,** or flower festival, on the second weekend in August. Street artists perform, wine is tasted, and gnomes invade the streets on floats of over 500,000 dahlias. It ends in a giant fireworks display. (Info at corso@ville-selestat.fr, or call the Service Culturel ✆ 03 88 58 85 75. €6.60, under 12 free.) Home to the first recorded Christmas tree in Europe, Sélestat decks itself in evergreen for the weeks leading to December 25.

◪ **DAYTRIP FROM SÉLESTAT: HAUT KOENIGSBOURG.** On a rocky outcropping far above the spreading *plaine d'Alsace,* this highly touristed **château** is an early 20th-century masterpiece of medieval forgery. When the people of Sélestat presented Germany's Kaiser Wilhelm II with the ruins of a 12th-century Hohenstaufen fortress demolished in the Thirty Years' War, he rebuilt the once-grand château on its original site. This towering recreation strikes a note of falseness with its undamaged gorgeousness—the unending stream of neck-craning tourists doesn't help—but there is no denying the appeal of the views from the towers, its marvelous architecture, its **Donjon,** and the 15th- to 17th-century collection of medieval weaponry. The gloriously appointed **Salle des Fêtes** dazzles with polished decadence. *(✆ 03 88 82 50 60. By car from Sélestat, take A35 to sortie (exit) 17 via Kintzheim or 18 via Saint-Hippolyte, then take N59 via Lièpvre. A taxi is about €20 each way from Sélestat. The Sélestat tourist office advises on other methods of travel. Open daily June-Aug. 9:30am-6:30pm; Apr.-May and Sept. 9:30am-5:30pm; Mar. and Oct. 9:45am-5pm; Nov.-Feb. 9:45am-noon and 1-5pm. Dungeon tours July-Aug. 10:45am, noon, 1:45, 3, 4:15pm; €1.50. Free brochures in English, German, and French. Audioguide €4. Free French tours 11am and 2:30pm. €7, ages 18-25 €4.50, under 18 free, first Su of month Oct.-Apr. free.)*

COLMAR

The largest town on the Route du Vin, Colmar (pop. 68,000) feels a bit like the afterworld limbo: while the city possesses its own charm, the enormous crowds are just waiting to get somewhere else. Though best used as a base for exploring smaller Route towns, Colmar itself still hosts a smattering of worthwhile diversions, including an entertaining museum devoted to its former resident Auguste Bartholdi, sculptor of the Statue of Liberty. Otherwise, the Alsatian pastel-colored *vieille ville* makes for an enjoyable (but hardly breathtaking) sojourn.

▣ TRANSPORTATION

Trains depart from pl. de la Gare (☎08 91 67 68 69) to: Lyon (4½-5½hr., 7 per day, €39.30); Mulhouse (19min., 36 per day, €6.20); Paris (5hr.; 21 per day, only one is direct; €47.90); and Strasbourg (40min., 36 per day, €9.50). Check the ticket office for info. (Open M-F 6:15am-8pm, Sa 8:30am-7pm, Su 8:30am-8:15pm. AmEx/MC/V.) Various **bus** companies on pl. de la Gare, right of the station exit, run 6am-7pm, to small towns on the Route du Vin, including Kaysersberg (9 per day, €5-10) and Riquewihr (10 per day, €6-11). Trace, on rue des Unterlinden, in a covered *galerie* to the right of the tourist office (☎03 89 20 80 80; open M-F 8:30am-12:15pm and 1:30-6:15pm, Sa 8:30am-12:15pm; tickets €0.90, *carnet* of 10 €6.40; buses run 6am-8pm) and infrequent night Somnabus (open M-Sa 9pm-midnight) provide public transportation. **Taxis**, pl. de la Gare (☎03 89 41 40 19 or 03 89 80 71 71) are available 24hr. **Rent bikes** from Colmar à Bicyclette, in the pl. Rapp near av. de la République. (☎03 89 41 37 90. €3 per half-day, €4.50 per day. €50 cash deposit and ID required. Helmets not rented except for children. Open daily Apr.-May and Oct. 9am-noon and 2-7pm; June-Sept. M-Tu and Th-F 8:30am-noon and 2-8pm, W and Sa-Su 8:30am-noon and 1-8pm.)

▣ PRACTICAL INFORMATION

To reach the **tourist office**, 4 rue des Unterlinden, from the train station, turn left on av. de la République until it becomes rue Kléber and curves right through pl. du 18 Novembre into the main pl. Unterlinden. German- and English-speaking staff has free, hard-to-follow maps, cash-only **currency exchange,** and reservations service with a night's deposit. Themed city tours are available in French and German, including *vieille ville*, Bartholdi, and Judaic history tours. (☎03 89 20 68 92; www.ot-colmar.fr. Open July-Aug. M-Sa 9am-7pm, Su 9:30am-2pm; Apr.-June and Sept.-Oct. M-Sa 9am-6pm, Su 10am-2pm; Nov.-Mar. M-Sa 9am-noon and 2-6pm, Su 10am-2pm.) The **police** are located at 6 rue du Chasseur (☎03 89 24 75 00), and the **Hôpital Pasteur** at 39 av. de la Liberté (☎03 89 12 40 00). **Internet** access is available at Infr@ Réseau, 12 rue du Rempart. (☎03 89 23 98 45. €3 per hr. Open during school year M 2-9pm, Tu and Th-F 10am-2pm and 3-9pm, W and Sa 10:30am-9pm, Su 2-8pm; school vacation M and Su 1:30-8pm, Tu-Sa 10am-noon and 1:30-9pm.) A **laundromat,** 1 rue Ruest, is open daily 7am-9pm. The **post office,** 36-38 av. de la République, across from the Champs de Mars, offers currency exchange, cyberposte, and an **ATM.** (☎03 89 24 62 00. Open M-F 8am-6:30pm, Sa 8:30am-noon. Branch office on the corner of rue Etroite and rue du Nord. OPen M-F 9am-6pm, Sa 9am-noon.) **Postal Code:** 68000.

▣ ACCOMMODATIONS AND CAMPING

Auberge de Jeunesse (HI), 2 rue Pasteur (☎03 89 80 57 39). Take bus #4 (dir: Europe) to Pont Rouge. Crowded dorm rooms and showers, but singles are a bargain. Breakfast included. Sheets €3.50. Reception Apr.-Sept. 7-10am and 5-11pm. Lockout 10am-5pm. Curfew 11pm. June-Aug. reserve in advance. Closed mid-Dec. to mid-Jan. 6- to 8-bed dorms €11.50; singles €16.50; doubles €28. MC/V. HI members only. ❶

Hôtel Kempf, 1 av. de la République (☎03 89 41 21 72; hotel.kempf.free.fr). Large, simple rooms with a homey atmosphere in the middle of the *vieille ville*. Breakfast €6. Reception 11am-1am. Closed mid-Jan. to end of Feb. and for 2 weeks June-July. Singles and doubles €28, with hall shower €30.50, with private shower €35; triples with bath and toilet €55. MC/V. ❸

Hôtel Primo, 5 rue des Ancêtres (☎03 89 24 22 24; www.hotel-primo.com), near pl. Unterlinden. A stone's throw from the town center, Primo offers styleless institutional comfort for the masses in a hotel that feels more like an overpriced hostel. Rooms have TV. Overpriced Internet at reception. Breakfast buffet €6. 24hr. reception. Wheelchair-accessible. Singles and doubles €29, with shower €39; triples €44-62. MC/V. ❸

La Chaumière, 74 av. de la République (☎03 89 41 08 99), near the station, 10min. from the center of town. Kind hostess lets somewhat small, slightly aged, but pleasant rooms with TV. Rooms around the cement balcony overlooking a courtyard are quietest; others overlook a busy street with frequent buses. Breakfast €5. Reception 7am-11pm. Single with small bed €28, singles and doubles with large bed €28-30, with shower €40-43. 4- to 5- person suite with bath €46. Jan.-Feb. prices €2 lower. MC/V. ❸

Camping: Camping de l'Ill, rte. de Neuf-Brisach (☎03 89 41 15 94; www.camping-alsace.com), is 2 laurel-scented kilometers from town on a wooded river in view of the Vosges. Take bus #1 (dir: Horbourg-Wihr) to Plage d'Ill. Reception July-Aug. 8am-noon and 2-9pm; Mar.-June and Sept.-Dec. 8-11am and 2-9pm. Open Mar.-Nov. Fills quickly in summer. €3 per person, under 10 €1.80, €3.30 per site. Electricity €2.40. ❶

ALSACE, LORRAINE, AND FRANCHE-COMTÉ

🍴 FOOD

Colmar has a wealth of gastronomic goodies for the thrifty diner. There is a **Monoprix supermarket** at pl. Unterlinden (open M-Sa 8am-8pm; AmEx/MC/V) and **markets** in pl. St-Joseph (Sa morning) and pl. de l'Ancienne Douane (Th morning), a popular cafe spot. **La Cassolette ❷**, 70 Grand'Rue, prepares cheap breakfasts as well as an exhaustive selection of delicious sandwiches and large salads (€7-11.50) on a meters-tall menu in its cozy, flower-filled interior. *Le choucroute comme chez grandmère* (€14), a house specialty, is sauerkraut prepared in the style of that Alsatian grandmother you never had. (☎03 89 23 66 30. Open M-Th 8am-7pm and F-Sa 8am-9:30pm; closed W afternoon. MC/V.) **Brasserie Schwendi ❷**, 23-25 Grand'Rue, is open late and serves generous portions of *tartes flambées* (€5.90-8.10) and other Alsatian staples, as well as a great selection of local beer and wine. (☎03 89 23 66 26. *Plats* €6.40-13. Open daily 10am-12:30am, hot food served noon-11pm. MC/V.) For those exploring the local viticulture, a friendly welcome, great selection of local wines (€3.90 and up), and a 400-year legacy await at **Robert Karcher et Fils,** 11 rue de l'Ours, in the *vieille ville.* (☎03 89 41 14 42; www.vins-karcher.com. Open daily 8am-noon and 2-7pm. MC/V.)

🔆 SIGHTS

A fair number of Colmar's sights are outdoors. Get acquainted with the (rather bizarre) traditional style of the Alsatian houses, glistening in Easter egg colors, that cluster thickly in the **quartier des Tanneurs** and **la petite Venise** (little Venice). On rue des Têtes, 105 grotesque stone heads stare out from the 1609 **Maison des Têtes,** a must-see for its sheer creepiness. It also houses a tasty but expensive restaurant. The 13th- to 14th-century **Collégiale St-Martin,** pl. de la Cathédrale, boasts an attractive, speckled exterior and 14th-century German stained glass.

MUSÉE D'UNTERLINDEN. Converted from an idyllic 13th-century Dominican convent, this museum of largely religious art holds Mathias Grünewald's and Nikolaus Haguenauer's *Issenheim Altarpiece* (1500-1516), which depicts scenes from Christ's life in stunning iconographic detail. The rest of this busy museum's collection is interesting for its wild variety, which includes a section of tiny 15th-century woodblock prints and 20th-century art. (*1 rue des Unterlinden. ☎03 89 20 15 58; www.musee-unterlinden.com. Open daily May-Oct. 9am-6pm; Nov.-Apr. M and W-Su 9am-noon and 2-5pm. Free audioguides in French, English, and German. €7, students and ages 12-17 €5, under 12 free. Last tickets sold 30 min. before closing. MC/V.*)

ÉGLISE DES DOMINICAINS. Originally built by the Dominican order, the minimalist interior reflects their strong attachment to poverty and spiritual austerity. Today the church is little more than a showroom for Martin Schongauer's exquisite *Virgin in the Rose Bower* (1473), a lushly colored panel overwhelmed by an outrageous neo-Gothic frame. Stolen in 1975, the story of its improbable discovery and return is narrated by multilingual panels within. German-captioned paintings on the walls date to the German occupation of Alsace during the Franco-Prussian War; their return was a provision of the Treaty of Versailles. *(Pl. des Dominicains. Open daily Apr.-Dec. 10am-1pm and 3-6pm. €1.30, students €1, ages 14-16 €0.50.)*

MUSÉE BARTHOLDI. Noted French sculptor Frédéric Auguste Bartholdi (1834-1904), best known for a 47m statue of his mother entitled *Liberty Enlightening the World* (often called the Statue of Liberty), has been memorialized in this peculiar museum, where drawings and models reveal the amusing and distressing fact that nearly all his figures sport a familiar pose, that of one arm raised. The giant plaster ear was a full-scale study for Ms. Liberty's. In 2004, to celebrate the centennial of Bartholdi's death, a 12m scale replica of the Statue of Liberty was unveiled at the northern point of the city. *(30 rue des Marchands. ☎03 89 41 90 60. Open Mar.-Dec. M and W-Su 10am-noon and 2-6pm. Brochures in English. €4, students €2.50.)*

MUSÉE DU JOUET ET DES PETITS TRAINS. The tiny Museum of Games and Little Trains is full of everything you ever wanted to play with but didn't have when you were a kid. It even comes with that same childhood frustration of not being able to touch. A town-sized population of dolls, a Cinderella's coach exhibit, and a 1000m network of button-activated model trains stand out among the diminutive collection. *(40 rue Vauban. ☎03 89 41 93 10; www.musee-jouet.com. Open daily July-Sept. 9am-6pm; Oct.-June M and W-Su 10am-noon and 2-6pm. €4, students €3, children under 8 €3.)*

🎵 🌿 ENTERTAINMENT AND FESTIVALS

A wide selection of pubs and bars dot the *vieille ville*, particularly around the cathedral and **Grand' Rue.** Snacks are available into the wee hours at **Brussel's Café,** 18 pl. de la Cathédrale, in a jovial atmosphere. (☎03 89 41 43 12. Beer from €2.80. Open daily 11am-1:30am, food service noon-3pm and 6:30-11pm. MC/V.)

The 10-day **Foire aux Vins d'Alsace** in mid-August is the region's largest wine fair. Popular European musicians hold concerts at 9pm; free tastings and exhibitions take place daily. (☎03 90 50 50 50; www.foire-colmar.com. Festival entrance until 5pm €2.50, after 5pm €5.50. Concerts €12-25.) In the first two weeks of July, the more highbrow **Festival International de Colmar** features two dozen concerts by some of the best names in classical music, with an annual tributary theme giving homage to one of the great composers. (☎03 89 20 68 97, tickets 03 89 41 05 36; www.festival-colmar.com. Tickets €9-56, under 25 €5-20.50.) The Collégiale St-Martin's organists play for the **Heures Musicales** (July-Aug. Tu 8:45pm; €8, students €6.50), and the **Soirées Folkloriques** offers up free folk music concerts Tuesday nights at 8:30pm in pl. de l'Ancienne Douane (call the tourist office for details).

MULHOUSE

Once a wealthy industrial powerhouse, Mulhouse (pop. 110,000) is now a thriving cultural center. Home not to museums of antiquity, but rather fabulous tributes to technology, Mulhouse can provide an intriguing break from Gothic churches and 17th-century architecture. There is a distinct sense that the city is living in the present—from nightlife to city life, Mulhouse's throbbing heart may be a mechanical one, but this is one pacemaker that can really get going.

▣ ▮ TRANSPORTATION AND PRACTICAL INFORMATION

Trains (☎03 89 36 11 03) run from 10 av. du Général Leclerc to Basel, Switzerland (20min., 7 per day, €5.90); Belfort (30min., 28 per day, €7.70); Paris (4½hr., 8 per day, €47.90); Strasbourg (1hr., 14 per day, €14.40). Local **buses** run from Porte Jeune, north of the pedestrian district. (☎03 89 66 77 77; www.solea.info. Most routes 7am-7pm; evening routes 8:30-11:30pm. Bus #17 goes by all major museums. Tickets €1.15, *carnet* of 10 €8.20, day pass €3. Tickets available at SNCF station, Porte Jeune office, or on the bus. MC/V in station and office.) For a **taxi**, call ☎03 89 45 80 00. (24hr. service. €10-16 from train station to hostel.) **Car rental** is available at Hertz, 94 rue de Bâle. (☎03 89 65 15 04. Open M-F 8am-noon and 2-6:30pm, Sa 8am-noon and 3:30-6:30. MC/V.)

The **tourist office**, 9 av. Foch, is two blocks ahead of the station, across from a park. Signs from the station are for driving only—and a circuitous route. Walk straight on av. Foch. Friendly English- and German-speaking staff provides reservations service and free detailed maps of the town. (☎03 89 35 48 48; www.tourism-mulhouse.com. Tours in French and English on request July-Aug. Tu and Sa 10:30am. €4, under 12 free. Main office open M-F 9am-noon and 2-6pm.) The annex is in the Hôtel de Ville. (☎03 89 66 93 13. Open July-Aug. 10am-7pm; Sept.-June M-Sa 10am-6pm, Su 10am-noon and 2-6pm.) Other services include: **banks** with **ATMs** and **currency exchange** around the city, especially pl. de la Réunion; a **laundromat** at 1bis rue des Halles (☎06 62 86 55 43; open daily 6:30am-8pm); **police** at 12 rue Coehorn (☎03 89 42 71 10; call here for the **pharmacie de garde**), off bd. de La Marseillaise; a **hospital** at 20 rue du Dr. Laënnec (☎03 89 64 62 72), behind the station; **Internet** at Noumatrouff, 57 rue de la Mertzau (☎03 89 32 94 17; free with reservation) and Brasserie Le Convivial, 5 rue de la Sinne. (☎03 89 46 11 06. €3.50 per hr. Open daily 9am-1am, closes W at 5pm. Opens at 2pm for 3 weeks in Aug.) The **post office**, 3 pl. de Gaulle, has **currency exchange** and an **ATM**. (☎03 89 56 94 11. Open M-F 8am-7pm, Sa 8am-noon.) A branch is at pl. de la Réunion. (☎03 89 46 83 50. Open M 1-6pm, Tu-F 10am-6pm, Sa 10am-noon.) **Postal Code:** 68100.

▮ ▮ ACCOMMODATIONS AND CAMPING

Dirt-cheap rooms in Mulhouse are elusive, but there are many comfortable and reasonably priced two-stars. Rates often drop on weekends. The newly refurbished **Auberge de Jeunesse (HI) ❶**, 37 rue d'Illberg, offers clean, sparse three-, four- and six-bed rooms with co-ed bathrooms. Take bus #2 (dir: Coteaux; bus #S1 after 8:30pm) to Salle des Sports. (☎03 89 42 63 28; mulhouse@fuaj.org. Breakfast included. Luggage storage. Linen €2.80. Reception daily 8am-noon and 5-11pm. Wheelchair-accessible. Dorms €12.50. MC/V. HI members only.) Homey, family-run **Hôtel St-Bernard ❸**, 3 rue des Fleurs, conveniently located near the town center, maintains small, bright rooms with showers, TVs, and cute accents. Guests have access to free high-speed Internet, bikes, a small library, a safe for valuables, and, most importantly, an irresistible Saint Bernard. (☎03 89 45 82 32; stbr@evhr.net. Breakfast €7. Reception daily 7am-9:30pm. Singles with shower €32; doubles with shower €33-47. Extra bed €9. AmEx/DC/MC/V.) **Hôtel de Bâle ❸**, 19-21 Passage Central, is a decent alternative with a friendly staff, pleasant rooms, and cable TV, but not the extra niceties. (☎03 89 46 19 87; www.ot.ville-mulhouse.fr. Breakfast €6, free for kids under 12. 24hr. reception. Singles with shower €35, with shower and toilet €48, with bath and toilet €52. Extra bed €8. MC/V.) The **Camping de l'Ill ❶**, rue Pierre de Coubertin, has an on-site grocery store. (☎03 89 06 20 66. Reception daily 8am-1pm and 3-9pm. Open Apr.-Oct. €3.40 per person, €3.40 per lot. Electricity €3.25. MC/V.)

🟥 FOOD

Mulhouse tries to price like the Swiss (steeply), but the student community necessitates the cheap kebab joints and pizzerias found on **rue de l'Arsenal.** A **Monoprix supermarket** at the corner of rue du Sauvage and rue des Maréchaux sells the usual staples. (Open M-F 8:15am-8pm and Sa 8:15am-7pm. MC/V.) A few doors down, **Le Globe** grocery also sells Alsatian *choucroute* (sauerkraut), local sausages, and delicacies from *pâté* to handmade marzipan. (☎03 89 36 50 50. Open M-Th 9:30am-6:30pm, F-Sa 9am-6:45pm. MC/V.) On a quiet street off the main drag, the unassuming facade of ▨**Le Maharadjah ❸,** 8 rue des Tanneurs, conceals a beautiful dining area and friendly service. Scrumptious *plats*, including chicken *tikka masala* (€13.25) and vegetarian curried potatoes *alu saag* (€12.25) are enormous. (☎03 89 56 48 21.; www.maharadjah.fr.fm. Vegetarian specialties €11.50-14.50, meat *plats* €11.25-16.25, *menu du jour* €9. Open daily 11:45am-2:30pm and 6:45-11:30pm; closed M lunch. MC/V.) **Auberge du Vieux Mulhouse ❸,** pl. de la Réunion, cooks up *La Mulhousienne*, a pork and saurkraut confection with apples (€12.30), in a timbered restaurant. (☎03 89 45 84 18. Weekday lunch *menu du jour* €10.80. Open daily 9:30am-10:30pm, F-Sa until 11pm. MC/V.) Gyros (€2.50-4), salads (€2.50-4), cold sandwiches (tuna, cheese, or shrimp; €2.50), and desserts (€2.50) await at **Le Bosphore ❶,** 13 av. de Colmar, the best quick-service joint in town. (☎03 89 45 16 00. Open daily 10am-midnight, sometimes later. MC/V.)

🔵 SIGHTS

Mulhouse's historic district centers around the **place de la Réunion,** named for the occasions in 1798 and 1918 when French troops reunited the city with France, though most museums are outside the *vieille ville* and accessible only by bus.

MUSÉE NATIONAL DE L'AUTOMOBILE. Worshippers of the internal combustion wonders of the automobile will be in heaven; others will at least find their interest piqued. The brothers Schlumpf once owned the 500-plus top-of-the-line automobiles on display. The staggering collection ranges from an 1878 steam-driven Jacquot à Vapeur to the bubbly electric cars of the future, all shined to a blindingly impressive polish. The room of *chefs d'œuvres* (masterpieces) contains cars once owned by the likes of Charlie Chaplin and Emperor Bao Dai. *(192 av. de Colmar. Take bus #1, 4, 11, 13, or 17 north to Musée Auto. ☎03 89 33 23 23; www.collection-schlumpf.com. Open daily Apr.-Oct. 9am-6pm, closes 6:30pm July-Aug.; Nov.-Mar. 10am-6pm. Free audioguides. Wheelchair-accessible. €10, students €7.50, ages 7-18 €5, under 7 free. MC/V.)*

MUSÉE FRANÇAIS DU CHEMIN DE FER. The slick engines and railway cars appeal to the slackjawed gawker in everyone. Peer into the perfectly restored compartments of such railroad legends as the Orient Express. Every hour a massive 1949 steam engine (the last of its kind) chugs away in place, to the delight of viewers. Closed for renovations until March 2005. *(2 rue Alfred de Glehn. Take bus #17 (dir: Musées) from Porte Jeune Place, or #18 (dir: Technopole) from the train station; 1 per hr. On Su, use line M. ☎03 89 42 83 33. Wheelchair-accessible. Open daily May-Sept. 10am-6pm; Oct.-Apr. 10am-5pm. €8, students and children 6-18 €4, under 6 free. MC/V.)*

ELECTROPOLIS. This zippy new museum introduces kids of all ages to the wonderful world of energy with scale models, hands-on exhibits, films, and historical collections. The *grande machine*, an enormous 170-ton room-sized power generator, supplied the city with electricity from 1901-1947. *(55 rue du Pâturage, next to the railway museum. ☎03 89 32 48 60; www.electropolis.tm.fr. Wheelchair-accessible. Open Tu-Su 10am-6pm. €7.50, students and children 6-18 €3.50, under 6 free. MC/V.)*

TEMPLE DE ST-ETIENNE. The bustling pl. de la Réunion centers on one of France's few Protestant Gothic cathedrals. If the church seems distinctly modern, it's because the Protestants acquired it from the Catholics in 1890, then tore it down and built it back up again. The temple's original 14th-century stained-glass windows were preserved and now line the galleries. (☎03 89 66 30 19. Open May-Sept. M and W-Su 10am-noon and 2-6pm, Sa 10am-noon and 2-5pm, Su 2-6pm. Free.)

MUSÉE DE L'IMPRESSION SUR ÉTOFFES. This homage to the printed textile industry is a fascinating trip into the world of hand-printing, dye-making, and mechanization. Luminaries from Dior to Paloma Picasso have come here, seeking inspiration for the future from the wealth of the past. For €5, you can print a t-shirt using 200-year-old hand-carved blocks. The gift shop will drain anyone's budget. (14 rue Jean-Jacques Henner. ☎03 89 46 83 00. Open daily 10am-noon and 2-6pm. Audioguide available in English, French, and German. €6, students €3, children 12-18 €2, under 12 free.)

OTHER SIGHTS. To escape the ubiquitous machinery in town, visit the blossoming gardens of the **Parc Zoologique et Botanique.** There are entertaining animal feedings, from the bears through the storks, at various times throughout the day 10:30am-4pm. Flower displays change with the seasons. (Take bus #12, dir: Moenschsberg, to Zoo. ☎03 89 31 85 10; www.zoo-mulhouse.com. Open daily May-Aug. 9am-7pm; Apr. and Sept. 9am-6pm; Mar. and Oct.-Nov. 9am-5pm; Dec.-Feb. 10am-4pm. Mar.-Oct. €8, Nov.-Feb. €4, students and ages 6-16 €4.) The tourist office lists Mulhouse's smaller museums.

■ ▧ NIGHTLIFE AND FESTIVALS

Fun-loving Mulhouse is especially busy in the center of town. **Rue Henriette** buzzes with pub chatter late into the night, and the area between **rue du Sauvage** and **place de la Réunion** boasts a high concentration of nightlife. Students flock to the crowded **O'Bryan Pub,** 5 pl. des Victoires, off rue du Sauvage. (☎03 89 56 25 58. Beer from €2.50; tasting of 4 beers €6. Open daily 10am-1:30am. MC/V.) There are a few gay-friendly bars in town, but the **Jet 7 Bar,** 2bis passage de l'Hôtel de Ville, is probably the friendliest, a sleek, happening spot with happy hour 6:30-8pm. (☎03 89 56 04 21. Open daily 4pm-1:30am. MC/V.) At the nightclub **Salle des Coffres,** 74 rue du Sauvage, right outside the *vieille ville,* a young crowd keeps it jumping late into the night each weekend. (☎03 89 56 34 98. Cover €8 with one drink, students €5. W-Sa 10pm-4am.) **J.H.,** 1 rue Ste-Thérèse just off quai du Forst, is the best gay club in town. Theme nights rotate throughout the week; some themes try to welcome more women. (☎03 89 32 00 08. M and Th free; F-Sa €18 with 2 drinks, €11 with 2 non-alcoholic drinks. Open M and Th-Su 10:30pm-4am.)

Throughout the year, especially in summer, Mulhouse comes alive with a number of **concerts** and **festivals.** The **Festival Automobile de Mulhouse** brings together autophiles from around Europe in mid-July. This homage to the car includes drive-in movies, rallies, exhibitions, a high-priced auction, a parade, and a different theme each year. **Bêtes de Scène,** in mid-July, brings a series of fringe rock concerts and underground DJs to venues across town. (For ticket info call ☎08 92 68 36 22 at €0.34 per min. or the tourist office for details. Ticket prices vary, some events free.) Every year, the city comes out for the **International Carnaval** party from late February to early March and for **street theater** in August. The tourist office has a full calendar.

FRANCHE-COMTÉ

BELFORT

Occupying a valley between the mountains of the Vosges and the Jura, the only chink in the eastern mountain-range defenses of the French nation, Belfort (pop. 50,000) has been a favorite target of invading armies for centuries. Known as the "city of three sieges" because of its history as the object of a trio of failed Prussian-led offenses in the 19th century, Belfort is defined by its sprawling mountaintop citadel. Although in recent years the old town has become an industrial power-house, home to the factories that produce TGV trains and Peugeot automobiles, this rejuvenating industrial development has managed to leave no trace on the charming *vieille ville* of bustling shops and strolling locals.

TRANSPORTATION AND PRACTICAL INFORMATION. Trains run to Besançon (1hr., 17 per day, €13.10); Mulhouse (30min., 17 per day, €7.70); Paris (4hr., 9 per day, €43.20); Strasbourg (1½hr., 8 per day, €19.40). The train station is open daily 4:45am-11pm. Buy tickets at the ticket office. (☎08 36 35 35 35. Open M-F 5:30am-8pm, Sa 8:40am-6:30pm, Su 8:50am-8pm. AmEx/MC/V.) **CTRB**, pl. Corbis, runs **buses** around Belfort. (☎03 84 21 08 08. Office open M-F 9am-12:15pm and 1:45-8:15pm. Lines run 6am-8pm. Tickets €1.10, *carnet* of 10 €8.) For **taxis**, call Radio Belfortains at 44 rue André Parant. (☎03 84 22 13 44. Base €1.25, €1.25-1.60 per km. 24hr.) **Car rental** is available at Budget, 63 faubourg de Montbéliard. (☎03 84 22 70 23. Open M-Sa 9am-noon and 2-6pm. MC/V.)

To get from the station to the **tourist office**, 2bis rue Clemenceau, head left down av. Wilson, then right on faubourg de France. When you see the river, turn left on faubourg des Ancêtres and follow it to rue Clemenceau; the office, set back from the road, is right of the mammoth Caisse d'Epargne. Friendly staff has free maps, *Le Petit Géni*, a guide to Belfort with discounts to local stores and restaurants, and *Spectacles*, a free guide to restaurants and clubs. (☎03 84 55 90 90. www.ot-belfort.com. Open late June-Aug. M-F 9am-12:30pm and 1:45-6:30pm, Sa 9am-12:30 and 1:45-6pm; Sept. to late June M-F 9am-noon and 1:45-6pm, Sa 9am-noon and 1:45-5:30pm.) There is an automatic **currency exchange** machine and **ATM** at Caisse d'Epargne, pl. de la Résistance (☎03 84 57 77 77), and other **banks** with currency exchange and ATMs on bd. Carnot and in the *vieille ville*. Other services include: a **laundromat** at 60 faubourg de Montbeliard (☎03 84 21 84 10; open daily 7am-9pm); **police** at 1 rue du Monnier (☎03 84 58 50 00; call here for the **pharmacie de garde**); a **hospital** at 14 rue de Mulhouse (☎03 84 57 40 00); **Internet** access at Belfort Information Jeunesse, 3 rue Jules Vallès (☎03 84 90 11 11. €2.50 per hr., reserve ahead; open M-F 10am-noon and 1:30-6pm, Sa 10am-noon and 2-5pm; closed Tu morning); and a **post office**, complete with ATM, at 19 faubourg des Ancêtres. (☎03 84 57 67 67. Open M-F 8am-7pm, Sa 8am-noon. MC/V.) **Postal Code:** 90000.

If traveling by train in Franche-Comté with more than one person, consider using SNCF's *VISI'ter Pass* (€10), which is usable by its owner and up to four others. The first three people travel at half-price; the last two get roundtrips for €1.(*Visit a SNCF Franche-Comté office or www.ter-sncf.com/franche_comte for more info. Pass is valid year-round on Sa-Su and holidays; daily July-Aug. Valid only for travel within Franche-Comté and round-trips from Franche-Comté to Dijon and Epinal.*)

ALSACE, LORRAINE, AND FRANCHE-COMTÉ

AU RELAIS D'ALSACE

Homesick or weary travelers should head directly to the **Hôtel au Relais d'Alsace ❸**, where a plain exterior gives way to brightly painted rooms and the warmest welcome on the face of the planet. Kim and Georges, the unbelievably friendly English-speaking Franco-Algerian couple who own and run the hotel, put their hearts and souls into making their little hotel everyone's home away from home.

You can't buy an environment like this: Kim's motherly enthusiasm is limitless, while Georges gives better advice than the tourist office about trails to take around town (ask for a map). The welcoming lobby is often filled with lively conversation, and adoring souvenir pictures drawn by past guests cover the walls. At breakfast, sip fresh-squeezed juice as you add your name to one of their lengthy guestbooks.

(5 av. de la Laurencie. ☎ 03 84 22 15 55; www.arahotel.com. From the station, take av. Wilson left until you hit Faubourg de France on the right. Take it to the vieille ville. At the cathedral, make a left onto rue Général Roussel, then a right onto Grande Rue, then left onto rue Grande Fontaine. Pass through the Porte de Brisach (an old gate) and continue straight. Av. de la Laurencie will be on the left. Breakfast €5.80. Washer, dryer, and free bike rentals available. All rooms with shower. Singles €28; doubles €36; triples €45; quads €53. Extra bed €6. MC/V.)

🏠 📷 ACCOMMODATIONS AND CAMPING. Belfort has a smattering of one- and two-star hotels, but few truly budget places, except for 🏠**Hôtel au Relais d'Alsace ❸**, 5 av. de la Laurencie (see **Hôtel au Relais D'Alsace**, left). **Résidence Madrid ❶**, 6 rue Madrid, a cheap option 10min. from the station away from the *centre ville*, provides dorm-style rooms and singles of adequate quality, a friendly international crowd of residents, co-ed toilets, and clean showers. From the train station, turn left onto av. Wilson, left again on rue Michelet, then right onto rue Parisot, which becomes av. Général Leclerc. Rue Madrid is on the left up 7min. Exercise caution on the street at night. (☎ 03 84 21 39 16; www.ufjt.org/adresse/belfort-madrid. Breakfast €2.50, full meal €6.90, main course €4.40. 24hr. reception. Dorms €14.30, with HI card €12. MC/V.) **Hôtel St-Christophe ❹**, pl. d'Armes, is in a prime location across from the cathedral in the heart of the *vieille ville*. The main hotel rents nice rooms with TV and bath at somewhat high prices; the annex across the square, equally comfortable, is a better deal. (☎ 03 84 55 88 88; fax 03 84 54 08 77. Breakfast €7.50. Reception daily 7am-11pm. Hotel: singles with shower €52; doubles with bath €60. Annex: singles €42; doubles €54. MC/V.) The three-star **Camping International de l'Etang des Forges ❶**, 4 rue du Général Bethouart, is ideally located on the Etang des Forges, a sparkling lake 10min. by car from the *centre ville*. The open grounds afford little privacy but plenty of space, good views, squeaky-clean bathrooms, and best of all, a free brand-new pool. (☎ 03 84 22 54 92; fax 03 84 22 76 55. Reception daily 8am-12:30pm and 2:30-10pm. Open mid-Apr. to late Sept. Mid-Apr. to May and Sept. €7 per tent, €3.10 per person, €2.50 ages 4-10. July-Aug. €8 per tent, €3.80 per person, €3.10 ages 4-10. Electricity €3.)

🍴 FOOD. The local pastry is the *belflore*, a light and fluffy raspberry-almond meringue tart. Finding food is delightfully easy along **Faubourg de France**, which cuts from the river to the train station, or nearly anywhere in the *vieille ville*. Cafes, *boulangeries*, and restaurants cluster around **place des Armes. Supermarket Petit Casino** is by the hostel at rue Léon Blum (☎ 03 84 21 20 88; open M-F 7am-12:30pm and 3-7pm, Sa 7am-12:30pm; MC/V) and there is a **Monoprix** at the corner of bd. Carnot and av. Foch. (☎ 03 84 21 47 67. Open M-F 8:30am-8pm, Sa 8:30am-7:30pm. MC/V.) Find good vegetarian dining at 🏠**Gazelle d'Or ❸**, 4 rue des 4 Vents, a quiet eatery off pl. des Armes which specializes in couscous. (☎ 03 84 58 02 87. *Menu* €8.50. Open M-Sa noon-1:30pm and 7-11pm. MC/V.) **Aux Crêpes d'Antan ❶**, 13 rue du Quai, presents a formidable but fairly usual selection of creamy, artistically folded crêpes and *galettes* (€2.40-9) in a Provençal-themed shop around the corner from the cathedral, with a little terrace on the plaza. (☎ 03 84 22 82 54. Open daily noon-2:30pm and 7-10:30pm. MC/V.) For a change of pace, **La Patate Gourmande ❷**, 12bis faubourg des Ancêtres, fills the stomach with garnished, baked, and au gratin potatoes (€7.50-15) and elaborate salads (€4.50-9.50). The restaurant resembles a cabin in the woods, only it's in a tiny alley. (☎ 03 84 21 88 44. *Franc-Comtoise* potato with melted *comté* cheese and sausage €12.20. Open M-F noon-2pm and 7-10pm, Sa-Su 7-11pm. MC/V.)

◙ **SIGHTS.** At the top of any list of Belfort's sights—and at the top of the hill overlooking the town, on the winding road from pl. des Bourgeois—sits its medieval **château,** which served as a military fortress during the Thirty Years' War but is now a scenic hodgepodge of historical attractions. A free tour of the grounds provides a lesson in military history; the site's fortifications have been beefed up four times throughout its turbulent history. The best place for a view of the valley below is the **terrace** above the museum. (☎ 03 84 54 25 51. Open daily Apr.-Sept. 10am-6:30pm; Oct.-Mar. 10am-5pm. Free tours in French daily July-Aug. every 30min. 10am-11am and 2-5pm. Special themed tours July-Aug. Sa and Su, call ahead for schedule.) A passageway on one of the lower levels leads to the viewing platform of the enormous **Belfort Lion,** a monument to the failure of the Prussians 1870-1871 siege, carved entirely of red Vosges sandstone by the man who crafted the Statue of Liberty. (Platform open daily June-Sept. 9am-7pm; Apr.-May 9am-noon and 2-7pm; Oct.-Mar. 10am-noon and 2-5pm. €5.60, students €4, under 18 free; includes the Musée d'Art et d'Histoire, Tour 46, and the Donation Jardot. MC/V.) Less impressive, but strange enough to be of interest, the **Musée d'Art et d'Histoire** displays an oddball collection of the town's history, from guns and bayonets to keys, woodprints, and scale models. (☎ 03 84 54 25 51. Open Apr.-Aug. M and W-Su 2-6pm; Sept.-Mar. M and W-Su 10am-noon and 2-6pm. €2.90, students €1.95, including Tour 46; 2nd Su of every month free. MC/V.) Along the route back into town, remnants of the octagonal fortifications that once surrounded the *vieille ville* remain intact, though not visitable.

The city has a pair of unique museums. **Tour 46,** on the corner of rue Bartholdi and rue Ancien Théâtre, presents special exhibits by great modern artists. (Open May-Sept. M and W-Su 10am-noon and 2-6pm. Call the château for info.) The **Donation Maurice Jardot,** 8 rue de Mulhouse, surrounded by the floral abundance of **square Emile Lechten,** has an impressive rotating collection of sketches and paintings by modern greats like Picasso, Braque, Léger, Chagall, and architect Le Corbusier. (☎ 03 84 90 40 70; www.mairie-belfort.fr. Open daily July-Sept. 10am-6pm; Apr.-June 10am-noon and 2-6pm; Oct-Mar. 10am-noon and 2-5pm. €3.81, students €2.29, under 18 free. Wheelchair-accessible. AmEx/MC/V.) Walk along av. Jean Jaurès away from the museum to find the dazzling flowers of the **Rosière Garden.**

Back in the *vieille ville*, on the other side of the ramparts from rue des Bons Enfants, Vauban's perfectly preserved 1687 **Porte de Brisach,** rue des Mobiles, bears the motto of the ever-humble Louis XIV: *Nec Pluribus Impar* ("superior to all others"), and his royal insignia of three fleurs-de-lis. The **Cathédrale St-Christophe** presides over pl. des Armes in the heart of Belfort. Made of the same Vosges sandstone as the château, its graceful classical facade shelters a chilling transept with paintings by Belfort native G. Dauphin.

The petit train touristique that departs from the Pl. d'Armes will let you take a lazy 45min. trip through the vieille ville to the top of the citadel. (☎ 03 89 73 74 24; www.petit-train.com. Daily May-Sept. 10am-6pm.)

🖥 🎭 ENTERTAINMENT AND FESTIVALS. Belfort's dance clubs are relegated to the suburbs; think long and hard about how you are going to get back to town once the buses have stopped. The center of town does, however, have several fun bars, including **Café Brussels**, 3 pl. des Armes, which is a good place for people-watching in the heart of the *vieille ville*. (☎03 84 38 06 01. Beer on tap €2.10-3.20, coffee €1.50. Open daily 7:30am-1am. MC/V.) Beer of all kinds can be had at **Bistro des Moines**, 22 rue Dreyfus Schmidt, a lively bar-restaurant with an extensive brewery selection. (☎03 84 21 86 40. Beer €2.20-6.40; meals €7.50-12.50. Open M-F 10:30am-1am, Sa 10:30am-2am. MC/V.)

The first Sunday of every month, Belfort hosts the largest flea market in the east of France, the **Grand Marché aux Puces,** in numerous locations in the *vieille ville*. The tourist office opens a bureau at the pl. d'Armes from 8am-noon on the day of the market. The château hosts free **jazz** in July and August (W 8:30pm) and the cathedral holds cheap classical **concerts** on Thursday nights. The tourist office has details. In the first weekend of July, 85,000 music fans from all over Europe descend upon Belfort for **Les Eurockéennes,** France's largest open-air rock festival. Recent lineups featured Radiohead, Massive Attack, the Roots, Belle and Sebastian, Korn, and nearly 60 other acts from rock to rap. Get tickets early. (Info ☎08 92 68 85 88 at €0.34 per min.; www.eurockeennes.fr. Tickets sold at FNAC stores.) At the beginning of June, over 2000 musicians from around the world hit town for the **Festival International de Musique Universitaire** (☎03 84 22 94 42; www.fimu.com), a three-day extravaganza offering over 200 concerts, many of them free, that run the gamut from classical and jazz to rock and world music. Reserve accommodations well in advance; rooms are next to impossible to find during the event. The tourist office has a free guide of other concerts and festivals throughout the summer. The last week of November brings the film festival **Entrevues,** which showcases both young directors and retrospectives. (For info on all festivals, call Cinéma d'Aujourd'hui ☎03 84 54 24 43.)

🅚 OUTDOOR ACTIVITIES. Belfort has nearly 550km of marked hiking trails. The tourist office has many pamphlets including *Country Walks* that list nearby walks, hikes, and biking trails. One popular route circles Bessoncourt, 4km to the east. The town is also the departure point for the daunting E5 trail that stretches from the Adriatic to the Atlantic, but following one of the many *petites randonnées* around the area provides a fairly flat 10-14km circuit (3-5 hours). To the north, the towering summit of the Ballon d'Alsace (1247m) is a meeting point for three major long-distance trails: the GR5, GR7, and GR59. The taxing 7km hike to the peak should only be attempted by the fit, and biked only by the insane, but the panoramic view of the glacial Doller Valley and the Rhine and Saône Valleys is spectacular.

The **Lac de Malsaucy,** west of Belfort, offers hiking, swimming, sunning, fishing, and outdoor performances. Small **boats, nautical bicycles,** and **mountain bikes** can be rented from the Base de Loisirs du Malsaucy, rue d'Evette (☎03 84 29 21 13). The nearby **Maison Départmentale de l'Environnement** (☎03 84 29 18 12) offers exhibits on everything from frogs to weather. Throughout the summer, puppeteers, acrobats, comedians, and musicians perform here. Outdoor movies are shown for a fee on Thursday nights in late July and August, but are free on Tuesdays at 10pm. To get to the lake, take bus #17 from town. (See bus schedule for details.) For more info on **fishing** in and around Belfort, contact the Fédération du Territoire de Belfort pour la Pêche (☎03 84 23 39 49; www.unpf.fr/90).

🅳 DAYTRIP FROM BELFORT. A 20min. train ride west, in the tiny village of **Ronchamp** (pop. 3000), Le Corbusier's famous 1954 🅒**Chapelle de Notre-Dame-du-Haut** stands on the site of a disastrous 1944 German attack. The mushroom-shaped chapel, which draws architecture students from all over the world, was built as a testament to hope in the wake of World War II. This is one building that shows there's still hope for creative construction with concrete. The chapel features beautiful, sloping lines, receding walls, and a sparsely decorated candlelit worship space "to create a space of silence, prayer, peace, and interior joy."

To reach Ronchamp, take the SNCF bus or train at the station in Belfort (20min.; M-F 9 per day, Sa 6 per day, Su 2 per day; €4.30 bus, €3.70 train). To reach the chapel from the train station, follow rue de la Gare left, turn left onto rue Le Corbusier, and left again onto rue de la Chapelle, then climb the steep, winding road for 1.5km. (☎03 84 20 65 13. Open daily Apr.-Sept. 9:30am-6:30pm; Oct.-Mar. 10am-4pm. €2, students €1.50, children 5-12 free. Wheelchair-accessible. MC/V over €15.) For those with neither car, bike, nor legs of steel, call taxi Guy Bourgogne (☎03 84 20 65 66), which will cost about €5 each way from the train or bus stop.

BESANÇON

The capital of the largely rural Franche-Comté region, Besançon (pop. 120,000) has never been tremendously wealthy, but it does have a unique sense of style. From the fountained and stone-tiled streets of the *vieille ville* to the stylish shops and classy eateries that line the main drag, Besançon feels like a town that knows how to live the good life. To keep the city intact, Louis XIV had his own military engineer, Vauban, fortify it with an enormous citadel. Though the citadel isn't particularly pretty, Besançon's slew of amazing museums and vibrant international student population prove that it's what inside that really counts. The friendly locals have great nightlife, with one of the best gay scenes in the east of France.

⌐ TRANSPORTATION

Trains: av. de la Paix. Office open M-F 5:10am-9:30pm, Sa 5:40am-8pm, Su 6:25am-9:30pm. To: **Belfort** (1hr., 18 per day, €13.10); **Dijon** (1hr., 22 per day, €12.40); **Lyon** (2½hr., 11 per day, €27.30); **Paris** (2hr., 8 per day, €55.10); **Strasbourg** (3hr., 8 per day, €28). Minor station at av. de Chardonnet, few useful trains. AmEx/MC/V.

Buses: Monts Jura, in the train station; office at 17 rue Proudhon (☎08 25 00 22 44). To **Pontarlier** (1hr., 5 per day, €7.30). Office open M-F 8:30am-noon and 2:30-6pm.

Public Transportation: Ginko, 4 pl. du 8 Septembre (☎08 25 00 22 44; www.ginko-bus.com). Open M-Sa 10am-12:45pm and 1:15-7pm. Night buses run sporadically until midnight. Tickets €0.90, *carnet* of 10 €7.80, 24hr. pass €3. Buy tickets on bus.

Taxis: (☎03 81 88 80 80). Min. charge €4.60. 24hr.

Bike Rental: Cycles Pro Shop, 18 av. Carnot (☎03 81 47 03 04). €9 per half-day, €12 per full day; helmet €3. ID deposit. Open M-Sa 9am-noon and 2-7pm. MC/V.

▟ ▟ ORIENTATION AND PRACTICAL INFORMATION

Most areas of interest in Besançon lie within a thumb-shaped and well-fortified turn of the Doubs River. To reach the tourist office, cross the train station's parking lot and head down the stairs. Follow av. de la Paix, which turns into av. Foch, but stay to the right. Continue to veer left at the river, and turn onto av. de l'Helvétie. Follow this to pl. de la Première Armée Française. The office is in the park to the right, and the *vieille ville* is across the bridge (10 minutes).

Tourist Office: 2 pl. de la 1ère Armée Française (☎08 20 32 07 82; www.besancon-tourisme.com). Provides free accommodations service, and the comprehensive student guide *La Besace*. Tours May-Sept. for individuals (in French; €6, students €4) and

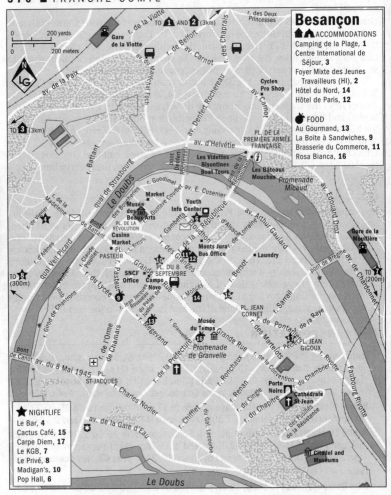

groups (in French, English, or German; by reservation). **Currency exchange** at the same rate as the banks. Open June-Sept. M-Sa 10am-9pm, Su 10am-7pm; Oct.-May M-Sa 9:30am-12:30pm and 3:30-5:30pm. MC/V.

English-Language Bookstore: Campo Novo, 50 Grande Rue (☎03 81 65 07 70), has a small selection of books in English. Open M 10am-7pm, Tu-Sa 9am-7pm. MC/V.

Youth Center: Centre Information Jeunesse (CIJ), 27 rue de la République (☎03 81 21 16 16; www.crijfc.com). Info on internships, jobs, events, and apartments. HI cards. Free Internet with a *Carte Avantage Jeunes* (€6 for a year membership. The card also gets discounts on everything from lodging to sights. Limit 2hr. per week.) Open M and Sa 1:30-6pm, Tu-F 10am-noon and 1:30-6pm.

Laundromat: Blanc-Matic, 54 rue Bersot (☎03 81 80 63 63), near the bus station. Also at 57 rue des Cras, near the Foyer Mixte. Both open daily 7am-8pm. Also **Salon Lavoire JTI,** 54 rue Battant (☎03 81 81 58 66). Open daily 7am-8pm.

Police: 2 av. de la Gare d'Eau (☎03 81 21 11 22). Near pl. St-Jacques.

Hospital: Centre Hospitalier Universitaire, 2 pl. St-Jacques (☎03 81 66 81 66).

Internet Access: At the CIJ (see **Youth Center**). **T@cybernet,** 18 rue de Pontarlier (☎03 81 81 15 74). €3.60 per hr., €2.40 with a *Carte Avantage Jeunes*. MC/V. Open M-Sa 11am-10pm, Su 2-8pm. **Foyer des Jeunes Travailleurs** has free access for guests.

Post Office: 4 rue Demangel (☎03 81 53 81 12). Open M-F 8am-7pm, Sa 8am-noon. Branches at 23 rue Proudhon (☎03 81 65 55 82; open M and Sa 8am-7pm, Tu-F 10am-noon and 1:30-6pm), off rue de la République, and at pl. Jouffroy d'Abbans (☎03 81 65 55 82; open M-F 9:30am-noon and 1:30-6:30pm, Sa 9am-noon). **Currency exchange** and Cyberposte.

Postal Code: 25000.

🏠 ACCOMMODATIONS AND CAMPING

Hostels are a trek from the *vieille ville* (30min.), but offer excellent facilities at a bargain. They are easily accessible by convenient daytime and nighttime bus lines (until midnight). Besançon's central hotels are closer to the action, but require advance reservations and aren't cheap.

Foyer Mixte des Jeunes Travailleurs (HI), 48 rue des Cras (☎03 81 40 32 00; fax 03 81 40 32 01). Take bus #7 (or night line A) from pl. Flore (dir: Orchamps; 3-5 per hr., €0.90). To pl. Flore, take av. de la Paix; keep left as the road turns into rue de Belfort. Turn right onto av. Carnot, then take a sharp left onto rue des Chaprais. The stop is on the same side of the street as a Casino grocery. Locals refer to it as "Foyer Les Oiseaux." Large rooms with private bathrooms are a great deal. Concerts, movies, and other special events. Free Internet. Breakfast included. Cafeteria meal €6.80. Reception daily 8:30am-8pm. Dec.-Feb. only 2 rooms available unless you call a day ahead. Singles €20, 2nd night €18; doubles €30/€27. AmEx/MC/V. ❷

Hôtel du Nord, 8-10 rue Moncey (☎03 81 81 35 56; www.hotel_du_nord_besancon.com), on a charming street in the old town. Rooms are enormous, with new mattresses, satellite TVs (some with video capacity), and sparkling, fully outfitted bathrooms. Tiny elevator runs through 4 stories. Breakfast €4.60. Parking. 24hr. reception. Check-in and check-out noon. Reserve far ahead. Singles and doubles with shower or bath €47-54; triples and quads with shower €60. AmEx/DC/MC/V. ❸

Hôtel de Paris, 33 rue des Granges (☎03 81 81 36 56; www.hotel-deparis.com). Step into the lap of luxury in these large, fully-equipped, spring-colored rooms overlooking a quiet courtyard garden. Free Internet for guests. Breakfast €7. 24hr. reception. Reserve in advance. High-season singles €47-52.54, low season (Sept.-Mar.) €38; doubles €55.50-61/€38; triples €78; quads and quints €82-88. AmEx/DC/MC/V. ❹

Centre International de Séjour, 19 rue Martin-du-Gard (☎03 81 50 07 54; cis.besancon@wanadoo.fr). Take bus #8 (dir: Campus, or the Campus night bus) from the Foch stop to Intermarché. Walk back up the hill and turn left at the hostel sign. Another friendly place with clean rooms and many non-backpackers. Restaurant, TV room, and foosball. Breakfast €4.40. Meals €6.40-10.40. Reception daily 7am-1am. Check-in 3pm, check-out 9am. Singles €18.50, with bath and TV €28; doubles €23.20/€31; triples (no shower) €25.80. AmEx/MC/V. ❷

🍴 FOOD

Besançon's dining options are plentiful and reasonably priced to accommodate the city's enormous student population. **Rue Claude Pouillet** and **rue des Granges** dish out many tempting options at tourist-level prices, while out-of-the-way eateries appeal to the student budget. For the do-it-yourself shopper, **place de la Révolution** hosts outdoor covered **markets.** (Open Tu and F 6am-12:30pm, Sa 6am-7pm.) Groceries are always available at one of the **Petit Casino supermarkets** that dot the city. (12 Grande Rue. Open M-Sa 8:30am-8pm. MC/V.) Sharp cheddar-like *comté* cheese is Besançon's speciality. Wash it down with *vin jaune*, one of the more famous Arbois wines. *Charcuteries* along rue des Granges sell *saucisse de Marteau*, a regional sausage specialty, while *chocolatiers* in the center of town will offer up *releuleu*, also known as *boulets de la Citadel*, a layered chocolate, nut, and sugar confection. Two lesser-known great deals are just south of the main drag. The gay pride sticker in the window and the broad selection of sandwiches make ▓**La Boîte à Sandwiches ❶,** 21 rue du Lycée, a friendly and casual environment for all orientations and palates. Hip tunes play in the background, while exotic ingredients like heart of palm grace the menu of over 50 wittily-named and unbelievably enormous sandwiches. (☎03 81 81 63 23. Sandwiches and salads €2.30-6.50. Wine €0.65 a glass. Open M-F 11:30am-2:30pm and 7pm-10:30, Sa 11:30am-2:30pm. MC/V.) ▓**Au Gourmand ❶,** 5 rue Megevand, serves an astonishing array of hearty meat-and-potatoes dishes at incredibly low prices. Canary-yellow walls, a garden gnome collection, and collections of teapots and cat figurines conjure images of the eccentric grandmother you never had. (☎03 81 81 40 56. Rice and pasta dishes €6-7.70; omelettes €3.10-5.40; warm salads with potatoes €4.60-6.10. Open Tu-F 11:30am-1:45pm and 6:45-8:30pm, Sa 11:30am-1:45pm. MC/V.) Pricier options include the vertically splendid **Brasserie du Commerce ❷,** 31 rue des Granges, where the two-story ceiling and ornate decor complement the regional delicacies on the menu. (☎03 81 81 33 11. *Andouilletes du Côté de Jura* with *crème vin jaune* €11; large salads €8-12.50. Open M-Sa 8am-midnight, Su 9am-midnight. AmEx/MC/V.) **Rosa Bianca ❸,** pl. Granville, is a *brasserie* with a park view and a sprawling terrace. With a white and pastel-blue decor, it brings a touch of class to your meal. Pastas (€9.50-12), pizzas (€8-11), and a slew of dinner-sized salads (€10-12) pack the menu. (☎03 81 81 05 60. Open daily 8am-1am. MC/V.)

◉ SIGHTS

Besançon's *vieille ville* is a bustling but walkable circuit, surrounded by the Doubs River and graced by a trio of worthwhile museums. Be sure to notice the remarkably well-preserved Renaissance buildings along the way.

▓**MUSÉE DU TEMPS.** Captain Hook would have hated this whirring and ticking homage to time, where hands-on experiments teach the principles of physics that underlie mechanical and quartz-based clock making. Clocks and related materials are displayed in a whimsical, high-tech, ultra-modern manner. Though most information is posted in French, quotation-shaped placards explain more significant holdings in both English and German. Completed just three years ago, the museum still feels a bit like a work in progress. *(Palais Granvelle, 96 Grande Rue. ☎03 81 87 81 50; musee-du-temps@besancon.com. Open May-Sept. Su and W-Sa 1-7pm; Oct.-Apr. 1-6pm. Wheelchair-accessible. €3, Sa €1.50, ticket valid 2 days. Students with ID free, everyone free on Su; English and German guides available at desk.)*

CITADEL. Built during the reign of Louis XIV, Vauban's military masterpiece, a Renaissance-style citadel, has since been converted to a host of delightful museums for children and adults alike. A visit requires a grueling trek from the town, but is worth every step. After passing through the free park overlooking the city, a first priority should be the ▓**Musée de la Résistance et de la Déportation.** One hundred members of the French Resistance were shot at the citadel in 1944, during the German occupation of Besançon. This comprehensive collection chronicles the untold stories of WWII from a distinctly French perspective. First-person letters and artifacts document all aspects of the war in France, from the occupation to the Vichy government, collaboration to resistance, and the Holocaust to liberation in a deeply affecting manner. Ask a guard to open the exhibition room on the third floor, which contains sculptures and drawings by two local men who were deported to concentration camps. Audioguides, available in English (€2), last 1½hr. and play survivors' recorded accounts. (☎ 03 81 65 07 55. No children under 10.)

More lighthearted and appealing to children is the fine **Natural History Museum** that features a number of smaller museums and exhibits, including an **Evolutionary Path** that illustrates Darwin's theory on the development of species. The back houses the always-entertaining primate wing, as well as a hands-on farm. The **insectarium** to the east is fascinating, but not for the weak-stomached: a kitchen exhibit reveals the little nasties that hide inside cupboards, while numerous ant colonies—in glass containers—plan for a winter that will never come. Rounding out the experience, an **aquarium**, a **climatorium**, and a **noctarium** make a significant attempt to be interactive—as in the fish "petting zoo," where dozens of fish crammed into a tiny tank are subjected to the grabby fingers of underage tourists.

More conventional in nature, but nevertheless of interest, are the informative **Salle de Vauban** and **Musée Comtois.** The former chronicles—in French only—the life of the citadel's famous creator, while the latter displays an assortment of archaeological finds from Franche-Comté. A floor is dedicated to the history of milk and milk products. Both lie near the **Tour de la Reine,** from which the countryside can be observed at a royal height. (Citadel ☎ 03 81 87 83 33; www.citadelle.com. Open daily July-Aug. 9am-7pm; Apr.-June and Sept.-Oct. 9am-6pm; Nov.-Mar. 10am-5pm; Nov.-Easter closed Tu. €6, students €5, under 14 €4, includes entrance to every museum and facility. 1hr. before closing, €3.50. Audioguide €2. Light show (son-et-lumière) weekends July-Aug at 9:30pm. €10 adults, €8 students and children. Most sites wheelchair-accessible. MC/V.)

CATHÉDRALE ST-JEAN. Perched beneath the citadel, this attractive cathedral boasts the **Horloge Astronomique,** a 30,000-part indoor clock visible only by tour. Fifty-seven faces provide information on the planets, eclipses, and more. The cathedral also features the elaborate **Rose de St-Jean,** a circular white marble altar dating back to the 11th century. A walk back into town on rue de la Convention passes through the **Porte Noire** (Black Gate), a triumphal arch from the reign of Marcus Aurelius that is covered in protective scaffolding. (Cathedral ☎ 03 81 83 34

THE LOCAL STORY

NATZWEILER-STRUTOF

From 1939-1945 over 10 million men, women, and children were brutally murdered by a Nazi regime bent on power and racial dominance. Most of these murders were committed in concentration camps in Poland and Germany, but Nazi death camps were spread as far west as Natzweiler-Strutof (30km from Obernai), the only concentration camp on French soil.

Ten to twelve thousand Jews, political dissidents, and French Resistance fighters were massacred at Natzweiler. In one of the most horrific acts of the Holocaust, hundreds of prisoners died in twisted scientific experiments in chemical warfare and diseases like hepatitis and typhus. Some prisoners were killed solely to provide skeletons for anatomical research.

The remains of the Natzweiler camp are open to the public, continuing to stand as a reminder of the brutal capacity of human cruelty. Visitors can see the guard towers, four crematoria, and the gas chamber. A museum converted from a barracks displays pictures, diagrams, and items that tell the intensely human side of the story of inhuman deportation and execution. It is simple but powerful, and well worth a visit.

(Natzweiler-Strutof can only be reached by car. From Obernai, take D426, D214, and D130, then follow signs for Camp du Strutof. €2.50.)

62. Open M and W-Su 9am-6pm except during Mass. Free. Horloge ☎03 81 81 12 76; www.monum.fr. Tours Apr.-Sept. M and W-Su 9:50, 10:50, 11:50am, 2:50, 3:50, 4:50, 5:50pm.; Oct.-Mar. no tours W. Closed Jan. €2.50, under 18 and students free.)

MUSÉE DES BEAUX ARTS ET D'ARCHÉOLOGIE. The oldest public museum in France houses an exceptional collection of more than 6000 works by Ingres, Van Dyck, Rubens, Matisse, Picasso, Renoir, and other masters in a capacious, well-presented space. With half the tourists of museums that are half as interesting, this museum should be high on any visitor's list. *(1 pl. de la Révolution. ☎03 81 87 80 49. Open June-Oct. M and W-F 9:30am-noon and 2-6pm, Sa-Su 9:30am-6pm; Nov.-May M and W-Su 9:30am-noon and 2-6pm. Tours in French for groups only; reserve at tourist office. Wheelchair-accessible. €3, students with ID free, Su and holidays free. MC/V.)*

BOAT TRIPS. Les Vedettes Bisontines runs boat cruises on the Doubs and the citadel canals from pont de la République, near the tourist office. *(☎03 81 68 13 25; www.sautdudoubs.fr. Operates Apr.-Oct. 1hr. 40min.; hours vary, usually 3-4 per day. €9.50, children €7.50.)* Or cross rue de la République to **Les Bâteaux Mouches.** *(Le Pont Battant. ☎03 81 68 05 34. Operates Apr.-Oct.; Nov.-Mar. by reservation only. 1¼hr.; 4-5 per day. €9.50, children €7.50. Days and tours vary; call ahead.)*

🄝 NIGHTLIFE

Most nights of the week, Besançon's students pack bars and discos until early morning, especially in the area from **rue Claude Pouillet** over **Pont Battant** to **place Jouffroy d'Arbans.** Small, friendly bars proliferate in the pedestrian section of town.

■ **Pop Hall,** 26 rue Proudhon (☎03 81 83 01 90), across from the post office, is the hippest pool hall in town. Nondescript facade hides antique chandeliers, gondolas, and cars appropriated from amusement parks. The high point is the bathrooms, which feature Victorian mirrors, cowhead sinks, and a toilet bowl lamp. Kitschy/casual/retro/cool, attracts all ages, but especially the young. Beer €2, cocktails €2.50-4.50. Happy hour 6-8pm, drinks half-price. Open M-Th and Su 2pm-1am, F-Sa 2pm-2am. MC/V.

Le Bar, 15 rue de Vignier (☎03 81 82 01 00), offers up 2 radically different environments for its discerning gay clientele. The upstairs bar is a casual pregame spot until about 2am, when everyone heads over to discotheque Le Privé. Downstairs is another story: from the all-porn video room to lockable "pleasure rooms," the theme is sex, and everyone is cruising. Women tend to be straight and accompanying gay friends. Ring bell to enter, but don't ring the bell of the family next door by accident. Beer on tap €2.50, cocktails €5. Open M-Th 8pm-1am, F-Su 9pm-2:30am. MC/V.

Le KGB, 8 av. de Chardonnet (☎03 81 61 17 49), about 1km from the tourist office, is the best of Besançon's dance clubs. A large dance floor with London Underground decor is surrounded by plush couches, 2 bars, and many drunken students. Different music in each room, plus **Le Lounge** for the 30-40 set. Be cautious on the poorly lit av. de Chardonnet. Cover €5, €10 with drink included. Th-Sa 10:30pm-5am. MC/V.

Le Privé, 1 rue Antide Janvier (☎03 81 81 48 57). Follow rue d'Arênes straight past the Lycée Condé to a stoplight. Go left onto rue A. Janvier. The club is on the right. The 22-year-old establishment feels like it never left the 80s, blasting a variety of French and American music from that fabled decade and sporting fluorescent green neon lights. Nicely packed on the weekends, with a 50/50 mix of men and women. Cover Tu-Th €8, F €9, Sa €10; includes one drink. Open Tu-Th 11pm-4am, F-Sa 11pm-5am.

Carpe Diem, 2 pl. Jean Gigoux (☎03 81 83 11 18). Run by a delightful owner according to his ideas on *le rôle sociale* of the pub, this much-appreciated hotspot brings together comrades and mere socialists alike for largely political drinks and discussion. Just don't tell them the revolution is never coming. Events, films, and concerts held regularly. Beer €2. Open M-Th 7am-1am, F-Sa 7am-2am, Su 8am-11pm. MC/V.

Madigan's, 17 pl. 8 Septembre (☎03 81 81 97 44), brings the Irish pub experience across the Channel. Students and tourists share in the Guinness drinking. Margaritas €2.50, half-pints Irish beer €2-3.10, full pints €4-6.50. Open M-Th, Su 7:30am-1am, F-Sa 7:30am-2:30am. MC/V.

🌸 FESTIVALS

The tourist office publishes several comprehensive lists of events; make sure to get *Les Temps Chauds de l'Été* for up-to-date summer information. In July and August, the city sponsors **Festiv'été,** with theater, music, dance, expositions, and a film festival. (Many events are free. Call the tourist office for info.) **Jazz en Franche-Comté** brings a flurry of concerts in June and July, uniting jazz musicians from across France and abroad. (Call ☎03 81 83 39 09 or visit www.multimania.com/festivaljazz for info. Most tickets €5-16, all with student discounts, many free.)

Les Concerts de Granvelle bring a wide range of free musical acts to the open-air Palais Granvelle Friday nights throughout July and August. (Call the tourist office for more info.) The **Festival International de Musique** fills the air with nightly classical concerts during mid-September. Orchestras from across Europe perform well-worn favorites as well as more recent compositions in 85 concerts, most of which are free. (☎03 81 25 05 80; contact@festival-besancon.com. Tickets €11-36 depending on locale, student discounts up to 25%.)

JURA MOUNTAINS

The Jura mountain range, an ancient ocean floor whose archaeological finds led to the naming of the Jurassic Era, is often overlooked by travelers who flock to the younger, pointier Alps farther south. Smoothed by the ravages of time, the Jura provide slightly easier but no less scenic hiking, biking, and skiing trails. The relatively untouristed surrounding cities provide enjoyable bases for exploration, with low prices you're unlikely to find anywhere else in France.

ARBOIS

Though Arbois's minute city center is tucked into the Jura mountains, great local wines, inexpensive regional cuisine, and an amazing chocolate shop make it a gastronomic giant. In spite of its large numbers of tourists, this peaceful wine-tasting center (pop. 3960) has not lost its down-to-earth feel: for every air-conditioned tour bus zipping by, a tractor rattles through town. Combined with a healthy splash of the locally produced *vin jaune*, the sandy-colored stones, medieval ramparts, and cascading river make it a picturesque as well as delicious visit.

🖩📶 TRANSPORTATION AND PRACTICAL INFORMATION. Trains and **SNCF buses** will take you to Besançon (45min., 11 per day, €7.40) and Dole (36min., 4 per day, €6.40). The largely abandoned train station is a good 20min. hike from the town center. Go straight from the station onto av. de la Gare, take the second left onto av. Pasteur, and follow it straight into town as it becomes rue de Courcelles and, a block later, Grande Rue, until it reaches the central pl. de la Liberté. The train station itself, with one ancient automatic ticket machine, only functions as a departure point for trains; the building has been closed for some time. The SNCF office inside the tourist office functions as the ticket/information center. Also note: while trains depart from the station, SNCF buses often depart from the center of town on rue des Fossés. Check with the office before heading to the station. (☎03 84 66 25 00. Open M-Sa 9am-noon and 2-6pm.)

To get to the **tourist office** and SNCF office, 10 rue de l'Hôtel de Ville, from the train station, follow the directions above to pl. de la Liberté. From there, turn right onto rue de l'Hôtel de Ville; both offices are on your right, just after the Hôtel de

Ville. Pick up a free map, a list of hotels and restaurants, and, in July and August, a free tour of the town in French. Audio tours available in English and German for €1.60 year-round. (☎03 84 66 55 50; www.arbois.com. Open May-Aug. M-Sa 9:30am-12:30pm and 2-6:30pm, Su 10am-noon; Sept.-Apr. 9am-noon and 2-6pm.) Banks with **ATMs** can be found along Grande Rue in the center of town. Other services include: **laundromat** (☎03 84 66 12 97) at 6 rue des Courcelles; **police** (☎03 84 66 14 25) at 17 av. Général-Delort; **hospital** at 23 rue de l'Hôpital (☎03 84 66 44 00; the **pharmacie de garde**'s number is posted on the window of any pharmacy); **Internet** access at the public **library**, 9 Grande Rue (☎03 84 37 41 90; €1 per hr; open Tu 10:30am-noon and 4-6:30pm, W and Sa 10:30am-noon and 2-6:30pm, Th 4:30-6pm, F 9am-noon and 4:30-6pm), and at Château Pécauld, rue des Fossés. (☎03 84 66 26 14. €1.60 per hr. Open Tu-Th afternoons. Call ahead.) The **post office** is on av. Général Delort just past the police station. (☎03 84 66 01 21. Open M-F 8:30am-noon and 2-6pm, Sa 8:30-noon.) **Postal Code:** 39600.

ACCOMMODATIONS AND FOOD. While some ritzy Arbois hotels reach ungodly prices (rooms begin at €125 at the four-star Château de Germigney outside of town), there are a few decent, affordable options. **Hôtel les Messageries ❸**, 2 rue de Courcelles, a Victorian-style establishment, has stone archways, bright rooms, and great views. (☎03 84 66 15 45. Breakfast €7. Reception daily 7am-10pm. Closed Dec.-Jan. and W night Sept.-Nov. and Feb.-June. Singles with hall shower €27, with private shower €33, with toilet €47; doubles €30/€36/€54. Extra bed €8, under 10 free. MC/V.) **Hôtel de la Poste ❷**, 71 Grande Rue, is the only truly inexpensive accommodation, with aged rooms and creaky stairwells above a bar. (☎03 84 66 13 22. Shower on first floor, toilets on every floor. Breakfast €5. Reception daily July-Aug. 7:30am-10pm; closed Tu, Sa afternoon, and Sept.-June. Doubles €22; triples and quads €27-33. MC/V.) The three-star, not-too-distant **Municipal des Vignes ❶** campsite, nearby on av. du Général Leclerc, offers 139 sites with modern amenities including hot showers, snack bar, nearby pool, laundry, and TV. (☎/fax 03 84 66 14 12. Reception open Apr.-Sept. 7am-noon and 4pm-10pm. July-Aug. 1-2 people €10.80; electricity €11.90. Apr.-June and Sept. 1-2 people €9.80; electricity €11. €1.50 per child. Bank cards and traveler's checks accepted.)

The mysteriously compelling *vin jaune*, fermented from Sauvignon grapes for six or more years in an oak cask, is the pride of Arbois. The more elaborate *vin de paille*, made from grapes that have been dried on beds of straw, is sweet and intense. Many *caves* in Arbois offer free *dégustations*, and upscale restaurants have local wines by the glass. For a free tour and tasting in a sophisticated barrels-and-stools setting, visit the *caves* of **Henri Maire**, pl. de la Liberté, one of the larger establishments in town. (☎ 08 11 45 39 39; www.henri-maire.fr. Open daily 7:30am-12:30pm, 3-7:30pm; closed Su afternoon. Tours given daily. Make reservations 2-3 days in advance. MC/V.) Not as glamorous, but much cheaper, are the exquisite wines at **Spar supermarket**, 55 Grande Rue, including a large selection of *vins jaunes*. (☎ 03 84 37 44 47. Open daily 7:30am-12:30pm and 3-7:30pm, closed Su afternoon. MC/V.) Outdoor **markets** are held every Friday just off pl. de la Liberté.

The homemade ice cream and chocolate at ◪**Hirsinger's Chocolatier and Salon de Thé ❷**, pl. de la Liberté, are to die for. Consistently ranked among the best chocolatiers in France, the Hirsinger family has been perfecting the art of chocolate-making since 1900. (☎03 84 66 06 97; www.chocolat-hirsinger.com. Open Sept.-June M-Tu and F-Su; daily July-Aug. and holidays.) A bit off the main drag, lively, friendly **Bar Le 33 ❶**, 43 pl. Faramand, prepares quick sandwiches for €2.45 or heartier grub for €6-6.80. (☎03 84 66 08 74. Open M and W-Su 8:30am-1am. MC/V.) Popular **La Balance ❸**, 47 rue de Courcelles, has a vegetarian *menu* and outdoor dining with a lovely fountain view. (☎03 84 37 45 00. Open Tu-Su noon-2pm and 7-

10pm, closed Su night Sept.-June. Closed for 3 weeks in Dec. and 2 weeks in June. Reservations recommended for summer. MC/V.) **La Cuisance ❷**, 62 rue de Faramand, with a patio view of the river, fills with locals who delight in the generous traditional *plats* (€6) and generously sized regional *menus* (€13.40-22.80), including a vegetarian *menu* (€12.80). Kids eat for €5.70. (☎03 84 37 40 74. Open M and Th-Su 9am-3pm and 5-11pm, Tu-W 9am-3pm. MC/V.) Bring a date with a sense of humor to the atmospheric **La Finette: Taverne d'Arbois ❸**, 22 av. Louis Pasteur, a rustic pub-cum-restaurant with candles, wooden tables, animal heads, shotguns, and €15.50 3-course meals. (☎03 84 66 06 78. Open daily 11am-midnight. AmEx/MC/V.)

◨▨ **SIGHTS AND FESTIVALS.** Arbois is proud to be known as Louis Pasteur's "favorite town." The enjoyable **Maison de Pasteur**, 83 rue de Courcelles, showcases Pasteur's childhood and summer home, restored by the renovations of his heirs. It continues to bottle wine under Pasteur's name. (☎03 84 66 11 72. Open daily June-Sept. 9:45-11:45am and 2-6pm; Apr.-May and Oct. 2:15-5:15pm. €5.35, children €2.75. MC/V.) Surrounded by model vineyards of both today and yesteryear, the **Musée de la Vigne et du Vin**, in **Château Pécauld** on rue des Fossés, explains the detailed processes by which regional wines are produced. (☎03 84 66 40 45. Open daily July-Aug. 10am-12:30pm and 2-6pm; Mar.-June and Sept.-Oct. 10am-noon and 2-6pm, closed Tu; Nov.-Feb. 2-6pm, closed Tu. July-Aug. guided tours available, with wine-tasting afterward for an extra €2.50-5. €3.30, students €2.50.) The tower of **Église St-Just** and the nearby 16th-century ramparts provide exquisite views. Don't miss the untouristed **Musée Hirsinger Chocolates**, in the basement of the shop and open only by appointment during store hours, which was assembled to commemorate the 100th anniversary of the store in 2004. Guided tours, given in French by Édouard's now-retired father, take visitors through the tasty 100-year-long history of the machines and methods of this succulent establishment.

Nightlife in Arbois consists of some quiet wine-sipping at a pub (most likely on pl. de la Liberté), but a series of events livens up the town in summer. The newly jazzed-up **Fête des Vins,** on the second to last weekend of July, pairs a little mood music with a lot of wine-tasting during the last two weekends in July. During the **Fête du Biou,** the first Sunday in September, a procession of *vignerons* (wine makers) offers the first grapes of the season to God, a tradition that took a break neither for the Godless revolution nor the two World Wars. If the outdoors are calling, the Arbois area supports 125km of marked **hiking trails** and nearly 60km of **mountain biking trails.** (Contact the tourist office for detailed maps and descriptions.)

PONTARLIER

Pontarlier (pop. 18,400), at an elevation of 840m, is the second-highest city in France, though it was likely at one time the highest—an extensive history of hallucinogenic absinthe production, still the pride of the town, made it the Amsterdam of its day until the liquor was banned in 1915. Now Pontarlier is a slow, not-so-happening town, where locals spend most of their time sitting in cafes and, well, watching other locals. As such, Pontarlier now serves best as a base for hiking, riding, skiing, and biking in the Jura, or for a trip to Switzerland, just 12km away.

▐▨ **TRANSPORTATION AND PRACTICAL INFORMATION.** The **train station** is on pl. de Villingen-Schweningen. (Open M-F 5am-12:30pm and 1:40-10:55pm, Sa 5am-12:30pm and 1:30-10:40pm, Su 7am-12:40pm and 1:30-10:40pm.) **Trains** go to: Dijon (1½hr., 5 per day, €18.70); Geneva (3hr., 5 per day, €33.50); and Paris (3½hr., 5 per day, €55.20) via bus connections. **Monts Jura buses** (☎03 81 39 88 80) leave from in front of the train station for Besançon (55min., 5 per day, €7.30). The **tourist office** is at 14bis rue de la Gare. From the train station, cross through the roundabout and head left one block on rue de la Gare. The office is left of the bus station, down rue Michaud. The staff has info on Pontarlier, hiking, and other outdoor sports, and free regional guides *Le Doubs: Massif de Jura* and *Guide Pratique*, which list cheap mountain lodgings. (☎ 03 81 46 48 33; www.pontarlier.org. Office open M-Sa 9am-7pm, July-Aug. also Su 10am-noon. Guides available in English and German.) Cycles Pernet, 23 rue de la République, rents **bikes.** (☎ 03 81 46 48 00. €15 per day, €36 for 3 days. Passport deposit. Open Tu-Sa 9am-noon and 2-7pm; May-Aug. also M 3-6pm. MC/V.) Other services include: banks with **ATMs** along rue de la République; a **laundromat** at 13 rue du Moulin Parnet (open daily 7am-9pm); **police** at 19 Rocade Georges Pompidou (☎ 03 81 38 51 10; call here for the **pharmacie de garde**); a **hospital** at 2 faubourg St-Etienne (☎ 03 81 38 53 60); and **Internet** access at Dimension Net, 5 rue Mirabeau. (☎ 03 81 39 70 82. Open Tu-Sa 11am-9pm, Su 2pm-9pm.) The **post office,** 17 rue de la Gare, has a Cyberposte. (☎ 03 81 38 49 44. Open M-F 8am-6:30pm and Sa 8am-noon.) **Postal Code:** 25300.

⛛⛶ ACCOMMODATIONS AND FOOD. The best deal in town is the quiet, centrally located **Auberge de Pontarlier (FUAJ) ❶,** 2 rue Jouffroy. From the tourist office, go left on rue Marpaud; the hostel is the white stucco building on the left. Sturdy rooms in bright colors make this a hostel a cut above the rest. The friendly reception organize hiking and skiing trips. Amenities include common room with big-screen TV and kitchen. Push-button showers can be cold. (☎ 03 81 39 06 57. Breakfast €3.25. Sheets €2.75. Reception daily 8am-noon and 5:30-10pm, though hours vary Sept.-June. Reservations advised for summer. Dorms €9.60 per bed. Members only.) TVs, wood paneling, spacious rooms, and a central location above a bar make the rooms of the **Hôtel de France ❷,** 8 rue de la Gare, another good bargain, although some rooms are quite dim. (☎ 03 81 39 05 20; fax 03 81 46 24 43. Breakfast €5. Reception daily 7am-9:30pm, though hours vary with bar downstairs. Singles with hall shower €20, with private shower €30; doubles €30; triples with no private shower €35; quads with shower €55. MC/V.) At the upscale **Hôtel St-Pierre ❸,** 3 pl. St-Pierre, guests enjoy bright, spacious, tastefully decorated rooms in a classy establishment, with a restaurant downstairs that serves everything from *croque monsieurs* (€3) to regional *comtoise menus* (€11). Reserve well in advance during summer. (☎ 03 81 46 50 80. Reception daily 7am-10pm. Singles and doubles €38-42; triples €52-58. MC/V.)

The most scenic accommodations are at the three-star **campground ❶** on rue du Tolombief. From the station, turn right onto Rocade Georges Pompidou, cross the river, and bear left onto rue de l'Industrie. Take the first right onto av. de Neuchâtel and follow the signs (20-25 minutes). Amenities include TV, ping-pong, a game room, and a bar. Many sites are next to either horse stables or livestock yards, though some are more isolated and slightly less, er, fragrant. (☎ 03 81 46 23 33; fax 03 81 46 23 34. Office open 8am-1pm and 4-10pm. July-Aug. tent and car €6.60, €2.80 per person, children €1.40. Sept.-June €6.25/€2.25/€1.15. Electricity €3.05. *Chalets* July-Aug. €54 per day for 2 people, Sept.-June €46; €366/€275 per week, €1250/€963 per month. Extra person €3.75. 6-person max.)

Although it may not pack the hallucinogenic punch for which it was once known, a modern version of **absinthe Pontarlier** is available at every bar and cafe for €3-4. Do as the Pontarliens do and buy food at the **Casino supermarket,** 75 rue de la République. (☎ 03 81 46 51 22. Open M-F 8:30am-12:30pm and 2:30-7pm, Sa 8:30am-7pm. MC/V.) Outdoor **markets** appear Thursday and Saturday mornings at pl. Jules Pagnier. Good restaurants are concentrated around the well-traveled **rue de la République.** Right in the thick of things, sprawling **Le Grand Café Francais ❷,** 36 rue de la République, gives a good bang for your buck. The *plat du jour* costs €7.20 and specialty *FlammeKüche* (a quiche-like dish) with Alsatian trimmings, cheese, and a salad goes for €7.10. (☎ 03 81 39 00 72. Open M-Sa 6:30am-10pm. MC/V.) The wood oven of **Le Gambetta ❷,** 15 rue Gambetta, off rue de la Gare, cooks over 20 varieties of pizza, ranging from pepperoni to eggs, tuna, and potatoes. Regional meat dishes and pasta can be made to go, but stay for the incredible chocolate mousse. (☎03 81 46 67 17. Pizza from €6, design-your-own €8.90; dinner salads €7-9; mousse €3.80. Open W-Su noon-2:30pm and 7-9:30pm. Closed much of Sept. MC/V.) Sample the *menu régional* (€12), which features *fondue au Comté* and local *saucisse de Marteau* at **La Pinte Comtoise ❸**, 4 rue Jeanne d'Arc, an inviting place just off rue de la République. (☎03 81 39 07 35. Open M-Tu and Th-Su noon-1:45pm and 7-9pm, closed Tu and Su afternoons. MC/V.)

⚡ OUTDOOR ACTIVITIES. The smooth, pine-covered Jura mountains are home to 74km of long-distance **cross-country skiing** trails. Nine trails on two slopes (**Le Larmont** and **Le Malmaison**) span every level of difficulty. An outline of all trails is free at the tourist office. (Daily pass for cross-country skiing €6, under 17 €3.50; for downhill skiing €11, under 12 €8. MC/V.) Le Larmont (☎03 81 46 55 20; www.cc-larmont.fr.), the alpine ski area nearest to Pontarlier, offers toboggan and snowshoe trails. For ski conditions, call **Info-Neige** (☎03 81 39 91 66), Massif de Jura. The Jura are much colder than the Alps; wear layers. **Sport et Neige**, zac des Grands Planchants, sud rue Mervil, is the nearest store that rents ski equipment. (☎03 81 39 04 69. €9 per day, €40 per week; children €7/€35. Open M-F 9:30am-noon and 2-7pm, Sa 9am-7pm. MC/V.) Prices are far cheaper than in the Alps, but the snow quality is less reliable. **Metabief Mont d'Or,** accessible by shuttle bus from Pontarlier, has day and night skiing. (☎03 81 46 47 47. Shuttle 30min., 3-4 per day from Mont Jura bus station, €2.70. Lift tickets €18 per day, under 12 €14. MC/V.)

In the summer, skiing gives way to fishing, hiking, and mountain biking. There are two **mountain bike** departure points in Pontarlier, one to the north just off rue Pompée and one to the south, about 2km west of Forges. Hikers can choose between the **GR5,** an international 262km trail accessible from Larmont, and the **GR6,** which leads to a narrow valley dominated by the dramatic **Château de Joux et Musée d'Armes Anciennes.** The massive 1000-year-old castle houses an extensive series of dungeons and a collection of rare arms. In July and Aug. it hosts concerts, theater, and merriment during the **Festival des Nuits de Joux,** held annually from late July to mid-August. (☎03 81 69 47 95; www.chateaudejoux.com. Open daily July-Aug. 9am-6pm; Sept.-May 10-11:30am and 2-4:30pm. €5.10, students €4.10.) The tourist office sells a map (€2.50) that has departure points for biking and hiking around town, including one near the train station at pl. St-Claude. More detailed maps can be found at **Librairie Rousseau,** 20 rue de la République. (☎03 81 39 10 28. Open M-Sa 9am-noon and 2-7pm, closed M afternoon. English books also available here. MC/V.) **Le Poney Club,** rue du Toulombief, adjacent to the campground, rents well-trained horses for riders of all skill levels. (☎03 81 46 71 67. Take bus #2, dir: Poney Club. €7 for 30min., €10 per hr. For rides with a free guide, call ahead.)

LONS-LE-SAUNIER

Lons-le-Saunier (pop. 20,000) is a green gem of a mountain town, though not quite so convenient a base as Pontarlier for exploring the Jura. Best known as the birthplace of Rouget de Lisle, composer of *la Marseillaise*, Lons is also an ancient Roman spa site, with preserved ruins and saltwater baths that are still its main attraction two millennia later.

🚊 TRANSPORTATION. Trains run to Besançon (11 per day, €11.70) and Lyon (7 per day, €15.80). **Local buses** run to outlying villages. (☎03 84 86 07 74, usually 6am-6pm. Inquire at the tourist office for a schedule.) **Taxis** are available outside the station. (☎03 84 24 11 16. €1.70 base fee; €1.30 per km before 7pm, €1.77 after 7pm. 24hr.) Rent **bikes** at Forestier, 44 carrefour de la Libération. (☎03 88 43 11 44. €16 per day, ID deposit required. Open M and W-Sa 9am-noon and 2-7pm.)

🛛 PRACTICAL INFORMATION. To get to the **tourist office,** pl. du 11 Novembre, cross the street in front of the station and head up rue Aristide Briand until it forks. Take the right fork (av. Thurel) to rue Rouget de Lisle on the left. Continue straight across rue Jean Jaurès. They offer free maps, hotel and restaurant listings, and guides to excursions in the Jura (available in English). The office leads French tours (€3) of the town and into the Jura on a highly variable schedule. (☎03 84 24 65 01; www.ville-lons-le-saunier.fr. Open M-F 8am-noon and 2-6pm, Sa 8am-noon and 2-5pm.) For info on countryside tours (available in English and German) with groups of ten or more, contact Juragence, 19 rue Jean Moulin. (☎03 84 47 27 27. Open M-Sa 8am-noon and 2-6pm, Sa closes at 5.) Other services include: banks with **ATMs** on rue Aristide Briand and pl. de la Liberté; a **laundromat** at Lavomatique, 26 rue des Cordeliers (☎06 80 92 08 37; open daily 7am-9pm; €4.50 for 5kg); **police** at 6 av. du 44ème R.I. (☎03 84 35 17 10; call here for the **pharmacie de garde**); a **hospital** at 55 rue Docteur Jean Michel (☎03 84 35 60 00); and **Internet** access at Car'Com, at the tourist office (€3.80 per hr.; open M-F 8am-noon and 2-6pm, Sa 10am-noon and 2-6pm) and Info Jeunesse, 2 pl. de la Liberté. (☎03 84 87 02 55. €3.80 per hr. Open M-F 10am-noon and 2-6pm, Sa 10am-noon.) Info Jeunesse also sells discount cards for museums, lodgings, cinemas, and concerts (€5 for those under 26). The **post office** is on av. Aristide Briand. (☎03 84 85 83 60. Open M-F 8am-7pm, Sa 8am-noon.) Poste Restante: 39021. **Postal Code:** 39000.

🛏 ACCOMMODATIONS. Lons has a few decent, less expensive hotels located near pl. de la Liberté, but no hostels to speak of. Reserve at least a week in advance during the summer. The central **Hôtel des Sports ❷,** at 21 rue St-Desiré, is the best, but that's not saying much. Go four blocks from the train station on av. Aristide Briand and follow it around an abrupt left, then right onto rue St-Desiré. Cramped, dark hallways and stairways give way to linoleum floors, faux wood wall paneling, and views of the building next door. (☎03 84 24 04 42. Breakfast €5. Reception M-Sa 6am-10pm, Su 9am-10pm. Singles and doubles with shower €25.50; triples €38.50. AmEx/MC/V.) At **Hôtel les Glaciers ❷,** 1 pl. Philibert de Chalon, nine bright though sparse rooms go for snap-'em-up rates. From rue St-Desiré, walk one block to pl. Liberté; diagonally across the *place* is rue du Commerce. Take this for two blocks to a fork at pl. de l'Hôtel de Ville, then veer to the left and continue to the end of the block. (☎03 84 47 26 89. Breakfast €5. Reception 7am-11pm, closed Su. Singles €20, with shower €25; doubles €23/€28. MC/V.)

🍴 FOOD. *Charcuteries, pâtisseries,* and *boulangeries* line **rue du Commerce.** A produce **market** appears at pl. Verdun each Thursday morning; find goodies the rest of the week at the local markets, cafes, and restaurants around the **place de la Liberté,** or at the **Casino supermarket,** 41 rue du Commerce. (☎03 84 24 48 64. Open M 8am-12:30pm and 3-7pm, Tu and Th-Sa 7:30am-12:30pm and 3-7:30pm, W 7:30am-12:30pm, Su 8-11:45am.) The cheerful market **La Ferme Comtoise,** 23 rue St-Desiré, will help indecisive customers find the perfect *miel de Jura* (honey) or *fromage de Comté.* (☎03 84 24 06 16. Open M-Sa 7am-7:30pm, Su 7:30am-1pm. MC/V.) Locals sip their *kirs* at the **Grand Café du Théâtre ❸,** 4 rue Jean-Jaurès on pl. de la Liberté, a classy *fin de siècle* eatery with a *Jurassienne* salad featuring *fromage de Comté* for €8.40. (☎03 84 24 49 30. Open daily 7am-1am. MC/V.) **Le Strasbourg ❸,** around the corner, next to the tourist office, offers up regional *plats* in a sleek dining area. (☎03 88 24 36 92. *L'assiette Franc-Comtoise,* with Marteau sausage and potatoes, €10.90. Open daily noon-2pm and 7-10pm. MC/V.)

◙ **SIGHTS.** Lons-le-Saunier has two important bases for exploration. Pl. de la Liberté, with its open promenade and glittering fountain, is the center of Lons's tiny universe. It is also the site of the old theater, where the Rococo facade, reconstructed in 1901 after a devastating fire, has been equipped with a clock that chimes a refrain from *la Marseillaise* on the hour. Just off the *place*, the houses of the bustling **rue du Commerce** were also rebuilt—in stone—after a great fire in 1637. A few blocks down av. Jean Moulin is the second base, the beautiful gardens of **Parc des Bains.** Within the tree-lined gates lies the popular **Thermes Ledonia,** a luxurious salt-water spa whose ancient spring water allegedly cures ailments like rheumatism and cellulite. Not merely a spring water source, this spa is the source of much of Lons's tourism and wealth: full-scale treatments cost thousands of euros, but €9 will buy a dip in the pool and a sauna session. (☎03 84 24 20 34; lons@villegiatherm.com. Open Apr.-Oct. M-Sa 1-8pm; closes at 7pm F-Sa. MC/V.)

The museums of Lons, while not the central reason for any visit, possess their own character and charm. To the left off rue du Commerce, **Musée des Beaux Arts,** pl. Philibert de Chalon boasts a splendid collection of Perraud statuary. Its highlight is the lifelike *L'Enfance de Bacchus.* (☎03 84 47 64 30. Open M and W-F 10am-noon and 2-6pm, Sa-Su 2-5pm. €2, students €1, under 18 free.) Following the rue du Commerce to its end and bearing right onto rue Richebourg leads to the stylish **Musée d'Archéologie,** 25 rue Richebourg. The Jura didn't lend its name to the Jurassic period for nothing: this tiny museum is home to France's oldest dinosaur skeleton, the Plateosaurus, a Jurassic creature typical of the ancient seabed. (☎03 84 47 12 13. Open M-F 10am-noon and 2-6pm, Sa-Su 2-5pm. €2, students €1, under 18 free; W and first Su of every month free.) Following rue Richebourg back toward the center of town from the Parc leads to **Promenade de la Chevalerie** and an astonished-looking statue of Rouget de Lisle sculpted by Bartholdi.

◪ **DAYTRIPS FROM LONS-LE-SAUNIER.** Nestled between some of the Jura's most breathtakingly beautiful peaks, 10km from Lons, lies the little town of **Baume-les-Messieurs** and its well-known **abbey.** (☎03 84 44 99 28. Open mid-June to mid-Sept. daily 10am-noon and 2-6pm.) **Monts Jura buses** run from Lons June through August. (☎03 84 86 08 80. Ask the tourist office for bus schedules.) There is a network of naturally formed caves with salt and calcium icicles near the town, with underground lakes and vaults up to 80m high. (☎03 84 48 23 02. Caves open daily Apr.-June and Sept. 10am-noon and 2-5pm; July-Aug 10am-6pm. €3.50, under 14 €2.50.) The cliffs surrounding Baume are an incredible sight by starlight; you can spend the night outdoors at **Campground La Toupe ❶,** a well-placed site with showers but no laundry service. (☎03 84 44 63 16. Apr.-Sept. reception 9-10am and 6-8pm. €2.50 per person, €2 per car or tent. Electricity €2.50.)

BURGUNDY
(BOURGOGNE)

Siding with the English during the Hundred Years' War—not for any love of the English, but to antagonize the French—the Burgundians betrayed young Joan of Arc and have never regretted it. Punctuated by bright-roofed villages nestled among hilly pastures and rich green vineyards, this largely agricultural area of France has long been saturated with a strong regional identity and an independent spirit. The people of Burgundy may be exceptionally open and welcoming, but don't mistake them for pushovers: these same friendly farmers and courteous winemakers were a hotbed of resistance to Nazi occupation.

The heartland of Roman Gaul in the first century BC, this fertile region was finally conquered in the fifth century by the Burgundians, a Germanic tribe who then modestly named the area after themselves. By the Middle Ages, the duchy of Burgundy had grown fat off the land, building itself magnificent cathedrals and palaces, collecting priceless works of art, funding powerful monasteries, and creating a legacy of winemaking with few equals in the modern world. For many years, Burgundian dukes were a greater power in Europe than the puny Parisian monarchy, and today the ducal palace and sumptuous museums of Dijon, the regional capital, reflect this decadent heritage.

You can taste another source of pride for this region by sampling the wines produced in this fertile area. Louis XIV called Burgundian wine *"le vin des rois, le roi des vins"* (the wine of kings, the king of wines) and allowed little else on his table. Connoisseurs esteem the wines of Burgundy's hillside Côte D'Or among the best in the world. The names of these winemaking towns roll off the salivating lips of drinkers of its precious Pinot Noirs and Chardonnays, who then shell out big bucks in search of the rare, exquisite, and extravagantly priced *Grand Crus*.

HIGHLIGHTS OF BURGUNDY

MONASTIC LIFE never looked so good as at the impeccably restored 12th-century monastery **Abbaye de Fontenay** (p. 394).

TAKE A SCENIC (AND CHEAP) TRAIN TRIP through the picturesque **Yonne Valley,** indulging in free samples of local cheese, biscuits, *pâté,* and wine along the way (p. 403).

ROAM in the 5km of underground *caves* at the **Patriarche Père et Fils** (p. 389), then sample the delicious products of this iconic Beaune winery.

DIJON

Once the center of secular power for all of France, Dijon is now simply the regional capital of Burgundy—but don't assume this means its ancient grandeur has faded. Dijon (pop. 150,000) manages to tread a precious middle ground between reverence for the past and enjoyment of a more irreverent present. From the terrace pub scene to the rockin' late night dance clubs, Dijon is a city of youth and vigor that just happens to party among fine museums, decadent churches, and the ducal seat of the most powerful men in 15th-century France. Few cities outside of Paris are this capable of providing ample entertainment at any hour.

GERMANY

Basel

Bern

Biel/
Bienne

Fribourg

Montreux

SWITZERLAND

Colmar

Rhine

Sélestat

St-Dié

Ribeauvillé

Metzeral

Thann

Mulhouse

Kruth

la Bresse

Bussang

Sewen

Belfort

Doubs

Lausanne

Lake Geneva (Lac Léman)

Evian

Thonon

Gérardmer

Flombières

Vesoul

Pontarlier

Divonne-les-Bains

St-Claude

Epinal

Vittel

Besançon

Mouchard

Arbois

Lons-le-Saunier

St-Amour

Neufchâteau

Langres

Dole

Pierre-de-Bresse

Louhans

Tournus

Chaumont

Marne

TO LYON

Aube

Dijon

Gevrey-
Chambertin

Clos de Vougeot

Nuits-St-Georges

Beaune

Chalon-sur-Saône

Chagny

Santenay

Mâcon

Bar-sur-Aube

Châtillon-sur-Seine

Abbaye de Fontenay

Montbard

Sémur-en-Auxois

Rochepot

Val Lamartinien

Cluny

Montceau-les-Mines

Paray-le-Monial

Troyes

Aube

Serein

Avallon

Chablis

Vézelay

Château-Chinon

Autun

Sens

Yonne

Auxerre

Toucy

Nevers

la Charité-sur-Loire

Moulins

Malesherbes

Montargis

Gien

Cosne

Loire

Bourges

Burgundy

TO PARIS

BURGUNDY

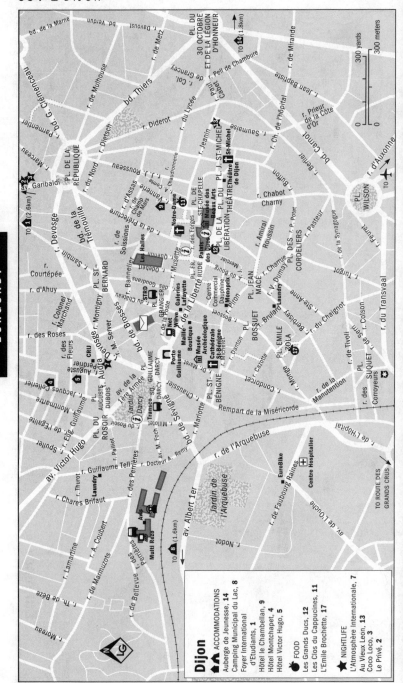

Dijon

▲ ACCOMMODATIONS
Auberge de Jeunesse, 14
Camping Municipal du Lac, 8
Foyer International
d'Étudiants, 1
Hôtel le Chambellan, 9
Hôtel Montchapet, 4
Hôtel Victor Hugo, 5

🍴 FOOD
Les Grands Ducs, 12
Les Clos du Cappucines, 11
L'Emile Brochette, 17

★ NIGHTLIFE
L'Atmosphère Internationale, 7
Au Vieux Leon, 13
Coco Loco, 3
Le Privé, 2

BURGUNDY

TRANSPORTATION

Trains: cours de la Gare, at the end of av. Maréchal Foch. Info office open M-F 9am-7pm, Sa 9am-6pm. To: **Beaune** (30min., 27 per day, €6); **Clermont-Ferrand** (4hr., 5 per day, €31.80); **Lyon** (2hr.; 5 trains, 2 TGV per day; €22.50); **Nice** (6-8hr.; 4 trains, 2 TGV per day; €63.70); **Paris** (1¾-3hr.; 7 trains, 13 TGV per day; €32.60). **SOS Voyageurs** (☎03 80 43 16 34), in the train station, has travel information. Open M-F 8:30am-6:30pm, Sa 8:30am-5pm. Luggage storage Sept.-June M-F 8am-7:15pm, Sa-Su 9am-12:30pm and 2-6pm; July-Aug. M-F 8am-7:15pm. €3 per bag, €5 for 2 bags.

Buses: TRANSCO, av. Maréchal Foch (☎03 80 42 11 00; www.cg21.fr), connected to the train station, left from the exit. Ticket and info office open M-F 5:30am-8:30pm, Sa 6:30am-12:30pm and 4-8:30pm, Su 9:30am-12:30pm and 4:40-8:30pm. Schedule posted outside the terminal. Tickets also available on the bus or at the *chef de gare's* office near the bus terminal. Confusingly, buses leaving Dijon can have the same number but be going to different places. Check with the driver to ensure you are on the correct bus. To **Beaune**, via **Gevrey Chambertin** and various stops in the **Côte D'Or** (Bus #44; 1hr.; M-Sa 9 per day 6:53am-7:25pm, Su 11:10am; €5.81).

Public Transportation: STRD (☎03 80 30 60 90), pl. Grangier. Office open M-F 7:15am-7:15pm, Sa 8:30am-noon and 2-7:15pm. Map at the tourist office. Tickets €0.80, 1-day pass €2.70, 12-trip pass €7, 1-week pass €7.30; all available on board. Buses run 6am-8pm; limited night bus service until 12:30am, Su morning until 1am.

Taxis: Taxi Dijon (☎03 80 41 41 12). 24hr. Under €10 from center to periphery.

Car Rental: Avis, Budget, and **Hertz** share an office at 7bis cours de la Gare (☎03 80 42 05 99; fax 03 80 41 87 84). €90 per day. 25+. Open M-F 8am-12:30pm, 2-8pm, and 8:30-9:30pm; Sa 8am-12:30pm and 2-6pm; Su 5:15-9:15pm. AmEx/MC/V.

Bike Rental: EuroBike, 4 rue du faubourg Raines (☎03 80 45 32 32), rents bikes, scooters, motorcycles, and in-line skates. €10-12 per half-day, €18-20 per day. Open Apr.-Oct. M-Sa 8am-noon and 2-6:30pm, Su 9:30-10:30am and 6:30-7pm; Nov.-Mar. M-Sa 9am-noon and 2-6pm. Low-season prices lower.

ORIENTATION AND PRACTICAL INFORMATION

The main axis of the *vieille ville*, the pedestrian **rue de la Liberté,** runs roughly from **place Darcy** (recognizable by its big arch) and the tourist office to **place St-Michel**. From the train station, follow av. Maréchal Foch. The pl. de la République, northeast of pl. Darcy, is the central roundabout for roads leading out of the city.

Tourist Office: pl. Guillame Darcy (☎03 80 44 11 44; www.dijon-tourism.com). Organizes themed city tours, some in English (daily June-Aug.; €6, students €3, under 18 €1; reserve ahead), and vineyard tours (www.vineatours.com; €45-95; reserve ahead). Accommodations service €2.30 plus 10% deposit. **Currency exchange.** Open May to mid-Oct. daily 9am-8pm; mid-Oct. to Apr. M-Sa 10am-6pm, Su 10am-noon and 2-6pm. Branch at 34 rue des Forges. Open May to mid-Oct. M-Sa 9am-1pm and 2-6pm; mid-Oct. to Apr. M-F 9am-noon and 2-6pm. Branch in the Palais des Ducs. Open M-F 8am-7pm, Sa 8am-12:30pm and 1:30-6pm, Su 9am-12:30pm and 1:30-6pm.

Youth Information: Centre Régional d'Information Jeunesse de Bourgogne (CRIJ), 18 rue Audra (☎03 80 44 18 44). Info, most in French, on lodging, classes, grape-picking, summer jobs, and travel. Open M-Tu and Th-F 10am-1pm and 2-6pm, W 10am-6pm.

Laundromats: 36 rue Guillaume Tell. Wash €3.50 per 8kg, dry €1 per 25min. Open daily 6am-9pm. Another at 28 rue Berbisey. Open daily 7am-9pm. Also at 8 pl. de la Banque. Open daily 7am-8:30pm.

Police: 2 pl. Suquet (☎03 80 44 55 00). Call here for the **pharmacie de garde.**

BURGUNDY

DIJON BY SEGWAY

In most cities, the touristy *petit train*—a vehicle that looks more like an amusement-park reject than a real mode of transport—is the only way to tour town.

The Dijon tourist office, recognizing the unattractiveness of a plastic train in a city of such sophistication, but also understanding the occassional laziness of even the most intrepid traveler, has come up with an elegant, fun alternative: touring via Segway.

The Segway, a masterpiece of engineering, is a two-wheeled self-balancing vehicle. The rider stands on a little platform suspended between the wheels, holds the upright handles, and leans in the direction he or she wants the cart to go. Tiny oscillating weights under the platform keep it astoundingly balanced, with the result that the rider remains steady and in complete control.

Tour guides in Dijon take visitors on voyages through the *vieille ville* or the city's beautiful parks. In a further expression of their wisdom, the tours involve large open spaces in which guides encourage you to see just what these amazing machines can do.

(Tours Apr. Sa-Su 3 and 4pm; May-June and Sept.-Oct. F-Su; July-Aug. M-Su, with extra trips Sa-Su 10 and 11:30am. Groups of 7+ can reserve custom times year-round. Reserve well in advance. €15, groups €12, children 12-16 €7, children under 12 prohibited for safety reasons.)

Medical Services: Centre Hospitalier Universitaire, 2 bd. Mar. de Lattre de Tassigny (☎03 80 29 30 31). **Médecins, Pharmaciens, Infirmiers et Dentistes de Garde,** pl. Suquet (☎03 80 44 55 00) has doctors and pharmacists on call during weekends and nights. **SOS Médecins** (☎03 80 59 80 80). Emergency doctors on call 24hr.

Internet Access: Multi Rezo, 21 cours de la Gare (☎03 80 42 13 89), in the bus station. Open M-Sa 9am-midnight, Su 2-10pm. €1 for 12min., €5 per hr., €10 for 3hr. **Net W@ve,** 10 rue de la Liberté (☎03 80 30 55 16). Open M-Sa 10am-10pm. €3 for 30min., €4 per hr.

Post Office: pl. Grangier (☎03 80 50 62 19), near pl. Darcy. **Currency exchange.** Open M-F 8am-7pm, Sa 8am-noon.

Postal Code: 21000.

🏠🏕 ACCOMMODATIONS AND CAMPING

Dijon's budget accommodations can be uninvitingly dark and impersonal, while its moderate hotels are universally charming. They are very popular; reserve ahead.

▧ **Hôtel Victor Hugo,** 23 rue des Fleurs (☎03 80 43 63 45; fax 03 80 42 13 01). The best of Dijon's budget accommodation, this hotel offers up friendly proprietors and tidy rooms. All with antiques and sparkling tiled shower or bath and toilet. Some have great views of the back garden. Breakfast €4.80. Reception 24hr. Reserve at least 2 weeks ahead. Singles €29-37.50, with shower €37.50-44; doubles €32.50-46. MC/V. ❸

▧ **Hôtel Montchapet,** 26 rue Jacques Cellerier (☎03 80 53 95 00; www.hotel-montchapet.com). In a quiet neighborhood, though traffic on the street can be loud. Genuinely friendly proprietors, electronic locks on doors, and TVs in every room. Breakfast €5. Reception 7am-10:30pm. Check-out 11am. Singles €26, with toilet €32, with shower €39; doubles €36/46; triples and quads with shower €54-59. AmEx/MC/V. ❷

Hotel le Chambellan, 92 rue Vannerie (☎03 80 67 12 67). On a quiet street by Église St-Michel, this dark wood hotel with a kind proprietress is a real bargain. All rooms with fans, TVs, and colorful carpets; some face the little courtyard (perfect for picnics). 4 stories with no elevator; shower on the top floor. Breakfast €5.35. Reception 6:30am-11pm. Singles with shower €28; doubles €26, with shower €34-48; triples €60. ❸

Foyer International d'Etudiants, 6 rue Maréchal Leclerc (☎03 80 71 70 00; fax 03 80 71 60 48). A very long walk (30-40min.) or bus #4 from pl. Darcy (dir: St-Apollinaire) to Parc des Sports will take you to this hostel. From av. Paul Doumer, turn right onto rue du Stade, then take the first left onto rue Maréchal Leclerc. An international crowd inhabits this colorless, dormitory-like hostel, which is also university housing. Rooms are a study in minimalism, featuring beds, small desks, and little else. TV rooms, ping-pong and tennis courts, laundry, kitchen, and common bathrooms. Cafeteria open daily during the school year, Oct.-June. Reception 24hr. Singles €15. AmEx/MC/V. ●

Camping: Camping Municipal du Lac, 3 bd. Kir (☎03 80 43 54 72). Exit the back of the station and turn right on av. Albert I. After 1km, turn left on bd. Kir and follow the signs; if you cross a bridge, you've gone too far. Or take bus #12 from pl. Darcy (dir: Fontaine d'Ouche) to Hôpital des Chartreux. Park and canal with bike path nearby. This grassy site gets crowded in the summer. Reception July-Aug. 8:30am-8pm; Apr.-June and Sept.-Oct. 15 8:30am-noon and 2:30-7pm; closed Oct. 15-Apr. 1. €2.65 per person, under 7 €1.45; €1.45 per car; €2.05 per site. Electricity €2.65. ●

FOOD

Dijon's reputation for *haute cuisine* is well deserved—and restaurant prices reflect it. *Charcuteries* are an economical way to sample specialties like *tarte bourguignonne*, mushroom quiche, and *jambon persillé* (ham with parsley).

If you're willing to pay €10-15, **rue Berbisey, rue Monge, rue Musette,** and **place Emile Zola** host a variety of delicious restaurants within your price range. The narrow pedestrian **rue Amiral Boussin,** behind the pl. de la Liberté, provides dining in a classic 17th-century setting. Shoppers can find local produce at a colorful **market** in the pedestrian area around **Les Halles.** (Open Tu and Th-F mornings, all day Sa.) There's a **supermarket** in the basement of **Galeries Lafayette,** 41 rue de la Liberté (open M-Sa 8:15am-7:45pm), and within **Monoprix,** 11 rue Piron, off pl. Jean Macé. (☎03 80 30 26 60. Open M-Sa 9am-8:45pm.)

You can't go wrong at ⬛**L'Emile Brochette** ❸, 16 pl. Emile Zola, where a you can feast on hearty platters with a *brochette* (kebab) theme. (☎03 80 65 83 03. Platters €10.50-17.90, dessert €5.50.) ⬛**Les Clos du Cappucines** ❸, 3 rue Jeanin, serves delicious *menus* of Burgundian masterpieces like *aspic de poulet* (chicken gelatin mold) in a romantic 17th-century courtyard. (☎03 80 65 83 03. 2-course *menu* €12.50, 3-course *menu* €16. Open Tu-F for lunch and dinner, M and Sa-Su dinner only.) The fantastic sprawling terrace at **Les Grands Ducs** ●, pl. de la Libération, features stained-glass of the Ducs themselves. Egg-centric quiche (€4.50) and omelettes (€3.70) make a great lunch. (☎03 80 30 25 30. Open daily 6am-2am.)

SIGHTS

⬛**MUSÉE DES BEAUX ARTS.** Most of the buildings in the palace are currently administrative offices, but the east wing houses the quite elegant Musée des Beaux-Arts, pl. de la Ste-Chapelle. The *Tomb of the Dukes,* which showcases the memorials for the 15th-century Valois dukes of Burgundy, is breathtakingly ornate. The section dedicated to modern art includes a Cézanne and 20th-century technicolor paintings by Lapicque. *(Pl. de la Libération, enter by cour de Bar. ☎03 80 74 52 70; museedesbeauxarts@ville-dijon.fr. Open daily May-Oct. M and W-Su 9:30am-6pm; Nov.-Apr. 10am-5pm, closed Tu. Modern art wing closed 11:30am-1:45pm. €3.40, groups and seniors €1.60, students with ID free, Su free.)*

PALAIS DES DUCS DE BOURGOGNE. The Dukes of Burgundy (1364-1477) were the best sort of rulers: fearless (Jean sans Peur), good (Philippe le Bon), and bold (Philippe le Hardi and Charles le Téméraire). At the center of the *vieille ville,* the 52m Tour Philippe le Bon is the most conspicuous vestige of ducal power, tower-

BURGUNDY

THE LOCAL STORY

UTTING THE MUSTARD

Mustard has been spicing up Burgundian palates since the Middle Ages, when it was also used as animal feed, oil, and fertilizer. To people in the mustard business, he biblical "seed of Senève" efers to mustard.

Locals love to tell the story of how mustard got its name. When Philip the Bold brought the Burgundian specialties of wine and mustard to his home in Flanders, his flag carried the words *"Moult me tard"* (I am in a hurry to return). Blowing in the wind, the flag read as "Moutard"—the first mustard advertising campaign.

The yellowish condiment is made by sifting, washing, and pressing the brown or black seeds, adding vinegar, and grinding it after a 48hr. storage period. Rich in vitamin C, mustard wards off scurvy and aids in the digestion of rich Burgundian cuisine. Mustard plaster placed on the chest is an old home remedy. For those who want to learn more and eat copious amounts of mustard seeds, the **Amora/Maille Factory** on quai Nicolas Rolin offers daily tours of its **Musée de Moutarde** in English and French at 3pm. Tickets (€3) are available at the tourist office.

No trip to Dijon would be complete without a stop at the source of Grey Poupon, the Maille Boutique, 32 rue de la Liberté, which sells 20 different mustards. (☎ 03 80 30 41 02. Open M-Sa 9am-7pm. MC/V.)

ing over all buildings in the city. A climb up the 316 steps of the 600-year-old tower for a panoramic view of the *vieille ville* is a good way to begin a Dijon visit. (☎ 03 80 74 51 51. Tours daily Easter to mid-Nov. every 45min. 9am-5:30pm; mid-Nov. to Easter W 2-6pm, Sa-Su 9-11am and 1:30-3:30pm. €2.30, students €1.20.)

MUSÉE ARCHÉOLOGIQUE. In the converted 11th-century Benedictine Abbey of Saint-Bénigne is the Musée Archéologique, with artifacts from the Côte d'Or's past, from pre-historic jewelry and Gallo-Roman sculpture to 17th-century pottery. Claus Sluter's emotionally arresting sculpture "Head of Christ" graces the first floor. (5 rue Dr. Maret. ☎ 03 80 30 86 23. Open daily mid-May to Sept. 8:55am-6pm, closed Tu; Oct. to mid-May 9am-12:30pm and 1:35-6pm, closed Tu. €2.20, students and Su free.)

ÉGLISE NOTRE-DAME. Built in only 20 years, from 1220 to 1240, this cathedral has an amazingly detailed and unified Gothic style, making it one of the most famous in all of France. The 11th-century cult statue of the Black Virgin in the cathedral is credited with the liberation of the city on two desperate occasions: in 1513 from a Swiss siege and in 1944 from the German occupation. Some 13th-century stained glass, among the oldest surviving in France, remains to the right of the altar, though most of the glass dates to the 19th century and famed artist Didron. The **Horloge à Jacquemart** clock atop the church tower, one of the famous symbols of the city, was hauled off as plunder by Philippe le Hardi after his 1382 victory over the Flemish. As you leave the church via rue de la Chouette, remember to rub the well-worn **chouette** (owl) with your left hand for good luck. (Pl. Notre Dame. ☎ 03 80 74 35 76. English pamphlet well worth the €0.50.)

ÉGLISE ST-MICHEL. While the inside of this church has the dark, vaulted interior of a Gothic cathedral, it switched style mid-construction, resulting in a hybrid colonnaded Renaissance facade. Like the Église Notre-Dame, it suffered severe damage during the Revolution, and much of its stained glass and original sculptures were destroyed. In the 19th century, it was lovingly restored by Abbé Deschamps, who is buried in one of the chapels. (Pl. St-Michel. ☎ 03 80 63 17 84.)

CATHÉDRALE ST-BÉNIGNE. Next door to the Musée Archéologique, this Gothic cathedral, recently renovated and recognizable by its distinctive brightly tiled Burgundian roof, was constructed in the 6th century over the tomb of local saint Bénigne. Four hundred years later, the powerful Abbey of Cluny had the church redone to make it the largest in Christendom.

Don't miss the 18th-century organ designed by Charles Joseph Riepp and the unusual circular crypt, which is pitch-black in places. *(Pl. St-Bénigne.* ☎ *03 80 30 39 33. Open daily 9am-7pm. Crypt €1.)*

🎧 NIGHTLIFE

Rue Berbisey is lined with bars and cafes. ▓**Le Privé,** 20 av. Garibaldi, just north of pl. de la République, pulses with late-night energy as students and 20-somethings lounge on leopard-skin couches in one room, or dance to techno and hip-hop. (☎ 03 80 73 39 57. M-Th and Su cover €5, with 1 drink €8; F-Sa cover €8, includes 1 drink. Open daily 11pm-5am.) The club starts rocking at 2am, after closing time at other bars like the Latin-themed **Coco Loco,** 18 av. Garibaldi—where jumping throngs of youngsters really go bananas. (☎ 03 80 73 29 44. Open Tu-Sa 5pm-2am.) ▓**Au Vieux Leon,** 52 rue Jeanin, attracts a merry Bohemian crowd. Discussion is the stimulant of choice, whether over beer at large outdoor picnic tables or in the trendy cafe full of angst-riddled intellectuals downstairs. The dress code is black, and more black, although tattered blue jeans make an occasional appearance. (☎ 03 80 30 98 29. Beer €3-4.) At **L'Atmosphère Internationale,** 7 rue Audra, local students let loose on the dance floor while aloof foreigners watch from the pool tables. The party starts late. (☎ 03 80 30 58 33. *Soirées internationales* W and Th night. No cover for international students with ID; Su-W free for everyone; Th-Sa cover €5, includes a drink. Open daily 5pm-5am. MC/V.)

🎭 🎋 ENTERTAINMENT AND FESTIVALS

The beautiful 18th-century **Théâtre de Dijon,** pl. du Théâtre, right next to St-Michel, puts on operas from mid-October to late April. (☎ 03 80 68 46 40. Office open M-F 1-7pm and Sa 4-7pm during production months. Tickets €21.40-42.70, students €9.20 1hr. before curtain.) Check out the plays (both classic and contemporary) at the **Nouveau Théâtre de Bourgogne,** Théâtre du Parvis St-Jean, rue Danton. (☎ 03 80 30 12 12. Open Oct.-June M-F 1-7pm, Sa 4-7pm; performances M and F-Sa 8:20pm, W 7:30pm.) Dijon's **Estivade** brings dance, music, and theater to the streets and indoor venues from late June to mid-July. Pick up a program at the tourist office. (☎ 03 80 30 31 00. Tickets both free and up to €8.) The city devotes a week in late summer to the **Fêtes de la Vigne** and the **Folkloriades Internationales,** a celebration of grapes accompanied by over 20 foreign dance and music troupes. (☎/fax 03 80 30 37 95. Tickets €10-46, most €10-15; ask about youth discounts.)

The internationally renowned **World Orchid Conference,** a celebration of one of the world's most elusive and expensive flowers held only once every three years, will dominate the city of Dijon from March 11-20, 2005. Reserve hotels well ahead. Details available through the tourist office, or at www.woc2005.org.

BEAUNE

The puns are easy enough to make—*le vin de Beaune, c'est du bon vin*—but the throngs of dapper 40-somethings and red-faced septuagenarians who come to this viticulture hot spot (pop. 24,000) often don't speak enough French to understand them. The crowds of visitors share with locals their deep love of the world-class wines that have been produced on the surrounding hillsides since Roman times.The atmosphere at Beaune is decidedly *bourgeois*: while the cobblestone streets are universally accessible, the prices at boutiques are not. Although prices at restaurants and for wine can be high by budget travel standards, the gastronomical delight that is Beaune makes a visit here well worth the splurge. More fiscally challenged travelers might find it an ideal daytrip.

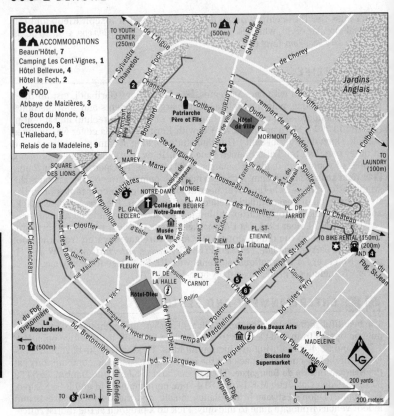

Beaune

♦♦♦ ACCOMMODATIONS
Beaun'Hôtel, **7**
Camping Les Cent-Vignes, **1**
Hôtel Bellevue, **4**
Hôtel le Foch, **2**

🍎 FOOD
Abbaye de Maizières, **3**
Le Bout du Monde, **6**
Crescendo, **8**
L'Hallebard, **5**
Relais de la Madeleine, **9**

BURGUNDY

⬛ TRANSPORTATION

Trains (☎ 03 80 22 13 13) depart av. du 8 Septembre for Dijon (25min.; 33 per day, 4 TGV; €5.70); Lyon (1½hr., 11 per day, €18.10); and Paris (2hr., 11 per day, €38.40). The info office is open M-F 10am-noon and 2-7pm. **TRANSCO buses** go to Dijon (1hr., 10 per day, €5.80) from rues Buttes, Clémenceau, Jules Ferry, Pasteur, and St-Nicolas. (☎ 03 80 42 11 00. Stops along the Côte d'Or; schedule at tourist office.) **Allo Beaune Taxi** (☎ 06 09 42 36 80) has 24hr. service. **Cars** can be rented at ADA, 26 av. du 8 Septembre, across from the train station. (☎ 03 80 22 72 90. Open M-Sa 8am-noon and 2-6pm. MC/V.) The staff at Bourgogne Randonnées, 7 av. du 8 Septembre, near the station, rents **bikes,** gives free maps with suggested routes, and stores luggage, space permitting. (☎ 03 80 22 06 03; www.bourgogne-randonnees.com. €3 per hr., €15 per day, €28 for 2 days, €75 per week. Credit card deposit. Open M-Sa 9am-noon and 1:30-7pm, Su 10am-noon and 2-7pm. MC/V.)

✳ 🔢 ORIENTATION AND PRACTICAL INFORMATION

The streets of the town center run in concentric rings around the **Basilique Notre-Dame.** Almost everything there is to see lies within the circular ramparts enclosing Beaune's *vieille ville.* From the station, head straight on av. du 8 Septembre, which becomes rue du Château. Turn left onto rue Thiers and follow it for about 10min. until you cross **rue de l'Hôtel-Dieu**, which leads to the Hôtel-Dieu and the **tourist office**, 1 rue de l'Hôtel-Dieu (15 minutes). The staff provides free maps, lists of *caves* (wine cellars), a reservations service with 10% deposit, tours of the *vieille ville* (daily July to mid-Sept. at noon; €6.50 per person, €10.50 per couple), a €15.15 *Pass Beaune* to three sights of choice, and **currency exchange** (€5) Sa-Su. They also offer 2½hr. winery tours by minibus for €41, leaving three times daily. (☎03 80 26 21 30; www.ot-beaune.fr. Open mid-Nov. to Mar. M-Sa 10am-6pm, Su 10am-12:30pm and 2-5pm; late Mar. to late June M-Sa 9:30am-7pm, Su 10am-12:30pm and 2-5pm; late June to mid-Nov. open an hour later.) The staff also runs an info booth at Porte Marie de Bourgogne, 6 bd. Perpeuil. (Open June-Nov. M-F 9:30am-noon and 2-6pm.) The **Point Information Jeunesse**, 8 av. de Salins, has info on work, study, and sports. (☎03 80 22 44 95. Open M-Th 1:30-6pm, F 1:30-5pm.) Other services include a **laundromat** at 19 rue faubourg St-Jean (☎03 80 24 09 78; open daily 6:30am-9pm), **police** at 5 av. du Général de Gaulle (☎03 80 25 09 25), a **hospital** at 120 av. Guigone de Salins, northeast of the town center (☎03 80 24 44 44), and 24hr. ambulance service (☎03 80 20 20 09). The **post office**, bd. St-Jacques, has **currency exchange** and incredibly slow **Internet** access for €7 per hr. (☎03 80 26 29 50. Open M-F 8am-7pm, Sa 8am-noon.) **Postal Code:** 21200.

ACCOMMODATIONS AND CAMPING

Visitors swarm to Beaune from April to November; reserve at least a week in advance. **Beaun'Hôtel ❸**, 55 faubourg Bretonnière, is southwest of the center, off bd. Clemenceau. It features bright rooms in yellow and blue, and some are quite large. (☎03 80 22 11 01; fax 03 80 22 46 66. Breakfast €6.50. Reception 8am-9pm; Su closed noon-5pm. Closed mid-Dec. to mid-Feb. Doubles €54-60; triples €66-72; family suite for 4-5 people €81. MC/V.) **Hôtel le Foch ❷**, 24 bd. Foch, has a friendly proprietress that lets colorful rooms with TV and large sinks. Close to the heart of downtown, but on the other side of the ramparts from the train station, next to a quiet park. (☎03 80 24 05 65; fax 03 80 24 75 59. Breakfast €5.40. Reception 7am-9pm, variable with the hours of the bar downstairs. Singles and doubles €25, with shower €33-54; triples €38. Extra bed €6. MC/V.) **Hôtel Bellevue ❷**, 5 rte. de Seurre, is a 10min. walk from the town center. From the station, make a left onto av. des Lyonnais and then another left onto rue Bellevue, and follow it to the corner (7 minutes). Above a large restaurant, a somewhat grouchy owner maintains clean, plain rooms for 2 people at a great price. (☎03 80 24 05 10. Doubles €30.)

To spend a night under the stars, **Les Cent-Vignes ❶**, 10 rue Dubois is a great campsite. (☎03 80 22 03 91), It's located 500m from town center off rue du faubourg St-Nicolas, Head north on rue Lorraine from pl. Monge to get there. Arrive early in summer. Gravel or grassy sites made private by hedges. Ping-pong, tennis, laundry, restaurant, and grocery store. Open mid-Mar. to end of Oct. Reception 8am-10pm. €3.20 per person, €4.20 per site, car included. Electricity €3.20. MC/V.

FOOD

The restaurants around **place Madeleine** and **place Carnot** serve the least exorbitantly priced *menus*, but even here prices for local wine are high. **Casino supermarkets** are at 28 rue du faubourg Madeleine (open M-Sa 8:30am-8pm); rue Carnot (open M 3-7pm, Tu-Sa 7:30am-12:30pm and 3-7:30pm, Su 8:30am-noon); and 15 rue Maufoux (open M-Sa 7:30am-12:30pm and 3-7:30pm). A large and popular open-air **market** opens on pl. de la Halle Wednesday and Saturday mornings, and Monday afternoons from June to mid-September. Those willing to dispense with formality can eat a full meal for under €9 at the locally popular cafeteria **Crescendo ❷**, Centre Commercial Champion, 9 av. Charles de Gaulle, 12min. from the center. (Open daily 11:30am-2:30pm; tea 9am-10pm.)

Monsieur Neaux, chef of ▒**Relais de la Madeleine ❷**, 44 pl. Madeleine, wants diners to try everything he cooks—he boisterously visits each table at the end of a meal to make sure his patrons are satisfied. A cut above the rest, Madeleine features house specialties like duck *pâté* with pistachio, a wondrous *mousse au chocolat*, and peppered trout—all of which can be sampled in the deluxe three-course €14.50 *menu*. (☎03 80 22 07 47. 3-course *menus* €11.50. Open Su-Tu and Th-Sa noon-2pm and 7-10pm. AmEx/MC/V.) For a tasty dinner that takes you back in time, head into the 12th-century wine cellar at **Abbaye de Maizières ❸**, 19 rue Maizières, near the Musée du Vin and the cathedral. (☎03 80 24 74 64; www.abbayedemaizieres.com. 3-course *menu* of regional specialties €16, 4 courses €23. Open daily noon-1:30pm and 7:30-9:30pm.) The traveler who hasn't yet had enough to drink can have an aperitif or a glass of wine at the wine bar **Le Bout Du Monde ❶**, 2 rue du faubourg Madeleine. (☎03 80 24 04 52. Wine €3-7+ per glass. Open daily 6pm-2am. MC/V.) The nearby German-themed **L'Hallebard ❶**, 25 rue d'Alsace, serves reasonably priced bar food and cherry-flavored beer in a garden setting (☎03 80 22 17 68. Beer €3-6. Open daily 1-11pm.)

❻ SIGHTS

▒**HÔTEL-DIEU.** In 1443, Nicolas Rolin, chancellor to the Duke of Burgundy, built this hospital to help the city's poor recover from the ravages of the famine that followed the end of the Hundred Years' War. Patients were treated here until 1971. Today, the building is the town's best non-drinkable tourist attraction. In the courtyard, visitors ogle the colorful roofs that make this one of France's architectural icons. In the *Salle des Pôvres*, the communal patients' room, mannequins of the nuns who served as nurses bend over velvet-curtained beds. The room's elegant decor explains why the hospital was called "the palace of the poor." The Hôtel's great treasures are its 16th century tapestries, as well as *The Last Judgment*, by Roger van der Weyden. Most info placards are in French, but English and German pamphlets are available. (2 rue de L'Hôtel Dieu. ☎03 80 24 45 00. Ticket office open daily Apr.-Nov. 9am-6:30pm; Dec.-Mar. 9-11:30am and 2-5:30pm; museum closes 1hr. after ticket office. €5.40, students €4.50, children 10-18 €2.60, under 10 free; tour €1.60.)

▒**PATRIARCHE PÈRE ET FILS.** At the foot of a winding staircase under a chapel, a labyrinth of wine bottles matures to perfection in Beaune's largest *cave*. Though not for experts, this 40min. audioguided tour serves as a great introduction to winemaking and winetasting in the region. Visitors can explore 5km of musty corridors lined with over four million bottles, a staggering fortune's worth of wine. In the final *caves*, a *dégustation* of 13 different wines is led by expert *sommeliers*, who will educate even the most ignorant visitors. Wines for purchase €14-35+. (5-7 rue du Collège. ☎03 80 24 53 78; www.patriarche.com. Open daily 9:30-11:30am and 2-5:30pm; arrive at least 1hr. before closing. €9; all proceeds to charity.)

OTHER SIGHTS. Inside the 15th-century Hôtel des Ducs de Bourgogne, the **Musée du Vin** offers visitors an amazingly detailed analysis of the Côte's *terroire* (territory), from the angles of the sun to the composition of the soil to the location of individual vineyard plots and their characteristics. Also on display is the stuff of winemaking itself: a wine cellar, vats, immense presses, labels, and bottles. Nearly all information is presented in French only. (Rue d'Enfer, off pl. Général

Leclerc. ☎ *03 80 22 08 19. Open daily Apr.-Nov. 9:30am-6pm; Dec.-Mar. W-Su 9:30am-5pm.
€5.10, students €3.10. Includes Musée des Beaux Arts and Musée Etienne-Jules Marey.)* In the
newly opened **La Moutarderie,** Fallot Mustards presents a bizarre hands-on history of mustard. Learn about the different types of mustard, from *Moutard au
pain d'épices de Dijon* to *Moutard à l'Ancienne,* and their varied histories.
Finish your gastronomical tour by mixing your own mustards and comparing
them to the "indominable" Fallot brand. *(31 faubourg Bretonniere. ☎ 03 80 26 21 30;
www.fallot.com. Guided tours only, at 9:30am and 11am. €10).* In addition to a small collection of Gallo-Roman sculpture, the **Musée des Beaux Arts** houses paintings by
15th- and 16th-century Dutch and Flemish artists and 18th- and 19th-century
French artists. *(Porte Marie de Bourgogne, 6 bd. Perpreuil. ☎ 03 80 24 56 92, weekends ☎ 03
80 24 98 70. Open daily. For admission, see Musée du Vin.)*

For three days around the last weekend in November, Beaune's moderate wine-
drinking becomes one debauched wine-soaked party (albeit for the same middle-
aged crowd) during **La Fête de la Vente du Vin,** a celebration of the bountiful wine
harvest. This family-oriented, Bacchus-inspired event promises clowns, folklore
plays, music, and wine *"à consommer sans modération"* (to drink without mod-
eration) throughout the pedestrian district.

CÔTE D'OR

The 60km of well-tended slopes that run from Dijon to the tiny village of Santenay,
20km south of Beaune, have nurtured grapes since 500 BC. Limestone-laced soil,
the right amount of rainfall, and perfect exposure and drainage, make it a godsend
for viticulturists—as well as some of the most valuable real estate in the world.

The **Côte d'Or** is divided into two regions, which by law can only bottle and sell
the wine of two kinds of grapes: the red Pinot Noir and the white Chardonnay. The
Côte de Nuits, stretching south from Dijon through **Nuits-St-Georges** to the village of
Corgoloin, is known for strong and flavorful reds, and has been nicknamed "The
Champs-Elysées of Burgundy." All the *Grand Crus* of Burgundy (except one) are
grown here in only 550 hectares.

Transportation around the vineyards is easy. The most intimate way to see
the vineyards near either Beaune or Dijon is to **bike** down the **Route des Grands
Crus.** Bike rental shops in both cities arrange tours of differing lengths that can
get you where you want to go. Renting a **car** in Dijon or Beaune (around €90
per day including tax, insurance, and gas) is the easiest way to the grapes, but
if you are planning on taking part in the wine tasting, this might not be the best
choice. **TRANSCO buses** (☎ 03 80 42 11 00) run frequently from Dijon to Beaune
(1hr.; 9 per day, Su only 11:10am; €5.80), and stop at all the great wine names
in between, including Gevrey-Chambertin (30min., 19 per day, €1.66) and
Nuits-St-Georges (45min.; 11 per day, Su only 12:34 and 6:24pm; €4). Many
buses are specially equipped to be wheelchair-accessible. Call ahead to determine their schedules. General schedules are available at the Dijon or Beaune
bus station. TRANSCO will take you from Beaune to Château de Rochepot (5
per day, fewer on Su; €3.20).

Lodging on the Côte, however, is expensive; your best bet—for both bargain
and experience—is to reserve a room days in advance at one of the many *chambres d'hôte* that dot the villages. The tourist office in Beaune or Gevrey-Chambertin will supply you with a copy of *Chambres et Tables d'hôte,* a comprehensive
list of bed and breakfasts. The Dijon and Beaune tourist offices also offer the
Bourgogne Hôtes guide, which lists almost every hotel and campsite in the
region. Accommodations in either Dijon or Beaune make a more convenient (and
cheaper) base from which to explore these rich viticultural areas.

ROUTE DES GRANDS CRUS

From Eurobike turn right on av. de l'Hôpital, bear left at the intersection to av. Jean Jaurès, then right at the Port du Canal. Follow the signs to Chenove or Route des Grands Crus. This heavenly, mostly flat road, which loses its congestion after a mile or two, winds through **Chenove, Marsannay, La Cote, Couchey, Fixin, Brochon,** and finally **Gevrey-Chambertin,** each village more enchanting than the next. Among the green hills speckled with church spires, omnipresent vineyards make the air intoxicating. Family-owned *caves* along the route offer free *dégustations*, but most will expect you to buy something. Drink and bike at your own risk. (Dijon to Gevrey-Chambertin by bike, about 1hr. By foot, about 2½hr.)

GEVREY-CHAMBERTIN

Perhaps the finest vineyards in all of France are around Gevrey-Chambertin, 10km south of Dijon. Nine of Burgundy's thirty-three *Grands Crus* are grown here. Perched atop the vineyards, the **Château de Gevrey-Chambertin** is a perfect place to unwind, especially after a long bike ride. The gracious proprietress will take you through her 13th-century château, built to protect the wine and the villagers (in that order). The tour ends with a taste of the prized vintages, which include both a *Premier Cru* and a *Grand Cru*, and cost at least €14. (☎03 80 51 84 85. Get off at the bus stop near the entrance to the village, go left up the hill, left again, and the château will be on your left. Open M and Th-F 10am-noon and 2-5pm, Sa-Su 11am-noon and 2-6pm. Tour €4.50, includes tasting. Tours in English on demand.)

The Gevrey-Chambertin **tourist office,** 1 rue Gaston Roupnel, is small, but very helpful. (☎03 80 34 38 40. Open M and Sa 9:30am-12:30pm and 1:30-5:30pm, Tu-F 9am-12:30pm and 1:30-6pm, Su 10am-12:30pm and 1:30-5pm; July-Aug. M and Sa open until 6pm.) Bunk down at the **Marchands ❸,** 1 pl. du Monument aux Morts, a three-bedroom B&B with a country feel. (☎03 80 34 38 13; fax 03 80 34 39 65. Singles €28; doubles €39-43; triples €54-59; quads €69-75. MC/V.) Reserve early in the summer.

Those who love wine are sure not to miss this little town's **Festival Musical des Grands Crus de Bourgogne,** held on weekends in September, where tastings of the precious just-harvested vintages are paired with exceptional classical music. Student tickets to combined tastings and shows are as low as €8. Inquire at the tourist office for further details.

■ ABBAYE DE FONTENAY

To get to Fontenay from Dijon, take the train from Dijon to Montbard (3-4 per day, €10). Taxis are usually waiting at the train station to take tourists on to the Abbey, but if you can't find one, ask at the station or the tourist office across the street for individual drivers' numbers (about €24 round-trip). Most other passengers who get off at Montbard are also heading to the Abbey—share a cab to cut the costs to a much more manageable fare.

If ever a single location could make a traveler yearn for the seclusion of a monastic life, the Abbaye de Fontenay is it. Lovingly restored in the early 20th century from the paper mill to which it had been converted following the Revolution, the Abbey now exists almost exactly as it did in the 12th century. The grounds, immaculately maintained by the Abbey's current private owners, convey the simplicity and precision of monastic life, but the bubbling fountains and towering buildings do little justice to the vows of poverty. From the majestic church—known for its **Virgin of Fontenay** statue—to the simple yet spacious dormitories, this out-of-the-way stop is well worth the time and effort it takes to get there. The forge, now recreated, is a landmark as the site of the first water-driven hammer; the whole Abbey is now a UNESCO World Heritage site. Adjacent to the grounds is a little museum, which includes the enormous and beautiful papal proclamation of the founding of

Fontenay. (☎03 80 92 15 00; www.abbayedefontenay.com. Open daily 10am-5:30pm Admission €8.50, students and senior citizens €4. 1hr. tours available, occasionally in English (call ahead), but most visitors choose to go it alone with multilingual pamphlets from the information office.)

CHÂTEAU DE ROCHEPOT

The **Château de Rochepot,** 15km southwest of Beaune, springs straight out of a (distinctly Burgundian) fairy tale, with its wooden drawbridge, slate roof, and pointed, colorfully-tiled turrets. "To enter, knock three times," declares the ancient sign. The 45min. tour of this 13th-century medieval fortress includes a peek at the Guard Room, the ingenious kitchens, the dining room, the old chapel, and the "Chinese" room, a gift of the last empress of China. (☎03 80 21 71 37. Open Apr.-June M and W-F and Su 10:30-11:30am and 2-5:30pm; July-Aug. 10am-6pm; Sept. 10-11:30am and 2-5:30pm; Oct. 10-11:30am and 2-4:30pm. €5.50.)

While lodging is scarce in this tiny town, ▧**Le Relais du Château ❸,** rte. de Nolay, has a friendly, English-speaking proprietor, and the bright, clean rooms are a fantastic deal. (☎03 80 21 71 32. Breakfast €6. Reception 7:30am-11pm. Restaurant *menus* €11-28. Doubles with shower €30, with bath €45. MC/V.)

CLUNY AND VAL LAMARTINIEN

These two gems of Southern Burgundy are easily accessible by **Mâcon,** an unimpressive town in its own right but extremely useful as a base for exploring. **Trains and buses** run from rue Bigonnet to Dijon (1¼hr., 19 per day, €15.90) and Lyon (1hr., 20 per day, €10). The info desk is open M-Th 5:15-8pm, F 5am-9pm, Sa 5:30am-7:40pm, Su 6am-9pm. **TGVs** stop at Mâcon-Loche, 6km away. SNCF bus #7 (dir: Chalon-sur-Saône) shuttles to the TGV station (12min., 4 per day, €1.80). Call ☎06 07 36 57 06 for a **taxi.** (24hr. About €15 from Mâcon-Loche to Mâcon.) Pro' Cycles, 45 rue Gambetta, **rents bikes.** (☎03 85 22 81 83. €14 per day, €70 per week. Open Tu-Sa 9am-noon and 2-7pm.)The town center is framed by rue Gambetta, rue Victor Hugo, cours Moreau, and the Saône. To reach the **tourist office,** 1 pl. St-Pierre, from the station, down rue Gambetta and left onto rue Carnot. The staff provides an accommodations service to take advantage Mâcon's of the less expensive hotel options while you explore Cluny and Val Lamartinien. (☎03 85 21 07 07; fax 03 85 40 96 00. Open M-Sa 10am-8:30pm, Su and holidays 3-8:30pm.)

CLUNY

At its height, **Cluny** and its nearly omnipotent abbot headed up a vast network of daughter abbeys. By virtue of the order's unique charter, it escaped the control of every ruler except the pope. The Romanesque abbey church, **Cluny III,** dedicated to St-Pierre and St-Paul, produced almost a dozen popes and was the largest church in the world until the construction of St. Peter's in Rome. During the Wars of Religion, the Revolution, and its aftermath, the abbey was looted, sold, and used as a quarry. A mental reconstruction of the abbey's scale requires some effort, but its former wealth is apparent in the ornamentation of the Gothic **Pope Gelasius** facade. The remains are now home to the **Ecole Nationale Supérieure d'Arts et Métiers,** whose central cloister is surrounded by student rooms. To get to the abbey from the tourist office, follow rue Mercière one block and turn right onto rue de la République. This area, particularly rue d'Avril and rue Lamartine, is home to the best of the well-preserved **maisons romanes** (medieval houses) which dot the city. (☎03 85 59 23 97; fax 03 85 59 16 34. Open daily May-Aug. 9:30am-6:30pm; Sept.-Apr. 9:30am-noon and 1:30-5pm. Closed May 1, Nov. 1, Nov. 11, Dec. 25, and Jan. 1. Abbey tours in English July-Aug. W and F 10:15am, 2:15, 4:15pm; tours also available in French. €5.50, under 26 €3.50. Ask about night tours July-Aug.)

Cluny has no train station and buses are a bit infrequent, so check schedules ahead. SNCF bus #7 runs to Cluny from Mâcon (40min., 6 per day, €4). Venturing by bike from Mâcon is also a feasible option for those up for the trip; take the scenic, car-free Voie Verte path from its terminus in Charnay-les-Mâcon, a 15min. ride from Mâcon. To get from the central Cluny bus stop to the **tourist office,** 6 rue Mercière (☎03 85 59 05 34; fax 03 85 59 06 95), walk against the traffic on rue Porte de Paris, turn right at pl. du Commerce, and continue for 5min. The office gives out a helpful map and a free guide pratique. (Open June-Sept. M-Sa 10am-7pm, Su and holidays 3-7pm; Mar.-May and Oct. M-Sa 10am-12:30pm and 1:30-6pm; Nov.-Feb. M-Sa 10am-12:30pm and 2-5pm. Tours mid-July to Aug., inquire at the Cluny Abbey info desk. Open daily May-Aug. 9:30am-6pm; Sept.-Apr. 9:30am-noon and 1:30-5pm.)

VAL LAMARTINIEN

The namesake of this lush area of southern Burgundy, Romantic poet Alphonse de Lamartine (1790-1869), makes his presence known even on roadside signs, which bear his famous verses. The verdant valley is replete with châteaux, most notably the privately owned ▓**Château de Cormatin,** complete with moat, formal gardens, aviary, and maze. The monumental open-well staircase in the north wing was the height of sophisticated engineering at the time of its construction (1605-1616). The Italian-style rooms, though unrestored, are well preserved. The tour features a plethora of eyebrow-raising historical details and even a brief meditation session. You can **bike** by taking car-free **la Voie Verte,** a 44km stretch of road devoted to bikers and bladers, which covers a good deal of fairly flat countryside near Cluny. Purchase a *Voie Verte* guide from the Mâcon, Cluny, or Cormatin tourist offices for €1.50. The **SNCF bus** # 7 from Cluny (25min., 6 per day 5:20am-8:13pm, €2.50) or Mâcon (1hr., 6 per day 7:58am-7:40pm, €5.70) stops right next to the château. (☎03 85 50 16 55; fax 03 85 50 72 06. Open daily mid-July to mid-Aug. 10am-5:30pm; June to mid-July and mid-Aug. to Sept. 10am-noon and 2-6:30pm; Apr. to mid-Nov. 10am-noon and 2-5:30pm. Tours in French with written English translation every 30min. €7.50, students ages 18-26 with ID €5, ages 10-17 €4. Park only €4.).

AUTUN

Lovers of antiquity will delight in Autun (pop. 18,000), originally Augustodunum, founded around 15 BC by Emperor Augustus as a "sister and rival of Rome" and still displays remnants of this now-distant glory. In addition to its collection of ancient rubble—which includes an impressive but decayed Roman theater as well towering Roman walls and lavishly ornate gates—Autun has (somewhat) more recent architectural prizes, including the 12th-century Cathédrale St-Lazare, erected to compete with nearby Vézelay in the lucrative medieval pilgrimage business. Still standing after the ravages of eight unkind centuries, the cathedral houses some of the most arresting Romanesque sculpture in the world. Despite these ancient gems, the town's contemporary life feels rather listless; visitors to Autun come to experience the life of yesteryear, not today.

🖫 🔁 TRANSPORTATION AND PRACTICAL INFORMATION. The main street, **avenue Charles de Gaulle,** connects the station to the central **place du Champ du Mars,** up a slow, steady hill (10 minutes). To get to the *vieille ville* from there, follow the signs from rue aux Cordeliers or rue St-Saulge.

Trains run from pl. de la Gare on av. de la République, but Autun is far from any major railway line and thus difficult to get to. Most journeys to and from Autun require a change at regional stops Châlon-sur-Saône or Etang, and many involve tortuous connections. It is possible to get to Dijon almost directly by train (2hr.; 9 per day, Su 5; €16) with an SNCF bus exchange via Etang. TGVs leave Gare Le

Creusot for Paris (1½hr., 5 per day, €41.90-55.30). The quickest way to get to Lyon is to catch a bus to regional hub Gare Le Creusot (45min., 5 per day, €5.40) and take the TGV from there (50min., 3 per day, €22.40). **SNCF buses** leave from outside the Autun station for Chalon-sur-Saône (2hr., 3 per day, €8.80). Check the station office. (Open M-F 7:05am-12:30pm and 12:50pm-7pm, Sa 9:05am-12:30pm and 2:30-6:30pm, Su 12:05-7:30pm.) **TRANSCO buses** (☎03 80 42 11 00) leave for Dijon from pl. de la Gare (2¼hr., daily 5:10pm, €12). For a **taxi**, call ☎03 85 52 04 83. (24hr.)

The **tourist office**, 2 av. Charles de Gaulle, off pl. du Champ de Mars, offers various themed city tours, as well as nocturnal tours of the *vieille ville* in summer that mix music and historical sketches. Self-guided city brochure in French €3. (☎03 85 86 80 38; www.autun.com. City tours €5.50, children €2.40. Night tours daily July-Aug. 9:30pm; €7.60, under 12 free. Bike tours €9.90. Office open May-Sept. M 2-6pm, Tu-Sa 10am-12:30pm, 2:30-6pm; Oct.-Apr. 10-11:30am, 2:30-6pm.) There's a branch office at 5 pl. du Terreau, next to the cathedral. (☎03 85 52 56 03. Open daily May-Sept. 9am-7pm.) The **hospital** is at 9 bd. Fr. Latouche (☎03 85 52 09 06). The **police** are at 29 av. Charles de Gaulle (☎03 85 52 14 22); call them for **pharmacie de garde** info. Do **laundry** at Salon Lavoir, 1 rue Guerin. (☎03 85 86 14 12. Wash and dry €4-5. Open daily 6am-8pm.) You can **exchange currency** at the **post office,** 8 rue Pernette. (☎03 85 86 58 10. Open M-F 8:30am-6:30pm, Sa 8:30am-noon.) **Postal Code:** 71400.

⌐C ACCOMMODATIONS AND FOOD. The city's two cheap hotels are across from the train station. Reserve a couple of weeks in advance in summer. The **Hôtel de France ❷**, 18 av. de la République, is a plain hotel across from the train station, over a quiet restaurant/bar, though the street below can be loud. Most rooms are bright but very basic; the little rooms under the slope of the roof are charming, if warm in summer. (☎03 85 52 14 00; www.hotel-de-france-autun.fr. Breakfast €4.70. Reception 8am-11pm. Singles and doubles €20-22, with toilet €24, with shower €26; triples €33-39; quads €39-46; quints €54. MC/V.) Next door are the inviting rooms of the **Hotel of Commerce and Touring ❷**, 20 av. de la République, which feature large bathrooms and TVs in small but well-decorated rooms. Rooms with bathtubs are particularly spacious. (☎03 85 52 17 90; fax 03 85 52 37 63. Breakfast €5. Reception 6:30am-11pm, Su by reservation only. Closed Jan. Singles and doubles €25, with shower €32-36, with bath €40-42; triples and quads €40. MC/V.) The **Camping Municipal de la Porte d'Arroux ❶**, located just an easy 20min. walk from town, rides the soft banks of a river in the fields. From the train station, turn left on av. de la République, left on rue de Paris, and go under the Porte d'Arroux. Cross the bridge and veer right on rte. de Saulieu; the campground is on your left. The standard, graveled sites have hedges for privacy. There is a restaurant (open June-Aug.) and a grocery store, as well as a common room with satellite TV; a few feet away is a small pond for fishing and swimming. (☎03 85 52 10 82; www.camping-autun.com. Open Apr.-Oct. Office open daily July-Aug. 7am-8pm; Apr.-June and Sept.-Oct. 9-11am and 6-9pm. Check-out noon. €2.50 per person, €3.50 per tent, €1.30 per car. Electricity €2.50.)

Autun's ruins are prime picnicking territory. Prepare your feast at **Intermarché,** pl. du Champ du Mars (open M-Th 8:30am-12:30pm and 2:30-7:30pm, F-Sa 8:30am-7:30pm), where some markets come Wednesday and Friday mornings. Bright little restaurants line the cobblestone streets of the upper city. **Le Petit Rolin ❷**, 12 pl. St-Louis, serves crêpes and salads for under €10 and drinks all day in the shadow of the cathedral, with romantic terrace seating at night. (☎03 85 86 15 55. *Menu* €15-25. Open daily 11am-3pm and 6-11pm. MC/V.)

◙ SIGHTS. At the top of the upper city, the **Cathédrale St-Lazare** rises above the Morvan countryside; the uphill walk from pl. du Champ de Mars feels like a pilgrimage. The stunning **tympanum** above the church doors, which depicts the Last

Judgement with expressive 12th-century figures, escaped the ravages of the Revolution. Covered in plaster following a clerical dispute in the 20th century, it has now been restored to full resplendent glory. Gislebertus, the artist's name, is visible below Jesus's feet. In the dimly lit nave, intricately carved capitals illustrate biblical scenes; to see them at eye level, climb up to the *salle capitulaire* above the sacristy. Beware the basilisk, an imaginary serpent whose gaze reputedly turns people to stone. (Open daily 8am-7pm.)

The **Théâtre Romain,** near the lake northeast of the *vieille ville*, is delightfully unrestored. Its remaining stones emerge from a grassy hillside, and picnickers relax where 12,000 enthralled spectators once sat. Today the theater faces the local soccer field and a pretty lake. During the first three weekends in August, 600 locals bring chariot races and Roman games to life in the much-hyped **Augustodunum** show, held in the original theater. (Info ☎ 03 85 86 80 13. €12, children under 12 €8. Tickets sold at tourist office.) From the back of the theater you see the **Pierre de Couhard,** a 30m pyramid-shaped pile of stone bricks. Its purpose remains unclear, although excavations recently unearthed a 1900-year-old plaque that cursed anyone who disturbed the man inside's eternal slumber. *Let's Go* does not recommend incurring dormant wrath. To reach the site, leave the *vieille ville* through the Porte de Breuil and climb into the hills.

The **Musée Rolin,** 3 rue des Bancs, next to the cathedral, features the true archaeological treasures of this ex-Roman city: beautiful mosaic floors harvested from the ruins, along with 12th- to 15th-century statues and paintings taken from St-Pierre for safekeeping. Miniature recreations and remnants of the original solemn mausoleum for the St-Pierre, which stood where the cathedral now stands, are well worth seeing. The real highlight, however, is Gislebertus's relief sculpture, *Eve at the Fall,* which scandalized audiences of its day for depicting female nudity and for imbuing the sinful foremother with real sadness. (☎ 03 85 52 09 76; fax 03 85 52 47 41. Open Apr.-Sept. M and W-Su 9:30am-noon and 1:30-6pm; Oct.-Mar. Su 10am-noon and 2:30-5pm. €3.20, students €1.60.)

There are a number of signs that Autun was once the largest city in Roman Gaul. The easiest way to see them is on the **petit train,** which leaves from pl. du Champ de Mars and from the tourist office annex near the cathedral. Tours are given in French, but the driver can give you an English translation sheet (45min.; June-Aug. 7 French tours per day 10am-6pm; €5, children €3). If you go solo, arm yourself with a free map from the tourist office, and prepare for a very long walk. Standing in the fields behind the train station, across the river Arroux, is the huge brick first-century **Temple de Janus.** The two remaining walls tower over cow pastures, white clouds drifting through their eroded, gaping windows. To reach them from the train station, walk northeast along av. de la République and take a left onto rue du faubourg d'Arroux, passing under one of the city's two remaining Roman gates: the still impressive, double-decker **Porte d'Arroux,** conveniently located near an idyllic river park. These two large arches for vehicles and two smaller ones for pedestrians led to the **Via Agrippa,** the main trade road between Lyon and Boulogne and the source of Autun's ancient wealth. Better preserved, the other gate, **Porte St-André,** is at the intersection of rue de la Croix Blanche and rue de Gaillon.

Autun's ramparts and towers are best seen from the hills above; to get there, take the path from near the cathedral to the Pierre de Couhard, or rent a **bike** from the Service du Sports on the far side of the lake. (☎ 03 85 86 95 80. €8.60 per half-day, €14.50 per day. Open July-Sept. 8:30am-6pm.) A part of the Morvan Valley, Autun has easy access to 2476km of marked mountain-biking trails, including one 8km easy-biking trail for the whole family. Ask at the tourist office for the guide *Le Morvan à VTT* or call the Morvan Park Authority for more information (☎ 03 86 78 71 77; morvanvtt@wanadoo.fr).

NEVERS

A budding tourist destination in western Burgundy, Nevers (pop. 50,000) is a relatively undiscovered city of medieval and Renaissance architecture, lush parks, and a scenic location on the banks of the Loire. Ravaged by WWII bombing, Nevers has rebounded with significant restorations. It is an ideal base for excursions to picturesque châteaux and for countless outdoor activities.

☎☑ TRANSPORTATION AND PRACTICAL INFORMATION. Trains pass through Nevers to: Bourges (38-55min., 7 per day, €9.70); Clermont-Ferrand (1½hr., 11 per day, €19.80); Paris (2¾ hr., 10 per day, €27.50). Ticket windows (☎03 92 35 35 35) open M 5:35am-9pm, Tu-Sa 6:05am-9pm, Su 6:45am-9pm. **Local buses** depart from rue de Charleville, left of the train station as you exit. (☎03 86 57 16 39. €1 to the city center. Transit maps available at the main office, 31 av. Pierre Bérégovoy.) For a **taxi**, call ☎03 86 57 19 19 (7am-11pm) or 03 86 59 58 00. To explore the region by **bike** or by **boat**, *Le Bureau des Guides de Loire*, 6 quai des Mariniers, rents bikes and canoes, complete with repair kit and helmet. (☎03 86 57 69 76. Bikes €12.50 per half day, €18 per day; canoes €15 per half-day, €21 per day; transport from destination included. Open M-Sa 8am-12:30pm and 1:30-7pm.) The town center is an easy 8min. walk from the station; head four blocks up av. du Général de Gaulle to Nevers's main square, **place Carnot.** Diagonally across the square from av. du Général de Gaulle is rue Sabatier, where the sleek multilingual **tourist office,** 4 rue Sabatier, has free maps of the city, a practical guide, directions for self-guided walking tours, and information on boat excursions, all in several languages. (☎03 86 68 46 00; www.ville-nevers.fr. Open Apr.-Sept. M-Sa 9am-6:30pm, Su 10am-1pm and 3-6pm; Oct.-Mar. M-Sa 9am-noon and 2-6pm, Su 10am-1pm and 3pm-6pm. July-Aug. city tours in French daily 10:30am, €5.) Other services include: **police** at 6bis av. Marceau (☎03 86 60 53 00); a **hospital** on bd. de l'Hôpital (☎03 86 93 70 00); a **pharmacie de garde** (☎03 86 60 53 00); **Internet** access at Pain et Friandises, 5 rue de la Pelleterie (☎03 86 59 26 69; €0.06 per min.; open M-Sa 9:30am-7pm), or Forum Espace Culture, a large bookstore at the corner of rue du Nièvre and rue de la Boucherie (☎03 86 59 93 40; €2.29 for 30min., €3.05 per hr.; open M 2-7pm, Tu-Sa 10am-7pm); and **currency exchange** at Crédit Municipal, pl. Carnot (open M 1:15-5:15pm, Tu-F 8:15-11:45am and 1:15-5:15pm, Sa 8:15-11am), and at the **post office,** 25bis av. Pierre Bérégovoy, which also has **ATMs** nearby. (☎03 86 59 87 00. Open M-F 8am-6:30pm, Sa 8am-noon.) **Postal Code:** 58019.

⚔ ACCOMMODATIONS. To get to quiet **Hôtel Beauséjour ❷,** 5bis rue St-Gildard, exit the train station, walk left, and then take a sharp right onto rue St-Gilard (10 minutes). The tidy rooms have firm beds and stenciled wooden furniture. (☎03 86 61 20 84; hbeausejour@wanadoo.fr. Breakfast €5.70. Reception daily 7am-10pm. Singles and doubles with sink €26, with shower €32, with shower and toilet €32-40. Extra bed €8. MC/V.) **Hôtel de Verdun ❸,** 4 rue de Lourdes, overlooking the Parc Salengro, has spacious, renovated rooms and English-speaking owners. (☎03 86 61 30 07; www.hoteldeverdun-nevers.com. Breakfast €5.50. Reception M-Sa 7am-9pm, Su 7am-noon. Singles €30-42; doubles €40-52. Extra bed €10. MC/V.)

⚑ FOOD. Skip the *brasseries* in the *vieille ville* for the cheaper, more interesting restaurants off pl. Carnot. The tourist office distributes a restaurant guide featuring the city's *toques Nivernais,* which offer reasonably priced gourmet menus. **Marché Carnot** hosts a covered **market** on av. du Général de Gaulle and rue St-Didier. (Tu-F 7am-12:30pm and 3-6:45pm, Sa 6:30am-7pm.) A **Champion supermarket,** 12 av. du Général de Gaulle, is ½ block from pl. Carnot. (Open M-F 9am-7:30pm, Sa 8:30am-7:30pm, Su 9am-noon. MC/V.) The sassy decor of **Tandem Café**

❷, 7 pl. Guy Coquille, complements its playfully color-coded *menus* of salads, *tartines*, and pastas. (☎ 03 86 59 24 15. *Menus* €9-10, including wine. Open M-W 8am-8pm, Th-Sa 8am-midnight. Food at lunch only, drinks only in the evening.) **Le Goemon Crêperie ❶**, 9 rue du 14 Juillet, serves omelettes and creative crêpes (€2.30-5.50) in a wood-trimmed dining room just off pl. Carnot. (☎ 03 86 59 54 99. Open Tu-Sa noon-2pm and 7-11. Closed Sept. MC/V.) **Autour du Monde ❸**, pl. Carnot, dishes up Greek and Turkish specialities like moussaka (€13) in a spirited setting. (☎ 03 86 57 68 72. Entrees €6.50-19. Open daily noon-11pm. MC/V.) For a special night out, try **La Cour Ste-Etienne ❹**, 33 rue Ste-Etienne, which has rotating *menus* (€15.50-27.50) fashionably presented in the courtyard of the Église Ste-Etienne. (☎ 03 86 36 74 57. Open Tu-Sa noon-1:30pm and 7:30-9:15. Closed Sept. MC/V.)

◪ **SIGHTS.** The most visible building in Nevers, the Renaissance **Cathédrale St-Cyr et Ste-Juliette,** off pl. Carnot and up rue du Doyenné, was nearly reduced to rubble in WWII. Astonishing reconstruction has restored it almost to its original splendor. The windows, striking reminders of the war's destruction, are intriguing examples of modern stained glass. (☎ 03 86 59 06 54. Open June-Sept. Tu-Sa 10am-noon and 2-7pm. Free tours M, W, F 3pm.) Opposite the cathedral, fairy-tale turrets ornament the 15th-century **Palais Ducal**, once the seat of regional government. A modest museum of local porcelain resides within, but the exquisite exterior is the real draw. (☎ 03 86 68 46 00. Open Apr.-Sept. M-Sa 9am-6:30pm, Su 10am-1pm and 3-6pm; Oct.-Mar. M-Sa 9am-noon and 2-6pm, Su 3pm-6pm. Enter from tourist office. Free.) To visit a neighborhood that flourished during the monastic boom of the 11th century, turn right on rue des Ourses from pl. Carnot, and follow it to the pedestrian rue François Mitterrand, lined with classy stores. On nearby rue Ste-Etienne, the nearly 1000-year-old **Église Ste-Etienne** is remarkably well-preserved.

◪▣ **OUTDOOR ACTIVITIES AND DAYTRIPS.** A walk through the gardens lining the Promenade des Remparts, from the Loire to av. Général de Gaulle, passes the crumbled remains of 12th-century Nevers. In the center of the city, just off pl. Carnot, the paths of Parc Roger Salengro winds through manicured flower gardens, groves of enormous trees and picnic-ready lawns. The scenic **Sentier Ver-Vert** footpath stretches 3.5km along the rolling banks of the Loire, with informative signs all long the way. To get there, follow rte. des Saulaies along the river east (dir: Magny) to Square Henri Virlogeux. Farther east of the city, along rte. D504 lies **Le Bec d'Allier,** the confluence of France's two wildest rivers. Peace-seekers and eco-enthusiasts can take advantage of the 1.5km nature trail that leads into the area around Le Bec, starting from the other side of the Loire in the town of Gimouille. To get there by car, leave Nevers by the Pont de la Loire on the N7 and take a right onto the D976 (dir: Bourges); signs direct you to the parking lot and trails on the right, about 10min. down the road. By bike, follow the trail that runs beside the **Canal Latéral de la Loire** to Gimouille.

Activities and sights near Nevers naturally center around its two rivers; the tourist office provides maps and information on a wide range of outdoor activities. **Le Bureau des Guides de la Loire** rents canoes, kayaks, bikes, and also offers guided canoe excursions down the Loire for either an afternoon or overnight trip. (☎ 03 86 57 69 76; www.L-o-i-r-e.com. Canoes Apr.-Sept. only. Call ahead to reserve for guided trips; 6 or more people necessary. Daytrip €45 per person, overnight €65. Unguided canoe rental €15 per half-day, €21 per day. Bikes €12.50/€18.)

A wonderful stop (or destination) for excursions from Nevers is the tiny, unassuming medieval village of ◪**Apremont-sur-Allier,** 16km southeast of the city. Set on the expansive banks of the Allier River, the town seems inured to the touch of the past centuries. Overgrown ivy drapes the ancient cottages, setting off the flowers which cluster on every windowsill. Apremont's real focal point follows the same

BURGUNDY

theme: **Le Parc Floral**, an vast, immaculately kept hybrid park-garden. Interspersed among rose-bowers sit whimsical sculptures and structures—including a painting-adorned Turkish pavilion in the middle of a pond—which mimic the 18th-century fad for out-of-character *follies*. (☎02 48 77 55 06. Open daily Apr.-Sept. 10:30am-12:30pm and 2:30-6:30pm; closed Tu in Sept. €7, under 12 €4.)

AUXERRE

A prime piece of riverfront real estate, the city of Auxerre (pop. 40,000) has always been defined by its location on the banks of the Yonne River, which has allowed it to accumulate substantial wealth through trade since the first century. Birthplace of the bishop Germain (AD 378-448), who was later made a saint, the church contains his tunic and embalmed remains became an important site of pilgrimage. Many of the city's most impressive sights still have ecclesiastical ties, but modern Auxerre also has a lively *centre ville* with timbered *ancien regime* houses, superb vineyards, pristine fishing areas, and a national champion soccer team.

📧📶 TRANSPORTATION AND PRACTICAL INFORMATION. Trains run from Gare Auxerre-St-Gervais, rue Paul Doumer, to east of the Yonne: Avallon (1hr., 10 per day, €8); Lyon (3-5hr., 19 per day, €35.70) via Dijon (2½hr. 10 per day, €20.20); Marseille via Laroche-Migenne (4 hr. TGV, 1 per day, €60.70); Paris (2hr., 12 per day, €20). (☎08 36 67 68 69. Info office open M-F 5:15am-8:30pm, Sa 6:15am-8:30pm, Su 6:45am-9:30pm. Hub for regional bus routes and regional trains. MC/V.) Get around town with Allo Le Bus, which runs local buses town M-Sa 7:30am-7:30pm (☎03 86 94 95 00; www.auxerre.com. Schedules and maps at tourist office. Tickets €1.10, *carnet* of 10 €8.30.) There is a taxi stand right in front of the train station (☎03 86 46 78 78).

To get to the **tourist office**, 1-2 quai de la République, follow signs from the train station to the *centre ville*, cross pont Bert, and take a right onto quai de la République. Office is 2 blocks down on the left. (12min.) Sells *Auxerre Privilèges* passport (€2), which gives half-price admission to most attractions in town, as well as half-price bike rental. Accommodations service (€2.30 plus 10% of the first night's cost up front), currency exchange Su only, walking tours (French only, except by reservation; daily June-Sept., Oct.-May Sa or Su by reservation; €4.50, students €3), and (☎03 86 52 06 19; www.ot-auxerre.fr. Open June 15 -Sept. 15 M-Sa 9am-1pm and 2-7pm, Su 9:30am-1pm and 3-6:30pm; Sept. 15-June 15 M-F 9:30am-12:30pm and 2-6pm, Sa 9:30am-12:30pm and 2-6:30pm, Su 10am-1pm. Other services include: **laundry** at 138 rue de Paris (open 7am-8pm); **police** at 32 bd. Vaulabelle (☎03 86 51 85 00.); a **hospital** at 2 bd. de Verdun (☎03 86 48 48 48.); **Internet** access at the Bureau d'Information Jeunesse de l'Yonne at 17 av. de St-Georges (☎03 86 51 63 84; €1.60 per 15min., 25 and under €0.80 per 30min.; open M-Tu and F 10:30am-12:30pm and 2-6pm, F until 5pm); and a **post office** at pl. Charles-Surugue with **currency exchange.** (☎03 86 72 68 60. Open M-F 8:30am-7pm, Sa 8:30am-noon. Branch location: 110 rue du Pont. Open M 1:30pm-6pm, Tu-F 9:30am-12:30pm, 1:30-6pm, Sa 9:30am-12:30pm and 1:30-6pm.) **Postal Code:** 89000.

👤📷 ACCOMMODATIONS AND CAMPING. At 🏨**Hôtel le Seignelay ❸**, 6 rue du Pont sparkling bathrooms, large windows, and 70s-inspired wallpaper make rooms feel just like Grandma's. Rooms open onto a courtyard, which doubles as a delicious restaurant at mealtimes. All rooms except some singles come with shower or bath. (☎03 86 52 03 48; www.leseignelay.com. Breakfast €6. 24hr. reception. Buzz to be let in 7pm-7am. Reserve ahead June-Aug. Closed Feb. Singles without shower €25, with shower or bath €38-41.50; doubles €45; triples €53; quads €64.50. AmEx/MC/V.) To get to the **Foyer des Jeunes Travailleurs (HI) ❶**, 16

BURGUNDY

bd. Vaulabelle, follow signs from the train station to the *centre ville*, cross pont Bert, and turn left on quai de la République; rue Vaulabelle is the first right. Walk down rue Vaulabelle about 15min; take a left at the alley after the Service Citroën. The apartment building is set back from the street. This out-of-the-way hostel offers dim hallways that lead to tiny, basic rooms with little furniture. Hall showers and toilets. (☎03 86 52 45 38; perso.wannadoo.fr/fjt. Breakfast included. Lunch €5.40. Reception daily 2-8pm. Singles €13.70, €253 per month.) Head to the **Hôtel La Poste ❸**, 9 rue d'Orbandelle at pl. de Cordeliers for a more central location. This hotel features small but homey rooms and a friendly proprietress. Though the hallways are a bit cramped, and the walls oddly carpeted, the rooms inside are bright, and some have a great view of the plaza. (☎03 86 52 12 02; fax 03 86 51 08 61. Breakfast €6. Reception M-Sa 6:30am-11pm. Closed Feb. Singles €32-50, doubles €36-54, triples €60, quads from €66. MC/V.) There is a **campsite ❶**, 8 rte. de Vaux, south of town on D163. (☎03 86 52 11 15. Reception 7am-10pm. Open Apr.-Sept. €2.50 per site, €2.90 per person. Electricity €2.30. V.)

◘ FOOD. Markets are held on pl. de l'Arquebuse (Tu and F), the *centre ville* (W), and on pl. Dégas, on the outskirts of town (Su morning). The **Monoprix supermarket,** 10 pl. Charles Surugue, in the heart of the old town, also operates a cheap cafeteria with a three-course *formule* for €6. (Supermarket open M-Sa 8:30am-8pm. Cafeteria open M-Sa 11:30am-6pm.) Rue du Pont has the best and widest variety of flavors and prices. Night owls will appreciate **◙La Tour d'Orbandelle ❷**, 34 pl. des Cordeliers, a refreshing Italian option. (☎03 86 52 31 46. Tasty pizza from €5.50, pasta from €8. Open daily 11:30am-11:30pm. AmEx/MC/V.) Locals, young and old alike, go to **Primavera ❸**, 39 rue du Pont, for its Greek-inspired menu (including souvlaki and moussaka), served in a classy outdoor setting. The *menu du jour* (€11.50) is a great value. (☎03 86 52 03 48. Fixed *menus* €9-24. Open M-Sa 12:30-2pm and 7:30-10pm. MC/V.) The amusing **Au Grand Gousier ❷**, 45 rue de Paris, has a children's menu *"pour les petits ogres"* (for the little ogres) among other witty touches. (☎03 86 51 04 80. *Escargot* starts at €5.20. Open M-Tu and F-Sa 12:15-2:30pm, 7:30-10pm; W-Th 12:15-2:30pm. MC/V.)

◙ SIGHTS. Utterly charming and picturesque, the petite **Passerelle footbridge** (up the quai de la République from Pont Bert) makes a perfect starting point for an exploration of Auxerre. The tourist office right across the road provides free guides in English, French, German, Italian, and Dutch to **The Thread of History,** a colored line on the ground that weaves past every monument in the city, although the weary traveler might curse its comprehensiveness.

The towering **Cathédrale St-Etienne,** begun in 1215 and featuring impossibly detailed stained glass, is a must-see. Its wounded facade still displays statuettes decapitated by Huguenots when they occupied the city in 1567. Inside, the hulking organ is an impressive sight, as is the 11th-century Romanesque crypt, which preserves an ochre fresco of Christ on horseback. The treasury on the south wall guards relics, illuminated manuscripts from the 15th century, hand-carved ivory triptychs, and St-Germain's 5th-century tunic. (Cathedral open April-Oct. M-Sa 7:30am-7pm, Su 2-6pm; Nov.-Mar. M-Sa 7:30am-5:30pm. Crypt €2.50, treasury €1.50, student entry to treasury free with payment for crypt, under 14 free. Light show *(son-et-lumière)* with audioguides in English and German, every night June-Sept. 10pm; €5. Call ☎03 86 52 23 29 for details. AmEx/MC/V.)

The Gothic **Abbaye St-Germain,** 2 pl. St-Germain, commissioned around AD 500 by Clothilde, attracts pilgrims and tourists to the tomb of the former bishop of Auxerre. While the church itself contains a crypt with some of France's oldest frescoes, the Abbaye itself, which now houses a museum, is the real scene-stealer. Featuring St. Germain's carefully preserved tunic, as well as relics from monastic life, the museum recreates Benedictine life in the quarters in which it was lived. (☎ 03 86 18 05 50. Open June-Sept. M and W-Su 10am-6:30pm; Oct.-May 10am-noon and 2-6pm. €4.20, students under 26 free. Parts are wheelchair-accessible.) Visitors wandering near pl. de l'Hôtel will certainly be charmed by the **Tour de l'Horloge**, a turreted 15th-century clock tower in white and gold, but they may be slightly unnerved by the boldly painted wooden statues of *auxerrois* celebrities that dot the area. Those with an interest in pottery and tapestries might enjoy the **Musée Leblanc-Duvernoy**, set in an 18th-century mansion at 9bis rue d'Egleny, with special exhibits each summer. (☎ 03 86 52 44 63. Open Su-M and W-Sa 2-6pm. €2, students under 26 free, first Su of every month free.)

> **TIP** **FRUIT OF THE LYONNE.** Stretching through northern Burgundy, the largely rural Yonne Valley features endless wineries, farms, and freshly made regional treats. The Lyonne tourist train lets you sample them all as it travels the 1½hr. scenic route from Auxerre to Avallon. At €8 round-trip for adults (€4 for groups and ages 12-25), it's even cheaper than a normal SNCF train, not to mention the free tastes of cheese, local biscuits, *pâté*, and wine. *(Reservations can be made through SNCF. For more info, contact the Yonne Office of Tourism ☎ 03 86 52 06 19; www.lyonne.com. Train runs mid-July to September Tu-Su, 1-3 per day.)*

⚅ 🎭 ENTERTAINMENT AND NIGHTLIFE. Concerts descend on Auxerre in the summer, beginning with the *"Garçon, la note!"* series July 1st through August. (Free concerts M-F 11pm in the city's terraces and cafes; call tourist office for details.) The **Cathédrale St-Etienne** presents free organ concerts in the summer. (July-Aug. Su 5-6pm.) Auxerre hosts a piano festival in September and an international music and film festival in November. (Ask tourist office for details.) The **Théâtre of Auxerre**, 54 rue Joubert (☎ 03 86 72 24 24), is closed during the summer, but from September to May it sings and dances with a variety of musical and dramatic events. (Prices vary widely depending on event.) Enthusiastic pub-crawlers can find satisfaction in any of the bars that line the rue du Pont, but none stay open much later than midnight.

Those more interested in outdoor sports can take advantage of the great fishing in Auxerre and the Yonne region. Contact the **Fédération de Pêche de l'Yonne**, 9-11 rue du 24 Août for fishing info (☎ 03 86 51 03 44; www.peche-yonne.com). The **Société Mycologique Auxerroise**, 5 bd. Vauban (☎ 03 86 46 65 96), organizes mushroom-hunting expeditions in spring and autumn.

AVALLON

Though the oldest section of town still lends itself to a pretty cobblestone stroll, Avallon proper (pop. 8560) is no tourist's dream destination. Centered around its train and bus station, it lacks both compelling sights and charming hotels. Despite this, however, Avallon retains a certain appeal: sitting high above the stunning Valée de Cousin, it is a central base from which to take breathtaking daytrips by car or by foot around the surrounding Morvan countryside. Nearby worthwhile sites include picturesque Burgundian towns, like Vézelay or Semur-en-Auxois, as well as numerous relatively untouristed vineyards and châteaux.

🏳 🎫 TRANSPORTATION AND PRACTICAL INFORMATION. Trains run To: Autun (1¾hr.; Su-Th and Sa 1 per day, F 2 per day; €11.50); Auxerre (1½hr., 5 per day, €8); Paris (2½-3hr., 7 per day, €24.60). SNCF buses run to Vézelay (July-Aug. daily 9:37am and 10:46am, return 5:24pm). Routes marked "car" on SNCF's schedule are serviced by buses. (☎ 03 86 34 01 01. Station open M-F 5:30am-noon

FROM THE ROAD

JUST EAT IT

As a *Let's Go* writer, I was used to going above and beyond the call of duty. But as a smiling waiter placed a dish of ice-cold gelatinous chicken-product in front of me one night in Dijon, I felt that rock-hard resolve wavering.

I had already vowed to try every French regional specialty on my route so I could report back on which ones deserved the real thumbpick. Tripe sausages in Troyes? Check. Vintage champagne at Moët & Chandon? Check. Cassis mustard in Beaune? Check. But cold chicken with the look of jello and the consistency of congealed fat? Gulp.

After a half-bottle of fine Pinot Noir to steel my will, I finally dug into that chicken. I wish I could tell you it was rewardingly delicious, but to this writer's palate, it just wasn't. It was exactly as terrible as I had imagined: cold and slimy all the way down. But as the next dish, a succulent beef bourguignon, arrived at my table, I realized that I had learned a valuable lesson—aside from "never order aspic de poulet au basilic again." If I never stretch myself beyond my comfort zone, I might never again be as disgusted as I was when that chicken came, but neither will I be as deeply satisfied as I was just minutes later as I devoured that delectable beef.

Ok, so I did eat some fast food the next night. But hey, "Le Quick Hamburger" is French food too, right?

— *Sarah Charlton*

and 1:15-8pm, Sa 5:30am-12:15pm and 1:15-7:15pm, Su 8:45am-noon and 3:30-8pm.) **TRANSCO buses** (☎03 80 42 11 00) depart from the train stations to: Dijon (2hr.; M-Sa 3 per day, Su 1 per day at 5:05pm; €15.20) via Semur-en-Auxois (45min.; M-Sa 3 per day, Su 1; €6.60). Purchase tickets on the bus, daily bus times are posted on wall at train station. The tourist office has full schedules; the train station does not. **Taxis** (☎03 86 34 31 08) can be reached 24hr. To rent **bikes,** stop by M. Gueneau, 26 rue de Paris (☎03 86 34 28 11. €16 per day. Open Tu-Sa 8am-noon and 2-6pm. AmEx/MC/V).

To get to the **tourist office,** 6 rue Bocquillot, head straight from the train station on av. du Président Doumer and turn right onto rue Carnot. At the large intersection, turn left on rue de Paris. Pass a large parking lot. The street becomes Grande Rue A. Briand, passes through the Tour de l'Horloge, and ends at the office. (☎03 86 34 14 19; www.avallonnais-tourisme.com. Internet access €3.10 per 15min. Accommodations service €2.30. Maps €0.50. Open daily July-Aug. 10am-1pm and 2-7pm; Sept.-June Tu-Sa 10am-12pm, 2-8pm; longer hours during holidays and festivals.) Other service include: **laundry** at 8 rue du Marché, off pl. du Général de Gaulle (☎06 14 93 24 86. Open daily 7am-9pm.); **police** at 2 av. Victor Hugo (☎03 86 34 17 17); a **hospital** at 1 rue de l'Hôpital (☎03 86 34 66 00. **Pharmacie de garde** is displayed at Pharmacie Rauscent Maratier, 4 Grande Rue, and in the window of the tourist office.); and a **post office** at 9 rue des Odebert. (☎03 86 34 91 08. **Currency exchange.** Open M-F 8am-12:30pm and 1:30-6pm, Sa 8am-noon.) **Postal Code:** 89200.

📷 ACCOMMODATIONS AND CAMPING. In the **Hôtel St-Vincent ❸,** 3 rue de Paris, 10min. from train station, the dark and musty stairwell gives way to homey blue and white seashell-themed rooms, tastefully decorated with antique armoires and bedside tables and complete with TV and shower. Windows are small and the road outside can be noisy, especially after bars close. (☎03 86 34 04 53. Breakfast €5.40. Reception 8am-11pm at *tabac* downstairs, closed Su. Doubles from €33.53; triples €36.60; quads €59.50. MC/V.) A professional staff welcomes travelers to the stately **Les Capuchins ❹,** 6 av. Paul Doumer, one block from the train station. It features double beds, classy decor, and sparkling bathrooms. Many rooms look out on a small backyard garden, and the restaurant downstairs has gourmet *menus* for €25. (☎03 86 34 06 52; fax 03 86 34 58 47. Breakfast €6. Reception 8am-10pm. Reservations suggested. Closed Tu-W and for 2 weeks at

Christmas. Doubles €49; triples €59; quads €67. AmEx/MC/V.) **Camping Municipal de Sous-Roche ❶**, 3km from the *centre ville* (☎03 86 34 10 39). Walk straight from the train station on av. du Président Doumer, left on rue Carnot, then straight through a big intersection. Follow the signs to "Camping." Head along rte. de Lourmes, bear left, and then veer left on rue de Sous Roche. to reach this quiet riverside campground. (Reception 8am-8pm. Open mid-Mar. to mid-Oct. €3 per person, €2 per site, €2 per car. Electricity €3.)

◘ FOOD. Head to ⊠**Relais des Gourmets ❸**, 45-47 rue de Paris, for a luxurious treat that won't bust your budget. The dining room, overflowing with *fleurs vibrantes* during the summer, offers a three-course traditional Burgundian *menu* for €16.50, with vegetarian plates starting at €18. (☎03 86 34 18 90. Food served daily noon-2pm and 7:15-9:15pm, Sa to 9:30pm; Sept.-June closed Su afternoon and M. Reservations required during summer and on weekends all year. AmEx/MC/V.)

At the top of town, **La Tour ❷**, 84 Grande Rue A. Briand, cooks up a variety of Italian and Burgundian food, from *escargot* to *jambon persillé*, in a warm, half-timbered 15th-century house behind the Tour de l'Horloge. (☎03 86 34 24 84. Big salads €4-7.50, pizzas €6-8.50, pastas €7.50-9. Open daily June-Aug. noon-2:30pm and 7-10:30pm; Sept.-May noon-2pm and 7-10pm, closed Su and M lunch. AmEx/MC/V.) Have the traditional low-cost French lunch at the centrally located **Crêperie ❶**, 35 rue de Paris, where you can eat a cheap hearty meal or indulge your sweet tooth. (☎03 86 34 30 67. Sugary selections from €2.50, meaty options €8.70.) The central watering hole is the **Café de l'Europe ❶**, 7 pl. Vauban. Watch all of Avallon walk by from this big, comfortable hangout. (☎03 86 34 04 45. Beer €2.50, sandwiches from €4. Open daily 7am-midnight.) **Le Palais de Pékin ❷**, 8 rue de Odebert, serves Chinese, Vietnamese, and Thai *menus*. (☎03 86 34 51 24. *Menus* €11.80, €12.80, and €14.80. Lunch *menu* €8. Open Su-Tu and Th-Sa noon-2:30pm and 7-10:30pm, W 7-10:30pm. MC/V.) For **groceries**, the **Petit Casino supermarket**, 31 rue de Paris, is a block away from the intersection with rue Carnot. (Open Tu-Sa 8am-12:30pm and 3:30-7:15pm, Su opens at 8:30.) Morning **markets** are held on pl. du Marché (Sa morning) and in the pl. du Général de Gaulle (Th morning).

◩ SIGHTS. Within Avallon, you can visit the uniquely enjoyable ⊠**Musée du Costume**, 6 rue Belgrand, off Grande Rue A. Briand, where historical narrative meets fashion show with rooms full of 18th- to 20th-century *haute couture* on amusingly up-close display. The mannequins strike witty poses, and the tour guides provide charming patter that will entertain both fashionistas and history lovers. (☎03 86 34 19 95. Open daily Easter-Nov. 10:30am-12:30pm and 1:30-5:30pm. Tours in French. €4, students and under-18 €2.50.) If you have more than a few hours to kill in Avallon itself, the rolling countryside surrounding the town makes for a great walk. More compelling than a tour of the town itself, a walk along the narrow paths of the western and southern ramparts reveals an excellent view of the dense forests, verdant pastures, and crumbling châteaux of the Vallée du Cousin. The tourist office provides a free map of an 8km walk covering the area's highlights. At the **Musée des Voitures de Chefs d'Etats**, at Château de Montjalin in nearby Sauvigny-le-Bois (7km east of Avallon), you can get a look at the wheels of famous presidents and prime ministers. This one-of-a-kind museum showcases cars formerly owned by JFK, Charles de Gaulle, and USSR General Secretary Brezhnev, among others. Though the actual cars aren't much to get excited about, how many chances do you get to check out a "Popemobile"? (☎03 86 34 46 42. Open daily 9am-7pm. Admission €2.50, free with *Passeport Coeur de Bourgogne*.)

BURGUNDY

VÉZELAY

High above the breathtaking Vallée de Cousin, Vézelay (pop. 492) is like all the perfections of small-town France distilled. Breathtaking views abound, as the tiny hilltop village watches over dense forests, golden wheat, and white flecks of cattle in distant pastures. Vézelay's small, shop-lined streets cater to tourists not in the tacky manner of less classy towns, but by selling nothing but local Burgundian produce and artisanal creations. All this, combined with splendid views, distinguishes Vézelay as one of the most beautiful villages in France.

▉▉ TRANSPORTATION AND PRACTICAL INFORMATION. There's no train station in Vézelay; **trains** run from Paris via Auxerre to Sermizelles (2½hr., 5 per day, €12.60). From here you can take **Taxi Vézelay** for the 10km ride to Vézelay (☎03 86 32 31 88 or 06 85 77 89 36. 24hr. Around €15). An easier option is to take the **SNCF bus,** which leaves the train station at Avallon for Vézelay. (Daily July-Aug. 9:37am and 10:46am, return 5:24pm.) **Taxis** from Avallon are around €25. Call **Alain Taxi** (☎03 86 34 31 08), which is open 24hr., or **Taxi Avallon** (☎03 86 34 09 79). Vézelay is also easily reached by **bike,** which is a great way to explore the nearby villages and countryside. The tiny **tourist office,** 12 rue St-Etienne, just down the street from the church, has free maps and a very helpful *guide pratique* that lists all local accommodations and businesses. The office also has **Internet** access (€2 per 10min.), group tours by reservation, and individual tours July-August (☎03 86 33 23 69; www.vezelaytourisme.com. Open daily May-Oct. 10am-1pm and 2-6pm; Nov.-Apr. closed Th.) For the **pharmacie de garde,** check the window of the Pharmacie Meslin at 25 rue St-Etienne. Renting **bikes** at A.B. Loisirs, rte. du Camping in nearby Saint-Père, requires a short downhill walk of 2km along D957, heading toward Avallon. (☎03 86 33 38 38; www.abloisirs.com. Bikes €16 per half-day, €23 per day. Open daily 9:30am-7pm.) The **post office,** rue St-Etienne, has both an **ATM** and **currency exchange.** (☎03 86 33 26 35. Open July-Aug. M-F 8:30am-12:30pm and 1:30-5pm, Sa 8:30am-noon; Sept.-May M-F 9am-noon and 2-5pm, Sa 8:30-11:30am.) **Postal Code:** 89450.

▉▉ ACCOMMODATIONS AND FOOD. With more than 100,000 visitors passing through each summer, Vézelay's accommodations fill up rapidly. Book a month in advance, particularly in the summer. Only a block away from the hilltop and the church, ▉**Maison Les Glycines ❸,** rue St-Pierre, is a three-star hotel with 11 attractive, spacious rooms, each with a full bath. An attached *salon de thé* offers a wisteria-shaded outdoor dining area and food from €7. (☎03 86 32 35 30. Breakfast €6. Reservations required. Singles €30-52; doubles €52-64. Extra bed €14. MC/V.) The **Auberge de Jeunesse (HI) ❶** shares space with **Camping de L'Ermitage ❶.** Both are a scenic 15min. stroll from downtown Vézelay. Follow the signs downhill from the bus stop on rte. de l'Etang. HI has dorm-style rooms of four to six beds and kitchen access; Camping has beautiful views, showers, bathrooms, and electricity. (☎03 86 33 24 18. Reception 10am-12pm, 7:30-10pm. Closed Jan. Beds €7-9, camping €2 per person, electricity €2.50.) An option used primarily by pilgrims, but open to all, is the **Centre Sainte Madeleine,** run by the Fraternité Monastique de Jerusalem and the sisters of Ste-Madeleine, who also organize days of prayer, silence, and study. (☎03 86 33 39 53. Singles €13.50; doubles €19; 12-bunk dorm €7 per bed.) Right by the bus stop, **Le Cheval Blanc ❷** offers travelers nine bright, tidy rooms. Attached to the hotel, a restaurant serves salads (€8-8.30) and three *menus* for €14-22.50. (☎03 86 33 22 12. Breakfast €6. Reservations required. Closed mid-Dec. to mid-Jan. Singles and doubles with shower and toilet €19-38. MC/V.) **La Terrace ❷,** pl. de la Basilique Sainte Madeleine, is a hotel-cafe-*brasserie* with a prime location right next to the church. Some rooms face the garden, while others have a tremendous view of the valley below. (☎03 86 33 25 50. Breakfast €5. Doubles €25-45; triples €50; quads €60. Extra bed €10. MC/V.)

With its ruddy tile floor and smoky fireplace, the rustic █Auberge de la Coquille ❷, 81 rue St-Pierre, perfectly suits the local specialties it serves, including spicy *escargot* (€12 for 12) and crumbling rounds of *fromage époisses* (€3.50). The *menu bourguignon* (€10.90)—a *galette bourguignon, crêpe miel* (honey), and a glass of red wine—makes a perfect light lunch. (☎03 86 33 35 57. 3- and 4-course *menus* €8-24.50. Reservations suggested June-Aug. Open daily noon-10pm. MC/V.) Vegetarians can dive into the four-course *menu végétarien* (€19) while their carnivorous friends enjoy a *menu* featuring *noix de porc à la moutarde* (pork with mustard; €15) at Le Bouganville ❸, 28 rue St-Etienne. (☎03 86 33 27 57. A la carte options from €10. Reservations suggested. Open Su-M and Th-Sa noon-2pm and 7-9pm. Closed Dec.-Jan. MC/V.) Casual types and those who just don't want to climb the hill should try À La Fortune du Pot ❸, pl. du Champ-de-Foire across from the bus stop, with *menus* of hearty favorites from *jambon* to *anduoillette* for €10.50. (☎03 86 33 32 56. Open 8am-11pm. MC/V.) Groceries can be found at the Vival supermarket, near the bottom of rue St-Etienne. (Open daily July-Aug. 8am-8pm, Sept.-June M-Sa 8:15am-8pm, Su 9am-8pm. MC/V.)

◪ SIGHTS. All roads in Vézelay converge at the famous hilltop Basilique Ste-Madeleine. The Gothic and Romanesque church stands as an impressive, if typical, member of medieval France's old-church club, with an intricately sculpted tympanum and a cavernous interior. A strange melange of camera-clad tourists and praying pilgrims fills the welcome center. The underground crypt housing the relics of Mary Magdalene would be otherworldly were it not for the tour guides and stage lighting. The basilica is also the site where St. Bernard of Clairvaux launched the Second Crusade and Richard the Lionheart set off for the Third Crusade. (☎03 86 33 39 50. Open daily sunrise to sunset. Closed during mass. Tours in English with reservation; pamphlets in English.) Concerts and performances take place in the basilica and all over town most nights throughout the summer months; call tourist office for details. A peaceful and attractive spot for a bit of fresh air or a snack can be found along the southern ramparts behind Ste-Madeleine, which look out over vineyards that have been producing Chardonnay, Mélon, and Pinot Noir since the 9th century. The *caves* (cellars) of local winery Caves du Pèlerin, 32 rue St-Etienne, offer a guided tour and tasting. (☎03 86 33 30 84. Multi-level tours daily July-Sept. 2-5pm; Oct.-June on weekends. €5, under 18 free. MC/V.) The Maison Jules Roy, rue des Ecoles (facing downhill from the church, turn right through parking lot and follow the signs), makes for a thoughtful visit to the ivy-covered home of the late Algerian-born French author known for denouncing France's treatment of Algeria and Indochina. Guest writers and literary readings take place here. Most information in French only. (☎03 86 33 35 01. Open Apr.-Oct. M and W-Su 2-6pm. Free.)

For a more adventurous way to return from Vézelay to Avallon, head downhill 2km to St-Père and drop by the Canoë-Kayak Club d'Avallon, on Rue des Graviers directly across from the St-Père campsite. By canoe, raft, or kayak, you can take a half-day trip downstream from St-Père to Sermizelles. A 25m swim test is required, and insurance is highly recommended. (☎03 86 33 35 64. Open daily May to mid-Oct. 9am-6pm. Credit card number and 40% deposit required to reserve.)

SÉMUR-EN-AUXOIS

The crumbling towers that protect the *vieille ville* of Sémur-en-Auxois (pop. 5100) and its seventh-century castle have long defined its identity over the years. The name of this 2000-year-old town is derived from its Roman appellation, *Sene*

Muros, meaning "old walls." Overlooking a bend in the Armençon River, the unspoiled provincial town provides serenity, but don't come here if you're looking for much more than a mild, relaxing night.

⊟ TRANSPORTATION. TRANSCO (☎ 03 80 42 11 00) runs **buses** from Semur to Avallon (45min.; M-Sa 8:25am, 1:46, 7:53pm, Su 12:46 and 10:02pm; €6.50) and Dijon (1¼hr.; 7:16am, 1, 6pm; €9.96). Schedules at the tourist office. For a **taxi,** call ☎ 03 80 96 60 18 or 03 80 97 34 67.

⚠ PRACTICAL INFORMATION. The **tourist office,** pl. Gaveau, where rue de la Liberté meets the gates of the *vieille ville,* has bus schedules, free maps, a list of hotels, and an SNCF info and reservation office. The info office staff runs group tours in English and French. (☎ 03 80 97 05 96; www.ville-semur-en-auxois.fr. Tourist office open mid-June to Sept. M-Sa 9am-7pm, Su 10am-noon and 3-6pm; Oct. to mid-June M 2-6pm, Tu-Sa 9am-noon and 2-6pm. SNCF info office open mid-June to Sept. Tu-F 9am-noon and 2-6pm, Sa 9am-noon and 2-5pm. Tours by reservation €3.10.) Other services include: **bike rental** at R.D.X., 2ter rue du Bourg Voisin (☎ 03 80 97 01 91; €7 per half-day, €11 per day. Open Tu-Sa June-Aug. 9am-noon and 2-7pm; Sept.-May 9:30am-6:30pm. MC/V.); **Laundromat La Buanderie** at the Centre Commercial Champlon (open daily 9am-7pm); **police** (☎ 03 80 97 11 17) and a **hospital** (☎ 03 80 89 64 64; 24hr.) on av. Pasteur, east of the center; a **pharmacie de garde,** which is listed on every pharmacy's window; **Internet** at the Cyber KFÉ inside the bar at the Hôtel du Commerce, 19 rue de la Liberté (☎ 03 80 96 64 40; KFÉ M-F 7:30am-8pm; €2 per 30min.); and **ATMs** and **banks** around pl. de l'Ancienne Comédie, which also has a **post office** with **currency exchange.** (☎ 03 80 89 93 06. Open M-F 8:30am-noon and 1:30-5:30pm, Sa 8:30am-noon.) **Postal Code:** 21140.

⌂⌂ ACCOMMODATIONS AND CAMPING. Hôtel du Commerce ❸, 19 rue de la Liberté, close to both the bus stop and the *vieille ville,* lets spacious rooms with TV, shower, sink, toilet, and access to a sleek terrace bar. (☎ 03 80 96 64 40; fax 03 80 97 00 18. Breakfast €5. Reception M-F 7am-9pm, Sa-Su by reservation only. Reservations suggested during summer. Most singles and doubles €35, some €45-55. AmEx/MC/V.) The **Hôtel des Gourmets ❷,** 4 rue Varenne, offers large, beautifully furnished rooms with large windows and high ceilings in an old house near the heart of the *vieille ville.* The attached restaurant serves local favorites from €14. (☎ 03 80 97 09 41; www.hotellesgourmets.fr.st. Breakfast €5.80. Free parking. Closed M-Tu and all Dec. Reservations suggested in summer for both hotel and restaurant. Singles €25.50-36.50; doubles €28.50-40; triples and quads €40; 6-person room €58. Extra bed €5. AmEx/MC/V.) **Hôtel des Cymaises ❹,** 7 rue du Renaudot, around the corner from rue Buffon, features cable TV, spacious rooms, immaculate wooden floors, and beautifully maintained grounds. (☎ 03 80 97 21 44; www.hotelcymaises.com. Breakfast €6.30. Reservations suggested. Singles and doubles equipped with shower, toilet, and sink €48.5-57.50; triples €68. MC/V.) **Camping Municipal du Lac de Pont ❶,** 3km south of Sémur, offers a three-star spot in the sun next to a scenic lake with a beach, tennis courts, bike rental, laundry, and a mini-mart. From pl. de l'Ancienne Comédie, follow signs to "camping." (☎ 03 80 97 01 26. Open May to mid-Sept. Reception 9am-noon and 4-8pm. €3.10 per person, €1.80 per site or child, €1.60 per car. Electricity €2.50.)

⊡ FOOD. A stroll along rue Buffon reveals a number of attractive dining options, although the tasty *crêpes bourguignonnes* (€7) make **◼La Goulue ❷,** 15 rue Buffon, a standout with colorful decor, outdoor dining, and huge portions. (☎ 03 80 97 28 97. Crêpes €5.50 and up, *tartiflettes* €7-18, 3-course *menu du marché* €9.50, dessert €4. Open 11:30am-2:30pm and 7-11pm. MC/V.) **Le Calibressane ❸,** 16 rue

Févret, located just around the corner from rue Buffon, provides a taste of California. Enjoy their special *chile con carne de Jill* (€12.25) served in a wood-trimmed dining room. (☎03 80 97 32 40. Fish from €11.50; *menus* from €17.50. Reservations suggested in summer. Open Tu-Th noon-2pm and 7-9:30pm, F until 10pm, Sa until 10:30pm. Closed Sa afternoon, Su night, and M. MC/V.) **Le Sagittaire ❷**, 15 rue de la Liberté, has inexpensive Italian dishes, including dependable pizzas (€5.50-8.20) and pastas. (☎03 80 97 23 91. 3-course weekday lunch *menu* €9. Open daily noon-2:30pm and 7-11pm. AmEx/MC/V.)

For **groceries**, stop in at the **Petit Casino** supermarket, located directly across from the church. (☎03 80 96 61 21. Open Su 9am-12:30pm, Tu-Sa 8am-12:30pm and 3-7:30pm. MC/V.) Small **markets** open at pl. Charles de Gaulle (Th morning), and at pl. Notre Dame (Su morning).

◙ SIGHTS. The tourist office schedules walking tours of the city, offers free brochures with self-guided itineraries, and also runs a 45min. *petit train* in the summer. (July-Aug. Su and Tu-Sa 5pm-10pm; Sept.-June for groups by reservation only. Groups must reserve in advance. €4, children €2.50.) Walk around the ramparts and the orchard-lined Armençon river. Romantics can take a moonlit walk down to the charming and little-touristed **Pont Pinard** for a breathtaking view of the illuminated *vieille ville*. (10min. on foot. From the rue du Rempart, walk away from Notre-Dame and make a left onto rue du Fourneau, then follow the signs. *Vieille ville* illuminated mid-June to Sept. 10pm-midnight.)

In the medieval town, down rue Buffon, mossy gargoyles menace the *place* from the 15th-century Gothic facade of the **Collégiale Notre-Dame**, which is currently getting a much-needed face-lift. The 13th-century tympanum on the **porte des Bleds** faces rue Notre Dame, and two sculpted snails slime their way to St. Thomas's feet on the skinnier left pillar—no doubt seeking divine intervention to save them from their likely fate in Alsace: a quick dip in a bowl of tasty butter-and-garlic sauce. Be sure to check out the church interior, if only for a glimpse of a surprising stained glass memorial to fallen American WWI soldiers, which features crossed American and French flags and portraits of the fallen. A **light show** (*son-et-lumière*) run by the church recounts the city's history. (☎03 80 97 05 96. Open daily 9am-noon and 2-6pm. Light show 45min. July-Aug. Su and F-Sa 10:30pm; Sept.-May by reservation.) Behind the church lies a quiet **park** perfect for a picnic.

The comprehensive **Musée**, rue Jean-Jacques Cottenot, dabbles in a bit of everything—the eerie zoology room is worth a look. (Open Su-M and W-Sa 2-6pm. €3.10, €1.10 for students.)

◪◪ ENTERTAINMENT AND NIGHTLIFE. At around 300 seats, the **Théâtre Municipale**, 11 rue du Rempart, is the smallest opera house in France. Stop by and enjoy the impressive acoustics and unique *architecture à l'italienne*. (Check the tourist office for the season's schedule.) To seek out bars and *brasseries* at night, walk the **rue Buffon** or **rue de la Liberté**.

With its absurd festivities, you won't want to miss the **Fêtes des Fous au Bourg Notre-Dame,** when locals recreate an ancient medieval festival that reversed the traditional social order, by electing a King and Queen of the Fous (the insane). Join the "crazy" locals and dance around bonfires dressed as a sorcerer, or arm yourself with fake medieval weapons and help them fight pretend dragons. Donkey rides all day for everyone. The festival is held from 8am to 11pm on a weekend day between late May and early June; call the tourist office for the 2005 dates.

BURGUNDY

RHÔNE-ALPS

As the Alps-bound train leaves the rolling countryside and begins its long climb into the mountains, riders abandon their newspapers to watch a stunning transformation. Hills give way to craggy peaks, riverbeds to stream-cut gorges, cows to mountain goats. In the high Alps, mountainsides blanketed with wildflowers stretch unendingly toward snowfields and glaciers. A trip to the region can hardly be complete without at least a glimpse of Mont Blanc, Western Europe's highest peak. In addition to these soaring mountains, the green Chartreuse and Vercors ranges are gentler but equally breathtaking. Summer and winter visitors will find the most dependable weather, accompanied, naturally, by the biggest crowds. Alpine air is an elixir for all city-weary souls, and skiers and hikers face a mind-boggling array of opportunities.

The Alps are split between two historical provinces: Savoie and the Dauphiné. Savoie, bearing the name of the oldest royal house in all of Europe, includes the peaks of Haute Savoie, the expansive Tarentaise Valley, and the awesome Vanoise National Park. The Dauphiné includes the Chartreuse Valley, Vercors Regional Park, Ecrins National Park, and the Belledonne and Oisans Mountains. The region first became independent in the 11th century, under Guiges I, and derived its name when his great-grandson Guiges IV took the surname "Dauphin" (dolphin). In the 14th century, when the last independent Dauphin finally sold all of his lands to France, the French monarchs adopted the practice of ceding the province to the heir to the throne, the Dauphin. In the 15th century, Louis XI established a permanent *parlement* (court) in Grenoble (p. 426), which has since become the area's cultural and intellectual capital.

HIGHLIGHTS OF RHÔNE-ALPS

CHILL WITH CHAMOIS (the antelope's smaller cousin) as you take in the amazing scenery along the many trails in the **Vanoise National Park** (p. 451), the Alps' premier wildlife preserve.

LEARN what just a little creativity and a lot of time can do at Hauterives's **Palais Idéal** (p. 433), a surreal fortress built over the course of 33 years by the local postman.

INDULGE in gourmet luxury in **Lyon** (p. 414), arguably France's finest culinary center.

LYON

Ultra-modern, ultra-friendly, and undeniably gourmet, Lyon (pop. 450,000) is more relaxed than Paris and claims a few centuries' more history. Connected by Roman roads to both Italy and the Atlantic, Lyon became a provincial capital of Gaul and its status has endured into modern times. During the Renaissance, encouraged by the city's tax-free permanent markets, foreign merchants and bankers set up shop; then, in the 15th century, Lyon became Europe's printing house. Silkworms imported from China in the 16th century solidified the city's position as an economic power. The ornate facades and elegant courtyards of the 16th-century townhouses in *Vieux Lyon*, spared from the urban renewal of the early 1960s, attest to this period of wealth. These buildings played a major role in Lyon's men-

RHÔNE-ALPS

Rhône-Alps

tion as a UNESCO World Heritage sight in 1998. Today Lyon is the stomping ground of world-renowned chefs Paul Bocuse and Georges Blanc, and an incubator of new culinary genius. There's no doubt one can eat well at one of the masters' spin-off restaurants, and just about anywhere else in this vibrant city.

◩ INTERCITY TRANSPORTATION

Flights: Aéroport Lyon-Saint-Exupéry (☎04 72 22 72 21). The TGV, which stops at the airport, is cheaper and more convenient than the daily flights to Paris. **Satobuses/ Navette Aéroport** (☎04 72 68 72 17) **shuttles** to Gare de la Part-Dieu, Gare de Perrache, and subway stops Grange-Blanche, Jean Mace, and Mermoz Pinel (every 20min., €8.50). **Air France,** 17 rue Victor Hugo, 2ème (☎08 20 82 08 20), has 6 daily flights to Paris's Orly and Roissy airports (€101-207).

Trains: Trains passing through Lyon stop at **Gare de la Part-Dieu,** bd. Marius Vivier-Merle (M: Part-Dieu), in the business district on the Rhône's east bank, and trains terminating in Lyon continue to **Gare de Perrache,** pl. Carnot (M: Perrache). SNCF trains go from both stations to: **Dijon** (2hr., 16 per day, €22.50); **Grenoble** (1¼hr., 19 per day 6:10am-12:20am, €16.30); **Marseille** (3hr., 17 per day, €35.20); **Nice** (6hr., 12 per day, €51); **Paris** (2hr., 26 TGV per day, €55-70); **Strasbourg** (5½hr., 5 per day, €42.30); **Geneva, Switzerland** (2hr., 13 per day, €19.90). Info desk at Gare de la Part-Dieu open M-F 9am-7pm and Sa 9am-6:30pm; ticket windows open M-Th and Sa 5:15am-11pm, F and Su 5:15am-midnight. Gare de Perrache open daily 5am-12:30am; ticket window open M-Sa 9am-7pm. Also, there is an **SNCF Boutique** at 2 pl. Bellecour, near the tourist office. Open M-F 9am-6:45pm, Sa 10am-6:30pm.

Buses: On the lowest level of the Gare de Perrache and at Gorge de Loup in the 9ème (☎04 72 61 72 61 for both). Domestic companies include **Philibert** (☎04 78 98 56 00) and **Transport Verney** (☎04 78 70 21 01), but it's almost always cheaper, faster, and simpler to take the train. **Eurolines** (☎04 72 56 95 30; fax 04 72 41 72 43) travels out of France; office on the main floor of Perrache M-Sa open 9am-9pm.

Bike Rentals: Holiday Bikes, 199 rue Vendôme, 3ème (☎04 78 60 11 10; www.holiday-bikes.com). €12 per day; €250 deposit. Open daily 9am-12:30pm and 3-7pm. AmEx/MC/V. Paths run along the Saône.

◩ ORIENTATION

Lyon is navigable thanks to its largely north-south running streets and the parallel rivers which separate the city into three major sections. Another good way to orient yourself is to use the **Fourvière,** a huge hill with a Basilica looming over *Vieux Lyon* in the west, and the **Tour du Crédit Lyonnais,** a reddish-brown "crayon" towering over Part-Dieu, in the east. Lyon has two major squares; **place Bellecour,** containing the tourist office and numerous bookstores, lies toward the south, while **place des Terraux,** with the Hôtel de Ville and its giant statue of four horses, lies about a 15min. walk to the north.

Lyon is divided into nine **arrondissements;** the 1er, 2ème, and 4ème lie on the **presqu'île** (peninsula), a narrow strip of land jutting south toward the confluence of the Saône and Rhône rivers. Starting in the south, the 2ème (the city center) includes the Perrache train station and place Bellecour, as well as most of the city's boutiques, hotels, and fast-food joints. The 1er is home to the nocturnal Terraux neighborhood, with its sidewalk cafes and student-packed bars. Farther north, the *presqu'île* widens into the 4ème and the Croix-Rousse, a residential neighborhood that once housed Lyon's silk industry. The main pedestrian arteries of the *presqu'île* are **rue de la République,** affectionately known as "la Ré," to the northeast of pl. Bellecour, and **rue Victor Hugo,** to the south of Bellecour.

To the west of the Saône lies the oldest part of the city, *Vieux Lyon*, with narrow cobblestone streets and a many traditional restaurants. Here you will also find the **Fourvière** hill, with a Roman theater, a basilica, and fabulous views. Most of Lyon's permanent population, however, live east of the Rhône in the *3ème* and *6ème-8ème*, home to the **Part-Dieu** train station and modern commercial complex.

Most trains terminating in Lyon stop at both the **Gare de Perrache** and the **Gare de la Part-Dieu**. Perrache is more central and considered safer at night, but Part-Dieu is larger and sees more long-distance trains. Both are connected to Lyon's highly efficient **metro**, which is the fastest way to the tourist office in the **tourist pavilion** on pl. Bellecour. To walk from Perrache, head straight onto pedestrian rue Victor Hugo and follow it until it terminates at pl. Bellecour; the tourist office will be on the right (15 minutes). From Part-Dieu, leave the station by the fountains and turn right, walk for three blocks and turn left onto cours Lafayette, cross the Rhône on pont Lafayette and continue as the street changes to pl. des Cordeliers, then turn left on rue de la République and follow it to pl. Bellecour (30 minutes). Lyon is a reasonably safe city, though travelers should watch out for pickpockets inside Perrache, at pl. des Terraux, and in pl. Bellecour's crowds.

⊫ LOCAL TRANSPORTATION

TCL (☎08 20 42 70 00; www.tcl.fr) has info offices at both bus stations and all major metro stops. *Plan de Poche* (pocket map) available from the tourist office or any TCL branch. Tickets are valid for all methods of mass transport, including the **metro, buses, funiculars,** and **trams**. Tickets €1.40; *carnet* of 10 €11.50, student discount includes 10 passes valid for 1 month €9.90. 1pass is valid 1hr. in 1 direction, connections included. *Ticket Liberté* day pass (€4.20) is a great deal for short-term visitors. The efficient **metro** runs 5am-midnight, as do **buses** and **trams**, which have 2 different lines; T1 connects Part-Dieu to Perrache directly. **Funiculars** (cable cars) swing between the Vieux Lyon metro stop, pl. St-Jean, and the top of Fourvière and St-Just until midnight.

Taxis: Taxi Radio de Lyon ☎04 72 10 86 86. Perrache to airport €36 during the day, €49 at night; Part-Dieu to airport €31/€49. 24hr. **Allô Taxi** ☎04 78 28 23 23.

⊠ PRACTICAL INFORMATION

TOURIST AND FINANCIAL SERVICES

Tourist Office: In the Pavilion, at pl. Bellecour, *2ème* (☎04 72 77 69 69; www.lyon-france.com). M: Bellecour. Staff is eager to help. Brochures and info on rooms and restaurants. Free, indispensable map and guide in 7 languages has museum listings, a subway map, and a blow-up of the city center. Ask about the wide range of excellent city tours in French (and English during the summer). Tours €9, students €5. 3hr. audio tours of the city are available in 4 languages; €6.10. Also available is an insightful book that describes walking tours through the 5 quarters included in the UNESCO World Heritage list (€5.35). Equally invaluable is the *Lyon City Card*, which authorizes unlimited public transportation along with admission to the 14 biggest museums, tours, audio tours, and boat tours. Valid for 1, 2, or 3 days; €18/€28/€38. Internet Access available but expensive. Open May-Oct. M-Sa 9am-7pm, Su 10am-6pm; Nov.-Apr. daily 10am-6pm. For info on entertainment and cinema, try the weekly *Lyon Poche* and *Guides de l'été de Lyon: Restaurant Nuits*, available in the tourist office, or the seasonal *Lyon Libertin* (€3), sold in many *tabacs*. For longer stays, pick up *Le Petit Paumé*, a free gold mine of all the city's goings-on. The office offers tours of the old city departing from in front of the Cathédrale St-Jean in *Vieux Lyon* (M: Vieux Lyon).

Bus Tours: Philibert (☎04 78 98 56 00; webescapes@philibert.fr). 1½hr. tour of Lyon, with audio guides in 6 languages. Tour starts at Perrache. Get on or off at any point and reconnect later on. Daily late Mar. to Oct. €15.

Consulates: Canada, 21 rue Bourgelat, 2ème (☎04 72 77 64 07), 1 block west of the Ampère-Victor Hugo metro. Open M-F 9am-noon. **Ireland,** 58 rue Victor Lagrange, 7ème (☎06 85 23 12 03). Open M-F by appointment only. **UK,** 24 rue Childebert, 2ème (☎04 72 77 81 70). M: Bellecour. Open M-F 9am-12:30pm and 2-5:30pm. **US,** 1 quai Jules Cormant, 2ème (☎04 78 38 33 03). Open daily by appointment only 10am-noon and 2-5pm.

Currency Exchange: no commission at **Goldfinger S.A.R.L.,** 81 rue de la République (☎04 72 40 06 00). Open M-Sa 9:30am-6:30pm.

LOCAL SERVICES

English-Language Bookstore: Decitre, 6 pl. Bellecour, 2ème (☎04 26 68 00 12; www.decitre.fr). Fantastic selection and Anglo staff. Open M-Sa 9:30am-7pm. MC/V.

Cultural Center: Centre Regionale d'Informations de Jeunesse (CRIJ), 9 quai des Célestins (☎04 72 77 00 66; www.j-net.org), lists jobs and apartments. Has Internet. Open M noon-7pm, Tu-F 10am-6pm, Sa 10am-1pm and 2-5pm. Closed Sa July-Aug.

Women's Center: Centre d'Information Féminine, 18 pl. Tolozan, 1er (☎04 78 39 32 25). Open M-F noon-1pm and 1:30-5pm.

Gay Support: Maison des Homosexualities, (☎04 78 27 10 10). Call for events schedule.

Laundromat: Laverie, 19 rue Ste-Hélène, north of pl. Ampère, 2ème. Open daily 7:30am-8:30pm. €3 wash. **Laverie,** 51 rue de la Charité, 2ème. Open daily 6am-10pm. €2.90 wash.

EMERGENCY AND COMMUNICATIONS

Police: 47 rue de la Charité (☎04 78 42 26 56).

Crisis Lines: SOS Amitié (☎04 78 29 88 88). **SOS Racisme** (☎04 78 39 24 44). Open Tu 6-8pm. **AIDS info service,** 2 rue Montebello, 3ème (toll-free ☎0800 840 800).

24hr. Pharmacy: Pharmacie Blanchet, 5 pl. des Cordeliers, 2ème (☎04 78 42 12 42).

Hospitals: All hospitals should have English-speaking doctors on call. **Hôpital Edouard Herriot,** 5 pl. Arsonval. M: Grange Blanche. Best for serious emergencies, but far from the center of town. More central is **Hôpital Hôtel-Dieu,** 1 pl. de l'Hôpital, 2ème, near quai du Rhône. The central city hospital line, ☎08 20 08 20 09, will tell you where to go. There's also **Hôpital Antiquaille,** rue de l'Antiquaille, in Roman Lyon.

Medical Assistance: SOS Médecins, 10 pl. Dumas de Loire (☎04 78 83 51 51), arranges home visits.

Internet Access: Internet stations and cafes cluster along rue de Marseille, in the 7ème, across the river from the Perrache station. **Taxiphone Communications,** 15-17 rue Montebello (☎04 78 14 54 25). €0.50 for 15min., €1 for 30min., €2 per hr. Open daily 8:30am-10:30pm. **Connectik Café,** 19 quai St-Antoine, 2ème (☎04 72 77 98 85). €6 divisible card allows 1hr. of use. Open M-Sa 10am-7pm.

Post Office: pl. Antonin Poncet, 2ème (☎04 72 40 65 22), next to pl. Bellecour. **Currency exchange.** Open M-F 8am-7pm, Sa 8am-12:30pm.

Postal Codes: 69001-69009; last digit indicates *arrondissement.*

◗ ACCOMMODATIONS AND CAMPING

France's second-largest financial center (after Paris, *bien sûr*) is filled on most weekday nights with businessmen who leave town on the weekends. Fall is the busiest season for accommodations in Lyon; it's easier and cheaper to find a place in the summer, but it is still prudent to make reservations ahead of time. Budget hotels cluster east of pl. Carnot; prices rise as one approaches pl. Bellecour, but there are some inexpensive options just north of pl. des Terraux. The accommodations in *Vieux Lyon*, aside from the hostel, tend to break budgets.

■ **Auberge de Jeunesse (HI),** 41-45 montée du Chemin Neuf (☎04 78 15 05 50; fax 04 78 15 05 51). M: Vieux Lyon. Panoramic views from the grassy terrace and a lively bar make this hostel the place to meet fellow backpackers in Lyon. It's a hike up the hill, and the bathrooms may be less than spotless, but a friendly staff and prime location in *Vieux Lyon* make up for any grit. Bar, laundry (€4.05), Internet (€2.25 per 15min.), and kitchen. Breakfast included. Sheets €2.80. Reception 24hr. Reservations recommended, especially in the summer season. Most rooms have 4 to 8 bunks, one has 14. €13.25 per bed. MC/V. HI members only. ❶

■ **Hôtel St-Vincent,** 9 rue Pareille, 1er (☎04 78 27 22 56; www.hotel-saintvincent.com), just off quai St-Vincent. The friendly owners rent airy, tastefully decorated rooms, within stumbling distance of much nightlife. Breakfast €5.50. Reception 24hr. Reserve ahead. Singles with shower €35, with toilet €40; doubles €38-47; triples €47. MC/V. ❸

Hôtel Iris, 36 rue de l'Arbre Sec (☎04 78 39 93 80; www.hoteliris.freesurf.fr). This cozy little convent-turned-hotel is often filled with return customers. The sunny yellow walls of the breakfast room reflect the refined taste of the artistic owner. Breakfast €5. Reservations recommended 2 weeks in advance during the summer. Singles €29-41; doubles €32-50, triples €51. MC/V. ❸

Hôtel de Paris, 16 rue de la Platière, 1er (☎04 78 28 00 95; www.hoteldeparis-lyon.com). Elegant and full of character, this hotel offers spacious, spotless rooms that range from classic to futuristic. The comfortable lobby is adorned with black-and-white Impressionist drawings of Lyon. Breakfast €6.50. Reception 24hr. Singles €42; doubles €49-68; triples €78; quads €81. AmEx/MC/V. ❹

Hôtel Vaubecour, 28 rue Vaubecour, 2ème (☎04 78 37 44 91; fax 04 78 42 90 17). Good spot hidden away on the 3rd floor of an antique building. Breakfast €3.70. Reception daily 7am-10pm. Reserve June-Aug. Singles from €30; doubles from €35. Extra bed €13. MC/V. ❸

Hôtel d'Ainay, 14 rue des Remparts d'Ainay, 2ème (☎04 78 42 43 42; fax 04 72 77 51 90). M: Ampère-Victor Hugo. The d'Ainay offers basic, cheap, airy rooms. No public shower for rooms without a private one. Breakfast €4.50. Reception daily 6am-10pm. Singles €26, with shower €40; doubles €31/€43. MC/V. ❸

Camping Dardilly, 10km from Lyon (☎04 78 35 64 55). From Hôtel de Ville, bus #19 (dir: Ecully-Dardilly) to Parc d'Affaires. Pool, TV, and restaurant. Reception daily 8am-10pm. €3.20 per person; tent €6.30, caravan €8.20, car free. Electricity €3. MC/V. ❶

◖ FOOD

The galaxy of Michelin stars adorning Lyon's restaurants confirms its status as the gastronomic capital of the Western world. Lyonnais food is bizarre, elegant, creative, and always delicious; one delicacy consists of cow's feet prepared in a subtle, creamy sauce. Best of all, one can dine in Lyon for a wide scope of prices and still enjoy uniformly excellent cuisine.

THE PRIDE OF LYON

The pinnacle of the Lyonnais food scene is ■**Chez Paul Bocuse** ❺, 9km out of town, where meals cost approximately the equivalent of Andorra's GNP. For Lyonnais master Jean-Paul Lacombe's cuisine, head to **Léon de Lyon** ❺, 1 rue Pléney, 1er. (☎04 72 10 11 12. *Menus* €57, €105, and €135. Open Tu-Sa noon-2pm and 7:30-10pm. MC/V.) For Philippe Chavent's, try **La Tour Rose** ❺, at 22 rue du Boeuf, 5ème. (☎04 78 92 69 26. *Menus* €53, €91, and €106. Open M-Sa noon-2:30pm and 7-11.

RHÔNE-ALPS

RHÔNE-ALPS

RHÔNE-ALPS

MC/V.) Some of these restaurants occasionally have more accessible weekend buffet brunches hovering around €30-40; check outside or call. However, gourmands need not sell their souls to enjoy Bocusian cuisine; the master has several spin-off restaurants in Lyon, themed around the four corners of the earth. At **Le Nord ❹**, 18 rue Neuve, *2ème*, Bocuse's traditional food graces the €18 *menu* in a famed century-old *brasserie*. (☎04 78 28 24 54; fax 04 72 10 69 68. Extravagant desserts €5-6. Open daily noon-2:30pm and 7pm-11pm, F-Sa until midnight. AmEx/ MC/V.) Bocuse's kitchens serve up Mediterranean fare at the appropriately named **Le Sud ❸**, 11 pl. Antonin Poncet, *2ème*, which has an €18 *menu*, plus pizza and pasta from around €11, in a beautiful formal setting. (☎04 72 77 80 00. Open daily noon-2:30pm and 7pm-11pm, F-Sa until midnight. AmEx/MC/V.) Whether you're heading north or south, reserve a few days ahead.

Locals snap up the tasty *cocons* (chocolates in marzipan), made in the grand *pâtisserie* ▨**Bernachon**, 42 cours F. Roosevelt.

OTHER FLEURS-DE-LYON

For a happy medium between *haute cuisine* and university canteens, try one of Lyon's many **bouchons**, descendants of the inns where travelers stopped to dine and have their horses *bouchonné* (rubbed down). These cozy restaurants serving local fare can be found along **rue Mercière** and **rue des Marronniers** in the *2ème*. Although frowned on by locals as touristy, most places in *Vieux Lyon* are sure to satisfy with style. The *bouchons* along **rue St-Jean** have €13-16 *menus*. The trendy locals eat at lantern-strewn **rue Mercerie;** dinner *menus* tend to be €16-20. Cheaper Chinese fast-food restaurants and *brasseries* line the wide streets off **rue de la République** (*2ème*), and dozens of kebab joints surround the Hôtel de Ville.

▨ **Chez Mounier,** 3 rue des Marronniers, *2ème* (☎04 78 37 79 26). Cheerful staff serve tasty, hearty traditional dishes in a sparsely decorated but cozy setting. 4-course *menus* €10, €14, and €15. Open Tu-Sa noon-2pm and 7-10:30pm, Su noon-1:30pm. MC/V. ❸

▨ **Chabert et Fils,** 11 rue des Marronniers, *2ème* (☎04 78 37 01 94). A well-known, well-loved *bouchon*, 1 of 4 on rue des Marroniers run by the same family. *Museau de bœuf* (snout of cattle) is one of many unique *lyonnais* concoctions on the €16.50 *menu*. For dessert, try the exquisite, creamy *guignol* (€5.40), but plan to take an after-dinner nap after this rich delight. Lunch *menus* €8-12.50, dinner *menus* €16.50-33. Open daily noon-2pm and 7-11pm, F-Sa until 11:30pm. MC/V. ❸

Chez Marie-Danielle, 29 rue des Remparts d'Ainay (☎04 78 37 65 60), offers refreshing change from the male-dominated chef scene in Lyon; Marie-Danielle receives dozens of awards for her *lyonnais* fare served in a *brasserie*-style dining hall. Lunch *menu* €14, dinner *menu* €21.50. Open Tu-Sa noon-2pm and 7:30-10pm. MC/V. ❹

L'Assiette St-Jean, 10 rue St-Jean, *5ème* (☎04 72 41 96 20). A great *bouchon*, with unusual, archaic decor. *Foies de volaille* (chicken liver) €8, *menus* €13.60. Open June-Aug. Tu-Su noon-2pm and 7-10:30pm; Sept.-May W-Su 7-10:30pm. AmEx/MC/V. ❷

L'Etoile de l'Orient, 31 rue des Remparts d'Ainay, *2ème* (☎04 72 41 07 87). M: Ampère-Victor Hugo. Be sure to have some tea at this intimate Tunisian restaurant, run by an exceptionally warm couple. *Tajine* lamb €12, couscous dishes €8.50-15. *Menus* €10-25; vegetarian *menu* €15. Open M noon-2pm, Tu-Su noon-2pm and 7-11pm. ❸

SUPERMARKETS

There are **markets** open on the quais of the Rhône and Saône every morning 8am-1pm, except for Mondays, and small **supermarkets** and **épiceries** are close to nearly every major square, including Bellecour, pl. St-Jean, and pl. des Terreux. Ultra-gourmet products are sold at **Maréchal Centre,** rue de la Platière at rue Lanterne,

1er. (☎04 72 98 24 00. Open M-Th 9am-12:30pm and 3pm-8:30pm, Sa and Su 9am-8:30pm.) Lyon's many university restaurants may not boast any culinary master-pieces, but they're sure to please the wallet.

👁 SIGHTS

VIEUX LYON

Stacked against the Saône at the foot of the Fourvière hill, *Vieux Lyon*'s narrow streets wind between lively cafes, tree-lined squares, and magnificent medieval and Renaissance homes. The colorful *hôtels particuliers*, with their delicate carvings and ornate turrets, sprang up between the 15th and 18th centuries, when Lyon controlled Europe's silk and printing industries. The regal homes around **rue St-Jean, rue du Bœuf,** and **rue Juiverie** have housed Lyon's elite for 400 years.

TRABOULES. The distinguishing features of *Vieux Lyon* townhouses are their **tra-boules,** tunnels connecting parallel streets through a maze of courtyards, often with vaulted ceilings and statuary niches. Although their original purpose is still debated, many of the later *traboules* were constructed to transport silk safely from looms to storage rooms. During WWII, the passageways proved invaluable as information-gathering and escape routes for the Resistance (though some *résistants* found their way blocked by Germans at the exits). Many are open to the public at specific hours, especially in the morning. An informative 1hr. tour beginning near the Cathédrale St-Jean is the ideal way to see them, or pick up a list of addresses from the tourist office. (*Tours in English and French in summer every few days at 2:30pm, irregular hours during rest of year; consult tourist office. €9, students €5.*)

CATHÉDRALE ST-JEAN. The southern end of *Vieux Lyon* is dominated by soaring columns of the St-Jean Cathedral. Some of its multicolored stained-glass windows are replacements of the ones destroyed by Lyon's exploding bridges during the Nazi's hasty retreat in 1944. In the gallery, the shift from Romanesque to Gothic style is evident where the rows of arches have pointed tops. Inside, every hour between noon and 4pm, automatons pop out of the 14th-century ▓astronomical clock in a charming reenactment of the Annunciation. (*Cathedral open M-F 8am-noon and 2-7:30pm, Sa-Su 8am-noon and 2-5pm.*)

MUSEUMS. Down rue St-Jean, turn left on rue de la Fronde before pl. du Change for the **Hôtel de Gadagne,** a typical 16th-century *Vieux Lyon* building, and its relatively minor museums. The better of the two is the **Musée de la Marionette,** which displays puppets from around the world, including models of **Guignol,** the famed local cynic, and his quite inebriated friend, Gnaffron. The Museums are currently undergoing extensive restoration, and are tentatively set to reopen in September 2005. (*Pl. du Petit Collège, 5ème. M: Vieux Lyon. Check ☎04 78 56 74 06 or www.museegada-gne.com for info on reopening.*)

FOURVIÈRE AND ROMAN LYON

From the corner of rue du Bœuf and rue de la Bombarde in *Vieux Lyon*, climb the stairs heading straight up to reach **Fourvière Hill,** the nucleus of **Roman Lyon,** with its wealth of visit-worthy sites. From the top of the stairs, continue up via the rose-lined **Chemin de la Rosaire,** a series of switchbacks that leads through a garden to the **esplanade Fourvière,** where a model of the city indicates local landmarks. Most prefer to take the less strenuous **funicular** (known as *la ficelle*) to the top of the hill. It leaves from the *Vieux Lyon* metro station, at the head of av. A. Max. The **Tour de l'Observatoire,** on the eastern edge of the hilltop basilica, offers a more acute angle on the city. On a clear day, scan for Mont Blanc, about 200km to the east. *(Jardin de la Rosaire open daily 6:30am-9:30pm. Tour de l'Observatoire open W-Su 10am-noon and 2-6:30pm. €2, under 15 €1.)*

■ **BASILIQUE NOTRE-DAME DE FOURVIÈRE.** During the Franco-Prussian War, Lyon's archbishop vowed to build a church if the city was spared from attack. Today, the basilica's white, meringue-like exterior looms over the entire city (gorgeous or bizarre, depending on taste). The highlight of its ornate, colorful interior is the group of shimmering mosaics that depict religious scenes like Joan of Arc at Orléans. The low, heavy crypt used for mass was conceived by the architect Pierre Bossan to contrast with the impossibly high Byzantine basilica above. *(Behind the Esplanade at very top of the hill. Chapel open daily 7am-7pm; basilica open daily 8am-7pm.)*

MUSÉE GALLO-ROMAIN. The rooms and corridors of this brilliant museum, housing a collection of arms, pottery, statues, and jewelry are cut deep into the historic hillside of Fourvière. Romaholics will appreciate six large, luminous mosaics, a bronze tablet inscribed with a speech by Lyon's favorite son, Emperor Claudius, and a huge, half-cracked eggshell pot. Artifacts are labeled in English and French. *(Open Tu-Su Mar.-Oct. 10am-6pm; Nov.-Feb. 10am-5pm. €3.80, students €2.30. Th free.)*

PARC ARCHÉOLOGIQUE. Just next to the Minimes/Théâtre Romain funicular stop, the Parc holds the almost-too-well restored 2000-year-old **Théâtre Romain** and the **Odéon,** discovered when modern developers dug into the hill. Wander along the huge slabs of rock and gaze out over the city, or, on summer evenings, relax and enjoy the show; both function as venues during the **Nuits de Fourvière** (see **Festivals,** p. 423). *(Open daily Apr. 15-Sept. 15 9am-9pm; Sept. 16-Apr. 14 7am-7pm. Free.)*

LA PRESQU'ÎLE AND LES TERREAUX

Monumental squares, statues, and fountains are the trademarks of the *presqu'île,* the lively area lying between the Rhône and the Saône. At its heart is **place Belle-cour,** home to the tourist office and linking Lyon's two main pedestrian arteries. **Rue Victor Hugo** heads south toward the Perrache station, lined with boutiques and bladers. To the north, crowded **rue de la République,** or "la Ré," is the urban aorta of Lyon. It runs through **place de la République** and ends at **place Louis Pradel** in the 1*er*, at the tip of the Terreaux district, once a marshy wasteland. The area has been filled with soil, creating a chic neighborhood of dry terraces *(terreaux)* where bars, clubs, and sidewalk cafes keep things hopping long into the night.

Just to the West, in **la place des Terreaux,** sits the spectacular 17th-century facade of the **Hôtel de Ville,** framed by an illuminated field of miniature geysers. The **Opéra** building behind the Hôtel de Ville is a 19th-century Neoclassical edifice supporting what looks like an outsized airplane hangar, lit alluringly crimson after dark.

■ **MUSÉE DES BEAUX-ARTS.** This unassuming but excellent museum includes a comprehensive archaeological wing, a distinguished collection of French, Dutch, and Spanish paintings, works by Picasso, a section devoted to the Italian Renaissance, and a lovely sculpture garden. Surrounded by all-star Impressionist collections, even the museum's esoteric local works are delightful. A few cool surprises await museum-goers, including a Rodin bust of national hero Victor Hugo at the end of his life (1883), and an unbelievably large French coin collection. The museum's courtyard, open to the public, provides a much-needed sanctuary from the commotion of the square outside. *(20 pl. des Terreaux. ☎04 72 10 17 40. Open M, W-Th, and Sa-Su 10am-6pm, F 10:30am-8pm. Sculptures closed noon-1pm; paintings closed 1-2pm. €6, under 26 €4, students under 26 with ID free.)*

RHÔNE-ALPS

LA CROIX-ROUSSE AND THE SILK INDUSTRY

Though mass silk manufacturing is based elsewhere today, Lyon is proud of its historical dominance of the industry in Europe. Lyon's few remaining silk workers perform delicate handiwork, reconstructing and replicating rare patterns for museum and château displays.

■ MUSÉE HISTORIQUE DES TISSUS. In dark rooms, rows of costumes recall skirt-flouting, bosom-baring characters of the past. The collection also includes examples of 18th-century elite garb (like Marie-Antoinette's Versailles winter wardrobe), scraps of Byzantine textiles, and silk wall-hangings resmbling stained-glass windows. Included in admission is the neighboring **Musée des Arts Décoratifs,** housed in an 18th-century **hôtel.** The fully furnished rooms showcase an astounding array of clocks, painted plates, silverware, and furniture dating from the Renaissance to the present *(34 rue de la Charité, 2ème. ☎ 04 78 38 42 00. Tissus open Tu-Su 10am-5:30pm. Arts Décoratifs open Tu-Su 10am-noon and 2-5:30pm. Maps in English. Tour in French Su 3pm. €5, students €3.)*

LA MAISON DES CANUTS. Some old silk looms in a tiny back room are all that remain of the weaving techniques of the *canuts* (silk weavers). The Maison's shop sells silk made by its own *canuts*. A scarf costs €30 and up, but silk enthusiasts can take home a silkworm cocoon for €7 or less, or maybe just a handkerchief for €7. *(10-12 rue d'Ivry, 4ème. ☎ 04 78 28 62 04; fax 04 78 28 16 93. Tours by arrangement. Open M-F 9am-noon and 2-6:30pm, Sa until 6pm. Closed M in Aug. €3.80, students €2.30.)*

EAST OF THE RHÔNE AND MODERN LYON

Lyon's newest train station and monstrous space-age mall form the core of the ultra-modern Part-Dieu district. Locals call the commercial **Tour du Crédit Lyonnais** *Le Crayon* for its unintentional resemblance to a giant pencil standing on end. Next to it, the shell-shaped **Auditorium Maurice Ravel** hosts major cultural events.

CENTRE D'HISTOIRE DE LA RÉSISTANCE ET DE LA DÉPORTATION. Housed in a building where Nazis tortured detainees during the Occupation, this museum presents an impressive but sobering collection of documents, photos, and films of the Resistance, which was based in Lyon. There's also an area set up for children. *(14 av. Berthelot, 7ème. M: Jean Macé. ☎ 04 78 72 23 11. Open W-Su 9am-5:30pm. €3.80, students €2, under 18 free. Admission includes an audioguide in French, English, or German.)*

MUSÉE D'ART CONTEMPORAIN. This extensive, entertaining mecca of modern art resides in the futuristic **Cité International de Lyon,** a super-modern complex with shops, theaters, and Interpol's world headquarters. All the museum's exhibits are temporary; even the walls are built anew for each installation. *(Quai Charles de Gaulle, next to Parc de la Tête d'Or, 6ème. Take bus #4 from M: Foch. ☎ 04 72 69 17 18; www.moca-lyon.org. Open Su and W-Sa noon-7pm. €5, students €2, under 18 free.)*

INSTITUT LUMIÈRE. A must for film buffs, the museum's exhibits chronicle the exploits of the brothers Lumière, who invented the motion picture in 1895. The small museum is full of intriguing factoids: Louis created a forerunner to holograms in 1920. The Institut's complex also includes a movie theater, "Le Hangar du Premier-Film." *(25 rue du Premier-Film, 8ème. M: Monplaisir Lumière. ☎ 04 78 78 18 95; www.institut-lumiere.org. Open Su and Tu-Sa 11am-7pm. €5.50, students €4.50.)*

PARC DE LA TÊTE D'OR. This massive park, one of the largest in Europe, sprawls over 259 acres. Its name derives from the legend that a golden head of Jesus lies buried somewhere on its grounds. In summer, paddle boats are available for a visit to its artificial green lake and island. Reindeer, elephants, and other animals fill the free zoo, and giant greenhouses encase a botanical garden. People can also enjoy a stroll along the 60,000-bush rose gardens that stretch magnificently along the Western side. *(M: Charpennes or Tram T1 from Perrache, dir: IUT-Feyssine. ☎ 04 78 89 02 03. Open daily mid-Apr. to mid-Oct. 6am-11pm; mid-Oct. to mid-Apr. 6am-9pm.)*

♫ ENTERTAINMENT

LIVE PERFORMANCES

Lyon's major stage theater is the **Théâtre des Célestins**, pl. des Célestins, 2ème. (☎ 04 72 77 40 00; box office open Tu-Sa noon-7pm. Tickets €8-29, discounts for under 26 and over 65.) **Closed for renovations until winter 2005.** The **Opéra**, pl. de la Comédie, 1er (☎ 04 72 00 45 45; www.opera-lyon.com), has pricey tickets (€5-80), but €8 tickets for those under 26 and over 65 go on sale 15min. before the show. (Reservations office open M-Sa noon-7pm.) The acclaimed **Orchestre National de Lyon** plays a full season, lasting from Oct.-June. (☎ 04 78 95 95 95. Tickets €15-50.) The **Maison de la Danse**, 8 av. Jean Mermoz, 8ème, keeps pace with the dance scene. (☎ 04 72 78 18 18; www.maisondeladanse.com. Tickets €12-35.)

CINEMA

As the birthplace of cinema, Lyon is a superb place to see quality film. Both the **Cinéma Opéra**, 6 rue J. Serlin (☎ 04 78 28 80 08), and **Le Cinéma**, 18 impasse St-Poly-carpe (☎ 04 78 39 09 72), specialize in black-and-white undubbed classics offered every night of the week. (€6.50, €5.50 for students; W night €5.50 for all.)

⬚ SHOPPING

Serious shoppers and awestruck admirers of French fashion will enjoy Lyon. The Centre Part-Dieu, across bd. Marius Vivier-Merle from Gare de la Part-Dieu, is the closest thing homesick Americans will find to the local **mall**, containing chain clothing stores, food shops, a movie theater, bowling alley, and a huge Galleries Lafayette. The 1er and 2ème *arrondissements*, particularly **rue de la République** and the charming **passage de l'Argue**, form a regular mecca of upscale brand-name stores. Funky ethnic **boutiques** and poster stores cluster around rue St-Jean in Vieux Lyon, and **bookstores** surround pl. Bellecour. Bargain-hunters will enjoy the massive **flea market** that sets up on Mondays on the quais to the east of the Saône.

♟ NIGHTLIFE

Nightlife in Lyon is fast and furious. There is a row of semi-exclusive joints off the Saône, on quais Romain Rolland, de Bondy, and Pierre Scize in *Vieux Lyon* (5ème), but the city's best and most accessible late-night spots are the riverboat dance clubs by the east bank of the Rhône. Students buzz in and out of a series of tiny, intimate bars on **rue Ste-Catherine** (1er) until 1am, before heading to the clubs. For those in search of a more mellow (and expensive) evening, the streets off **rue Mercerie** host several **jazz and piano bars**. When school is out of session for the summer, the scene is only lively on weekends. More suggestions can be found in *Lyon Libertin* (€3) and *Guides de l'Été de Lyon: Restaurant/Nuits*, available at *tabacs* and the tourist office, respectively. The tourist office's city guide lists spots that cater to Lyon's active gay community, and *Le Petit Paumé* offers superb tips. The most popular gay spots are in the 1er.

■ **Le Fish,** across from 21 quai Augagneur (☎ 04 72 84 98 98), plays salsa, jungle, hip-hop, disco, and house on a swank boat. This club is the choice spot for *les jeunes de Lyon*. F-Sa cover €11 includes 1st drink, free before 11pm. Open W-Th 10pm-5am, F-Sa 10pm-6am. Students only.

Ayers Rock Café, 2 rue Désirée (☎ 04 78 29 13 45), an Aussie bar is a melange of international 20-somethings. Right next door, the **Cosmopolitan** (☎ 04 72 07 09 80), serves New York-themed drinks. Both are usually packed with students, and offer shooters for €3 and cocktails starting at €6. Cosmo is a little darker, a little less international, and a little more restrained. Ayers open daily 9pm-3am; Cosmo open M-Sa 8pm-3am; Tu student nights have happy hour all night.

Tavern of the Drunken Parrot, next door to Le Chantier on rue Ste-Catherine (☎04 78 28 01 39), serves homemade, extremely potent rum drinks (€2); try the citron or coco. Combined with the ship motif, the drinks have eager customers treading toward the edge of the plank. Open Su-Th 6pm-1am, F-Sa 6pm-3am.

Le Funambule, 29 rue de l'Arbre Sec (☎04 72 07 86 70), is a darkly lit, hip bar for the late-20s crowd. Wine €2-4 per glass. Open Tu-Th 7pm-1am, F-Sa 7pm-3am.

Le Chantier, 20 rue Ste-Catherine (☎04 78 39 05 56), offers 12 tequila shots for €15.25. Slip down a spiral slide to reach the dance floor downstairs, which is filled with students and locals. Open M-Sa 8pm-3am, sometimes later.

La Marquise (☎04 78 71 78 71; www.marquise.net), next door to Le Fish, spends less on the boat but more on big-name jungle and house DJs. Cover €6 for occasional soirées à thème. Open W-Sa 11pm-dawn.

L'United Café, impasse de la Pêcherie (☎04 78 29 93 18), in an alley off quai de la Pêcherie. The weekend club circuit starts here around midnight, with American and Latino dance hits. Theme nights range from post office to beach party—and there are lip-shaped urinals to boot. Drinks €3-6. Open daily 10:30pm-5am.

DV1, 6 rue Violi (☎04 72 07 72 62), off rue Royale, north of pl. Louis Pradel. Drag queens nightly, with a huge dance floor. A mostly male, mid-20s to mid-30s crowd. Drinks €3.50-4. Open T-Su 11:30pm-5am.

▓ FESTIVALS

During the summer, Lyon has a festival or special event nearly every week. The **Fête de la Musique** (June 21) and **Bastille Day** (July 14) naturally entail major partying. The end of June launches the two-week, nearby **Festival du Jazz à Vienne** (p. 426). **Les Nuits de Fourvière** is a three-month summer festival held in the ancient Théâtre Romain at Lyon, from mid-June through mid-Sept. Popular performers are in the mix with classical concerts, movies, dance, and plays. (☎04 72 32 00 00; www.nuitsdefourviere.fr. €10-35 tickets and info at the Théâtre Romain or the FNAC shop on rue de la République.)

The biennial **Festival de Musique du Vieux Lyon,** 5 pl. du Petit Collège, 5ème, brings artists from around the world to perform in Lyon's old town in early and mid-December. (☎04 78 38 09 09. Tickets €15-36.) Every December 8, locals place candles in their windows and ascend with tapers to the basilica for the **Fête des Lumières.**

▶ DAYTRIPS FROM LYON

▓PÉROUGES

Trains run from Lyon (30min.; M-Sa 18 per day, Su 9 per day; €5.80) to Mexiemeux-Pérouges. From the station, turn left and follow the road around the curve to the round-about. From there, take a left and continue until the intersection at the Gendarmerie; take a right, following the sign for Pérouges. Follow the road up the hill and take a right onto a steep dirt pedestrian road, which runs right to the city gates (15min. from station). Arriving in the morning is the best chance before tour groups flood the main square.

This tiny, historic hilltop hamlet is such a source of pride for Europe that it was the site of the G-7 summit in 1996. Pérouges's streets, affectionately called **galets,** are made with age-worn stones collected from nearby rivers whose shape and muted colors blend with the town's masonry. Exquisitely preserved, the houses, streets, and gardens, complemented by draping flora, invoke romantic visions of royalty. While legend has it that Pérouges was built by a tribe of Gauls from Italy, the town has changed nationalities many times due to various feuds between dukes and kings. Most of the buildings date to the 15th century, a period of prosperity during which weaving dominated. The town's culinary specialty is *galette de Pérouges* (a doughy pastry made with sugar and butter), which is served with *cerdon*, a magnificent wine.

A superb way to see the evolution of the area's history is to stop in at the **Musée de Vieux Pérouges,** in the Maison des Princes, which showcases ancient wares donated by citizens. The museum turret has a fabulous view of the rooftops below. (Open June-Oct. M-F 10am-noon and 2-6pm, Sa-Su 10am-7pm. €4, children €2.) The **tourist office** can assist in getting around. (☎ 04 74 61 01 14. Open May-Sept. M-F 9am-noon and 2-5pm. Call ahead during the low season.)

BEAUJOLAIS VALLEY

The most beautiful and authentic areas in the Beaujolais are difficult to access by public transportation; trains run between Mâcon and Lyon, but stop mostly in uninteresting industrial towns like Villefranche. The best option is to rent a car in Lyon or Mâcon. Venturing in by bike is more difficult, but equally rewarding; rent a cycle in Lyon (Holiday Bikes, ☎ 04 78 60 11 10) or Mâcon (Pro' Cycles, ☎ 03 85 22 81 82) and use one of the midpoint train stops on the Lyon-Mâcon line as a starting point (bikes are welcome on the train). Brochures with maps and descriptions of the area are available at both the Lyon and Mâcon tourist offices, and given out by many hotels in the area.

Every mention of Beaujolais provokes a thirst for the cool, fruity wine that this region exports. Between the Loire and the Saône rivers, with Lyon at its foot and Mâcon at its head, the Beaujolais houses an important textile and lumber industry; however, its claim to fame lies solely in its vineyards. The most touristed spot is in the town of Romaneche-Thorins, called "Le Hameau," which offers exhibits, tastings, and a *vinothèque*. (☎ 03 85 35 22 22.) Tourist offices dotting the countryside can provide suggested bike or car routes that wind through endless vineyards, sleepy villages, and medieval châteaux, with a couple of *dégustations* (tastings) thrown in for good measure. Devoted wine enthusiasts, though, are better off getting a list of serious wine growers.

VIENNE

In the days of the Roman Empire, Vienne was made a Roman colony, which entitled her inhabitants to all the privileges of Roman citizens. The impressive remnants of those glory days cluster in the town center and spread along a giant stretch of land across the Rhône river. The town's name has become immediately linked with the world-renowned **Festival du Jazz à Vienne,** a two-week party starting at the end of June each year. During the festival, musicians from all corners of the globe come to play at both pricey and free venues, and to consume gallons of Côtes du Rhône wine. The town's revered Roman ruins again fill with spectators and performers, proving that people here can still get down like Caesar's fun-loving subjects even after all these years.

▐▐ TRANSPORTATION AND PRACTICAL INFORMATION. Trains leave from pl. de Pierre-Semard at the end of Cours Brillier to both of Lyon's stations (20-30min., 40 per day, €5.40). The ticket booth is open daily (5:15am-8pm, Su until 10:15am). **Buses** are to the left after the train station. Taxi Mounier **taxis** (☎ 06 80 59 37 17) congregate in front of the station. From the station, walk straight on cours Brillier to the river to get to the **tourist office.** The helpful staff has free maps, brochures, and sporadic themed city tours (July-Aug. 2 per week; Sept.-June 1 per month). They can help with railroad schedules, accommodations, and, of course, tickets to the jazz festival. (☎04 74 53 80 30; www.vienne-tourisme.com. Open M-Sa 9am-noon and 1:30-6pm, Su 10am-noon and 2-5pm.) Above and behind the train station is Mt. Pipet, with the Roman amphitheater, while St-Romain-en-Gal and its treasure trove of ruins sit directly across the Rhône. An **Internet** cafe is at 16 rue des Clercs. (Open M-F 11am-8pm, Sa 2pm-midnight. €1.50 per 15min., €3 per hr.)

⌂⌂ ACCOMMODATIONS AND FOOD. To reach the **Auberge de Jeunesse ❶**, 11 quai Rondet, 5min. from the tourist office, take a left along the river. Huge, co-ed dorms and bathrooms create a social atmosphere on three floors overlooking the Rhône. (☎04 74 53 21 97; mjcvienne@wanadoo.fr. Breakfast €3.30. Sheets €2.80. Reception daily July to mid-Sept. 6pm-9pm; mid-Sept. to June closed Sa and Su. Dorms €8.40.) The tourist office has a list and directions to Vienne's other hotels, which are mostly very close to the *centre ville*.

Cafes and *brasseries* line **cours Brillier** toward the station, while **cours Romestang** has dozens of *pâtisseries* and *salon de thés* serving sandwiches and drinks. For picnics among the Roman ruins or in the Jardin de Ville, a mid-sized **Spar supermarket** is just around the corner from the train station, at 50 bd. de la République. (Open daily 7:30am-9pm.) Those craving nearby Lyon's delicacies should head to **La Potin'noise ❷**, 14 Rue Henry Jacquier, an appealing restaurant tucked away on a street above the Hôtel de Ville. (☎04 74 78 19 19. 4-course *lyonnais menu* €16, other *menus* €23 and €26. Open Tu-F noon-2pm, W-Su 7-9pm. MC/V.) **La Medina ❷**, 71 rue de Bourogne, a popular Moroccan restaurant, has couscous dishes for €8-12.50 and *tajines* for €11.50. (☎04 74 53 51 35. Open daily noon-2pm and 7-11pm. Closed M-Tu lunch. MC/V.)

◙ SIGHTS. The most spectacular of Vienne's Roman ruins is the well-preserved **Temple of Augustus and Livia**, which rises in the middle of a square in the heart of the pedestrian district. On the hillside, at the foot of Mt. Pipet, the steeply plunging **Théâtre Romain** hosts dozens of outdoor concerts and is worth a visit just for the sight. The flat top of **Mont Pipet** above offers spectacular views over the whole valley and its various hillside ruins. From the theater, continue 15min. up steep rue Pipet and take a left at the sign. Below the amphitheater, the **Jardin Archéologique de Cybèle** contains remnants of archways from the old Roman forum, and is a pleasant picnic venue for early-evening jazz concerts. The small **Pyramide du Cirque Romain** rises sharply above the traffic on bd. Fernand-Point, not far from the hostel, the only vestige of a vast Roman circus.

The granddaddy of them all is the **Gallo-Roman city,** across the river at **St-Roman-en-Gal,** accessible by a pedestrian walkway from the quai or by the bridge at place du Jeu-de-Paume. The area contains the remains of a forum, main streets, public bathrooms, baths, and underground storerooms. Analysis of amphorae found here revealed the date of the Italian vintage inside to be AD 124. Restored fountains gurgle amid the ancient streets. The **museum** contains an impressive collection of restored mosaics, recovered cutlery, amphorae, old coins, and a hall for rotating exhibits. The museum recently drew raves with a show that compared Andy Warhol's pop art to the mass production of images for political propaganda in ancient Rome. (☎04 74 53 74 01. Open Mar.-Oct. Tu-Su 10am-6pm; Nov.-Feb. 10am-5pm. Museum and sites €3.80, students €2.30, Th free. You can buy a €6 day pass at any of Vienne's museums.)

Impressive churches cluster around the *centre ville*. The cavernous **Cathédrale St-Maurice** has an intricate, somewhat decaying facade and an array of Romanesque capitals. (Open daily 6am-6pm.) **Église St-Pierre,** at pl. St-Pierre, from the 5th century AD, now has a small archaeological museum with a lovely collection of Gallo-Roman sculptures and artifacts. North of the temple, **St-André-le-Bas,**

RHÔNE-ALPS

has a peaceful cloister and several revolving exhibits. (St-Pierre ☎04 74 85 20 35; St-André ☎04 74 85 18 49. Both open Nov.-Mar. Tu-F 9:30am-12:30pm and 2-5pm, Sa-Su 2-6pm; Apr.-Oct. Tu-Su 9:30am-1pm and 2-6pm. Admission for each €2.50.)

■ ■ **ENTERTAINMENT AND FESTIVALS.** During the two-week summer **jazz festival,** mainline concerts featuring world-renowned artists take place at 8:30pm in the **amphitheater.** Tickets are €26-28, but *musique gratuite* that bookend the main shows make the festival accessible to all. Schedules are available at the box office or tourist office. Free music, often featuring young bands or singers, comes every evening at about 7:30pm to a makeshift stage at the **Jardins de Cybèle.** Another bandstand gives musicians a chance to serenade onlookers even earlier (6pm) at **L'Académie,** part of a square right in front of the **Hôtel de Ville.** At midnight, the free ■**Club de Minuit** sets up in the Théâtre de Vienne, behind the Cybèle gardens, packing awestruck crowds into an intimate, cabaret-style venue. Schedules and tickets are available at the tourist office, the amphitheater box office inside the amphitheater entrance (☎08 99 27 02 07), the Théâtre de Vienne (☎04 74 85 00 05), various music stores across France, and at www.jazzavienne.com. The amphitheater hosts pop, jazz, and classical artists all summer as well; the tourist office and the theater box office both have concert schedules.

Popular bars and cafes cluster on rue du Musée, cours Romenstang, and rue Orfèvres. **Almodobar,** 17 rue du Musée, is a Spanish-themed bar and cafe that serves *tapas* for €4-8. (☎04 74 85 78 85. Open 1pm-midnight.)

GRENOBLE

A dynamic university town full of nightlife, earnest politics, shaggy radicals, and charming sidewalk cafes, Grenoble (pop. 153,000) is cherished by hikers, skiers, bikers, aesthetes, and set designers for its snow-capped peaks and sapphire-blue rivers. An influx of immigrants to France in the 1960s gave Grenoble a sizable North and West African population, which helped to establish the cosmopolitan feel of the unoffical capital of the Alps. During the school year, a thriving foreign exchange program fills the city with young scholars from all corners of the globe.

RHÔNE-ALPS

■ TRANSPORTATION

Flights: Aéroport de Grenoble St-Geoirs, St-Etienne de St-Geoirs (☎04 76 65 48 48), 41km from city center. Buses leave 1¼hr. before each flight from bus station (€3.80). Domestic flights only.

Trains: Gare Europole, pl. de la Gare. Open daily 6am-9pm. To: **Annecy** (2hr., 18 per day, €15); **Lyon** (1½hr., 27 per day, €16.30); **Marseille** (2½-4½hr., 15 per day, €34.60); **Nice** (5-6½hr., 5 per day, €55.60); **Paris** (3hr., 10 per day, €60-80).

Buses: Exit the train station and turn left. Open M-Sa 6:15am-7pm, Su 7:15am-7pm. **VFD** (☎08 20 83 38 33; www.vfd.fr) runs to **Aéroport Lyon-Saint-Exupéry** (1 hr., 10 per day, €20); **Geneva,** Switzerland (3hr., 1 per day, €25.50); **Nice** (10hr., 1 per day, €52.40). Frequent service to ski resorts and outdoor areas.

Public Transportation: Transports Agglomération Grenobloise (TAG; ☎04 76 20 66 66; www.semitag.com). Grenoble's extensive tram and bus network is only really useful for transport to and from the *gare* and to the youth hostel, as the city center is very walkable. Info desk in the tourist office open Sept.-June M-F 8:30am-6:30pm, Sa 9am-6pm; July-Aug. M-Sa 9am-6pm. Ticket €1.20, *carnet* of 10 €9.50. Day pass €5, 5-day pass €14. 4 lines run Th-Sa 6am-8:30pm and 9pm-midnight; the 2 tram lines run Su-W 5am-midnight about every 5-10min.

Taxis: (☎04 76 54 42 54). 24hr. €55 to the airport.

Car Rental: Self Car, 24 rue Emile Gueymard (☎04 76 50 96 96), located by the train station. Insurance included. 21+. Open July-Aug. M-F 8am-noon and 2-6 pm, Sa 8am-noon; Sept.-June M-F 7:30am-noon and 1:30-6:30pm, Sa 8am-noon. AmEx/MC/V.

◼ 🔟 ORIENTATION AND PRACTICAL INFORMATION

Getting to the tourist office and the center of town is a 15min. walk. Turn right from the station onto **place de la Gare** and take the third left onto **avenue Alsace-Lorraine,** following the tram tracks. Continue along the tracks on **rue Félix Poulat** and **rue Blanchard;** the tourist complex will be on the left, just before the tracks fork. The primarily pedestrian *vieille ville* stretches from the tourist office to the river, bounded by the **Jardin de Ville** and **Musée de Grenoble.** The winding streets intersect with innumerable *places* and squares, making it tricky to navigate the city. The **Bastille** looms over the town from its perch across the river.

Tourist Office: 14 rue de la République (☎04 76 42 41 41; www.grenoble-isere.info). From the train station, tram lines A and B (dir: Echirolles or Universités) run to Hubert Dubedout-Maison du Tourisme. Hosts an SNCF counter, local bus office, and post office. Good maps, hotel info, and train and bus schedules. Daily tours of the *vieille ville* July-Aug. 10:30am; Sept.-June 2 per month (€6.80). 1hr. audio tour €6.10. Also offers *Multipass' Grenoble* daypass, including entry to museums, round-trip up the Bastille, guided tour of the old city, and unlimited use of trams and buses; €16. Open M-Sa 9am-6:30pm, Su 10am-1pm and 2-5pm.

Hiking Information: Bureau Information Montagne, 3 rue Raoul Blanchard (☎04 76 42 45 90; infos.montagne@grande-traversee-alpes.com), across from the tourist office. Extensive info on hiking, mountaineering, and biking. Free brochures, maps, and expert advice. Sells detailed guides and topographic maps. Open M-F 9am-6pm, Sa 10am-1pm and 2-5pm. **Weather:** ☎08 36 68 02 38. **Snow info:** ☎08 92 68 10 20.

Ski and Climbing Equipment Rental: Borel Sport, 42 rue Alsace-Lorraine (☎04 76 46 47 46; fax 04 76 46 00 75). Skis, boots, and poles €13 per day. Snowboard package €16 per day. Cross-country package €8 per day. Via Ferrata climbing ensemble (harness, cord, helmet) €11 per day. Snowshoes €5-7 per day. Open daily Sept.-May 9am-noon and 2-7pm; June-Aug. Tu-Sa 10am-noon and 2-6pm. MC/V.

Budget Travel: Voyages Wasteels, 7 rue Thiers (☎04 76 47 07 13; www.wasteels.fr). Student travel packages. Open M-F 10am-6pm, Sa 9am-1pm. MC/V.

GLBT Resources: www.grenoble-lgbt.com.

Laundromat: Lavomatique, 14 rue Thiers (☎04 76 96 28 03). Open daily 7am-10pm.

Police: 36 bd. Maréchal Leclerc (☎04 76 60 40 40). Take bus #31 (dir: Malpertuis) to Hôtel de Police.

Hospital: Centre Hospitalier Régional de Grenoble, La Tronche av. du Maquis du Grésivaudan (☎04 76 76 75 75).

Internet Access: E-toile, 15 rue Jean-Jacques Rousseau (☎04 76 00 13 60.) €1.50 for 15min., €2 for 30min., €3 per hr. Open M-Th 10am-11pm, F-Sa 10am-midnight, Su noon-10pm. **Celciuscafe.com,** on rue Gutéal next to the Casino cafeteria (☎04 76 46 43 36). Friendly owner welcomes a truly international crowd and offers the cheapest prices in town. American keyboards on request. €1 for 15min., €2 for 30min., €2.50 per hr. Drinks €1. Open daily 9am-11pm.

Post Office: 7 bd. Maréchal Lyautey (☎04 76 43 51 39). Open M-F 8am-7pm, Sa 8am-noon. Branch office, 12 rue de la République (☎04 76 63 32 70), adjacent to the tourist complex. Open Sept. to mid-July M 8am-5:45pm, Tu-F 8am-6pm, Sa 8am-noon; mid-July to Aug. M-F 9am-noon and 2-5:30pm, Sa 9am-noon.

Postal Code: 38000.

RHÔNE-ALPS

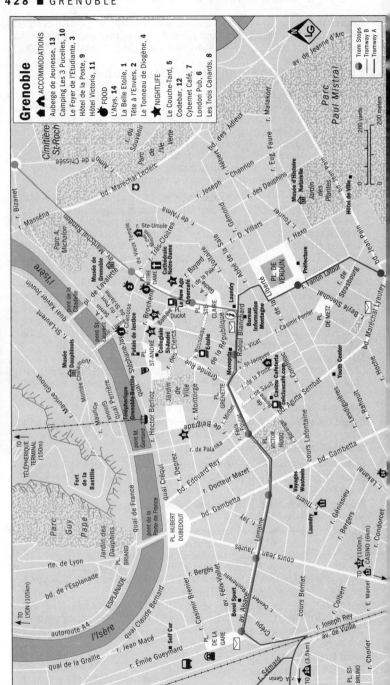

Grenoble

♠ ACCOMMODATIONS
Auberge de Jeunesse, 13
Camping Les 3 Pucelles, 10
Le Foyer de l'Etudiante, 3
Hôtel de la Poste, 9
Hôtel Victoria, 11

● FOOD
L'Atys, 14
La Belle Etoile, 1
Tête à l'Envers, 2
Le Tonneau de Diogène, 4

★ NIGHTLIFE
Le Couche-Tard, 5
Codebar, 12
Cybernet Café, 7
London Pub, 6
Les Trois Canards, 8

Tram Stops ●
Tramway B ▬
Tramway A ▬

ACCOMMODATIONS AND CAMPING

Budget hotels dot downtown Grenoble. It's wise to call ahead. The student guide *Le Guide de l'Etudiant*, free at the tourist office, has info on long-term stays.

Le Foyer de l'Etudiante, 4 rue Ste-Ursule (☎ 04 76 42 00 84; www.multimania.com/foyeretudiante). A budget traveler's best bet for June-Aug. when it ceases to be a dorm and welcomes tourists, but be advised that Oct.-June this hostel is women only. The stately old building encloses a courtyard where backpackers and students mix. Spacious rooms with desks and high ceilings. Large kitchen, piano, laundry facilities and free Internet. Sheets €10. Laundry €2.20. 24hr. reception. July-Sept. 3-night min. for room; 5-night max. for dorm. Dorm €8. June-Sept. singles €15; doubles €24. Oct.-May 6-month min. stay, singles €255 per month; doubles €380. MC/V. ❶

HI Auberge de Jeunesse, 10 ave. du Grèsivaudan. (☎ 04 76 09 33 52, www.fuaj.org). Take bus #1 (dir: Pont Rouge) from the corner of rue Alsace-Lorraine and cours Jean Jaurès to the stop "Quinzaine," in front of a large shopping plaza; facing back toward Grenoble, take a left onto av. du Grèsivaudan. The Auberge is 3 buildings down on the right. Or take tram A (dir: Echirolles) to "la Rampe," and follow the "Auberge de Jeunesse" signs past the bowling alley down av. de Grugliasco through several intersections, past the Casino supermarket. (15min.) Bar, patio, kitchen, and beautiful 4-8 bed dorms, most with their own shower and toilet. Nearby bus stop and grocery store make up for relative distance from the city. 24hr. keycard access. Breakfast included. Sheets €2.80. Reception 7:30am-11pm. Dorms €13.25. MC/V. HI Members only. ❶

Hôtel de la Poste, 25 rue de la Poste (☎/fax 04 76 46 67 25), in the pedestrian zone. Cheap rooms have antiquated charm at this homey refuge. Those in showerless rooms should get comfortable with the owner and friendly staff: the only public shower is 4 ft. from the reception desk. 24hr. reception daily. Singles €22, with shower and TV €28; doubles €28/€35; triples €32; quads €37. MC/V. ❷

Hôtel Victoria, 17 rue Thiers (☎ 04 76 46 06 36; fax 04 76 43 00 14). Friendly owner takes good care of visitors at this super-clean, flower-decorated hotel. Though a bit dark, rooms are spacious and have firm beds. Breakfast €5.80. Reception daily 7am-11:30pm. Curfew 11:30pm. Closed Aug. Singles €31, with shower €36; doubles €36/43; triples €51; quads €55. MC/V. ❸

Camping: Les 3 Pucelles, 58 rue des Allobroges (☎ 04 76 96 45 73; www.camping-trois-pucelles.com), in Seyssins. Take tram A (dir: Fontaine-La Poya) to Louis Maisonnat, then take bus #51 (dir: Les Nalettes) to Mas des Iles; turn left and the site is a couple of blocks down. Small and suburban, this is the closest campsite to town and the only one open all year. Reception daily 7:30am-11pm. Laundry €2.30. Call ahead June-Aug. 1 person, tent, and car €7.50. Extra person €3. Electricity €2.20. MC/V. ❶

FOOD

The most lively of Grenoble's 16 markets can be found on **place St-André, place St-Bruno, place Ste-Claire,** and **place aux Herbes.** (All Tu-Su 6am-1pm; pl. Ste-Claire also F 3-8pm.) A particularly well-stocked **Monoprix supermarket** is across from the tourist office (open daily 8:30am-8pm); a **Casino** with a cafeteria is at 46 cours Jean Jaurès, just up the street from the HI hostel. (Open M-Sa 8:30am-8pm; cafeteria open daily 11am-11:30pm.) Grenoble boasts many affordable restaurants, some with discounts and student *menus*. **University Restaurants (URs)** (☎ 04 76 57 44 00) sell meal tickets (€2.40) during the school year. Two URs are in Grenoble *ville:* 5 rue d'Arsonval (open M-F 11:30am-1:30pm and 6:30-7:45pm) and rue Maurice Gignoux. (Open daily noon-1:15pm and 6:30-7:50pm.) There's also a **Casino Cafeteria** on rue Guétal for cheap meals and fast service. (Salads €2.20-4.50, appetizers €1-3.80, hot dishes €3.50-6.40. Open daily 11am-9:30pm.)

Cafes and restaurants cluster around **place Notre-Dame** and pl. St-André, in the heart of the *vieille ville*. Regional restaurants cater to locals around **place de Gordes,** between pl. St-André and the Jardin de Ville. Asian eateries abound between pl. Notre-Dame and the river and **rue Condorcet;** *pâtisseries* and North African establishments congregate around **rue Chenoise** and **rue Lionne,** between the pedestrian area and river. Cheap pizzerias line **quai Perrière** across the river.

■**Tête à l'Envers,** 12 rue Chenoise (☎04 76 51 13 42). This 7-table gem specializes in a melange of international cuisine. Menu changes daily, depending on what's fresh at the market and in the creative mind of the expert chef. Guess the identity of 5 of the 6 desserts and win a prize. Mention *Let's Go* for a free coffee or *digéstif.* Entrees €8.90, *plats du jour* €11, dessert €8.90, lunch *menu* €15-17. Reservations recommended. Open Tu-F noon-3pm and 7:30pm-1am, Sa 7:30pm-1am. MC/V. ❸

■**L'Atys,** 2 rue Lazare-Carnot (☎ 04 76 43 84 13, www.latys.com), off rue Lesdiguières. Vegetarianism with a North African twist gives traditional *dauphinois* fare a run for its money. The walls of the green-themed dining room are decorated with silk paintings done by the owner, a vegetarian artist-poet-musician. Deliciously spiced salads €5.50-8.50, entrees €5.50-8.50, *plats* €10.50, desserts €6.50, all made with organic produce. Open Tu-Sa 11am-2pm and 7pm-11pm. AmEx/MC/V. ❷

La Belle Etoile, 2 rue Lionne (☎04 76 51 00 40). This family establishment specializes in Tunisian cuisine, with excellent couscous and other North African specialties (€7.40-13). Large salads €2.30-8.40, omelettes €2.60-5.60, *tagines* €9.50. Closed mid-July to mid-Aug. Open Tu-Su noon-2pm and 7-11pm. AmEx/MC/V. ❷

Le Tonneau de Diogène, 6 pl. Notre-Dame (☎04 76 42 38 40). Nothing beats the weekly philosophical discussions held by local intellectuals Sept. to mid-July; check storefront for times and topics. Salads €6.10-7.50, omelettes €3.50-5, meat dishes €2.90-9.40, 3-course *menu* €6.50. Open daily 11:30am-midnight. A set of back stairs leads to **Le Sphinx** (☎04 76 44 55 08), Grenoble's finest philosophy library/bookstore. Open M-F noon-8:30pm, Sa 10am-7pm. AmEx/MC/V. ❶

◔ SIGHTS

■**TÉLÉPHÉRIQUE GRENOBLE-BASTILLE.** The icons of Grenoble, these gondolas depart from the city every 10min. and head for the **Bastille,** a 16th-century fort perched 475m above the city. From the top, on a clear day, visitors can look north toward the Lyon valley and its two converging rivers, or east over the ridge of mountains to the distant peak of Mont Blanc. History buffs can continue 1hr. up to **Mont-Jalla,** where a flower-studded memorial tells the story of Alpine soldiers through the centuries. At the cable station, practice alpine climbing skills on the **Via Ferrata,** the first urban climbing site in the world, or walk down through the **Parc Guy Pape** through the other end of the fortress to the Jardin des Dauphins (1 hour). Be cautious: the trail is isolated and passes through several dark tunnels. *(Téléphérique: quai Stéphane-Jay. ☎04 76 44 33 65. Open July-Aug. M 11am-12:15am, Tu-Su 9:15am-12:15am; Nov.-Feb. M 11am-6:30pm, Tu-Su 10:45am-6:30pm; Mar.-May and Oct. M 11am-7:25pm, Tu-Sa 9:15am-11:45pm, Su 9:15am-7:25pm; June and Sept. M 11am-11:45pm, Tu-Sa 9:15am-11:45pm, Su 9:15am-7:25pm. Closed mid-Jan. One-way €3.80, students €3; round-trip €5.50/€4.40.)*

■**MUSÉE DE GRENOBLE.** Art lovers will swoon over one of France's most prestigious collections of fine art. Its masterpieces include larger-than-life canvases by Rubens, de la Tour, and Zubararàn, and a great 20th-century collection with an entire room devoted to Matisse. A fair amount of space is devoted to local artists' depictions of the mountains, perfect for drumming up enthusiasm for outdoor pursuits. *(5 pl. de Lavalette. ☎04 76 63 44 44; www.museedegrenoble.fr. Open 10am-6:30pm. Closed Tu. €5, students €2. Guided 1½hr. visits in French Sa-Su 3pm, €3.)*

⊠ MUSÉE D'HISTOIRE NATURELLE DE GRENOBLE. Children in particular love this museum, with dioramas of alpine animals (including lynx, bears, and birds) lining a stately wooden hall. The second floor presents exotic insects from around the world and a glittering array of gems. Many of the exhibits have English descriptions, but the beautiful displays need little introduction. *(1 rue Dolomieu. ☎04 76 44 05 35; www.museum-grenoble.fr. Open M-F 9:30am-noon and 1:30-5:30pm, Sa-Su 2-6pm. €2.20, under 18 free. Oct.-May W afternoon free.)*

MUSÉE DAUPHINOIS. Transformed from convent to prison to Catholic school to historic site, this regional ethnographic museum merits a visit from anyone with a penchant for archaeology. Situated on the north bank of the Isère in a beautiful 17th-century convent, it boasts multimedia extravagance and futuristic sound effects. The two permanent exhibits have English explanations. *The Gens de l'Alpe* (People of the Alps) explores the history of the hearty souls who first carved out a livelihood in the mountains. Check out *La Grande Histoire du Ski* (The Great History of Skiing), featuring a vast collection of early and modern skis. *(30 rue Maurice Gignoux. Cross the Pont St-Laurent and go up Montée Chalemont. ☎04 76 85 19 01; www.musee-dauphinois.fr. Open June-Sept. M and W-Su 10am-7pm; Oct.-May 10am-6pm. €3.20, under 25 free. W afternoon free.)*

VIEILLE VILLE. Built over 17 centuries, Grenoble's *vieille ville* is a motley but charming collection of old-time squares, fountains, and parks. Vestiges of the Roman ramparts are most visible near the town's historic center, pl. St-André, now transformed into Grenoble's most popular student hangout. The 13th-century **Collégiale Saint-André** was the traditional burial place for Dauphins before the French crown acquired both land and title in 1349. *(Open 8am-5pm.)* Directly across, you can't miss the flamboyant Gothic **Palais de Justice,** built by Dauphin prince and future king Louis XI in 1453 to house the Dauphiné region's parliament. *(Tours depart from the tourist office Jul.-Aug. Su-F 10:15am. €6.80, students €5.30.)* The **Café de la Table Ronde,** built in 1739, is the second-oldest coffee shop in France. *(☎04 76 44 51 41. Open M-Sa 9am-1am. Coffee €1.)*

🎵 🎭 ENTERTAINMENT AND FESTIVALS

Grenoble's main **theater** features plays and classical music performances throughout the year; info and tickets at the **Billetterie** next to the theatre in pl. André. (☎04 76 42 96 02. Open Tu-Sa 1pm-6pm.) Info and tickets for most events are available in the **Fnac Billetterie,** in a huge superstore on rue Felix Poulat across from the church. (Open M-Sa 10am-7pm. www.fnac.com.) The weekly *Le Petit Bulletin,* free in cinemas and some restaurants, has full movie schedules.

Travelers feeling Grenoble's student-dominated vibe won't be surprised to learned that the city hosts many art, music, and dance festivals, mainly in summer. **Cabaret Frappe** celebrates singers and songwriters from around the world, from late June to early July with both free outdoor and €11 indoor concerts. The **Festival du Court Métrage** celebrates short films in early July; contact the **Cinémathèque,** 4 rue Hector Berlioz (☎04 76 54 43 51). Also in July, the **Festival de Théâtre Européen** hams it up. (Info ☎04 76 44 60 92. Admission free and up to €16.) On July 14, Grenoble blazes with fireworks over its Bastille. In late November, the two-week **Festival 38ème Rugissants** (info ☎04 76 51 12 92) features contemporary music.

🎷 NIGHTLIFE

Grenoble has all the funky cafes and raucous bars of a true college town, most located in the area between pl. St-André and pl. Notre-Dame. Covers for clubs range €8-10, and drinks are nearly as much. Hours listed here are for the school year; most places have more limited hours in summer. Grenoble's **Maison de la Culture,** located on rue Paul Claudel about 15min. from the *centre ville* is so hip it calls itself **Le CARGO.** (☎ 04 76 00 79 00; www.mc2grenoble.fr. Open Sept.-June Tu-Sa 9am-6:30pm.)

Le Couche-Tard, 1 rue du Palais (☎ 04 76 44 18 79), a small bar with graffiti-covered walls, neon lights, and a dance area, is where drunken scholars mix it up. Happy hour M-Sa 7-10pm, cocktails €2. Open M-Sa 7pm-2am. AmEx/MC/V.

Les Trois Canards, 2 av. Felix Viallet (☎ 04 76 46 74 74), by the Jardin de Ville, has €1.60 shooters and a mind-boggling selection of flavored vodka (€4) for students and 20-somethings. Spacious interior with a flower-draped ceiling and a disco ball, or break it down to a live DJ. Open daily 7am-3pm and 5pm-2am; July-Aug. closed Su. MC/V.

Cybernet Café, 3 rue Bayard (☎ 04 76 51 73 18), is a funky bar with a misleading name—you won't find a computer here. A laid-back crowd loves this artfully decorated spot, and the delicious choices on the drink menu will keep you coming back. Happy hour 6-8:30pm, drinks €2-4. Cocktails €5-13. Open Tu-Sa 6pm-1am. AmEx/MC/V.

London Pub, 11 rue Brocherie (☎ 04 76 44 41 90), is a slightly kitschy, friendly home-away-from-home for expats of all kinds, with a more local crowd in the student-deprived summer. The 2-floor establishment has an outgoing staff and flag-adorned interior. After a few drinks, the bar area morphs into a *de facto* dance floor. Happy hour daily 6-9pm; pints from €3.80, shots €1.60. Open M-Sa 6pm-1am.

Le Codebar, 9 rue Etienne Marcel (☎ 04 76 43 58 91, http://lecodebar.free.fr), a right off rue Jean Jaurès about 5min. from its intersection with av. Alsace-Lorraine. This gay-and lesbian-friendly bar boasts a fun cocktail menu and frequent theme nights.

🅗 HIKING

A number of popular hikes lie just a short bus ride away. Before setting out, pick up the free trail map, *La Carte des Sentiers des Franges Vertes*, at the Bureau Info Montagne (p. 427). In Vercors, views from the top of **Le Moucherotte** (1901m) are unparalleled. Take VFD bus #510 (dir: Plateau du Vercors) to St-Nizier du Moucherotte (40min., 1-3 per day, €2.70) and head to the center of town. In front of the church, an easy trail starts to the right of the orientation table and quickly joins the **GR91,** passing the remains of an old *téléphérique* before reaching the mountain's summit via a former ski trail. Descend along the same route. (4hr. round-trip.) To the north, in the heart of the Chartreuse park, a steeper trail reaches the summit of the **Chamechaude** (2082m). Take VFD bus #7140 to Col de Porte (3 per day, €2.70), then follow the dirt trail leading from behind Hôtel Garin to the right until reaching the middle of a field; to the left, a second trail leads into the forest and joins the main path, a zig-zag ascent up to the **source des Bachassons.**

🅢 SKIING

Rent equipment in town to avoid high prices at the resorts. The biggest ski areas are to the east in **Oisans.** The **Alpe d'Huez,** rising above one of the most challenging legs of the Tour de France, boasts an enormous 3330m vertical drop and sunny, south-facing slopes; 220km of trails span all difficulty levels. (Tourist office ☎ 04 76 11 44 44; www.alpedhuez.com. Ski area: ☎ 04 76 80 30 30. Lift tickets €33.50 per day, €202 per week.) Popular with advanced skiers, **Les Deux Alpes** has the largest skiable glacier in Europe, limited summer skiing, and a slope-side youth hostel. Its lift system, including two gondolas, runs up the 2000m vertical. (Tourist office ☎ 04 76 79 22 00; www.les2alpes.com. Ski area ☎ 04 76 79 75 00. Youth hostel ☎ 04 76 79 22 80; fax 04 76 79 26 15. Lift tickets €32 per day, €137.70-153 per week.)

The **Belledonne** region, northeast of Grenoble, lacks the towering heights and ideal conditions of the Oisans but compensates with lower prices. **Chamrousse** is its biggest and most popular ski area, offering a lively atmosphere and a youth hostel. If conditions are right, there's plenty of good alpine and cross-country skiing at a great value, especially for beginners. (Tourist office ☎ 04 76 89 92 65; fax 04 76 89 98 06. Youth hostel ☎ 04 76 89 91 31; fax 04 76 89 96 66. Lift tickets €24 per day, €108-139 per week.) Only 30min. from Grenoble, the resort makes for an ideal daytrip in the summer (bus ride €3.80, 6 per day). Chamrousse maintains four **mountain bike** routes of varying difficulty in addition to a 230km network of **hiking** trails. In January, the town plays host to a renowned comedy film festival.

The neighborly slopes of the **Vercors** region, south of Grenoble, are popular with locals. In traditional villages with small ski resorts like **Gresse-en-Vercors,** vertical drops range around 1000m. Rock-bottom prices make the area a stress-free option for beginners or those looking to escape the hassles of the major resorts. The drive from Grenoble takes about 40min. (Tourist office ☎ 04 76 34 33 40. Tickets €9.10-12.60 per day, €54.50-74.30 per week.)

⚡ DAYTRIP FROM GRENOBLE

HAUTERIVES

To reach the site, take the train from Grenoble to Romans (1hr., 11 per day, €10.90), then pick up a Régie Voyages Drôme bus to Hauterives. (☎ 04 75 02 30 42. 30min.; July-Aug. W 8am and 4pm, F 7:15, 8, 11:30am, 4pm; Sept.-June M-Tu and Th 6:15pm, F 9:30, 11:30am, 4pm, 6:15pm; €4.70.) Call to be sure there is a bus back the same day. A better option, for those traveling by car, is to make the 1hr. drive from Grenoble. Take A48 north; at Voreppe, switch to A49 toward Romans. At Romans, take D538 north to Hauterives. From Lyon, head south on A7 and change to D538 at Vienne.

This village has put itself on the map with a whimsical palace and the intriguing story behind it. In 1879, the local postman, Ferdinand Cheval, tripped over an oddly shaped rock while on his daily rounds. He began to collect piles of odd little rocks and over the next 33 years, he shaped them into a fantasy palace outside the village. Rock by rock, the structure grew into an unbelievably detailed world of grimacing giants, frozen palms, and swirling staircases. When Cheval finally laid down his trowel, the █**Palais Idéal** (Ideal Palace) was almost 80m long and over two stories high. An indescribable mix of fantasy visions, Middle Eastern architecture, and phantasmagoric creatures, the palace has become a national monument. Visitors can climb all over it to explore the caves and crevices, mottoes and mysteries sculpted by the postman's two hands and unshakable faith. (☎ 04 75 68 81 19; www.facteurcheval.com. Open daily July-Aug. 9am-12:30pm and 1:30-7:30pm; Sept. and Apr.-June 9am-12:30pm and 1:30-6:30pm; Oct.-Nov. and Feb.-Mar. 9:30am-12:30pm and 1:30-5:30pm; Dec.-Jan. 9:30am-12:30pm and 1:30-4:30pm. Admission €5, students €4, under 16 €3.50.)

Hauterives's tourist office, next to the entry to the palace, provides info on the Palais and the surrounding region. (☎ 04 75 68 86 82; fax 04 75 68 92 96. Open daily Apr.-Sept. 10am-12:30pm and 1:30-6pm; Oct.-Nov. and Feb.-Mar. 10am-12:30pm and 1:30-5:30pm; Dec.-Jan. 10am-12:30pm and 1:30-4:30pm.)

MEGÈVE

Nestled in a lush valley, shopping and gambling mecca Megève is one of the poshest resorts in the Alps, ideal for beginning skiers and those who prefer an off-slopes experience in a chic French town. The town's cobblestone alleyways and rushing mountain streams somewhat redeem its heavy tourism, and visitors don't

RHÔNE-ALPS

have to part with (all) their fortunes to enjoy its charms. During the winter holiday season, twinkling lights and fresh snow combine to transform Megève into a picturesque winter paradise.

◻ TRANSPORTATION

Megève itself has no train station, only a bus depot at 116 rte. 212 with an SNCF window. (Outside the *centre ville*; open M-F 9am-noon and 2pm-6:15pm.) The closest train station is **Sallanches,** 12 km away, on the St-Gervais line. **Trains** run from Sallanches to St-Gervais (7min., 10-12 per day, €4); Annecy (1½hr., 7 per day, €10.50); Lyon (4hr., 11 per day, €26.30); and Paris (4½hr., 12 per day, €65.20). **Geneva International Airport** is 1hr. away. €32 bus rides from the airport to Sallanches are available twice daily through S.A.T. **Buses** (☎04 50 21 23 42, office open daily 9am-noon and 2-6:15pm) run directly from the 116 rte. 212 bus depot, and go to Sallanches (1hr., 4 per day; €8.50) and Chamonix (1¼hr., 1 per day; €8.70). **Taxis** wait at the bus station. (☎04 50 21 28 20, 24hr.)

◼◻ ORIENTATION AND PRACTICAL INFORMATION

The **place de l'Église,** with its oft-photographed spire, serves as a central square of sorts. On one side, pedestrian **avenue Charles Feige** and **rue St-François** run past lively cafés, shops, and bars on the way to **rue Edmund Rothschild,** which leads to **Mt. d'Arbois:** the golf course, hotel, *téléphérique*, and ski area. In the summer a marked footpath cuts up the hill; in the winter the best way to reach the summit is to take the linked Chamois and Rocharbois **gondolas.**

On the other side of the *place*, **rue Monseigneur Conseil** goes to the tourist office, 70 rue Monseignuer Conseil. The staff provides maps and info on hiking, skiing, camping, and *chambres d'hôtes*, Internet access (€2.30 for 15min. with an ATM card), accommodations booking (☎04 50 21 29 52; reservation@megeve.com), and **currency exchange** with €5 commission. (☎04 50 21 27 28; megeve@megeve.com. Open mid-June to early Aug. and mid-Dec to late Apr. daily 9am-7pm; late Apr. to mid-June and early Aug. to mid-Dec. M-Sa 9am-12:30pm and 2-6:30pm.) **Internet Access** is also available at Bar des Alpes, 273 rue de la Poste (☎04 50 93 08 15), across from post office. Other services include: **police** off pl. de l'Église (☎04 50 93 29 22), **mountain rescue** (☎04 50 91 28 18), and a **post office,** 276 rue de la Poste (☎04 50 21 04 64), down the street from the bus station, that **exchanges currency** at good rates. (Open M-F 8:30am-noon and 2-5pm, Sa 8am-noon.) **Postal Code:** 74120.

> **ALPINE SPRING.** The French Alps have not only two high seasons (one skiing, one hiking) but two (very) low seasons as well, when many establishments close and some high-season hubs become veritable ghost towns. Ski season tends to run from late November to mid-April, while hiking trails are typically passable from July to mid-September. If you are planning to visit the Alps from April to early July or from September to November, be sure to call local tourist offices first to check the availability of bus service, ski/hiking conditions, and how many restaurants and accommodations will be open.

◼◼ ACCOMMODATIONS AND CAMPING

In the busy winter months Megève's many hotels and resorts easily handle long-term stays and large groups. Many hotels charge the same for singles as for doubles; the best deals are doubles and ski apartments for multiple people. Most cheaper hotels are about a 20min. walk outside the *centre ville*, toward either Sallanches or Rochebrune. Camping is an inexpensive summer option, while in the winter, reserving a *demi-pension* may save money. Since Megève does not have a hostel, the best deal by far for groups of two is to take a room at one of several local **chambres d'hôtes**, which tend to charge less than €30 per person per night with breakfast included. Arrangements must be made well in advance through the Megève reservation office (see **Practical Infomation**). Because this is a ski town, rates rise and fall with snow. Always call ahead for winter reservations. Those traveling Apr.-June or Sept.-Dec. are advised to call the tourist office to verify the opening dates of hotels.

The English-speaking management at **Hôtel le Rond-Point d'Arbois** ❸, 111 rte. Edmund Rothschild, rents airy doubles, some with balconies, on the road up to Mt. d'Arbois near the skibus stops. (☎44 12 23 47 76; www.stanfordskiing.co.uk. Breakfast €5. Doubles from €49. MC/V.) **La Croix du Savoie** ❹ offers spacious modern apartments with small kitchens and bathrooms in the Demi Quartier neighborhood, a 25min. walk out of town along rte. 212 toward Sallanches. (☎04 50 21 67 37. Breakfast included. Closed in May and November. Doubles from €49; family friendly 3- to 4-person suites from €62. Winter price-hikes are quite steep. MC/V.)

A 30min. walk from town, **Camping Bornand** ❶ has small sites, some graveled, and a playground. From rte. 212, toward Sallanches, turn right at the sign for "Télécabine Princesse." Follow signs for "camping." (☎04 50 93 00 86; camping.bornand@tiscali.fr. Open May-Sept. €3.40 per person, €3.80 per site. MC/V.)

🞂 FOOD

For a day of hiking the mountains or *après-ski* cravings, store-bought goodies hit the spot. Along the streets of the *centre ville*, dozens of *épiceries* and *crèmeries* specializing in Savoyard food open their doors. There are also multiple supermarkets, the most centrally located of which is **Sherpa**, 150 rue Ambroise Martin (☎04 50 21 46 92. Open M-Sa 9am-12:15pm and 4-7pm, Su 9am-12:15pm). There is a **Petit Casino** across from the tourist office, and several large supermarkets on rte. 212 toward Sallanches. *Brasseries* with less expensive *menus* abound on the main pedestrian streets; those in the mood for serious upscale dining can kiss their budget goodbye at one of the town's famously top-notch hotels.The **🞖Chalet du Mont d'Arbois** ❺, 447 chemin de la Rocaille, has been a Megève institution for nearly a century. (☎04 50 21 25 03. Reservations required. *Plats* from €28, *menus* €45-55. Open late June to Sept. and mid-Dec. to Mar. only noon-2pm and 7:30-10pm. AmEx/MC/V.) If you want to eat without breaking your budget, **Petite Crêperie Bretonne** ❷, 4 rue Charles Feige, is located in a charming wooden alleyway near the place de l'Église. (☎04 50 58 92 30. Takeout crêpes €3, sit-down *menu* with salad, *galette*, and sweet crêpe €10. Open M-Sa noon-10pm.)

🞂 OUTDOOR ACTIVITIES

The **ski areas** surrounding Megève offer solid intermediate terrain. The largest complex, **Mt. d'Arbois/Mt. Joly**, offers the most varied and challenging terrain, much of it above tree line, through a large network of lifts. It is serviced from either the Princesse or Mt. d'Arbois *téléphériques*. Skiing is also available in the nearby hamlets of **Rochebrune, Jaillet,** and **Combloux,** connected by lifts from St-Gervais. From the town center, the **Chamois lift** enables skiers to head to the Rochebrune or Mt. d'Arbois areas. The base areas are connected by a **skibus,** which is included in Megève lift passes. At the **Maison de la Montagne,** behind the tourist office on rue de la Poste, a bulletin board and ski map list lift and trail openings and closings.

RHÔNE-ALPS

Because the town is a giant base for several **ski schools,** it attracts beginners and families in droves. Two main ski schools compete for Megève children: the **École de Ski Français** in the Maison de La Montagne (☎04 50 21 00 97), and the **École de Ski Internationale** (☎04 50 58 78 88), which meets under the Mt. d'Arbois cable car. Both offer private and group lessons, including multi-day morning packages for skiing, snowboarding, and ski racing. Several smaller ski schools meet as well; ask at the tourist office.

Ski rental is in dozens of places throughout town and is best done by the week. Budget travelers might want to rent skis in Megève's neighboring towns for better deals. The cost of **ski passes** depends on ability. A simple Megève pass includes all the areas listed above for €30 per day, children €24. For beginners, there's a pass that serves only the Jaillet and Combloux resorts for €20 per day, children €16. Multi-day passes save about €4 per day. For those who want access to the real *hors-piste* stuff, a 6 or 7 day Mt. Blanc pass provides access to the slopes in nearby Chamonix and Courmayer, Italy. (6 day pass €151, children €121.)

During the **summer,** three principal *téléphériques* offer hikers and visitors expansive mountain views and hiking opportunities. (**Mt. d'Arbois gondola:** ☎04 50 21 22 07. Mid-June to Aug. one-way €5.50, round-trip €9. **Jaillet gondola:** ☎04 50 21 01 50. Late June to mid-Sept. €4.70/€9. **Rochebrune cable car:** ☎04 50 21 01 51. Late June to early Aug. €5.50/€9.70.)

The tourist office sells an IGN topographic trail map for €6 and has a free French or English brochures that describe popular hikes in the area. The Compagnie des Guides, in the Maison de la Montagne, offers **guided multi-day hikes, alpinism courses, climbing, mountain biking,** and **canyoning.** Several facilities are available for **horseback riding, tennis,** and **golf;** there are also four or five **spas** and a **swimming pool.** The magazine *Megève Eté,* free at the tourist offices in Megève or in Chamonix, has an extensive list of activities.

♪ ❀ ENTERTAINMENT AND FESTIVALS

Upscale *après-ski* and late-night options await skiers on **rte. Edmund de Rothschild.** The **Pallas** disco, 96 rte. Edmund de Rothschild (☎04 50 91 82 70), is one of the more popular clubs in town. (Cover €9. Open during ski season nightly 11pm-5am.) Trendy nightspot **Wake Up,** 131 rte. Edmund de Rothschild, is another busy bar, and serves *tapas* and sushi as well as drinks. (☎04 50 58 25 79. Beer €3.30-6.50. Open daily June-Aug. 7pm-3am and Sept.-May 6pm-3am.) Most night spots in the center of town are found on rue Ambrose Martin and rue Charles Feige. Intimate and quirky, the **5 Rues Jazz Club,** *quartier* des 5 Rues (☎04 50 91 90 69), off pl. de l'Église in the basement of an old stone building, draws crowds and luminaries during ski season. The **Cargo Club,** 30 rue Ambrose Martin, often brings in DJs from around the region for Friday and Saturday night parties. (☎04 50 58 78 70. Cover €7-12. Open in winter Th-Sa 11pm-3am; in summer call for hours.) A **casino,** 199 rue Charles Freige, beckons with the usual slot machines, poker, roulette, and blackjack. (☎04 50 93 01 83. Open daily 1pm-2am, Sa-Su until 3am. MC/V.) **Cinémas Rochebrune** (☎04 50 21 03 52) plays movies July-Aug. and Dec.-Apr. **Le Canadien Bowling Alley** is at 370 rte. de Sallanches, in the *demi-quartier.* (☎04 50 21 18 40. Open Jan.-May and July-Dec. 2pm-2am.)

Summer brings great jazz music to Megève. In the middle of July is the annual **Megève Jazz Contest,** with over fifty free open-air concerts, while August heralds the week-long **Megève Jazz Festival.** More information available at the tourist office.

ANNECY

In the *vieille ville* of Annecy (pop. 50,300), far from the noisy thoroughfares and high-rises of downtown, narrow cobblestone streets, winding canals and turreted castles seem more the makings of a fairy-tale than a modern city. Massive moun-

RHÔNE-ALPS

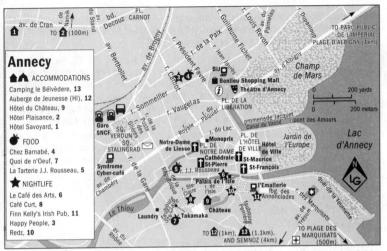

Annecy

🏠🏠 ACCOMMODATIONS

Camping le Bélvèdere, 13
Auberge de Jeunesse (HI), 12
Hôtel du Château, 9
Hôtel Plaisance, 2
Hôtel Savoyard, 1

🍎 FOOD

Chez Barnabé, 4
Quoi de n'Oeuf, 7
La Tarterie J.J. Rousseau, 5

⭐ NIGHTLIFE

Le Café des Arts, 6
Café Curt, 8
Finn Kelly's Irish Pub, 11
Happy People, 3
Redz, 10

tains and one of the purest lakes in Europe surround the manmade charms of this "Venice of the Alps," providing a stunning sight for both the windsurfers below and paragliders above.

TRANSPORTATION

Trains: pl. de la Gare. Open daily 5am-9pm. Ticket window open M-Sa 6am-8:45pm, Su and holidays 7:40am-8:30pm. To: **Chamonix** (2½hr., 6 per day, €17.70); **Grenoble** (2hr., 7 per day, €15); **Lyon** (2hr., 9 per day, €19.20); **Nice** (7-9hr., 7 per day with a change at Lyon, €67); **Paris** (4hr., 6 per day, €70.20).

Buses: adjacent to the train station. Office open M-F 7:45-11am and 2-7:15pm, Sa 7:45-11am. **Autocars Frossard** (☎04 50 45 73 90) runs to **Geneva, Switzerland** (1¼hr., 6 per day, €9.40).

Public Transportation: SIBRA (☎04 50 10 04 04). Info booth across from the train station at the southwest corner of rue de la Gare, open M-F 8:30am-7pm, Sa 8:30am-6pm. Extensive service; July-Aug. and weekends in June a summer line stops at the HI hostel when the D line bus stops just down the hill, (dir: Semnoz; 7am-6:30pm; July-Aug. daily 6 per day, June and Sept. Sa-Su 6 per day).) Tickets €1, *carnet* of 8 €6.50.

Taxis: at the station (☎04 50 45 05 67). 24hr. About €7 to the Auberge de Jeunesse.

Bike, Ski, and In-line Skate Rental:

Roul' ma Poule, 4 rue des Marquisats (04 50 27 86 83), next to the port. Bikes €7 per half-day, €11 per day. Inline skates €8 per half day, €12 per day. Open daily July-Aug. 8am-7pm; Sept.-June 8am-12:30pm and 2pm-7pm.

Little Big Shop, 38 av. de la Maveria-Annecy-le-Vieux (☎04 50 67 42 13), in front of the Maveria bus stop on line 1 (dir: Poisy). Bikes €10.50 per half-day, €15 per day. Ski, boot, and pole packages €14.50-25.50 per day. Open Tu-Sa 9am-noon and 2-7pm. MC/V.

Golf Miniature de l'Imperial, 2 av. du Petit Port (☎04 50 66 04 99), beside plage d'Albigny. Ask about a reduction if you're staying at the Auberge de Jeunesee. In-line skates €5 per hr., €8 per half-day, €9 per day. Bicycles €5 per hour, €14 per day. Open daily 9am-7pm.

ORIENTATION AND PRACTICAL INFORMATION

Most activity centers around the lake southeast of the train station. The canal runs east-west through the old town; the elevated château is on one side and the main shopping area, closer to the center of Annecy, is on the other. To reach the tourist

office from the train station, take the underground pedestrian passage to rue Sommeiller. Turn left onto rue Vaugelas and follow it for four blocks. The tourist office
is straight ahead in the large Bonlieu shopping mall.

Tourist Office: 1 rue J. Jaurès (☎04 50 45 00 33 or 04 50 45 56 66; ancy-
tour@noos.fr), at pl. de la Libération. Detailed maps of the city, info on hiking, climbing,
excursions, and lodging. The bilingual Annecy Guide describes nearby sights. Sentiers
Forestiers (€3.10) details hiking paths in the Semnoz forest. Comprehensive French
topo-guide of the region (€9.60). **Tours** of the *vieille ville* (2hr.; July-Aug. French tours
M-Sa 3:30pm, English tours M and F 4pm; €5.20). Office open daily 9am-6:30pm.

Youth Center: Bureau Information Jeunesse, 1 rue Jean Jaurès (☎04 50 33 87 40;
infojeunes@ville-annecy.fr), in the Bonlieu Center. Friendly staff offers advice and info
on study options, housing, jobs, and leisure activities. Free **Internet**, though expect a
wait. Open M 3-7pm, Tu-F 12:30-7pm, Sa 10am-noon.

Laundromat: Lav'Confort Express, 6 rue de la Gare, across the canal. Wash €4.50, dry
€0.50 per 5min. Open daily 7am-9pm.

Police: 17 rue des Marquisats (☎04 50 52 32 00).

Hospital: 1 av. de Trésum (☎04 50 88 33 33).

Internet Access: Free at the **Youth Center. Syndrome Cyber-café,** 3bis av. de Chevenes
(☎04 50 45 39 75), around the corner from the train station. €2 per 15min., €6 per
hr. Open daily July-Aug. noon-10pm; Sept.-June M-W noon-7:30pm, Th-Sa noon-10pm.
L'Emailerie, faubourg des Annonciades (☎04 50 10 18 91), in the *vieille ville*, has
American keyboards. €1.50 per 15min., €6 per hr. Open daily June-Aug. 10am-8pm;
Sept.-May M-Sa 10:30am-12:30pm and 2:30-7:30pm.

Post Office: entrance on rue des Glières (☎04 50 33 68 20), down the street from the
train station. **Currency exchange** at good rates, no commission. Open M-F 8:30am-
6:30pm and Sa 8am-noon. **Poste Restante:** 74011.

Postal Code: 74000.

ACCOMMODATIONS AND CAMPING

Annecy's priciest accommodations are in the charming *vieille ville* and by the
lake. Reservations are recommended, especially during ski season and in summer.

■ **Auberge de Jeunesse "La Grande Jeanne" (HI),** rte. de Semnoz (☎04 50 45 33 19;
annecy@fuaj.org). See **Public Transportation.** Or, take bus #1 (dir: Marquisats) from
the station to Hôpital, in front of the police station. Walk straight on av. de Tresum,
away from the lake, and follow the signs to Semnoz. Take a left onto bd. de la Corniche
and a right onto the small chemin du Belvédère for the ascent to the hostel (15 min. by
bus, 25min. by foot from train station.) This auberge makes up for its relative distance
from the *centre ville* in both views and value. Tiny, quiet dorms, with showers. Single-sex
rooms available. Game room, kitchen, TV room, bar and laundry. Breakfast included.
Dinner €9. Sheets €2.90. Reception Apr.-Nov. 8am-noon and 3-10pm; mid-Jan. to Mar.
8am-noon and 5-10pm. Reservations via the Internet at www.iyhf.org suggested June-
Aug., must pay in advance. Closed Dec. to mid-Jan. Bunks €13.90. MC/V. ❶

Hôtel Savoyard, 41 av. de Cran (☎04 50 57 08 08). The spacious rooms in this
Savoyard mansion are a bargain, and the managers attend to their clientele with infinite
care. Breakfast €4. Reception daily 7am-10pm. Open May-Oct. Singles and doubles
€20, with shower and bath €27-35; triples €30/€33-41; quads with bath €45. ❷

Hôtel Plaisance, 17 rue de Narvik (☎/fax 04 50 57 30 42), off av. de Cran, 5 min. from
the train station. Charming manager offers intimate, quiet rooms, a cozy breakfast area,
and a TV salon. Breakfast €3.90. Showers €2. Reception daily 7am-midnight. Singles
and doubles €24, with shower and toilet €32; triples €39; quads €45.80-49. Reservations recommended, especially during festivals. MC/V. ❷

Hôtel du Château, 16 rampe du Château (☎04 50 45 27 66; hotelduchatea@noos.fr). Spectacular views and pristine white rooms make this the best option in the *vieille ville*. All rooms have shower and bath. Free Internet access for guests. Breakfast € 7. Reception daily 7am-9pm. Open mid-Dec to mid-Nov. Singles €48; doubles €58-62; triples €65; quads €75. MC/V. ❹

Camping: Camping le Bélvèdere, 8 rte. de Semnoz (☎04 50 45 48 30; camping@ville-annecy.fr), uphill from the youth hostel. Open campsites dot a grassy hill overlooking the lake. Small grocery store, phone booth, TV, ping-pong, pétanque, and extensive hiking trails nearby. Reception. 8:30 am-2pm, 5pm-8pm. July-Aug. reserve via email or fax. Open mid-Apr. to mid-Oct. Sept.-June 1-2 people with tent and car €10-11; July-Aug. €13.70. Extra person €3.90-4.70, extra tent €1.70-2.40. Electricity €2.50. Laundry €5.50 wash/€2.60 dry. Bike rental €7 per half-day, €12 per day. MC/V. ❶

FOOD

Annecy's *vieille ville* is lined with restaurants that charm the eye, palate, and pocketbook. Fill a picnic basket with the soft local *reblochon* cheese at the **markets** on pl. Ste-Claire (Tu, F, and Su 8am-noon) and on bd. Taine. (Sa 8am-noon), or cool mid-afternoon crankiness with sorbet from one of countless *glaciers*. A **Monoprix supermarket** fills most of pl. de Notre-Dame. (☎04 50 45 23 60. Open M-Sa 8:30am-7:30pm.) A **Petit Casino** supermarket is at 10 rue des Glières, across from the post office. (☎04 50 51 38 31. Open M-F 8am-12:15pm and 3-7:30pm, Sa 8am-12:15pm and 3-7pm.) The best options for budget-conscious gourmands are the tiny restaurants along faubourg Ste-Claire. The popular ⚫**Quoi de n'Oeuf ❸**, 19 faubourg Ste-Claire, serves meals of plentiful tartiflettes, salads and desserts, starting at €10.50. (☎04 50 45 75 42. Open M-Sa noon-2pm and 7-9:45pm. MC/V.)

For an escape from fondue, try **La Tarterie J.J. Rousseau ❷**, 14 rue J. J. Rousseau. The €10.20 *menu* includes *tarte salée* (in salmon, chicken, vegetarian, and cheese variations), *tarte sucrée*, and drink. (☎04 50 45 36 25. Open M-Tu noon-2pm, W-Sa noon-2pm and 7-9pm. MC/V.) With so many lovely gardens around, picnics are a great option. Paper-bag it at **Chez Barnabé ❶**, 29 rue Sommeiller. (☎04 50 45 90 62. Salad bar €2.70-€5.30, homemade hot dishes €2.10-€5.30, sandwiches €2.50-€3.10, pizza €1.60-€2. Open M-Sa 10am-7:15pm.)

SIGHTS

VIEILLE VILLE. A stroll through the *vieille ville* will cost you several rolls of film. **The Palais de l'Isle,** is a 13th-century château first occupied by the Counts of Geneva after their hometown came under Episcopal control, is a beautiful building, located strategically on a narrow island in the canal. It served as a prison, most recently for WWII Resistance fighters, whose impassioned carvings mark the walls. (☎04 50 33 87 30. Open daily June-Sept. 10:30am-6pm; Oct.-May Su-M and W-Sa 10am-noon and 2-5pm. €3.20, students €0.90.) Beneath the towers of the castle on the opposite side of the canal, **quai Perrière, rue de l'Isle,** and **faubourg Ste-Claire** are some of Annecy's most charming streets, despite abundant arcades and crowds of visitors.

Straddling the town's narrowest canal, the large and bare church **Église St-Maurice,** consecrated in 1442, is well-known for the rare 15th-century painting that marks the tomb of Philibert de Monthoux, a one-time Annecy noble; look for it on the choir's left wall as you enter. This macabre mural of a decomposing corpse—finished a whole two years before its patron's death—is thought to reflect anxiety over the Hundred Years' War.

THE LAKE. A brisk swim in Annecy's crystalline, Mediterranean-blue lake might just hit the spot after a long afternoon in the *ville*. With a spectacular view and grassy expanses, ⚫**plage d'Albigny,** 3km up av. d'Albigny, draws tourists and locals in the summer for windsurfing, sailing, and kayaking, as well as dining in lakeside restaurants.

The smaller and more crowded **plage des Marquisats,** south of the city down rue des Marquisats, also permits swimming. The Club de Voile Française on the lake rents a limited selection of watercraft. Rent **pedal boats** at one of the numerous companies along the port or, for better deals, on the south side of the Champ de Mars. *(€8 for 30min., €12 per hr.; lake tours €6-14.)* For €3.50, the young at heart can frolic in the **Parc Public de l'Impérial,** an aquatic wonderland with waterslides, sailing, tennis, swimming, and a casino. *(20min. up av. d'Albigny beside plage d'Albigny. ☎04 50 23 11 82. Open daily May-Sept. 11am-7:30pm.)* Views of the lake from above are as breathtaking as plunging into its depths. Annecy is one of the best places in the world for **paragliding** *(parapenting)*, and plenty of companies help fuel this reputation, most with comparable prices. **Takamaka,** 17 faubourg Ste-Claire, helps little Daedali fly above the crystal-blue waters. *(☎04 50 45 60 61; www.takamaka.fr.* Hikes €30 per half-day, €45 per day. Canyoning €47-95. Sign up the night before. Tandem paragliding €80, 5-day course €480. Open daily July-Aug. 9am-7pm; Sept.- June M-F 9am-noon and 2-6pm. MC/V.)

GARDENS. Graced by manicured hedges, fountains, and the occasional long-necked swan, the shaded **Jardin de l'Europe** is Annecy's pride and joy. At its north side, the **Pont des Amours** (Lover's Bridge) connects the European gardens to the **Champ de Mars,** a grassy esplanade frequented by picnickers, sunbathers, and frisbee-throwers. Residents aren't quick to gloat, but such gardens have won it victory in the national *Ville Fleurie* (Flower City) contest three times in the last decade.

CHÂTEAU. The 12th-century château, a short, steep climb from the *vieille ville*, towers over Annecy. Once a stronghold of the Genevan Counts, the castle and its imposing parapets now contain archaeological and artistic exhibits. In the main building, the museum's welcome desk occupies an enormous hearth. Exhibit rooms present a melange of objects and architecture, from Medieval Savoyan furniture to contemporary art. In the rear of the castle, the **Observatoire Régional des Lacs Alpins** has an aquarium of local fish and extensive exhibits about regional ecology and archeology. A large model of the Lac and its surrounding mountains gives a bird's eye view for those who never ascend higher than the Château. *(☎04 50 33 87 30. Open June-Sept. daily 10:30am-6pm; Oct.-May Su-M and W-Sa 10am-noon and 2-5pm. Château €4.70, students €1.60 1.50. Entrance to grounds free.)*

🎵 🎇 **ENTERTAINMENT AND FESTIVALS**

Relaxing bars line the canal in the *vieille ville*, creating a scene that tends to revolve more around mellow outdoor drinking than wild dancing. Artsy bar **Le Café des Arts,** 4 pass. de l'Isle, has a prime spot next to the cathedral. *(☎04 50 51 56 40. Beer €3.10-4. Open daily 8:30am-2am.)* Easy-going **Café Curt,** 35 rue Ste-Claire, is crowded with students and backpackers. *(Wine €1.30-3, Kronenbourg €2, cognac €5-55. Open daily June-Sept. 10am-2am; Oct.-May 10am-1am.)* The most beloved bar in town is **Finn Kelly's Irish Pub,** 10 faubourg des Annonciades, where locals chat by the bar and Anglos converge at outdoor tables. *(☎04 50 51 29 40. Beer €3-5. Open daily 4:30pm-2am.)* Annecy's flashiest bar is **Redz,** 14 rue Perrière, which puffs smoke out of its perpetually open doors. It draws an older clientele with theme nights and DJs nightly June-Aug. *(☎04 50 45 17 13. Beer €3-6, cocktails €9-16. Open daily Apr.-Oct. 11am-3am; Nov.-Mar. 5pm-3am.)*

Happy People, 48 rue Carnot, lives up to its name; wild nights are the norm at this gay and lesbian-friendly disco, with a dark lounge in the back perfect for romantic breaks from the dance floor. *(☎04 50 51 08 66. Drinks €9-12. Cover F-Sa €12, includes one drink. Open daily 6pm-5am.)*

Performing arts and films can be found at the **Théâtre d'Annecy** in the Bonlieu Mall across from the tourist office. (☎ 04 50 33 44 11. Tickets €15-23, students €11.50-20.) Pick up festival schedules at the tourist office. There's a film festival the first weekend of June, but the biggest party is the **Fête du Lac,** with fireworks and water shows every first Saturday in August (€6-41.50).

◤ HIKING

Annecy's nearby Alpine forests shelter excellent hiking and biking trails. Dozens of hikes begin on the **Semnoz,** a limestone mountain south of the city. The **Office National des Forêts** (☎ 04 50 23 84 10) distributes a color map, *Sentiers Forestiers*, with several routes (€3.10 at the tourist office or hostel). The *Guide Pratique* also has lots of info on outdoor recreation. One of the best hikes begins at the **Basilique de la Visitation,** a 5min. walk from the hostel and campground. From town, take bus A to its terminus, Visitation. From the basilica, continue along the road until you reach a small parking lot. Follow signs for "*La Forêt du Crêt du Maure*." The trailhead has a large map of trails, all color coded. The gently graded perimeter trail, well marked with blue blazes, follows a meandering 2hr. circle around the Semnoz forest, leading past breathtaking views. After about an hour, the trail intersects with the red-and-yellow-marked **GR96,** on which long-haulers sometimes opt for a 38km circuit of the lake. Turn around or continue the blue-marked loop, which terminates at a second trailhead just above the hostel and campgrounds. A short road above the campgrounds leads back to the start.

For those who prefer to cover more ground, an exquisite 16km *piste cyclable* (bike route) hugs the level, eastern shore of the lake. An entire circuit of the lake can be completed by cycling on the main road (D909a), but be prepared for the hills of the western shore and be vigilant of traffic. The tourist office has a free map of the lake that includes the bike route and some departure points for hikes.

The **Bureau des Guides** and **Takamaka** run excursions for mountaineering activities, that include hiking, biking, rock-climbing, paragliding, and canyoning.

Performing arts and films can be found at the **Théâtre d'Annecy** in the Bonlieu Mall across from the tourist office. (☎ 04 50 33 44 11. Tickets €15-23, students €11.50-20.) Pick up festival schedules at the tourist office. There's a film festival the first weekend of June, but the biggest party is the **Fête du Lac,** with fireworks and water shows every first Saturday in August (€6-41.50).

AROUND LAC D'ANNECY

The smaller, more peaceful villages on the Lac d'Annecy, within 20km of Annecy, are accessible by bus and boat and make excellent daytrips. Voyages Crolard **buses,** departing from the train station and stopping in front of the tourist office and near the plage d'Albigny, circle the lake. (☎ 04 50 45 08 12; www.voyages-crolard.com. 10 per day, Su less frequently. Tickets €2.70-3.10.) The tourist office in Annecy can help avoid confusion about bus schedules, which tend to vary on the weekends. In the summer, the Compagnie des Bateaux runs three lake buses per day, departing from the main port of Annecy and stopping around the lake at Veyrier, Methon, Talloires, Doussard, Duingt, Saint-Joriez, and Sevrier. (☎ 04 50 51 08 40. €12.30 for the whole circuit.)

· The spectacular **Gorges du Fier** is a canyon etched by water erosion, 10km west of Annecy. The 256m long suspended walkway across the gorges yields spectacular views. (Info ☎ 04 50 46 23 07. www.gorgesdufier.com. Open daily mid-June to mid-Sept. 9am-7pm; mid-Mar. to mid-June and early Sept. to mid-Oct. 9am-noon and 2-6pm. €4.50.)

Château de Montrottier, 5min. from the canyon entrance, was formerly owned by the region's foremost art collectors and displays centuries-old Asian costumes, armor, and pottery. (☎ 04 50 46 23 02. Open daily June-Aug. 10am-1pm and 2-7pm; mid-Mar.-May and Sept. Su-M and W-Sa 10am-1pm and 2-6pm; early Oct.-June Su-M and W-Sa 2-6pm. €6, students €5.20.) To get there, take SIBRA minibus A from the train station to **Poisy-Moiry** (30min., 5 per day, €1) and walk away from the town center, following signs for Lovagny to the gorges. (40min., 3km.) The route is poorly marked at first: walkers should remember to head away from the town center and get directions from the bus driver or tourist office. For those who would rather avoid the walk, Voyages Crolard runs a **bus** tour that includes admission to the gorges and the château. (☎ 04 50 45 00 56. July-Aug. W 2pm, returns 7pm. €18.)

🗹**Talloires,** 13km from Annecy, claims panoramic views over the lake, excellent dining, a beautiful public beach and, to top it off, access to multiple "*curiosités naturelles.*" A 40min. hike to the point of **le Roc de Chère,** declared a natural reserve in 1977, passes through a forest of unique flora and fauna and ends with unparalleled views of the whole region. To reach the trail, follow rue Noblemaire which traverses the town to its terminus, take a left (toward Annecy), and after the haripin bend turn off on the stairs in a stone wall on the left. As if the view of Talloires wasn't enough, continue on to try the 1hr. hike to the impressive waterfalls at **La Cascade d'Angon,** the **Pont de Fées,** and the beautiful gardens of the **Ermitage de St-Germain.** Take the Closettaz path out of the village, which is a right up the hill, and follow the signs. The hike begins behind the Talloires Écoles bus stop. At the trail's first division, about 40min. into the climb, make a sharp right through an old iron gate to skirt the side of the gorge and view the cascade with (perhaps) canyoners rappelling down its sides. Those looking for a more hard-core day of hiking should inquire about the route that ascends the mountain which looms over the town, la Tournette (2351m). Talloires's tourist office (☎ 04 50 60 70 64; fax 04 50 60 76 5; open M-F 9:00am-12:30pm and 2pm-6pm, Sa 9am-12:30pm) distributes maps, written directions, and friendly advice on the town's many sights. The town is accessible by Voyage Crolard Buses running seven times per day except Sunday and holidays (see above listing).

South of Annecy, **Doussard** is noteworthy for being Lac d'Annecy's source and for its surrounding nature preserves. (Tourist office ☎ 04 50 44 30 45; fax 04 50 44 81 75.) Nearby **St-Jorioz** is known for its great mountain views. (Tourist office ☎ 04 50 68 61 82; fax 04 50 68 96 11.)

Across the lake from Annecy, **Menthon** holds a hidden marvel in the opulent 12th-century **château de Menthon.** The castle marks the birthplace of St-Bernard de Menthon, who made his name in the business of dog breeding. His ridiculously wealthy descendants still live in the spacious abode, but the lower floors—including a walnut-paneled library, music salon, and 14th-century bedroom—are open to the public. (☎ 04 50 60 12 05. Open July-Aug. daily noon-6pm; May-June and Sept. F-Su 2-6pm. €6, weekend tours in period dress €7.)

The nearest **ski resort** is **La Clusaz,** 32km away, with 130km of trails and 56 lifts. Contact the **tourist office** in La Clusaz for info. (☎ 04 50 32 65 00.) The international youth hostel **La Grande Jeanne ❶,** outside La Clusaz on rte. du Col de la Croix Fry, has mostly quads with showers. (☎ 04 50 02 41 73; fax 04 50 02 65 85. Breakfast included. Reception daily 8am-noon and 5-8pm. Open mid-Dec. to mid-Sept. Mid-May to mid-Sept. dorms €15. Mid-Dec. to mid-May weekly stays only; *demi-pension* €289, full *pension* €329. MC/V.)

CHAMONIX

The train station is named "Chamonix-Mt. Blanc" for more than convenience: the towering snow-capped mountain and the city in its shadow have an intimate connection. Chamonix (pop. 10,000) hosted the first Winter Olympics in 1924 and never extinguished the torch. Whether they're drawn to the skiing, hiking, cycling, or rock-climbing, it's clear that people here always have mountains on their minds. Those who glance away from Western Europe's tallest peak will notice a friendly, easily navigable town with authentic chalets, bustling pedestrian streets, and a bilingual population.

TRANSPORTATION

Trains: av. de la Gare (☎ 04 50 53 12 98). A special local train runs from **St-Gervais** to **Martigny,** stopping at Chamonix. Ticket sales daily 6:10am-8:10pm. Info kiosk daily July-Aug. 9:20am-noon and 1:15-6:18pm. From St-Gervais to: **Annecy** (2½hr., 6 per day, €18); **Geneva airport** (2½hr., 7 per day, €45); **Grenoble** (4hr., 5 per day, €26); **Lyon** (4hr., 6 per day, €32); **Paris** (6-7hr., 7 per day, €50-70).

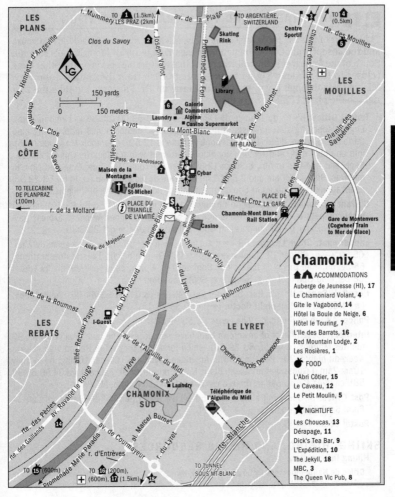

RHÔNE-ALPS

Chamonix

🏠🏕 ACCOMMODATIONS

Auberge de Jeunesse (HI), **17**
Le Chamoniard Volant, **4**
Gîte le Vagabond, **14**
Hôtel la Boule de Neige, **6**
Hôtel le Touring, **7**
L'Ile des Barrats, **16**
Red Mountain Lodge, **2**
Les Rosières, **1**

🍴 FOOD

L'Abri Côtier, **15**
Le Caveau, **12**
Le Petit Moulin, **5**

⭐ NIGHTLIFE

Les Choucas, **13**
Dérapage, **11**
Dick's Tea Bar, **9**
L'Expédition, **10**
The Jekyll, **18**
MBC, **3**
The Queen Vic Pub, **8**

Buses: Société Alpes Transports, at the train station (☎04 50 53 01 15). Ticket office open July-Aug. M-Sa 7:45-8:15am, 9:30am-12:15pm, and 1:20-6:30pm; Su 8-8:30am, 9:30am-12:15pm, and 2-6:15pm. Call for office hours during low season. To: **Courmayeur,** Italy (50min.; July-Aug. 6 per day, Sept.-June M-Sa 2 per day; €9.50), and **Geneva,** Switzerland (1hr.; July-Aug. M-Sa 3 per day, Su 1 per day; Sept.-Nov. and May-June M-Sa 1 per day; Dec.-Apr. M-F 4 per day, Sa-Su 5 per day; €33 to town, €33 to airport). **Voyages Crolard** (☎04 50 45 08 12) runs to **Annecy** (2¼hr., M-F 1 per day, €15).

Public Transportation: Chamonix Bus (☎04 50 53 05 55) runs to ski slopes and hiking trails. Follow signs from pl. de l'Église to the main bus stop. Chamonix hotels and *gîtes* dispense the **Carte d'Hôte,** which gives free travel on all buses. Tickets €1.50.

Taxis: at the station (☎04 50 53 13 94). **Alp Taxi Rochaix** (☎04 50 54 00 48). 24hr. About €12 to the Auberge de Jeunesse.

ORIENTATION AND PRACTICAL INFORMATION

The center of town is the intersection of av. Michel Croz, rue du Docteur Paccard, and rue Joseph Vallot, each named for a past conqueror of Mont Blanc's summit. South of the **Arve** river is the train station. Most everything else is on the other bank (closer to the slopes). To get to the tourist office from the station, follow av. Michel Croz through town, turn left onto rue du Dr. Paccard, and take the first right to the pl. de l'Église (5 minutes).

Tourist Office: 85 pl. du Triangle de l'Amitié (☎04 50 53 00 24; www.chamonix.com). English-speaking staff has lists of accommodations, campgrounds map, hiking map *Carte des Sentiers d'Eté* (€4, guidebook with maps 12.50), *Chamonix Magazine* (free), info on cable cars, and weather conditions. **Internet** with a *télécarte*. Open daily July-Sept. and mid-Dec to Apr. 8:30am-12:30pm and 2-7pm; May-June, Oct., and Nov. to mid-Dec. 9am-12:30pm and 2-6:30 pm. **Centrale de Reservation** (☎04 59 53 23 33; reservation@chamonix.com) books apartments or hotels for stays of 2 nights or more.

Currency Exchange: Comptoir de Change, 21 pl. Balmat (☎04 50 55 88 40), has the most competitive rates. 24hr. **exchange** machine. Also changes American Express traveler's checks for €7.60 commission Open daily 8am-noon and 1:30-6:30.

Laundromat: Cham'Laverie, 98 via d'Aoste, located just off of av. de l'Aiguille du Midi. €5.50 wash, €2 per 12 minutes dry. Open daily 9am-midnight. **Laverie Automatique,** 65 av. du Mont Blanc, in the Galerie Commerciale Alpina, does your laundry for you at €8 per load Open Jul.-Aug. 8am-7pm, Sept.-June 9am-noon, 2pm-7:30pm.

Hospital: Centre Hospitalier, 509 rte. des Pèlerins (☎04 50 53 84 00). **Ambulance:** (☎04 50 53 84 00); **night doctor** (☎04 50 53 48 48).

Police: 48 rue de l'Hôtel de Ville (☎04 50 55 99 58).

Internet Access: Plenty of downtown bars have web access. The best deal is **Cybar,** 80 rue des Moulins (☎04 50 53 69 70), which turns into Dick's Tea Bar on high season weekend nights. 20+ PCs, some with American keyboards, €1 per 10min., open daily 10am-2am. **I-Guest,** in the Galerie Blanc Neige, off rue du Dr. Paccard, (☎04 50 55 98 58), charges €7.50 per hr. Open daily 10am-1pm and 4-8pm. MC/V.

Post Office: pl. Jacques-Balmat (☎04 50 53 15 90). Open M-F 8:30am-noon and 2-6pm, Sa 8:30am-noon.

Postal Code: 74400.

SKIING, BIKING, AND HIKING RESOURCES
Hiking Information:

Office de Haute-Montagne (☎04 50 53 22 08; www.ohm-chamonix.com), on the 3rd floor of the Maison de la Montagne, across from the tourist office. An expert staff helps plan your adventures, gives info on weather conditions, and sells detailed maps (€4-9). Extensive printed resources, including magazines and recent travel-logs, line shelves for perusal. Open daily July-Aug. 9am-noon and 3-6pm; closed Su Sept.-June and Sa Oct.-Nov.

Club Alpin Français, 136 av. Michel Croz (☎ 04 50 53 16 03; infos@clubalpin-chamonix.com). Best source of info on mountain *refuges* and road conditions. Guides available: register 6-7:30pm the day before hikes. Bulletin board matches drivers, riders, and hiking partners. Hikers from far and wide convene in the office to plan the weekend's trips and excursions (F 7pm). **Members only;** email to inquire about membership. Open July-Aug. M-Sa 9:30am-noon and 3:30-7:30pm, closed W morning; M-Tu and Th-F 3:30-7pm, Sa 9am-noon.

Skiing and Hiking Lessons and Info: École du Ski (☎ 04 50 53 22 57), on the 2nd floor of the Maison de la Montagne. Half-day group lessons €60; 2hr. private lesson €105; guided group descent of Vallée Blanche €62. Open Dec.-Apr. daily 8:15am-7pm. On the main floor, the **Compagnie des Guides** (☎ 04 50 53 00 88; www.cieguides-chamonix.com) gives skiing and climbing lessons and leads guided summer hikes and winter ski trips of varying difficulties. Group ski excursions €60 per person. Register by 5:30pm the evening before. Open daily Jan.-Mar. and July-Aug. 8:30am-noon and 3:30-7:30pm; Sept.-Dec. and Apr.-June Mon-Sa 9am-noon and 2:30pm-7pm.

Cycling Information: Pick up the free, invaluable map and guide, *Itinéraires Autorisés aux Vélos Tout Terrain,* at the tourist office or at mountain bike rental shops.

Weather Conditions: at Maison de la Montagne, Club Alpin Français, and the tourist office. Call ☎ 08 92 68 02 74 for a French recording of road and weather conditions.

Mountain Rescue: PGHM Secours en Montagne, 69 rte. de la Mollard (☎ 04 50 53 16 89). 24hr. emergency service.

Hiking Equipment: Outdoor outfitters abound in Chamonix's main shopping areas. **Snell Sports,** 104 rue Paccard (04 50 53 02 17, www.cham3s.com) has a massive stock of skiing and hiking gear and clothing. Rentals of everything from boots (€7 per day) and backpacks (€ 8 per day), to a "Mont Blanc" kit of boots, crampons, and ice axes (€16 per day). Open high season 9am-12:30pm and 2:30pm-7:30pm; low season 9am-noon and 2:30pm-7pm. AmEx/MC/V.

Bike and Ski Rental: Dozens of places rent skis, snowboards, bikes, and climbing equipment. Skis should not be more than €8-16 per day or €40-65 per week, depending on quality. Snowboards should not exceed €16 per day and €80 per week.

■■ ACCOMMODATIONS AND CAMPING

Chamonix's hotels tend to be expensive, but the *gîtes* and dormitories are quite cheap. The hardest time to get a room is early February, when the city hosts a car race. Call the tourist office for available places; the accommodations listed by *Let's Go* fill up fast, especially in the high seasons, which last from January to April and mid-June to late August. Prices often rise and fall with the crowds.

The area's far-flung mountain *refuges* tend to be remote, with few facilities, and are frequently unattended. For info on these mountain *refuges,* see the **Outdoors** section of Chamonix (p. 448). The tourist office and the Club Alpin both have listings of refuge openings and price-lists.

☒ Red Mountain Lodge, 435 rue Joseph Vallot (☎ 04 50 53 94 97). From the station, walk down av. Michel Croz and turn right onto rue Joseph Vallot. Spacious *chalet* turned backpacker's haven, where 2-night stays quickly stretch into 2 weeks. Friendly, hard-working staff helps facilitate a homey warm atmosphere. Breakfast included. Reserve well in advance, especially in the high seasons. Dorms €16; private rooms €20-30. ❷

Gîte le Vagabond, 365 av. Ravanel le Rouge (☎ 04 50 53 15 43; gitevagabond@hotmail.com). This friendly *gîte,* near the center of town, has cozy wooden bunkrooms that encourage bonding, as well as a popular bar, climbing wall and Internet cafe (€0.15

per min). Breakfast €5. Dinner €10.50. Kitchen. Luggage storage. Laundry €7.70. Reception 8am-10am, 4:39-midnight. 4-to 8-bunk dorms €12.90. Renovated bed and breakfast doubles, with bathroom and sitting room, €60. Credit card deposit. MC/V. ❶

Auberge de Jeunesse (HI), 127 montée Jacques Balmat (☎04 50 53 14 52), in Les Pélerins, at the foot of the Glacier de Bossons. Take the bus from the train station or pl. Mont Blanc (dir: Pélerins) to Pélerins École (€1.50), and follow the signs uphill to the hostel. On the special train, get off at Les Pélerins and follow the signs. By foot, walk down rte. des Pélerins. (30min.) The hostel is situated in a beautiful modern *chalet* practically on top of a glacier, but the atmosphere is a bit impersonal. The 2-to 6-person bunks are in a separate building. Ask about reductions on all-inclusive ski packages (€415 and up), equipment rental, and other special guest values in town. Breakfast included. Dinner €8. Sheets €3. Reception 8am-noon and 5-10pm. Dorms €14.20; singles €15.30; with shower €16; doubles €30.60/€32. MC/V. ❶

Le Chamoniard Volant, 45 rte. de la Frasse (☎04 50 53 14 09; www.chamoniard.com), 15min. from the center of town. From the station, turn right, go under the bridge, and turn right across the tracks, left on chemin des Cristalliers, and right on rte. de la Frasse. This *gîte* has a rustic, camplike atmosphere with wooden walls, 4, 6, or 8-person bunkrooms, red-checked tablecloths, and lots of ski paraphernalia. Internet €9 per hr. Breakfast €4.50. Dinner €10.50. Sheets €4. Reception 10am-10pm. Reservations required; call or check the website. Dorms, €12; demi-pension €27. MC/V. ❶

Hôtel la Boule de Neige, 362 rue Joseph Vallot (☎04 50 53 04 48; laboule@claranet.fr). Cute, ski instructor-run alpine *chalet* with small but spotless rooms and firm beds, above a bar in a busy part of town. Breakfast €6. Reception 7am-noon and 5-7pm. Dec.-Feb. reserve 2 months in advance. Singles €35, with bath €40-50; doubles €55-60; triples €50-60; quads with bath €75-85. MC/V. ❸

Hôtel le Touring, 95 rue Joseph Vallot (☎04 50 53 59 18; www.hoteltouring-chamonix.com). Large hotel with English-speaking staff, charming alpine decor, and spacious rooms. It's almost always packed with groups Dec.-Apr. Breakfast €8. Reception 8am-10pm. Singles with shower €44; doubles with bath €54-72, 3rd bed €15, 4th bed €10. Late Aug. to mid-July prices €10-15 lower. MC/V. ❹

Camping:

L'Ile des Barrats, 185 chemin de l'Ile des Barrats (☎/fax 04 50 53 51 44), off rte. des Pèlerins, has great views and amiable crowds. Friendly manager keeps a well-maintained, grassy site. With your back to the cable car, turn left, pass the busy roundabout, continue 5min., and look right. Luggage storage. Open May-Sept. Reception daily July-Aug. 8am-10pm; May-June and Sept. 9am-noon and 4-7pm. Laundry, €5 wash, €3 dry. €5.40 per person, €4.90 per tent, €2.20 per car. Electricity €3. ❶

Les Rosières, 121 clos des Rosières (☎04 50 53 10 42; www.campinglesrosieres.com), off rte. de Praz, is close to les *Praz* and often has room. Small sites among chalets with stunning views. Follow rue Vallot for 1.5km or take a bus to Les Nants. Reception daily July-Aug. 8am-9pm; Sept.-June 9am-noon and 2-7pm. Open early Feb. to *late Sepy.* €5.80 per person, €3 per tent, €3 per car. Electricity €2.80. Prices slightly lower in the low seasons. ❶

🄵 FOOD

Tourist-driven Chamonix has a wider gamut of restaurants than one might expect. Bars and ski lodges serve decent meals, and in the town's many bistros regional fare like fondue and *raclette* shares menu space with international ski staples. There is a **Super U,** 117 rue Joseph Vallot (☎04 50 53 12 50; open M-Sa 8:15am-7:30pm, Su 8:30am-noon), and a **Casino** supermarket at 17 av. du Mont Blanc, inside the Galerie Commerciale Alpina. (☎04 50 53 11 85. Open M-Sa 8:30am-7:30pm; July-Aug. also Su 8:30am-12:30pm.) A morning **market** is held on pl. du Mont Blanc. (Sa 7:30am-1pm.)

RESTAURANTS

▨ **Le Petit Moulin,** 65 rue des Moulins (☎04 50 53 50 03), has a creative *tapas*-style menu featuring such diverse dishes as falafel salad, tandoori chicken, steak, ale pie, and marsala duck (€5–6.50), as well as massive sandwiches and baked potatoes for lunch (€4-5.50). Dinner *plats* €11-13.50. Closed 1½ weeks in Oct. Open M-F noon-2pm and 7-10:30pm, Sa-Su 8:30am-2pm and 7-10:30pm. MC/V. ❸

▨ **Le Caveau,** 13 rue du Dr. Paccard (☎04 50 55 86 18). This 300-year-old former wine and cheese cellar serves tasty, large brick-oven pizzas (€6.90-11.80), vegetarian options (€8.50-9.80), and Swedish specialties like meatballs (€12.90). The Swedish owner claims to serve the world's best garlic bread. Open Dec. to mid-June and mid-July to Sept. daily 6:30pm-2am; Oct.-Nov. Su-M and W-Sa 6:30pm-2am. MC/V. ❷

L'Abri Côtier, 67 promenade Marie Paradis (☎04 50 53 42 97), offers regional specialties and traditional cuisine under a ceiling of hanging baskets. Try the excellent fondues and *raclettes*. Lunch *menu* €12.50, lunch and dinner *menus* €15.50 and 24.50. Open daily 11:30am-3pm and 5:30-10:30pm. Closed for 2 weeks in late May. MC/V. ❸

RESTAURANT AND BARS

▨ **The Jekyll,** 71 rte. des Pèlerins (☎04 50 55 99 70). In an old stone barn, this popular Irish pub serves huge portions of hearty, traditional Irish and international food, with live music on many weekend nights. A new cocktail bar downstairs, called the Hyde (!), promises to keep the party going. Happy hour 5pm-6pm. Entrees €12-19. Open daily Dec.-Apr. 4pm-2am; July-Oct. M-Sa 6pm-2am; July-Aug. closed Su. MC/V. ❷

▨ **MBC Micro Brasserie de Chamonix,** 350 rte. du Bouchet (☎04 50 53 61 59). A 10min. walk from the center of town, just across from the Centre Sportif. Anglo and French locals rave about this mellow, untouristed micro-brewery with 3 ales and lots of food. Lounge on couches beneath Christmas lights and canoe paddles, and drink maple leaf ale made in the huge brewing vats behind the bar. *Plats* €10.50-13.50, pints €4.50, pitchers €12. Open daily 4pm-2am. ❷

▨ NIGHTLIFE

Chamonix's nightclubs and pubs are especially popular in the winter when people shake what's left of their ski-weary bodies. Pubs are open year-round, although they can be eerily empty during the low seasons. Locals offer great tips on where to drink, but even the newest visitors to the town won't have to crawl far between beverages on bar-filled **rue des Moulins.**

▨ **L'Expédition,** 26 rue des Moulins (☎04 50 53 57 68). A chic crowd of ski instructors, *hôteliers*, and guides schmooze in this mainstay's small, intimate interior. Frequent theme nights, including "Beach Party" and "Gangsta." Draft beer €5.50, cocktails €4.20-7.80. Open daily 6pm-2am.

▨ **The Queen Vic Pub,** 74 rue des Moulins (☎04 50 53 91 98). Energetic English pub draws a young, mixed crowd. Pool tables, sports viewing, and loud music in a 2-floor *chalet*. Beer €2.50. Happy hour 6-9pm. Open daily 6pm-2am.

Le Dérapage, 17 pl. Jacques-Balmat (☎ 04 50 53 36 41), across from the post office. Run by British brothers, this laid-back bar makes for a relaxed night. 17 kinds of home-flavored vodkas line the walls behind the bar, including kiwi, toffee, and (masochistic) chili pepper. Ask the bartenders for recommendations, or try 1 of the tempting cocktails (banana daiquiri, €8). Shots €3, wine €3-3.50. Happy hour 5pm-6pm and 9pm-10pm. Open daily 4pm-2am, 8pm-2am in mid-fall and late spring. MC/V.

RHÔNE-ALPS

Les Choucas, 206 rue du Dr. Paccard (☎04 50 53 03 23). Alpine swank in a revamped *chalet.* Cow-skin lounges and giant TV screen showing extreme skiing. Beer €3.40 before 10pm. Cocktails €7-10.50, including "Multiple Orgasm up Against the Wall." Open Dec.-Sept. daily 3pm-4am; Oct.-Dec. and May-June F-Sa only.

Dick's Tea Bar, 80 rue des Moulins (☎04 50 53 19 10), is the flagship of this bar-saturated street. London DJs keep the dance floor thumping at this hot spot, 1 of 3 Dick's in the Alps. Shots €4-5. Dec.-Apr. cover €11 after 11pm, including one drink. Open daily Dec.-Apr. 10pm-4am; July-Aug. open Fr and Sa only.

⚠ OUTDOOR ACTIVITIES

Whether you've come to climb mountains or ski down them, expect a challenge; steep grades, potential avalanches, and unique terrain make this entire region ill-suited for beginners. However, with adequate gear and planning, expeditions up into the mountains are utterly (and literally) breathtaking. The low seasons, in October to November and May to late June, have less outdoor options; snow covers the mountains at elevations over 2000m while the lower altitudes are green, limiting hiking and skiing.

TÉLÉPHÉRIQUES. Hikers and skiers will probably need to take a *téléphérique* (cable car) during their stay in Chamonix, and others will probably want to take the ride just for the views. A board on pl. de l'Église lists the lifts that are currently open; many close in the low season from early May to late June. Those who desire a spectacular trip should consider taking the **Aiguille du Midi** (see **L'Aiguille du Midi,** p. 450).

High-altitude escapades don't end with a view of Europe's tallest peak; from the Aiguille du Midi summit, hikers continue to **Helbronner,** where they can stride along the French-Italian border (May-Sept. only; round-trip €50, ages 12-15 €42.50) and eat a picnic lunch on the Glacier Géant. The slightly rickety four-person gondolas run into the glacial heart of the Alps and provide views of the **Matterhorn** and **Mont Blanc.** From Helbronner, a final *téléphérique* descends into Italy to **La Palud,** near the resort town of **Courmayeur.** Bring a passport and cash—the Italian side doesn't accept credit cards for the cable car. Check at the tourist office that the entire *téléphérique* route is in operation before setting out for this trip.

Several *téléphériques* run year-round to the opposite side of the valley (away from Mt. Blanc), which is known for popular hiking trails and panoramic restaurants. Cars to **Le Brévent** (2525m), stopping at the mid-station Planpraz, leave from the corner of rte. Henriette and La Mollard, up the street from the tourist office (☎04 50 53 13 18.) Open daily July-Aug. 8am-6pm; Sept.-June 9am-5pm. One-way €12.50, round-trip €15.50.) Another great option is **La Flégère,** 2km east of the city in Les Praz, on rue Joseph Vallot. The car stops at an eponymous plateau on the way to **l'Index** (2595m), a starting point for most ice climbs in the area. (☎04 50 53 18 58. One-way €12.50, round-trip €15.50. Open daily July-Aug. 7:40am-5:50pm; June and Sept. daily 8:40am-4:50pm.)

A special train (not a *téléphérique*) runs up to the **Mer de Glace,** France's largest glacier (97km long). The train departs from a small station next to the main one. (☎04 50 53 12 54. Daily July-Aug. every 20min. 8am-6pm; May-June and early to mid-Sept. every 30min. 8:30am-5pm; mid-Sept. to Apr. every hr. 10am-4pm. €10.50, round-trip €14) From the Mer, a cable car runs to an **ice cave** that is carved afresh every year—the glacier slides 30m per year, so last year's cave is farther down the wall of ice (car descent €2.50, cave admittance €3.50). Consider riding the train to the Mer and taking the downhill hike back, or, if you're up for a workout with great views, doing the opposite (see **Hiking,** p. 450).

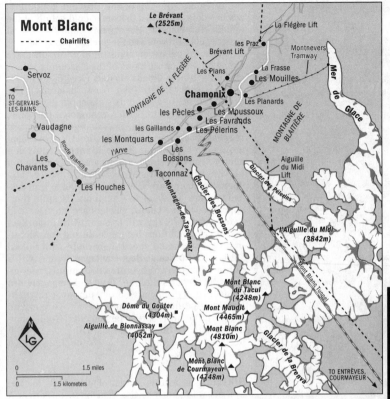

Mont Blanc
- - - - - - - **Chairlifts**

Le Brévent
▲ (2525m)

La Flégère Lift

les Praz
Brévant Lift

Montnevers
Tramway

MONTAGNE DE LA FLÉGÈRE

Servoz

Les Plans

La Frasse
Les Mouilles

TO
ST-GERVAIS-
LES-BAINS

Chamonix

Les Planards

Vaudagne

les Pècles

Les Moussoux
Les Favrands

MONTAGNE DE
BLATIÈRE

Mer

de

Glace

les Gaillands

Les Pélerins

l'Arve

Les Montquarts

Route Blanche

Les
Bossons

Aiguille
du Midi
Lift

Les
Chavants

Taconnaz

Glacier des Pélerins

Les Houches

Montagne de Taconnaz

Glacier des Bossons

l'Aiguille du Midi
(3842m)

Mont Blanc
du Tacul
(4248m)

Mont Blanc tunnel

Dôme du Goûter
(4304m)

Mont Maudit
(4465m)

Aiguille de Bionnassay
(4052m)

Mont Blanc
(4810m)

Glacier de la Brenva

N
LG

Mont Blanc
de Courmayeur
(4748m)

TO ENTRÈVES,
COURMAYEUR

0   1.5 miles
0   1.5 kilometers

RHÔNE-ALPS

SKIING. Those aiming to ski for only a few days should buy daily lift tickets at the different ski areas—one area is more than enough for each day. If your plans extend to a week, buy a **Cham'Ski** pass, available at the tourist office or major *téléphériques* (Brévent, Flégère, Aiguille du Midi). The ticket gives unlimited access to the Chamonix Valley, excluding the small Les Houches area, and one day in Courmayeur-Val-Veny, Italy (€176; passport photo required). Get to lifts early during peak times to avoid unbearable lines.

Chamonix is surrounded by skiable mountains. The **southern side** of the valley opposite Mont Blanc, drenched in sunlight during the morning, offers terrain for all abilities. In the afternoon, the sun and extreme skiers head over to the death-defying **north face,** which has mostly advanced, off-*piste*, and glacial terrain. Public buses (free to Cham'Ski holders) and the trains of the Mont Blanc tramway connect the valley's string of resort villages, from Les Bossons to Le Tour.

At the bottom of the valley, near the Swiss border, **Le Tour-Col de Balme** (☎ 04 50 54 00 58), above the village of **Le Tour,** is the first of Chamonix's ski areas. Its sunny trails are the most suitable for beginning to intermediate skiers (day pass €27). More dramatic runs for the non-expert can be found around the **Brévent** and **Flégère** *téléphériques* closer to town. Connected by a cable car, Brévent and Flégère together constitute Chamonix's largest ski area; located a few steps from the tourist office, the Brévent *téléphérique* is particularly convenient. Note, however, that

THE BIG SPLURGE

L'AIGUILLE DU MIDI

With a touch of pride, Chamonix residents boast that more people ascend the *Aiguille du Midi* (Needle of the South) cable car than the Eiffel Tower. Those with acrophobia (fear of heights) or argentophobia (fear of expenditure) might be tempted to avoid the 20min., €34 ride over towering forests and snowy peaks, but few who make the journey are ever disappointed. (Closed Nov. and part of May. Open 6:30-8am, closes 3:30-4:30pm. One-way €29, ages 12-15 €24.50/€29.)

Peak-worshippers should head out early, as clouds and crowds often gather by mid-morning. The first stop, **Plan de l'Aiguille** (€13, round-trip €15; ages 12-15 €11/€12.50), is a great starting and ending point for hikes (see **Hiking,** right), but is otherwise not worthwhile. For the best views, as well as a look at ice-climbers, summer skiers, and other hardcore adventurers, continue to **l'Aiguille du Midi,** which is nearly twice as high as the first stop. The panorama is breathtaking, as is the head-lightening 3842m high air; warm clothes are essential for the trip. A touch of wooziness might set in; take it slow up the stairs to the *terrasse.* For an additional €3, an elevator will take you right to the summit, where there's a glorious 360° view. Take some once-in-a-lifetime pictures and forget about your newly emptied wallet; things are supposed to be lighter at this altitude anyway.

the terrain at the top of the Brévent gondola is advanced; less confident skiers should get off at the middle stop **Planpraz,** the starting point for several easier trails. (Brévent and Flégère day pass €30.)

There are plenty of opportunities for off-*piste* skiing on the opposite side of the Chamonix valley, starting with **Les Grands Montets** (☎04 50 54 00 71; 3275m), in Argentière (8km from Chamonix). The *grande dame* of Chamonix's ski spots is virtually all advanced terrain. With a remodeled half-pipe, Les Grands Montets is now also geared toward **snowboarding.** (Day pass €36). Directly above Chamonix, the infamous **Vallée Blanche** requires a hearty dose of courage and insanity. From the top of the Aiguille du Midi *téléphérique,* the ungroomed, unmarked, unpatrolled 20km trail cascades down a glacier to Chamonix. Despite their appearance from below, glaciers are more icefield than snowfield. Stay within sight of trail markers and check conditions before venturing out. All off-*piste* skiers should check their route with the **ski patrol** or the **Office de Haut Montagne.** Skiing with a guide who knows the terrain is highly recommended. Never ski alone. Try the **Compagnie des Guides.** (p. 445; from €55 per person.) English-speaking guides tailor the itinerary to you and make all the necessary arrangements, from equipment rental to lift reservations. Otherwise, you'll need to reserve a spot on the *téléphérique* in high season (☎08 92 68 00 67).

HIKING. Chamonix has 350km of hiking trails, marked by signs, with terrain ranging from forests to glaciers. A map, available at the tourist office, lists all the mountain *refuges* and gives departure points and estimated lengths for all the trails (€4). Climbers should buy the **IGN topographic map** (p. 444), available at the **Office de Haute Montagne** and local bookstores (€9.50).

The following are several recommendations for intermediate level hikes that are easily accessible from Chamonix. Grades are often steep, but using cable cars for either the trip up or back saves time and energy. Most hikes can be extended by avoiding the cable cars. Walkers who would rather just look at the mountains can meander the trail that follows the Arve River through the valley, which begins by the river next to the sports center.

Chalet Floria is the perfect introduction to the mountains surrounding Chamonix. Turning left on rue Mummery, follow the signs to an uphill track that eventually becomes a narrow trail. The walk is 45-50min. to an adorable restaurant with red umbrellas, hundreds of colorful flowers planted by the owners, and views of Mt. Blanc. The botanical owners allow picnics with the purchase of a drink (€3), but the price is really for the gorgeous setting. (1½-2hr. round-trip.)

The **Mer de Glace**, in which numerous picturesque trails ascend to the largest glacier in France. One outstanding 2½hr. trip begins 900m beyond the station, below the telesiege de Planards. Follow signs to Rochets des Mottets on the wide, moderately graded trail. After reaching the Rochets cabin (1½hr.), turn right onto the steeper, more narrow trail which climbs to the train station of the Mer (1 hour). The train can whisk tired hikers back to Chamonix, while day-trippers can extend the trip by heading under the tracks toward the glacier's **Hôtel Montenvers** (☎04 50 53 87 70; breakfast and dinner included; open mid-June to mid-Sept.; €35), and then following the sign toward the **Refuge du Plan de l'Aiguille**. (☎06 65 64 27 53. Open mid-June to mid-Sept. Breakfast and dinner €19. Rooms €10.) The wild-flower studded trail that crosses toward the refuge is the **Grand Balcon Nord**, one of the many mountain traverses that was planned and constructed in the 1920s by famous alpinist Joseph Vallot and his mountain-loving friends. After reaching the refuge (2½hr. from the Glace de Mer), ascend a short trail to the midpoint stop of the Aiguille du Midi cable and ride down, or descend from the refuge along the left or right-hand trails, both of which lead back to Chamonix (2½ hours). Total hiking time for the whole circuit is about 7-8hr. The Balcon Nord may not be passable until late June; ask at the Office de Haute Montagne for up-to-date reports.

On the south side of the valley, a vast network of trails wind near and above the ski *pistes*, offering unparalleled views across to Mont Blanc and its offshoot glaciers. A great starting point for hikes is the **Flégère téléphérique** station in les Praz. Ascend to the mid-station either by taking the cable car or by climbing the ski slopes on the trail that starts behind the nearby golf course (2½ hours). From the station, a number of hikes lead along or further up into the craggy range. Heading east from la Flégère, the ▨**Grand Balcon Sud** is a spectacular, wildflower studded trail which traverses its way gently to **Planpraz**, the mid-station of the Brévent *téléphérique* (2 hours). From there, you can hike or ride back to town, or embark on the steep, gorgeous ascent to the **Col de Brévent** (2368m), the top of the Brévent lift (2 hours). Even the hardiest hikers will want to take the lift all the way back to central Chamonix. Alternatively, from the top of the Flégère cable car station, follow the signs on a breathless 1¾hr. ascent to **Lac Blanc**, a turquoise alpine lake that stays frozen through June. Hikers can picnic, sun themselves on rocks, and watch ice climbers descend a steep bowl. Those with spending money can sit at tables in the restaurant at **Refuge du Lac Blanc**, which offers rooms with breakfast and dinner for €44.50. (☎04 50 53 49 14. Reservations required.)

Experienced mountain climbers, of course, come to Chamonix to ascend **Mont Blanc** (4810m), a two or three day climb. Don't try it solo. Climbers can be caught by vicious blizzards, even in August. The Maison de la Montagne, the Compagnie des Guides, and the Club Alpin Français all have info on this most classic of alpine climbs (see **Skiing, Biking, and Hiking Resources**).

VAL D'ISÈRE

Although less accessible than other ski towns in the Alps, Val d'Isère (pop. 1750) attracts visitors from all over the world for unparalleled hiking, almost year-round skiing, and other excellent outdoor options. Frequenters of this world-class ski resort worship its snow, the surrounding *hautes montagnes*, and native son Jean-Claude Killy, who walked away with the gold in every men's downhill event in the 1968 Grenoble Olympics. As a spokesman for the area, Killy brought Olympic events to Val d'Isère in 1992, which transformed the town's main street into a tourist-laden strip of expensive hotels, restaurants, and ski boutiques.

During the spring and summer, as the turquoise river Isère emerges spectacularly from under melting snow, prices drop, and bikers, hikers, and climbers fill the few open hotels. The town officially "opens" in late June and then again in early December, but can be eerily quiet during the low season. Mid-December is a particularly crazy time due to the Criterium de la Première Neige, one of the first international competitions of the season.

▐ TRANSPORTATION

Trains: pl. de la Gare in **Bourg-St-Maurice.** Open daily 5am-10:30pm. To: **Annecy** (3hr., 2 per day, €22.78); **Chambry** (2 hr., 10 per day, €13.80); **Grenoble** (3hr., 2 per day, €21.10); **Lyon** (3-4hr., 5 per day, €27.40).

Buses: Autocars Martin (☎04 79 06 00 42), at the bus station by the roundabout, 150m down the main drag from the tourist office. Open Dec.-Apr. M-F 9:30-11:30am and 1:15pm-7:30pm, Sa 6:30am-7pm, Su 7:30-11:30am and 1:15-7:30 pm; July-Aug. M 5-8pm, Tu and W-F 9:30-10:30am and 1:45-8pm, Sa 6:45-10am and 12:45-7:30pm. **Main office** at pl. de la Gare in Bourg-St-Maurice (☎04 79 07 04 49). Open daily 7:30am-noon and 2-7pm. Buses from Bourg-St.-Maurice to: **Geneva,** Switzerland (4-4½hr.; M-F 3 per day, Sa 7 per day, Su 4 per day; €48.50); and **Lyon airport** (4hr.; M-F 2 per day, Sa 4 per day, Su 3 per day; €44, ages 12-24 €33). Buses run from Bourg St. Maurice to Tignes and Val Village (see **Orientation and Practical Information**), and upon request, from Val Village to the hostel in **Les Boisses** (15min., 2-4 per day, €10.30). **SNCF** info and reservation desks (☎04 79 06 03 55) are in the same building as the bus station. Open Dec.-Apr. Tu-Sa 10am-noon and 1-6:30pm; July-Aug. M-F 9:15am-12:15pm and 2-6pm.

Public Transportation: Val d'Isère runs **free shuttles** (navettes) around town during the ski season and again in July and August. **Train Rouge** runs between La Daille and Le Fornet (Dec.-Apr. every 5-30min. 8:30am-2am, Jul.-Aug. every 20-30 min. 9am-8pm), while **Train Vert** runs from the tourist office and the bus station up to the Manchet Sports complex and the entrance to the Vanoise national park (Dec.-Apr. every 30 min. 10am-8pm; Jul.-Aug. every 15 minutes 8:15am-7pm). Both shave time off trips to the refuges.

Taxis: ABC ☎06 22 73 05 31; **Altitude Espace Taxi** ☎06 07 41 11 53. €46-68 to the train station in Bourg St-Maurice. €15 from Val to the hostel.

Bike and Ski Rental: About 30 locations in town offer rental; ask at the tourist office.

▮✚▮ ORIENTATION AND PRACTICAL INFORMATION

Val d'Isère has no train station. The nearest one is in **Bourg-St-Maurice,** 30km to the north; a bus leaves there for Val d'Isère 3 times a day (Apr.-Nov. last bus 6:35pm, Dec.-Mar. extended weekend service and hours; €11.50). To get to the hostel, get off at **Tignes-Les-Boisses,** 7km from Val d'Isère (€10.30). The Val d'Isère mega-resort is made up of three villages in a line along the river Isère: **Le Fornet** at the top, **La Daille** below at the valley's entrance, and **Val Village** in the middle, home to most accommodations and the **tourist office.** Unless otherwise stated, listings below are in Val Village, the most substantial of the three towns. Although street names are neither used nor clearly indicated, the town is navigable with the tourist office's *Practical Guide* map.

Tourist Office: (☎04 79 06 06 60; www.valdisere.com), in Val Village. From the bus station, it's a 5min. walk along the main road toward Le Fornet. The office is on the left at the roundabout. Distributes practical guides in six languages that detail prices and schedules and suggest where to hike and ski. Open Dec.-Apr. Su-F 8:30am-7:30pm, Sa 8:30am-8pm; July-Aug. daily 8:30am-7:30pm; May-June and Sept.-Nov. M-F 9am-noon and 2-6pm, Sa-Su

10am-12pm and 3pm-6pm. Information is also available at the **Annex** (☎04 79 06 19 67) at the town entrance; it's a small wooden hut to the right on the way up from La Daille. Open daily July-Aug. 9am-noon and 3-6pm; Dec.-Apr. Sa-Su 9am-noon and 2-6pm.

Laundromat: Laverie Automatique, just above the Spar supermarket, on the way up the roundabout. **Laverie Linge** (☎06 11 84 29 33), on the right about 300m down from the bus station.

Weather, Ski, and Road Info: Call the tourist office or listen to French-language **Radio Val** (96.1FM; ☎04 79 06 18 66). **Weather forecast:** ☎08 92 68 02 73. **Ski Lifts:** ☎04 79 06 00 35. **Ski Patrol:** ☎04 79 06 02 10.

Police: (☎04 79 06 03 41), above the tourist office, across from Casino supermarket.

Hospital: (☎04 79 41 79 79), in Bourg-St-Maurice.

Internet Access: Lodge Bar (☎04 79 06 19 31). Turn right at roundabout above the bus station. €3 for 15min., €5.50 for 30min. Open daily mid-Nov.-Apr. 4pm-2am; July-Aug. 5pm-2am.

Post Office: (☎04 79 06 06 99), across from the tourist office on a side street. **Currency exchange** with good rates. Open Dec.-Apr. M-F 8:30am-noon and 2-6pm, Sa 8:30am-noon; July-Aug. M-F 9am-noon and 1:30-4:30pm, Sa 8:30-11:30am; Sept.-Nov. and May-June M-F 10am-noon and 1pm-2:30pm, Sa 9:30-11am.

Postal Code: 73150.

ACCOMMODATIONS AND CAMPING

With world-class slopes feet away from the town, it can be tough to find a room in winter. An inexpensive option for groups during non-peak times is to rent an apartment or "tourist residence" in one of the many *chalets* in town. **Val Location** at the tourist office does the booking. The hotels that remain open in the low season maintain very reasonable prices. The cheapest beds are at the *refuges*, **Le Prariond** and **Le Fond Des Fours**, each at least a 2hr. hike from downtown (see **Hiking,** p. 455), and cheaper **gîtes** in Le Fornet offer an alternative to downtown hotels. The **tourist office** has a complete list. During the ski season, **Moris Pub** (☎04 79 06 22 11), 75m up from the tourist office, rents bright rooms upstairs for super-cheap prices.

Gîtes Bonnevie (☎04 79 06 06 26; fax 04 79 06 16 65), in Le Fornet. Accessible by the Train Rouge or by foot; (see **Hiking,** p. 455), just across the bridge on the right. Gorgeous wood-trimmed studios for 2 or 10 people, all with bathroom, kitchen, TV, and splendid views that make you feel like you're at your own alpine *chalet*. About as cheap as it gets. Apr.-Nov. €20 per person. Dec.-Mar. weekly rentals only: doubles €310; 10-man €1448. Winter prices fluctuate; call to verify. ❷

Auberge de Jeunesse "Les Clarines" (HI) (☎04 79 06 35 07, reservations 04 79 41 01 93; tignes@fuaj.org), in the village of Les Boisses. Call ahead to see if the trail is open. Or take the Tignes/Val Claret bus to Les Boisses from Bourg-St-Maurice (€11.50) or Val d'Isère (€6.40). Wooden rooms for 4-6 people off of bright orange hallways, all but 3 with toilets. Friendly staff. Safe atmosphere overlooking the Lac du Chevril. Discounts on rentals. **Skiing, hiking, biking,** and **watersports** packages (from €10-30 per day). Reception daily 8-10am and 5-10pm; entry code after 10pm. Reserve far in advance. Closed May to mid-June and Oct. to mid-Nov. June-Aug. bed and breakfast €13.20, with dinner €21.80; week with *demi-pension* €134.20. €2.90 extra for non-members. ❶

Hôtel Sakura (☎04 79 06 04 08; www.sakura7.com). Turn right at the roundabout above the bus station. Spacious rooms with wood furniture, shower or bath, toilet, TV, telephone, and kitchen. Breakfast €6. Reception daily 8am-8pm. Open July-Aug. and Dec.-May. July-Aug. singles €55; doubles €56; triples and quads €100; quints €110. Dec.-May singles and doubles €100; triples and quads €169; quints €184. MC/V. ❹

SUMMER SKIING

At 1pm on a sunny afternoon, a horde of ski- and snowboard-toting youngsters gathers in the parking lot in Tignes to board the homebound bus. The scene suggests a normal winter day on the slopes, but the temperature tells a different story. It's early July, the surrounding mountains are specked with wildflowers, and everyone else sports hiking boots or biker shorts. Here in the (highest) heart of the Alps, the skiing never stops. The glaciers looming behind the villages of Le Fornet and Tignes often retain their snow into September, making Val d'Isère a national center of *ski d'été* (summer skiing).

Summer skiers rouse themselves at 6am and hit the snow hard by 7 or 7:30am. By 1pm, it's all over; the snow deteriorates until it's, as the French say, *"comme la soupe."* On a typical morning, small, teenager-heavy French ski teams practice their slalom and downhill skills, boarders cruise over jumps in the snow park, and elite groups of skiers train with year-round instructors. For die-hard skiers and snowboarders, *ski d'été* offers a real thrill; those less inclined to participate can tan at the base of the slopes and watch their friends fly down the glacier.

(Rental at the base of the slopes €20-30 per day; lift passes €22.50 per day. Hostelers can arrange rental and lift packages through the hostel in Tignes. See p. 453)

Le Relais du Ski (☎04 79 06 02 06; www.valdisere.com/lerelaisduski), 500m up from the tourist office, on the left. Small, wood-paneled rooms with hall showers. Breakfast €10, automatically included. Dinner €20. 24hr. reception. Dec.-Apr. singles €57-115; doubles €67-135; triples €77-160; quads €82-195. June-Sept. singles €56-75; doubles €53-80; triples €58-96; quads €73-112. AmEx/MC/V. ❹

Camping: Camping les Richardes (☎/fax 04 79 06 26 60), 1km up from the tourist office. Take the free Train Rouge shuttle to Les Richardes. Plain campground in a beautiful valley close to town. Crowded mid-Aug. during the 4x4 competitions. Reception daily July-Aug. 7:30am-12:30pm and 2-8pm; June and Sept. open fewer hours, but someone is always near. Open mid-June to mid-Sept. €2.80 per person, €1.60 per tent, €1.50 per car. Electricity €1.90-3.80. Shower €1 for 5 min. MC/V above €15. ❶

🍴 FOOD

A **Sherpa** across from the bus station is open all year. (☎ 04 79 06 01 98, M-Sa 9am-12:30pm and 4:30pm-7:30pm, Su 9am-1pm.) There is also a **Spar** in the *centre ville*, just up the roundabout by the bus station. (☎04 79 06 02 66. Open daily Dec.-Apr. 7:30am-1pm and 2:30-8:30pm; July-Aug. 7:30am-1pm and 3:30-8pm.) In the low season, only a few *brasseries* and standard restaurants remain open; ask at the tourist office for a list of openings and hours.

🦐 **Le Bananas** (☎04 79 06 04 23) is up the roundabout and near the base of the *téléphériques*. Ski instructors and wannabes pack this rockin' *chalet* for delicious Tex-Mex bites and beers inches from the slopes. Quesadillas €18, salads €5-10, *menus* from €16. Happy hour Dec.-Apr. 7-8pm. Open daily 1pm-midnight. MC/V. ❸

La Casserole (☎04 79 41 15 71) is just up the roundabout. Enjoy Savoyard specialties like *tartiflettes* (€13-20) in a dark wood *chalet* with animal skins hanging on the walls. Meat dishes €14-22, salads €3.50-11.50. Open July-Aug. Tu-Sa noon-1:45pm and 6:30-10pm, Su noon-1:45pm; daily Dec.-Apr. 6:30pm-midnight. AmEx/MC/V. ❸

Maison Chevallot (☎04 79 06 02 42) is 20m up from the bus station. Delicious homemade options like *tourte au beaufort, quiche lorraine, tartiflette, fougasse,* and sandwiches are served with a salad (€6.50). For dessert, don't miss the excellent pastries, including nut cake (€2.50) and *fondant chocolat* (€2.70). Open daily 6:30am-7:45pm; May-June and Oct.-Nov. closed 1-3pm. MC/V. ❶

Le Canyon (☎04 79 06 18 19). Across the street from the bus station and to the left. Keeps itself in business as the only restaurant in town open almost all year. Serves locally endorsed Savoyard specialties like *gratin dauphinois* (€13.50), in addition to salads, pastas, and pizzas. For sandwiches and crêpes (€3-6), ask for their lighter menu. Entrees €4-14. Open daily 8am-midnight. MC/V. ❸

ENTERTAINMENT

In addition to being a haven for pizzerias, the roundabout above the bus station serves as Val d'Isère's unofficial nightlife strip. Start a night of drinking at **Lodge Bar.** (See **Internet Access,** p. 453.) Happy hour 5-7pm; beer €1.50-3. DJ 1 night per week in winter.) Then breeze up the block to **Café Face** (☎04 79 06 29 80) and groove to the sounds of DJs and sax players. Across the street, **Dick's Tea Bar** (☎04 79 06 14 87) offers a great late-night option. A touristy crowd packs the dance floor of this Val mainstay. Across from the bus station, **Le "XV"** serves drinks in beach chairs on the terrace, making it an enticing summer option. Drinks €3-8. (☎04 79 41 90 55. Open late June to Sept. and Dec.-Apr. 9am-2am. **Café Fats** or **Le Bananas** also stay busy long into the night.

OUTDOOR ACTIVITIES

SKIING. Over 100 lifts, several of them originating right in Val d'Isère and Tignes, provide access to 300km of trails. One can ski for a day without returning to the same base area, and for a week without repeating a run. Lift tickets are valid on the entire Espace Killy, which includes all lifts and runs from Val d'Isère to Tignes, a ski station 7km away. The mountains are generally skiable from late November to early May, with optimum conditions in mid-winter. (Lift tickets €27 per half-day, €38 per day, €206 per week.)

Most good beginner runs begin at the higher altitudes, around the Marmottes and Borsat lifts on the south side of Bellevarde (take the Bellevarde lift up) and in the super-scenic **Pissaillas** area (take the Solaise cable car, then the Glacier and Leissier lifts). Intermediate and advanced skiers frequent the slopes surrounding Tignes, while the north side of Bellevarde is known for expert runs. There's a giant **snow park** between Val and Tignes; a classic snowboard run starts at the top of the Mont Blanc lift and whirls its way down to La Daille, where a Funival car whisks boarders back to the Bellevarde summit for an encore.

Val d'Isère is most proud of its off-*piste* opportunities. Skiers of the **col Pers** region, accessible from the Pissaillas glacier, speed past wildlife in the Gorges de Malpassaet. Check weather conditions, leave an itinerary with the ski patrol, and never go alone. Hire a **guide** (☎04 79 06 02 34) if unfamiliar with the area.

Late June to mid-July, **Pissaillas** and **La Grande Motte** in Tignes offer **summer skiing** (see **Summer Skiing,** opposite page).

HIKING. With expansive alpine meadows, plunging gorges, snow-covered glaciers, and free-ranging Ibex, the mountains surrounding the Val offer some of the most spectacular hiking in the Alps. The mountains are dotted with **refuges,** most of which offer full board in July and August; with proper planning, backpackers can hike all day and sleep in style. The Val serves as an entry-point for hikes in the ▧**Vanoise National Park,** which extends to the Italian border and is France's premier wildlife reserve. Before setting out for any trip, check ahead to make sure *refuges* and trails are open, check the weather report, and bring warm clothing— snowstorms and winter weather strike even in summer. Many of the more advanced routes are suitable only for those with the proper equipment and experience. Trails around Val are well-marked with blazes and signs, but hikers should buy the detailed *Val d'Isère—Balades et Sentiers* (€4) and a hiking map at the tourist office (€6.90), which describes over 40 routes spanning 100km. Not all hiking is based in Val: several *refuge* hikes in the Vanoise also depart from Tignes, from both the upper town and the hostel. A map is available in the Tignes tourist office, and staff at the hostel have loads of advice for guests.

Until the construction of modern ski areas in the 1960s, **Le Fornet** (1950m) was the highest continuously inhabited village in the French Alps. The easy trail leading up the valley starts from the church in Val Village (3km one-way, 1 hr., 100m vertical). Following the signs for Le Fornet, walk though the *Vieux Val* to a pedestrian road that briefly joins up with the **GR5** before forking again toward Le Fornet. Just before the village, the trail allows hikers to double back via the 45min. **sentier écologique,** which meets up with the GR5 once again and returns to town.

The stunning **Refuge de Prariond** (3km one-way, 2 hr., 300m vertical) hike leads into the heart of the Vanoise and is a must for animal lovers; acrobatic *bouquetin* (ibex), *chamois* (the antelope's smaller cousin), and furry marmots roam the areas around the trail. From the center of Le Fornet, cross the bridge and follow the signs to **pont St-Charles** (30 minutes). At the back of the parking lot near the pont, a marked trail climbs high above the Isère river, ascending steeply to the **Gorges du Malpasset.** The trail plateaus and continues though an alpine meadow to the Refuge Prariond. (*Refuge* ☎ 04 79 06 06 02. Staffed late Mar. to mid-May and mid-June to mid-Sept. During unstaffed months, wood, gas, utensils, covers, and a tin box are provided with payment. Breakfast €6.40, *demi-pension* €32, students €28.50. Shower €2. Sleeping sacks €2.50. Reserve and get directions at the tourist office. €11.80 per person, students €8.50.)

The intermediate **Refuge des Fours** (1¾hr. one-way, 560m vertical). hike starts at the Manchet entrance to the Vanoise; take the free Train Vert shuttle to Le Manchet (see **Public Transportation**) and continue up the road to the beginning of the trail, which is near a cluster of old stone farmhouses. Take the trail on the right marked *"refuge des fours;"* from there, it's a steady climb to the hut in a high valley across from the **Méan Martin** glacier and alpine lakes. (*Refuge* ☎ 04 79 06 16 90; Staffed late Mar. to mid-May and mid-June to mid-Sept. *Demi-pension* €32. Showers €2.80. €11.80 per person, students €8.50.) To return to Val, one option is to cross the **Col des Fours** pass and head back to town via the **GR5.** Continue along the trail that runs to the *refuge*, then turn left onto the path that ascends the neckline between the 3135m **Pelou Blanc** and the 3072m **Pointe des Fours** (1¼hr., 450m vertical). Where the trail ends, hang a left on the red-and-white marked **GR5** for a scenic descent to town on the **Col d'Iseran,** a popular leg of the Tour de France (6km, 1½-2hr., 900m vertical).

The full-day **Lac de la Sassière** advanced trek starts at the Fornet *téléphérique* (12.25km round-trip, 7hr., 940m vertical). From the station, descend slightly and turn right at the trail marker for the **Balcon des Barmettes**. At the Balcon, head right on Trail #36, the **Bailletta,** which climbs steeply for 800m to the small **Lac de la Bailletta** (2½hr.), where the trail reaches a pass and then descends gradually to the larger **Lac de la Sassière.** This man-made lake is packed with trout and surrounded by *chamois*, ibex, and marmots.

OTHER OUTDOOR ACTIVITIES. Mountain Guides (☎ 04 79 06 06 60) teaches ice climbing (morning session €76) and rock climbing (afternoon session €28), and leads full-day canyoning trips (€64). Nature expeditions are offered for all levels.

For a relaxing trip to the summit of Val d'Isère, take a *téléphérique* (cable car) over peaks, glaciers, and valleys up to the top of the mountain. In the summer, a chairlift runs to **Solaise,** a small summit surrounded by a lake and easy hiking trails, and to the higher **Bellevarde,** site of the 1992 Olympic downhill. (Cable cars to Solaise and Bellevarde Dec.-Apr. and July-Aug. Summer €6 round-trip, winter (with ski pass) €39.) Before attempting uncharted mountains, advanced **climbers** should call the **Bureau des Guides** (☎04 79 06 06 60). Beginners will appreciate **Via Ferrata** in La Daille. This 3hr. climb (360m vertical) uses metal footholds and ropes and hugs the side of the mountain facing the valley; there is also a more demanding 4-6hr. climb that requires a guide.

MASSIF CENTRAL

 Many claustrophobic travelers escape from Paris to the coastal regions of Provence and the Riviera, but the lucky few who penetrate the Auvergne, in the very heart of the country, will find rugged unadulterated beauty. Giant lava needles, extinct volcanic craters, and aromatic pine forests rise out of the Massif Central. Although fairly quiet, Auvergne has picturesque scenery and a wealth of outdoor adventures. The towering Puy-de-Dôme (p. 464) offers prime views of the Volcanic Park, though the real hiking (and skiing) mecca is Le Mont-Dore (p. 465), nestled in the shadow of a string of dormant volcanoes. The Massif's varied terrain also caters to the less adventurous. In Le Puy-en-Velay (p. 468), pumice-paved streets wind among Renaissance houses and statue-topped volcanic needles. The mineral waters of Le Mont-Dore, Bourbelle, and Vichy (p. 473), a city stuck in the *Belle Époque*, attract both the *curistes* (those who believe in the healing powers of the springs) and the curious. During World War II, the region was the seat of the Nazi-controlled French government, but nevertheless teemed with small bands of Resistance fighters.

HIGHLIGHTS OF THE MASSIF CENTRAL

CLIMB the gigantic, temple-topped lava needle **St-Michel d'Aiguilhe** (p. 468) in Le Puy-en-Velay.

TREAT YOUR AILMENTS with (small) sips of **Vichy**'s (p. 473) potent mineral water.

BE INSPIRED at Clermont-Ferrand's **Cathédral Notre Dame de l'Assomption** (p. 463), where 13th-century workers used lava-stones to build the spire sky-high.

CLERMONT-FERRAND

During the Middle Ages, Clermont-Ferrand (pop. 137,000) was two distinct cities, Clermont and Montferrand. Economic and political rivalry festered between them until Louis XIII ordered their merger in 1630. Clermont got a better deal: the "combined" city's walls excluded Montferrand. Forty minutes away by foot, the outcast city is now nearly forgotten. During the 20th century, Clermont became synonymous with Michelin tires (rubber was first used in bike tires here) and the revered *Red Guides*, thanks to brothers André and Edouard Michelin. Even with college-town appeal and cobblestone streets, Clermont-Ferrand perhaps best serves travelers as a base for trips to the surrounding mountains.

■ TRANSPORTATION

Trains: av. de l'Union Soviétique. Info office open M-F 4:45am-11:30pm, Sa 5:30am-11:30pm, Su 7am-11:30pm. To: **Le Puy** (2½hr., 7 per day, €18.10); **Lyon** (3hr., 10 per day, €25.30); **Paris** (3½hr., 7 per day, €40.20).

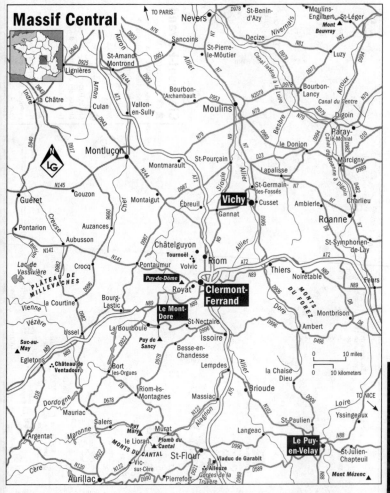

Massif Central

TO PARIS

Buses: 69 bd. F. Mitterrand (☎04 73 93 13 61), near the Jardin Lecoq. Buses to destinations throughout the Auvergne, including **Vichy** (1¾hr., 2 per day, €10.20). Office open M-Sa 8:30am-6:30pm.

Public Transportation: 15-17 bd. Robert Schumann (☎04 73 28 56 56; www.t2c.fr). Buses cover the city 5am-10pm. Ticket €1.30, day pass €4.80; available from vending machines at pl. de Jaude and throughout the city.

Taxis: **Taxi 63** (☎04 73 31 53 15), **Taxis Radio** (☎04 73 19 53 53).

Bike Rental: **Léovélo,** 20 pl. Renoux or 43 av. de l'Union Soviétique, across from the train station (both ☎04 73 14 12 30; www.leovelo.com). Open M-Sa 7am-7pm. Amazing rates at €1.50 per hr., €5 per day, €13 per week. Reduced prices for students.

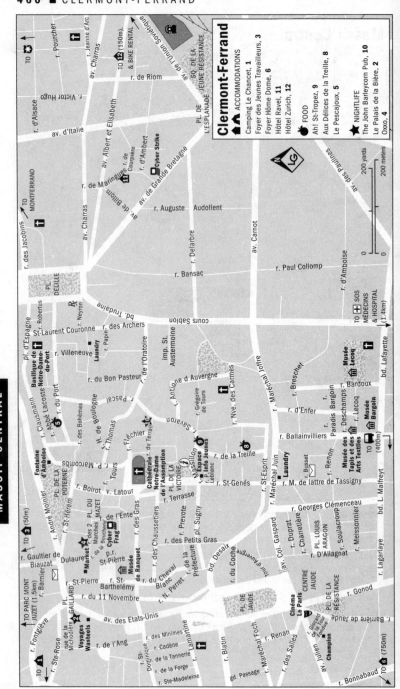

Clermont-Ferrand

🏠 ACCOMMODATIONS
Camping Le Chancet, **1**
Foyer des Jeunes Travailleurs, **3**
Foyer Hôme Dome, **6**
Hôtel Ravel, **11**
Hôtel Zurich, **12**

🍴 FOOD
Ah! St-Tropez, **9**
Aux Délices de la Treille, **8**
Le Pescajoux, **5**

★ NIGHTLIFE
The John Barleycorn Pub, **10**
Le Palais de la Bière, **2**
Oxoo, **4**

MASSIF CENTRAL

▆▐ ORIENTATION AND PRACTICAL INFORMATION

The *centre ville* of Clermont-Ferrand is in Clermont, between pl. Delille and pl.de Jaude. The train station is a 20min. walk from the city center, but buses #2, 4, and 14 travel from the station to **place de Jaude.** Several restaurants, a theater, and the monstrous shopping complex, **Centre Jaude,** surround the *place.* From the station, go left onto av. de l'Union Soviétique, left again onto bd. Fleury, and take a quick right onto av. Carnot. Continue on this road through several name-changes to pl. de Jaude. Pick up a map at the information desk in the train station.

Tourist Office: pl. de la Victoire (☎ 04 73 98 65 00). From the train station, make a left onto av. de l'Union Soviétique. Take a left at pl. de l'Esplanade and a quick right onto av. Carnot (changes names several times), walk about 10min., and make a right onto rue St-Gènes. The office will be on the right, before the cathedral. (20min.) Excellent map, bus schedules, and helpful staff. French and English walking tours of Montferrand, July to mid-Sept. Tu, Th, Sa 3pm. €5.70, students €3.10. Office open May-Sept. M-F 9am-7pm, Sa-Su 10am-7pm; Oct.-Apr. 9am-6pm, Sa 10am-1pm and 2-6pm, Su 9:30am-12:30pm and 2-6pm. Located in the same building, **L'Espace Massif Central** has further info on natural attractions in the Auvergne, including an impressive selection of maps and outdoor activity guides for sale or perusal. Open M-F 10am-7pm, Sa 10am-1pm and 2-6:30pm.

Budget Travel: Voyages Wasteels, 11 av. des Etats-Unis (☎ 04 73 19 07 95). Open M-F 9:30am-noon and 2-6pm, Sa 9:30am-noon.

Youth Center: Espace Info Jeunes, 5 av. St-Genès (☎ 04 73 92 30 50; www.crij.org/auvergne). Open M-F 10am-6pm, Sa 10am-1pm. Info on jobs, travel, and schools.

Laundromat: 55 rue du Port. Open daily 7am-11pm. Also at 6 pl. Hippolyte Renoux. Open daily 7am-8:30pm.

Police: 2 rue Pélissier (☎ 04 73 98 42 42).

Poison Control: ☎ 04 72 11 69 11.

24hr. Pharmacy: Pharmacie Ducher, 1 pl. Delille (☎ 04 73 91 31 77). Night fee €3.90 (10pm-7am).

Hospital: Centre Hospitalier Universitaire de Clermont-Ferrand, rue Montalembert (☎ 04 73 75 07 50). 24hr. **SOS Médecins,** 28 av. Léon Blum (☎ 04 73 42 22 22).

Internet Access: Cyber Strike, 31 av. de Grande Bretagne. Incredible €2 per hr. Open daily 11am-midnight. In the *vieille ville,* try **Cyber Frag,** 3 rue de la Boucherie. €2.50 per hr. Open daily 11am-11pm.

Post Office: 1 rue Busset (☎ 04 73 30 65 00). **Currency exchange** and Cyberposte. Open M-F 8am-7pm, Sa 8am-noon. Branch at 2 pl. Gaillard (☎ 04 73 31 70 00). Open M-F 9am-7pm, Sa 8am-noon.

Postal Code: 63000.

▐▐ ACCOMMODATIONS AND CAMPING

Most inexpensive hotels are located just outside of the center of town, about halfway between the train station and the *vieille ville.* Several older, less attractive hotels, along with the youth hostel, cluster near the train station.

▩ **Foyer des Jeunes Travailleurs (Corum Saint Jean),** 17 rue Gauthier de Biauzat (☎ 04 73 31 57 00; fax 04 73 31 59 99). With a prime location near the *vieille ville* and college-worthy array of resources, this is a best bet. Modern complex has simple, airy rooms (some with private showers), bar, cafeteria-style restaurant, a climbing wall, Internet access

(€2.50 per hr.), and laundry facilities (€3). Breakfast included. Meals €5.50. Reception daily 8am-6:30pm. Often full during school year; call 2-3 days ahead. Singles or doubles €17-23 per person. ❷

Foyer Hôme Dome, 12 pl. de Regensburg (☎ 04 73 29 40 70; www.chez.com/homedome). From the intersection of av. Carnot and av. d'Italie, just down from the station, take bus #13 (dir: Perignat) to Regensburg. Or, from pl. de Jaude, follow rue Jaude to pl. Gallieni, cross and follow rue des Salins and take the 4th right onto rue de L'Etang. Beautiful new *jeunes travailleurs* establishment in a quiet residential area offers singles, doubles, and suites, all with toilet and shower. Restaurant, computer lab, and laundry facilities. Breakfast included. 2-night min. stay. 24hr. reception. Singles and doubles €18 per person. Reduced rates for stays over 3 nights. MC/V. ❶

Hôtel Ravel, 8 rue de Maringues (☎04 73 91 51 33; hotelravel63@wanadoo.fr). Has an anglophone owner and an intricate mosaic facade. This hôtel sits just outside Clermont-Ferrand's charming city center. All rooms have shower and bathroom. Breakfast €5. Singles €35; doubles €42; triples €50; quads €60. MC/V. ❸

Hôtel Zurich, 65 av. de l'Union Soviétique (☎04 73 91 97 98), to the right of the train station, past the hostel. Dark but homey rooms have plush red curtains and gold bedspreads. Reception after 3pm. 1 single at €18; other singles and doubles €23-27, with shower €23-35. Reduced rates for stays over 1 week. ❸

Camping: Le Chancet, av. Jean-Baptiste Marrou (☎04 73 61 30 73). 6km outside Clermont, on the Nationale 89 (dir: Bordeaux). From the station, take bus #4C (dir: Ceyrat) to Préguille. 3-star rated site has biking and hiking excursions during the summer. Laundry. Reception daily July-Aug. 9am-8pm. €2.80 per person, ages 4-10 €2; €5.20 per tent; €1.70 per car. Caravan site with electricity €9.50. ❶

▐ FOOD

Michelin may have created the most influential French restaurant guide, but Clermont-Ferrand is not generally known for its cuisine. A few quaint restaurants are tucked along side-streets in the city center, fast-food joints cluster on av. des Etats-Unis, and some *brasseries* surround the tourist office and cathedral. A **Champion supermarket** takes up much of rue Giscard de la Tour Fondue. To get there from the train station, make a left at pl. de la Résistance and take a right onto rue Giscard de la Tour Fondue. (Open M-Sa 8:30am-8:30pm, Su 9am-12:30pm.) Local produce and cheese are sold at the **Marché Couvert/Espace St-Pierre,** off pl. Gaillard, a huge covered **market** selling hundreds of regional specialties (open M-Sa 7am-7:30pm), and nearby rue de la Boucherie has a lovely **fruit market.**

    Aux Délices de la Treille ❸, 33 rue de la Treille, prepares delicious regional *menus* (€11-22) in a quirky restaurant that toes the delicate line between tacky and cool. Yannick, the charismatic owner, happily chats up his customers. (☎04 73 91 26 90. Open daily 11:30am-2:30pm and 6-11pm.) **Ah! St-Tropez ❹,** 10 rue Massillon, near pl. de Victoire, serves tasty, gourmet *menus* (€15-18, lunch *menu* €12) against a vibrant backdrop of playful Provençal murals. (☎04 73 90 44 64. Open Tu-Sa noon-11pm. MC/V.) **Le Pescajoux ❶,** 13 rue du Port, has over 160 types of delicious crêpes from basic nutella (€3) to the "Popeye" (€6.70), with fresh spinach. (☎04 73 92 12 26. Open M-F noon-2pm and from 7:30pm, Sa from 7:30pm. MC/V.)

◉ SIGHTS

The *vieille ville* of Clermont, called the **Ville Noire** (Black City) for its black-stone buildings, blends typical French country architecture with volcanic stone. The city's museums touch on archaeology, sociology, and natural history; some of the best sights, however, lie in the surrounding mountains. The **Passe Découverte** (€10) allows entry into each of the five major museums. All museums give free admission the first Sunday of each month.

▧ CATHÉDRALE NOTRE-DAME DE L'ASSOMPTION. First built in AD 450 and completely reconstructed in the Gothic style between 1248 and 1295, this church now commands attention from miles away. The lava-based material allowed the architects to elongate the church's jet black spires to a height of 100m; climb the 252-step tower for a panoramic view. Within the dark, airy interior, three huge rose windows gleam brilliantly. (*Pl. de la Victoire. http://cathedrale-catholique-clermont.cef.fr. Open June to mid-Sept. M-Sa 7:30am-6pm, Su 11:15am-6pm; mid-Sept. to late May 8am-noon and 2-6pm. Info available in 11 languages. Tower open 10am-6pm. €1.50.*)

BASILIQUE DE NOTRE-DAME-DU-PORT. This 12th-century church was built in the local Auvergnat Romanesque style; its intricately carved capitals depict Bible stories. Pope Urban II is believed to have urged the First Crusade here. After May 14, pilgrims come to see the icon of the Black Virgin. (*Pl. Notre-Dame-du-Port. ☎04 73 91 32 94. Open daily 8am-7pm. French tours July-Aug. W and F at 3pm.*)

PARC DE MONTJUZET. This beautifully groomed park spreads across a hill high above Clermont (486m), offering spectacular views of the city and its surrounding mountains, including Puy-de-Dôme to the west. Numerous shaded paths, grassy hillsides, and various playgrounds (including a huge rope jungle gym) make it a lovely spot for a picnic or a (breathless) jog. (*☎04 73 42 62 27. Northwest of the main city. Main entrance and parking on rue du parc Monjuzet; secondary pedestrian entrance closer to the vieille ville on rue des Aubepines. A 15min. walk from the cathedral; ask at the tourist office for directions. Open 7am-8pm.*)

MONTFERRAND. Montferrand's best sights are its inconspicuous *hôtels particuliers*, private mansions which date from the Middle Ages and the Renaissance. The best way to visit the town, which is a 40min. walk up av. de la République, is to take the tourist office's 2hr. walking tour. (Tu, Th, Sa 3pm from pl. Louis Deteix; €5, students €3.10) Take bus #17 (dir: Blanzat or Cébazat) or bus #10M (dir: Aulnat) from the train station. Like Clermont, this town also boasts a volcanic stone church. **Notre-Dame-de-Prospérité** stands on the site of the long-demolished château of the Auvergnat counts.

MUSÉE DES TAPIS ET DES ARTS TEXTILES. This museum has exhibits on the various uses, techniques, and international differences of textile art. *(45 rue Ballainvilliers. Bargoin ☎ 04 73 91 37 31, Tapis ☎ 04 73 90 57 48. Both open Tu-Su 10am-6pm, closed Su in Aug. Info available in French, English, and Braille. Each museum €4, students €2.50.)*

🎵🍷 ENTERTAINMENT AND NIGHTLIFE

Clermont's students complain that the city's nightlife is sluggish, but a few popular nightspots hide away on side-streets; check *Le Guide de l'Etudiant Clermont-Ferrand* (available at the tourist office) for complete listings. Pool tables and cheap beer are the main attractions at the many bars across from the train station.

Le Palais de la Bière, 3 rue de la Michodière, on the corner of pl. Galliard and av. des Etats-Unis, lacks a little in ambience, but compensates with diverse beers and late-night *brasserie* fare. (☎ 04 73 37 15 51. Open Tu-Sa 7pm-12:30am. Closed Aug.) Imbibe with students and townies at **The John Barleycorn Pub,** 9 rue du Terrail, on a cobblestone side-street of the *vieille ville.* The bearded and tattooed bartender entertains with wild stories. (☎ 04 73 92 31 67. Open daily 5pm-2am.) For a late night of clubbing, **Oxxo,** 16 rue de Deux Marchés, has two dance floors that stay bumping until the early morning. (☎ 04 73 14 11 11. Cover Th €2; F-Sa €7 with drink, €5 without. Open W 10pm-4am, Th-Sa 10pm-5am.)

During the first week of February, European filmmakers gather for Clermont-Ferrand's annual **Festival International du Court Métrage,** considered the Cannes of the short film. For more info, contact La Jetée, 6 pl. Michel de l'Hospital. (☎ 04 73 91 65 73; www.clermont-filmfest.com. Pass for 5-6 films €2.50.)

🏞️ DAYTRIP FROM CLERMONT-FERRAND

PUY-DE-DÔME. Clermont-Ferrand's greatest attraction is its proximity to a terrain of extinct volcanoes, crater lakes, and famed mountains. Puy-de-Dôme, the mountain dominating the middle, is part of the **Parc Naturel Régional des Volcans d'Auvergne,** west of Clermont-Ferrand. (☎ 04 73 65 64 00; fax 04 73 65 66 78.) Hikers, bikers, and skiers alike enjoy the unspoiled terrain of one of France's largest parks. A booklet available at the Clermont-Ferrand tourist office indicates hiking paths in the area. There are three main sections in the protected area: the **Mont-Dore,** the **Monts du Cantal,** and the **Monts Dômes,** which makes the best base for exploring the mountains.

On a clear day, the sweeping view from the top of flat-topped **Puy-de-Dôme** (1465m) includes the teacup-shaped **Chaîne des Puys,** a lush ridge of extinct volcanoes which runs north-south. In late autumn, a *mer de nuages* (sea of clouds), obscures the plains below such that only isolated peaks protrude into the sky. (Puy-de-Dôme open mid-June to Aug. 7am-10pm; Apr. to mid-June and Sept. 7am-7:30pm; Mar. and Oct. 8am-7pm; Nov. 8am-6pm, weather permitting. Call ☎ 04 73 62 12 18 to see if the road to the top is open.)

Although Puy-de-Dôme is only 12km from Clermont-Ferrand, getting there takes some planning. The Clermont tourist office's **L'Espace Massif Central** desk has info on how best to make the trip. A bus service of *navettes* circulates three times daily from the Clermont train station to the summit, and also to the nearby Vulcania natural area. (☎ 08 00 50 05 24. 35min. Daily in June-Aug.; weekends and holidays in May-June and Sept. €5 round-trip including connecting shuttles with Vulcania.) For more intrepid folk, the best bet is to hike or drive. Hikers should take bus line #14 to Royat from the stop at Place Allard. Follow the signs for the Hôtel Paradis to reach the first yellow markers that guide the rest of the wide, graveled 3hr. hike along the PR Chamina to the summit. Buy a good map (the IGN *Chaîne des Puys*) and listen to the weather forecast for the day, as conditions change rapidly. The summit is only car-accessible at certain times: from 10am to 6pm in July and Aug., and weekends and holidays in May-June and Sept.-Oct. Drivers must leave their cars at the base and take a bus to the top (last bus descends at 7pm; round-trip €3.50; free parking at base and summit); otherwise, the toll is €4.50.

LE MONT-DORE

Located in an isolated valley amid primordial scenery, Le Mont-Dore (pop. 1700) sits at the foot of the largest volcano in a dormant range. Elephants, rhinos, and tigers once roamed through bamboo forests here, and their fossils remain encrusted in the area's volcanic rock. A premier ski resort in the winter and a hiking mecca year-round, Le Mont-Dore also attracts summer *curistes* seeking rejuvenation in the warm, mineral-rich waters that seep up through cracks in the lava.

▣☎ TRANSPORTATION AND PRACTICAL INFORMATION. Trains and SNCF **buses** run from pl. de la Gare (☎04 73 65 00 02) to Clermont-Ferrand (1½hr., 6 per day, €10.40) and Paris (6 per day, €47.40). Info desk open M-Th 5:50am-7:15pm, F-Sa until 7pm, Su 9:30am-noon and 2-6pm. **Taxis** are operated by Claude Taxi (☎04 73 99 80 61) and Taxi Sepchat (☎04 73 65 09 38). Rent **bikes** and **skis** at **Bessac Sports,** rue de Maréchal Juin, near the top of the hill. (☎04 73 65 02 25. Bikes €12 per half-day, €18 per day. Skis €7-24 per day. Passport deposit. Snowboards and hiking equipment also available. Open daily July-Aug. 9:30am-noon and 2-7pm; Sept.-June during school vacations Sa-Su 8:30am-7pm. MC/V.)

From the train station, head up av. Michel Bertrand and follow the signs to the **tourist office,** av. de la Libération, behind the ice-skating rink across the Dordogne. Staffers distribute a practical city guide, help with accommodations booking (for stays over 3 days), and organize summer hikes and bike tours. **Internet** access with France Téléecom *télécartes.* (☎04 73 65 20 21; fax 04 73 65 05 71. Open daily July-Aug. 9am-1pm and 2-7pm; Sept.-June M-F 9am-12:30pm and 2-6:30pm, Su 10am-noon and 2-4pm. Hikes €10.) Other services include: **police** (☎04 73 65 01 70 or 17) on av. M. Bertrand; a **hospital** at 2 rue du Capitaine-Chazotte (☎04 73 65 33 33), off pl. Charles de Gaulle; a **laverie** in pl. de la République (open daily 9am-7pm); the **Pharmacie du Parc** at 17 rue Meynadier. (☎04 73 65 02 86 or 06 03 78 20 93. Open M-Sa 9am-12:15pm and 2:30-7:15pm.) The **pharmacie de garde** alternates between **Parc** or **Pharmacie de l'Etablissement,** 1 pl. du Panthéon (☎04 73 65 05 21; after 7pm 04 73 81 08 98). The **post office,** pl. Charles de Gaulle, **exchanges currency** and has an **ATM** just outside. (☎04 73 65 37 10. Open M-F 9am-12:30pm and 2-6pm, Sa 9am-12:30pm.) **Postal Code:** 63240.

▐☎ ACCOMMODATIONS AND CAMPING. With tourism as its major industry, Le Mont-Dore has over a dozen hotels with rooms starting in the low €20s, making it relatively easy to find an affordable bed. Even so, reservations are usually recommended during summer and peak skiing periods. **Hôtel Le Parking ❷,** 19 av. de la Libération, behind the tourist office, has sizable, comfortable rooms and spectacular views. (☎04 73 65 03 43. Breakfast €4. Reception daily 8am-7pm. Closed Nov. Singles €18.50-26; doubles €21.40-43; triples with bath €39-47. MC/V.) Modern wood paneling creates a clean, bright feel at **Castel Medicis ❷,** 5 rue Duchatel, at the top of the main part of town. (☎04 73 65 30 50; www.castel-medicis.com. Breakfast included. Reception daily 8am-8pm. Doubles €20, with shower €28, with bath €32. Extra bed €8. MC/V.) In the center of town, **Grand Hôtel ❸,** 2 rue Meyandier, looks like a castle, and offers simple rooms for a happily-ever-after evening. (☎04 73 65 02 64; fax 04 73 65 27 72. Breakfast €5. Singles and doubles with toilets €25, with shower €30; triples and quads with bath €35. MC/V.) **Hôtel de Londres ❸**, 45 rue Meyandier, overlooks the city park. This moderately priced hotel has fresh and clean rooms, some with balconies. (☎ 04 73 65 01 12. Reception 7:30am-9pm. Check-in after 1pm. Closed in Apr. Singles and doubles with bath €35-41; triples and quads €43-54. MC/V.) **Auberge de Jeunesse "Le Grand Volcan" (HI) ❶**, rte. du Sancy, is 4km from town. From the station, climb av. Guyot-Dessaigne, which becomes av. des Belges. Continue on D983 (through several name changes) into the countryside. The hostel is on the right, after the ski lifts.Local buses run to the hostel from behind the tourist office four times per day. The spartan one- to seven-bed rooms could be more appealing, but the idyllic setting at the foot of Puy de Sancy, just steps from skiing and hiking trails, makes up for all that. (☎ 04 73 65 03 53; fax 04 73 65 26 39. Outdoor kitchen, bar, and Internet kiosk. Ski and snowboard packages €11-13. Reception daily June-Aug. 8am-2pm and 6-9pm; Sept.-May 8am-noon and 6-9pm. Breakfast and bunk €12.30. HI members only.) The most convenient of the four campsites in Le Mont-Dore **Des Crouzets ❶**, av. des Crouzets, is across from the station in a crowded hollow on the Dordogne. (☎/fax 04 73 65 21 60. Office open M-Sa 9am-noon and 3-6pm, Su 9:30am-noon. Open mid-Dec. to mid.-Oct. €2.70 per person, €2.40 per site. Electricity €2.60.)

❒ FOOD. Restaurants take a backseat to outdoor pursuits in Le Mont-Dore. However, the small spots serving regional dishes like potato and cheese *truffade*, or its creamed cousin *aligot*, are ideal after a day of exploring. Many restaurants in Le Mont-Dore are affiliated with a hotel and give discounts to guests. Most *menus* begin at €11; the good ones run €13-15. **Le Bougnat ❸**, 23 rue Georges Clemenceau, serves regional fare in a flower-trimmed stone building toward the top of town. The delicious *aligot* goes for €12.50. (☎ 04 73 65 28 19. Entrees €11-13. Open Tu-Sa noon-2pm and 7:30-11pm. MC/V.) In a 1920s salon, **Café de Paris ❷**, pl. du Panthéon, cooks up local cafe food (*truffade*, €9) on a quiet street, and sometimes has an evening piano bar. (☎ 04 73 65 01 79. Open daily 8am-8pm; meals only served noon-3pm.) Mountaintop picnics make the most scenic meals: pick up a wedge of St-Nectaire cheese and a link of uniquely flavored dry sausage from one of the streetside shops specializing in local food, or try the **Utile supermarket** on rue du Cap-Chazzotte. (Open July-Aug. M-Sa 7am-7:30pm, Su 7am-12:30pm and 3-7:30pm; Sept.-June M-Sa 7am-12:30pm and 4-7:30pm, Su 8am-12:30pm.)

◲ SIGHTS. Every morning in the May-October thermal season, *curistes* seeking the healing power of Le Mont-Dore's springs descend upon the ornate **Etablissement Thermal**, 1 pl. du Panthéon. Five springs used today were channeled by the Romans, who discovered that the pure water did wonders for their horses' sinuses. Today, a French-led tour of the *thermes* ends with a dose of the celebrated *douche nasale gazeuse*, a tiny blast of carbon and helium that evacuates sinuses more effectively than any sneeze. (☎ 04 73 65 05 10. Tours M-Sa every hr. 2-5pm. €3.) Down the hill on av. Michel Bertrand, the **Musée Joseph Forêt** honors the celebrated art editor and Le Mont-Dore native who bequeathed his collection to the town in 1985. Before his death, Forêt recruited seven painters and seven writers to collaborate in the publication of the world's largest book, *Le Livre de l'Apocalyps*. The final product, weighing a quarter-ton, incorporates works by Dalí and Cocteau and had to be sold in bits to pay for printing. A copy is displayed in the back of the museum. (☎ 04 73 65 00 91. Call 12:30-3pm to set up a visit. €2.)

◪ ▩ HIKING AND BIKING. Trails through the volcanic mountains span dense forests, rushing waterfalls, and jagged rocks, then plunge into verdant valleys. Scaling the peaks is relatively easy—the summit of **Puy de Sancy** (1775m) awaits at the end of a moderate 2hr. climb—and day-long rambles along the lush ridges yield a wonderfully varied landscape. Those embarking on an extended hike should review their route with the tourist office, which has maps and multilingual guidance. Leave an itinerary of multi-day routes with the *peloton de montagne* (mountain police; ☎04 73 65 04 06), on rue des Chaussers at the base of Puy de Sancy. All hikers should acquire maps and weather reports—mist in the valley often signifies hail or snow in the peaks. The tourist office's pocket-sized *Massif du Sancy* (€7) maps out hiking circuits. The *Massif du Sancy et Artense guide* (€14.40) covers 47 hikes originating in all areas of Le Sancy. An **IGN map** (either Massif du Sancy or the larger Chaîne des Puys) is essential for any serious trek (€6).

For all the views without all the exertion, the **téléphérique** runs from the base by the hostel to a station just below the Puy de Sancy; a climb up wooden stairs leads to the summit. (☎08 20 82 09 48. Departs daily July-Aug. every 10min. 9am-6pm; May-June and Sept. 9am-12:30pm and 1:30-5pm; Oct.-Apr. 8:45am-4:45pm, Oct. and Nov. open Sa-Su only. One-way €5.20, round-trip €6.50.) Farther north, the **funicular** departs from near the tourist office to Salon des Capucin, a rocky outcropping high above town. (Departs July-Aug. Tu-Su every 20min. 9am-6:40pm; May and Sept. 10am-noon and 2pm-6:30pm. One-way €3.30, round-trip €4.20.) Both can be used to launch other hikes, or to save weary knees from a final descent.

Bikers and drivers should check out the calm volcanic lakes, like **Lac Servière** (15km northeast), which pool in the craters of the Le Mont-Dore region. Most of the lakes have small pebble beaches and are suitable for windsurfing, sailing, and swimming. **Lac d'Aydat,** to the northeast, offers paddle-boats and other amusements, as does **Lac Chambon,** 20km east of Le Mont-Dore via D996E, near Murol.

Hikes are indicated by yellow trail signs, often accompanied by detailed maps of the surrounding area. The following recommendations are only a few; innumerable routes can be planned with a good map. Distances and times given are for round-trips. A lovely hike, ▓**La Grande Cascade** (3.5km, 1½hr., 200m vertical), starts from the center of town and packs in a variety of sights, ending in a lush field with views of the whole Sancy range. From the *thermes*, follow rue des Desportes a few meters to the right and climb the stairs on the left to the chemin de Melki Rose, which joins the rte. de Besse and becomes the chemin de la Grande Cascade. After crossing a road, the trail winds up a narrow gorge. A quick climb up the metal stairway leads to the top of the waterfall and the field stretching above.

THE BIG SPLURGE

SOAKING IT UP

The mineral-water springs of Auvergne's volcanic region have long drawn flocks of cure-seeking patients. Discovered by the Romans, the *thermes* were forgotten until the late 1700s and early 1800s, when Byzantine-style bath houses were built in a small string of cities throughout the Auvergne. Now these institutions bring a rich clientele to the mountains for weeks of treatment, providing France's quietest region with a much-needed economic boost.

Dedicated *curistes*, doctors' notes in hand, line up as early as 6:30am for their daily cures, which involve everything from inhaling the springs' vapors to being sprayed with a large hose. The majority of bathers are on three-week prescriptions.

Newcomers eager to test the waters can try the **Etablissement Thermal** in Le Mont-Dore. Even without a prescription, visitors can opt for a morning *découverte* package (€45), which includes treatments like a high-powered whirlpool, a precisely placed vapor shower, a nasal humidifier, and a sauna. "Patients" in thick robes are whisked from one tiled room to the next for various water cures. For those recovering from the previous day's hike, it may be just what the doctor ordered.

(1 pl. du Panthéon. ☎04 73 65 05 10; fax 04 73 65 09 37. Reservations recommended.)

Ascending to the Massif's highest peak the ◨**Puy de Sancy** (8km, 3-4hr., 560m vertical), is an utter pleasure. The 360° view from the platform on the summit includes the entire Auvergne region and, on cloudless days, the distant Alps. Begin the hike at the base of the Puy de Sancy and ascend the mountain via the picturesque, cow-inhabited Val de Courre, which starts about a 2min. walk to the right of *téléphérique* no. 2. At Puy Redon, the trail joins the GR30, which winds to the left and eventually climbs a series of wooden steps to reach the summit of Puy de Sancy. It's possible to make a loop by following the GR4E down the other side back to the base, but aesthetes will want to retrace their steps down the Val de Courre instead of suffering through the marked ski trails.

☒ **SKIING.** It's not every day that skiers find themselves slicing down hardened magma fields, and Le Mont-Dore offers as spectacular a winter wonderland as any area outside the Alps. Like most visitors to Auvergne, skiers and snowboarders will encounter pleasantly smaller crowds (and shorter lift-lines) than elsewhere in France. The network of ski trails covers much of the Massif du Sancy, with the possibility of skiing down the other side of the valley into ritzy Super-Besse on clear days. Ski-rental shops by the dozen fill the main village; rental packages should generally cost no more than €10-15 per day. Lift tickets for the entire Mont- Dore and Super-Besse area are €15.70 per half-day, €20 per day. At the base of the Puy de Sancy lifts is a ski school (☎04 73 65 07 43). The area also boasts an extensive network of cross-country skiing trails; ask at the tourist office or call ☎04 73 65 20 21 for information.

▶ **DAYTRIPS FROM LE MONT-DORE: LA BOURBOULE.** The region surrounding Le Mont-Dore has a number of small, picturesque towns within easy driving or hiking range. La Bourboule, which can also be reached by a shuttle service from Le Mont-Dore, was established in 1875 upon the discovery of its thermal springs and became a widely popular destination in the 1920s. The city, just 15min. from Le Mont-Dore, maintains its "Roaring Twenties" atmosphere with exquisite Art Nouveau architecture, glamorous plazas, and charming hotels and restaurants. Information on thermal visits, shuttles from Le Mont-Dore, and lodging is available at the tourist office, pl. de la République. (☎04 73 65 57 71; www.bourboule.com. Open June-Aug. daily 9am-7pm; Sept.-May 9am-12:30pm and 2-7pm.)

LE PUY-EN-VELAY

Jutting crags of volcanic rock pierce the sky near Le Puy (pop. 20,500), punctuating a horizon dominated by endless expanses of green. Ever since the first churches were built atop these natural skyscrapers, Le Puy has claimed thousands of pilgrims per year by serving as the starting point for the 1600km *Via Podiensis* trail, which ends in Santiago de Compostela, Spain. Today it is a popular tourist destination as well, drawing people to its lava-stone streets lined with countless traditional lace-making shops. Although the town is predominantly tranquil, the Fête de la Musique on June 21 launches a busy festival season that ends with a bang: September's Renaissance extravaganza, La Roi de l'Oiseau.

▥ TRANSPORTATION

Trains: pl. Maréchal Leclerc. Info and ticket offices open M 4:25am-7pm, Tu-Sa 5:40am-7pm, Su 10:05am-8:10pm. To: **Clermont-Ferrand** (2½hr., M-F 6 per day, €18.10*)*; **Lyon** (2½hr., M-F 4 per day, €18.10); **St-Etienne-Châteaucreux** (1¼hr., M-F 7 per day,

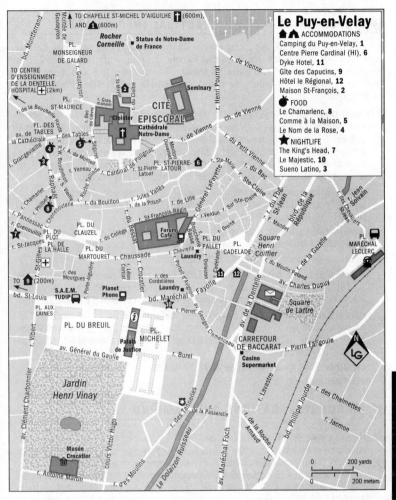

Le Puy-en-Velay

▲⌂ ACCOMMODATIONS
Camping du Puy-en-Velay, **1**
Centre Pierre Cardinal (HI), **6**
Dyke Hotel, **11**
Gîte des Capucins, **9**
Hôtel le Régional, **12**
Maison St-François, **2**

🍎 FOOD
Le Chamarlenc, **8**
Comme à la Maison, **5**
Le Nom de la Rose, **4**

★ NIGHTLIFE
The King's Head, **7**
Le Majestic, **10**
Sueno Latino, **3**

MASSIF CENTRAL

€11.80). Most trains arriving from the south or from Clermont-Ferrand require a change at Brioude; trains from Lyon or Paris change at St-Etienne-Châteaucreux. Trains marked "car" are buses.

Buses: pl. Maréchal Leclerc (☎04 71 09 25 60), next to the train station. Open M-F 8am-noon. Transportation by bus can be spotty. Buses run to **St-Etienne** (2¼hr., M-Sa 2 per day, €9). Those traveling south should bus to **Langogne** (2hr., M-F 3 per day, €7.50) to catch a train. Buy tickets on bus.

Public Transportation: S.A.E.M. TUDIP, pl. du Breuil. Info and map at the tourist office. Tickets on bus €1, *carnet* of 10 at the tourist office €7. Runs daily 7am-7:25pm.

Taxis: Radio-Taxis, pl. du Breuil (☎04 71 05 42 43). 24hr.

■ ⚡ ORIENTATION AND PRACTICAL INFORMATION

From the station, walk left along **avenue Charles Dupuy**, cross **square H. Coiffier**, and turn left onto **boulevard Maréchal Fayolle**. A 5min. walk leads to adjacent squares **place Michelet** and **place du Breuil**. The tourist office and most hotels are here and on bd. St-Louis; the cathedral, hostels, and *vieille ville* are uphill to the right.

Tourist Office: pl. du Breuil (☎04 71 09 38 41; www.ot-lepuyenvelay.fr). Free accommodations service. Free, well-marked map with 3 walking tours. Open July-Aug. M-Sa 8:30am-7:30pm, Su 9am-noon and 2-6pm; Sept.-June M-Sa 8:30am-noon and 1:30-6:15pm, Su 9:30am-12:30pm and 2-6pm; Oct.-Mar. Su 10am-noon only. Daily guided tours of the cathedral or the nearby geological sites are given early July to early Sept.; weekly tours on Sa at 3pm during the rest of the year. €5, €3 students.

Currency Exchange: Western Union office with small commission. Cyberposte. Open M-F 8am-7pm, Sa 8:30am-noon. Branch office: 49 bd. St-Louis (☎04 71 09 77 61). Open M-F 9am-noon and 2-5:30pm, Sa 9am-noon.

Laundromat: Lavo-Self, 12 rue Chèvrerie. Open M-Sa 7:45am-noon and 1-7pm. **Lav'Flash,** 24 rue Portail d'Avignon. Open M-Sa 8am-7pm, Su 9:15am-6:30pm.

Police: rue de la Passerelle (☎04 71 04 04 22).

Medical Assistance: Centre Hospitalier Emile Roux, bd. Dr. Chantemesse (☎04 71 04 32 10). 24hr. **Clinique Bon Secours,** 67bis av. M. Foch (☎04 71 09 87 00). **Ambulance** ☎04 71 90 30 34. For the **pharmacie de garde,** call ☎04 71 04 04 22.

Internet Access: Forum Café, 5 rue Général LaFayette (☎04 71 04 04 98), is dirt cheap at €1.50 per hr. Open Tu-Sa 1-6pm; school vacations 2pm-7pm. **Planet Phone,** 33 pl. du Breuil (☎06 25 10 17 13), has an international phone booth. €1.50 per 30min. Open daily 9am-11pm.

Post Office: 8 av. de la Dentelle (☎04 71 07 02 05).

Postal Code: 43000.

■ ■ ACCOMMODATIONS AND CAMPING

Gite des Capucins, 29 rue des Capucins (☎04 71 04 28 74), off bd. St-Louis. White boards on every door encourage guests to make their own nameplates at this small, extremely friendly stop. Immaculate 4- to 6-bed dorms, each with private bath. Kitchen facilities and a beautiful little garden in back. Breakfast €4.60. Sheets €1.60. Reception until late; there is usually someone around to answer calls. Check-out by 10am. Beds €12.50. Well-furnished, colorful 2-person apartments €51.80; 4-person apartments €64; 6-person apartment €76.20. ❶

Centre Pierre Cardinal (HI), 9 rue Jules Vallès (☎04 71 05 52 40; fax 04 71 05 61 24). Numerous quads and 1 18-bed dorm in clean former barracks. Excellent kitchen. Breakfast €3.20. Sheets €3.50. Reception M-Sa 2pm-11:30pm, Su 8pm-10pm. Lock-out Su 10am-8pm. Curfew 11:30pm. Closed holidays, Christmas vacation, weekends from Oct.-Mar. and during the July *Festival des Musicales*. Bunks €7. AmEx/MC/V. HI members only. ❶

Maison St-François, rue St-Mayol (☎04 71 05 98 86; fax 04 71 05 98 87). Soothing peach- and white-trimmed rooms, practically in the cathedral. Kitchen, convent garden, and joyful common room. Caters primarily to pilgrims in summer, but other travelers are welcome. Breakfast included. Meals €10. No sheets available. Reception 2-8pm. Check-out by 8:30am. Call a few days ahead. Beds €16. ❶

Hôtel le Régional, 36 bd. Maréchal Fayolle (☎04 71 09 37 74), near pl. Michelet. Noisy area near train station. Large, clean, colorful rooms with sound-proof windows attached to small cafe. Breakfast €4.50. Reception daily 7am-10pm. Singles and doubles €21.50, with shower from €26; triples from €28; quads €41.50. AmEx/MC/V. ❷

Dyke Hotel, 37 bd. Maréchal-Fayolle (☎04 71 09 05 30; fax 04 71 02 58 66). The name, pronounced deek, refers to tall points of rock in Le Puy. Modern, wood-paneled rooms painted in cheerful yellow tones. Breakfast €5.35. Singles and doubles with shower €31-45. MC/V. ❸

Camping: Camping du Puy-en-Velay, chemin de Bouthezard (☎04 71 09 55 09), near the Chapelle St-Michel and the river. Walk up bd. St-Louis, continue on bd. Carnot, turn right at the dead end onto av. d'Aiguille; the campground is on the left. (15min.) Or take bus #6 (dir: Mondon) from pl. Michelet (10min., 1 per hr., €1). Grassy, pleasant sites, but not very private. Reception daily 8am-9pm. Open Easter to Sept. €8.79 for 2 people, site, and car. Electricity €2.95. ❶

◪ FOOD

Recognized by the French government as a city with exceptional local cuisine, Le-Puy-en-Velay's many restaurants and markets provide mouth-watering regional specialties. Nearly every restaurant serves *lentilles vertes et saussicon*, as lentils are grown in mass, quality-controlled quantities around the region. Complete a meal with Verveine, an alcoholic *digéstif* with a sweet mint flavor, made from local herbs and honey (€10-22 per bottle); the distillery down the road gives tours and tastings. (☎04 71 03 04 11; www.verveine.com. Open daily 10am-noon and 1:30-6:30pm. €5.30, students €4.) Inexpensive restaurants line the side-streets off **place du Breuil**. A **Casino supermarket** occupies the corner of av. de la Dentelle and rue Farigoule (open M-Sa 8:30am-8pm). On Saturdays (6am-12:30pm), farmers set up fresh produce **markets** in practically every square. The **market** in pl. du Plot also sells cheese, mushrooms, and a few live chickens and rabbits; the adjacent pl. du Clauzel hosts an antique market. (Open Sa 7:30am-1pm.)

◪**Le Nom de la Rose ❷**, 48 rue Raphaël, serves an unusual but eminently satisfying combination of French-cooked Mexican food. (☎04 71 05 90 04. *Menu* €14.10, *chili con carne* €7.55, *quesadillas* €5.35. Open M-Sa noon-3pm and 7pm-midnight; closed M in winter. MC/V.) In a tastefully renovated 17th-century house, small, hip **Comme à la Maison ❸**,

BIRD'S THE WORD

Come mid-September, the normally quiet streets of Le Puy-en Velay into a lively 16th century fair. Over 30,000 visitors come for the annual Fêtes Renaissance du Roi de L'Oiseau, a lavish week-long celebration that has become France's largest costume party.

Though the festival took its current form in 1986, it revives a 400-year-old tradition. In 1524 a group of young archers designed a contest to pierce a cloth bird through the heart. The winner gained the title *roi de l'oiseau* (king of the bird) and was given royal privileges, including keys to the city, for a full year. Today, a crowd still watches as archers take their chance at becoming the new *roi*. Anyone can try their hand, provided they sign up the previous day (€2 bow and arrows provided).

For a full five days, the streets and squares of le Puy fill with Renaissance-themed events put on by more than 3000 costumed actors: jugglers and minstrels stoll the streets, and a huge 16th century market sells wares galore. At night, an ancient tunnel system carved into the rock below the *vieille ville* is opened and turned into a party hall where beer and wine flow all night among bonnet and legging-sporting gentlefolk.

(Information at ☎04 71 02 84 84; www.roideloiseau.com or www.ot-lepuyenvelay.fr. For costume rental, call ☎04 71 09 16 53. Activities €2-5, free for those in costume.)

7 rue Séguret, serves simple, delicious *menus du jour* (€12-16) named after local celebrities. (☎04 71 02 94 73. Open M-Sa noon-3pm and 7-11pm. MC/V.) At wood-decorated **Le Chamarlenc ❸**, 19 rue Raphaël, diners sample fresh cheeses and yogurts. Daily *menus* (€9-14) feature local farm products. (☎04 71 02 17 72. Open Tu-W noon-4:30pm, Th-Sa noon-11pm. MC/V.)

◉ SIGHTS

CHAPELLE ST-MICHEL D'AIGUILHE. Just outside the old city, this primitive chapel crowns an 80m spike of volcanic rock. Its stained glass dimly illuminates a faded 12th-century fresco and the almost voodoo-like 10th-century woodcut crucifix uncovered during excavations. The chapel was built in 950 by the first pilgrim to complete the Chemin de St-Jacques, a trail that still sees hundreds of pilgrims each year. (☎04 71 09 50 03. Open daily May-Sept. 9am-6:30pm; Feb. to late Mar. 2-4pm; late Mar. to late Apr. and Oct. to mid-Nov. 9:30am-noon and 2-5pm. €2.50, under 14 €1.)

CATHÉDRALE NOTRE-DAME. Towering over the city, the **Cité Episcopale** stands on a rock known as "le puy," where, legend holds, the Virgin Mary appeared and healed a woman in the fifth century. The church has attracted pilgrims and tourists for over 1000 years, largely for its famous statue of **la Vierge Noir** (Black Virgin), who looks serenely out from atop an elaborate base. The influence of the cathedral's Muslim builders is apparent on the doors to either side of the entrance, where "There is only one true God" is written in Arabic. A side chapel displays the celebrated Renaissance mural *Les Arts Libéraux*. It is thought to be unfinished: of the seven arts, only Grammar, Logic, Rhetoric, and Music are represented. (☎04 71 05 98 74. Open daily 7am-8pm. Free tours are offered early July to late Aug.)

CLOISTER. The most remarkable of the sights near the cathedral, the cloister's black, white, and peach stone arcades reflect an Islamic influence from Spain. Beneath flame-red tiling and black volcanic rock is an intricate frieze of grinning faces and mythical beasts. Amid the Byzantine arches of the **salle capitulaire**, a vivid and well-preserved 13th-century fresco depicts the Crucifixion. The entry ticket also allows a peek at the **Trésor d'Art Religieux**, which contains walnut statues and jeweled capes. (☎04 71 05 45 52. Both open daily July-Sept. 9am-6:30pm; May-June 9am-noon and 2-6pm; Oct.-Mar. 9am-noon and 2-5pm. €4.60, ages 18-25 with ID €3.10.)

STATUE DE NOTRE-DAME DE FRANCE. The pinnacle of the *vieille ville* is the **Rocher Corneille**, the pointy, eroded core of a volcano. The summit overlooks a dreamscape of jagged crags and manicured gardens. For a dizzying view through windows below the Virgin's arm, climb the winding stairs inside the 16m **Notre-Dame de France,** a giant statue cast from cannons captured during the Crimean war. Notre-Dame earned national fame in 1942, when 20,000 young people came here to pray for the liberation of France. (Open daily July-Aug. 9am-7:30pm; mid-Mar. to Apr. 9am-6pm; May-June and Sept. 9am-7pm; Oct. to mid-Mar. 10am-7pm. €3, students €1.20.)

MUSÉE CROZATIER. This broad-sweeping cultural history museum has a different theme to every floor: local craftsmanship like *dentelle* (lace-making), fine arts, and natural history. After perusing some of the early patented designs of native son Emile Reynaud, who invented the precursor to the film projector, check upstairs on the stuffed kangaroo. The museum overlooks the beautifully manicured **Jardin Henri Vinay,** which has a small zoo, duck pond, ample shade, and a peacock made of shaped bushes and flowers. (☎04 71 06 62 40. Open May-Sept. M and W-Su 10am-noon and 2-6pm; Oct.-Apr. M and W-Su 10am-noon and 2-4pm, Su 2-4pm. €3, students and under 25 €1.20, under 18 free.)

🅿️ 🌿 NIGHTLIFE AND FESTIVALS

Of Le Puy's many bars, one of the best is ▧**The King's Head,** 17 rue Grenouillit, a relaxed English pub that serves beer (€2.50-6) and fish and chips, in addition to curries and whatever else the friendly owner concocts. Ask for Dave's special cocktail, €5. (☎04 71 02 50 35. Open M-Th 4:30pm-1am, F 4:30pm-2am, Sa 4:30pm-midnight.) **Sueno Latino Café,** 37 rue Raphaël, cultivates a chic, low-key, dimly lit environment, where locals chat amiably over Latin rhythms and jazz. (☎04 71 02 23 02. Beer €2-2.50, cocktails €4. Open M-Th 5pm-1am, F-Sa 5pm-2am.) **Le Majestic,** 8 bd. Maréchal Fayolle, is a *brasserie* by day but spills out onto a terrace at night. Art exhibits and low, colorful chairs give this nightspot a creative flair. (☎04 71 09 06 30. Techno F-Sa. Open M-Sa 7am-1am, Su 10am-1am.) Although the **Municipal Theater** is closed until 2005, information on theater and dance performances can be found at the **Centre Culturel de Vals,** av. Charles Massot (☎04 71 05 61 24). A **cinéma** is located at 29 pl. du Breuil. (☎04 71 09 00 35. €6.40, students €5.30.)

From early July, Le Puy hosts a different festival each week, ranging from music to theater and culminating at the mid-September **Fête Renaissance du Roi de L'Oiseau.** From mid-August to early September, the world-renowned classical **Festival de la Chaise-Dieu,** featuring choral groups from all corners of the globe, has concerts in Le Puy and in nearby Chaise-Dieu. (Info and tickets ☎04 71 00 01 16; www.chaise-dieu.com. Tickets €10-75.) The tourist office gives out free copies of *Sortir,* a guide to the festival season, and can provide more specific info.

VICHY

With lacy ironwork, and resplendent Belle Époque architecture, Vichy (pop. 78,000) remains wedded to its identity as a city whose mineral-rich water once drew royals, celebrities, and the wealthy. Despite its splendor, Vichy's past is darkened by its years as the capital of France from 1940 to 1944. Forced to evacuate Paris, the French administration selected Vichy, with its large hotels and strong cultural life, as the seat of the Nazi-overseen government, under the leadership of Maréchal Philippe Pétain, a WWI hero. Amidst Art Nouveau promenades and *confiseries,* the absence of major WWII monuments and museums to designate buildings used by Pétain's government creates an eerie historical gap.

📠🔢 TRANSPORTATION AND PRACTICAL INFORMATION. The **train** station on pl. de la Gare sends trains to: Clermont-Ferrand (35min., 11 per day, €8.10); Nevers (1hr., 15 per day, €14.50); Paris (3hr., 6 per day, €36.20). Ticket counters open M-Th 5:40am-8:50pm, F 5:40am-9:50pm, Sa 6:30am-8:50pm, Su 6:45am-9:50pm; info desk open M-Sa 9:40am-5:50pm and Su June-Aug. The **bus station** is in a brick building next to the train station. (Office open M-F 8am-noon and 2-6pm. Reduced hours during the July-Aug. school vacation.) **Public buses** run through town from 6:30am to 8pm (€1). Schedules are available at the tourist office and at the Bus Inter **kiosk** (☎04 70 97 81 29; open M-Th 8:30-11:30am and 1-6pm, F 8:30-11:30am and 1-5pm), on pl. Charles de Gaulle near the post office. Purchase tickets on the bus or in kiosks around town. For cabs, call **Vichy Taxis** (☎04 70 98 69 69).

Both Vichy's well-managed **tourist office,** 19 rue du Parc, and the popular natural springs sit in the **Parc des Sources.** From the station, walk straight on rue de Paris; turn left at the fork onto rue Clemenceau, then right onto rue Sornin. The tourist office is 10min. away straight across the park, in the Hôtel du Parc, which once housed Pétain's government. The staff provides a good map, a list of hotels and restaurants, free accommodations service, and themed French walking tours. (☎04 70 98 71 94; www.ville-vichy.fr. Office open July-Aug. M-Sa 9am-7:30pm, Su

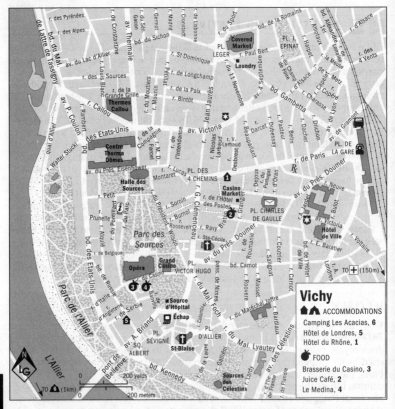

Vichy

🏠🏠 ACCOMMODATIONS

Camping Les Acacias, **6**
Hôtel de Londres, **5**
Hôtel du Rhône, **1**

🍎 FOOD

Brasserie du Casino, **3**
Juice Café, **2**
Le Medina, **4**

9:30am-12:30pm and 3-7pm; Apr.-June and Sept. M-Sa 9am-12:30pm and 1:30-7pm, Su 9:30am-12:30pm and 3-7pm; Oct.-Mar. M-F 9am-noon and 1:30-6pm, Sa 9am-noon and 2-6pm, Su 2:30-5:30pm.) Other services include: **police**, 35 av. Victoria (☎04 70 96 11 11); the **Centre Hospitalier**, 15 bd. Denière (☎04 70 97 33 33); **La Grande Pharmacie**, 46 rue de Paris (☎04 70 98 23 01; open M 2:30-7:15pm, Tu-Sa 9:30am-12:15pm and 2-7:15pm); a **pharmacie de garde** (dial ☎15); a **Wash'n Dry** at 3 bd. Gambetta (☎06 78 78 08 9; open daily 7am-9pm); **Internet** access at Echape, 12 rue Source de l'Hôpital, across from the Source d'Hôpital (☎04 70 32 28 57; open T-Sa noon-midnight, Su 2pm-midnight; €3 per 30min., €4 per hour). The **post office** at pl. Charles de Gaulle **exchanges currency** at 1.5% commission. (☎04 70 30 10 75. Open M-F 8am-6:30pm, Sa 8am-noon.) **Postal Code:** 03200.

🏠 **ACCOMMODATIONS.** In keeping with Vichy's long-standing tradition of pampering its guests, even its budget hostels are deluxe. Hotels jostle for business on; rooms start around €22. The historic, restored **Hôtel de Londres ❷**, 7 bd. de Russie, offers large, clean rooms around a flower-filled courtyard. (☎04 70 98 29 27; hotel.londres@wanadoo.fr. Breakfast €6. Open Jan.-late Oct. Singles, some with shower €21-25; doubles €23-28. Extra bed €7.50. MC/V.) The friendly, multilingual owner of **Hôtel du Rhône ❸**, 8 rue de Paris, between the train station and the *thermes*, offers well-decorated doubles and triples and an air-conditioned salon.

Let's Go readers staying more than two nights receive a free breakfast. (☎04 70 97 73 00; fax 04 70 97 48 25. Breakfast €3. 24hr. reception. Singles and doubles with shower €25-39; triples €36-68; deluxe rooms with bath €54-79. AmEx/MC/V.)

The four-star, riverside **Camping Les Acacias ❷** has a market, pool, and laundry facilities. Take bus #7 from the train station (dir: La Tour) to Charles de Gaulle, then bus #3 to Les Acacias; it's 3.5km on foot. (☎04 70 32 36 22; www.camping-aca-cias.com. Reception daily 8am-10pm. Open Apr. to mid-Oct. €4.90 per person, €4.80 per tent. Electricity €2.90. Prices lower Apr.-June and Sept.-Oct. MC/V.)

☐ **FOOD.** A **Casino supermarket** sits at the corner of pl. Charles de Gaulle and rue de l'Hôtel des Postes. (Open M-Sa 8:30am-12:30pm and 2:30-7:30pm, Su 9am-noon.) A covered morning **market** is on pl. Léger where rue Jean Jaurès and bd. Gambetta intersect. (Open Tu-Sa.)

Most restaurants in Vichy are affiliated with hotels and, in contrast to the rooms, tend to be fairly expensive. **La Medina ❸**, 7 rue de Banville, serves delicious Moroc-can food in a beautiful North African salon, complete with petal-strewn tables. (☎04 70 98 54 03. Couscous and *tijanes* €10-13. Open Sept.-June Tu-Su 5-11pm. MC/V.) For a satisfying smoothie or snack in a sunny interior, the **Juice Café ❶**, 16 rue Ravy Breton, whips up fruit-filled concoctions. (☎04 70 97 93 86. Smoothies €5, pasta with pesto or tomatoes, €7. Open daily June-Aug. noon-7pm. Sept.-May closed M.) For an evening worthy of the Belle Époque, cross the street from the opera and sit down in **Brasserie du Casino ❹**, 4 rue du Casino, which serves *haute cuisine* in a plush dining room lined with photos of old Vichy. (☎04 70 98 23 06. *Menus* €15-25. Open M and Th-Su noon-1:15pm and 7:30-9:15pm. MC/V.)

◨◪ **SIGHTS AND ENTERTAINMENT.** The only evident mark of Vichy's dark years is a small memorial across from the tourist office commemorating the 1942 deportation of 6500 Jews to Auschwitz. Significant buildings of the World War II era are not marked, and information on the period is difficult to find. The best way to see Pétain's Vichy is to take a French **tour** from the tourist office. (Tours depart at 3:30pm. July-Aug. W and Sa; June and Sept. W only. €5.)

A sip of Vichy's nectar makes one wonder how the town ever made it big—the water tastes disgusting. However, the *sources* made, and sustain, the town's main attraction, pulling visitors and *curistes* from all corners of the globe. Source-hopping, even out of sheer curiosity, provides a vision of the city's strangely magnetic phenomena. The *sources* bubble free of charge at the cold springs of **Sources des Célestins** on bd. Kennedy. (Open Apr.-Sept. M-Sa 6:15am-8:30pm, Su 7:45am-8:30pm; Oct.-Mar. daily 8am-6pm.) The heart of the action, though, is the **Halle des Sources** at the edge of the **Parc des Sources.** Any-one can drink for €1.60. Regulars bring their own glass encased in a special woven carrying basket, available for purchase at Vichy pharmacies for €7.50, though visitors may purchase a less classy plastic cup for €0.15. (☎04 70 97 39 59. Open M-Sa 6:15am-8:30pm, Su 7:45am-8:30pm.) If you go, take small swigs—it looks like plain water, but it's powerful stuff. Célestins is easiest to digest and was proven to relieve arthritis in a 1992 study by the Hôpital Cochimin in Paris. Parc is tougher on the stomach, and Lucas is chock-full of sulphur, hence the rotten-egg smell. Still thirsty? The **hot springs** are even more vile. (Open M-Sa 6:30am-8:30pm, Su 7:45am-8:30pm.) **Hôpital,** which also flows freely behind the Grand Casino (open M-Sa 6:30am-8:30pm, Su 7:45-8:30pm), is used for stomach problems—**Chomel** is the most popular; **Grand Grille** is the most potent. Visitors can recover with older *curistes* in the Parc des Sources; surrounded by a wrought-iron Art Nouveau promenade and flanked by the Opéra, the space exemplifies Vichy elegance.

Manicured floral displays and thick shade trees fill the English-style gardens in the elegant riverside **Parc de l'Allier,** commissioned by Napoleon III. Across the river and a brisk 20-25min. walk along the promenade to the right of Pont de Bellerive lies Vichy's ultimate recreational facility.

Cheap gaming thrills beckon at the **Grand Casino** in the Parc des Sources. (Open daily noon-4am.) **Operas** and **concerts** take place during the summer in the beautiful **Opéra,** 1 rue du Casino. (☎ 04 70 30 50 30. Box Office on rue du Parc open Tu-Sa 1:30-6:30pm, until curtain time on performance nights; by phone only Tu-F 10am-12:30pm. Operas €30-60, under 25 €28-54; concerts €21-42/€18-26.)

DORDOGNE, PÉRIGORD, AND LIMOUSIN

 A landlocked position and lack of well-known attractions have long left this region out of the limelight. As a result, its many sights are relatively undiscovered, offering a welcome respite from the ceaseless crowds at the Loire châteaux. The region's unadulterated countryside hides villages set among oak-woods, tranquil cities, and châteaux galore. During the 15th-century English occupation of Paris, Bourges (p. 477), now the area's largest city, served as France's capital and benefited from the lavish attentions of the king's financier, Jacques Cœur. Before being imprisoned for embezzlement, the flamboyant Cœur built a string of châteaux through the heart of Berry, most of which remain inhabited but open to visitors. Found along the Route Jacques Cœur, they are easily accessible from Bourges or the medieval St-Amand-Montrond (p. 483). The region has also long been an artistic breeding ground, producing painter Auguste Renoir, dramatist Jean Giraudoux, and novelist George Sand. In a different twist on the artistic trend, medieval Limoges (p. 485) produces France's finest porcelain. Périgord, where green countryside is splashed with yellow sunflowers, steep chalk cliffs, and ducks paddling through shady rivers, boasts exceptional historical remnants of the Neolithic, Roman, and medieval varieties.

HIGHLIGHTS OF DORDOGNE, PÉRIGORD, AND LIMOUSIN

GET IN TOUCH with your Cro-Magnon side at the caves of the **Vézère Valley** (p. 495).

THE STUNNING STAINED GLASS at Bourges's **Cathédral St-Etienne** (p. 482) gives Paris's Notre Dame a run for its money.

THE GHOST TOWN of **Oradour-sur-Glane** (p. 489), untouched since Nazis systematically massacred its residents because of suspected Resistance activity, remains a deeply moving testament to the human capacity for brutality.

LIMOUSIN

BOURGES

Snug in the heart of the lower Loire valley, Bourges (pop. 72,000) attracts visitors with its Flamboyant Gothic architecture, half-timbered houses, and charming medieval streets. Bourges' wealth originated in 1433, when Jacques Cœur, financier of Charles VII, chose the humble city as the site for his palatial home. The region around Bourges is replete with exquisite, secluded châteaux, all tucked away into a thick forest. The city is also a convenient base for daytrips to the beautiful villages of Charité-sur-Loire and Mehun-sur Yèvre.

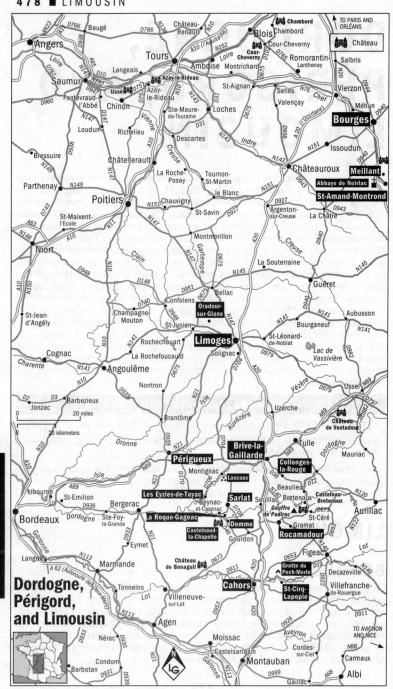

TO PARIS AND ORLÉANS

🏰 Château

🏰 Chambord
Chambord

Baugé
Château-Renault
Blois
Cour-Cheverny
🏰 Cour-Cheverny
Romorantin-Lanthenay
Salbris

Angers
Loire
Tours
Amboise
Montrichard
D765
Vierzon
Méhun

Langeais
🏰 Azay-le-Rideau
St-Aignan
Selles
Cher
Cher

Saumur
Ussé 🏰
Azay-le-Rideau
Loches
Valençay
BOURGES

Fontevraud-l'Abbé
Chinon
Vienne
Ste-Maure-de-Touraine
Indre
D956
A 20 (l'Occitane)

Loudun
Richelieu
Descartes
Issoudun

Bressuire
Châtellerault
Creuse
Tournon-St-Martin
le Blanc
Châteauroux
Meillant

Parthenay
La Roche-Posay
Abbaye de Noirlac
St-Amand-Montrond

Poitiers
Chauvigny
St-Savin
D927
Argenton-sur-Creuse
La Châtre

St-Maixent-l'École
Montmorillon
Creuse

Niort
Clain
Gartempe
La Souterraine
N145

St-Jean-d'Angély
Confolens
Bellac
Guéret
Aubusson

Champagne-Mouton
St-Junien
Oradour-sur-Glane
Bourganeuf
N141

Cognac
Rochechouart
Limoges
St-Léonard-de-Noblat
Lac de Vassivière

Charente
La Rochefoucauld
Solignac
Ussel

Angoulême
Nontron
Vézère
Uzerche

Barbezieux
Brantôme
Auvézère
Château de Ventadour

Jonzac
0   20 miles
Dronne
Tulle
Mauriac

20 kilometers
Périgueux
Montignac
Brive-la-Gaillarde
Collonges-la-Rouge

Libourne
St-Émilion
Lascaux
Beaulieu
Castelnau-Bretenoux

Bordeaux
Bergerac
Les Eyzies-de-Tayac
Beynac-et-Cazenac
Sarlat
Souillac
Bretenoux
Aurillac

Ste-Foy-la-Grande
La Roque-Gageac
Gouffre de Padirac
St-Céré

Eymet
Castelnaud-la-Chapelle
Domme
Gourdon
Gramat
Rocamadour

Langon
Marmande
Château de Bonaguil
Figeac
Lot

Tonneins
Grotte du Pech-Merle
Decazeville
Villefranche-de-Rouergue

Cahors
St-Cirq-Lapopie

Agen
Villeneuve-sur-Lot
Lot

Dordogne, Périgord, and Limousin

Nérac
Aveyron
Cordes-sur-Ciel

Condom
Barbotan
Castelsarrasin
Montauban
Gaillac
Albi

TO AVIGNON AND NICE

TRANSPORTATION

Trains: pl. du Général Leclerc (☎08 92 35 35 35). Info office open M-F 9:30am-7pm, Sa 9:30am-6pm. Ticket office open M 4:25am-8:35pm, Tu-Th and Sa 5:50am-8:20pm, F 5:35am-9:30pm, Su 7am-9:35pm. To: **Nevers** (1hr., 11 per day, €9.70); **Paris** (2½hr., 5-8 per day, €25.60); **Tours** (1½hr., 12 per day, €17.90). Many trains require a change at nearby **Vierzon.**

Buses: rue du Champ de Foire (☎02 48 24 36 42). Office open M-Tu and Th-F 8-9:30am and 4-6pm, W and Sa 8am-noon. To: **Châteauroux** (1¾hr., 1-3 per day, €4.40); **Vierzon** (1¼hr., 3 per day, €3.20). Most buses stop at the train station as well.

Public Transportation: CTB (☎02 48 50 82 82) serves all areas of the city. Tickets €1.15, *carnet* of 10 €8. Buses also run to nearby villages; the most popular is **St-Germain** (take bus #4 from La Nation; 2-4 per day), which has a bowling alley and several pubs. All schedules are posted at the bus stops and available at the tourist office. Tickets €1.35, *carnet* of 10 €10.10.

Taxis: (☎02 48 24 50 00). 24hr. €5 from the train station to tourist office.

Car Rentals: Hertz, 4 av. Henri Laudier (☎02 48 70 22 92), near train station. Cars from €46 per day. Under 25 €26 fee per day. 21+. Open M-F 8am-noon and 2-6pm. AmEx/MC/V. Ucar, 21 av. Jean Jaurès (☎02 48 70 63 63), halfway between the station and the *centre ville*. Cars from €30 per day. Open M-F 8am-noon and 2-6pm, Sa 8am-noon. MC/V.

Bike Rental: Narcy, 39 av. Marx-Dormoy (☎02 48 70 15 84; fax 02 48 70 02 61). €8 per day, €16 per weekend. Credit card deposit. Open Tu-Sa 9am-noon and 2-7pm, Su 9am-noon and 2-6pm.

PRACTICAL INFORMATION

Tourist Office: 21 rue Victor Hugo (☎02 48 23 02 60; www.bourges-tourisme.com), facing rue Moyenne near the cathedral. Cross the street in front of station and follow av. Henri Laudier into the *vieille ville* as it becomes av. Jean Jaurès. Bear left onto rue du Commerce and continue straight as it becomes rue Moyenne. (18min.) Or catch bus #1 (dir: Val d'Auron, €1.15) to Victor Hugo. Staff gives out an excellent map of the city, information on museums and festivals, and advice on daytrips. **Accommodations booking** €1. Themed **walking tours** in French daily July-Sept. 10:30am and 3pm; €5.50, students €3. Self-guided illuminated night tours mid-July to mid-Aug. at sunset. Office open Apr.-Sept. M-Sa 9am-7pm, until 7:30pm: Jul.-Aug. Su 10am-7pm; Oct.-Mar. M-Sa 9am-6pm, Su 2-5pm.

Laundromat: Laveromatique, 117 rue Edouard Valliant (☎06 72 77 32 05), and 15 bd. Juranville (☎02 48 67 41 49). Open daily 8am-8:30pm.

Police: (☎02 48 55 85 00), rue Mayet Genetry.

Crisis Lines: Medical SOS Médecin, ☎02 48 23 33 33. **Women SOS Femmes Victimes de Violence, ☎**02 48 21 05 34.

Pharmacy: Pharmacie du Progrès, 27 rue Moyenne (☎02 48 24 00 41), on the corner near the post office. Open M 2-7pm, Tu-F 9am-12:30pm and 2-7pm, Sa 9am-noon and 2-6pm. The pharmacie de garde is posted in the windows of all pharmacies.

Hospital: 145 rue François Mitterrand (☎02 48 48 48 48).

Internet Access: Free at the public library **Médiathèque** (☎02 48 23 22 50) on bd. Lamarck close to the hostel, 10min. from the tourist office. 30min. limit. Open July-Aug. Tu-F 12:30-6:30pm, Sa 9am-noon; Sept.-June M-W 12:30-6:30pm, Th 12:30-8pm, F 12:30-6:30pm, Sa 10am-5pm. **Le Tie Break,** 78 av. Jean Baffier (☎02 48 67 94 58), about 12min. from the tourist office away from the station. Open M-F 11am-10:30pm, Sa-Su 4-10:30pm. €4.80 per hr. MC/V.

Post Office: 29 rue Moyenne (☎02 48 68 82 82). **Currency exchange.** Cyberposte. Open M-F 8am-7pm, Sa 8am-noon.

Postal Code: 18000.

ACCOMMODATIONS AND CAMPING

Bourges' cheapest hotels are outside the city center. Summer visitors should phone ahead for reservations.

Hôtel St-Jean, 23 av. Marx-Dormoy (☎02 48 24 70 45; fax 02 48 24 79 98), an equidistant 10min. walk from the train station and the center of town. A gracious owner lets clean, carpeted rooms with excellent showers. Elevator. Breakfast €5.50. Reception 7am-9:30pm. Singles with bath €28.50; doubles €34.60, with bath 39.70; triples with bath €42.70; 1 quad for €51. MC/V. ❷

Centre International de Séjour: La Charmille, 17 rue Félix-Chédin (☎02 48 23 07 40; fax 02 48 69 01 21). From station, cross over the tracks, and walk 5min. up rue Félix-Chédin. Buses #1 and 2 run by it to the *centre ville* (dir: Golf or Hôpital, respectively). A skater's heaven, with bowls, ramps, and classes in summer. Social atmosphere among an interesting range of guests, mostly teenagers and 20-somethings. Clean, basic rooms, all with shower. Breakfast included. Meals €8.60. Laundry. Singles €15; larger rooms €11.95 per person. One-time adherence fee €4, good for a year. MC/V. ❶

Auberge de Jeunesse (HI), 22 rue Henri Sellier (☎02 48 24 58 09; bourges@fuaj.org), 10min. from town center. From station, take av. Henri Laudier to av. Jean Jaurès, and then to pl. Planchat. Follow rue des Arènes as it becomes rue Fernault. At the intersection, cross to rue René Ménard. Turn left at rue Henri Sellier; walk approx. 1 block. Hostel is on the right, behind a brown and white building. (25-30min.) Or, take bus #1 (dir: Val d'Auron; daily 6am-6pm) to Conde. Cross the parking lot; take the footpath to the left through the park, down rue Vieil Castel. Hostel is across the street, 30m down a driveway to right. Bar, laundry, kitchen, parking, and bare but clean 3- to 8-bunk rooms, some with showers. Quiet, grassy yard overlooks a small river. Breakfast €3.30. Sheets €2.80. Reception daily 8-10am and 5-10pm. Beds €8.90. MC/V. HI Members only. ❶

Le Cygne, 10 pl. du Général Leclerc (☎02 48 70 51 05; www.lecygne.com). Across from the train station, a 15min. walk from the center of town. Rooms off bright yellow hallways are cozy and well kept, with shower and toilet. Elevator and attached restaurant. Breakfast €5.50. Parking €3. Singles and doubles €27.50-38; triples €45; quads €53; *demi-pension* for 1 person €40, 2 people €52. MC/V. ❸

Camping: Camping Municipal, 26 bd. de l'Industrie (☎02 48 20 16 85; fax 02 48 50 32 39). Follow directions to *Auberge de Jeunesse* (see above). Continue on rue Henri Sellier, then turn right on bd. de l'Industrie. Landscaped campground in a riverside residential neighborhood, a 10min. walk from the city center. Free swimming pool nearby. Reception daily June-Aug. 7am-10pm; Sept.-June 8am-9pm. Open mid-Mar. to mid-Nov. €3.20 per person, €1.80 per child, €3.20 per tent. Electricity €2.70-4.20. ❶

FOOD

The outdoor tables on **place Gordaine** and **rue des Beaux-Arts** fill with locals during the spring and summer. For a touch of elegance, try the tasty regional cuisine in the many timber-framed restaurants on **rue Bourbonneux** or **rue Girard.** Look for specialties like *poulet en barbouille* (chicken roasted in aromatic red wine) and *oeufs en meurette* (eggs in red wine). The largest **market** is held on pl. de la Nation (Sa morning); another livens up pl. des Marronniers (Th until 1pm). There is a smaller, permanent **covered market** at pl. St-Bonnet. (Tu-Th 8am-12:45pm and 3:30-7:30pm, F-Sa 8am-1pm and 3-7:30pm, Su 8am-1pm.) The huge

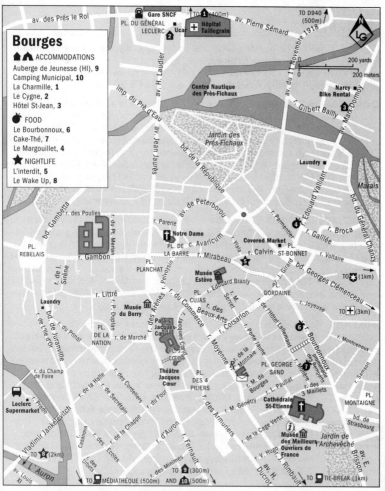

Leclerc supermarket, rue Prado off bd. Juranville, next to the bus station, provides supplies for ambitious chefs. (Open M-F 9:15am-7:50pm, Sa 8:30am-7:20pm.) Hidden gem ⚡**Cake-Thé ❶,** 74 promenade des Remparts, is a storybook tearoom nestled along a lavender-lined passage between rue Bourbonnoux and rue Molière. Delicious desserts (€3.90-4.60) are accompanied by flowers, lace, and gentle music. (☎02 48 24 94 60; www.cak-t.com. Tea €1.90-3, coffee €3. Open Sept.-July Tu-Sa 3-7pm.) Vibrantly colored **Le Margouillet ❸,** 53 rue Edouard Vaillant, serves up Caribbean cuisine in an airy island atmosphere. The specialty is créole fish (€11.50-14), but *menus* (€14.50-21) change weekly. (☎02 48 24 08 13. Open M and Sa 7:30pm-11pm, Tu-F noon-2pm and 7:30-11pm. MC/V.) On a charming street full of half-timbered houses, **Le Bourbonnoux ❹,** 44 rue Bourbonneux, serves rotating regional gourmet *menus* (€12-28) in a stately fashion. (☎02 48 24 14 76. Open M-Th noon-2pm and 7:30-9:45pm, Sa 7:30-9:45pm, Su noon-2pm. July-Aug. Su also 7:30-9:45pm. MC/V.)

◉ SIGHTS

Bourges's *vieille ville* boasts a delightful variety of museums and sights, most of which are contained enough to be explored in an hour or so. The three paid-entry sites (two of which are part of the cathedral) sell a combined *billet jumelé*, which saves money and individual tickets (€8.50, students €5.50).

▓ **CATHÉDRALE ST-ETIENNE.** 13th-century St-Etienne is a magnificent example of the ornate French Gothic style, comparable to Paris' Notre Dame. Stunning stained-glass windows illuminate the marble interior with red and blue tones. The church is free, though tickets are required to visit the cathedral crypt and climb St-Etienne's northern tower for its splendid view of the city. *(Cathedral open daily Apr.-Sept. 8:30am-7:15pm; Oct.-Mar. 9am-5:45pm. Closed to tourists Su morning. Mass June-Aug. M-F 6:30pm; Sept.-May M 6:30pm and F 9am. Mass year-round Su 11am. Crypt and tower open daily July-Aug. 9:30am-6pm; May to mid-June M-Sa 9:30am-12:15pm and 2-6pm, Su 2-6pm; Sept.-Apr. 9:30am-12:15pm and 2-5:15pm. €6.10, students €4.10; tower only, €4.60/€3.10.)*

PALAIS JACQUES-CŒUR. This palace was commissioned in 1443 by Jacques Cœur, finance minister to Charles VII. It was intended to flaunt his personal fortune to his high-society guests, but he was imprisoned for embezzlement in 1451, years before its completion. The palace still lies unfurnished, but exquisite carved mantelpieces, gargoyles, and a heavily decorated chapel remain. *(10bis rue Jacques-Cœur. ☎ 02 48 24 06 87. Visit by guided French tour only. Open daily July-Aug. 9:30am-5:45pm, tours every 45min.; Sept.-Apr. 9:45am-4:15pm, tours every hr.; May-June 9:45am-5:15pm, tours every hr. English text available. €6.10, ages 18-24 €4.10, under 18 free.)*

MUSEUMS. Bourges has several small, free museums with regionally focused exhibits. The **Musée des Meilleurs Ouvriers de France,** within the Hôtel de Ville, puts a unique twist on local craftsmanship. Each year the French government bestows a medal of honor, the Meilleur Ouvrier, on a select number of artists and workers who produce exceptional work in fields ranging from hairstyling to cuisine to leatherwork; the museum highlights recent winners within a particular craft. The focus for 2005 is "l'Art de la Table." *(Pl. Etienne Dolet. ☎ 02 48 57 82 45. Open daily July-Aug. 10am-6pm; Sept.-June Tu-Sa 10am-noon and 2-6pm.)* The **Musée Estève** displays the colorful modern paintings and drawings by the local contemporary artist of the same name. *(13 rue Edouard Branly. ☎ 02 48 24 75 38. Open M and W-Sa 10am-noon and 2-6pm, Su 2-6pm. English explanations.)* The **Musée du Berry** showcases pre-historic, Gallo-Roman, and medieval artifacts excavated from the region. *(4 rue des Arènes. ☎ 02 48 70 41 92. Open M and W-Sa 10am-noon and 2-6pm, Su 2-6pm.)*

♫ ▓ ENTERTAINMENT AND FESTIVALS

Bars and cafes cluster in the *vieille ville,* but the nightlife is fairly subdued. Electronic and 80s music sets the scene at **L'interdit,** 5 rue Calvin, a small, social club frequented mainly, though not exclusively, by gay men. Knock or buzz to be let in through the locked door. *(☎ 02 48 65 90 57. Open W-Su 5pm-2am.)* At **Le Wake Up,** 147 chemin de Villeneuve, a live DJ spins techno and pop rock for teens and early 20-somethings. Play laser tag in the 500m maze of ramps and walls. *(☎ 02 48 67 90 46. Open daily 4pm-1am.)*

End an evening with **Les Nuits Lumière de Bourges,** a lovely self-guided tour of Bourges. This tour begins with music and a slide-show on local history, then follows a predetermined route along streets lined with blue lampposts. The major monuments are playfully illuminated in different colors for a fantastic nighttime effect. Tours start at the Jardin de l'Archevêché. (June-Oct. Free.)

Over 200,000 ears perk up in April for the **Festival Printemps de Bourges** (☎02 48 70 61 11; www.printemps-bourges.com). Most tickets cost €7-28, but some informal folk, jazz, classical, and rock concerts are free.

ROUTE JACQUES CŒUR

Jacques may have left his *cœur* in Bourges, but his ego spilled far into the surrounding countryside. The Route Jacques Cœur consists of a string of 17 châteaux (along with a 12th-century abbey), from La Buissière in the north to Culan in the south. Less ostentatious than those of the Loire, these castles see much less tourism. Many are still inhabited by the families who made them famous, and who often delight in giving personal tours. Most of the châteaux in this section can be seen only by tour; the guide often doubles as ticket seller. Those who arrive while a tour is in progress will have to wait at the ticket booth until the tour guide returns. Written English explanations are usually available, but not English tours.

Châteaux make for relaxing daytrips, but most can be reached only by car or bike. Fortunately, the routes are usually well marked. Arrange lodging in advance. The tourist offices in Bourges (p. 477) and St-Amand-Montrond (see below) have free English maps of the route and info on excursions. Although *Let's Go* specifically lists several fabulous châteaux here, the area is a treasure-trove of sights; this list should be considered a starting point for further exploration.

ST-AMAND-MONTROND

Forty-five kilometers south of Bourges, St-Amand-Montrond (pop. 12,000) is an excellent, accessible starting point for explorations of the southern stretch of the route. To get there, take the **train** from Bourges (1¾hr.; M-Sa 6 per day, Su 3 per day; €8.60), or drive south from Bourges on the N144 or the A71. From St-Amand, a short bike or car ride reaches the nearby sights. Though the surrounding châteaux and hectares of forest are the real draw, St. Amand itself also merits a visit. A walking tour organized by the tourist office takes visitors past the city's two medieval churches, **Paroisse de St-Amand** and **Église St-Roche.** The ruins of the ancient **Forteresse de Montrond** can be seen from afar, or up close by reservation. (Call ☎02 48 96 79 64 to schedule a visit.) The **tourist office**, pl. de la République, sells maps indicating sights both within the city and its surroundings (€1). From the train station, follow av. de la Gare and its continuation, av. Jean Jaurès, which becomes rue Henri Barbusse, to the town center. After 20min., the road runs into pl. de la République; the tourist office is on the left. (☎02 48 96 16 86; fax 02 48 96 46 64. Open M-Sa 9am-noon and 2-6:45pm.) **Bike rental** is available at Vélo & Oxygen, 72 av. Général Charles de Gaulle (☎02 48 96 00 80). Head toward the tourist office from the station and turn left off av. Jean Jaurès onto rue 14 Juillet; at the T-intersection with N144, turn left (dir: Bourges) and walk for about 5min. The shop is on the right, before the supermarket. (Open Tu-Sa 9am-noon and 2-7pm. Bikes €5 per hr., €10 per 4hr., €12 per 8hr. Credit card deposit. MC/V.)

CHÂTEAU DE MEILLANT

A beautiful 8km bike ride from St-Amand through the **Fôret de Meillant** leads to the foot of this imposing, heavily spired Renaissance building. It was purchased by the Amboise family, in the 15th century, who imported Italian architects, sculptors, and decorators. Its ornate stone carvings are especially visible on the **Tour du Lion,** the upper part of which was designed by Leonardo da Vinci. Next to the château, a small building contains surprisingly intricate miniature representations of life from the Middle Ages to the 18th century. To get to Meillant from **St-Amand,** take rue Nationale from near the tourist office north to the D10. (☎02 48 63 32 05. Open mid-May to mid-Sept. 9:30am-6pm; Feb. to mid-May and mid-Sept. to mid.-Nov. 9:30-noon and 2-5:30pm; closed Dec. and Jan. Visits by French guided tour only; English info available. Château and gardens €7, students €4, ages 5-15 €3.)

ABBAYE DE NOIRLAC

Just 4km west of St-Amand-Montrond, the Abbaye de Noirlac sits peacefully next to a field of grazing cattle. The typically Cistercian abbey has spacious, spartan rooms, and geometric stained-glass windows. The cloister at the center is framed by gorgeous arches and fringed by roses. Most of the monks' **chapter house** dates from the original 12th-century construction; the rest was renovated in the 18th century. The abbey hosts annual exhibits on regional arts and specialties.

During the summer, the popular **L'Eté de Noirlac** fills the abbey's spacious rooms with an excellent selection of live music. (☎08 10 02 01 00; www.festivalde-noirlac.com. Tickets €8-22.) To get there from nearby St-Amand, take rue Henri Barbusse to the rue 14 Juillet. After crossing the river, turn left onto the N144 (dir: Bourges); the well-marked turn-off for the abbey is on the left. Be careful of traffic if you are on a bike. (☎02 48 62 01 01. Open daily July-Aug. 9:45am-6:30pm; Apr.-June and Sept. 9:45am-12:30pm and 2-6:30pm; Oct.-Mar. 9:45am-12:30 and 2-5pm; ticket office closes 1hr. before closing. Self-guided tours optional. French tours every hr. starting 10am; July-Aug. no tours noon-2pm. English explanations available; call ahead for a tour in English. €5.50, students €4, under 16 €3.)

LA VERRERIE

The 15th-century La Verrerie, set on a gorgeous lake in the Ivoy Forest 45km north of Bourges, is one of the most elegant and popular châteaux on the Route. To get to La Verrerie from Bourges, take N940 (dir: Montargis). At La Chapelle, turn right toward Auxerre on rte. 926. After 10km, signs for La Verrerie will appear. Eighteenth-century Beauvais tapestries and hand-carved 16th- and 17th-century tables create an elegant interior. (☎02 48 81 51 60; www.chateaux-france.com/~verre-rie.fr. Open daily June-Aug. 9am-6pm; Apr.-May and Oct. to mid-Nov. M and W-Su 10am-6pm. €7, students €5, under 7 free.) Those willing to shell out the money can spend a night in the château for €150-350. Call ahead for reservations. For significantly less, **La Maison d'Héléne ❺**, a lovely restaurant next to the château, serves regional *menus* (€22-36) and a special *carte blanche* (€40), where the chef creates innovative, one-of-a-kind meals. (☎02 48 81 51 60. Open Th-Tu noon-2pm and 7:30-10pm. MC/V.)

MENETOU-SALON AND MAUPAS

A bit closer to Bourges and easy to reach by bike, Maupas and Menetou-Salon combine to make the perfect daytrip. Begin with **Menetou-Salon**, 20km north of Bourges; take the D940 (av. du Général de Gaulle in the city) north for 5km and bear right onto D11, then follow the signs to Menetou-Salon. The urban sprawl quickly recedes, replaced by endlessly rolling vineyards, many of which offer tours and direct sales. The Menetou-Salon castle regally overlooks them, and has a fascinating life-story. Jacques bought the estate in 1448, but his subsequent imprisonment, and later the Revolution, left the castle temporarily in ruins. In the 19th century, the Prince of Arenburg stepped in and decided to complete it. Though the current prince lives in New York and only visits his hunting lodge four times a year, his personal touches make Menetou a real treat. A guided French tour unveils the antique splendor of the home with its 297 windows, 24 chimneys, and multiple secret bathrooms. (Estate ☎02 48 64 08 61. Open daily July-Aug. 10:30am-6:30pm; May-June and Sept. Sa-Su 2pm-6pm (last tour departs 5pm). Wine tastings available. €8.50, students €4, under 12 free.)

To continue another 7km to **Maupas**, follow the signs to Parassy and Morogues, passing through scenic vineyard-covered countryside. The château is on the left, about 1km before Morogues; look for the white gates tucked away on the curbside. This small but exquisitely preserved 13th-century castle is decorated with antique furniture and *faïences* collected by Antoine Agard, whose family has lived there since 1686. A 45min. French tour starts with a staircase whose walls are decorated by over 800 painted plates and leads through the rooms of the Comte de Chambord, the last legitimate Bourbon pretender to the throne. (Estate ☎02 48 64 41 71. English translations available. Open daily mid-July to mid-Sept. 10am-noon and 2-7pm; Easter to mid-July and mid-Sept. to mid-Oct. M-Sa 2-7pm, Su and holidays 10am-noon and 2-7pm. Tours available by telephone reservation during the rest of the year. €6.50, students €4.50, ages 7-15 €4. Wine-tasting available for groups, €7.50 per person.)

LIMOGES

For centuries, Limoges (pop. 133,000) has manufactured porcelain and enamel for the French upper class. The trade and its proceeds have given Limoges a graceful beauty; traces of the city's trademark craft can be seen on its porcelain mosaic fountains, in the small artisan boutiques lining its older streets, and in the intricate carvings on its cathedral.

▐ TRANSPORTATION

Trains: Gare des Bénédictins (☎05 55 11 11 88), pl. Maison-Dieu, off av. du Général de Gaulle, has been restored to its 1920s Art Nouveau splendor. Info and ticket office open daily 5:15am-11pm. To: **Bordeaux** (3hr., 7 per day, €26.40); **Brive** (1hr., 15 per day, €13.60); **Lyon** (6hr., 1:13am and 1:13pm, €4.80); **Paris** (3-4hr., 5 per day, €40.90); **Poitiers** (2hr., 3 per day, €18.30); **Toulouse** (3½hr., 5 per day, €34.20). An **SNCF Boutique** is on rue Othon Péconnet, near pl. de la Motte. Open M noon-7pm, Tu-Sa 9am-7pm.

Buses: ☎05 55 04 91 95, in the train station. **Equival,** 14 rue de l'Amphithéâtre (☎05 55 10 10 03; office open M-F 9am-5pm) runs buses throughout the region. Tickets can be purchased at the office, at the SNCF station, or on the buses. Most buses stop at the main train station as well as around Limoges before leaving the city.

Public Transportation: TCL (☎05 55 32 46 46) runs around the city. Info office at 10 pl. Léon Betoulle, across from town hall. Open M 1:30-6pm, Tu-F 8:30am-12:30pm and 1:30-6pm, Sa 8:30am-12:30pm. Ticket €1, *carnet* of 10 €8.50. Tickets available onboard.

Taxis: Taxis Limoges (☎05 55 37 81 81 or 05 55 38 38 38). 24hr.

Car Rental: Avis (☎05 55 79 78 25; www.avis.com) is also in the train station. Open M-F 9:45am-1:30pm and 4-6:30pm, Sa 9:45am-1:30pm and 4-6pm. **Europcar** (☎05 55 04 13 25), in the train station. Open M-Sa 8am-noon and 2-7pm.

✳ ▐ ORIENTATION AND PRACTICAL INFORMATION

Limoges was originally separated by medieval fortifications into two villages: **la Cité** and **le Château.** Today, divided only by one city block, the two villages have become the main commercial and tourist sectors of the city. The cobblestone-paved Cité, surrounding the Cathédrale St-Etienne along the Vienne River, holds the municipal museum and gardens, while restaurants, clothing boutiques, and small porcelain shops fill le Château.

Tourist Office: 12 bd. de Fleurus (☎05 55 34 46 87; www.tourismelimoges.com), near pl. Wilson. From the train station, walk left down av. du Général de Gaulle. Cut across pl. Jourdan onto bd. de Fleurus. English-speaking staff has maps and a *guide pratique* that lists restaurants and accommodations. **Currency exchange** €1. Themed walking tours daily July-Aug. Tours in English Tu 3:30pm; 1½hr.; €5, children under 12 €2. Office open mid-June to mid-Sept. M-Sa 9am-7pm, Su 10am-6pm; mid-Sept. to mid-June M-Sa 9am-noon and 2-7pm.

Bank: Banque de France, 8 bd. Carnot (☎05 55 11 53 00). **Currency exchange** open M-F 8:45am-noon. No commission and good rates.

Laundromat: Le Forum des Lavendières, 14 rue des Charseix. Open daily 8am-9pm. **Laverie,** 31 rue de François Chinieux. Open daily 7am-9pm.

Police: 84 av. Emile Labussière (☎05 55 14 30 00 or 05 55 04 50 50).

Crisis Hotlines: SOS Medecin, ☎08 03 06 70 00; Poison Control, ☎05 56 96 40 80.

Hospital: 2 av. Martin Luther King (☎05 55 05 61 23).

Internet Access: Free at **Bibliothèque Francophone Multimédia de Limoges,** 2 rue L. Longequeue (☎05 55 45 96 00), beyond the Hôtel de Ville. Often long lines. Open W 10am-7pm and Sa 10am-6pm. **Net Center,** 5 bd. Victor Hugo (☎05 55 10 93 61). €2 per 30min., €3.80 per hr. Open M-Th 8:45am-4am, F 8:45-6am, Sa 9:45am-6am, Su 2pm-4am. **Pointcyber,** 7 av. du Général de Gaulle (☎05 55 79 03 28), near the train station. €2 per 30min., €3.50 per hr. Open M-Th 9:30am-4am, F-Sa 9:30am-6am, Su 2pm-midnight; open from 11am M-Sa in July and Aug.

Post Office: av. Garibaldi, part of the huge St-Martial shopping complex. **Currency exchange** with no commission. Open M 2-7pm, Tu-F 10am-7pm, Sa 10am-6:30pm.

Postal Code: 87000.

ACCOMMODATIONS AND CAMPING

Hôtel de Paris, 5 cours Vergnaud (☎05 55 77 56 96). From the train station, walk up av. du Général de Gaulle 200 ft. and veer right onto cours Bugeaud, then right again onto cours Vergnaud. Recently renovated, most rooms large with tall windows, clean bathrooms, and a charming Victorian air. Breakfast €5. 1 single with no shower €23; singles and doubles with shower and toilet €30-46; triples €51-54. AmEx/MC/V. ❷

Foyer des Jeunes Travailleurs, 20 rue Encombe Vineuse (☎05 55 77 63 97; fjt.acceuil-2000@wanadoo.fr). From the train station, descend the stairs to the right, then cut across the grass to the street. Rue Théodore Bac is across the street on the left. Walk to pl. Carnot, turn left onto av. Adrien Tarrade, then left onto rue Encombe Vineuse. (15min.) Simple singles and doubles with sinks, some with small refrigerators; showers and toilets at the end of each hall. Communal TV room, kitchen, and elevator. Breakfast included. 24hr. reception. Call ahead. Open July-Aug., and the rest of the year if there is room. Singles €14; doubles €20. ❶

Hôtel de la Gare, 2 Cours Guy-Lussac (☎05 55 77 36 46), 2min. from the station. Basic, cheap rooms with shared showers and toilets in each hallway, over a calm bar. Breakfast €4.50. Reception M 11:30am-7pm, Tu-W and Su 9am-11pm, Th-Sa 9-1:45am. Singles and doubles €23.40. MC/V. ❷.

Hôtel de la Paix, 25 pl. Jourdan (☎05 55 34 36 00; fax 05 55 32 37 06). Walk left down av. du Général de Gaulle away from the train station. The hotel is on the far side of pl. Jourdan, close to the tourist office. The spotless hallways and eccentrically decorated rooms of this "Musée du Phonograph" are filled with 1920s paraphernalia and photos. Breakfast €6. 24hr. reception. Single with shower €36; singles and doubles with shower and toilet €47-60. AmEx/MC/V. ❸

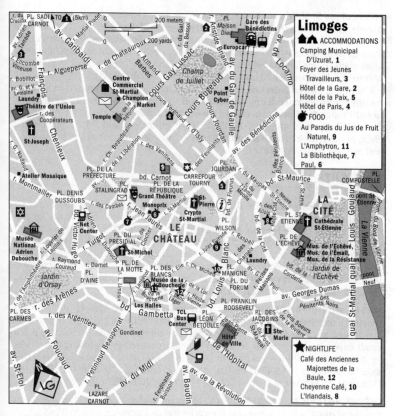

Limoges

⌂▲ ACCOMMODATIONS

Camping Municipal
  D'Uzurat, **1**
Foyer des Jeunes
  Travailleurs, **3**
Hôtel de la Gare, **2**
Hôtel de la Paix, **5**
Hôtel de Paris, **4**

🍴 FOOD

Au Paradis du Jus de Fruit
  Naturel, **9**
L'Amphytron, **11**
La Bibliothèque, **7**
Paul, **6**

★ NIGHTLIFE

Café des Anciennes
  Majorettes de la
  Baule, **12**
Cheyenne Café, **10**
L'Irlandais, **8**

Camping: Camping Municipal D'Uzurat, 40 av. d'Uzurat (☎ 05 55 38 49 43; fax 05 55 37 32 78). From the train station, take bus #20 (dir: Beaubreuil; M-Sa 6am-8:30pm) to L. Armand. On Sundays, take bus #2 (dir: Beaubreuil) to Uzurat. By foot, take av. Général Leclerc from pl. Carnot and follow signs to Uzurat. (1hr.) Walk down av. d'Uzurat until reaching the campground. 5km north of Limoges, beside Lake Uzurat, this is the closest site. Access to tennis courts, mini-golf, and hiking trails. 2 people with tent and car €9.90, extra person €2.45, child €1.30. Electricity €3-4. **❶**

🍴 FOOD

Perhaps the best option for hungry visitors, the stalls of the central Les Halles **indoor market,** facing pl. de la Motte, overflow with fresh cheeses, produce, meat, fish, and baked goods. (Open daily 8am-noon, fewer stalls open on Su.) A larger market (Sa mornings) brightens pl. Carnot. A **Monoprix supermarket** is at 11 pl. de la République. (Open M-Sa 8:30am-8:30pm.) A huge **Champion** is on av. Garibaldi in the St-Martial shopping mall on the north side of town. (Open M-Sa 8:30am-8pm.) The most interesting restaurants are well hidden. Among them, **⊠Au Paradis du Jus de Fruit Naturel ❶,** 5 rue Jules Guesde, serves excellent fresh juices (€2.50-6) with playful straws. The friendly owner suggests the best fruit combinations. (☎ 05 55 11 98 46. Open M-F 10am-noon and 2-7pm, Sa until 7:30pm. MC/V.) **Paul ❶,** on the corner of rue St-Martial and rue Jean Jaurès, is an excellent bakery with a range of breads, sandwiches (€3-6.50), and pastries. (☎05 55 34 60 82. Open M-Sa 7am-8pm.) Restaurant by day and busy bar by night, ■**La Bibliothèque ❸**, 7 rue Turgot, lives up to its name with chic mahogany stools, candelabra chandeliers, and shelf after shelf of leather-bound books. (☎05 55 11 00 47. Tasty pastas, salads, and entrees €8-17. Open daily 11am-2am, F until 4am. AmEx/MC/V.)

Charming, flower-bedecked restaurants around the medieval rue de la Boucherie offer more gourmet dining. **L'Amphytron ❸**, 26 rue de la Boucherie, serves traditional French food in a converted 13th-century home. (☎05 55 33 36 39. *Menus* from €16. Open M and Sa 7-10:30pm, Tu-F noon-2pm and 7-10:30pm.) For a cheaper meal, look to **rue Haute-Cité**, near the cathedral, for *crêperies, brasseries*, and even an Indian restaurant.

👁 SIGHTS

■**MUSÉE NATIONAL ADRIEN DUBOUCHE.** Founded in the early 20th century by a wealthy Cognac merchant, this beautiful national museum houses the largest ceramics collection in Europe. An excellent video presentation traces modern porcelain production from clay to gilded decoration. The large Chinese plate with a dragon in its center, dating from 1345, is one of the most valuable pieces of china in the world. (*8bis pl. Winston Churchill.* ☎*05 55 33 08 50; www.musee-adriendubouche.fr. Open July-Aug. Sa-M and W-Su 10am-5:45pm; Sept.-June 10am-12:35pm and 2-5:40pm. €4, ages 18-25 and Su €2.60; 1st Su of the month and under 18 free.*)

MUSÉE MUNICIPAL DE L'EVÊCHÉ. Also known as the Musée de l'Email (enamel), this 18th-century bishop's palace is filled with the city's impressive collections of enameled art dating from the 12th century. The museum also has a small collection of Egyptian art and 19th-century paintings, including five works by Auguste Renoir, who was born in Limoges in 1841. (*Next to the cathedral in la Cité.* ☎*05 55 34 44 09 or 05 55 45 61 75. Open daily July to mid-Sept. 10am-noon and 2-6pm; June M and W-Su 10-11:45am and 2-6pm; Oct.-May M and W-Su 10-11:45am and 2-5pm. Free.*)

EVÊCHÉ BOTANICAL GARDENS. Stroll along on the banks of the Vienne through this floral oasis, which surrounds the cathedral and museums. (☎*05 55 45 62 67. Tours by appointment.*) An idyllic "promenade" along the river also passes the gardens.

OTHER SIGHTS. The magnificent Gothic **Cathédrale St-Etienne**, built on the site of a Roman temple, took over 600 years to complete. (*Pl. St-Etienne. Ask the tourist office for directions. Free French tours M-Sa 11am. Open M-Sa 10am-5pm, Su 2-6:30pm.*) For a slice of life as a butcher, visit the **Maison Traditionelle de la Boucherie**, 36 rue de la Boucherie. Guides lead French and broken English tours through a house. (☎*05 55 34 46 87. Open daily July-Sept. 10am-1pm and 3-7pm. Free.*) Across the street, the 15th-century **Chapel St-Aurelien** still lights candles to honor the patron saint of butchers. Limoges's famous ceramics decorate several remarkable structures, including Les Halles, the nearby Pavilion de Verdurier, and the fountain in front of the Mairie. To learn more about porcelain production, the **Manufacture Bernardaud** offers tours of the factory. (*27 av. Albert Thomas.* ☎*05 55 10 55 91. Tours daily June-Sept. 9-11am and 1-4pm; Oct.-May by reservation only. €4. Boutique open June-Sept. 9am-7pm, Oct.-May M-Sa 9:30am-6:30pm.*) Another facet of the ceramics tradition thrives at **Atelier Mosaïque**, 17 rue Montmailler, one of the hidden treasures of Limoges. Here, Mr. Soubeyrand de St-Exupery makes and sells delicate mosaics. Mosaics-in-progress surround his work area and finished projects adorn the walls in the form of mirrors, jewelry boxes, clocks, and more. (☎*05 55 77 73 05. Open M-Sa 9:30am-10:30pm. 2-week seminars offered continuously.*)

ENTERTAINMENT AND NIGHTLIFE

At night the streets of Limoges seem to empty out, though a handful of popular bars and clubs dot the center of town. Most *brasseries* serve as social hangouts in the evening. The **Cheyenne Café,** 4 rue Charles-Michels, is usually the loudest and most crowded. (☎05 55 32 32 62. Open Tu-W 6pm-1am, Th-Sa 6pm-2am.) Artsy older people and hip young locals socialize over French music in the spacious interior of **Café des Anciennes Majorettes de la Baule,** 27 rue Haute-Vienne. Paintings by local artists and shelves of used books decorate the walls. (☎05 55 34 34 16. Open Tu-Th 10am-1am, F-Sa 10pm-2am.) Communal picnic tables spill onto the sidewalk terrace of **L'Irlandais,** 2 rue Haute-Cité, near the cathedral, which becomes an Irish pub at night. Regular live music provides the evening's soundtrack. (☎05 55 32 46 47. Open Tu-Sa 4pm-1am, Su 3pm-midnight. Pints. €4.50-6.)

The **Grand Théâtre,** 48 rue Jean Jaurès, presents 60 ballet, orchestral, operatic, and choral productions every season, which runs between September and early June. (Reservations ☎05 55 34 12 12. Box office open daily 10am-6pm, closed July-Aug. €5-35. MC/V.) The **Théâtre de l'Union,** 20 rue des Coopérateurs (☎05 55 79 90 00), also has a season from September to May. On weekdays, the five **Centres Culturels Municipaux** put on a diverse array of concerts, theater productions, and films; contact the **Centre Culturel Jean-Moulin,** 76 rue des Sagnes (☎05 55 35 04 10).

FESTIVALS

The **Fête de St-Jean,** also known as the **Fête des Ponts,** held at the end of June every year, brings diving, fireworks, water shows, dancing, and musical performances. The popular **Festival Urb'Aka** (info ☎05 55 45 63 85; http://lejouretlanuit.com) heats up the last three days in June with street performances, nightly fireworks, and concerts. At the end of September, the **Festival International des Théâtres Francophones** features 15,000 French Canadians, French-speaking Africans, and Francophones from all over the world. (☎05 55 10 90 10; www.lesfrancophonies.com.)

DAYTRIP FROM LIMOGES

ORADOUR-SUR-GLANE

Not without hesitation, a new Oradour (pop. 2000) has been built next to its obliterated precursor. Equival runs a daily bus (line #12) from Limoges (train station, pl. Carmes, or pl. Winston Churchill) to the Centre de la Mémoire. (30min., 4-6 per day, €3.10. During July-Aug., buses run to the new town rather than directly to the center.) Schedules are available at the tourist office and the train station.

On June 10, 1944, in a heinous act of brutality, Nazi SS troops massacred all the inhabitants of the farming village **Oradour-sur-Glane,** without warning or provocation, in their relentless quest to rid the countryside of resistors. The Nazis entered at 2pm and corralled the women and children into the church and the men into six barns. At 4pm, a shot was fired, ordering the troops to begin the massacre. The women and children in the church were burned alive; the men were shot, then burned. By 7pm, 642 people, including 205 children, had been slaughtered. Most of the SS troops participating in the attack were tried in 1953, found guilty, and then immediately freed as the result of a general amnesty by the French government. Heinz Barth, commander of the unit, is currently serving a life sentence in a German jail. Plaques with heartbreaking messages and pictures adorn two glass tombs that contain the bones and ashes of the dead. The town remains in disturbingly untouched ruins. Train wires dangle from slanting poles and 50-year-old skeletons of cars rust next to crumbling walls. Visitors can walk freely along the main thoroughfare and peer into remnants of homes. Signs indicate the name and profession of each former resident. A small memorial between the cemetery and town displays bicycles, toys, and watches that were all stopped at the same moment by the heat of the fire. Access to the town is gained through **Le Centre de la Mémoire,** an incredible museum that places the massacre in the context of the Nazi regime with artifacts, timelines, and an informative film, all with English subtitles. (☎05 55 43 04 30. Museum and town open daily mid-May to mid-Sept. 9am-7pm; mid-Sept. to Oct., mid-Mar. to mid-May, Feb. to mid-Mar., and Nov.-Dec. 9am-5pm. Museum €6, students and children €4. Free entry to town.)

PÉRIGORD

PÉRIGUEUX

High above the Isle River, the towering steeple and five massive cupolas of the Cathédrale St-Front dominate the skyline of the city of Périgueux (pop. 65,000). Beneath the awesome church lies the town center which, though rather quiet during the afternoon, is packed with students enjoying the city's bars and clubs come evening. Rich with both ancient and medieval tradition as well as gourmet cuisine, the lovely neighborhoods of Périgueux are a true microcosm of the French countryside. Travelers with cars might consider daytripping to the caves of Périgord from here rather than from Les Eyzies-de-Tayac.

▐ TRANSPORTATION

Trains: rue Denis Papin. Info office (☎05 53 35 35 23) open M-Sa 8:25am-7:25pm, ticket booth open M 4:50am-8pm, Tu-Th 5:40am-8pm, F 5:40am-10:15pm, Sa-Su 6:10am-10:15pm. To: **Bordeaux** (1½hr., 12 per day, €16.30); **Brive** (1hr., 3 per day, €10.30); **Limoges** (1-1½hr., 8 per day, €13.30); **Lyon** (6-8hr., 2 per day, €46.80); **Paris** (4-6hr.; 12 per day; €45.90, more if switching trains); **Sarlat** (1½hr., 5 per day, €12); **Toulouse** (4hr., 8 per day, €37) via **Agen.**

Buses: In the midst of reorganization, Périgueux's bus service does not have a central office. Buses depart from various stops around town. To **Angoulême** (1½hr.; M, F, Su, 2nd Th of every month 1 per day; €12.70; stops at the train station; call ☎05 53 08 43 13 for info) and **Sarlat** (1½hr., F-Sa 2 per day, €7.70).

Taxis: Taxi Périgueux, pl. Bugeaud (☎05 53 09 09 09). 24hr.

Car Rental: Avis, 18 rue du Président Wilson (☎05 53 53 39 02). Open M-F 8am-noon and 2-7pm, Sa 8am-noon and 2-6pm. AmEx/DC/MC/V. **Hertz,** 20 cours Michel Montaigne (☎05 53 53 88 88), a few blocks from pl. Général de Gaulle. Open M-F 8am-noon and 2-7pm, Sa 8am-noon and 2-6pm. AmEx/DC/MC/V.

▐ ORIENTATION AND PRACTICAL INFORMATION

To reach the *vieille ville* and tourist office from the train station, turn right onto rue Denis Papin and left onto rue des Mobiles-de-Coulmiers, which becomes rue du Président Wilson. Take the right just after the Monoprix and walk one block. The tourist office is on the left, beside the stone Mataguerre Tower (15 minutes).

Tourist Office: 26 pl. Francheville (☎05 53 53 10 63; www.ville-perigueux.fr). Free map and info on walking, *petit train,* and bike tours. Walking tours can be long but provide entry to otherwise inaccessible buildings. Tours mid-June to mid-Sept. M-Sa 10:30am,

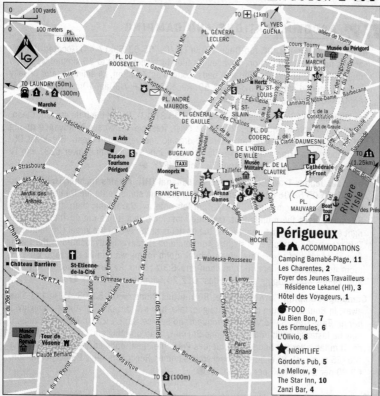

Périgueux

🏠🏕 ACCOMMODATIONS
Camping Barnabé-Plage, **11**
Les Charentes, **2**
Foyer des Jeunes Travailleurs
Résidence Lekanel (HI), **3**
Hôtel des Voyageurs, **1**

🍎 FOOD
Au Bien Bon, **7**
Les Formules, **6**
L'Olivio, **8**

⭐ NIGHTLIFE
Gordon's Pub, **5**
Le Mellow, **9**
The Star Inn, **10**
Zanzi Bar, **4**

2:30, 4pm, additional tour M 9pm; mid-Sept. to mid-June M-Sa 2:30pm. €5, students €3.80. Office open mid-June to mid-Sept. M-Sa 9am-6pm, Su 10am-1pm and 2-6pm; mid-Sept. to mid-June M-Sa 9am-1pm and 2-6pm, Su 10am-1pm and 2-6pm. **Espace Tourisme Périgord,** 25 rue du Président Wilson (☎05 53 35 50 24), has excellent topographic maps and info on travel in Périgord, campgrounds, *gîtes,* and *chambres d'hôtes.* Open M and F 9am-noon and 2-5pm, Tu-Th 9am-noon and 2-5:15pm.

Banks: Banque Tarneaud, 17 rue du Président Wilson (☎05 53 02 46 02) has **currency exchange.** Open M-F 8:35am-12:10pm and 2-6pm. **Société Général,** 16 cours Michel Montaigne (☎05 53 02 57 00), offers **currency exchange** with €5.40 commission. Open M-F 8:30am-12:15pm and 1:30-5pm.

Laundromat: Lav'matic, 20 rue Mobiles de Coulmiers, near rond-point Lanxade on the way to the train station. Wash €3-8, dry €1 per 9min. Open daily 8am-9pm.

Police: rue du 4 Septembre (☎05 53 06 44 44), near the post office.

Hospital: Centre Hospitalier, 80 av. Georges Pompidou (☎05 53 07 70 00).

Internet Access: Surf the net in a medieval mansion at **Arena Games,** 11 rue des Farges (☎05 53 53 75 21). Take a sharp left after the tourist office onto rue de la Bride, which becomes rue des Farges. €1 for 15min., €3 per hr. Open daily 11am-midnight.

Post Office: 1 rue du 4 Septembre (☎05 53 03 61 12). Offers **currency exchange.** Open M-F 8am-6:30pm, Sa 8am-noon.

Postal Code: 24070.

♠ ♣ ACCOMMODATIONS AND CAMPING

Hôtel des Voyageurs, 26 rue Denis Papin (☎/fax 05 53 53 17 44), located directly across from the train station. Voyageurs's friendly owner tends to 15 simple, well-worn rooms at great prices. Comfortable beds, convenient location, cleanliness, and privacy make it a good value. Breakfast €3.50. Reception M-F 7:30am-10pm. Singles €14; doubles €16, with shower €19. ❶

Les Charentes, 16 rue Denis Papin (☎05 53 53 37 13), facing the train station. Clean, comfortable rooms with a quirky 1970s twist. Reserve 1-2 weeks in advance during summer. Restaurant serves an extensive organic and vegetarian menu. Breakfast €5. Reception 7am-10pm. Closed late Dec. to early Jan. Singles with shower €23, with TV €28, with toilet €33. Extra person €5. AmEx/MC/V. ❷

Foyer des Jeunes Travailleurs Résidence Lakanal (HI), rue des Thermes (☎05 53 06 81 40; fax 05 53 06 81 49). Turn right from the train station onto rue Denis Papin and follow it as it becomes rue Chanzy. Turn left onto av. Cavaignac, then right onto rue Romain. Across the roundabout, take rue Mosaïque until it hits rue de Thermes. Turn right and walk along the train tracks; the hostel is at the end of the street (25 minutes). This cramped dormitory in a slightly worn building is conveniently located in the Gallo-Roman section of town. Tiny, clean 4-bunk dorm rooms with small showers. Busy TV room downstairs. Reception 9am-noon and 6:30-10pm. Reserve ahead for July and Aug. Dorms with bedding and breakfast €12.20, with dinner €18.90. ❶

Camping: Camping Barnabé-Plage, 80 rue des Bains (☎05 53 53 41 45), 1.5km away, in Boulazac. From cours Montaigne, take bus #8 (dir: Cité Bel Air; M-F roughly 1 per hr. 7am-7pm, Sa service less frequent, no service Su; €1.25) to Rue des Bains. It may be faster to walk; from Cathédrale St-Front, head downhill and cross Pont des Barris. Turn left after the bridge onto rue des Prés. The street ends at rue des Bains at the site (25 minutes). Riverside site packed in summer. Reception 24hr. €3.40 per person, €2.90 per tent, €4.90 per car. MC/V. ❶

♦ FOOD

The labyrinth of narrow stone streets between cours M. Montaigne and rue Taillefer is lined with regional culinary treasures: *foie gras*, walnuts, *cèpe* and *girolle* mushrooms, and fruit liqueurs. A stroll down rue Salinière and rue Limogeanne reveals an assortment of *charcuteries, pâtisseries, boulangeries*, and *sandwicheries*. While restaurants in this area can be slightly pricey, the other side of rue Taillefer is more reasonable. There are morning **markets** on pl. du Coderc, pl. de l'Hôtel de Ville, and a larger one on pl. de la Clautre, near the cathedral. (Open daily, with larger versions W and Sa 8am-1pm.) The behemoth **Monoprix**, pl. Bugeaud in the town center, is impossible to miss. (Open M-Sa 7am-9pm, Su 8am-1pm. MC/V.) For **groceries**, visit **Marché Plus**, 55 rue du Président Wilson. (Open M-Sa 7am-9pm, Su 8am-1pm. MC/V.) ☒**Au Bien Bon ❸**, 15 rue Aubergerie, serves exceptional regional cuisine, specializing in a variety of meat dishes like *filet du porc avec sauce bleu*. Try the lunch *menu* with appetizer, main course, and dessert for €14. Outdoor tables overlook a quiet, winding street. (☎05 53 09 69 91. Open Tu-F noon-2pm and 7:30-10pm, Sa noon-2pm. MC/V.) Personalize a *menu* with generous portions for €10, €13, or €16 at **Les Formules ❷**, 16 rue des Farges. The herring with potato salad makes a delicious meal, though all their *plats* are wonderful. Diners can also choose to sit in a pleasant courtyard out back. (☎05 53 03 46 56. Open M-Sa noon-2pm and 7-10:30pm. MC/V.) Those looking for lighter fare should check out **L'Olivio**

❷, 14 rue ed l'Aubergine, a quaint pizzeria with outdoor seating underneath a large archway. (Pizzas from €7. Open M-Sa noon-2:30pm and 7-10:30pm. MC/V.)

🔵 SIGHTS

Gabarre de Périgueux (☎05 53 24 58 80) offers 50min. boat tours of the city from mid-June to mid-September, departing from the base of Cathédrale St-Front (€6.50). Boats depart daily at 2:15, 3:30, 4:45, and 6pm, and in July and August at 11am as well. The tourist office provides an excellent walking tour guide to Gallo-Romain, medieval, and Renaissance Périgueux. The only way to get inside the *hôtels particuliers* and monuments is to take one of these tours.

MEDIEVAL AND RENAISSANCE PÉRIGUEUX
The massive **Cathédrale St-Front,** which dominates the skyline above the river, is the end product of nearly 1500 years of renovation and restoration. Five immense Byzantine cupolas in the shape of a cross (like St. Mark's in Venice) make the interior feel light and open. The cathedral incorporates parts of a 10th-century church, and Romanesque frescoes dot the walls. In the late 1800s, the structure inspired Paul Abadie in his design of the Basilique Sacré-Cœur in Paris. (Open daily 8am-noon and 2:30-7pm.) Down rue St-Front from the cathedral, the **Musée du Périgord,** 22 cours Tourny, is home to one of France's most important collections of pre-historic artifacts, including fossils from Les Eyzies, 2m long mammoth tusks, and an Egyptian mummy whose bare toe bones peek out from crusty coverings. There's also a small collection of modern art, fine art, and regional medieval art. (☎05 53 06 40 70. Open Apr.-Sept. M and W-F 10:30am-5:30pm, Sa-Su 1-6pm; Oct.-Mar. M and W-F 10am-5pm. €4, students €2, under 18 free.) Walk back to the tourist office to find the crumbling **Tour Mataguerre.** It derives its name from an English captain held in its dungeons for 17 years during the Hundred Years' War.

GALLO-ROMAN PÉRIGUEUX
The few remains of Gallo-Roman Périgueux lie west of the *vieille ville,* down rue de la Cité from pl. Francheville. The crumbling, but still impressive **Tour de Vésone,** built in the first century AD and once part of a huge temple dedicated to Vésone's patron god, stands adjacent to the Musée Gallo-Romain. The tower itself was a *cella,* the center of worship in Roman temples, though now it's little more than a crumbling stone wall. About a quarter of the weighty

ON THE MENU

DUCK, DUCK, GOOSE

Périgord prides itself on its *cuisine du canard* and the excellence of its *foie gras,* and with good reason: it all tastes delicious. Duck and goose appear on every menu from Périgueux to Cahors. Here is a quick cheat sheet on the many ways to serve these birds.

The bird can be bought whole at *marchés au gras,* but popular cuts are commonly served at restaurants. The most sought-after is the *magret,* duck or goose breast, which can be served grilled, sliced, and covered in a pepper sauce with delicious *pommes sarladaises* (sautéed potatoes). *Confit,* cooked thighs and wings preserved in fat, can be bought at any duck gourmet shop in the region, though they are also easy to make and store at home. They are often served sautéed in garlic. *Mique* is a traditional dumpling soup with duck stock.

The indisputed delicacy of the region, though, is *foie gras,* a gourmand's dream come true. As part of an age-old method, *foie gras,* fattened goose or duck liver, is produced by force-feeding ducks a few weeks before they are sent to the butcher's block. The prized treat is often served in a *terrine de foie gras,* marinated in liqueur and baked slowly or lightly fried. Poultry lovers rejoice—and give those chicken-weary tastebuds a rest.

structure was demolished, supposedly by the last fleeing demons of paganism, although it was more likely dismantled to create the city's defensive wall. (Park grounds open daily Apr.-Sept. 7:30am-9pm; Oct.-Mar. 7:30am-6:30pm.) Next door, the **⬛Musée Gallo-Romain,** 20 rue du 26ème Régiment d'Infanterie, has built an intricate walkway over the excavated ruins of the Domus de Vésone, once the lavish home of a wealthy Roman merchant. Look closely—the windows sometimes do not touch the ground; the building is supported by columns and cables to protect the site. The museum contains an impressive array of Roman artifacts, murals, and stonework. (☎ 05 53 53 00 92. Open daily July and Aug. 10am-7pm; Apr.-June and Sept. Tu-Su 10am-6pm; Oct. to mid-Nov. 10am-12:30pm and 2-6pm; Feb.-Mar. and mid-Nov. to Dec. Tu-Su 10am-12:30pm and 2-5:30pm. Closed Jan. €5.50, under 12 €3.50. Tours in French daily July-Aug. €2. Audioguide in English €2.) Cross the bridge from the Tour de Vésone and turn left down rue Romaine to reach a cluster of architectural vestiges from the first century through the high Middle Ages. Flowers sprout through the crevices of the **Château Barrière,** a four-story late-Gothic castle. The Romanesque house next door is an example of the use of *spolia*—chunks of ruins incorporated decoratively into new buildings. Both buildings were constructed on the remains of the Roman wall built around the city in AD 275 to defend against the first Norman and barbarian attacks. A fragment of this wall, the **Porte Normande** was one of the only three doors in the city wall in ancient times.

Up rue Romaine, the 11th-century **Église St-Etienne-de-la-Cité** was the seat of the bishopric until Calvinist attackers destroyed all but the choir and one-third of the nave in 1577. Its two simple but stately cupolas are punctuated by small Romanesque windows. (Open M-Sa 8am-7pm.) Forty meters beyond the church, up rue de l'Ancien Evêché, the crumbling foundations of a **Roman amphitheater** have found new life as a public park, complete with archways and an inviting fountain that becomes a makeshift swimming pool during the summer. (Open daily Apr.-Sept. 7:30am-9pm; Oct.-Mar. 7:30am-6:30pm.)

🎵 🎎 ENTERTAINMENT AND FESTIVALS

While the streets may be sleepy, Périgueux's *places* jump with activity. **Place St-Silain** and **place St-Louis** are centers of the city's nightlife with music and outdoor cafes; **place du Marché au Bois** hosts frequent concerts. Bars line the lively cobblestone **rue de la Sagesse.** The sophisticated **⬛Le Mellow,** 4 rue de la Sagesse, is the coolest place to unwind with a martini. The contemporary lounge also features a cigar bar and upbeat music. (☎ 05 53 08 53 97. Cocktails €5.50-6.10. MC/V.) **⬛The Star Inn,** 17 rue des Drapeaux, is a classic Irish pub run by native English speakers in three large rooms in a restored Renaissance house. Outdoor seating also available. (☎ 05 53 08 56 83. Drinks from €2.20. Happy hour 8-9pm. Open July-Aug. M-Sa 8pm-2am; Sept-June 8pm-1am.) **Zanzi Bar,** 2 rue Condé, serves jungle-inspired cocktails (from €4.80) and exotic *tapas* (€6) in a tropical ambiance. Kick things up a notch with their salsa lessons (€5) on Wednesday nights. (☎ 05 53 53 28 99. Salsa class W 8-9:30pm. Open Tu-Sa 6:30pm-1am. MC/V.) **Gordon's Pub,** 12 rue Condé, off rue Taillefer, is an Irish-style pub with a small terrace and a warm welcome for all. A young, energetic crowd packs the bar late. (Beer €2. Open M-Sa noon-2am. MC/V.)

Macadam Jazz presents free outdoor concerts on Tuesdays in July and August. **Son-et-Lumière de Périgueux: La Légende de Saint-Front** is a light show that illuminates Cathédrale St-Front with an artistic exploration of the area's history. (☎ 05 53 53 18 71. Late July to mid-Aug. W 10:30pm. €13, students €10.) The town quiets down during the first week of August for **Mimos,** the world's leading mime festival. Mime companies from all over the world give phenomenal performances. The big events cost money, but there are free performances and public workshops all over town. (☎ 05 53 53 18 71. Ticketed events €10, students €8.)

LES EYZIES-DE-TAYAC

Les Eyzies-de-Tayac (pop. 900) is the picture-perfect base for travel to the Vézère valley's famous caves (except for Lascaux); most of them are less than 20min. from the town center by foot. The beautiful Vézère River nearby is ideal for post-spelunking relaxation. Reserve a visit weeks in advance, as cave access is limited. In town itself there are two prestigious museums and the official information center for the region's pre-historic sites, and the sites are also good sources of information about Neolithic art. The village abounds with pre-historic-themed hotels, duck specialties, and Bergerac wines. The medieval château of the lords of Tayac can be seen from the cliff above the town.

■ ☑ ORIENTATION AND PRACTICAL INFORMATION. Trains (☎ 05 53 06 97 22) run to Paris (6-8hr., 3 per day, €48.70) via Limoges; Périgueux (30min., 5 per day, €6.30); and Sarlat (1hr.; 3 per day, change at Le Buisson; €7.50). Open M-F 8am-6pm, Sa-Su 10am-6pm. Facing away from the station, turn right and walk 500m down the town's only street, av. de la Préhistoire, to reach the town center (5 minutes). For a **taxi** to the caves, call Taxi Tardieu at ☎ 05 53 06 93 06. The **tourist office**, at pl. de la Mairie, rents **bikes** (€8 per half-day, €14 per day; ID or €20 deposit), offers summer tours to sights within walking distance (€4.50, children €2), lists of caves and *gîtes d'étapes*, **Internet** (€1.60 per 15min.), accommodations booking (€1.50), and **currency exchange** at no commission. (☎ 05 53 06 97 05; www.leseyzies.com. Open July-Aug. M-Sa 9am-7pm, Su 10am-noon and 2-6pm; Apr.-June and Sept. M-Sa 9am-noon and 2-6pm, Su 10am-noon and 2-5pm; Oct.-Mar. M-Sa 9am-noon and 2-6pm.) Other services include an **ATM** next to the tourist office, **police** (☎ 05 53 30 80 00) in nearby St-Cyprien, a **laundromat** at the eastern end of town, just at the beginning of rte. de Sarlat (open M-Sa 9am-noon and 2:30-7pm), and a **post office** on av. de la Préhistoire past the tourist office, which provides **currency exchange**. (☎ 05 53 06 94 11. Open M-Tu and Th-F 8:30am-noon and 2-4pm, W 9:30am-noon and 2-4pm, Sa 9-11:30am.) **Postal Code:** 24620.

☐ ☐ ACCOMMODATIONS AND FOOD. Rooms tend to be expensive. The tourist office has a list of private B&Bs in the surrounding area (€25-32 for 1-2 people). Drivers will notice signs along the main roads advertising *fermes* (farms) with camping space (€3-8). Some village homes rent rooms for €23-46 during the summer; look for *chambres* signs, especially on the east end of the town. The Demaison family runs an exceptional **◪chambre d'hôte ❸**, rte. de Sarlat, 3min. outside town. From the train station, go through town and follow signs to Sarlat; the house is a few houses past the laundromat on the right. Twelve charming rooms are available in their timbered home on the edge of the forest. Rooms are immaculately clean. (☎ 05 53 06 91 43. Breakfast €5. Free parking. Reservations required. Singles and doubles €25-36; triples and quads €48. All rooms with bath and toilet, except for one with shower and toilet.) In town, try the **Hôtel des Falaises ❸**, av. de la Préhistoire. Spotless rooms have royal blue furnishings and plenty of space. All rooms come with bath; larger rooms have a balcony overlooking the garden. The hotel offers more private and homey lodgings in the **annex**, about 100m down the road toward Font-de-Gaume in a large half-timbered building. (☎ 05 53 06 97 35. Breakfast €5. Reception in the bar downstairs 8am-6pm. Doubles €30-35; triples €40. Annex prices same as hotel. MC/V.) For **Camping La Rivière ❶**, rte. de Périgueux, turn left from the tourist office on av. de la Préhistoire. Follow the road for 5min., cross the bridge, and take another left at the gas station. The site offers a snack bar, restaurant, bike rental, laundry, Internet, athletic facilities, kitchen, and a pool. (☎05 53 06 97 14; www.campings-dordogne.com/la-riviere. Reception daily 8am-10pm. Open Apr.-Oct. €3-4.70 per person; €5.20-7.40 per site; price varies with season. Electricity €3.) Attached to the campsite, a small but luxurious **hotel ❸** inside a 16th-century Périgordian home lets fresh, well-furnished rooms. (Breakfast €4.50. Doubles with bath €32-37; quads with bath €45-50. MC/V.)

From April to October, a **market** runs the length of town every Monday 9am-1pm. **Halle des Eyzies,** just past the center of town on rte. de Sarlat, is full of expensive boutiques hawking *foie gras*, Bergerac wine, and walnut products. Wonderful local art, oils, cookies, and cakes are also for sale here, in addition to every duck, goose, and pork product imaginable. The *gâteau aux noix* and *foie gras* are not to be missed. (Open mid-June to mid-Sept. daily 8am-1pm.) A large convenience store, **Relais de Mousquetaires,** a bit up rte. de Sarlat, sells **groceries.** (Open M-Sa 8:30am-12:30pm and 3-7pm.) Most restaurants in Les Eyzies are expensive but extremely good. **La Grignotière ❷,** facing the tourist office, serves cheap drinks and sandwiches (€3.20-4.50) all day long and a three-course *menu* (€10.40 or €11.40) during mealtimes. The omelettes (€5-8) and salads are particularly delectable. (☎05 53 06 91 67. Open daily 7:30am-midnight. MC/V.) **La Milanaise ❸,** av. de la Préhistoire, serves delicious thin-crust pizzas, salads full of *gésiers* and walnuts, and duck plates. Try the inventive Pizza Antilles topped with mango. (☎05 53 35 43 97. Salad €3.50-12, pizza €6-11.30, *plats* €10-15, *menus* €15.50 and €22.50. Open daily July-Aug. 11am-2pm and 6:30-10:30pm; Mar.-Nov. M and W-Su. MC/V.)

🖸 **SIGHTS.** For information on visiting nearby **caves,** see p. 500. The **Musée L'Abri Pataud** is the site of a pre-historic *abri* (shelter), where reindeer hunters lived over a span of 20,000 years. The museum provides an informative and in-depth explanation of the archaeological finds of the region and the types of dwellings built by these early humans. The 18,600-year-old remains of a teenage girl found on the site may represent a transitional link between Neanderthal and Cro-Magnon man. The site is not currently active, but it is also not complete; bones and artifacts can still be seen in the surrounding rock wall. (☎05 53 06 92 46; pataud@mnhn.fr. Open daily July-Aug. 10am-6pm; Sept.-June Tu-Th and Su 10-11:30am and 2-5pm. 1hr. visits leave every 30min. Groups must reserve ahead. Tours in English on demand, generally 1 per day, come early to find the time. €5.20, ages 6-12 €3.20.)

The **Musée National de Préhistoire,** in a château overlooking the village, is a walk through the pre-historic discoveries in the many caves around Les Eyzies. The remains of a Neanderthal infant lie next to etchings of bison. Learn how archaeologists study these objects and see the actual hearths cavemen used to work with fire. English guide cards are displayed at the entrance of each room. (☎05 53 06 45 45. Open daily July-Aug. 9:30am-6:30pm; Sept.-June M and W-Su 9:30am-12:30pm and 2-5:30pm. Tours 1hr.; 3 per day in French, 1 per day in English at 2pm; €4.50, ages 18-25 €3, under 18 free.)

SARLAT

Sarlat (pop. 10,500) was an unknown, average hamlet until 1962, when Minister of Culture André Malraux, inspired by the architectural unity and lack of modernization in the *vieille ville*, selected it for a massive restoration project. Three years later, a new Sarlat emerged—handsomely restored and surprisingly medieval. Since then it has been the setting for films like *Cyrano de Bergerac* and *Manon des Sources.* Sarlat merits a full day's visit and is the best base from which to explore the Lower Dordogne and Lascaux (p. 499).

█⁊ TRANSPORTATION AND PRACTICAL INFORMATION. Trains (☎05 53 59 00 21) rumble from av. de la Gare to Bordeaux (2½hr., 4 per day 6am-7:30pm, €20.60) and Périgueux (3hr., 2 per day M-F 6am and Sa 5:40pm, €12.30), both via le Buisson. (Info booths open daily 6am-12:30pm and 1:15-7pm.) **CFTA**, 15 av. Aristide Briand (☎05 53 59 01 48), and **Trans-Périgord** run **buses** from the train station to Souillac, a stop on the Paris-Toulouse line (40 min., 8-10 per day, €4.70), Brive (1½hr.; 1 per day July-Aug. Tu, Th, and Sa noon; Sept.-June M-F 6:30am; €6.40) and from pl. Pasteur to Périgueux via Montignac (1½hr., 1 per day M-F 6am, €10.35). **Sarlat Bus** runs **local buses** on two routes; line A stops at the train station, line B at the roundabout one block down rue Dubois. (☎05 53 59 01 48. Open M-Sa 8:30am-5pm.) For a **taxi** call ☎05 53 59 06 27. (24hr.) **Car rental** is available from Europcar at pl. Tassigny, down the hill from the train station and to the left along av. Thiers walking away from the city. (☎05 53 30 30 40. Open M-F 8am-noon and 2-6:30pm, Sa 8am-noon and 2-6pm. AmEx/MC/V.) To rent **bikes**, try Cycles Sarladais, av. Aristide Briand near the station (☎05 53 28 51 87; open M-Sa 9am-noon and 2-7pm, Sept.-June closed M; €13 per day, €35 for three days; MC/V) or Cum's Bikes, 8 av. de Selves, a block from the hostel away from town. (☎05 53 53 31 56. Open Tu-F 9am-noon and 2-7pm, Sa until 6pm. €8 per half-day, €13 per day. MC/V.)

To reach the **tourist office**, off rue Tourny in the *centre ville*, follow av. de la Gare downhill and turn right on av. Thiers, which becomes av. Général. Leclerc, then rue de la République. Bear right on rue Lakanal and left on rue de la Liberté, which leads to the Cathédrale St-Sacerdos. Next door is the tourist office, in the Ancien Evêché (15 minutes) The staff offers accommodations booking (€2), **currency exchange** when banks are closed, city tours, and a walking guide in English. (☎05 53 31 45 45; www.ot-sarlat-perigord.fr. Open Apr.-Oct. M-Sa 9am-7pm, Su 10am-noon and 2-6pm; Nov.-Mar. M-Sa 9am-noon and 2-7pm. Tours in English Apr.-Sept. W 2pm. 1-3 tours in French per day. €5, children €3.) All **banks** in Sarlat exchange currency, including Crédit Lyonnais, 15 rue de la République. (☎05 53 59 20 31. Open Tu-F 8:15am-noon and 1:45-5:15pm, Sa 8:15am-12:15pm.) An **ATM** is opposite the Bishop's Palace on rue Tourny. Other services include: a **laundromat** at 24 av. de Selves (open daily 7am-9pm); **police** at pl. Salvador Allende (☎05 53 31 53 17); a **hospital** on rue Jean Leclaire (☎05 53 31 75 75); and **Internet** at Le Taverne du Web, 17 av. Gambetta. (☎05 53 30 80 77. Open M-Sa 10am-10pm, Su 2-9pm. €3.20 for 30min., €5.50 per hr.) The **post office**, pl. du 14 Juillet, has **currency exchange**. (☎05 53 31 73 10. Open M 9am-5:30pm, Tu-F 8:30am-5:30pm, Sa 8:30am-noon.) **Postal Code:** 24200.

█▀ ACCOMMODATIONS AND CAMPING. Sarlat's hotels are typically quite expensive, and the small hostel fills quickly in summer. The best option is to book a room at one of the *chambre d'hôtes* (€25-40), close to the city center. The tourist office has a complete list that also includes *gîtes*, farms, and campgrounds in the surrounding countryside.

The simple, laid-back **Auberge de Jeunesse ❶**, 77 av. de Selves, is 40min. from the station, but only 5-10min. from the *vieille ville*. Follow rue de la République though the old city until it becomes av. Gambetta; bear left at the fork onto av. de Selves. By bus, walk downhill on rue Dubois and catch line B (dir: Hôpital) to La Pologue. The *auberge* consists of 16 beds in three co-ed rooms in a large, wooden cabin. There is also a grassy yard for **campers**. Clean bathrooms, a rustic common room, and a stocked kitchen make for an enjoyable, if do-it-yourself, stay. (☎05 53 59 47 59 or 05 53 30 21 27. Kitchen access. Reception 6pm-9pm. Reserve ahead. Open mid-Mar. to Nov. Bunks €10 the first night, then €9 per night. Camping €6/€5.) **Hôtel de la Mairie ❹**, 13 pl. de la Liberté, in a lovely, medieval building in the heart of the *centre ville*, offers large, wood-trimmed rooms with clean baths. (☎05

53 59 05 71. Breakfast €5.50. Singles and doubles with shower €40-50; triples €65; quads €75; quints €85. Extra bed €10. AmEx/MC/V.) For a quieter night's sleep, the **Hôtel Le Lion D'Or ❹**, 48 av. Gambetta, has refined, spacious rooms, private baths, and high ceilings. (☎05 53 59 00 83. Reception 6am-8pm. Breakfast €5. Closed Dec. to mid-Mar. Singles €38; doubles and triples €40-46; quad €53. MC/V.) The campground **Le Montant ❶**, 4km from town on D57 toward Bergerac, has hot showers, a bar, laundry, and two pools. (☎05 53 59 18 50 or 05 53 29 45 85; fax 05 53 59 37 73. Reception daily 9am-8pm. Open Easter-Sept. €5 per person, €3.20 per child, €6 per tent, including vehicle. Electricity €2.70.)

🗋 FOOD. Most regional delicacies—*foie gras, confit de canard*, truffles, walnut oil, strawberries, Bergerac wine—can be purchased directly from their sources for lower prices than in town. *Pâtisseries* and *confiseries* sell decorated breads, walnut-and-chocolate tarts, *gâteaux aux noix* (walnut cookies), and chocolate-dipped meringue *boules* the size of grapefruits. A Saturday **market** takes over the city (open 8:30am-6pm); a smaller one fills pl. de la Liberté (W 8:30am-1pm). Follow av. de Selves away from the town center to the enormous **Champion supermarket** near the hostel on rte. de Montignac. (Open M-Sa 9am-7:45pm.) You can also stock up at the **Petit Casino**, 32 rue de la République. (Open M-Sa 8am-7:15pm and Su 9am-7pm.) The narrow streets of Sarlat's *vieille ville* host a variety of excellent, slightly pricey restaurants. The **Auberge des Lys D'Or ❷**, pl. André Malraux, behind the Maison de la Boétie, offers fish or duck specialties in a gourmet atmosphere. Their two-course *formule* (€10), with a *plat* and dessert, available until 8pm, is a good deal among Sarlat's largely pricey options. Try the *canard aux pêches* for a taste of regional cuisine. (☎05 53 31 24 77. Open M-Tu and F-Su noon-10:30pm, W noon-2pm. *Menus* €13, €16, and €22. MC/V.) **Le Petit Borie ❸**, 3 rue des Oliviers, hidden in one of the crooked *centre ville* alleys, crafts delicious, home-style favorites like sautéed potatoes and spicy mustard over ham. (☎05 53 31 23 69. Open M-Sa noon-2pm and 7-11pm. *Plats* €7-19, *menus* €10.80-27. MC/V.)

◙ SIGHTS. The golden stone buildings of the *vieille ville* are the city's most compelling features, but the landscaped forest and fountains of the **Jardin Public du Plantier**, bd. Henri Arlet, run a close second. Most sights are to the right off rue de la République when entering the town from the station. The 16th-century neo-Gothic **Cathédrale St-Sacerdos**, to the right of the tourist office, was recently renovated; it was originally part of a Benedictine abbey. Behind it, the conical **Lanterne des Morts** (Lantern of the Dead) has served as a chapel, charnel-house, election site for city consuls, and gunpowder magazine. Across the street from the bishop's palace, the **Maison de la Boétie**, a tall, gabled house, has carved pilasters typical of the Italian Renaissance. The windows are composed of hundreds of tiny glass panels. The building was the birthplace of writer Etienne de la Boétie, a key figure in Renaissance efforts to reconcile Catholics and Protestants.

🎝 🎬 ENTERTAINMENT AND FESTIVALS. Every weekend, street performers and musicians converge on pl. de la Liberté, crowding cafes with boisterous audiences. Young locals meet in the polished ◙**Le Bataclan,** 31 rue de la République, a glitzy bar and *brasserie* with delicious, inexpensive food. Noisy rock and a carefree crowd spill onto the streets from within. (☎05 53 28 54 34. Drinks €3-5, *plats* €6-9. Open daily 8am-2am. MC/V.) **CinéRex**, av. Thiers, occasionally screens foreign films in their original language. (☎08 92 68 69 24. Foreign films €5.50, French films €7. Cheaper M and W and on the 25th of every month.) During the last two weeks of July and the first week of August, Sarlat hosts the **Festival des Jeux du Théâtre**, which features open-air performances, comedies, musicals, and panel discussions. (☎ 05 53 31 10 83. Tickets €15-25. Students get 20% off with ID.) The second weekend in September brings the flower contests and picnics of the **Fête des Fleurs** to the Jardin Public du Plantier.

⚡ DAYTRIPS FROM SARLAT. Castelnaud-la-Chapelle, 10km south of Sarlat on D57, snoozes on the Dordogne in the shadow of its yellow-stone château, the largest in the region. To visit the castle, climb the hill from the post office parking lot and through the village, following signs for *piétons* (10 minutes). By car, take the winding sign-posted road on the right just after crossing the bridge. The castle houses a 13th- to 17th-century armory and a behemoth catapult. Videos demonstrate the uses of these weapons, while full-scale replicas surround the castle outside. Tour guides share gruesome tales of warfare in the Middle Ages, and audience members can dress in medieval garb during live demonstrations. (☎ 05 53 31 30 00; www.castelnaud.com. July-Aug. 6 tours in French per day, 2-3 tours in English per day. Call in advance for low season English tours. Demonstrations daily July-Aug. 11:30am-1:30pm and 3-5:45pm. Open daily July-Aug. 9am-8pm; Feb.-Apr. and Oct to mid-Nov. 10am-6pm; mid-Nov. to Jan. 2-5pm; Dec. 10am-5pm. Château and museum €6.60, ages 10-17 €3.30, under 10 free; adults €5.60 before 1pm.) Halfway down the hill from the castle lies the Eco-Musée de la Noix de Périgord, a restored farmhouse which showcases the history and inner workings of the region's famous walnut industry. Nut-lovers can purchase homemade walnut products galore and enjoy the shade of the walnut groves. (☎ 05 53 59 69 63. Open daily Apr.-Oct. 10am-7pm. €4, children €3.)

The elegant Renaissance **Château des Milandes,** 5km from Castelnaud, was built by François de Caumont in 1489 to satisfy his wife, who wanted a more stylish home than the outdated fortress of Castelnaud. Centuries later, cabaret singer Josephine Baker fell in love with the neglected château's pointed roofs and gables, purchased the property, and created a "world village" to house and care for children she had adopted on her international tours. Tours of her living space include a museum devoted to her life and times. A falconry show, complete with handlers in medieval garb, takes place 2-4 times per day on the lawns. (☎ 05 53 59 31 21; www.milandes.com. Open daily July-Aug. 9:30am-7:30pm; Mar-Apr. and Oct. 10am-6:15pm; May-June and Sept. 10am-6:30pm. Tours off-season only. Falconry show Apr.-Oct.; call for schedule. €7.50, students €6.50, ages 4-15 €5.50.)

For those seeking riverside rambles, ancient caves, or more medieval marvels, the nearby towns of Roque-la-Guignac and Domme make for lovely stops, as do the many picnic-worthy beaches on the banks of the Dordogne.

CAVES OF THE VÉZÈRE VALLEY

LASCAUX

The world's most famous pre-historic cave paintings line the ceilings of Lascaux, "the Sistine Chapel of prehistory." A couple of teenagers stumbled upon them in 1940 while chasing after their runaway dog. Lascaux closed to the public in 1963 because the humidity from the breath of millions of visitors bred algae and ministalactites that ravaged the paintings that nature had preserved for 17,000 years. Today, visitors line up Disneyland-style to see **Lascaux II,** which duplicates practically every inch of the original. The new paintings of 5m tall bulls, horses, and bison are brighter than their ancient counterparts, but were crafted with identical natural powders, derived from the soil in the original caves. While there is a distinct lack of ancient mystery, Lascaux II compensates with one of the best guided cave tours in the valley. Watch for a deer whose eyes seem to follow the viewer, a horse sprawled on his back on a nearby rock, and a herd of galloping elk. Many of the paintings are superimposed within each other (the same curve serving as the belly for two animals), making for a compellingly subtle panorama. Interspersed among the paintings are hundreds of unidentifiable symbols suggesting the existence of an ancient written language.

The Lascaux caves are 2km up a winding road from **Montignac** (pop. 3000), 25km north of Sarlat along D704 and 23km northeast of Les Eyzies on D706. The Montignac **tourist office** (☎05 53 51 95 03), pl. Bertram-de-Born, shares a building with the Lascaux II **ticket office**. (☎05 53 05 65 65. Advance tickets 05 53 51 95 03. Reserving 1-2 weeks ahead assures entry, though those who arrive early can usually get tickets for later in the day. Ticket office open from 9am until tickets sell out. French and English cave tours run July-Aug. 9am-7pm; Feb.-June and Sept.-Dec. Tu-Su 10am-noon and 2-5:30pm. 40min; €8, ages 6-12 €4.50. MC/V.)

In the nearby town of **Thonac, Le Thot Espace Cro-Magnon,** rte. D706, is a museum that serves as a great introduction to Lascaux and pre-historic discoveries in the area. The center paints a sweeping picture of ancient life, from family groups and hunting scenes to the making of cave art. An informative short film in French with English subtitles explains how Lascaux II was constructed. Engaging displays and an animal park behind the complex are perfect for children. The museum was closed in 2004 for construction, with indefinite plans to reopen in 2005; animal exhibits free with a Lascaux ticket. (☎05 53 05 65 65; www.semitour.com. Open daily July-Aug. 10am-7pm; Feb.-June and Sept.-Dec. 10am-noon and 2-5:30pm.

The **train station** nearest to Montignac is 10km away at Le Lardin. **Taxis** (☎05 53 50 86 61) wait here, and, during the school year (Sept.-June), **CFTA** (info ☎05 55 86 07 07) runs **buses** from Brive, Périgueux, and Sarlat; call or check at the stations for times and prices. July and August see fewer buses, most of which stop at Montignac on the Sarlat-Périgueux route. **Découverte et Loisirs** in Sarlat runs a **minibus tour** to Lascaux and the Thot Museum once per week. (☎05 65 37 19 00 for reservations and schedule. May-Sept. 1 per week. €42 includes admission to the cave.) Renting a **car** in Sarlat is the easiest option, though making the trip by **bike** is possible for those who can handle the endlessly rolling countryside and the steep climb from Montignac to Lascaux. Numerous **campgrounds** dot the Vézère Valley near Montignac; the tourist office has a complete list. Close to the *centre ville* is **Le Moulin du Bluefond,** with 83 spots and a pool (☎05 53 51 83 95. Open Apr.-Oct. €4.45 per person, €5.40 per tent. Electricity €2.80. Prices lower Sept.-June.)

NEAR LES EYZIES-DE-TAYAC

CAVES WITHIN WALKING DISTANCE OF LES-EYZIES. The **Grotte de Font-de-Gaume,** on the D47 1km east of Les Eyzies (10min. by foot), has faded but spectacular 15,000-year-old friezes, completed over the course of hundreds of years. They are quite technically advanced, using the natural contours of the cave for relief. This is the last cave in the Aquitaine basin with polychrome (multi-colored) paintings that is still open to the public. Locals discovered the paintings in the 18th century but did not realize their importance until two centuries later, by which time several murals had decayed or had been defaced by graffiti. Consequently, the most brilliant colors are deep in the cavern. The scene of a black reindeer licking the nose of its kneeling red cousin is amazingly expressive, but the *vôute* (vault), where 12 bison stampede across the ceiling, is the undisputed highlight. The cave can be chilly; visitors should bring an extra layer. (☎05 53 06 86 00; www.leseyzies.com/grottes-ornees. Open daily mid-May to mid-Sept. 9:30am-5:30pm; mid-Sept. to mid-May M-F and Su 9:30am-12:30pm and 2-5:30pm. July-Aug. reserve 4 weeks in advance; Sept.-early June 2 weeks in advance. Cave access is limited to 180 per day, but 50 same-day tickets go on sale at 9:30am every morning. Be sure to be at the door well before 9:30 in high season. €6.10, ages 18-25 €4.10, under 18 free. 1hr. tours available in English.)

The **Grotte des Combarelles,** 2km farther down, has lost its paintings to humidity, but the etchings in the "Lascaux of engravings" are spectacular even without color. Over 600 surprisingly realistic carvings depict a range of species, including donkeys, cave lions, and rhinos. Fifty human figures keep watch from the narrow halls of the cave. Small, six-person tours are more personalized than the larger groups at Font-de-Gaume; the tour guides are wonderfully flexible. Reserve far in advance for the summer, and the ticket office also recommends bringing an extra layer. *(Tickets and reservations ☎05 53 06 86 00. Reservations required. Hours, prices, and website same as Font-de-Gaume. 1hr. tours in French, or in English if the majority of the group speaks English.)*

The **Gorge d'Enfer,** just upstream from Grand Roc and 2km from Les Eyzies, is filled with waterfalls, lagoons, and blooming flora. Inside is the **Abri du Poisson,** a shelter which contains the oldest drawing of a fish in France—a 25,000-year-old, meter-long "beaked" salmon. The rendering is so detailed that the salmon's upturned jaw, a sign of exhaustion after spawning, is distinctly visible. *(☎05 53 06 86 00. Same hours as Font-de-Gaume. Reservations required. €2.50, under 18 free.)*

Using various models and documents, the **Musée Spéléologie,** 24 l'Aegerie, just north of Les Eyzies, explores the region's cave history. Displays include cliff carvings above the Vézère Valley by English soldiers during the Hundred Years' War. *(☎05 53 05 71 74. Open daily 2-6pm. €3, under 16 €1.50, under 10 free.)*

NEARBY NATURAL CAVES. Many nearby caves have fascinating natural sights, especially the ▣**Grotte du Grand Roc,** 1.5km northwest of town along the road to Périgueux. A footpath by the road makes it easy to walk there (10 minutes). Halfway up the chalk cliffs, the cave commands a spectacular view of the valley and Tayac's fortified church. It is filled with millions of stalactites, stalagmites, and *eccentriques*—small calcite accretions that grow neither straight down nor straight up. The most remarkable of these formations are a thin, cross-shaped stalactite and an eroded column that resembles Bigfoot's footprint. The cave is naturally a constant, pleasant 16°C (61°F), though its humidity is an unpleasant 95%. *(☎05 53 06 92 70. Open daily July-Aug. 9:30am-7pm; Apr.-June and Sept.-Oct. 10am-6pm; Feb.-Mar. and Nov. 10am-5pm. Closed early Nov.-Jan., except during Christmas vacation. 30min. tour in French, or in both French and English should there be demand; also written guides in English. €7, children €3.50.)*

CAVES ACCESSIBLE BY CAR OR BIKE. Fifteen kilometers northwest of Les Eyzies in Rouffignac, on the road to Périgueux, **La Grotte de Rouffignac,** or **La Grotte aux Cent Mammouths,** houses 250 engravings and paintings. Etchings of rhinos and horses are interspersed with striking representations of shaggy mammoths. It is one of the longest caves in the area. The guided tour (via train) lasts an hour. *(☎05 53 05 41 71; fax 05 53 35 44 71. Wheelchair-accessible. Open daily July-Aug. 9-11:30am and 2-6pm; late Mar.-June and Sept.-Oct. 10am-11:30am and 2-5pm. €5.80, children €3.60.)*

Only 12 indistinct figures, less detailed than those in Font-de-Gaume, are visible on the sculptured frieze **Abri du Cap-Blanc,** 7km northeast of Eyzies on D48, but they are outstandingly well-preserved. Hunters etched horses, bison, and reindeer onto the thick limestone walls 15,000 years ago. The centerpiece is a 2m long herd of shuffling animals. *(☎05 53 59 21 74; www.leseyzies.com/cap-blanc. Open daily July-Aug. 10am-7pm; Apr.-June and Sept.-Oct. 10am-noon and 2-6pm. Reservations necessary July-Aug. 40min. tours in French with English translations available. €4.80, children €3.50.)*

Northeast of Les Eyzies on route D66, the ▣**Roque St-Christophe** is the most extensive cave dwelling yet discovered. Five floors of limestone terraces with about 100 cave shelters rise 80m and stretch over 400m. From 40,000 BC until the Middle Ages, this fascinating sanctuary served as a defensive fort and housed over 3000 people. A pulley system demonstrates how cave dwellers experimented with civil engineering to move objects into the caves. Visit the 11th-century kitchen and peer over the 60m cliff where Protestants sought shelter from a Catholic army in 1580. A 45min. tour describes the cave's ovens, monastic remains, and military defenses. (☎05 53 50 70 45; www.roque-st-christophe.com. Open daily July-Aug. 10am-7pm; Mar.-Apr. and Oct. 10am-6pm; May-June and Sept. 10am-6:30pm; Nov.-Feb. 11am-5pm. Last entry 45min. before closing. €6, students €5, ages 13-18 €4, ages 5-13 €3.)

DORDOGNE VALLEY

Dramatic cliffs and poplar thickets overlook the lazy waters of the Dordogne, which in the Hundred Years' War provided a natural boundary between France and English Aquitaine. Numerous châteaux, not as regal as those of the Loire, were built here to keep an eye on the enemy.

During the summer, the valley brims with tourists on bikes and in cars, and the river is rarely canoe-less. The fertile area south of Brive abounds with tiny hamlets that have never seen a tour bus. A world away from the area north, its terrain ranges from deep valleys amid rolling hills to towering cliffs of white rock and fields of tall grass. Though renting a car is the wisest option, biking the area is feasible—though expect a good workout. If you rely on trains, make sure your boots are made for walking.

TRANSPORTATION. The valley stretches west from Bergerac, 15km south of Sarlat. Exiting Sarlat, take av. de la Dordogne and, at the roundabout, head southwest on D57 toward Beynac, or south on the less hilly D46 toward Domme. Expect to rent a car or get a good bike workout to explore the area well. **Car** rentals are available in Périgueux, Brive, and Sarlat. For **bikers,** Sarlat is the best starting point. It's about 4-6km between each village, and once out of Sarlat, the bike ride along the Dordogne is fairly level. Most villages are built on hills or cliffs, with the châteaux at the top; the easiest way to see them is to park bikes at the bottom and walk up. Alternatively, Découverte et Loisirs **minibuses** run through the valley several times a week from Sarlat. (☎05 65 37 19 00. €30-44 per person, call for schedule.) Innumerable campgrounds and companies along the river rent **canoes** and **kayaks.** At the Pont de Vitrac, near Domme, try Canoës-Loisirs (☎05 53 28 23 43; www.perigord-insolite.com). Canoës-Dordogne (☎05 53 29 58 50; www.canoe-dordogne.com) and Canoë Vacances (☎05 53 28 17 07) are at La Roque Gageac, with a base also in Cénac, the riverside town below Domme. Tourist offices have schedules and info; prices average €11 per person per half-day, €16 per day. After a course down the river, most companies will pick up customers and return them to the starting point free of charge.

DOMME AND LA ROQUE GAGEAC

Domme (pop. 1000), built by King Philip the Bold in 1280 as a defensive stronghold, can be reached by bike or car on a winding 2.5km ascent from Cérac, which is 10km from Sarlat on the D46. The **tourist office,** pl. de la Halle, sells tickets for the village's attractions, many of which are accessible only on guided tours. (☎05 53 31 71 00. Open daily July-Aug. 10am-7pm; Sept.-June 10am-noon and 2-6pm; phone ahead for Jan. hours.) From pl. de la Halle, a 45min. cave tour descends into the ■Grottes de la Halle. Discovered almost a hundred years ago, this astoundingly beautiful network of caves sits literally underneath the city and brims with stalactites and stalagmites. Animal bones, an underground pool, and a variety of cave environments make for a varied visit. (☎05 53 31 71 00. Cave tours in French with English explanations July-Aug. every 30min. 10:15am-7pm; Apr.-June and Sept. every 45min. 10:15am-noon and 2-6pm; Feb.-Mar. and Oct. every hr. 2-5pm. €6, students €5, children €3.50.) Excellent guided tours in French explore the dilapidated **Porte des Tours**. Seventy Templar Knights were imprisoned there in 1307 and tortured for nearly 20 years by King Philip IV, who wanted the secret of their hidden treasure. The artistic graffiti they scratched into the walls with their teeth, hands, and fingernails remains a combination of idiosyncratic Christian iconography and the Islamic and Jewish motifs encountered by the Templars in the Holy Land. (Tours 1hr. July-Aug. 2-3 per day; Sept.-June 1 per day. €6, students €5, children under 16 €3.50.)

Downstream, **La Roque Gageac** juts out from the base of a sheer cliff. Its steep, twisting streets are lined with medieval stone houses and untraditional vegetation, from bamboos to palm trees. A tour on a **gabare**, a traditional wooden boat, affords a perfect view of the châteaux along the Dordogne. (☎05 53 31 61 94; www.norbet.fr. 1hr.; every 15min. 10am-6pm. English-speaking guides available. €7.20, children €4.20.) The 12th-century **Fort Troglodytique Aérien**, high above La Roque, commands a spectacular view of the Dordogne river valley. Its position made it an ideal defensive structure which withstood all British assaults during the Hundred Years' War. (☎05 53 31 61 94. Open daily July-Aug. 10am-7pm; Apr.-June and Sept. to mid-Nov. M-F and Su 10am-6pm. €4, students €3, ages 10-16 €2.)

The shores of the Dordogne abound with campgrounds, some of which have small dorm-style *gîtes* as well. The tourist office in Sarlat has a complete list, as does the one in Domme.

BRIVE-LA-GAILLARDE

When the courageous citizens of Brive (pop. 50,000) repelled English forces during the Hundred Years' War, they earned their town the nickname, *"la Gaillarde"* (the Bold), an appellation which was reaffirmed when Brive became the first French town to liberate itself from the German occupation in 1944. Unpretentious and untouristed, Brive has engaging museums and a peaceful *centre ville*. The melange of 12th- to 19th-century houses and 1970s highrises creates an unusual cityscape that provides an inexpensive base for exploring the ancient villages in the Quercy region.

⑦ PRACTICAL INFORMATION. Trains depart from av. Jean Jaurès to: Bordeaux (2hr., M-Sa 4 per day, €23.60); Limoges (1hr., 5 per day, €13.60); Sarlat (1hr. including bus from Souillac to Sarlat, 3 per day, €9.60); Toulouse (2½hr., 5 per day, €24.60) via Cahors (1hr., 5 per day, €13.60) and Lyon (6hr., 1 per day, €42.00). (Ticket windows open M-F 4:30am-8:50pm, Sa 5:35am-9pm, Su 6:40am-10:10pm. Info office open M-F 9am-7pm and Sa 9am-6:30pm.) **Buses** stop at the train station and in pl. de Lattre de Tassigny, next to the post office. **STUB** runs public buses in the city (tickets €1, *carnet* of 10 €6.50), **CFTA** to surrounding areas like Collonges-la-Rouge. (Office at pl. du 14 Juillet. ☎05 55 74 20 13. Info desk open M-Sa 8:15am-12:15pm and 2-6:15pm.) **Trans-Périgord** buses (☎05 53 09 24 08) go to Sarlat via Souillac (1½hr., 1 per day, €9). **Taxis** wait at 9 av. Jean Jaurès. (☎05 55 24 24 24. 24hr.) At 52-56 av. Jean Jaurès are **car rental** agencies Hertz (☎05 55 24 26 75; open M-Sa 8am-noon and 2-6:30pm, Sa 9am-noon and 2-6pm) and Avis (☎05 55 24 51 00; open M-F 8am-noon and 2-6pm, Sa 9-11:30am and 2:30-5:30pm). **Bikes** can be rented at Vélo & Oxygen, 26 av. Ribot, 15min. from the *centre ville* (☎05 55 87 27 26; open Tu-Sa 8am-noon and 2-7pm; €7 per half day, €15 per day, €55 cash deposit), and at Sports Bike, 142 av. Georges Pompidou, a 20min. walk down av. Thiers. (☎05 55 17 00 84. MC/V.)

To get to the **tourist office**, pl. du 14 Juillet (☎05 55 24 08 80; www.brive-tourisme.com), from the station, head down av. Jean Jaurès and its continuation to the cathedral and cut diagonally across the *place*. Veer left onto rue Toulzac, which becomes av. de Paris, and cross the large parking lot. The staff provides maps, an English audio sights guide, bus schedules, information on the surrounding region, and

DORDOGNE, PÉRIGORD, AND LIMOUSIN

city tours. (Tours Tu and Th 10:30am, W 9pm; €4. Audioguides €6. Open July-Aug. M-Sa 9am-7pm, Su 10am-1pm; Apr.-June and Sept. M-Sa 9am-12:30pm and 1:30-6:30pm; Oct.-Mar. M-Sa 9am-noon and 2-6pm.) Other services include: **currency exchange** at Banque de France, bd. Général Koenig (☎05 55 92 37 00; open M-F 9:30am-noon); a **laundromat** at Lavarie, 39 rue Dubois (open daily 6:30am-9:30pm); **police** at 4 bd. Anatole France (☎05 55 17 46 00); a **hospital** (☎05 55 92 60 00) at bd. Docteur Verlhac; **Internet** access at Le Mulot, 4 bd. Général Koenig (☎05 55 17 56 26; €2 per hr., 30min. minimum. Open M-Sa 9am-10pm, Su 11:30am-10pm) and at Ax'tion, 33 bd. Général Koenig (☎05 55 17 14 15; €2.30 for 15min., €9 per hr; open M 10:30am-7pm, Tu-Sa 9am-7pm). The **post office**, pl. Winston Churchill, **exchanges currency** with no commission. (☎05 55 18 33 10. Open M-F 8am-6:45pm, Sa 8am-noon.) **Postal Code:** 19100.

⌂ ACCOMMODATIONS. To get to the **Auberge de Jeunesse (HI) ❶**, 56 av. du Maréchal Bugeaud, from the station, walk the length of av. Jean Jaurès, cross the street at the bottom, take rue de l'Hôtel de Ville into the old town, and turn right on rue du Dr. Massenat. Go left onto bd. du Salan, then right on av. du Maréchal Bugeaud (15 minutes). Located in a quiet neighborhood next to the public pool and minutes from the *centre ville*, the hostel boasts small two- to four-bunk rooms with firm mattresses, clean hall bathrooms, and a lovely dining area. Kitchen, TV room, and Internet (€5 per hr.) are also available. (☎05 55 24 34 00; brive@fuaj.org. Breakfast €3.30. Sheets €3.80. Reception M-F 8am-noon and 2-10pm, Sa-Su 8am-noon and 6-10pm. Bunks €9.30. MC/V. HI members only.) Next to the station, **Hôtel de la Gare ❷**, 65 av. Jean Jaurès, provides small, quiet rooms with pastel decor and clean hall showers. (☎05 55 74 14 49. Singles and doubles with sink €19-21, with shower €26; triples €33. MC/V.) The amiable proprietor of **Hôtel Le Chêne Vert ❸**, 24 bd. Jules Ferry, rents spacious rooms with tidy bathrooms, some with balconies. (☎05 55 24 10 07. Singles and doubles with sink €26, with shower €32-35; triples €40-48; quads €50. MC/V.)

❑ FOOD. Regional fare like *foie gras*, duck, walnuts, truffles, apples, and cheese are featured on most menus, and the town's *centre ville* abounds with gourmet food shops. Brive's renowned open-air **market** is at pl. du 14 Juillet and pl. Thiers, just outside the tourist office. (Open Tu, Th, and Sa 8am-noon.) A **Casino supermarket** is in the shopping complex at the intersection of bd. Général Koenig and av. de Paris. (Open M-Sa 8:30am-7:30pm.) Cheap restaurants concentrate around **place Anatole Briand** and the cathedral side of **place Charles de Gaulle.** Elegant, family-run **▧Le Corrèze ❸**, 3 rue de Corrèze, prepares wholesome regional fare at great prices (☎05 55 24 14 07. 2-course *menus* €8.50, 4-course *menus* €11, €15, and €25. MC/V. Open M-Sa noon-2pm and 7-10:15pm.) **La Saladière ❷**, 13 rue de l'Hôtel de Ville, touts such goodies as tomatoes, blue cheese, and hummus. (Salads €5.30-9.30, *menus* €15 and €20, lunch *menu* €9.60. Open M-Sa noon-2pm and 7-10pm. MC/V.) Laid-back, Parisian-style bistro **Chez Francis ❹**, 61 av. de Paris, has a gourmet attitude and walls signed by satisfied customers. (☎05 55 74 41 72. *Plats* €9, *menus* €14-21. Closed M and Su. Reservations required. MC/V.)

◙ SIGHTS. The **▧Musée Labenche**, 26bis bd. Jules Ferry, in the beautiful 16th-century **Hôtel de Labenche**, is a lovely example of southern French Renaissance architecture. The red stone exterior, secluded courtyard, and wide galleries make it one of Brive's most compelling spots, and its collections deserve at least a peek. Combining art, natural history, and interior decorating, exhibits include ancient coins, busts, old accordions, 17th-century English tapestries, and contemporary art. All signs are in French. (☎05 55 92 39 39. Open Apr.-Oct. M and W-Su 10am-6:30pm; Nov.-Mar. 10am-noon and 1:30-6pm. Tours in French €2. Temporary exhibits free. €4.50, students €2.50, under 16 and last Su of the month free.)

From pl. de la République, rue Emile Zola leads to the **Centre National de la Résistance et de la Déportation Edmond Michelet,** 4 rue Champanatier. Take bd. Général Koenig to pl. de la République, turn right on rue Emile Zola, then left on rue Hue, and right onto rue Champanatier. Michelet, a Brive native and Resistance leader, survived internment at the Dachau concentration camp for over a year, then went on to become a minister under de Gaulle. The museum displays photos of women and children on their way to the gas chambers, heartbreaking last letters to loved ones, and other mementos. (☎ 05 55 74 06 08; www.centremichelet.org. Open M-Sa 10am-noon and 2-6pm. Free audioguides available in French and English. Free.)

The unassuming, beautiful 12th-century **Église Collégiale St-Martin,** pl. Charles de Gaulle in the center of town, is named for the iconoclastic Spaniard who introduced Christianity to Brive in the fourth century. Martin was beheaded by angry town members in 407; his sarcophagus rests in the church's crypt.

ENTERTAINMENT AND FESTIVALS. Evenings in Brive are pleasant but fairly calm. **Pub le Watson** livens rue des Echevins with boisterous beer-drinkers on the terrace. (☎ 05 55 17 12 09. Beer €2.50-4. Open Tu-Sa 5pm-2am.) At chilled-out **Brasserie de l'Europe,** 21 av. de Paris, smooth drinks pass the night away. (☎ 05 55 24 19 55. Drinks €3. Open M-Sa 8am-2am. MC/V.) After midnight, 20-somethings fill **La Charette,** across the river at 33 av. Ribot, for tepid techno and disco beats. (☎ 05 55 87 65 73. Cover €9.50, Th-F women free. Open Tu-Sa until 3am.)

Brive and its surrounding villages host a stream of performances all summer long. In mid-August, **Orchestrades Universelles** attracts orchestras, bands, and choirs from all over the world for a celebration of classical, traditional, and jazz music. All performances are free until 9pm on the last evening, when a spectacular gala celebrates 750 young musicians in l'Espace de Trois Provinces. (☎ 05 55 92 39 39. Tickets €3.10-15.30.) During the first weekend in November, pl. du 14 Juillet and Salle Georges Brassens swarm with authors from all over France for the **Foire des Livres** (☎ 05 55 92 39 39). Four times a year from December to February, the streets of Brive host **La Fois Grasses,** a market with the delicacies that make Brive famous: *champignons* (mushrooms), truffles, chocolate, and *foie gras.*

DAYTRIPS FROM BRIVE. Twenty kilometers southeast of Brive, the exquisite, red-rock **Collonges-la-Rouge** makes visitors wonder if the village is real. Cylindrical towers dangle grapevines as pastures and orchards bask in sunlight. There's nothing to do here but peek around, though one look is enough to understand why this village has been ranked one of the most beautiful in France. For those dead-set on visiting sights, the **Maison de la Sirène** displays a beautiful 18th-century painting of a blonde siren. The *maison* also houses a museum of local history that doesn't quite live up to the splendor of the town. The 12th-century church in the town center got a face lift during the religious wars. To get there, take CFTA buses, line #4, which depart from pl. Thiers in Brive (M-F 3 4 per day, Sa 2 per day, fewer buses July-Aug. 7:40am and 12:20pm; one-way €3.10, students under 26 €1.50).

Built dramatically into a steep hillside 15km south of Brive, **Turenne** carries a long legacy of power. In the 13th and 14th centuries, it served as the fortified seat of the region's viscount, who controlled more than 1200 villages in the surrounding territory. In the 17th century, with the wars of religion ravaging the country, Turenne became a bastion of Protestantism, virtually unthreatened. However, the town eventually proved too invincible for its own good; in 1738 Louis XV bought it from its indebted count and, in an assertion of royal power, had the castle largely dismantled. Today, Turenne remains nearly untouched by modernization and retains ample vestiges of its long lasting heyday. Narrow medieval streets wind upward, cutting between flower-draped houses, and at the pinnacle of the hill stands the remains of the **château.** Visitors can tour the fireplace-dominated keep, wander through the garden, and climb the uneven steps of the intact watchtower for an unparalleled view over the region. (Open July-Aug. M-Sa 10am-7pm and Su 2-5pm; daily Sept.-June 10am-noon and 2-6pm. €3.20, under 18 free. Written explanation available in English.) At the base of the town, Turenne's tiny **tourist office** gives out maps, offers guided tours of the city (W and F 9:30am and 5pm, €4), and rents bikes for €10 per day. (☎ 05 55 24 08 80. Open Easter-Oct. Tu-Su 10am-12:30pm and 3-6pm; daily July-Aug. 9am-12:30pm and 3-6:30pm.) Getting from Brive to Turenne can be tricky, since buses run infrequently; ask at the CFTA office at pl. du 14 Juillet for schedules. The better bet is to drive or to bike. From Brive, take av. Alsace-Lorraine (D38), which quickly climbs out of the city. After 10km, at the roundabout, bear right onto D8, which leads directly to Turenne. Paleontology lovers can take a quick detour at the roundabout by following the signs to Gouffre de la Fage, a stalactite-adorned limestone cave. (☎ 05 55 85 80 35; www.gouffre-de-la-fage.com. Open daily July-Aug. 9:30am-1pm and 2-7pm, Sept.-June M-Tu and Th-Su 2-6pm.)

ROCAMADOUR

Trains run from Brive to Rocamadour, stopping at the old train station, 4km from town on rte. N140 (40min.; M-Sa 5 per day 8:50am-7:50pm, Su 3 per day; return M-Sa 8:50am-8:50pm; €11.30). The tourist offices provide schedules and tickets, which can also be purchased onboard. From the station, a flat, winding road leads to the top of town. (45min.) For a taxi call ☎ 05 65 33 63 10 or 05 65 33 73 31.

Tiny Rocamadour (pop. 638) sets itself off from the surrounding countryside as a "verticity," carved into stunningly large chalk cliffs in three sections, one above the other. In the late 12th century, the perfectly preserved body of St-Amadour was unearthed near the town's chapel. St-Amadour was reputed to have been the biblical Zacchaeus, a tax collector who mended his ways after dining with Jesus. As the story grew, so did the miracles, and the town evolved into an important pilgrimage site. Although badly damaged in the turmoil of the Wars of Religion, Rocamadour bounced back to become one of the most beautiful villages in France, replete with holy sites and stunning views. Today, it attracts far more tourists than pilgrims, and its compact architecture makes for crowded summer afternoons; peace-seekers should arrive early.

At the top of the three-tiered city lies the 12th-century **Cité Religieuse,** an enclosed courtyard that encompasses seven chapels, two of which can be visited without a guide. Its nucleus is the **⊠Chapelle Nôtre-Dame,** a silent place of prayer which contains a black model ship that honors shipwreck victims under the watchful eye of the rare 12th-century Black Madonna. (Chapel ☎ 05 65 33 23 23. Cité open daily July-Aug. 9am-6pm and 6:30-10pm; Sept.-June 8am-6pm. Mass daily at 11am.) Under Notre-Dame lies the **Crypte St-Amadour,** where the saint's body rested undisturbed until a Protestant tried to set it ablaze during the Wars of Religion. Though apparently immune to fire, the saint's body could not withstand the assailant's back-up plan—an axe. The remains are preserved next door in the **Musée d'Art Sacré,** alongside paintings, colorful statues, illuminated manuscripts, and other religious art. (☎ 05 65 33 23 30. Open daily July-Aug. 9am-7pm; Sept.-June 10am-noon and 2-6pm. €4.70, students €2.60.) Adjacent to the chapel, the **Basilique St-Sauveur** attracts visitors to its gilt wooden altar. A French-led **tour** takes visitors to the **Crypte St-Amadour** and the **Chapelle St-Michel.** (☎ 05 65 33 62 61. Tours 45min.; 3 per day 10:30am-2:30pm; €5.30, children €3. Open Apr.-Oct. M-Sa 9am-noon and 2-6pm. Free.)

Next to the Cité is the **Chemin de Croix,** which depicts the 14 stations of the cross. The weak-kneed will appreciate the elevator. (☎ 05 65 33 67 79. Elevators operate daily July-Aug. 8am-10pm; May-June and Sept. 8am-7pm; Oct.-Apr. 8:30am-6pm. Round-trip from the lower city to the top of the *chemin* €4;

round-trip from the lower city to the Cité Réligieuse €3.) At the summit is the 14th-century **château,** home to the chaplains of Rocamadour and closed to the public. Walk along the **ramparts** for great views. (☎05 65 33 23 23. Open daily 8am-8pm. €2.60.) A road that runs through the Cité Réligieuse links the château to the lower villages.

The **Grotte des Merveilles,** beside the upper tourist office, is a cave of stalactite formations and remnants of pre-historic paintings. Guided French tours (45min.) point out the paintings. (☎05 65 33 67 92. Open daily July-Aug. 9:30am-7pm; Apr.-June and Sept.-Nov. 10am-noon and 2-6pm. €5, children €3.) Signs from the upper tourist office point the way (300m) to **La Féerie du Rail,** a fantastic fairground with all the traditional attractions made miniature. Every detail down to the last door-knob was constructed by one man over 45,000 hours. Song and dance shows in French with English subtitles (45min.) sell out quickly, so go early. (☎05 65 33 71 06; fax 05 65 33 71 37. Apr.-Sept. 4-9 shows per day; Oct.-Nov. 2 per day 2:45 and 4:15pm. Tickets sold daily mid-July to late Aug. 9am-noon and 2-7pm; late Aug.-early Nov. and Easter to mid-July 10am-noon and 2-6pm. €7, children under 12 €4.50.) The **Rocher des Aigles** shares the plateau with the castle and hosts a 45min. show featuring trained birds of prey. (☎05 65 33 65 45; www.rocherdesaigles.com. Open daily July-Aug. 11am-6pm, 5 shows; Apr.-June and Sept. M-Sa 1-5pm and Su 1-6pm, 3 shows; Oct.-Nov. M-Sa 2-4pm and Su 2-5pm, 1 show at 3pm. €6.50, children under 16 €4.50.)

Separate **tourist offices** serve the cliff's top and bottom. Each has town guides, accommodations booking, maps (€1), and **currency exchange** at nefarious rates. The lower office is in the old Hôtel de Ville, the upper in l'Hospitalet, on rte. de Lacave. (Upper office ☎05 65 33 22 00; fax 05 65 33 22 01. Open Nov.-Mar. M-F 10am-noon and 2-5:30pm; Apr. and Sept.-Oct. M-F 10am-noon and 2-6pm, Sa 2-6pm; daily May-Aug. 10am-12:30pm and 2-6:30pm, without interruption mid-July to Aug. Lower office ☎05 65 33 62 59; www.rocamadour.com. Open Nov.-Mar. 2-5pm; Apr. 10am-12:30pm and 1:30-6pm; May-Aug. 10am-12:30pm and 1:30-6:30pm; Sept-Oct. 10am-noon and 2-5:30pm.) Other services include **police** (☎05 65 33 60 17) and a **post office** near the lower tourist office. (☎05 65 33 62 21. Open M-F 9:30-11:30am and 2-4pm; Apr.-Oct. also Sa 9am-noon.) **Postal Code:** 46500.

LOT VALLEY

The emerald-green Lot Valley snakes from Cahors to Cajarc, sheltering sunflowers and vineyards between steep cliffs. Bus traffic is infrequent, so exploration inevitably involves some hiking—often upwards of 5km. The easiest way to travel the area is by car. The tourist office sells hiking maps (€4.60) of the entire Lot Valley.

CAHORS

Nestled in the crook of the Lot River, Cahors (pop. 20,000) is a budget-friendly base for daytrips to the beautiful villages, vineyards, cliffs, and caves of the Lot Valley. Those who spend a day exploring the town itself, however, will be entranced by its 14th-century Valentré Bridge and medieval quarter.

🖂🔊 TRANSPORTATION AND PRACTICAL INFORMATION. Trains leave from av. Jean Jaurès (info booth open daily 6am-8:30pm) to Brive (1½hr., 10 per day, €13.20); Limoges (2hr., 6 per day, €23.30); Montauban (45min., 10 per day, €8.90); and Toulouse (1½hr., 9 per day, €14.70). Call Allo-Taxi, 742 chemin des Junies (☎05 65 22 19 42), for a **taxi** (24 hours). Rent **cars** at Avis in pl. de la Gare. (☎05 65 30 13 10. Open M-F 8am-noon and 2-6pm; Sa 8am-noon. AmEx/MC/V.)

To get to the **tourist office,** pl. Mitterrand, bear right on av. Jean Jaurès from the station, cross the street, and head up rue Anatole France. At the end of the street, turn left onto rue du Président Wilson, then right onto **boulevard Gambetta,** the main thoroughfare separating the *vieille ville* from the rest of Cahors. The office will be around the corner on the right (15 minutes). The staff books rooms (€0.90) and gives **city tours** in French. (☎05 65 53 20 65; www.mairie-cahors.fr. Call ahead for tour times and for English tour schedule. €5.50. Open July-Aug. M-F 9am-6:30pm, Sa 9am-6pm, Su 10am-1pm; Sept.-June M-Sa 9am-12:30pm and 1:30-6pm.) Bureau Information Jeunesse, in the Foyer des Jeunes, 20 rue Frédéric Suisse, offers **Internet,** European travel planning, and resume assistance. (☎05 65 23 95 90. Internet €0.75 per 15min., free on W and Sa. Open M 2-6pm, Tu-F 9am-noon and 2-6pm, Sa 9am-noon.) Other services include: **currency exchange** and 24hr. **ATMs** at Banque Populaire, 26 bd. Gambetta (☎05 65 23 50 50; Tu-F 8:30am-12:10pm and 1:30-5:40pm, Sa 8:30am-12:20pm); **laundromats** at 208 rue Clemenceau (wash €3.40-6.90, dry €0.30 per 5min.; open daily 7am-9pm), 265 rue Nationale (wash €3.30, dry €1 per 10min.; open daily 7:30am-9:30pm), and Lavomatic, in pl. de la Libération, next to Hôtel aux Perdreaux (wash €3.40-6.40, dry €0.20 per 2min.; open daily 7am-9pm); **police** next to the Musée de la Résistance at pl. Bessières (☎05 65 23 17 17); a **hospital** at 449 rue du Président Wilson (☎05 65 20 50 50); and **Internet** at the youth center Les Docks, 430 allées des Soupirs (☎05 65 22 36 38; €2 per hr; open Tu-Sa 2-6pm, Tu and Th-F also 8-11pm). The **post office,** 257 rue Wilson, has **currency exchange.** (☎05 65 23 35 00. Open M-F 8:30am-6:30pm, Sa 8:30am-noon.) **Postal Code:** 46000.

╔╦╗ ACCOMMODATIONS AND CAMPING. To reach the ▨Foyer des Jeunes Travailleurs Frédéric Suisse (HI) ❶, 20 rue Frédéric Suisse, from the station, bear right onto rue Anatole France (ignore the Auberge de Jeunesse sign) and turn left onto rue Frédéric Suisse (10 minutes). Close to all the sights, this 17th-century building has co-ed dorms, comfortable private rooms, and large multi-room suites. (☎05 65 35 64 71; fax 05 65 35 95 92. Breakfast €3.30, lunch or dinner €8. Sheets €3.30. Reception M-F 10:30am-noon, 2-7:30pm, and 8-10pm, after 10pm for those with reservations; Sa-Su 9am-12:30pm, 1-7:30pm, and 8-10pm, after 10pm for those with reservations. 8- to 12-bunk dorms €9 for members; singles and doubles €9 per person.) To get to Hôtel aux Perdreaux ❸, 137 rue de Portail Alban, from the station, follow rue Joachim to bd. Gambetta. Cross the street to rue Portail Alban (15 minutes). Large, clean rooms have shower and toilet, and some have balconies. (☎05 65 35 03 50. Breakfast €5. Reserve July-Aug. Singles and doubles €28-32. MC/V.) Camping "Rivière de Cabessut" ❶, rue de la Rivière, is a three-star campground near the town center with bar, laundry, pool, athletic facilities, and mini-golf. From pl. de la Libération, take the second left to rue Pelegry, and turn right at rue du Pont Neuf; turn left and continue along the river (35 minutes). Or, take city bus #5 (dir: Terre Rouge) from the station to Stade Lucien Desprats (8min., M-Sa, €0.75) and walk the remaining 10min. along the river. (☎05 65 30 06 30; www.cabessut.com. Open Apr.-Sept. Reception daily 8am-10pm. Reserve ahead in summer. €3 per person, €2 per child, €8 per site. Electricity €2.)

▢ FOOD. Open-air markets liven up pl. Chapou every Wednesday and Saturday (8am-noon). The first and third Saturdays of the month are particularly grand. The smaller **covered market** is just off the square. (Tu-Sa 7:30am-12:30pm and 3-7pm, Su 9am-noon.) **Casino supermarket** is on pl. du Général de Gaulle. (Open July-Aug. M-Sa 9am-12:30pm and 3-7:30pm, Su 9am-12:30pm; Sept.-June closed Su.)

▨Au Coeur du Lot ❷, 71 rue du Château du Roi, offers delicious crêpes and *galettes* in a hidden courtyard and cave cellar rooms. Ask for any concoction in any language: they will translate it into wonderful food. (☎05 65 22 30 67. *Galettes*

€4.80-8, dessert €2.50-6, salad from €3. Open Tu-Sa noon-2pm and 7-10:30pm. MC/V.) Off the beaten path, **Le Mephisto ❸**, 448 rue du Président Wilson, serves hearty food for measly prices. A raucous staff ensures a warm welcome and a fun meal. Pick from salads (€7-11), omelettes (€4.50-6), or four-course *menus* (€9, €12, €15, €18) that include wine and regional duck specialties. (☎ 05 65 53 00 77. Open M-Sa 6:50am-7:30pm, Tu-F until 10:30pm in summer. MC/V.) **Le Lemparo ❸**, 76 rue Clemenceau, serves pizzas (€7.40-9.20), pots full of pasta (€6.80-8.70), and traditional French meat dishes with plenty of crowded outdoor and indoor tables. (☎ 05 65 35 25 93. *Menu* €14.90. Open M-Sa noon-3pm and 7-11pm. MC/V.)

◪ SIGHTS. The monumental 14th-century ▨**Pont Valentré**, credited with staving off invaders during the 1580 Siege of Cahors, is the city's most impressive sight. Legend holds that its architect, dismayed by construction delays, sold his soul to the devil for building materials. When it came time to give the devil his due, the architect killed all the town's roosters to stop them from announcing the dawn; caught unawares, the devil was turned to stone by the sunrise. Look carefully to see the devil clutching a corner of the central tower. Hike 5min. up the trail on the other side of the bridge to spectacular views of the city. 12th-century **Cathédrale St-Etienne**, pl. Chapou, is topped by three Byzantine-like cupolas and decorated with mosaics and wide medieval murals. The cathedral also often hosts classical concerts. (☎ 05 65 35 27 80. Open daily Easter-Oct. 8am-7pm; Oct.-Easter 8:30am-6pm.)

The grim but poignant **Musée de la Résistance, de la Déportation, et de la Libération du Lot,** located in the former Bessières barracks in pl. du Général de Gaulle, catalogues the town of Cahors's role in the fight against the German occupation of France, in part through a series of quite graphic photos. A pamphlet is available in English. (☎ 05 65 22 14 25. Open daily 2-6pm. Free.) In addition to ultra-modern Cahors-themed photography and video art, the **Musée Henri Martin,** 792 rue Emile Zola, displays a small number of modern art exhibits, including classically Pointillist interpretations of Cahors by the Toulouse-born student of Delacroix, Henri Martin. (☎ 05 65 20 88 66. Open M and W-Sa 11am-6pm, Su 2-6pm. €3, ages 7-18 and over 60 €1.50, under 6 free, first Su of the month free.)

▧ FESTIVALS. During the middle of July, Cahors taps its toes to American blues during the **Festival de Blues.** Afternoon and evening blues "appetizers" in coffee shops and bars throughout town are free, as are many of the more formal concerts. (☎ 05 65 35 99 99; www.cahorsbluesfestival.com. Try to purchase tickets in advance.) **Festival de Saint-Céré** features classical music from the end of July through mid-August. (☎ 05 65 38 28 08; www.festival-saint-cere.com.)

ST-CIRQ-LAPOPIE

One of the most beautiful villages in France, as the placard on the road leading to the town attests, tiny St-Cirq-Lapopie (pop. 200), 36km east of Cahors, is built on a cliff ledge, along streets so steep that the roof of one timbered house begins where its neighbor's garden ends. The incredible view from the town's perch recalls St-Cirq's role as a defensive fortress during the 16th century. The entire village of picturesque stone houses dates from the 17th century and is classified as a historical monument, and draws the inevitable hordes of tourists. Escape the crowds at **Château Lapopie,** the highest point in town, which offers an impressive view. The village's cultural center, the ▨**Maison de la Fourdonne,** chronicles St-Cirq's rocky history. (☎/fax 05 65 31 21 51. Guided tours M, W, F 3pm or by advance reservation. Open June-Sept. Tu-Su 10am-noon and 2-7pm; Oct. to mid-Nov. and mid-Mar. to May 10am-noon and 2-6pm; closed mid-Nov. to mid-Mar. €2, students €1.)

To get to St-Cirq-Lapopie by car, follow D653 out of Cahors; turn right onto D662 when you reach Vers. **SNCF buses** run past St-Cirq-Lapopie from Cahors on the way to Figeac (line #10; 45min.; 5 per day, 4 on Su; €4.90). Ask to get out at Tour de Faure. Cross the bridge and hike 2km uphill to the village (30 minutes). The **tourist office,** pl. de Sombral, in the main square, offers self-guided tours in English, French walking tours, and a complete list of hotel vacancies. (☎05 65 31 29 06. Open daily Apr.-June and Sept.-Oct. 10am-1pm and 2:30-6:30pm; July-Aug. 10am-1pm and 2:30-7pm; call ahead for Nov.-Mar. hours.)

The best beds in St-Cirq are at the *gîte d'étape* ◪**La Maison de la Fourdonne ❶,** a restored 16th-century home with a stocked kitchenette and timbered common room. Pine-paneled three- to five-bed rooms all have baths; some have balconies. (☎/fax 05 65 31 21 51. Bring sheets. Reception same as museum hours. Closed mid-Nov. to mid-Mar., but takes reservations. Reservations highly recommended July-Aug. Dorms €11.) **Auberge du Sombral ❹,** in front of the tourist office, has eight elegant rooms with bed-and-breakfast appeal. (☎05 65 31 26 08; fax 05 65 30 26 08. Breakfast €7.20. Singles with shower €50; doubles with shower €65, with bath €72. MC/V.) Between the town and the bus stop, the riverside ◪**Camping de la Plage ❶** is close to hiking, swimming, and kayaking sites. (☎05 65 30 29 51; camping.laplage@wanadoo.fr. €5 per person. July-Aug. €6 per site; Sept.-June €5 per site. Electricity €3-4. Bungalows available, call for prices. MC/V.) Kalapca Loisirs offers **kayak rental** and books two- to six-day trips with camping or *gîte d'étape* packages with advanced reservation. (☎05 65 30 29 51; www.kalapca.com. Canoe €5 per hr. Kayak €7 per hr. MC/V.) For a good meal, try **L'Atelier,** just before the village on the main road into town. Food is served in a shaded courtyard with a great view of the valley. (☎05 65 31 22 34. Open M and Th-Su noon-3pm and 7-10pm, Tu noon-3pm. Closed Jan.)

A few kilometers past St-Cirq-Lapopie, on the road from Cahors, is the turn-off for D653 and the **Grotte du Pech-Merle,** one of the best-preserved pre-historic caves open to the public. Unfortunately, as the nearest bus stop is 7km away in Bouzies, you'll need a cab or some form of private transportation to reach the cave. Discovered by local teenagers in 1922, the 4km gallery contains paintings between 18,000 and 30,000 years old. Bring a jacket. Reserve one week ahead June through August. English pamphlets are available. (*Grotte* ☎05 65 31 27 05; www.pech-merle.com. Both museum and *grotte* open daily early Apr.-early Nov. 9:30am-noon and 1:30-5pm. Visits last 1½hr. Tours in French July-Aug. every 30min. Mid-June to mid-Sept. Admission to *grotte* and museum €7, children €4.50; in low season €6, children €3.80.) *Gîtes d'étape* and campgrounds line the road to Pech-Merle.

POITOU-CHARENTES

After adopting Christianity in the fourth century, Poitou-Charentes emerged as an influential political and religious center. The eighth century saw Charles "the Hammer" Martel fend off Moorish attempts to conquer the region, only to have the British rule it for 300 years, starting with Eleanor of Aquitaine's marriage to England's Henry II in the 12th century. In the 17th century, Cardinal Richelieu attacked the Protestant stronghold of La Rochelle, thereby relegating it to a century of obscurity until trade with the New World finally restored it to prosperity. The region now quietly busies itself with fishing, sunbathing, and drinking the region's excellent wine.

Poitou-Charentes could be France's best-kept secret. Distinctly influenced by its proximity to the Atlantic Ocean, it is a brilliant collage of coastal fishing towns, pristine wetland preserves, and the wilds of its countless islands. Though rich in history, with medieval towns and countless châteaux, the region also offers distinctly modern diversions at the technologically advanced Futuroscope theme park (p. 517) or in Angoulême (p. 519), French capital of comic books.

HIGHLIGHTS OF POITOU-CHARENTES

STUFF YOURSELF with boatloads of seafood in coastal **La Rochelle** (p. 535), where locals aren't stingy with their *fruits de mer.* Work it all off with a hike around the wilds of nearby Île d'Aix (p. 542) or take a nap on a pristine beach.

MARVEL at the region's unique natural beauty as you set off in a canoe from picturesque **Coulon** (p. 545) into the wetlands preserve of the **Marais Poitevin** (p. 543).

EXPLORE the great cathedrals of **Poitiers** (p. 511), where churches bear the marks of over 1000 years of French history and provide ample opportunities for confession after enjoying this university's town vivacious nightlife.

POITIERS

The many renowned churches of Poitiers (pop. 83,000) stand as a testament to the power of the Catholic Church here during the early Middle Ages. It was here that Clovis won one for Christianity by defeating the Visigoths in AD 507 and Charles Martel repulsed the Moors in AD 732. In 1432, when Poitiers was still the capital of France, Charles VII founded the Université de Poitiers. Today, this city is now a business-oriented metropolis, with nightlife and cultural events that complement the peace and tranquility that characterize the surrounding region.

▊ TRANSPORTATION

Trains: bd. du Grand Cerf. Ticket/Information office open M-Sa 6am-10pm, Su 7am-10:20pm. To: **Bordeaux** (2hr., 17 per day, €27); **La Rochelle** (1¾hr., 8 per day, €18.10); **Paris** (2hr., 6 per day, €44.10); **Tours** (45min., 5 per day, €13.10).

Public Transportation: R.T.P., 6 rue du Chaudron-d'Or (☎05 49 44 77 00 or 05 49 44 66 88). Open mid-Aug. to mid-July M-F 9:30am-12:30pm and 1:30-6:30pm; Jul. 14-Aug. 15 M-F 1:30-6:30pm. Buses criss-cross the city during the day and are replaced by night buses late in the evening. One night bus (line #2) runs around the *centre ville* and to the University of Poitiers' campus. Timetables are at the tourist office and train station. Tickets valid 1hr. €1.20, *carnet* of 5 (available only at *tabacs*) €4.

Taxis: Radio Taxis, 22 rue Carnot (☎05 49 88 12 34). €10-11 to hostel. Phone operator 24hr. Office open M-F 7:30am-7pm and Sa 9am-noon, 2-6pm; school vacations 9am-6pm.

Car Rental: ADA, 19 bd. du Grand Cerf (☎05 49 50 30 20). From €45 per day. Open M-Sa 8am-6pm. MC/V. **Europcar,** 48 bd. du Grand Cerf (☎05 49 58 25 34). Open M-F 8am-noon and 2-6pm, Sa 8am-noon. AmEx/MC/V. **Avis,** 135 bd. du Grand Cerf (☎05 49 58 13 00). Open M-F 8am-7pm, Sa 8am-noon and 2-5pm. AmEx/DC/MC/V.

Bike Rental: Atelier Cyclaman, 60bis bd. Pont Achard (☎05 49 88 13 25). €9.10 per half-day, €14 per day. ID deposit. Open Tu-Sa 9am-12:30pm and 3-7pm.

■✻ ⓘ ORIENTATION AND PRACTICAL INFORMATION

Poitiers centers around **pl. Maréchal Leclerc, pl. Charles de Gaulle,** and the res-taurant- and shop-filled streets in between. Buses run from opposite the train station to the **Hôtel de Ville,** pl. Maréchal Leclerc. The *centre ville* is bordered by the Le Clain and La Boivre rivers; parks dot the city's outskirts. *Poitiers et ses environs à pied et à VTT*, available from the tourist office, has hiking and biking trail maps.

Tourist Office: 45 pl. Charles de Gaulle (☎05 49 41 21 24; fax 05 49 88 65 84). Well-labeled maps and lists of hotels and campgrounds. Ask for the brochure *Laissez-vous conter Poitiers.* Excellent free walking guide with 3 different circuits around the city available in English. Hotel reservations free. City tours in French (1½hr.) July-Sept. at 11am and 3pm, each covering different monuments and neighborhoods; English tours Sa afternoons (€5.40, under 25 €3). Open June 21-Sept. 21 M-Sa 10am-7pm, Su 10am-6pm; Sept. 22-June 20 M-Sa 10am-6pm.

Currency Exchange: Caisse d'Epargne, 7 rue Victor Hugo (☎05 49 60 65 56), has **ATMs** and **currency exchange** services. Open Tu-F 9am-12:15pm and 1:30-5:45pm, Sa 9am-12:45pm.

English-Language Bookstore: Librairie de l'Université, 70 rue Gambetta (☎05 49 41 02 05), off pl. M. Leclerc. Wide selection of 20th-century classics, popular fiction, and a bit of Chaucer and Shakespeare. Open M-Sa 9am-7:30pm. AmEx/DC/MC/V.

Youth Information: Centre Regionale Information Jeunesse (CRIJ), 64 rue Gambetta (☎05 49 60 68 68), near pl. M. Leclerc. Help with jobs, lodging, budget travel, and activity planning. Internet for students €0.80 per 30 min., €1.50 per hr. Open M-F 10am-1pm and 2-6pm; Internet only M, Tu, Th 2-6pm.

Laundromat: 2bis rue de la Tranchée. Open daily 7am-8:30pm.

Police: 38 rue de la Marne (☎05 49 60 60 00).

Hospital: 350 av. Jacques Caire (☎05 49 44 44 44), on the road to Limoges.

Internet Access: at the **CRIJ** (see **Youth information**). **Cybercafé LRM,** 71 Grande Rue (☎05 49 39 51 87). €6 per hr., with student ID €4. Open M 10am-8pm, Tu-F 10am-10pm, Sa 10:30am-8pm, Su 4-7pm.

Post Office: 16 rue Arthur Ranc (☎05 49 55 50 00). **Currency exchange** with no com-mission. Open M-F 8:30am-7pm, Sa 8:30am-noon.

Postal Code: 86000.

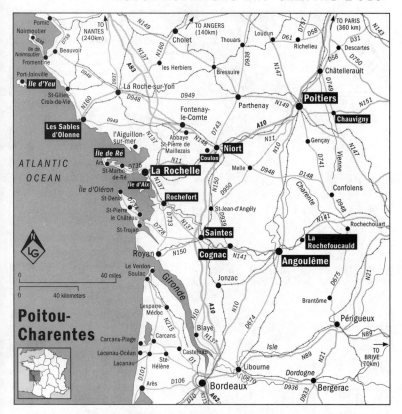

Poitou-Charentes

▊▊ ACCOMMODATIONS AND CAMPING

The hostel and campgrounds are far from town, but cheap, respectable hotels in the city center and near the train station are reasonable alternatives.

▧ **Hôtel de l'Europe,** 39 rue Carnot (☎05 49 88 12 00). Sophisticated, spacious rooms with dark wood furnishings face a large inner courtyard or a garden in the back. Breakfast €6.70. Singles and doubles with bath in old wing €48-55; singles, doubles, and triples in fancier new wing €66-85. AmEx/MC/V. ❹

Auberge de Jeunesse (HI), 1 allée Tagault (☎05 49 30 09 70; fax 05 49 30 09 79). Turn right at the train station and follow bd. du Pont Achard to av. de la Libération. At the fork, take a right onto rue B. Pascal, then right onto rue de la Jeunesse and left onto allée Tagault. The hostel will be ahead on the left. (35min.) Or, take bus #7 (dir: Pierre Loti) to Cap Sud from the stop to the right of the train station (M-Sa every 30min. until 7:50pm, €1.20). Family-oriented, clean hostel with modest communal facilities, a stocked kitchenette, pool table, Internet, bike rental, and proximity to local stores. A large grassy area is a favorite for picnicking, soccer, and volleyball games. Breakfast €2.30, lunch and dinner €8.60. Sheets €2.70. Reception M-F 7am-noon and 4-11pm, Sa-Su 7am-noon and 6-11pm. Bunks in 4-bed rooms €9.30. Tents and groundpad available for camping in backyard €5.60. Members only. MC/V. ❶

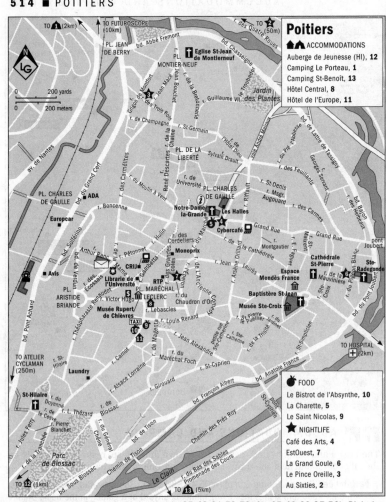

Poitiers

⌂⌂ ACCOMMODATIONS
Auberge de Jeunesse (HI), **12**
Camping Le Porteau, **1**
Camping St-Benoît, **13**
Hôtel Central, **8**
Hôtel de l'Europe, **11**

🍅 FOOD
Le Bistrot de l'Absynthe, **10**
La Charette, **5**
Le Saint Nicolas, **9**

★ NIGHTLIFE
Café des Arts, **4**
EstOuest, **7**
La Grand Goule, **6**
Le Pince Oreille, **3**
Au Sixties, **2**

Hotel Central, 35 pl. du M. Leclerc (☎05 49 01 79 79; fax 05 49 60 27 56). Right in the center of Poitiers, this well-equipped hotel offers a cheaper alternative to the usually pricey luxury hotels in the city. All rooms with TV, telephone. Breakfast €6. Single room with shower €32, with toilet and shower €41, with toilet, shower and bathtub €45; doubles €35/€45/€49. Add €10 for an extra bed. MC/V. ❸

Camping:

Le Porteau, rue de Porteau (☎05 49 41 44 88), 2km from town. Take bus #7 from near the station (dir: Centre de Gros; 7:15am-7:20pm, €1.20) to Porteau. Tiny, rocky field encircled by roads. Reception daily 7am-10pm. Open July-Aug. 2-person site €7.60, extra person €2.40. Electricity €1.60-2.40. ❶

Camping St-Benoit, rte. de Passelourdin (☎05 49 88 48 55), 5km from Poitiers. Slightly better than Le Porteau (there's grass), but hard to reach by public transportation. From the station, take bus #2, 3, 6, 8, 7, 9, or 11 to Hôtel de Ville. Walk to the bus stop at the corner of rue Carnot and pl. Maréchal Leclerc and take bus #5 (dir: La Varenne; 9:30am-7:20pm) to Rue du Clain. Cross the Rocade Sud-Est and follow rte. de Passelourdin for 1km until reaching the campground. Or take a taxi from the train station (€16-20). Reception M-F 7:30am-10pm, Sa-Su 8:30am-2pm and 6-10pm. Open July-Aug. 2-person site €7.60, extra person €1.60. Electricity €1.70-2.40. ❶

▐ FOOD

In Poitiers, it's easy to find local specialties including chèvre, macaroons, the wines of Haut-Poitou, or lamb from nearby Montmarillon. The problem is finding a budget-friendly *menu*—most hover around €15-30. Many hotel bars post adequate three-course *menus* for €10.50-15, and inexpensive pizzerias line the pedestrian streets between pl. Leclerc and Notre-Dame-la-Grande. There is a **market** at **Les Halles**, pl. Charles de Gaulle, which expands to epic proportions on Saturdays (open M-Sa 7am-1pm) and a **Monoprix** supermarket at Île des Cordeliers on rue des Grandes Écoles (open M-F 9am-9pm, Sa 9am-8pm). Hidden in a back alley lined with bamboo plants and ivy, **Le Saint Nicolas** ❸, 7 rue Carnot, prepares delicious French cuisine in the local market. An attentive host and an inventive menu make for a great meal (☎ 05 49 41 44 48. *Menus* €14.80 or €18.60, *plats* from €7.40. Open M-Tu and Th-Su noon-2pm and 7:30pm-10pm. MC/V.) Those on a slightly tighter budget should try **La Charette** ❷, 15 rue du Marché, a *crêperie* bustling with patrons sitting outside across from Notre Dame-la-Grande. (☎ 05 49 41 03 26. Specialty *galettes* €9.15. Open Tu-Sa noon-2pm and 7-10:15pm. MC/V.) For a formal meal, the elegant **Le Bistrot de l'Absynthe** ❸, 6 rue Carnot, serves upscale French favorites like *escargot, cuisses de grenouille* (frog legs), and absinthe, either straight-up or on a sundae. The chefs go for very creative combinations, such as an appetizer pairing coffee and almonds. (☎ 05 46 28 37 44. *Plats* €11.50, lunch *menu* €8.50, 3-course *menu* €20, absinthe €3.80. Open M-F noon-2pm and 7:30-10pm, Sa 7:30-10pm. MC/V.)

◉ SIGHTS

Poitiers's churches, by far the city's most impressive attractions, date from France's conversion to Catholicism in the 4th century. (All open daily 9am-6pm. Free.) Many hold organ concerts in July and August; check the *Guide des Manifestations* or call *Les Nuits en Musique* (☎ 05 49 41 21 24) or *Les Concerts du Marché* (☎ 05 49 41 34 18) for schedules. In addition to the churches, Poitiers's Renaissance buildings make it an excellent place to wander.

▓ **CATHÉDRALE ST-PIERRE.** In 1162, the construction of the cavernous St-Pierre was funded by Eleanor of Aquitaine and her husband King Henry II Plantagenêt, who lived in the current Palais de Justice. During two hundred years of construction, builders remained faithful to the original plan, constructing a uniformly 12th-century Angevin Gothic cathedral. The church's Cliquot organ (1787-1791) is one of only two extant that predate the Revolution, and its central stained-glass window contains one of France's oldest crucifixion scenes. The interior extends in a seeming eternity of light, space, and clean lines. A careful examination of the columns and the junctions of the wall and the ceiling will reveal 267 of the church's original carvings of people and animals. *(Pl. de la Cathédrale, off rue de la Cathédrale.)*

▓ **PARC DE BLOSSAC.** This classic 18th-century French-and-English-style garden is one of the most beautiful in the region. The park's borders afford spectacular views of the town and valley below. Immaculately tended lawns and trees line scenic walkways, making the park an ideal place to picnic after a busy day. A small but noisy zoological garden houses various birds and Asian mountain goats. *(Rue de Blossac, down rue Carnot, near the river Clain. Open daily Apr.-Sept. 7am-10:30pm; Oct.-Mar. 7am-9:30pm. Jardin Anglais open daily Apr.-Sept. 7am-8pm; Oct.-Mar. 8am-sundown.)*

NOTRE-DAME-LA-GRANDE. Though small, this is one of France's most important Romanesque churches. A scant amount of light filters beautifully through small stained-glass windows, illuminating a vast array of paintings in an otherwise windowless nave. Inside, an original fresco on the choir ceiling depicts Christ in Glory, the Virgin and Child, and the Lamb of God in a cruciform. The rest of the interior has been restored in a different style. During the summer, a not-to-be-missed **☀light show** *(son-et-lumière)* projects the original polychrome detail onto the facade, reviving the splendor of the original colors and details. *(Pl. de Gaulle, off Grande Rue. Projections daily June 21-Sept. 1 10:30pm; early-to mid-Sept. 9:30pm.)*

ÉGLISE STE-RADEGONDE. The church's belltower porch was built atop the ravaged foundations of a 6th-century chapel erected by Saint Radegonde, a Thuringian princess who fled to the church when she was forced to marry a brutish Frankish prince. She later established the first female convent in Gaul. Although its exterior is now nearly in ruins, the church's interior holds the tomb of Radegonde. In AD 587, Christ appeared to Radegonde on this site and foretold her imminent death, calling her "one of the most precious diamonds in His crown." He left a footprint in the stone floor before vanishing, providing the doomed nun with proof for her story and the abbey with centuries of pilgrims and tourist allure. Today the outside of the church is slightly worn, but the frescoes near the altar are still impressive. *(Off rue de la Mauvinière, down the street from the cathedral.)*

BAPTISTÈRE ST-JEAN. This fourth-century baptistry is the oldest Christian structure in France. Today, the Baptistère is now a museum filled with Roman, Merovingian, and Carolingian sarcophagi and capitals, which were kept by the earliest Christians when they destroyed Poitiers's Roman baths, arches, and amphitheater. The interior still contains a fourth-century octagonal baptismal pool surrounded by 12th-century Romanesque frescoes. *(Rue Jean Jaurès, near the cathedral. Open daily July-Aug. 10:30am-12:30pm and 3-6pm; Apr.-June and Sept. Su-M and W-Sa 10:30am-12:30pm and 3-6pm; Oct.-Mar. Su-M and W-Sa 2:30-4:30pm. €1, under 12 and groups €0.50.)*

MUSÉE STE-CROIX. This eclectic museum spans four millennia, displaying everything from pre-historic artifacts to Roman coins, medieval sepulchres, and a permanent collection of art which dates back to the Renaissance. Hidden in the basement is a Roman excavation site with the original walls and foundations of ancient homes. The museum also frequently rotates modern art exhibits, and admission includes Musée Rupert de Chièvres. *(3bis rue Jean-Jaurès. ☎ 05 49 41 07 53. Open June-Sept. M 1:15-6pm, Tu 10am-noon and 1:15-8pm, W-F 10am-noon and 1:15-6pm, Sa-Su 10am-noon and 2-6pm; Oct.-May M 1:15-5pm, Tu 10am-5pm, W-F 10am-noon and 1:15-5pm, Sa-Su 2-6pm. €3.60, students and under 18 free; Tu and the 1st Su of each month free. Guided tours in French on Tu.)*

ÉGLISE ST-JEAN DE MONTIERNEUF. This magnificent church lies away from the center of Poitiers and is often overlooked. This church was built by William VIII, Count of Poitou, known best for a victory of the Saracens in Spain in 1063. The result is an enormous Gothic church with some of the most striking stained-glass windows and paintings in the city. *(Off Pl. Montier-Neuf.)*

OTHER SIGHTS. The **Musée Rupert de Chièvres** displays a collection of Dutch, Flemish, and Italian paintings, many by anonymous artists, and scientific antiquities like the earliest Diderot encyclopedia. *(9 rue Victor Hugo. ☎ 05 49 41 07 53. Open June-Sept. M-F 10am-noon and 1:15-6pm, Sa-Su 10am-noon and 2:15-6pm, Oct.-May M-F 10am-noon and 1:15-5pm, Sa-Su 2-6pm. €3.50; students, under 18 free; free Tu and the 1st Su of each month, and June-Sept. Th 6-9pm. Admission includes Musée Ste-Croix. Guided tours in French once weekly, €1.50-3.50. Schedule varies; call for more information.)*

🎵 🎭 ENTERTAINMENT AND NIGHTLIFE

Nightlife in Poitiers is livelier than its size would suggest, particularly during the school year. Locals and students frequent the pubs and restaurants along the side-streets of pl. Leclerc. Pick up the booklet *Café-Concerts, Bars avec Animations* at the tourist office for more info.

The **Festival du Cinéma** in March draws film students from international schools for independent and mainstream offerings. Throughout July and August, rock, opera, jazz, and fireworks thunder through town during the **Places à l'Eté** festival. Concerts, mostly free, begin around 9pm three nights per week. A relatively new summer tradition, **La Nuit des Orgues**, organizes a series of mostly free organ performances in local churches from May to October. Contact the tourist office for tickets and details. In late August and early September, a more formal organ festival, **Voix Orgues**, hosts organ players from all over the region. (Call ☎ 05 49 47 13 61 for more info. Tickets €9-15; book in advance.) *Le guide des manifestations*, free at the tourist office, lists all the concerts and shows in the city.

EstOuest, 10 rue l'Eperon (☎ 05 49 41 13 36; www.estouest.net), is a lively pub with an extensive beer list, pool tables, and karaoke with popular French and American tunes. A steady flow of customers cheers on many a boisterous rendition of "I Will Survive." Karaoke every night, and whenever else desired. Beer from €2.10. Open M-F 11am-2am, Sa 3pm-2am. MC/V.

Café des Arts, 5 pl. Charles de Gaulle (☎ 05 49 41 14 61), attracts trendy students and couples to its relaxed environment. Patrons people-watch from the bar, with jazz music in the background and a rum punch in hand. Punch €1.90, drinks €1.90-4.75. Teas also served. Open M-Sa 8:30am-2am.

Le Pince Oreille, 11 rue des Trois Rois (☎ 05 49 60 25 99), puts its stage to good use, hosting jazz bands, stand-up comedy, and jam-sessions for any musician with the guts to play. Armchairs and painted walls create a welcoming, though dimly lit, atmosphere for a predominantly student crowd. Concerts Th-Sa (€6); free jam-sessions every Tu and W. The bar opens select at 5:30pm for a "philosophical cabaret" discussion. Drinks from €2.30. Open Tu-Th 5pm-2am, F 5pm-3am, Sa 9pm-3am.

La Grand Goule, 46 rue du Pigeon Blanc (☎ 05 49 50 41 36; www.lagoule.fr). Poitiers's most popular nightclub pumps house beats beneath the stately Église Ste-Radegonde, packing in teens early on and an older crowd later in the evening. Cover from €4; no cover for women before midnight, nor for women or students M-Tu and Su. Drinks from €2. Open daily 11pm-4am.

Au Sixties, 1 rue des Quatres Roues (☎ 05 49 52 19 44), is a gay dance club that draws a mix of people. It hosts art exhibits for up-and-coming artists several times a year. Glitzy cabaret shows the 1st Su of every month. Drinks €5-8. Cover varies. Open Tu-Su 10:30pm-2am.

▶ DAYTRIPS FROM POITIERS

FUTUROSCOPE

10km north of Poitiers, near Chasseneuil. ☎ 05 49 49 30 80; www.futuroscope.com. Take bus #9 (20min; M-F every 20min., Sa every 30min., Su only 3 departures) from Poitiers's Hôtel de Ville or across the street from the train station, in front of the Printania Bar-Hôtel. Schedules are subject to change. For info, contact RTP, 6 rue du Chaudron d'Or (☎ 05 49 44 66 88) or the tourist office. Buy tickets from the bus driver. Get off at Parc de Loisirs and follow directions to the park entrance. By car, follow A10 (dir: Paris-Châtellerault) to exit 28. The park is also accessible by TGV from Bordeaux (1½hr., 1-2 per day, €35) and Paris (80min., 2-3 per day, €37.50). Open Apr.-mid-Nov.; hours vary, consult the website or the tourist office in Poitiers. €30, children €22; low season €21/€16. All main attractions are included in the price, but the video games on Cyber Avenue require additional tokens.

The Futuroscope amusement park is a slick collection of high-tech film theaters including spherical and hemispherical screens, virtual reality, high-definition 3-D simulation rides, and the occasional straight-up film experience. A whole building is dedicated to the latest video games. A headset obtained in the Maison de Vienne near the entrance provides the English translation for many films. Those enticed by the late-night laser show will miss the last bus to Poitiers, but hotels and restaurants surround the park.

CHAUVIGNY

SNCF buses leave Poitiers for Chauvigny from outside the station (dir: Châteauroux; 30min.; 5 per day, Su at 4:20 and 8:50pm only; €4.40). Buy tickets in the SNCF train station in Poitiers, on board for return. The bus will stop at pl. de la Poste in the center of modern-day Chauvigny. The cité médiévale, encompassing all the castle ruins, lies up on the hill. To get there, walk back on rue du Marché in the direction the bus came from. At the end of pl. du Marché, turn right onto rue de Châtellerault. At the end of rue de Châtellerault, turn right onto bd. des Châteaux, which will run to the cité médiévale. The tourist office is on rue St-Pierre, a left off of bd. des Châteaux. (☎/fax 05 49 46 39 01. Open daily July-Aug. 10am-1pm and 2-7pm; June, Sept. Tu-Su 10:30am-12:30pm and 2-6:30pm; Oct.-Mar. Tu-F 2-6pm; Apr.-May W-Su 2-6pm. Tours July-Aug. M and W-Su 2:30pm and 4:15pm; €3.10, students €1.60. Call ☎ 05 49 46 35 45 in advance for English tours.)

Chauvigny, 23km from Poitiers, was conquered four times during the Hundred Years' War, razed during the Wars of Religion, and shelled by the retreating German army in 1944. Today the beautiful town's tiny medieval citadel and pretty, restaurant-lined walkways around the tranquil pl. du Donjon make a worthwhile half-day escape from bustling Poitiers.

Five ruined 11th- to 15th-century châteaux create Chauvigny's striking skyline. Among these, the 12th-century **Église St-Pierre** is known for its choir capitals, which are engraved with dragons, vultures, and images of Satan. The ultra-modern **Espace d'Archéologie Industrielle,** nestled under a glass ceiling in the ruins of the Gouzon keep, showcases regional quarrying, porcelain-firing, milling, and steam-engine activity. The museum's glass elevator affords a cool view of the city and countryside below. (☎ 05 49 46 35 45. Open daily June 15-Aug. 31 M-F 10am-12:30pm and 2:30-6:30pm, Sa 2:30-6:30pm, Su 11am-6:30pm; Apr. 1-June 15 and Sept.-Oct. 2-6pm; Nov.-Mar. Sa-Su 2-6pm. €4.60, students €3.05, under 14 free. Tours in French July-Aug. Su-M and W-Sa 4:15pm.) The crumbling walls of **Les Géants du Ciel** (☎ 05 49 46 47 48; fax 05 49 44 10 45), once home to Chauvigny's bishops, now host 60 eagles, falcons, vultures, owls, buzzards, storks, parrots, and countless other winged species. The squeamish should avoid the dark room of *chauves* (bats) that fly unrestrained among visitors. The highlight is a bird show in which the flock swoops over the city just above the heads of the audience. (Open daily Apr. to early Nov. Shows daily July-Aug. at 11:15am, 2:30, 4, 5:30pm; Apr.-June and Sept.-Nov. at 2:30 and 4pm, with additional shows Sa-Su at 11:15am and 5:30pm. €8.50, students €5.50; ruins €3 if no show.)

For a truly unique glimpse of the countryside, take a ride on the **Vélo-Rails,** 10 rue de la Folie. These rail contraptions, powered by pedaling, take passengers along the viaduct that traverses the Vienne River on a 17km loop around the Chauvigny valley. Reservations must be made at least one day in advance. (☎ 05 49 41 08 28. To get there from pl. de la Poste, walk down rue du Marché, cross the Vienne River and continue straight as the road becomes rue de Poitiers. After reaching rue de la Verrerie, turn right, then left onto rue de la Folie. Open daily July-Aug. 10am-9pm; Sept. and May-June 2-7pm; 2hr. ride €21.50.)

From June to October, the **Festival d'Eté** (☎05 49 45 99 10) fills the city with (occasionally free) jazz, dance, and theater performances. Purchase tickets in advance at the tourist office.

ANGOULÊME

A gem unblemished by tourist hordes, Angoulême (pop. 46,000) sits high on a plateau and affords a magnificent view of the Charente River. The cradle of the French paper industry in the 1600s, the town and its ready supply of writing pads brought Jean Calvin here in 1534. Wood pulp is no less an obsession today, for Angoulême reigns supreme as the capital of French comic strip production; countless Lucky Luke and Astérix volumes roll off the town's presses each year. The fixation even permeates the cityscape, where visible sides of buildings are decorated with swaths of cartoons, incorporating elements of reality—windows for example—into the world of fantasy. In addition to the town's attractions for the comic-obsessed, the winding hilly streets of the *vieille ville* are filled with hip and crowded bars and cafes, attracting young and old alike.

▐ TRANSPORTATION

Trains: pl. de la Gare. Info office open M-F 9:30am-7pm, Sa 9:30am-6pm, ticket windows open M-Th 5:15am-8:50pm, F 5:15am-9:20pm, Sa 6:40am-8pm, Su 7:10am-9:30pm. To: **Bordeaux** (1hr.; 10 per day; €17, €18.70 TGV); **Paris** (2½hr., 7 per day, €52.80); **Poitiers** (45min.; 5 per day; €14.70, €16.40 TGV); **Saintes** (1hr., 10 per day, €10.60).

Buses: Autobus Citram goes to **Cognac** (1hr., 8 per day, €6.95) and **La Rochelle** (3hr., 2 per day, €16.35). Buses stop at pl. du Champ de Mars. Buy tickets on board. Info at the **Cartrans** office, pl. du Champ de Mars (☎05 45 95 95 99). Open mid-July to mid-Aug. M-F 2-6:15pm; mid-Aug. to mid-July M-F 9:15am-12:15pm and 2-6:15pm. **CFTA Périgord** (☎05 53 08 43 13) goes from the train station to **Périgueux** (1½hr.; 1 per day M, F, Su, and every 2nd Th of the month; €12.70).

Public Transportation: STGA office, in a kiosk on pl. du Champ de Mars. Maps available. Open 7th-27th of each month M-F 1-6pm, Sa 9am-12:30pm; 1st-6th and 28th-31st of each month M-Sa 8:30am-6pm. Tickets €1.20, *carnet* of 10 €8.40, 1-week pass €10.10. Buses run M-Sa 6am-8pm and are a good way to get to many of the museums on the edge of town.

Taxis: Radio Taxi (☎05 45 95 55 55), in front of train station. Meter base €2.24; €1.24 per km during day, €2.84 per km at night. €7-8 to Auberge de Jeunesse. 24hr.

Car Rental: Ada, 19 pl. de la Gare (☎05 45 92 65 29), right across from the train station, rents cars from €45 per day. Open M-Sa 8am-noon and 2-7pm. **Europcar** a few doors down at 15 pl. de la Gare (☎05 45 92 02 02), has a 10% student discount. Rates from €41.50 per day. 21+. Can be returned at other locations. Open M-F 8am-noon and 2-7pm, Sa 8am-noon and 2-6pm. AmEx/MC/V.

▌ ▐ ORIENTATION AND PRACTICAL INFORMATION

The *vieille ville* sits among the ramparts just south of the Charente and southwest of the train station. It is easy to get lost in its maze of streets; grab a map from the tourist office kiosk outside the station.

Tourist Office: 7bis rue du Chat, pl. des Halles (☎05 45 95 16 84; fax 05 45 95 91 76). Provides indispensable info on restaurants, hotels, museums, and outdoor activities; available only in French, though a few English paragraphs describe the *vieille ville*. To get to the main

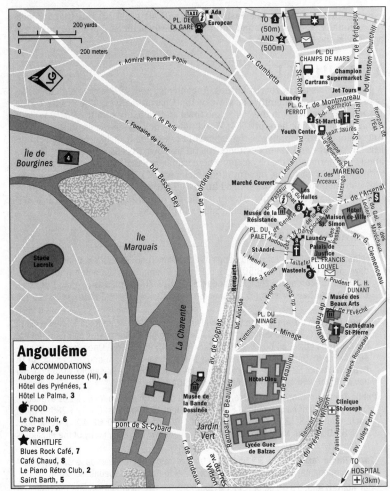

Angoulême

🔺 **ACCOMMODATIONS**
Auberge de Jeunesse (HI), **4**
Hôtel des Pyrénées, **1**
Hôtel Le Palma, **3**

🍴 **FOOD**
Le Chat Noir, **6**
Chez Paul, **9**

⭐ **NIGHTLIFE**
Blues Rock Café, **7**
Café Chaud, **8**
Le Piano Rétro Club, **2**
Saint Barth, **5**

office at pl. des Halles, follow av. Gambetta right and uphill to pl. G. Perrot, continue straight up the rampe d'Aguesseau, and turn right onto bd. Pasteur. Keeping close to the rail overlooking the valley, pass the market building on your left, and turn left onto rue du Chat; the office will be on your right. Open July-Aug. M-Sa 9:30am-7pm, Su 10am-noon and 2-5pm; Sept.-June M-F 9am-6pm, Sa 10am-noon and 2-5pm, Su 10am-noon. Kiosk by the train station open July and Aug. Tu 1:30-6:30pm, W-Sa 10am-12:30pm and 1:30-6:30pm.

City Tours: Day and night tours offered through the Hôtel de Ville's **Service Patrimoine** (☎ 05 45 38 70 79; patrimoine@mairie-angouleme.fr). Enter the main gates of the Hôtel de Ville and cross the courtyard; the office is on the left. 2hr. daytrips (1hr. for tour of Hôtel de Ville, 1hr. for tour of *vieille ville*) leave Apr.-May and Oct. Sa and Su 3pm; daily June and Sept. 3pm; July-Aug. 3 times per day; Nov.-Mar. 3pm on select weekends. Those who only want to tour the *vieille ville* can join the tour at 4pm. €5 for both tours, children €3.50; €4 for only 1 tour, children €2.50, family €9. English tours available, sometimes at slightly higher rates; call in advance.

Budget Travel: Voyages Wasteels, 2 pl. Francis Louvel (☎05 45 92 21 45). Student discounts available. Open M-F 9am-noon and 2-6pm, Sa 10am-12:30pm. **Jet tours,** 5bis rue de Perigeux (☎05 45 92 07 94), also arranges cheap trips with excellent deals on airfare. Open M-Sa 9:30am-12:30pm and 2-6:30pm, Sa closes at 6pm.

Currency Exchange: The post office (see below) exchanges money with no commission. For other monetary needs, the **Banque de France** is at 1 rue de Général Leclerc (☎05 45 97 60 00), on pl. de l'Hôtel de Ville. Open M-F 8:40am-noon and 1:30-3:30pm.

Youth Center: Centre Information Jeunesse, inside the Espace Franquin building, 1 bd. Berthelot (☎05 45 37 07 30; www.info-jeunesse16.com), off the rampe d'Aguesseau. Friendly staff provides advice, info on jobs, cheap concert tickets, and free condoms. Open Tu-F 9am-6pm and Sa 2-6pm. Internet €2 for the 1st hr. (€1.50 for 30min, €0.75 for 15min.), but after requires a €10 1 year membership.

Laundromat: Lavomatique, 3 rue Ludovic Trarieux. Wash €3-6.50, dry €0.50 per 5 min. Open daily 7am-9pm. **Washmatic,** 11 rue St-Roch. Wash €3-5.50, dry €1.60, dry cleaning €1.40-6.40 per item. Open M-Sa 9am-12:30pm and 2-7pm.

Police: pl. du Champs de Mars (☎05 45 39 38 37), next to post office.

Hospital: Hôpital de Girac, rte. de Bordeaux (☎05 45 24 40 40), not to be confused with rue de Bordeaux. Take the #1 bus (dir: La Couronne Galands) or #8 bus (dir: La Couronne Mairie) from the Hôtel de Ville or pl. du Champ de Mars and get off at the Girac stop. Closer to town is private **Clinique St-Joseph,** 51 av. Président Wilson (☎05 45 38 67 00).

Internet Access: The **Musée de la Bande Dessinée** (p. 522) has 10 Internet terminals that can be used free with a museum ticket or for €2 per hr. without one. Closer to town is the **Centre Information Jeunesse** (see **Youth Center**). Directly below the youth center, in the basement of the Espace Franquin building, the **Espace Culture Multimedia** ☎05 45 37 07 32) rents movies and allows tourists 2hr. free Internet, after which they have to buy a €10 1-year pass. Open Tu, Th, Sa 1-6pm, W, F 1-8pm.

Post Office: pl. du Champs de Mars (☎05 45 66 66 00; fax 05 45 66 66 17). Open M-F 8am-6:30pm, Sa 8am-noon. Branch office at pl. Francis Louvel, near the Palais de Justice (☎05 45 90 14 30). Open M-F 8am-6:45pm, Sa 8:30am-12:30pm. Both offer **currency exchange** with no commission for US dollars.

Postal Code: 16000.

ACCOMMODATIONS

Cheap hotels are clustered near the intersection of av. Gambetta and the pedestrian district, which slopes downhill from the *vieille ville*.

Hôtel des Pyrénées, 80 rue St-Roch (☎05 45 95 20 45; fax 05 45 92 16 95), off pl. du Champ de Mars. From the train station, follow rue Gambetta until the 2nd large intersection, and take a sharp left. Hotel is at the end of the road on your left (10 minutes). Spacious rooms with colorful wallpaper and spotless bathrooms. Breakfast €5, in room €5.50. Reception 7am-10:30pm. Singles and doubles €24-27, with shower and TV €31-37, with shower, TV, and toilet €34-43; triples with shower, TV, and toilet €40-46. The upper range of prices is reserved for festival season. Extra bed €7. MC/V. ❷

Hôtel Le Palma, 4 rampe d'Aguesseau (☎05 45 95 22 89; fax 05 45 94 26 66), near the Église St-Martial, about 3 blocks up the hill from the train station. 10 rooms decorated with antique furniture lie along a dark, narrow staircase. Quiet atmosphere with friendly owners and an excellent location—5min. from both the train station and the center of town—make up for the grimy hall shower and shaky door handles. Breakfast €4.50. Reception M-Sa only; call in advance for Su. Singles €21.50, with shower €28; doubles €26/€33-37. AmEx/DC/MC/V. ❷

Auberge de Jeunesse (HI), (☎05 45 92 45 80; fax 05 45 92 27 50), on the Île de Bourgines in the Charente. By foot, turn left out of the train station onto av. de Lattre de Tassigny and take the 1st left onto bd. du 8 Mai 1945. Cross the railroad tracks. Before the big bridge turn left onto bd. Besson Bey and cross the footbridge. Follow the dirt path beside the river to the left; the hostel is just ahead. (30min.) To get there by bus, leave the station, turn right onto av. Gambetta, and right again onto rue Denis Papin, which crosses over the tracks. Continue straight onto Passage Lamaud, a pedestrian shortcut that leads to rue de Paris. (5-10min.) Turn right onto rue de Paris and take bus #7 (dir: Le Treuil, last bus 8pm, €1.20) to St-Antoine. Bleak modern cement hostel amid parking lots but also grassy fields on an island in the Charente. 2- to 6-bed rooms have maroon metal beds and fiendish press-and-repeat showers. Breakfast €3.30. Sheets €2.80. Lockout 10am-2pm. Reception M-F 8am-10pm, Sa-Su 8-10am and 5-10pm. Call ahead in summer. Dorms €9.30; doubles €11.30. ❶

🍴 FOOD

The local specialty, *cagouilles à la charentaise* (snails prepared first with garlic and parsley, then with sausage, smoked ham, and spices), can be found in the restaurants of the *vieille ville*. A favorite sweet is the flower-shaped *marguerite* chocolate, named for the sister of François I, Marguerite de Valois. Bars, cafes, and bakeries line **rue de St-Martial** and **rue Marengo,** but the food becomes funkier and the crowds more interesting along the narrow streets of the quadrant formed by Les Halles, pl. du Palet, Église St-André, and the Hôtel de Ville. The recently renovated covered **market** on pl. des Halles sells the town's freshest produce two blocks down rue de Gaulle from the Hôtel de Ville. (Open daily 7:30am-1pm.) There is a **Champion supermarket,** 19 rue Périgueux, right by the Champ de Mars. (Open M-Sa 8:30am-7:15pm, Su 9-11:45am. MC/V.) For a light meal, **Le Chat Noir** ❶ on pl. des Halles serves bruschetta made with the freshest ingredients (€5.25-7), in addition to a variety of sandwiches (€2.40-4.70) and dessert crêpes (€2.20-3.40). The drink menu is also extensive, with a large selection of local vintages. (☎05 45 75 26 27. Open 7:30am-2am. AmEx/MC/V.) **Chez Paul** ❸, 8 pl. Francis Louvel, has an unassuming exterior, but opens out to a paradise-themed garden with flowers, candles, sculptures, and a miniature river running through the middle. Excellent regional food served in a three-course *menu* (€23), or less expensive lunch *menus*. The *brasserie* also hosts amateur theater every Friday on the stage upstairs. (☎05 45 90 04 61. Open daily noon-3pm, 6pm-2am. AmEx/MC/V.)

👁 SIGHTS

🏛**MUSÉE DE LA BANDE DESSINÉE.** Housed in the **Centre Nationale de la Bande Dessinée et de L'Image (CNBDI),** this museum is a tribute to Angoulême's leading role in the development of computerized graphics and the *B.D.—la bande dessinée* (comic strips). Presented in colorful rooms that resemble comic books, the exhibits feature French and international cartoons from the 19th and 20th centuries, including favorites like Tintin, Astérix, and Popeye. Entrance to the museum also gives free access to its library and one free hour of Internet access. The extensive bookshop filled with comics from all over the world is by far the best asset of the CNBDI. (*121 rue de Bordeaux. From pl. du Champ de Mars and pl. de l'Hôtel de Ville, take bus #3 or 5 to "Nil-CNBDI" or walk along the ramparts, following the signs. (10min.) ☎05 45 38 65 65; cnbdi@cnbdi.fr. Open July-Aug. M-F 10am-7pm, Sa-Su 2-7pm; Sept.-June Tu-F 10am-6pm, Sa-Su 2-6pm. €5, students €3.50, children €2.50, under 6 free.*)

MUSÉE DE LA RÉSISTANCE ET DE LA DÉPORTATION. Occupying the one-time home of 16th-century religious reformer Jean Calvin, this museum now chronicles Angoulême's experience under the Nazi occupation, in particular the development and courageous actions of the French Resistance fighters, many of whom were captured and tortured to death by the Nazis. The horrifying photographs on the second floor illustrate the tragic experience of the 1180 Jews deported from the Charente region during WWII, documenting life and death in concentration camps. The exhibits are all in French, with limited English texts available. *(34 rue de Genève. ☎ 05 45 38 76 87; fax 05 45 93 12 66. Open M-F 2-6pm, 9am-noon by appointment only. €2.50, students €1.50, children free.)*

MUSÉE DES BEAUX ARTS. Occupying a restored 12th-century bishop's palace, the museum displays a pleasing melange of media. A labyrinth of 16th- to 19th-century paintings, 19th-century *charentais* archaeological digs, North and West African pottery, and locally created sculptures surround one of the museum's prized possessions, Etienne Barthélémy's 1800 *Grief of Priam's Family*. Under renovation at the time of publication, the museum plans to reopen in 2005. *(1 rue Friedland, behind the cathedral. ☎ 05 45 95 07 69; fax 05 45 95 98 26. Open M-F noon-6pm, Sa-Su 2-6pm. €3, students and children under 18 free, free for all visitors noon-2pm.)*

CATHÉDRALE ST-PIERRE. The elegant 12th-century cathedral of Angoulême is textbook Romanesque but for one main element: the structure was built without internal columns in order to permit an uninterrupted view of the interior. The original 6th-century structure also lacked windows. Before Byzantine renovations bathed the transept in pale blue light, it was lit only by lanterns. The edifice exerted a considerable architectural influence during the height of religious power, not only on other churches in the diocese, but also on more distant buildings like Fontevraud in the Loire and Notre-Dame-la-Grande of Poitiers. The intricate facade depicting the Ascension of Christ and scenes from the Last Judgment opens up to a comparatively barren but architecturally impressive interior. *(Pl. St-Pierre. ☎ 05 45 95 44 83. Open daily 9am-5pm.)*

ÉGLISE ST-ANDRÉ. The 12th-century church, originally Romanesque, was reworked in a Gothic style. Today it combines paintings from the 16th to 19th centuries with a massive altarpiece and a superb Baroque oak pulpit. The facade was redone in the early 19th century, but the church still retains its tower and entrance. *(8 rue Taillefer, on the pl. de Palet in the town center. Open daily 9am-7pm.)*

GARDENS AND SPORTS. Angoulême's ramparts and green riverside areas are a refreshing escape from the bustle of the town. At the bottom of av. du Président Wilson, beneath the meandering paths of the park, the waterfalls of the **Jardin Vert** calm visitors. The 4th-century ramparts that surround the town provide a view of the red-roofed houses of the city. To kayak (4-14km) on the Charente, call **SCA Angoulême**. *(☎ 05 45 94 68 91. €9.10-18.10 per person.)* For water skiing, call **CAM's water skiing**. *(☎ 05 45 92 76 22. €9 per session. Open June-Oct. daily noon-8pm.)* The tourist office has information on outdoor sports like water skiing and tennis.

🅢 NIGHTLIFE

As the sun sets, folks move toward the cafes on rue Massillon and pl. des Halles, and av. Gambetta comes alive with numerous bars and restaurants. Have a hot coffee or a cold drink at the two-story **Café Chaud**, 1 rue Ludovic Trarieux. Around a wooden spiral staircase, the orange-striped seats hold mostly locals amid lively music. *(☎ 05 45 38 18 24. Open daily 1pm-2am.)* **Blues Rock Café**, 19 rue de Genève on the pl. des Halles, caters to a mixed crowd of young and old, tourists and locals, and packs the square outside with drinks, smoke, laughter, and live music every

Thursday during the summer months. (☎05 45 94 05 98. Extensive salad menu €4.50-7.50; beer €2.40. Open daily 10am-2am.) Further down rue de Genève, the trendy bar at **Saint Barth** has a DJ every night and occasional live music. Crowds rest their drinks on old oak wine barrels in homage to the region's primary industry. (Open daily 11am-2am. Beer €2.40. Theme nights from time to time.) A lively crowd and exciting atmosphere justify the hike out to **Le Piano Rétro Club**, near pl. Victor Hugo. (☎05 45 38 16 04. Open W-Sa 11pm-5am. W-Th no cover, F-Sa €10 cover with drink, ladies free before midnight.)

⚜ FESTIVALS

Every year, the world-famous **Salon International de la Bande-Dessinée** breezes into town the last weekend in January. Over 200,000 visitors spend four days admiring comic strip exhibits throughout town, where Astérix and Obélix can occasionally be sighted. (☎05 45 97 86 50; www.labd.com. For tickets, call ☎08 92 69 00 32 or visit the Hôtel de Ville. €9.20 for 1 day, €18.30 for all 4 days, children ages 7-18 €4.60, under 7 free.) The **Festival Musiques Métisses,** 6 rue du point-du-Jour, features live French-African and Caribbean music each year during the feast of the Ascension. (☎05 45 95 43 42. Tourist office sells tickets. 4 nights €60, students and ages 16-18 €45, ages 10-15 €35, under 10 free.) The popular **Circuit des Remparts,** 2 rue Fontgrave, revs its engine in mid-September, when antique cars hold free races and exhibitions for three days in the town center (☎05 45 94 95 67), and international pianists of all genres participate in the two-week long installments of the **Festival International de Piano, "Piano en Valois,"** in October and November. (☎05 45 92 11 11. Concerts €12-25, under 26 free.)

In November, **Gastronomades,** a celebration of culinary arts, offers cooking lessons, food displays, and free tastings (☎05 45 67 39 30), and **Ludoland** celebrates children's toys and video games. (☎05 45 21 29 02; www.ludo-angouleme.com. 3-day pass €8.) Like many French cities, Angoulême also welcomes all sorts of artistic festivities in the summertime. Call the tourist office after mid-June for info about the **Eté au Ciné,** a series of outdoor films shown during summer evenings, and the **Jeux de Rue,** an open-air theater festival with free outdoor performances every Thursday during July and August.

For those who love to wine and dine to the gentle sway of the river, **Les Croisières au pays d'Angoulême** are a series of themed cruises that run July to August. Themes include the paper cruise, which makes a stop at the paper museum, the wine cruise, and the chocoholic cruise. Breakfast, lunch, and dinner cruises are also available. The themes tend to change each summer, but may include fireworks or a Spanish fiesta. Prices range from €15-40, children €5-25. Call the tourist office for info and reservations.

DAYTRIP FROM ANGOULÊME

LA ROCHEFOUCAULD

Get to La Rochefoucauld by train (25min.; M-Sa 5 per day, Su 2 per day; €4.70). From the back of the train station, cross the parking lot to the traffic circle. Go halfway around the traffic circle and keep walking straight for 4 blocks through the town center. The château is straight ahead. (8min.) Tourist office is 1 rue des Tanneurs. (☎05 45 63 07 45. Open daily June-Sept. 10am-1pm and 3-7pm; Oct.-May M-Sa 9:30am-12:30pm and 2-6pm.)

La Rochefoucauld (pop. 3200) has been home to more than 43 generations of the aristocratic Foucauld family. The present **château,** known as the "pearl of Angoumois," was built by Duke Francis II in 1528 on a feudal-era foundation, with twin towers, a medieval fortress, and an elegant chapel on a plateau overlooking the

town. The magnificent central spiral staircase, built in 1520 and designed by Leonardo Da Vinci, is a perfect work of Renaissance art. (☎05 45 62 07 42. Open daily Apr.-Jan. 10am-7pm. Open year-round for groups by appointment. €7, ages 4-12 €3.) The surrounding village, which takes its name from the family ("La Roche à Foucauld" or "The Rock of Foucauld"), houses a well-preserved 14th-century cloister, **Le Couvent des Carmes,** and a church with an impressive and deeply colored stained glass window, which dates from 1266.

COGNAC

Originally a small medieval town known only as the birthplace of King François I, Cognac (pop. 20,000) was completely transformed in the 17th century with the invention of double distillation. French lawmakers decided that only crops produced in the Cognac region are fit to become the liquor that bears the Cognac name, and today distilleries here give tours and samples of the prized beverage. The small town is perfect for a daytrip from nearby Saintes, or even Angoulême, but spending more time in the town's manicured gardens and enjoying the scent of cognac vapor in the *vieille ville* may merit an overnight stay.

◨ ◪ ORIENTATION AND PRACTICAL INFORMATION. Trains come from Angoulême (40min., 5 per day, €7.60) and Saintes (20min., 6 per day, €4.40). To get to the **tourist office,** 16 rue du 14 Juillet, follow av. du Maréchal Leclerc out of the train station to the first circle and take a right, following signs to the town center. Turn right on rue Bayard and go straight across pl. Bayard onto rue du 14 Juillet (15 minutes). The tourist office provides information, maps, and free accommodations booking. It is also the departure point for *petit train* tours (May-Sept. every 45min. 11:15am-5:15pm; €5, ages 5-15 €3) and trips to the local bottle and cask making factories. (☎05 45 82 10 71; fax 05 45 82 34 47; office.tourisme.cognac@wanadoo.fr. Open July-Aug. M-Sa 9am-7pm, Su 10am-4pm; Sept. and May-June M-Sa 9:30am-5:30pm; Oct.-Apr. M-Sa 10am-5pm.) Other services include the **hospital** (☎05 45 36 75 75) and **police** (☎05 45 82 38 48). The **CIC Banque CIO,** 36 bd. Denfert-Rochereau, exchanges money with a 3% commission (min. €6 fee) and has **ATMs** outside. (☎05 45 36 84 84. Open Tu-F 8:45am-12:30pm and 1:45-6pm, Sa 8:45am-12:30pm.) For even better rates, the **post office,** 2 pl. Bayard, exchanges money with a 2% commission. (☎05 45 36 31 70. Open M-F 8am-6pm, Sa 8am-noon.) **Postal Code:** 16100.

◪ ◪ ACCOMMODATIONS AND CAMPING. Staying the night in Cognac, which has no budget accommodations, will be a bit of a splurge for the backpacking set. Directly across from the train station and to the left, the one-story **Hotel de la Gare ❹** offers clean, spacious, modern rooms, all with TV and telephone, for the cheapest prices in the city. Ask about free passes to the Hennessy distillery. (☎05 45 82 04 15; fax 05 45 82 64 44; hoteldelagare1@tiscali.fr. Breakfast €5. Reservations recommended. Wheelchair-accessible. Singles with bath €37; doubles €44; triples €52. Extra bed €8. MC/V.) Three-star **Cognac Camping ❶,** bd. de Châtenay, on rte. de Ste-Sévère, is a 30min. walk from town. In July and August, lines A-C run from the pl. François I (☎05 45 82 01 99; July-Aug. 2 per day; €1, round-trip €1.20). Get off at Camping. (☎05 45 32 13 32. Pool, playground, fishing, and laundry. Open mid-Apr. to mid-Oct. July-Aug. 2 people with site, showers, and electricity €12.10; Apr.-June and Sept.-Oct. €10. 3 people with site €17.60/€13. 4- to 6-person mobile homes July-Aug. €440 per week. MC/V.)

◖ FOOD. Sampling Cognac's famous product doesn't necessarily mean drinking it. Restaurants around **place François I** serve pricey local specialties drenched in it. **Le Cellier ❸,** 4 et 6 rue du 14 Juillet, just off place François I, is a local favorite, packing in customers at lunch and serving generous portions of meat and fish. (☎ 05 45 82 25 46. *Plats* €7.50-16.10, lunch *menu* of the *plat du jour* and dessert €8, dinner *menus* €13.90-€24.70. Open M-F noon-2pm and 7-10pm, July-Sept. open Sa nights. MC/V.) **La Boune Goule ❷**, 42 allées de la Corderie, is right in the town center at the intersection with rue Aristide Briande. Huge, fresh portions of local cuisine served in an American diner-style setting. (☎ 05 45 82 06 37. Appetizers €3.90-12.20, meat and fish €5.35-15.50, lunch/weekday dinner *menu* €11.50. Open daily July-Aug. 9am-2am, food served noon-3pm and 7-10pm; Sept.-June open Tu-Sa only. MC/V.) More basic needs can be satisfied at **Supermarket Eco**, on pl. Bayard, right down the street from the tourist office. (Open M-Sa 9am-12:30pm and 3-7:30pm, Su 9-11:45am.) There is an **indoor market** at pl. d'Armes (Tu-Su 8am-1pm), and a lively **outdoor market** brightens pl. du Marché on the second Saturday of each month.

📷 **COGNAC DISTILLERIES.** The joy of visiting Cognac lies in traveling from one brandy producer to the next, watching films on the history of each house, touring the warehouses and collecting gift-wrapped bottles of liqueur. In the summer, most houses regularly give tours in English; call in advance during the winter. Listed below are the distilleries in the city center; **Rémy Martin** and **Camus** also lie within a short walk of the *centre ville*.

Hennessy, quai Richard Hennessy (☎ 05 45 35 72 68; fax 05 45 35 79 49; quais@hennessy.fr). Those with time for only 1 distillery visit should make this their stop. The industry's biggest player has the longest and most interesting presentation, which includes a trip to "paradise," where the oldest cognacs are kept, a short boat ride along the Charente River and movies accompanied by the most dramatic soundtracks since *Titanic*. Tours daily June-Sept. 10am-6pm; Mar.-May and Oct.-Dec. 10am-5pm; Jan.-Feb. call ahead for a reservation. Several English tours per day, call ahead for times. €9 (includes taste of 2 vintages), €6 (1 vintage), children under 16 free.

Otard and the Château François I, 127 bd. Denfert-Rochereau (☎ 05 45 36 88 86), in the Château de Cognac, where François I was born in 1494. The 50min. tour led by guides dressed in medieval costumes begins with the history of the building and ends with a visit to the damp castle cellar where the cognac is produced and stored. Many cool facts on the informative tour, right down to the booze-hound fungus on the wall, that consumes 23,000 bottles worth of vapor each year. Open daily July-Aug. 10am-7pm; Apr.-Dec. 10am-noon and 2-6pm; Jan.-Mar. call ahead for reservations. Last tour leaves 1hr. before closing. €5, ages 12-18 €2.50, under 12 free, families €10.

Martell, pl. Edouard Martell (☎ 05 45 36 33 33; www.martell.com), is the oldest of the major cognac houses and ships to cities around the world. The interesting hi-tech tour features a replica of an 18th-century exporting ship and a visit to the founder's elegant and perfectly preserved cottage. Open for tours June-Sept. M-F 9:30am-5pm, Sa-Su 11am-5pm; Oct. and Apr.-May 10, 11am, 2:30, 3:45pm, 5pm Nov.-Mar. call ahead to reserve. English tours given daily; call for times. €4, students €2 (not advertised; be sure to ask for the discount at the ticket desk), under 16 free.

📷📷 **SIGHTS AND FESTIVALS.** The **Musée d'Art et d'Histoire du Cognac,** 48 bd. Denfert-Rochereau, details the history of Cognac with regional clothing, ceramics, and viticulture tools. Its newly opened sister museum the **Musée des Arts du Cognac,** pl. de la Salle Verte, near the river, has exhibits dedicated to the spirit which made the town famous. (☎ 05 45 32 07 25; musee.cognac@alien.fr. Open daily May-Sept. 10am-6pm; Mar.-Apr. and Oct. Tu-Su 11am-12:30pm and 1:30-6pm; Nov.-Feb. Tu-Su 2:30-5:30pm. €4.50 for admission to both museums, students €3.) The Hennessy distillery hosts a **film festival** every April.

⚑ OUTDOORS. Cognac's valley provides great **hiking** among vineyards, fields, groves, and forests. The tourist office provides four *Sentiers de Randonnées* maps (€2.30 each, €9.20 for all four) with paths (2-18km) around Cognac that vary in difficulty; off-trail discoveries include a 13th-century crypt, abbeys, and châteaux. The tourist office also has info on canoe and kayak rental. Parks in Cognac include the **Jardin de l'Hôtel de Ville** around the museum, and the tree-lined **Parc François I,** northwest of the center between allée Bassée and allée des Charentes. (Garden open May-Sept. 7am-9pm, Oct.-Apr. 7am-7pm. Park open 24hr.)

SAINTES

Saintes (pop. 26,000) began as the ancient Roman city of *Mediolanum Santonum*, named for the local Gallic Santon tribe, was founded in the first century AD. Located along the Charente River and connected by a major road to Lyon, this wealthy city served as the capital of Aquitaine for nearly 100 years. It converted to Christianity early and with conviction, and was nearly destroyed in the Wars of Religion. Today Saintes's first-century ruins and impressive cathedrals bear testament to the city's importance during both Roman and medieval times. With great restaurants and relaxing outdoor options, Saintes is a great place to dine in style and take a breath of fresh air on the way to larger tourist hubs.

▐ TRANSPORTATION

Trains: station on pl. Pierre Senard. Info and ticket office open M-Sa 5:30am-8pm, Su 8am-10pm. To: **Bordeaux** (1½hr., 5 per day, €15.70); **Cognac** (20min., 5 per day, €4.40); **La Rochelle** (50min., 5 per day, €10.20); **Niort** (1hr., 5 per day, €10); **Paris** (2¼hr., 6 per day, €58.40); **Poitiers** (1½hr., 6 per day, €21.90); **Royan** (30min., 6-7 per day, €5.80).

Buses: Autobus Aunnis et Saintonage, 2 rue des Oeillets (☎05 46 97 52 00). To **Royan** (1½hr., 4 per day, €5.70). Office open M-F 8:30am-noon and 2-5:30pm.

Public Transportation: Tickets €0.85 valid for 1hr. after purchase. Last train leaves the "Théâtre" stop daily at 7:30pm. Schedules at tourist office or at **Boutique Bus** (☎05 46 93 50 50) in the Galerie du Bois d'Amour. Open M-Sa 8am-12:30pm and 1:15-7pm.

Taxis: at the train station (☎05 46 74 24 24). €2 plus €0.62 per km.

Car Rental: Budget, 43 av. de la Marne (☎05 46 74 28 11). €185+ per week. Discount on weekends. €750 deposit. AmEx/MC/V. 21+. Open M-Sa 8am-noon and 2-6:30pm. **Europcar,** 41 av. de la Marne (☎05 46 92 56 10). €214+ per week. €534 deposit. 21+. Open M-F 8am-noon and 2-7pm, Sa 8am-noon and 2-6:30pm.

Bike Rental: Groleau, 9 cours Reverseaux (☎05 46 74 19 03). €10 per day. Prices decrease with multi-day rentals. €225 deposit required. Open Tu-Sa 9am-noon and 2-7pm, summer months open Sa until 6pm.

▰▰ ORIENTATION AND PRACTICAL INFORMATION

Saintes lies on the Charente River, 25km from Cognac along the La Rochelle-Bordeaux railway line. To get to the tourist office, take a sharp left upon leaving the train station and follow av. de la Marne until you hit lively av. Gambetta. Turn right and follow it to the river; the Arc Germanicus will be on your left. Cross the bridge at pont Palissy and continue straight on **cours National.** The tourist office is on your right in a villa set back from the street (20 minutes). The hub of the mellifluous pedestrian district is **rue Victor Hugo,** three blocks to the left after the bridge.

Tourist Office: 62 cours National (☎05 46 74 23 82; www.ot-saintes.fr), in Villa Musso. Free maps. Organizes walking tours of the city, abbey, and Roman ruins. 1 Internet terminal; €7.40 for 50min., €14.75 for 2hr. Open July-Aug. M-Sa 9am-1pm and 2-7pm, Su 10am-1pm and 2-6pm; May-June and Sept. 9am-12:30pm and 2-6pm, 1st 3 Su of Sept. 10am-1pm and 2-6pm; Oct.-Apr. M-Sa 9:30am-12:30pm and 2:15-6pm. Tours in French mid-June to mid-Sept. M-Sa. €6 for 1 tour, €10 for 2, €13 for all 3; under 16 free.

Bank: Banque de France, 1 cours Lemercier (☎05 46 93 40 33). Open M-F 9am-12:10pm and 2-3:45pm.

Laundromat: L'Arc de Triomphe, 9 rue Arc de Triomphe (☎06 19 17 00 34). Wash €2.30-5.60, dry €0.80 per 10min. Open daily 7am-9pm. **Laverie et Cie,** 46 cours Reverseaux (☎05 46 74 34 79). Wash €3.20-€8, dry €1 per 10min. €10 washing, drying, and folding service. Open Tu-Sa 10am-12:30pm and 3:30-7pm.

Police: pl. du Bastion (☎05 46 90 30 40), or **Gendarmerie,** 17 rue du Chermignac (☎05 46 93 01 19).

Hospital: pl. du 11 Novembre (☎05 46 92 76 76).

Post Office: 6 cours National (☎05 46 93 84 53). **Currency exchange** with no commission. Internet €7 per hr. Open M and W-F 8:30am-6pm, Tu 9am-6pm, Sa 8:30am-noon.

Postal Code: 17100.

ACCOMMODATIONS AND CAMPING

Hotels fill for the festivals from early to mid-July; rooms should be easy to find otherwise. The cheaper accommodations are on the train station side of the Charente.

Auberge de Jeunesse (HI), 2 pl. Geoffrey-Martel (☎05 46 92 14 92; fax 05 46 92 97 82), next to the Abbaye-aux-Dames. From the station, take a left onto av. de la Marne and then turn right onto av. Gambetta, left onto rue du Pérat, and right onto rue St-Pallais. Turn left through the archway into the courtyard of the abbey. Go straight through the courtyard and out through the arch at the back. The hostel will be on the right. (15min.) A clean, renovated building that feels like part of the abbey itself. Cozy, cabin-like rooms. Breakfast included. Sheets €3.10. Reception June-Sept. M-Sa 7:30am-noon and 5-11pm, Su 7:30-10am and 6-10:30pm; Oct.-May until 10:30pm. 2- to 6-bed dorms (single-sex) with bath €11.45. MC/V. HI members only. ❶

Au Bleu Nuit, 1 rue Pasteur (☎05 46 93 01 72; fax 05 46 74 43 80; au-bleu-nuit@t3a.com). Follow directions to the tourist office but continue walking straight on cours National until you arrive at a small rotary. The hotel will be across from you on the corner of rue Pasteur and rue Lemercier. All rooms have long, white curtains, bright bedsheets, and TVs. Rooms vary in size; some are enormous and come with their own personal terrace. Breakfast €5.50. Parking €4.80. Reservations recommended in the summer. Singles with toilet €29, with shower and toilet €36; doubles with shower, and toilet €40, with bath and toilet €41.50, with 2 beds, shower and toilet €42; triple with 2 beds, shower, and toilet €49. Extra bed €8. AmEx/MC/V. ❸

Le Parisien, 29 rue Frédéric-Mestreau (☎05 46 74 28 92), by the train station. Run by a friendly couple, this hotel has small but homey rooms surrounding a somewhat unkempt garden. Breakfast €3-4.50. Reception 7am-10pm. Call several weeks ahead for July-Aug. Singles €22, with shower €25; doubles with showers €32 (€22 in low season). Extra bed €7. MC/V. ❷

Camping: Camping Au Fil de L'Eau, 6 rue de Courbiac (☎05 46 93 08 00; fax 05 46 93 61 88), 1km from the town center. From the train station, follow directions to the hostel until av. Gambetta and turn right onto quai de l'Yser after crossing the bridge. The campsite is ½mi. farther on the right. (25-30min.) By bus, take #2 (dir: Ormeau le Pied)

Saintes

▲■ ACCOMMODATIONS
Au Bleu Nuit, **4**
Auberge de
Jeunesse (HI), **9**

Camping Au Fil de L'Eau, **1**
Le Parisien, **2**

🍴 FOOD
Cafétéria du
Bois-d'Amour, **3**
Le Gourmandin, **6**

★ NIGHTLIFE
Bar Le Palissy, **7**
Billiard Saintais, **8**
Le Santon, **5**

from the train station; get off at Théâtre and catch the #3 (dir: Magezy), to Port Larousselle/Piscine (25min., €0.85). 3-star site by the Charente, next to pool (free for campers) and mini-golf (€4). Fence gives feeling of seclusion and security. Individual lots are crowded, but there is an on site market and *brasserie*. Convenient location is a plus, only 10-15min. walk from the *centre ville*. Some buildings wheelchair-accessible. Reception July-Aug. 8am-1pm and 3-9pm; mid-May to June and early to mid-Sept. 9am-noon and 4-8pm. €4.20 per person, €2.10 per child, €4.30 per site; car included. Electricity €3.20. Locked parking €3.30. Lockout for cars 10pm-7am. MC/V. ●

🍴 FOOD

Menus in Saintes flaunt the region's seafood, *escargot* dishes, and *mojettes* (white beans cooked in Charenté). Start things off with *pineau*, a sweeter relative of Cognac. Saintes is blessed with plenty of family-run restaurants and bars, especially in the pedestrian district by rue Victor Hugo. The town also holds **markets** at pl. du 11 Novembre, off cours Reverseaux (Tu and F), near Cathédrale St-Pierre (W and Sa), and on av. de la Marne and av. Gambetta (Th and Su), all 7am-1pm. On the first Monday of every month, the cours National and the av. Gambetta host **Le Grand Foire,** an open-air market that sells everything, including clothes, sunglasses, and purses. A huge **Leclerc supermarket** and general store are on cours de Gaulle near the hostel. (Open M-Th and Sa 8:30am-7:45pm, F 8:30am-8:15pm.) A smaller **Co-op** supermarket can be found on both rue Urbain Loyer, off cours National (open M-Sa 8:30am-12:30pm and 3-7:30pm), and at 162 av. Gambetta, near the train station. (Open M-Sa 8am-1pm and 3:30-8pm, Su 8am-1pm and 5:30-8pm.)

For sit-down fare, try the friendly **Le Gourmandin ❸,** av. de la Marne, near the station. In nice weather, the enclosed outdoor seating provides a respite from the city commotion, and can make for a romantic evening dinner. Sit under an umbrella in a quiet courtyard next to a small man-made waterfall. (☎ 05 46 93 01 16; fax 05 46 74 37 90. *Menus* €15, €21, €25. Open M and Sa 7-9pm, Tu-F and Su noon-1:30pm and 7-9pm. MC/V.) A cheap hot meal is available at **Cafétéria du Bois-d'Amour ❶,** 7 rue du Bois-d'Amour, off cours National in the Galérie Marchandise, a pay-by-the-plate cafeteria, offering €1-4.90 appetizers and €4.20-6.50 *plats*. (☎ 05 46 97 26 54.

HEADY FASHION

Many distinctive headdresses have evolved throughout France over the centuries. While French cities are known for their *haute couture*, country tailors have also been known to let loose, completely unconstrained by city fashions. The remarkable adornments visible in old photographs and famous paintings are the impressive result.

One of the most enduring of these are the headdresses that were worn by French women until well after WWII: the white *quichenotte*. The *quichenotte* has become a trademark of the area along the coast of the Gironde, and can be viewed in any local museum that features old rural clothing. Made of lace or thin cloth, the bonnets served to protect female farmers' delicate skin from the hot coastal sun and were popular from field workers in Italy to oyster collectors in Brittany.

Legend has it that the *quichenottes* got their name when invading English soldiers burst into the vineyards of the Angoumois and Saintonge regions and surprised the women working in the fields. In an effort to defend themselves from the advances of the aggressive soldiers, the story goes, the women pulled the large wings of their headdresses over their mouths and screamed "kiss not!" in their best English. In honor of these chaste farmers, the name *quichenotte* was given to the famous white bonnets.

Open daily 11:30am-12:30pm and 7-9:30pm, 11:30am-10pm for salad. 5% student discount with student ID. MC/V.)

◎ SIGHTS

Built in AD 18 as a gateway into the city, the Roman **Arc Germanicus** rises on the right bank of the river in honor of Emperor Tiberius and his nephews Drusus and Germanicus. Although originally located at the entrance to a bridge that crossed the Charente, the arc was moved to the right bank of the river when it began to lose its stability in 1843.

A little farther down the river is the flower-filled **Jardin Public,** where travelers can rest on shaded benches and kids will be entertained by a free petting zoo. Next door, on esplanade André Malraux, the small **Musée Archéologique** displays a collection of Roman funeral monuments and marble statues, as well as the remains of a first-century chariot. Impressive (and free) Roman ruins exhibition just outside. (☎05 46 74 20 97. Open daily June-Sept. 10am-6pm; Oct.-May 10am-5pm. €1.50, or €4 ticket that includes year-long admission to the **Musée du Présidial,** the **Musée de L'Echevinage,** and the **Musée Dupuy-Mestreau;** under 18 free.)

Rue Arc de Triomphe, which becomes rue St-Pallais, leads to the Romanesque **Abbaye-aux-Dames.** Built in 1047 as a convent for Benedictine nuns, the abbey led a quiet life for a while—some Gothic touch-ups here, another gallery there—until plagues, fires, and wars prompted centuries of constant construction and renovation. During the antireligious fervor of the Revolution, the abbey was shut down and temporarily used as a prison. Today, it serves as the musical and cultural center, displaying frequent exhibitions by local artists in its bright **Salle Capitulaire.** The pinecone-shaped belltower of the connected **Église Notre-Dame** dates from the 12th century, when Eleanor of Aquitaine aided the nuns during renovations. Climb to the top to scan the stunning horizon or check out contemporary tapestries depicting the six days of the Creation. In the spaces typically reserved for stained-glass windows or paintings, this church features modern art tapestries. See the *L'Abbaye aux Dames: Eté* pamphlet at the tourist office for information on the weeklong music festival held every July. (☎05 46 97 48 48. Exhibit and ramparts open Apr.-Sept. 10am-7pm; Oct.-Mar. 1-6pm. Church free. Abbey €3, under 16 free. Tours in French early May to late June Sa-Su 3:15pm; late June to mid-Sept. daily 2:15pm and 4:15pm. €6. Concerts €12-45.)

Across the flower-lined pedestrian bridge on rue St-Pierre the impressive **Cathédrale St-Pierre** towers over the town. Renovations transforming the 12th-century Romanesque church into the Gothic style were halted by the Wars of Religion; the steeple and portal were left unfinished. (☎ 05 46 93 09 92. Open daily 9am-7pm.) Turn away from the center of town and descend the steps of less traveled rue St-Eutrope, which crawls through tree-lined fields to the **crypt** of the saint who is the road's namesake. Known as the saint of recovery, **St-Eutrope** lies in a crypt treasured by many for its healing powers. Joseph de Compostela paid a visit to the crypt on his way to Santiago. (Open daily 9am-7pm.)

ENTERTAINMENT AND NIGHTLIFE

Late in the day, Saintes's cafes and pubs are great places to unwind with an evening of conversation and sunset-watching. Enjoy a game (€1) and a beer (€2) at **Billiard Saintais,** 126 av. Gambetta. (☎ 06 83 46 02 37. Open Tu-Su 2pm-2am.) Where rue Gambetta runs into pont Palissy you'll find **Bar Le Palissy,** a gathering place for students who listen to jazz or rock. The bar also offers karaoke on Thursdays and occasional live music. (☎ 05 46 74 30 65. Beer €2. Open M-Sa 11am-2pm, Su 3pm-2am. AmEx/MC/V.) Those with cars can dance up a storm with partying students at **Le Santon,** Ste-Vegas, on rte. de Royan. In summer, the adjoining **swimming pool** provides a respite from the steamy dance floor. (☎ 05 46 97 00 00. Cover for both club and pool Su-Th €4, F €9 with an alcoholic drink and ladies free, Sa €11 with an alcoholic drink. Open daily 10:30pm-5am.)

FESTIVALS

For ten days in mid-July, the **Festival de Folklore en Charente Maritime** celebrates international folk music, food, and dance. The Arènes Gallo-Romaines host the opening and closing events. (☎ 05 46 97 04 35. Some events free, others up to €30.) At the same time, be sure to join the **Académies Musicales** celebration, in which more than 28 classical music concerts are packed into 10 days at the Abbaye aux Dames. (☎ 05 46 97 48 48; www.festival-saintes.org. Tickets €12-45. Childcare is offered at €3.32 per hr.; ☎ 05 46 92 59 96. Reserve 24 hr. in advance.)

LA ROCHELLE

Though it cannot boast of beautiful beaches or sandy shores, La Rochelle (pop. 76,000) does have one great claim to fame—fish, and lots of it. The town's reputation as one of France's best-sheltered seaports helped to create its fortune, but it also nearly destroyed it: France and England fought over the town during the Thirty Years' War, and Cardinal Richelieu was so upset with the city's support of England during the 17th-century invasion of the Île de Ré that he besieged the town for 15 months, starving three quarters of its citizens. Having survived its rocky past, La Rochelle now entices visitors with medieval architecture, pristine offshore islands, quirky museums, and excellent seafood restaurants.

TRANSPORTATION

Trains: station on bd. Maréchal Joffre. Info office open M-F 9am-7:30pm, Sa 9am-6:30pm. To: **Bordeaux** (2½hr., 5 per day, €22.50); **Nantes** (2hr., 6 per day, €21); **Paris** (3hr., 5 per day, €54.80); **Poitiers** (1½hr., 8 per day, €19.80).

POITOU-CHARENTES

Buses: Océcars (☎05 46 00 95 15) sends buses from pl. de Verdun to **Royan** (2½hr., 3 per day, €12.30) and **Saintes** (4 per day, €9.60) via **Rochefort.** Buy tickets from driver. Info office at pl. de Verdun open M-F 8:30-noon and 2:45-6:15pm.

Ferries: Croisières Océanes, office on cours des Dames (☎05 46 50 68 44; fax 05 46 44 52 69) runs boats to **Île d'Aix** (**Inter Iles** ☎05 46 50 51 88; fax 05 46 50 18 97). See Île d'Aix (p. 542) for prices. **Bus de Mer** (☎05 46 34 02 22) shuttles between the old port and les Minimes (July-Aug. every 30min., 9am-11:30pm, €1.70; Apr.-June and Sept. every hr. 10am-7pm, €1.50, children under 5 free). **Le Passeur** (☎05 46 34 02 22) provides transportation between the 2 Bus de Mer stations (daily June-Sept. every few min. 7:45am-midnight; Apr.-May 7:45am-10pm; Oct.-Mar. 7:45am-8pm; €0.60.)

Public Transportation: Autoplus (☎05 46 34 02 22) serves the campgrounds, hostel, and town center (every 20min. 7am-8pm, €1.20), and nearby towns. Tickets for rides within the city can be bought from the driver, but traveling farther away requires a stop at the pl. de Verdun office. Maps and schedules available. Open M-Sa 7am-7:30pm.

Taxis: pl. de Verdun (☎05 46 41 55 55 or 05 46 41 22 22). €7 from train to hostel.

Car Rental: On av. Général de Gaulle, under 50m from the train station: **ADA** (☎05 46 41 02 17; www.ada.fr). Open M-Sa 8am-noon and 2-7pm, MC/V. **Budget** (☎05 46 41 35 53; fax 05 46 41 55 26). Open M-F 8am-noon and 2-7pm, Sa 8am-noon and 2-6pm. AmEx/MC/V. **Hertz** (☎05 46 41 02 31). Open M-F 8am-noon and 2-7pm, Sa 8am-noon and 2-6pm. AmEx/MC/V. **Rent-A-Car** (☎05 46 27 27 27; fax 05 46 28 33 66). Open M-F 8am-noon and 2-7pm, Sa 8am-1pm and 2-6pm. Expect to pay €30 per day at each establishment.

Bike Rental: Vélos Municipaux Autoplus (☎05 46 34 02 22), off quai Valin (open May-Sept. M-Sa 7am-7:30pm, Su 1-7pm) or in pl. de Verdun, near the bus station (open daily July-Aug. 7:30am-7:30pm; Sept.-June M-Sa 7:30am-7pm and Su 1:15-7pm). Free with ID deposit for 2hr., €1 per hr. thereafter.

◼◼ ◼ ORIENTATION AND PRACTICAL INFORMATION

La Rochelle spreads from cafe-lined **quai Duperré** in the **vieux port** to the boutique-filled **vieille ville** inland. Opposite the *vieille ville*, to the south is the more modern area of **la ville en bois** (Wooden Village), which, despite its name, is a complex of industrial buildings, storage for boats, and several museums, including the excellent **aquarium** (see **Sights,** p. 535). Farther to the south is a little strip of beachfront, **Les Minimes.** It's a 5min. walk from the train station to the tourist office; head up av. du Général de Gaulle to the first square, pl. de la Motte Rouge, and turn left onto quai du Gabut. The tourist office is on the left, in the quartier du Gabut.

Tourist Office: pl. de la Petite Sirène, quartier du Gabut (☎05 46 41 14 68; www.larochelle-tourisme.com). Multilingual staff sells a useful French brochure with maps and info (€0.60) and an abbreviated version in English and 8 other languages (€0.20). Sign in window lists festivities. 2hr. **walking tours** of the *vieille ville* July-Aug. M-Sa 10:30am (€6, children €4) and 1hr. horse-and-carriage tours daily 2:30pm (€8, children €6). Night visits led by costume-clad locals every Th July to mid-Sept. (2hr.; 8:30pm, 9pm; €10, students and children €6). Reservations are required for the carriage and night tours. Most tours are in French, but English tours can occasionally be arranged in advance. Also offers hotel reservation service for an additional €2. Open July-Aug. M-Sa 9am-8pm, Su 10:30am-5:30pm; June and Sept. M-Sa 9am-7pm, Su 10:30am-5:30pm; Oct.-May M-Sa 9am-6pm, Su 10am-1pm.

Bank: Banque de France, on the corner of rue Réamur and rue Léance Vieljeux (☎05 46 51 48 00), has an ATM. Open M-F 8:30am-noon and 1:30-3:30pm. **Crédit Lyonnais,** 19 rue du Palais, also 24hr. **ATMs.**

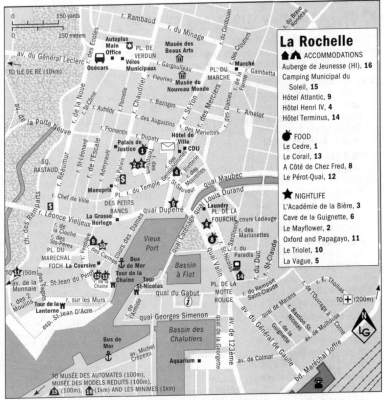

Youth Center: Centre Départemental d'Information Jeunesse (CDIJ), 2 rue des Gentilshommes (☎05 46 41 16 36; cdij17@yahoo.fr). Apartment and job listings. Open M 2-6pm, Tu-F 10am-12:30pm and 1:30-6pm. Internet €1 for 30min., €2 for 1hr., €10 for unlimited use for 1 year.

Laundromat: Laverie Vague Bleue, 4bis quai Louis Durand, corner of rue St-Nicolas. Open daily 8:30am-8:30pm. Wash 8kg load €3.80, 16kg load €6.90. Dry €1. W 8:30am-12:30pm; prices €3.10-€6.10.

Police: 2 pl. de Verdun (☎05 46 51 36 36).

Hospital: rue du Dr. Schweitzer, 24hr. emergency entrance on bd. Joffre (☎05 46 45 50 50). English-speaking staff.

Internet Access: Cyber Squat, 63 rue St-Nicolas (☎05 46 34 53 67). €0.76 connection fee, €0.10 per min. Also has video games and a fax machine (€2 for the 1st page, €1.80 after that). Open Sept.-June. M-Sa noon-10pm; July-Aug., M-Sa 11am-10pm.

Post Office: 52 av. Mulhouse (☎05 46 51 25 03), 50m from the train station. **Currency exchange** offered free of charge, outdoor ATM, and Cyberposte. Open M-F 8:30am-7pm, Sa 8:30am-noon. Branch at 6 pl. de l'Hôtel de Ville (☎05 46 30 41 30), open M-F 8:30am-6:30pm, Sa 8am-noon. **Poste Restante:** Hôtel de Ville, 17021 La Rochelle.

Postal Code: 17000.

🏠 🏠 ACCOMMODATIONS AND CAMPING

Cheap beds in town are limited, especially during the summer, when rates are higher; make reservations in early June for trips in July and August when festivals crowd the city. The rates listed below are for the high season.

🏨 **Hôtel Terminus,** pl. de la Motte-Rouge (☎05 46 50 69 69; www.tourisme-francais.com/hotels/terminus). Victorian wallpaper and cascading white curtains create a romantic ambience, complete with a sunny lounge on the 1st fl. and an elegant breakfast room. Breakfast €6. Enclosed private parking available. Reception 24hr. Singles and doubles with bath and TV €39-64; triples and quads with bath and TV €58-72. Prices vary with season. AmEx/MC/V. ❹

Hôtel Atlantic, 23 rue Verdière (☎05 46 41 16 68; fax 05 46 41 25 69). Despite its drippy faucets, the 2-star Atlantic features bright rooms and friendly service. Excellent location and unbeatable prices make it one of the best bargains in town. Breakfast €5. Open mid-Mar. to Nov. Singles and doubles €26, with shower €31-37, with shower and toilet €36-43, with shower, bath, and toilet €45-48; doubles and triples with 2 beds, shower and bathroom €49; quads with 2 beds, shower, and toilet €53. No showers available for those in showerless rooms. MC/V. ❷

Hôtel Henri IV, 31 rue des Gentilshommes (☎05 46 41 25 79; fax 05 46 41 78 64; henri-iv@wanadoo.fr), on pl. de la Caille, off rue du Temple, in the heart of the *vieille ville.* Spacious, modern rooms are available right in the *centre ville* in this newly renovated hotel. Cheery sunflower-themed dining room. Breakfast €5.50. Singles and doubles €40-54 with 1 bed; doubles with 2 beds €50-77; triples with 2 beds €65-96; quads with 2 beds €70-120. Price vary with season. AmEx/MC/V. ❸

Centre International de Séjour, Auberge de Jeunesse (HI), av. des Minimes (☎05 46 44 43 11; fax 05 46 45 41 48). A 30min. walk along the water from the SNCF station. Keep to the port edges, navigate through the marina, and look for the white 2-story building on your left. No signs are visible. Note the markings on the boat docks; the hostel is just past dock #36. Pick up a map from the tourist office. Alternatively, take bus #10 (dir: Port des Minimes) from av. de Colmar, 1 block from the station, to "Lycée Hôtelier" (M-Sa every 20min. 7am-7:45pm, €1.20). Take a right onto av. des Minimes and look for the *auberge* set back from road on the right. Enormous and impersonal, the hostel offers dimly lit 2- to 6-bunk dorms. Ample supply of plants tries to brighten the mood. Internet €0.20 per min. Breakfast included (7-9am). Reception July-Aug. 8am-10pm; Sept.-June 8am-noon and 2-10pm. Reserve ahead. 6-bed dorm €13; 4-bed dorm €15.50; single or double room €18.50. MC/V. ❶

Camping: Camping Municipal du Soleil, av. Michel Crépeau (☎05 46 44 42 53). A 10min. walk from the city center along the quai, following av. Marillac to the left at its junction with allée des Tamaris. Or catch bus #10 (dir: Port des Minimes). Crowded, friendly, and close to the port. Facility does a good job keeping a natural feel. Open mid-June to mid-Sept. Reservations recommended. 1 person and car €7; extra person €3.20; children €2.20. Electricity €3.70. Free showers. ❶

🍴 FOOD

The *fruits de mer* are always ripe in La Rochelle; follow the fishy smell to the **covered market** at pl. du Marché for fresh seafood and produce. (Open daily 7am-1pm.) **Monoprix** is on rue de Palais, near the clock tower. (Open July-Aug. M-Sa 8:30am-9pm, Su 9am-noon; Sept.-June M-Sa 8:30am-8pm.) **Co-ops** operate at 41 rue Sardinerie (open M 3:30-8pm, Tu and Th-Sa 8:30am-1pm and 3:30-8pm, W 8:30am-1pm, and Su 9am-1pm and 5-8pm). and at 17 rue Amelot (open M 3:30-7:45pm, Tu-Sa 8:30am-12:45pm and 3:30-7:45pm, Su 9am-12:30pm). Restaurants crowd the *vieille ville* along **rue St-Jean** and the quai.

■ **Restaurant Le Corail,** 10 pl. de la Chaîne (☎05 46 50 59 69). Classic seafood restaurant has plenty of outdoor seating, but it's main claim to fame is the boatloads of seafood it serves—literally. The restaurant serves seafood in boats over 2ft. long, a 1ft. high, and overflowing with crabs, lobster, mussels, clams, oysters, and countless other *fruits de mer* (€35.60). For those on a tighter budget, the restaurant offers a 3-course *menu* for €9.80, and 4-course *menu* for €14.40, with further upgrades for more expensive items. Open daily noon-2pm and 7-10pm. MC/V. ❸

A Côté de Chez Fred, 30-32 rue St-Nicolas (☎05 46 41 65 76). This little seafood place physically surrounds its market supplier; you can watch the fish being prepared through an open window. *Plats* €8.50-25, *menu* available for €17. Open M-Sa 12:15-2:30pm and 7-10:30pm. MC/V. ❸

Le Pérot-Quai, 15 rue St-Jean du Pérot (☎05 46 41 43 68). This newly opened ultra-chic restaurant serves up seafood dishes in an inventive style. Silver minimalist decor, funky dishware, and a well-dressed staff add to the trendy ambience. *Plats* €8.50-13.50. Open Tu-Su 12:30-2pm and 7:30-10pm. MC/V. ❸

Le Cedre, 22 rue des Templiers (☎05 46 41 03 89). This Lebanese restaurant offers fresh vegetables, quality bread, and a shaded outdoor seating area perfect for people-watching. A variety of sandwiches, kebabs, and hamburgers €2.20-€5.40; shish kebab pita €3.40; shish kebab platter with fries and veggies €5.50. Open daily 11am-2am. ❶

◉ SIGHTS

A mere €6.60 buys combined admission to the Musées du Nouveau Monde and the Musée des Beaux Arts. Joint tickets are available at the tourist office or at any of the three museums, and are valid for one month.

■ AQUARIUM. This not-to-be missed, thematically decorated aquarium is home to a whopping 10,000 marine animals, kept in habitats that simulate environments from the French Atlantic coast to the tropical rainforest. Audio tours offered in French, Spanish, German, and English (€3.50) provide fascinating fish tales to accompany the awe-inspiring visual displays. The aquarium makes a perfect rainy-day activity, but be prepared for crowds of people with the same idea. Be sure not to step on a turtle in the tropical room, where they are allowed to mosey freely. (*Bassin des Grande Yacht, next to the Musée Maritime. ☎05 46 34 00 00. Open daily July-Aug. 9am-11pm; Apr.-June and Sept. 9am-8pm; Oct.-Mar. 10am-8pm. Free parking. €12, students and children €9. Slightly discounted rates for groups over 20. Wheelchair-accessible.*)

OLD TOWN. The pedestrian *vieille ville*, dating from the 17th and 18th centuries, stretches beyond the whitewashed townhouses of the harbor to a glitzy inland shopping district sprinkled with museums, making a perfect place to grab an outdoor meal. The 14th-century **grosse horloge** (great clock) is worth strolling by, but the archaeological exhibit inside has little to offer. Also of note is the intricately decorated white stone facade of the Renaissance **Hôtel de Ville,** with the prominent statue of its builder, Henry IV. (*45min. French tours of the interior daily June-Sept. 3pm; Oct.-May Sa-Su 3pm. €3, students and children €1.50.*)

TOUR ST-NICOLAS AND TOUR DE LA CHAÎNE. Now the defining characteristic of La Rochelle's landscape, these 14th-century towers on the port once guarded the town from attack. When hostile ships approached, guards closed the harbor by raising a chain between the two towers. Now the 800-year-old chain lines the path leading from rue de la Chaîne to the tower. Tour St-Nicolas, on the left as you face the harbor, continues to impress visitors with its thick fortifications and narrow, dizzying staircases. Tour de la Chaîne houses a fascinating timeline of the city's history (in French only) with a model of the town in Richelieu's day. (*St-Nicolas ☎ 05 46 41 74 13, Chaîne 05 46 34 11 81; fax 05 46 34 11 83. Both towers open daily July-Aug. 10am-7pm; mid-May to June and early to mid-Sept. 10am-1pm and 2-6:30pm; mid-Sept. to mid-May Tu-Su 10am-12:30pm and 2-5:30pm. Last entrance 30min. before closing. €4.60, ages 18-25 €3.10, under 18 free. Combined ticket including Tour de la Lanterne, with ferry passage between the 2 towers €10, ages 18-25 €6.50; Oct.-Mar. free first Su of the month.*)

TOUR DE LA LANTERNE. Accessible from the Tour de la Chaîne by a low rampart, this 70m high tower was France's first lighthouse. The 15th-century structure has a morbid history. It became known as the **Tour des Prêtres** after 13 priests were thrown from the steeple during the Wars of Religion. In 1822, four Carbonari sergeants were imprisoned here before being executed in Paris for conspiring against the monarch. Along the 162 steps to the top hold the stone walls are carved with intricate graffiti that provides remarkable historical documentation of castles and shipwrecks, recorded by the tower's detainees. At the summit, only 3in. of stone protect visitors from free-falls, but on a sunny day, the view extends all the way to the Île d'Oléron. Historical exhibitions are also on display on the various floors on the way up. (*☎ 05 46 41 56 04. Same hours and prices as the Tour St-Nicolas.*)

MUSÉE DU NOUVEAU MONDE. This museum explores European perceptions of the New World during the Age of Exploration. Antique maps, paintings of slaves and Native Americans, and other artifacts are on display alongside a few classically decorated French salons. (*10 rue Fleuriau. ☎ 05 46 41 46 50. Open M and W-Sa 10am-12:30pm and 2-6pm, Su 2:30-6pm. €3.50, students and children under 18 free.*)

MUSÉE DES BEAUX ARTS. This museum has works by Rembrandt and Delacroix, and a nice Fromentin series which appears on the town's postcards. Look for Signac's 18th-century painting of the lively city harbor. (*28 rue Gargoulleau. ☎ 05 46 34 76 55. Open Su-M and W-Sa 2-5pm. €3.50, students and children under 18 free. English guidebook available at the desk.*) A newer gallery downstairs contains rotating exhibits of modern art. (*Opening hours and contact information changes with the exhibits.*)

🎵 🌿 ENTERTAINMENT AND FESTIVALS

La Coursive, 4 rue St-Jean-du-Perot, hosts operas, jazz and classical music concerts, traditional and experimental plays, dance performances, and art films. (*☎ 05 46 51 54 00; fax 05 46 51 54 01. Info office open M 5-8pm, Tu-Sa 1-8pm, Su 2-8pm.*) During the summer, **quai Duperré** and **cours des Dames** are closed to cars and open to mimes, jugglers, musicians, and an outdoor market. (Open daily July-Sept. 8pm-midnight, May-June Su noon-8pm.)

La Rochelle's popular festivals attract art-loving, sun-seeking crowds like nowhere else. During the last week of June and the first week of July, the city becomes the Cannes of the Atlantic with its **Festival International du Film de La Rochelle.** Fans come from Paris to stay up all night watching movies. (Information ☎ 05 46 51 54 00, reservations 01 48 06 16 66; fax 05 46 28 28 29. All 100 films €80; students, those under 25, and unemployed €60; 3 films €15; students, those under 25, and unemployed €10; one film €6. Visit www.larochelle-tourisme.com and www.larochelle.fr for more information.) Without batting an eyelash, La Rochelle turns around and holds its **FrancoFolies,** a massive six-day music festival in mid-July that draws francophone performers from around the world. (*☎ 05 46 50 55 77; www.francofolies.fr. Some afternoon performances cost only €4,* evening concerts €22-38.) To round out the month, the end of July brings a 10-day **theater festival** on quai Simenon. (☎05 46 34 33 75.) During the 2nd week of September, hundreds of boats in the Port des Minimes open their immaculate interiors to the public for the **Grand Pavois,** a boat competition known as "the foremost floating boat show in Europe." (☎05 46 44 46 39; www.grand-pavois.com.) The town has recently added **Festival de Jazz de La Rochelle** to its repertoire, which takes place in the beginning of October. (☎05 46 27 11 19 for more information.) To cap the busy summer and fall seasons, the **marathon** runs through town at the end of November. (☎05 46 44 42 19. For information, write to Res le Platin, 2 Perspective de l'Océan, BP 97.)

▓ NIGHTLIFE

No visit to La Rochelle is complete without a visit to ◼**Cave de la Guignette,** 8 rue St-Nicolas. This bar has been in operation since 1933, when it stocked fishing boats with barrels of wine for their long voyages, and now is an extremely popular student hangout. The bar is well-known for it's house specialty, "la Guignette," a white wine infused with fruit flavorings (1L bottle €8). Other wines by the glass €2. (Open Tu 4-8pm, W 10am-1pm and 4-8pm, Th-Sa 10am-1pm and 3-8pm.) Though its name may raise expectations of port-swilling patrons discussing 17th-century philosophy, **L'Académie de la Bière** on the rue des Templiers is actually a lively cross between an Irish pub and a French outdoor cafe, with plenty of outdoor seating for people-watching, and a dark, cramped inside for rocking out. (☎05 46 42 43 78. Beers €2.40-2.80. Open daily 10am-2am.) Next door, relaxed **Le Mayflower,** sells a large, potent rum concoction (€3.80) in a bar reminiscent of an English pub. (☎05 46 50 51 39. Open daily 6pm-2am.) Along the waters of the old port, the dressed-down folks at **La Vague,** 16 quai Duperré, sip cocktails amid the surf boards and parasols. (☎05 46 30 53 19. Open daily 8:30am-2am.) For a cool place to hang out on a summer night, head to the **cour du Temple,** a lively square tucked away off rue des Templiers.

The crowd is young at the twin nightclubs **Oxford** and **Papagayo Discothèque,** behind the restaurant Richard Coutanceau on the plage de la Concurrence. Oxford offers a wild night of dancing under a giant disco ball, while Papagayo is a fun-filled party complete with fake palm trees and 80s music. The streets leading to the clubs near the Tour de Lanterne are dark and isolated at night; they should not be traveled alone. (☎05 46 41 51 81. Cover €10 with 1 alcoholic drink, or 2 non-alcoholic drinks, M-Th and Su clubbers can pay €5 with no drinks. Open Su-M and W-Sa 11pm-5am.) Two floors and two bars decked with gaudy palm trees and mirrors, **Le Triolet,** 8 rue des Carmes, gets yuppies very tipsy on 94 different kinds of whiskey. This discotheque's eclectic soundtrack doesn't heat up the dance floor until late. (☎05 46 41 03 58. €10 cover includes 1 alcoholic drink or 2 non-alcoholic. Open M-Sa 11pm-5am; July-Aug. also open Su.) The tourist office offers a brochure, *Gay-Friendly La Rochelle*, to find gay- and lesbian-friendly nightlife.

▶ DAYTRIP FROM LA ROCHELLE

ROCHEFORT

Trains connect Rochefort with Bordeaux (2hr., 6 per day, €19.90) and La Rochelle (20min., 5 per day, €4.90), Saintes (30min., 7 per day, €6.80). Rochefort is also easily accessible by taking Ocecars, which shuttle between the gare routière and La Rochelle (line #51; 1hr.; M-Sa 8 per day, Su 2 per day; €5.10) and Saintes (line #60, 1hr., M-Sa 6 per day, €6.70). Citram Littoral buses, pl. de Verdun, bring travelers to Le Château on l'Ile d'Oléron (☎05 46 82 31 30; line #10; 1½hr.; M-Sa 8 per day, Su 2 per day; €6.50.)

For more information, the tourist office on av. Sadi Carnot is extremely helpful. (☎ 05 46 99 08 60. Open mid-June to mid-Sept. 9:30am-7pm, mid-Sept. to mid-June 9:30am-12:30pm and 2-6:30pm.) The tourist office offers a promotion called the carte sesamé available at any museum. It offers reduced admission to all Rochefort's museums.

The modern town of Rochefort (pop. 27,000) was a sparsely populated marsh along the Charente River until Louis XIV took possession of it in the 17th century and transformed it into the greatest royal dockyard in France.

In homage to their naval past, residents of Rochefort have begun construction of an exact replica of ◪**L'Hermione,** the vessel which transported Marquis de Lafayette to the aid of George Washington and the American colonies in 1780. Great pains have been taken to ensure the replica's authenticity, with the changes only being made to satisfy modern maritime standards. The reconstruction is expected to be finished in 2007 and will sail to Boston in either 2008 or 2009. Scaffolding is in place in the oversized tent in which the boat in being constructed so that visitors can see it from every angle, watching the builders at work. Guided tours of the worksite demonstrate the craft of 18th-century blacksmiths and carpenters. (☎ 05 46 87 01 90. €4.60; students, retirees, and unemployed €4; ages 8-16 €2; under 8 free. Tours July and Aug. continuously 9am-7pm; Apr.-June and Sept. 11:30am, 2:30, 4:30pm, Oct.-Dec. M-F 2, 4pm, Sa-Su 11am, 2, 4pm; Jan.-Mar. M-F 2:30, 4:30pm, Sa-Su 11:30 am, 2:30, 4:30pm. Entrance with guided tour €6, students retirees and unemployed €5.50, ages 8-16 €3, under 8 free.)

Perhaps the most fascinating of Rochefort's smaller museums is the **Maison Pierre Loti,** 141 rue Pierre Loti, which exhibits the exotic collection of curiosities accumulated by the magician and naval officer, Loti. Eccentric to the extreme, this Rochefort resident transformed the rooms of his house into a Turkish lounge, an Islamic mosque, and a Gothic chamber. The museum can only be seen through guided tours. (☎ 05 46 99 16 88. Tours daily 1hr. July to mid-Sept. every 30min. 10am-5:30pm; mid-Sept. to June Su-M and W-Sa 10:30, 11:30am, 2:30, 3:30, 4:30pm. €7.65, students and children 8-18 €3.90.) The **Musée National de la Marine,** 1 place de la Galissonnière, next to the Hermione, is dedicated to the nautical history of Rochefort, and displays countless model ships, while rotating other nautically themed exhibits. (☎ 05 46 99 86 57. Open daily Apr.-Sept. 15 10am-6:30pm, Feb.-Mar. and Sept. 15-Dec.15 Tu-Su 10am-noon and 2-6pm. Closed Dec. 15-Jan. 31. €4.60, students €1.50, under 18 free.) Detailed dioramas at the **Musée des Commerces d'Autrefois,** 12 rue Lesson, depict the average day of various French workers between 1890 and 1940. Scenes include the grocery store, barber shop, pharmacy, and bar. (☎ 05 46 83 91 50; www.museedescommerces.com. Open daily July-Aug. 10am-8pm; Apr.-June and Sept.-Oct. 10am-noon and 2-7pm; Nov.-Mar. 10am-noon and 2-6pm.) The impressive 176m long steel and iron **Pont Transbordeur,** 10 rue du Docteur Pujos, stands farther down the Charente. Designed by engineering genius Ferdinand Arnodin, the bridge was built in 1900 from the same materials as the Eiffel Tower.

For those who choose to stay the night, the two-star hotel ◪**Roca-Fortis ❸,** 14 rue de la République, offers quiet, sunny, impeccably clean and tastefully decorated rooms, the larger fit for kings. (☎ 05 46 99 26 32; www.hotel-rocafortis.com. Breakfast €5.50, can be served in room. Reserve ahead in July and August. Extra bed €8. Singles and doubles with TV and shower €35, with TV, shower, and toilet €39; extra-large rooms with TV, shower, bath, and toilet €48. AmEx/MC/V.) For a tasty meal, Rochefort locals recommend **Le Cap Nell ❸,** 1 quai Bellot, overlooking the small boat-filled harbor. The combined bistro and grill serves fresh seafood, along with duck and peppered steak. Three-course *menus* are €14.90 or €21.

(☎ 05 46 87 31 77. Open daily July-Aug. noon-2pm and 7:30-10pm; Sept.-June Su-M and Th-Sa noon-2pm and 5-7pm, Tu-W noon-2pm. AmEx/MC/V.)

ÎLE DE RÉ

Île de Ré, dubbed "Ré La Blanche" for its 70km of fine, white sand beaches, is a sunny paradise just 10km from La Rochelle. Connected by a bridge to the mainland, the 30km long island combines one of Europe's largest nature preserves, with extensive paved bike paths, pine forests, farmland, vineyards, and bustling towns with huge stretches of untouched sand. Though only 15,000 people live on the island year-round, July and August bring crowds to the main town of **St-Martin-de-Ré** and to the beaches on the island's southern coast. Though far more touristed than nearby Île d'Aix, this popular Parisian weekend getaway spot offers plenty of easily accessible pristine beaches and nature trails while maintaining the lively atmosphere of a booming resort town.

Île de Ré

Phare des Baleines
Plage de la Conche des Baleines
St-Clément-des-Baleines
D101
Les Portes-en-Ré
Ars-en-Ré
Plage du Petit Bec
ATLANTIC OCEAN
RD735
0   2 miles
0   2 kilometers
Plage des Prises
Loix
Plage du Peu Ragot
La Couarde-sur-Mer
Plage des Aneries
Plage du Petit Sergent
Le Bois-Plage-en-Ré
St-Martin-de-Ré
Plage des Gollandières
RD735
Plage du Pas des Boeufs
Plage de Gros Jonc
D201
La Flotte
Abbaye des Châtelliers
Oyster beds (écluses)
La Noue
Ste-Marie-de-Ré
D201
D103
RD735
Fort de la Prée
FRANCE
Île de Ré
Rivedoux beach
D201
Plage Sud
Sablanceaux
TO MAINLAND (4km)
Pont La Pallice

TRANSPORTATION. Driving across **pont La Pallice** costs a steep €16.50 in round-trip tolls from June to mid-September. (Mid-Sept. to May €9; €2 for motorcycles and scooters year-round.) **Walking** and **biking** are easy alternatives to driving, and cycling from La Rochelle to Sablanceaux takes less than an hour. The ride is a bit tough going up the 4km long bridge, but well worth it, as the trails on the island are marvelous, with great coastal views. From pl. de Verdun in La Rochelle, head west on av. Maréchal Leclerc and follow road signs to Île de Ré until the bike path appears on the left.

The city **buses** also provide a viable means of transportation. Line #50 goes as far as Sablanceaux, the first beach on the island after the bridge. Make sure the bus is going to Sablanceaux: some buses on lines 1 and 21 stop before crossing the bridge. (Hours and frequency change with the season. Off-season no buses go to Sablanceaux, and in early and late summer, buses only operate on certain days. Check the schedule ahead of time. €1.50.) For ventures beyond Sablanceaux, **Rébus** is a convenient way to travel between pl. de Verdun and the villages on Ré, including St-Martin (45min., 9 per day, €4.80) and Les Portes (1½hr., 4 per day, €8.20), at the northern tip of the island. (☎ 05 46 09 20 15. Info office at 36 av. Charles de Gaulle in St-Martin. Open M-F 8:30am-noon and 2-5:30pm.)

Once on Île de Ré, there are plenty of places to rent bikes in each village. **Cycland** has branches in Rivedoux, La Flotte, St-Martin (just off rue Sully), Le Bois-Plage, Ars, Les Portes, St-Clément, and La Couarde. (☎ 05 46 09 08 66. Bikes €3.50-5 per hr., €5.50-€7 per half-day, €7-9 per day; price depends on style of bike rented. Deposit €100-200 by check or cash, or ID deposit. Monetary deposit required for those wishing to drop off bikes in another location. Open daily July-Aug. 9am-7pm; Sept.-June 9:30am-12:30pm and 2-7pm. MC/V.)

POITOU-CHARENTES

🛈 PRACTICAL INFORMATION. The largest and most centrally located town on the island, **St-Martin-de-Ré** (pop. 2650) is the best starting place for exploring Île de Ré. St-Martin's **tourist office,** on quai Nicolas Baudin, has a free map of the island's bike trails. Walking tours (90min.; mid-June to mid-Sept. Tu 10:30am; €5.50, children €2) depart from the tourist office. Horse-and-carriage tours (1½hr.; mid-June to mid-Sept. Th at 10am; €8.50, children €5) begin at the **Parking Vauban.** (☎05 46 09 20 06; fax 05 46 09 06 18; ot.st.martin@wanadoo.fr. Open July-Aug. M-Sa 10am-7pm, Su 10am-1pm; Sept.-June M-Sa 10am-noon and 2-6pm, Su 10am-1pm.) The best location for **currency exchange,** with a 1% commission, is at **Crédit Agricole,** 4 quai Foran, on the port. (☎05 46 09 20 14. Open Tu-F 9am-12:15pm and 1:30-6pm, Sa 8:45am-12:45pm.) Other services include: **police** (☎05 46 09 21 17); **Pharmacie Dubreuil,** 7 rue de Sully (☎05 46 09 20 43; open M-Sa 9am-12:30pm and 2:30-7:30pm); and the **post office,** pl. de la République. (☎05 46 09 20 14. Open M-F 9am-noon and 1:30-3:30pm, Sa 9am-noon.) **Postal Code:** 17410.

🛏🛏 ACCOMMODATIONS AND CAMPING. The attractive prices of the hotels in Ré go way up in summer, as hotel owners know there will be a steady stream of tourists ready to pay higher fees. St-Martin's understaffed **Hôtel Le Sully ❸,** 19 rue Jean Jaurès, offers wood-paneled rooms on a busy street for the island's cheapest prices. (☎05 46 09 26 94; fax 05 46 09 06 85. Breakfast €5.20. Reservations recommended. Singles or doubles with shower €35-39, with toilet and shower or bath €45-48; doubles with 2 beds, toilet, and shower €48-52; quads with toilet and shower €62-64. Extra bed €8. MC/V.) The smaller surrounding towns also provide suitable accommodations. **L'Hippocampe ❸,** 16 rue Château des Mauléons, in **La Flotte,** 4km east of St-Martin and 9km north of Sablanceaux, has small, modest rooms. (☎05 46 09 60 68. Breakfast €5. Reserve months ahead. Reception open only 5-7pm. Singles and doubles €35, with shower €40, with bath €45. MC/V.) Campsites are plentiful on Île de Ré, but those between the bridge and St-Martin-de-Ré become crowded in July and August. Travelers seeking solitude should head to beachside **La Plage ❶,** 408 rte. du Chaume, near St-Clément. (☎05 46 29 42 62. Open Apr.-Sept. Reserve months in advance. In the summer, campers can stay only by the week. Up to three people with tent €241, each extra person €64.50. Car included. Electricity €32 per week.) Gorgeous, thickly forested **Camping Tamaris ❶,** 4 rue du Comte D'Hastrel, is right near **Rivedoux**'s center and one of the island's popular spots. (☎05 46 09 81 28. Open Easter-Sept. 1-3 people €12.50, €4.20 per extra person, children under 7 €2.10. Electricity €3.60.)

🍴 FOOD. Most towns have pizzerias and *crêperies* as well as **morning markets,** which are listed in full in Ré's tourist packet. St-Martin's indoor market is off rue Jean Jaurès, by the port. (Open daily high season 7am-1pm, in low season closed M and W.) Two **supermarkets** sit just east of St-Martin on the road to La Flotte across the street from one another: **Intermarché,** 4 av. des Corsaires (☎05 46 09 42 02; open M-Sa 9am-7:30pm, Su 9-11:45am) and **Super U,** 23 rue des Salières (☎05 46 09 42 80; open M-Sa 9am-7:30pm, Su 9-11:45am). A cluster of tasty, albeit pricey, restaurants surround the port in St-Martin and overlook the colorful fleet of fishing boats below. The **Marco Polo,** 6 quai de Bernonville, offers a superb penne with black olives (€6.30) in addition to a selection of fresh seafood and an array of traditional desserts. (☎05 46 09 15 92. Three-course *menu* €12.90. Open daily 9:30am-4pm and 6-11pm.)

🔆 SIGHTS. Between Sablanceaux and beachy La Flotte are the ruins of the 13th-century **Abbaye des Châteliers.** First built in 1156, the abbey was destroyed during the Wars of Religion as Ré passed back and forth between Catholic and Protestant hands. The abbey was abandoned in 1574, and many of its stones were taken to build the Fort de la Prée in 1625. The ruins, composed of the walls of the nave and a gaping window frame now stand in an isolated field, visible from the bus from Sablanceaux to La Flotte. **La Flotte** (pop. 2700) is the island's most typical fishing town, with a bustling port and pedestrian area. **Maison du Platin,** av. du front de Mer, 4 cours Félix Faure, details the history of the island's fish and salt industries and features photographs of Ré's earliest residents. The museum conducts walking tours in French of the old quarters, port, and nearby oyster farms (€4.60, children €2.60), as well as bike tours of the **Abbey des Chateliers** and the **Fort de la Prée** (90min.; €5, children €2.60). Schedules vary; call for information. (☎05 46 09 61 39. Open Apr.-Oct. M-F 10:30am-12:30pm and 2:30-6pm, Su 2:30-5:30pm. €3.60, ages 6-18 €2, under 6 free.) Hour-long tours of the medieval fishing beds, the **écluses à poissons,** in Ste-Marie de Ré, teach visitors about the island's fishing traditions. The stone walls of the beds, which lie along the southern coast's beaches off Sablanceaux, were erected to trap fish with the waning tides. Wear boots! (8 bis de la Terre Rouge. Times vary with tides. Call ☎05 46 30 25 28 for a schedule.)

St-Martin lays claim to a port built by Vauban and a citadel built by Louis XIV in order to protect Ré from the invading English. The citadel now serves as an active prison, with around 500 inmates. The 15th- to 17th-century Renaissance gallery of the **Hôtel Clerjotte,** on av. Victor-Bouthilier, houses the **Musée Ernest Cognacq,** which is devoted to the history of the island and displays such exhibits as model ships, old paintings, and archaeological finds including an enormous elephant skull. (☎05 46 09 21 22. Open July-Aug. M and W-Su 10am-7pm; Sept.-June M and W-F 10am-noon and 2-6pm, Sa-Su 2-6pm.) Just up the hill from the quai rests the imposing 15th-century **Église St-Martin.** Originally constructed in the Romanesque style, the church has been built and destroyed so many times in religious wars that its outside and interior now have no stylistic relation. The decor inside is nonetheless magnificent, drawing a large crowd. At sunset the view of the entire island from the top of the belltower is even more breathtaking than usual. (Open daily July-Aug. 9:30am-11:30pm; Oct.-Mar. 9:30am-sunset; Apr.-June and Sept. M-F 9:30am-sunset, Sa-Su and holidays 9:30am-11pm. Admission to church free, belltower €1.50, ages 11-15 €0.75, under 11 free. Guided tours €2.30, children 11-15 €1.50. Binoculars are available for €0.75 with an ID deposit.) On the way up the island, stop by **Ars** to admire its 17 windmills, dismantled in the 19th century when a phyloxera plague wiped out the island's chief crop. Nearing **St-Clément-des-Baleines,** watch for the blinking red light of the **Phare des Baleines,** built in 1854. Standing 60m high, the lighthouse is one of the tallest in France and directs boats over 50km away. Climb its 257 stairs for a great view of the ocean. (☎05 46 29 18 23. Open daily Apr.-June 10am-6:45pm; July-Aug. 9:30am-7:15pm; Sept. noon-6:15pm; Oct.-Mar. 10:30am-5:15pm. €2.20, ages 7-12 €1.10.)

🎵 **NIGHTLIFE.** St-Martin has a surprisingly outsized nightlife for its diminutive size. Port-side vendors stay open until 11pm or midnight during the summer to accommodate the late-night tourists, while locals shuttle between the bars and discos all night. **Le Cubana,** on Venelle de la Fosse Braye, is a lively bar with rum-infused drinks that accompany thumping Latin rhythms. (☎05 46 09 93 49. Open July-Aug. daily 10pm-2am; Mar.-June and Sept.-Oct. M-Sa 10pm-2am; Nov.-Feb. F-Sa 10pm-2am.) Behind a mysterious locked door next to Le Cubana, the **Boucquingham** blasts techno and hip-hop into the wee hours of the morning. (☎05 46 09 01 20. Drinks €8. Cover €10, includes one drink. Open daily 11pm-5am.) Farther down the island, on Rivedoux plage, **La Rive,** pl. de la République, cranks out the beats daily from 11pm to 5am in July and August and Sa-Su during other months. (☎05 46 68 54 16. €10 cover includes one drink.)

▓ ▟ BIKING AND BEACHES. It's easy and affordable to rent a bike in any island town and pedal along the paths, coastal sidewalks, and wooded lanes spread out across the island. Although trails to St-Martin along the southern half of Île de Ré are often packed, crowds thin out to the north. The *Guide des Itinéraires Cyclables*, available from island tourist offices, describes five 10-22km paths. One of the island's best trails begins in Le Martray, just east of Ars, and runs along the northern coast through the island's trademark salt marsh and bird preserve, a wetlands sanctuary home to herons and rare blue-throated thrushes. The marsh is worth visiting in the summer, but winter's really the time to see it—20,000 birds stop by on their migration from Siberia and Canada to Africa. Other bike paths lead through forests, beside beaches, and to other island landmarks.

The major attraction of the island is, of course, its splendid beaches. Slather on some sunscreen and shake off all inhibitions at the bathing-suit-optional **plage du Petit Bec** in **Les Portes-en-Ré.** To avoid that full-body glow, head to the pine-fringed dunes of **plage de la Conche des Baleines,** near the lighthouse just off the Gare Bec. Both beaches, at the northern tip of the island, are huge and free from the crowds that fill beaches on the western coast. The sea off the exposed north coast tends to be dangerous, and the shores rocky; for better swimming, try the long strip of beach along the southern shore beginning at **La Couarde.**

ÎLE D'AIX

Smaller and less accessible than Ré, Aix (pop. 200) is almost entirely free of the souvenir shops and fast food stands that cover most towns in this region. Aix sees its fair share of visitors (300,000 per year), but this island maintains the feel of unspoiled wilderness. Just 3km long and barely 600m wide, the island has backwoods trails perfect for quiet hiking and tiny coves set into the rocky, shell-covered coastline. The best beaches are along the southwest coast near the lighthouses, though the *plage aux coquillages* is most sheltered from the wind, and has the bluest water. As one of the only coastal islands with no highway to the mainland, Aix rarely sees any cars. To get here, it's ferry or bust.

On the island, stop at the **Point Accueil** if it is open (hours vary), immediately on your right as you leave the port, and pick up a free map and brochure. If not, head to the **tourist office** at 6 rue Gourgaud, straight past the horse carriages. (☎05 46 83 01 82. Open daily Apr.-June and Sept. 10am-noon; July-Aug. 10am-noon and 2-5pm.) Île d'Aix also holds the bragging rights as the smallest town in France with a tourist office. **Horse carriages** lie just past the Point Accueil and conduct historical tours of the island in French. (☎05 46 84 07 18. 50min.; €6, under age 10 €5.) *Crêperies* and snack shops in town rent **bicycles** to tourists who want to explore the island. (Approx. €3.50 per hr., €8.50 per day. ID deposit.) Additionally, pedestrians can walk around the island in a mere 2hr., and some of the most beautiful spots are accessible only by foot.

One of the most striking sites dates from the time Aix hosted Napoleon in 1815 three days before he was exiled to the island of Ste-Hélène. The house in which he stayed was transformed into the **Musée Napoléonien** in 1928. Today it contains a small but impressive collection of portraits and Napoleon relics, including a dress worn by his first wife, Josephine, and 40 clocks stopped at 5:49, the time of his death. The **Musée Africain** next door presents an ethnographical and zoological exhibition on Napoleon's Egyptian campaign and contains African war booty, including a stuffed dodo bird. (☎05 46 84 66 40. Both open daily June-Sept. 9:30am-6pm; Apr.-May and Oct. Su-M and W-Sa 9:30am-12:30pm and 2-6pm; Nov.-Mar. Su-M and W-Sa 9:30-11:30am and 2-4:30pm. Separate admission €3, ages 18-25 €2.30, under 18 free. Combined admission €4, ages 18-25 €3.) The **Fort Liedot,** built by Napoleon to protect this tiny but strategically located island off the coast of

France, housed German prisoners during World Wars I and II and was later used as a summer camp for children, until the government purchased it in 1980 for use as a historical monument. (July-Aug. tours in French available through the tourist office, 5 per day 11am-5pm; 1hr.; €3.)

Île d'Aix's only hotel, **Hôtel Napoleon ④**, on the corner of rue Gourgaud and the place Austerlitz, is expensive, but the rooms are spacious and peaceful. (☎ 05 46 84 66 02; fax 05 46 84 69 70. Breakfast €6.50. Reception until 8pm. Singles and doubles with shower €56, with shower and toilet €62, with bath and toilet €64; *demi-pension* for two people €90-110 depending on room.) Next to the port, quiet **Camping le Fort de la Rade ①** offers a uniquely picturesque camping experience inside the red poppy-filled ruins of a fort. (☎ 05 46 84 28 28; fax 05 46 84 00 44. Open Apr.-Sept. Visitors arriving after reception is closed are welcome to enter on their own but must be sure to pay in the morning. Pool facilities available. €4.10 per person in July/Aug., €3.60 low season, €2.60/2.10 per child ages 2-10. Animals €2.10/€1.60. July-Aug. €5.60-7.70 per tent, €3.60-6.70 low season.)

The few restaurants on Aix tend to be pricey. The **bakery** on rue Gourgaud sells cheap sandwiches, and a little grocery store just across the street has all the essentials. In the middle of the island, on rue Le Bois Joly, the classy restaurant **Les Paillotes ④** beckons. Satisfied diners feast upon lamb and fresh seafood in an elegant shaded courtyard. (☎ 05 46 84 66 24; fax 05 46 84 23 25. 3-course *menu* €14.90-€25.50. Open daily 9am-2am. AmEx/MC/V.) The cheerful and always packed restaurant **Pressoir ③**, just down rue Le Bois Joly, is run by a bunch of young fishermen with perpetual five o'clock shadows. Enjoy fresh *moules frites* on the terrace for €10.50. *Menus* €16.90-22.90. Reserve ahead if possible. (☎ 05 46 84 09 37. Open daily July-Aug. noon-2pm and 7-11pm; May-June and Sept. noon-2pm and Sa-Su also 7-11pm. AmEx/MC/V.)

MARAIS POITEVIN

Stretching from Niort to the Atlantic just north of La Rochelle, this natural preserve of marshland has been nicknamed *la Venise Verte* (the Green Venice) for the serene canals that wind through it. Visitors biking along the banks or punting on the canals pass weeping willows, purple irises, herds of cattle, and the occasional rustic home. At its origin by the Sèvre Niortaise river, trees form an overhanging canopy, and duckweed carpets the water's surface, making the canals look like grassy paths. Canals control flooding, ensuring that small-scale farming remains the region's primary industry.

Though well worth the trouble, the Marais is not a very convenient daytrip from Poitiers; visitors should consider spending the night there. Most towns are inaccessible by public transportation. From **Coulon,** travelers can rent bikes or boats to travel along the river, visit other towns, and see the landscape of the wetlands. The tourist office in Coulon provides info and sells a great walking and biking map.

NIORT

A small city which combines modern store-filled pedestrian zones with windy and hilly residential streets, Niort (pop. 16,000) is a relaxing place to spend a day, as well as a convenient base for exploring the Marais.

⬛ TRANSPORTATION. Trains run from Niort to La Rochelle (45min., 9 per day, €9.50, TGV €11.20); Poitiers (1hr., 14 per day, €10.90, TGV €12.60); and Saintes (1hr., 10 per day, €10). Ticket windows are open M-Th 5:45am-8pm, F 5:45am-8:45pm, Sa 5:45am-7:30pm, Su 7:20am-10pm. Next to the station at the *gare* *routière*, **CASA buses** run to La Garette and Coulon (see Coulon, p. 545). For 24hr. **taxis**, call Taxi ABCD at ☎ 05 49 26 10 00. Niort has numerous **car rental** agencies all within one block of the train station.

■■☎ ORIENTATION AND PRACTICAL INFORMATION. To get to the **tourist office**, 16 rue du Petit St-Jean, from the station, walk down rue de la Gare, turn right onto rue du 14 Juillet, then left after reaching pl. de la Brèche. Circle around the place and take a left onto rue Ricard, which becomes rue Victor Hugo. After pl. des Halles, take a left onto rue Thiers; the office will be up the block on the left next to the Hôtel de Ville. The staff provides boating, biking and hiking maps of the Marais (€7.95), and walking and biking tours of Niort (free). Boat and bike tours of the Marais are available. (☎ 05 49 24 18 79; www.niortourisme.com. Open July-Aug. M-Sa 9:30am-7pm, Su 10am-12:30pm; Mar.-June and Sept.-Nov. M-Sa 9:30am-6:30pm; Dec.-Feb. M-F 9:30am-6pm, Sa 9:30am-6:30pm.) Other services include a **laundromat** at 48 rue Saint Gelais, off Place Pilori (open daily 7am-9pm); **police** at 2 rue de la Préfecture (☎ 05 49 28 72 00); a **hospital** on av. Charles de Gaulle (☎ 05 49 32 79 79); **Internet** Access at Medi@click, 6 rue Porte St-Jean, near pl. St-Jean d'Angely (☎ 05 49 28 31 31; €3 for 30min., €4 per hr., €1 less for those under 18; open M-Sa 2-7pm); and a **post office** at 4 rue Ernest Perochon. (☎ 05 49 06 33 33. Open M-F 8am-7pm, Sa 8am-noon.) **Postal Code: 79000.**

☎☎☎ ACCOMMODATIONS AND CAMPING. Niort has a plenty of hotel options to fit all budgets. **☒Hôtel St-Jean ❷**, 21 av. St-Jean d'Angely, lies just 12min. outside the center of town. From the station, walk up rue de la Gare, which will become rue du 24 Février. At pl. St-Jean, turn left onto av. St-Jean. Clean, basic furnishings, floral wallpaper, and a warm dining room with terra-cotta walls make visitors feel at home. (☎ 05 49 79 20 76; fax 05 49 35 03 27; hotelsaintJean@wanadoo.fr. Breakfast €5.50. Singles €22 with sink, €26 with shower, €28 with shower and toilet; doubles €25/€29/€31. MC/V.) **Hôtel de L'Univers ❷**, 22 rue Mazagran, across from the station, contains large rooms with TV, and a pleasant courtyard. (☎ 05 49 24 41 70; fax 05 49 77 09 52. Breakfast €5. Reception 7am-10:45pm. Singles €25-31 with shower, €34 with shower and toilet, €39 with bath and toilet; doubles €34/€39/€44; triples €39 with shower, €44 with shower and toilet.) Closer to the *centre ville*, **Grand Hôtel ❹**, 32 av. de Paris, has elegant rooms for a hefty price. The enormous lobby and terrace garden charm guests. (☎ 05 49 24 22 21; fax 05 49 24 42 41. Breakfast €8. 24hr. Reception. Singles €58 with shower, €65 with bath; doubles €70/€80; triples €84/94. MC/V.) **Camping Municipal ❶**, 21 av. Salvador-Allende, is a grassy campsite along the river 2km from town. Take TAN bus #2 from pl. de la Brèche to Tour Chabot; €1.15 per person, *carnet* of 10 €8.60. (☎ 05 49 79 05 06 or 05 49 78 71 00; fax 05 49 79 05 06. Reception daily 7am-10pm. Campgrounds open Apr.-Oct. Reserve ahead July-Aug. €2.80 per person, €1.70 per child, €1.15 for the first car, €2.80 for each after. Tents €1.10 each. Electricity €2.50.)

☎☎☎ FOOD AND NIGHTLIFE. Restaurants and cafes line the **place de la Brèche.** Purchase local goods at the **Marché Plus supermarket,** rue Victor Hugo, before Place des Halles (open M-Sa 7am-9pm), or the covered **market** in **Les Halles.** (☎ 05 49 24 29 66; www.halles-de-niort.fr. Daily 9am-1pm, larger version Th and Sa.)

Starry-eyed couples and gourmands will appreciate the carefully prepared classic French dishes under wooden beams at **☒Les Deux Chèvres ❸**, 2 rue du Pont. (☎ 05 49 05 10 44. *Plats* from €8, *menu* €19, lunch *menu* €9.50. Open M-F noon-2pm and 7-10pm. MC/V.) A small number of pubs and cafes draw crowds, especially around place de la Brèche. **Le Grand Café,** on the corner of rue Ricard and av. de la République, has been entertaining Niort crowds since 1940. (☎ 05 49 24 64 33.

Beer €2.40, cocktails €2.50-5.50. Open 8am-2am. MC/V.) **Les Remparts,** 3 av. de la République, attracts a youthful crowd with pumping music at the open air cafe. (☎05 49 24 10 33. Beer from €2.80, cocktails from €2.60. Open 8am-2am. MC/V.)

◙ SIGHTS. While you're here, you can pay a visit to the 15th-century **Église Notre-Dame,** the finest religious building in the region, that is home to a splendid stained glass front window. (☎05 49 28 14 28. Open May to mid-Sept. M and W-Su 9am-noon and 2-6pm; mid-Sept.-Apr. 9am-noon and 2-5pm. €3, W free, students and seniors free.)

COULON

The winding streets of tiny Coulon (pop. 2200) run alongside the canals of the Marais, making the town an ideal launch for a boat ride into the Marais.

◪ TRANSPORTATION. CASA Autocars, 11-13 chemin du Fief Binard (☎05 49 24 93 47), arrive from Niort's *gare routière* (next to the train station) and its central pl. de la Brèche (30min.; 4 per day, more on W, Sa, and during school vacations, none Su and holidays; €2.40, students €1.80). Take bus #20 (dir: Coulon/Marais Poitevin). Once in Coulon, the most practical way to delve farther into the Marais is by **boat** or **bike.** Though many hitch, *Let's Go* does not recommend it.

Though more expensive than bikes, boats merit the extra money and are the best way to experience the Marais. Boats are rented in 15 different boat rental locations in the 12 towns along the river. Although most explore the area on their own, a few companies offer guides who instruct travelers in the marsh's history and secrets. Stirring the waters releases methane gas trapped below; theatrical guides will prod the water to light a fire right on the surface. In Coulon, Le Trigale, 6 rue de l'Église (☎05 49 35 14 14), will supply a private boat and boatsman, though none of the guides speaks English. (1-2½hr., 1-7 people €26-45.) The nautically inclined can rent a boat and navigate themselves. (1-7hr., €13-48. MC/V.) Many other vendors offer similar deals, usually €1-2 cheaper down the river.

⚨ PRACTICAL INFORMATION. Head to the **tourist office,** 31 rue Gabriel Auchier, for general info about hiking and bicycling tours and for a complete list of the area's chambre d'hôtes and campsites. (☎05 49 35 99 29. Open June M-Sa 10am-1pm and 2-5:30pm, Su 10am-1pm; July-Aug. M-Sa 10am-1pm and 2-6pm, Su 10am-1pm; call for low-season hours. Hotel and chambres d'hôtes reservation service €1.) Bike, canoe, and punt rental locations are everywhere in town, especially along the river. An **ATM** is located at Crédit Agricole, pl. de l'Église. The **post office,** 17 rue Gabriel Auchier, next to the tourist office, offers currency exchange. (☎05 49 35 90 11. Open M-F 8:30am-noon and 3-5pm, Sa 9-11:30am.)

◪◪ ACCOMMODATIONS AND CAMPING. Hotels are expensive in Coulon, but many chambres d'hôte are available from €40 for two people. **Le Central ❹,** 4 rue d'Autre-mont, is the least expensive hotel in town and has classic, cottage-style decor and a location close to the city center. (☎05 49 35 90 20. Breakfast €6. Make reservations Tu-Sa. Singles and doubles €43. V.) Three-star **Camping de la Venise Verte ❶,** 2km outside of town, is embedded in lush greenery. Follow the river west from Coulon to reach the campground. Hiking and biking tours are organized through the campground. Canal-side sites, a pool and canoe and bike rental are available. (☎05 49 35 90 36; fax 05 49 35 84 69. Reception daily July-Aug. 8:30am-noon and 2-8:30pm; Sept.-Oct. and Apr.-June 8:30am-12:30pm and 3-7pm. Open Apr.-Oct. Tours €5. 2 adults, car, tent, and electricity €19; low season €14.50. Children €1.50-4.20. 4 to 5 person bungalows €225-580 per night, depending on the season. MC/V.) **Camping de La Garette ❶** is another well-equipped campground with showers, a pool, laundromat, and a location right on the water, 3km south of Coulon. (☎05 49 35 00 33. Bike and canoe rental available. Reception daily 8:30am-1pm and 2-8pm; Sept. 9:30am-noon and 3-7pm. Open April to late Sept. €3 per site. €3 per person, €2 per child, €1.50 per car. Electricity €2.50.) An 8km hike through marshy forests starts next to the campsite and past the two-door houses (one for land, one for water) unique to the area. La Garette is just after Coulon on CASA bus #20. Get off at La Garette-Centre des Loisirs. Continue walking in the direction of the bus, past the horse stables, until reaching the camp.

◖◗ ◪ SIGHTS AND ENTERTAINMENT. While in Coulon, take a moment to visit **La Maison des Marais Mouillés,** pl. de la Coutume, for a comprehensive look at the history and development of the Marais wetlands region, presented through artifacts, botanical displays, old photographs, and art exhibits. During July and August, the *maison* also offers a half-day guided boat tour of the Marais in French with a 45min. boat segment and a 6.5km walk through the wetlands. (☎05 49 35 81 04 or 05 49 35 83 26. Reservations required for tour. Open daily July-Aug. 10am-8pm; May-June and Sept. M-Sa 10am-1pm and 2-5:30pm, Su 10am-1pm; daily Nov. 2-7pm; daily Dec.-Feb. 10am-noon and 2-7pm. €5, students €3.80, children €2.20. Boat tours €14, under 16 €8.)

Every August, the **Festival du Marais Poitevin** brings music and dancing to a different town each weekend. (☎05 49 35 99 29. Ticket prices vary; some events are free. Call for detailed schedule.) In the first week of July, the **Fête Maraîchine** features a parade of traditional boats down the river. The **Rally canoë-kayak** attracts 2000 boats racing down the Marais during one day at the end of June.

OTHER SIGHTS OF THE MARAIS

About 35km from Niort, the ruins of the 12th-century **Abbaye St-Pierre de Maillezais** peep out from among the trees. Within the crumbled walls, on uneven and shifting marshland, are the monks' ruined 13th-century kitchen and living quarters, as well as the tombs of several dukes of Aquitaine. The closest public transportation is the train station in **Fontenay-le-Comte,** which is accessible by **SNCF buses** from the *gare routière* in Niort. (50min., M-Sa 8 per day, €5.60.) Once in Fontenay-le-Comte, take a taxi the remaining 12km. The only alternative is to rent a car in Niort and follow N148 (dir: Nantes). About 7min. past Oulmes, signs point to the parking lot for the abbey on the left. (☎02 51 50 43 00. Open daily June-Sept. 10am-7pm; Oct.-May 9:30am-12:30pm and 1:30-6pm. Free tours in French every hr. in July and Aug.) Farther west, just north of La Rochelle, is the little inlet known as the **Baie de l'Aiguillon,** one of the largest shellfish-producing regions of France; oyster-and mussel-collecting still supply its livelihood. Bordered by a nature reserve to the east and by sparkling water to the west, **Aiguillon-sur-mer** is a small vacation resort set amid salt marshes and swamps. Aiguillon is serviced by **Sovetours** (☎02 51 95 18 71) and is accessible by bus from La Rochelle, although the schedule makes it impossible to take a daytrip, so visitors may have to camp out. (Bus 1¾hr.; 6:50pm, return 10:20am; €14.) Just east of Aiguillon sits a **nature reserve** at St-Denis-du-Payre, with trails to the winter residence of greylag geese and wigeons, and the summer home of storks, redshanks, and the occasional spoonbill. Thousands of birds drop by during spring and autumn migratory periods. Campsites which serve as bases for the bay and the nature reserve. The **municipal campgrounds,** rte. de Lyon, are just outside of town on a lake. (☎ 02 51 56 40 70. Reception daily July-Aug. 8am-1pm and 2-7pm; Apr.-June and Sept. 11:30am-noon and 2-4:30pm. Open Apr.-Sept. €4.70 per person, €3.20 per child, €4.70 per site. Electricity €3.70.)

LES SABLES D'OLONNE

Les Sables d'Olonne was once a port outlet for Olonne, the region's capital, but the city abandoned it when the harbor silted up and it became useless for shipping. Les Sables today is popular with French vacationers for its beautiful beaches, hotels, and restaurants, though it is especially enjoyable as a center for water-sports, fishing excursions, and hikes through the marshlands. With ocean to the west, secluded surf to the north and south, and marshlands to the east, this beach town has a landscape for every taste.

📠🚆 TRANSPORTATION AND PRACTICAL INFORMATION. The **train station** is on rue de la Bauduère. (Open M-F 6:40am-7:45pm, Sa 6:40am-7:50pm, Su 6:55am-8:30pm.) To: La Rochelle (2hr., 5 per day, €17.60) via La Roche-sur-Lyon; Nantes (1½hr., 6-7 per day, €15.20); Paris (5hr., 6 per day, €69.90). The bus station is next door. **Sovetours** (☎ 02 51 95 18 71) sends **buses** to La Rochelle (3¼hr., 9am, €22) and Fromentine. (2hr., 2 per day, €10. Office open M-F 8:30am-12:30pm and 2:30-6:30pm, Sa 9:30am-noon.) **La Sabia**, 95bis rue de la Croix Blanche (☎ 02 51 23 54 88), runs **ferries** to l'Île d'Yeu. (1hr.; Apr.-Sept. 3 departures daily 7:30am-7pm; call for times and low season schedule; round-trip €33, children €22.) Local **TUSCO buses** run to beaches. (☎ 02 51 32 95 95. Buses 7:30am-7:30pm. Ask at the tourist office for a map and schedule. €1.10, *carnet* of 10 €7.70.) For **taxis**, call Radiotaxi Sablais (☎ 02 51 95 40 80). Cross the small canal dividing Les Sables from La Chaume on **La Chaumoise**, a **water taxi** that ferries back and forth on demand. (Leaves from quai Guiné. Service around 6am-2am. €0.75 one-way.) Holiday Bikes, 66 prom. Clemenceau, rents **bikes.** (☎ 02 51 32 64 15. Bikes €9-10 per day, scooters €38-€48, motorbikes €55-€120; €800 deposit. Open daily July-Aug. 9am-11pm, June and Sept. 9am-12:30pm and 2-11pm.)

The **tourist office,** 1 promenade du Maréchal Joffre, a 15min. walk from the train station, provides excellent regional and local maps, as well as thorough city and walking tour guides. The *Randonées* brochure is full of info on 16 area hiking and bike excursions. The office also books boat tours. (☎ 02 51 96 85 85; www.ot-les-sablesdolonne.fr. Boat tours daily July-Aug. 3pm and 4pm. Open daily July-Aug. 9am-7pm; Sept.-June M-Sa 9am-12:30pm and 1:30-6pm. F opens 10am, Su 10:30am-noon and 3:30-5:30pm.) The **Centre d'Information Jeunesse**, in the Hôtel de Ville at pl. du Poilu, has services ranging from **Internet** (with *télécarte*) to apartment list-ings. (☎ 02 51 23 16 83. Open M-F 9am-noon and 2-6pm.) Crédit Industriel de L'Ouest, 1 av. Carnot, **exchanges** traveler's checks at good rates. (☎ 02 51 96 82 11. Open Tu-F 8:45am-12:30pm and 1:45-6pm, Sa 8:45am-12:30pm.) Other services include: **laundry** at Lavarie des Salines, 3 rue Nicot (☎ 06 89 63 45 23; open daily 7am-9pm), and 33 bd. de Castelnau (open daily 7am-9pm); **police** at 1 bd. Blaise Pascal (☎ 02 51 21 19 91); a **hospital** at 75 av. d'Aquitaine (☎ 02 51 21 85 85); and **Internet** access at Hot Blues Café, 24 prom. Clemenceau, where "broken English is spoken." A drink is supposedly required to log on, but the policy is not always enforced. (☎ 02 51 95 91 01; hotbluescafe@hotmail.fr. €1 for 15min. Open daily July-Aug. noon-2am; Sept.-June Tu-Su noon-1am.) Le Quizz Café, 32 av. Alcide Gabaret, also has Internet. (☎ 02 51 22 14 81. €2 for 15min., €1.80 per hr. Open daily mid-June to mid-Sept. 10am-2am.) The **post office,** 65 rue Nicot, **exchanges cur-rency** and has Cyberposte, fax, photocopies, and a **Western Union.** (☎ 02 51 21 82 82. Open M-F 8:30am-5:45pm, Sa 8:30am-noon.) **Postal Code:** 85100.

Les Sables d'Olonne

🏠 ACCOMMODATIONS
Hôtel L'Etoile, 4
Hôtel les Voyageurs, 1

🍴 FOOD
L'Albatros, 5
Le Port, 2

⭐ NIGHTLIFE
Casino des Atlantes, 3

⌂ ACCOMMODATIONS. Lodgings in Les Sables are on the expensive side, especially when tourists flock here in the summer months. On the street left of the train station, **Hôtel les Voyageurs ❸**, 16-17 rue de la Bauduère, at pl. de la Gare, has modern rooms with wood floors, bright vinyl furniture, and tiny, clean bathrooms. Les Voyageurs overlooks a nice restaurant (*menus* €9.50-23.20) and lies about 8min. from the beach. (☎02 51 95 11 49; www.les-voyageurs.net. Breakfast €5.40. Reception 6:45am-3pm and 5:30pm-10pm; ring bell if restaurant closed. Closed last 2 weeks of the year. Singles and doubles with shower and toilet €40-50; triples with bath €65-72; quads €86. Extra bed €5-10. MC/V.) For a comparatively inexpensive hotel along the water, one block from the beach, try the **Hôtel L'Etoile ❸**, 67 cours Blossac, where mid-sized, somewhat run-down rooms are nonetheless adequate, with walls papered in a large old-fashioned floral print. (☎02 51 32 02 05. Breakfast €5.50. Reception 8am-10pm. Call ahead for reservations. Open Easter to mid-Sept. Mid-July to Aug. singles and doubles with sink €35, with shower €43, with shower and toilet €49, with shower, toilet, and TV €55; triples with shower and toilet €55-59; quads with shower and toilet €65-70. Prices €9-15 lower in low season. MC/V.) **Hotel Les Olonnes ❸**, 25 rue de la Patrie, 50m from both the town and the beach, has modern bathrooms, cheery decor, and TV. (☎02 51 32 04 12; www.chez.com/olonnes. Breakfast €5.50. Reception 8am-10pm. Open Apr.-Oct. Doubles €38, with shower and toilet €50. AmEx/MC/V.) Les Sables's many **campsites** are listed at the tourist office.

⌂ FOOD. There's a covered **market** in the 19th-century Art Nouveau **Les Halles**, between rue des Halles and rue du Palais. (Open daily late June to mid-Sept. 8am-1pm; mid-Sept. to late June closed M.) There is also a **Champion supermarket** on bd. de Castelnau (open M-Sa 8:30am-8pm, Su 8:30am-1pm) and an **Intermarché** on bd. de l'Île Vertime. (Open M-Sa 9am-8pm, Su 8:30am-1pm.) The *brasseries* and *crêperies* along the plage du Remblai serve the cheapest food in town, though many of them have fairly low culinary standards. For a more complete meal, try the Porte de Pêche and its nearby quais, which overflow with restaurants serving whatever the boats have brought in. **Le Port ❷**, 24 prom. Georges V, just across the water in La Chaume, specializes in grilled fish (from €13) and has affordable *plats* (€7-15) as well. (☎02 51 32 07 52. Appetizers €7-8. Open daily 12:15-2pm and 7-

10pm. AmEx/MC/V.) For a good plate of traditional French cuisine, beachside **L'Albatros ❸**, 8 pl. de Strasbourg, serves a *menu* of grilled fish and delightful salads in a romantic atmosphere. (☎ 02 51 32 03 80; fax 02 51 22 07 41. *Plats* €10-16, *menus* €7.50-31.50. MC/V.)

◘ 🎵 SIGHTS AND ENTERTAINMENT. There are a few interesting sights hidden among the postcard racks and plastic beach toys, although they pale before the lure of the beach on a sunny day. The **Musée du Coquillage**, 8 rue du Maréchal Leclerc, near the Porte de Pêche, is one-of-a-kind. The overstuffed glass cases display over 45,000 intricate, beautifully colored shells and corals gathered by a local sea diver for his once-private collection, the result of twenty years of diving in almost all of the world's seas. Especially impressive is the *crabe de cocotier*—the crustacean can tear apart coconuts, its dietary staple, fiber by fiber. While many specimens appear painted, all are entirely natural. (☎ 02 51 23 50 00; museum-du-coquillage.com. Open daily May-Aug. 9am-8pm; Sept.-Apr. 9:30am-12:30pm and 2-6:30pm; Sept.-June closed Su morning. €6, ages 4-11 €4.) The **Musée de l'Abbaye Ste-Croix**, rue de Verdun, occupies a wing of a restored 17th-century Benedictine abbey and presents a hodgepodge of regional artifacts, folk crafts, and modern and contemporary art, most notably the work of writer/ painter/jack-of-all trades Victor Brauner and surrealist Gaston Chaissac. Temporary exhibits are designed to showcase up-and-coming artists. (☎ 02 51 32 01 16; fax 02 51 32 01 17; musee-lessables@wanadoo.fr. Open mid-June to Sept. Tu-Su 10am-noon and 2:30-6:30pm; Oct. to mid-June 2:30-5:30pm. €4.60, children €2.30, first Su of every month free.) **La Chaume,** the promontory across the channel from the center of town, has two monuments along its quais: the 18th-century **Château St-Clair,** where the cloud-scraping Tour d'Arundel is visible from a distance, and the restored **Prieuré St-Nicolas,** an 18th-century fort and contemporary art gallery. On the mainland, **Notre-Dame-de-Bon-Port,** pl. de l'Église, is a rare blend of Gothic and Baroque style.

Nightly during the summer, **Les Remblais,** the widest strip of the boardwalk, becomes a pedestrian walkway with organized concerts, outdoor theater, jugglers, clowns, and marionette shows. The tourist office distributes a complete schedule of events. For the big spender, the nearby **Casino des Atlantes,** 3 bd. Franklin Roosevelt, features blackjack tables, slot machines, and a piano bar. During the summer, the casino puts on ritzy shows with dinner on most nights. Ask at the tourist office or call for a schedule. (☎ 02 51 32 05 40. Open daily 10am-4am.)

🏞 ⛱ OUTDOOR ACTIVITIES AND BEACHES. Sables Tours (☎ 02 51 96 85 85) books regional excursions, sports, and entertainment. The tourist office distributes a free brochure in French with about 10 hiking and biking trails, detailing jaunts that traverse its dunes, forests, and beaches. In July and August, the office also posts daily listings of local tennis tournaments, concerts, and organized beach volleyball games. Guided boat trips, canoeing, surfing, sailing, diving, and other watersports are also available. The closest **hiking** trail to Les Sables starts about 1km north of the train station. From the station, follow rue Georges Clemenceau until it intersects rue du Doctor Charcot; signs indicate the beginning of an 18km trail that winds through the Vendée countryside and its tiny villages to a beautiful church at Olonne-sur-Mer.

The city's beaches live up to the town's name (*sable* is French for sand). **La Grande Plage,** a beautiful 3km strip of beach close to the *centre ville*, is the largest and most crowded of Les Sables's offerings. A popular surfing spot, **plage de Tanchet,** is right beyond La Grande Plage, when walking along the beach away from the tourist office. Bus #8 also runs to Tanchet. For more solitude, take bus #2 to La Chaume's **plage de la Paracou** (disembark at Le Large), another good beach for surfing, though it is known for its dangerous waters. Following the coast north from Paracou, beachgoers will encounter two uncrowded beaches with great surf. **Plage de Sauveterre** is 1.5km north of Paracou, while **plage des Granges** is another kilometer farther. ▨**Nudity** lies everywhere in between. Adventurers may enjoy the **Forêt Domaniale d'Olonne** just east of here, where huge dunes span all the way from dry woodlands into the sea.

ÎLE D'YEU

Bordered on all sides by clear water, the Île d'Yeu (pop. 5000) has a vast array of landscapes crammed onto one island—dense mini-forests, wide, flat beaches and stony paths. Despite the rush of tourists who flood the island in July and August, many secluded spots remain away from the public beaches. Ferries unload passengers from the mainland at Port Joinville, home of marine-wear souvenir shops, retiree-filled restaurants, worthwhile boutiques, and transportation rental: all the prerequisites for a day out on the island.

◨◧ TRANSPORTATION AND PRACTICAL INFORMATION. The small seaside town of **Fromentine** is the easiest base from which to reach the island, although if in Les Sables, it's usually more practical to take a direct ferry. **Sovetours buses** run between Fromentine and Les Sables. (☎02 51 95 18 71. 2hr., 2 per day 8am-6pm, €12.30.) To get from the *gare routière* to the *gare maritime*, where **ferries** depart, cross pl. de la Gare and turn left onto the av. de l'Estacade. The *gare maritime* is at the end of this road. Three ferry companies shuttle visitors from Fromentine to Île d'Yeu: **Vedettes Inter-Îles Vendéenes (VIIV),** 9 av. de l'Estacade (☎02 51 39 00 00; www.ile-yeu.com; 2-4 per day; round-trip €27-29, students €13.50-14.50, children €19; MC/V) and **Compagnie Yeu Continent,** 3 av. de l'Estacade, near the *gare maritime.* (☎08 25 85 30 00; www.compagnie-yeu-continent.fr. Office open M-F 9:30am-noon and 2-5pm, Sa 9:30-11:30am. 1hr.; 4 per day; round-trip €27, students and seniors €21.80, children €19.30. AmEx/MC/V.) Rates change for overnight stays. **SABIA boats** leave Les Sables from quai Rousseau-Méchin in Port Olona for Île d'Yeu. (☎02 51 23 54 88; fax 02 51 21 33 85. Apr.-Sept. 1hr.; 2 per day 7-10am; round-trip €33, children €22.) Make reservations and buy tickets online, through company ticket offices, or at tourist offices in Fromentine, Nantes, and Les Sables.

Biking is the best means by which to explore; the entire island can be covered in 4-5hr. if the temptation to stop and swim can be resisted. The numerous paths range from sandy to boulder-strewn; fortunately, bikes in Port-Joinville are built for the back roads. Expect to pay €5 per hour or €8-14 per day. La Roue Libre, 4 rue Calypso rents bikes in many different sizes and scooters as well. (☎02 51 59 20 70. Bikes €8.90 per day, scooters €49 per day. Open daily Apr.-Sept. 8:30am-7pm; Oct.-Mar 9am-noon and 2-6pm. MC/V.) Another spot to rent bikes is La Trottinette, right next to the docks on rue de la Chaume. (☎02 51 58 70 42. Open daily Apr.-Sept. 9am-7pm. Bikes €6 per hr., €9 per day. MC/V.) Rent **cars** at Cantin, 1 quai de la Mairie. (☎02 51 58 33 80 25. Cars from €62 per day. Open daily 9am-noon. Call if closed. MC/V.) Most rental places will store bags and provide a map of suggested routes. The **tourist office,** pl. du Marché, distributes biking and hiking itineraries of varying lengths, with directions and historical descriptions of sights in English and French, and provides an accommodations service. (☎02 51 58 32 58, accommodations 02 51 58 40 48; tourisme@ile-yeu.fr. Open M-Sa 9am-1pm and 2-7pm, Su 9am-12:30pm.) **Internet** access is available on the right side of the port at Oy@net, 12 rue des Quais (☎06 15 37 05 76; www.oyanet.com. €0.10 per min., €1 for 15min., €4 per hr. Open daily 9:30am-12:30pm and 2-7pm. Closed Su afternoon.)

ACCOMMODATIONS AND FOOD. Though accommodations on Île d'Yeu are expensive, some are worth the price. The charming two-star **Hôtel L'Escale ❸**, 14 rue de la Croix du Port, is about a 5min. walk from the quai at Port Joinville on a quiet street. Sunny, rustic rooms look out on a grassy courtyard filled with roses and folding chairs. Kids will love the family rooms with lofts. (☎ 02 51 58 50 28; http://site.voila.fr/yeu_escale. Breakfast €6.20. Reception 7:30am-1pm and 5-8pm. Call if absent. Closed 3 weeks in Nov. Singles and doubles with shower and toilet €30-35, with bath, telephone, toilet, and satellite TV €45.70-61; triples and quads €38.20-53.20/€61.60-73.30. Prices vary with season. Extra bed €6.90. MC/V.) The island's crowded **campground ❶** is near the beach at Pointe de Gilberge, 2km from the port, enclosed by a calm expanse of beach on one side and tennis courts and horse stables on the other. (☎ 02 51 58 34 20. 4 people with 2 tents €10, €1.80 per extra person, €2.50 per car.) During the summer, many visitors camp illegally, though *Let's Go* does not recommend it. Fresh food is available from the **outdoor market** on pl. de la Norveige, by the docks. (Open daily 9am-1pm.) The **Casino supermarket,** 31 rue Calypso, is 2min. from the port. (Open Tu-F 9am-1pm and 2:30-7:45pm, M and Sa 9am-7:45pm, Su 9:30am-12:30pm.)

There are seven campsites in **Fromentine;** its tourist office (across the street from the bus station) has a list. **Camping la Grande Côte ❶**, on the rte. de la Grande Côte, 100m from Fromentine and the beach, has a pool, bike rental, laundry, food services, and a full activities calendar. This popular site gets crowded in the summer. (☎ 02 51 68 51 89; www.campeoles.fr. Wheelchair-accessible. Open May to mid-Sept. 2 people and car €9.80-17, additional person €3.40-5. Electricity €3.20.)

OUTDOOR ACTIVITIES. Île de Yeu's tourist office skillfully lays out three easy **bike circuits** of the island, all originating from Port Joinville. The shortest, a 12km path, runs to the island's southern port and back in 2½hr. Its highlights are **Port Meule,** with its 11th-century chapel and tiny dock, and ■**Pointe du Châtelet,** a beautiful seascape vista overlooking the tall ruins of the 14th-century **Vieux-Château.** The château, which frequently changed hands between the French and English, was used as a fortress in the 16th century until it was ultimately abandoned by Louis XIV. The remnants stand crumbling on the craggy coast, accessible by bike path alone. (Tours in French daily July-Aug. 9am-7pm; late June and Sept. noon-5:30pm. €2.80, children €1.30.) The longest route (5½hr.) circles the island, passing Renaissance churches, serene ports, and ■**plage des Conches,** a perfect stretch of shore with soft sand and calm waters that goes on for miles. One of the most popular bike routes (4½hr.) travels into the center of the island, stopping 2km southeast of Port Joinville at the 18th-century church in **St-Sauveur,** where bright stained-glass windows illuminate a dark, musty interior. Along this route lies the flat, sparkling **plage des Sapins,** very popular with windsurfers. The route then curves around to the south coast, where cliffs rise in all directions. **Plage Anse des Soux,** enclosed by looming cliffs, is a great place for an early afternoon siesta. The path then leads back to Joinville, but bikers can also continue west to the **Grand Phare,** a 20m tall lighthouse on the island's highest "hill," to get a view of the island from above. All coastal paths are reserved for pedestrians.

AQUITAINE AND PAYS BASQUE

At the geographical extremities of both France and Spain, Aquitaine and the Pays Basque are diverse in landscape and culture. Aquitaine was in English hands from the 12th to 15th centuries, and the Pays Basque was part of Basse-Navarre until its ruler inherited the French throne in 1598 as Henri IV. A small Basque separatist minority still maintains that their *Euzkadi* homeland is independent of French and Spanish authority.

In Aquitaine, sprawling vineyards surround Bordeaux, while the pine forest of Les Landes opens onto the windswept sands of the west coast, beaches known for stunning beauty and, farther south, the perhaps equally stunning exploits of local surfers. Closer to the Spanish border, the clinking of cowbells mixes with the sharp scent of seafood closer to the water, and villages perch among the towering peaks of the Pyrenees. The entire area is known for three critical traits: sun, food, and, of course, wine. When locals aren't enjoying the beach or lush inland parks, they can be found relishing the regional cuisine. The Pays Basque cooks up some of France's best seafood, along with *jambon cru* (cured ham) and the ubiquitous *piperade* (omelette with green peppers, onions, tomatoes, and thyme). In Gascony, Moulard duck and Roquefort cheese are menu essentials, accompanied by *Armagnac*, a local brandy. Aquitaine flavors its cuisine with the elusive *truffe noir* (black truffle), but its glory is in its wine. The world-famous vineyards of Bordeaux produce some of the best vintages in the world.

HIGHLIGHTS OF AQUITANE AND PAYS BASQUE

THE MOST INTENSE BEACH EXPERIENCE this side of a tsunami awaits in Arachon, where you can hike (or hang glide) on Europe's tallest sand dune, the **Dune du Pyla** (p. 563).

HIT THE TRAILS and check out another country while you're at it—hike from France into Spain past towering waterfalls at the **Parc Nationale des Pyrénées** (p. 591).

AN OLD ROMAN FAVORITE, the wineries of **St-Emilion** (p. 560) keep pumping out the goods in an idyllic rural setting.

AQUITAINE

BORDEAUX

Bordeaux's aromatic wines are grown on the *bords d'eaux* (riverbanks) of the Garonne and Dordogne. Without them, Bordeaux (pop. 215,000) might never have thrived. Until someone, probably an ancient Roman, discovered that the soil was perfect for growing grapes, the sandy, rocky land around the city was useless. Today, the city hosts summer wine festivals and provides a base for tours of legendary vineyards like St-Emilion, Médoc, Sauternes, and Graves. A university town, Bordeaux's diverse, youthful atmosphere makes for great nightlife.

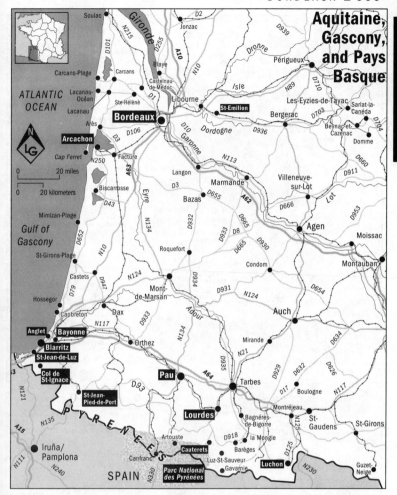

Aquitaine, Gascony, and Pays Basque

TRANSPORTATION

Flights: Airport in **Mérignac** (☎05 56 34 50 44), 11km west of Bordeaux. A shuttle bus (☎05 56 34 50 50) connects the airport to the train station and the pl. Gambetta (45min.; daily every 45min. 6am-9:45pm; €6.50, students, under age 26, over 60, and families of 3 €5 each). **Air France** (☎08 20 82 08 20) flies one plane to **London** daily for €590. Main office in Bordeaux makes reservations and provides flight schedules. 37 av. de Tourny. Open M-F 9:30am-6:30pm, Sa 9:30am-1:15pm. AmEx/MC/V.

Trains: Gare St-Jean, rue Charles Domercq. Info office open M-Sa 9am-7pm. To: **Lyon** (8-10hr., 4 per day, €56.70); **Marseille** (6-7hr., 5 per day, €59.60); **Nantes** (4hr., 5 per day, €38.30); **Nice** (9-10hr., 2 per day, €74.10); **Paris** (3hr., 15-25 per day, €60.40); **Poitiers** (2hr., 10-20 per day, €29.40); **Rennes** (6hr., 1 per day, €49.40); **Toulouse** (2-3hr., 11 per day, €28.40).

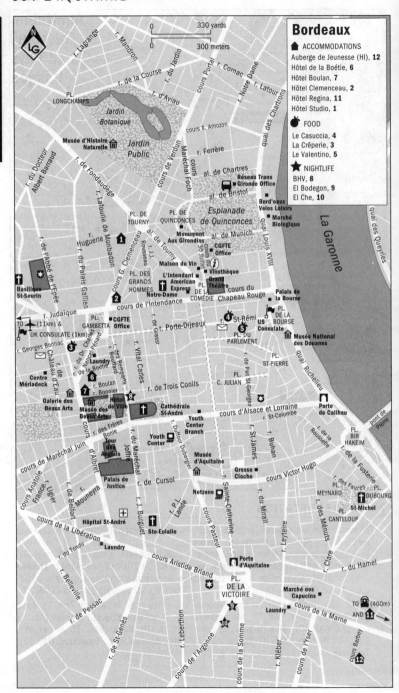

Bordeaux

🏠 ACCOMMODATIONS
Auberge de Jeunesse (HI), **12**
Hôtel de la Boétie, **6**
Hôtel Boulan, **7**
Hôtel Clemenceau, **2**
Hôtel Regina, **11**
Hôtel Studio, **1**

🍴 FOOD
Le Casuccia, **4**
La Crêperie, **3**
Le Valentino, **5**

⭐ NIGHTLIFE
BHV, **8**
El Bodegon, **9**
El Che, **10**

Buses: Réseau Trans Gironde, pl. de Quinconces. Buses travel to over 50 small towns surrounding Bordeaux, including Martillac and Pauillac.

Public Transportation: The **CGFTE bus system** (☎05 57 57 88 88) serves the city and suburbs. Maps at the train station and info offices at 9 pl. Gambetta (M-Sa 10am-6pm) and at pl. de Quinconces (M-Sa 7am-7pm). 3 new **tram** lines have recently been added (daily 5am-1pm). The *Carte Bordeaux Découverte* allows unlimited city bus and tram use (1-day €3.75, 3-day €8.40); otherwise, fare for both is €1.30.

Taxis: Taxi Télé (☎05 56 96 00 34), in front of the train station. €2 starting fee, €1.16 per km during the day, €1.74 at night. €30/€45 to the airport.

Car Rental: Europcar, 35 rue Charles Domercq (☎08 25 00 42 46; fax 05 56 31 26 94), connected to the train station. €229+ per week, with a €650 deposit. 21+. Open M-F 7am-11pm, Sa 8am-8pm, Su 10am-noon and 1:30-7:30pm. AmEx/MC/V.

Bike Rental: Free at allée de Tourny with ID deposit on the first Su of the month. **Bord'eaux Vélos Loisir,** quai Louis XVIII (☎05 56 44 77 31), facing the pl. des Quinconces, rents bikes, in-line skates, electric bikes, and "talking bikes" that give a brief historical overview of 16 major landmarks in 4 languages. Bikes and in-line skates €9 for 4hr., €15 for the day. Talking bikes €15 for 2hr. €150-200 and ID as deposit. Open Tu-Sa 1-8pm, Su 10am-8pm, and other times if you call 24hr. in advance. AmEx/MC/V.

◼◼ ORIENTATION AND PRACTICAL INFORMATION

It takes about 30min. to walk from the train station to the *centre ville*, the oldest and most picturesque part of town. Follow **cours de la Marne** from the station. This busy thoroughfare will take you past the **Marché des Capucins** on your right and into the **place de la Victoire.** Nearby, the huge stone arch of the **porte d'Aquitaine** towers above the surrounding bars and clubs that serve crowds of students from the nearby **Domaine Universitaire.** From here, turn right under the arch of the *porte* onto the pedestrian **rue Ste-Catherine.** The patterned brick sidewalk leads to Vieux Bordeaux, the hub of the city, where shops and restaurants draw tourists and locals alike. After 10-15min., you'll cross the wide **cours de l'Intendance** and enter the **place Comédie** as the street you're on becomes the **cours du 30 Juillet.** The tourist office is ahead on the right, just beyond the Grand Théâtre. The bus depot is right in front of the station. The new tramway, line C, runs from the station to pl. des Quinconces. Tram line B runs to pl. Gambetta from there. Bus #16 also runs from the station to pl. Gambetta but not from it (every 10min. 5am-9pm, €1.30). **Place Gambetta,** as well as **place des Quinconces,** are in the middle of the old town, and are important transportation hubs. Treat Bordeaux as a big city; there are many poorly lit and quiet streets at night. Be aware of your surroundings and use caution, especially in the neighborhood around the train station.

Tourist Office: 12 cours du 30 juillet (☎05 56 00 66 00; www.bordeaux-tourisme.com). Well stocked with maps and brochures; also makes hotel reservations. Open July-Aug. M-Sa 9am-7:30pm, Su 9:30am-6:30pm; Sept.-Oct. and May-June M-Sa 9am-7pm, Su 9:30am-6:30pm; Nov.-Apr. M-Sa 9am-6:30pm, Su 9:45am-4:30pm. Branch at train station (☎05 56 91 64 70) makes hotel reservations. Open M-Sa 9am-7pm.

Tours: The tourist office offers several in French and English. Walking tours of city Apr. to mid-Nov. M-Tu, Th-F, and Su 10am, with an extra tour daily at 3pm; mid-Nov. to Mar. daily 10am. 2hr. bus tours Apr. to mid-Nov. W and Sa 10am. €6.50, students €6. Also arranges local vineyard tours half-day bus tour daily Apr. to mid-Nov. 1:30pm; mid-Nov. to Mar. W and Sa 1:30pm. €26, students and seniors €23. Each day of the week is a different vineyard, call in advance to verify the day of a region of interest.

AQUITAINE AND PAYS BASQUE

A REAL CORKER

Since the 17th century, bottled wine has been closed with a cork. Corks, made from natural cork-ree bark, are incredibly elastic and are thus a perfect material for sealing bottles tightly and keeping wine fresh. In recent years, however, conflict over the best way to seal wine has torn apart the industry.

The problem with real cork lies in spoilage. A cork infected with the chemical TCA (trichloroanisole) can affect the wine, leading to the foul taste of "cork taint." It's to detect this common phenomenon that connoisseurs ritualistically sniff a cork before consuming a bottle of wine.

Providing an air-tight seal and immunity to cork taint, screw caps—"Stelvin Caps" to the wine industry—are a perfect, if inelegant, solution, but many wine-makers fear that the air-tight seal of the Stelvin, as opposed to the slightly imperfect seal of the cork, will affect the long-term aging of their vintage reds.

In 2003, André Lurton of Bordeaux made waves in the French winemaking industry when he announced that one of his *Grand Cru* whites would now be sealed with a Stelvin. While it remains to be seen if Burgundy's precious longer-aging reds will ever see the end of the cork, in the near future most young French wines will probably no longer need corkscrews. Another revolution, it seems, is brewing in France.

Budget Travel: Wasteels, 13 pl. de Casablanca (☎05 56 31 11 74; fax 05 56 31 91 48), across the street from the station, books charter flights. Open M-F 9am-1pm and 2-6pm, Sa 9:30am-12:30pm. MC/V.

Consulates: UK, 353 bd. du Président Wilson (☎05 57 22 21 10; fax 05 56 08 33 12). Open M-F 9am-12:30pm and 2-5pm. **US,** 10 pl. de la Bourse (☎05 56 48 63 80; fax 05 56 51 61 97). For security reasons, the office is only open by reservation. To reach other foreign consulates, contact the tourist office.

American Express: 11 cours de l'Intendance (☎05 56 00 63 36). Open M-F 9:30am-12:30pm and 1:30-5pm. For 24hr. refund assistance, call ☎08 00 90 86 00 for lost traveler's checks, 01 47 77 72 00 for credit cards).

Youth Center: Centre d'Information Jeunesse d'Aquitaine, 5 rue Duffour Dubergier (☎05 56 56 00 56). Information about activities, jobs, and GLBT services. Open M-Th 9:30am-6pm, F 9:30am-5pm. Free Internet for up to 10min. Branch half a block away at 125 cours d'Alsace Lorraine (☎05 56 56 00 41), sells train tickets and provides free Internet use for 45min. Open M-Th 9:30am-6pm, F 9:30am-5pm.

Laundromat: 57 cours de la Marne. Wash €3-7, dry €0.50-1, detergent €0.50. Open daily 7am-10pm. Also at 26 rue Docteur Charles Nancel-Penard. Wash €3.50-7, dry €0.50 per 6min., detergent €0.50. Open daily 7:30am-9:30pm. Also at 43 cours de la Libération. Wash €3.50-6, dry €1 per 9min., detergent €0.50. Open daily 7am-9pm.

Police: 23 rue François de Sourdis (☎05 57 85 77 77). Branch at train station.

Hospital: 1 rue Jean Burguet (☎05 56 79 56 79).

Internet Access: Netzone, 209 rue Ste-Catherine (☎05 57 59 01 25), 3 blocks from pl. de la Victoire. €3 per hr., students €2. Open M-Sa 9:30am-midnight, Su noon-midnight. Free Internet at the 2 **youth centers;** available for a small fee at the **Hôtel Studio** and the **post office** (see listings).

Post Office: 52 rue Georges Bonnac (☎05 57 78 85 25), off pl. Gambetta. **Currency exchange** with no commission. Open M-F 8:30am-6:30pm, Sa 8:30am-noon. Cyberposte. Branch (☎05 57 14 32 00) at the corner of rue St-Rémi and rue des Piliers-de-Tutelle is open M 2-6pm, Tu-F 10am-6pm, Sa 10am-12:30pm.

Postal Code: 33065.

🏠 ACCOMMODATIONS

Despite being in the run-down outskirts of town, Bordeaux's modern hostel is close to the train station. Some great deals can be found on streets around the pl. Gambetta and the cours d'Albret. Reserve a few days in advance in summer.

Hôtel Studio, 26 rue Huguerie (☎05 56 48 00 14; www.hotel-bordeaux.com), is a backpacker favorite. Walk 1 block down rue Clemenceau from pl. Gambetta, turn left on rue Lafaurie de Montbadon, and left on rue Huguerie. The tiny, clean rooms have telephone, bath, and cable TV at the lowest prices around. The rooms are a little dark on the lower floors, but with all the perks and the comfortable beds you might not even notice. Internet: hotel guests €2.25 per hr., others €4.50. Breakfast €4. Reception 7am-midnight. Reserve ahead. Singles of varying size €16-24; doubles of varying size €20-27; call ahead for prices on larger rooms. MC/V. ❷

Hôtel de la Boétie, 4 rue de la Boétie (☎05 56 81 76 68; fax 05 56 81 24 72). Check-in is at Hôtel Bristol around the corner, 4 rue Bouffard. Run by the same family as Hôtel Studio, La Boétie offers similar amenities. Each plain room comes with shower, cable TV, telephone. Breakfast €4. Reception 7am-midnight. Singles and doubles €24; triples €30.50. Larger rooms available. AmEx/MC/V. ❷

Hôtel Boulan, 28 rue Boulan (☎05 56 52 23 62; fax 05 56 44 91 65). Take tramway B to pl. Gambetta. Right around the corner from the Musée des Beaux Arts. Several of the 16 simple white rooms have hardwood floors and balconies overlooking the quiet street, and some have cable TV. Breakfast €4. Singles €19.25-25.25, with shower and TV €28.25, with bath and TV €32.25; doubles €23-25.50/€28.50/€32.50; triples €30.75/€33.75/€37.40. MC/V. ❷

Hôtel Clemenceau, 4 cours Georges Clemenceau (☎05 56 52 98 98; clemenceau@hotel-bordeaux.com). In the heart of old Bordeaux, 20m from pl. Gambetta. This 2-star hotel was built during the 18th century, but has since been modernized to include cable TV, A/C, telephones, mini-bars, and showers in every room. Elevator. Breakfast €4.50. Reception 7am-midnight; after-hours ask for code. M-Th and Su singles €29-39; doubles €35-42. F-Sa singles €26; doubles €31. AmEx/MC/V. ❸

Hôtel Regina, 34 rue Charles Domercq (☎05 56 91 66 07; fax 05 56 91 32 88). Beautiful old white building across from the train station. Noise from the street and the bus stop may be bothersome. Breakfast €5.50. Singles with shower €26, with shower and TV €30, with shower and toilet €34, with shower, toilet, and TV €37, with bath, toilet, and TV €40. Extra people €5 each, maximum of 3 per single. MC/V. ❷

Auberge de Jeunesse (HI), 22 cours Barbey (☎05 56 33 00 70; fax 05 56 33 00 71). Large modern rooms are decorated with shiny metal furniture and patches of bright colors. Near the station, the hostel is in a student-filled but somewhat run-down neighborhood; travelers, especially those alone, should exercise caution. Almost all rooms with shower, some with toilet. TV and foosball available. Wheelchair-accessible. Unlimited Internet access for €2. Breakfast and sheets included. Lockout 10am-4pm. Curfew 2am. 2- to 6-person dorm rooms €17.25, non-members €18.77. MC/V. ❶

🍴 FOOD

Center of the self-proclaimed *"région de bien manger et de bien vivre"* (region of fine eating and living), Bordeaux takes its food as seriously as its wine. Local specialties include oysters, *foie gras*, and beef braised in wine sauce. Most restaurants are scattered around the **rue St-Rémi** and **place St-Pierre**. Most *Bordelais* don't eat before 9pm in the summer, and restaurants usually serve until 11pm or midnight. For **markets,** there's fish at the Marché des Capucins (Tu-Su 6am-1pm), and organic food throughout the week at pl. Vème République (Tu 8am-1:30pm), on quai des Chartrons (Th 7am-2pm), at pl. Lucien Victor Meunier (F 6:30am-1pm), and at Caudéran pl. Saint-Armand Côté rue de l'église (Sa 6am-2pm). For pre-packaged goods, try the enormous **Auchan supermarket,** near the post office at the huge Centre Meriadeck mall on rue Claude Bonnier. (Open M-Sa 8:30am-10pm.)

La Casuccia ❷, 49 rue St-Rémi is a romantic Italian restaurant, reminiscent of a wine cellar. Especially good are their pizzas (€5.50-10) and *gratin d'avocat au crabe* (crab avocado au gratin) for €8.50. (☎05 56 51 17 70. *Menus* €10-18. Open

Tu-Su noon-3pm and 7-11:30pm. Taking the food to go is 10% cheaper. MC/V.) **Le Valentino ❸**, 6 rue des Lauriers, is an inexpensive oasis in the pricey quarter of Bordeaux, combining Italian and local specialties. The beautifully presented cuisine tastes just as good as it looks. (☎05 56 48 11 56. Appetizers €6.50-12, *plats* €8-15, 3-course *menu* €12-22. Open daily noon-2pm and 7-11pm. AmEx/MC/V.) The delicious dessert crêpes (€2.20-7.20) at **La Crêperie ❶**, 20 rue Georges Bonnac, take the French staple to a whole new level, while saltier *galettes* (€2.20-9.15) are bursting at the seams. (☎05 56 51 02 33; www.lacreperie.com. Salads €2-6.80. Open daily noon-midnight. MC/V.)

 QUIT HOGGING THE TRUFFLES! If you see a group of diners in a French restaurant with their napkins over their heads, don't be alarmed. They're merely savoring the delicate aroma of the most sought-after mushroom in the world—the *truffe noir* (black truffle), which grows in the roots of oak and hazelnut trees. Picked fresh, a truffle is worth its weight in gold. Why so dear? Truffles hide underground and defy systematic cultivation. Fortunately, nature has blessed the French with the truffle-hunter *par excellence*. Pigs, which are attracted to the truffle's enticing odor, can snuffle out these delicacies in no time.

◉ SIGHTS

Admission to all museums in Bordeaux is free on the first Sunday of every month.

CATHÉDRALE ST-ANDRÉ. Nearly nine centuries after its consecration by Pope Urban II and one century since its renovation, this building is still the centerpiece of Gothic Bordeaux. On the facade of the church are statues of angels and apostles surrounding reliefs from the life of Christ. The cathedral hosted the wedding of Eleanor of Aquitaine and the future Louis VII in 1137, as well as the marriage of Louis XIII and Princess Anne of Austria in 1615. *(Pl. Pey-Berland. ☎05 56 52 68 10. Open M 10-11:30am and 2-6:30pm, Tu-F 7:30-11:30am and 2-6:30pm, Sa 9-11:30am and 2-7pm, Su 9am-12:30pm and 2:30-8:30pm. Sept.-June closed Su afternoon except for the first Su of the month. Guided tours available at 3pm and 5pm; other times if you call in advance.)* Its bell tower, the **Tour Pey-Berland,** juts 50m into the sky, with a large statue on top for good measure. The tower was placed 15m away from the cathedral, Italian-style, because its masons feared that the vibrations of the massive bells might make the cathedral collapse. Climb the 229 spiraling steps for a great view. *(☎05 56 81 26 25. Open daily June-Sept. 10am-1:15pm and 2-6pm; Oct.-May Tu-Su 10am-12:30pm and 2-5:30pm. Last trip up 30min. before closing. €4.60, under 25 and seniors €3.10.)*

MUSÉE DES BEAUX ARTS. Originally used to display Napoleon's captured war booty, Bordeaux's impressive fine arts museum now houses a multitude of great works by painters like Titian, Caravaggio, Rubens, Matisse, Picasso, Seurat, and Renoir. The permanent collection is in the two buildings that frame the Hôtel de Ville; the temporary exhibits are across the street in the **Galeries des Beaux Arts.** *(20 cours d'Albret, near the cathedral. ☎05 56 10 20 56. Open M and W-Su 11am-6pm. Guided tours in French W 12:30pm. Joint ticket for the temporary and permanent collection €5.50, over 65 €3; ticket solely for the permanent collection €4/€2.50; students and under 18 free.)*

ÉGLISE ST-MICHEL. The best cityscape of Bordeaux can be seen from the 114m tower of the Église St-Michel. At ground level, you can catch even more of the world sitting in one of the many cafes that surround the church or browsing the different markets that fill the courtyard each morning. This is the most Bohemian district of Bordeaux, the place where students chill and sip mint tea with friends. *(Church open M-Sa 9am-6pm, Su 9am-12:30pm. Free. Tower open June-Sept. M and Sa-Su 2-7pm, Tu-F 10:30am-7pm. €2.50, under 12 free.)*

MONUMENT AUX GIRONDINS. Several avenues in Bordeaux converge on pl. de Quinconces, at the center of which is a much-adorned marble pole topped by a stone Lady Liberty. The monument commemorates the moderate group of Girondin leaders—so named because they came from towns bordering the Gironde—who were guillotined in 1797 by their political rivals. Before losing their heads, they produced the Revolution's most important document, the **Declaration of the Rights of Man.** The event is commemorated by the bicentennial date (1989) inscribed on the monument's side. The 100-year-old monument is filled with symbols: the three women on the side facing town represent Bordeaux, the Dordogne, and the Garonne, and empty pedestals recall the murdered Girondins.

GRAND THÉÂTRE. The rather austere Neoclassical facade of this 18th-century opera house conceals a breathtakingly intricate interior. Probably the most strictly classical opera house in the world, it is certainly one of the grandest. Attend an opera, concert, or play, or take a daytime tour conducted in English. *(On pl. de la Comédie. Tickets ☎ 05 56 00 85 95; www.opera-bordeaux.com. Open Tu-Sa 11am-6pm. 1hr. tours through tourist office ☎ 05 56 00 66 00, frequency depends on theater's production schedule. Tickets €8-70, 50% discount for those under 25. €5; students, children, and over 65 €4.)*

PALAIS DE LA BOURSE. The construction of the Palais de la Bourse (Stock Exchange), with its ornately adorned pillars, fountain, and wrought-iron facades, was the most important step in the 18th-century modernization of Bordeaux. To the left of the building, the interesting **Musée National des Douanes** (National Customs Museum) houses quirky exhibits devoted to tariffs and excise taxation that require an understanding of French to be appreciated. *(☎ 05 56 48 82 82. Open Tu-Su 10am-6pm. €3; students under 25, ages 10-18 and over 60 €1.50.)*

▣ NIGHTLIFE

Youthful Bordeaux's lively bars and nightclubs seem endless. *Clubs and Concerts*, a free brochure at the tourist office, gives an overview of them. Pl. de la Victoire and pl. Gambetta are mobbed by 70,000 students during the school year and continue to serve as entertainment hotspots during the summer. St-Michel has a more mellow atmosphere, with locals gathering at cafe tables around 6pm and often staying until midnight. After the clubs close, you can eat and drink at pl. Marché des Capucins and hang out with early-morning market workers. In addition, Bordeaux's gay scene is one of the best in France.

El Bodegon, on the pl. de la Victoire (☎ 05 56 94 74 02). Dominating the nightlife in this popular square, enormous El Bodegon draws wild students. On W nights, crowds come for karaoke at 10:30pm. Theme nights with free give-aways every weekend. M brings special deals. Beer €2.50. Happy hour 6-8pm. Open M-Sa 7am-2am, Su 2pm-2am.

BHV (Bar de l'Hôtel de Ville), 4 rue de l'Hôtel de Ville (☎ 05 56 44 05 08), across from the Hôtel de Ville. Flashing lights spin off the mirrors in this small but fashionable gay bar, which is full most nights of the week. Beer €3.50. Theme nights W, daily July-Aug. Drag shows Sept.-June one Su per month at 10pm. Open daily 6pm-2am. MC/V.

El Che, 34 cours de l'Argonne (☎ 05 56 92 33 98). A funky Afro-Cuban bar-*rhumerie* near pl. de la Victoire. Sip on homemade rum cocktails (€3.50) in this bit of tropical Île des Antilles transported to the gray streets of Bordeaux. Free salsa lessons Sept.-May W and F 8:30pm. Beer €2.50. Currently open M-Sa 7pm-2am; daily once street construction is finished. MC/V.

◢ WINERIES AND VINEYARDS

A HISTORY OF CLARET

Bordeaux's reputation for wine is the product of 20 centuries of shameless (but justifiable) self-promotion. The wines were of variable color and quality until Louis IX snatched the port of La Rochelle from the English in 1226. Not to be deprived of his claret (as the English call red Bordeaux wine), King Henry II bestowed generous shipping rights on Bordeaux, making it England's wine cellar. At first citizens simply shipped out wines produced farther up the Garonne River, but the money flowing in sparked a local planting mania. Soon Bordeaux's port made the decision to ensure its monopoly over the market by refusing to accommodate other wines. As consumption grew in the 18th century, the vineyards spread from the Médoc region to areas south of the Dordogne. Today, the region produce almost 500 million bottles per year.

TASTING IN BORDEAUX

If you're just in town for a day or two and are desperate for the full wine experience, head to the **Maison du Vin/CIVB,** 1 cours du 30 juillet, where there's a wine bar, professionals on hand to tell you what you're drinking, and even a tasting course. The 2hr. "Initiation to Wine Tasting" program, available in English, teaches the subtle art of oenophilia through comparative tasting and will leave you confident enough to waltz into any four-star restaurant. (☎ 05 56 00 22 88; www.vins-bordeaux.fr. Open M-F 9am-5:30pm. Wine-tasting course twice weekly mid-June to mid-Sept., €20. Longer courses available throughout the year; contact the Maison for more information.) Locals buy their wine and crystal pitchers at the classy **Vinothèque,** 8 cours du 30 Juillet. (☎ 05 56 52 32 05. Open M 2-7:30pm, Tu-Sa 10am-7:30pm. AmEx/MC/V.) Across the street at 2 allée de Tourny, the smaller and more intimate **L'Intendant** is run by a knowledgeable and helpful owner. (☎ 05 56 48 01 29. Open M-Sa 10am-7:30pm. AmEx/MC/V.)

VISITING THE CHÂTEAUX

It's easiest to explore the area with a car, but some vineyards are accessible by train—St-Emilion and Pauillac in particular make good daytrips. The tourist office gives English tours of the more popular vineyards. (Daily Apr. to mid-Nov. 1:30pm; mid-Nov. to Mar. W and Sa 1:30pm. St-Emilion tours W and Su, Médoc tours Th and Sa, Graves and Sauternes F. €26, students and seniors €23.) Bring a good map if you're biking or walking; local roads are hard to navigate. The owners of the châteaux are usually happy to give private tours, but call ahead or ask the tourist office to call for you. All of the châteaux sell wine directly.

ST-EMILION

The viticulturists of St-Emilion (pop. 2850), just 35km northeast of Bordeaux, have been refining their technique since Roman times; theirs is, not surprisingly, among the best appellations in France. Today they gently crush 12,850 acres of grapes to produce 23 million liters of wine annually. Quite apart from its main industry, the medieval village's yellow stone buildings, twisting narrow streets, and religious monuments are a pleasure to visit. The **Église Monolithe,** carved by Benedictine monks over three centuries, is the largest subterranean church in all of Europe. The damp underground **catacombs** nearby served as the burial place for a series of Augustine monks when the cemetery became too small. As a tribute to its religious origins, the town also proudly holds the hermitage of **St-Emilion** himself. The three monuments can only be accessed through the guided visits that depart from the tourist office. (Tours 45min. 10, 10:45, 11:30am, 2, 2:45, 3:30, 4:15, 5, 5:45, and 6:30pm. Normally in French, but English guides can be reserved in advance. €5.50, students and children ages 12-17 €2.90.)

The **Maison du Vin de St-Emilion,** pl. Pierre Meyrat, offers a 1hr. course on local wines in French and English. Their wine shop has wholesale prices and a free exhibit. (☎05 57 55 50 55; www.vins-saint-emilion.com. Open daily Aug. 9:30am-7pm; Apr.-July and Sept.-Oct. 9:30am-12:30pm and 2-6:30pm; Nov.-Mar. 10am-12:30pm and 2-6pm. Wine course daily mid-July to mid-Sept. 11am. €17. MC/V.)

The **tourist office,** near the church tower at pl. des Créneaux, distributes the *Grandes Heures de St-Emilion,* a list of **classical concerts** and **wine tastings** hosted by nearby châteaux. To get to the tourist office, take a right on the main road from the station; when you reach town, walk 2km up rue de la Porte Bouqueyre toward the tower. (☎05 57 55 28 28; www.saint-emilion-tourisme.com. Open daily July-Aug. 9:30am-8pm; mid- to late June and early to mid-Sept. 9:30am-7pm; Apr. to mid-June and mid-Sept. to Oct. 9:30am-12:30pm and 1:45-6:30pm; Nov.-Mar. 9:30am-12:30pm and 1:45-6pm.) In addition to renting **bikes,** they offer tours in English to local châteaux. (Bikes €10 per half-day, €14 per day; credit card deposit required. Tours July-Aug. M-Sa 2 and 4:15pm; May-June and Sept. 3:30pm. €9, children €6.) **Trains** come here from Bordeaux (35min., 4 per day, €7.20). Watch carefully: it's the second stop from Bordeaux and the tiny station is poorly marked. The only train back to Bordeaux after 8am is at 6:26pm; plan accordingly.

MÉDOC, GRAVES, AND SAUTERNES REGIONS

Though St-Emilion is probably the best vineyard for a first visit, there are other worthwhile options near Bordeaux. The **Médoc** area north of Bordeaux, between the Gironde Estuary and the ocean, gets its name from the Latin *medio-acquae,* meaning "between the waters." This region is home to some of the world's most famous red wines: Lafite-Rothschild, Latour, Margaux, Haut-Brion, and Mouton-Rothschild. To access the vineyards, book one of the organized tours that depart from Bordeaux, or take the **Réseau Trans Gironde** from the depot in the pl. de Quinconces to Pauillac, the most renowned village of the region (1hr., M-Sa 8 per day). The **tourist office,** at La Verrerie, can provide free maps, suggest hiking trails, and help make reservations to visit local châteaux. (☎05 56 59 03 08; www.pauillac-medoc.com. Open daily July-Aug. 9:30am-7:30pm; Sept.-June M-Sa 9:30am-12:30pm and 2-6pm, Su 10:30am-12:30pm and 2:30-6pm.)

South of the Garonne is the **Graves** region, named for its gravelly topsoil. Graves's dry and semi-sweet wines were the drink of choice in the time of Eleanor of Aquitaine, before the reds of Médoc overtook them 300 years ago. In the southeastern end of Graves is the **Sauternes** region, celebrated for its sweet white wines.

The charming château **Smith Haut Lafitte,** in the town of Martillac, is located less than a 20min. drive from Bordeaux. Proprietors Daniel and Florence Cathiard bought the crumbling vineyard in 1990 and saved it from corporate ownership. Now a small but luxurious château with peacocks strolling in its garden, Smith Haut Lafitte gives detailed tours and tastings by reservation (☎05 57 83 11 22; www.smith-haut-lafitte.com).

Across the street from the vineyards, the four-star luxury hotel **Les Sources des Caudalie,** run by the friendly Cathiard daughters, overindulges the likes of Madonna and Princess Caroline of Monaco (among others) with a revolutionary *vinothérapie* spa. (☎05 57 83 82 82; www.caudalie.com. 30min. barrel bath in grape extract €51. Bath, massage, jet shower, and honey and wine wrap €135. Reservations must be made 3 weeks to 1 month in advance.)

ARCACHON

Arcachon (pop. 11,450) is one of the best in a chain of beach towns on the Côte d'Argent (Silver Coast), the thin strip of sand which runs along 200km of France's southern Atlantic seaboard. It's known in particular for two sandy landmarks: the Dune du Pyla, Europe's highest sand dune, and the Banc d'Arguin, a 1000-acre sand bar. Arcachon is a resort town at heart, full of vacationing families in summer and despondent hotel owners in the winter. During its high season, the town is a perfect daytrip—easygoing, unpretentious, and naturally stunning.

🖥🔢 TRANSPORTATION AND PRACTICAL INFORMATION. Trains go only to Bordeaux (55min.; 10-20 per day, last train M-Sa 8:15pm, Su and holidays 9:51pm; €8.80.), with the occasional TGV to Paris (4hr., 1-3 per day, €63.80). They leave from pl. Roosevelt. Check the ticket office (open M-F 7am-9:55pm, Sa 7:40am-9:55pm, Su 8:40am-9:55pm). **City bus** #611 runs from a stop in front of the train station to "Pyla-sur-Mer," site of the dune. (25min.; July-Aug. 15 per day, Sept.-June 8 per day; €2.70.) The office is at 47 bd. du Général Leclerc (☎05 57 72 45 00.) Locabeach 33, 326 bd. de la Plage, rents **bikes, scooters,** and **mopeds.** (☎05 56 83 39 64; www.locabeach.com. Open daily July-Aug. 9am-8pm; Sept.-June 9am-12:30pm and 2-7pm; hours are flexible and depend on the weather. Bikes €7-10 per half-day, €10-13 per day; deposit €130-155. Scooters and mopeds €39-59 per day; driver's license required; deposit €760-1200 with an ID card. AmEx/MC/V.)

Arcachon's **tourist office,** pl. Georges Pompidou, is one block left of the station. (☎05 57 52 97 97; tourisme@arcachon.com. Open daily July-Aug. 9am-7pm; June and Sept. M-Sa 9am-6:30pm, Su 10am-1pm and 2-5pm; Oct.-May M-Sa 9am-6:30pm.) Wash beach towels at the **laundromat** on the corner of bd. du Général Leclerc and rue Molière. (Wash €5-8, dry €0.50 per 3min., detergent €0.50. Open daily May-Sept. 7am-10pm; Sept.-June 7am-8pm.) The **police** (☎05 57 72 29 30) are on pl. de Verdun. The **hospital** (☎05 57 52 90 00) is on bd. Louis Lignon. The **post office,** 1 pl. Franklin Roosevelt, opposite the tourist office, has a **currency exchange** with no commission for US$. (☎05 57 52 53 88. Cyberposte. Open M-F 8:30am-6pm, Sa 8:30am-noon.) **Postal Code:** 33120.

🛏🏕 ACCOMMODATIONS AND CAMPING. In the summer, rooms here start at €36 for a double; even in the low season, the prices begin at €27. Don't expect to find any deals, and reservations are essential in the summer. The best value in town seems to be at **Le Bordeaux ❹,** 39 bd. du Général Leclerc, a two-star hotel 20m from the train station and 300m from the beach. Directly over a bar and restaurant, Le Bordeaux offers 14 modest rooms complete with bath and TV. (☎05 56 83 80 30; le.bordeaux@discali.fr. Breakfast €6. Reserve a week in advance. July-Aug. singles €50; doubles €70. Prices lower Sept.-June. AmEx/MC/V.) **The Auberge de Jeunesse (HI) ❶,** 87 av. de Bordeaux, is in Cap-Ferrat. To get there, take a ferry from Arcachon's Jetée Thiers on av. Gambetta. (☎05 56 54 92 78. Daily July-Aug. at least 1 per hr. 9am-7pm; one-way €6, children €4, bikes €3; round-trip €10/€5/€4.) From the Cap-Ferrat ferry pier, take av. de l'Océan and continue as it becomes rue des Bouvreuils after the roundabout (15 minutes). Turn left onto av. de Bordeaux; the hostel will be on your right after a few minutes. (☎05 56 60 64 62. Reception 8am-1pm and 6-9pm. Open July-Aug. €8. HI members only.)

In Arcachon, the very social **Camping Club d'Arcachon ❷,** 5 allée de la Galaxie, lies in the middle of a beautiful pine forest 2km from the beach. The three-star site has a two-tiered pool, jacuzzi, billiards table, and a bar-restaurant. (☎05 56 83 24 15; www.camping-arcachon.com. Laundry €4-5. Check-out noon. Closed mid-Nov. to mid-Dec. July-Aug. €4-6 per person, €1 per child, €10-13 per tent, €2-4 per car. Bungalows €400-550 per week; mobile homes €450-630; *chalets* €550. Electricity

€4. All prices are significantly cheaper Sept.-June. AmEx/MC/V.) There are five campsites within a few kilometers of each other in **Pyla-sur-Mer** along the rte. de Biscarrosse, although it's quite a trek to any of these from town. One of the closest is the three-star **Camping de la Dune ❷**, 300m from the beach on rte. de Biscarrosse. Take bus #611 from the SNCF station of Arcachon to Camping de la Dune (dir: Le Pyla; 4 per day go directly to the campsite, 6 others stop at the Dune du Pyla, more in July-Aug.; €2.70). A pool, tennis court, bar, grocery store, and laundromat are located on the campsite. Frequent shows and events (including karaoke) July-Aug. (☎05 56 22 72 17; www.campingdeladune.fr. Open late-Apr. to late-Sept. Two people with a tent and car late June to mid-July €17; mid-July to late Aug. €23; late Apr. to late June and Sept. €12; mobile home €20/€26/€15; extra person €6/€8/€4. Electricity and showers included. MC/V.)

🍴 FOOD. It would be a crime to leave Arcachon without savoring some of the 15,000 tons of oysters gathered here annually. Beach cafes line **avenue Gambetta** and **boulevard de la Plage,** offering copious seafood platters and €10 *moules frites* (mussels and fries). **Le Commerce ❷**, 9 av. Gambetta, spills into the street, providing a perfect vantage point for munching on shellfish while watching sunbathers strut by. (☎05 56 83 05 17. Fish €7.50-17.50, meat €6.50-14, salad €3-8. *Menus* €12.50-19. Open daily 7am-1am. AmEx/MC/V.) A bit of a splurge, **Le Pavillon d'Arguin ❹**, 63 bd. du Général Leclerc across the street from the tourist office, serves fresh and plentiful seafood platters, duck, and veal with asparagus for €16-28. (☎05 56 83 46 96. Open July-Aug. noon-2:30pm and 7-10:30pm; Sept.-June Su 7-10:30pm, Tu-Sa noon-2:30pm and 7-10:30pm. Sa-Su reservations recommended. AmEx/MC/V.) A cheaper option chosen by many French tourists is to buy bread from one of the many *boulangers artisanals* and produce from the **market,** rue Jehenne. (Open daily 8am-1pm.)

◉ 🎭 SIGHTS AND ENTERTAINMENT. Rising suddenly from the edge of a pine forest, the 117m **◼Dune du Pyla** looks more like a transplanted section of the Sahara than a French beach. The wind races furiously across the face of the dune, creating an ocean of white sand unblemished by vegetation. For courageous souls who are willing to cross the entire dune, there is a protected area at the edge where wading is possible, although a fierce undertow makes deeper swims too dangerous. Farther along the water, there are separate beaches for the clothed and the nude. From the bus stop at Dune du Pyla, head into the park and continue past the shops for about 500m to reach the staircase to the top. The École Professionnelle de Vol Libre du Pyla (EPVLP) has **hang gliding** from the dune; ask at the tourist office. (☎05 56 22 15 02. €61 per flight, €400 per week.)

Arcachon's bird sanctuaries and nature parks attract flocks of tourists. **UBA boats** take 2hr. excursions to the Dune du Pyla, the Cap-Ferrat lighthouse, and the oyster beds around **L'île aux Oiseaux** (Apr.-Oct. 3 per day, with 3 extra July-Aug.; €13, children €9). The same company also offers trips to **Arguin Sandbar** from the Jetée Thiers pier. (☎05 56 54 92 78. Daily July-Aug. 11am; June and Sept. W, Sa and Su. €15, children €10.) About 15km out of town, the **Parc Ornithologique du Teich** shelters 260 species of migrating birds in one of France's most important sanctuaries. (☎05 56 22 80 93; www.parc-ornithologique-du-teich.com. Open daily June-Aug. 10am-8pm; Sept.-May 10am-6pm. Binoculars and seeds available. Guided visits with a reservation. €6.40, ages 5-14 €4.60.)

In the hilly town of Arcachon itself, **Ville d'Hiver** (Winter Village), a district of turn-of-the-century villas, lies across from the **Parc Mauresque** north of the beach. Doctors designed the neighborhood's curving streets to protect invalids from the ocean winds; it is 2°C warmer on average than its beachfront counterpart. Now the fairy-tale villas, which range in style from faux Swiss chalet to pseudo-Gothic castle, make up a quiet suburban neighborhood, removed from the tourist rat race below. The village is accessible by foot or in a tacky *petit train.* (Office at 47 bd. du Général Leclerc. ☎05 57 72 45 00. Tours 35min.; July-Aug. 11am, 3, 4, 5, and 6pm. June and Sept. reserve in advance. €4, children €3.) The **Ste-Cécile** observatory, across the park on the way back from the Ville d'Hiver, offers a stunning view of Arcachon. The spiral staircase is not easy to climb and worse to descend, as the stairs are hung from cables and can sway. (Open 9am-7pm. Free.)

Arcachon's younger set run to several beachfront discotheques as soon as night falls. There's also the **Casino d'Arcachon,** 163 bd. de la Plage, a fairy-tale creation containing, besides the obvious, several bars and a nightclub. Strict dress code prohibits flip-flops, sleeveless t-shirts, frayed jeans, and beach attire. (☎05 56 83 28 67; casino-arcachon@g-partouche.fr. 18+. Nightclub open 11:30pm-4:30am; slot machines open daily 10am-4am, Sept.-June until 5am; roulette, blackjack, and stud poker open daily with 2 days of closure for each game: M-Tu for boule, W-Th for blackjack and roulette. 9:30pm-4am. AmEx/MC/V.)

PAYS BASQUE

BIARRITZ

Once a minor whaling village, the town of Biarritz, at the base of the Pyrenees, became the playground of aristocrats in the mid-19th century. Napoleon III, Alphonse XIII of Spain, Nicholas II of Russia, and the Shah of Persia were all drawn to the town's shores by its natural beauty and the fashionable reputation persists to this day. Still glistening with money, grandiose and sleek Biarritz remains an opulent getaway for both the rich and famous but offers plenty in the way of sparkling beaches, phenomenal vistas, and flower-lined paths for luxury and budget travelers alike.

◪ TRANSPORTATION

Flights: Aéroport de Parme, 7 esplanade de l'Europe (☎05 59 43 83 83). M-Sa take bus #6 (dir: Bayonne Gare) from Hôtel de Ville to Parme Aéroport (every 30min. 7am-7:20pm), Su take bus C (dir: Aéroport; 4 buses depart before 1pm, then every 30min. noon-8pm). **Ryanair** (☎05 59 43 83 93) flies to **London** daily for €32-55 one-way.

Trains: Biarritz-la-Négresse (☎05 59 50 83 07), 3km from town. Information desk open daily 7:45am-8pm. To: **Bayonne** (10min.; 17 per day; €2.10, TGV €3.80); **Bordeaux** (2hr.; 7per day; €24.20, TGV €25.90); **Paris** (5hr., 5 per day, €73.70); **Pau** (2hr., 4 per day, €15.30); **Toulouse** (4hr., 4 per day, €35). SNCF office, 13 av. Foch. Open M-F 9-11:45am and 2-5:45pm.

Buses: ATCRB (☎05 59 26 06 99) shuttles over to **St-Jean-de-Luz** (€2.80) and **Hendaye** (€4.90), connecting to the EuskoTren to **San Sebastian.** Main office in St-Jean-de-Luz. Bus stops on rue Joseph Petit, next to the tourist office. Buy tickets on the bus.

Public Transportation: STAB (☎05 59 52 59 52). Office with maps and schedules on rue Louis-Barthou, near the tourist office (☎05 59 24 26 53; open M-Sa 8:15am-noon and 1:30-6pm). 10min. to **Anglet** and 25-30min. to **Bayonne** (M-Sa 6am-8:30pm bus #1, 2, or 6; Su 7:30am-8:30pm bus A, B, or C). 1hr. tickets €1.20; *carnet* of 5 €4.75; *carnet* of 10 €9.50, local students during school year €8.

Taxis: Atlantic Taxi Radio (☎05 59 03 18 18). 24hr. €2 base fare, €0.64 per km during the day, €0.85 per km at night. Approximately €10 from the taxi stand to either the train station or the airport; approximately €15 to Bayonne.

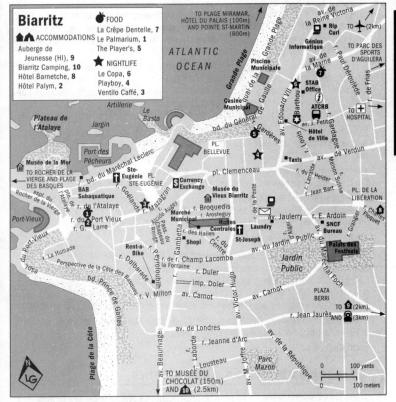

Biarritz

🍎 **FOOD**

La Crêpe Dentelle, 7
Le Palmarium, 1
The Player's, 5

⭐ **NIGHTLIFE**

Le Copa, 6
Playboy, 4
Ventilo Caffé, 3

🏠🏠⛰ **ACCOMMODATIONS**

Auberge de
  Jeunesse (HI), 9
Biarritz Camping, 10
Hôtel Barnetche, 8
Hôtel Palym, 2

Bike and Scooter Rental: Rent-a-Bike, 24 rue Peyroloubilh (☎05 59 24 94 47 or 06 80 71 72 88; sobilo.location@wanadoo.fr). Bikes €12 per day, €5 for *Let's Go* users. Scooters €31 per day, in-line skates €12, Harley Davidsons €230. Deposit €75-150. Open daily 9am-7pm. MC/V.

Surfboard Rental: Rip Curl Surf Shop, 2 av. Reine Victoria (☎05 59 24 38 40), 1 block from Grande Plage. €10 per half-day, €15 per day, €85 per week; ID or €300 deposit. Open daily July-Aug. 10am-8pm; Sept.-June M-Sa 10am-1pm and 3-7pm. For lessons, contact Rip Curl (☎05 59 24 62 86). One 2hr. lesson €35; three 2hr. lessons €90; six 2hr. lessons €160.

✈🚌 ORIENTATION AND PRACTICAL INFORMATION

The train station is 3km from the *centre ville*, so buses are more convenient when coming from areas around Biarritz. For traveling from greater distances, buses #2 (dir: Sainsontan) and 9 (dir: La Barre or Ste-Madeleine) run from the train station to the city center and the tourist office (every 20min. M-Sa 6:30am-9pm, €1.20). On Sundays, bus B (dir: Sainsontan) travels the same route (every 30min. 8am-8pm). Arriving from Biarritz-la-Négresse, turn left onto **allée du Moura,** which becomes av. du Président Kennedy. Turn left a few kilometers later onto **avenue du Maréchal Foch,** which continues to **place Clemenceau,** at the *centre ville* (30 minutes).

AQUITAINE AND PAYS BASQUE

Tourist Office: 1 sq. d'Ixelles (☎05 59 22 37 10; biarritz.tourisme@biarritz.fr), off av. Edouard VII. Staff tracks down same-night hotel rooms or campsites for free. Pick up the free *Biarritzscope* for monthly events listings. Open daily July-Aug. 8am-8pm; Sept.-June M-Sa 9am-6pm, Su 10am-5pm.

Tours: Guided walking tours of the town center (in French) depart from the tourist office July-Aug. M 10am and F 6pm. The **petit train** (☎06 07 97 16 35 or 05 59 03 44 03) also offers 30min. French guided train rides of the Port des Pêcheurs, the Hôtel de Palais, the Port Vieux, and the Jardin Public Departs every 30min. from the Grand Plage. Daily July-Aug. 11am-11pm; Apr.-June and Sept.-Oct. 2-6pm, but hours depend on the weather. Open year-round for groups with reservation. €5.

Currency Exchange: Change Plus, 9 rue Mazagran (☎05 59 24 82 47). No commission. Good rates. Open July-Aug. M-Sa 9am-7pm; Sept.-June 9am-noon and 2-6pm.

Laundromat: Le Lavoir, 4 av. Jaulerry, by the post office. Open daily 7am-9pm. Wash €4-7, dry €0.30 per 5min., detergent €0.60.

Beach Emergencies: Grande Plage ☎05 59 22 22 22. **Plage Marbella** ☎05 59 23 01 20. **Plage de la Milady** ☎05 59 23 63 93. **Plage Miramar** ☎05 59 24 34 98. **Plage du Port Vieux** ☎05 59 24 05 84.

Police: av. Joseph Petit (☎05 59 01 22 22).

Hospital: Hôpital de la Côte Basque, av. Interne Jacques Loëb (☎05 59 44 35 35).

Internet Access: Génius Informatique, 60 av. Edouard VII, in the back of a toy store (☎05 59 24 39 07). €5 per hr., €9 per 2hr. Color photocopies €1.50 per page, black and white €0.30. Fax €1.50 per page. Open daily July-Aug. 9am-9pm; Sept.-June 10am-9pm. Internet available at the **post office** and at the **Hotel Palym** (see listings).

Post Office: 17 rue de la Poste (☎05 59 22 41 10). **Currency exchange** open M-F 8:30am-6:30pm, Sa 8:30am-noon. Cyberposte.

Postal Code: 64200.

🖈 🖈 ACCOMMODATIONS AND CAMPING

Bargains do exist, but it's best to plan at least a month ahead for stays in July and August, or enlist the help of the tourist office. The best-priced hotels are off rue Mazagran, around rue du Port-Vieux. The youth hostel is newly renovated but far from the city center; all other hotels listed are centrally located.

🌊 **Auberge de Jeunesse (HI),** 8 rue de Chiquito de Cambo (☎05 59 41 76 00; aubergejeune.biarritz@wanadoo.fr), a 40min. walk or a 15min. bus ride from Biarritz. From the town center, take bus #2 (dir: Gare SNCF) to Francis Jammes or #9 (dir: Labourd; mid-June to mid-Sept.) to Bois de Boulogne. Walking, take av. Maréchal Foch; as it becomes av. du Président J. F. Kennedy. Turn right on rue Philippe Veyrin. Hostel is at the bottom of the hill on the right. From train station, walk out to the left, continue past the viaduct, make the first left on the other side, and continue until the end of the street. (10 min.) Situated near a beautiful lake. Social hostel povides a well-stocked bar mid-June to Sept. Sunny rooms have lockable cabinets. Internet €0.50 per 10min. Breakfast included. Dinner €8.40. Laundry. Reception 8:30am-12:30pm and 6pm-10pm. 2- to 4-bed dorms €16.70-17.70 the first night, subsequent nights €13.90-14.90. Non-HI members €2.90 extra per night. AmEx/MC/V. ❶

Hôtel Palym, 7 rue du Port Vieux (☎05 59 24 16 56; www.le-palmarium.com). Antique wood furnishings in clean rooms about 50m from the ocean. More expensive rooms with cable TV. Internet €10 per hr. Breakfast €4.50. Reception 8am-8pm. Singles and doubles €37-40; with shower €45, with bath €50-65; triples with bath €65-75; quads with bath €75-90. MC/V. ❸

Hôtel Barnetche, 5bis rue Charles-Floquet (☎05 59 24 22 25; www.hotel-barnetche.fr), in the center of town. From pl. Clemenceau, take rue du Helder through pl. Libération to rue Charles Floquet. 12-bed dorm room perfect for travelers on a budget, as well as more expensive individual rooms. No-nonsense, energetic owner keeps everything ship-shape. Obligatory breakfast (with homemade croissants) €6. Reception 7:30am-10:30pm. Reservations recommended. Open May-Sept. Dorms €20 per person. Singles €40; doubles €50, with toilet €60, with *demi-pension* €54-92 per person. ❸

Camping: Biarritz, 28 rue d'Harcet (☎05 59 23 00 12; www.biarritz-camping.fr). A 10min. walk from Milady and the beach, and 30min. from town. Take the Navette-des-Plages bus (#9; mid-June to mid-Sept.) or walk down av. du Président J. F. Kennedy from the station following signs. Quiet, unshaded plots separated by perfect hedges. Restaurant, bar, washing machines, jacuzzi, and heated pool on-site. Wheelchair-accessible. Reception 8am-9:30pm. Reservations are mandatory early July to late Aug. Open early May to late Sept. Early July-late Aug. 2 people with tent €19.50, mobile homes €485-580 per week, electricity €3.50; start of July and end of Aug. €17/€350-450/€3; May-June and Sept. €13.50/€215-270/€2.30. MC/V and traveler's checks. ❶

☐ FOOD

In dining, as with everything in Biarritz, style trumps substance. Expect impressive elegance and high prices around **Grande Plage** and **place Ste-Eugénie.** More mid-priced eateries can be found on **avenue de la Marne** as it splits from av. Edouard VII. Cheap crêpes and sandwiches can be found along **rue Mazagran** and **place Clemenceau.** The **market** on rue des Halles offers local produce and an abundance of specialties. (Open daily 8am-2pm.) Next door is a **Shopi supermarket,** 2 rue du Centre. (☎05 59 24 18 01. Open M-Sa 9am-8pm, Su 9am-12:30pm. MC/V.)

Le Palmarium ❸, 7 rue du Port Vieux, serves up a wide variety of meals, including pizzas (€6.50-10) and meat or fish dishes (€8-14), in a palm-filled courtyard; but the best choice on the menu is the paella (evenings only)—the house specialty. Cooked in huge pans out front, diners get as much rice, chicken and shellfish as they can eat for only €12. (☎05 59 24 25 83. Open daily 10am-11pm. MC/V.) **La Crêpe Dentelle ❷,** 6 av. de la Marne, offers delicious crêpes derived from the owner's imagination and modeled on traditional Breton recipes. From July to January, the restaurant prepares crêpes topped with fresh mussels and shrimp imported directly from nearby Brittany. (☎05 59 22 28 29. Lunch *menu* €10. Crêpes €2-8.30. Open M-Sa noon-2:30pm and 7pm-10:30pm. MC/V.) Perfectly situated next to the Grand Plage and the casino, **The Player's ❷,** 2 rue Gardères, serves tasty food for reasonable prices. The delicious homemade *tarte aux pommes* (€5) with buttery crust and whipped cream comes especially recommended. (☎05 59 24 19 60. Meat and fish €6.50-16.50; filling pizzas €6-9.50; pitchers of local sangria €6. Open Dec.-Oct. noon-midnight. MC/V.)

☐ ☐ SIGHTS AND BEACHES

All of Biarritz is designed in consideration of its beaches. The **Grande Plage** is nearly covered in summer by thousands of perfect bodies and talented surfers. On the walkway behind the beach is the immaculate white **Casino Municipal.** Walk left along av. de l'Impératrice to reach the **Pointe St-Martin** and the tall lighthouse, **Le Phare de Biarritz.** From here, it is possible to see the sands of the Landes region separating from the rocky coast of the Basque country. Inland, the **Hôtel du Palais** overlooks the **Plage Miramar.** Constructed in 1845 by Emperor Napoleon III for Princess Eugénie, the E-shaped palace has since been converted into a hotel. Rooms begin at €250 in the low season, and climb as high as €500 per night, but those without such royal wallets can soak up the atmosphere of Biarritz's best four-star hotel in the terrace cafe with a cup of coffee (€4-5.50), or to splurge, a bottle of Cristal champagne (€168). Across av. de l'Impératrice is the old **Hôtel Continental,** where Russian nobles fled after the 1917 Bolshevik Revolution.

The best way to soak in all Biarritz has to offer is to take a stroll along the shoreline. On the other side of the Grande Plage, jagged rock formations provide shelter in the **Port des Pêcheurs** for small fishing boats. **BAB Subaquatique,** near the Port des Pêcheurs, organizes scuba excursions. (☎ 05 59 24 80 40. Open July-Aug. €18, with guide €21, for beginners €28. Diving excursions to the *Vieux Port* and nighttime trips available. Cash and traveler's checks only.) Continue down the coast and over the steel bridge and through the **Rocher de la Vierge,** a tooth-like rock with a statue of the Virgin Mary, to gaze at breathtaking sunsets.

Finally, make the worthwhile trek out of town to the **Musée du Chocolat,** 14 av. Beaurivage, to learn about the history of chocolate and consume delicious handmade samples. The chocolate maker **Henriet** sits next door. (☎ 05 59 41 54 64. Open daily July-Aug. and school vacations 10am-6pm; Sept.-June M-Sa 10am-noon and 2:30-6pm. Guided tours in French or English usually depart every 15min. If there are not enough visitors, the museum will give out hand-held audioguides instead. Wheelchair-accessible. €6, students and ages 13-18 €5, ages 4-12 €3.50.)

NIGHTLIFE AND FESTIVALS

Casino Barrière de Biarritz gloats over the Grande Plage in all its Art Deco glory, but in order to enter the ocean of slot machines, gamblers must leave their flip flops, ripped jeans, and beach gear at the door. (1 av. Edouard VII. ☎ 05 59 22 77 77. 18+. Open daily July-Aug. 10am-4am; Sept.-June M-Th and Su 10am-3am, F-Sa until 4am. Tables open M-F 7:30pm-close; Sa-Su 6pm-close. €11 to enter table rooms.) Hang out around the Port des Pêcheurs until 11pm or midnight, when the rich and reckless strap on their party boots. Things pick up early at the **Ventilo Caffé,** 30 rue Mazagran, a popular bar where a young crowd drinks and chats. (☎ 05 59 24 31 42. Beer €2.50, alcohol €5. Open daily 8am-3am. MC/V.) Once all the local bars close at 2am, the more persistent party-goers flock to the town's two main nightclubs. Lively **Le Copa,** 24 av. Edouard VII, has a large tropical bar on its main floor, outdoor and indoor tables, and a dance club downstairs that plays Latin music, techno, and hip-hop (☎ 05 59 24 65 39. Beer and alcoholic drinks €8, glass of champagne €10. Bar open daily 3pm-8am, dance club midnight-6am, €8.) A few streets away, the competing nightclub **Playboy,** 15 pl. Clemenceau, attracts a younger crowd by blasting rap and dance music until the early morning hours. (☎ 06 63 60 39 20. Beer €5, alcohol €8. €10 cover with drink. Open midnight-6am, although no one comes until 2am.) On weekend nights, many head for cheaper, wilder **San Sebastian** just over the border in Spain.

The **International Festival of Biarritz** celebrates the cinema and culture of Latin America during the first week of October. Throughout September, **Le Temps d'Aimer** will please the culturally inclined with music, ballet, and art exhibits. (Tickets at the tourist office; student discounts.) In July and August, *pelote* and Basque dancing hit **Parc Mazon** Mondays at 9pm. Two *cesta punta* tournaments animate the **Fronton Euskal-Jai** in the **Parc des Sports d'Aguiléra.** For two weeks in mid-July, Biarritz hosts the international **Biarritz Masters Jaï-Alaï** tournament, and at the end of August the town is taken over by the **Gant d'Or,** a tournament among big-name players. The winning teams from each tournament compete for the **Trophée du Super Champion** in mid-September. (For all 3, call tourist office ☎ 05 59 22 44 66. Tickets €10-20.) As a tribute to its other primary sport, Biarritz hosts a **Surf Festival** for two weeks in July and the **Junior Pro Competition** at the end of August. The city also celebrates its ethnic heritage year-round with free **Basque music concerts** (pl. des Halles, 3rd Sa of month 11:30am) and **dance shows** (at the esplanade Casino Municipal, 1st Su of month 11:30am).

BAYONNE

Although only a few kilometers from the center of Biarritz, Bayonne (pop. 42,000) seems hundreds of years removed from its more fashionable neighbor. The pace of life has not changed here since the 17th century, which is reflected even in the language of the region: the verb for "walk" is *flâner* (meaning "stroll"). Bayonne rises early, when lively markets crowd the banks of the Nive and shoppers roam throughout the streets of the *vieille ville*, but then slows down again in the afternoon as people retreat indoors behind exposed wooden beams and colorful shutters. Towering above it all, the grand Gothic cathedral marks the lazy passing of time with the tolling of its bells. It is only in the middle of July and August that things pick up, when hurried tourists flock to Bayonne for festivals, bullfights, and sports matches, as well as more modern jazz concerts and artistic events.

⌐ TRANSPORTATION

Trains: pl. de la Gare. Info office open M-Sa 9am-7pm. To: **Biarritz** (10min., 11 per day, €2.10); **Bordeaux** (2hr., 9 per day, €23.30); **Paris** (5hr., 7 TGV per day, €73.70); **Toulouse** (4hr., 5 per day, €34.30). Also to **San Sebastian, Spain** via **Hendaye** (1½hr.; M-F 6 per day, Sa-Su 5 per day; €8) *Passe Basque* has round-trip tickets to anywhere between Bayonne and San Sebastien for €8.50, valid for 24hr.

Public Transportation: STAB, Hôtel de Ville (☎05 59 59 04 61). Office open M-Sa 8:15am-noon and 1:30-6pm. Buses run every 20-30min. Lines #1, 2, and 6 serve **Biarritz.** Lines #1, 2, and 7 stop in the center of **Anglet.** Line #4 follows the Adour river through Anglet. Buses run around 6:30am-8pm (7pm on Su). 1hr. ticket €1.20; *carnet* of 5 €4.75, *carnet of* 10 €9.50.

Taxis: Both **Radio Taxi** and **Taxi Gare** are stationed outside the train station and at pl. Charles de Gaulle (☎05 59 59 48 48). €2 starting cost, €1.24 per km during the day, €1.85 per km at night. Around €12-20 to get to Biarritz. 24hr.

✦ 🛈 ORIENTATION AND PRACTICAL INFORMATION

Bayonne is on two rivers that join to split the city into three sections. The train station is in **St-Esprit,** on the northern side of the wide Adour river. From here, the pont St-Esprit, usually lined with fishermen, connects to budget-friendly **Petit-Bayonne,** home of Bayonne's museums and smaller restaurants. Five small bridges from Petit-Bayonne cross the much narrower Nive to **Grand-Bayonne** on the west bank. This oldest part of town has a buzzing pedestrian zone where red-shuttered *arceaux* (houses) perch over ground-floor shops and *pâtisseries*. The center of town is manageable on foot, and an excellent bus system makes Anglet and Biarritz a snap to reach. To get to the tourist office from the train station, follow the signs to the *centre ville*, crossing the main bridge (pont St-Esprit) to Petit-Bayonne. Continue through pl. du Réduit and cross the next bridge on the right over to Grand-Bayonne. Take a slight right onto rue Bernède, and continue walking 300m as the street becomes av. Bonnat. The tourist office is on the left (10 minutes).

Tourist Office: pl. des Basques (☎05 59 46 01 46; www.bayonne-tourisme.com). Free city map, hotel reservations, and *Fêtes en Pays Basque* brochures. Organizes 2hr. walking tours of neighborhoods and old ramparts. (July-Sept. M-F 10am; Oct.-June Sa 3pm in French; tours given in English July-Aug. Th 10am. €5, children under 12 free.) Office open July-Aug. M-Sa 9am-7pm, Su 10am-1pm; Sept.-June M-F 9am-6:30pm, Sa 10am-6pm. **Bâteau le Bayonne,** allée Boufflers (☎06 80 74 21 51), runs 2hr. guided boat trips along the Adour River. Excursions leave year-round upon demand; call for departure times. €15, group members €13, ages 5-12 €7.50.

Budget Travel: Pascal Voyages, 8 allées Boufflers (☎05 59 25 48 48). Open M-F 8:30am-6:30pm, Sa 9am-noon.

Bank: BNP Paribas, 1 pl. de la Liberté (☎08 02 35 58 71). €5.40 commission for cash, no commission on traveler's checks. Open for exchange M-Tu and Th 8:30am-noon and 1:30-5:15pm. **ATMs** outside.

Laundromat: Lavopratic, 57 rue Bourg-Neuf (☎06 82 02 41 55). Wash €3.40-6.80, dry €0.40 per 5min. Ironing available daily 8am-noon and 2-5:30pm (T-shirt €0.60, long-sleeved shirt €0.75, jeans €0.90); closed W afternoon. Open daily 8am-8pm.

Police: av. de Marhum (☎05 59 46 22 22).

Hospital: 13 av. Interne Jacques Loëb (☎05 59 44 35 35), St-Léon.

Internet Access: In St-Esprit, **Cyber-net Café,** 9 pl. de la République (☎05 59 50 85 10). €0.15 per min., €4.50 per hr. Open M-Sa 7am-9pm, Su 10am-9pm. Also available at the **post office** (see below).

Post Office: 11 rue Jules Labat (☎05 59 46 33 60), Grand-Bayonne. **Currency exchange** with no commission. Open M-F 8am-6pm, Sa 8am-noon. Cyberposte. Branch office on the corner of bd. Alsace-Lorraine and rue de l'Este (☎05 59 50 32 90). Open M-F 9am-5:30pm, Sa 8:30am-noon.

Postal Code: 64100.

ACCOMMODATIONS

Reasonably priced lodgings dot St-Esprit's train station area. Hotels in Grand-Bayonne are pricier; hunt around **place Paul Bert** in Petit-Bayonne, but expect a noisy night near nightlife. Hotels fill quickly in festival season—reserve ahead. The closest hostels are in Anglet (p. 574) and Biarritz (p. 564), each a 20min. bus ride away. **Hôtel Paris-Madrid ❷,** pl. de la Gare, is located to the left of the train station, a 3min. walk from Petit-Bayonne. Large individualized rooms are decorated with old wooden furniture. The 4th floor has personal balconies overlooking pl. de la Gare. Gracious, English-speaking husband and wife are more knowledgeable and forthcoming than 20 tourist offices. (☎05 59 55 13 98; sorbois@wanadoo.fr. TV and reading room. Breakfast €4. In-room TV €1. Reception 6:30am-12:30am. Singles €17-22, with shower €26, with bath €29-45; doubles €22, with shower €26, with bath €29-45; triples and quads with bath €41-45. MC/V.) **Hôtel Monte-Carlo ❷,** 1 rue Hugues, is located just to the right of the train station. Check in at the lively restaurant-bar next door. Colorful rooms are decorated with old local posters and most come with a TV. (☎05 59 55 02 68; fax 05 59 55 19 47. Breakfast €4.60. Reception July-Sept. 6am-2am; Oct.-June 6:30am-9pm. Singles with shower July-Sept. €25, Oct.-June €22; doubles €31/€25, with shower €35/€32; quads with shower €48/€45. MC/V.)

FOOD

At the very beginning of the 18th century, the Spanish monarchy heightened its anti-Semitic laws and expelled all non-Christians from its borders. Jews escaped by the hundreds on ships and landed in the first French port they encountered—Bayonne. As many of the deportees had previously been chocolate-makers, they introduced their skills to the region and quickly established an enormous candy market. Today, Bayonne is known as the chocolate capital of France and honors this title with its large array of chocolate shops. Along with its desserts, the city

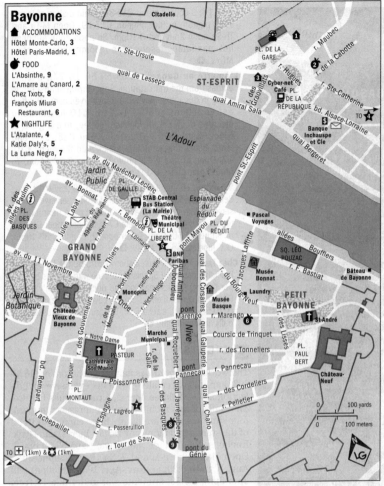

Bayonne

⌂ ACCOMMODATIONS
Hôtel Monte-Carlo, **3**
Hôtel Paris-Madrid, **1**
🍎 FOOD
L'Absinthe, **9**
L'Amarre au Canard, **2**
Chez Txotx, **8**
François Miura
  Restaurant, **6**
★ NIGHTLIFE
L'Atalante, **4**
Katie Daly's, **5**
La Luna Negra, **7**

has also borrowed most of its meat and fish recipes from Spain. The narrow streets of Petit-Bayonne and St-Esprit offer €8-10 *menus* of *jambon de Bayonne* (dry-cured ham) and *poulet à la basquaise* (chicken wrapped in large peppers). Grand-Bayonne, the city's cloth-napkin zone, serves regional specialties in a less budget-oriented atmosphere. Vendors sell meats, fish, cheese, and produce at the **marché municipal,** on quai Roquebert. (Open M-Th 7am-1pm, F 7am-1pm and 3:30-7pm, Sa 6am-2pm.) There is also a **Monoprix supermarket** on the corner of rue Orbe and rue Port Neuf. (☎ 05 59 59 00 33. Open M-Sa 8:30am-7:30pm. AmEx/MC/V.)

▨ François Miura Restaurant, 24 rue Marengo (☎ 05 59 59 49 89). In terms of luxury and decadence, this restaurant is far and away the best in Bayonne. Amid fresh roses and modern art, patrons dine on sophisticated Basque food like squid marinated in its own ink and pork juice (€16). Tucked away down a street; look for a foggy glass door decorated with the recommendation stickers of a dozen different travel guides. Appetizers

BASQUE CASE

In Bayonne, the capital of France's Basque region, restaurants post signs reading *"Euskara badikigu."* Years of Latin lessons won't help you discover that this means "Basque spoken here;" Basque is the only non-Indo-European language spoken in Western Europe. Basque might not be the language of Babel, as believed in the 18th century, but Basques are tied to the ancient past—geneticists have found a link between Basques and Celts, suggesting both are descendants of European pre-farming communities.

Recent talk of Basque identity, however, has focused on the ETA (Basque Homeland and Liberty), a radical movement based in Spain that organizes attacks in the name of independence. As violence continues in Spain, France has cracked down on ETA training cells and imprisoned members for acts of terrorism.

Yet only 10% of French Basques vote for Basque parties, and even fewer support the ETA's radical ideology. How has France escaped Spain's problems? French Basques did not experience the cultural oppression their Spanish counterparts did under Franco, and scholars suggest that tolerance toward French Basques has actually aided in their identification with the larger nation. The Pays Basque remains the middle ground, balancing its cultural identity between extremes of separatism and assimilation.

€14-17; 3-course *menu* €19-30; main dishes of lamb, veal, pigeon, or filet mignon €17-19. Open M-Tu and Th-Sa noon-2pm and 8-10pm, Su noon-2pm. Although not mandatory, reservations recommended. AmEx/MC/V. ❹

L'Amarre au Canard, (☎05 59 50 16 77), directly across from the train station. Specializing almost exclusively in duck, this new restaurant serves over 20 different variations (€6.90-14.20). €10 lunch *menu* includes duck platter, dessert, coffee, and a glass of wine. Salad €6.90, 3-course *menu* €15, beef and lamb dishes that somehow snuck onto the menu €10-12. Open M and W-Sa noon-2pm and 7:30-11pm, Tu noon-2pm, Su 7:30-11pm. MC/V. ❸

L'Absinthe, 15 quai Jauréguiberry (☎05 59 25 60 13), has delicate cuisine in small, intensely flavorful servings. Dinner served within the purple and yellow art deco room or on a terrace by the river. Appetizers €7-8, fish and meat €13-20, absinthe €4.50. Open Tu-Su noon-2pm and 7:30-10pm; Oct.-June closed Su. MC/V. ❹

Chez Txotx, 49 quai Jauréguiberry (☎05 59 59 16 80). This bullfighting-themed Spanish *brasserie* with a *tapas* bar (€1 per *tartine*) fills its seats on the dock with a lively crowd. Fresh fish come directly from the covered market next door (€10.50-13.50). Paella €14. Occasional live music. Open daily noon-midnight. ❸

🄶 SIGHTS

The works of *bayonnais* painter Léon Bonnat (1833-1922) are displayed along with his extensive art collection at the ◪**Musée Bonnat,** 5 rue Jacques Laffitte. The walls of this architecturally impressive modern, four-story museum are hardly large enough to fit all of the stunning paintings by Dégas, Ingrès, Van Dyck, Reubens, Rembrandt, and Goya. (☎05 59 59 08 52. Open May-Oct. Su-M and W-Sa 10am-6:30pm, July-Aug. W until 9:30pm; Nov.-Apr. 10am-12:30pm and 2pm-6pm. €5.50, students €3, under age 18 free. Entrance is free Sept.-June the first Su of each month and July-Aug. W evenings 6:30-9:30pm.) Holding the title of world's largest ethnographic museum on the Pays Basque, the **Musée Basque,** 37 quai des Corsaires, includes exhibits on dance, clothing, jai alai, transportation, cooking, and history, and features a few multimedia presentations. Explanations are in French, Basque, and Spanish. (☎05 59 46 61 90; www.musee-basque.com. Open May-Oct. Tu-Su 10am-6:30pm, W until 9:30pm; Nov.-Apr. Tu-Su 10am-12:30pm and 2-6pm. The tourist office leads French guided visits through the museum July-Sept. F at 3pm. Combined ticket for the Basque Museum and the Bonnat Museum €9, students €4.50. €5.50, students €3, under 18 free. Entrance is free Sept.-June the first Su of each month and July-Aug. W 6:30-9:30pm.) On Sundays at 10:30am, the **Église St-André** (☎ 05 59 59 18 72) holds a traditional mass with Basque chants.

The 13th-century **Cathédrale Ste-Marie,** pl. Pasteur, where spiny steeples pierce the sky above Bayonne, seems disproportionately tall in relation to the town it serves. Although the church has endured sporadic fires, weathered a brief stint as a cemetery, and suffered massive destruction during the secularizing zeal of the Revolution, renovations have completely erased all traces of decay. (☎ 05 59 59 17 82. Church open M-Sa 7:30am-noon and 3-7pm, Su 3:30-8pm. Cloister open daily 9am-12:30pm and 2-6pm; Oct.-May closes at 5pm. Entry to both is free.) The prison block of the **Château-Vieux de Bayonne** on nearby rue des Gouverneurs has held such notorious villains as Don Pedro of Castille. The fort, however, is now occupied by the army and is closed to the public. Around the corner on av. du 11 Novembre, Bayonne's refreshing **botanical gardens** flourish atop the battlements with 1000 species of Japanese flora, including a miniature bamboo forest. (Open daily mid-Apr. to mid-Oct. 9:30am-noon and 2-6pm.)

Those looking for a beach that is more secluded than the crowded plots of sand in Anglet or Biarritz should try the **Metro plage** in Tarnos; take bus #10 from the train station (every 20min. M-Sa 7:20am-7:25pm). Lifeguards are only on duty during July and August, but the beach is beautiful all year.

🎵 🌿 ENTERTAINMENT AND FESTIVALS

Nightlife is nearly nonexistent in this quiet town of long afternoons and short evenings. The main bars grouped on the streets between **place Paul Bert** and **quai Galuperie** in Petit-Bayonne cater mostly to aging local men. Travelers seeking a more lively atmosphere often take the 10min. bus ride to Biarritz or head across the border to San Sebastian. In Bayonne, the Irish pub **Katie Daly's,** 3 pl. de la Liberté, serves expensive pints to animated crowds on the weekends. A large screen is set up by the door so that locals can watch soccer games while drinking. (☎ 05 59 59 09 14. Pints of Guinness €6, €5 7-9pm. Live pop and rock music F-Sa. Open M-Sa 5pm-2am, Su 6pm-2am.) **La Luna Negra,** in an alleyway off rue de la Salie, presents a cornucopia of music styles at its cabaret-style bar and stage. Wednesday is blues night; Thursday through Saturday entertainment ranges from salsa to jazz to storytellers to classical concerts. (Blues night €3-4, other shows €5-10, student discounts available for some shows; beer €2.50. Bar open W-Sa 5pm-2am, shows start 9-9:30pm.) **L'Atalante,** 7 rue Denis Etcheverry, in St-Esprit, shows artsy international films in their original language. (☎ 05 59 55 76 63; www.cinema-atalante.org. Wheelchair-accessible. €5.70, students and children €3.80, €25 for 5 tickets. Daily screening at 6:30 or 7pm, €5. Closed 2 weeks in early Aug.)

Bayonne's festivals take over the city from the end of June to the very beginning of October. The orchestra **Harmonie Bayonnaise** stages jazz and traditional Basque concerts in the pl. de Gaulle gazebo. (July-Aug. Th 9:30pm. Free.) After the first Wednesday in August, unrestrained hedonism breaks out during the **Fêtes Traditionelles,** as the locals immerse themselves in five days of concerts, bullfights, fireworks, and a chaotic cow race. The *fête* is noted as one of the world's five biggest festivals. July through September, Bayonne holds several bullfights or *corridas* in the **Plaza de Toros** (☎ 05 59 46 61 00). Tickets (€15-93.50) sell out fast, but the cheap section usually has seats available on fight days. The Hôtel de Ville, on rue Bernède, provides information about local bullfights at the **Bureau des Arènes** (☎ 05 59 46 61 00) and about the city's festivals at the **Bureau d'Information Municipale** (☎ 05 59 46 61 00). Both are open Monday to Friday 10am-1pm and 4-7pm. In some seasons, the **Théâtre Municipale** hosts various musical performances. (☎05 59 59 07 27. Ticket office open Tu-F 1-6pm, Sa 10am-1pm and 3-6pm. Tickets approximately €10-20, although they vary for every show.)

⚡ DAYTRIP FROM BAYONNE OR BIARRITZ

ANGLET. Known as the surfing capital of France, Anglet's *raison d'être* is its 4km of fine-grained white sand, parcelled out into nine sparkling beaches. The waves are strongest at the **plage des Cavaliers,** where most of Anglet's surfing competitions are held, but swimmers all along the coast should be wary of the strong undertow. When in doubt, swim near a lifeguard (they're on all the beaches except the plage du Club and the plage des Dunes). Pine needles cover the walking trails at the **Fôret du Chilberta,** which has a newly con-structed adventure and ropes course. Contact Evolution 2 Pays Basque, 130 av. de l'Adour, which runs the course and offers **river-rafting trips** (€24.50 per half-day), **scuba diving** (€28 per 2hr.), and **surfing lessons** (€30 per 1½hr.) at sepa-rate locations within an hour's drive of Anglet. (☎05 59 42 03 06; www.evolution2.com/paysbasque. Open mid-May to Oct. Beginner's ropes course for children ages 3-5 €5, ages 5-10 €8; 1½hr. intermediate course for adults €19; 2hr. advanced course €25.) Sailing is also offered right next to the office afternoons 2-6pm for €30. (Office open daily July to mid-Sept. 10am-8pm; Apr.-June and mid-Sept.-Oct. Sa-Su 2-6pm.) Along the coast, professional surf competitions are held throughout the summer and are free for spectators. Starting off the season in the beginning of August, the **O'Neill Pro Competition** is held for six days on the plage des Cavaliers. About a week later, pro and ama-teur surfers demonstrate their skills at the **Quicksilver Air Show.** The qualifying rounds take place during the day at the Sables d'Or, followed by the final match-up at 9pm. For five days at the end of August, women take over the scene to compete in the longboard and bodyboard divisions of the **Kana Miss Cup.** Prepare for these title challenges by renting a board and taking lessons at one of the many surf shops along the beaches. At 22 av. des Dauphins, Free-style provides surfboards, wetsuits, bikes, beach cruisers, and skis, depending on the season. (☎05 59 03 27 24; freestyle.surfacademy@wanadoo.com. 1½hr. lessons €30, €150 for 6 people. Surfboards €9 per half-day, €15 per day, €75 per week; wetsuits €5-6/€8-10/€40-50; skis and snowboards with boots €140 per week. Photocopy of credit card required as a deposit. Open daily June to mid-Oct. 9:30am-7pm; mid-Sept. to May 10am-12:30pm and 2:30-7pm.) Anglet Olympique Canoe Kayak on pl. du Docteurs Gentilhe also rents out **jet skis** and **sea kayaks,** both €12 per hr. and €34 per day. (☎06 15 54 60 41. Open July-Aug. daily 10am-5pm; Sept.-June W and Sa 2-6pm.)

Those too sunburned to stand another day at the beach can head over to the town's **skating rink,** 299 av. de l'Adour, near the ropes course. (☎05 59 57 17 30. Visitors €2, skaters €3.50, skate rentals €2.50. Open July-Aug. M-Sa 3-5:30pm and 9-11:30pm, Su 10am-noon and 3-5:30pm; Sept. to early May M and W-Th 2-5pm, Tu 2-5pm and 9-11pm, F 2-5pm and 9pm-midnight, Sa 2-6pm, Su 9:30-11am and 2-6pm. Closed early May-June.)

In the Fôret du Chilberta, the Club Hippique provides **riding lessons** and **horse-back tours** of the forest. The stables are on rue du Petit Palais, off Promenade de la Barre. (☎05 59 63 83 45; fax 05 59 63 95 59; clubhippique@wanadoo.fr. 1hr. lesson €20, forest-walk €18, on ponies both €18. Horseback excursions €33-48 per half-day, €43-46 per day. Open July-Aug. M-W and F 9am-noon and 4-8pm, Th 10am-noon and 4-8pm, Sa 9am-noon and 3-6pm; Sept.-June M-W and F-Su. If there is no one at the office, speak to a stable hand. Reservations are mandatory.)

The well-equipped **tourist office,** 1 av. de la Chambre d'Amour in pl. Général Leclerc, is a good 10-15min. walk from the sea. (☎05 59 03 77 01; fax 05 59 03 55 91. Open July to mid-Sept. M-Sa 9am-7pm; mid-Sept. to June M 9:30am-12:30pm and 2:30-6pm, Tu-F 9am-12:30pm and 2-6pm, Sa 9am-12:30pm.) There is an annex closer to the shore on av. des Dauphins. (Open daily July to mid-Sept. 10am-7pm; Apr. 10:30am-1pm and 3-6:30pm; mid-Sept. to Mar. and May-June Sa-Su 10:30am-1pm and 3-6:30pm.) **STAB buses** (€1.20) run throughout Anglet about every 15min., less frequently on Sundays and holidays. Get a map or schedule from the tourist office in Anglet, or the train stations in Biarritz and Bayonne. From these two neighboring towns, buses the #1, 2, 6, and 7 Monday through Saturday and the A and B buses on Sunday travel to the center of Anglet, while buses #9, 7, and C run along its coast.

ST-JEAN-DE-LUZ

St-Jean-de-Luz (pop. 13,000; Basque name Donibane Lohitzun) has always lived off the sea. Its early wealth came from whaling and the Basque *corsaires* (pirates) who raided British merchants throughout the 1600s. These maritime riches are responsible for the fine examples of Basque architecture, from the octagonal bell-tower above Ravel's birthplace to the elaborate interior of the Église St-Jean-Baptiste. This Basque town is certainly worth a visit for its charm and architecture, as well as its great beaches, but budget travelers may want to daytrip from the more affordable Bayonne.

🚆 TRANSPORTATION

Trains: bd. du Commandant Passicot. Info office open daily 7:45am-6:50pm. To: **Bayonne** (30min.; 10 per day; €4, TGV €5.70); **Biarritz** (15min.; 10 per day; €2.60, TGV €4.30); **Paris** (5½hr., 10 per day, €74.30); **Pau** (2½ hr., 5 per day, €16.70).

Buses: across from the train station. **ATCRB** (☎05 59 26 06 99) runs to **Bayonne** (40min-1hr., 15 per day, €3.60) and **Biarritz** (40min., 17 per day, €2.80). Buy tickets on bus. Office open M-F 9am-noon and 2-6pm.

Taxis: at the train station (☎05 59 26 10 11). €6.50 flat rate to anywhere in town. Approximately €26 to get to Biarritz during the day, €32 at night. 24hr.

Car Rental: Avis (☎05 59 36 76 66; fax 05 59 26 19 42), at the station. €230 per week and up. Copy of credit card required as a deposit. Can return at other locations. 25+. Office open M-F 8am-noon and 2-6pm, Sa 9am-noon and 2-6pm. AmEx/MC/V.

Bike Rental: Fun-Bike Location (☎05 59 26 75 76 or 06 27 26 83 01), at the train station. Bikes €12 for half-day, €15 for 24hr., €69 per week in summer (€61 with reservation), €200 deposit; scooters €21-27 per half-day, €41 for 24hr., €400-700 deposit. Prices lower Sept.-June. Open daily 9am-7pm. Call in advance Sept.-June because the owner will often leave the office if there is a lack of customers. MC/V.

🔁🛈 ORIENTATION AND PRACTICAL INFORMATION

From the train station, bear left diagonally across the roundabout onto bd. du Commandant Passicot. The **tourist office,** pl. Foch, is on the right, just past the 2nd rotary. From pl. Foch, rue de la République runs two short blocks to **place Louis XIV,** the center of town. The beach is 50m straight ahead, and the pedestrian **rue Gambetta** runs perpendicular to the right. **Ciboure,** the section of St-Jean-de-Luz on the other side of the Nivelle River, can be reached by crossing the pont Charles de Gaulle.

AQUITAINE AND
PAYS BASQUE

Tourist Office: pl. Foch (☎05 59 26 03 16; fax 05 59 26 21 47). Maps and info on accommodations, events, and excursions. 2hr. tours of the town offered in French July-Aug. Tu and F at 10am, Apr.-June and Sept.-Oct. Tu 10am. Reserve in advance for English tours. €5, children €2.50. Open July-Aug. M-Sa 9am-7:30pm, Su 10am-1pm and 3-7pm; Sept.-June M-Sa 9am-12:30pm and 2:30-7:30pm, Su 10am-1pm.

Currency Exchange: Banque Inchauspé et Cie, 16 bd. Victor Hugo (☎05 59 26 24 71). Good exchange rates and no commission. Open Tu-Th 8:30am-12:15pm and 1:45-5:15pm, F 8:30am-12:20pm and 1:45-5:45pm, Sa 8:30am-12:30pm. **ATMs** directly across the street.

Laundromat: Laverie Automatique, at the intersection of bd. Victor Hugo and rue Chauvin Dragon. Wash €4-7, dry €0.40 per 4min., detergent €0.50. Open daily 8am-10pm.

Surf Shop: Le Spot, 16 rue Gambetta (☎05 59 26 07 93). 2hr. lesson €35. Wet-suit €7 per half-day, €12 per day; bodyboard €6/€10; surfboard €10/€15. Deposit: ID plus value of object. Open July-Aug. M-Sa 10am-1pm and 3-8pm, Su 11am-1pm and 3:30-7:30pm; Sept.-June M 3-7pm, Tu-Sa 10am-12:30pm and 3-7:30pm. AmEx/MC/V.

Police: av. André Ithurralde (☎05 59 51 22 22).

Hospital: 19 av. André Ithurralde (☎05 59 51 45 45). 24hr. emergency service at the private hospital **Polyclinique,** 10 av. de Layats (☎05 59 51 63 63).

Post Office: 44 bd. Victor Hugo (☎05 59 51 66 54). Open July-Aug. M-F 8:45am-5:30pm, Sa 8:45am-noon; Sept.-June M-F 8:45am-noon and 1:45-5:30pm, Sa 8:45am-noon. **ATM** outside.

Postal Code: 64500.

ACCOMMODATIONS AND CAMPING

Hotels are expensive and fill up rapidly in summer. Reserve early, especially in August. It may be best to commute from Bayonne or Biarritz. However, those who do stay in St-Jean-de-Luz can expect nice rooms and good service for the prices.

Hôtel Bolivar, 18 rue Sopite (☎05 59 26 02 00; fax 05 59 26 38 28), on a central but quiet street near the beach. Sparkling rooms are rented by a no-nonsense owner. Breakfast €6. Reception 7:30am-9:30pm. Open May-Sept. Singles with toilet €34, with toilet and shower €52; doubles €40/€65; triples with bath, toilet, and TV €70. May-June and Sept. prices slightly lower. AmEx/MC/V. ❸

Hôtel Verdun, 13 av. de Verdun (☎05 59 26 02 55), across from the train station. Well-kept, pastel-colored rooms with huge bathrooms for the lowest prices in St-Jean. Breakfast €4. July-Sept. singles and doubles €39, with shower €43; triples and quads with shower €45, with bath €50 Jan-Apr. and Nov.-Dec. 1-4 people €23-28, May-June and Oct. 1-4 people €26-32. Reception 9am-11pm. MC/V. ❸

Camping: There are 17 campsites in St-Jean-de-Luz and 13 more nearby. All are separated from the city center, behind the plage D'Erromardie. The tourist office has the addresses and phone numbers of the sites and can make recommendations. To walk to the sites, take bd. Victor Hugo from the center of town, continue along the road as it turns into av. André Ithurralde, then veer left onto chemin d'Erromardie. (20min.) Or take an ATCRB bus headed to Biarritz or Bayonne and ask to get off near the camping. For a quiet and sheltered location, the **Camping Iratzia,** on chemin d'Erromardie (☎05 59 26 14 89; fax 05 59 26 69 69), offers grassy sites 300m away from the beach. Reception 8:30am-8pm. Those arriving when the office is closed may set up their tents in an open spot, and return to the reception later. Open May-Sept. Aug. €5.50 per person, €3.10 per car, €7 per site; July and Sept. €4/€2.50/€5; May-June €3.50/€2/€4. Mobile home for 4 people May-June and Sept. €260; July-Aug. €390-550. Electricity €3.50. Showers included. ❶

FOOD

St-Jean-de-Luz has the best Basque and Spanish specialties north of the border. The port's famous seafood awaits in every restaurant along the rue de la République and pl. Louis XIV, but expect to pay upwards of €13 per meal. There is a large **market** at pl. des Halles. (Open daily July to mid-Sept. 8am-1pm; mid-Sept. to June closed Su.) For groceries, stop at the **Shopi supermarket,** 87 rue Gambetta (open July-Aug. M-Sa 9am-8pm, Su 9am-noon; Sept.-June M-Sa 9am-12:30pm and 3-7:15pm; MC/V), or at **Casino,** 46 bd. Victor Hugo (open M-Sa 8:30am-7:30pm, Su 8:30am-12:30pm and 4:30-7:30pm; MC/V).

■ **Buvette de la Halle,** bd. Victor Hugo-Marché de St-Jean-de-Luz (☎05 59 26 73 59), has been in the same family for over 70 years and refuses to alter its original menu—not even to include modern additions like ketchup. Although unimpressive at first glance, it serves the freshest seafood and vegetables in St-Jean. Grilled sardines €6, *gambas* (large shrimp) €12, *gâteaux Basques* €4, and *Patxaran,* a wild prune aperitif €3. Open daily July-Aug. noon-3pm and 7-11pm; Sept.-June closed on Su. ❷

■ **Pil-Pil Enea,** 3 rue Sallagoity (☎05 59 51 20 80) near the post office, is a tiny restaurant serving the finest *merlu* (hake fish) caught by Europe's only female captain and cooked by her husband. The environmentalist fisherwoman catches all her fish by line, rather than by net. *Menu* €23, appetizers €6-10, fish and meat €11-17. Open M-Sa noon-2pm and 8-10pm, Su noon-2pm. AmEx/MC/V. ❸

Txantxangorri, 30 rue Chauvin Dragon (☎05 59 26 04 32), dishes up traditional basque *plats* and seafood atop blue-and white-striped tablecloths. This new restaurant has a great €10 *menu* including either appetizer and *plat* or *plat* and dessert, salad, and fruit salad. Open M-Sa noon-2pm and 7:30-10pm, Su 7:30-10pm. ❷

Etchebaster Frères, 42 rue Gambetta (☎05 59 26 00 80), caters to your sweet tooth with cherry jam and cream-filled *gâteaux Basques* (€6.50-14). The traditional pistachio *guernikas* (€1.70) and frosted *gâteaux des rois* (€5.90-11.80) also come highly recommended by the owner. Open July-Aug. Tu-Sa 8:30am-1pm and 3:30-7:30pm, Su 8am-1pm and 4-7pm; Sept.-June Tu-Su 8:30am-12:30pm and 3:30-7pm. MC/V. ❷

SIGHTS

To see St-Jean-de-Luz at its most striking, follow the walkway on the beachfront away from the river Nivelle to the end of the **Grande Plage.** The path up toward the **Chapelle Van Bree** takes you on a *balade à pied* (footpath) along the edge of St-Jean's cliffs. From the lookout points, gaze out across the river Nivell over to Hendaye and the Spanish border beyond. In town, the 15th-century **Église St-Jean-Baptiste,** rue Gambetta, has a plain exterior but is decorated inside with enormous gold sculptures of saints and apostles. (☎05 59 26 08 81. Open daily 10am-noon and 2-6pm. Mass is held Su 10:30am, Sa 7pm.) It was in this church that Louis XIV married the Spanish princess Maria-Teresa, according to the terms of the 1659 Treaty of the Pyrenees. The treaty was worked out after months of negotiations by Cardinal Mazarin and the Spanish prime minister on the nearby Île des Faisans or "island of conferences," jointly owned by France and Spain.

Owned by the same family for over 350 years, the elaborate royal furniture inside the **Maison Louis XIV** has been frozen in time, seemingly awaiting the return of its most famous boarder. It was here that Louis XIV stayed while Mazarin negotiated, and here that he consummated his marriage with Maria-Teresa. Unlike the average royal marriage, this one proved successful; upon the queen's death, the king lamented, *"C'est le premier chagrin qu'elle me cause"* (This is the first sorrow she has caused me). (☎/fax 05 59 26 01 56. Free 30min. guided tour in French leaves every 30min. July to mid-Sept. Written explanations in English and audioguides in French available upon request. Open July-Aug. M-Sa 10:30am-12:30pm and 2:30-6:30pm, Su 2:30-6:30pm; Sept. and June M-Sa closes at 5:30pm, Su 10:30am-noon. €4.60, students €3.80.)

🧭 BEACHES

From 1954 to 1956, St-Jean-de-Luz was France's primary supplier of tuna. Fishing boats still leave regularly from quai de l'Infante and quai Maréchal Leclerc, although they are not as fruitful as they once were. To get in on the fun at sea level, stop by the docks near the Maison Louis XIV, where Marie Rose offers a four-hour **fishing trip** from 8am to noon. (☎ 05 59 26 39 84 or 06 08 25 49 74; www.bateau-marie-rose.com. Trips leave every other day July-Aug. and less frequently, often dependent on weather, Sept.-June. €25, children €13. Reservations recommended.) If you prefer to leave the fish alive, **Promenade Jacques Thibaud,** sheltered by dikes, provides some of the best **sailing** and **windsurfing** in the Basque region. Farther down the coast, the most popular surfing spot in St-Jean-de-Luz lies beyond the crowded beaches on **plage d'Erromardi.**

🎊 FESTIVALS

Summer is packed with concerts, Basque festivals, and the heavily anticipated championship match of *cesta punta* (jai alai) featuring the fastest moving ball in any sport. (www.cestapunta.com. Qualifying series and finals July-Aug. Tu and F at 9pm. Tickets at the tourist office; €8-18.50, students €5-11, under 12 free.) Other festivals in town focus on St-Jean's history and culture. The biggest annual festival is the three-day **Fête de St-Jean,** held on a weekend in late June, when singing and dancing fills the streets. Nearly continuous performances by amateurs and professionals alike liven the *fronton* (arena), while spectators consume fruity sangria and barbecued Basque dishes. **Toro de Fuego** heats up summer nights in pl. Louis XIV with pyrotechnics, dancing, and bull costumes. (July-Aug. W 10:30pm, and occasionally Su 11pm.) Show love for fish as St-Jean celebrates tuna at the **Fête du Thon** (the first Sa in July beginning at 6pm), when the town gathers around the harbor to eat tuna and toss confetti (fish, *gâteau basque*, and wine €10). The homage to fish continues the second Saturday of July with the all-you-can-eat **Nuit de la Sardine** at the Campos-Berri, next to the *cesta punta* stadium (☎ 05 59 26 02 87 for info). The last festival of the year, the **Fête du Toro,** held on an early Saturday in September, celebrates the region's excellent fish soup.

🚌 DAYTRIP FROM ST-JEAN-DE-LUZ

COL DE ST-IGNACE

Basque Bondissant (☎ 05 59 26 30 74) runs buses to Col de St-Ignace from the green-rimmed bus terminal facing the train station in St-Jean-de-Luz (20min.; July-Aug. M-Sa 3 per day, Sept.-June M-Tu and Th-F 3 per day, W 2 per day; round-trip €4, including train to top €15, children 4-10 €8.50. Office open M-F 8:30am-noon and 1:30-6pm.)

Ten kilometers southeast of St-Jean-de-Luz, the miniscule village of **Col de St-Ignace** serves as a base for the Basque country's loveliest vantage point. Trains from Col de St-Ignace crawl at a snail's pace along an authentic 1924 *chemin de fer* (railroad) up the mountainside to the 900m summit of **La Rhune.** Each hair-raising turn reveals a postcard-perfect display of forests hovering above farmland, as *pottoks* (wild Basque ponies) return your curious stares and sheep bound down the mountainside. At the peak, chilly air and gusty winds prevail even in summer.

(Trains operated by **Le Petit Train de la Rhune.** ☎05 59 54 20 26; www.rhune.com. Open mid-Mar. to early Nov.; first train up 9:30am, last train up 4:30pm. €11 round-trip. Cash and traveler's checks.) La Rhune *(Larun)* is Spanish soil; shop owners slip easily between French and their native tongue. Those who decide to walk back down from La Rhune should take the roundabout route, as loose rocks on the path make for treacherous footing. Take the well-marked trail to the left of the tracks down to the village of **Ascain** instead of trying to return directly to St-Ignace. Then hike the remaining 3km on D4 back to Col de St-Ignace (1½hr.); or set out directly for St-Jean-de-Luz from Ascain along the busy highway (5km).

ST-JEAN-PIED-DE-PORT

St-Jean-Pied-de-Port is the last stop before the tortuous mountain pass of Ron-cevaux on the pilgrimage to the tomb of St. James in Santiago de Compostela, Spain. Ever since the 10th century, pilgrims have passed through this medieval vil-lage nestled in the middle of the red Pyrenean hills. First built by Sancho the Strong in the 13th century, the walls of St-Jean-Pied-de-Port have withstood attack from Visigoths, Charlemagne, the Moors, and the Spanish army. The city is now a popular tourist spot and features flower-lined stone-arch bridges, Basque craft stores, and a citadel. Outside the now-crumbling ramparts, visitors can set off on numerous hikes into the gorgeous French and Spanish Pyrenees. The Fôret d'Iraty, a mecca for hikers and cross-country skiers, is only 25km away.

◪◪ TRANSPORTATION AND PRACTICAL INFORMATION. Trains leave for Bayonne (1hr.; 5 per day; last train July-Aug. 6:50pm, Sept.-June 4:43pm; €7.50) from the station on av. Renaud. (☎05 59 37 02 00. Info office open M-Sa 6:30am-noon and 1-6:45pm, Su 9am-noon and 2-7pm.) Rent **bikes** at Garazi Cycles, 32 bis au Jaï-Alaï. (☎05 59 37 21 79; jean-jacques.etchardy@wanadoo.fr. Bikes €9.50 per half-day, €14 per day; scooters €18.50/€30; motorcycles €35/€50. Passport or ID deposit. Open daily 9am-noon and 2-7pm; closed W morning.) From the station, turn left and then immediately right on av. Renaud, follow it uphill, and turn right at its end on av. de Gaulle. 40m on the left, the **tourist office**, 14 av. de Gaulle, gives out small maps of the town and sells hiking guides (€6.10) charting the 25 trails in the surrounding region. (☎05 59 37 03 57; saint.jean.pied.de.port@wanadoo.fr. Open July-Aug. M-Sa 9am-7pm, Su 10am-4pm; Sept.-June M-Sa 9am-noon and 2-5pm, Su 10am-noon and 2-4pm.) The **police** (☎05 59 49 20 10) are on rue d'Ugagne, and the Clinique Luro in Ispoure handles **medical emergencies** (☎05 59 37 00 55). The **post office** (☎05 59 37 90 00), rue de la Poste, has **currency exchange** with no commission. (Open M-F 9am-noon and 2-5pm, Sa 9am-noon.) **Postal Code:** 64220.

◪◪ ACCOMMODATIONS AND CAMPING. St-Jean offers beautiful rooms at unbecoming prices; you won't find much under €31 per night. Furthermore, hotels in the summer fill up quickly, so those looking for privacy should book well in advance. There are however, a glut of *gîtes* in town, thanks to the city's position along the popular pilgrimage to Santiago de Compostela in Spain. Many are clus-tered on rue de la Citadelle. The best option is to stay at Mme. Etchegoin's **gîte d'étape ❶**, a popular stopover for pilgrims following the chemin de St-Jacques. The lodging is just outside the city walls, 9 rte. d'Uhart. From the tourist office, walk downhill, cross the bridge, and take the first right on the opposite bank. The street becomes rte. d'Uhart after the city gates. (5min., follow signs to Bayonne.) Twelve spartan bunks await in this 18th-century house, as do six attractive *chambres d'hôte* with handmade quilts, antique furnishings, and hardwood floors. All rooms have either personal showers, or access to a communal one. (☎05 59 37 12 08. Open Mar.-Nov. Breakfast €4 for those in dorms, included for those in rooms.

Sheets or sleeping bag €2. Reception 8am-10:30pm. Mme. Etchegoin prefers that you call in advance so that she can be home for your arrival. Dorms €9; singles €30; doubles €38; triples €48.) **Hôtel des Remparts ❸**, 16 pl. Floquet, is on the same road as Mme. Etchegoin's *gîte*, but inside the city walls. Large, pastel rooms come equipped with bath, TV, and telephone. (☎05 59 37 13 79; fax 05 59 37 33 44. Breakfast €6. Reception daily 7am-8pm. Singles and doubles €36.50-50. MC/V.)

Quiet **Camping Municipal ❶** rests against a low ivy-covered stone wall by the Nive, 5min. from the center of town, on av. du Fronton. For its price, the campsite has the most central and convenient location of any lodging in St-Jean. From the porte St-Jacques, follow the river upstream 50m to the next bridge. Cross the river; the site is on the left on av. du Fronton. (☎05 59 37 11 19; fax 05 59 37 99 78. Open daily Apr.-Oct. 9am-11pm and 5-7pm. €2 per person, €1.50 per child, €1.50 per tent, €2.50 per car. Electricity €2. Bathrooms and showers are free.)

◘ FOOD. Farmers bring *ardigazna* (tangy, dry sheep's-milk cheese) to the **market** on pl. de Gaulle. (Open M 9am-6pm.) In July and August, there are also local fairs that bring produce from nearby villages; ask for the dates at the tourist office. Bread, cheese, and wine are all available at any one of the many small shops that line **rue d'Espagne**. For everyday food, the **Relais de Mousquetaires supermarket** is on the corner of rue d'Espagne and rue d'Uhart. (☎05 59 37 00 47. Open M 9am-12:30pm and 3-7:30pm, Tu-Sa 9:30am-12:30pm and 4-7:30pm. MC/V.) None of the cheap restaurants in St-Jean-Pied-du-Port are spectacular, but there are several cafes and *crêperies* along the **rue de Zuharpeta** that offer budget-friendly meals and refreshing sangria. If splurging is an option, the charming little **Restaurant Etche Ona ❺**, on pl. Floquet, serves delicious food amid starched white tablecloths and crystal wine glasses. Expertly cooked and garnished with traditional Basque sauces, the duck, lamb, and rabbit (€12) are truly superb. (☎05 59 37 01 14; fax 05 59 37 35 69. 3-course *menu* €28, *plats* €12. Open daily July-Sept. 10am-2pm and 7:30-10pm; Oct.-June closed F. MC/V.) For those looking for something more affordable, across the street sits **Lizarra Ostatua ❷**, pl. Floquet, which serves a variety of pizzas, along with a delicious paella dish. (☎05 59 37 00 99. Pizzas €6.50-8.50, paella €10, *plat du jour* €9. *Menus* €11.50-24. Open daily noon-3pm and 7pm-midnight for meals, with snacks served throughout the day. MC/V.)

◙ SIGHTS. Bounded by **Porte d'Espagne** and **Porte St-Jacques**, the ancient *haute ville* of St-Jean consists of one narrow street, **rue de la Citadelle**, which is bordered by houses made from regional crimson stone. The well-preserved remains of the **Citadelle de Vauban** rest at the top of this narrow street, towering over the town and its surrounding farmland. Originally built by the knight Antoine Deville in 1628, the fortress was later reinforced by Vauban during the reign of Louis XIV. In 1750, the citadel housed an impressive 2000 soldiers and actively protected Bayonne and Orthez from the feisty Spaniards lurking across the border. Although the interior of the stronghold has since been converted into an elementary school, visitors can still climb to the top and catch a breathtaking view of both the town below and its surrounding mountain, as well as picnic on the grassy ramparts. Standing below the walls of the fortress is the 13th-century **Prison des Evêques**, 41 rue de la Citadelle. Originally built as a municipal prison, the building was used to discipline unruly citadel soldiers during the 19th century and torture French escapees during the Nazi occupation. Today, the prison has been converted into a small museum dedicated to the pilgrimage of St-Jacques. (☎05 59 37 00 92. Open daily July-Aug. 10am-7pm; Easter-June and Sept.-Oct. M-W and F-Su 11am-12:30pm and 2:30-6:30pm. €3, children under 10 free.) Rue de la Citadelle returns to the rear of the

Église Notre-Dame-du-Bout-du-Pont, fused with the Porte St-Jacques. Once a fortress, the church betrays its past with rocky, low-lit crevices. Carefully patterned stained glass casts a mist of light over the rest of the simple edifice. (Open daily 7am-9pm.)

🔝 **HIKING THE PILGRIM'S ROUTE.** The Spanish border is only a 7-8hr. walk from St-Jean-Pied-de-Port along a clearly marked trail. The **GR65** leads you through the Pyrenees toward the Pass of Roncevaux and, a quick 800km later, to Santiago de Compostela and St. James' tomb. To get on the trail from St-Jean, take the rue d'Espagne out from the Porte de l'Église. When the road forks, take a slight left onto rte. du St-Michel and continue straight until it becomes rte. Napoleon. You will start to see red and white stripes on the telephone poles, the symbol of the GR65. The narrow paved road slopes up the mountainside, past family farms and then into the Pyrenees, where sheep and horses wander. The **Fontaine de Roland** and the **col de Bentarte** signal entry onto land claimed by both France and Spain; the French maintain that the border lies ahead at Col de Roncevaux. The round-trip hike takes about 8hr. to Bentarte, and scales 1100m up into the Pyrenees (to Roncevaux about 14hr. round-trip); if it becomes too late to turn back, there is lodging near the pass of Roncevaux, about a 2hr. walk past the col de Bentarte. **Amis du Chemin de Saint-Jacques de Pyrénées Atlantiques,** 39 rue de la Citadelle, in St-Jean, offers help, advice, and lodging exclusively for hikers. (☎ 05 59 37 05 09. Open daily Mar. to mid-Nov. 7:30am-12:30pm and 2:30-10pm; July-Aug. 7am-1pm and 2:30-10pm. Shelter available for €7 per night.)

PAU

Once the seat of the kings of Navarre, Pau (pop. 78,000) has transformed itself into a bustling modern little metropolis. While the château of native son Henri "Edict of Nantes" VI remains in near-perfect condition, the surrounding city is filled with good shopping and lively streets. Thanks to the nearby Pyrenees, Pau benefits from good weather and access to several centers of mountain sports. As the capital of the Béarn region, Pau is also the capital of *Béarnais* cuisine—the city now holds more than 150 restaurants, each serving regional delicacies fit for a king.

📺 **TRANSPORTATION.** The **train station,** on av. Gaston Lacoste, is at the base of the hill by the château. (Info and ticket office open M 5am-8:35pm, Tu-Th and Sa 5:15am-8:35pm, F 5:15am-11:35pm, Su 7:15am-11:30pm.) **Trains** go to: Bayonne (1¼hr., 7 per day, €14); Biarritz (1½hr., 6-7 per day, €15.30); Bordeaux (2½hr.; 9 per day; €26.30, TGV €27.80); Lourdes (30min., 14 per day, €6.30); St-Jean-de-Luz (2½hr., 4 per day, €16.70). **CITRAM,** 30 rue Gachet (☎ 05 59 27 22 22), runs **buses** to Agen (3hr., 1 per day, €26). Office open M-F 9am-noon and 2-6pm. **Société TPR** (☎ 05 59 27 45 98), on rue Gachet, goes to Bayonne (2½hr.; M-Sa 2-3 per day, Su 1 per day; €15.10); Biarritz (2¾hr.; M-Sa 2-3 per day, Su 1 per day; €15.60); Lourdes (1¼hr.; M-Sa 5 per day, Su 2 per day; €7.20, under 6 free). Office open M-F 9am-noon and 2-6pm. **STAP** runs **local buses** (tickets €1, day pass €2.50, *carnet* of 8 €5.50). First bus in any direction M-Sa 6:30am, Su 1:15pm; last bus in any direction M-Sa 8:20pm, Su 7:40pm. The new **Noctambus** is run by the same company but circulates on fewer routes 8-9:30pm or 11:30pm depending on the route. The office is on rue Gachet. (☎ 05 59 27 69 78. Open M-F 8:30am-12:30pm and 1:30-6pm, Sa 9am-noon.) There is also a kiosk on pl. Clemenceau. (☎ 05 59 14 15 16. Open M-F 9am-noon and 2-6pm.) **Taxis** depart from the train station, pl. Clemenceau, pl. Verdun, the hospital, and the airport. (☎ 05 59 02 22 22. During the day €1.24 per km, at night €1.70, starting rate €2. Approximately €23-25 to go from the train station to the airport. 24hr.) Romano Sport, on the corner of rue Jean-Réveil and rue Castetnau, rents **bikes** (€10 per day), mountain bikes (€22 per day), in-line skates (€7 per day), hiking boots, and mountain equipment. (☎05 59 98 48 56. Deposit €100-600 or ID. Open M-Sa 9am-noon and 3-7pm.)

⑦ PRACTICAL INFORMATION. To get to the tourist office and town center from the station, ride the free Funicular to bd. des Pyrénées (every 3min.; M-Sa 6:45am-12:10pm, 12:35-7:50pm, and 8:15-9:40pm; Su 1:30-7:50pm and 8:15-9pm), or climb the steep zig-zagging path outlined in white fences to the top of the hill. At the top, the **tourist office** is at the far end of pl. Royale, across the tree-lined park from the funicular. They have maps and an accommodations service, both of which are free. (☎05 59 27 27 08; www.pau.fr. Open July-Aug. M-Sa 9am-6pm, Su 9:30am-1pm and 2-6pm; Sept.-June M-Sa 9am-6pm, Su 9:30am-1pm.) Service des Gîtes Ruraux, on the corner of rue Maréchal Joffre and rue Gassion in the Cité Administrative, gives advice on mountain lodgings and makes reservations for a commission. (☎05 59 11 20 64; fax 05 59 11 20 60. *Chambres d'hôte* reservation €3, *gîtes* €15. Open M-F 8:30am-6pm, Sa 8:30am-4:30pm.)

Other services include a **laundromat** on rue Gambetta (open daily 7:30am-10pm; wash €4-7, dry €0.30 per 4min.) and a **dry-cleaning service** at Pressing, near the marketplace, at 7 pl. du Foirail. (☎05 59 30 92 75. €3.20 per item. Open M-F 9:30am-12:30pm and 3-7pm, Sa 9:30am-12:30pm.). The **police** (☎05 59 98 22 22) are on rue O'Quin; the **hospital** is at 4 bd. Hauterive (☎05 59 92 48 48). Consult the tourist office or the signs posted on every pharmacy's door for the rotating **pharmacie de garde.** Access the **Internet** at C Cyber, 20 rue Lamothe, past the post office. (☎05 59 82 89 40. €0.80 per 10min., €4.80 per hr. Open M-Sa 10am-2am, Su 2pm-midnight.) The **post office,** on cours Bosquet at rue Gambetta, has **currency exchange** with no commission, and a Cyberposte. (☎05 59 98 98 98. Photocopies €0.10 per page. Fax services available. Open M-F 8am-6:30pm, Sa 8am-noon.) **Postal Code:** 64000.

⑤ ACCOMMODATIONS. Hôtel de la Pomme d'Or ❷, 11 rue Maréchal Foch, offers bare, somewhat run-down rooms in the center of town at low prices. Turn left from the tourist office onto rue Louis Barthou and left again on rue A. de Lassence. Walk through pl. Clemenceau and turn right onto rue Maréchal Foch. Most rooms have TVs, but for the less expensive, it comes with a €3.50 charge. (☎05 59 11 23 23; fax 05 59 11 23 24. Breakfast €3.50. 24hr. reception. Singles €19-20, with shower €24, with shower and toilet, €25-30; doubles €23/€28-32/€33-38; triples with shower €36-37, with bath €41-42; quads with shower €39-40.) The Pomme d'Or provides the cheapest rooms in town, but couples or larger families may want to try the more upscale two-star **Hôtel Central ❸,** 15 rue Léon Daran. From the tourist office, take a right and walk down rue Louis Barthou until you see rue Léon Daran. The 28 large, spotless rooms are individually decorated and quiet, and looked after by a caring owner. The renowned author of *Le Petit Prince*, Antoine de Saint-Exupéry, stayed in room #7 before his rise to fame. All rooms come with shower and TV, and a billiard room and bar with cable TV are available. (☎05 59 27 72 75. Breakfast €6. Reception 7am-11pm. Reservations recommended. Singles €38-46.20, with bath instead of shower €48.50; doubles €38-49.80, with bath instead of shower €55; with 2 beds €59-60. Some rooms with kitchenette and fridge. Extra bed €8. MC/V.) Deeper in the heart of the city is the three-star **Hôtel Montpensier ❹,** 36 rue Montpensier, a large pink stucco building. Follow the directions to the Hôtel Pomme d'Or, but instead of turning right onto Maréchal Foch, continue straight through pl. Clemenceau to rue Serviez, which becomes rue Léon Daran. The rooms are cheery and are equipped with shower, toilet, TV, telephone and mini-fridge. Air-conditioning is available. (☎05 59 27 42 72; fax 05 59 27 70 95. Breakfast €6. Reception 6:45am-1am. Reserve well in advance for the cheapest rooms. Singles €35-55; doubles €45-60; triples €65 and quads €70. MC/V.) About

3km from the train station, the hostel **Logis des Jeunes ❶**, outside Pau, is in Gelos. Shell out €7 to get there by taxi, or take bus #1 (dir: Larrious Mazères-Lezon) to Mairie de Gelos (€1). With three bedrooms, this tiny hostel can only support five people at a time. (☎05 59 35 09 99. Reception daily 5-9pm. Reservations taken only up to 1 week in advance. Dorms €8.55, non-HI members €14.)

◘ FOOD. The region that brought you tangy *béarnaise* sauce has no paucity of specialties: salmon, pike, *oie* (goose), *canard* (duck), and *assiette béarnaise*, a succulent platter that can include gizzards, duck hearts, and asparagus. The area around the château, including **rue Sully** and **rue du Château,** has elegant regional restaurants (*plats* €9, *menus* €16). Down the hill, the Quartier du Hédas offers more expensive fare in a fancier setting. Inexpensive pizzerias, kebab joints, and Vietnamese eateries can be found on rue Léon Daran and adjoining streets.

For lunch, the modern restaurant **◙Ciel and Chocolat,** 11 rue Maréchal Foch, is not to be missed. The €7 lunch *menu* includes quiche with a large side salad, dessert (the chocolate mousse is excellent), and espresso. (☎05 59 27 44 15. Salad lunch *menu* with large salad, dessert, and espresso €9. Open M-Sa 9am-4pm.) Overlooking the pl. de la Liberté and the Église Saint-Jacques, the modern **Le Saint Vincent ❷**, 4 rue Gassiot, serves €8 *moules frites* and €9 *escargots*. (☎05 59 27 75 44. *Menus* €11-18, couscous €10, fish and meat dishes €10-15. Open M-Sa noon-2:45pm and 7-8:30pm. MC/V.) On a cobblestoned street by the château, **Au Fruit Défondu ❸**, 3 rue Sully, serves 10 kinds of fondue—many including typical *béarnaise* fare (€12-15). Don't forget to leave room for the divine chocolate fondue (€12.20), which is meant for two people. (☎05 59 27 26 05. Open Th-Tu 7pm-midnight. MC/V.) The sprawling, Olympic-sized **Champion supermarket** sits in the new **Centre Bosquet** megaplex on cours Bosquet. (Open M-Sa 9am-7pm.) The equally enormous **market** at **Les Halles,** pl. de la République, is a maze of vegetable, meat, and cheese stalls. (Open M-Sa 6am-1pm. Many vendors choose to shut down during the afternoon slot.) The **Marché Biologique,** pl. du Foirail, offers a variety of organic produce to the health-conscious. (Open W and Sa 8am-noon.)

◙ SIGHTS. Originally built as a fortress in the 12th century, the **Château d'Henri IV** was reshaped and remodeled by a succession of *béarnais* viscounts and famous *navaresse* kings. Henri IV, Napoleon III, and Louis-Philippe all made their mark on the castle, leaving behind a large array of velvet furniture, ornate ceilings, and crystal chandeliers. Now a national museum, the castle displays Henri IV's enormous tortoise-shell crib along with a collection of beautiful Gobelin tapestries. The château is accessible only through 1hr. French guided tours that depart every 15min. (☎05 59 82 38 19. Open daily mid-June to mid-Sept. 9:30am-12:15pm and 1:30-5:45pm; Apr. to mid-June and mid-Sept. to Oct. 9:30-11:45am and 2-5pm; Nov.-Mar. 9:30-11:45am and 2-4:15pm. Last tour 1hr. before closing; English tours by appointment. English brochure available. €4.50, ages 18-25 €3, under 18 free.) The local obsession with Henry IV becomes clear with a visit to the **Musée des Beaux-Arts,** on rue Mathieu Lalanne, where a staircase leads to an enormous tableau of his birth and then to a wall-length depiction of his 1598 coronation. The rest of the museum contains a small collection of modern art and a more impressive collection of 17th- to 19th-century European paintings. (☎05 59 27 33 02. French and English guides available if requested in advance. Open M and W-Su 10am-noon and 2-6pm. €3, students €1.50, under 18 free.)

The mild climate makes Pau conducive to botanical flights of fancy, and for a good part of the year the town is covered in flowers and trees of every color and origin, from America to Japan. The best place to sample some of this biodiversity is around the pond in the **parc Beaumont.** Follow the bd. des Pyrenees away from the castle to the Palais Beaumont; the park is just behind the Palais.

⛶ ☙ ENTERTAINMENT AND FESTIVALS. Cinéma le Méliès, 6 rue Bargoin, shows artsy films, some in English. (☎05 59 27 60 52; www.cinefil.com. Tickets €5.40, students €4.30, under 12 €3. Closed 4 days in mid-Aug.) Throughout the summer, Pau remains active with numerous festivals and cultural presentations. Starting in mid-June, the **Festival de Pau** brings three weeks of theater, music, ballet, and poetry to the Palais Beaumont and to the Théâtre St-Louis. (Reservations at the tourist office from FNAC ☎05 59 98 90 00. €16-36 per concert, €9-15 per child under 12.) The weekend of Pentecost, cars race about the town center during the Formula 3 **Grand Prix de Pau.** Speedy bikes replace cars in mid-July when the **Tour de France** passes through the city and spectators line the streets to cheer on the competitors. At around the same time, the **Ciné Cité** hosts a month of musical concerts and outdoor films. Salsa, blues, and jazz bands perform at around 9pm and are quickly followed by either a recent popular film or an old classic. Contact the tourist office for movie and concert schedules. From mid-July to mid-August, the city hosts a series of strength competitions every Monday and Thursday night during the **Festival de Pelote Basque.** The **Festival International des Pyrénées** occurs 35km south of Pau in Oloron every other year during the first week of August, when ballet troupes from 25 countries storm the city in a celebration of dance. (Info and tickets from the Oloron tourist office ☎05 59 39 98 98; www.danseaveclemonde.com. Festival will be held in Oloron in 2006. Tickets around €11.). Trains run to Oloron from Pau's train station (35-45min., 10 per day, €6).

⛶ NIGHTLIFE. While clubs in the town center cater to an older and more sedate crowd, the foreign bar scene on bd. des Pyrenees is an outlet for the young and lively. The two-story **Galway,** 20 bd. des Pyrenees, provides good Irish folk music to a mostly anglophone crowd. (☎05 59 82 94 66. Pints of beer from €4. Live music twice a month. Open daily July-Sept. 1pm-3am; Oct.-June 1pm-2am.) Next door an Australian bar, an Irish *brasserie*, and a Russian cafe serve a stylish mixed crowd of youngsters and 30-somethings. After a drink, be sure to stroll along the beautiful flower-lined boulevard.

LOURDES

In 1858, 14-year-old Bernadette Soubirous reported seeing the first of what would total 18 visions of the Virgin Mary in the Massabielle Grotto in Lourdes (pop. 16,300). Eventually, the Virgin Mary instructed her to "go tell the priests to build a chapel here so that people may come in procession." Today, over five million visitors from 100 countries come annually to this pilgrimage center, toting rosaries and hoping for miracles as they solemnly march, or are wheeled, to the Blessing of the Sick. Lourdes's secular wonders include the medieval fortress that rises from the center of town and the panoramic views from the summit of nearby Pic du Jer.

⌐ TRANSPORTATION

Trains (☎05 62 42 55 53; info office open daily 6am-8:50pm) go from 33 av. de la Gare to Bayonne (2hr., 5 per day, €18.40); Bordeaux (3hr., 7 per day, €29.50, TGV €31); Paris (7-9hr., 5 per day, TGV €88.40); Pau (30min., 16 per day, €6.30); and Toulouse (2½hr., 8 per day, €21.50). **SNCF buses** run from the station to Cauterets (50min., 3-6 per day, €6.20). Local buses (☎05 62 94 10 78) run from all points in the city to the grotto, the Pic du Jer (from which the funicular departs), and the Lac de Lourdes (daily Easter-Oct. every 20min. 7am-6:30pm, Sept.-June Tu, Th, Sa only; €1.50). **Taxis** wait at the train station (☎05 62 94 31 30) and the grotto from

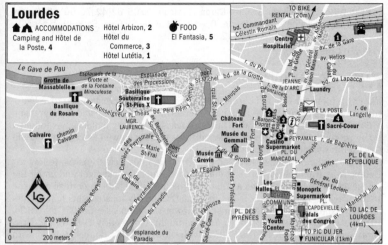

Lourdes

▲ ACCOMMODATIONS
Camping and Hôtel de
  la Poste, **4**

Hôtel Arbizon, **2**
Hôtel du
  Commerce, **3**
Hôtel Lutétia, **1**

🍎 FOOD
El Fantasia, **5**

Easter to October. Rent **bikes** at Cycles Antonio Oliveria, 14 av. Alexandre Marqui, near the train station. (☎05 62 42 24 24. €9.20 per half-day, €18.30 per day, €73 per week. Open Tu-F 9:30am-noon and 2-7pm, Sa 9:30am-noon and 2-6pm. MC/V.)

▓▌ ORIENTATION AND PRACTICAL INFORMATION

The train station is on the northern edge of town, 10min. from the town center. To get from the station to the tourist office, turn right on av. de la Gare, then bear left on the busy av. du Général Baron Maransin at the first intersection, cross a bridge above bd. du Lapacca, and proceed uphill. The office is in a modern glass complex on the right (5 minutes). The religious heart of Lourdes is at the **grotto.** Follow av. de la Gare through the intersection, turn left onto bd. de la Grotte, and follow it as it snakes right at pl. Jeanne d'Arc. Cross the river Gave to reach the Esplanade des Processions, the Basilique St-Pius X, and the grotto (10 minutes).

Tourist Office: pl. Peyramale (☎05 62 42 77 40; www.lourdes-infotourisme.com). Friendly multilingual staff distributes maps, info on religious ceremonies, a list of hotels, and brochures about the nearby Pyrenees. Open May-Oct. M-Sa 9am-7pm; early to mid-Nov. and mid-Mar. to Apr. 9am-noon and 2-7pm; mid-Nov. to mid-Mar. 9am-noon and 2-6pm. Bernadette-related sights are managed by the Church-affiliated **Sanctuaires de Notre-Dame de Lourdes** (☎05 62 42 78 78), which has a **Forum d'Info** to the left, in front of the basilica. Open daily 8:30am-12:15pm and 1:45-7pm.

Youth Center: Forum Lourdes/Bureau Information Jeunesse, pl. de Champ Commun (☎05 62 94 94 00), in a red building beyond Les Halles. Helpful info for young travelers, though with a somewhat religious spin. Open M-F 9am-noon and 2-6pm. **Police:** 7 rue Baron Duprat (☎05 62 42 72 72). Open daily 9am-noon and 3-8pm.

Laundromat: Laverie GTI, 10 av. du Général Baron Maransin. Wash €3.50-8. Open daily 8am-7pm.

Hospital: Centre Hospitalier, 3 av. Alexandre Marqui (☎05 62 42 42 42), at the intersection of av. de la Gare, av. Marqui, and av. du Général Baron Maransin. **Medical emergency,** 2 av. Marqui (☎05 62 42 44 36).

Disabled Services: Pavillon Handicapés (☎05 62 42 79 92), bd. Remy Sempe.

Internet Access: In the **Youth Center.** €3 per hr. Open M-F 9am-noon and 2-6pm.

Post Office: 31 av. du Général Baron Maransin (☎05 62 42 72 00). **Currency exchange** (bills only). Cyberposte. Open M-F 8:30am-6:30pm, Sa 8:30am-noon; in summer sometimes closed from 12:30-1:30pm.

Postal Code: 65100.

⚑ ACCOMMODATIONS AND CAMPING

Finding a room for €22 in Lourdes is easy. Similar hotels are grouped together—the cheap ones on rue Basse, and the two-stars on av. de la Gare and rue Maransin. Most hotels are clean but drab. The city's massive healing industry has induced many proprietors to improve wheelchair accessibility as well as construct facilities for the visually and hearing impaired.

To get to the affordable **Hôtel Arbizon ❶**, 37 rue des Petits Fossés, follow av. Helios away from the station as it curves down the hill. Bear right and under the bridge ahead on bd. du Lapacca. Take the first left uphill after the bridge onto rue Basse; rue des Petits Fossés is the first right. Centrally located, this hotel offers small. No showers available for those in shower-less rooms. (☎/fax 05 62 94 29 36. Breakfast €3.97. Reception daily 7am-midnight. Open early Feb. to mid-Nov. *Demi-pension* €20-22. Singles €13.72, with shower €14.48; doubles €19.06, with shower €19.82; triples €23.63 with or without shower.) **Hôtel Lutétia ❷**, 19 av. de la Gare, is a pleasant if somewhat bland mock-château to the right heading away from the train station. Clean, comfortable rooms with sink, table, and telephone fill quickly in the summer; be sure to call ahead. Pricier rooms come with TV. (☎05 62 94 22 85;info@lutetialourdes.com. Elevator and free parking. Singles €17.50, with toilet €24.50, with shower €30-36, with bath €37; doubles €24.50-74, depending on room type and season. MC/V.) **Hôtel du Commerce ❸**, 11 rue Basse, faces the tourist office with a pizzeria on the first floor. It's bright, renovated rooms, all com with a full bath. The back rooms have view of the château. (☎05 62 94 59 23; hotel-commerce-et-navarre@wanadoo.fr). Singles €32; doubles €40; triples €45; quads €55; quints €75. With breakfast rooms €35/€45/€56/€71/€80. Prices slightly lower in low season. MC/V.) **Camping and Hôtel de la Poste ❶**, 26 rue de Langelle is a small, backyard campground 2min. beyond the post office. It has large spaces with grass shaded by trees. The campground also lets eight pristine rooms in the attached hotel. (☎05 62 94 40 35. Breakfast €4.50. Open Easter to mid-Oct. Doubles €22, with bath €25; triples €29, with shower and toilet €32; quads with bath €40. Camping €2.60 per person, €3.80 per site. Electricity €2.50. Shower €1.30.)

◖ FOOD

Find expensive groceries at **Casino supermarket**, 9 pl. Peyramale (☎05 62 94 03 87; open Tu-F 8:30am-1pm and 3:30-8pm, Sa 8:30am-1pm and 3-8pm, Su 8am-1pm), or at the larger **Monoprix supermarket**, 9 pl. du Champ Commun. (☎05 62 94 63 44. Open M-Sa 8:30am-7:30pm, Su 8:30am-12:30pm.) Produce, flowers, second-hand clothing, books, and cheap pizza are all sold daily at the **market** at **Les Halles**, pl. du Champ Commun. (Open daily 8am-1pm, every other Th until 5pm.)

Restaurants not affiliated with hotels are few and far between. On the main strip of the **boulevard de la Grotte,** many similar restaurants charge similar prices for similar food. Meals will cost €9-12. Slightly cheaper *plats du jour* and *menus* can be found around the tourist office and on **rue de la Fontaine;** just don't expect gourmet fare. Slightly swankier—if still touristy—restaurants are down the steps on both sides of the river Gave, with the nicest views and breeze in town. **El Fantasia ❸**, 5 rue Basse, has a tiny, basic, wholesome Moroccan menu (*tagines* €9.50) to relieve *brasserie*-tired palates. (Open daily noon-2pm and 7pm-10pm.)

👁 SIGHTS

Most of the religious sights are amazing not in themselves, but for the fervent reactions they incite among pilgrims. **Passeport Visa Lourdes** (€34, children €17) provides access to four Bernadette-related museums, the Fortified Castle and its museum, the funicular to Pic du Jer, and a tourist train ride through town. Ask for details at the tourist office. **Carte Lourdes Pass,** free at the tourist office, grants entrance to two of the previous sights or activities after you visit five others.

GROTTE DE MASSABIELLE. Visitors from around the world shuffle past this small dark crevice in the mountainside at the edge of town, touching its cold rock walls, whispering prayers, and waiting to receive a blessing from the priest on duty. Lines are longest in the late afternoon. Nearby, water from the spring where Bernadette washed her face is available for drinking, bathing, and bringing home, hence the numerous water bottles sold here. The cave lies by the river on the right side of two superimposed churches, the Basilique du Rosaire and the upper basilica. *(No shorts, tank tops, or food. Fountain and grotto open daily 5am-midnight.)*

BASILICAS. The **Basilique du Rosaire** and **upper basilica** were built double-decker style above Bernadette's grotto. Their pointed steeples, soft grey color, and flags are reminiscent of a fairy tale and look striking against the mountains. The interiors are less elegant. In the **Rosaire,** completed in 1889, an enormous Virgin Mary strikes a maternal pose. Modern, bright mosaics decorate the side chapels. The **upper basilica,** consecrated in 1876, has a more traditional, Gothic interior. The most remarkable space for prayer is the **Basilique St-Pius X,** which is hidden underground, in front of the other two basilicas and to the left of the Esplanade des Processions. Accessible by several wide, unmarked passages, it's a stadium-sized concrete echo chamber in the form of an upturned ship. It won an international design prize in 1958. When filled with singing it can be quite gorgeous, though some think it looks more like the parking garage of the Starship Enterprise. Covering 12,000 square meters, this concrete cavern fits 20,000 souls with room to spare. *(All 3 open daily Easter-Oct. 6am-7pm; Nov.-Easter 8am-6pm, excluding masses at 11am and 5pm, which can be respectfully observed.)*

PROCESSIONS AND BLESSINGS. The **Procession of the Blessed Sacrament** and the **Blessing of the Sick** are huge affairs held daily at 5pm, starting in the Basilica St-Pius X. One by one, wheelchair-bound or otherwise infirm pilgrims—often escorted by nuns—receive their blessing. Observers can stand, squeeze onto a bench, or watch from the upper basilica's balcony. "One-day pilgrims" join the procession and march along the esplanade behind rolling ranks of wheelchairs. *(Meet other pilgrims July-Sept. at 8:30am at the "Crowned Virgin" statue in front of the basilica.)* A solemn **torchlit procession** blazes from the grotto to the esplanade nightly, from April through late October at 9pm. Pilgrims from all over the world recite "Hail Mary" in six languages and proudly hold banners proclaiming church names and nationalities. *(Mass in English Apr.-Oct. daily 9am at the Hémicycle, just across the river from the cave in a cavernous concrete building.)*

CHÂTEAU FORT. Practically the only sight in town without a religious connection, the feudal castle overlooks Lourdes from atop a rocky crag. A shuttlecock in territorial disputes between France and England during the Middle Ages, the building dates from the 14th century. The high square tower and well-preserved walls of the château now offer unequaled panoramas of surrounding Lourdes and guard the strange collection of the **Musée Pyrénéen.** The museum displays a series of regional objects including wine barrels, decorated plates, and butter churns. *(☎05 62 42 37 37. Enter by elevator. Open daily mid-Apr. to mid-Oct. 9am-noon and 1:30-6:30pm; mid-Oct. to mid-Apr. 9am-noon and 2-6pm. €5.)*

FUNICULAIRE. Just outside of town, a track climbs 1000m up the **Pic du Jer.** Local buses lead to the bottom of the track. Taking this 6min. ride and walking the extra 10min. up to the observatory at the summit gives a stunning 360° view of the surrounding countryside and the town below. Energetic folk can hike up the mountain using the map from the ticket booth. Beware of rapidly descending mountain bikers. Both car and hike are wheelchair-accessible. (☎05 62 94 00 41. Buses depart daily every 30min. 10am-6pm, July and Aug. 10am-7pm. Last ride up 1hr. before closing, last ride down 15min. before closing. €8, children €5.50, except noon-1pm, when prices drop to €6 and children under 14 are free. Open late Mar.-mid Nov. Depot on the southern edge of town, at the base of the mountain. Follow the main road, rue St-Pierre, 2km from the center of town by the tourist office. There's also a bus from the ticket booth at the intersection of rue de la Grotte and rue de la Tour de Brie. Round-trip €3.)

LAC DE LOURDES. Local bus #7 runs to a large, peaceful lake 4km from the center of town, where locals flip off the dock and eat ice cream in the waterside cafe. A relief from the summer humidity, the lake is a good follow-up to morning tours of the grotto and sanctuaries. (Buses July-Aug. 4 per day 8:25am-6:30pm; Sept.-June Tu, Th, Sa only, less frequently. By foot, take av. du Général Baron Maransin toward the train station and turn left onto bd. Romain. The street becomes av. Béguere and then rte. de Pontacq. Take a left onto chemin du Lac to reach the water. 30min.)

MUSEUMS. The **Musée de Gemmail** reproduces famous works of art in the thick, multi-layered stained-glass technique that gives the museum its name. There's an equally large annex near pont St-Michel. (72 rue de la Grotte. ☎05 62 94 13 15. Open daily Apr.-Oct. 9am-noon and 1-7pm. Free.) Down the street, the **Musée Grevin** is as close as it gets to a Catholic Disneyland. One hundred uncannily life-like wax figures act out the lives of Bernadette and Jesus. Most impressive is the life-size replica of Leonardo da Vinci's *Last Supper.* (87 rue de la Grotte. ☎05 62 94 33 74. Open daily mid-July to late Aug. 8:30am-10pm; Apr.-Oct. 9-11:40am and 1:30-6:30pm. €5.70, students €4.60.)

CAUTERETS

Every morning in Cauterets (pop. 1300) sugared vapors of *berlingots* waft through the air while the mist slowly rolls off the surrounding mountains. Nestled 930m up in a narrow, breathtaking valley among near-vertical peaks, sleepy Cauterets awakes in May and June to the sounds of a turquoise river rushing beneath its bridges. The melting snows of early summer bring wilderness lovers here to this town on the edge of Parc National des Pyrénées Occidentales. For serious hikers, the sharply contrasting French and Spanish sides of the Pyrenees are both accessible from Cauterets, and there are dozens of day hikes that range from 1½ to 8 hours. When hiking becomes overly taxing, the town's *thermes* offer a relaxation program of *remise en forme*, bringing hikers back to their former selves.

■ ♫ ORIENTATION AND PRACTICAL INFORMATION. Cauterets runs lengthwise along the river Gave and is small enough to walk across in 5min. It is accessible only by bus from Lourdes. From the bus station, turn right and follow av. du Général Leclerc up a steep hill to the tourist office at pl. Foch. **SNCF buses** (☎05 62 92 53 70) run from pl. de la Gare to Lourdes (1hr., 8 per day, €6.20; office open daily 9am-12:30pm and 3-7pm). Rent **bikes** at Le Grenier, 4 av. du Mamelon Vert. Bikes €22-53 for a full-day, €16-39 for a half-day. (☎05 62 92 55 71. Open daily 8am-1pm and 3-8pm.) Bernard Sports-tifs, 2 rue Richelieu, next to the tourist office, offers good prices on **alpine ski rentals** and gives discounts to American students. (☎05 62 92 06 23; www.bernardsports-tifs.com. From €12 per day for boots, skis, and poles; from €62 for 6 days.)

The **tourist office,** pl. Foch, has a list of hotels, a useful map, and a *Guide Pratique.* (☎05 62 92 50 50; www.cauterets.com. Open July-Aug. M-Sa 9am-12:30pm and 2-7pm, Su 9am-12:30pm and 3-6pm; Sept.-June M-Sa 9am-noon and 2-6pm, Su 9am-noon.) Their hiking map, *Sentiers du Lavedon* (€5), is the best dayhike resource for English speakers, owing to its colorful, logical format. For more hiking info, drop by the **Parc National des Pyrénées** office at pl. de la Gare. The **police** are on av. du Docteur Domer (☎05 62 92 51 13). For **medical emergencies,** call ☎05 62 92 14 00. Access the **Internet** at Pizzeria Giovanni, 5 rue de la Raillère (☎05 62 92 57 80; €3.20 per hr.; open daily July-Aug. noon-3pm and 7-11pm; Sept.-June Th-Su only), or in the basement of the **public library,** 2 esplanade des Oeufs. (☎05 62 92 59 96. €5 per hr. Open W and Sa 3-6:45pm, Th-F 4:45-6:45pm, during school vacations W-Sa 3-6:45pm.) The **post office,** at the corner of rue Belfort and rue des Combattants, offers **currency exchange.** (☎05 62 92 53 93. Open M-F 9am-12:30pm and 2-4:30pm; Sa 9am-noon.) **Postal Code:** 65110.

🛈 **ACCOMMODATIONS.** ▨Gîte d'Etape UCJG ❶, av. du Docteur Domer, 7min. from the town center, is the best accommodation for real mountain travelers in Cauterets. From the Parc National office, cross the parking lot and street and turn left uphill on a footpath underneath the funicular depot. The *gîte* is just beyond the tennis courts. Gloriously located with welcoming hosts, this *gîte* has 60 beds in every possible set-up, from canvas barracks to the eaves of an attic, in addition to leafy campsites. Run by a friendly pastor who has the answers to all questions and who introduces guests to one another. Fridge available for use. (☎05 62 92 52 95. Kitchen, shower, and sheets included. Reception daily, but hours vary. Open mid-June to mid-Sept. Dorms €8; €3.50 per tent; €6.50 for space in the *gîte's* tent; bed in bungalow €8.50.) **Hôtel Christian ❸,** 10 rue Richelieu, offers a view of the Pyrenees, darts, and *bocce* for somewhat steep prices, but breakfast is included. The incredibly gracious owner, whose family has run the hotel for generations, is eager to chat with guests. Cheaper rooms on the top floor are smaller and darker than the others. (☎05 62 92 50 04; www.hotel-christian.fr. Reception daily 7:30am-10pm. Closed early Oct. to late Dec. Singles €42.50-44; doubles €54-56; triples €70.20-73; quads €85.40-88.40. MC/V.) Every room at **Hôtel Bigorre ❷,** 15 rue de Belfort, has a balcony with a tremendous view of the surrounding mountains. The rooms are old but spacious, and back-country travelers can leave luggage here for a few days. Rue de Belfort runs between pl. de la Gare

THE LOCAL STORY

SWEET AND SULFUR

Two smells permeate the high Pyrenees from early morning until nightfall. One is the overpowering smell of sulfur that rises from natural springs, now home to the famed *thermes* of Cauterets and Luchon. The other is the sweet smell of *berlingots* candy that comes from the *confiseries* that dot the town's main thorough fares.

These two vastly different smells are historically connected. "Taking the cure" in hot sulfur springs was thought to improve the health of rheumatics, consumptives, and arthritics. The cure included everything from having one's sinuses cleaned with small brushes to taking the water up through the nose and expelling it from the mouth. Around 1840 doctors decided that the healing process would be helped if the patient held a morsel of sugar in the mouth while gargling the hot water. The innovation endured and France's *thermes* were soon surrounded by *confiseries.*

Today, the *thermes* have gone from healing pain to pure pleasure. While some of them remain strictly for rheumatics, most offer healing massage therapy, saunas, and relaxing pools for everyone. Others even have small spa and gym areas. Yet the main streets leading toward the sulfurous springs remain sweet with the dozens of shops making and selling *berlingots,* which are worth a taste either in their hard form as lollipops, or by the pound.

and pl. Foch, near the tourist office. (☎ 05 62 92 52 81; www.bigorrehotel.com. Reception daily 7:30am-10pm. Open daily late May-early Nov.; early Nov.-late May on weekends and school holidays only. Singles €15.80, with shower €25.50; doubles €33/€43; triples and quads €48/€65.) **Hôtel de Paris ❸**, 1 pl. Foch, is as close to the action in town as one can get in Cauterets. Decently priced doubles have plush carpets, TVs, and large bathrooms. (☎ 05 62 92 53 85; fax 05 62 92 02 23. Breakfast €5.80. Reception daily 7:30am-midnight. Doubles €40-44; triples €50-58; quads €54-58. AmEx/MC/V.)

❐ FOOD. The small, beautifully old-fashioned **Halles market**, a few doors down from the tourist office on av. du Général Leclerc, has fresh produce. (Open daily June-Sept. 7:30am-1pm and 4-8pm; Oct.-May M-Sa 9am-1pm and Su 8am-1pm.) An **open-air market** is held in the parking lot next to the Casino. (Open mid-June to mid-Sept. for food Th 8:30am-1pm and for food and clothing F 8:30am-1pm.) The local specialty is the *berlingot*, a hard sugar candy originally used by patients visiting the *thermes* to contribute to "the cure." Thirty-five flavors of the candy are prepared by hand and cranked through a magical candy-making machine to the delight of watching customers at **A la Reine Margot ❶**, pl. de la Mairie Crown. (€1.60 per 100g. Delicious swirly lollipops €0.75-1.70. Open daily 10am-midnight.) The jovial and welcoming husband and wife team at **Chez Gillou ❶**, 3 rue de la Raillère, specializes in blueberry and almond cakes known respectively as *tourtes myrtilles* and *pastis des Pyrénées*. (☎ 05 62 92 56 58. Cakes €5.50. Open daily July-Aug. and Feb.-Mar. 7am-1pm and 3-7pm; Mar., Apr., June, Sept., and Dec.-Jan. daily 7:30am-12:30pm and 3:30-7pm; closed May, Oct.-Nov.) Stock up on meats for hiking and all kinds of homemade confitures at **Au "Mille Pâtes,"** 5 rue de la Raillère. (☎ 05 62 92 04 83. Open daily July-Aug. and Feb. 8am-12:30pm and 4-8pm; Jan., Mar.-Apr., June, Sept., Dec. Th-Tu 8am-12:30pm and 4-8pm; closed May, Oct.-Nov.) *Foie gras* and other fancy regional products are sold with a smile at **Chez Gailhou Durdos ❷**, 8 rue de Belfort. (☎ 05 62 82 01 10. *Foie gras* from €7.10. Open daily 9:30am-12:30pm and 4-7:30pm. AmEx/DC/MC/V.)

There are few gourmet restaurants in Cauterets, but plenty of hearty food. Several small restaurants with outdoor seating line **rue Verdun**. Crêpes and every other kind of snack food imaginable make **Le Ski Bar ❷**, pl. Foch, a popular spot with hikers—or maybe it's the pitchers of sangria. (☎ 05 62 92 53 85. Main dishes and snacks €3-10. Open daily 7:30am-midnight. AmEx/MC/V.) **La Crêperie Basque ❷**, 8 rue Richelieu, serves simple, delicious *galettes* and crêpes, along with homestyle *plats* under a pale blue ceiling on a quiet street. (☎ 05 62 92 51 79. Entrees €6-12, crêpes €3-7. Four-course *menu* with wine €11. Open daily 11am-midnight. MC/V.)

◙ ⚑ SIGHTS AND OUTDOOR ACTIVITIES. From av. du Docteur Domer, the **Téléphérique du Lys** cable car (☎ 05 62 92 03 59) races overhead every 30min. into the nearby mountains. From there, trails lead across the ridge to the breathtaking Lac d'Ilhéou (1½ hours). In July and August and during the ski season, the **Télésiège du Grand Barbat** chairlift runs from the top of the *Téléphérique* to the **Crête du Lys**, over 1000m above Cauterets. (€9.50 round-trip, €8 one-way to Crête du Lys, €7.50 round-trip on the *téléphérique*.) The hike back down from **Crête du Lys** is a medium difficulty trek that passes Lac d'Ilhéou (3 hours). Opens at 9am, last possibility for full round-trip at 4:30pm.

HIKES. Multiple half-day hikes depart directly from Cauterets at a **trailhead** behind the Thermes du César. These include the tough climbs to the **Col du Lisey** and the **Col de Riou,** both of which provide startling views of several valleys (both 3hr. round-trip) and the more relaxing trek to the **Cascade du Lutour** (2hr. round-trip). The deservedly popular **Chemin du Cascades** is a steep but waterfall-laden 2½hr.

climb from Cauterets. It begins on a staircase on the hill to the right of the Casino (a map is posted here as well), and ends in the national park at the Pont d'Espagne. The €5 round-trip **navettes** that depart directly for the Pont d'Espagne make other hikes in the national park easily accessible (see **Parc National**, p. 591).

SULFUR SPRINGS. Cauterets's natural sulfur springs have been credited over the years with curing everything from sterility to consumption. But it's no bubble bath—the doctors here have taken to heart the maxim of "no pain, no gain." The *thermes* also offer a relaxing program of massage for those who don't have what it takes to undergo the full process. For info on the *thermes*, contact **Thermes de César**, av. Docteur Domer. (☎05 62 92 51 60. Aerobath-sauna-hydrojet pool €9.50 for 20min., hydromassage jet showers €8 for 15min. Open M-Sa 7-11:30am and 2:30-8pm.) **The Balneo Aladin Spa**, 11 av. du Général Leclerc, has cheaper access to a pool and solarium (€15), as well as a jacuzzi, sauna, and hammam. (☎05 62 92 60 00; www.hotel-balneo-aladin.com. Open daily June-Sept. 10am-noon and 3-8pm.)

⚡ ENTERTAINMENT. Esplanade des Oeufs offers a casual **cinema** (☎05 62 92 52 14) that plays French and foreign films (the latter are mostly popular American imports in English) and a **casino.** (☎05 62 92 52 14. Open daily 11am-3am, tables open at 9:30pm.) The **patinoire** (skating rink) hosts skating nights year-round, mostly near the end of the week, according to a complicated schedule provided by the tourist office. The rink itself can be reached through the parking lot of the train station. (☎05 62 92 58 48. €5.50, children €3; skate rental €2.50.)

PARC NATIONAL DES PYRÉNÉES OCCIDENTALES

One of France's seven national parks, the **Parc National des Pyrénées** shelters endangered brown bears and lynxes, 200 threatened colonies of marmots, 118 lakes, and 160 unique plant species in its snowcapped mountains and lush valleys. Punctuated by sulfurous springs and unattainable peaks, the Pyrenees change dramatically with the seasons, never failing to awe a constant stream of visitors. To get a full sense of the extent and variety of the mountain range, hikers should experience both the lush French and barren Spanish sides of the Pyrenees (a 4- to 5-day round trip hike from Cauterets). But there are plenty of more modest opportunities as well. Jaw-dropping views are just an hour or two away from civilization, satisfying those who do not have time to venture too far afield.

AT A GLANCE

AREA: Narrow 100km long swath along the Franco-Spanish border

CLIMATE: Misty in France, arid in Spain

GATEWAYS: Gavarnie; Luz-St-Sauveur; Ainsa, Spain

DAY HIKES: Turquoise Lac de Gaube (5-6hr. round-trip from Cauterets), Chemin des Cascades (4hr. from Cauterets)

LONG HIKES: Cirque de Gavarnie, passing through waterfalls and lush forests (2- to 3-day hike from Cauterets); or continuing into Spain (4-5 days from Cauterets)

ACCOMMODATIONS: *Gîtes* (around €11) are available in towns along the GR10; 1-night camping permitted in areas at least 1hr. away from major highways

⚑ PRACTICAL INFORMATION. Touch base with the friendly, helpful staff of the **Parc National Office,** Maison du Parc, pl. de la Gare, in Cauterets before braving the wilderness. They provide free info on the park and the 14 different trails beginning and ending in Cauterets. Trails in the park are designed for a range of abilities, from novices to rugged outdoor enthusiasts. The Haute Randonnée Pyrénées (HRP) trails offer a more challenging mountain experience. Speak with the folks at the Parc National Office before attempting these treks. Documentary films in French feature aerial views of the local mountains and show 2-3 times per week, generally on bad weather days, to teach hikers about the area. (☎05 62 92 52 56; www.parc-pyrenees.com. Open daily June to mid-Sept. 9:30am-noon and 3-7pm; mid-Sept. to May hours vary, but are generally M-Tu and F-Sa 9:30am-12:30pm and 3-6pm, Th 3-6pm; call ahead to make sure they are open.)

The **maps** sold at the Parc National Office are probably sufficient. (Day-hike maps €6.40, topographical maps €8.99.) For the Cauterets region, use the #1647 Vignemale map of the Institut de Géographie Nationale. The Bureau des Guides, pl. de la Mairie on tiny rue Verdun in Cauterets, runs tours and guides for **rock-climbing, canyoning, hiking,** and **skiing.** Medium-difficulty tours are €14-30.50 per person; harder ones €46-140. Tours depart the Cauterets tourist office. (☎05 62 92 59 83. Open M-F 9am-noon and 2-5pm, Sa 9am-noon.)

Gîtes in the park average €11 per night and are generally located in towns along the GR10. Reserve at least two days ahead, especially in July and August when the mountains teem with hikers. The Parc National Office in Cauterets will help plan an itinerary while the **Service des Gîtes Ruraux** (☎05 59 11 20 64) in Pau makes *gîte* reservations. The general rule is that people can camp anywhere in the wilderness for one night, provided they are more than an hour's hike from the nearest highway. Long-term camping in one place is not allowed. Those looking to stay in one place for a couple of days should find a camp zone near a *refuge*. Listen to Météo-Montagne for a French **weather forecast** for nearby mountains (☎08 92 68 02 65; updated twice daily). For **Mountain Rescue,** call ☎05 62 92 41 41.

◪ **HIKING.** The **GR10** meanders across the Pyrenees, connecting the Atlantic with the Mediterranean and looping through most major towns. Both major and minor hikes intersect with and run along it; for either level of trail, pick up one of the purple maps at the park office (€8.99). The most spectacular local hikes begin at the **Pont d'Espagne** (a 2½hr. walk or 20min. drive from Cauterets). Several **buses** run daily in July and August (every 2hr. 8am-6pm; €3.50, round-trip €5); inquire at **Bordenave Excursions** (☎05 62 92 53 68). The rest of the year, call a **taxi.** (☎06 71 01 46 86. Around €17.) One of the most popular trails follows the GR10 to the turquoise **Lac de Gaube** (1hr.) and then to the end of the stony glacial valley (2hr. past the lake), where hikers can spend the night 2km in the air at **Refuge des Oulettes ❶.** (☎05 62 92 62 97. Open June-Sept. Dorms €13.50, *demi-pension* €32.) The trail leading up is crowded through Lac de Gaube, but the crowd thins a bit past the restaurant. Ten minutes past the Lac de Gaube *hôtellerie* brings hikers to the far side of the lake, a much more pristine spot, sometimes popular with fishermen. Forty-five minutes farther up the trail is the **Cascade Esplumouse,** a stunning waterfall, with great views of it from just below. Day hikers may want to consider hiking all the way back to Cauterets, just 90min. down past Pont d'Espagne, on a trail that boasts waterfall after waterfall, including a sulfur spring at La Raillère. Another day hike option is to begin at the trailhead just behind Thermes du César in Cauterets and follow the trail up to **Lac d'Estom,** about 3½hr. one-way. The trail inclines steeply out of town, leading to great views of the city, and waterfalls line the trail up to the blue mountain lake. A greener hike lies one valley over along the **Vallée du Marcadau;** the **Refuge Wallon Marcadau ❶** provides shelter here. (☎05 62 92 64 28. Open June to late Sept. Breakfast €2.30. Dorms €12.50, *demi-pension* €33.90.) Both hikes are popular as daytrips. The *refuge* is an ideal base for numerous dayhikes to other lakes and *cols* in the area. In May or June, when melting snow swells the streams, the **Chemin des Cascades** (waterfall trail), which leads from the Pont d'Espagne to La Raillère, is sensational. The 4hr. round-trip from Cauterets is a moderate afternoon hike—those who lose the path should keep the river on their left as they ascend the mountain. The **Circuit des Lacs** is an 8hr. hike that includes the Vallée du Marcadau as well as three beautiful mountain lakes.

🎿 **SKIING.** There is a weekend's worth of skiing available in the Crête du Lys area, accessible by the *téléphérique* in Cauterets (☎05 62 92 03 59). The Cauterets tourist office has free *plans des pistes* (maps of ski paths for all skill levels). Many area resorts are accessible by **SNCF bus** from Cauterets or Lourdes. **Luz-Ardiden** offers downhill and cross-country skiing. (☎05 62 92 30 30; fax 05 62 92 87 19. €25 per day, students €13.) Farther away, **Barèges** (☎05 62 92 16 01) and **La Mongie** (☎05 62 95 81 81) offer joint tickets (€29 per day during school vacation, €27.50 other times; students €23/€22).

CIRCUIT DE GAVARNIE

From Cauterets, the GR10 connects to Luz-St-Sauveur over the mountain and then on to Gavarnie, another day's hike up the valley; the round-trip from Cauterets to Gavarnie and back is known as the **circuit de Gavarnie.** These towns are also accessible by **SNCF bus** (1hr. from Cauterets to Luz, 6 per day, €6.20; 2 per day from Luz to Gavernie, €5.30). The Luz tourist office is at pl. du 8 Mai 45 (☎05 62 92 30 30). Circling counter-clockwise from Cauterets to Luz-St-Sauveur, the **Refuge Des Oulettes ❶** (see **Hiking**) is the first shelter past the Lac de Gaube. Another option for day one is to hike to Lac d'Estom (see **Hiking**), and continue from there; the trails merge soon after. It is important to note that the trek from Lac d'Estom is technically challenging, and is impossible in the winter. Dipping into the Vallée Lutour, the **Refuge Estom ❶** rests peacefully near Lac d'Estom. (☎05 62 92 07 18. Open June-Sept. €9 per night, *demi-pension* €27.) The **Refuge Jan Da Lo ❶** is in Gavarnie, near the halfway mark of the loop, at the culmination of the hiking. (☎05 62 92 40 66. Dorms €8.40, *demi-pension* €22.20.) There are *refuges* between d'Estom/des Oulettes and Jan Da Lo for those looking for an easier trip. From Gavarnie, hop on a horse offered by the *refuge* (€15 round-trip) for a 2hr. trek to the grandiose, snow-covered **Cirque de Gavarnie** and its misty waterfall. During the third week in July, the **Festival des Pyrénées** animates the foot of the Cirque, as nightly performances begin while the sun sets over the mountains. Afterwards, torches are distributed to light the way back to the village. (Tickets available from the tourist office in Gavarnie. €20, students €17.)

INTO SPAIN AND BACK

Both the Spanish and French sides of the range must be experienced in order to get a full sense of the diversity of these mountains. The desiccated red rock of the Spanish side and the misty forests of the French side are accessible on a four- to five-day hike from Cauterets. Confer with the tourist office in Ainsa, Spain (☎34 974 50 07 67), for reservations at the Spanish *refuges* before attempting this trek. A one- to two-day hike from Pont d'Espagne runs up and over the Spanish border. Descend the far side of the Pyrenees to the village of Torla and hop on one of the buses to the **refuge de Goriz.** (☎34 974 34 12 01. Open year-round, call ahead to reserve.) A magnificent hike to the snow-capped mountain peaks of **Brèche de Roland,** on the edge of the Cirque de Gavarnie, will start hikers' returns to France the following day. Cut the hike short here at four to five days and take a bus back from Gavarnie to Luz and then to Cauteret. Climb from the Vallée d'Ossoue to camp among the clouds of the **Refuge de Bayssellance** in view of Mount Montferrat before returning to Cauterets along the Vallée de Lutour.

LUCHON

More grandiose and cosmopolitan than other Pyrenean mountain towns, Luchon (pop. 2900) has attracted the rich and famous to its celebrated *thermes* for over two centuries. The baths are the town's main attraction, and the number of senior citizens in the tourist population is correspondingly large. But families, Chanel-swaddled women, and cigarette-toting teenagers all stroll along the boulevards. Hikers will appreciate that the numerous trails in the surrounding mountains are less crowded than those of the Parc National. A *télécabine* (gondola) ferries skiers and hikers from the town center to the nearby mountain Superbagnères.

■ ⁊ TRANSPORTATION AND PRACTICAL INFORMATION. The train station, av. de Toulouse, runs **trains** and **SNCF buses** to Montréjeau (50min., 4-5 per day, €5.80), where connections await to Bayonne, Paris, St-Gaudens, Toulouse, and other cities. Trains also run directly to Toulouse (2hr., 1-2 per day, €17.80). Check the info office (open M-Sa 6am-8:30pm and Su 6am-8pm).

From the station, turn left on av. de Toulouse and bear right at the fork to follow av. Maréchal Foch. At the lions, cross the rotary and bear left, following signs for the *centre ville*. The main **allée d'Etigny** will unfold to the left. A few blocks down on the right is the **tourist office**, 18 allée d'Etigny, which lists nearby hikes and mountain bike trails, as well as a map of the town. (☎ 05 61 79 21 21; www.luchon.com. Open daily July-Aug. 9am-7pm; Sept.-Nov. and Apr.-June 9am-12:30pm and 1:30-7pm; Dec.-Mar. 8:30am-7pm.) For ambitious outdoor excursions, check in at the Bureau des Guides, next to the tourist office, which has info on **biking, hiking, rock climbing,** and **canyon scaling** nearby and in Spain. Guided hikes run around €140 per day or €80 per half-day for a group of 12; canyoning and climbing €235; €135 for half-day. (☎ 05 61 79 69 38; bureaudesguides@free.fr. Open daily July-Aug. 10am-noon and 3-7pm; Sept.-June M-Sa 10am-noon and 4-6pm.) **Bike rental** at Malvina Europe, 55 av. Foch, is €15 per half-day, €25 per day for performance mountain bikes with a credit card deposit. They also provide **Internet** for €5 per hr. (☎ 05 61 79 46 99; malvina@nem.net. Open M-Sa 9am-noon and 2-7:15pm. MC/V.) It's not a bad idea to shop around for **extreme sports;** at least half a dozen outdoor companies base themselves within a half-mile of the tourist office, offering everything from rafting to paragliding. Other town services include a **laundromat**, 66 av. M. Foch (wash €5-8, dry €3; open M-Sa 8am-8pm); **police**, at the Hôtel de Ville (☎ 05 61 94 68 81); a **medical emergency center**, 5 cours de Quinconces (☎ 05 61 79 93 00); and **Internet** at the **post office**, 26 allée d'Etigny, located on the corner of allée and av. Gallieni. (☎ 05 61 94 74 50. Open M-F 8:45am-noon and 2-5:45pm, Sa 8:45am-noon.) **Postal Code:** 31110.

⁊ ACCOMMODATIONS. Standard budget hotels with rooms under €25 abound in the town center; the tourist office has a list. For cheaper accommodations, the closest *gîte*, **Gîte Skioura ❶**, is 2km uphill from the tourist office en route to Superbagnères. Call ahead to be picked up. Otherwise, follow cours des Quinconces out of town and up the mountain. During the week (mornings only), it's more convenient to catch the *car thermal* from the train station allée d'Etigny to the *thermes* and get off at the camping stop (15min., free). Keep walking uphill for 10min. Five large rooms have 40 beds and a fireplace large enough to heat a castle. Some privacy is afforded by cloth partitions between every two beds. During the high season, the *gîte* is dominated by groups. (☎ 05 61 79 60 59. Breakfast €4. Sheets €2.50. Dorms €12.95.) **La Demeure de Venasque ❶**, located some 3km up the road from Gîte Skioura, in a large house in the middle of an open field, offers more homey dorm accommodations and every kind of facility imaginable to travelers, including a basketball court, foosball, and a music room. (☎ 05 61 94 31 96; fax 05 61 94 31 96. Breakfast €4. Dorms €11.)

Hôtel de Sports ❸, 12 av. Maréchal Foch, just 5min. from the station, has simple but spotless rooms and caring owners who help guests check email, store luggage, and make reservations for hiking and mountain biking. Almost all rooms have shower and bath. (☎05 61 79 97 80. Breakfast €5.50. Singles and doubles €30-45. Prices lower in the low season.)

🍴 **FOOD.** The town **market** is held on Wednesday and Saturday mornings (8am-1pm) at pl. Rovy. The **Casino supermarket** at 45 av. Maréchal Foch is on the way from the train station. (Open July-Aug. M-Sa 8:30am-12:30pm and 3-8pm, Su 9am-noon; Sept.-June M-Sa 8:30am-12:30pm and 3-7:30pm.) For a treat, head to the *pâtisserie* **Rino Marseglia ❶,** 9 av. Carnot, for savory quiches and tarts, including the exquisite *tarte aux myrtilles* (blueberry tart). Most of their selections are under €2. (☎05 61 79 18 95. Open M-Sa 6am-1pm and 3-8pm.) For a fuller meal, head to **alleé d'Etigny,** where €8-12 *menus* are available at any of the nondescript *brasseries* that line the street, many of which become lively bars late at night. For a slightly more upscale—if not entirely gourmet—experience, try **L'Arbesquines ❹,** 47 allée d'Etigny, which serves fondues from all different regions of France, particularly the Pyrenees, in a cozy atmosphere. (☎05 61 79 33 69. *Menus* €16-30, fondues €13-18. Open M-Tu and Th-Su 12:15-1:45pm and 7:15-10pm. MC/V.)

📷🥾 **SIGHTS AND HIKES.** The tourist office has information about hiking paths (1-2½hr.) and mountain bike trails that leave from the **Parc Thermal,** just behind the *thermes* at the end of allées d'Etigny on Superbagnères. An easier option is a 2hr. ramble leading from the Parc to the town market. The truly hardcore can make the 3hr. haul to the top. Alternatively, the **Altiservice** runs a **télécabine** that transports hikers and bikers to the top of Superbagnères. (☎05 61 79 97 00. One-way €4.90, round-trip €7.50. Open daily July-Aug. 9:45am-12:15pm and 1:30-6pm; Apr.-Sept. Sa-Su 1:30-5pm; ski season daily 8:30am-6pm.) The tourist office has two free hiking and biking maps that indicate the way back down. Also check the Bureau des Guides (see **Practical Information**). Enjoy a soak in the **thermes,** located in the appropriately lavish white marble building at the end of allées d'Etigny. €13 buys access to the 32°C pool and the **Vaporarium,** a natural underground sauna unique to Europe. For this and other programs, inquire at **Vitaline,** found in the Greek temple-like bathhouse of the *thermes.* Tours of the adjacent 18th-century *thermes* depart Tuesdays at 2pm, June through September. (Reservations and info ☎05 61 79 22 97; www.luchon.com. Open mid-Dec. to mid-Oct. Info office open daily 9am-noon and 3-8pm. Vaporarium open daily early July-early Sept. and mid-Dec.-late Mar. 3:30-8pm; late Mar.-early July and early Sept.-Oct. 3:30-7pm. Closed occasional Su in spring.)

LANGUEDOC-ROUSSILLON

Occitania, independent of both France and Spain, once stretched from the Rhône valley to the foothills of the Pyrenees. Its people spoke the *langue d'oc*, a Romance language whose name comes from their word for "yes." In the mid-12th century, Occitanians adopted the heretical Cathar brand of Christianity, which triggered the Church's Albigensian Crusade (named for the Cathar stronghold of Albi) against the so-called heretics; the slaughter that followed resulted in Occitania's political and linguistic integration into France.

Roussillon, in the far southwest corner of France, was historically part of Catalunya, not France, and Perpignan (p. 619) was the capital of the Kings of Majorca. Today, Roussillon's locals identify with Barcelona more than with Paris. Many speak Catalan, a relative of the *langue d'oc*, which sounds like a hybrid of French and Spanish. Architecture, food, and nightlife all bear the marks of its Spanish neighbors, giving them an added zest that make for a very lively stop. Perfectly situated between the sandy coasts of the Mediterranean and the gorgeous peaks of the Pyrenees, with everything from beachside resort towns to fortified mountain villages, the region has inspired the likes of Matisse and Picasso and now attracts an interesting mix of sunbathers and backpackers. Medieval ramparts and one-street towns look like they come straight from the pages of a fairy tale, while natural attractions outside of Millau (p. 626) provide lively adventure sports.

HIGHLIGHTS OF LANGUEDOC-ROUSSILLON

YOU MAY THINK you've died and gone to heaven as you approach **Cordes-sur-Ciel** (p. 607); the hilltop medieval town is often shrouded in clouds and has a museum dedicated to the "art of sugar."

SPLASH AROUND with every watersport under the sun in the waters of the **Gorges du Tarn** (p. 629).

TAKE A BREAK from the world-class art at the Musée d'Art Moderne in **Céret** (p. 637) to stroll in the town's prized cherry orchards.

TOULOUSE

Sassy, headstrong Toulouse (pop. 390,000) is known as *la ville en rose* (the city in pink)—the place to come when all French towns begin to look alike. The city's magnificent buildings, from the stately homes of 16th-century pastel merchants to the striped Capitole, are built of local rose-colored bricks. Many of them are trimmed with white marble, giving Toulouse a grandeur befitting France's 4th-largest city. Politically, Toulouse has always been a free-thinking place. Its powerful counts made life miserable for French kings in the Middle Ages, and it wasn't until the Revolution that France finally got a firm grip on the *capitouls* (town councillors) of Toulouse's unique government. Still pushing the frontiers of knowledge, this university town, where Thomas Aquinas made Aristotle palatable to medieval

theologians, now serves as the capital of France's aerospace industry. During the school year, 100,000 students flood the pizzerias of rue du Taur, the city's countless museums, and the quais of the Garonne.

▐ TRANSPORTATION

Flights: Aéroport Blagnac (☎05 61 42 44 00). **Air France** (☎08 02 80 28 02) flies to **London** (2 per day, round-trip from €210) and **Paris** (25 per day, round-trip from €115). **Navettes Aérocar** (☎05 34 60 64 00; www.navettevia-toulouse.com) serves the airport from the bus station and allée Jean Jaurès (30min.; every 20min.; €3.90, under 25 €3).

Trains: Gare Matabiau, 64 bd. Pierre Sémard. To: **Bordeaux** (2-3hr., 14 per day, €27.70); **Lyon** (6½hr., 3-4 per day, €51); **Carcassonne** (24 per day, €12.10); **Marseille** (4½hr., 8 per day, €40.60); **Paris** (8-9hr., 4 per day, €59.90); **Perpignan** (2½hr., 6 per day, €23.90). Ticket office open M 5:10am-9:30pm, Tu-Th and Sa 5:40am-9:30pm, F 5:40am-10:30pm, Su 6:10am-10:30pm.

Buses: Gare Routière, 68-70 bd. Pierre Sémard (☎05 61 61 67 67), next to the train station. Open M-Sa 7am-7pm, Su 8am-7pm. To: **Albi** (1½hr., 4 per day, €11.60); **Carcassonne** (2¼hr., 1 per day, €11); **Foix** (2hr., 2 per day, €9.20); **Montauban** (70min.,

4 per day, €6.70). Buy tickets on the bus. **Eurolines** (☎05 61 26 40 04; www.euro-lines.fr) with an office in the station, runs buses to most major cities in Europe. Open M-F 9:30am-6:30pm, Sa 9:30am-5pm.

Metro: SEMVAT, 49 rue de Gironis (☎05 61 41 70 70 or 05 62 11 26 11). Buy tickets just inside the station (€1.30 per ticket). Maps at ticket booths and tourist office. Open daily 5am-midnight.

Taxis: Capitole Taxi (☎ 05 34 25 02 50). €25 to the airport.

Bike Rental: In front of the tourist office. €1 per half-day, €2 per day. €260 deposit required. Open daily 9am-7pm.

■✳ 🛈 ORIENTATION AND PRACTICAL INFORMATION

While residential Toulouse sprawls ever outward along both sides of the Garonne, tourist Toulouse, along with the thriving student quarter, is within a small section east of the river, bounded by **rue de Metz** in the south and by **boulevard Strasbourg** and **boulevard Carnot** to the north and east. The metro is useful for reaching your hotel from the train station, but after you've dropped off your pack, there should be no need to venture underground again. Even the walk from the train station to the main part of town takes only about 15min. The center is the huge stone plaza known as the **Capitole.**

Tourist Office: Donjon du Capitole, on rue Lafayette at pl. Charles de Gaulle (☎05 61 11 02 22; www.ot-toulouse.fr), in the park behind the Capitole. From the station, take the metro to Capitole or turn left along the canal, then right onto allée Jean Jaurès. Walk two-thirds of the way around pl. Wilson (bearing right), then right onto rue Lafayette. Office is in a small park on the left of the intersection with rue d'Alsace-Lorraine. Free accommodations service. City tours in English (June-Sept. Tu, Sa at 2pm, €7; in French M-F 2 per day). Lists of hotels, restaurants, and cultural events. Office open June-Sept. M-Sa 9am-7pm, Su 10am-1pm and 2-6:15pm; Oct.-May M-Sa 9am-6pm, Su 9am-5pm.

Budget Travel: OTU Voyage, 60 rue de Taur (☎05 61 12 18 88). Cheap fares for students. Open M-F 9am-6:30pm, Sa 10am-1pm and 2-5pm. **Nouvelles Frontières,** 2 pl. St-Sernin (☎05 61 21 74 14, national 08 25 00 08 25). Open M-Sa 9am-7pm, Sa closes at 6pm. AmEx/MC/V.

Consulates: US, 25 allées Jean Jaurès (☎05 34 41 36 50). Open by appointment only.

Currency Exchange: Banque de France, 4 rue Deville (☎05 61 61 35 35). No commission, good rates. Open M-F 9am-12:20pm and 1:20-3:30pm.

English-Language Bookstore: The Bookshop, 17 rue Lakanal (☎05 61 22 99 92). Collection of novels, French history books, and travel guides. Open M-Sa 10am-7pm. AmEx/MC/V.

Youth Center: CRIJ (Centre Regional d'Info Jeunesse), 17 rue de Metz (☎05 61 21 20 20). Info on travel, work, and study. Open daily July-Aug. 10am-noon and 2-6pm; Sept.-June 10am-1pm and 2-7pm.

Laundromat: Laverie St-Sernin, 14 rue Emile Cartailhac. Wash €3.30-6.50, dry €0.50 per 6min. Open daily 7am-10pm.

Late-Night Pharmacy: 70-76 allées Jean Jaurès (☎05 61 62 38 05). Open daily 8pm-8am, open until 9am Su and holidays.

Hospital: CHR de Rangueil, av. du Prof. Jean Poulhes (☎05 61 55 44 92).

Police: Commissariat Central, bd. Embouchure (☎05 61 12 74 74).

Internet Access: Nethouse, 1 rue des 3 Renards (☎05 61 21 98 42). €3 per hr. Open M-Sa 9am-11pm, Su noon-6pm. **Adéclik,** 5 pl. St-Pierre. €2 per hr. Open Sept.-June M-Sa 10am-midnight, Su 2-11pm; July-Aug. M-F noon-10pm, Sa-Su 4-10pm.

Post Office: 9 rue Lafayette (☎ 05 34 45 70 51). **Currency exchange** with good rates. Open M-F 8am-7pm and Sa 8am-noon. **Poste Restante:** 31049 Toulouse Cedex. **Postal Code:** 31000.

🏠 🏕 ACCOMMODATIONS AND CAMPING

Hotels line the blocks near the train station, but cheaper, more comfortable hotels can be found in the city center or on the outskirts of town. A host of welcoming, hostel-priced hotels make up for Toulouse's lack of a youth hostel.

🏨 **Hôtel des Arts,** 1bis rue Cantegril (☎ 05 61 23 36 21; fax 05 61 12 22 37). M: pl. Esquirol. Low prices and spacious rooms in perfect location. Breakfast €5. Reception daily 7am-11pm. Singles €23-26, with shower €28.50-30.50; doubles €28-33.50/ €31.50-38. Extra bed €5. MC/V. ❷

CASSOULET DE CASTELNAUDARY

For rich, phenomenally flavorful eats, no one can beat the best of French cuisine, and few French meals are more savory than Languedoc *cassoulet*, a thick hearty stew of white beans and meat. Pays Cathar residents are proud of their native *cassoulet*, and top-notch chefs feature it front and center on their menus. The dish originated in Castelnaudary, a small town located between Toulouse and Carcassonne, which is denoted on the highway by a small icon symbolizing *cassoulet*: delicious fumes wafting toward the sky.

Requiring days of preparation and a rich variety of ingredients, *cassoulet de Castelnaudary* can be rather difficult and quite expensive to make. The hopeful gourmet chef must soak 800g of white beans (*haricots blancs*) in water for 12hr., cook them with lard and onions, and then add garlic and an assortment of meat. A leading French culinary society has proclaimed that authentic *cassoulet* must contain at least 30% *saucisson de Toulouse* (a pork sausage), goose or duck liver, or mutton. The remaining ingredients include pork rinds, stock, and aromatic vegetables and herbs. The whole concoction is simmered in layers for up to three days. Finally, it is placed in a pan and cooked for 2½hr. until there's a fine *croustillant*, or crust, on top. It is eaten warm with salad and a strong red wine.

Hôtel Beauséjour, 4 rue Caffarelli (☎/fax 05 61 62 77 59), just off allée Jean Jaurès, close to the station. Bright rooms with new beds at the lowest prices. Ask about tiny singles that usually go to long-term guests (€15). Breakfast €4. Shower €1. Reception daily until 11pm, but someone is always present. Huge singles and doubles €20, with bath €27; rooms with 2 beds €28, with shower €31, with bath €33. MC/V. ❷

Hôtel Anatole France, 46 pl. Anatole France (☎05 61 23 19 96; fax 05 61 21 47 66). In a calm *place* next to the student quarter. Bright, airy rooms. Breakfast €4. Singles and doubles €22, with shower €25, with shower and TV €28, with bath and TV €33. Extra bed €5. MC/V. ❷

Camping:

Pont de Rupé, 21 chemin du Pont de Rupé (☎05 61 70 07 35; fax 05 61 70 00 71), at av. des Etats-Unis (N20 north). Take bus #59 (dir: Camping) from pl. Jeanne d'Arc to Rupé. Restaurant, bar, and laundry. €9.50 per person, €3.50 per additional person. ❶

La Bouriette, 199 chemin de Tournefeuille (☎05 61 49 64 46), 5km outside Toulouse along N124 in St-Martin-du-Touch. Take bus #64 (dir: Colomiers) from metro stop Arène and ask for "St-Martin-du-Touch." Open year-round. €8.50 per person, car included. ❶

FOOD

Any budget traveler should head directly to the **rue du Taur** in the student quarter, where cheap eateries serve meals for €5.50-10. Lebanese, Chinese, and Mexican restaurants fill the storefronts on **rue des Filatiers** and **rue Paradoux.** On Wednesdays and Saturdays (6am-noon), **place du Capitole** becomes an open-air department store. Other **markets** are held at pl. Victor Hugo, pl. des Carmes, and bd. de Strasbourg. (Open Tu-Su 6am-1pm.) There's a **Monoprix supermarket** at 39 rue Alsace-Lorraine (open M-Sa 9am-10pm) and a **Casino** near pl. Occitane at the Centre Commerciale St-Georges. (Open M-Sa 9am-7:30pm.) Students who want a good, hot meal at low rates (€2.40) should head to the **restaurants universitaires.** The nearest student cafeteria to town is the **Arsenal Restaurant Universitaire,** 2 bd. Armand Duportal, near rue du Taur (☎05 61 23 98 48). For info on the 13 other student cafeterias scattered around Toulouse, head to the **CROUS,** 58 rue du Taur. (☎05 61 12 54 00. Open M-F 8:30am-5:30pm; cafeteria hours vary. ISIC required.) The *brâsseries* that crowd busy **place Wilson** offer €8.50-15 *menus.*

Le Grand Rideau ❸, 75 rue du Taur, a cross between small restaurant, art gallery, and theater, serves regional food in a three-course lunch (€9.10) and a generous evening *menu* (€16). Dishes have names like "Shakespeare" and "Molière." Some concerts are planned, but impromptu performances spring up all the time. (☎05 61 23 90 10. Special summer dinner *menu* €10.30. Open M noon-2pm, Tu-F noon-2pm and 7:30-10pm.) **Jour de Fête ❷**, 43 rue du Taur, right down the street from Rideau, serves a large *plat du jour* (€6.70) and salad (€4.70) in a relaxed *brâsserie* with brick walls and old posters. Crowds pack in night and day. (☎05 61 23 36 48. Open daily 11am-midnight.) With a simple veggie-heavy menu, omelettes, and pastas, **La Faim des Haricots ❸**, rue du Puits Vert, between pl. Capitole and the student quarter, is a vegetarian's heaven. (☎05 61 22 49 25. *Menus* €8-11, including all-you-can-eat salad bar option. Open M-Sa noon-2:30, Th-Sa also 7:30-10:30pm.)

🌐 SIGHTS

Toulouse is famous for the red-brick **stone mansions** of the town's wealthy 15th- and 16th-century dye merchants. These houses can be seen on the tourist office's 2hr. tour. (In French. W and Sa 3pm. €8.80, students €7.30.) From local artists to canonized painters, the diversity of Toulouse's art makes for a nice afternoon of museum-hopping. Most museums are free to students. Multi-sight passes are sold at all museums: €5 gives entry to any three museums, €8 to any six.

LE CAPITOLE. The city's most prominent monument is its mammoth brick palace and the huge stone plaza in front, which is ideal for people-watching. The building was once home to the bourgeois *capitouls*, who unofficially ruled the city (technically controlled by counts) for many years. All people in Toulouse who marry must pass through the **Salle des Illustres,** beside the Mairie. **La Salle Henri Martin,** next door, includes 10 post-Impressionist *tableaux* by Henri Martin, representing Toulouse in all four seasons. *(Salles open daily 9am-7pm. Free.)*

BASILIQUE ST-SERNIN. St-Sernin is the longest Romanesque structure in the world, but its most visible feature is an enormous brick steeple that rises skyward in five ever-narrowing double-arched terraces like a massive wedding cake. St-Dominic, head of the Dominican order of friars, made the church his base in the early 13th century, though he departed a bit from the ascetic monastic traditions. The impressive altar is the highlight of the visit, surrounded by vivid frescoes. Behind the left side of the ornate altar in the back of the church, the crypt conceals a treasure trove of holy relics, from engraved silver chests to golden goblets, some from the time of Charlemagne. *(☎05 61 21 70 18. Church open July-Sept. M-Sa 8:30am-6:30pm, Su 8:30am-7:30pm; Oct.-June M-Sa 8:30-11:45am and 2-5:45pm, Su 8:30am-12:30pm and 2-7:30pm. Tours in French July-Aug. 2 per day. €5.40. Crypt open July-Sept. M-Sa 10am-6pm, Su 11:30am-6pm; Oct.-June M-Sa 10-11:30am and 2:30-5pm, Su 2:30-5pm. €2.)*

RÉFECTOIRE DES JACOBINS AND CHURCH. This 13th-century southern Gothic church is the final resting place of St. Thomas Aquinas. His ashes take center stage in an elevated, under-lit tomb. Be sure to notice the ceiling, whose vaults look like palm trees. *(Rue Lakanal. Open daily 9am-7pm. Occasional summer piano concert. Tickets at tourist office. Cloister €2.20.)*

MUSEUMS. The huge **Musée des Augustins** displays an unsurpassed assemblage of Romanesque and Gothic sculptures, including 15 snickering gargoyles, in a gorgeous redone Augustine monastery. Highlights include the nightmare sculpture at the bottom of the stairway and the church's giant rose window. *(21 rue de Metz, off rue des Arts. ☎05 61 22 21 82. Free organ concert W 8-8:30pm. Open M and W-Su 10am-6pm, W until 9pm. €2.40, students free.)* The striking **Hôtel d'Assezat** hosts the Fondation Bemberg, which displays 28 Bonnards, a modest collection of Dufys, Pissarros, and Gauguins, as well as the odd Picasso, Renoir, and Matisse. The gorgeous rose-brick building also makes it worth a stop. *(Pl. d'Assézat. ☎05 61 12 06 89. Fondation*

☎05 61 12 06 89. Open Tu and F-Su 10am-12:30pm and 1:30-6pm, Th 10am-12:30pm and 1:30-9pm. €4.60, students €2.75.) The **Musée St-Raymond** holds a decent collection of archaeological finds. (Pl. St-Sernin. ☎05 61 22 31 44. Open daily June-Aug. 10am-7pm; Sept.-May 10am-6pm. English text available. €2.40, students free.) **Les Abbatoirs** is a vast space dedicated to cutting-edge revolving exhibits of contemporary art, reached by walking across the St-Pierre bridge. (76 allées Charles-de-Fitte. ☎05 62 48 58 00. Open Tu-Su noon-8pm. €6.10, students €3.05, prices lower when no exhibits are on display.)

🎵 🌺 ENTERTAINMENT AND FESTIVALS

Toulouse has something to please almost any nocturnal whim, although the city is liveliest from October to May, when students come out in full force. The numerous cafes, *glaciers*, and pizzerias flanking **place St-Georges** and pl. du Capitole are open late, as are the bars off rue des Filatiders and **rue de la Colombette.** Locals like to cafe-hop, drinking *kir* and beer all afternoon, take a break for dinner, and then hit the bars and clubs hard at night. During the school year, students head to **place St-Pierre** to watch rugby in one of the small bars while drinking *pastis.* From September to June, the weekly *Flash* keeps up on the latest in restaurants, bars, and clubs (€1 at tabacs). The July-August issue *Flash Eté* has a big festival listing. CD and book megalith **FNAC**, at the intersection of bd. Strasbourg and bd. Carnot, has cultural pamphlets, club advertisements, and tickets to large concerts. (☎05 61 11 01 01. Open M-Sa 9:30am-7:30pm.)

🍷**Au Père Louis**, 45 rue des Tourneurs, is always packed by well-dressed crowds who drink the regional wines by the glass (€2.30)—and bottle (€10). Try the house specialty, the aperitif *quinquina*. The *maison* (with a lunchtime restaurant) has been around since 1889. (☎05 61 21 33 45. Open M-Sa 8:30am-2:30pm and 5-10:30pm.) **Café Populaire,** 9 rue de la Colombette, is a hot and smoky destination for the financially strapped. Groups come here for the cheapest beer in Toulouse. A box of 13 bottles of beer costs €19, or a mere €13 on Mondays. (☎05 61 63 07 00. Happy hour 7:30-8:30pm: buy one *pastis*, get one free. Open M-F 9pm-2am, Sa 2pm-4am.) **Bodega-Bodega,** 1 rue Gabriel Péri, just off bd. Lazare Carnot, a wildly popular destination for young crowds, is a bar that turns into a club after the clock strikes twelve. It's hard to guard your money when the poker chips given as change make it easy to buy another drink. (☎05 61 63 03 63. Beer €2.50, margaritas €6, *tapas* €3.50-9 until midnight. €6 min. Th-Sa 10pm-2am. Open M-Su 7pm-2am, Sa 7pm-6am. MC/V.)

Cave Poésie, 71 rue du Taur, hosts plays and performances. The full moon is the catalyst for an "open door" night (starting around 9pm) of comedians, poets, and musicians. Pick up their schedule outside the door or at the tourist office (☎05 61 23 62 00. Tickets €12, students €7.) **Cour de l'École des Beaux Arts,** ☎05 61 22 29 89 quai de la Daurade, occasionally stages classic plays with a modern twist. Most of Toulouse's **movie theaters** are located in and around pl. Wilson. **UGC,** 9 allée du Président Roosevelt (☎05 62 30 28 30), plays mostly American new releases, some of them dubbed in French. Everything is shown in its original language at **Utopia Cinemas,** 23 rue Montardy (☎05 61 23 66 20), including independent films from around the world.

From July to September, **Toulouse d'Eté** brings classical concerts, jazz, gospel, and ballet to a variety of outdoor settings, including the Jacobins courtyard and the Halle aux Grains. Tickets are sold at concert halls and the tourist office (€15). Traditional music and dance groups parade through the streets on the last Sunday in June for the festival known as the **Grand Fénétra** (☎05 62 22 29 22). The **Festival International de Piano aux Jacobins** tickles Toulousian ivories every couple of days at 8:30pm during September at the Jacobins cloister. (Bureau du Festival ☎05 61 22 40 05; www.pianojacobins.com. Tickets available at the Bureau or the tourist office. €16-28, students €9.)

DAYTRIPS FROM TOULOUSE

CASTRES

The train station, av. Albert I (open M 5:40am-7:15pm, Tu-F 6:25am-7:15pm, Sa 7:55am-12:10pm and 1:30-6:30pm, Su 10:10am-12:10pm and 2:30-9:20pm), has service to Toulouse (1hr., 9 per day, €11.60). Though trains from Albi do eventually arrive in Castres, buses are cheaper and more direct. They run from the bus station, pl. Soult (☎05 63 35 37 31), to Albi (45-55min., 8 per day, €6) and Toulouse (1hr., 7 per day, €10.60).

When Castres (pop. 48,000) acquired the 11th-century bones of St-Vincent, the city became an essential pilgrimage stop for those en route to Santiago de Compostela. This prominence ended when the basilica was destroyed during the Wars of Religion. The city compensated by constructing two museums, each worth their own brief pilgrimage—the **Musée Goya** and the **Centre National et Musée Jean Jaurès.**

In front of the shrubs of the perfectly groomed **Jardin de l'Evêché**, the **Musée Goya** houses a large collection of Spanish paintings, along with works by Catalan and Aragonese masters. The works inside the ancient Episcopal palace are centered around four series of Goya's sardonic engravings on subjects as diverse as the horrors of war and the humor of daily life. (☎05 63 71 59 27. Open daily July-Aug. 10am-6pm; Sept.-June Tu-Sa 9am-noon and 2-6pm, Su 10am-noon and 2-6pm. €2.30, students €1.15, under 18 free.)

While art lovers enjoy the Goya museum, the **Centre National et Musée Jean Jaurès**, 2 pl. Pélisson, caters to those interested in France's social history—or those just curious about why every single town in the country seems to have an avenue Jean Jaurès. A brilliant scholar and professor of philosophy, prominent socialist Jaurès led the striking glass-workers of Carmaux in 1896 and vehemently supported Alfred Dreyfus, a Jewish officer framed as a traitor by the army, before being assassinated in 1914. The modern, sleek building is packed with political cartoons, photographs, and newspaper articles that recount the spirited life and rhetoric of the man himself, as well as occasional small temporary exhibitions. (☎05 63 72 01 01. Open daily July-Aug. 10am-noon and 2-6pm; Apr.-June and Sept.-Oct. Tu-Su 10am-noon and 2-6pm; Nov.-Mar. Tu-Sa 10am-noon and 2-5pm. €1.50, students €0.75.) The **Centre d'Art Contemporain,** 35 rue Chambre de l'Edit, is an intimate space for temporary exhibits of current artists. (Open daily July-Aug. 10am-1pm and 2-6pm; Sept.-June M and Sa-Su 3-6pm, Tu-F 10am-noon and 1-5:30pm. €1, students free.) The Musée Goya and Musée Jaurès both sell a €4 ticket for adults that allows admission to all three of Castres's museums.

For two weeks in mid-July, the **Extravadanses** festival celebrates international Hispanic culture with concerts, exhibitions, flamenco, and ballet performances. Many events are free; tickets to others are available at the tourist office or by calling the **Théâtre Municipale.** (☎05 63 71 56 57. Open M-F 10:30am-12:30pm and 3-6:30pm.) The city also hosts a multicultural festival in mid-August with free concerts and dances around the city.

When hunger strikes, try the **markets** on pl. Jean Jaurès (Tu and Th-Sa 7:30am-noon) and pl. de l'Albinque. (Covered market Tu-Sa 7am-1pm, Su 7am-noon; open market Tu, F 7am-1pm, Th 7am-1pm and 4-8pm. Tu flea market also.) **Monoprix supermaket** is on rue Sabatier at pl. Jean Jaurès. (Open M-Sa 8:30am-7:30pm.) There are a few bakeries on **rue Gambetta** and **rue Victor Hugo** in the town center, while restaurants surround the **Pont Vieux**, pl. Jean Jaurès, and **rue Villegoudou.** For a sit-down meal, try **La Mandragore ❸**, behind pl. Jean Jaurès on rue Malpas. The restaurant serves regional French cuisine with an extra touch of flavor—try the *crème brûlée* perfumed with lavender. (☎05 63 59 51 27. Three-course *menu* with wine €12. Open Tu-Sa noon-2pm and 7:30-10pm.) Traditional *Nougatines Cas-*

traises (€9.20 for 200g) are the specialty of **Cormary ❶**, 13 rue Victor Hugo, which also sculpts fine chocolates, marzipan, and pastries into animal shapes. (☎05 63 59 27 09. Open Tu-Sa 6am-1pm and 1:30-7:30pm, Su 6am-1pm. MC/V.)

Getting around Castres is easy, and all the sights are within a 5min. walk of one another; but since the tourist office allows visitors to use their bikes free for two hours, it's worth taking a spin through the pedestrian streets.

To get to the **tourist office**, 3 rue Milhau Ducommun, from the train station, turn left onto av. Albert I and then bear right onto bd. Henri Sizaire. At pl. Alsace-Lorraine, continue straight over the bridge, ignoring signs for the *centre ville* (following signs and bearing left will take you right to the Musée Goya). Turn left onto bd. Raymond Vittoz, then turn left onto rue Villegoudou and veer right onto rue Leris. It's on the right at the very end of the street (20 minutes). Across the river is pl. Jean Jaurès. From the bus station, walk across pl. Soult and continue straight on rue Villegoudou, then see the directions from the train station above. (☎05 63 71 37 00 or 05 63 62 63 62; www.ville-castres.fr. Open July-Aug. M-Sa 9am-12:30pm and 1:30-6:30pm, Su 10:30am-noon and 2:30-5pm; Sept.-June M-Sa 9:30am-12:30pm and 2-6pm, Su 2:30-4:30pm.)

MONTAUBAN

Accessible from Toulouse by train (25min.; every hr.; €7.60; info office open M-F 7am-7:30pm, Sa 9am-7:30pm) and by bus (☎05 63 22 55 00; 1hr.; 6 per day; €6.70). Local buses are run by Transports Montalbanais, bd. Midi-Pyrénées (☎05 63 63 60 60; 7:30am-7pm; €0.90, carnet of 10 €7). Catch taxis at the train station or call ☎05 63 66 99 99.

The ochre-tinted medieval architecture of the city (pop. 55,000) dates back to 1144, when the Count of Toulouse incited local artisans to sack the wealthy abbey at Montauriol ("golden mountain") and use its stones to start construction of present-day Montauban. Never on good terms with mainstream Catholicism, Montauban was one of the last bastions of Protestantism in France following the revocation of the Edict of Nantes in 1685. The birthplace of celebrated 19th-century painter Jean-Auguste Dominique Ingres, the town merits a stop for its impressive **Musée Ingres**, 19 rue de l'Hôtel de Ville, which occupies the 17th-century Bishop's palace. While the museum is not exclusively devoted to the Neoclassical painter and his predilection for nude female forms, its upper floors spotlight hundreds of his sketches and some minor paintings. The highlight of the museum is the large, vaulted medieval hall—the only remnant of the château built by the Black Prince in 1362. (☎05 63 22 12 91. Open daily July-Aug. 10am-6pm; Sept.-June Tu-Su 10am-noon and 2-6pm; mid-Oct. to mid-Apr. closed Su mornings. Tours in French daily July-Aug. 2:30pm, €7. Museum €4, students free, 1st Su of month free.)

Just after revoking the Edict of Nantes, Louis XIV spitefully constructed Montauban's classical cathedral, ⬛**Notre Dame de l'Assomption**. Four enormous sculptures of the Evangelists keep solemn watch over *Le Vœu de Louis XIII*, one of the most impressive religious works by Ingresi, located in the left transept. Detailed murals decorate the smaller side chapels, and the entrance facade is the highest in Europe. (Open daily 10am-noon and 2-6pm.)

Alors Chante is a festival where revelers play traditional French tunes for one week at the end of May or the beginning of June, beginning the Tuesday preceding Ascension and finishing on that Sunday (☎05 63 63 02 36; tickets €15-50), while a **Jazz Festival** swings through during the second week of July. Big-name concerts are all ticketed events, but during the festival the streets of the *vieille ville* resound with free concerts, usually held at noon and 7pm. (Info ☎05 63 63 60 60; www.jazzmontauban.com. Tickets available at tourist office. €15-45, students €10-15.)

ALBI

Dominated by the magnificent Cathédrale Ste-Cécile, the narrow, cobblestone streets of Albi (pop. 50,000) twist down to the tree-lined Tarn River. Native son Henri de Toulouse-Lautrec was lured away by the lights of Paris and the Moulin Rouge, though visitors to Albi will wonder why he left. Those who come for the cathedral and the Toulouse-Lautrec Museum often end up staying longer than planned, entranced by the peaceful, relatively untouristed city.

TRANSPORTATION

Trains run from pl. Stalingrad to Castres (1½hr., 8 per day, €13.30) via St-Sulpice; and Toulouse (1hr., 15 per day, €10.60). Check the info office for times. (Open M-F 5:30am-9:45pm, Sa 6am-9:45pm, Su 6:15am-10:10pm.) **Buses** depart pl. Jean Jaurès (☎05 63 54 58 61) for Castres (1hr., M-Sa 8 per day, €5.50). **Local transportation** is run by Espace Albibus, 14 rue de l'Hôtel de Ville. (☎05 63 38 43 43. M-F 8:45am-noon and 2:30-6pm; €0.80.) **Albi Taxi Radio,** 64 impasse Jean de la Fontaine (☎05 63 54 85 03), waits at the station.

PRACTICAL INFORMATION

To reach the **tourist office,** Palais de la Berbie, at pl. Ste-Cécile, turn left from the station onto av. Maréchal Joffre, then left on av. du Général de Gaulle. Bear left over pl. Lapérouse to the pedestrian *vieille ville.* Rue de Verdusse leads to pl. Ste-Cécile; signs point the way from there (10 minutes). The office books rooms (€2) and offers guides to the city, tours in French (July-Sept. M-Sa 12:15pm, €4), and **currency exchange** on bank holidays. (☎05 63 49 48 80; www.albitourisme.com. Open July-Aug. M-Sa 9am-7pm, Su 10am-12:30pm and 2:30-6:30pm; May-June and Sept. M-Sa 9am-12:30pm and 2-6:30pm, Su 10am-12:30pm and 2:30-6:30pm; Oct.-Apr. M-Sa 9am-12:30pm and 2-6pm, Su 10am-12:30pm and 2:30-5pm.) Other services include: **ATMs** and **currency exchange** at Crédit Agricole, pl. du Vigan (☎05 63 92 66 11; open Tu-Th 9am-noon and 1:45-5:30pm, F 9am-noon and 1:45-6:30pm, Sa 9am-1pm and 1:45-4pm); a **laundromat** at 8 rue Emile Grand, off Lices Georges Pompidou (☎05 63 54 51 14; open daily 7am-9pm); **police** at 23 rue Lices Georges Pompidou (☎05 63 43 74 60); a **hospital** on rue de la Berchère (☎05 63 47 47 47); and **Internet** access at Ludi.com, 62 rue Séré-de-Rivière. (☎05 63 43 34 24. €4.60 per hr. Open M-Sa 11am-midnight.) The **post office,** pl. du Vigan, offers **currency exchange.** (☎05 63 48 15 63. Open M-F 8am-7pm, Sa 8am-noon.) **Postal Code:** 81000.

ACCOMMODATIONS AND FOOD

Be sure to reserve ahead, especially for summer weekends. For info on *gîtes d'étape* and rural camping, call **ATTER** (☎05 63 48 83 01; fax 05 63 48 83 12). The antiquated ◪**Hôtel La Régence ❷,** 27 av. Maréchal Joffre, near the train station, is a good deal with its brightly wallpapered rooms and homey feel. All rooms have TV. (☎05 63 54 01 42; fax 05 63 54 80 48. Breakfast €5. Singles €21-23, with shower €24-27; doubles with shower €28-32, with shower and toilet €33-42. Extra bed €8. MC/V.) Elegant **Hôtel Saint-Clair ❹,** 8 rue St-Clair, has large, immaculate rooms overlooking a small courtyard. (☎05 63 54 25 66; andrieu.michele.free.fr. Breakfast €7. Reception daily 8am-9pm. Singles and doubles with shower and toilet €36-60, triples €63; quads €65. MC/V.) **Camp** near the municipal pool at **Parc de Caussels ❶,** 2km east of the town center, toward Millau on D999. Take bus #5 from pl. Jean

Jaurès to "Camping" (M-Sa every hr. until 7pm). Or walk (30min.), leaving town on rue de la République and following the signs. (Reception daily 7am-10pm. Open Apr. to mid-Oct. €8 for 1 person, €11 for 2 people with car, extra person €3.)

Near Albi, the vast region of **Gaillac** shelters *vignoble* estates that prepare some of the best wines of the southwest. Due to temporary construction work, almost all **markets** have been relocated to pl. Lapérouse (Tu-Su 8am-noon). An additional flea market is held Sa 8am-noon at pl. du Forail. Stock up on **groceries** at **Casino,** 39 rue Lices Georges Pompidou. (Open M-Sa 9am-7:30pm.) ✪**La Table du Sommelier** ❸, 20 rue Porta, a wine cellar and restaurant, serves carefully prepared, modern cuisine. A courtyard in the back greets visitors, and is the perfect place to enjoy one of the extensive varieties of wine offered. (☎05 63 46 20 10. *Plats* €10, 2-course meal €12.50, 3-course €15. Open Tu-Sa 12:15-2pm and 7:15-11pm. MC/V.) Regional specialties like *foie gras*, duck salads, and creative grilled meats are presented at **La Tête de l'Art** ❸, 7 rue de la Piale. Try the local tripe flavored with saffron. (☎05 63 38 44 75. *Menus* €14-28, *plats* €12-23. Open July-Aug. daily noon-2pm and 7:30-9:30pm; Sept.-June closed Tu-W. MC/V.) **Le Tournesol** ❷, 11 rue de l'Ort en Salvy, a popular vegetarian restaurant behind pl. du Vigan, has vegan *pâté*, as well as hummus, cheese, and heavenly homemade desserts. (☎05 63 38 38 14. *Plat du jour* €8.10. Open Tu-Sa noon-2pm. MC/V.)

◉ SIGHTS

The pride of Albi, eclipsing even the Lautrec museum, is the ✪**Cathédrale Ste-Cécile.** Stained-glass windows, lavish gold and blue walls, and graphic frescoed depictions of hell combine to create an imposing physical manifestation of the power of the Church. It was built between the 13th and 15th centuries as a fortress cathedral to enforce "the one true religion" after the Church's Albigensian Crusade stamped out the Cathar sect. Carvings line the choir walls in patterns so intricate they look like lace. The bright, unrestored fresco covering the entire ceiling, painted in 1512, is the largest Italian painting in France. (☎05 63 43 23 43. Open daily June-Sept. 9am-6:30pm; Oct.-May 9am-noon and 2-6:30pm. Services Su-F 6:20pm; Sa 11:15am and 6pm. Free. Choir €1; treasury €3, ages 12-25 €2. Free organ concert in mid-July and Aug. W 5pm and Su 4pm. Tours July-early Sept. daily 2:30pm, mid-July to Aug also at 10am. €5, English audioguide €3.)

The **Palais de la Berbie,** the 13th-century bishop's palace, was constructed in a similar defensive style owing to the tense relations between the church and the ruling family. The fortress showcased the clergy's wealth and power and served as both the tribunal courts and prison for those charged of crimes by the church. Beautiful gardens and walkways, crafted after the building was converted into a residence, offer splendid views of the Tarn River. (Gardens open daily July-Aug. 9am-7pm; Sept.-June 8am-noon and 2-6pm. Free.) The palace now contains the ✪**Musée Toulouse-Lautrec.** The son of the Count of Toulouse by his cousin and wife, **Henri de Toulouse-Lautrec** (1864-1901) suffered from a congenital bone defect that left him significantly shorter than average. He moved to Paris to witness and experience the high life of cafes, nightclubs, and brothels, capturing the essence of the late 19th-century city in his gripping sketches and paintings. The museum's impressive collection of his oil paintings and ink prints includes all 31 of the famous posters of Montmartre nightclubs. Sculptures and paintings by Dégas, Dufy, Matisse, and Rodin are displayed upstairs. (☎05 63 49 48 78. Open daily July-Aug. 9am-6pm; Apr.-June and Sept. 10am-noon and 2-6pm; Nov.-Mar. M and W-Su 10am-noon and 2-5pm; Oct. M and W-Su 10am-noon and 2-5:30pm. €4.50, students €2.50. Tourist office gives tours June-Sept. 8 at 11am and 4pm. €8.50, students €6.50, audioguide in English €3.)

🎵 🎎 ENTERTAINMENT AND FESTIVALS

When the sun goes down, the crowds come out along **place de l'Archevêché** in front of the Palais de la Berbie and on **Lices Georges Pompidou** near pl. du Vigan. Salsa and merengue flows from **Le Patio Latino**, 10 rue de l'Ort en Salvy, with its brightly colored cafe and dance floor. (☎05 63 38 68 16. Drinks €3-6. Lessons Th 9pm (€6, €10 per couple). Rock and pop W. Open Tu-Su 9pm-2am, July-Aug. opens at 10pm. MC/V.) Popular **Café Le Grand Pontie**, pl. du Vigan, doles out beer, sundaes, loud music, and billiards amid stream-lined booths and neon signs. (☎05 63 49 70 75. Beers €2.80-3.30, pizzas and pastas €8.50. Open daily 7am-2am. MC/V.) Innovative plays organized by the **Théâtre de la Croix Blanche**, 14 rue de Croix Blanche, take place in various town centers during the first two weeks of July. (☎05 63 54 18 63 for schedules. Tickets around €11.) **L'Athanor Scène Nationale**, pl. de l'Amitié Entre les Peuples, off bd. Carnot and opposite Parc Rochegude, often screens foreign art films. (☎05 63 38 55 56. Open Tu-F 2-7pm, Sa 10am-noon and 2-7pm. Movies generally start at 8:30pm. €6.50, M and W students and seniors €4.50.)

Albi's festivals are currently on hiatus due to construction work in town, but to compensate, the city is funding free musical performances around the town for the summer. Albi revels in an abundance of celebrations, all listed in *Sortir à Albi*, which is available at the tourist office.

🏃 DAYTRIPS FROM ALBI

CORDES-SUR-CIEL

Sudcar Rolland (☎05 63 54 11 93) runs two buses from Albi to Cordes (M-F only, last return bus 4:45pm; €4.80). Trains from Albi go via Tessonnières to Vindrac (1hr., 5 per day, €6.70), where travelers can avoid the nightmarish walk by calling the Barrois minibus (☎05 63 56 14 80), which runs the last 5km to Cordes (M-Sa €4.15, Su €5.85).

True to its name, medieval Cordes-sur-Ciel is a celestial city. Perched among the clouds and bounded by a crumbling double wall that sprouts flowers between its stones, the tiny city 24km from Albi rises to a summit accessible only by a steep, cobblestoned street.

Much of the town's medieval architecture was preserved by the efforts of archaeologist Charles Portal. **Museé Charles Portal**, located in Portail Peint when first approaching from pl. de la Bouteillerie, chronicles the town's history with a varied collection of his finds. (Call tourist office for info ☎05 63 56 06 11. Open daily July-Aug. 11am-12:30pm and 3:30-6:30pm; Apr.-June and Sept.-Oct. Sa, Su, and holidays 3-6pm. €2.30, ages 10-14 €1.10, under 10 free.) The **Musée de l'Art du Sucre**, a few steps farther down Grande Rue Raymond VII, sells all kinds of sweet treats and intricate sugar models. (☎05 63 56 02 40. Open daily Feb.-Dec. 10am-noon and 2:30-6:30pm. €2.30.)

Across the street, **place de la Bride** once served as the town's defensive platform in place of a more formal central fort. Today it provides a panoramic view of the countryside. Next to **Église St-Michel**, the highest point in town. (open daily 3-5:30pm), rests the **Puits de la Halle**, a 114m deep well constructed in 1222 by tunnelling through an entire mountain. The bottomless oasis supplied Albi with water during sieges of the area.

For a few days around July 14th, fire-eaters play to a costumed crowd during the **Fête du Grand Fauconnier**, which offers plays, concerts, magic shows, banquets, and a medieval market. (Reservations and info ☎05 63 56 49 13. Entrance €8, children €3, free if costumed.) The **Festival Musique** sponsors classical music concerts during late July. (For information, call ☎05 63 56 00 75. Tickets €15-25, students €10.)

The **tourist office,** pl. de Halle in Maison Fontpeyrouse, offers guided tours and books rooms. (☎05 63 56 00 52; www.cordes-sur-ciel.org. Tours July-Aug. Su-F 4pm, additional evening tours M and Th; €3.80. Open daily July-Aug. 10am-1pm and 2-7pm; Sept.-June 10:30am-12:30pm and 2-6pm.) There is also an annex in the lower city, in the Maison du Pays Cordais. (Open daily July-Aug. 10:30am-12:30pm and 2-6pm, Sept.-June open periodically.) A **navette** shuttles between the annex in the *haute ville* and the lower part of Cordes. (Departs daily every 12min. €2, children €1.30.) A **market** takes place at the bottom of the hill. (Sa 8am-noon.)

CARCASSONNE

Carcassonne (pop. 46,000) is where Cinderella lost her glass slipper, Beauty nursed the Beast, and Jack's giant lived a happy life until that whole beanstalk affair. Round towers capped by red-tiled roofs and an undulating double wall guard the approach to the *vieille ville.* As you walk past the stone portals and through the medieval drawbridge, the ramparts still seem to resound with the clinking of armor and sharpening of steel. The dream, though, fades fast once you clear the city walls. The "battle sounds" are actually the shouts of thousands of photo-taking visitors jostling for space on the narrow streets. Carcassonne has become one of France's largest tourist traps, for a reason. Up to 800,000 daytrippers flock to Carcassonne in July, where Bastille Day brings one of France's most spectacular firework displays. Try to experience the town late in the evening, when the streets are clear of crowds and the flood-lit fortress echoes with free concerts.

▌ TRANSPORTATION

Trains: behind Jardin St-Chenier (☎04 68 71 79 14). Info office open M-Sa 9am-noon and 1:30-6:15pm. To: **Lyon** (3½hr., 2 per day, €49.30); **Marseille** (3hr., every 2hr., €35.10); **Montpellier** (1½hr., 9 per day, €19.50); **Nice** (6hr., 5 per day, €52); **Nîmes** (2hr., 9 per day, €24.60); **Perpignan** (2hr., 17 per day, change at Narbonne, €17); **Toulouse** (50min., 20 per day, €13.20).

Buses: Regional buses leave from the *gare routière* on bd. de Varsovie. From the train station, cross the canal, turn right onto bd. Omer Sarrut, and then left at the fork. Check schedules at the station. **Cars Teissier** (☎04 68 25 85 45) runs to **Lourdes** (€23). **Trans'Aude** (☎04 68 25 13 74) covers western Roussillon.

Public Transportation: a **navette** (shuttle) takes you from sq. Gambetta (in the lower city) to the citadel gates. (☎04 68 47 82 22. Mid-June to mid-Sept. every 15min. M 2:30-7:30pm, Tu-Sa 8:30am-12:30pm and 2-6pm. €1 roundtrip.) **Agglo'Bus,** sq. Gambetta (☎04 68 77 73 21), runs **buses** through the city, including from the train station to the citadel gates and campground. To get from station to the *cité*, take bus #4 (dir: Gambetta) and then bus #2 (dir: La Cité, M-Sa every 20-40min. 7am-7pm, €0.90).

Taxis: Radio Taxi Services (☎04 68 71 50 50). At the train station or across the canal by Jardin St-Chenier. 24hr. €6-7 from the station to the *cité.*

▌ ▌ ORIENTATION AND PRACTICAL INFORMATION

The **Bastide St-Louis,** once known as the *basse ville* (lower town), recently changed its name to recruit daytrippers who might otherwise pass it over. Its main attractions are shops, hotels, the cathedral, the **train station,** and most importantly the **shuttle** and **TOUC,** which both run to the citadel. Otherwise, it's a pleasant but steep 30min. hike. To get from the station to the *cité,* walk straight down av. de Maréchal Joffre, which turns into rue G. Clemenceau. Just past the clearing of pl. Carnot, turn left on rue Verdun, and past the **tourist office.** Bear right through sq.

LANGUEDOC-ROUSSILLON

Gambetta, and turn left up the narrow road that leads to Pont Vieux. Continue straight up the hill to the *cité*. The tourist office annex will be on the right as you enter the castle.

Tourist Office: 28 rue de Verdun (☎ 04 68 10 24 30; www.carcassonne-tourisme.com), near the main post office. Map, comprehensive English guide *Round and About Carcassonne*, accommodations service, and lots of brochures; all free. Guided visits to Bastide St-Louis. Mid-June to mid-Oct. Tu and Th 9:30pm (€5, children €2). In low season, audioguides (€3). Organizes excursions of region as well (€13-30); call the office for info. Open daily July-Aug. 9am-7pm; Sept.-June 9am-6pm. Annexes in the *cité's* Porte Narbonnaise, same hours (☎ 04 68 10 24 36); and near the station on av. de Maréchal Joffre (☎ 04 68 25 94 81). Open July-Aug. 9am-1pm and 2-7pm.; Apr.-May 2-6pm; June and Sept.-Oct. 9am-1pm and 2-6pm; Hours change frequently, so call ahead.

Police: Commissariat, 4 bd. Barbès (☎ 04 68 11 26 00).

Medical Assistance: Centre Hospitalier, rte. de Ste-Hilaire (☎ 04 68 24 24 24).

Internet Access: All are located in the Bastide St-Louis. **Alerte Rouge,** 73 rue de Verdun (☎ 04 68 25 20 39). €4 per hr. Open M-Sa 10am-11pm. **Call World,** 32 rue de la République (☎ 04 68 72 89 00). €3.50 per hr. Open M-Sa 10am-2pm and 3-11pm, Su 2-10pm. **Logigames,** 35 bd. de Varsovie (☎ 04 68 72 67 04). €4 per hr. Open Tu-Sa 10am-10pm, Su 2-10pm.

Post Office: 40 rue Jean Bringer (☎04 68 11 71 00). **Currency exchange.** Open M-F 8am-7pm, Sa 8am-noon. Branch office (☎04 68 47 95 45) also offers currency exchange on rue de Comte Roger and rue Viollet-le-Duc. Poste Restante: 11012.

Postal Code: 11000.

ACCOMMODATIONS AND CAMPING

Carcassonne's comfortable hostel is a gift from above to budgeteers, with 120 beds right in the middle of the *cité*. Hotels in Bastide St-Louis, a hefty walk from the sights of the *cité*, are surprisingly cheap; those in the *cité* itself are expensive. If you find crowds unbearable, the Sidsmums hostel is in the beautiful countryside 10km outside the city.

■ Auberge de Jeunesse (HI), rue de Vicomte Trencavel (☎04 68 25 23 16; carcas-sonne@fuaj.org). A friendly staff welcomes visitors to this jewel, nested in the very heart of the *cité*. In summer, regional excursions are organized (€10-20), and free concerts take place on the hostel's peaceful interior courtyard. Bunkbeds with shower and sink in large, clean 4- to 6-bedrooms. Kitchen. Snack bar. Free bike rack. Bike rental €8 per day. Internet €3 per hr. Breakfast and sheets included. Laundry (€5 wash and dry). Lockout 10am-3pm. 24hr. reception. Reserve a few days ahead, earlier in July-Aug. Bunks €15.50, €18.40 for non-members. MC/V. ❷

■ Sidsmums Travelers Retreat, 11 chemin de la Croix d'Achille (☎04 68 26 94 49 or 06 16 86 85 00; www.sidsmums.com). Call for pick-up from the station (€5) or take the bus headed for Limoux from the canal side of the *gare routière* (ask for Preixan; 4-6 per day, last bus at 6:15pm). This 10-bed hostel, set in the country in the peaceful town of Preixan, will seem like paradise after the crowds in town. Sid and his Mum will offer you advice on the best hikes in the area, drive you to nearby pubs (free minibus lifts to Car-cassonne twice daily), or serve you cool lemonade in the garden. For privacy, book one of the four 2- to 4-person wooden cabins. Kitchen. Bikes €8 per day. 24hr. reception. Reserve ahead. Bunks €18; 1 double €38, cabins start at €40. ❷

Hôtel Le Cathare, 53 rue Jean Bringer (☎04 68 25 65 92; fax 04 68 47 15 02), near the post office in the lower town. This family-run hotel-restaurant offers clean, conve-nient accommodations. Older rooms are cheap, but the bright, well-renovated rooms are worth the extra money. Hallway shower. Breakfast €5. Reception daily 8am-mid-night. 3-tiny, aging singles for €19; renovated singles and doubles €21, with shower €29; huge triple/quad €45. MC/V. ❷

Hôtel Montmercy, 2 rue Camille St-Saens (☎04 68 11 96 70; le.montmercy@wana-doo.fr), right below the parking lot at the gates to the *cité*. Spacious, comfortable rooms equipped with satellite TV, phone, safes, and large bathrooms. Heated pool, jacuzzi, cafe, and quiet garden steps away from the *cité*. 5-year renovation should be com-pleted in 2005. Triples and quads are good for groups. For a splurge, stay in one of the palatial, flat-screen TV-equipped doubles overlooking pool. Breakfast €6.50. Reception daily 8am-8pm. Reserve ahead July-Aug. Unrenovated doubles €46; renovated doubles €62; luxury doubles €180; triples and quads €75-92. AmEx/D/MC/V. ❹

Camping: Camping de la Cité, rte. de Ste-Hilaire (☎04 68 25 11 77; cpllac-ite@atciat.com), has lots of wide open grassy—but shadeless—space across the Aude. From the lower town, cross Pont Vieux and turn right down rue du Jardin; follow the foot-path, past the sunflower field. (45min.) Or, take the shuttle from the train station (15min.; 5-9 per day, last one 6:33pm). English-speaking staff. Pool, tennis courts, snackbar, barbecue, and grocery store in modern, well-kept site. Karaoke, dancing nights, bike excursions, and darts tournaments. Internet €8 per hr. Reception daily 8am-9pm. Open mid-Mar. to early Oct. Mid-June to early July and late Aug. to mid-Sept.

€16.50 per site, €4.60 per extra person; early July to late Aug. €18.90 per site, €4.70 per extra person; mid-Mar. to mid-June and mid Sept. to early Oct. €13.50 per site and 1-2 people, €3.80 per extra person. Electricity €3.30. ❷

🗂 FOOD

The grassy and shady banks of the Aude, near the Pont Vieux, provide ideal sites for those wanting to **picnic.** Carcassonne's specialty is the inexpensive *cassoulet* (see **Cassoulet de Castelnaudary,** p. 600). There is a food **market** on pl. Carnot (open Tu, Th, and Sa 7am-1pm) and a **Monoprix supermarket** on rue G. Clemenceau at rue de la République. (Open M-Sa 8:30am-8pm and Su 9am-noon.) Restaurants on **rue du Plô** offer €8.50-10 *menus;* save room for dessert at one of the outdoor *crêperies* on **place Marcou.** Restaurants in the *cité* tend to close in winter. Simple and affordable options line **boulevard Omer Sarraut** in the lower city. Serving traditional French cuisine, **🔲Les Fontaines du Soleil ❷,** 32 rue du Plô, is one of Carcassonne's most lauded eateries. Much of this gourmet restaurant's charm lies in its a sunny courtyard, but the €9.50 weekly lunch *menu,* which includes a salad, *cassoulet,* and a pitcher of wine, also adds some budget appeal. Dinner *menus* are significantly more expensive—up to €45. (☎ 04 68 47 87 06. Open daily 11:30am-3pm and 7-10:30pm. MC/V.) **🔲 Blanche de Castille ❶** is a *salon de thé* next to the tourist office annex at the Porte Narbonnaise, serving what seems like the only frozen coffee in France (€3.50). Ice cream, *tartes* (€3.50), crêpes (€2-7), and *foie gras* with toast (€11.50) are served on a secluded terrace. Blanche's biggest secret, however, is its wide selection of teas (€2.90-3.30)—from jasmine to the more creative *thé des amants* (lovers' tea), with recipes guarded carefully by the owners. (☎04 68 25 17 80. Open daily 9am-8pm. MC/V.) **Le Bar à Vins ❶,** 6 rue du Plô, has snacks and *tapas* platters (€11) as well as a sizeable wine selection (€2 per glass, €13 per bottle), all served in a courtyard with a large outdoor bar and a laid-back atmosphere. Be sure to stop by late at night for the only real nightlife in the *cité.* (☎04 68 47 38 38. Open daily Feb.-Nov. 9am-2am. MC/V.)

🔘 SIGHTS

The entire *cité* (pop. 120), with its turrets, ramparts, and windy streets, is a sight in itself. The walls and **fortifications** date back to the first century, unsurprising since this hill above the sea road to Toulouse is a strategically valuable spot. After centuries of unsuccessful sieges, Carcassonne came under control of the French crown, and in 1844, it was restored by the controversial architect Viollet-le-Duc. The 52 **watchtowers** retrace the history of the fortified town from Roman times to the Renaissance. A *petit train* takes visitors around the ramparts (Apr.-Nov. 10am-5pm; €5, students €4); while a **calèche,** or horse-drawn carriage, crosses the drawbridge and goes inside the fortified town (€5.50, under 12 €4). Both tours depart from the main entrance of the *cité.*

Intended at the time of its construction in the 12th century to be a palace, the **Château Comtal,** 1 rue Viollet-le-Duc, was transformed into a citadel when Carcassonne submitted to royal control in 1226. In the 19th century, the castle went through a controversial restoration project, giving the towers cone-shaped roofs instead of preserving its medieval architecture. Entrance to the outer walls is free, but you can enter the château's inner walls only on a paid tour. The **Cour du Midi,** the first stop on the visit, holds the remains of a Gallo-Roman villa, once home to the troubadours for which Carcassonne's court was famous. The **Tour de la Justice**'s treacherous staircase, which ends in a dead end, was a stairway to heaven (or hell) for ill-fated invaders who rushed upstairs to find themselves trapped. At the red-brick **Tour du Four Saint-Nazaire,** 45min. tours in French and

English (mid-June to mid-Sept. 11:30am, 2:30, 3:30, and 4:30pm) take place daily. (☎ 04 68 25 01 66; fax 04 68 25 65 32. Open daily Apr.-Sept. 9:30am-6pm; Oct.-Mar. 9:30am-5pm. €6.10, ages 18-25 €4.10.)

The Romanesque nave and Gothic choir of the **Basilique St-Nazaire and St-Celse**, at the end of rue St-Louis, is an interesting juxtaposition of architecture. On a sunny day the 13th- and 14th-century rose windows on either side of the transept are especially eye-catching. From July to mid-September, during the **Estivales d'Orgue de la Cité**, organ concerts take place every Sunday at 5pm. (Open M-Sa 9-11:45am and 1:45-6pm, Su 9-10:45am and 2-4:30pm.)

The *cité* of Carcassonne is filled with small museums, most of which are kitsch shops in disguise. One exception is the **Musée de l'École**, 3 rue du Plo, in the city's old schoolhouse. In reconstructed classrooms, the museum displays a fascinating collection of historical textbooks, photographs, certificates, and letters from the late 1800s, when Jules Ferry made primary education free, compulsory, and secular. (☎ 04 68 25 95 14. Open daily July-Aug. 10am-7pm; Sept.-June 10am-6pm. €4, students €3, under 12 free.) Set in a medieval house, the **Maison Hantée** (Haunted House) is an entertaining way to experience the *cité*. (☎ 06 03 84 13 86. Open daily July-Aug. 10am-10pm; June and Sept. 10am-7pm; Oct.-May 10am-6pm. €6.)

The lower town—the **Bastide St-Louis**—was born when Louis IX, afraid enemy troops might find shelter close to his fortress, burned the houses that clung to the city's outside walls and relocated their residents, to whom he gave their very own walled fortifications and church. Converted into a fortress after the Black Prince razed Carcassonne during the Hundred Years' War in 1355, the *basse ville*'s **Cathédrale St-Michel**, on rue Voltaire, still sports fortifications on its southern side facing bd. Barbès. The church's back entrance opens into a small but meticulously kept garden. Don't miss the gargoyles snarling down from their high perches. (Open M-Sa 7am-noon and 2-7pm, Su 9:30am-noon.)

ENTERTAINMENT AND NIGHTLIFE

The evening is the best time for wandering the streets of Carcassonne's *cité* and relaxing in the cafes in **place Marcou**. Bars and cafes along **boulevard Omer Sarraut** and **place Verdun** are open until midnight. Grab a Guinness (€5.50 per pint) at **O'Sheridans**, 13 rue Victor Hugo off pl. Carnot, a friendly Irish pub filled with French and anglo crowds. (☎ 04 68 72 06 58. Live music Th and Sa. Half-priced whiskeys during daily happy hour, 6-8pm. Open daily 4pm-2am; in summer 5pm-2am. MC/V.) Nocturnal locals dance the night away at **La Bulle**, 115 rue Barbacane, the only club within walking distance of the *cité*. (☎ 04 68 72 47 70. €9 cover includes first drink. Open F-Sa until dawn.)

FESTIVALS

In July, the month-long **Festival de Carcassonne** brings dance, opera, theater, and concerts to the Château Comtal and the ancient amphitheater, both of which are known for having great acoustics. (Info and reservations ☎ 04 68 11 59 15; www.festivaldecarcassonne.com. €23-60.50, most shows €13 for students.) The **Festival Off** showcases smaller bands as well as mildly alternative free comedy and dance performances in the *places* of the *cité* and in the Bastide St-Louis. On **Bastille Day**, deep red floodlights and smoke set the entire *cité* ablaze in remembrance of the villages burned by the inquisitorial jury headquartered here in the Tour de l'Inquisition. The fireworks display is the second best in France. For two weeks in mid-August, the entire *cité* returns to the Middle Ages for the **Spectacles Médiévaux**. Locals dressed in medieval garb talk to visitors, display their crafts, and pretend nothing has changed in eight centuries. Every afternoon at 3 and 4:45pm, there is an equestrian show with mock jousting and pitched battles (July-Aug.; €10, children €5, under 7 free). Even non-French speakers will enjoy the nightly 9:30pm spectacle—a huge multimedia drama that brings the 13th century to life (mid-Aug.; €12, children €8, under 7 free). For ticket info, contact Compagnie Mystère Baiffe (☎06 12 54 83 75). During the **Fiesta y Toros,** horse shows, traditional dances, *abrivados* and *corridas* mark a week-long celebration of Spanish culture.

FOIX

Il était une fois (once upon a time, as French fairy-tales begin), the powerful counts of Foix decided to show their might by building a massive château overlooking their small village. Today, the magnificent château looks down on the marketplace below, cobblestoned streets lead through a maze of red-roofed houses, and nearby caves and grottoes still bear the marks of the pre-historic peoples who first settled the Ariège region. The city is a good base for hiking and kayaking nearby. Strongly consider renting a car—the Château de Montségur, pre-historic caves, and serene Ariège passes are served poorly by public transportation.

⊟⁊ TRANSPORTATION AND PRACTICAL INFORMATION. The train station (☎05 61 02 03 64), av. Pierre Sémard, is north of town off the N20. (Info and ticket windows open M 5:50am-12:20pm and 1:20-8:30pm, Tu-Sa 8am-12:20pm and 1:20-8:30pm, Su 8:15am-1:50pm and 2:20-10:20pm.) Trains go to Toulouse (1hr., 10 per day, €11.60). By bus, **Salt Autocars,** 2 rue des Cheminots (☎05 61 48 61 51), also runs to Toulouse (2hr., 2 per day, €8).

To reach the **tourist office,** 29 rue Théophile Delcassé, leave the train station and turn right. Follow the street until you reach the main road (N20). Follow this highway to the first bridge, cross it, take the second left and walk to the end of the street, about three blocks. The office provides a free small map and tons of information on exploring the region. (☎05 61 65 12 12; www.ot-foix.fr. Open July-Aug. M-Sa 9am-7pm, Su 9:30am-12:30pm and 2-6pm; Sept.-June M-Sa 9am-noon and 2-6pm.) For **police,** call ☎05 61 05 43 00. The **hospital** (☎05 61 03 30 30) is 5km out of town in St-Jean de Verges. For **Internet,** drop by the **Bureau d'Information Jeunesse (BIJ),** pl. Parmentier. (☎05 61 02 86 10. €2.50 per hr. Open M 1-5pm, Tu 10am-6pm, W and F 10am-noon and 1-5pm, Th 10am-noon and 1-6pm.) There is a **laundromat** at 32 rue de la Faurie. (☎05 61 02 72 15. Open daily 8am-8:30pm.) The **post office,** 4 rue Laffont, has **currency exchange.** (☎05 61 02 01 02. Open M-F 8am-7pm, Sa 8am-noon.) **Postal Code:** 09000.

⊓⊡ ACCOMMODATIONS AND FOOD. The best option for budget travelers is unquestionably the ▧**Foyer Léo Lagrange ❶,** 16 rue Peyrevidal. To get there, turn right onto cours Gabriel Fauré out of the tourist office and right again onto rue Peyrevidal just after the Halle Aux Grains; the *foyer* will be on your right. A cross between a nice hotel and a friendly hostel, it offers privacy and sociability in 22 clean 1- to 4-bed rooms, each equipped with a sink, desk, and private shower. Rooms facing the street in back have impressive views of the château. (☎05 61 65 09 04; fax 05 61 02 63 87. Kitchen available. Reception daily 8am-11pm; call ahead if arriving late. €15 per person.) Opposite the *foyer* is centrally located **Hôtel Eychenne ❸,** 11 rue Peyrevidal, which rents large rooms above a smoky but lively bar. (☎05 61 65 00 04; fax 05 61 65 56 63. Breakfast €4.60. Reception 8am-8pm; call ahead if arriving late. Singles and doubles with shower and toilet €40; triples or quads with shower €55. MC/V.) Classy **La Barbacane du Château ❸,** 1 av. de Lérida, is just past the flowered roundabout to the right on cours Gabriel Fauré, about 5min. from the tourist office. The price is reasonable for the elegance of mahogany, large beds, sparkling bathrooms, and glossed tables. Several rooms have excellent views of the château. (☎ 05 61 65 50 44; fax 05 61 02 74 33. Elevator. Breakfast €7. Reception daily Apr.-Oct. 7:30am-11pm. Singles and doubles €35, with bath €37, with bath, toilet, and TV €45-72. AmEx/D/MC/V.) **Camping du Lac/Labarre ❶** is a three-star site on a lake 3km up N20 toward Toulouse. Buses from Toulouse stop at the camp. From the train station, head left along N20 until you see the signs for the campground on your left. Rent canoes and kayaks from lakefront Base Nautique (half-day €8) down the street. (☎ 05 61 65 11 58; www.campingdulac.com. July-Aug. €7 per person, €17 for 2 people, car, tent, and electricity; Oct.-May €3.50 per person, €11 for 2 people, car, tent, and electricity; June and Sept. €5.50/€13.)

Foix's restaurants serve specialties of the Ariège region. Try *truite à l'ariègeoise* (trout), *cassoulet* (white-bean and duck stew), or the wonderfully messy *écrevisses* (crayfish). Restaurants with moderately priced local specialties line **rue de la Faurie.** For regular supplies, head to the **Casino supermarket,** rue Laffont. (Open M-Sa 9am-7pm.) On Fridays and the first, third, and fifth Mondays of the month, **open-air markets** sprout up all over Foix, with meat and cheese at the Halle aux Grains, fruit and vegetables at pl. St-Volusien, and clothing along the allées de Villote. (Food 9am-12:30pm, clothes 9am-4pm.) The star restaurant in town is undoubtedly **La Sainte Marthe ❹,** pl. Lazema, which exudes an air of mastery over every dish made with water-fowl. Menus featuring dishes like *foie gras, magret de canard,* and, of course, *cassoulet,* aren't cheap, but the array of culinary awards in the window make them seem like bargains. (☎ 05 61 02 87 87. *Menus* €22-51, *cassoulet* €16. Open daily noon-2:30pm and 7-10pm. AmEx/D/MC/V.) For good prices on regional food, try the casual **Le Jeu de l'Oie ❷,** 17 rue de la Faurie. €6.90 will get you a generous *plat du jour;* the three-course lunch *menu* (€9.50) allows you to sample the taste of local cuisine. (☎ 05 61 02 69 39. Open July-Aug. M-Sa noon-2:30pm and 7-10:30pm; Sept.-June M noon-2:30pm, Tu-F noon-2:30pm and 7-10:30pm, Sa 7-10:30pm. MC/V.) For those who want to escape the *cassoulet* glut, **l'Atlas ❸,** 14 pl. Pyrène, serves many varieties of couscous and *tagines* (a casserole of lamb and vegetables) under Moroccan tapestries and a vine canopy. (☎ 05 61 65 04 04. 3-course lunch *menu* €10. Open daily noon-2pm and 7-10pm.)

🔲 🔲 **SIGHTS AND EXCURSIONS.** The **Château de Foix,** the prototypical medieval castle, is unique for its collection of three stunning towers, all perched protectively on a high point above the city. The towers were built centuries apart. The round tower, from the 15th century, is a particularly impressive piece of architecture. Inside the well-preserved castle, a small part of the regional **Musée de l'Ariège** displays a collection of armor, stone carvings, and artifacts from the Roman Empire to the Middle Ages. After its glory days, the castle was used as a garrison and later a prison: inside the round tower, graffiti written by desperate prisoners is still legible. Be sure to take the free tour in English, which is full of historical details. After the tour, visitors haul themselves up the towers of the castle for an impressive panoramic view of the Pyrenean foothills. (☎ 05 34 09 83 83. Both open daily July-Aug. 9:45am-6:30pm; June and Sept. 9:45am-noon and 2-6pm; Oct.-May W-Su 10:30am-noon and 2-5:30pm. Included with admission are tours in French every hr. or 30min., in English 1pm. €4.20, students €3.10.) Down the hill at pl. St-Volusien, the 9th-century **Abbaye Saint-Volusien** pre-dates the château by a couple of hundred years. The streets radiating out from in front of it indicate its once-central location; in medieval times it dominated the religious life of the region. Now its large, simple interior, boasting a large organ, and a few large canvases are worth a visit. (Church open daily 8am-8pm.)

The Ariège region boasts some of the most spectacular **caves** in France. The **Grotte de Niaux** would be a stunning cave in its own right, but it becomes spectacular when lanterns illuminate the pre-historic wall drawings of bison, horses, and ibex that date from around 12,000 BC. Reservations are required to enter the cave. Twenty kilometers south of Foix, the grotto is only accessible by car. (☎ 05 61 05 88 37. Open daily Apr.-Oct.; Nov.-Mar. Tu-Su. €9.40, students €7.50, children €5.60.) An hour-long boat ride navigates the **Rivière Souterraine de Labouiche,** the longest navigable underground river in Europe. Six kilometers from town, the small metal boat cruises through galleries of stalactites and stalagmites, pulled along by wisecracking guides who can give the tour in both French and English. There is no public transportation to this site. Arrive before 3:30pm to avoid extreme crowds. (☎ 05 61 65 04 11. Open daily July-Aug. 9:30am-5pm (last visit); daily June and Sept. 10am-11am (last visit) and 2-5pm (last visit); Oct. to mid-Nov. Sa-Su 10am-11am (last visit) and 2-5pm (last visit). €7.50, children €5.50.)

FESTIVALS. From the end of July though the middle of August on weekends at 10pm, an extravagant medieval spectacle, **Si L'Ariège m'était Contée,** enlivens the area around Foix's château. Villagers wrestle bears, fight battles, and shoot off more fireworks than some major cities use on Bastille Day. (For info and tickets call the Théâtre de Verdure de l'Espinet ☎ 05 61 02 88 26. €10-23, students €5-12.) In the second week of July, the **Résistances** festival brings 100 art films—many of which premiere in Cannes—to Foix. (☎ 05 61 05 13 30; www.cine-resistances.com. €5 per film, €70 per week; students half-price.) There's also a **jazz festival** at the end of July, with concerts nightly at 9pm and jazz playing from speakers around the *centre ville* all day. (☎ 05 61 01 18 30; www.jazzafoix.com. €20 per night, students €15; weekly pass €120, students €60.)

VILLEFRANCHE-DE-CONFLENT

Deep in the mountains of the Conflent range lies the miniscule Villefranche-de-Conflent (pop. 230). For almost 300 years, the walled city kept an active garrison to protect the borders arbitrated by Louis XIV in the 1659 Treaty of the Pyrenees. Since its decline in military importance, the idyllic town has gained recognition for its impregnable fortress, preserved medieval ramparts, and nearby stalagmite caves. The gorgeous surrounding Pyrenees and their scenic mountain trails also make Villefranche a perfect base for hikers.

PRACTICAL INFORMATION. Buses and trains (☎ 04 68 96 63 62) run from Perpignan to the outskirts of Villefranche. (Buses: 1 hr., 7 per day, €9.60 or free with tourist pass; Trains: 50min., 8 per day, €7.10.) From the station, cross the bridge and bear right along the highway to reach the town center (5 minutes). Surrounding the city, the rampart walls have two open gates that lead to the town's parallel main streets. The left gate will bring you to the rue St-Jacques; the right gate opens onto the rue St-Jean. The **tourist office,** 32bis rue St-Jacques, has lodging info, free town maps, and sells IGN hiking maps for €9-11. When the office is closed, info and brochures can be obtained from the ramparts' booth. (☎ 04 68 96 22 96; fax 04 68 96 07 24. Open daily July-Aug. 10am-8pm; June and Sept. 10am-7pm; Oct.-Dec. and Feb.-May 10:30am-12:30pm and 2-5pm; closed Jan.)

Running 63km through the Pyrenees, the tiny *train jaune* links Villefranche to Latour-de-Carol (2½-3hr., 3-8 per day depending on the season, €16.50). The train runs over deep mountain valleys on spectacular viaducts, stopping at over 20 small towns along the way. From Latour you can either turn around and head back to Villefranche or switch to a regular train and continue on to Toulouse (2¾hr. from Latour-de-Carol, 6 per day, €20.10) or Barcelona. If you don't have too much time to spare, shorter scenic trips can be made for €3.20 and up. During the winter, the train also hauls **skiers** off to the fashionable **Font-Romeu** (30min., 3-8 per day, €9.80). Equipped with snow machines and chair lifts, this resort offers first-rate skiing. (**Tourist office** in Font Romeu ☎ 04 68 30 68 30). The *train jaune* does not take reservations, so arrive at the station at least an hour in advance (2hr. mid-July to mid-August) to ensure a spot. Children 4-12 are half-price.

⎵ ACCOMMODATIONS. Villefranche has few hotels, all of which fill quickly during the summer. Conveniently located between the village and the gare SNCF, ▨ **L'Auberge du Cèdre ❷** takes its name from the cedar tree that shades the front garden. The charming private house lets ten large, bright rooms, with TVs, antique furnishing, and individual baths. Some have sizeable balconies offering great views. The owner takes pleasure in cooking Catalan specialities for clients who opt for the *demi-pension* (€20). (☎ 04 68 96 05 05; fax 04 68 96 35 39. Breakfast €5. Reservations recommended. Singles and doubles €41; triples €56; quads €66. AmEx/MC/V.) The *mairie* (town hall) on pl. de l'Église rents out small studio apartments in the center of the village. All come with kitchens and antique furniture. However, to take advantage of these **gîtes communaux ❷**, you must stay for a full week (July-Aug. Sa-Sa, any one week period the rest of the year)—or at least pay the weekly rate. (☎ 04 68 96 10 78. Town hall open M-Tu and F 3-6pm. July-Aug. €155 for 2 people, €205-220 for 4-6 people; Sept.-June €130/€170-180.) If you succumb completely to the lure of the Pyrenees and the tiny *train jaune*, continue on from Villefranche to the stop Thuès Carança (30min., 5 per day, €5 from Villefranche). 15km from Villefranche, the *gîte-camping* **Mas de Bordes ❶** is perched beside a crumbling church in a canyon nook, right by a natural hot spring. (☎ 04 68 97 05 00. Supper €13. Small bungalows with kitchen access €10-35; camping €4 per person, €1 per tent.) The *gîte* is a 3hr. walk from an entrance to the **GR10**, the hiking trail which stretches from the Atlantic to the Mediterranean.

◧ ⛰ SIGHTS AND OUTDOOR ACTIVITIES. Built into the mountainside high above the town, the impressive **Fort Liberia** takes the form of two overlapping hexagons, meant to prevent attacks from the front and back of the building. The stronghold was constructed in 1681 by Vauban in order to protect Villefranche and the rest of the Catalan region from Spanish attacks, and was later fortified again by Napoleon III in the mid-nineteenth century. Vauban left towers to climb and *meurtrières*-filled passageways to navigate, but it is the view of the impossibly picturesque Villefranche from above that makes the trip worthwhile. There are actually only 826 steps in the subterranean "Staircase of 1000 Steps," which leads back down to the city. It remains the longest publicly accessible underground tunnel in the world. To reach Fort Liberia's fortified heights, hike 30min., catch the *navette* from the Porte de France (10min.; July-Aug. every 30min.; Sept.-June request at the St-Jacques info desk; round-trip €2.50, ages 5-11 €1.50), or climb the seemingly endless staircase built inside the mountain. Buy tickets at the info desk inside the town, next to the tourist office on rue St-Jacques. (☎ 04 68 96 34 01; fax 04 68 05 21 78. Open daily Apr.-Oct. 10am-8pm, Nov.-Mar. 10am-7pm. Guided tours every half-hour in July and August. €5.50, students €4.60, ages 5-11 €2.60.)

Accessible from the tourist office, the 11th-century fortified **ramparts** of Villefranche offer more bare rock passageways to wander around in. Be careful not to get lost in the maze of stone tunnels, as the endless walls and empty rooms all begin to look alike after a while. (☎ 04 68 96 16 40. Open daily July and Aug. 10am-8pm; June and Sept. 10am-7pm; Oct.-Dec. and Feb.-May 10:30am-12:30pm and 2-5pm; closed Jan. Guided visits in French July-Aug. 11am and 3pm. 1hr. cassette tour in English or French €3. Admission €3.50, students €2.50, under 10 free.) Created by an underground river ten million years ago, the magnificent site of the **Grandes Canalettes** reveals water-eroded galleries, stalactite-filled grottoes, underground lakes, and a bottomless pit—actually an underground cavity formed under the cave. In July and August, a sound-and-light show is held nightly in an auditorium located at the heart of the caves. (☎ 04 68 96 23 11; www.grotte-grandes-canalettes.com. Open daily mid-June to mid-Sept. 10am-6pm; mid-Sept. to Oct. and Apr.-June 10am-5:30pm; Nov.-Mar. Su 2-5pm. Guided tour and sound and light show (*son-et-lumière*) €11. €8, children €4.)

▓ **FESTIVALS.** Celebrated throughout the Catalonian region on June 23, the **Fête des Feux de St-Jean** burns brightly in Villefranche. Torches lit on the Canigou mountain return sacred fire to the village, where locals dance the traditional *sardane*, drink wine, and leap over bonfires. People dressed as giants appear in the village every Sunday in April in recognition of **Pâques.** Instead of Bastille Day, Villefranche-de-Conflent celebrates the **Fête de St-Jacques** during the third weekend in July with fireworks and traditional Catalan dancing.

The biggest festival in the area is in the nearby city of **Prades,** which for 23 years was home to the great Catalan cellist Pablo Casals during his political exile from Franco's Spain. The annual **Festival Pablo Casals,** from the late July through the middle of August, attracts international musicians for three weeks of chamber music and workshops. The **Bureau du Festival Pablo Casals** in Prades sells tickets. (☎ 04 68 96 33 07; www.prades-festival-casals.com. Open M-F 9am-noon and 2-6pm. Tickets €15-30, students €12-25, under 13 €7-13. *Pass* €250. MC/V.)

COLLIOURE

Collioure (pop. 2930) is nestled at the idyllic spot where the Pyrenees tumble through emerald vineyards and orchards to meet the shores of the Mediterranean. The rocky harbor of this small port captured the interest of Greeks and Phoenicians long before it modeled for Matisse, who baptized the town an artist's mecca in 1905. Matisse was soon followed by Dérain, Dufy, Dalí, and Picasso, who fell in love with Collioure's expansive sea and late afternoon sun. Today, tiny art galleries fill up the streets. On market days, fishermen and farmers offer organic products direct from the boat or the homestead.

▐▓ **TRANSPORTATION AND PRACTICAL INFORMATION.** The **train station** (☎ 04 68 82 05 89), at the top of av. Aristide Maillol, sends trains north to Perpignan (20min., 16 per day, €4.80). You can also travel south to Port Bou (30min., 7 per day, €2.90) and then catch a train to Barcelona (3¾hr., 5 per day, €12.10). The ticket office and info desk are open daily (6:40am-9pm). **Cars Inter 66** (☎ 04 68 35 29 02) travels to nearby coastal towns and Perpignan (45min.; 5 per day; €6.60, free with pass). X-Trem Bike, 5 rue de la Tour d'Auvergne, has good prices on **bike rentals.** (July-Aug. ☎ 04 68 82 59 77, Sept.-June 06 23 01 93 01. Open daily 8:30am-12:30pm, 1:30-2:30pm, and 6-7pm. Half-day €10, full day €18, week €85; €100 deposit.) Departing from pl. du Maréchal Leclerc, a *petit train* offers a 45min. tour of the vineyards up to Fort St-Elme and Port-Vendes. (www.le-petit-train-touristique.com. July-Aug. 10am-8pm. Departures every hr., Apr.-June and Sept.-Oct. 10am-6pm.) Taxis can be reached at ☎ 04 68 82 09 30.

To get to the tourist office from the train station, walk downhill on av. Aristide Maillol until you reach pl. du Maréchal Leclerc. Continue down along the canal and take a left onto pl. du 18 Juin. The friendly staff provides free maps of the town, a guide to hiking in the region (€5.50), and suggestions for 1-7hr. hiking trails. (☎ 04 68 82 15 47; www.collioure.com. Open July-Aug. M-Sa 9am-8pm, Su 10am-6pm; Sept.-June M 2-6pm, Tu-F 9am-noon and 2-6pm, Sa 9am-noon.) A **pharmacy** is on av. de la République. (Open M-Sa 9am-12:15pm and 3-7:15pm.) The **police station** (☎ 04 68 82 09 53) and the **post office** are on rue de la République. The post office **exchanges currency** without a commission and has **ATMs** outside. (☎04 68 98 36 00. Open M-Tu and Th-F 8:30am-noon and 1:30-4pm, W 8:30am-12:30pm, Sa 8:30-11:30am.) **Postal Code:** 66190.

ⒻⒸ ACCOMMODATIONS AND FOOD. Collioure fills its hotels and beaches to the brim during July and August. Don't bother looking for cheap accommodations: in the summer, the cheapest rooms are €35-45. The ⓈHostellerie des Templiers ❹ on av. Camille Pelletan (mailing address: 12 quai de l'Amirauté), a block away from the tourist office, is more than a hotel—it's a living museum. Since 1898, Templiers has accommodated famous artists like Matisse, Picasso, and Dalí, all of whom left original paintings behind. Tiled stairways lead to hallways covered top to bottom with over 2000 original paintings. The rooms come equipped with original works of art, TV, A/C, toilet, and shower. Two annexes offer cheaper rooms but fewer amenities. The post office annex, located on the central *place*, features modern rooms in white and blue tones; while the Colbert annex, right behind the main building, offers exquisite furniture and paintings. (☎04 68 98 31 10; www.hotel-templiers.com. Breakfast €6. Reception daily 8am-midnight. Wheelchair-accesible. Closed early Jan. to early Feb. July-Sept. doubles €62-75; quads €93-112; annex doubles €36-50. Apr.-June and Oct. €55-65/ €83-88/€34-47. Nov.-Mar. €46-55/€73-78/€39-41. AmEx/MC/V.) **Hôtel Triton ❸**, 1 rue Jean Bart, is in a bright pink villa on the waterfront. The charming rooms have A/C, TVs, soundproof windows, and showers for comparably low prices. The extra €10 for a balcony overlooking the seashore is well worth the splurge. From the train station, follow av. Aristide Maillol to pl. du Maréchal Leclerc and turn right over the bridge on rue de la République. At the small rotary, take a left on av. du Général de Gaulle and follow this street down to the beach. (☎04 68 98 39 39; www.aswfrance.com/hotel-triton. Breakfast €6. Reception daily 8am-7pm. Reserve ahead July-Aug. One double with shower €36, with toilet €48, with view of the sea €58; triples with toilets and a view of the sea €70; quads €80. AmEx/DC/MC/V.) **Camping la Girelle ❷**, on plage de l'Ouille, is a scenic 15min. hike from the town center. Nestled between two protective hills, the campsite is located on an idyllic beach. Restaurant, bar, and two hot showers available. (☎04 68 81 25 56; campinglagirelle.66@wanadoo.fr. Reception daily 9am-noon and 5-8pm. Open Apr.-Sept. and July-Aug. €19 for 2 people and tent; Apr.-June and Sept. €17. Electricity €3.80.)

Local produce is sold at a fantastic **market** centered around pl. du Maréchal Leclerc and spilling out along the canal toward the Château Royal. (Open W and Su 8am-1pm.) Reasonably priced *crêperies*, pizzerias, and cafes crowd **rue St-Vincent** near the port. For pre-packaged goods, head to the **Shopi supermarket**, 18 av. de la République. (Open July-Aug. M-Sa 8:30am-7:30pm, Su 8:30am-1pm and 4-8pm; Sept.-June M-Sa 8:30am-12:30pm and 3:30-7:15pm.) On bd. Boramar, the **San Vincens ❹** cafe provides cushioned chairs that spill out onto the rocky beach. Local seafood specialties include Catalan *bouillabaisse* (€21), paella for two (€35), and mussels with creamy garlic sauce (€9.50). The breathtaking view of the nearby mountains, harbor, and châteaux compensates for inflated prices. (☎04 68 82 05 12; fax 04 68 82 15 69. *Menus* €17-27. Open daily 9am-2am. Closed mid-Oct. to mid-Jan. AmEx/MC/V.) For an equally impressive view at a lesser price, try next door at the **Copacabana ❸**. This tourist-filled restaurant serves expensive seafood, but also some cheaper dishes. The oversized and surprisingly affordable *salade de crudités* (€7.50) should fill you up. Just make sure not to order a cocktail (€8.50) with your meal. (☎04 68 82 06 74; fax 04 68 82 24. *Menus* start at €17. Open July-Aug. 9am-2am; Apr.-June and Sept.-Nov. 9am-midnight.)

◪ **SIGHTS.** The **Église Notre-Dame des Anges,** whose foundations lie deep in the Mediterranean, is Collioure's most fascinating sight. This architectural wonder is characterized by its richly decorated side chapels as well as its monumental Baroque main altar. (Open daily 9am-noon and 2-5:30pm. €1 to light main altar. Free.) Extending from pl. du 8 Mai 1945 to the port, the hulking white stone **Château Royal** sheltered the kings of Majorca in the 13th century and was later fortified by both French and Spanish kings during the unending border wars. Every architectural element—from the shape of the towers to the design of the ramparts—was designed to guarantee the utmost protection. The walk over the ramparts takes visitors from the medieval castle to the 17th-century fortress. The château is worth a visit for its spooky underground tunnels and its spectacular view of the harbor. In summer, the main courtyard hosts a variety of performances. (☎04 68 82 06 43; www.cg66.fr. Open daily July-Aug. 10am-7pm; June and Sept. 10am-6pm; Oct.-May 9am-5pm. 1¼hr. tours in French and English available in the summer, other months by reservation. €4, students and ages 12-18 €2, under 12 free.)

A 30min. hike through the **Parc Pams,** behind the Musée d'Art Moderne, will give a good view of the 16th-century **Fort Saint Elme.** Back across the bay, a walkway built into the bottom of the cliffs continues for several kilometers along an isolated coastline and leads to the town of **Argelès.** Hikers can get info from the tourist office on these and other magnificent trails nearby.

To retrace the steps of Matisse and Dérain, follow the **Chemin du Fauvisme.** Masterpiece reproductions are displayed exactly where they were originally painted. The *chemin* begins and ends in front of the tourist office, where you can pick up a free map and itinerary. In the small ivy-covered Villa Pams on rte. de Port-Vendres, the **Musée d'Art Moderne-Fonds Peské** houses a modest collection of ceramics as well as a few paintings by minor 20th-century artists. (☎04 68 82 10 19. Open daily July-Aug. 10am-noon and 2-6pm; Sept.-June M and W-Su 10am-noon and 2-5pm; Oct.-May 10am-noon and 2-5pm. €2, students €1.50, under 12 free.)

Those with a taste for the harbor should stop by **Les Anchois Roque,** on the corner of av. du Général de Gaulle and rte. d'Argelès. Besides selling anchovies, the store allows visitors to watch them being prepared and to taste a series of anchovies preserved in vinegar with flavors like Catalan sauce and *provençal* herbs. (☎04 68 82 04 99. Open M-F 9am-noon and 2-5pm. Free visit and *dégustation.*)

◪◪ **OUTDOOR ACTIVITIES AND FESTIVALS.** The **Centre International de Plongée,** 15 rue de la Tour d'Auvergne, offers scuba lessons and rents underwater equipment. (☎04 68 82 07 16; www.cip-collioure.com. Initation lesson for beginners (ages 8 and up) €39, second lesson in the ocean €45, combined price for 2 lessons €75. 8-session course during July or August €250; ages 14 and up only. €21 per dive with scuba card, €26 per dive with scuba card and guide. Open Apr.-Christmas M-Sa 10am-noon and 3-7pm, Su 10:30am-noon and 5:30-7pm. MC/V.)

From August 14 to 18, the streets of Collioure fill with traditional dance and music for the **Festival de St-Vincent.** Midway through the folklore festival, on August 16, a **corrida** (bullfight) at the arena is followed by a fireworks display over the sea. Every Friday in July and August, Collioure rocks to the sounds of **Vendredis du Jazz.** Jazz concerts take place in both the castle and other venues.

PERPIGNAN

The hot and crowded city of Perpignan (pop. 105,000) is only a few kilometers from the transparent waters of the Mediterranean and 27 km from the Spanish border, but the distance feels much larger when you're stuck in the middle of this congested city. The Catalan influence permeates the town; brilliant "blood and gold" flags hanging everywhere. There is little to see or do in central Perpig-

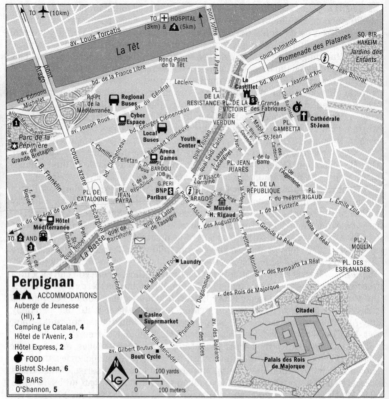

Perpignan

🏠🏠 ACCOMMODATIONS

Auberge de Jeunesse
(HI), **1**
Camping Le Catalan, **4**
Hôtel de l'Avenir, **3**
Hôtel Express, **2**

🍴 FOOD
Bistrot St-Jean, **6**

🍺 BARS
O'Shannon, **5**

nan, so a daytrip is plenty of time to experience the Palais des Rois de Majorque and the Cathédrale St-Jean, the city's two most interesting sights. However, with its cheap accommodations and friendly locals, Perpignan is a great base for visits to the more beautiful—and more pricey—Collioure or Canet-Plage.

▐ TRANSPORTATION

Flights: Aéroport de Perpignan-Rivesaltes, 4km northwest of the town center, just outside of town along D117 (info and reception desk ☎04 68 52 60 70; aeroport@perpignan.cci.fr). **Ryanair** (☎04 68 71 96 65; www.ryanair.com) offers the cheapest flights to **London** (€60 or more depending on date and availability). **Navette Aéroport** runs shuttles from the SNCF train station, pl. Catalogne, and the *gare routière* to the airport. (☎04 68 55 68 00. Around 5-6 per day, depending on the flight schedule. €4.50, ages 4-10 and groups €3.)

Trains: rue Courteline. Info office open M-Sa 8am-6:30pm. To: **Carcassonne** (1½hr.; 21 per day, change at Narbonne; €16.10); **Lyon** (5½hr., 4-5 per day, €43.70); **Montpellier** (1½-2hr.; 24 per day, change at Narbonne; €19.90); **Paris** (5hr., 4 per day, €74.80); **Toulouse** (3hr.; 22 per day, change at Narbonne; €24.50); **Marseille** (5hr., 6 per day, change at Narbonne; €35.40).

Buses: Regional buses depart the *gare routière*, 17 av. Général Leclerc (☎04 68 35 29 02) to: **Céret** (45 min., 8 per day, €5.90); **Collioure** (45min., 5 per day, €6.60); **Villefranche-de-Conflent** (1hr., 7 per day, €9.60). Office open M-Sa 7am-6:45pm. They also offer a **free tourist pass** good for 8 days within the *département*. Bring your passport and ride regional buses for free (non-renewable). From June to September, the **Cars Verts Voyages,** 10 rue Jeanne d'Arc (☎04 68 51 19 47), organizes **daytrips** to: **Carcassonne** (€23), **Andorra** (€27), **Barcelona** (€28-33), and the peak of nearby **Mt. Canigou** (€39).

Public Transportation: CTP, 27 bd. Clemenceau (☎04 68 61 01 13), runs **buses** throughout Perpignan and **shuttles** over to Canet-Plage. Tickets within Perpignan €1, *carnet* of 10 €7.80. First bus in any direction 6am, last bus around 8:30pm. Office open M-F 7:30am-12:30pm and 1:30-6:30pm, Sa 8:30am-noon.

Taxis: Accueil Perpignan Taxi (☎06 68 35 15 15), by the train station. 24hr. €2.30 starting fee, €1.24 per km. Around €12-15 to the airport, €20-25 to Canet-Plage.

Car Rental: Europcar (☎04 68 34 89 80) is located inside the train station. Car rentals from €296 per week with a €600 deposit. Cars can be returned elsewhere. 21+. Open M-F 8am-7pm, Sa 8am-noon and 2-6pm. AmEx/DC/MC/V. **Hertz** (☎04 68 61 18 77) rents cars at the airport. Cheapest car is €300 per week with a €730 deposit. Cars can be returned elsewhere. 21+. Open Su-F 8am-noon, 1-6:30pm, and 8:30-11pm, Sa closed during the late-night shift. MC/V.

Bike Rental: Bouti Cycle, 20 av. Gilbert Brutus (☎04 68 85 02 71). €38 for 5 days, €54 per week. 5-day min. rental. €120 deposit. Open Tu-Sa 9am-12:30pm and 2:30-7:15pm. AmEx/DC/MC/V.

ORIENTATION AND PRACTICAL INFORMATION

Perpignan's train station, once referred to as "the center of the world" by a rather off-center Salvador Dalí, is almost constantly packed with weary travelers, making connections to Catalonia, Spain, 50km to the south, and to the Pyrenees, where foothills begin rolling 30km to the west. The city itself stretches for a long way from the station, but most of the action takes place in the labyrinth of small streets in the heart of the *vieille ville*. The area makes a triangle, bounded on the far side by the regional tourist office, the **place de Catalogne** up the canal toward the train station, and the **Palais des Rois de Majorque** to the south. Avoid **Quartier St-Jacques,** near the intersection of bd. Jean Bourrat and bd. Anatole France, at night.

Tourist Office: Palais des Congrès, pl. Armand Lanoux (☎04 68 66 30 30; www.perpignantourisme.com), at the opposite end of town from the train station. From the train station, follow av. de Gaulle to pl. de Catalogne, then take bd. Georges Clemenceau to pl. de la Résistance. Go left on cours Palmarole and continue until you see a large glass-paneled building in the middle of the garden on your right. (20min.) Multilingual staff offers comprehensive tours in French (2½hr.; June-Sept. M and W at 5pm, F 10am; €4, under 14 free) and English (June-Sept.; Tu 5pm and Th 10am; same prices). The city can also be visited on a night tour, with music and dance animations (info ☎04 68 66 24 98; some July-Aug. Tu 9:30pm, €6). Tours available by reservation. Office open mid-June to mid-Sept. M-Sa 9am-7pm, Su 10am-4pm; mid-Sept. to mid-June M-Sa 9am-6pm, Su 10am-4pm. Branch at the Espace Palmarium on pl. Arago, in the center of town. Open June-Sept. M-Sa 10am-7pm; Oct.-May Tu-Sa 10am-6pm.

Laundromat: Laverie Foch, 23 rue Maréchal Foch. Open daily 7am-8:30pm. Wash €2.80-€6.50, dry €0.50 for 7min. **Clean Discount,** 60 rue Maréchal Foch. Open M-F 7:30am-7pm, Sa 8pm-7pm. €3.30 per piece of clothing.

Police: av. de Grande Bretagne (☎04 68 35 70 00).

Hospital: av. du Languedoc (☎04 68 61 66 33).

24hr. Pharmacy: The local newspaper *L'Indépendant* (€1.30), sold at every *tabac,* lists the rotating **pharmacie de garde.**

Internet Access: Cyber Espace, 45bis av. du Général Leclerc, facing the *gare routière* (☎04 68 35 36 29). Two floors hold 46 PCs equipped with games. €2 per 30min., €3 per hr., €9 for a 8am-1pm, 1-6pm, or 8pm-1am slot. Open July-Aug. M-F noon-1am, Sa noon-1am, Su 1-8pm; Sept.-June M-F 8am-1am, Sa noon-1am, Su 1-8pm. **Hôtel Méditerranée,** 62bis av. du Général de Gaulle (☎04 68 34 87 48). €4 per hr., after 9pm €2. Open daily 7am-2am. There's also **Arena Games,** 9 bis rue du docteur Pouce (☎04 68 34 26 22). €3 per hr. Open daily 3pm-1am.

Post Office: quai de Barcelone (☎04 68 51 99 12). **Currency exchange** with good rates. Cyberposte. Open M-Tu and Th-F 8am-7pm, W-Th 9am-7pm, Sa 8am-noon. Poste Restante: 66020.

Postal Code: 66000.

ACCOMMODATIONS AND CAMPING

Perpignan has many surprisingly affordable accommodations, making the town a great base to explore surrounding villages. The cheapest hotels are near the train station on av. du Général de Gaulle. From these hotels and the nearby Auberge de Jeunesse, it's only about a 10min. walk to the city center.

Hôtel de l'Avenir, 11 rue de l'Avenir (☎04 68 34 20 30; www.avenirhotel.com), off av. du Général de Gaulle. Colorful rooms, terraces, and a rooftop garden give the feel of a beautiful summer home, with furnishings and wall decorations painted by the jovial owner. Immaculate hallway bathrooms and shower. Breakfast €4.20. Shower €3. Reception M-Sa 7am-11pm, Su 7-11am and 6-11pm. Reserve ahead, especially in July-Aug. Singles €16; doubles and larger singles €19-23, with toilet €24.90, with bath €33.60; triples with shower €36.90; quads with shower €39.70. Extra bed €5.60. Except singles, all prices drop €1.50-2.30 mid-Sept. to mid-June. AmEx/MC/V. ❷

Auberge de Jeunesse La Pépinière (HI), allée Marc-Pierre (☎04 68 34 63 32; fax 04 68 51 16 02), on the edge of town between the highway and the police station. From the train station, go down av. du Général de Gaulle and turn left on rue Valette. At the end, turn right on av. de Grande Bretagne, left on rue Claude Marty (rue de la Rivière on some maps) before the police station, and right on allée Marc-Pierre. (10 min.) 6-8 small metal bunks are crowded into each room of this old stucco building. Most windows open onto the highway. Hostel's outdoor terrace provides a refreshing break from the somber bedrooms. Kitchen available daily 7:30-11am and 5-11pm. Breakfast €3.30. Sheets €2.80. Check-out 10am, strictly enforced. Lockout 10am-5pm. Closed mid-Nov. to late Feb. Bunks €9.10, €12.40 for non-HI members. ❶

Hôtel Express, 3 av. du Général de Gaulle (☎04 68 34 89 96). A block from the train station. Clean, functional rooms come with wooden floors and old furniture. The one quad is a good deal. Breakfast €4.50. Shower €2.50. 24hr. reception. Often full during the summer; call ahead. Singles €18, with shower €21; doubles €20, with shower €24, with TV €29-32; triples €37-43; quad €43. MC/V. ❷

Camping: Camping Le Catalan, rte. de Bompas (☎04 68 63 16 92; fax 04 68 63 34 57). Take the bus (dir: Bompas) from the *gare routière* and ask to be let out at Camping Le Catalan (15min.; every 30min., last bus 7pm; €1). 94 spots have access to a snack bar, pool, playground, and hot showers. Wheelchair-accessible. Laundry. Closed late Oct. to Mar. July-Aug. 2 people with car €14.90, extra person €4, electricity €2.45-3.05; Apr.-June and Sept.-Oct. €11.10/€3/€2.60-3.80. MC/V. ❶

◘ FOOD

Perpignan's best culinary feature is its reasonably priced restaurants, which serve Catalan specialties. If you've been waiting to try *escargots*, don't slither an inch farther; *cargolade* smothers your shell-wearing garden friends with garlic *aïoli*. The local *charcuterie* is also a must, with Catalan *pâté*. The specialty *touron* nougat is available in flavors like caramel, almond, and dried fruit. **Place de la Loge, place Arago,** and **place de Verdun** in the *vieille ville* are filled with restaurants and cafes that stay lively at night. Pricier options and candle-lit tables line **quai Vauban** along the canal, while **avenue du Général de Gaulle,** in front of the train station, has cheaper alternatives. A wide variety of fresh produce can be found at the **open-air markets** on pl. Cassanyes (open daily 7am-12:30pm) and pl. de la République (open Tu-Sa 7am-12:30pm and 4:30-7:30pm, Su 7am-1pm; M 7am-1pm fruits and vegetables only). Place de la République also holds an assortment of fruit stores, *charcuteries*, and bakeries, as well as the **Marché République.** (Open Tu-Su 7am-1pm and 4-7:30pm.) A huge **Casino supermarket** stockpiles food on bd. Félix Mercader. (☎04 68 34 74 42. Open M-Sa 8:30am-8pm.)

The best location in the city is held by the ▧**Bistrot St-Jean** ❸, 1 rue Cité Bartissol, which is set at the foot of the cathedral. Sit at a table next to the wall and enjoy a view of the 12th-century bell tower. Try their specialty, the *pause terroir* (€9.50), a hearty concoction of grilled bread smothered with cheese and toppings, including onions, potatoes, and anchovies. *La Tartine Saint-Jean*, topped with homemade *foie gras*, is also a treat (€11.50). An expansive *carte des vins* is also available. (☎04 68 51 22 25. *Menus* €17-19; *tartines* €9.50-11, meat and fish dishes €12-20, desserts €4-7. Open daily July-Aug. noon-2pm and 7-10:30pm; Sept.-June closed M-Tu. MC/V.)

◙ SIGHTS

A **museum passport,** valid for one week (€6), allows entrance to the Musée Hyacinthe Rigaud; the Casa Pairal; the Musée Numismatique Joseph Puig, 42 av. de Grande Bretagne (☎04 68 66 24 86); and the Musée d'Histoire Naturelle, 12 rue Fontaine Neuve (☎04 68 66 33 68). Purchase at any of the listed museums.

An uphill walk across the *vieille ville* brings you to the sloping red-rock walls of Perpignan's 15th-century Spanish **citadel.** Concealed inside is the 13th-century **Palais des Rois de Majorque,** where the kings of the short-lived Majorcan Dynasty (1272-1344) had settled. The thick walls, sparse openings, and high watchtower leave no doubt about their purpose. While the castle's main chambers are bare and generally unimpressive, comprehensive guided tours attempt to recreate life in the succession of chambers and antechambers. The Ste-Croix chapel, whose beautiful white and pink marble facade testifies to Italian, French, and Moorish architectural influences, is a notable exception. The palace's large courtyard serves as a concert hall throughout July, hosting a variety of plays and musical performances; tickets cost €12-49 and can be purchased next to the tourist office, at the Palais des Congrès. (Enter from av. G. Brutus. Palais ☎04 68 34 48 29. Open daily June-Sept. 10am-6pm; Oct.-May 9am-5pm. 1hr. French tours available every 30min. in summer, other times of the year if reserved in advance. Ticket sales end 45min. before closing. €4, students €2, under 12 free.)

Back in the *vieille ville*, the **Musée Hyacinthe Rigaud,** 16 rue de l'Ange, contains a small but impressive collection of Gothic paintings by 13th-century Spanish and Catalan masters, as well as canvases by Rigaud, Ingres, Picasso, and Miró. On the bottom floor is a painting by 5-year old Colette Pous, which Picasso compared to some of the most beautiful Fauvist works. (☎04 68 35 43 40. Wheelchair-accessible. Open M and W-Su noon-7pm. €4, students and ages 15-18 €2, under 15 free.)

Partly supported by a macabre pillar depicting the severed head of John the Baptist, the striking **Cathédrale St-Jean** is a paragon of Gothic architecture. Consecrated in 1509, the grandiose cathedral is characterized by its internal buttresses, an 80m long nave, and high cellars. Stunning oil paintings, colorful stained glass, and crystal chandeliers are designed in Renaissance, Baroque, and 19th-century religious styles. The 12th-century tower, once part of the Romanesque church nearby, houses a newly restored 46-bell carillon. (☎04 68 51 33 72. Open daily 7:30am-noon and 3-7pm. Su mass 8 and 10:30am.) Guarding the entrance to the city's center, **Le Castillet**, originally built in 1368 by the Spanish, was intended to repel French invaders. After the Treaty of the Pyrenees in 1659, the small castle was transformed into a prison and torture chamber for those who refused to acknowledge the victorious French crown. Now that relations between France and Spain are slightly less hostile, the Castillet is used to hold the small **Casa Pairal,** a museum of Catalan domestic ware and religious relics. Visit meticulous reconstructions of old Catalan houses as well as the giant statues of the King and Queen of Majorca guarding the museum entrance. The statues are paraded around Barcelona during Catalan festivals. The small, wind-swept platform on the top of the tower offers a panoramic view of the city. (☎04 68 35 42 05. Open M and W-Su May-Sept. 10am-7pm; Oct.-Apr. 11am-5:30pm. French guided tours in summer around twice a month; call for exact dates. Admission €4, students €2, under 15 free.)

🎵 🎎 ENTERTAINMENT AND FESTIVALS

Perpignan is a big city that keeps small-town hours. Everything seems to shut down by 8pm, and even the restaurants usher out their last customers around 10:30pm. If you're looking for a night on the town, prepare yourself for a calm and cafe-centric experience. A few bars, scattered in the tiny streets around the Castillet, keep a small crowd entertained until early morning hours. **O'Shannon,** 3 rue de l'Incendie, is Perpignan's quintessential Irish pub. From September to May, the place hosts occasional concerts by local bands. (☎04 68 35 12 48. Pint €6, half-pint €3.70. Open M-Sa 6pm-2am, Su 7pm-2am.) The open-till-dawn clubs lining the beaches at nearby **Canet-Plage** constitute the wildest nightlife, but unless you can make the night last until 6:50am, getting back to Perpignan will mean paying €20-25 for a taxi. In the summer, however, a **bus service** (€1 round-trip) runs every Saturday night between Perpignan and the clubs at Canet (buses leave from pl. Arago 12:40am, 1:40, and 11:40pm; return from Canet-Plage 1:10, 3:20, and 5:10am. Check with tourist office for most up-to-date schedules). In July and August, during the **Jeudis de Perpignan,** the town hosts free musical performances and traditional Catalonian dancing at various locations every Thursday from 7:30 to 11:30pm. **Procession de la Sanche** takes over the streets of the *vieille ville* on Good Friday in April. As in most of southwestern France, sacred fire is brought down from Mt. Canigou on June 23 for the **Fête de la St-Jean.** (☎04 68 35 07 60. Office open daily 5-8pm.) Known as the **Festa Major** (Main Fest), the two weeks surrounding the celebrated day are filled with traditional dancing, music concerts, and food tasting, culminating in a sound-and-light show. For two nights at the end of June, **La Fête des Vins** makes the entire town a little more jolly. Between bd. Wilson and the cours Palmarole, over 50 stands hand out wine samples. Cheese, *foie gras,* and Catalan lamb are also available. (☎04 68 51 59 99; fax 04 68 51 62 06. Empty glass at entrance €3.) Throughout the month of July, the **Estivales de Perpignan** brings world-renowned theater and dance to town. Recent performers have included Lambert Wilson. (Tickets €12-49, students and under 21 €11-29. Tickets can be purchased next to the tourist office, at the Palais de Congrès, online or by calling ☎08 92 70 53 05.) During the first two weeks in September, Perpignan hosts **Visa Pour l'Image**, an international festival of photojournalism which brings a large share of foreigners (☎04 68 62 38 00; www.visapourlimage.com).

◢ DAYTRIP FROM PERPIGNAN

LANGUEDOC-ROUSSILLON

CÉRET

Buses run from the train station and gare routière in Perpignan to the center of Céret (45min., 8 per day, €5.90). Pick up a schedule at gare routière office. (☎04 68 35 29 02. Open M-Sa 7am-6:45pm.) From the bus stop on av. Clemenceau, the tourist office, 1 av. Georges Clemenceau (☎04 68 87 00 53; www.ot-ceret.fr), is 2 blocks up the hill on the right. Make sure your bus stops in the town center—some buses stop about 2km from town, in which leaves a 20min. hike. The office provides a free map of hikes and gives tours in French and English by reservation. (Tours €3.50. Open July-Sept. M-Sa 9am-12:30pm and 2-7pm, Su 10am-1pm; Oct.-Mar. M-F 10am-noon and 2-5pm, Sa 9:30am-12:30pm; Apr.-June M-Sa M-Sa 9am-noon and 2-6pm.) The post office in the town center is open M-W and F 9am-noon and 2-5pm, Th 9am-noon and 2:30-5pm, Sa 9am-noon.

In the foothills of the Pyrenees, Céret blossoms in the spring. Each season the first cherries from its prized orchards are sent to the President of France. The town square is not just known for its cherry markets, but also for being the "Cubist Mecca," beloved by Chagall, Picasso, Manolo, and Herbin, and home to one of the best modern art museums in France. Céret also has many remarkable art galleries that sell works by these artists. Far enough into the hills to allow spectacular hiking, Céret has plenty to offer any naturalist or artist.

The ◪ **Musée d'Art Moderne**, 8 bd. Maréchal Joffre, is located up the hill from the tourist office. The collections in this modern glass building are composed primarily of personal gifts to the museum by artists including Picasso, Matisse, Braque, Chagall, and Miró. Rotating every three months, the temporary exhibits are usually minor during the off-season and superb from mid-June to mid-September. Although subject to change, the museum expects to house several galleries of Matisse's work in 2005. (☎04 68 87 27 76; www.musee-ceret.com. Open daily July to mid-Sept. 10am-7pm; May-June and late Sept. 10am-6pm; Oct.-Apr. M and W-Su 10am-6pm. Guided visits available daily July-Aug., year-round upon reservation; €3.50. Wheelchair-accessible. €5.50, students €3.50, under 12 free; more expensive for temporary exhibits in the summer.) According to legend, the **pont du Diable** (Bridge of Satan), which links the town center to its outskirts, couldn't be successfully built until the devil agreed to aid in its construction. Satan demanded the right to the first soul to cross the bridge, but the villagers foiled him by sending a sacrificial black cat across it. Back in the town center, the marble fountain situated in the middle of **place des Neuf-Jets** serves as a reminder of the town's dual Spanish and French roots. The Castillian lion that graces the top symbolizes France's 1659 victory over Spain. Other sights include the **Musée de l'Archéologie** (☎04 68 87 00 53; open daily July-Aug. 10am-noon and 1-6pm, Sept-June M-F 10am-noon and 2-5pm), the **Vieux-Céret**, and the single-naved **Église Saint-Pierre**, the largest baroque Church in Roussillon.

The weekend after Pentecost, Céret celebrates the **Grande Fête de la Cerise** with two days of cherry markets and Catalonian songs. Late in June, the **Querencias—Festival de Musique de Céret** features musical and dance performances. (☎04 68 87 00 53. Tickets €15, €25 for 2 days.) The most raucous *féria*, **Céret de Toros**, occurs every year for three days in the middle of July. During the boisterous festival, the town hosts two bullfights, and music livens the streets well into the night. (☎04 68 87 47 47; www.ceret-de-toros.com. Tickets €34-82 for each *corrida*, €27-56 for the *novillada*. Children under 14 get half-price tickets.) For five days toward the end of July, the **Festival de la Sardane** commemorates traditional Catalan folkdancing with concerts and processions through town. The festival culminates with the *"concours de Sardanes,"* where talented Sardane groups compete against one another in the annual dance tournament and amateurs practice almost continuously in the streets. (Entrance to contest €12.) In mid-September, the **Festa major de sant ferriol** brings long-distance runners to town for 6.5 and 20km runs. The two-day event also features a traditional market.

MILLAU

Located in a small valley between the Tarn and Dourbie rivers, Millau (pop. 25,000) originally put itself on the map as a Roman industrial center acclaimed for its sturdy red pottery. Several centuries later, the town shifted its focus to the production of fine leather and continues to export its handmade gloves to elegant shops in Paris and New York City. Visitors now come mainly for the town's gorgeous hiking trails, abundant mountain sports, spectacular views, and more recently, to see the famed viaduct, the soon-to-be world's tallest bridge. Positioned in the center of the idyllic Parc Naturel Régional des Grands Causses, the modern town of Millau provides a reasonably priced home base for nature lovers and adventure-seekers alike. Nearby, Roquefort's cheese factories and the canyons in Gorges du Tarn make perfect daytrips.

▣🛂 TRANSPORTATION AND PRACTICAL INFORMATION. Infrequent **trains** travel to: Béziers (2hr., 3 per day, €15.60); Montpellier (2½hr., 2 per day, €22.40); Paris (10hr., 2 per day, €59.60). Information and ticket desk (☎05 65 61 56 63) open daily 7am-8pm. More convenient **buses** run from outside the Millau train station to Montpellier (2hr., 6 per day, €14.40-15.60) and Toulouse (4hr., 1 per day, €23). The information desk is inside the train station. (☎05 65 59 89 33. Open M-Tu and Th 8:30am-noon and 2:30-6:30pm, W and F 8:30am-12:30pm and 2:30-6:30pm, Sa 9am-noon.) **Taxis** (☎06 73 00 53 58 or 06 85 74 05 07) are sometimes outside the train station. **Europcar**, 3 pl. Frédéric Bompaire, **rents cars.** (☎05 65 59 19 19; www.europcar.fr. Cars from €255 per week, €725 per month. 21+. Open M-F 8:30am-noon and 2:30-7pm, Sa 9am-noon. AmEx/MC/V.)

To get to the center of town, take a right out of the train station and walk a block down rue Georges Pompidou until you see rue du Barry on your left. As this street turns into rue Droite, you will find the **tourist office** on your left, at 1 pl. du Beffroi. The helpful staff makes hotel reservations and provides free maps. (☎05 65 60 02 42; www.ot-millau.fr. Open July-Aug. M-Sa 9am-7pm; Sept.-June M-Sa 9am-12:30pm and 2-6:30pm, Su 10am-12:30pm and 3-6:30pm; Oct.-Easter closed Su.) The tourist office also offers tours from the last week in June until the first week in September. (M 10am and Th 4:30pm. €5.) The **police** can be found at 14 rue de la Condamine (☎05 65 61 23 00), while the **hospital** is located at 265 bd. Achille Souquest. (Info ☎05 65 59 30 00, emergencies 05 65 59 31 35.) The **pharmacie de garde** is posted outside the tourist office or in the local *Midi Libre* newspaper. There is a **laundromat** at 14 av. Gambetta. (Open daily 7am-9pm. Wash €3-6, dry €0.50 per 5min., detergent €0.50.) The cheapest **dry-cleaning** service is at 66 rue Jean Jaurès. (☎05 65 61 16 28. Pants €5, shirt €4.60, dress €6.10. Open M 2-4:40pm, Tu-F 8:45am-noon and 1:45-7pm, Sa 9am-noon.) Get on the Internet at **Posanis**, 5 rue Droite. (☎05 65 60 68 53. €3 per hr.; photocopies €0.15 per page. Open M-Sa July-Aug. 10am-10pm; Sept.-June 2-10pm.) The **post office**, 12 Alfred Merle, has a **Western Union** desk and **ATMs**. It also offers **currency exchange** with good rates. (☎05 65 59 20 50. Open M-F 8am-7pm, Sa 8am-noon.) **Postal Code:** 12100.

ACCOMMODATIONS AND CAMPING. Most of the hotels in Millau are expensive and thoroughly unimpressive. One exception to the rule is the **Hôtel de Paris et de la Poste ❷**, 10 av. de Alfred Merle, across from the train station. This hotel's colorful rooms have antique furniture and large sunny windows. (☎05 65 60 00 52; fax 05 65 60 71 34. Breakfast €6. Reception varies, call ahead to assure a room. Reserve 1 week in advance in August. Singles and doubles €25, with shower and TV €35, with bath €38-42. Extra bed €6. MC/V.) Another good deal can be found at the two-star **Hôtel du Commerce ❷**, 8 pl. de Mandarous. From the train station, walk straight on av. de Alfred Merle and turn right onto av. de la République. The hotel is at the end of this street, on the fourth floor of a small office building. Although plain and nondescript, the rooms are clean and come with TVs, and the hotel is right in the center of town. (☎05 65 60 00 56. Breakfast €4.50. Reception M-F 7am-1pm and 3:30-11pm, Sa-Su 7:45am-1pm and 3:30-11pm. Reserve 1 week in advance in July and August. Singles and doubles €24.50, with toilet and shower €31, with toilet and bath €34; triples with toilet and bath €44; quads with toilet and bath €50. Extra bed €8. Wheelchair-accessible. AmEx/D/MC/V.) Those that reserve ahead may just be lucky enough to ensure a spot at the **Gîte de la Maladrerie ❶**, av. Louis Balsan. This small cottage offers homey 2- to 8-bed rooms with great views of the valley. Stop at the tourist office for a map, as the *gîte* is far from the center of town. (☎05 65 61 41 84 or 05 65 60 41 84; fax 05 65 60 26 02. Reception daily 6-8pm. Beds €10, plus €1 the first night.) There is also an **Auberge de Jeunesse ❶**, 26 rue Lucien Costes, on the outskirts of town. The hostel is located in a modern cement building, and boasts a pastel decor. Rooms are basic, but are equipped with refrigerators. (☎05 65 61 27 74; fax 05 65 61 90 58. Sheets €2.80. Reception M-Th 8am-7:30pm, F 8am-6:30pm, Sa 3-7pm and additionally Sa 7-9pm and Su 9-10pm for those who have reserved rooms in advance. 2- to 5-bed rooms €11 per person. HI members only.) For a night of luxury, check into the **Château de Creissels**, rte. de Ste-Affrique, a converted medieval fort.

There are also six campsites on the other side of the Tarn River, about 5min. from the town center. About 500m from the pont de Cureplat, the four-star **Camping Les Rivages ❶**, av. de l'Aigoual, is the best site in Millau. Catering to a wide range of interests, the shaded grounds offer two badminton courts, three ping-pong tables, two pools, three tennis courts, three squash courts, a volleyball net, a basketball court, a river beach, a playground, and a

IN RECENT NEWS

STANDING TALL IN MILLAU

At first glance, the sleepy town of Millau looks like many other mountain towns, but it now has another claim to fame as the site of the world's tallest bridge. When completed in early 2005, the bridge will span the Tarn Valley as a part of the A75 highway that connects Paris to Barcelona and the rest of Spain.

The viaduct spans 2.5km, and the roadway sits up to 270m above the valley floor. The tallest pillar is 340m, and when all the necessary additions are in place, it will stand taller than the Eiffel Tower (324m). In fact, the bridge is being built by the Eiffage Group, the same company that built the Tower over 110 years ago.

Many opposed the construction of such a large structure in the otherwise scenic mountain area, but Millau's mayor got the project pushed through, some say due to his friendship with French President Jacques Chirac. Construction has been costly, with a total price tag of €310 million. Nonetheless, the viaduct is set to ease traffic and even boost tourism as its grand presence draws engineering buffs and curious travelers alike.

(Visitor Center in nearby Cazalous, a 5min. drive from Millau on D992 (dir: Albi), with exhibits on the bridge construction. Tours are also available for €10; contact the tourist office in Millau.)

jacuzzi. (☎ 05 65 61 01 07; www.campinglesrivages.com. Reception daily July-Aug. 8am-9pm.; May-June and Sept. 8am-7pm. Open May-Sept. July-Aug. 2 people and tent with electricity €24, with water €26, 4-person mobile home €380-570 per week; late June and early Sept. €19.50/€20.50, 4-person mobile home €39-56 per night; May to mid-June and late Sept. €15.50/€17.50/€31-45. MC/V.)

🍴 FOOD. There is an enormous **Super U** on av. du Pont Lerouge, on the other side of the Tarn river. (Open M-Sa 8:30am-8pm, Su 8:30am-1pm.) In the center of town, there is a smaller **Petit Casino,** 11 av. Jean Jaurès. (Open M 3:30-7:30pm, Tu-Sa 7:30am-12:30pm and 3:30-7:30pm, Su 8am-12:30pm.) At pl. Foche, pl. Emma Calvé and pl. des Halles, **markets** provide fresh meat and vegetables (W and F 7am-noon). Selling over 100 varieties of cheese, **Le Buron,** 18 rue Droite, has a variety of pungent Roquefort and other regional cheeses among its crowded shelves. (☎ 05 65 60 39 88. Open M 9am-noon and 3-7pm, Tu-Sa 8am-12:30pm and 3-7:30pm. MC/V.)

Although more expensive than along the coast, restaurants in Millau offer gourmet food produced with fresh local ingredients and an abundance of Roquefort cheese. In the heart of the *vieille ville*, bd. and rue de la Capelle have a pleasing mixture of elegant restaurants and cheap pizzerias. **Le Chien à la Fenêtre ❶,** 10 rue Peyrollerie, serves elaborate *galettes* (€2-7.50) topped with salmon, cheese, or duck. For dessert, the sugary *crêpes* (€2-5.30) come with bananas, chocolate, coconut, and ice cream. The open kitchen lets diners watch their food being prepared. (☎ 05 65 60 49 22. Salads €3.20-7.50. Open Tu-Sa noon-2pm and 7-10pm. MC/V). **Mand-Arielle ❷,** 6 rue du Mandarous, serves filling portions of pizza (€5.80-7.80) and homemade pasta (€6.50-7.30) for the cheapest prices around. The €12 *menu* includes a drink, pizza, and movie ticket to the nearby cinema. (☎ 05 65 60 66 25. *Menus* €11-14, meat or fish dishes €6-11.20. Open daily July-Aug. noon-2:30pm and 7-11pm; Sept.-June closed Su lunch and M. MC/V.) The upscale restaurant **Capion ❸,** 3 rue Jean-François Almeras, serves regional specialties made entirely with locally grown produce. The delicious *foie gras* and duck breast come especially recommended. (☎ 05 65 60 00 91; fax 05 65 60 42 13. *Menus* €11-19, fish or meat dishes €10-16. Open M and Th-Su 9am-4pm and 6pm-midnight, Tu 9am-4pm. Closed the last 3 weeks in July. MC/V.)

🔷 SIGHTS. Occupying one corner of pl. Maréchal Foch, the interesting **Musée de Millau** displays local artifacts dating back to the pre-historic period. Fossilized dinosaur footprints and primitive skulls line the basement walls, including a giant reptile skeleton, while the top floor is covered with an extensive exhibit on glovemaking. The exhibit includes a film with sometimes graphic depictions of the process of turning animal skin into leather. (☎ 05 65 59 01 08; fax 05 65 61 26 91. Open daily July-Aug. 10am-6:30pm; daily May-June and Sept. 10am-noon and 2-6pm; Oct.-Apr. closed Su. €5, ages 19-25 €3.50, under 18 free.)

Three blocks farther down rue Droite, the ancient tower of the **Beffroi** looms high above the city. Originally built in the 12th century as a medieval *donjon*, the belfry remained an active prison until just after the French Revolution. Today visitors can wander through the ancient jail cells and observe the tower's enormous iron bell. A steep climb up the narrow, crumbling staircases leads to a breathtaking view of the orange roof tiles of Millau, and the surrounding mountains and plateaus. (July-Aug. guided visits at 10 and 11am, self-guided visits 2:30-6pm; late June and most of Sept. guided visits at 3, 4, and 5pm; Oct.-May open by reservation only. Guided tours €3.50, self-guided €2.50, under 18 free.)

The ruined Roman pottery factories are 2km from the city at **Gaufresenque.** During the 1st century BC, the red ceramic bowls and vases produced here were exported from England to India. Today, all that remains of this mighty industrial center are the low stone walls that outline the ancient town's foundations. (☎ 05 65

60 11 37. Open daily May to mid-Sept. 9am-noon and 2-6:30pm; mid-Sept. to Oct. and mid-Nov. to late Dec. 10am-noon and 2-6pm. €4, ages 19-25 €2.50, under 18 free. Combined ticket to the Gaufresenque and the Musée de Millau €6.)

☐ ※ ENTERTAINMENT AND FESTIVALS. The town of Millau does not offer much in terms of nightlife. Catering to an older crowd, several cafe-bars sprinkled at the ends of **boulevard de Bonald** serve drinks in a calm, subdued atmosphere. Farther from the heart of the city, the popular **Locomative,** 33 av. Gambetta, offers refuge for young locals and foreigners. Fondly referred to as "Le Loco," the bar hosts concerts every Friday year-round, and also every Wednesday in July and August. (☎ 05 65 61 19 83. Beer €2, other alcohol from €1.50. Happy hour Th 6:30-7:30pm. Open M-Sa 4pm-1am, Su 5pm-1am. MC/V.)

For six days in the middle of August, thousands of *pétanque* players from around the country fly to Millau to compete in the town's annual **Mondial Pétanque** tournament. In an effort to raise female participation, two days are now devoted entirely to women competitors, while the last day consists of a mixed gender tournament. The tournament is free to viewers. In the middle of July, the **Millau en Jazz** festival brings eight days of musical concerts. (☎ 05 65 60 82 47; www.millauen-jazz.net. Tickets €19 to one concert and €35 to three; sold at the tourist office.)

☒ OUTDOOR ACTIVITIES. The town's greatest asset is the beautiful **Parc Naturel Régional des Grands Causses** that stretches throughout the region and centers around Millau. Primitive humans first discovered this idyllic region over 200,000 years ago and left behind various carved statues and cave paintings as proof of their inhabitancy. Today the 315,000-hectare park offers excellent mountain trails as well as an unlimited number of sporting activities. The tourist office sells hiking maps (€9) and mountain-biking maps (€6.10), while the park's office, 71 bd. de l'Ayrolle, can answer any ecological questions you might have. (☎ 05 65 61 35 50. Open M-F May-Sept. 9am-12:30pm and 2-6pm; Oct.-Apr. 9am-noon and 2-5pm.)

Taking advantage of the park's natural beauty, companies fill Millau to the brim, advertising every sporting activity imaginable. Providing the largest selection in town, **Antipodes,** 6 pl. des Halles, organizes underground cave-climbing, mountain biking, ropes courses, rafting, kayaking, bungee jumping, and hang gliding. (☎ 05 65 60 72 03; www.antipodes-millau.com. Hang gliding €65 per person; bungee jumping €35; ropes course €10-18. Office open M 2:30-7:30pm, Tu-Sa 9:30am-12:30pm and 2:30-7:30pm. AmEx/MC/V.) **Horizon Millau Vol Libre,** 6 pl. Luciéne Grégoire, just off pl. Maréchal Foch, offers most of the same activities, but specializes in hang gliding. (☎ 05 65 59 78 60; www.horizon-millau.com. Hanggliding €50-65, 5-session initiation course €350. Office open daily July-Aug. 8am-noon and 2-6pm; Mar.-June and Sept. to mid-Nov. 10am-noon and 2-5pm.) **Organisation Roc et Canyon,** 55 av. Jean Jaurès, stands out from the masses by providing paintball for those with their own means of transportation. (☎ 05 65 61 17 77; www.roc-et-canyon.com. Paintball €23 per person; rafting €24; 5-8km kayak trip €17-20; 5-17km canoe trip €25-42; mountain biking €16 for a half-day; 50m bungee jumping €39; cave climb €29; 120m rock climb €34. Open daily mid-June to Sept. 8am-8pm; Oct. to mid-June 9am-6pm.)

☑ DAYTRIPS FROM MILLAU. Surrounded by herds of white goats, the small town of **Roquefort** (pop. 800) has become famous for its beautiful countryside and pungent blue cheese. Granted the sole right to produce cheese under the prestigious Roquefort label, the tiny village somehow churns out enough moldy goat milk to support the entire nation. This impressive feat is accomplished by seven main producers, the largest of which is the well-respected Société. Guided tours of the caves lead visitors to where the cheese is wrapped and stored on wooden shelves. After walking through a museum on Roquefort's history, the tour ends with a sampling of three cheeses. (☎05 65 59 93 30; www.roquefort-societe.com. Open daily mid-July to Aug. 9:30am-6:30pm; Sept. to mid-July hours fluctuate every few weeks, call ahead for specific times. 1hr. tour €3, students €1.60, under 16 free.)

In a similar presentation, the **Papillon** company, rue de la Fontaine, takes visitors through each phase of the cheese process and provides free samples. A documentary summarizes the effects of past political leaders upon the town of Roquefort and its famous product. (☎05 65 58 50 08; fax 05 65 58 50 31. Guided tours free. Caves open daily July-Aug. 9:30am-6:30pm; Apr.-June and Sept. 9:30-11:30am and 1:30-5:30pm; Oct.-Mar. 9:30-11:30am and 1:30-4:30pm.)

For information on moldy blue cheese, visit the **tourist office** on av. de Lauras. (☎05 65 58 56 00; www.roquefort.com. Open daily July-Aug. 9:30am-7:30pm; Apr.-June and Sept.-Oct. M-Sa 9am-6pm; Nov.-Mar. M-F 10am-5pm.) Although it is easy to find your way around the tiny town of Roquefort, getting there is a more difficult matter. Buses going in the direction of Toulouse can drop you off at Lauras, a town 3km away from Roquefort (25min., M-Sa 7am and 12:35pm, €4.80). From there, walk uphill through pastures while paying close attention to road signs.

A second worthwhile jaunt from Millau is a daytrip to the **Gorges du Tarn.** With its base only 10km away from Millau, the Gorges du Tarn slice dramatically through the rocky mountainside above. Considered to be a small, vegetated version of the Grand Canyon, the Gorges attract visitors with their natural beauty and plentiful water activities. The canyon is lined by several old villages, each a blur of red-tiled roofs and crumbling cobblestone streets. The farthest from Millau, **Ste-Enimie,** also happens to be the largest and most infused with tourists. At the intersection of Gorges du Tarn and Gorges de la Jonte, the tiny town of **Rozier** benefits from both the Tarn and Jonte Rivers. Closer to Millau, **Aguessac** and **Rivière-sur-Tarn** make beautiful 10-15km hikes.

The best way to see the canyon is to float right down the middle. On rte. des Gorges du Tarn in Aguessac, Escapade rents **canoes** and **kayaks,** among many other modes of transportation. (July-Aug. ☎05 65 59 72 03, Sept.-June 06 87 01 02 94; fax 05 65 59 08 70; c-escapade@wanadoo.fr. 7-14km canoe trip €22-27, 7-14km kayak trip €14-18. Open daily July-Aug. 9am-7pm; Sept.-June by appointment.) Another option is to rent **horses, ponies,** or **donkeys** from Ferme Equestre du Puech Capel, in Rivière-sur-Tarn. The stables take riders for short walks or long excursions lasting up to 15 days. (☎05 65 59 86 32; fax 05 65 60 41 74; ferme-de-puech-capel@wanadoo.fr. €11 per hr., under 6 €5 for 30min. Excursions €40 per day.)

For a change, the **Grotte de Dargilan** allows visitors to view its rock formations from the inside. The natural underground cave offers a mile-long trail of breathtaking stalagmites and rock columns. (☎04 66 45 60 20; www.dargilan.com. Open daily July-Aug. 10am-6:30pm; Apr.-June and Sept. 10am-noon and 2-5:30pm; Oct. 10am-noon and 2-4:30pm. Closed Nov.-Easter. €8, students €7, ages 6-18 €5.)

For a list of hotels and campsites, visit the **tourist office** on rte. des Gorges du Tarn in Rivière-sur-Tarn. The friendly staff hands out maps and lists of water activities. (☎05 65 59 74 28; www.ot-gorgesdutarn.com. Open daily mid-June to mid-Sept. 10am-12:30pm and 3:30-7pm; mid-Sept. to mid-June M-F 9am-noon and 2-5pm.) From Millau, **buses** run to the tourist office (25min., 1 or 2 per day, €3), as well as to the towns of Aguessac, Rozier, Meyrueis, and Ste-Enimie. Prices and travel time vary greatly depending on the distance.

MONTPELLIER

College town Montpellier (pop. 225,000), the capital of Languedoc, has rightfully earned its reputation as the most light-hearted place in the south. The city prides itself on a young, laid-back population of party-goers who enjoy year-round nightlife. Amateur theatrical and live musical performances sprout up on every street, academics and poseurs browse fabulous bookstores, and the city puts together a

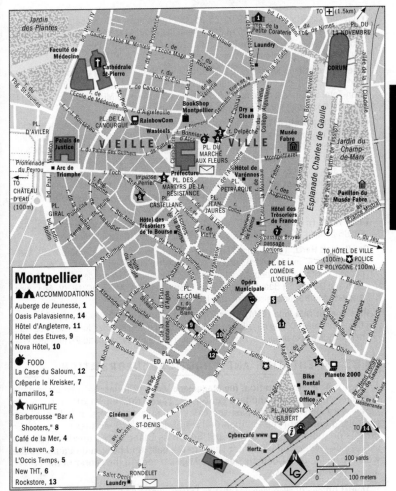

Montpellier

🏠🏠 ACCOMMODATIONS

Auberge de Jeunesse, **1**
Oasis Palavasienne, **14**
Hôtel d'Angleterre, **11**
Hôtel des Etuves, **9**
Nova Hôtel, **10**

🍴 FOOD

La Case du Saloum, **12**
Crêperie le Kreisker, **7**
Tamarillos, **2**

★ NIGHTLIFE

Barberousse "Bar A
    Shooters," **8**
Café de la Mer, **4**
Le Heaven, **5**
L'Occis Temps, **5**
New THT, **6**
Rockstore, **13**

vibrant annual avant-garde dance festival. Cafes on pl. de la Comédie, fondly known as *l'Oeuf* (the egg), sell expensive coffee with complimentary people-watching. Stores on every street cater to the trendy and the retro alike. Come sundown, students hit the bars around pl. Jean Jaurès and in the many streets of the *vieille ville*. The city floods with tourists during the summer, but the wide, tree-lined avenues and sunny streets maintain a relaxed and airy feeling.

▐ TRANSPORTATION

Flights: Planes take off from the **Aéroport Montpellier Méditerranée** (☎ 04 67 20 85 00; fax 04 67 20 86 44), in nearby Mauguio. **Air France** flies to London daily. Info office in the Polygone (☎ 08 20 82 08 20; www.airfrance.fr). **La Navette Aéroport** shuttles between the airport and the *gare routière* on rue du Grand St-Jean (20min., 13 per day, €4.80). Contact the TAM office (see **Public Transportation**) for a bus schedule.

Trains: pl. Auguste Gibert (☎08 92 35 35 35). Office open daily 5:15am-midnight. To: **Avignon** (1 hr., 12 per day, €13.30); **Marseille** (1¾hr., 12 per day, €21.50); **Nice** (4hr., 3 per day, €40.30); **Paris** (3½hr., 12 per day, €83.30); **Perpignan** (1½hr., 17 per day, €19.90); **Toulouse** (2½hr., 13 per day, €27.50).

Buses: rue du Grand St-Jean (☎04 67 92 01 43), on the 2nd floor of a parking garage next to the train station, access through track "A" in the station. Info office open M-F 7am-7pm, Sa-Su 7am-noon and 2-6:30pm. **Les Courriers du Midi** (☎08 25 34 01 34) travel to **Béziers** (1¾hr.; M-Sa 8 per day, Su 4 per day; €11.10).

Public Transportation: TAM, 6 rue Jules Ferry (☎04 67 22 87 87; www.tam-way.com), operates the local buses and a tramway that connects the city center to its outskirts. Trams every 10-20min. 5am-1am; buses less regular, only until 6-9pm. 1hr. tickets for trams and buses €1.20, 24hr. pass €3, weekly pass €11.20. Buy bus tickets from the driver and tram tickets from automated dispensers at the train stops. **Rabelais** connects the city center and the train station 9pm-1am. **L'Amigo** connects Corum (near the city center) to 12 popular night clubs on the outskirts of town. Buses leave Corum Th-Sa midnight, 12:45, and 1:30am, and return at 2:30, 3:30, and 5am.

Taxis: TRAM (☎04 67 58 10 10) wait at the train station. €1.24 per km during the day, €1.86 at night, €1.70 starting fee. €8-10 from station to hostel. 24hr.

Car Rental: Hertz, 18 rue Jules Ferry (☎04 67 58 65 18; fax 04 67 58 63 15). Walk along track "A" inside the train station and follow the signs from there. Cars from €237 per week, with a €620 deposit. 21+. Under-25 surcharge €25 per day. Open M-F 8am-1pm and 2-7pm, Sa 8am-noon and 2-6pm, Su noon-6pm. AmEx/DC/MC/V. **Ada, Avis, Budget,** and **National** also share this location.

Bike Rental: TAM Vélo (TAM), 27 rue Maguelone (☎04 67 92 92 67). €1.50 per hr., €3 per half-day, €6 per day. ID and €150 deposit. Electric bicycles for same price. Tandem bicycles also available. Open M-Sa 9am-7pm, Su 9am-1pm and 2-7pm. MC/V.

◾✦ 🛈 ORIENTATION AND PRACTICAL INFORMATION

Across from the train station, **rue Maguelone** leads to fountain-filled **place de la Comédie,** Montpellier's modern center. To reach the tourist office from the *place,* turn right and walk past the cafes and street vendors. It is behind the right-hand corner of the Pavillon de l'Hôtel de Ville (10 minutes). The *vieille ville* is bounded by bd. Pasteur and bd. Louis Blanc to the north, esplanade Charles de Gaulle and bd. Victor Hugo to the east, and bd. Jeu de Paume to the west. From pl. de la Comédie, **rue de la Loge** ascends to the center of the *vieille ville,* **place Jean Jaurès.**

Tourist Office: 30 allée Jean de Lattre de Tassigny (☎04 67 60 60 60; www.ot-montpellier.fr). Free maps and same-night hotel reservation service. Distributes the weekly *Sortir à Montpellier* and *L'INDIC,* a student guide published in October. **Currency exchange** with no commission. Wheelchair-accessible. Open July-Aug. M-F 9am-7:30pm, Sa 10am-6pm, Su 9:30am-1pm and 2:30-6pm; Sept.-June M-F 9am-6:30pm, Sa 10am-6pm, Su 10am-1pm and 2-5pm. Branch office (☎04 67 92 90 03) at the train station. Open July-Aug. M-F 9:30am-1pm and 2-6pm.

Tours: 2hr. city tours in English June Sa at 3:30pm; July-Aug. Tu and Sa 10:30am; Sept. Sa 10:30am. French tours depart daily Oct.-May 5pm. €6.50, students €5.50. There is a *petit train* that leaves from pl. de la Comédie, near the Gaumont movie theater. 30min. tours of the *vieille ville* given daily mid-June to mid-Oct. 2pm-7pm. €4.20.

Budget Travel: Wasteels, 1 rue Cambacérès, offers good plane, train, and bus prices. Open mid-Sept. to June M-F 9:30am-12:30pm and 2-6:30pm, Sa 9:30am-1pm; July to mid-Sept. closed Sa. Branch at 6 rue Faubourg de la Sauverie.

Currency Exchange: Banque Courtois, pl. de la Comédie (☎04 67 06 26 16; fax 04 67 92 65 49), exchanges money with no commission. 1.1% commission on traveler's checks. Open M-Tu and Th-F 9am-noon and 2-4pm.

English-Language Bookstore: BookShop Montpellier, 6 rue de l'Université (☎04 67 6 09 08). Browse bestsellers while sipping complimentary coffee. Open Sept.-July M-Sa 9:30am-1pm and 2:30-7pm; closed M in Aug. **As You Like It,** 8 rue du Bras de Fer (☎04 67 66 22 90; ayli@wanadoo.fr). Tea room. Open Tu-Sa 10am-6:30pm.

Gay Organization: RainbowCom, 2 rue Fournarié (☎04 67 91 20 75), supplies information about gay life in Montpellier and other towns in the south. They also write the free *IB News* magazine, which lists all upcoming gay events. Office open M-Sa 2-7pm.

Laundromat: Lavo Sud, 70 rue des Écoles Laïques. Open daily 7am-9pm. **Laverie Repasserie,** 12 rue St-Denis. Open daily 7:30am-9pm. For both: wash €3-6.80, dry €0.50 per 5min. There is also a dry-cleaning service at **Pressing Notre Dame,** 51 rue de l'Aiguillerie (☎04 67 60 67 38). Pants and shirts €5.20, dresses €8.80. Open M 2-7pm, Tu-Sa 8am-noon and 2-7pm.

Police: In the Hôtel de Ville (☎04 67 34 71 00).

Hospital: 191 av. du Doyen Guiraud (☎04 67 33 81 67).

Internet Access: On every street corner in Montpellier. Those listed are the cheapest options, but many offer comparable prices. Check the tourist office. **Cybercafé www,** 12bis rue Jules Ferry (☎04 67 06 59 52), across from the train station. €0.80 for 30min., €1.50 per hr. Fax, photocopier, and scanner available. Open daily 9:30am-1am. **Planète 2000,** 21 rue de Verdun (☎04 99 13 35 15 or 04 99 13 35 16). €1.80 per hr. Open M-Sa 9:30am-midnight, Su noon-midnight.

Post Office: Pl. Rondelet (☎04 67 34 50 00). **Currency exchange** with no commission. **Western Union** office. Open M-F 8am-7pm, Sa 8am-noon. Branch office at pl. des Martyrs de la Résistance (☎04 67 60 03 60). Open M-F 8am-6:30pm, Sa 8:30am-noon.

Postal Code: 34000.

ACCOMMODATIONS AND CAMPING

Except for the campsite, all listings are in the large *vieille ville*. The cheapest is the youth hostel, although several hotels offer great bargains as well. Search **rue Aristide Olivier, rue du Gal. Campredon** (off cours Gambetta and rue A. Michell), and **rue A. Broussonnet** (off pl. Albert I) for other reasonably priced hotels.

Nova Hôtel, 8 rue Richelieu (☎04 67 60 79 85; hotelnova@free.fr). From the train station bear left on rue de la République. Turn right onto bd. Victor Hugo, left onto rue Diderot, and right onto rue Richelieu. (5min.) Don't let the unappealing facade mislead you: this family-run hotel hides large, comfortable (if slightly worn) rooms. Breakfast €4.60. Reception M-Sa 7am-1am, Su 7am-11am and 7pm-1am. Reserve several weeks in advance in the summer, earlier in festival season. Singles €20.90; doubles €23.90, with shower €27.70-34.10, with bath and TV €35.85-40.85; triples with shower €40, with bath and TV €52.55; quads with bath and TV €60.40. 5% discount with *Let's Go.* AmEx/MC/V. ❷

Hôtel d'Angleterre, 7 rue Maguelone (☎04 67 58 59 50; www.hotel-d-angleterre.com), right off pl. de la Comédie. Perfect location between train station and the Oeuf means some of these sunny rooms overlook the busy street where tramways run late into night. Elevator, cable TV, and 24hr. bar justify slightly expensive prices. Breakfast €5.50. Reception 24hr. Singles with shower and TV €30; doubles with shower and TV €40, with bath €45. 5% discount with *Let's Go.* AmEx/DC/MC/V. ❸

Hôtel des Etuves, 24 rue des Etuves (☎/fax 04 67 60 78 19; www.hoteldesetuves.fr). From train station, follow directions to Novel Hôtel, then turn left off rue Richelieu and continue straight on rue des Etuves. Nice owner keeps 13 plain but comfortable rooms, all with wooden furniture and bath. Fax/email €1. Breakfast €4.20. Reception daily 7am-11pm, closed Su noon-6pm. Reserve 1 week in advance. Singles €21.50-28, with TV €33; doubles €34-36; triples €48-55. ❷

Auberge de Jeunesse (HI), 2 impasse de la Petite Corraterie (☎04 67 60 32 22; montpellier@fuaj.org). From the train station, go straight on rue Maguelone and across pl. de la Comédie onto rue de la Loge. Turn right on rue Jacques Cœur. Continue until the end of the *vieille ville.* Turn right on impasse de la Petite Corraterie, before bd. Louis Blanc. (20min.) Good location and prices almost compensate for unappealing dorms and bathrooms, and pesky 2am curfew. 90 beds in 2- to 10-person single-sex rooms. Pool table €2 per game. Internet €3 for 30min., €5 per hr. Breakfast €3.30. Lockers €0.50. Sheets €2.80 per week. Reception daily 8am-noon and 1pm-midnight. Lockout 10am-1pm. Reserve in advance, online reservations only. Dorms €8.90. MC/V. ❶

Camping: Oasis Palavasienne, rte. de Palavas (☎04 67 15 11 61; http://oasis-pala-vasienne.com). To reach l'Oasis, take the Tram (dir: Odysseum) to the Port Marianne stop. From there, switch to bus #17 and get off at Oasis Palavasienne in Lattes. (20 min.) 4-star campsite with sauna, gym, bar, and restaurant overlooking a beautiful swimming pool. In the summer, the site fills up with teenagers and young students. Free shuttle takes campers to nearby beaches and back twice a day at no charge. Bike rental €10 per day, €48 per week. Reception M-F 8:15am-12:30pm and 2:30-7:30pm, Sa-Su 8:15am-7:30pm. Mid-July to mid-Aug. €26; mid-Aug. to mid-July €17-23. Extra person €5/€2.50-3.50). ❷

🍴 FOOD

Montpellier has many friendly, reasonably priced restaurants. Standard French cuisine dominates the *places* of the *vieille ville.* Great bargains abound near the **rue des Écoles Laïques** with low-priced Greek, Egyptian, Italian, Moroccan, and Lebanese choices. Students frequent the eateries on **rue de Faubourg Boutonnet,** halfway between the *vieille ville* and the university. Morning **markets** set up daily at Les Halles Castellane, on rue de la Loge, and Plan Cabanes, on cours Gambetta. The excellent **supermarket INNO,** in the basement of the Polygone commercial center, just past the tourist office, offers great bargains. (Open M-Sa 9am-8:30pm.)

Crêperie le Kreisker ❷, 3 passage Bruyas, near pl. de la Comédie, serves over 50 tasty meal crêpes (€3.20-6.60) topped with buttered snails, mushrooms, artichokes, seafood, and bacon. Speedy, attentive English-speaking staff also dishes out large salads (€5.80-6.60), 30 types of dessert crêpes (€1.90-5.70), and a stunning choice of ice cream flavors. (☎04 67 60 82 50. Open M-Sa 11:45am-2pm and 7-11pm. MC/V.) Hip, unassuming **La Case du Saloum** ❷, 18 rue Diderot, serves authentic Senegalese dishes in a small dining room and quiet interior courtyard. Cuisine with a twist features such delicacies as veal with peanut butter sauce and "Tiapi," a grilled exotic fish. Knock yourself out with their specialty drink, ginger punch (€3), made from natural ginger, orange juice, and rum. (☎04 67 02 88 94. *Plats* €9, desserts €4. Open M-Sa 11:30am-1am. AmEx/MC/V.) Located in a blossoming town square, upscale **Tamarillos** ❹, 2 pl. du Marché au Fleurs, creates elaborate dishes garnished with fruit and flowers. Creative selections include *foie gras* with chocolate sauce and warm apples (€22). Vegetarian options are available upon request. If you can't make the splurge, try the lunch *menus,* which start at €16. (☎04 67 60 06 00. Appetizers €14-22, meat and fish dishes €16-25, desserts €11. Open daily noon-3pm and 8am-midnight. MC/V.)

⊙ SIGHTS

Built on a site where Molière performed between 1654-55, the gigantic **Musée Fabre**, at 39 bd. Bonne Nouvelle (☎04 67 14 83 00), holds one of the largest collections of fine art outside of Paris. Focusing on 17th- to 19th-century painting, the museum features works by Courbet, Ingres, Poussin, and Delacroix. Although the museum is closed for renovations until 2006, the small pavilion annex on the other side of Esplanade Charles de Gaulle continues to house temporary exhibits. Recent displays have included a tribute to French painter Zao Wou-Ki. (☎04 67 66 13 46; fax 04 67 66 09 20. Call in advance: hours and ticket prices vary with exhibits. 1st Su of each month free.) Right beside the pavilion, small **ponies** can be rented for a 10min. stroll around the Esplanade gardens for €3. (Open June-Sept. daily 2-8pm.)

The old city's pedestrian streets and bookstores as well as its sprawling pl. de la Comédie have some of the best entertainment in Montpellier. The secret courtyards and intricate staircases of 17th- and 18th-century *hôtels particuliers* hide behind grandiose oak doors. The **Hôtel de Varennes**, 2 pl. Petrarque, holds two small (and free) museums: the **Musée du Vieux Montpellier** on the first floor retraces Montpellier's history through furniture, maps, ceramics, and other artifacts (☎04 67 66 02 94. Open Tu-Su 9:30am-noon and 1:30-5pm; free); the second-floor **Musée Fougau** reconstructs 19th-century lifestyles in Montpellier (W-Th 3-6pm; free). The **Hôtel des Trésoriers de France**, rue Jacques Cœur, is occupied by the **Musée Languedocien**, the city's archaeological museum. (☎04 67 52 93 03. Open M-Sa Sept.-May 2-5pm, July-Aug. 3-6pm. €5.) The **Hôtel des Trésoriers de la Bourse**, 4 rue des Trésoriers de la Bourse, is notable for its quiet garden and 16th-century architecture. The tourist office distributes a walking guide to help visitors find the most impressive *hôtels*. Rue Foch, off pl. des Martyrs in the northwest corner of the old city, leads to the grassy **promenade du Peyrou**, which links the **Arc de Triomphe**, erected in 1691 to honor Louis XIV, to the **Château d'Eau**, the arched terminal of an aqueduct. Locals may tell you it dates back to antiquity, but it only just turned 100. Boulevard Henri IV leads to the **Jardin des Plantes**, France's first botanical garden. (Open June-Sept. M-Sa noon-8pm; Oct.-Mar. M-Sa noon-6pm. Free.)

If you're tired of sights and shopping, the sandy **plage de Palavas** provides a relaxing refuge. Take the tram (dir: Odysseum) to Port Marianne, switch to bus #17 or 28, walk from the *gare routière* in Palavas (20 minutes).

GAY MONTPELLIER

With its vibrant nightlife, Montpellier has become one of France's unofficial gay capitals.

1 **IB News** is a journal on the gay scene in southern France, and can answer any questions about the hottest beaches, bars, and buns.

2 Shop for club wear at **Le Village**, 3 rue Fornarié (☎04 67 60 29 05), a hip boutique.

3 **Le Renouveau**, rue Delpeche (☎04 67 63 33 49), is a gay-friendly restaurant with traditional French fare. Open M-Sa noon-3pm and 7pm-midnight, Su 7pm-midnight. MC/V. ❸

4 The terrace of **Café de la Mer** is ideal for people-watching over a post-dinner coffee. It's the unofficial rendez-vous point for gay partiers.

5 At **New THT**, the first gay bar in Montpellier, a crowd of young clubbers rock to disco.

6 **Le Heaven** serves the same crowd as THT, but with more drinking and less dancing.

🎵 🌼 ENTERTAINMENT AND FESTIVALS

The **Corum**, at the far end of Esplanade Charles de Gaulle, hosts weekly theatrical performances and concerts. (☎04 67 61 67 61. Office open M-F 8am-7pm. Operas and philharmonic orchestras €14-23, students and children €11-18; plays €8-46.50/€7-40.50. Prices can vary, so call ahead.)

During the last two weeks of June and the first week of July, the open-air **Printemps des Comédiens** arrives in Montpellier, featuring theatrical and dance performances. For details, contact the Opéra Comédie, pl. de la Comédie. (Info ☎04 67 63 66 67, reservations 04 67 63 66 66; www.printempsdescomediens.com. Tickets €6-21, under 25 and seniors €6-18.) From late June to early July, the **Festival International Montpellier Danse** organizes performances, workshops, and films on local stages and screens. (☎04 67 60 83 60, reservations 04 67 60 07 40. Tickets €3.80-27.50.) The rest of July is taken up by over 100 music performances in the **Festival de Radio France et de Montpellier.** (Info and tickets ☎04 67 02 02 01; www.festivalradiofrancemontpellier.com. Most concerts free; others cost €11-34, students and seniors €6-25.) For more than two decades, October has brought the **Festival International du Cinéma Méditerranéen.** Featuring over 250 films and related events, this international gathering brings close to 100,000 film-lovers every year.

🍸 NIGHTLIFE

The most animated bars are scattered along **place Jean-Jaurès.** At sundown, **rue de la Loge** fills with vendors, musicians, and stilt-walkers. The packed and popular ▨**Barberousse "Bar A Shooters,"** 6 rue Boussairolles, just off pl. de la Comédie, sells 73 different flavors of rum for €2 each. (☎04 67 58 03 66. Beer €3 and up. Happy hour 7pm-8:30pm. Open M-Sa 7pm-2am.) Montpellier's own brewery, **L'Occis Temps,** 2 impasse Perrier, near pl. des martyrs de la Résistance, serves homemade, all-natural beer inside a 13th-century cellar vault. From September to June, concerts draw student crowds. (☎/fax 04 67 54 59 96. Pint €5.40-€5.60. Happy hour for beer cocktails 6-8pm. Open W-Sa noon-2am, Tu 2:30pm-2am. MC/V.) **Fizz,** 4 rue Cauzit, is a hot live-music dance club. Foreign and local students meet each other on the first floor and dance closely on the second. (☎04 67 66 22 89. Beer €5.50, hard stuff €6.50. Cover F-Sa €8, includes one drink; Tu-Th free. Open July-Aug. Tu-Su midnight-4am; Sept.-June midnight-5am.) At the dance spot **Rockstore,** 20 rue de Verdun, a young crowd grinds to hip-hop on the first floor and gyrates to techno music above. The disco also hosts live concerts 3-5 times per week from Sept. to June. (☎04 67 06 80 00. Beer €2. Bar open M-Sa July-Sept. 6pm-6am; Oct.-June 6pm-4am. Disco opens at 11:30pm.)

There is vibrant **gay nightlife** in Montpellier. The best discos, including **La Villa Rouge,** rte. de Palavas (☎04 67 06 52 15 or 04 67 06 52 58), in Lattes, lie on the outskirts of town; L'Amigo buses (p. 632) are a good way to get there. Gay bars are sprinkled throughout the *vieille ville* (see **Gay Montpellier,** p. 635). Pre-party at **Café de la Mer,** 5 pl. du Marché aux Fleurs, known as the gay hub of Montpellier. (☎04 67 60 79 65. Open M-Sa 8am-2am, Su 3pm-2am.) **New THT,** 10 rue St-Firmin, off rue Foch, becomes very popular during the later hours. (☎04 67 66 12 52. No cover. Beer €3.10, straight liquor €5.40. 2-for-1 happy hour 8-10pm. Open daily mid-June to mid-Sept. 9am-1am; mid-Sept. to mid-June 8pm-1am.) Wilder **Le Heaven,** 1 rue Delpech, provides a perfect atmosphere for meeting men. (☎04 67 60 44 18. Beer €3, liquor €5.50. Open daily 9pm-2am.)

🔁 DAYTRIPS FROM MONTPELLIER

SÈTE

The train station, quai M. Joffre, sends trains to: Béziers (30min., 34 per day, €6.90); and Montpellier (20min., 34 per day, €4.70). Info office is open M-F 5:50am-7:45pm, Sa-Su 6:40am-7:45pm. Taxis wait at the train station. (☎04 67 20 49 00. €1.24 per km during the day, €1.82 at night, €1.07 starting fee. Approximately €7 to the hostel.) Sétoise buses shuttle passengers throughout town until 6:30-8:45pm. (☎04 67 74 18 77; 1hr. ticket €1.) Some lines don't run on weekend; pick up a schedule at the tourist office. Bus #2 goes from the train station to the tourist office; ask to get off at La Marine; to continue on to both beaches, get off at Les Quilles. If you need to walk, cross the bridge facing the station and take Ave. Victor Hugo. Then, make a left on quai Louis Pasteur and follow signs to office du tourisme and centre ville from there. (20 min.)

Strategically situated between the Mediterranean and the Bassin Thau, Sète (pop. 42,000), was founded in 1666 as a port town. It is now the largest Mediterranean fishing town in France. Its hybrid Italian-French culture, the result of an early 20th-century exodus from the Italian village of Gaet during the depression in Italy, produces unusual maritime festivals and the lovely *Sétois* accent made famous by folk singer Georges Brassens. Heavy machinery blots the otherwise picture-perfect shoreline, though there is a certain industrial poetry in the rusty ships and screeching gulls—appropriately enough, since the town gave birth to Paul Valéry, one of France's greatest modern poets. Nearby, the two local beaches offer a sunny respite from the bustle of everyday life.

Sète's **tourist office,** 60 rue Mario Roustan, behind quai Général Durand, provides €1 maps, free city guides, free accommodation services, and daily themed tours in French July and August, including a nighttime boat ride on the canal. In low season, audioguided tours of the city are available for €7. (☎04 67 74 71 71. Office open daily July-Aug. 9:30am-7:30pm; Sept-May 9:30am-6pm. **Currency exchange** open M-F 9:30am-noon and 2:30-6pm, Sa 9:30am-noon. Tours vary in price €4.50-10, children €2-5.) A *petit train* departs from quai Général Durand, taking visitors on a 30min. guided tour of the city. Longer themed visits are offered in the summer. (Daily July-Aug. 10am-11pm; Apr.-May and Oct. Sa-Su 2:30-5:30pm; daily June and Sept. 2:30-5:30pm. €4.50, children under 12 €2.50.)

🗋 **FOOD.** During festivals and holidays, *frescati* can be found on every dessert menu. The sweet raisin biscuit is soaked in rum and topped with a layer of coffee cream and soft meringue. Invented in Sète, *tielle* was originally given to fishermen about to embark on long sea voyages. The round pie contains octopus, tomatoes, and spices in a flaky crust. Vendors on the canal offer them for €2. The restaurants lining **Promenade J. B. Marty,** at the end of rue Mario Roustan near the *vieux port,* serve the catch of the day in unusual ways for €9 and up. Cheaper pizza, pasta, and seafood are the specialties of the less touristy eateries on **rue Gambetta** and its offshoots. The **Monoprix supermarket** is located at 7 quai de la Résistance. (☎04 67 74 39 38. Open M-Sa 8:30am-8pm, Su 8:30am-noon.) The **daily market** at Les Halles, just off rue Alsace-Lorraine, provides an abundance of fresh vegetables and fruits, local specialties, and fish freshly unloaded from the boat (5am-1pm).

☑ **SIGHTS.** The **Société Nautique de Sète,** on Môle St-Louis, at the southern end of town, is one of France's oldest yacht clubs. All summer, yacht races, including the famed **Tour de France à la Voile,** sail by the Môle. The best place to watch is in front of the cafe **L'American's Club.** The **plage de la Corniche,** in the southwest corner of town, starts off a 12km stretch of sandy beaches, accessible by bus #6 (departs from the Môle Saint-Louis July-Aug. daily 10am-7pm) and #7 (departs from the Hôtel de Ville year-round W and Sa 8:35-11:25am). Bus #2 stops a few blocks away from the beach at Les Quilles. (Departs from quai de la Résistance, the train station, and Pont de Pierre year-round M-Sa 7am-7:30pm, Su 2:30-7pm.) All buses are €1. The tourist office has a full list of beach activities, including **scuba diving, jet skiing,** and **sailboat rentals.** Sète Croisières offers **boat rides, underwater viewing,** and **fishing excursions** in July and August. (Quai Général Durand. ☎ 04 67 46 00 46; www.setecroisiers.com. 1hr. canal ride €10, ages 3-12 €5; 1-day excursion along the Canal du Midi or in Aigues-Mortes €29/€19; underwater viewing of oyster and mussel beds along the coast €13/€8; 4hr. sea-fishing trip with bait and equipment included €19, ages 8-12 €15. Reserve 2 days in advance.)

A walk to the *vieux port* and up the hill along rue Haute gets you to the **maritime cemetery,** on oasis of calm overlooking the sea that inspired Valéry's poem *Le Cimetière Marin.* The poet himself is interred here. (Open daily July-Sept. 8am-7pm; Oct.-June 8am-6pm.) The **Musée Paul Valéry,** rue François Desnoyer, retraces the history and culture of Sète since its 17th-century beginnings. The modern museum also pays modest tribute to French poet Paul Valéry. (☎ 04 67 46 20 98. Open daily July-Aug. 10am-noon and 2-6pm; Sept.-June M and W-Su. €4.60, Sept.-June €3. Students and children 12-18 €1.50, first Su of each month free.) From the museum, take the Grande rue Haute to reach the **Décanale Saint-Louis,** the oldest standing structure in town. Built at the end of Louis XIV's reign, the classical-styled church celebrated its 300th anniversary in 2003. (Open M-F 9am-noon and 2-6pm. Free 45min. guided tours June-Sept. 10:30am and 3pm. English tours upon request.) On the other side of the city is **L'Espace Georges Brassens,** 67 bd. Camille Blanc, a multimedia museum that pays homage to the irreverent folk singer from Sète. Brassens's grave can be found in the nearby **cimetiére le Py.** (☎ 04 67 53 32 77; www.ville-sete.fr/brassens. Take bus #2 or 3. Open daily July-Aug. 10am-noon and 2-7pm; Sept.-June 10am-noon and 2-6pm; Oct.-May. closed M. €5, students €2.)

If you're in good shape, climb chemin de Biscan-Pas from the hostel to the top of **Mont St-Clair** (183m) for a great view of Sète and the sea (15minutes). The church **Notre Dame de la Salette,** with wall murals from the 1950s, is the destination of fishermen's wives on a pilgrimage in late September for the **Feu de la St-Jean.**

🎵 🎭 **ENTERTAINMENT AND FESTIVALS.** Every evening the popular **Piano-Bar la Bodega,** 21 quai Noel Guignon, plays live music, from Brazilian jazz to hip-hop, and serves over 25 types of whiskeys and 100 cocktails. (☎ 04 67 74 47 50; http://webfrance.fr/la-bodega.htm. Open daily June-Sept. 10pm-4am; Oct.-May closed Su.) **La Dolce Vita,** 21 quai Rhin et Danube, offers dancing, and live music. (☎ 04 67 74 80 73. Open Tu-Su 10pm-3am.) At pl. Edouard Herriot, **Casino de Sète** opens its slot machines early for the morning gamblers. (☎ 04 67 46 65 65. 18+. Roulette and blackjack open Tu-Sa at 9pm. Piano bar daily July-Aug. 10:30pm; Sept.-June F-Sa 10:30pm. Casino open daily 10am-4am; Sept.-July M-F from 3am. ID compulsory.)

In the summer, Sète is festival-rich. For six days in late August, locals celebrate ◙**La Fête de St-Louis,** Sètes's major festival, with fireworks, concerts, dances, and street performances. The festival centers around the animated **Tournois de Joutes Nautiques,** in which participants joust from oversized rowboats. Arrive early to secure a spot on quai de la Résistance for the competition. On most other summer weekends at 2:30pm, gladiators from the various jousting societies stage exposition battles in preparation for the tournament. **La Fête de St-Pierre,** the first weekend in July, brings solemn religious rites in the morning, and loud festivities at night. On Sunday morning, during the **Bénédiction de la Mer,** fishermen invite the crowds onto their decorated boats and throw flowers into the water to commemorate those lost at sea. For five days in July, Sète draws a few big names to its annual jazz festival, **Jazz à Sète.** (☎04 67 51 18 11; www.jazzasete.com. Tickets €22-25, students €18-20.) Later in the month, the **festival de chanson francaise "Quand je pense a Fernande"** takes over town, drawing musicians from all corners of France.

ST-GUILHEM-LE-DÉSERT

Hérault Transport (☎08 25 34 01 34) sends buses from the Gare Routière in Montpellier to Gignac. From Gignac, take the bus to St-Guilhem (1hr., 2 per day, €5.10). Buses depart M-Sa 10am and 12:25pm, Su 10am and 11:05am. Your original bus ticket entitles you to a €1.30 discount on the connecting bus. Last bus returning to Montpellier leaves St-Guilhem for Montpellier at 5pm (4:40pm on Su).

With its dramatic cliffs and picturesque streets, **St-Guilhem-le-désert** (pop. 200) has been a favorite among tourists since the 19th century. Unlike what its name suggests, St-Guilhem is far from being a desert—as a matter of fact, the village suffers from giant floods. As outside visitors flock to town in the summer, local craftsmen open their tiny boutiques, selling anything from pottery to soap to candles. Despite the tourist frenzy, this perched hamlet is a pleasant—and very romantic—daytrip.

St-Guilhem's main attraction is the **Abbaye de Gellone.** Founded early in the ninth century by Charlemagne's cousin Guillaume, the abbey celebrated its 1200th anniversary in 2004. The Abbaye traces Romanesque, Gothic, Baroque and Classic architecture. For centuries now, pilgrims on their way to Saint-Jacques de Compostelle continue to make a stop at Gellone. Gilles Nicaise, a St-Guilhem native, offers highly recommended tours of the religious edifice (July-Aug. only). Unfortunately, much of the site remains in poor shape: floods have caused severe damage, but the biggest blow was the sale of Gellone's unique 8-gallery vaulted cloister around 1850 for a mere US$4000—now on display at the cloisters' museum in New York. (Open July-Aug. M-F 8am-12:15pm and 2:30-6:20pm, Sa-Su 8-10:45am and 2:30-6:30pm; Sept.-June M-F 8-11:50am and 2-5:40pm, Sa-Su 8:30-10:40am and 2:30-5:40pm. 1½hr. guided tours €2. Free.) The **Grottes de Clamouse,** 3km from the village, tour the flora and fauna of St-Guilhem's underground caverns. Make sure to stop at the tiny booth in the village for a €1.30 discount on the price of entry tickets. (☎04 67 57 71 05; www.clamouse.com. Open daily July-Aug. 10am-7pm; June and Sept. 10am-6pm; Feb.-May and Oct. 10am-5pm; Nov.-Jan. noon-5pm. 1hr. guided tour €7.50, students €5.50.) Those feeling sporty can kayak down the 12km rapids. **Kayapuna,** and a few other companies at the village entrance, offer similar services. (☎04 67 57 30 25. €42 to rent a 2-person canoe for 4hr., €20 for a 1hr. version. Cheaper with 24hr. reservations. ID deposit.)

If you plan to spend the night in St-Guilhem, the ◪**Gîte de la Tour ❶,** 38 rue de la Font du Portal, is your best bet. The simple attic rooms, with their dark wooden furniture, offer a kind of rustic charm. A kitchen is available for use by all guests. (☎/fax 04 67 57 34 00; gitedelatour@free.fr. Breakfast €5, dinner €11. Sheets €2.50. Dorms €11; doubles €24. MC/V.) **Le Petit Jardin ❷,** at the village's exit, is a convenient dining option, serving delicious regional dishes on a shaded terrace. (Open Apr.-Sept. noon-3:30pm and 7:30-11pm. *Menus* €9-23.)

From the bus stop in the parking lot, walk 100m uphill, past Canoé Rapide to the **tourist office.** Staff provides free English maps, a comprehensive town guide, and advice on trekking. Guided tours of the village and the abbey are available all year. (☎/fax 04 67 57 44 33; www.saint-guilhem-le-desert.com. Open daily July-Aug. 9:30am-7pm; Oct.-Mar. 10am-1pm and 2-5pm; Apr.-June and Sept. 9:30am-1pm and 2-6pm.) There's an **ATM** on pl. Gérard Calmel. Make sure to withdraw enough cash, almost no shops in Guilhem take credit cards.

PROVENCE

From its tiny vineyards that stretch into fields of sunflowers to vibrant North African fabrics and spices sold in its marketplaces, Provence greets travelers with picture-perfect views and a warmer welcome than the hottest days of July.

The secret to Provence's appeal lies partly in the diversity of its offerings. Roman relics are interspersed with Arabic food stalls, and artists continually find inspiration in Provence's varied landscape, including the astonishing red, yellow, and orange cliffs of the ochre hills; the jewel-green resort towns near Marseille; and the perfumed fields of lavender. Fierce *mistral* winds cut through the olive groves and tranquil fountains in the north, while pink flamingoes, black bulls, and white horses run free in the marshy Camargue (p. 685) to the south. With 2600 years of history, Marseille (p. 640) is France's second-largest city and an energetic melting pot of French, African, and Middle Eastern cultures. The former stomping ground of medieval popes, Avignon (p. 661) combines rich history with a lively arts scene and a world-renowned theater festival. Throughout the Lubéron and the Vaucluse, the smaller towns are most popular for their festivals and picturesque charm, though they also provide excellent bases for exploring the area's mountains and forests.

HIGHLIGHTS OF PROVENCE

THE ROOMS JUST KEEP COMING as you stroll through the **Palais des Papes** (p. 666), the monstrous Gothic palace built by the popes during their tenure in Avignon.

YOU MAY WATCH an unforgettable piece at the **Théâtre Antique** (p. 680) in Orange, but you can't take one home with you. Its wall is one of only three Roman stage walls still intact today.

LEAVE YOUR WHITE SNEAKERS BEHIND and walk through the Sentier des Ochres, where you can appreciate the red-orange of **Roussillon** (p. 673).

MARSEILLE

Marseille (pop. 800,000), France's second-largest city, is like the *bouillabaisse* soup for which it is famous, with a little bit of everything mixed in. A blend of color and commotion, the city that Alexandre Dumas once called "the meeting place of the entire world" remains an alluring center of international influence. Although Marseille does inherit a history similar to that of many French cities, complete with Roman ruins, crumbling forts, and traditional 18th-century art workshops, a walk through the side streets is punctuated by the vibrant colors of West African fabrics for sale in markets, the sounds of Arabic music from car stereos, and the smells of North African cuisine wafting out of hole-in-the-wall restaurants. A true immigrant city, Marseille offers a taste of both the ancient and modern cultures of the entire Mediterranean.

▐ TRANSPORTATION

Flights: Aéroport Marseille-Provence (☎04 42 14 14 14; www.marseille.aeroport.fr). Flights to: **Corsica** (**Air Littoral,** ☎08 25 83 48 34; **Air Lib Express,** 08 25 80 58 05); **Lyon** (**Air France,** ☎08 20 82 08 20); **Paris** (Air France and Air Lib Express). Shuttle buses (☎04 91 50 59 34) connect airport to Gare St-Charles every 20min. 5:30am-9:50pm, €8.50. Taxis from the *centre ville* to airport €36 during the day, €45 at night.

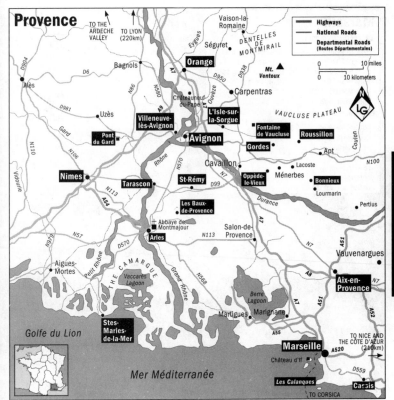

Provence

TO THE ARDECHE VALLEY
TO LYON (220km)

Vaison-la-Romaine

Eygues · Séguret

DENTELLES DE MONTMIRAIL

Orange

D950

Mt. Ventoux ▲

D38

Bagnols

A7

N86

N580

A9

Châteauneuf-du-Pape

L'Isle-sur-la-Sorgue

·Carpentras

VAUCLUSE PLATEAU

Alès

D904

D6

D981

·Uzès

Gard

N110

N106

Villeneuve-lès-Avignon

Pont du Gard

Rhône

Avignon

Fontaine de Vaucluse

Roussillon

Gordes

Coulon

·Apt

Légende:
— Highways
···· National Roads
▭ Departmental Roads (Routes Départementales)

0   10 miles
0   10 kilometers

N

LG

Vidourle

D975

N570

Cavaillon

·Lacoste

N100

Nimes ·

N113

Tarascon

St-Rémy

D99

N7

Oppède-le-Vieux

·Ménerbes

Bonnieux

·Lourmarin

·Pertius

A54

N57

D570

Les Baux-de-Provence

Durance

■ Abbaye de Montmajour

Arles

N113

Salon-de-Provence

A7

N7

A51

Vauvenargues

Aigues-Mortes

Petit Rhône

THE CAMARGUE

Vaccarès Lagoon

Grand Rhône

N568

Berre Lagoon

Martigues · Marignane

A7

A51

A8

Aix-en-Provence

N7

A52

Stes-Maries-de-la-Mer

Golfe du Lion

A55

A520

Marseille

TO NICE AND THE CÔTE D'AZUR (210km)

Château d'If ■

D559

Mer Méditerranée

Les Calanques

Cassis

TO CORSICA

PROVENCE

Trains: Gare St-Charles, pl. Victor Hugo (☎08 92 35 35 35). M: Gare St-Charles. Info and ticket counters open daily 4:30am-1am. To: **Lyon** (1½hr., at least 21 per day, €47.50); **Nice** (2¾hr., 21 per day, €24.50); **Paris** (3hr., 18 per day, €68). Baggage service open daily 7:15am-11pm (€3.40-7 per bag, held r up to 72 hours). **SOS Voyageurs** (☎04 91 62 12 80), in the station, helps tourists find lodgings and offers general assistance for any confused travelers. Open M-Sa 9am-7pm. Routes marked "car" on SNCF's schedule are serviced by buses.

Buses: Gare Routière, pl. Victor Hugo (☎04 91 08 16 40), near the train station. M: Gare St-Charles. Ticket counters open M-F 6:15am-7:30pm, Sa 6:30am-6:30pm, Su 7:30am-12:30pm and 1:30-6:30pm. **Cartreize** is an organization of local operators. Buy tickets on the bus (except to Nice) with exact change. To: **Aix-en-Provence** (every 20min., €4.70); **Arles** (2-3hr., 7 per day, €15); **Avignon** (2hr., 5 per day, €15); **Cannes** (2¼-3hr., 4 per day, €21); **Nice** (2¾hr., 1 per day, €22.50). **Eurolines** also makes international trips to destinations in Western Europe. Open M-Sa 9am-12:30pm and 1:30-6pm.

Ferries: SNCM, 61 bd. des Dames (☎04 91 56 32 00). M: Joliette. To: **Algeria** (24hr., €92-250); **Corsica** (12hr.; €35-53, students €20-40); **Sardinia** (20hr., €59-69/€50-€65); **Tunisia** (24hr., €144). Prices vary according to season and port of arrival. Open M-F 8am-6pm, Sa 8am-noon and 2-5:30pm.

PROVENCE

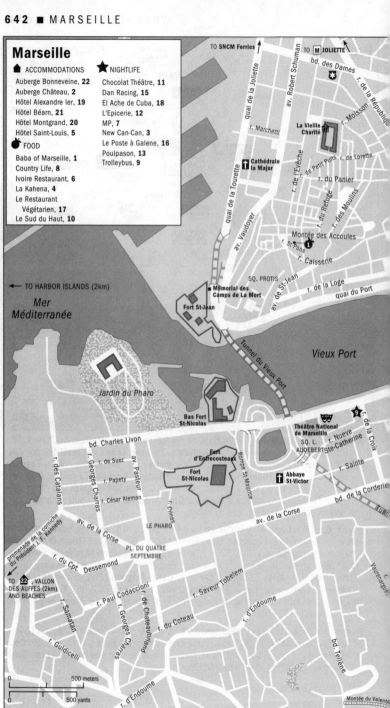

Marseille

ACCOMMODATIONS

Auberge Bonneveine, **22**
Auberge Château, **2**
Hôtel Alexandre Ier, **19**
Hôtel Béarn, **21**
Hôtel Montgrand, **20**
Hôtel Saint-Louis, **5**

FOOD

Baba of Marseille, **1**
Country Life, **8**
Ivoire Restaurant, **6**
La Kahena, **4**
Le Restaurant
  Végétarien, **17**
Le Sud du Haut, **10**

NIGHTLIFE

Chocolat Théâtre, **11**
Dan Racing, **15**
El Ache de Cuba, **18**
L'Epicerie, **12**
MP, **7**
New Can-Can, **3**
Le Poste à Galene, **16**
Poulpason, **13**
Trolleybus, **9**

TO SNCM Ferries

TO M JOLIETTE

bd. des Dames
quai de la Joliette
av. Robert Schuman
r. de la République
r. Moisson

La Vieille
Charité

r. Marchetti

Cathédrale
la Major

r. de l'Evêche
r. de Petit Puits
r. de Lorette
r. du Panier
r. du Refuge
r. des Moulins

quai de la Tourette

av. Vaudoyer

Montée des Accoules
r. St-Fons
r. Caisserie

SQ. PROTIS

r. de la Loge
quai du Port

Mémorial des
Camps de La Mort

av. de St-Jean

Fort St-Jean

TO HARBOR ISLANDS (2km)

*Mer
Méditerranée*

Tunnel du Vieux Port

Vieux Port

Jardin du Pharo

Bas Fort
St-Nicolas

Théâtre National
de Marseille
r. de la Croix
r. Nueve
SQ. L.
AUDEBERT Ste-Catherine

bd. Charles Livon

Fort
d'Entrecosteaux

Fort
St-Nicolas

r. Sainte

Abbaye
St-Victor

bd. de la Corderie

r. des Catalans
r. de Suez
av. Georges Charras
av. Pasteur
r. Papety
r. César Aleman
r. Chimas

Rampe St-Maurice

av. de la Corse

LE PHARO

promenade de la corniche
du Président J. F. Kennedy

r. du Cpt. Dessemond

PL. DU QUATRE
SEPTEMBRE

TO VALLON
DES AUFFES (2km)
AND BEACHES

r. Samatan

r. Guidicelli

r. Paul Codaccioni

r. Georges Charras

r. de Chateaubriand

r. du Coteau

r. Saveur Tobelem

r. d'Endoume

bd. Tellene

bd. de la Valenti

0   500 meters
0   500 yards

r. d'Endoume

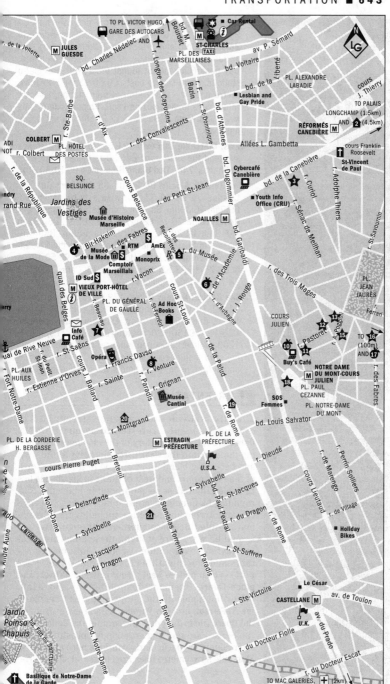

PROVENCE

TO PL. VICTOR HUGO,
GARE DES AUTOCARS

bd. M. Bourdet

ST-CHARLES
TAXI
Car Rental

av. P. Sémard

r. de la Joliette

JULES GUESDE

bd. Charles Nédelec AND

r. Longue des Capucins

PL. DES MARSEILLAISES

bd. Voltaire

av. de la Liberté

PL. ALEXANDRE LABADIE

cours J. Thierry

TO PALAIS LONGCHAMP (1.5km) AND (4.5km)

r. Ste-Barbe

r. F. Bazin

r. St-Dominique

bd. d'Athènes

Lesbian and Gay Pride

RÉFORMÉS CANEBIÈRE

ADI NOT

COLBERT

r. Colbert

PL. HÔTEL DES POSTES

r. d'Aix

r. des Convalescents

Allées L. Gambetta

cours Franklin Roosevelt

St-Vincent de Paul

r. de la République

rand Rue

SQ. BELSUNCE

cours Belsunce

r. du Petit St-Jean

bd. Dugommier

Cybercafé Canebière

bd. de la Canebière

r. Curiol

r. Adolphe Thiers

r. St-Savournin

Jardins des Vestiges

Musée d'Histoire Marseille

NOAILLES

Youth Info Office (CRIJ)

r. des Récollettes

Bir-Hakeim

r. des Fabres

RTM

AmEx

r. du Musée

r. de l'Académie

bd. Garibaldi

r. Sénac de Meilhan

quai des Belges

Musée de la Mode

Comptoir Marseillais

Monoprix

r. Vacon

ID Sud

VIEUX PORT-HÔTEL DE VILLE

PL. DU GÉNÉRAL DE GAULLE

r. Beauvau

Ad Hoc Books

cours St-Louis

r. Senac

r. d'Aubagne

r. F. J. Rouge

r. des Trois Mages

PL. JEAN JAURÈS

r. Ferrari

arry

Info Café

r. St-Saëns

cours J. Ballard

Opéra

r. Francis Davso

r. Venture

r. de la Palud

COURS JULIEN

r. Pastoret

r. Bussy

Buy's Café

NOTRE DAME DU MONT-COURS JULIEN

TO (100m) AND

r. des Fabres

PL. AUX HUILES

Fort Notre-Dame

r. du Petit St-Jean

r. Estienne d'Orves J. Ballard

r. Sainte

r. Paradis

r. Grignan

Musée Cantini

SOS Femmes

PL. PAUL CEZANNE

PL. NOTRE-DAME DU MONT

r. Venture

bd. Louis Salvator

r. Montgrand

ESTRAGIN PRÉFECTURE

PL. DE LA PRÉFECTURE

U.S.A.

r. Dieudé

cours Lieutaud

r. Perrin Solliers

PL. DE LA CORDERIE H. BERGASSE

cours Pierre Puget

r. Breteuil

r. Sylvabelle

bd. Paul Peytral

r. du Dragon

r. de Rome

r. de Marengo

r. de Village

Holiday Bikes

bd. Notre-Dame

r. E. Delanglade

r. Sylvabelle

r. Stanislas Torrents

r. St-Jacques

r. Paradis

r. St-Suffren

r. St-Jacques

r. du Dragon

Le César

CASTELLANE

av. de Toulon

Jardin Poinso Chapus

bd. Notre-Dame

r. Breteuil

bd. Notre-Dame

r. Ste-Victoire

U.K.

av. du Prado

r. du Docteur Fiolle

r. du Docteur Escat

Basilique de Notre-Dame de la Garde

TO MAC GALERIES, (2km)

PANIER PANNED

In June, a festival packs every square in Marseille's Panier district with music, dancing, and local cuisine, giving this tense, high-crime neighborhood a chance to relax and celebrate. But in summer 2004, Jean-Noel Guerini, president of the Conseil Général, was forced to cancel the event. Hundreds of tables remained empty; half-constructed concert shells were abandoned.

Guerini's decision came after protests over outside workers. In previous years, the city hired local workers to string lights and build stages. Additionally, well-known Panier inhabitants were recruited as a makeshift security force. Unfortunately, after several reports of stolen items and vandalism in recent years, 2004's committee decided to employ a professional Parisian task force to oversee the the year's festivities. Outraged, Panier locals threatened to set fire to restaurants and shops unless the workers returned to Paris. The Conseil Général eventually decided to cancel everything.

The silent squares in June 2004 characterize the many racial and ethnic issues at the forefront of French politics. Primarily Muslim and North-African, the often marginalized Panier inhabitants viewed the intervention as a slap in the face. With an already tenuous relationship with the city and the nation as a whole, this mixed *quartier* is still struggling to forge a common identity.

Public Transportation: RTM, 6 rue des Fabres (☎04 91 91 92 10). Office open M-F 8:30am-6pm, Sa 9am-12:30pm and 2-5:30pm. Tickets (€1.50) sold at bus and metro stations, or exact change on board. Day pass (€4) sold at tourist office, bus and metro stations. *Carte Liberté* costs €6.50-13 for 5-11 trips. **Metro** lines #1 and 2 stop at train station. Line #1 (blue) goes to the *vieux port* (dir: Timone). Metro runs M-Th 5am-9pm, F-Su 5am-12:30am. Tourist office has map.

Taxis: Marseille Taxi (☎04 91 02 20 20). Taxi stands surround the *vieux port.* €20-30 to hostels from Gare St-Charles. 24hr. **Taxi Blanc Bleu** (☎04 91 51 50 00).

Car Rental: Avis (☎08 20 05 05 05, from Gare St-Charles 04 91 64 71 00; www.avis.fr). Open M-F 6:30am-10:30pm, Sa 7am-8pm. **National/Alamo Car Rental** (☎08 25 16 12 12/☎04 91 05 90 86). Open M-F 8am-10:30pm, Sa-Su 8:30am-8pm. Both are located to the left of the main entrance to the Gare St-Charles. **Europcar,** in the Hôtel Ibis (☎04 91 50 12 76 or 08 25 35 23 52; www.europcar.fr). Call☎04 91 78 78 78 for road conditions.

Bike Rental: Holiday Bikes, 129 cours Lieutaud (☎04 91 92 76 04; www.holiday-bikes.com). M: Cours Julien. Bikes €12 per day, €65 per week; mopeds €25-120/€150-720; motorcycles €53-215/€300-1200. Helmet, unlimited mileage, maintenance, towing, and insurance included. Open Tu-Sa 9am-noon and 3-7pm, or any other time if you call ahead.

ORIENTATION

The city is divided along major streets into 16 *arrondissements,* referred to as quartiers. **La Canebière** is the main artery of the city center, funneling directly into the **vieux port** (old port) to the west and becoming bland urban sprawl to the east. North of the *vieux port* and west of **rue de la République** lies **Le Panier,** the oldest neighborhood in Marseille. Surrounding La Canebière are several *Maghreb,* or African and Arabic communities, including the African-market-filled **Belsunce quartier.** Although travelers should be wary here at night, these areas are great for daytime exploration. Upscale outdoor restaurants and chic nightlife cluster around the *vieux port* on **quai de Rive Neuve, cour Estienne d'Orves,** and **place Thiers.** Big-name fashion brands and small, pricey boutiques fill the shops along La Canebière, **rue St-Ferreol,** and **rue Paradis.** The areas in front of the **Opéra** (near the port) and around **rue Curiol** (near rue Sénac) are meeting grounds for prostitutes and their clients; be particularly cautious here after dark. Marseille's two metro lines are clean and simple. The bus system is much more thorough but complex—a route map from the tourist office helps enormously. Use the buses to access the beach and the *calanques*, which stretch along the coast southwest of the *vieux port*.

⁊ PRACTICAL INFORMATION

Tourist Office: 4 bd. de la Canebière (☎04 91 13 89 00; www.marseille-tourisme.com). Multilingual staff provides brochures of walking tours, free maps, accommodation booking, excursions, and RTM day pass for use on metro and bus lines. City tours daily at regular intervals, €16 by bus and €5 by open-car train. Open July-Aug. M-Sa 9am-7:30pm, Su 10am-6pm; Oct.-June M-Sa 9am-7pm, Su and holidays 10am-5pm. Annex (☎04 91 50 59 18) at train station. Open daily 10am-6pm, Sa-Su closed 3-4pm.

Consulates: UK, 24 av. du Prado (☎04 91 15 72 10). **US,** 12 bd. Paul Peytral (☎04 91 54 92 00). Both open by appt. M-F 9am-noon and 2-5pm.

Currency Exchange: ID SUD, 3 pl. Général de Gaulle (☎04 91 13 09 00). Open M-F 9am-6pm, Sa 9am-5:30pm. **Comptoir Marseillais de Bourse,** 22 bd. de la Canebière (☎04 91 54 93 94). Only accepts traveler's checks and cash. Open M-Sa 9am-6pm. Both with good rates and no commission. **ATMs** line rue Canebière.

American Express, 39 bd. de la Canebière (☎04 91 13 71 21), located in Afat Voyages. Open M-F 9am-5:30pm, Sa 9am-noon and 2-5pm.

English-Language Bookstore: Ad Hoc Books, 8 rue Pisançon (☎04 91 33 51 92; ad.hoc.books@wanadoo.fr). Open M-Sa 10am-7pm. Small but well-stocked English-language bookstore tucked on a side street off cours St-Louis.

Cultural Center: L'Espace Culture, 42 rue de la Canebière (☎04 96 11 04 60; www.espaceculture.net). Provides detailed information on current cultural events, from the major festivals to the most obscure independent performances. A knowledgeable staff can help visitors book tickets at many performances. Open M-Sa 10am-6:45pm.

Gay Support: Lesbian & Gay Pride, 8 bd. de la Liberté (☎04 95 08 21 72).

Youth Information: Centre Régional Information Jeunesse, 96 La Canebière (☎04 91 24 33 50; www.crijpa.com). Info on sports, short-term employment, leisure activities, vacation planning, and services for the disabled. Bulletin board advertises baby-sitters and other personal notices. Open July-Aug. M-F 9am-1pm; Sept.-June M and W-F 10am-5pm, Tu 1-5pm. **CROUS,** 42 rue du 141ème R.I.A. (☎04 91 62 83 60), has info on housing, work, and travel. Open M-F 9am-12:30pm and 1:30-4:30pm.

Laundromat: Point Laverie, 56 bd. de la Libération and 6 rue Méry. Wash €3.50-7, dry €0.60 per 6min. Open daily 7am-8pm. Also at 8 rue Breteuil. Open daily 6:30am-8pm.

Police: 2 rue du Commissaire Becker (☎04 91 39 80 00). Also in the train station on esplanade St-Charles (☎04 91 14 29 97).

Traveler Emergency: SOS Traveler, Gare St-Charles (☎04 91 62 12 80). **Lost and Found** (☎04 91 90 99 37). Open M-F 8am-2pm.

Crisis Line: SOS Femmes, 30 rue Nationale (☎04 91 90 79 07), a rape hotline. 24hr.

Pharmacy: Pharmacie le Cours Saint-Louis, 5 cours Saint-Louis (☎04 91 54 04 58). Open daily 8:30am-7:30pm. Serves as 1 of 5 rotating **pharmacies de garde;** check pharmacy windows, the front page of *La Provence,* or with the police for up-to-date info.

Hospital: Hôpital Timone, 246 rue Saint Pierre (☎04 91 38 60 00). M: Timone. **SOS Médecins** (☎04 91 52 91 52) and **SOS Dentist** (☎04 91 85 39 39) have on-call doctors.

Poison Control: ☎04 91 90 79 07.

Internet Access: Cyber Café de la Canebière, 87 rue de la Canebière (☎04 91 05 94 24). €2 per hr. Open daily 8:30am-11pm. **Info Café,** 1 quai Rive Neuve (☎04 91 33 53 05). €3.80 per hr. Open M-Sa 9am-10pm.

PROVENCE

Post Office: 1 pl. Hôtel des Postes (☎04 91 15 47 00). Follow rue de la Canebière toward the sea and turn right on rue Reine Elisabeth as it becomes pl. Hôtel des Postes. **Currency exchange** at this branch only. Open M-F 8am-7pm, Sa 8am-noon. Branch office at 13 cours Jean Ballard (☎04 96 11 23 60), just off the quai des Belges. **Postal Code:** 13001.

ACCOMMODATIONS

Marseille has a range of hotel options, from pricey three- and four-star hotels sprinkled throughout the *vieux port* to the less reputable but temptingly cheap options in the *quartier* Belsunce. Some hostels are located far from the city center, offering an escape from traffic and noise, but infrequent bus service make them less accessible. On weekends and in the summer; call at least a week in advance. Signs posted throughout the city provide directions to the major hotels.

Hôtel Saint-Louis, 2 rue des Recollettes (☎04 91 54 02 74; www.hotel-st-louis.com). Brightly painted, spacious rooms match a cheerful lobby just off busy rue de la Canebière. Nearly all with satellite TV. Wireless Internet access throughout the building, free Internet kiosk in lobby. Breakfast €5, in bed €6. Reception 24hr. Singles €32; doubles with bath €40-49; triples €57. Extra bed €7. AmEx/V. ❸

Hôtel Montgrand, 50 rue Montgrand (☎04 91 00 35 20; www.hotel-montgrand-marseille.com). Proximity to the *vieux port* and soundproof rooms make this newly renovated hotel a great choice for those staying in Marseille. Chatty, gracious husband-and-wife team ensures that the bright, comfortable rooms are kept spotless. Breakfast €5. Reserve ahead for Aug. Singles €36 or €43, depending on size of room; doubles €43, €47 with 2 beds; triples and quads €49/€61. MC/V. ❸

Hôtel Alexandre Ier, 111 rue de Rome (☎04 91 48 67 13; fax 04 91 42 11 14). Spacious, red-toned rooms in a neighborhood just southeast of the *vieux port,* all with shower and pleasantly cushy pillows. Traffic roars past rooms on the cours St-Louis; light sleepers should ask for options on the other side. Breakfast €5. Reception 24hr. Singles €37; doubles €38-40; triples €49; quads €65. MC/V. ❸

Auberge de Jeunesse Bonneveine (HI), impasse Bonfils (☎04 91 17 63 30; fuaj.net/homepage/marseille), off av. J. Vidal. From the station, take metro #2 to Rond-Point du Prado, and transfer (keeping your ticket) to bus #44 to pl. Bonnefon. At the bus stop, walk back toward the traffic circle and turn left at J. Vidal. Turn left onto impasse Bonfils; the hostel is at the end of the street on the left. Modern building houses bar, restaurant, outdoor terrace, Internet (€0.15 per min.), pool table, and vending machines. Rooms are basic but adequate. Breakfast included. Laundry facilities. Bike rental €10 for 4hr. July-Aug. 6-night max. stay. Reception 9am-noon and 2-6pm. Curfew 1am. Guests under 18 must be accompanied by an adult. Closed late Dec.-Jan. Dorms Apr.-Aug. €14 1st night, €12.10 thereafter; doubles €16.70/€14.80. Feb.-Mar. and Sept.-Dec. dorms €13.40/€11.50; doubles €15.60/€13.70. MC/V. HI members only. ❶

Auberge de Jeunesse Château de Bois-Luzy (HI), allée des Primevères (☎04 91 49 06 18). Take metro #1 to Réformés-Canebière, then transfer to bus #6 from cours J. Thierry at the top of La Canebière to Marius Richard. 10m up the hill from the bus stop, turn right onto bd. de l'Amandière to the soccer fields. Follow the road down the right and around the fields to the hostel. A beautiful 19th-century château provides 90 beds for youths and families. Quiet hilltop location in a suburb east of Marseille offers panoramic views of the city and sea below. Guests can cook meals in a small but well-equipped kitchen. Mostly 3- to 6-bed dorms and a few doubles. Breakfast €3.20. Dinner and lunch €8.50, €8.90 for picnic. Luggage storage free for guests 1st day, after that €2 per bag per day. Sheets €2.50. 4-night max. stay. Reception 7:30am-noon and 5-10:30pm. Lockout noon-5pm. Curfew 10:30pm. Dorms €11.40 for 1st night, €8.90 thereafter; singles €15.50/€13; doubles €12.50/€10. HI members only. ❶

Hôtel Béarn, 63 rue Sylvabelle (☎04 91 37 75 83; hotelbearn@aol.com). On a quiet side street between rue Paradis and rue Breteuil. Small but homey rooms have high ceilings, large windows, and dolphin-patterned wallpaper on the bathroom doors. Organized scuba diving excursions (with reduced rates) most weekends in the summer; ask at reception. Breakfast (with homemade jam from a local monastery) €4. Reception 7am-11pm. Singles €25, with toilet and shower €35, with toilet and bath €43; doubles €29/€40/€50; triples with bath €60; quads €70. AmEx/MC/V. ❸

⬛ FOOD

Marseille's restaurants reflect the city's cultural diversity. From the small African eateries and kebab stands along **cours St-Louis** to the Provençal places lining **rue St-Saens** and **rue Fortia,** diners can choose among the finest flavors from around the world. The streets surrounding the *vieux port* are packed with countless restaurants serving steaming dishes of the city's trademark *bouillabaisse* (a full meal comprising various Mediterranean fish, fish broth, and a spicy red sauce called *rouille,* or "rust"). **Cours Julien** offers a more eclectic collection of restaurants along the side streets and beside the fountains on the main pedestrian mall. A daily **fish market** on quai des Belges (8am-1pm) supplies locals with fresh ingredients for their homemade *bouillabaisse,* while **vegetable and fruit markets** on cours Pierre Puget (M-Sa 8am) and at Noailles on bd. de la Canebière (M-Sa 8am) provide the fixings. Before heading to hostels, stock up at the **Monoprix supermarket,** bd. de la Canebière, across from the American Express office. (Open M-Sa 8:30am-8:30pm.)

Baba of Marseille, 14 rue St-Pons (☎04 91 90 66 36). Baba has won a loyal clientele with generous portions of delicious Provençal dishes spiced according to the season. Photos of past diners as well as an eclectic collection of paper lanterns and glass chandeliers give this restaurant a homey feel. The *mille feuille d'agneau* (lamb and pastry) with tapenade (€17) is just 1 of the many tempting dishes presented by an affable staff. Look for the owner's baby picture on the menu. Open W-Sa 8pm-midnight. ❹

Ivoire Restaurant, 57 rue d'Aubagne (☎04 91 33 75 33). Loyal patrons come to this no-frills restaurant for authentic West African cuisine and helpful advice from "Mama Africa," the exuberant, caring owner. The Cote d'Ivoire specialties include *maffé* (meat or fish in a heavy peanut sauce, €7) and *gingembre,* a refreshing dessert liquor and a natural West African aphrodisiac. Open daily noon-midnight. ❷

Le Sud du Haut, 80 cours Julien (☎04 91 92 66 64). M: Cours Julien. Inviting decor and outdoor seating make this place ideal for a leisurely meal of beautiful, traditional Provençal cuisine. Short but enticing *menus* are presented on individual chalkboards. The *Saint Marcellin Rôti* (roast cheese dish, €13) are highly recommended. Funky bathrooms supply markers and paper so patrons can add their words of praise to the glowing reviews on the walls. Open M-Sa noon-1:30pm and 8-12:30pm. AmEx/MC/V. ❸

La Kahena, 2 rue de la République (☎04 91 90 61 93). M: Vieux Port. Tasty couscous dishes (€8-14) served on hand-painted plates at this sunny Tunisian restaurant on the corner of the *vieux port.* Blue tile mosaics, a Berber tent, and smells of warm spices create a decidedly North African aura. Open daily noon-2:30pm and 7-11:30pm. MC/V. ❸

Le Restaurant Végétarien, 63 rue St-Pierre (04 91 42 61 15 06). M: Cours Julien. Steps from cours Julien, tables in a quiet outdoor courtyard provide a respite from the city. Appetizing *plats du jour* or salads (€10-13) and delicious homemade desserts (€4.30-5) from the full vegetarian menu make for a pleasant meal. Open M-Sa noon-2pm and 6:30-10:30pm. MC/V. ❸

Country Life, 14 rue Venture (☎04 96 11 28 00), off rue Paradis. Appetizing vegetarian buffet with creative hot and cold selections. Tastefully decorated dining room has an upscale cafeteria feel. Big buffet plate €7.50; small plate €4.50. Open M-F 11:30am-2:30pm; health food store open M-Th 9am-6:30pm, F 9am-3pm. MC/V. ❷

🔍 SIGHTS

A walk through the city's streets tops any other sights-oriented itinerary, providing glimpses of the influences of lively African and Arabic communities amidst ancient Roman ruins and 17th-century forts. Walking trips are easily planned with maps and suggestions from the tourist office, and an extensive bus and rail network makes daytrips quite easy. The *petit train*, which gives tours of the city, departs on two different circuits from quai Belges every hour. (☎04 91 40 17 75. 10:15am-5pm. €5, children €3.) Though it is usually packed with tourists, this open-air ride does take a direct route to the must-see monuments throughout the city. Check www.museum-paca.org for info on museums and current exhibits. Unless otherwise noted, all the museums listed below have the same hours: June-Sept. Tu-Sa 11am-6pm; Oct.-May 10am-5pm.

🔳 **BASILIQUE DE NOTRE DAME DE LA GARDE.** A stunning view of the city, surrounding mountains, and island-studded bay make this a must-see for visitors today. In WWII, during the liberation of Marseille, a fierce battle raged for days before French Resistance forces regained the imposing basilica. The east face of the church remains pocked with bullet holes and shrapnel scars. Climb the stairs to the small basilica to see intricate mosaics and touching *ex votos*, symbolic objects presented by the faithful in thanks for protection and safety. Shipwreck survivors offer detailed models of ships that hang from the ceiling on frayed ropes. Towering nearly 230m above the city, the church's golden statue of Madonna cradling the infant Christ, known affectionately as *la bonne mère*, is regarded by many as the symbol of Marseille. Visit in the early evening, when crowds are few and the setting sun lends an unforgettable glow to the red roofs of the city below. *(Take bus #60 (dir: Notre Dame) or, from the tourist office, walk up rue Breteuil and turn left onto rue Grignon, which becomes bd. de la Corderie. Turn left onto bd. André Aune and you will see the basilica's huge staircase. ☎04 91 13 40 80. Open daily in summer 7am-8pm; in winter 7am-7pm.)*

HARBOR ISLANDS. Resembling a child's sandcastle come to life, the **Château d'If** guards the city from its rocky perch outside the harbor. The history of this "perfect prison" is varied. For years, the rowdy sons of noble families were straightened out by a year or two's stay at the château. Tempting views of the sparkling sea must have only added to the torture of the drafty stone cells. The tiny island's most famous resident was of course the fictional Count of Monte Christo. Nearby, the **Ile Frioul** quarantined plague victims for two centuries, beginning in the 1600s. It was only marginally successful, as an outbreak in 1720 killed half of the city's 80,000 citizens. Here the **Hôpital Corine** burned down several years ago and is now being restored as a public monument. In June, crowds enjoy open-air jazz concerts and occasional parties among the starlit, crumbling walls. (All events are weather and ferry schedule dependent—check with the tourist office or *L'Espace Culture* for details.) A handful of small shops and restaurants, combined with tiny inlets perfect for swimming, make this an excellent and convenient escape from the city. The short ride out to the islands takes you between the batteries of **Fort St-Jean,** whose original tower guarded a giant chain that successfully closed the harbor off in times of trouble, until King Aragon of Spain took it back home as a trophy for his victory in a 14th-century war. *(Reserve in advance in the high season. Boats depart from quai des Belges for both islands. Call the Groupement des Armateurs Côtiers at ☎04 91 55 50 09. Château ☎04 91 59 02 30. Round-trip 20min.; €10 for each island, €15 for both. Boats* *leave for the islands June-Aug. daily 9am-5pm; Sept.-May Tu-Su 9am-3:30pm. Adults must pay an additional €4.60 to enter the Château itself, visitors 18-25 €3.10. Children under 18 must be accompanied by an adult.)*

LA VIEILLE CHARITÉ. A formidable example of the famous 17th-century work of local architect Pierre Puget, La Charité was constructed to house the hundreds of beggars that were congesting the entrances of churches throughout Marseille in the 17th century. Later, the building served as a hospice center to provide aid for orphans and the elderly. Parents could leave their unwanted children in front of the church, where a wooden turnstile near the gate kept the nuns inside from seeing their faces. Now a national historic monument and home to many of Marseille's cultural organizations, it contains several of the city's museums. Egyptian, pre-historic, and anthropological collections are held in the **Musée des Arts Africains, Océaniens et Amérindiens.** Temporary art exhibits are displayed beneath a soaring oval dome in the central baroque chapel, and the **Musée d'Archéologie Méditerranée** houses the city's premier collection of Egyptian artifacts. The blank exterior walls facing the **Panier** district disguise the complexity of the splendid interior courtyard, which boasts a grand colonnade. *(2 rue de la Charité. ☎04 91 14 58 80. Temporary exhibits €3, permanent collections €2, students with ID half-price.)*

MUSÉE CANTINI. This memorable museum chronicles the region's artistic successes of the last century. Major Fauvist and Surrealist collections, including limited works by Henri Matisse and Paul Signac, are located throughout the building. *(19 rue Grignan. ☎04 91 54 77 75. €3, students €1.50, over 65 and under 10 free.)*

MÉMORIAL DES CAMPS DE LA MORT. The poignant exhibits at this small museum are exhibited in a blockhouse built by the Germans during their occupation of Marseille. A collection of photos and news articles recalls the death camps of World War II and the deportation of thousands of Jews from the *vieux port* in 1943. The glass panels on the first level are engraved with song lyrics and quotes by Primo Levi, Elie Wiesel, and Anne Frank, while photographs and an arresting collection of ashes provoke reflection on the third floor. *(Quai de la Tourette. ☎04 91 90 73 15. Open Tu-Su Sept.-May 10am-5pm; June-Aug. 11am-6pm. Free.)*

ABBAYE ST-VICTOR. St-Victor, an abbey fortified against pirates and Saracen invaders, is one of the oldest Christian sites in Europe. Its construction in the 5th century brought the first traces of Chris-

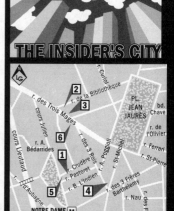

COURS JULIEN

An eclectic collection of murals, vintage music and clothing shops, bookstores, theaters, and countless cafes and restaurants make cours Julien the perfect place to stroll for a bargain. Many shops are closed on Sundays and Mondays.

1 Street artists have turned **rue Pastoret** and **rue Crudère** into impromptu outdoor galleries with cartoonish, bright spray-paint murals.

2 **Black Music,** 2 rue de la Bibliothèque, has a large assortment of soul and hip-hop.

3 **Kaleidoscope,** 3 rue des Trois Mages, offers eclectic used records and CDs.

4 Tiny **Baluchon Boutique,** 11 rue des Trois Rois, has the best vintage digs.

5 Peruse dusty paperbacks at **Librairie du Cours Julien,** 51 cours Julien.

6 **La Passerelle,** 26 rue des Trois Mages, features comic books and a snappy cafe.

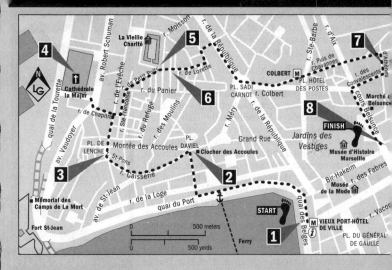

1 QUAI DES BELGES. Every morning the smell of fish fills the air as fishmongers sell the freshest of the day's catch along the entrances to the *vieux port*. Around noon the city cleans up with large firehoses.

START: quai des Belges
FINISH: bd, de la Canebière
DISTANCE: 2.7km/1¾ mi.
DURATION: 3-4hr.

2 CLOCHER DES ACCOULES. Follow the quai du Port to the passage Petécontore, and head up the stairs to the remains of one of Marseille's oldest churches. The towering 11th-century clock h. become the symbol of the Panier district.

3 PLACE DE LENCHE. Though it is now filled with small cafes and *brasseries,* this square presumed to be the site of the ancient Greek city center. It offers an excellent view, throu modern buildings, of Notre-Dame-de-la-Garde and the *vieux port.*

4 CATHÉDRALE DE LA MAJOR. From pl. de Lenche, bear right on rue de l'Evêché and follo it for three blocks, passing some tiny bakeries, then go left on rue de Chapitre. The hu Roman-Byzantine cathedral appears suddenly on the coast. Built under the direction of you Napoleon III, it contains beautiful mosaics.

5 VIEILLE CHARITÉ. Built between 1671 and 1749, the Vieille Charité formerly served as a orphanage and a shelter for the poor. It now houses the **Musée d'Archéologie,** the **Mus d'Arts Africain, Océanien, et Amérindien,** and a small cinema.

6 ARTERRA. One of many shops on rue Petit Puits continuing the 200-year-old Marseille tra tion of *santon* making. This traditional workshop demonstrates how *santons* (tiny nativity fig rines) are made, from the initial mold to the final detailed painting. (3 rue Petit Puits. ☎ 04 9 91 03 31. Open M-F 9am-1pm and 2-6pm, Sa hours vary.)

7 RUE DU BAIGNOIR. Head past rue d'Aix and the miniature Arc de Triomphe on rue Pu de Chavannes, which changes to rue des Dominicaines, until you arrive at rue du Baignoir. T small shops in this neighborhood sell goods from North Africa, ranging from vibrant fabrics fragrant incense.

8 MARCHÉ DE BELSUNCE. Cut down rue Nationale to this daily market known for its Me terranean imports as well as pungent stalls overflowing with fresh garlic.

tianity to the pagan inhabitants of Marseille. The eerie, expansive 5th-century catacombs and basilica hold the remains of two 3rd-century martyrs. The bright gold reliquaries near the altar contain remnants of St. Victor, who was martyred in 304. The abbey hosts a concert festival each year from March to December. *(Perched on rue Sainte at the end of quai de Rive Neuve. Follow the signs from the quai. ☎04 96 11 22 60. Open daily 9am-7pm. €2 for crypt entrance. Call ☎04 91 05 84 48 for festival info. Tickets €26, students €23.)*

PALAIS LONGCHAMP. The sweeping columns, majestic statues, and imposing stone facades of the palace were constructed in 1869 to honor the completion of a canal which brought fresh water to the plague-ridden city. Today, the complex includes two museums, a park, and an observatory. The **Musée des Beaux-Arts** features dramatic biblical works and two particularly gruesome paintings depicting the 1720-1723 plague outbreak. The galleries of the **Musée de l'Histoire Naturelle** are filled with a wide assortment of stuffed wildlife and temporary exhibits on subjects as diverse as the histories of dinosaurs and milk. *(Take metro #1 to Cinq Avenues Longchamps. Musée des Beaux-Arts ☎04 91 14 59 30. €2, students €1. Musée de l'Histoire Naturelle ☎04 91 14 59 50. Open Tu-Su Oct.-May 10am-5pm; June-Sept. 11am-6pm. €3.20.)*

OTHER SIGHTS. The rotating exhibits at the **Musée de la Mode** feature international clothing designers from different fashion periods. *(Espace Mode Méditerranée, 11 La Canebière. ☎04 91 56 59 57. Free tours in French Sa-Su 4pm. €1.50, students €1, over 65 free.)* At the nearby **Musée d'Histoire de Marseille**, Greek, Phoenician, and modern-day artifacts reveal Marseille's lively past. One of many highlights is a skeleton of a 6th century fishing boat. The museum ticket also gives access to the adjacent **Jardin des Vestiges**, marked by quiet, crumbling medieval foundations. *(Enter through the lowest level of the Centre Bourse mall. Museum ☎04 91 90 42 22. Open M-Sa 12-7pm. €2, students €1 with ID, over 65 and under 10 free.)* The **MAC, Galeries Contemporaines des Musées de Marseille,** features art from the 1960s to today, including works by César and Wegman. *(69 av. d'Haifa, off av. Hambourg. ☎04 91 25 01 07; dgac-mac@mairie.marseille.fr. Bus #23 or 45. Open Tu-Su 11am-6pm. €3, students €1.50.)*

🎵 🎭 ENTERTAINMENT AND NIGHTLIFE

Late-night restaurants and a few nightclubs center around **place Thiers,** near the *vieux port.* On weekends, there's a rush for seats at the bar tables that spill out onto the sidewalk along the **quai de Rive Neuve,** but a more eclectic crowd likes to unwind along the **cours Julien.** Tourists should exercise caution at night, particularly on the dimly lit streets of the Panier and Belsunce *quartiers* and in the more far-flung areas of the city since night buses are scarce, taxis expensive, and the metro closes early (M-Th and Su 9pm, F-Sa midnight).

Marseille offers the best of international theater, music, and art. Throughout the city, a number of independent theaters and music venues assures Marseille's reputation as a cultural treasure trove. *L'Espace Culture* (see **Practical Information,** p. 645) provides information and tickets. For classic and contemporary performances, theater buffs should check out the program at the **Théâtre National de Marseille La Criée,** 30 quai de Rive Neuve. (☎04 91 54 70 54; www.theatre-lacriee.com. Tickets €9-25. Box office open by telephone Tu-Sa 10am-7pm, in person 1-7pm, Su when there is a show 1:45-7pm.) Music lovers will not be disappointed by **L'Opéra de Marseille,** 2 rue Molière (☎04 91 55 11 10; http://opera.mairie-marseille.fr.), which, in addition to presenting annual seasons of spectacular opera, serves as the home of the **Philharmonic Orchestra of Marseille.** (Tickets €8-82, 15% discount for those under 25. Open Tu-F and Su 10am-5:30pm.) Smaller theaters present a wide range of performances for all ages and tastes. Check out **Marseille Théâtre Municipal, L'Odéon,** 162 bd. de la Canebière (☎04 96 12 52 70), and

Théâtre Gymnase, 4 rue du Théâtre Français. (☎04 91 24 35 24. Box office open Sept.-July M-Sa noon-6pm. Call from 11am-6pm. Tickets €20-28, students €12.) **Cité de la Musique,** 4 rue Bernard du Bois (☎04 91 39 28 28; www.citemusique-marseille.com), offers monthly programs. Unwind with the latest French and American films at **Le César,** 4 pl. Castellane (☎04 91 37 12 80. €6.50), or **Variétés,** 37 rue Vincent Scotto, just off rue Canebière. (☎04 96 11 61 61. €6.50.) Pick up a copy of *Ventilo* at the tourist office or any museum for up-to-date information regarding weekly cultural events, movies, and specific museum exhibits.

BARS AND CLUBS

El Ache de Cuba, 9 pl. Paul Cézanne (☎04 91 42 99 79). An enormous plaster head watches over this little slice of Havana, where partiers down liters of the "House Punch"—a deadly concoction of sangria, white wine, exotic fruits, and cane sugar syrup (€2 per cup, €15 per L). Mismatched chairs and a faux-bamboo bar provide a casual background for weekly Latin and Spanish dance lessons. You must buy a card (€2) to order something. Afterwards, drinks run about €2.50. Open Th-Sa 5pm-2am.

Trolleybus, 24 quai de Rive Neuve (☎04 91 54 30 45; www.letrolley.com). Known affectionately as "Le Trolley," this mega-club is a Marseille institution that has to be seen to be believed. 3 separate rooms for pop-rock, techno, and soul-funk-salsa, each with its own nickname and decor, keep a hip crowd in the groove. The club is housed in an 18th-century warehouse, and stone walls, narrow hallways, and dark corners give an anti-commercial feel. The French and international DJs who have been spinning here for 15 years make sure every party is a hit. Beer from €5, drinks €6-7. Sa cover €10, includes 1 drink. Open July-Aug. M-Sa 11pm-7am; Sept.-June Tu and Th-Sa.

Dan Racing, 17 rue André Poggioli (☎06 09 17 04 07). M: Cours Julien. Let your inner rock star run wild at this fun, casual bar, where drunken revelers can hop onstage for impromptu jam sessions. 15 guitars, 2 drum sets, and countless other instruments provide the makings for an ear-splitting insta-band. Auto-racing decor adds to the personality of this hilarious, happening spot. €2.50-3.50. Open M-Sa 9pm-2am.

Poulpason, 2 rue André Poggioli (☎04 91 48 85 67). M: Cours Julien. DJs spin rock, techno, and electro-house at the Poulpason, where a giant eyelash-sporting octopus reaches out from the wall. Wave mosaics and a black-lit aquarium complete the trippy underwater theme. Drinks €2.50-5. M-Sa 10pm-2am.

MP, 10 rue Beauvau (☎04 91 33 64 79). Both men and women relax on plushy velour couches at this quiet gay bar. Tall stools, red runner lights, and elaborate metal sconces add class to this laid-back hangout. Patrons can snack on *paella* or couscous and use the free Internet kiosk near the bar. Drinks €2.50-6.50. Open daily from 5:30pm.

Aux 3 G's, 3 rue St-Pierre (☎04 91 48 76 36; www.aux3g.com). M: Cours Julien. Nude Barbies star in a humorous, off-color window display outside this social lesbian bar. Come late evening, patrons shove aside rainbow furniture and groove to techno and house music. Drinks €2.60-4. Open Th and Su 6:30pm-midnight, F-Sa 6:30pm-2am.

New Can-Can, 3 rue Sénac (☎04 91 48 59 76). A perpetual weekend party for the city's gay community. Swanky discotheque set-up with full-length mirrors, a small stage, and low-slung red leather couches. Drinks €7-8. F free before midnight, then €13; Sa €8 before midnight, €14 after. Open daily from 10pm.

LIVE PERFORMANCE

L'Epicerie, 17 rue Pastoret (☎04 91 42 16 33). M: Cours Julien. A creative showcase for budding artists, this funky new theater, gallery, cafe, and bar features everything from jazz and poetry performances to tango lessons and art conferences. Open W-Sa 4-11pm in the summer; noon-10pm in the winter.

Chocolat Théâtre, 59 cours Julien (☎04 91 42 19 29). Live comic relief at a perfect dinner-and-theater combo. Open Tu-Sa 11:30am-1am. Tickets Tu-Th €14, F-Su €15.50. Dinner and show €30-34; students Tu-Th €10, F-Su €15.50.

La Poste à Galene, 103 rue Ferrari (☎04 91 47 57 99). A concert space that features popular local groups. Heavy metal, techno, and everything else. Buy a €1 membership card for entry; tickets €5-17 after that. Open M-Sa from 8:30pm, shows at 9:30pm.

 ## ALONG THE SHORE

From the Palais du Pharo to the av. du Prado, the **promenade de la corniche du Président J. F. Kennedy** runs along Marseille's most beautiful stretch of beaches. The typically heavy traffic is made bearable by the picturesque views of the Mediterranean and nearby islands. Make a stop at **Vallon des Auffes,** a hidden cove where residents used to spin fishing nets by hand from coconut fiber. Today the nets are synthetic, but little else has changed. Rows of brightly painted dories still dip and pull at their moorings as they have for years. Pedestrians take bus #83 from the *vieux port* (dir: Rond-Point du Prado) to Vallon des Auffes.

Bus #83 continues on to Marseille's **public beaches.** Get off just after it rounds the statue of David and turns away from the coast (20-30 minutes). Or take #19 (dir: Madrague) from M: Castellane or M: Rond-Point du Prado. Both the north and south **plages du Prado** offer sandy stretches, clear water, and good views of Marseille's surrounding cliffs. In June, the adjacent fields are overrun with children for the **Jours de Sport,** a five-day exposition where youngsters try their hand at every athletic competition imaginable. Rock climbing, kayaking, BMX, frisbee, and sailing are just a few of the offerings. Check with the tourist office or visit www.joursdesport.com for details. **Supermarché Casino et Cafeteria,** across from the statue, provides for the traveler's every need. (Open M-Sa 8:30am-9:30pm. Cafeteria open daily 8:30am-10pm.)

FESTIVALS

From city-wide, month-long celebrations to local weekend *fêtes*, festivals showcase Marseille's cultural best. **Ciné Plein-Air** presents free outdoor movies in locations throughout the city at 9:30pm from June to August. Experience the **International Documentary Film Festival** in June and the **Lesbian and Gay Pride March** in late June and early July. Mid-summer also brings **Jazz des Cinq Continents,** with jazz artists from all over the world. The **Festival Folklore du Château-Gombert** highlights regional folkloric traditions. The **Festival de Marseille Méditerranée** keeps Marseille full of music, dance, and theater throughout July. From September to December, visitors can enjoy the **Festival de Musique,** a week-long jubilee of jazz, classical, and pop music at l'Abbaye de St-Victor. Pick up a Festival Guide from the tourist office or *L'Espace Culture* (see **Practical Information,** p. 645) for info.

 ## DAYTRIPS FROM MARSEILLE

LES CALANQUES

Centuries ago, glacial erosion, sea level fluctuations, and climactic change shaped the southern coasts of this region into a string of magnificent rock formations. Today, the *calanques* stretch from Marseille to Toulon and provide spectacular natural scenery. Plunging limestone cliffs shelter a fragile balance of terrestrial and marine animals and plants, including foxes, bats, and peregrine falcons. They also serve as Marseille's largest outdoor playground, where scuba divers, mountain climbers, and cliff divers all come to test their skills. **Massilia Spirit Adventure** (☎ 06 12 39 59 39) and **G2 Guides des Goudes** (☎ 06 65 67 40 48) both offer gear and guided adventures for climbers of all skill levels. If heights aren't your thing, get your thrills by going *au naturel* at one of the many nude beaches along the coast.

A marvelous way to view the *calanques* from the water is with **G.A.C.M.,** 1 quai des Belges (☎ 04 91 55 50 09; fax 04 91 55 60 23), which operates 4hr. **boat trips** along the *calanques* to Cassis and back. (Daily mid-June to Sept.; mid-July to Sept. W 9:30am and 2pm, Sa-Su 2pm. €25, children ages 3-5 half-price.) **Hiking** is possible, though only recommended for those with considerable experience. The GR98, a national trail, links Marseille to Cassis over 28km of steep, rough trails. Those interested should check with the tourist office for local conditions. An easier option is to take bus #23 (dir: Sormiou; €1.50) from M: Rond-point du Prado, which stops near the *calanques* **Morgiou** and **Sormiou.**

CASSIS

Just 23km from Marseille, Cassis is easily accessible by bus and train. Both options are convenient, though the bus is less expensive. Buses leave from the bus station at M: Castellane. (40min.-1hr., 9 per day 9:15am-7:30pm, €3.30 one-way.) Trains, however, run at later hours (15-20min.; 29 each day from Marseille 6am-11:06pm; 26 each day from Cassis 5:17am-10:04pm; €4.40, students €3.50.) For a taxi from the train station to town (about €8-10), call ☎ 04 42 01 78 96 or 06 81 60 48 51, or take the #2 shuttle (dir: Gendarmerie, €0.80). From the bus stop, take a right onto av. du Professeur Lariche. Walk down towards the beach for 5min. On your right, just at the water, you will find the tourist office, quai des Moulins. (☎ 04 42 01 71 17; fax 04 42 01 28 31. Open June-Sept. M-F 9am-12:30pm and 2-7pm, Sa-Su 9:30am-12:30pm and 3-6pm; Mar.-May and Oct. M-F 9:30am-12:30pm and 2-6pm, Sa 10am-noon and 2-5pm, Su 10am-noon; Nov.-Feb. M-F 9:30am-12:30pm and 2-5pm, Sa 10am-noon and 2-5pm, Su 10am-noon.)

The charming resort town of Cassis clings to a hillside overlooking the Mediterranean. Between immaculate white villas surrounding the slopes above and an emerald-green port below, the town is a network of winding staircases, slender alleyways, and thick gardens. Every afternoon, locals compete in rowdy games of *pétanque* in the *boulodrome* at the center of town. Don't step through their courts, or you may find yourself at the center of a heated argument. Instead, grab an ice cream cone from one of the many *glaceries* crowding the port and find a shady spot to chill at a safe distance. Wine enthusiasts will enjoy sampling delicate *rosés* from the 14 vineyards that surround the town. Pick up a map from the tourist office and follow the signs to the **Calanque de Port-Pin,** about an 1¼hr. east of town. From there, scramble up the rocky trails to reach the stunning **Calanque En Vau** and beach. Though the trail is steep and offers little shade, the view of limestone cliffs dropping thousands of feet into turquoise seas makes every step worth it. The trail is marked by green, red, and white blazes; the beach can usually be reached in 45min. Both spots are perfect for a picnic lunch and a leisurely swim.

Explore the crystalline water with a kayak at **Club Sports Loisirs Nautiques,** plage de la Grande Mer (☎ 04 42 01 80 01; culturel.cassis@wanadoo.fr; single kayak €40 per day, double €65), or see the cliffs on a boat tour. (☎ 04 42 01 90 83. 45min.-1½hr. Feb. to mid-Nov. boats leave regularly from port. €9-12, €6-8 for children under 10.) The *calanques* are also known for great diving; for information, contact **Diving Cassis Services Plongée,** 3 rue Michel Arnaud. (☎ 04 42 01 89 16; www.cassis-services-plongee.fr. €28.50 per trip, €43 with equipment rental.)

AIX-EN-PROVENCE

Aix (pronounced "X"; pop. 134,000) is one of those rare cities that caters to tourists yet remains unspoiled by their influence. The *Aixois* are proud to share their streets, and rightly so: this is the city of Paul Cézanne, Victor Vasarely, and Emile

Aix-en-Provence

ACCOMMODATIONS
Arc-en-Ciel, 16
Chantecler, 15
Hôtel des Arts, 6
Hôtel La Caravelle, 14
Hôtel du Globe, 2

FOOD
L'Atlas, 1
Chez Maxime, 9
Patisserie Riederer, 10
Le P'tit Bistro, 3
Le Villon, 8
Le Zinc d'Hugo, 7

NIGHTLIFE
Bistro Aixois, 4
Le Cuba Libre, 13
Le Mistral, 12
O'Neill's, 11
Le Scat, 5

TO ✈ (300m)

Atelier Paul Cézanne

chemin de la Pâquerette

av. Paul Cézanne

av. de la Violette

r. Notre Dame

r. des Nations

r. de Grassi

av. Pasteur

tr. Gianotti

r. E. Signoret

bd. Aristide Briand

cours de la Trinité

PL. BELLEGARDE bd. Zola

av. Sainte Victoire

av. du Doct

r. de Silvacanne

bd. Jean Jaurès

r. des Étuves

r. de Jacques

r. des Guerriers

r. de la Roque

St-Sauver

Musée des Tapisseries

PL. DE L'UNIVERSITÉ

r. Cure

r. Lisse Bellegarde

r. du Puits Neuf

r. Mignet

cours St-Louis

Parc Rambot

TO AVIGNON

r. de la Molle

Thermes Sextius

Pavillon et Jardin Vendôme

r. du Bon Pasteur

r. du Carreau

r. Merindol

r. de la Treille

r. Venel

Musée du Vieil Aix

PL. DES MARTYRS DE LA RÉSISTANCE

Casino Supermarket

r. Bédarrides

r. Constantin

r. Bouteau

r. Matheron

r. Lisse St-Louis

r. Suffren

cours des Arts et Métiers

r. Célony

VanLoo

r. de la Treille

Virtu@us

PL. DES CARDEURS

Hôtel de Ville

PL. DE L'HÔTEL DE VILLE

Hub Lot

r. Granet

La Madeleine

PL. DES PRÊCHEURS

r. Chastel

r. Lacépède

r. Fondérie

bd. Carnot

Laundry

cours Sextius

r. Lisse des Cordeliers

r. du 11 Novembre

r. des Cordeliers

r. Lieutaud

r. des Magnans

Foch

PL. RICHELME

Pôle Judiciare

Palais de Justice

PL. DE VERDUN

r. Fontaine d'Argent

r. Manuel

bd. de la République

r. de Brueys

r. des Tanneurs

PL. RAMUS

r. d'Esparriat

Marius Reinaud

r. des Carmes

r. Fabrot

r. Thiers

Emeric David

Fontaine David

r. de la Mule Noire

r. de l'Opéra

r. des Bernardines

r. Victor Leydet

PL. NIOLLON

av. Bonaparte

Book in Bar

cours Mirabeau

Renoir

r. Papassaudi

r. Nazarin

r. Aude

r. de la Masse

r. Laroque

r. Cabassol

r. Frédéric Mistral

PL. FORBIN.

Chapelle des Oblats

r. M. Joffre

r. Pavillon

PL. DE LA LIBÉRATION (LA ROTONDE)

PL. DU GÉNÉRAL DE GAULLE

r. de Villars

r. Mazarine

r. Goyrand

r. du 4 Septembre

Casino Supermarket

St-Jean de Malte

av. N. Froment

r. Lapierre

Bike Rental

r. Gombard

av. Victor Hugo

r. Cardinale

r. Malherbe

av. Benjamin Abram

Collège Mignet

r. Roux Alpheran

r. Sallier

cours Gambetta

av. Mozart

av. des Belges

r. de l'Europe

TO CITÉ DU LIVRE

r. G. Desplaces

Callssons Leonard Parlrin

impasse Gustave Desplace

bd. du Roy René

av. Anatole France

cours d'Orbielle

chemin Robert

TO 15 & 16 (3km)

bd. Albert Charrier

av. M. Blondel

av. St-Jerome

av. d'Oraison

av. de Craponne

TO 🏛 FONDATION VASARÉLY (3km)

bd. Paul d'Ollone

av. Reine Astrid

r. de la Poudrière

Parc Joseph Jourdan

av. Jules Ferry

N

LG

0   200 yards

0   200 meters

PROVENCE

Zola, where nearly every golden facade or dusty cafe has had a brush with artistic greatness. It's not hard to see why they were so inspired—charming fountains and lively squares are tucked amid narrow, picturesque streets. Though highly conscious of its past, Aix manages to keep up with the latest cultural traditions thanks to its large student population. Hip nightlife keeps things rolling all year long, and annual summer dance, opera, jazz, and classical music festivals showcase the finest culture in the region.

▐ TRANSPORTATION

Trains: at the end of av. Victor Hugo, off impasse Gustave Desplace. Ticket window open M-F 5am-9:20pm, Sa-Su 6am-9:20pm. Reservations and info offices open M-F 8am-7:30pm, Sa 8am-7pm; be prepared for a long wait. Almost every train goes through Marseille; info on schedules can be found in the waiting area. To: **Cannes** (3½hr., 8 per day 5:10am-9pm, €25.10); **Marseille** (38min., 27 per day 5:10am-9pm, €6); **Nice** (3-4hr., 8 per day 6:44am-9:25pm, €30). Routes marked "car" on SNCF's schedule are serviced by buses. The **Gare d'Aix-en-Provence TGV,** 20min. outside of the city, connects travelers to major cities throughout France via the TGV. To: **Paris Aéroport Charles de Gaulle** (3½hr., 4 per day 5:36am-5:32pm, €88.50). The TGV station can be reached by shuttles running every 15min. from the bus station (20min., €3.70).

Buses: av. de l'Europe (☎04 42 91 26 80), off av. des Belges. Info desk open M-F 7:30am-7:30pm, Sa 7:30am-6:30pm. Ticket window open M-F 6:15am-7:30pm, Sa 6:30am-6:30pm, Su 7:30am-12:30pm and 1:30-6:30pm. Companies compete for the heavy commuter traffic to **Marseille,** with buses almost every 10min. (€4.20). **Phocéens Cars** (☎04 93 85 66 61) goes to **Cannes** (1¾hr., 4 per day, €21) and **Nice** (2¼hr., 4 per day, €22.50). **C.A.P.** (☎04 42 97 52 12) runs to **Arles** (1¾hr.; M-Sa 7 per day, 1 on Su; €11.40). Under-26 student discounts for Nice or Cannes (with ISIC).

Public Transportation: Aix-en-Bus (☎04 42 26 37 28) runs buses around the city. Maps and *carnets* available at the tourist office M-Sa 8:30am-5pm (€1.10, *carnet* of 10 €7.70).

Taxis: Radio Aixois (☎04 42 27 71 11). €10 from train station to hostel 3km west of *centre ville.* 24hr.

Bike Rental: La Rotonde, 2 av. des Belges (☎04 42 26 78 92), at the back of the furniture exchange store. Bikes €15 per day, €60 per week; students and children under 12 €13/€55. Includes helmet, pump, and repair kit. ID and deposit required. Open M-Sa 9:30am-12:30pm and 2:30-6:30pm.

◼✦ ▐ ORIENTATION AND PRACTICAL INFORMATION

The **cours Mirabeau** sweeps through the center of town, linking **La Rotonde** (a.k.a. **place du Général de Gaulle**) to the west with **place Forbin** to the east. Traffic rolls past a series of richly-decorated fountains, separating countless cafes on one side from classy shops and banks on the other. The predominantly pedestrian *vieille ville* snuggles inside the **périphérique**—a ring of boulevards including **boulevard Carnot, cours Sextius,** and **boulevard du Roy René.** In the twisting side streets north of the cours Mirabeau, boutiques and restaurants abound.

Tourist Office: 2 pl. du Général de Gaulle (☎04 42 16 11 61; www.aixenprovencetourism.com), on the left, between av. des Belges and av. Victor Hugo. To get there from the bus station, go up av. de l'Europe, take a left onto av. des Belges, and follow it to La Rotonde. The tourist office will be on the right. Provides multilingual guides to Aix, *Visa pour Aix* card (€2) with reduced rates to museums, and city tours, some in English (€8,

€4 with *Visa pour Aix*). Accommodation booking June-Aug. M-F 9am-6:30pm, Sa 9am-12:30pm and 1:30-5pm. Office open July-Aug. M-Sa 8:30am-8pm, Su 10am-1pm and 2-6pm; Sept.-June M-Sa 8:30am-7pm, Su 8:30am-1pm and 2-6pm.

Currency Exchange: L'Agence, in Afat Voyages, 15 cours Mirabeau (☎04 42 26 93 93; fax 04 42 26 79 03). American Express affiliate; takes Travelers Cheques. Open July-Aug. M-Sa 9am-12:30pm and 1:30-7:30pm, Su 10am-2pm; Sept.-June M-F 9am-6:30pm, Sa 9am-2:30pm and 1:30-5pm. 24hr. **ATMs** line cours Mirabeau.

English-Language Bookstore: Book in Bar, 1 rue Cabassol (☎04 42 26 60 07), just off cours Mirabeau. Also a cafe. Hosts weekly English-language events, a bilingual book club, and live music. Monthly exhibitions on the cafe walls feature local artists. Open M-Sa 9am-7pm. Closed Aug. 1-15. Also, visit the **Cité du Livre** (see **Sights,** p. 659).

Laundromat: Laverie, 35 cours Sextius. Wash €2.90-6.10, dry €0.30 per 15min. Open Tu-Su 7am-8pm. Also on 15 rue Jacques de la Iroquois (☎06 08 01 02 13). Open daily 7am-8pm. Also at 3 rue Fonderie (open Tu-Su 7am-8pm) and 3 rue Fernand Dol (open Tu-Su 7am-8pm).

Police: 10 av. de l'Europe (☎04 42 93 97 00), near the Cité du Livre.

Crisis Lines: SIDA Info Service (☎08 00 84 08 00) is an AIDS hotline. **SOS Viol** (☎04 91 33 16 60) and **SOS Femmes Battues** (☎04 91 24 61 50) are hotlines for rape victims and battered women, respectively. Call **SOS Médecins** (☎04 42 26 24 00) for medical advice (24hr). **Urgence 24** (☎04 42 96 66 00) can address any emergency on weekends and holidays. **Service des Etrangers** (☎04 42 96 89 48) aids foreigners.

Pharmacy: 17 cours Mirabeau (☎ 04 42 93 63 60). Open M-Sa 8:30am-8pm. Also operates a rotating 24hr. **pharmacie de garde** (☎04 42 26 40 40).

Hospital: Centre Hospitalier Général du Pays d'Aix, av. Tamaris (☎04 42 33 50 00). **Ambulance** ☎04 42 21 37 37 or 04 42 21 14 15.

Poison Control: ☎04 91 75 25 25.

Internet Access: Virtu@us, 40 rue des Cordeliers (☎04 42 26 02 30; fax 04 42 93 26 08). €2.30 per 30min., €3.80 per hr. Open M-F 9am-1am, Sa-Su noon-1am. Also **Hub Lot Cybercafé,** 17 rue Paul BERT (☎04 42 21 37 31). €0.06 per min., €3.60 per hr. No min. time usage. Open daily 9am-midnight.

Post Office: 2 rue Lapierre (☎04 42 16 01 50), just off La Rotonde. Open M-F 8:30am-6:45pm, Sa 8:30am-noon. **Currency exchange** for small commission. 24hr. **ATM** to the right of the main entrance. The annex, 1 pl. de l'Hôtel de Ville (☎04 42 63 04 66), has the same services. Open M and Th-F 8am-6:30pm, Sa 8am-noon.

Postal Code: 13100.

▚▚ ACCOMMODATIONS AND CAMPING

There are few inexpensive hotels near the city center, and during festival season all ranges of accommodations may be fully booked. Travelers hoping to find lodging during July should reserve as early as March or April, or hope for cancellations. The tourist office can reserve rooms and provide information on guest houses and nearby châteaux. Visit www.aixenprovencetourism.com to make your own reservations. Campgrounds and basic chain hotels are on the outskirts of Aix.

▨ **Hôtel du Globe,** 74 cours Sextius (☎04 42 26 03 58; fax 04 42 26 13 68). Hôtel du Globe sets a high standard for mid-price accommodations in Aix with small, thoughtful touches like flower-stenciled tiles and wooden bath stools. Rooms are spacious and well lit, with colorful decor, pristine bathrooms, and TV. Some balconies. Breakfast €8. Reception 24hr. Singles €30, with shower €39; doubles with shower €54, with bath €59; 2 small beds with shower €54, with bath €57; triples with bath €63-69; quads with bath €85. Extra bed €9. June-Aug. add €4 to all rooms for A/C. AmEx/MC/V. ❹

Hôtel La Caravelle, 29 bd. du Roy-René (☎04 42 21 53 05; fax 04 42 96 55 46). Cheery, moderately sized rooms overlooking a small, tangled garden southeast of the *centre ville.* Enormous windows on the street-side rooms let in plenty of light and fresh air. Some rooms with A/C, those without are equipped with fans. Breakfast €6.50. Reception 24hr. Singles €39, some with toilets down the hall; doubles €43-61; doubles with garden view €69; quad €72. AmEx/MC/V. ❹

Hôtel des Arts, 69 bd. Carnot at rue Portalis (☎04 42 38 11 77; fax 04 42 26 77 31). A blue neon sign directs travelers to this hotel on the eastern edge of the city. Identical rooms are compact but clean. All have bath, phone, and TV. Amiable owners eagerly brush up on English with guests. Breakfast included. 24hr. reception. Singles €34 or €39, depending on whether the room faces bd. Carnot; doubles €40/€45. MC/V. ❸

Camping:

Arc-en-Ciel, rte. de Nice (☎04 42 26 14 28), is 2km from the city center. Take bus #3 from La Rotonde to the Trois Sautets stop. The Roman Pont des Trois Sautets, immortalized in Cézanne's painting, spans the river near the center of the grounds. Multilingual management organizes spirited fishing, badminton, and ping pong competitions. Swimming pool. Reception 8:30am-12pm and 2-7pm daily. €5.90 per person, €5.40 per site. Parking included. ❶

Chantecler, av. St-André (☎04 42 26 12 98; www.airotel-chantecler.com), by rte. de Nice, is 2km from the city center. Take bus #3 from La Rotonde at the Office de Tourisme stop. Sites are on a quiet, wooded hill; several have views of Mont Ste-Victoire. Newly renovated pool, hot showers, and restrooms, restaurant, bar, and bike rental services. Theme parties in the bar 2 times a week. Reception daily June 8am-1am; July-Aug. 8am-3am; Sept.-May 8am-11pm. €5.40 per person, €6.40 per site. Low season €5.20/€5.90. Mobile homes and darling *chalets* with full kitchen, living room, and bath available for rent. €500-630 per week. ❶

🟦 FOOD

Though Aix boasts a comprehensive selection of Provençal and international cuisine, the local sweets are the true gastronomic delights. The city's bonbon is the *calisson d'Aix,* a small iced almond-and-candied-melon treat. Other specialties include *merveilles de Provence* (pralines flavored with kirsch and covered with chocolate) and soft nougat candies. You can stop by **Pâtisserie Riederer,** 67 cours Mirabeau, to sample *merveilles.* At dinnertime, tables and chairs crowd **rue de la Verrerie, rue Lieutaud,** and **place Richelme.** Markets with fruits and vegetables, and regional products are on pl. de la Madeleine (Tu, Th, Sa 7am-1pm) and pl. Richelme (daily, same times). Three **Petit Casinos** serve **supermarket** shoppers: 3 cours d'Orbitelle (☎04 42 27 61 43; open M-Sa 8am-1pm and 4-7:30pm); 16 rue d'Italie (open Tu-Sa 8am-8pm, Su 8am-1pm); 5 rue Sapora (open Tu-Sa 8:30am-7:30pm, Su 8:30am-12:30pm). To see and be seen, nothing is better than a leisurely lunch at the cafes lining **cours Mirabeau.** Prime real estate, however, comes at a high price. If you can't resist, grab coffee (€1.80) at the historic **Café des Deux Garçons ❶,** the former watering hole of Cézanne and Zola. (☎04 42 26 00 51. Open daily 7am-2am.)

Le Villon, 14 rue Félibre Gaut (☎04 42 27 35 27), off rue des Cordeliers. Quiet outdoor seating, a friendly waitstaff, and an excellent *tarte citron* (lemon pie, €5.00). Inside, candlelight reveals wooden beams and a large fireplace. Lunch *menu* €9.60, dinner *menu* €11.50-19. Open M-Sa noon-2pm and 7-11pm. MC/V. ❸

Chez Maxime, 12 pl. Ramus, (☎04 42 26 28 51). Excellent Provençal cuisine dons a pinkish glow under Maxime's red canopy. Delicious fresh meats and wine menu, and the lavender *créme brûlée* (€6.80) is not to be missed. €13-20; *menus* €21-28. Open M 6pm-midnight, Tu-Sa noon-midnight. MC/V. ❹

Le Zinc d'Hugo, 22 rue Lieutaud (☎04 42 27 69 69). Traditional *Aixois* food with a modern twist. Try creative dishes on a quiet street. *Plats* €8.50-14, *menus* €12-24. Open Tu-Sa noon-midnight. MC/V. ❸

Le P'tit Bistrot, 38 rue Lieutaud (☎04 42 27 52 20), at the back of pl. des Cardeurs. Locals and expats devour dishes of *tartines* (grilled bread with cheese and other toppings). Try the *tartine provençale*, with house-made tapenade. *Tartines* €9.20-11.20. Open Tu-Sa 9am-3pm and 6pm-1am. MC/V. ❸

L'Atlas, 18 rue Boulegon (☎04 42 96 91 76), near the pl. de l'Hôtel de Ville. Generous helpings of savory Moroccan fare in a cozy setting. Most couscous dishes €11-19; *menus* €16.90-24.80. Open daily noon-4pm and 6pm-midnight. MC/V. ❸

🎯 SIGHTS

Nearly every corner of Aix is marked by a timeworn mansion, an elaborate facade, or a bubbling fountain. Individual exploration is the best way to savor Aix's charm. Narrative maps from the tourist office provide interesting facts on the city's various squares, markets, and fountains. The *Visa pour Aix* (€2), sold at the tourist office or participating museums, gives reduced admission at museums, and halves the price of the tourist office's town tour.

PROVENCE

FONDATION VASARELY. This trippy black-and-white museum stands in stark contrast to the rolling green hills of the surrounding countryside. Designed in the 1970s by Hungarian-born artist Victor Vasarely, the father of optical illusion art, the building resembles a beehive from above and displays some of Vasarely's most monumental work in eight huge hexagonal spaces. The audioguide probes Vasarely's attempts to create a "polychromatic city of happiness." The museum also serves as a research center for artists exploring the fields of urbanism, computer research, and industrial design. *(Av. Marcel-Pagnol, Jas-de-Bouffan, next to the youth hostel; take bus #4 or 10 from the Casino stop on av. Bonaparte. ☎04 42 20 01 09. Open June-Sept. M-Sa 11am-7pm; Oct.-May closes at 6pm. €7, students and ages 7-18 €4, under 7 free.)*

CHEMIN DE CÉZANNE. Golden markers trace the footsteps of the artist on a self-guided 2hr. walking tour. Explore the many haunts of Aix's most famous son, including his birthplace and favorite cafes. In his studio, the **Atelier Paul Cézanne,** the artist's overcoat and beret still hang in the corner, and a lunch bag slung casually over a chair makes a visitor feel as though Cézanne might step inside from the garden at any moment to pick it up. Windows thrown open to the countryside let in the natural light the artist revered. The catalogue of his most famous works matches painted objects to the originals on the shelves. In summer, music and projected images fill the garden at night. *(Walking tours maps available at the tourist office. Atelier at 9 av. Paul Cézanne. Take bus #1 from the St-Christophe stop at la Rotonde, or just walk 10min. uphill on av. Paul Cézanne. ☎04 42 21 06 53; www.atelier-cezanne.com. Open daily mid-June to Sept. 10am-6:30pm; Oct.-Mar. 10am-noon and 2-5pm; Apr. to mid-June 10am-noon and 2:30-6pm. €5.50, students €2, children under 16 and seniors free.)*

CATHÉDRALE ST-SAVEUR. An eclectic mix of Romanesque, Gothic, and Baroque naves built on (and with) stones from a preexisting Roman site, this church is pure architectural whimsy. During the Revolution, angry *Aixois* defiantly chopped off the marble heads of the statues. They were recapitated in the 19th century, albeit without necks. Ask the guide to open the 12th-century cloister, where you'll have a picture-perfect view of the octagonal bell tower between ornate columns depicting religious scenes. *(Rue Gaston de Saporta, on pl. de l'Université. ☎04 42 23 45 65. Open daily 8am-noon and 2-6pm, except during services.)*

CITÉ DU LIVRE. Huge steel replicas of major French classics mark the entry to this former match factory, now a cultural center with three major sections. The **Bibliothèque Méjanes** is the second largest library in the region and contains ancient volumes from the personal collection of the Marquis de Méjanes, as well as British and American literature. A wide selection of music from around the world is available for rent in the **Discotheque** section. At the air-conditioned **Videothèque d'Art Lyrique,** visitors can watch videos of operas, ballets, and concerts of past **Festivals d'Aix** and admire original opera costumes. *(8-10 rue des Allumettes, southeast of La Rotonde. ☎04 42 91 98 88. Open Tu and Th-F noon-6pm, W and Sa 10am-6pm. Borrowing from the Bibliothèque requires a €25 membership.)*

OTHER SIGHTS. For fans of city history, the **Musée du Vieil Aix,** 17 rue Gaston de Saporta, highlights a somewhat haphazard assortment of Aixois treasures, from screens depicting a procession of the famous *Fête Dieu* to a collection of traditional wooden marionettes. *(☎04 42 21 43 55. Open Apr.-Oct. Tu-Su 10am-noon and 2:30-6pm; Nov.-Mar. 10am-noon and 2-5pm. €4.)* A fine collection of 17th- and 18th-century tapestries hangs in the **Musée des Tapisseries,** the former seat of the illustrious clergy of Aix. The highlight is the series depicting the misadventures of Don Quixote. *(Palais Archiépiscopal, 2nd fl., 28 pl. des Martyrs de la Résistance. ☎04 42 23 09 91. Open M and W-Su 10am-6pm. €2, under 25 free. July-Aug. free tours in French and English. Call ☎04 42 21 05 78 for info on tours.)* Antique lovers might enjoy the 17th-century **Pavillon de Vendôme,** originally the lavish residence of a noble. Today, it is a small museum which houses paintings and furniture from the turn of the 18th century. Plane trees lining the courtyard provide the perfect spot for a shady picnic. *(32 rue Célony. ☎04 42 21 05 78. Museum open Apr.-Sept. M and W-Su 10am-noon and 2-6pm; Feb.-Mar. and Oct. 10am-noon and 1:30-5:30pm; Nov.-Jan. 10am-noon and 1-5pm. €2, under 26 free. Gardens open daily 9am-5:30pm. Free.)*

▣ NIGHTLIFE

Crowds of students during the year and festival-goers in summertime ensure that partying is a year-round pastime in Aix. **Rue de la Verrerie** has the highest concentration of bars and clubs; lanterns sway in the breeze at cafes along the **Forum des Cardeurs,** behind the Hôtel de Ville. At **Bistro Aixois,** 37 cours Sextius, loads of international students guzzle *les girafes,* enormous plastic tubes that hold up to 5L of beer. Revelers dance on the Caribbean-inspired bar in this compact space. (☎04 42 27 50 10. Open Tu-Sa 6:30pm-4am. MC/V.) A sophisticated older crowd enjoys live jazz and rock on low, funky couches at **Le Scat,** 11 rue Verrerie. (☎04 42 23 00 23; scatclub.free.fr. Nightly free concerts M-Sa 1am. Open Tu-Sa 11pm-5:30am.) Get down to techno, dance, R&B, and house at **Le Mistral,** a chic dance club at 3 rue F. Mistral that has kept Aix hopping for the past 55 years; don't show up in shorts, jeans, or sandals. (☎04 42 38 16 49. €10 cover, €16 on weekends includes one drink. Tu women free with open bar all night. Open Tu-Sa 11:30pm-5am.) For salsa, hip-hop, and rock, **Le Cuba Libre,** 4 bd. Carnot, transports partiers to the happening island with Cuban cigars and tropical mixed drinks. (☎04 42 26 01 38. Drinks €2.50-5. Happy hour 5-10pm. Open M-Sa 5pm-2am.) Pack into **O'Neill's,** 15 rue d'Italie, to party with a vibrant, youthful crowd. (☎04 42 26 03 38. Weekly theme parties. Drinks €5. Open daily 5pm-2am.) **Ciné Mazarin,** 6 rue Laroque, off cours Mirabeau, and **Renoir,** 24 cours Mirabeau, screen French and foreign films, all in the original language with French subtitles. (Both ☎04 42 26 61 51. €7.50, students €6, under 6 €4.50.)

▨ FESTIVALS

The week-long **Cinestival** kicks things off in June, when screenings of hundreds of French and international films cost just €3, all accessible with the free *billet scoop* from the tourist office. Famous performers and rising stars descend on Aix for the **Festival d'Aix-en-Provence,** a series of operas and orchestral concerts that lasts from June to July. (Ticket office at 11 rue Gaston de Sapora. ☎04 42 16 11 70; www.festival-aix.com. Tickets start at €6.) For two weeks at the end of July and the beginning of August, the city hosts **Danse à Aix,** which features ballet, jazz, and modern dance at venues across the city. (☎04 42 96 05 01. Call M-F 2-5pm. €11-38, students €11-30.) Tickets are available at the tourist office or at 1 pl. John Rewald. (M-Sa 9am-noon and 2-6pm.) In early July, the city puts on a two-week **Jazz Festival** (tickets €20). **Aix-en-Musique,** 3 pl. John Rewald (☎04 42 21 69 69), sponsors concerts year-round, including "Music on Saturday" programs for children.

AVIGNON

With its bridge memorialized by the children's song "Sur le pont d'Avignon," the city of Avignon (pop. 85,000) is a medieval maze of fashionable boutiques, intriguing museums, and the unparalleled Palais des Papes, a sprawling Gothic fortress known in its time as "the biggest and strongest house in the world." Some 700 years ago, political dissent in Italy led the homesick French pontiff Clement V to shift the papacy to Avignon. During this period, seven popes erected and expanded Avignon's Palais, making the city a Rome away from Rome, so to speak. Gregory XI returned the papacy to Rome in 1377, but the town remained Papal territory until the Revolution.

PROVENCE

⮕ TRANSPORTATION

Airport: Aéroport Avignon Caumont (☎04 90 81 51 51; www.avignon.aeroport.fr), 8km. from town. Direct flights to Paris (4 per day), with connections to major French and international destinations.

Trains:

Gare Centrale: bd. St-Roch, porte de la République (☎04 90 27 81 89). Info desk and ticket counters open daily 4:30am-10pm. To: **Arles** (30min., 19 per day, €5.70); **Lyon** (2hr., 7 per day, €25.40); **Marseille** (70min., 18 per day, €15.50); **Montpellier** (1hr., 15 per day, €13); **Nice** (3-4 hr., 5 per day, €34.80); **Nîmes** (30min., 16 per day, €7.40).

TGV: departs from a second train station outside of town, in quartier de Courtine. A Navette **shuttle** bus (€1.10) runs every 20min. between the 2 train stations; it also stops just in front of the post office on rue de la République. Fewer buses on Su. **TGV** ticket counters open daily 5:40am-10pm. To: **Dijon** (2¾hr., 16 per day, €41); **Lyon** (1hr., 5-7 per day, €35.70); **Paris** (3½hr., 17 per day, €79.20).

Regional Buses: *Gare Routière,* bd. St-Roch. Turn right from the train station. Info desk (☎04 90 82 07 35) open M-F 10:15am-1pm and 2-6pm. Buy tickets on bus. **CTM** goes to: **Arles** (45min., 5 per day, €8.50); **Les Baux** (1hr., 5 per day July-Aug., €6.60); **Marseille** (2hr., 1 per day, €16.40); **St-Rémy** (45min., 9 per day, €4). Buses are less frequent Sept.-June.

Public Transportation: TCRA, av. de Lattre de Tassigny (☎04 32 74 18 32; www.tcra.fr), near porte de la République. Office open M-F 8:30am-12:30pm and 1:30-6pm. Tickets (€1.10) sold on the bus, *carnet* of 10 (€8.20) sold at the office. Maps available at the tourist office.

Boat Shuttle: Navette Fluviale (☎04 90 80 80 00). Follow the signs to the right of Pont d'Avignon. Runs a free shuttle across the Rhône mid-Feb. to Dec. every 15min. Schedule varies by month; the tourist office has up-to-date information.

Taxis: Radio Taxi, pl. Pie (☎04 90 82 20 20). 24hr.

Car Rental: Most offices are located at one of the two stations. **Car Go,** 141 rue des Rémouleurs (☎04 90 800 700; www.cargo.fr), at the TGV station, will drive customers to and from their hotels. Smart car from €9 per day, €0.32 per km, or €198 for 5 days and 500km. Larger vehicles available. Open M 7:30am-noon and 2-6pm, Tu-Sa 8-

PROVENCE

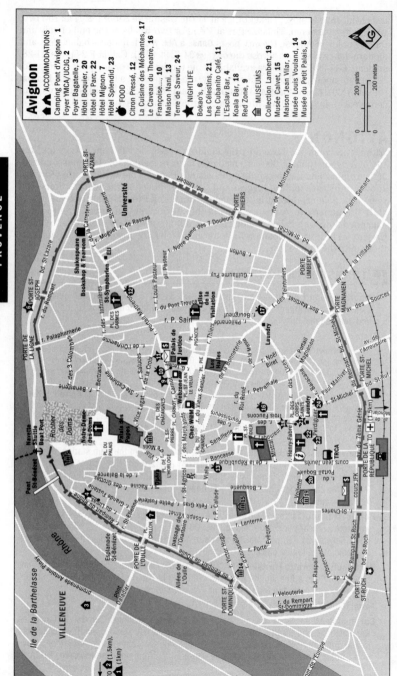

Avignon

ACCOMMODATIONS
Camping Pont d'Avignon, **1**
Foyer YMCA/UCJG, **2**
Foyer Bagatelle, **3**
Hôtel Boquier, **20**
Hôtel du Parc, **22**
Hôtel Mignon, **7**
Hôtel Splendid, **23**

FOOD
Citron Pressé, **12**
La Cuisine des Méchantes, **17**
Le Caveau du Theatre, **16**
Françoise..., **10**
Maison Nani, **13**
Terre de Saveur, **24**

NIGHTLIFE
Bokao's, **6**
Les Célestins, **21**
The Cubanito Café, **11**
L'Esclav Bar, **4**
Koala Bar, **18**
Red Zone, **9**

MUSEUMS
Collection Lambert, **19**
Musée Calvet, **15**
Maison Jean Vilar, **8**
Musée Louis Vouland, **14**
Musée du Petit Palais, **5**

10am and 2-6pm. **National/Citer**, at both the *Gare Centrale* (☎04 90 85 96 47; open M-Sa 9:30am-12:30pm and 1:30-5:30pm) and the TGV station (☎04 90 27 30 07; open M-W and Sa-Su 8:30am-10pm, Th-F 8:30am-11pm). Basic car €248 for 5 days.

Bike Rental: Provence Bike, 52 bd. St Roch (☎04 90 27 92 61; www.provence-bike.com) rents bikes and motorbikes at competitive prices. Open daily 9am-12:30pm and 3-7pm (reduced hours Su). Bikes €10 per day, €40 per week, €10 per extra week; mountain bikes €15 per day, €75 per week. Motorbike rental from €35 per day. AmEx/MC/V. **Aymard Cycles Peugeot**, 80 rue Guillaume Puy (☎04 90 86 32 49). Open Tu-Sa 8am-noon and 2-7pm. €12.96 per day, €35.83 per week. €120 deposit. MC/V.

✷ ⁊ ORIENTATION AND PRACTICAL INFORMATION

Avignon's 14th-century ramparts enclose a labyrinth of alleyways, squares, and cramped cobblestoned streets that is excellent for exploring. To reach the tourist office from the train station, walk straight through porte de la République onto cours Jean Jaurès. The tourist office is about 200m uphill on the right. Cours Jean Jaurès becomes rue de la République and leads directly to **place de l'Horloge**, Avignon's central square, below the looming Palais des Papes.

At night, lone travelers should stay on well-lit paths and avoid pedestrian streets, as well as the area around rue Thiers and rue Philonarde. During the July festival season, the town becomes a haven for car thieves and pickpockets.

Tourist Office: 41 cours Jean Jaurès (☎04 32 74 32 74; www.ot-avignon.fr). Knowledgeable and friendly staff provides maps and walking tours of the city's historical landmarks. (2hr. tours in several languages Apr.-Oct. Tu, Th, Sa 10am. €10, students €7. Themed tours offered during the Festival d'Avignon and for children.) Open July M-Sa 9am-7pm, Su 10am-5pm; Apr.-June and Aug.-Oct. M-Sa 9am-6pm, Su 10am-5pm; Nov.-Mar. M-F 9am-6pm, Sa 9am-5pm, Su 10am-noon.

Tours:

Train Tours: Les Trains Touristiques (☎06 11 35 06 66) provides a 45min. tour of the old town, ramparts, and the Rocher des Doms garden (€7). Trains leave from the Palais des Papes every 20min. Tours run daily mid-Mar. to mid-Oct. 10am-7pm. (July and Aug. until 8pm.)

Bus Tours: Autocars Lieutaud (☎04 90 86 36 75; www.cars-lieutaud.fr) runs excursions to the **Alpilles, La Camargue, Nimes, Arles**, the **Lubéron, Pont-du-Gard** and **Orange**. Tickets (€15-28) can be bought from the tourist office. All buses leave from the Grand Hôtel near the train station (Apr.-early Nov.) **Les Provençales** (☎04 90 14 70 00, www.provence-reservation.com) also tours nearby locales. All tours leave from Grand Hôtel. (€20-40. June-late Sept. 10% discount on second purchased tour.) True to its name, **Lavender Tours** (☎04 90 14 70 02) tours lavender areas and the lavender museum in Coustellet (June-Aug., €50-60 for half-day tours and €90-120 for full-day tours, €140 for a 50min. flight over lavender fields).

Boat Tours: Bâteau Bus (☎04 90 85 62 25; www.avignon-et-provence.com/mireio) offers boat trips along the Rhône (1-2hr.; July-Aug. 6 per day; €7.50, children €4). A dinner cruise is offered nightly (1½ hr.; July-Aug.; €23.50, children €12). For longer river cruises, **Compagnie G.B.P.** (☎04 90 85 62 25; same web address) rides up and down the Rhône, stopping in Arles, Tarascon, Châteauneuf-du-Pape, and the Camargue, among others. (Options alternate throughout the year. €45-57, €28.70 cruise only, €45-57 depending on meals and length.) **Les Provençales** (☎04 90 14 70 00; www.provence-reservation.com) provides 3hr. cruises that take tourists from Avignon to Arles. (€60, includes lunch and visit to sites painted by Van Gogh. W.)

Lost and Found: at Municipal Police Office, 13 quai St-Lazare (☎04 32 76 01 73).

English-Language Bookstore: Shakespeare Bookshop and Tearoom, 155 rue de la Carreterie (☎04 90 27 38 50), down rue Carnot toward ramparts. English-cream teas and great homemade brownies (€1.30). Open Tu-Sa 9:30am-12:30pm and 2-6:30pm.

Youth Information: Espace Info-Jeunes, 102 rue de la Carreterie (☎04 90 14 04 05). Info on jobs, study, health care, housing, work. Open M-F 8:30am-noon and 1-5pm.

Laundromat: 66 pl. des Corps Saints. Also 48 rue Carreterie. Both open daily 7am-8pm. For an exciting way to pass the time doing laundry, **Le Café Lavoir,** 101 rue de la Bonneterie (☎04 90 27 91 06; le-cafe-lavoir@wanadoo.fr), is a funky cafe and laundromat, complete with a tiny art gallery. Wash €4-8, dry €1 per 15min. Open daily 10am-8pm.

Police: bd. St-Roch (☎04 90 16 81 00), left of the train station.

Pharmacy: 11-13 rue St-Agricol (☎04 90 82 14 20). Open daily 8am-7:15pm. For the nightly **pharmacie de garde,** call the police.

Hospital: 305 rue Raoul Follereau (☎04 32 75 33 33), south of the town center. 24hr.

Internet Access: Webzone, 3 rue St-Jean le Vieux (☎04 32 76 29 47), at pl. Pie. Fair number of computers and chatty English-speaking staff. €2.50 for 30min., €4 per hr. Open M-Sa 9am-midnight, Su noon-8pm. **Chez W@M,** 41 rue du Vieux Sextier (☎04 90 86 19 03). New computers. €3.50 per hr. Open M-F 8am-1am, Sa-Su noon-1am.

Post Office: cours JFK (☎04 90 27 54 00), near porte de la République. **Currency exchange.** Western Union. Open M-F 8am-7pm, Sa 8am-noon. Branch office on pl. Pie (☎04 32 74 67 40). Open M-F 8:30am-6:30pm, Sa 8:30am-noon.

Postal Code: 84000.

ACCOMMODATIONS AND CAMPING

In general, Avignon's budget offerings are pleasant and plentiful. Unfortunately, unreserved beds vanish once the theater troupes hit town. All prices increase (often by €10 for hotels) during festival season. Reserve up to six months in advance for July and August. The tourist office lists organizations that set up cheap housing during the festival; if hotels are full, festival-goers might consider staying in Arles, Nîmes, Orange, or Tarascon and commuting by train (€5.50-7.10).

Hotel Boquier, 6 rue du Portail Boquier (☎04 90 82 34 43; fax 04 90 86 14 07), near the tourist office. Comfortable rooms with antique wooden ceilings in a charming 18th-century home. Private bath, phone, and TV. Triples are decorated with objects from the owner's many travels. Breakfast €6. Reception 7:30am-9:30pm. Reserve well ahead. Singles €40; doubles €45-52; triples €70-72; quads €80. Extra bed €10. 5% discount with *Let's Go* (except in July). Prices increase by €10 in July. MC/V. ❹

Hôtel du Parc, 18 rue Perdiguier (☎04 90 82 71 55; fax 04 90 85 64 86). Modern, comfortable rooms with handmade bedspreads and curtains offer a beautiful view of the park. Breakfast (€6.50) cooked daily by the owner gives a homey feel. Hallway shower €2. Reception 6am-10pm. Reserve well ahead. Singles €28, with shower €35; doubles €35, with bath €42; triples with bath €65. €1.50 discount with *Let's Go* mid-Nov. to mid-Mar. Prices increase (€10-14) in July festival season. MC/V. ❸

Hôtel Splendid, 17 rue Perdiguier (☎04 90 86 14 46; www.avignon-splendid-hotel.com), near the tourist office, 5min. from the *Gare Centrale* and Palais des Papes. Bright, recently redone rooms with new wooden furniture. The smallest rooms are cramped and a bit dark. Breakfast €6. Reception 7am-11pm. Singles €30, with shower €37, with bath €40; doubles with bath €50-58; triples €70-75. A spacious apartment with kitchen and private garden available for €60-80 a night. Extra bed €15. From Nov.-Mar. *Let's Go* holders get one free breakfast per room, or a €3 discount. All prices increase by €10 in July. MC/V. ❸

Hôtel Mignon, 12 rue Joseph Vernet (☎04 90 82 17 30; www.hotel-mignon.com). Charming hotel on a chic, busy street near great shopping. Provençal fabrics adorn each comfortable, well-equipped room. Phone, TV, and WIFI Internet (€8 per hour). Breakfast included. Singles €33; doubles with shower €50; triples with shower €61; quads €79. Rates increase by €4-5 July-Aug. MC/V. ❸

Foyer Bagatelle, Ile de la Barthelasse (☎04 90 86 30 39 or 04 90 85 78 45; aub-erge.bagatelle@wanadoo.fr). Take bus #10 or 11 to La Barthelasse. 10min. walk to downtown Avignon. Incomparable view of city. Simple 2-, 4-, 6-, or 8-bed rooms with minimal furnishing. Supermarket, 2 cafeterias, and bike rental (€13 per day with ID deposit). Internet €1 for the first min., and €0.15 per extra min. Breakfast priced a la carte. Reception 8am-8:30pm. Lockout 2-5pm. Dorms €11; doubles €24-31; triples €37; quads €47. Prices increase by 10% during festival season. Basic, crowded **camping** facilities available in the dense shade of plane trees, though lots are small, and the grass is spotty at times. Reception 8:30am-8:30pm. 1 person and tent €7.86-9.66, 2 people and tent €10.20. Electricity €2.50. Water €1.30-1.50. MC/V. ❶

Foyer YMCA/UCJG, 7bis chemin de la Justice, Villeneuve (☎04 90 25 46 20; info@ymca-avignon.com). From the train station, turn left and follow the city wall; cross second bridge (pont Daladier) and Ile Barthelasse. Continue straight 200m, take a left onto chemin de la Justice; the foyer is up the hill on your left. (30min.) From the post office, take bus #10 (dir: Les Angles-Grand Angles) to Général Leclerc or #11 (dir: Villeneuve-Grand Terme) to Pont d'Avignon. Sparsely decorated, slightly worn rooms with terraces. Great views of the Palais, the surrounding countryside, or the inviting pool. Internet €2.80 per hr. Breakfast €5. *Demi-pension obligatory in July (€12 extra).* Reception 8:30am-6pm; July-Aug. F-Su reception at on-site restaurant. Reserve ahead. Apr.-Oct. singles €22 per person, with shower and toilet €33; doubles €28-42; triples and quads €33-51. Rates drop 20% in other months. MC/V. ❷

▨ **Camping: Pont d'Avignon,** 300 Ile de la Barthelasse (☎04 90 80 63 50; www.camping-avignon.com), 10min. past Foyer Bagatelle. Showers, laundry, restaurant, market, pool, and tennis courts in a 4-star site that feels like a hotel. 300 large, shady sites in a quiet, well-maintained park. Boat shuttles to Avignon. Internet access €9 per hour. Open Mar.-Oct. Reception July-Aug. 8am-10pm; June and Sept. 8am-8pm; Mar.-May and Oct. 8:30am-6:30pm. July 1 person and tent €14.30; 2 people and tent €20.50; extra person €4.10. Electricity €2.50-3. Prices up to 60% less in low season. MC/V. ❶

🄵 FOOD

There's a delicious selection of lively, creative restaurants on the crooked **rue des Teinturiers.** The Vietnamese restaurants on side-streets throughout the city are often great budget options. The **Parc du Rocher des Doms,** overlooking the Rhône, provides good picnic spots and has an outdoor cafe near the pond. **Les Halles,** the large indoor **market** on pl. Pie, promises endless amounts of regional produce, chèvre, meats, olives, and wines. (Tu-F 6am-1:30pm, Sa-Su 6am-2pm.) Food may be less expensive at the **open-air markets** outside the city walls near porte St-Michel (Sa-Su 7am-1pm) and on pl. Crillon (F 7am-1pm). **Shopi supermarket,** rue de la République, about 100m from the tourist office, offers quick grocery fixes (open M-Sa 8:30am-8pm), as does the reliable **Petit Casino** on rue St-Agricol (open M-Sa 8am-8pm, Su 9am-8pm) and at 3 rue Corps Saints. (Open M-Sa 8am-noon and 3-7:30pm.) Most restaurants stay open an hour or two later and seven days a week during the festivals.

▨ **La Cuisine des Méchantes,** 68 rue de la Bonneterie (☎04 90 86 14 81). Hidden from the tourist traps of pl. de l'Horloge, this gem specializes in *tartines,* served hot (€4.50) or cold (€4.30). The 2 chatty owners serve cheerful regulars in their tastefully decorated kitchen. Complete a meal with the homemade *dessert du jour* (€3.50). If you stay late enough, you might get a chance to hear Silvère, the restaurant's talented bard. Open daily noon-2pm and 7:30pm-1:30am; noon-3am during the July festival season. ❶

▨ **Françoise...,** 6 rue Général Leclerc (☎04 32 76 24 77), near pl. Pie. Gourmet home-style meals. Lots of vegetarian options, sandwiches, salads, and soups (all €2-4.50), as well as full meals (€8-10). The owner welcomes diners with home-like touches, including apple-raspberry crumble (€3) served in little baskets with wooden "silver-ware." Open daily 11:30am-7pm; 10am-midnight during the July festival season. ❷

Maison Nani, rue de la République (☎04 90 82 60 90), near H&M. Jovial regulars satisfy their appetites with heaping salads (€9), *carpaccios* (€10), and homemade desserts (€4-5) at this lively restaurant amidst the action of rue de la République. Try the *Don Nani salade de penne* (€8.90). Open M-Sa 11:30am-2:30pm, F-Sa 7-11pm. ❸

Le Caveau du Theatre, 16 rue des Trois Faucons (☎04 90 82 60 91; lecaveau.dutheatre@wanadoo.fr). Regulars and tourists alike flock to this restaurant, which serves gourmet Provençal cuisine with a twist. The *menu* changes according to season. Lunch *menu* €10.60, dinner *menus* €14 or €18. Open M-F noon-2pm and 7-10pm, Sa 7-10pm; daily during the July festival season. MC/V. ❸

Terre de Saveur, 1 rue St-Michel (☎04 90 86 68 72), just off pl. des Corps Saints. Homey Provençal restaurant serves hearty dishes with organic veggies in a cozy dining room filled with locals. Vegetarian *menu* €13; omnivore version €15. *Plats* €9-11.50. Open M-Sa 11:30am-2:30pm; F-Sa and nightly during festival 7-9:30pm. MC/V. ❸

Citron Pressé, 38 rue Carreterie (☎04 90 86 09 29). This small restaurant offers tasty Lebanese and Indian fare at astonishing prices (€3.50-6). Chatty, smiling owners keep customers coming back with homemade *plats du jour* (€6.80). Open Sept.-June M-Sa noon-2pm, Th-F also 7:30-11:30pm, Sa also 7:30pm-2am; daily July noon-2am. ❶

🔘 SIGHTS

Most of Avignon's sights operate on a pass system. Pay full admission for entrance to a monument or museum, and pay a reduced price at sights visited for 15 days thereafter. The pass also entitles visitors to discounts on guided tours of town (30% off) and tourist transportation (up to 20% off).

▩ PALAIS DES PAPES. This golden Gothic palace, the largest in Europe, thrusts gargoyles over the city and the Rhône. Begun in 1335 by the third pope of Avignon, Benoît XII, it was completed less than twenty years later by his successor Clément VI. The papal palace is neatly divided into two sections marked by the contrasting styles of their builders: the strict, spare grandeur of the Cistercian Benoît and the astonishing scale and ostentation of the aristocratic Clément. Following the political unrest of the late 18th century, the castle was turned into a prison (1790) and served as barracks until 1906, when it was finally restored and opened for public viewing. Although Revolutionary looting stripped the interior of its lavish furnishings, the giant rooms and their frescoed walls are still remarkable, with brightly colored tiles and slowly flaking paint in some of the inner chambers. The Great Chapel, whose single nave is 52m long, 15m wide and 20m tall, is representative of the palace's gigantic dimensions. What dazzles the viewer most is the way the palace unrolls almost endlessly, chamber after chamber. Since 2004, the formerly bare rooms have become home to the Musée de l'Œuvre, a permanent display retracing the history of the papacy in Avignon. (☎04 90 27 50 74; www.palais-des-papes.com. Open daily July 9am-9pm; Aug.-Sept. 9am-8pm; Oct.-June 9am-7pm. Last entrance 1hr. before closing. Palace and exhibition €9.50, with pass €7.50.)

PONT ST-BÉNÉZET. This 12th-century bridge is known to all French children as the "Pont d'Avignon," immortalized in the famous song. In 1177, Bénézet, a shepherd boy, was commanded by angels to build a bridge across the Rhône. He announced his intentions to the population of Avignon, but the people, thinking he was crazy, laughed at him. The Archbishop, pointing to a gigantic boulder, told Bénézet that he would have to place the first stone himself. Miraculously, the shepherd heaved the rock onto his shoulder and tossed it into the river. The holy shot-put convinced the townspeople, who responded quickly with shovels and mortar, finishing the bridge in 1185. Despite the divinely chosen location, the bridge has suffered at the hands of warfare and the once-turbulent Rhône, now extending only partway across the river. It costs €3.50 (with pass €3) to walk on the wind-swept bridge; there is no extra charge for dancing to the song playing on your audioguide. (☎04 90 85 60 16. Includes a detailed audioguide in 7 languages. Open daily Apr.-Sept. 9am-7pm; Oct.-Mar. 9:30am-5:30pm.) Farther down the river, **Pont Daladier** makes it all the way across the river to the campgrounds, offering free views of the broken bridge and the Palais along the way.

MUSÉE DU PETIT PALAIS. Avignon's most significant museum, housed in a 600-year old palace, displays a prolific collection of Medieval and Renaissance paintings as well as unique Romanesque and Gothic sculptures. (Palais des Archevêques, pl. du Palais des Papes. ☎04 90 86 44 58; musee.petitpalais@wanadoo.fr. Written guides available in English, German, and Italian for €2. Open June-Sept. M and W-Su 10am-1pm and 2-6pm; Oct.-May 9:30am-1pm and 2-5:30pm. €6, with pass €3.)

COLLECTION LAMBERT. Highlighting the oft-misunderstood art of the period from the late 1960s through the present, this excellent museum presents three exhibits per year. Past artists have included Sol LeWitt and Jean-Michel Basquiat. The museum displays two permanent pieces: a digitized message from Jenny Holzer, and a throbbing red neon room. (5 rue Violette. ☎04 90 16 56 20; www.collection-lambert.com. Open daily July-Aug. 11am-7pm; Nov.-Feb. Tu-Su until 6pm. €5.50, with pass €4.)

OTHER SIGHTS. On the hill above the Palais, the beautifully sculpted **Rocher des Doms Park** has vistas of Mont Ventoux, St-Bénézet, and the fortifications of Villeneuve. (Open during daylight hours.) Next to the Palais, the 12th-century **Cathédrale Notre-Dame-des-Doms** contains the dramatically lit Gothic tomb of Pope John XXII. (Open daily 10am-7pm.) Avignon's oldest museum, the elegant 18th-century **Musée Calvet**, highlights French artists from the 15th to 20th century. Works by Vernet, Claudel, and David are part of the permanent collection. (65 rue Joseph Vernet. ☎04 90 86 33 84. Open M and W-Su 10am-1pm and 2-6pm. €6, with pass €3.)

🎵 🎭 ENTERTAINMENT AND FESTIVALS

From October to June, opera, drama, and classical music performances take place in the **Opéra d'Avignon**, pl. de l'Horloge (☎04 90 82 81 40). **Rue des Teinturiers** is lined with theaters holding performances from early afternoon through the wee hours of the morning. These include the **Théâtre du Chien qui Fume**, 75 rue des Teinturiers (☎04 90 85 25 87), the **Théâtre du Balcon**, 38 rue Guillaume Puy (☎04 90 85 00 80), and the **Théâtre du Chêne Noir**, 8bis rue Ste-Catherine (☎04 90 86 58 11). The popular **Utopia Cinéma**, behind the Palais des Papes, on 4 rue des Escaliers Ste-Anne, is an independent theater that screens a wide variety of documentaries and movies. (☎04 90 82 65 36. €5, 10 showings €40, early birds €3.)

Although the festival means that bars, cafes, shops, and restaurants stay open until early in the morning, the rest of the year still promises nighttime amusement that is only slightly tamer. *Brasseries* on **cours Jean Jaurès** and **rue de la République** stay open late to entertain quiet crowds on their terraces. A few lively bars color **place des Corps Saints**. A favorite among young tourists, **The Cubanito Café**, 52 rue Carnot, features nightly dancing to Cuban music in a boisterous atmosphere. (☎04 90 27 90 59. Beers from €2.20. Free salsa lessons Tu-Sa 9-10pm. Open daily 8am-1am.) **Les Célestins**, 38 pl. des Corps Saints, is a mosaic-tiled cafe whose fun-loving crowd overflows the *place*. (Beer from €2, drinks €3-5. Open daily 9am-1am.) For those seeking black-lit dance floors and chic drinking, **Bokao's**, 9bis bd. St-Lazare, just outside the porte St-Lazare, is filled with glowing white lanterns and palm trees. (☎04 90 82 47 95. Drinks from €5. Cover Sa only, €10. Open W-Sa 10pm-5am.) **L'Esclav Bar**, 12 rue du Limas, near the Pont d'Avignon, has heavy techno and house with a bouncer who enforces the private club policy. (☎04 90 85 14 91.

Cover €5, includes a drink. Open daily from 11pm.) **Red Zone,** 25 rue Carnot, fulfills its role as a student club with later hours and music ranging from salsa to R&B. (☎04 90 27 02 44. Open daily 9am-3am; closed Su Nov.-Feb.) Cheap beer and pool draw a talkative crowd to the **Koala Bar,** 2 pl. des Corps Saints. (☎04 90 86 80 87. Beer from €2.50, drinks from €2. Happy hour daily 7-10pm. Open 8:30pm-1:30am, until 1am Nov.-Feb.)

July brings the definite highlight of Avignon's calendar, a month filled with more theater than is imaginable. During the riotous ■**Festival d'Avignon,** Gregorian chanters rub shoulders with all-night *Odyssey* readers and African dancers. The official festival, known as the **IN,** is the most prestigious theatrical gathering in Europe, and uses at least 30 different venues from factories to cloisters to palaces. (Info and tickets ☎04 90 14 14 14, festival office ☎04 90 14 14 60; www.festival-avignon.com. Tickets free-€33. Reservations accepted after mid-June. Rush tickets at venue 45min. before the show; students and those under 25 get a 50% discount, 30% discount on every performance with the *carte IN,* sold at the tourist office for €8.) The cheaper and more experimental (although equally established) **Festival OFF** presents over 700 pieces, some in English, over the course of three weeks in July. (OFFice on pl. du Palais. ☎01 48 05 01 19; www.avignon-off.org. Tickets free-€16; purchased at the venue or the OFFice, not available over the phone. 30% discount on every performance with the *carte OFF,* sold at the OFFice for €13.) Tickets aren't necessary to get in on the act—fun, free theater overflows into the streets during the day and even more so night. The Centre Franco-Américain de Provence sponsors the **Euro-American Film Workshop** in late June at the Cinéma Vox. The festival showcases feature and short films directed by young French and American aspirants. Meals, parties, and lectures make for good schmoozing with the next big thing. French and English subtitles are provided. (☎04 90 25 93 23. Night showings €6, morning films €1.50, day pass €55.)

■ DAYTRIP FROM AVIGNON

VILLENEUVE-LÈS-AVIGNON

From Avignon, bus #11 (every 20min.) to Villeneuve tourist office. Or, a 25-30min. walk over the Le Pont Daladier, just below Pont d'Avignon, provides scenic views along the Rhône. Follow the signs to Villeneuve. The Bâteau Bus boat, allées de l'Oulle, near the Pont Daladier, cruises past Pont St-Bénézet and docks at Villeneuve. A free petit train will take you to the town center. (☎04 90 85 62 25. July-Aug. 6 per day 10:30am-6:30pm. Round-trip €7.50, children €4; 20% off with pass. Tickets on board or at tourist office in Avignon and Villeneuve.)

Founded in the 13th century to intimidate France's Provençal neighbors, Villeneuve-lès-Avignon ("new town by Avignon") sits on a hill overlooking Avignon. The so-called City of Cardinals was the home of many dignitaries and attendants to the papal court. Today, the imposing towers of Fort Saint-André and Tour Philippe le Bel offer panoramic views of Avignon and the Rhône Valley.

Chartreuse du Val de Bénédiction, rue de la République, is one of the largest Carthusian monasteries in France, housing three cloisters and 40 cells. The beautiful *trompe-l'oeil* frescoes testify to the monastery's wealth throughout the Middle Ages. Abandoned in 1790, the Chartreuse has become home to the Centre National des Ecritures du Spectacle, which hosts artists and creative performances throughout the year. The collapsed back wall of the 14th-century Gothic church affords a dramatic view of Fort St-André. (☎04 90 15 24 24; www.chartreuse.org. Open daily Apr.-Sept. 9am-6:30pm; Oct.-Mar. 9:30am-5:30pm. Guided tours daily July 3pm, and sometimes Aug. €6.10, students and those with pass €4.10, Chartreuse/Fort Saint-André combo €5.50 with pass.) Info regarding regular and special events is available at the front desk.

The **Musée Pierre de Luxembourg**, also on the rue de la République, has a small yet interesting collection of sacred art. A 14th-century ivory sculpture of the Virgin Mary and a few works by French painter Pierre de Champaigne are all part of the collection. The highlight, however, is Enguerrand Quarton's *The Crowning of the Virgin*, a large Medieval painting depicting the three-layered Christian universe. (☎04 90 27 49 66. Open Apr.-Sept. Tu-Su 10am-12:30pm and 2-6:30pm; Oct.-Mar. Tu-Su 10am-noon and 2-5pm. €3, €2 for pass holders.)

A steep path leads to Gothic **Fort Saint-André,** built by King Philip le Bel (the Fair) in the 14th century. The towers of this large, windowless citadel served as prisons after losing their strategic value; the stone floors and walls still bear traces of the prisoners' desperate carvings. (☎04 90 25 45 35. Open daily Apr.-Sept. 10am-1pm and 2-6pm; Oct.-Mar. 10am-1pm and 2-5pm. €4.60, students and with pass €3.10.)

Situated within the fortress is the Benedictine **Abbaye St-André.** Now in ruins, the once-prosperous abbey was home to as many as 90 monks in the 14th century. Excavations have unearthed the remains of two churches erected in the 11th and 12th centuries, and evidence suggests that more remains lie underneath. Although the original buildings were mostly destroyed during the Revolution, they have been replaced with multi-layered Italian-style gardens complete with purple lilies, olive trees. Between the fountains and arcades of cypresses are views of the Rhône Valley and Avignon. (☎04 90 25 55 95. Open Apr.-Sept. Tu-Su 10am-12:30pm and 2-6pm; Oct.-Mar. Tu-Su 10am-12:30pm and 2-5pm. €4, with pass €3.)

The Gothic **Tour Philippe le Bel,** located right at the intersection of av. Gabriel Péri and Montée de la Tour, is not for the faint of the heart. Its seemingly endless spiral staircase can easily make your head spin, though the view from the tower's wind-swept platform is worth the climb. (☎04 32 70 08 57. Tower open Apr.-Sept. Tu-Su 10am-12:30pm and 2-6:30pm; Oct.-Mar. Tu-Su 10am-noon and 2-5pm. €1.60, students and pass €1.)

Be sure to visit the **tourist office,** pl. Charles David (☎04 90 25 61 33; www.ville-neuvelesavignon.fr/tourisme), which offers free maps, information on boat shuttles, and more. English brochures are scarce, but the friendly staff may unearth a few if you ask. A city **pass** (€6.86) allows you to visit virtually every major historical sight in Villeneuve. Guided tours of the *vieille ville* are offered in July and August. (2hr. tours in French; Tu, Th 5pm. Open Aug.-June M-Sa 9am-12:30pm and 2-6pm; daily July 10am-7pm. €4.50, under 18 and with pass €3.50.)

THE LUBÉRON AND THE VAUCLUSE

This region fulfills every romanticized vision of sunny French countryside. The Parc Naturel Régional du Lubéron and the Vaucluse stretch over neat rows of vineyards and radiant fields of lavender, dotted with haunting medieval châteaux and tiny villages on rocky cliffs. For centuries this mini-Eden has been a home and inspiration to writers, from Petrarch to the Marquis de Sade to Samuel Beckett. Small wonder—from the fiery reds of the ochre hills to the deep greens of the olive farms, this is Provence's living poetry. Although *Let's Go* lists a few famous beauties here, this region is ideal for discovering hidden surprises on one's own.

TRANSPORTATION AND PRACTICAL INFORMATION. The majority of the Lubéron can easily be covered in two to three days by **car**—by far the easiest option. Avignon is filled with rental companies happy to provide maps and suggestions. N100 blows right through the middle of the Lubéron park and branches off to the smaller towns. While the twisting, narrow roads from one town to the next are usually far more picturesque, drivers should stay away from them. Expect to pay €2-4 for parking in most villages. Combining occasional bus trips with walks or bike rides between towns (usually 7-15km) will let you experience Provence at its pristine finest, albeit in more time. Biking, though common, is not for the faint of heart, as the mountains climb steeply here. A few of the bike rental companies offer to drop renters off at cities that allow for strategic downhill coasting. While the town may not merit a visit, the **Maison du Parc** in Apt (on N100, accessible from Avignon with Autocars Barlatier ☎04 90 73 23 59) is a major base for exploring the natural wonders in this area. It has information desk that can answer questions about various **hiking, canoeing,** and **biking** routes throughout the Lubéron National Park with maps and natural guide books for sale. (☎04 90 04 42 00. Open Apr.-Sept. M-Sa 8:30am-noon and 1:30-7pm; Oct.-Mar. M-F 8:30am-noon and 1:30-6pm.) Locals sometimes choose to hitch, but rides for tourists are difficult to come by and *Let's Go* does not recommend hitchhiking at any time. Avignon **buses** leave from the central bus terminal by the train station. **Voyages Arnaud** (☎04 90 38 15 58) runs buses from Avignon to **L'Isle-sur-la-Sorgue** (40min., 8 per day, €3.10) and **Fontaine de Vaucluse** (55min., 2 per day, €3.90). **Les Express de la Durance** (☎04 90 71 03 00) buses head to **Cavaillon** (40min., 12 per day, €3.10), which also serves as a hub for bus excursions. **TransVaucluse** (☎04 90 82 07 35) covers most of the Vaucluse and Lubéron. Schedules change regularly; information is posted at the *gare routière* in Avignon. **Autocars Barlatier** (☎04 90 73 23 59) goes to the **train station** at **Bonnieux** (1hr., 6 per day, €5.30). However you choose to travel, good walking shoes are a must for the hilly, often unpaved roads.

L'ISLE-SUR-LA-SORGUE

L'Isle-sur-la-Sorgue (pop. 17,500), birthplace of notorious Surrealist poet René Char (1907-1988), is the first step from Avignon into the Vaucluse countryside. Entangled in the green ribbon of its river, this tranquil town echoes with the rushing currents of water that twist around the *centre ville*. The sparklingly clear, shallow waters of the Sorgue are split into numerous channels to the east of the city, surrounding and running beneath the town center, aptly nicknamed "the Venice of Vaucluse." Founded in the 12th century, L'Isle-sur-la-Sorgue has long depended on its narrow waterways for fish, industry, and now tourism. For travelers, the gardens along the river, particularly the **Jardin Public,** provide idyllic views for a picnic. The third largest center for antiques in Europe, L'Isle-sur-la-Sorgue counts over 300 **antique shops** housed in seven "antique dealers' villages" scattered throughout the city. Art collectors, flock to the tiny village for a world-famous **antique fair** that brings over 500 dealers every year (at Easter and in mid-August).

Delectable fruits and vegetables are sold weekly in the **open-air market,** one of the town's main attractions (Th and Su 8am-1pm). On the first Sunday of August, the **floating market** *(marché flottant)* crowds the Sorgue with small boats full of hawkers' wares (9am-noon). Merchants sell local products, including homemade tapenade and cheeses, directly from their boats. Every third Sunday in July, at the **Marché Provençal,** merchants dressed in traditional garb take part in fishing events (8am-1pm). Also in July, the city and its neighbors host the **Festival de la Sorgue,** celebrating the river with water jousting, singing contests, and concerts. The **tourist office,** in the church on pl. de la Liberté, supplies maps (free or €1) and comprehensive info on festivals, markets, lodging, shopping, and outdoor activities for the entire region around the town and in the Vaucluse. Starting in June, half-day tours of the *vieille ville* and single-day tours of Vaucluse are offered—inquire at the office. (☎04 90 38 04 78. Open July-Aug. M-Sa 9am-12:30pm and 2-6pm, Su 9:30am-1pm; Sept.-June M-Sa 9am-12:30pm and 2:30-6pm, Su 9am-12:30pm.)

Restaurants abound near the Pont Gambetta, many with terraces overlooking the Sorgue. **Le Potager de Louise ❷,** 9 quai Rouget de L'Isle, has many vegetarian options. The lunch *menu* is a deal (€11), and the homemade chèvre-spinach lasagna (€10) is worth a try. (☎04 90 20 96 56. Open M-Sa noon-3pm and 7-10:30pm, Su noon-3pm. Salads €9-12, *plats* €9-18, desserts €5. V.)

The easiest way to L'Isle-sur-la-Sorgue is by the TransVaucluse **train** from Avignon (☎04 90 82 07 35; about 20min., 9-10 per day, €4). Cheaper accommodations are mostly located on the outskirts of L'Isle-sur-la-Sorgue. The tourist office provides an excellent guide to the hotels, B&Bs, and campgrounds in the region. **La Gueulardière ❹**, 1 cours René Char, near the rotary, offers five quiet, large, well-kept rooms in a dignified old hotel where tree leaves flutter in the breeze and old paintings decorate the walls. (☎04 90 38 10 52; fax 04 90 20 83 70. Breakfast €7.50. Reception 8am-9pm. Doubles €54. AmEx/MC/V.) Camping at ▨**La Sorguette ❶**, on rte. d'Apt (RN100), along the river 2km north of the town center, is a great base for exploring the Vaucluse. The award-winning campsite has an unusually large number of well-maintained facilities, lacking only a swimming pool. (☎04 90 38 05 71; www.camping-sorguette.com. Free hot showers, laundry, snack bar, Internet, children's playground, tennis, ping-pong, *boules*, fishing, and volleyball. July-Aug. kayaks €8 per hr., €16 per half-day. Foreign newspapers available at the reception 8:15am-7:30pm. Open mid-Mar. to mid-Oct. 2 people with car €14.70-18.20. Extra person €4.70-6.30, visitors €2.50. Electricity €3.50-6.)

Tendil/Moto-Cycles, on 10 av. de la Gare right outside the train station, rents **bikes.** (☎04 90 38 19 12. Open Tu-Sa 8am-noon and 2-7pm. €13 per day. Passport deposit.) Family-run **Provence Vélos Location,** a friendly, English-speaking rental place, will drop off customers with their rental bikes in the village of their choice to avoid painful uphill climbs. (☎/fax 04 90 60 28 07; www.guideweb.com/provence-velos. Check their website for their four locations in Provence, including Isle-sur-la-Sorgue. €14.50 per day. 10% reduction for groups of three or more. All offices open daily 7am-7pm.) Crédit Agricole, 7 quai Jean Jaurès, has a 24hr. **ATM** across the river from the post office. There is a **laundromat** on Pl. Victor Hugo, and an **Internet cafe** at 10 Rue A. Autheman. (☎04 90 38 15 87. Tu-Su 10am-7pm. €4.50 per hr.) **Taxi** services can be reached at ☎06 08 09 19 49. For the **police station,** quai Jean Jaurès, call ☎04 90 20 81 20. For medical needs, use the small **Hôpital de l'Isle-sur-la-Sorgue** (☎04 90 21 34 00) and **ambulance** service (☎04 90 38 00 00). The **Pharmacie de la Sorgue** is on rue de la République (open M-Sa 8:30am-12:15pm and 2:15-7:15), and the **pharmacie de garde** can be found by calling ☎04 90 78 58 00. The **post office,** av. de Quatre Otages, across from the Jardin Public, provides **currency exchange.** (☎04 90 21 28 44. Open M-F 8:30am-noon and 1:30-5:30pm, Sa 8:30am-noon.) **Postal Code:** 84800.

FONTAINE DE VAUCLUSE

Tucked into the base of 230m cliffs, with an emerald spring so clear that it gives off an otherworldly glow, Fontaine de Vaucluse (pop. 500) is a refreshing oasis. The Sorgue rushes full-speed here from **Le Gouffre,** one of the largest river sources in the world. At its spring peak, Le Gouffre pours 70 to 90m^3 of water per second into the Sorgue. The underground cavern of water gushes below the cliffs to unknown depths; neither Jacques Cousteau and his team of explorers nor modern robotics have discovered the bottom of this mysterious water source. Equally fruitless were the quests of Petrarch, who pined on the banks of the river after "Laura," his enduring muse. After spotting the young woman in an Avignon church on April 6, 1327, Petrarch spent two decades composing sonnets in Fontaine—a melancholy time recounted in *De Vita Solitaria.* In July and August, tourists swarm into Fontaine only a little less ferociously than its river does, bringing out the worst of Provençal kitsch. Luckily, the pure, unadulterated beauty of the diaphanous fountain and the hum of cicadas wipe out the plastic impression left by this tourist trap.

The 10m **Colonne** in the center of town commemorates Petrarch's life and labor, as does the small **Musée Petrarque** across the bridge. The museum, which is believed to lie on the site of Petrarch's 14th-century dwelling, holds rare editions of the poet's works. A small modern art collection attests to the enduring influence of the Italian literary figure in Western culture. (☎04 90 20 37 20; musee-biblio-petrarque@cg84.fr. Open June-Sept. M and W-Su 9:30am-noon and 2-6pm; early Apr.-May and early Oct. M and W-Su 10am-noon and 2-6pm; Mar. to early Apr. and late Oct. Sa-Su 10am-noon and 2-6pm; Nov.-Mar. closed except to groups. €3.50, students €1.50.) The opposite side of the river is scattered with several small museums, including the fascinating **Musée**

d'Histoire. Holding a permanent collection of over 10,000 objects and documents, the museum vividly reconstructs the *années noires* (dark years) under Vichy rule. Sleek exhibits include a redone classroom, complete with chalkboard, desks, and Vichy propaganda books. An allegory of the war's horror, Matisse's gouache painting *The Fall of Icarus* is the museum's most precious jewel. (☎ 04 90 20 24 00; musee-appel-liberte@cg84.fr. Audioguides available. Open June-Sept. M and W-Su 10am-6pm; Apr.-May M and W-Su 10am-noon and 2-6pm; early Oct. M and W-Su 10am-noon and 2-5pm; mid-Oct. to Dec. Sa-Su 10am-noon and 2-5pm; Mar. to mid-Apr. Sa-Su 10am-noon and 2-6pm. €3.50, students €1.50, under 12 free.)

Le Monde Souterrain offers underground strolls through caverns that have been reconstructed for tourists. While the site looks a bit artificial, the visit is surprisingly informative: guided tours are given by professional speleologists, whose passion for caves is strangely contagious. The museum displays a stunning collection of 400 stalactities and crystallizations, kept under protective glass. (☎ 04 90 20 34 13. Open May-June 10am-noon and 2-6pm; July-Aug. 10am-noon and 2-7:30pm; Feb.-Apr. and Sept.-Nov. 10am-noon and 2-5pm. Last tour 1hr. before closing. 40min. tours in French with written English translation €5, under 18 €3.30.) The **tourist office,** along the chemin de la Fontaine toward the Gouffre, has helpful hotel and camping listings as well as English information about activities in the area. (☎ 04 90 20 32 22; officetourisme.vaucluse@wanadoo.fr. Open M-Sa 9am-1pm and 2-7pm. Office hours are variable.)

Surprisingly inexpensive lodgings can be found at the ▣**Hôtel Font de Lauro ❸**, 1.5km from Fontaine de Vaucluse, right off the road to L'Isle-sur-la-Sorgue. The sign is small, so be on the lookout. A friendly owner who takes great care of her guests gives the place a homey feel. The quiet, simply furnished rooms have views of vineyards. A pool completes this bargain package. Satisfied clients have sent postcards from all over the world. (☎/fax 04 90 20 31 49. Breakfast €5.70. Gate closes at midnight. July-Aug. reservations required. Doubles with shower €27, with bath €38; one triple with bath €50. MC/V.) The rural **Auberge de Jeunesse (HI) ❶**, chemin de la Vignasse, 1km from town, is not your typical hostel. Wake to a chorus of roosters in this rustic, spacious stone country house. A diverse international crowd of adventurous backpackers gives the place a friendly feel. (☎ 04 90 20 31 65; fontaine@fuaj.org. Breakfast €3.20. Dinner €8.40. Kitchen access, payphones. Sheets €2.70. Laundry €3.20. Reception 8-10am and 5:30-11pm. Curfew 11pm. Open Feb. to mid-Nov. Bunks €8.90, camping €5. HI members only.) The hostel also offers suggestions for hiking in the Lubéron, especially on the nearby national hiking trails GR6 and GR91, although hiking is sometimes prohibited in July and August for fear of fires.

The outfitting company **Kayak Vert,** located about 500m from Fontaine on the road to L'Isle-sur-la-Sorgue, rents kayaks for the 8km trip down to L'Isle-sur-la-Sorgue. A friendly (and mandatory) guide escorts you down, and a minibus takes you back up to Fontaine. The Sorgue is a Class I river, meaning it's safe and suitable for all skill levels. Ask for a membership card, free after your first kayaking trip, for a 10% discount at 12 river sites in Provence. (☎ 04 90 20 35 44; www.canoefrance.com. 2-person canoes €36; 1-person kayak €18, university students with ID €14. Open mid-Apr. to Oct., weather permitting. Reserve ahead.) There is a **post office** with a rare **ATM** up the street from the Colonne, away from the river. (Open M-F 9am-noon and 2-5pm, Sa 8:30-11:30am.) A **mini-market** is across the street. (Open July-Aug. Tu-Su and holidays 8:15am-8pm; low season daily 7:15am-12:30pm and 3:30-7pm, closed W afternoon.)

OPPÈDE-LE-VIEUX

The tiny village of Oppède-le-Vieux clings to the mountainside below an exquisitely ruined château and above gardened terraces of lavender and olive groves. Formerly a papal residence (1271-1506) and bustling market town, Oppède was slowly abandoned in the 16th century for more agriculturally advantageous regions. Early in the 20th century, the village was completely deserted following a violent earthquake that destroyed several houses. In 1943, descendants of the Marquis de Sade returned to the empty village, which now counts 30 to 50 inhabitants. Oppède-le-Vieux has recently begun to restore the ancient ruins, some of which predate the 13th century. Parking is compulsory below the village (€2), from which small, handpainted signs direct pedestrians up a winding path to the 11th-century **Église Notre-Dame d'Alidon,** next to the **château.** The walk through vine-covered ruins provides stunning views of the tidy vineyards in the valley below. Warning signs around the castle should be heeded: overhanging arches and clifftop towers have been known to drop loose stones on unaware trespassers.

⊠L'Echaugette ❷, the only restaurant in Oppède-le-Vieux, offers a delicious *poulet au citron* (lemon chicken) to hungry visitors. (☎04 90 76 83 68. *Plats* around €8-10.) Purchase a fascinating guide retracing the village's past (€5), or ask the owners about the strange modern art that lies on the path to the church.

BONNIEUX

Bonnieux (pop. 1430), though only slightly larger than its neighbors, is the capital of the Lubéron. Flowers burst from the balconies and windows of the well-restored stone houses that cluster along the hillside of this village, which also offers stunning views over the Vaucluse. Bonnieux's charm lies in its two churches. Perched at the top of the village, the 12th-century *vieille église* (old church) can only be reached through a steep 86-stair staircase. The *église neuve* (new church), in contrast, was built in 1870 at the bottom of the village and is easily accessible. To remember the infamous residents of this region, visit the ruined château of the infamous Marquis de Sade, only 10km away in Lacoste.

A good base to explore the surrounding villages, Bonnieux hosts the **tourist office** for Lacoste, Ménerbes, and Oppède (☎04 90 75 91 90. Open M-Sa 9am-12:30pm and 2-6pm. **Currency exchange** desk. Hours flexible, so call ahead.) The town has many *maisons d'hôtes,* but the cheapest accommodation is the **Camping Municipal du Vallon ❶,** located right outside the city on the road leading to Lacoste. The campsite, located within a forest, is particularly quiet and peaceful. (☎/fax 04 90 75 86 14. Reception daily 9am-noon and after 6pm. Open Apr.-Nov. 1-2 people, car, and tent €8.60; €2.25 per additional person. Electricity €2.60.) **Rent bikes** and **motorbikes** at Mountain Bike Lubéron, rue Marceau, which organizes free delivery within 15km of Bonnieux, including Lacoste. (☎04 90 75 89 96; mobile 06 83 25 48 07. €8 per half-day, €14 per day, €74 per week; motorbikes €30 per day. Open Mar.-Nov. 8:30am-noon and 1:30-6:30pm.) For a **taxi,** call Claude at ☎04 90 75 91 65 or 06 81 75 87 13. A **post office** is located behind the *église neuve,* and has an **ATM.**

⊠ROUSSILLON

Radiant oranges, bright yellows, and earthy reds have made Roussillon (pop. 1200) the most famous of the ochre villages. Its stunning natural ochre park, a wild, red-orange incision in the otherwise gray-green countryside, can be seen from as far away as Gordes. According to local legend, the intense red that colors Roussillon comes from the bleeding body of Dame Sermonde, who jumped from the *castrum* (the highest point in town) after her husband discovered her infidelity. More pragmatic minds have argued that the village is built on the world's largest vein of natural ochre. Whatever the reason, every doorway, windowsill, and wall in Roussillon is tinted with warm and vibrant shades of the earth. While one might be tempted to remove some of the richly colored sand, doing so is strictly prohibited and could result in a hefty fine. Ochre pigments can be purchased in local stores.

An exploration of the ⊠**Sentier des Ochres,** one of the many amazing walking trails in Roussillon, is indispensable: visitors can walk through a vast, dusty ochre deposit between steep, wind-sculpted cliffs. White shoes and clothing will change colors after a few minutes here. (Open daily July-Aug. 9am-7:30pm; Mar.-June and Sept. to mid-Nov. M-Sa 9:30am-5:30pm, Su 9:30am-6pm. €2. Closed on rainy days for safety's sake.) Just 1km outside the town, the **Conservatoire des Ocres et Pigments Appliqués**, rte. d'Apt, has restored an old pigment-making factory and offers tours (€5) and classes (prices vary) throughout the year. Short-term classes for children and adults range from painting and photography to fabricating dyes from natural resources. A large bookstore and a pigment store are next to the conservatory. (☎/fax 04 90 05 66 69; www.okhra.com. 30min. tour; times vary but are frequent in summer. Open July-Aug. Tu-Su 9am-7pm; Sept.-June Su and Tu-Sa 9am-6pm.) Enjoy a panoramic view of the ochre-colored landscape from the **observation table.** The villages of St-Saturnin, Gordes, Joucas, and Cavaillon, as well as the Monts de Vaucluse, can be seen from the highest point in Roussillon.

The **tourist office,** pl. de la Poste, has hotel listings and sells a bilingual French/ English guide, *Balades en Lubéron: Roussillon,* offering detailed information on walking trails (€5). Information on the annual Samuel Beckett event, a tribute to the author, who completed *Waiting for Godot* in Roussillon, is also available. Past summer events have included art exhibits, readings, and performances of the Irishman's most celebrated plays. (☎ 04 90 05 60 25; www.roussillon-provence.com. Open daily June-Aug. 9am-noon and 1:30-6:30pm; Sept.-May M-Sa 10am-noon and 2-5:30pm.)

There's **currency exchange** and a 24hr. **ATM** at the **post office** next door. (Open Apr. to mid-Nov. M-F 9am-noon and 2-5pm, Sa 9-11:30am; mid-Dec. to Feb. 9am-noon and 2-4:30pm.) A **pharmacy** is located in pl. du Pasquier. (☎ 04 90 05 66 15. Open M-Sa 9am-noon and 2:30-7pm.)

The first Sunday of September, a yearly **marché potier** attracts crowds of tourists and locals alike. Now in its 30th season, the **Festival International de Quatuors a Cordes** brings the best of chamber music every year from late May to early September. (☎ 04 90 75 89 60; www.festival-quatuors-luberon.com. €20, students €15, children 12-17 €8, under 12 free.)

GORDES

Considered by many to be the most picturesque of the hillside towns, Gordes (pop. 2050) is perched precariously over remarkable views that seem to stretch to the ocean. Sprinkled with a few small shops and cafes, the village attracts a large (and wealthy) population of tourists. Expect prices to be significantly higher than in Lacoste, Bonnieux, and even Fontaine de Vaucluse.

Gordes and its surroundings are particularly recognized for its **bories,** drystone huts and dwellings built through the skillful placement of stone upon stone without the use of mortar. Often seen in the middle of fields or lost in the tangled undergrowth of the hills, they predate the Romans but continued to be built and used by the locals until the 18th century. The **Village des Bories** outside town is a unique hamlet of *bories* inhabited until a little over 150 years ago. Once inhabited by Ligurians, the village of Gallic huts is complete with sheep-pens, barns, a wine cistern, and several dwellings. (☎ 04 90 72 03 48. Open daily 9am to around sunset. €5.50, ages 10-17 €3.) A 4km twisting, narrow, and particularly dangerous drive beyond Gordes leads to the **Sénanque Abbey,** an active Cistercian community surrounded by perfumed fields of lavender. The exceedingly touristed site was occupied by monks from AD 1148 until the Revolution, then repopulated and restored in the mid-19th century. Today the abbey's popular shop sells prayer books, honey, lavender products, and *sénacole,* a liqueur produced by the local monks. Despite recent efforts to curb tourist intrusions (including reduced hours, mandatory guided tours, and restrictions on groups), visitors continue to flock to this postcard-perfect abbey. It is, however, a place of prayer. Visitors are required to dress conservatively and respect the peace of the abbey. Masses are still held daily in the *Église Abbatiale.* (☎ 04 90 72 05 72. Visits by tour only (in French); times vary by season. The information office can provide detailed schedules. €6, under 18 €2.50, clergy free.) Although well-preserved and restored, the **château** in the middle of town cannot be visited. Originally erected in the 11th century, the medieval fortress was modernized in 1525 and boasts one of the largest *salle d'honneur* in France, as well as a remarkable 16th-century fireplace. Successively used as a barracks, a prison, and a stable, the former Romanesque structure now houses the Hôtel de Ville, the tourist office, and a collection of 200 sensual paintings and photo montages in the **Musée Pol Mara.** Signed works by the contemporary Flemish artist can be purchased on-site for €500-600. (Open daily 10am-noon and 2-6pm. €4, ages 10-17 €3.) Other sights include the **Musée de l'Histoire du Verre et du Vitrail,** which retraces the history of glass-making, and the **Musée du Moulin des Bouillons,** where traditional oil presses are on display. (☎04 90 72 22 11. Apr.-Oct. M and W-Su 10am-noon and 2-6pm. Wheelchair-accessible. €4.50 for each museum, €7 for both.)

A large **market** surrounds the château on Tuesday mornings, selling everything from pottery and paintings to sausage and socks. L'Église St-Firmin, just below the château, has unusual, brightly painted walls in turquoise and brick-red, punctuated with framed paintings and frescoes. Above the château, the Charité St-Europe hosts the annual **Bazart** sale in July and August featuring the work of 32 young artists. (€60-170; www.bazart.com has information on the traveling exhibition as well as works for sale.)

Many of the restaurants in Gordes are filled with tourists, but **Le Bouquet de Basilic ❸**, rte. de Murs, just above the château, serves changing dishes deliciously laden with basil (€9-12) in a peaceful, shady garden terrace. (☎04 90 72 06 98. Open daily noon-2:30pm and 7:15-11pm, closed Th lunch. MC/V.) Accommodations in Gordes are pricey (€60-400), and most visitors elect to stay in villages nearby.

Held in August, **Soirées d'Eté** is a festival that brings world-renowned artists to town for a series of concerts, theatrical performances, and poetry readings.

The **tourist office** is in the château. (☎04 90 72 02 75; www.gordes-village.com. Open M-Sa 9am-noon and 2-6pm, Su 10am-noon and 2-6pm.) There's a 24hr. **ATM** in the *place* in front of it. The **post office** is located in the center of town and **exchanges currency.** (Open M-F 9am-noon and 2-5pm, Su 10am-noon and 2-6pm.) A **pharmacy,** 2 rue de l'Église, faces the church. (☎04 90 72 02 10. Open M-Sa 9am-12:30pm and 2-7pm, Su 10am-12:30pm.) **Taxis,** though expensive, are available at ☎04 90 72 61 43 or 04 90 72 11 24.

ARLES

Each street in Arles (pop. 35,000) seems to run into or out of the great Roman arena. The one-time political capital of Roman Gaul, Arles was nearly destroyed by invasions in the Middle Ages. Since the 12th century, however, the city has remained an important commercial and cultural center. With enthusiastic locals and numerous horse-riding events and *camarguaises* (bull races) in the Arènes, Arles is a favorite among visitors to Provence. The town is also known as a magnet for artists: Van Gogh lost two years and an ear here; Picasso loved Arles's bullfights enough to produce over 150 drawings in 35 days (he donated 70 to the city); and the annual International Photography Festival fills every nook and cranny with exhibits. For the adventurous, the hills of the Alpilles and the Camargue marshlands are an easy daytrip away.

▐ TRANSPORTATION

Trains: av. P. Talabot. Tickets M-F 5:50am-9:50pm, Sa 6:05am-9:50pm, Su 7am-9:30pm. To: **Avignon** (20min., 17 per day, €5.80); **Marseille** (50min., 20 per day, €11.90); **Montpellier** (1hr., 5 per day, €12.50); **Nîmes** (20min., 7 per day, €6.70).

Buses: av. P. Talabot (☎04 90 49 38 01), outside the train station. Info desk open M-F 9am-4pm. **Les Cars de Camargue,** 24 rue Clemenceau (☎04 90 96 36 25). To **Nîmes** (1hr., M-Sa 6 per day, €5.20). **Cars Ceyte et Fils** and **CTM,** 21 chemin du Temple

(☎04 90 93 74 90), go to **Avignon** (45min.; M-Sa 7 per day, Su 2 per day; €8.10). Buses may drop passengers at bd. Georges Clemenceau rather than the *gare routière*. Info desk open M-Th 8:15am-noon and 2-5:30pm, F 8:15am-noon and 2-4:30pm.

Public Transportation: (☎08 10 00 08 16; www.star-arles.fr). Serves both central Arles and the local suburbs.

Taxis: A.A.A. Arles Taxis (☎04 90 93 31 16). **Arles Taxis Radio** (☎04 90 96 90 03).

Car Rental: National/Citer, 4 av. Paulin Talabot (☎04 90 93 02 17; fax 04 90 93 18 83). Located a block from the train station toward the city center.

Bike Rental: Peugeot Cycles, 15 rue du Pont (☎04 90 96 03 77). €14 per day. Open Tu-Su 8am-noon and 2-7pm.

▚ 🔢 ORIENTATION AND PRACTICAL INFORMATION

Arles follows the curve of the Rhône River in the north near the train station. The tourist office, bd. des Lices, south of the old city center, divides the commercial areas from the residential areas farther south.

Tourist Office: Espl. Charles de Gaulle, bd. des Lices (☎04 90 18 41 20; www.tourisme.ville-arles.fr). Turn left outside the train station and walk to pl. Lamartine; after the Monoprix turn left down bd. Emile Courbes. Continue to the big intersection by the southeast old city tower, then turn right onto bd. des Lices. Excellent free maps and brochures. Accommodations service €1 plus down payment. Guided tours of the city are offered in English July-Sept. M 5pm (€4, €1.60 students). (☎08 92 68 25 11, ext. 016003. €0.34 per min.) From Apr. to Oct., a *petit train* leaves from the tourist office on a 35min. tour of the *vieille ville* (daily 10am-7pm; €6, under 10 €3). Open daily Apr.-Sept. 9am-6:45pm; Oct.-Nov. M-Sa 9am-5:45pm, Su 10:30am-2:15pm; Dec.-Mar. M-Sa 9am-4:45pm, Su 10:30am-2:15pm. Branch in the train station (☎04 90 18 41 20). Open M-Sa 9am-1pm.

Currency Exchange: Arène Change, 22bis rond-point des Arènes (☎04 90 93 34 66). No commission on US$. Accepts traveler's checks. Open Apr.-Oct. M-Sa 9am-6:45pm, closed in winter. Several 24hr. **ATMs** surround pl. de la République.

Police: on the corner of bd. des Lices and av. des Alyscamps (☎04 90 18 45 00).

Luggage Storage: 1 pl. Lamartine (☎ 04 90 96 01 24). From the train station, ½ block toward the city center at Hôtel de France (see **Accommodations and Camping, p. 677**). €10 per day.

Laundromat: Lincoln Laverie, 6 rue de la Cavalerie. Wash €3.50-7.50. Open daily 7am-9pm.

Ambulance: 7bis bd. Emilie Combes (☎04 90 49 79 79 or 04 90 96 04 27).

Poison Control: ☎04 91 74 66 66.

AIDS Info Service: ☎08 00 23 13 13.

SOS Femme: Marseille-based women's health and rape hotline (☎04 90 24 61 50).

Pharmacy: Pharmacie de l'Hôtel de Ville, 31 rue de l'Hôtel de Ville (☎04 90 96 01 46). Open M-Sa 8:30am-7:30pm. Arles's **garde de ville** (24hr. pharmacy) changes each weekend; call the police for info.

Hospital: Centre Hospitalier J. Imbert, quartier Fourchon (☎04 90 49 29 29).

Internet Access: Cyber City, 41 rue du 4 Septembre (☎04 90 96 87 76) offers Internet services at competitive prices. €3 per hr. Open daily 10am-11pm. **Point Web,** 10 rue du 4 Septembre (☎04 90 18 91 54; www.hexaworld.net/pointweb). €1 for 10min. Open M-Sa 9am-7pm.

Post Office: 5 bd. des Lices (☎04 90 18 41 10), between the tourist office and the police station. **Currency exchange.** $100 bills not accepted. Open M-F 8:30am-6:30pm, Sa 8:30am-12:30pm.

Postal Code: 13200.

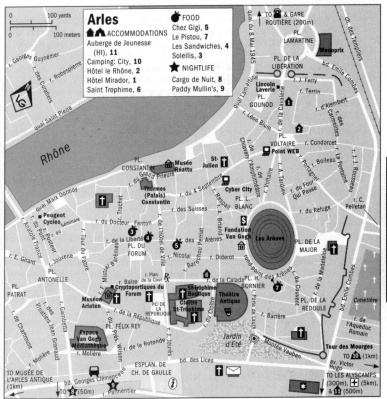

ACCOMMODATIONS AND CAMPING

Arles has plenty of inexpensive hotels, especially in the area around **rue de l'Hôtel de Ville** and **place Voltaire.** The tourist office provides guides to accommodations, as well as *chambres d'hôtes* and camping options. Reservations are crucial during the photography festival in July and should be made a month or two in advance.

Saint Trophime, 16 rue de la Calade (☎ 04 90 96 88 38; st.trophime@wanadoo.fr). Set in a 15th-century private mansion, the 20 fairy-tale rooms of this hotel come in lively colors with high ceilings. Ideally located within steps of the Arènes and the city center. Breakfast €5.95. 24hr. reception. Reserve well in advance in summer. Singles €35-40; doubles €50, with bath €50-55; triples and quads €70. AmEx/MC/V. ❹

Hôtel le Rhône, 11 pl. Voltaire (☎ 04 90 96 43 70; http://perso.wanadoo.fr/hotel_rhone). Inviting breakfast loft and charming Provençal pastel-painted rooms, some with TV or balcony. Though not well-equipped, the cheaper rooms are both spacious and spotless. Free, comprehensive guide of the region available at reception. Breakfast €5. Reception 8am-8:30pm. Reservations recommended. Singles and doubles €26, with shower €31-33; triples with toilet €43. MC/V. ❸

Hôtel Mirador, 3 rue Voltaire (☎ 04 90 96 28 05; www.hotel-mirador.com). Large, simply furnished rooms, each with TV, phone, and spacious bath. Internet €7 per hr. Breakfast €4.30. Garage €4 a day. Reception 7am-11pm. High-season singles and doubles with shower €30-38, with bath €41; low-season €30-35/€38. Extra bed €9.20. AmEx/MC/V. ❹

Auberge de Jeunesse (HI), 20 av. Maréchal Foch (☎04 90 96 18 25; fax 04 90 96 31 26), 10min. from the center and 20min. from the station. From the station, take the Starlette bus to Clemenceau, then take the #4 bus (dir: l'Aurélienne) to Foch (€0.80). There are no Starlettes on Su. Last bus leaves Clemenceau at 6:34pm. From the station, follow directions to the tourist office, but on bd. des Lices cross and continue down av. des Alyscamps; follow the signs. Modern 8-bed dorms and a few 3-, 4-, and 5-bed rooms. Breakfast included. Bar open until midnight. Reception 7-10am and 5-11pm. Lockout 10am-5pm. Curfew 11pm in winter, midnight in summer. Reservation (by letter or fax) recommended Apr.-June. Bunks €13.70, €11.80 after 1st night. MC/V. ❶

Camping: City, 67 rte. de Crau (☎04 90 93 08 86; www.camping-city.com). Take Starlette bus #2 from station to Clemenceau. Then take bus #2 (dir: Pont de Crau) to Hermite (€0.80). Closest site to town; 15-20min. walk to downtown Arles. Small 2-star with pool, hot showers, laundry, bar, and restaurant. Bike €10 per day. Mobile home €150 for 3 nights. Reception daily 8am-8pm; July-Aug. 24hr. Open Apr.-Oct. €15.50 for person, car, and site; €4.50 per extra person; €3 per child under 7. Electricity €4. ❶

◖ FOOD

Situated on the edge of the Camargue, Arles's cuisine benefits from both fresh seafood and hearty Camargue *taureau* (bull) meat. Restaurants serving these are tucked into the small squares and the narrow streets, particularly in **place du Forum** and around the **Arènes.** Regional produce fills the **open-air markets** on bd. Emile Combes (W 7am-1pm) and bd. des Lices (Sa 7am-1pm). There are two **supermarkets** in town: **Monoprix** on pl. Lamartine, close to the train station and the city gates (open M-Th 8:30am-7:30pm, F-Sa 8:30am-8pm), and **Petit Casino,** 26 rue Président Wilson, off bd. des Lices toward the center of town. (Open Tu-Sa 7:30am-12:30pm and 3:30-7:30pm, Su 8:30am-12:30pm; July-Aug. also open M 8:30am-12:30pm.)

▩ Soleilis, 9 rue Docteur Fanton (☎04 90 93 30 76). After dinner, try a *boule* or two of perhaps the most delicious ice cream in all of Provence. €1.80 for one scoop and homemade waffle cone, €1 for regular cone. Mountainous sundaes €5.20. Open daily July-Aug. 2-7pm and 8:30-10:30pm or later; Mar.-June and Sept.-Oct. 2-7pm. ❶

Les Sandwiches, 46 rue des Arènes. Behind forest-green shutters, this sandwich counter serves an ideal alternative to the *paninis* found at most cafes. Ingredients include fresh basil and olive oil. Sandwiches €2-4. Open Tu-F 11am-12:30pm and 4-6pm. ❶

Chez Gigi, 49 rue des Arnènes. Hearty Provençal food and rustic interiors draw a regular crowd. Cast 2 dice before your meal: a double draw gets you a free aperitif. Appetizers €7-8, entrees €8.50-12.50. Open for lunch and dinner Tu-Su. MC/V. ❸

Le Pistou, 30bis rond-point des Arènes (☎04 90 18 20 92; www.lepistou.com). Overlooking the Roman amphitheater, Pistou's gourmet cuisine matches its magical setting. Local specialties, including an excellent *gardienne de taureau* (bull meat cooked in a wine sauce). Entrees €9-20, *menus* €18-25. Open noon-3pm and 6-11pm. MC/V. ❸

◖ SIGHTS

It takes two or three days to see the city's major sights. Ancient Roman ruins hide below the surface of the 17th- and 18th-century architecture of the *centre ville*. The city's *Pass Monuments* (€13.50, students and under 18 €12) will give you access to all the major sights in Arles, including Les Arènes, Cryptoportiques, Musée Réattu, Muséon Arlaten, Musée de l'Arles Antique, Théâtre Antique, Les Alyscamps, and Cloître St-Trôphime.

▩ MUSÉE DE L'ARLES ANTIQUE. Housed inside an ultra-modern blue building, the awe-inspiring archeological museum retraces the evolution of Camargue from pre-historic times through the decline of the Roman empire in the 6th century AD.

A 200-year effort has uncovered spectacular 2nd-century mosaics, countless amphoras, statues, and pieces of jewelry, and the second-best collection of antique sarcophagi in the world. Check out the large scale models of Roman architecture, including the ingenious pontoon bridge that was once the symbol of Arles. *(Av. de la 1ère D.F.L. ☎04 90 18 88 80; www.arles-antique.org.cg13.com. 10min. from the center of town. With your back to the tourist office, turn left, walk along bd. Georges Clémenceau to its end, and follow the signs. Alternatively, take bus #1 to Musée from bd. Georges Clémenceau. Open daily Mar.-Oct. 9am-7pm; Nov.-Feb. 10am-5pm. Detailed English brochures and excellent guided tours July-Sept. M 2pm (English or French); Oct.-June Su 3pm. €5.50, students €4.)*

■ **MUSÉON ARLATEN.** Founded by turn-of-the-century poet Frédéric Mistral, who dedicated his life to safeguarding local traditions in the region, this museum features the most important collection of Provençal objects in the world. Museum guards don traditional 19th-century costumes, and visitors stroll through galleries of handcrafts, domestic furniture, jewelry, and a series of stunning dioramas depicting daily Provençal life. *(29 rue de la République. ☎04 90 93 58 11. Open daily June-Aug. 9:30am-1pm and 2-6:30pm; Apr.-May and Sept. Tu-Su 9:30am-12:30pm and 2-6pm; Oct.-Mar. Tu-Su 9:30am-12:30pm and 2-5pm. Comprehensive videoguides in French, Provençal, English, German, and Italian €2. €4, students €3; free last W and 1st Su of every month.)*

LES ARÈNES. Every street in Arles's medieval maze seems to lead to the towering layered arches of its Roman amphitheater. Built in the first century AD, this structure—the largest of its kind surviving in France—was so cleverly designed that it could evacuate all 20,000 spectators in 5min. In the 8th century, homes were built on and in the original structure, converting it into a fortified village, and two towers built during that era still remain. Later, when villagers were forced to leave, the amphitheater was used to celebrate the conquest of Algeria around 1830. The smaller tower, however, offers a nice view of all of Arles—and a heavenly breeze on hot summer days. Bullfights and bull races are staged here from Easter through September, and are as exciting as anything the Romans watched. The owner of the *buvette* inside the amphitheater is a gold mine of information on Arles's history. Guided tours are offered daily at 10am in summer. *(Arènes ☎04 90 49 36 86; Bullfights 04 90 96 03 70. Open daily May-Sept. 9am-6pm; Mar.-Apr. and Oct. 9am-5:30pm; Nov.-Feb. 10am-4:30pm. €4, children and students €3. Bullfights from €12, children €6.)*

MUSÉE RÉATTU. Once a stronghold of the knights of St-John, this spacious museum now houses an intriguing collection of modern art that contrasts with the gargoyles and arched ceilings of the medieval building. At the heart of the museum, near exhibits of work by Henri Rousseau and Réattu, are the 57 drawings with which Picasso honored Arles in 1971. The Cubist works attempt to capture the many "faces" (literally) of the town. *(Rue du Grand Prieuré. ☎04 90 49 37 58. Open daily May-Sept. 10am-12:30pm and 2-7pm; Mar.-Apr. and Oct. 10am-12:30pm and 2-5:30pm; Nov.-Feb. 1-5:30pm. €4, students €3. More expensive when there are temporary exhibits.)*

FONDATION VAN GOGH. You'll find no Van Goghs here—only tributes to him by other artists. From innovative sculpture and paintings to creative musical compositions and poetry, the pieces here reflect the tremendous impact Van Gogh continues to have on the art world. Highlights include a Liechtenstein interpretation of Van Gogh's *Sewer with Setting Sun*. *(Palais de Luppé, 24bis rond-point des Arènes. ☎04 90 49 94 04; www.fondationvangogh-arles.org. Open daily Apr.-Oct. 10:30am-8pm; Nov.-Mar. Tu-Su 11am-7pm. €7, students and children 8-18 €5.)*

CRYPTOPORTIQUES DU FORUM. A visit to the underground galleries of this former Roman forum, 6m below the modern city, is an eerie walk through history. Dating from the first century BC, the seemingly endless corridors run under the pl. du Forum to the city hall, revealing the extent of the ancient foundations of the Roman forum. Water still seeps down from the vaulted ceilings and makes for a muddy walk. *(Rue Balze. Open daily May-Sept. 9am-noon and 2-6pm. Mar.-Apr. and Oct. 9-11:30am and 2-5:30pm; Nov.-Feb. 10-11:30am and 2-4:30pm. Guided tours July-Sept. M, F 3pm; €4, €1.60 students. Admission €3.50, students and under 18 €2.60.)*

CLOÎTRE ST-TRÔPHIME. Named after Arles's first bishop, this small medieval cloister is an oasis of calm and shade. Each carved column in its arcades is topped by lions in brushwood, saints in stone leaves, and the occasional fluttering bird. From July to September, the bare chambers of the Episcopal complex showcase different photographs. *(Pl. de la République. ☎04 90 49 33 53. Open daily May-Sept. 9am-6pm; Mar.-Apr. and Oct. 9am-5:30pm; Nov.-Feb. 10am-4:30pm. Guided tours July-Sept. Tu, Th 11:30am; €4, students €1.60. Cloister €3.50, students €2.60. Masses daily. Church free.)*

THÉÂTRE ANTIQUE. Squeezed between the amphitheater and the gardens, this partially ruined Roman theater was erected in the first century BC. Though smaller and not nearly as well-preserved as Orange's *théâtre antique*, Arles's theater is a reminder of the art-loving side of Roman culture. Capitals lie haphazardly around the flower-filled backstage, and only two columns of the stage wall stand, but enough remains for modern productions to take advantage of the theater's magnificent acoustics and monumental atmosphere. *(Rue de la Calade. For reservations call the Théâtre de la Calade at ☎04 90 93 05 23 or the tourist office. Open daily May-Sept. 9am-6pm; Nov.-Feb. and Oct. 10-11:30am and 2-4:30pm; Mar.-Apr. 9-11:30am and 2-5:30pm. €3, students and children €2.20.)*

ALYSCAMPS. Meriting mention in Dante's *Inferno*, one of the most famous burial grounds from Roman times until the late Middle Ages was at Alyscamps, a twist on the name Champs-Elysées (Elysian Fields.) Consecrated by St-Trôphime, first bishop of Arles, it now holds 80 generations of locals. Van Gogh enjoyed strolling amid the unbreakable peace of the poplar avenues and the 12th-century abbey at their end. Sadly, the most elaborate sarcophagi have been either destroyed or removed. *(10min. from the center of town. From the tourist office, head east on bd. des Lices to its intersection with bd. Emile Courbes. Turn left onto av. des Alyscamps and cross the tracks. ☎04 90 49 36 87. Open daily May-Sept. 9am-6pm; Mar.-Apr. and Oct. 9-11:30am and 2-5:30pm; Nov.-Feb. 10-11:30am and 2-4:30pm. Guided tours July-Sept. M-Su at 5pm; €4, €1.60 students. Admission €3.50, students and under 18 €2.60.)*

🎵 🎭 ENTERTAINMENT AND NIGHTLIFE

For theater-goers, the Théâtre d'Arles, bd. Georges Clemenceau (☎04 90 52 51 55; accueil@theatre-arles.com), showcases drama, dance, circus, and musical performance from October to June (€11-14, students €8-9).

Although Arles is hardly a town for night owls, the cafes along bd. Georges Clemenceau attract an animated crowd for drinks and music at night. **Paddy Mullin's**, 5 bd. Clémenceau, is a popular Irish pub for 20-somethings, with 10 beers on tap and daily happy hour from 5-8pm. (☎04 90 49 67 25. Pint €5.25, €4 during happy hour. Open M-Sa 7am-2am, Su 5pm-2am.) A 2min. walk should lead you to **Cargo de Nuit**, 7 av. Sadi Carnot, the only nightclub in the central city. The cargo-ship-themed hotspot attracts locals and visitors with a wide range of music and a small art gallery. (☎04 90 49 55 99; www.cargodenuit.com. Drinks €3.80-4.50. Open daily noon-4pm for lunch, Th-Sa 8pm-3am for dancing.)

❉ FESTIVALS

Deep respect for traditional culture is evident in the many local Provençal festivals and celebrations held throughout the year. The biggest of these, the weeks-long **Fête d'Arles,** begins with the lighting of a midsummer's fire on the Solstice. Every three years, the city elects the Queen of Arles and her six ladies, who represent the city's language, customs, and history at local events and international exchanges. Other local festivals include the **Fête des Gardians** on May 1, which celebrates the brotherhood of herders of the Camargue's wild horses, and the several *férias*, or bullfights, held on Easter and during early September in the Arènes. (Tickets €15-85. For more info, contact the Bureau des Arènes at ☎04 90 96 03 70; www.label-camargue.com.) Those who stop in Arles outside the festival season can check out the weekly **bull races** (June-Aug. W 5pm; €6, children €3). Held in mid-November, the traditional **Marché de Noël** (Christmas market) draws large crowds into town. At the same time, the festival **Provence Prestige** showcases Provençal culture to 25,000 yearly visitors for five days. Call the tourist office for more info, or check www.provenceprestige.com.

The major draw for tourists is the annual **Rencontres Internationales de la Photographie**, held at the beginning of July. Undiscovered photographers court agents by roaming around town with portfolios under their arms, while established photographers present their work and nightly slide shows (€12). When the festival crowd departs, the remarkable exhibits are left behind. (€5 per exhibit, all exhibits €28; students €20, under 16 free.) For more info, contact Rencontres, 10 rondpoint des Arènes (☎04 90 96 76 06; www.rencontres-arles.com). During the festival, tickets can be bought in the Espace Van Gogh.

ALPILLES

Home to traces of Roman history, several famous artists and poets, and the tidy fields of olive groves and vineyards, the hills of the Alpilles are a tranquil tourist retreat. Its small towns provide clear vistas similar to those of the Vaucluse to the north and the relaxed atmosphere of Arles and Nîmes to the south.

⎚ TRANSPORTATION. Buses connect the major villages and towns to the *gare routière* in Avignon. **Rapides du Sud-Est** (☎04 32 76 00 40) goes to **Les Baux-de-Provence** and **St-Rémy** (40 and 55min., 5 per day,), while **STDG** sends buses to Tarascon (35 min., 6 per day) **Trains** leave frequently from **Avignon** for **Saint-Rémy** as well as **Tarascon** (13 per day, €3.60). A **car** is handy but it isn't necessary to visit the Alpilles.

▨ LES BAUX-DE-PROVENCE

Les Baux-de-Provence is known chiefly for its immense medieval ruins and for its breathtaking panoramas of the vineyards and villages below. The village sits 245m up on a defensively strategic rocky spur of the Alpilles. Traces of human habitations dating back to 2000 BC were found in the village, but the Middle Ages marked a period of exponential growth. The Baux lords plundered medieval Provence from this eagle's nest of a town, managing at one point to hold 72 towns in the region. Even Dante came to their court—it's thought that he found inspiration for his *Inferno* in the twisted gorges of the Val de l'Enfer (Valley of Hell), so named for the tortuous cliffs below the castle. The Baux line died out in the 14th century, and Louis XIII humiliated the town by destroying its castle and ramparts in 1632. In 1791, the Baux received the last blow: the village, which had shrunk to less than 400 inhabitants, was bought and became part of France. A narrated, self-paced tour of Les Baux takes tourists through the remaining ruins, an impressive testament to the powerful lords who once inhabited the immense stone structures.

The ruined halls and towers of the mountaintop **Château des Baux** cover an area five times that of the village below. Treacherously slim limestone stairs offer brave visitors a magnificent view of the cliffs and farmland in the valley below. A giant *trébuchet*, the largest and most powerful medieval siege warfare engine, stands out on the plateau. Hold on to children and lighter possessions, as gusting *Mistral* winds are strong on the unprotected cliff. Housed in a cool Romanesque chapel inside the château's gates, the tiny **Chapelle St-Blaise** has a delightful slideshow of Gauguin, Van Gogh, and Cézanne's paintings. In July and August, visitors can try themselves at crossbow archery with the help of a professional instructor, as well as enjoy a variety of shows centered around medieval warfare. (☎04 90 54 55 56; www.chateau-baux-provence.com. Open daily July-Aug. 9am-8:30pm; Dec.-Feb. 9am-5pm; Sept.-Nov. 9am-6:30pm, Mar.-June 9am-7pm. Thorough audioguide in 7 languages. €7, students €5.50, under 17 €3.50.) Les Baux is also known for its limestone quarries, one of which has been converted into the unique ■Cathédrale d'Images. From the bus stop, continue down the hill, turn right at the crossroads, and follow the sign. As visitors stroll through the 3000m² of galleries, dozens of projectors splash a slide show of 3000 images into gigantic walls cut deep into the limestone, offering an unparalleled sensory experience. New shows come every year— 2005 should bring a series of photographs from sacred sites around the world. Bring a jacket, as the caverns tend to be particularly cold. (☎04 90 54 38 65; www.cathedrale-images.com. Open daily 10am-7pm, last show at 6:15pm. €7, ages 8-18 €4.10.) Walk down the hill to the **Fondation Louis Jou**, rue Frédéric Mistral, which commemorates Les Baux's favorite son with major works by the printmaker himself as well as engravings by Dürer, Rembrandt, and Goya. Print-making workshops are also organized within the Fondation from time to time. If it seems shut down, continue 50m and inquire at the small shop carved into the stone; it may not really be closed. (☎04 90 54 34 17. Open Apr.-Oct. M and F-Su 2-5pm, Tu-Th by reservation; Nov.-Mar. by reservation. €3, students €1.50.) Other sights include a museum dedicated to contemporary figurative painter **Yves Brayer**. (☎04 90 54 36 99; www.yvesbrayer.com/pages/fr/baux/baux.htm. Open daily Apr.-Sept. 10am-12:30pm and 2-6:30pm; Oct.-Mar. 10am-12:30pm and 2pm-5pm; closed Jan. to mid-Feb. €4.)

The last two weeks of July welcome **Musique et Dance**, a yearly festival of ballet, classical music, and dance. Some performances take place in the Cathédrale d'Images. Call the tourist office for scheduling information and ticket sales. (☎04 90 54 34 39. €25-40, under 20 €10-20.)

■**Mas de la Fontaine ❹,** at the foot of the village in the Val d'Enfer, offers seven elegant and fashionably decorated rooms, with exquisite wooden furniture in a traditional *mas* (Provençal farm). A peaceful garden and a swimming pool add to this hotel's rustic charm. This place is worth the splurge, and travelers know it, so make reservations. Follow signs to the Gendarmerie; the hotel is then 2min. downhill on your right. (☎04 90 54 34 13. Breakfast €6. Open mid-Mar. to Oct. Doubles with shower €42-50, with bath €54-58; triples €66. Extra bed €10.) Most backpackers bring picnics to the Cité Morte for picturesque meals atop the hill; for picnic supplies, the small **bakery** in the parking lot has fresh breads, fruit, and sandwiches. (Open daily Mar.-Dec. 8:30am-8pm; Jan.-Feb. 10:30am-5pm.)

The **tourist office**, about halfway up the hill between the parking lot and the Cité Morte, gives out a free map and short history of the city, as well as lodging and transportation info. (☎04 90 54 34 39. Open daily Apr.-Sept. 9am-7pm; Oct.-Mar. 9am-12:30pm and 1:30-6pm.) Conseil Général des Bouches-du-Rhône has **bus** service between Avignon, St-Rémy, and Les Baux. (☎04 32 76 00 40. 1hr. Runs daily July-Aug. 7:40am-4:20pm; June and Sept. Sa-Su only; May and Oct. Su only. €5.40.) **Taxis** can be called at ☎06 80 27 60 92.

TARASCON

Tarascon (pop. 13,000) is intimately linked to Provençal folklore through its namesake, *la tarasque,* a legendary monster that once terrorized the village. For four days over the last weekend of June, during the **Fête de la Tarasque,** a replica of the monster is paraded through the town. Inaugurated in 1474, the *fête* has grown over the last 500 years and it now features concerts, bullfights, horse shows, and dancing. When Tarascon is not *en fête,* it is a quiet southern town with calm cobbled streets, refreshing breezes off the Rhône, and serious *boules* games in the municipal courts. While Tarascon is not the most exciting Provençal town, its proximity to Arles (17km), Avignon (23km), and Nîmes (24km), as well as less expensive lodgings make it a good base from which to explore the surrounding cities.

The prize of Tarascon is the imposing 15th-century ▧**Château de Tarascon,** perched above a wedge of the Rhône. This late medieval citadel, whose massive stone walls are punctuated by occasional grilled apertures, saw few years of warfare. Under the reign of René I (1434-1480), the stronghold was transformed into a Renaissance palace complete with Flamboyant Gothic carvings. After Provence lost its autonomy in 1481, the fortress palace became a short-term residence for French noblemen. Starting in the 18th century, and until as late as 1926, it was used as a prison. As a result, Tarascon's château is well maintained, with the star-painted ceiling in the Queen's chambers still easily visible. Surrounded by a now-dry grassy moat, it boasts a lovely Provençal garden, stunning ogival ceilings, and detailed tapestries. Prisoners' inscriptions, carved deep into stone, can be found on many of the walls. A climb to the roof (45m high) reveals a picture-perfect view of Tarascon's rival château, the ruined Château de Beaucaire, across the river, and of the surrounding countryside clear to the Camargue. (☎04 90 91 01 93. Open daily Apr.-Aug. 10am-7pm; Sept.-Mar. 10:30am-5pm. Guided tours offered 3 times a day during the summer. €6.10, ages 18-25 €4.10, under 18 free.)

During the last weekend in August, Tarascon goes back in time with the **Médiévales.** Life in the Middle Ages is recreated in the form of a life-size medieval camp set up on the pl. du Château. Knights' tournaments, theatrical performances, and dances go on all day, to the satisfaction of both locals and visitors.

To reach the **Auberge de Jeunesse (HI) ❶,** 31 bd. Gambetta, from the train station, turn right on Bd. du Viaduc, then make a left at Place Eimshorn and follow Bd. Gambetta—you should see signs indicating the hostel. It has comfortable beds in eight- to 12-bed dorms, kitchen facilities, a secure bike area, and free parking. Reservations are accepted by email, but this gem of a hostel is rarely full. (☎04 90 91 04 08; tarascon@fuaj.org. Breakfast €3.30, obligatory first morning. Sheets €2.70. Reception 7:30-10am and 5:30-10:30pm. Lockout 10am-5:30pm. Open Mar.-Dec. Beds €8.90. HI members only.) **Hôtel du Viaduc ❷,** 9 rue du Viaduc, is in a quiet street by the city walls. From the train station, cross under the tracks and head left. The hotel has large, comfortable rooms (some of them newly renovated) and a tranquil terrace where visitors often choose to be served their breakfast (€2.50). Popular with cyclists, the place maintains a locked bike area and free parking. Jovial proprietors, who speak some English, generate a convivial atmosphere. (☎04 90 91 16 67; http://perso.wanadoo.fr/hotelduviaduc. Internet €3 per 30min. Breakfast €5. Check-in 9am-10pm. Doubles €22-26, with shower €27-33, with toilet €34-38; family room €40-44.) **Camping Tartarin ❶,** bd. du Roy René, behind the château on the Rhône, is a simple site with a bar, snack stand, restaurant (*menu* €10), free showers, and lots of shade. Campers appreciate the quiet yet central location. (☎04 90 91 01 46; fax 04 90 91 10 70. Reception 9am-noon and 3-7pm; after-hours until 11pm try the bar. Open Apr.-Oct. €3.40 per person, €3 per tent, €1.70 per car. Electricity €2.70. MC/V.)

Bistrot des Anges ❸, located in the pl. du Marché, serves up daily Provençal *menus* (€16) and extraordinary chocolate cake (€3.90) on a bright, sunlit terrace. Fresh products are bought and prepared with care by a master chef. Work by local artists is displayed in the cozy dining room. (☎04 90 91 05 11. Open M-Sa noon-2pm. MC/V.) The **bakery** across from the tourist office, 56 rue des Halles, serves up melt-in-your-mouth treats, including *bésuquettes*, patented hazelnut truffles shaped like the *tarasque*. (☎04 90 91 01 17. Open Tu-Su 6:30am-1pm and 3-7:30pm. €5.30 for 100g.) There's also a **Petit Casino market** on the pl. du Marché. (Open M-Tu and Th-Sa 7:30am-12:30pm and 3:30-7:30pm, Su 8-12:30pm.)

Trains from Tarascon go to Arles (10min., 4 per day, €2.60) or Avignon (10min., 8-9 per day, €3.50). (Ticket window open M 6:10am-7pm, Tu-F 6:20am-7pm, Sa 6:40am-7pm, Su 9:35am-noon and 1:25-6pm.) **Cévennes Cars** (☎04 66 84 96 86) sends **buses** from the train station to **Avignon** (35min., M-Sa 4 per day 6:50am-6:20pm, €7.60) and **St-Rémy** (25min.; M-F 3 per day 7:55am-6:05pm, Sa 2 per day; €3.10). In a pinch, call **Accord Taxi** (☎06 08 40 75 31 or 04 90 91 34 50). For the **pharmacie de garde,** call the **police,** 3 rue du Viaduc (☎04 90 91 52 90). The multilingual staff of the **tourist office,** 59 rue des Halles, provides free guides and maps. From the train station, walk across the common, turn left on cours A. Briand; walk for two minutes, and rue des Halles will be on your right. (☎04 90 91 03 52; www.tarascon.org. Open Sept.-June M-Sa 9am-noon and 2-6pm; July-Aug. M-Sa 9am-7pm, Su 9:30am-12:30pm.) There are no currency exchange bureaus in town, but a 24hr. **ATM** lies just to the left of the tourist office. The **post office** is to the left of the train station. (☎04 90 91 52 00. Open M-F 8:30am-5:30pm, Sa 8:30am-noon.) **Postal Code:** 13150.

ST-RÉMY

A little town approached through luminous arcades of plane trees, St-Rémy's artistic flair shines through in its numerous boutiques, artists' galleries, and the oft-told stories of Van Gogh's years here. Just outside the maze of charming streets that makes up the *centre ville* lie a small group of Roman remnants and the ancient city of Glanum, now a major archaeological site.

The **Centre d'Art Présence Van Gogh,** housed in the 253-year-old Hôtel Estrine, 8 rue Estrine, is one of the small museums nested in the heart of town. Although it lacks original Van Gogh paintings, the Centre d'Art features rotating exhibits on contemporary artists who draw their inspiration from the master's work. The high-quality photographic reproductions of Van Gogh's masterpieces, however, fail to convey the feelings inspired by the originals. (☎04 90 92 34 72; fax 04 90 92 36 73. Open Tu-Su 10:30am-12:30pm and 2:30-6:30pm. €3.20, students and seniors €2.30.) The 15th-century **Hôtel de Sade,** rue de Parage, is unrelated to the infamous Marquis. The archaeological museum holds all the best finds from nearby Glanum, including well-preserved glasswork and pottery. (☎04 90 92 64 04; fax 04 90 92 64 02. Open daily July-Aug. 11am-6pm; Apr.-June and Sept. 10am-noon and 2-6pm; Jan.-Mar. 10am-noon and 2-5pm. €2.50, under 18 free.)

Glanum, a settlement from the 7th century BC, lies nearly 1km south of the town center, past the tourist office on av. Vincent Van Gogh. Discovered 80 years ago, the sprawling collection of houses, temples, springs, and sacred wells unearthed here are still being studied. The on-site archaeological team believes that the vestiges of the city spread over a surface 6 or 7 times larger than the one which has been unearthed. Glanum once prospered as a stop on the main road from Spain to Italy (the *Via Domitia*) and now provides fascinating insight into the hybrid Gallo-Roman culture that emerged in Provence. (☎04 90 92 23 79. Open daily Apr.-Sept. 9am-7pm; Oct.-Mar. 9am-noon and 2-5pm. €5.50, ages 12-25 €3.50.) Standing in solitary splendor across the street are the well-preserved **Antiques,** a commemorative arch and mausoleum. Built during the reign of Augustus, the two monuments marked the entrance to the Roman town of Glanum. The intricately carved bas-reliefs are reminiscent of those found in Orange's famous arch. Across the street, the still-functioning **Saint-Paul de Mausole,** chemin des Carrières, offers calm gardens and breezy corridors to visitors and residents of the therapeutic center where Van Gogh spent over a year producing over 100 drawings and 150 paintings, including some of his most famous. The renowned *L'Oliveraie* was most likely painted somewhere on the path that leads to the former monastery, as evidenced by the olive trees that continue to grow there. Above the flowered 11th-century cloister, visitors can tour the three rooms in which the artist spent the last year of his life. A small gallery now shows very creative exhibits by current patients. (☎04 90 92 77 00. Open daily Apr.-Oct. 9:30am-7pm; Nov.-Mar. 10:15am-4:45pm. €3.40, students €2.30, under 12 free.)

Restaurants are on the pricier side here. ⌘**Lou Planet ❶**, 7 pl. Favier, serves fresh produce-filled crêpes and salads (€4.80-7) in an umbrella-topped courtyard. The *légumes de saison et chèvre* crêpe (€6.50) gives an excellent taste of the season's finest veggies. (☎04 90 92 19 81. Open daily Apr.-Oct. noon-2:30pm and 7-10pm.) For slightly more expensive and substantial dining, **Bistrot Découverte ❸**, 19 bd. Victor Hugo, serves full Provençal meals like *pavé de taureau* (bull) on a terrace overlooking a busy intersection. The restaurant also offers a large selection of regional wines. (☎04 90 92 34 49. Open Tu-Su noon-2pm and 7-10pm. Appetizers €5.50-8.50, *plats* €10-14, desserts €4-6. MC/V.) Near the statue of Nostradamus are a handful of good *brasseries* and a **Petit Casino supermarket** on rue de la Résistance. (Open M-W and F-Sa 7:30am-12:30pm and 3:30-7:30pm, Su 8am-noon.) A **laundromat** can be found near the train station. (☎04 90 92 56 91. Open 6 days a week.) To take in the vistas that Van Gogh loved, get the pamphlet that includes the *Promenade sur les lieux peints par Van Gogh* from the **tourist office**, pl. Jean Jaurès. From the bus stop, walk up av. Durand Maillane; the office will be on the left, in a parking lot, next to the **police station** (☎04 90 92 58 11). The tourist office provides info on housing, restaurants, and local activities, and conducts daily group tours in English, German, and Spanish from late April to mid-September. (☎04 90 92 05 22; fax 04 90 92 38 52. Free map. Tours of old St-Rémy and Vincent's sights €6.50, not including St-Paul entrance fee. Open daily early Apr.-Oct. 9am-12:30pm and 2-7pm; Nov.-early Apr. 9am-noon and 2-6pm.) **Buses** (☎04 90 82 07 35) come from Avignon (45min., 8 per day 7:15am-5:15pm, €5.20). The **Pharmacie Cendres,** 4 bd. Mirabeau (☎04 32 60 16 43) has up-to-date info on the **pharmacie de garde,** as do the **police** at ☎04 90 92 58 11. For health emergencies, an **ambulance** can be reached at ☎04 90 92 11 88. **Taxis** are available at ☎06 09 52 71 54.

CAMARGUE

In stark contrast to the Provençal hills to the north, the Camargue is a vast, humid delta lined with tall grasses and prowled by all manner of wildlife. Pink flamingos, black bulls, and the famous local white horses roam freely across the flat expanse of wild marshland, protected by the confines of the national park. The Camargue is anchored in the north by Arles and in the south by Stes-Maries-de-la-Mer;

STES-MARIES-DE-LA-MER

According to legend, in AD 40 Mary Magdalene, Mary Salomé (mother of the Apostles John and James), Mary Jacobé (Jesus's aunt), and their servant Sara were put to sea to die. Their ship washed ashore here. Stes-Maries's dark, fortified church was built to house their relics. The tourist traffic it attracts has made Stes-Maries (pop. 2500; 25,000 in the summer) into a sort of monster, surrounded by a honky-tonk collection of overpriced snack trailers and stores willing to cast anything Provençal in plastic. The town, with its network of narrow pedestrian streets, is worth a visit nevertheless—besides possessing the aforementioned church, Stes-Maries is the official capital of the Camargue, and most expeditions into that strange wilderness depart from here.

■■ **ORIENTATION AND PRACTICAL INFORMATION.** The town is wedged between untouched conservation land to the north, sea to the south, and marshes to the east. **Buses** leave from Arles (50-55min.; 7:50am-6:10pm daily, M-Sa 5 per day, Su 4 per day; €4.80); contact **Autocars Telleschi/Cartreize** (☎04 42 28 40 22) for info. The bus stop in Stes-Maries-de-la-Mer lies in pl. Mireille. Once here, **rent bikes** at Le Vélo Saintois, 19 rue de la République. (☎04 90 97 74 56. €9 per half-day, €15 per day, €61 per week; passport or ID deposit. Free bike delivery to downtown hotels. Open daily July-Aug. 8am-7pm; Sept.-Nov. and Feb.-June 9am-6:30pm.) A few minutes up the road at the town entrance, Le Vélociste, rte. d'Arles, offers the same prices for rentals, as well as packages that include horse rides for €35 and kayaking for €28. (☎04 90 97 83 26. Passport or ID deposit. Open M and W-Su 9am-12:30pm and 2-7pm.) If you get stuck in the Camargue's mud, call **Allô Taxi** at ☎04 90 97 94 49 or 06 18 63 08 59. (From center of town to Musée Camarguais €32, to Auberge de Jeunesse €13-17.) A good way to visit the region is to ride the *petit train*, a 50min. tour of the village and its surroundings. (☎06 09 96 02 65. Apr.-Oct. €6. Daily departures in front of the tourist office.)

To get to the **tourist office**, 5 av. Van Gogh, walk toward the ocean down rue de la République from the bus station or down rue Victor Hugo from the church. (☎04 90 97 82 55; www.saintesmaries.com. Open daily July-Aug. 9am-8pm; Apr.-June and Sept. 9am-7pm; Oct.-Feb. 9am-5pm.) Crédit Agricole, on pl. Mireille, also has a 24hr. **ATM** outside the tourist office. **Pharmacie Cambon-Neuville-Corus** is at 18 rue Victor Hugo. (☎04 90 97 83 02. Call for service on off-hours. Open M-Sa 9am-12:30pm and 3-7:30pm, Su 9am-12:30pm.) The **police** are on av. Van Gogh (☎04 90 97 89 50), next to *les arènes*. The **post office** is at 6 av. Gambetta. (☎04 90 97 96 00. Open M-F 9am-noon and 1:30-4:30pm, Sa 8:30am-11:30pm.) **Postal Code:** 13460.

ACCOMMODATIONS AND CAMPING. Rooms fill quickly in summer, and most are over €35; the town may be cheaper as a daytrip from Arles. The ▮**Hôtel Méditerranée ❹**, 4 av. Frédéric Mistral, is a pretty, quiet hotel blooming with flowers. Fourteen pastel-colored rooms with rustic furniture and hand-painted motifs open into charming private terraces. (☎04 90 97 82 09; www.mediterraneehotel.com. Breakfast €5. 24hr. reception. Reserve ahead in summer. Closed for part of Jan. Doubles €40-50; triples €68; quads €65. About €4 cheaper in the low season. MC/V.) 10km north of Stes-Maries, in the heart of the Camargue, is the **Auberge de Jeunesse Hameau de Pioch Badet (HI) ❷**. To get there, take the bus that runs between Stes-Maries and Arles to Pioch Badet (from Stes-Maries 10min., 6 per day, €1.70; from Arles 40min., €4.50). This quiet, camp-style hostel fills early in summer, so take the first bus you can. The friendly owner goes out of his way to help clients. (☎04 90 97 51 72. Bike rental €10.70 per day plus passport deposit. Horse tours €11 per hr., €53.50 per day. Laundry €3. Sheets €2.80. Reception daily 7:30-10:30am and 5-11pm; call ahead if you plan to arrive later. Lockout 10:30am-5pm. July-Aug. curfew midnight; extended during festivals. Reserved primarily for groups Nov.-Jan. Obligatory *demi-pension*. Package includes bunk, breakfast, dinner, and sheets €24.40. HI members only.) If you're in the mood for a splurge, a night at the three-star **Mangio Fango ❺**, on the rte. d'Arles will allow you to live in splendor. The exquisite rooms have a private balcony or patio. Enjoy air-conditioning, a heated pool, outdoor terrace, and garden—at a price. (☎04 90 97 80 56, mangio.fango@wanadoo.fr. Breakfast €9.50. Reception 9am-9pm. High-season doubles €84-107, low season €58-88. AmEx/MC/V.)

The starry sky of the Camargue may be more fun to sleep under than a roof: in that case, **camp** at **La Brise ❶**, an expansive 3-star site crossed by watery ditches and stands of reeds dotted with purple-pink trees. Take the bus from Arles to La Brise, 5min. east of the city center. The site comes complete with a large pool, a supermarket, a snack bar, laundry, Internet, and direct access to the beach. In summer, the campsite organizes water polo and soccer games, karaoke nights, scuba diving. Be warned: the Camargue breeds mosquitoes. (☎04 90 97 84 67; labrise@laposste.net. Reception 8:30am-8:30pm. July-Aug. 2 people with car €18.90, €6.90 per extra person, children under 7 €3.90; Apr.-June €18/€6.50/€3.70. Mobile-homes starting at €523 per week. Bungalows at €468. Prices lower by 30-50% in low season. Electricity €4. AmEx/DC/MC/V.)

['] FOOD. The Camargue's main crop is a sweet, fat-grained rice; you will find it in gelatinous cakes sold at *pâtisseries*, at local restaurants, and on the shelves of **supermarkets** like the **Petit Casino** on av. Victor Hugo. (☎04 90 97 90 60. Open in summer daily 8am-8pm; in winter 8am-noon and 4-8pm.) A **market** fills pl. des Gitanes on Mondays and Fridays (7am-noon). Restaurants cluster near the waterfront and around **rue Victor Hugo**, especially on **place Esprit Pioch**, where they serve seafood, heaping portions of paella, *pavé de taureau* (bull), and refreshing sangria. Most *menus* start around €12, but €9 is reasonable for lunch. Near the beach, **Le Piccolo ❷**, 7 rue Leon Gambetta (☎04 90 97 82 82), serves fresh *coquillage* (mussels and oysters; €6.50-13) amid cool ocean breezes and chandeliers made of colored bottles. Every Friday evening from June to September the restaurant offers an-all-you-can-eat paella and Gypsy show combo for €15. The *buffet camarguais*, which includes *chorizo, pâté, taureau* meat, and more, is also a popular option. (Reservations recommended. Open daily noon-11:30pm. MC/V.)

[◎] SIGHTS. The only major sight in town, and the focus of Stes-Maries, is the gray 12th-century **church** looming above the town's menagerie of snack bars. Despite its imposing stone walls and windowless facade, the dark Romanesque interior offers a cool respite from the heat, and a picturesque view of the surrounding sea and marshland awaits those who climb the vertigo-inducing staircase. (☎04 90 97 87 60. Church open daily 8am-12:30pm and 2-7pm; masses held daily July-Aug. at 6pm. Roof and tower open daily in summer 10am-8pm; in winter 10am-noon and 2-5pm. €2, children under 12, €1.30.)

[※] FESTIVALS. According to legend, the family chief of the region's native Gypsies, Sara, greeted the Stes-Maries when they arrived, asking that they baptize her and her people as Christians. The **Pèlerinage des Gitans** is a yearly event uniting Gypsy pilgrims from all over Europe (May 24-25). A costumed procession from the church to the sea bears statues of the saints and reenacts their landing. The two days are otherwise filled with prayers, services, and a significant number of tourists. A pilgrimage on the weekend around October 22 honors the Maries, with similar ceremonies for non-Roman pilgrims. Around July 14th, the 3-day **Féria du Cheval** brings horses from around the world for shows, competitions, and rodeos at the Stes-Maries and Méjanes arenas. (For details, call the Arènes in Saintes-Maries at ☎04 90 97 85 86, or in Méjanes at ☎04 90 97 10 60. €24-70. Prices vary from year to year.) During July, August, and September, bullfights, bull games, and horse shows occur regularly at the modern arenas. (Call the Arènes ☎04 90 97 85 86. Tickets from €5-7.)

[⚠] OUTDOOR ACTIVITIES. Stes-Maries is the capital of the Camargue, and most organized visits to the region leave from here. While some tours are listed here, the tourist office is teeming with more information. The best way to see the Camargue is on **horseback**. The region is dotted with stables offering tours throughout the park. These animals can go far into the marshes, wading through deep water into the range of birds and bulls inaccessible by any other means. Most rides are oriented toward novices. For the sake of mosquito protection and comfort, most riding places recommend wearing long pants and sneakers or boots. The stables are all united under a single association, the Association Camarguaise de Tourisme Equestre, and their prices remain within a few euros of one another. A brochure with a list of stables is available from the tourist office. (☎04 90 97 10 40; www.parc-camargue.fr. €13-16 per hr., €26-30 for 2hr., €35-40 for a half-day, €55-80 per day; picnic usually included on daytrips.)

Although most of the trails are open only to horseback riders and walkers, **bicycle touring** is a great way to see much of the area. Trail maps indicating length, level of difficulty, and danger spots are available from the Stes-Maries tourist office and from bike rental shops. Bring an ample supply of fresh water—it's hot and there are few bathroom stops along the way. A 2hr. pedal will reveal some of the area, but you'll need a whole day if you plan to stop along the wide, deserted white-sand beaches that line the trail. Aspiring botanists and zoologists should stop at the **Maison du Parc Naturel Régional de Camargue (PNRC),** on the bus line between Stes-Maries and Arles, which distributes info on the region's unusual flora and fauna and offers panoramic views of the marshes. (Pont de Gau, 10min. from Stes-Maries. ☎ 04 90 97 86 32. Open daily Apr.-Sept. 10am-6pm; Oct.-Mar. M-Th and Sa-Su 9:30am-5pm.) Next door, the **Parc Ornithologique du Pont de Gau** provides several paths through the marshes and offers views of birds and grazing bulls. (☎ 04 90 97 82 62. Park open daily Apr.-Sept. 9am-sunset; Oct.-Mar. 10am-sunset. Reception office opens at 10am. €6, under age 17 €3.)

The final two options for visiting the area are by boat or Jeep. Camargue, 5 rue des Launes, sends **boats** from Port Gardian deep into the Petit Rhône for up-close bird- and bull-watching. (☎ 04 90 97 84 72; bateau.camargue@wanadoo.fr. Open Mar.-Nov. 1½hr.; Mar.-Sept. 3-4 per day, Oct. 2 per day. July-Aug. first departure 10:45am, last departure 5:55pm; Sept.-May last departure 4:10pm. €10, children €5.) En Camargue (☎ 04 90 97 70 10; www.lesquatremaries.com) and Tiki 3 (☎ 04 90 97 81 68; www.tiki3.fr) provide similar tours at comparable prices. For **Jeep safaris,** contact Le Gitan, 17 av. de la République, in Stes-Maries. Safaris explore the banks of the Grand and Petit Rhône. The jeeps hold 7-8 people. (☎ 04 90 97 89 33; legitansafari@libertysurf.fr. 2hr. trips €31 per person; 4hr. trips €37. July-Sept. trips depart between 10am-6pm; low season the last trip leaves at 4pm. Open daily 9am-8pm.) Camargue Safaris Gallon, 22 av. Van Gogh (facing the Arènes), has similar excursions throughout the year. (☎ 04 90 97 86 93 or 06 10 17 58 75; www.camargue.fr/safari4x4.html. Trips depart in morning and afternoon. 1hr. trip €13, 2½hr. €31, 4hr. €46.)

NÎMES

It is the Spanish feel of Nîmes (pop. 133,000) that draws so many vacationing French. They flock here in particular for the *férias*, with their bull runs, bullfights, flamenco dancing, and other hot-blooded Latin activities. Nîmes also serves as an excellent base for short excursions to some of the Roman ruins in the area, including the architecturally impressive Pont du Gard aqueduct. Despite the lively *féria* season, however, Nîmes doesn't otherwise merit a long-term stay, lacking both the intimacy of other Provençal cities and the glitz of the Côte d'Azur.

◾ TRANSPORTATION

Trains: bd. Talabot. Info office open M-F 5:45am-9:30pm, Sa 6am-9:30pm, Su 6am-10pm. To: **Arles** (20min., 8 per day, €6.70); **Bordeaux** (5hr., 4 per day €51.10); **Marseille** (1¼hr., 9 per day, €16.70); **Montpellier** (30min., 50 per day, €7.70); **Paris** (3hr., 12 per day, €70.80); **Toulouse** (3hr., 8 per day, €31.90).

Buses: rue Ste-Félicité (☎ 04 66 29 52 00), behind the train station. Info office just inside the train station open M-F 8am-noon and 2-6pm. **Lignes du Gard** (☎ 04 66 29 27 29) runs to **Avignon** (1½hr., 4 per day, €7.30) and **Montpellier** (M-Sa 2 per day, €8.50). **Cars de Camargue** (☎ 04 90 96 36 25) serves **Arles** (M-F 5 per day, 3 on Sa, €5.50).

Public Transportation: T.C.N. (☎ 04 66 38 15 40). Maps and schedules available at the tourist office. Buses stop running at 9:30pm. Tickets good for 1hr. Ticket €1, *carnet* of 5 €4. Single tickets available on the bus, *carnets* at the station kiosks near the Station Esplanade or the *gare routière*.

Taxis: TRAN office (☎ 04 66 29 40 11) in train station. Base €1.80; €0.58 per km until 7pm, €0.83 per km after 7pm. 24hr.

⊕ 🛈 ORIENTATION AND PRACTICAL INFORMATION

Nîmes's shops, museums, and cafes cluster in the *vieille ville* between bd. Victor Hugo and bd. Admiral Courbet. To get there from the train station, follow av. Feuchères, veer left around the park, then clockwise around the arena. To reach the tourist office, follow the signs and go straight on bd. Victor Hugo for five blocks until you reach the Maison Carrée, a Roman temple in the middle of pl. Comédie, which is opposite rue Auguste and the tourist office.

Tourist Office: 6 rue Auguste (☎04 66 58 38 00; www.ot-nimes.fr). Free accommodations service, detailed map, festival info, and guided English tours of the city (July-Aug. Sa 10am, €5.50). In low season, audioguided tours of the city are available for €8. Themed tours offered sporadically Apr.-Sept., call for info. The free *Nîmescope* lists events. Info on bus and train excursions to Pont du Gard, the Camargue, and nearby towns. Open July-Aug. M-F 8:30am-8pm, Sa 9am-7pm, Su 10am-6pm; May and Sept. M-F 8am-7pm, Sa 9am-7pm, Su 10am-6pm.

Tours: Le Petit Train (☎04 66 70 26 92). Leaves almost every hr. from esplanade Charles de Gaulle, in front of the Palais de Justice. Daily mid-July to mid-Aug. 9:30am-7:30pm; Apr.-June and Sept.-Oct. 10-11:30am and 2:30-5:30pm. €5, ages 2-11 €2.

Budget Travel: Nouvelles Frontières, 1 bd. de Prague (☎04 66 67 38 94; fax 04 66 78 38 62). Open M-F 9am-7pm, Sa 9pm-6pm.

Laundromat: Lavomatique, 5 rue des Halles and 23 rue Pierre Sémard. Open daily 7am-8pm. **Laverie Libre Service,** 22 rue de Vérone. Open daily 7am-9pm.

Youth Center: Bureau Information Jeunesse, 8 rue de l'Horloge (☎04 66 36 56 86). Provides information on employment, education, and travel opportunities geared toward students. Free Internet by reservation only. Open Tu-F 9am-6pm, Sa 2-6pm.

Police: 3 rue du Colysée (☎04 66 02 56 00).

Hospital: Hôpital Caremeau (☎04 66 68 68 68), 246 chemin du Carreau de Lanes.

SOS Médecins: Emergency doctor ☎04 66 23 69 23. On-call doctor ☎04 66 76 11 11.

Internet Access: Virtual Station, 25 rue de l'Horloge, pl. de la Maison Carrée (☎04 66 36 36 16), is packed with videogame-playing teens. €2 for 30min., €3 per hr. Open daily 10am-midnight. Also available at dark and smoky **PC Gamer,** 2 rue Nationale (☎04 66 76 27 85). €4 per hr., 10am-noon €3 per hr. Open M-Sa 9:30am-1am, Su 2pm-1am.

Post Office: 1 bd. de Bruxelles (☎04 66 76 69 50), across from the park at the end of av. Feuchères. **Currency exchange** with no commission. Open M-F 8am-7pm, Sa 8am-noon. Branch offices: 19 bd. Gambetta and 11 pl. Belle Croix.

Postal Code: 30000 and 30900.

🏠 📷 ACCOMMODATIONS AND CAMPING

Though the *vieille ville* is dotted with pricey hotels, a handful of affordable options also lies in the heart of the city. If you're up for a long walk or bus ride every morning, the hostel is unquestionably the best option. Reserve a couple of weeks in advance during festivals and summer concerts.

🏩 **Auberge de Jeunesse (HI),** 257 chemin de l'Auberge de la Jeunesse (☎04 66 68 03 20; fax 04 66 68 03 21), off chemin de la Cigale, 1.5km from quai de la Fontaine. On foot, pass the Maison Carrée on bd. Victor Hugo. Continue straight on bd. A. Daudet. Go left at sq. Antonin onto quai de la Fontaine. The Jardins de la Fontaine will be on the right; continue by the garden straight on av. Roosevelt. Follow the signs for the Auberge. (45min.) Or take bus #1 (dir: Alès) to Stade, rte. d'Alès, and follow the signs. Buses stop running at 8pm; the hostel minibus (call ahead to arrange) will pick you up at the station for free. It will also bring you back to the sta-

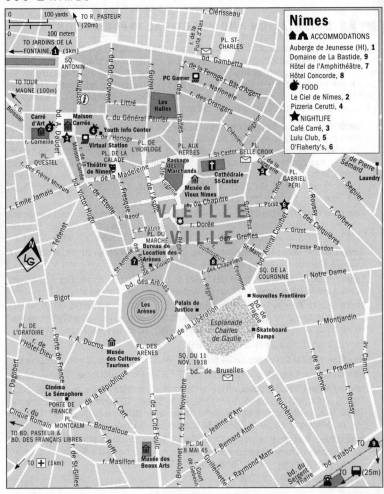

Nîmes

🏠🏠 **ACCOMMODATIONS**
Auberge de Jeunesse (HI), **1**
Domaine de La Bastide, **9**
Hôtel de l'Amphithéâtre, **7**
Hôtel Concorde, **8**

🍎 **FOOD**
Le Ciel de Nîmes, **2**
Pizzeria Cerutti, **4**

⭐ **NIGHTLIFE**
Café Carré, **3**
Lulu Club, **5**
O'Flaherty's, **6**

tion in the morning for €1.30. Delightfully modern and friendly hostel. Jovial manager keeps comfortable dorms, surrounded by botanical gardens. 4- to 6-bed dorms, some with bath and key-card access. Some family rooms available. Breakfast €3.30. Dinner €9.10; a la carte dinner €2.80-€5.50. Sheets €2.70 per week. Individual, locking cupboards for luggage. 24hr. reception Mar.-Sept. Reservations advised. Bunks €9.50. **Camping** €5.50, with tent rental €7.50. HI members only. MC/V. ❶

Hôtel de l'Amphithéâtre, 4 rue des Arènes (☎04 66 67 28 51; http://perso.wana-doo.fr/hotel-amphitheatre). Tucked into two 18th-century mansions, this centrally located hotel offers an elegant alternative to travelers willing to splurge. 16 charming, well-equipped rooms—TV, large bath, A/C—are named after French writers and artists. Breakfast €6. Reception 7am-10:30pm. Singles €32; doubles €41-55 depending on size and if it has a balcony; triples €51-58.Extra bed €17. Rates increase by €5-10 in high season, and by as much as €15 during the *férias*. MC/V. ❸

Hôtel Concorde, 3 rue des Chapeliers (☎/fax 04 66 67 91 03), off rue Régale. A friendly staff cares for clean but tiny rooms in this small, family-owned hotel. Just around the corner from *les arènes.* Breakfast €4. Singles €19-24, with shower and TV €26-29; doubles €22-35; triples with shower €35-43; quads €48. *Let's Go* users get a 5% discount. MC/V. ❷

Camping: Domaine de La Bastide, rte. de Générac (☎/fax 04 66 38 09 21), 5km south of the train station. Take bus D (dir: La Bastide, last bus 8pm) to its terminus. By car, drive toward Montpellier and get off at rte. de Générac. Unrenovated site with restaurant and laundry. Most clients are long-term residents who live and work nearby. No recreational facilities. €7.50 per person, €11.85 for 2. Caravan with electricity €10.70 per person, €15 for 2. MC/V. ❶

🔲 FOOD

Local chefs employ generous amounts of *herbes de Provence* (a mixture of local spices) and *aïoli* (a thick sauce of garlic and olive oil). Nîmes specializes in *la brandade de morue,* dried cod crushed with olive oil and packed in a turnover, pastry, or soufflé. Unfortunately, even the more expensive restaurants in Nîmes are unspectacular. If you have access to a kitchen, you can prepare better meals yourself, with fresh produce from the various markets. Stock up at the **open-air market** on bd. Jean-Jaurès (F 7am-1pm), the **market** in Les Halles (daily 6am-1pm), or the large **Marché U,** 19 rue d'Alès, just down the hill from the hostel. (Open M-Sa 8am-12:45pm and 3:30-8pm.) The terraced herb gardens and ponds on the back slopes of the **Jardins de la Fontaine** are great places to bring a picnic basket.

Caladons, honey cookies with almonds, are Nîmes's favorite sweet. Cafes and bakeries line the squares; *brasseries* dominate **boulevard Victor Hugo, boulevard Admiral Courbet,** and the arena. Terraced **place du Marché** with its crocodile fountain reverberates with laughter late into the night. On the third floor of the Carré d'Art, **Le Ciel de Nîmes ❸** serves artful delights before a beautiful view of the entire city. (☎ 04 66 36 71 70. *Entrées* €12-14, excellent salads, and fresh juices. Open Tu-Su 10am-8pm. MC/V.) At **Pizzeria Cerutti ❷,** 25 rue de l'Horloge, a friendly staff serves hearty Italian fare at great prices. Fresh pastas (€7-8) and pizzas (€7) with homemade sauces are cooked before your eyes in the large oven. (☎ 04 66 21 54 88. Open W-Su noon-2pm, 7pm-1am; M-Tu and Th-Su same hours in the summer.)

🔲 SIGHTS

A three-day pass to all sights is sold at every sight (€10, students €5).

JARDINS DE LA FONTAINE. Originally designed in the 18th century, the Jardins de la Fontaine remain typically French. They are ideal for strolling or a picnic, offering plenty of shade and a slight breeze on hot summer days. Full of secret nooks and luxuriant flora, the gardens are among the most beautiful in Southern France. *(Off pl. Foch to the left along the canals from the Maison. Garden open daily Apr. to mid-Sept. 7:30am-10pm; mid-Sept. to Nov. 7:30am-6:30pm; Nov.-Mar. 8am-7pm. Free.)* Rising majestically above the park is the **Tour Magne.** Built in the Iron Age and modified by Augustus in 15 BC, this massive tower, essentially a blunt stone spike, once represented a corner of the Roman Empire. Now the eroded ruins offer an exhilarating view of Nîmes and the surrounding countryside. *(☎ 04 66 67 65 56. Open daily July-Aug. 9am-7pm; Sept.-June 9am-5pm. €2.40, students €1.90.)*

LES ARÈNES. The city's pride and joy is the best-preserved Roman amphitheater in France. Impressive when empty, the amphitheater is awesome when packed with screaming crowds during its concerts and bullfights. The elliptical stone arena, built in AD 50, seats 23,000 people. *(☎04 66 76 72 77. Guided tours daily mid-July to Aug. 10am-12:30pm and 3-5:30pm. Open summer M-F 9am-7pm; winter 10am-6pm. Closed on days of* férias *or concerts; call in advance to verify. €4.65, students €3.40.)*

MAISON CARRÉE AND CARRÉ D'ART. Built from limestone rock, the imposing rectangular temple known as the **Maison Carrée** served as the center of public life in the first century of Roman rule. Louis XIV liked it so much that he almost ordered it to be brought to Versailles as a lawn ornament. In 1992 the roof was renovated to be an exact replica of the original large flat tiles. The former temple now houses a set of ancient statues and two Roman mosaics, as well as a few informative text panels in English and French explaining the history of the building. *(☎04 66 36 26 76. Open daily June-Sept. 9am-7pm; Oct.-May 10am-6pm. Free.)* The Maison Carrée is gracefully counter-balanced from across the square by Norman Foster's ultra-modern glass cube, housing the city library and the **Carré d'Art,** which displays impressive traveling exhibits in a fresh, cool setting. The museum also holds contemporary works from monochromatic painting to pop-art. *(☎04 65 76 35 35; carreart@mnet.fr. Open Tu-Su 10am-6pm. Guided tours Sa-Su 3 and 4:30pm, extra tours in summer Tu-F 11am and 4:30pm. €4.65, students €3.40.)*

MUSÉE DES CULTURES TAURINES. This new museum offers a playful and compelling glimpse into the culture of bullfights and the importance of the *férias* to the city and the surrounding region, especially if you're able to read the French text. Videos, images, clothing, and even mounted bulls' heads from ancient and modern *férias* describe in vivid detail the various components of the bullfighting culture, from the types of bulls in the region to the role of female *toreras*. *(6 rue Alexandre Ducros. ☎04 66 36 83 77; musee.taureau@ville-nimes.fr. Open May-Oct. Tu-Su 10am-6pm, until 10pm on* féria *days and during the Jeudis de Nimes. Guided tours June and Sept.-Oct. Sa 11am; July-Aug. Th 6pm. €4.65, students €3.40.)*

MUSÉE DES BEAUX ARTS AND MUSÉE DU VIEUX NÎMES. The **Musée de Beaux Arts,** a Neoclassical building accented with marble pillars and Roman mosaic floors, features paintings of the French, Italian, Flemish, and Dutch schools from the 15th to 18th centuries. The **Musée du Vieux Nimes,** in a 17th-century Episcopal palace, displays artifacts from the Middle Ages through the 19th century, as well as a great exhibit on the history of blue jeans that honors Nîmes as the birthplace of denim. *(Beaux-Arts: rue de la cité Foule. ☎04 66 67 38 21. Vieux Nîmes: pl. aux Herbes, next to the cathedral. ☎04 66 36 00 64. Both open July-Aug. Tu-Su 10am-6pm. €4.30, students €3.)*

▶ ⬛ ENTERTAINMENT AND FESTIVALS

Outside of the festival season, Nîmes is a pretty lousy place to party. Bars are lively during the *férias* (see below), but otherwise they shut down relatively early. In summer, however, the city comes alive with the weekly **Jeudis de Nimes,** when craftsmen, painters, artists, and musicians fill every street corner late into the night. Ask the tourist office for a map and detailed schedule of events (July-Aug. Th 7-11pm). On other nights, check out the cafes along the pl. du Marché. Bustling **O'Flaherty's,** 21 bd. Amiral Courbet, has €3.50-5 pints of beer and live music on Thursday nights in winter. The dart-filled, Guinness-sloppy bar is a favorite of both anglophone visitors and friendly *Nîmois.* *(☎04 66 67 22 63. Open M-F 11am-2am, Sa-Su 5pm-2am.)* Locals fill the outside tables at the **Café Carré,** 1 pl. de la Maison Carrée, which is a cafe overlooking the Maison Carrée by day and a lively bar at night. *(☎04 66 67 50 05. Drinks €1.50-3. Open daily 7am-2am.)* **Lulu Club,** 10 impasse de la Curaterie, off rue de la Curaterie, is a gay dance bar. Theme nights, some without cover. *(☎04 66 36 28 20. Mixed drinks €4; straight alcohol €8. €10 cover includes 1 drink. Open Th-Su midnight onward.)* **Cinéma Le Sémaphore,** 25 rue Porte de France, plays non-French films in their original languages. *(☎04 66 67 83 11. €5.50, under 25 €4.60, noon shows €4.)*

Students in Nîmes head for the beach in summer, where temporarily constructed restaurant-bars open in June and entertain until early September. Although it is difficult to get there and even harder to find a cheap way back to Nîmes, bus #6 runs along the plage de la Corniches. Party-goers can get off at Les Passantes or Les Amours d'Antan.

Concerts, movies, plays, and operas take place at *les arènes* throughout the year. Summer acts have included Phil Collins and Peter Gabriel. For info and reservations, contact the **Bureau de Location des Arènes,** 4 rue de la Violette. (☎08 91 79 12 01; www.arenesdenimes.com. Open M-F 9:30am-noon and 1:30-6pm.) The **Théâtre de Nîmes,** 1 pl. de la Calade, offers over 70 shows per year, ranging from theater to dance to musical performances. (☎04 66 36 65 00. Oct.-June only. Tickets €10-27, with some reduced rates for students.)

It is worth changing travel plans to see one of the famous *férias*. Nîmes holds three important *férias:* the **Féria de Primavera** in mid-February, the **Féria des Vendanges** in mid-September, and the most boisterous, the **Féria de Pentecôte** (during Pentecost). For five days, the streets resound with the clattering of hooves as bulls are herded to *les arènes* for combat, and the nights are full of revelry.

The **Courses Camarguaises,** held at varying dates in June, July, and August, provide more humane entertainment. Fighters strip decorations from the bulls' horns, narrowly avoiding the lethal points, and then vault over barriers to safety. (Purchase tickets at the arena ticket office, 4 rue de la Violette. Cheap seats usually available on the day of the event. €10.50-53.50.)

▶ DAYTRIP FROM NÎMES

PONT DU GARD. The Pont du Gard is the centerpiece of a 50km Roman aqueduct that once supplied Nîmes with water. Its three diminishing levels of arches bridge the 275m wide valley of the Gardon River at a height of 48m. Built in 19 BC under the direction of Roman engineers to transport water from the springs near Uzès to Nîmes, the entire aqueduct, an architectural *coup de grace*, slopes at a mere rate of 25cm per km, at an average gradient of 0.34 degrees. Close to 90% of the aqueduct is underground, a Roman feat of near-perfect construction.

Although a walk across the bridge itself is free, the helpful welcome center houses several interpretive activities, including a sleek, educational multimedia museum (€6), a 25min. film in English and French about the construction of the bridge (€3, screening times available at the information desk), and a children's learning center (€4.50). Guided tours of the bridge are available in several languages (€5). Packages of all four activities are available for €10, and €9 for students. Swimming in the refreshing river below the Pont du Gard offers a cool view of the bridge; stairs down to the rocky beach are on either side of the bridge itself.

If you have a whole day to spare, the best way to experience the Pont du Gard is to start from **Collias,** 6km toward Uzès. **Kayak Vert** rents canoes, kayaks, and bikes. The pleasant two- to three-hour paddle takes you down river past the Château de St-Privat to the Pont du Gard, where a bus shuttles you back to Collias. (☎04 66 22 80 76. Kayak/canoe rental €18 per day, bikes €15 per day. 10% discount for students, €4 discount for guests of the hostel in Nîmes.)

The **STDG** (☎04 66 29 27 29) runs **buses** from the bus station to the Pont du Gard (40min.; 7 per day; €5.60). Buses also leave for the Pont du Gard from Avignon (45min., 6per day, €6). From September to June the bus stops at the roundabout by the Hôtel L'Auberge Blanche—a.k.a., the middle of nowhere; in July and August the bus stops at the Pont du Gard Welcome Center.

Camping le Barralet ❶, rue des Aires in Collias, offers a pool and hot showers in addition to river bathing. (☎04 66 22 84 52; fax 04 66 22 89 17. Open Mar.-Sept. €8-12 per person. MC/V.) A grocery store is 200m away.

ORANGE

Despite its name, this northern Provençal town (pop. 29,000) hasn't harbored a single citrus grove in all of its colorful two-millennia history. *Orange* is actually a perversion of the original Roman name of the city: *Arausio*. Orange's juice, the Côtes du Rhône vintage, originates in its renowned vineyards, not in groves: *caves* throughout the region offer *dégustations* of the fine liquid. An immense first-century AD Roman theater, an intricately decorated triumphal arch, and certain summer festivals are the chief reasons for making a visit to this provincial town.

TRANSPORTATION. Trains run from av. Frédéric Mistral to **Avignon** (20min.; M-Sa 19 per day, Su 13 per day; €4.70); **Marseille** (1¼hr., 11 per day, €18.20); **Lyon** (2½hr.; M-Sa 7 per day, Su 4 per day; €23); and **Paris** (3½hr., 2 TGV per day, €68). The info office is open daily 5:30am-8:20pm. **Buses** (☎04 90 34 15 59) run from cours Pourtoules to **Avignon** (45 min.; M-Sa 4 per day, Su 2 per day; €4.80). The ticket office is open M-Tu and Th-F 8am-12:30pm and 3-5pm, W 8am-noon and 2-4pm. For a **taxi,** call **Taxi Monge** at ☎04 90 51 00 00.

ORIENTATION AND PRACTICAL INFORMATION. To reach the **tourist office,** 5 cours A. Briand, from the station, follow the signs along av. Frédéric Mistral to the *centre ville;* keep left as the road becomes rue de la République, then rue St. Martin. Multilingual staff provides maps, daytrip ideas, and free hotel booking. (☎04 90 34 70 88; fax 04 90 34 99 62. Open Apr.-Sept. M-Sa 9:30am-7pm, Su 10am-6pm; Oct.-Mar. M-Sa 10am-1pm and 2-5pm. Branch office, pl. des Frères Mounet, opposite Théâtre Antique. Open Apr.-June and Sept. M-Sa 10am-1pm and 2:15-6pm, Su 10am-12:30pm and 2:30-6pm; July-Aug. M-Sa 10am-1pm and 2:15-7pm, Su 10am-12:30pm and 2:30-6pm.) Other services include: a **laundromat** at 5 rue St-Florent, off bd. E. Daladier (open daily 7:30am-8pm); **police** at 427 bd. E. Daladier (☎04 90 51 55 55); the Louis Giorgi **hospital** at chemin de l'Abrian, near av. H. Fabré (☎04 90 11 22 22); **ambulances** at ☎04 90 34 02 66. **Pharmacie St-Martin** is at 18 rue St-Martin. (☎04 90 34 02 82. Open M 2-7:15pm, Tu-Sa 8:45am-12:15pm and 2-7:15pm.) For late-night pharmacies, check the list on the front door. **Internet** access is available at Atlas Télécom, 22 rue V. Hugo (☎04 90 11 04 60. €3.50 per hr.; open daily 10am-10:30pm), which has international phones. There is a **post office** with **currency exchange** at 679 bd. E. Daladier, cours Pourtoules. (☎04 90 11 11 00. Open M-F 8am-6:30pm, Sa 8am-noon.) **Postal Code:** 84100.

ACCOMMODATIONS AND FOOD. Orange's hotels fill up fast in July and August for the Festival d'Avignon, and prices increase accordingly. ■Hôtel St-Florent ❸, 4 rue du Mazeau, near pl. aux Herbes, is a charming, brightly colored establishment. All 17 rooms are beautifully furnished in B&B style. The Provençal frescoes and numerous paintings adorning the walls were all made by the owners and their children. St-Florent is definitely worth the splurge. (☎04 90 34 18 53; http://hotelsaintflorent.free.fr. Buffet breakfast €6. Garage €6. Open Mar.-Nov. Singles €22, with shower €35; doubles €35-60; triples €55; family suites with bath €60-70. Extra bed €8. July-Aug. €5-7 higher. MC/V.) Arcôtel ❷, 8 pl. aux Herbes, rents simple but comfortable rooms. The 20-room hotel is close to both the central *place* and the Roman theater. Singles and one-bed doubles are a great bargain, and some triples and quads are particularly big. (☎04 90 34 09 23; fax 04 90 51 61 12. Breakfast €6. Parking €4. TV €3.50. Reception 7am-10pm. Singles €20; doubles €27-38; triples with bath €45; quads with bath €55. MC/V.) The camping at Le Jonquier ❶, on rue A. Carrel, is a hike. From the tourist office, walk toward the autoroute, make a right on rue A. Rigord and continue down rue A. Carrel until you reach the campsite. The three-star site is conveniently located, but facilities are a worn and prices slightly expensive. A small pool, two tennis courts, mini-golf, horseback riding and a mini-mart are available. Mobile home/tent/cottage rental is also offered. (☎04 90 34 49 48; www.campinglejonquier.com. Reception daily 8am-8pm. Open Apr.-Sept. 1-2 people, car, and tent €17.50-21.50; €4 per additional person. Electricity €4. MC/V.)

The eateries on pl. aux Herbes and pl. de la République serve standard cafe fare, from goat cheese salads to steaming pizzas. For **groceries,** head to the **Petit Casino,** 16 rue de la République. (Open M-Sa 7:30am-12:30pm and 3:30-7:30pm, Su 3:30-7:30pm.) Pl. République, pl. Clemenceau, and cours A. Briand host an **open-air market** selling everything from produce (Th 7am-1pm) to handmade jewelry at a "food-less" Provençal market (June-Aug., Sa 10am-3pm). A *brocante* (garage sale) is also held on Saturdays near the Arc de Triomphe. **The Festival Café ❸,** 5 pl. de la République, serves copious *menus* (€16-26), including large salads and an incredible *mousse au chocolat* on a purple-trimmed terrace. Service can vary in quality. (☎04 90 34 65 58. Salads €9-13, *plats* €10-16, desserts €5-6. Open daily 7:30am-midnight. MC/V.)

◨ 🄳 SIGHTS AND ENTERTAINMENT. Built in the first century, Orange's striking **Théâtre Antique** is the best-preserved Roman theater in Europe. Its 3811 ft.^{2} stage wall is one of three remaining in the world; Louis XIV is said to have called it the most beautiful wall in his kingdom. The theater originally held 10,000 spectators and was connected to a gymnasium complete with running tracks, combat platform, sauna, and temple. After the fall of Rome, this locus of pagan entertainment fell into disrepair. In the mid-19th century, engineers rediscovered its great acoustics and used the three remaining rows as a template for reconstructing the seating area. Since 1869, Orange's Roman theater has again been home to various open-air performances. Explore with the free multilingual audioguide and finish with a film retracing the monument's history. On your way out, make sure to stop at the Taberna d'Arausio for a wine *dégustation* (€2, free with any purchase).

Above the theater, amid the ragged remnants of the Prince of Orange's castle, **Colline St-Eutrope** (St-Eutrope the Hill) offers a stunning view of the city and its surroundings. Queen Juliana of Netherlands, of Orange's old royal family, even planted a famous oak on the grounds of this overgrown park. Colline St-Eutrope provides free, though acoustically poor, standing room for concerts.

Across the street, a ticket to the theater provides access to the **Musée Municipal.** The small museum retraces the history of Orange, which was successively a Roman colony, a princedom linked to the Netherlands (1583-1702), and finally a French town. The historical museum dedicates exhibits to the city's recent past as well as to antique objects uncovered in the area. Fragments of its *cadastres*, the most complete Roman land register ever found, are displayed on the walls of the first floor. In the same room, a stunningly preserved mosaic from the 2nd century AD can be observed. (☎04 90 51 17 60 for both theater and museum. Open daily June-Aug. 9am-8pm; Apr.-May and Sept. 9am-7pm; Mar. and Oct. 9am-6pm; Jan.-Feb. and Nov.-Dec. 9am-5pm. Combined ticket €7.50, students €5.50.) Orange's other major monument, the **Arc de Triomphe,** stands on the Via Agrippa, which once connected Arles to Lyon. Built during Augustus's time, the 19m stone structure is a tribute to those who founded the colony of Arausio. The arch's remarkably well-preserved facades, depict victories over the Gauls.

From early July to August, the Théâtre Antique regains its original function with the **Chorégies,** a series of grand operas, choral productions, and symphonic concerts. Info available from the Maison des Chorégies, 18 pl. Sylvain, next to the theater. (☎04 90 34 24 24; www.choregies.asso.fr. Open June-Aug. M-Sa 10am-7pm; Feb.-May M-F 11am-1pm and 2-5pm. Tickets €5-180; students under 25 can buy tickets for as little as €2.) Orange hosts two smaller festivals: **Les Rencontres Classiques d'Orange** celebrates theater and the **Orange se met au Jazz** is dedicated to jazz. Both take place in late June to July and feature free performances. In August, concerts, films, and variety shows take the stage. For info, call the **Service Culturel,** next door to Maison des Chorégies. (☎04 90 51 57 57. Open M-Th 8:30am-noon and 1:30-6pm, F 8:30am-noon and 1:30-4:30pm, and on the nights of performances.)

P R O V E N C E

THE CÔTE
D'AZUR

A sunny place for shady people.
—Somerset Maugham

Between Marseille and the Italian border, sun-drenched beaches and warm Mediterranean waters form the backdrop for this fabled playground of the rich and famous. Sunbathers bronze *au naturel* on pebbly beaches, high rollers drop millions in casinos, and cultural types wander abandoned coastal fortifications. At nightfall, the Riviera's true pastime begins: non-stop partying in Europe's most exclusive, extravagant nightclubs.

Now one of the most touristed parts of France, the Côte d'Azur began as a Greco-Roman commercial base. Prosperous villages sprang up here around 600 BC, only to be razed by barbarian invaders toward the middle of the first millennium. With the 16th-century arrival of the French monarchy, the region started to take its modern form. The Riviera's resort status began to develop when English and Russian aristocrats took up the habit of wintering on the Côte in order to escape their abominable weather. Nice soon drew a steady crowd of the idle rich. In the 1920s, Coco Chanel popularized the Provençal farmer's healthy tan; parasols went down, hemlines went up, and ritual sun-worship began.

The Riviera has been the passion and the death of many a famous artist, including F. Scott Fitzgerald, Picasso, and Renoir. Most towns along the eastern stretch boast a chapel, room, or wall decorated by Matisse, Chagall, and playwright and painter Jean Cocteau. The ultimate celebrity accessory is a vacation home in St-Tropez, and each May high society makes its yearly pilgrimage to the Cannes Film Festival and the Monte-Carlo Grand Prix. Even in the smaller towns, idyllic villas tucked among scrubby vegetation on plunging cliffs are reminders that the Riviera is an international luxury resort. Less exclusive are Nice's raucous *Carnaval* in February and various summer jazz festivals. Penny-pinchers can soak up the spectacle, as well as plenty of sun, sea, and crowded sand.

HIGHLIGHTS OF THE CÔTE D'AZUR

PARTY THE NIGHT AWAY in the exclusive nightclubs of **St-Tropez** (p. 748), where celebrity sightings are a dime a dozen and drinks are approximately €800 a dozen.

FOR DAYTIME THRILLS, head to the **Grand Canyon de Verdon** (p. 741)—an outdoors adventure mecca that offers every watersport you can imagine and many you haven't.

RAMBLE through the medieval streets of **St-Paul** (p. 709), where a stroll along the ramparts provides a cultured respite from the fast life along the coast.

NICE

Sizzling Nice (pop. 340,000) is the unofficial capital of the Riviera. The former vacation haunt of dukes and czarinas continues to seduce tourists with nonstop parties, shopping, and first-rate museums. No matter the season, the maze of pedestrian streets buzzes with shoppers by day and lively bar-goers by night. Nice

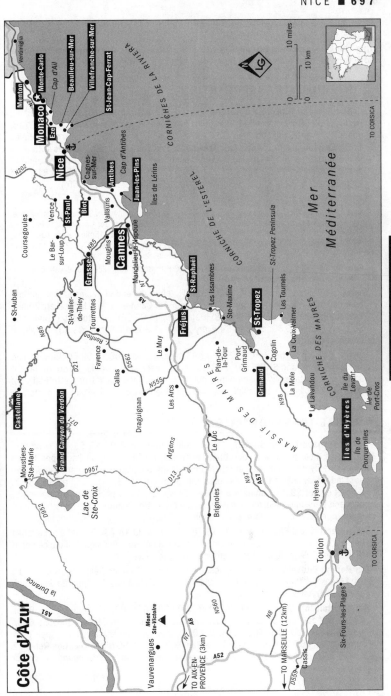

Côte d'Azur

CÔTE D'AZUR

is a budget traveler's paradise: excellent transportation, budget lodgings, and reasonable restaurants make France fifth-largest city an inexpensive base for sampling the Côte d'Azur's pricier delights. Be prepared to make new friends, hear more English than French, and have more fun than you'll be able to remember.

✈ INTERCITY TRANSPORTATION

Flights: Aéroport Nice-Côte d'Azur (☎08 20 42 33 33). **Air France,** 10 av. Félix Faure (☎08 20 82 08 20). Open M-F 9am-6pm. Outbound flights to **Bastia** in Corsica (€116; under 25, over 60, and couples €59) and **Paris** (€93; under 25, over 60, and couples €50). **EasyJet** flies to **London** (see **Travelling from the UK,** p. 20). **Sunbus** #23 goes to the airport. (☎04 93 13 53 13. Every 15min. 6am-9:15pm, €1.30.) The pricier **ANT** airport bus runs from the bus station. (☎04 92 29 88 88; fax 04 92 29 88 81. M-Sa every 20min. 5:35am-8:50pm, Su every 30min. 5:35am-8:30pm; €3.50.)

Trains: There are 2 primary train stations in town:

Gare SNCF Nice-Ville, av. Thiers (☎04 93 14 82 12, call M-F 9am-noon or 3-6pm for lost luggage, missed trains, and special assistance). Open daily 5am-12:30am. To: **Cannes** (35min., every 20min., €5.30); **Marseille** (2½hr., 16 per day, €25.60); **Monaco** (15min., every 10-30min., €3.10); **Paris** (5½hr., 9 per day, €83.40). Same-day ticket office open daily 5:20am-11:20pm; info and reservation center open M-Sa 8:30am-6:30pm, Su 9am-6pm.

Gare du Sud, 4bis rue Alfred Binet (☎04 97 03 80 80), 800m from Nice-Ville. Private outbound trains to **Digne-les-Bains** and **Plan-du-Var.**

Buses: 5 bd. Jean Jaurès (☎04 93 85 61 81), left at the end of av. Jean Médecin. Info booth open M-F 8:30am-5:30pm, Sa 9am-4pm. To: **Cannes** (1½hr.; M-Sa every 20min. 6:10am-9:45pm, Su every 30min. 8:30am-9:40pm; €5.90) and **Monaco** (45min.; M-Sa every 15min. 6:30am-8pm, Su every 20min. 6:30am-7:50pm; €3.80). Purchase tickets onboard.

Ferries: Corsica Ferries (☎04 92 00 42 93, reservations ☎08 25 09 50 95; www.corsicaferries.com) and **SNCM** (☎04 93 13 66 66, reservations 04 93 13 66 99; fax 04 93 13 66 91) take high-speed ferries out of the port. Take bus #1 or 2 (dir: Port). To: **Corsica** (€40, bikes €10, small cars €40-57). See **Corsica** (p. 754) for more info.

⬛ LOCAL TRANSPORTATION

Public Transportation: Sunbus, 10 av. Félix Faure (☎04 93 13 53 13; www.sunbus.com), near pl. Leclerc. Info booth open M-F 7:15am-7pm, Sa 8am-6pm. Buses operate daily 7am-8pm; tourist office provides the Sunplan bus map and *Guide Info-bus.* Individual tickets €1.30, day pass €4, 5-day pass €13, week-long pass €16.77, 8-ticket *carnet* €8.29. Purchase individual tickets and 1-day pass on board; *carnet,* 5-day, and week-long pass only available at the office. **Noctambus,** (night service) runs 4 routes daily 9:10pm-1:10am. Use caution when traveling around Nice after dark.

Taxis: Central Taxi Riviera (☎04 93 13 78 78; fax 04 93 13 78 79). Get a price range before boarding and make sure the meter is turned on. From the airport to the center of Nice €15-25. Night fares (7pm-7am) are more expensive.

Car Rental: Budget Rent-a-Car, opposite the station, 23 rue de Belgique. (☎04 93 16 24 16; fax 04 93 82 41 29), Open M-F 8am-12:15pm and 2-6:30pm, Sa 9am-noon and 2-5pm. AmEx/MC/V.

Bike Rental: JML Location, 34 av. Auber (☎04 93 16 07 00), opposite station. Bikes €7 per half-day, €11 per day, €56 per week; €228 credit card deposit. Scooters €25/€33/€203/€900. Cars €29 for 8hr., €0.13 each km over 200km. 23+. Open daily July-Aug. 9am-6:30pm; Sept-June M-Sa 9am-6:30pm. MC/V. **Nicea Location Rent,** 12 rue de Belgique (☎04 93 82 42 71; www.nicealocationrent.com), around the corner from the station. Bikes €5 per hr., €15 per day, €70 per week. Scooter €35 per day, €220 per week. Deposit €1000 and up. Also rents in-line skates. 5-10% student discount, 10% if you reserve by email. Open daily Feb.-Nov. 9am-6pm. AmEx/MC/V.

▐ ▐ ORIENTATION AND PRACTICAL INFORMATION

The train station, **Gare Nice-Ville**, is surrounded by a rough-and-tumble neighborhood with street after street of cheap restaurants, budget hotels, and X-rated video stores. As you exit the station, to the left is **avenue Jean Médecin**, a main artery lined with snack stands, shops, and *brasseries*. The traffic-choked street eventually meets the water at **place Masséna** (10 minutes). To the right is **boulevard Gambetta**, the other main water-bound thoroughfare. The **promenade des Anglais**, which becomes **quai des États-Unis** east of av. Jean Médecin, hugs the coast and is a people-watcher's paradise, as are the boutiques and pricey outdoor restaurants west of bd. Jean Medecin in the **rue Masséna** pedestrian zone. Below and to the left of Jean Médecin lies the pulsating **Vieux Nice**. Continuing along past the old city, you'll find **Port Lympia**, a small harbor bordered by clubs and bars on the **quai de Lunel.**

Unfortunately, Nice's big-city appeal also means big-city crime. Women should avoid walking alone at night, and everyone should **exercise caution** around the train station, in Vieux Nice, and on the Promenade des Anglais. Be especially careful not to put your bags down when enjoying a meal at an outdoor cafe; expert thieves are looking to lighten your load.

Tourist Office: av. Thiers (☎08 92 70 74 07; www.nicetourisme.com), next to the train station. English-speaking staff makes reservations for hotels and provides the English-language *Nice: A Practical Guide* and map. The *Semaine des Spectacles* (€0.80 at *tabacs*) lists entertainment for the Côte. *Le Pitchoun* is a free booklet published by local students with favorite restaurants, nightlife, and activities. Open June-Sept. M-Sa 8am-8pm, Su 9am-7pm; Oct.-May M-Sa 8am-7pm. Branches: 5 promenade des Anglais (☎08 92 70 74 07). Same hours, but closed on Su Oct.-May. Also at Airport Terminal 1 (☎08 92 70 74 07). Open daily June-Sept. 8am-10pm; closed Su Oct.-May.

Budget Travel Offices: OTU, 48 rue de France (☎04 97 03 60 90; nice.ville@otu.fr). Books cheap international flights as well as bike and bus tours within France, and offers car rental reductions. Arranges language courses and themed outdoor excursions (sailing, kitesurfing, rafting). ISICs available for purchase. Open M 9:30am-1pm and 2:15-6pm, Tu 9:30am-6pm, W-F 9:30am-6:30pm, Sa 10am-1pm and 2-5pm.

Consulates: Canada, 10 rue Lamartine (☎04 93 92 93 22). Open M-F 9am-noon. **UK,** 26 av. Notre Dame (☎04 91 15 72 10). Open M-F 9am-noon and 2-5pm. **US,** 7 av. Gustave V (☎04 93 88 89 55; fax 04 93 87 07 38). Open M-F 9-11:30am and 1:30-4:30pm.

Currency Exchange: Office Provençal, 17 av. Thiers (☎04 93 88 56 80), opposite the train station. 4% commission on European traveler's checks. Open daily 7:30am-8pm. **Flamme et Fumée,** 16 av. Félix Faure (☎04 93 62 18 31). Open daily 7:30am-8pm. **Travelex,** 12 av. Thiers (☎04 93 82 13 00), outside the train station. Open daily 7am-8pm. Also located at pl. Masséna (☎04 93 88 59 99). Open daily 10am-10pm.

American Express, 11 promenade des Anglais (☎04 93 16 53 53; fax 04 93 16 21 67), at the corner of rue des Congrès. Open M-F 9:15am-5:30pm.

English-Language Bookstore: The Cat's Whiskers, 30 rue Lamartine (☎04 93 80 02 66). Great selection, from bestsellers to cookbooks and books-on-tape. Plenty of regional-interest titles, travel guides, and maps. Open July-Aug. M-Sa 10am-1pm and 3-7pm; Sept.-June M-Sa 9:30am-noon and 2-7pm. AmEx/MC/V.

Laundromat: Lavomatique, 7 rue d'Italie (☎04 93 85 88 14), near Basilique Notre Dame. Wash €4, dry €1 per 18min. Open daily 7am-9pm.

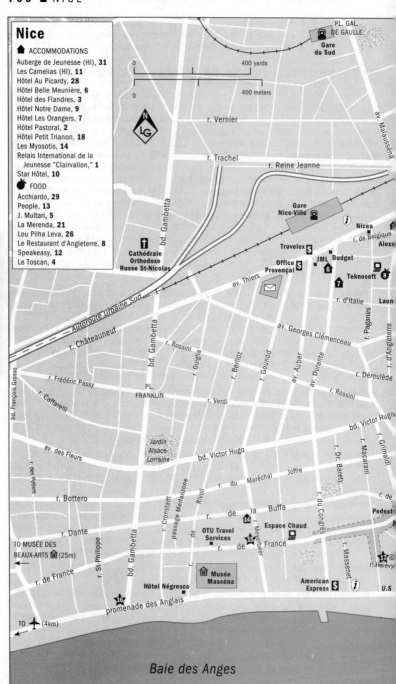

Nice

🏠 ACCOMMODATIONS

Auberge de Jeunesse (HI), **31**
Les Camelias (HI), **11**
Hôtel Au Picardy, **28**
Hôtel Belle Meunière, **6**
Hôtel des Flandres, **3**
Hôtel Notre Dame, **9**
Hôtel Les Orangers, **7**
Hôtel Pastoral, **2**
Hôtel Petit Trianon, **18**
Les Myosotis, **14**
Relais International de la
 Jeunesse "Clairvallon," **1**
Star Hôtel, **10**

🍽 FOOD

Acchiardo, **29**
People, **13**
J. Multari, **5**
La Merenda, **21**
Lou Pilha Leva, **26**
Le Restaurant d'Angleterre, **8**
Speakeasy, **12**
Le Toscan, **4**

CÔTE D'AZUR

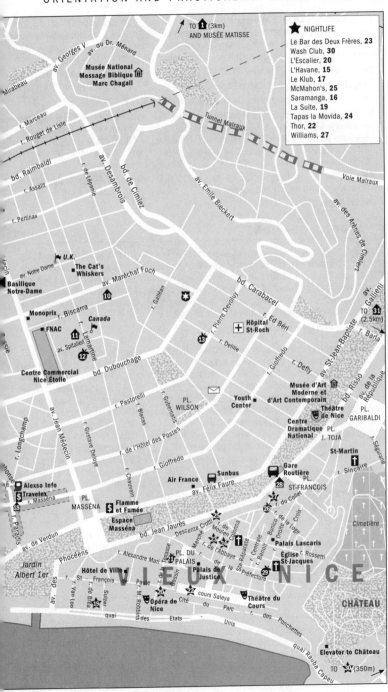

★ NIGHTLIFE
Le Bar des Deux Frères, **23**
Wash Club, **30**
L'Escalier, **20**
L'Havane, **15**
Le Klub, **17**
McMahon's, **25**
Saramanga, **16**
La Suite, **19**
Tapas la Movida, **24**
Thor, **22**
Williams, **27**

CÔTE D'AZUR

Youth Center: Centre d'Information Jeunesse, 19 rue Gioffredo (☎04 93 80 93 93; www.crij.org/nice), near the Museum of Contemporary Art. Posts student summer jobs and provides info on housing, study abroad, and recreational activities. Free 30min. Internet use with ID. Most useful if you speak French. Open M-F 10am-7pm.

Police: 1 av. Maréchal Foch (☎04 92 17 22 22), opposite end from bd. Jean Médecin.

24hr. Pharmacy: 7 rue Masséna (☎04 93 87 78 94).

Hospital: St-Roch, 5 rue Pierre Devoluy (☎04 92 03 33 75).

Internet Access: Centre d'Information Jeunesse, (see above). **Teknosoft,** 16 rue Paganini (☎04 93 16 89 81). €3 per hr. Open daily 8:30am-11pm. **Alexso Info,** 2 rue de Belgique (☎04 93 88 65 00). Open daily 10am-10pm. €0.80 per 10 min., €2.35 for 30min., €3.90 per hr. Also at 2 pl. Magenta, near pl. Masséna (☎04 93 82 29 69). Open M-Sa 10am-9pm, Su 1-9pm. €3.80 for 30min., €6 per hr.

Post Office: 23 av. Thiers (☎04 93 82 65 22; fax 04 93 88 78 46), near the station. Open M-F 8am-7pm, Sa 8am-noon.

Postal Code: 06033.

ACCOMMODATIONS

This budget-friendly city draws an annual crowd of international visitors, and hostels are often full. For economizing travelers, the city offers two clusters of hotels. Those near the train station are badly located but much newer than those closer to Vieux Nice and the beach. Particularly those traveling alone or planning to sample Nice's nightlife would be wise to stay near Vieux Nice, as a rough population tends to hassle travelers near the train station at night.

HOSTELS (OUTSKIRTS OF NICE)

Relais International de la Jeunesse "Clairvallon," 26 av. Scudéri (☎04 93 81 27 63; clajpaca@cote-dazur.com), in Cimiez, 4km from town. Take bus #15 to Scudéri (dir: Rimiez; 20min., every 20min., €1.30) from train station or pl. Masséna; after 9pm, take N2 bus from pl. Masséna. Turn left uphill and take 1st left. Or from the station, turn left and left again on av. Jean Médecin, then right before the overpass. Turn right on av. Comboul, left on bd. Carabacel, which becomes bd. de Cimiez, then right on av. de Flirey, uphill until av. Scudéri. Turn left and follow the signs (50min.). Friendly staff manages this clean hostel. 160 basic rooms with well-kept bathrooms and beds. Sports field, TV room, small bar (open 5-11pm, beer €1.30), and pool (open 5-7 or 8pm). 4- to 10-bed rooms. Breakfast included. 4-course dinner €9. Lockers available, €0.50 deposit. Laundry €4, dryer €2 for 20min. Check-in after 5pm, but luggage can be dropped off anytime. Lockout 9:30am-5pm. Curfew 11pm. After 3 nights guests are expected to pay *demi-pension* (€23.50). Dorms €14.60. ❶

Auberge de Jeunesse (HI), rte. Forestière du Mont-Alban (☎04 93 89 23 64; fax 04 92 04 03 10), 4km from the city center. From bus station, take #14 (dir: Mont Boron) to l'Auberge (2 per hr.; last bus 7:45pm). From train station, take #17 and switch to #14 at the Sunbus station. Ultra-clean hostel draws friendly crowd. 4- to 8-bed co-ed dorms. Internet €2 for 15min., €5 per hr. Kitchen (5-9:30pm). Breakfast included. Lockers in dorms, €5 deposit. Sheets €2.70. Laundry €6. Reception 6:30-10am and 5pm-midnight. Lockout 10am-5pm. Curfew 12:30am. Dorms €14.50. HI members only. ❶

Auberge de Jeunesse (HI) Les Camelias, 3 rue Spitalieri (☎04 93 62 15 54; nice-camelias@fuaj.org), near the Centre Commercial Nice Étoile. Brand-new hostel ideally located between train station and Vieux Nice. 165 beds, kitchen facilities, laundry service, and a restaurant. Breakfast included. Picnic lunches available. Reception 24hr. Currently under construction. Call starting April 2005. ❶

NEAR THE TRAIN STATION

Hôtel Belle Meunière, 21 av. Durante (☎04 93 88 66 15; fax 04 93 82 51 76), opposite train station. According to legend, one of Napoleon's generals gave this stunning mansion as a gift to his mistress. Today it hosts a relaxed crowd in 4- to 5-bed co-ed dorms. Single beds, large windows, and free breakfast in the courtyard make this stop a favorite for budget-travel. Showers €2. Luggage storage €2. Laundry €5.50-9.50 with drying and folding. Reception 7:30am-midnight, access code after hours. Dorms €15, with shower €20; doubles with shower €49.50; triples €60; quads €80. MC/V. ❷

Hôtel Pastoral, 27 rue Assalit (☎04 93 85 17 22), on the far side of av. Jean Médecin near the train station. Popular with students for basic rooms at reasonable prices. Hardwood furniture spruces up the plain decor. Breakfast (€3) in bed, but there's no sleeping-in: you must be out of your room by 10am. Mini-fridge. Free luggage storage. Reception 8am-8pm. Reservations essential. Singles with shower €20; doubles €25, with bath €30; triples €37.50/€47.50; quads €50. Extra bed €10. ❷

Hôtel Notre Dame, 22 rue de Russie (☎04 93 88 70 44; jyung@caramail.com), at the corner of rue d'Italie, 1 block west of av. Jean Médecin. Coastal colors fill the large, elegant rooms, each with sparkling shower, TV, Wi/Fi access, and direct-line phones. Friendly owners serve breakfast in bed (€4) and proudly maintain every aspect of their ultra-clean hotel. Free luggage storage. Reception 6am-11pm. Singles €39; doubles €46; triples €60; quads €71. Extra bed €10. MC/V. ❹

Hôtel des Flandres, 6 rue de Belgique (☎04 93 88 78 94; fax 04 93 88 74 90), 100m from the train station and 800m from the beach. Dark-stained wood accents add a touch of refinement. 40 large rooms with bath, TV, and direct-line phones. Eating in the hotel rooms is strictly forbidden. Breakfast €5. 24hr. reception. Singles €35-45; doubles €45-51; triples €60; quads €67; quints €84. Extra bed €12. MC/V. ❹

Hôtel Les Orangers, 10bis av. Durante (☎04 93 87 51 41; fax 04 93 82 57 82), across from Hôtel Belle Meunière. Orange facade welcomes tired guests to this hotel, housed in a 120-year-old building. Co-ed dorms are slightly worn but very clean, with showers and fridges (hot plates on request). Considerate, multilingual owner loans beach mats and helps travelers find accommodations when his hotel is full. Free luggage storage (non-guests €2). July-Aug. 2-night min. Reception 7am-9pm, key access after hours. Lockout June-Aug. 11am-1pm. Reserve in advance for July-Aug. Closed Nov. Dorms €16; singles €25-30; doubles €45; triples €54; quads €64. MC/V. ❶

NEAR VIEUX NICE AND THE BEACH

Hôtel Au Picardy, 10 bd. Jean Jaurès (☎/fax 04 93 85 75 51). 11 good-size rooms just steps from Vieux Nice and the bus station. Homey breakfast area is filled with family knick-knacks. Rooms overlooking bd. Jean Jaurès have soundproof windows. Breakfast €3. Reception 8am-8pm. Reserve in advance, especially in summer. Singles €25, with bath €33-35; doubles €40; triples €43; quads €49. Extra bed €5. ❷

Hôtel Petit Trianon, 11 rue Paradis (☎04 93 87 50 46; hotel.nice.lepetittrianon@wanadoo.fr), left off pl. Masséna. A charming owner lets 8 elegant rooms. Laundry service (€10 for 5kg) and free Internet. Free beach-towel loan. Breakfast €5. Reservations essential. Singles €30, with bath €35; doubles €40-43/€50-53; triples €66-75; quads €80-100. Extra bed €8. 10% reduction on stays longer than a week. MC/V. ❸

Star Hôtel, 14 rue Biscarra (☎04 93 85 19 03; www.hotel-star.com), between the station and Vieux Nice. Quiet, and full of charming touches like stained-glass windows. TV, A/C, phone, and soundproof windows. Open Jan.-Oct. Singles €38; doubles with shower €48, with bath €53; triples with bath €63. May-Sept. €10-€15. ❹

Backpackers Les Myosotis, 19 rue Meyerbeer (☎04 93 88 30 88 or 06 24 72 49 36), on the corner of rue Meyerbeer and rue de la Buffa. Friendly hotel minutes from the beach. Clean 2- and 4-bed dorms have showers and mini-fridges. Non-stop kitchen access, 24hr. key entry, and late check-out (1pm). Sheets €1.20. 4 days max. stay. 24hr. reception. Reserve in advance. Dorms €18. ❶

🔾 FOOD

Nice offers the typical big-city repertoire of restaurants, from four-star establishments to basic *brasseries* and tiny holes-in-the-wall. The city's true pride and joy is its authentic *Niçois* cuisine, flavored with Mediterranean spices. Try the crusty *pan bagnat*, a round loaf of bread topped with tuna, sardines, vegetables, and olive oil; *pissaladière* pizza loaded with onions, anchovies, and olives; *socca* (see **Socca,** opposite page), *or tourta de blea*, a thin tart with pine nuts. The *salade niçoise* combines tuna, olives, eggs, potatoes, tomatoes, and mustard dressing. Tomato, eggplant, and zucchini are baked to form *ratatouille*, and the local population also enjoys zucchini flowers breaded and fried to form *beignets* (doughnuts). Ask the tourist office for a list of restaurants that serve traditional *niçois* dishes.

The cafes along the promenade des Anglais offer pricey *menus*. Save your euros for the **market** at cours Saleya, and pick up fresh olives, cheeses, and melons (Tu-Su 7am-1pm.) Cours Saleya is also home to a stunning **flower market.** (Tu-Su 7am-1pm.) Stop by just before it closes for bargain blossoms. A produce **market** also springs up on av. Maché de la Libération. (Tu-Su 7am-1pm.) In the evening, tourists descend on the unremarkable *brasseries* and pizzerias on rue Masséna, which offer nothing cheaper than €9 pizza and €10 pasta dishes. Avenue Jean Médecin features reasonable *brasseries*, *panini* vendors, and kebab stands. Load up on groceries from the *épicerie* at **Monoprix,** av. Jean Médecin, next to the Centre Commercial Nice Étoile. (☎04 92 47 72 62. Open M-Sa 8:30am-8:50pm. MC/V.)

🔳 **La Merenda,** 4 rue de la Terrasse. Savor the work of a culinary master who turned his back on one of Nice's most renowned restaurants to open this affordable 12-table gem. Outstanding regional dishes like fried zucchini flowers, stockfish, and veal head. The chef recommends *pâtes au pistou* (€10). Reserve in the morning, in person, for dinner. 2 seatings at 7 and 9pm. *Plats* €10-15. Open M-F noon-1:30pm and 7-9pm. ❸

🔳 **Lou Pilha Leva,** 10-13 rue du Collet (☎04 93 13 99 08), in Vieux Nice. When you hear the cry "LA SOCCA, EN COMMANDE," head to the counter for a piping hot portion of this local dish. A lively staff keep things moving, dishing out plate after plate of *socca* (€2), *pissaladière* (€2), and *salade niçoise* (€7). Huge green awnings provide the perfect corner spot for enjoying the best grub at lunch or dinner. Open daily 8am-midnight. ❶

Le Restaurant d'Angleterre, 25 rue d'Angleterre (☎04 93 88 64 49), near the train station. Loyal crowd of elderly locals frequents this pleasant restaurant for delicious French specialties. The *menu sâge* (€12) includes bread, large salad, entree, side dish, dessert, and after-dinner cordial. Open Tu-Sa 11:45am-2pm and 6:45-9:55pm. ❸

People, 12 rue Pastorelli (☎04 93 85 08 43). A trendy setting for traditional cuisine, well worth the short walk from Vieux Nice. Tasty dishes like *risotto aux truffes* (€13) and *magret de canard* with *foie gras* (filet of duck with *foie gras*, €17) fill enormous chalkboard menus. Plenty of ambience to go with the excellent wines suggested by a friendly staff. *Plats* €9-17. Open M-Sa noon-2:30pm and 5:30-11pm. AmEx/MC/V. ❸

Acchiardo, 38 rue Droite (☎04 93 85 51 16), in Vieux Nice. A loyal clientele fills the family-style tables for simple Italian and French dishes. Try the *escalope maison* (€13.50), a side of veal in mouthwatering Provençal sauce. Pastas (€6), classic French meats (€12-13), and regional specialties like *soupe au pistou* (€6) and *salade niçoise* (€7). Open Sept.-June M-F noon-1:30pm and 7-10pm; July M-F 7-10pm; closed Aug. ❶

Speakeasy, 7 rue Lamartine (☎04 93 85 59 50). The stiffest drink at this hole-in-the-wall is fresh carrot juice—the perfect aperitif to delectable vegan options. American chef/animal-rights activist presides over the intimate setting. Daily specialties (€7) and desserts satisfy even the staunchest carnivores and convert along the way. Testimonials of famous vegetarians from Gandhi to Brigitte Bardot painted at the entrance. €11-12 for 2 courses and dessert. Open M-F noon-2:15pm and 7-9:15pm, Sa noon-2:15pm. ❸

J. Multari, 58bis av. Jean Médecin (☎04 93 92 01 99). Excellent, inexpensive fare offered among marble countertops and polished wood tables. Try a goat cheese, chicken, or ham sandwich (€3.30), pizza (€1.50), or crêpe with Corsican jam (€5). 4 other locations: 2 rue Alphonse Karr (☎04 93 87 45 90); 22 rue Gioffredo (☎04 93 80 00 31); 13 cours Saleya (☎04 93 62 31 33); and 8 bd. Jean Jaurès (☎04 93 62 10 39, takeout only). Open M-Sa 6am-8:30pm. ❶

Le Toscan, 1 rue de Belgique (☎04 93 88 40 54), near the train station. The Tuscan heritage of Elida, the chef's wife, inspires the delicious cooking. The couple constructs generous 4-course *menus* of fresh produce purchased that morning. Menus €12-€20; *plats* €8.50-16. Open Tu-Sa 11:45am-2pm and 6:45-10pm. MC/V. ❹

🔅 SIGHTS

One look at Nice's bright blue waves and you may be tempted to spend your entire stay stretched out on the beach. Though all that sun-worshipping and people-watching has its merits, azur waters and topless sunbathers are not Nice's only attractions. Put your clothes back on for a tour of the city's impressive museums. We promise your tan won't fade *that* quickly.

🖼MUSÉE NATIONAL MESSAGE BIBLIQUE MARC CHAGALL. This extraordinary museum was

founded by Chagall to showcase an assortment of biblical-themed pieces which he gave to the French State in 1966. 12 canvases illustrating the first two books of the Old Testament are hung based on color relations (rather than temporal development), in accordance with the artist's wishes. The museum also includes a breathtaking auditorium with stained-glass panels illustrating

ON THE MENU

SOCCA

The origins of this crispy, golden snack are murky, but its popularity is undeniable. While some *socca*-makers place its creation in Turkey and others are convinced that it was first developed right in Nice, the dish is so firmly entrenched in local traditions that its origins hardly matter.

Socca's simple batter is composed of chickpea flour, olive oil water, and salt. The ingredients are mixed together and then left to stand for 24hr., after which the batter reaches a thick, floury consistency. Olive oil and water are gradually added back to the crumbly mixture until it is smooth enough to be poured (in a very thin layer) into enormous copper pans. Five minutes at 400°F is all it takes for socca to be cooked completely; the edges turn delightfully crispy and the golden brown center remains doughy and soft. *Socca* is best enjoyed piping hot, and it is never eaten with silverware. Some *Niçois* will top it with roasted pepper, but most prefer to eat it plain.

Local fishermen were the first to eat *socca* on a regular basis; its easy preparation made it perfect after a long day on the water. Soon *socca* stands all over Nice began to serve the cheap, filling treat to hungry citizens. To try the snack, find a stand in Vieux Nice and squeeze onto the wooden benches with everybody else. Just don't ask for a fork!

the creation of the world. The auditorium occasionally stages concerts and lectures, ask at the entrance for program information. (Av. du Dr. Ménard. 15min. walk north of the station, or take bus #15 (dir: Rimiez) to Musée Chagall. ☎04 93 53 87 20; www.musee-chagall.fr. Open July-Sept. M and W-Su 10am-5:50pm; Oct.-June 10am-4:50pm. Last tickets sold 30min. before closing. €6.70, students 18-25 €5.20, under 18 and first Su of the month free.)

■ **MUSÉE MATISSE.** A 17th-century Genoese villa surrounded by olive, pine, and cypress trees is the setting for Matisse's three-dimensional work, including lost-wax bronze reliefs and dozens of paper-cutting tableaux. The museum also contains several early masterpieces, notably La Nature Mort aux Livres, considered his very first painting. Furniture and other personal items lend a personal touch to the galleries. (164 av. des Arènes de Cimiez. Take bus #15, 17, 20, 22, or 25 to Arènes. Free bus tickets between Musée Chagall and Musée Matisse; ask at either ticket counter. ☎04 93 81 08 08. Open Apr.-Sept. M and W-Su 10am-6pm; Oct.-Mar. 10am-5pm. Guided tours in English available by reservation (€3). Call for info on lectures. €4, students with ID €2.50.)

■ **VIEUX NICE.** Hand-painted awnings, pristine churches, and lively squares await at every turn in Vieux Nice. Though the tourism industry brings the inevitable slew of souvenir shops, Vieux Nice remains the historical heart of the city. **Rue Droigt** enjoys various handmade furniture stores and mosaic studios. At **Les Trois Étoiles,** 26 rue Pairoliere, you can fill a glass bottle with homemade vinegar, olive oil, or dessert liqueur. (☎04 93 92 30 83; Open M-Sa 10am-8pm.) **Terres Dorees,** 8 rue du Pont Vieux, offers fresh-scented handmade soaps and bath products, created using regional herbs (☎04 93 76 66 75. Open July-Aug. M and W-Su 10am-7:30pm; Sept.-June M and W-Su 10am-noon and 2:30-7:30pm.) For ice cream, line up with the locals at **Fenocchio,** on pl. Rosetti. Nice's best-loved ice cream shop offers over 54 flavors, including unusual choices like tomato basil, beer, thyme, olive, and calisson. (1 scoop in homemade cone €2, 2 scoops €3.50. Open daily 10:30am-2am.)

MUSÉE D'ART MODERNE ET D'ART CONTEMPORAIN. An impressive glass facade welcome visitors to this museum, which houses the work of French new Realists and American pop artists like Lichtenstein and Warhol. The minimalist galleries pay homage to avant-garde creations like the fantastic statues of Niki de St. Phalle and 'color field' pieces by Yves Klein. (promenade des Arts, at the intersection of av. St-Jean Baptiste and Traverse Garibaldi. Take bus #5 (dir: St-Charles) to Musée Promenade des Arts. The museum is behind the bus station. ☎04 93 62 61 62; www.mamac-nice.org. Open Tu-Su 10am-6pm. Guided tours in English (€7) available July-Aug. by reservation. €4, students €2.50, under 18 and the 1st and 3rd Su of every month free.)

LE CHÂTEAU. Le Château—the remains of an 11th-century cathedral—marks the site of the city's birthplace. For years, Celto-Ligurian tribes called the hillside home until they were finally ousted by the Romans in 154 BC. Centuries later, the counts of Provence built a castle and the Cathédrale Ste-Marie on top of the hill as a symbol of their authority over the developing village below. The château and fortress were methodically destroyed by Louis XIV in 1706; all that remains today is a pleasant green hillside park and a few stone ruins. In the summer, an outdoor theater hosts orchestral and vocal musicians. (☎04 93 56 51 35. Info booth open July-Aug. Tu-F 9:30am-12:30pm and 1:30-6pm. Purchase tickets at the FNAC in the Nice Étoile shopping center. Park open June-Aug. 8am-8pm; Sept. 8am-7pm; Oct.-Mar. 8am-6pm; Apr.-May 8am-7pm. Elevator runs June-Aug. 9am-8pm; Sept.-Mar 10am-6pm; Apr.-Sept. 9am-7pm. €1.)

CATHÉDRALE ORTHODOXE RUSSE ST-NICOLAS. Also known as the **Église Russe,** this cathedral was commissioned by Empress Marie Feodorovna in memory of her first husband, Tsar Nicholas Alexandrovich. The cathedral stands on the former site of the Tsar's villa, where he died in 1865. The ornate gold interior quickly became a home for exiled Russian nobles. The cathedral also houses a mysterious icon of St-Nicholas. Years of exposure to the elements had turned it completely black, but when it was finally brought inside the cathedral in 1915 it miraculously returned to its original state. *(17 bd. du Tsarevitch, off bd. Gambetta. ☎ 04 93 96 88 02. Open daily June-Sept. 9am-noon and 2:30-6pm; Oct.-May 9:30am-noon and 2:30-5pm. €2.50.)*

MUSÉE DES BEAUX-ARTS. The former villa of Ukraine's Princess Kotschoubey has been converted into a varied celebration of French and Italian Academic painting, with works by Van Loo, Fragonard, Chéret, and Raoul Dufy. Dufy, Nice's second-greatest painter, celebrated the spontaneity of his city with sensational pictures of the town at rest and play. *(33 av. Baumettes. Take bus #38 to Musée Chéret or #12 to Grosso. ☎ 04 92 15 28 28. Open Tu-Su 10am-6pm. €4, students €2.50.)*

JARDIN ALBERT I AND ESPACE MASSÉNA. Jardin Albert I is the city's oldest park, below the pl. Masséna. The outdoor Théâtre de Verdun presents jazz and plays in summer. (Contact tourist office.) Unfortunately, the picturesque park is one of the most dangerous spots in Nice after nightfall. Tourists should avoid crossing the park at night and instead stick to the well-lit *zone piétonne* on pl. Masséna and av. de Verdun. *(Between av. Verdun and bd. Jaurès, off promenade des Anglais and quai des Etats-Unis. Box office open daily 10:30am-noon and 3:30-6:30pm.)*

OTHER SIGHTS. Named by the rich English community that commissioned it, the **promenade des Anglais,** a posh, palm-lined seaside boulevard, is Nice's answer to Paris, London, and New York. From dawn to dusk, the promenade is filled with ambling tourists, locals, and posh hotels. The stately **Hôtel Négresco** (toward the west end), presents the best of Belle Époque luxury with coffered ceilings, crystal chandeliers, and an extensive collection of valuable artwork. The staff still dons 19th-century uniforms.

The seashore between bd. Gambetta and the Opéra alternates **private beaches** with crowded public strands, but a large section west of bd. Gambetta is reserved entirely for public use. Many travelers are surprised to find that the Baie des Anges is not lined with soft golden sand, but stretches of rock. Bring your beach mat.

🎵 📷 ENTERTAINMENT AND NIGHTLIFE

In Nice, lazy days in the sun mean wild nights on the town. The bars and nightclubs around rue Masséna, Vieux Nice, and Port Lympia cater to all musical tastes with house, jazz, and rock. As night falls, the promenade des Anglais fills with street performers, musicians, and pedestrians. Local men have a reputation for harassing people on the promenade, around the train station, and in the Jardin Albert I at night: lone women beware. Avoid untrafficked streets and walking in the city alone. At night, tourists should be extremely cautious on the beach itself.

The **Théâtre du Cours,** 5 rue Poissonnerie in Vieux Nice, stages traditional drama. (☎ 04 93 80 12 67. €12.20, students €9.20.) The grand **Théâtre National de Nice,** on the promenade des Arts, hosts professional dramatic productions, as well as various concerts. (☎ 04 93 13 90 90; contact@theatredenice.org. €10-30, students €7.50-28. Box office open June-July Tu-Sa 1-7pm; Aug.-May Tu-Sa 2-7pm; open Su at 1pm for same-day tickets only.) The **Opéra de Nice,** 4-6 rue St-François de Paule, stages productions from Sept.-May and hosts visiting symphony orchestras and soloists throughout the year. (☎ 04 93 13 98 53 or 04 92 17 40 79. Ticket window open Tu-Sa 10am-5pm. €8-40.) The **FNAC,** 24 av. Jean Médecin in the Nice Étoile shopping center, sells tickets for virtually every musical or theatrical event in town. (☎ 04 92 17 77 77; www.fnac.com. Open M-Sa 10am-7pm.)

CÔTE D'AZUR

The dress code at all bars and clubs is simple: look good. Almost all clubs will turn away people in shorts, sandals, sneakers, or baseball caps. Dressing *classé* ("in good taste") is paramount. So leave the fishnets on the beach.

BARS

McMahon's, 50 bd. Jean Jaurès (☎04 93 13 84 07). From Sangria Sunday (€10 pitchers) to Cheap Tuesday (€2 vodka, whiskey, or gin cocktails), any night is guaranteed to have great reductions and a killer crowd. Happy hour daily 6-9pm; €3.30 pints and €2 wine. Cocktail hour 9-10pm with €4 drinks. Open daily 6:30pm-2am.

Thor, 32 cours Saleya (☎04 93 62 49 90; www.thor-pub.com). This raucous Scandinavian pub is a favorite among Nice residents in the know. The most popular decoration is the svelte blonde staff that pours pints and shots of fiery *sma gra* (vodka with Turkish pepper, €2.50) for a playful, young crowd. Live music daily from 10pm Happy hour 6-9pm; €4.50 pints. Open daily 6pm-2:30am.

L'Havane, 32 rue de France (☎04 93 16 36 16). A mid-20s crowd enjoys free *tapas* with mojitos (€7.60) and *caipiranhas* (€7.60). Painted "windows," wicker chairs, and bamboo accents complete the Caribbean feel. Around 10pm, the relaxed crowd turns wild when live salsa bands fill the small bar with Cuban beats. Open daily 5pm-2:30am.

Le Bar des Deux Frères, 1 rue du Moulin (☎04 93 80 77 61; barles2freres@wanadoo.fr). Vinyl records cover the walls of this hip local favorite. Tequila (€3) and beer on tap (€5) draw plenty of lively students to the smoky interior. June-Sept. live DJ daily. Happy hour Tu-Sa 9-10pm with all drinks €1.60-4. Open Tu-Sa 9pm-2:30am.

L'Escalier, 10 rue de la Terrasse (☎04 93 92 64 39). DJs spin R&B, funk, and hip-hop for a lively mix of locals late into the night. In early evening, a relaxed crowd comes to shoot pool and sip gin fizz (€8), but the real party starts around 1am. Beer €3.50-8, cocktails €8-10. F and Sa €10 cover after 1am. Open daily 10pm-5am.

Williams, 4 rue Centrale (☎04 93 62 99 63). This split-personality spot looks like a traditional English pub but acts like a wild French discothèque. A tourist-heavy crowd guzzles €4 beers and dances to live house and techno. Cocktails €6.50; vodka, whiskey, and gin €60 per bottle. Live music F-Sa. Open daily M-Sa 11pm-5am.

Tapas la Movida, 2bis rue de l'Abbaye (☎04 93 62 27 46). This basement bar resembles a secret revolutionary meeting spot, but the only plotting you'll do is figure out how to crawl home after the *bar-o-mètre* (€15), a meter-long box of shots. Live reggae, rock, and ska concerts M-Th (€2). Theme parties with DJ F-Sa. Open M-Sa 9pm-12:30am.

NIGHTCLUBS

Exorbitant covers and expensive drinks can make for pricey partying, but reductions are generally offered on Thursdays, Sundays, all days before midnight, and to all well-dressed females. Cover usually includes the first drink. The scene in Nice is in constant flux: new clubs replace old ones almost daily and the hot spot shifts rapidly, so keep in touch with locals, expats, and the backpacking crowd to make sure you're hitting up the latest and greatest *boîtes de nuit*.

Wash Club, 26 quai Lunel (☎04 93 26 54 79). Brand-new to the Nice party scene. White vinyl stools and blank tile walls provide the perfect set for the young and the fashion-conscious. Dress to impress; this crowd isn't thrilled by t-shirts and jeans. DJs spin house music nightly. Cover €15, includes 1 drink. Open Th-Su midnight-5am.

La Suite, 2 rue Bréa (☎04 93 92 92 91). With velvet theater curtains and tall white candles, this small luxe club is for well-dressed and well-moneyed. Though swanky, the atmosphere is hardly tame: on weekends, La Suite brings in go-go dancers to pick up the party pace. Beer €6-7, cocktails €12. Cover €13. Open Tu-Su 11pm-2:30am.

Saramanga, 45-47 promenade des Anglais (☎04 93 96 68 00). Topless showgirls dance in enormous metal cages at this hot club. Hawaiian-shirted bartenders keep things wild with rounds of exotic drinks. Beer €6, alcohol €8. Cover €15, includes 1 drink. Open July-Aug. Th-Sa 11am-5am; Sept.-June F-Sa 11pm-5am.

Le Klub, 6 rue Halévy (☎04 93 16 87 26). Nice's most popular gay club caters to a gorgeous, well-tanned crowd with a sleek upstairs lounge and live video on the dance floor. On Sa nights, Le Klub's resident DJ is joined by a visiting artist. Cocktails €5-10. Cover €11 on Sa. Open July-Aug. Tu-Su midnight-5am; Sept.-June W-Su. W night men only.

FESTIVALS

In mid-July, the **Nice Jazz Festival** attracts 45,000 visitors, who enjoy over 500 musicians in 75 concerts over an 8-day period. The olive and palm trees of the quiet suburb of Cimiez provide an unforgettable setting for over 120 hours of fabulous international music. Ticket holders can attend nightly concerts. Concerts 7pm-midnight. (Arènes et Jardins de Cimiez. ☎08 20 80 04 00 or 08 92 70 75 07; www.nicejazzfest.com. Tickets €33 per night; 3-day pass €84, 8-day €163.) During the Lenten **Carnaval** (Feb. 11-27), Nice gives Rio a run for its money when the promenade des Anglais and the quai des États-Unis host two weeks of parades, fireworks, and concerts. Confetti battles, masked balls, and floral processions fill the city with color by day, and endless partying livens up the night (www.nicecarnaval.com; tickets €10-30.) Call the tourist office for more info.

DAYTRIP FROM NICE

ST-PAUL

SAP Buses (☎04 93 58 37 60) sends buses #400-410 to Vence and St-Paul from Nice (60min.; 28 per day; €4.20 to St-Paul, €4.70 to Vence). To get to St-Paul from Cannes, take the train to Cagnes-sur-Mer and change to bus #400-410 (€1.50). The last of the #400-410 buses leave St-Paul for Nice and Cagnes-sur-Mer at 7:20pm from the stop just outside the town entrance. The trip from Vence to St-Paul costs €1.30.

If you visit one medieval village on the Côte D'Azur, make it St-Paul. This clifftop hamlet draws more than two million visitors per year to its ivy-covered, cobbled streets. Though well touristed, the village remains a pedestrian delight. A walk along the rambling streets reveals incredible views of the surrounding countryside. Divine smells waft from basement restaurants, while colorful artwork brightens the doorways of tiny galleries. An artist's paradise, St-Paul attracted a veritable colony of creation when Chagall, Matisse, Léger, Picasso, and several others came to the hilltop for inspiration. Many contemporary artists have followed in their footsteps. Today, more than 80 galleries sell their wares in the somber 13th-century **Église Collégiale.** The wide vaulted interior of this church is home to the mounted skull of St-Etienne. (Open daily 9am-8pm.) A quiet **cemetery** just outside the village walls at the southeast end is the resting place of Marc Chagall. As you descend the first steps, his gravestone is the second on the right. (Cemetery open daily July-Aug. 7:30am-8pm; Sept.-June 8am-5pm.)

Though the medieval village is brimming with galleries, St-Paul's most impressive collection of art is in nearby **Fondation Maeght,** 1km from the town center. From the St-Paul bus stop, take a right onto chemin de St-Claire and head back downhill. Blue signs will direct you to the foundation (10 minutes). The fantastic galleries, designed by Joseph Sert to showcase modern and contemporary art, are the perfect backdrop for a stunning collection of works by Miró, Chagall, Léger, Giacometti, Calder, and Arp. Highlights include Miró's whimsical garden labyrinth, the Giacometti courtyard, and a lively steel fountain piece by Bury. (☎ 04 93 32 81 63; www.fondation-maeght.com. Open daily July-Sept. 10am-7pm; Oct.-June 10am-12:30pm and 2:30-6pm. €11, students €9, under 10 free. Photography permit €2.50.)

The **tourist office,** 2 rue Grande, is tucked inside the village walls just after the arched entryway. A friendly, knowledgeable staff dispenses free maps and info on galleries. (☎ 04 93 32 86 95; fax 04 93 32 60 27; artdevivre@wanadoo.fr. Open daily June-Sept. 10am-7pm; Oct.-May 10am-6pm.) Themed 1hr. "discovery" tours are available in English on request. (10am-6pm. €8 per person, under 12 free.) You can also rent balls for a game of *pétanque* for €3 per person per hr. or schedule a game with an experienced tourist office liaison (€8 per person, under 12 free).

THE CORNICHES

A perfect panorama of rocky shores, pebble beaches, and luxurious villas line the coast between hectic Nice and high-rolling Monaco. More relaxing and less touristed than their glam-fab neighbors, these tiny towns sparkle quietly with interesting museums, architectural finds, and unbelievably breathtaking countryside. Each unpretentious village is linked to the next by a magnificent rocky landscape, broken only by the occasional curve of unspoiled beaches. The train offers an exceptional glimpse of the coast's clustered towns, while buses maneuvering along the high roads of the *corniches* provide views of the cliffs and sea below.

▐ TRANSPORTATION. Trains and buses between Nice and Monaco serve most of the Corniche towns. With about two departures every hour, **trains** from Nice to Monaco stop at Villefranche-sur-Mer (8min., €1.40), Beaulieu-sur-Mer (12min., €1.70), and Eze-sur-Mer (20min., €2.60).

Several numbered **RCA buses** (☎ 04 93 85 64 44; www.rca.tm.fr) run between Nice and Monaco, making stops along the way. #100 leaves Nice every 15 min., stopping in Villefranche-sur-Mer (10min., €1.70), Beaulieu-sur-Mer (20min., €2.10), Monaco-Ville (40min., €3.80), and Monte-Carlo (45min., €3.80). #111 serves St - Jean-Cap-Ferrat from Nice (25min., M-Sa 9:10am and 12:15pm, €2.10), while Eze-le-Village can be reached by #112 (20min.; M-Sa 7 per day; Su 9am, noon, and 5pm; €2.50). Most tickets include free same-day return, though you should make sure. Last buses from the Corniches to Nice (M-Sa) leave Villefranche-sur-Mer at 8:55pm; Monaco-Ville at 8:35pm, Monte-Carlo at 8:30pm, St-Jean-Cap Ferrat at 7:50pm, and Eze-le-Village at 5:25pm.

VILLEFRANCHE-SUR-MER

The stairwayed streets and pastel houses of 700-year-old Villefranche-sur-Mer have earned the town a reputation as one of the Riviera's most photogenic. The backdrop for dozens of films, including a James Bond installation, *Dirty Rotten Scoundrels,* and movies by Hitchcock, the town has enchanted artists and writers from Aldous Huxley to Katherine Mansfield. Despite the celebrity presence, Villefranche remains refreshingly relaxed and unpretentious.

As you walk from the station along quai Courbet, a sign for the *vieille ville* directs you along the 13th-century **rue Obscure,** the oldest street in Villefranche. The low stone arches and shrunken doors served as an eery backdrop for Jean Cocteau's 1959 film *La Testament d'Orphée.* As you walk along the covered street, pale yellow lanterns throw creepy, long shadows, even at midday. A right at the end of rue Obscure takes you to the pl. de l'Église, a tiny square entirely occupied by the **Église Saint-Michel.** In addition to the lofty clock tower, the church contains an impressive wooden statue of the martyred Christ carved by an anonymous galley slave. At the end of the quai stands the pink and yellow 14th-century **Chapelle St-Pierre,** decorated from floor to ceiling by Jean Cocteau. His simple, trademark style fills the chapel, though an occasional burst of green and yellow (especially on exotic ceramic figures by the door) appear throughout. (☎04 93 76 90 70. Open Tu-Su summer 10am-noon and 4-8:30pm; autumn 9:30am-noon and 2-6pm; winter 9:30am-noon and 2-5pm; spring 9:30am-noon and 3-7pm. €2.)

Above the port sits the rather dull 16th-century **Citadelle,** which houses three small museums. The most interesting is the rustic **Musée Volti,** dedicated to Antoniucci Volti, who created curvaceous female forms out of bronze, clay, canvas, and copper. The **Musée Goetz-Boumeester** holds pastels by Henri Goetz, while a grouping of tiny figurines sculpted by Arlette Roux forms the **Collection Roux.** (☎04 93 76 33 27; musees@villefranche-sur-mer.fr. Open July-Aug. M and W-Sa 10am-noon and 2:30-7pm, Su 2:30-7pm; June and Sept. M and W-Sa 9am-noon and 2:30-6pm, Su 2:30-6pm; Oct.-May W-Sa 9am-noon and 2-5:30pm, Su 1:30-6pm. Free.)

Though a day in the peaceful Corniches might leave you in no hurry to get back to bustling, budget-friendly Nice, Villefranche has few reasonable accommodations options. Family-owned **La Régence ❹,** 2 av. Maréchal Foch, has nine good-sized rooms on top of a late-night *brasserie* along the main drag. The plain but well-kept rooms all come with double windows, bath, and phone. (☎/fax 04 93 01 70 91; laregence@caramail.com. Internet €6 per 30min., €9 per hr. Breakfast €5. Reception 6am-2am. Singles and doubles €44-49; triples €54. Extra bed €6.10.)

A fun Australian/French couple serves up beer, smoothies, and plenty of wit to a laid-back anglo crowd at **Chez Net,** pl. du Marché, behind Hôtel Welcome. This friendly Australian bar, Internet cafe, and DVD rental store is the one-stop nightlife location in Villefranche. Don't miss the double-chocolate macadamia nut cookies (€1.50); the owners have them sent all the way from the Land Down Under itself. (☎04 93 01 83 06. Beer €5 per pint, wine €2.50 per glass. Open daily 2pm-2:30am. Internet cafe €5 per hr. DVD rentals €3 for 24hr. 25% discount with *Let's Go.*) One awning over, the red-checked tables at **Loco Loco ❷** fill with hungry locals eager for delicious food at great prices. You can't go wrong with a heaping plate of mussels (€11), but fresh *paninis* (€4-4.50) and sandwiches (€4-4.50) will satisfy a smaller appetite. (Open Tu-Su 11:30am-3pm and 7-11pm. Closed Apr.-Oct.)

To reach the **tourist office** from the train station, exit on quai 1 and head inland on av. Georges Clemenceau. At the pl. Charles II d'Anjou, continue on the right side of av. Sadi Carnot. The office is at the end of the street, at the edge of the Jardin François Binon. It distributes a walking tour of town and suggests excursions to nearby villages. Guided 1¾min. walking tours of the citadelle and *vieille ville* are available in English July-August. (☎04 93 01 73 68; www.villefranche-sur-mer.com. Open daily June-Sept. 9am-7pm; Oct.-May M-Sa 9am-noon and 2-6pm.)

EZE-SUR-MER

Centuries ago Théodore de Banville explained that "to reach Eze one has to climb up from the sea or drop down from the sky." Today, roads make the Roman-village-turned-medieval-citadel at **Eze-le-Village** far more accessible. From the top of the Corniches, the village is a tangle of arches, ivy-covered walls, and blooming jasmine. In spaces carved into 429m cliffs over the sea, the houses in Eze have been inhabited for over 25 centuries by everyone from the Moors to Piedmontese. Now only 15 of Eze's 3000 residents live there. Most live below in **Col d'Eze** or even farther down the mountain in the seaside town **Eze Bord-de-Mer** (also called **Eze-sur-Mer**). The pretty stretch is popular with celebrities; U2 and Princess Antoinette Grimaldi (Prince Rainier III of Monaco's sister) both frequent nearby villas.

A favorite of photo-snapping tourists, Eze-le-Village recounts the Riviera's tumultous past with a series of unusual remains. The **Porte des Maures**, a short doorway carved into the cliff-face, was the Moors's golden ticket into Eze during their nonstop 10th-century destruction of Provence. Their surprise attack proved highly successful; they ended up maintaining control of the village for the following 70 years. Nearby, the **Chapelle de la Saint-Croix**, also known as the Chapelle des Penitents Blancs, is the oldest building in the village. The austere facade of the **Église Paroissial**, an 18th-century structure, conceals an elaborate baroque interior adorned with *trompe-l'oeil* frescoes and Phoenecian crosses. (☎ 04 93 41 00 38. Open daily July-Aug. 9:30am-7:30pm; Sept.-June 9:30am-6pm.) The **Jardin Exotique**, which offers fabulous views of the sea and the Cap d'Antibes, is planted around a Savoy fortress that was razed in 1706 by the armies of Louis XIV. Over 400 species of cacti and exotic plants dot the rocky hillside. (☎ 04 93 41 10 30. Open daily Sept.-June 9am-noon and 2-6pm; July-Aug. 9am-8pm. €3, students €2.)

Eze-le-Village offers more than narrow streets and nice vistas—the second-largest factory of the **Fragonard Parfumerie** is located here. Perfumes are sold at warehouse prices and free 15min. tours in English, Spanish, German, Italian, Russian, or Dutch explain the perfume, cosmetic, and soap-making processes. (☎ 04 93 41 05 05; www.fragonard.com. Open daily Apr.-Oct. 8:15am-6:30pm; Nov.-Mar. 8:30am-noon and 2-6pm.) The more intimate **Parfumerie Galimard** has a free museum and guided visits. (☎ 04 93 41 10 70. Open daily 9am-6:30pm.)

The long, slow climb from the seaside to Eze-le-Village provided Nietzsche with plenty of inspiration: it was on this rocky trail that he composed the third part of Thus Spake Zarathustra. Follow the 1hr. climb to the top along the winding Sentier Friedrich Nietzsche. The trail begins in Eze Bord-de-Mer, 100m east of the train station, and ends at the base of the medieval city, near the parfumerie. If you give it a go, wear hiking shoes and bring water and a camera. For those with less to contemplate, bus #112 connects Nice, Eze-le-Village, and Beausoleil seven times per day. From May-Oct., a daily municipal shuttle also connects Eze-le-Village and Eze-sur-Mer (8 per day 9:35am-6:30pm; one-way €3.80, round-trip €6.85).

Over 30 other trails criss-cross the landscape, taking robust hikers between the seaside, the Moyenne Corniche, and the Grand Corniche. They range in length and difficulty; most take about 1hr. and require sturdy shoes, water, and a map. The tourist office provides maps and info, but for detailed descriptions contact Eze Randonnées (☎ 04 93 01 51 52). Some of the paths have fallen into disuse so be sure to check with a knowledgeable source before you hit the trail.

In late July, Eze turns back the clock to the Middle Ages for **Eze d'Antan,** a three-day festival during which inhabitants dress up in period costumes and restaurants serve traditional medieval fare. Each year the village focuses on a different theme: recent years' themes have included "Charms and Magic Spells of the Middle Ages" and "Saracein Invasions." For details call the tourist office.

The friendly English-speaking staff at the **tourist office**, pl. de Gaulle, provides free maps and info. (☎ 04 93 41 26 00; www.eze-riviera.com. Open daily Apr.-Oct. 9am-7pm; Nov.-Mar. 9am-6:30pm.) Guided 1hr. tours of the medieval village and garden are offered by request. (€6 per person, children €3.70; 2-person minimum.) To get there, take the Navette minibus from the train station. An annex right next to the station also provides info. (☎ 04 93 01 52 00. Open May-Oct. 10am-1pm and 3-6:30pm.)

To get to Eze, take the **train** from Nice (20min., €2.10). The train station is in Eze-Bord-de-Mer, but from May-September a Navette **minibus** connects Eze's three tiers, stopping in Eze Bord-de-Mer and in Eze-le-Village where the main road meets the path to the medieval city (8 per day 9:35am-6:30pm; one-way €3.80, round-trip €6.90). If you miss the bus, a **taxi** (☎ 06 18 44 77 93) to the top costs about €20.

BEAULIEU-SUR-MER

Apparently Napoleon's creativity failed him when he named this seaside resort; he simply called it "bellolocco" or "beau lieu," (beautiful place). In the late 19th century, elite English and French visitors who shared Napoleon's sentiment flooded the small town, building Belle Époque villas, a classy casino, and four-star waterfront hotels. Today, the big money has long since moved on to quieter mansions in nearby St-Jean-Cap-Ferrat, but Beaulieu still attracts a few stars who dock their sleek yachts in its 800-boat marina. The main justification for a visit to this relatively uninteresting town is its spectacular Greek villa. Beaulieu also serves as a nice starting point for the lovely seaside walk to Saint-Jean-Cap-Ferrat.

On a plateau overlooking the sparkling Baie des Fourmis, Renaissance man Theodore Reinach built his dream villa, ■**Kérylos,** which today stands as proof that money can, in fact, buy happiness. The monumental home perfectly imitates a Greek dwelling from the second century BC, though modern comforts are cleverly hidden throughout the structure. Reinach made sure that no detail was ignored, installing artificially aged mosaics, gold-leaf cedarwood ceilings, and an enormous sundial. The eccentric millionaire and his wife ate on reclining, woven, Greek-style beds, took baths in enormous tubs made entirely of Carrara marble, and showered in a clever open-air space designed to catch rainwater in exactly the same fashion as the showers of ancient Greece. Though his lifestyle was certainly odd, visitors today can enjoy the magnificent result of his obsession. A 90min. audiotour explores the elaborate mansion, with stops in the colonnade-filled courtyard, mosaic bath house, and mysterious anti-chamber. The statue-encircled gardens provide unforgettable views of the Mediterranean. (Tours only. 90min. audio guide in English, German, Italian, or French. Open daily July-Aug. 10am-7pm; early Feb.-June and Sept.-early Nov. 10am-6pm; early Nov.-early Feb. M-F 2-6pm, Sa-Su 10am-6pm. Last admission 30min. before closing. €7.50, students €5.50, under 7 free.)

Beaulieu offers little in the way of budget accommodations; if you're dead-set on sleeping here, your best option is probably **La Riviera ❹,** 6 rue Paul Doumer. Eleven rooms have rich carpets, immaculate bathrooms, and bright Provençal decor. All rooms have bath, A/C, TV, and phone. (☎04 93 01 04 92; contact@hotel-riviera.fr. Breakfast €6. Reception 7:30am-noon and 4-8pm. Singles and doubles €52-60; triples €65, with bath €75. Prices €10-15 lower Sept.-Apr. AmEx/MC/V.)

Waterfront cafes and restaurants are expensive; a few *brasseries* in town offer more affordable but unremarkable meals. Most locals prefer **Le Petit Paris ❸,** bd. Marinoni, just off the pl. du Général de Gaulle. The airy purple cafe is the most popular in town, offering a €12.50 lunch *formule,* fresh pizzas (€7-8.40), and tasty pasta (€8-9) and meat (€12-15) dishes. (☎04 93 01 69 91. Open M-F 8am-2pm.)

A promenade along the waterfront passes by the major hotels and the large Port de Plaisance, home to an impressive collection of private sailboats and yachts. Further along the waterfront lies the **plage des Fourmis,** a perfect crescent of sand that draws an animated crowd of bathers. If you'd rather walk than gawk, the **tourist office,** pl. Georges Clemenceau, next to the train station, suggests scenic routes to nearby towns and provides free maps. (☎04 93 01 02 21; www.ot-beaulieu-sur-mer.fr. Open July-Aug. M-Sa 9am-12:30pm and 2-7pm, Su 9am-12:30pm; Sept.-June M-F 9am-12:15pm and 2-6pm, Sa 9am-12:15pm and 2-5pm.)

ST-JEAN-CAP-FERRAT

As if the Riviera needed a trump card! Quietly wealthy St-Jean-Cap-Ferrat is a haven for the upper-class—for years, the King of Belgium made an annual appearance. The Cap's well-to-do come to this peaceful haven for pure, uninterrupted R&R. The town is serviced by **bus #111,** but nothing compares to the 30min. ■**sea-**

CÔTE D'AZUR

side walk from Beaulieu (access the path in front of the Beaulieu casino). Lavish villas, rocky beaches, and once-beautiful docks provide endless photo opportunities. As you stroll along, don't forget to glance back toward Beaulieu, where the rugged mountain coastline drops gracefully into the sparkling sea.

The **Fondation Ephrussi de Rothschild** is just off av. D. Semeria, between the tourist office and the Nice-Monaco road. The villa, completed in 1912, holds the furniture and art collections of the eccentric Baroness de Rothschild and her famous father. The upstairs rooms contain a small collection of paintings by Boucher and ink sketches by his student, Fragonard. The villa's exquisite gardens form the shape of a ship's prow. From her perch on the villa's *loggia*, the offbeat Baroness liked to pretend she was at the helm of a magnificent ship. Obedient gardeners perpetuated her make-believe world; all were required to wear bright sailor costumes whenever they worked on the grounds. The villa can be accessed directly from Beaulieu. Follow the shore path toward St-Jean, turning right after the three-pronged tree and before the pink villa that separates the path from the Mediterranean. From the top of this walled shore access, turn left and follow the road uphill, turning right at the sign to the Fondation. (☎ 04 93 01 45 90; www.villa-ephrussi.com. A guided tour in French is the only way to see the first floor: 11:30am, 2:30, 3:30, 4:30pm; €2. Open daily July-Aug. 10am-7pm; Sept.-Oct. and mid-Feb. to June daily 10am-6pm; Nov. to mid-Feb. M-F 2-6pm, Sa-Su 10am-6pm, gardens until 6:30pm. Last admission 30min. before closing. €8.50, students €6.50.)

St-Jean's **beaches** have earned the area the nickname *presqu'île des rêves*, "peninsula of dreams." With so many options, you'll want to pass by the aptly named **plage Passable,** an unremarkable stretch on the western side just down the hill from the tourist office. Instead, hit Cap's most popular beach, the wide **plage Paloma,** past the port at the end of av. Jean Mermoz. For a more solitary sunbath, make a right off the end of av. Mermoz and head down the stone steps to the peaceful crescents at **Les Fossettes** and, farther on, **Les Fosses.** The view is just as nice from the water as it is from the beach: for more active types, the École Francaise de Voile at the Nouveau Port rents **sailboats, kayaks,** and **windsurfing** equipment for public use. (☎ 04 93 76 10 08. Single kayaks €10 per hr., €16 per 2 hr., €20 per 3 hr., €4 per day; double kayaks €13/€22/€28/€55. Sailboats €40 per person per hr., includes instruction. Experienced skippers can rent boats for €30-39 per hr. or €51-68 per 2 hr. Windsurfing equipment €25 per hr. Open daily June-Aug. 9am-6pm; Sept.-May M-Sa 9am-noon and 2-6pm.)

Three coastal *sentiers* (trails) border the peninsula, offering secluded sunbathing spots and sublime vistas. The easiest stretches are from Beaulieu to the Nouveau Port, and can be completed in 30min. A tour of the Pointe de St-Hospice reveals a dramatic view of the exquisite eastern coastline (40min.), but the stunning chemin de la Carrière provides a taste of both coasts on a 1½hr. rocky tour that stretches all the way down to the Pointe Malalongue.

The tiny **tourist office,** 59 av. Denis Séméria, sits in the middle of the peninsula along the winding street that runs from Nice and Monaco to the port. It distributes free maps and tours of the peninsula's 10km of *sentiers.* (☎ 04 93 76 08 90; fax 04 93 76 16 67. Open July-Aug. M-Sa 9am-6pm, Su 9am-5:30pm; Sept.-June M-Sa 10am-4pm.)

MONACO AND MONTE-CARLO

In 1297, François Grimaldi of Genoa established his family as Monaco's (pop. 7106) rulers, overthrowing the town with a few henchmen disguised as monks. The tiny principality has since jealously guarded its independence and exclusivity.

Although the rest of the Côte d'Azur may be defined by conspicuous consumption, Monaco doesn't flaunt its glamor as prominently as its neighbors do. It proves its wealth aptly enough with its ubiquitous surveillance cameras, high-speed luxury cars, multi-million dollar yachts, and the famous casino in Monaco's capital city of Monte-Carlo. The sheer spectacle of it all—not to mention the tabloid allure of Monaco's royal family—is definitely worth the daytrip from Nice.

⌐ TRANSPORTATION

Trains: The new **Gare SNCF** has 4 points of access: galerie Prince Pierre (behind the old train station), pl. Ste-Dévote, bd. de Belgique (at the intersection of bd. du Jardin Exotique), and bd. Princesse Charlotte. Open daily 4am-1am; info desk and ticket window open M-F 5:50am-8:30pm, Sa-Su 5:50am-8:05pm. To: **Antibes** (1hr., every 30min., €6.40); **Cannes** (65min., every 30min., €7.50); **Menton** (11min., every 30min., €1.80); **Nice** (23min., every 30min., €3.10).

Buses: Buses leave from bd. des Moulins and av. Princesse Alice, both near the tourist office. 2 lines: **TAM** and **RCA** (☎04 93 85 64 44). To: **Nice** (45min., every 15min., €3.80) and **Menton** (25min., every 15min., €2.10). **Cap d'Ail, Eze-sur-Mer, Beaulieu-sur-Mer, Villefranche-sur-Mer,** and **St-Jean-Cap-Ferrat** accessible via Nice route. Same day return tickets to Monaco free.

Public Transportation: (☎97 70 22 22; www.cam.mc.) 5 bus routes serve the entire principality (M-Sa every 11min. 7am-9pm, Su and holidays every 20min. 7:30am-9pm). Bus #4 links the Ste-Dévote train station entrance to casino; bus #2 connects the *vieille ville* and *jardin exotique* via pl. d'Armes; lines #5 and 6 connect Fontvielle with the rest of the city. Tickets €1.40, *carnet* of 4 €3.30, *carnet* of 8 €5.35. The €3.30 *carte touristique* offers unlimited travel on day of purchase. Tickets on board.

Taxis: ☎93 15 01 01. 24hr. 11 taxi stands, including the Casino, pl. des Moulins, and the Ste-Dévote train station exit. Consult the tourist office for a complete list. €10 min. charge; €12.20-15.30 to the Relais de Jeunesse in Cap d'Ail.

Car Rental: Avis, 9 av. d'Ostende (☎93 30 17 53). Open M-Sa 8am-noon and 2-7pm, Su 9am-noon. AmEx/D/MC/V. **Europcar,** 47 av. de Grande-Bretagne (☎93 50 74 95; www.europcar.fr). Open M-Sa 8am-noon and 2-6pm. AmEx/D/MC/V. **Hertz,** 27 bd. Albert I (☎93 50 79 60; fax 93 25 47 58). Open M-Sa 8:30am-noon and 2- 6:30pm, Su 8:30am-1pm. AmEx/D/MC/V.

Scooter Rental: Auto-Moto Garage, 7 rue de Millo (☎93 50 10 80; fax 93 50 10 82). Open M-F 8am-noon and 2-7pm, Sa 8am-noon. €35 for 9am-7pm, €40 for 24hr., €245 per week. €1000 credit card or check deposit. AmEx/D/MC/V.

◼◪ ORIENTATION AND PRACTICAL INFORMATION

This jam-packed principality can be divided into four neighborhoods (from east to west): **Fontvieille, Monaco-Ville, La Condamine,** and **Monte-Carlo/Larvotto.** Fontvieille is home to a small, quiet port. The enormous *rocher de Monaco* (rock of Monaco) looms over the harbor, with Monaco-Ville at the top. The historical and legislative heart of the city lies immediately adjacent, home to both the **Palais Princier** and the **Cathédrale de Monaco.** La Condamine sits just below Monaco-Ville, along the main port, and is the busiest area of the principality. Monaco's glitziest section is concentrated in Monte-Carlo. There you can find the fabled tables of the Monte-Carlo Casino and the **Carré d'Or,** a cluster of thoroughfares lined with luxury boutiques. Monte-Carlo/Larvotto also boasts Monaco's only beach, the **plage du Larvotto.** A 5min. walk uphill from the casino takes you across the border and away from Easy Street to **Beausoleil,** France, where you will find reasonably-priced hotels and restaurants a stone's throw from the *richesse* of the pl. du Casino.

Tourist Office: 2a bd. des Moulins (☎92 16 61 16), near the casino. A friendly, English-speaking staff provides city maps, events brochures, and same-day hotel reservations free of charge. Open M-Sa 9am-7pm, Su and holidays 10am-noon. There are annexes in the train station at the av. Prince Pierre exit, in the Chemin des Pecheurs parking garage, and in the port mid-June to Aug.

Tours: ☎92 05 64 38. Mini-train tours to the port, palace, and casino depart from the Oceanography Museum. 30min. tickets €6, children under 5 free. Open June-Sept. 10am-5pm; Oct.-May 10:30am-5pm; closed Jan. and mid-Nov. to late Dec.

Embassies and Consulates: Canada, 1 av. Henry Dunant (☎97 70 62 42); **United Kingdom,** 33 bd. Princesse Charlotte (☎93 50 99 66); **France,** 1 Chemin du Ténao (☎92 16 54 60). The nearest **US** consulate is in Nice (☎04 93 88 89 55).

Currency Exchange: Compagnie Monégasque de Change, parking du chemin des Pêcheurs, av. de la Quarantaine (☎93 25 02 50), at the end of the port, has reasonable rates. Open June-Sept. M-Sa 10am-5pm; Oct.-May 10am-noon and 2-4pm. Cash advance on MC/V available for amounts greater than €50 with 8% commission. 6% commission on traveler's checks, 4% for *Let's Go* readers.

ATMs: ATMs can be found throughout Monaco, principally on bd. Albert I along the main port and on rue Grimaldi, in the shopping district.

American Express, 35 bd. Princesse Charlotte (☎93 25 74 75). Open M-Sa 9:30am-6:30pm.

English-Language Bookstore: Scruples, 9 rue Princesse Caroline (☎/fax 93 50 43 52). Open June-Aug. M and W-F 10am-7pm, Tu 10am-12:30pm and 2:30-7pm, Sa 10am-12:30pm and 2:30-6:30pm; Sept.-May M-F 9:30am-12:30pm and 2:30-7pm, Sa 9:30am-12:30pm and 2:30-6pm. AmEx/MC/V.

Police: 3 rue Louis Notari (☎93 15 30 15). 5 other stations throughout the principality.

24hr. Pharmacy: Monaco has a rotating schedule of *pharmacies de garde*. Call the police station or look in the daily *Monaco-Matin*.

Hospital: Centre Hospitalier Princesse Grace, av. Pasteur (☎97 98 99 00; emergency 97 98 97 69), near the Jardin Exotique. Accessible by bus line #5.

Internet Access: Phone@Home, 3 rue du Marché (☎04 93 41 99 99; fax 04 93 41 93 44), next to the Hôtel Diana and Hotel Cosmopolite in Beausoleil. Owner speaks English, French, and Italian. Fax, phone, and photocopying; international calling cards sold. Internet €4 for 30min., €6.50 per hr. Faxes in France €2, within Europe €2.50, international €3.50. Open daily 8:30am-10pm. **Stars 'N' Bars,** 6 quai Antoine I (☎97 97 95 95; www.starsnbars.com). €6 for 30min. Open daily 11am-midnight.

Post Office: Palais de la Scala (☎97 97 25 25). Monaco issues its own stamps; French stamps not used there. Branch office across from Hôtel Terminus at the av. Prince Pierre train station exit. 5 additional branches. All offices open M-F 8am-7pm, Sa 8am-noon.

Postal Code: MC 98000 Monaco.

PHONING TO AND FROM MONACO	Monaco's country code is 377. To telephone Monaco from France, dial 00377, then the 8-digit Monaco number. To call France from Monaco, dial 0033, and drop the first zero of the French number. French phone cards will not work in Monaco's public phones, but cards purchased in Monaco will work throughout Europe.

ACCOMMODATIONS

If you choose to stay near the casino, you've either gotten really lucky at the slot machines or you've completely forgotten your children's college plans. Your best bet is to stay just across the border in Beausoleil, where prices are nearly

Monaco and Monte-Carlo

ACCOMMODATIONS
Hôtel Cosmopolite, 5
Hôtel Diana, 6
Hôtel Villa Boeri, 3

FOOD
Café Costa Rica, 4
Lina's, 11
Prince's Tea, 12
Le Regina, 7
Il Triangolo, 10

NIGHTLIFE
Black Diamond, 1
Café Grand Prix, 13
Jimmy'z, 2
McCarthy's, 9
Point Rouge, 8
Stars N' Bars (also Internet), 14

TO PLAGE DU LARVOTTO (100m), EUROPCAR, AND FRANCE (800m)

Grimaldi Forum
du Portier
Jardin Japonais
elevator to beach
Musée National de Monaco
Église St-Paul
av. de Verdun
av. de Grande-Bretagne
bd. du Larvotto
av. Princesse Grace

MONTE-CARLO

Phone @Home
Bernadette de Ste-Moreville
AmEx
bd. Princesse Charlotte
PL. DE LA CRÉMAILLÈRE
Marché U
Gale Force Computing
bd. Princesse Charlotte
av. St-Michel
U.K.
Église St-Charles
Centre Commercial Le Métropole
Monafinances
av. de la Madone
Parc des Boulingrins
Café de Paris
PL. DU CASINO
Monte Carlo Casino
Centre de Congrès Auditorium

BEAUSOLEIL
FRANCE
MONACO

r. Bellevue
r. Bel Respiro
av. Princesse Alice
Henry Dunant
Canada
Palais de la Scala
av. de la Costa
av. de Suisse
Avis
av. de la Madone
av. d'Ostende

Mer Méditerranée

route de la Moyenne Corniche

Gare SNCF
train station tunnel entrances
Ste-Dévote
PL. STE-DÉVOTE
Hertz
ACM
Casino Supermarket
Municipal Pool
Port de Monaco

bd. des Moneghetti
bd. du Jardin Exotique
bd. Rainier III
Gare SNCF

Louis Notari
SQ. T-GASTAUD
Scruples Bookstore
Auto-Moto Garage
r. de Millo
r. des Açores
r. Saige
av. du Port

LA CONDAMINE

Fort Antoine
quai Antoine I
av. de la Quarantaine
av. de la Porte Neuve
av. des Pins
av. St-Martin

MONACO-VILLE

Compagnie Monégasque de Change
Princess Caroline's Villa
Musée Océanographique
Jardin St-Martin

Parc Princesse Antoinette
Église St-Martin
bd. de Belgique
av. Prince Pierre de Monaco
r. Grimaldi
r. Suffren Reymond
PL. D'ARMES
Carrefour
La Notarie
Mairie
r. Basse
r. Comte Félix Gastaldi
r. Émile Loth
Palais de Justice
Cathédrale de Monaco

Jardin Exotique
Palais Princier
PL. DU PALAIS
PL. DU CANTON
Musée des Souvenirs Napoléoniens et Collection des Archives Historiques du Palais

bd. du Jardin Exotique
bd. Rainier III
av. Charles III
av. Pasteur
bd. Charles III

Centre Hospitalier Princesse Grace
The Private Collection of Antique Cars of H.S.H. Prince Ranier III

Port de Fontvieille
quai Jean-Charles-Rey

av. Prince Héréditaire Albert
Fontvieille
Stade Louis-II
FONTVIEILLE
Espace Fontvieille

0   200 yards
0   200 meters

CÔTE D'AZUR

halved. The hotels here are closer to the casino and the best nightlife than some in Monaco itself. The only other viable options are in La Condamine, along rue de la Turbie, rue Grimaldi, and av. Prince Pierre, just near the train tracks. Simple, clean rooms fill the genial **Hôtel Cosmopolite** ❹, 19 bd. du Général Leclerc, in Beausoleil, next door to Hôtel Diana. Rooms range from compact to enormous, each well equipped with A/C, TV, minibar, and direct phone. (☎04 93 78 36 00. Breakfast €7. Reception 7am-midnight. Singles with shower €42, Sept.-June €34, with bath €59-74/€51-66. Doubles with shower and toilet €68-88/€60-80. Triples €84-93/€76-85. Quads €94. AmEx/MC/V.) To reach **Hôtel Villa Boeri** ❹, 29 bd. du Général Leclerc, in Beausoleil, 10min. from the casino leave the train station at bd. Princesse Charlotte and keep to the left. Bd. de France changes to bd. du Général Leclerc in Beausoleil. The English-speaking owner rents a variety of rooms, from luxe doubles with huge bathtubs to singles with double bed and shower. All rooms have A/C, TV, hairdryer, and phone. (☎ 04 93 78 38 10; fax 04 93 41 90 95. Breakfast €5. 24hr. reception. Singles €46, with bath €50, in private pavilion €91; doubles €53/€60/€91; triples €62/€69/€91; quads €81/€122. AmEx/MC/V.) **Hôtel Diana** ❸, 17 bd. du Général Leclerc, is probably the only hotel on the Riviera with the same rates year-round. Despite a bit of wear and tear, rooms have firm beds, A/C, TV, and phone. Balconies facing Monaco have views of the city below. (☎04 93 78 47 58; www.monte-carlo.mc/hotel-diana-beausoleil. Breakfast €6. Reception 6am-8pm. Reservations required. Singles €35, with shower €38, with bath €46; doubles with 1 bed €35, with shower €45, with bath €56-61; triples €63, with bath €65. AmEx/MC/V.)

🄵 FOOD

Not surprisingly, most of Monaco has little budget fare. Try behind the pl. du Palais (**rue Comte Felix, rue Gastaldi,** and **rue Emile de Loth**) for reasonable prices. Fresh food awaits at the fruit and flower **market** on pl. d'Armes at the end of av. Prince Pierre (open daily 6am-1pm), the **Casino supermarket,** bd. Albert I (☎93 30 56 78; open July-Aug. M-Sa 8:30am-midnight, Su 9am-1pm; Sept.-June 8:30am-10pm), or **Marché U** at 30 bd. Princesse Charlotte. (☎93 50 68 60. Open M-Sa 8:30am-7:15pm.) Plow through the enormous **Carrefour** in Fontvieille's shopping plaza (☎92 05 57 00; open M-Sa 8:30am-10pm) for anything else you forgot (or didn't) at home.

Monaco enjoys an inordinate number of Italian restaurants and pizzerias. Bright and bustling 🄲**Café Costa Rica** ❷, 40 bd. des Moulins, serves bruschetta, salads, and other Italian staples to hungry crowds with record speed. After 3pm the sunny interior transforms into a welcoming *salon de thé* and *crêperie*, but come at lunchtime for the fabulous *farfalle bersagliera* (€8) and other pasta dishes between €8 and €11. (☎93 25 44 45. *Plats du jour* €10-11. Open July-Aug. M-F 8am-8pm, Sa-Su 8am-3pm; daily Sept.-June 8am-7pm. Lunch noon-2:45pm. Closed Aug. 1-15. V.) At 🄲**Le Regina** ❸, 13-15 bd. des Moulins, the charming English-, Italian-, and French-speaking owner knows everyone by name. This simple cafe serves delicious pizzas (€9-12), salads (€10-12), and pasta for €10-€12. (☎93 50 05 05. Open M-Sa 8am-9pm. MC/V.) Settle into the small corner terrace at **Il Triangolo** ❸, 1 av. de La Madone, where a friendly staff serves enormous, heavenly pizzas (€10-13) and generous pasta dishes (€12-16) to local regulars. (☎93 30 67 30. Open M-F noon-2:30pm and 7pm-1am, Sa and Su closed for lunch. Pizzas available at dinner. MC/V.) Tiny but charming **Prince's Tea** ❷, 26 av. de la Costa, offers regal desserts at—thankfully—pauper's prices (€1-2.50 each). The *salon de thé* is located near the tourist office. (☎93 50 63 91. Open July-Aug. M-Sa 7:30am-8pm; Sept.-June M-F

7:30am-8pm, Sa 8am-1pm and 3-8pm. DC/MC/V.) Put down your shopping bags and pick up a sandwich at **Lina's ❶**, in Le Métropole shopping center. Upscale offerings like pear-flavored cider (€3.10) and smoked-salmon *panini* (€7) are all reasonable. (☎93 25 86 10. €3.90-6.80. Open M-Sa 9am-7:30pm.)

👁 SIGHTS

▨MONTE-CARLO CASINO. The long history of this famous gambling house is peppered with legends and wild anecdotes. Its position along the rocky coast is convenient for suicide, an end once sought by as many as four high-stakes losers in one week. High rollers, too have their legendary habits: Cornelius Vanderbilt insisted on having his entire family present while he placed 40,000 francs on the table. Boost your own chances with a stop in the lobby of the **Hotel de Paris** next door to rub the knee of the bronze horse statue, rumored to bring good luck. While optimists tempt fate at **slot machines** (daily July-Aug. from noon; Sept.-June M-F from 2pm, Sa-Su from noon), **blackjack,** and **roulette** (daily from noon), the less intrepid can check out the **Atrium du Casino** theater. Though all casinos frown upon shorts, sneakers, sandals, and jeans, a fancier **dress code** is not in effect until 8pm. Exclusive *salons privés* require coat and tie and charge a €10 cover. The **Café de Paris** next door opens for gambling at noon with no cover. The 18+ rule is strictly enforced; bring a passport. (*☎92 16 20 00; www.casino-monte-carlo.com. €10.*)

▨PALAIS PRINCIER. Perched on *le rocher*, the lavish palace is the occasional home of Prince Rainier and his tabloid-darling family. The stoic palace guard that nominally protects the entrance changes shift with great fanfare daily (11:55am), and only when the prince is away does the flag above the palace lower and the doors open to tourists. Audioguides lead visitors along opulent silk walls, gilt furniture, and Venetian crystal chandeliers. Memorable stops include the courtyard's grand staircase, the hall of mirrors, the throne room, Princess Grace's official state portrait, and the chamber where the Duke of York died. (*☎93 25 18 31. Open daily June-Sept. 9:30am-6pm; Oct. 10am-5pm. €6, students with ID and children 8-14 €3.*)

PLAGE DU LARVOTTO. Though Monaco's beaches can't compare to the rest of the Riviera, residents and tourists fill this umbrella-speckled spot. Apartment buildings and coastline cliffs make a stunning background. (*Off av. Princesse Grace. The public elevator from the bd. des Moulins drops passengers off just to the right of the beach.*)

MUSÉE OCÉANOGRAPHIQUE. An educational break from Monaco's excesses, the oceanographic museum was founded by Jacques Cousteau and prince-cum-marine biologist Albert I. The museum's main attraction is a 90-tank aquarium featuring Mediterranean and tropical sealife. An innovative system pumps 250,000L of seawater directly from the harbor each day to fill the tanks. Kids will enjoy the reconstructed coral reef, shark lagoon, and 1.9m green moray eel, the largest on display in the world. (*Av. St-Martin. ☎93 15 36 00. Open daily Apr.-Aug. 9:30am-7:30pm; Sept. 9:30am-7pm; Oct.-Mar. 10am-6pm. €11, students with ID and children 6-18 €6.*)

CATHÉDRALE DE MONACO. Thirty-five generations of Grimaldis rest inside this white neo-Romanesque-Byzantine church, which hosted the 1956 wedding of Prince Rainier and Grace Kelly. The majestic interior includes an intricate marble floor, a quadruple organ, and an Episcopal throne constructed entirely of white Carrara marble. Princess Grace lies in a tomb behind the altar emblazoned with her Latin name, "Patritia Gracia." Citizens still adorn the tomb with fresh flowers and hand-written notes. (*Pl. St-Martin, near the Palais. ☎93 30 87 70; fax 93 25 32 59. Open daily Mar.-Oct. 8am-7pm; Nov.-Feb. 8am-6pm. Mass Su 10:30am and Sa 6pm. Free.*)

CÔTE D'AZUR

JARDIN EXOTIQUE. Though Monaco is hardly a desert locale, innumerable species of cacti that were imported from America in the 16th century thrive in this meticulous garden. Stone caves and tiny ponds covered with lily pads offer sweeping views of the entire principality. Free tours descend 300 steps into the cliffside, where visitors explore stalagmites and stalactites in damp grottoes. (*62 bd. du Jardin Exotique, up the public elevators on bd. de Belgique. The last stop on the #2 bus line. ☎ 93 15 29 80; www.monte-carlo.mc/jardinexotique. Open daily mid-May to mid-Sept. 9am-7pm; mid-Sept. to mid-May 9am-6pm or until sundown. €6.60, students and children 6-18 €3.20, under 6 free.*)

CAR COLLECTION. If you thought those hot wheels taking up the prime parking spots in front of the Casino were impressive, think again. The **Private Collection of Antique Cars of H.S.H. Prince Rainier III** easily puts them all to shame. One hundred of the sexiest cars in the world are on display here, gathered by the Prince himself. Gawk at a perfectly restored 1924 Model T, the 1956 Rolls Royce Silver Cloud that carried Prince Rainier and Grace Kelly on their wedding day, and the auto that captured the first Grand Prix de Monaco in 1929. (*Terrasses de Fontvieille. ☎ 92 05 28 56; fax 92 05 96 09. Open daily 10am-6pm. €6, students with ID and children 8-14 €3.*)

OTHER SIGHTS. The dolls you played with as a kid were nothing like the fantastic wood-and-porcelain creations at the **Musée National de Monaco.** Housed in a pink villa designed by Charles Garnier, the collection of 18th- and 19th-century dolls features several "automatons" that move and talk, including an illusionist who makes his head disappear. Upstairs, an enormous grouping of 180 *santons* depicts life in a traditional village at the end of the 18th century. (*17 av. Princesse Grace. Elevator from pl. des Moulins drops pedestrians off right next to the entrance. ☎ 93 30 91 26; fax 92 16 73 61. Automatons demonstrated at 11am and on the hr. from 2:30-5:30pm. Open daily May-Oct. 10am-6:30pm; Nov.-Apr. 10am-12:15pm and 2:30-6:30pm. €6, students with ID and children 8-14 €3.50.*) History buffs will love the crowded cases at the **Musée des Souvenirs Napoléoniens et Collection des Archives Historiques du Palais,** just to the left of the palace entrance. The jam-packed museum was assembled by Prince Louis II, the great-grandson of Napoleon's adopted daughter. The mezzanine level contains the general's legendary cocked hat and a locket containing a strand of his hair. The rest of the collection, devoted to the history of Monaco, illustrates the principality's warfare-ridden history. (*Next to the Palais Princier entrance. ☎ 93 25 18 31. Open daily June-Sept. 9:30am-6pm; Oct. 10am-5pm; Dec.-May Tu-Su 10:30am-12:30pm and 2-5pm. €4, students with ID €2.*) If a big loss at the casino has left you raging, find your center at the **Jardin Japonais,** a tranquil seaside spot next to the Grimaldi Forum. Cherry trees, bamboo fountains, and a traditional tea house invite visitors to "purify mind and body." (*Open daily 9am-sunset. Free.*) Fashionistas who love the big-name labels but not the big-time prices should check out **Second Hand Bernadette de Sainte Moreville** in Beausoleil, where racks stock (nearly) affordable secondhand Chanel, Dior, Armani, and Gucci threads. (*9 bd. Général Léclerc. ☎ 04 93 78 31 53. Open M-F 10:30am-1:30pm and 4-7:30pm, Sa 10:30am-1:30pm. Jeans €60-70, jackets €85-430, accessories €90-110, blouses €45-75.*) Stroll through the seaside **Jardin St-Martin,** next to the Oceanographic Museum. The pleasant grounds offer excellent views of the coast amid flowering trees and a beautiful wood trellis. (*Open daily 9am-sunset.*) Keep your eyes peeled for **Princess Caroline's villa,** a pink oasis just outside the gardens between the cathedral and the oceanography museum. It may be difficult to spot between the rows of trees, but the monk insignia on its gates should tip you off.

▣ NIGHTLIFE

Hope you've got that gold-sequined dress, because Monaco is the place to see and be seen. Its chic nightlife is accordingly *très cher*, but certainly not to be missed.

Stars N' Bars, 6 quai Antoine I (☎97 97 95 95; www.starsnbars.com). Poi rant by day and lively club by night. A young crowd relaxes over pool and v then heads upstairs to the dance floor. Bar stools with "legs" make for the I town. Restaurant open daily 11am-midnight. DJ spins nightly 10pm-1am. open daily July-Aug. 12:30am-5am; Sept.-June F-Sa 12:30am-5am.

Le Point Rouge, 11 rue du Portier (☎97 77 03 04; www.pointrouge.mc), street from McCarthy's. Faux-torches and imposing columns lead the way to this ultra-sleek club. If you don't want to shell out big bucks (€23 per drink), settle down on the terrace for more reasonable cocktails. Beer €6, cocktails €13. Bar open Tu-Th 8pm-midnight, F-Sa 8pm-1am. Club open Th-Sa 11pm-6am. AmEx/D/MC/V.

McCarthy's, 7 rue du Portier (☎93 25 87 67). Ogle at passing glitterati over Guinness or tasty Irish cocktails at this ritzy Monaco address. Live music daily July-Aug. at midnight; Sept.-June Th-Sa at midnight. Check *By Night* for details. Guinness €6, Irish cocktails €12. Happy hour 6-9pm with drinks reduced 30%. 18+. Open daily 6pm-dawn.

Café Grand Prix, 1 quai Antoine I (☎93 25 56 90), a short stroll down from Stars N' Bars. Cozy bar honors Monaco's famous race with sleek stools, racing-print etched glass, and deep red walls. Beer €5-8, cocktails €11.50-13. Live music 11pm. Happy hour daily 6-9pm with drinks half-price. Open daily 10am-5am. AmEx/DC/MC/V.

Jimmy'z, 26 av. Princesse Grace (☎92 16 22 77; www.montecarloresort.com). In case you missed the buzz, neon signs and blaring music are there to remind you that Jimmy'z has been Monaco's hotspot for the past 30 years. The floor is lit from below and surrounded by tables of classy clientele. Open daily from 11pm until the party stops.

Black Diamond, 11 av. Princesse Grace (☎97 77 00 24; www.blackdiamondcafe.com). Disco music and a swanky interior draws sophisticates. Though pricey cocktails and the crystal chandelier may intimidate, the bartenders are friendly, the outdoor seating relaxed, and the DJ obliging. Beer €8, cocktails €13-16. Happy hour daily 6-9pm. Open daily July-Aug. 5pm-3am; Sept.-June M-Sa 5pm-3am. AmEx/D/MC/V.

 FESTIVALS

Each January, Monaco kicks off the new year with the **Festival International du Cirque** (☎92 05 26 00), an exhibition of the world's best circus acts, then follows with the **Flower-Arranging Competition** in mid-May (call the Garden Club of Monaco ☎93 30 02 04 for details). But the real party starts at the end of May with the prestigious **Formula One-Grand Prix,** a jewel in the crown of the World Drivers' Championship. For four days, the roads surrounding the *vieux port* are transformed into a harrowing track where the world's best drivers test their skills. Sparkling white yachts in the bay provide a perfect backdrop, as do throngs of celebrities and tourists who come to cheer. If exhaust fumes, snazzy paint jobs, and bright jumpsuits aren't your thing, think twice about visiting during the race; tourist attractions close, waterfront access is limited, and hotel prices skyrocket. (Purchase tickets at booking office of ACM, 23 bd. Albert I. ☎93 15 26 24; location@acm.mc. Tickets €50-420.)

MENTON

Often called the "Secret Riviera," Menton (pop. 30,000) remains blissfully removed from the glitter and glare of nearby tourist traps but still offers the picturesque white-sand beaches, lush gardens, and medieval alleys that have made the Riviera famous. On France's eastern border, the town is flavored with hints of nearby Italy; shopkeepers and beach-goers speak French with a decidedly Italian accent, and many restaurants offer Italian *menus* to go with the typical French cuisine.

■ TRANSPORTATION

Trains: pl. de la Gare. Trains operate 5am-midnight. Reservations 9:15am-6:20pm; self-service machines at other times. Trains leave every 30min. to: **Cannes** (1¼hr., €8.10); **Monaco** (11min., €1.80); **Nice** (35min., €4). Also to: **Ventimiglia** (10min., €2.10) and **Genoa** (2½-3hr., 11-14 per day, €18.20) in Italy.

Buses: promenade Maréchal Leclerc (☎04 93 35 93 60); walk from the train station and take a left at the first major intersection. Open M-F 8:30am-noon and 1:30-6pm, Sa 10am-noon. Buses operate 6:30am-7:30pm. **Rapides Côte d'Azur** (☎04 97 00 07 00) runs buses every 15min. to **Monaco** (€2.10, same day return included) and **Nice** (€5.10).

Taxis: (☎04 92 10 47 02). 5 central taxi stands serve the city from 5am-11pm; reserve in advance by phone during off hours. Taxi from the train station to the hostel costs €8, more depending on baggage.

Bike Rental: L'Escale du 2 Roues, 105 av. de Sospel (☎04 93 28 86 05). €13 per day. Open Tu-Sa 8:30am-noon and 3-7pm. Holiday Bikes, 4 espl. G. Pompidou (☎04 92 10 99 98; www.holiday-bikes.com). Scooters, motorcycles, and cars also available. Bikes €13+ per day, €60+ per week, with a €230 deposit. Scooters €30+ per day with a €500 deposit. Open M-F 9:30-noon and 3-7pm, Sa 9:30-noon and 5-7pm. AmEx/MC/V.

■ ORIENTATION AND PRACTICAL INFORMATION

Menton is divided into the *vieille ville*, the new town, and the beach. **Avenue du Verdun** or **avenue Boyer** (depending on the side of the street) is the main thoroughfare of the new town, and ends at a casino right on the water. A left turn at the casino leads to shops and boutiques on **avenue Felix Faure,** and finally to the crowded pedestrian **rue St-Michel** and the heart of the *vieille ville*. The palm-lined **promenade du Soleil** runs the length of the bay between the old and new towns, funneling into the quai de Monleon at the edge of the *vieux port*. The liveliest beach is **plage des Sablettes,** located below the Basilique St-Michel.

Tourist Office: 8 av. Boyer (☎04 92 41 76 76; www.villedementon.com). From train station, walk onto av. de la Gare. Cross av. de Verdun, then turn right on av. Boyer. English-speaking staff provides free maps and guidebooks. Open July-Aug. M-Sa 9am-5pm, Su 9:30am-12:30pm; Sept.-June M-F 8:30am-12:30pm and 2-6pm, Sa 9am-noon and 2-6pm.

Garden Tours: Service du Patrimoine, 24 rue St-Michel (☎04 92 10 97 10). Two 2½hr. tours daily at 10am and 2:30pm. In French only; M, W, and F (€5-8). Call ahead for schedules and departure times.

Currency Exchange: Société Générale (☎04 92 10 54 54), av. Boyer, just down the street from the tourist office. Open M-F 8:30am-noon and 1:30-5:15pm.

Police: 9 rue Partouneaux, (☎04 93 28 66 00). The **local police** (☎04 92 10 50 50) are located on rue de la République.

Hospital: La Palmosa, rue Antoine Péglion (☎04 93 28 77 77). For emergencies, call ☎04 93 28 72 40.

Internet Access: Passion Informatique, 2 av. Thiers (☎04 92 10 32 80). 5 computers with fast connections. €1.50 for 15min., €5 per hr.

Post Office: cours George V (☎04 93 28 64 87), facing tourist office. **Currency exchange.** Open M-W and F 8am-6:30pm, Th 8am-6pm, Sa 8:30am-noon.

Postal Code: 06500.

⚑⚒ ACCOMMODATIONS AND CAMPING

⚏Hôtel de Belgique, 1 av. de la Gare (☎04 93 35 72 66; hoteldebelgique@wanadoo.fr). English-speaking owner greets new guests like old friends, ushering them to 20 spacious, attractively furnished rooms that come with TV, phone, and double windows. Breakfast €5. Reception 6am-3pm and 5-10pm. Singles with toilet €29.50; doubles €38, with bath €48; triples €59; quads €72. Extra bed €12. MC/V. ❸

Hôtel Beauregard, 10 rue Albert I (☎04 93 28 63 63; beauregard.menton@wanadoo.fr). Turn right out of train station and go down steps behind Le Chou Chou brasserie. Turn right; the hotel is 80m down. Quiet rooms with TV, near the train station. Friendly staff offers useful info. Breakfast €5. Reception daily 8am-9pm. Reserve ahead July-Aug. Singles and doubles €32, with toilet and shower €40; triples with toilet and bath €46-52. Extra bed €9. Prices €3-5 lower Sept.-June. MC/V. ❸

Hôtel Richelieu, 26 rue Partouneux (☎04 93 35 74 71; www.hotelrichelieumenton.com). Turn left off av. Boyer before tourist office; the hotel is 3 blocks down. A marble staircase lends a touch of elegance. 29 rooms have bath and TV; some A/C. Wi/Fi access. Breakfast included. Singles with bath €44; doubles €51-85; triples €76-100, with bath €90-120. Extra bed €15. Prices €11-40 lower Sept.-May. AmEx/MC/V. ❹

Auberge de Jeunesse (HI), plateau St-Michel (☎04 93 35 93 14; menton@fuaj.org). Take bus #6 (8:40, 11:10am, 2, 5pm; €1.20). Compensates for remoteness with friendliness. Fabulous vistas and free breakfast. (7:30-8:45am). Single-sex rooms are clean, each with 8 sturdy wooden bunks and small window. Bar serves cheap drinks (beer €2; open daily 5-11pm). Internet €5 for 30min., €7 per hr. Dinner (7pm) €4.90 (pay in advance). Sleepsack €2.80. Showers 6:30-9:30am and 5-10pm. Laundry €6. Max. stay 3 days. Reception 7-10am and 5-10pm. Strict midnight curfew. Open Feb.-Oct. Beds €14.40. HI members only. ❶

Camping: Camping Municipal du Plateau St-Michel, rte. des Ciappes de Castellar (☎04 93 35 81 23; fax 04 93 57 12 35), 50 steps shy of the hostel. Olive trees shade rows of tents at this isolated spot. On-site restaurant-bar offers affordable pizzas (€8-9), pastas (€8), and meat dishes (€10-13.50), as well as foosball and pool tables. Reception M-Sa 8:30am-12:30pm and 3-7pm, Su 8:30am-12:30pm and 5-7pm. €3.55 per person, €3.85 per small tent, €4.80 per large tent; €3.65 per car. Electricity €2.40. Laundry July-Sept. Prices €0.30-0.60 higher mid-June to mid-Sept. MC/V. ❶

◖ FOOD

Menton prides itself on quality fruits and vegetables—not too surprising for a city with the slogan "my town is a garden." Test the freshness of *mentonnaise* produce at one of the town's three **markets:** the small **Marché Carëi** (av. Sospel at the end of av. Boyer; open daily 7am-12:30pm), **Marché Couvert** or **Les Halles** (quai de Monléon, off rue St-Michel; open every morning), and **Marché du Bastion** (near the Musée Jean Cocteau, quai Napoléon III; open Sa mornings). Waterfront restaurants dot the **promenade du Soleil,** but **place du Cap** and **rue St-Michel** in the *vieille ville* offer lively alternatives at rock-bottom prices. Street vendors bring an Italian flair, selling *panini* and *glace italienne* (Italian ice cream). Pick up delicious homemade jam at ⚏**L'Arche des Confitures** (☎04 93 57 20 29), 2 rue du Vieux College. Combinations like coconut clementine and hazelnut fig are produced daily in the small kitchen. Stop by in the morning to watch the cooks at work. (Open M-Sa 9:15am-12:30pm and 3:15-7pm. Guided visits of the kitchen on W at 10:30am.)

CÔTE D'AZUR

Settle into a squishy green booth at **Le Café des Arts ❷**, 16 rue de la République, where friendly, English-speaking waitstaff serve delicious salads (€7-8), pastas (€7-9), or reasonably-priced (€8-10) *plats du jour*. (☎04 93 35 78 67; www.cafedesarts.com. Open M-Sa 7:30am-10pm.) Painted knights, faux-stone walls, and cross-shaped menus pay homage to medieval Europe in eccentric **L'Occitan ❸**, 7 rue Marins, just off pl. aux Herves. Enjoy delicious *plats* like melon-mint soup and *carpaccio* of duck breast. (☎04 93 41 67 76; www.occi-tan.fr.st. *Menus* €10, €14, or €20; meat €10-12; fish €12-14; *foie gras* €10-15. Open Tu-Su 2-4pm and 7-10:30pm. MC/V.)

🃏 🌺 SIGHTS AND FESTIVALS

The *vieille ville* is reason enough to venture into Menton. Plentiful but rocky beaches stretch along the coast from quai Napoléon III west to Monaco. **Plage du Borrigo, plage du Casino,** and **plage du Marché** combine to form Menton's longest stretch, but if you want sand, head east of quai Napoléon to local favorite **plage des Sablettes.** Also on quai Napoléon is Menton's main attraction, the **Musée Jean Cocteau,** also known as the **Bastion.** This fort was originally constructed by the Prince of Monaco in 1616 to ward off French invasions. (☎04 93 57 72 30. Open M and W-Su 10am-noon and 2-6pm. €3, students under 25 €2.25, 18 and under free. First Su of the month free.) The **Salle des Mariages** in the Hôtel de Ville, is an unusual state marriage site. Jean Cocteau decorated this windowless room as a Greek temple and then added leopard rugs and velvet chairs for a Vegas-like effect. (☎04 92 10 50 00. Open M-F 8:30am-12:30pm and 2-5pm. €1.50, students €1.15, under 18 free.)

The bell tower of the **Basilique St-Michel** rises majestically above rue St-Michel in the *vieille ville*. From rue St-Michel, take a left onto rue des Logettes, and then ascend the steps of rue des Écoles Pie. The Baroque facade hides a beautiful nave, a gold-and-marble altar, and a gruesome secret: until 1850 Menton did not have a single cemetery, so paupers were buried in a common grave below the cathedral. (Open M-F and Su 10am-noon and 3-5:15pm. Mass Su 10:30am.) Next door is the charming **Chapelle des Pénitents Blancs,** unconventionally decorated with shellfish. (Open M 3-5pm.) From the **place St-Michel,** between the two churches, an opening in the bright red roofs provides the perfect frame for a view of the plage des Sablettes and the coast of the Italian Riviera.

Climb 225m above the city to the **Monastère Annonciade.** Here, a small terrace provides views of the city and sea below. To reach the monastery, turn left on av. Riviera (just west of the bus station) from av. de Sospel. Follow the road uphill until you reach the **Chemin de Rosaire,** which leads all the way to the top. Though the hike is 30min. uphill, 15 chapels depicting the stations of the cross can help you count to the top. The chapels were built by Princess Isabelle of Monaco in gratitude to the Virgin of the Annonciade for curing her leprosy. Bus #4 leaves from the *gare routière* four times per day (8:30, 11:40am, 2:30, 6:35pm; €1.20) and heads directly for the top. (☎04 93 35 76 92. Open daily 8am-noon and 2-6pm. Mass July-Aug. M-Sa 7:30am, Su 10am; Sept.-June M-Sa 11:15am, Su 10am.)

Plant lovers will appreciate Menton's gardens—the small town's pride and joy. Beginning in the late 18th century, winter residents began planting elaborate and exotic gardens. Among the most exceptional is **Serre de la Madone,** 74 rte. de Gorbio (☎04 93 57 73 90; www.serredelamadone.com), at the Mer and Monts stop on the #7 bus (10min., €1.20). After designing the famous gardens at Hidcote Manor in England, the Parisian-born American resident Lawrence Johnston turned his attention toward Menton. Today, the garden is a designated *monument historique*. (Open Feb.-Sept. Tu-Su by guided visit only, at 9:30am and 3pm. €8, 15 and under free.) June is Menton's official "month of gardens," when private gardens open to the public. Contact the Service du Patrimoine to make reservations.

Each February brings some 250,000 visitors sweet on sour fruit to the **Fête du Citron** (Lemon Festival). What began as a small flower and citrus exhibition in 1929 has now become a joyful 15-day occasion, culminating in a parade of floats decorated with 120 tons of citrus. Annual themes test the builders' creativity; "Asterix in the Land of the Lemon" and "Alice in Wonderland" were two recent choices.

ANTIBES

While most Riviera towns flaunt sun and sand like cheap costume jewelry, demure Antibes (pop. 72,000) is the real gem of the coast. Though blessed with beautiful beaches, a charming *vieille ville*, and a renowned Picasso museum, the city is less touristed than Nice and more relaxed than St-Tropez. On the unforgettable Cap d'Antibes, the scent of pine and sea air floats over the rooftops of luxurious villas, hidden in scrubby forest off sleepy, winding streets. Wild locals, wealthy expatriots, and a recent inundation of young Anglophones make for scandalous summer nights in the neighboring town of Juan-les-Pins.

⎚ TRANSPORTATION

Trains: pl. Pierre Semard. Ticket desk open daily 5:30am-10:45pm; info desk open 9am-8pm. Station open daily 5:25am-12:05am. To: **Avignon** (1¾hr., 3 per day, €34.10); **Cannes** (15min., 23 per day, €2.30); **Marseille** (2¼hr., 12 per day, €23.70); **Monaco** (1hr., 5 per day, €6.20); **Nice** (15min., 25 per day, €3.50).

Regional Buses: RCA (☎04 93 39 11 39) sends buses from pl. de Gaulle to: **Cannes** (20min., every 20min. 7am-10:40pm, €2.50); **Nice** (45min., every 20min. 6:15am-8:38pm, €4.10); the **Nice airport** (30min., every 20min. 6:15am-9pm, €7). Bus schedules available at the tourist office.

Public Transportation: Local buses leave from the *gare routière*, on pl. Guynemer (☎04 93 34 37 60). On-site office provides transit maps. Tickets €1.10, *carnet* of 10 €8; unlimited 1-day pass €3, unlimited 3-day pass €10. Office open June-Aug. M-F 8:30am-noon and 2:30-5:45pm, Sa 10am-12:30pm and 2-4:30pm; Sept.-May 7:30am-9pm. Free **Minibus** connects travelers to various points in the city, including beaches, train and bus station, and *vieille ville* (every 15min. 7:30am-7:30pm). Ask for a route map at the tourist station or look for "minibus gratuit" signs throughout town.

Taxis: Allô Taxi Antibes (☎04 93 67 67 67) wait at the train station. Around €12-15 from the train station to Juan-les-Pins. 24hr.

Car Rental: Europcar, 26 bd. Foch (☎04 93 34 79 79; www.europcar.fr.). From €319 per week with a €500 deposit. 21+. Cars can be returned elsewhere. Open May-Sept. M-Sa 8am-noon and 2-7pm; Oct.-Apr. M-Sa 8am-noon and 2-6pm. AmEx/D/MC/V.

Bike and Scooter Rental: ScootAzur, 43 bd. Wilson (☎04 93 67 45 25; fax 04 93 67 45 26). Bikes from €12 per day, €56 per week; €150 deposit. Scooters €30-45/ €175-270/€900. Open M-Sa 9am-noon and 3-7pm. MC/V.

◼ ⁊ ORIENTATION AND PRACTICAL INFORMATION

Av. Robert Soleau connects the train station with **place de Gaulle** and the tourist office. From here, a short walk along rue de la République passes the bus station and heads into **Vieux Antibes,** below the *vieux port* along the eastern shore. **Boulevard du President Wilson** stretches from the pl. de Gaulle across the peninsula, funneling into the center of Juan-les-Pins. Follow bd. Albert I from pl. de Gaulle and turn right at the water to reach a long stretch of beach and the beginning of **Cap d'Antibes** (15 minutes). The tip of the peninsula is 30min. from the base of the Cap.

Tourist Office: 11 pl. de Gaulle (☎ 04 92 90 53 00; www.antibes-juanlespins.com). Free maps, info on restaurants, camping, and festivals, and help with hotel reservations. Open daily July-Aug. 9am-7pm; Sept.-June M-F 9am-12:30pm and 1:30-6pm, Sa 9am-noon and 2-6pm. Branch at the train station (☎ 04 97 21 04 48). Open daily July-Aug. 9am-7pm; Sept.-June M-F 9am-12:30pm and 1:30-5pm.

Tours: Tours (☎ 06 14 13 73 60) of the *vieille ville* depart from the Archaeology Museum every Tu 9:30am. Longer excursions around Cap d'Antibes leave from the Garoupe Beach every W 9:30am. (Both are conducted in French and take 2½-3hr. English tours by reservation. €7.50). Mid-July to Aug. additional 2hr. tours are offered M and W-Su at 10am and 2:30pm (€2, under 18 free). Consult the tourist office for more information.

Currency Exchange: Delta Change, 17 bd. Albert I (☎ 04 93 34 12 76; fax 04 93 34 67 44). No commission on foreign currencies. Open July-Aug. M-Sa 9:30am-12:30pm and 2-7pm; Sept.-June 9am-noon and 2-5pm. **Eurochange,** 4 rue G. Clemenceau (☎ 04 93 34 48 30). Open M-Sa Apr.-Oct. 9am-7pm; Nov.-Mar. 9am-6pm. Those with a *Let's Go* guide do not have to pay the 4% commission.

English-Language Bookstore: Heidi's English Bookshop, 24 rue Aubernon (☎/fax 04 93 34 74 11). Large English bookstore, with budget-friendly used-book section (€2.50-6.50). Open daily 10am-7pm. MC/V.

Laundromat: Lave Plus, 44 bd. Wilson (☎ 06 61 86 06 19). Wash €3.40-7.70, dry €0.50 per 5min., detergent €0.40. Wash, dry, and fold service €10 for 5kg, with ironing €20. Open daily 7am-8:30pm.

Police: 33 bd. Wilson (☎ 04 92 90 78 00).

24hr. Pharmacy: Call the police or consult the local *Nice Matin* newspaper.

Hospital: Chemin des Quatres Chemins (☎ 04 92 91 77 77).

Internet Access: Xtreme Cyber, 8 bd. d'Aguillon (☎ 04 93 34 09 96, cyber-xiimbal@yahoo.com), at the Galérie du Port. €0.12 per min., €5 for 1hr. Happy hour from 2-3pm lets you double your time block for free. Open M-F 9am-9pm, Sa 10am-6pm.

Post Office: pl. des Martyrs de la Résistance (☎ 04 92 90 61 00), behind the playground on rue de la République. Open M-F 8am-7pm, Sa 8am-noon.

Postal Code: 06600.

ACCOMMODATIONS

Antibes has a few affordable accommodations, most of which are sprinkled between the new town and the *vieux port*. Budget-friendly beds are harder to come by here than in Nice and Cannes, so those interested in only a few of Antibes's attractions may want to daytrip it. Serious sightseers should stay in the *vieille ville*; those looking for beach and nightlife should stay in Juan-les-Pins.

The Crew House, 1 av. St-Roch (☎ 04 92 90 49 39; workstation_fr@yahoo.com). From the train station, walk down av. de la Libération until it turns into av. de Verdun, then make a right onto av. St-Roch. Anglos congregate in the bright rooms with 4-8 metal bunks. Laid-back, friendly atmosphere near the Port Vauban. Internet €0.12 per min., €5.40 per hr. Lockers; bring your own lock. Reception M-F 9am-7pm, Sa-Su 10am-6pm. Dorms Apr.-Oct. €20, €100 per week; Nov.-Mar. €15/€75. MC/V. ❷

Stella's, 5 av. Paul Arène (☎ 04 93 34 12 14). From the station, cross the street and take av. de la Libération toward the port until the 3rd right after the roundabout, av. Paul Arène. For 10 years, Stella has opened the top floor of her beautiful home to backpackers and boat-handlers alike. 8-10 beds in 2 bright, co-ed dorms provide a quiet place for some sleep. No reservations, but there are usually vacancies; call M-F 10am-12pm and 5-7pm to be sure. Open Mar. 15-Oct. 30. Dorms €22, €132 per week. ❷

Hôtel Mediterranée, 6 av. Marechal Reille (☎04 93 34 14 84; http://hotel.mediterranee.free.fr). An accommodating staff maintains modern rooms, each with A/C, TV, telephone, soundproof windows, and bath. Breakfast (€6) is served on a beautiful terrace. Reception daily 8am-10pm. Reserve one month ahead July-Aug. Closed most of Dec. May-Sept. singles €42; doubles €55-61; triples €69; quads €77. Extra bed €5. Oct.-Apr. prices €7-12 lower. Reduced prices for stays of more than 7 days. MC/V. ❹

Nouvel Hôtel, 1 av. du 24 Août (☎04 93 34 44 07; fax 04 93 34 44 08). A chipper owner manages plain rooms with TVs and the lively corner *brasserie* below. Rooms are compact but comfortable, with new beds, individual safes, and large windows. Breakfast €4.60. Reception daily 6am-8pm. Singles €32.50; doubles €48-52, with shower €55, with bath €58-62. Extra bed €16. V. ❸

◪ FOOD

Vieux Antibes offers an extensive selection of popular restaurants. Stop by **Cours Masséna** for cheap pizza and local crafts, including vibrant paintings and ceramics. Nearby, the famous **marché Provençal** is considered one of the best on the Côte d'Azur. Colorful stalls display everything from ripe fruits to handmade wax candles. A variety of tempting restaurants set up outdoor tables along **boulevard d'Aguillon,** behind the vieux port. For cheaper prices and great people-watching, head off to lively **place Nationale,** a few blocks away. The largest local **supermarket** is **Intermarché,** 1 bd. Albert I. (☎04 93 34 19 10. Open M-Sa 8:15am-8pm.) The packed ◪**Le Brulot ❸,** 3 rue Frédéric Isnard, right off av. G. Clemenceau, specializes in wood-fired cuisine. Try the shrimp *au pastis* (€28.50), or choose from several meat (€12.50-21) and fish (€18-28.50) options. Stop by the day before and reserve the outstanding *bouillabaisse.* (☎04 93 34 17 76; www.brulot.com. Appetizers €7-11, *menus* €18-35. Open daily July and Sept. 7pm-midnight; Oct.-June M-W 7pm-midnight, Th-Su 1:30am-3pm and 7pm-midnight. AmEx/MC/V.) The low-key ◪**Le Broc en Bouche ❸,** 8 rue des Palmiers, just off rue Aubernon, serves delicious food worthy of the most glamorous locale, like melon and fig *carpaccio* with ham (€12). Wine-tasting is offered in the *cave* below. (☎04 93 34 75 60. Open July-Aug. M-Th 8-10pm, F-Sa 8-11:30pm; Sept.-June Tu-Sa noon-2pm and 8-10pm. MC/V.)

THE HIDDEN DEAL

WATER INTO WINE

France pumps out vast quantities of wine for unbeatable prices. That €4 *bouteille de vin* from the supermarket may seem to be a good deal now, but a visit to the **Cave Raymond** will forever transform frugal palates. Disguised behind a classy store front and expensive bottles of local *pastis,* the owners keep three enormous vats of red, white, and *rosé* wines. From these metal barrels, customers use a garden hose to transfer the store's wine into their own empty bottles for a mere €1.80 per liter. If you're worried about the quality of the wine you're getting, you can taste it first.

In order to conserve glass, the *cave* requires its patrons to use a specific wine bottle decorated with elevated glass stars. First-time customers can look for the appropriate bottle at the supermarket, or pay an extra €0.30 to buy an empty bottle from the *cave.* Super-thrifty wine lovers can bring in any sort of glass container (even Perrier bottles are approved), and the most desperate sorts can fill a plastic water bottle, though beware: the plastic taste can leech into the wine.

Cave Raymond has been emptying its vats to customers for the past 60 years at least. Unfortunately, this once-common practice is increasingly rare, so fill your bottles while you can.

LEFT OUT

The life of a highly talented artist is never easy. For Henri Bouchard, however, an artistic error cost him three years and, according to legend, his life.

The enormous statue of a French soldier that stands atop the Fort Carré was sculpted by Bouchard between 1924 and 1927 to serve as a commemoration of the thousands of young men who lost their lives in WWI. The statue (and others like it throughout France) is known as "La Poilu," a nickname for the French soldiers who were unable to shave and therefore came home very *poilu* (hairy).

While constructing the 22m statue, Bouchard apparently forgot to take into account mirror effect, or perhaps he just never learned to tell his right hand from his left. Whatever the case, the resulting figure was carved holding his weapon in his left hand—an extraordinarily glaring error, since even lefties carried guns in their right hands during WWI. The gigantic mistake stood above the city for everyone to see, a sky-high reminder of his *faux pas*.

Upon discovering his error, Bouchard reportedly climbed to the top of the statue and immediately jumped to his death. Some locals swear by the accuracy of the story, while others consider it a passing myth surrounding the flaw. Either way, Bouchard's name lives on through the enormous blunder towering over Antibes.

◙ SIGHTS

Popular with artists, Antibes was once home to Pablo Picasso, Graham Greene, and Max Ernst. A surprising variety of museums appeals to art-lovers and historians alike. A **combined ticket** allows entrance to Musée Picasso, Musée Archéologique, Fort Carré, Musée Napoléonien, and Musée de la Tour. (€10, valid for 7 days, available at all 6 museums.) ◙**Musée Picasso,** pl. Mariejol, in the Château Grimaldi, displays an excellent collection of Picasso's paintings and sculptures, as well as photos of the artist at work. (☎04 92 90 54 20; fax 04 92 90 54 21. Open mid-June to mid-Sept. Tu-Su 10am-6pm; July-Aug. until 8pm on Tu and F; mid-Sept. to mid-June 10am-noon and 2-6pm. Audioguide in English €3. Admission €3, students €1.50, under 18 free.) **Musée Archéologique,** on the waterfront in the Bastion St-André-sur-les-Remparts, showcases exhibits on the history of ancient Antibes. (☎04 93 34 00 39. Same hours as Musée Picasso. 45min. guided tours in French F 3pm. €3, students €1.50, under 18 free.)

The largest private marina on the Mediterranean, **Port Vauban** harbors 2400 spectacular white yachts. The new dock, for enormous mega-yachts, is affectionately known as "Millionaire's Row," named for the wealthy financiers who financed its construction. The 16th-century **Fort Carré** guards the entrance to the port. Outside, a statue of a French soldier honors the citizens of Antibes who died in WWI and serves as an inadvertent commemoration of the sculptor himself (See **Left Out,** left). (☎06 14 89 17 45. Fort accessible only by guided tours every 30min. in French or English. Open Tu-Su mid-June to mid-Sept. 10:15am-5:30pm; mid-Sept. to mid-June 10:15am-4pm. €3, students and seniors €1.50, under 18 free.)

The attractive **Musée Napoléonien,** bd. Kennedy in Cap d'Antibes, is housed in an old battery tower built by Napoleon in 1794, before his *coup d'état.* Take bus #2A from pl. Guynemer to Eden Roc (every 40min. M-Sa 6:50am-7:30pm, €1). Two galleries display a range of Bonapartist paraphernalia, including a bronze casting of the dictator's hand. (☎04 93 61 45 32. Open mid-June to mid-Sept. Tu-Sa 10am-6pm; mid-Sept. to mid-June 10am-4:30pm. €3, students €1.50, under 18 free.) Next door, the list of clientele at the super-posh, world-renowned **Hôtel du Cap-Eden-Roc** reads like a Who's Who: Celebrity guide—everyone from the Kennedys to the Shah of Afghanistan. (☎04 93 61 39 01. Beer €6-7, alcohol €15-35, bellinis €24. Reserve for July-Aug. in Jan. Closed mid-Oct. to mid-Apr. Singles €230-infinity.)

Beginning across from the Port de la Salis, the Chemin du Calvaire is decorated with the Twelve Stations of the Cross, dedicated to Christ's last struggle. The stations lead up to the small chapel of **Notre-Dame du Bon-Port,** which overlooks the Garoupe beaches. According to an ancient legend, an old man went to the church on a stormy night and saw the Virgin Mary drenched in seawater. Antibes locals have dressed up in nautical costumes every year since 1016 on the first Thursday in July to carry the Virgin statue down to the shore.

A small city of **theme parks** has emerged 3km up the northern shore on rte. de Biot. **Aquasplash** has a salt-water wave pool and 13 enormous water slides. (☎04 93 33 49 49. Ticket office open daily mid-June to mid-Sept. 9:30am-6pm. €18, ages 3-12 €15.) Dolphins, killer whales, and sea lions perform impressive tricks at **Marineland.** (☎04 93 33 49 49; www.marineland.fr. Ticket office open daily Feb.-Dec. 10am-10:30pm. €32, ages 3-12 €23. Oct.-Mar. prices €6 lower.) At night, **Antibesland** lights up carnival-style with a few small roller coasters, bumper cars, and cotton candy stands. (Open July-Aug. M-Sa 4pm-2am, Su 2pm-2am; Sept. Sa-Su 4pm-2am; Apr.-May Sa-Su 2-7pm; June M-F 8:30pm-2am, Sa 4pm-2am, Su 2pm-2am. Entrance free, rides from €1.50.) Take bus #200 (dir: Nice) from pl. de Gaulle to Biot Gare (every 20min. 6:15am-8:38pm, €1). From there, keep walking in the same direction along rte. de Nice and turn left at the roundabout.

█ ▒ NIGHTLIFE AND FESTIVALS

Most partiers head to **Juan-les-Pins** (see p. 731) at night, but the Antibes bars provide a low-key atmosphere to get your buzz started before hitting the discotheques. The bars and pubs along **boulevard d'Aguillon** hold happy hours (usually around 6pm) for a cosmopolitan crowd of Anglophones. **Cinéma Casino,** across from the bus station at 6 bd. du 24 Août, shows several modern films in English. (☎04 93 34 04 37; www.cinefil.com. €7.50, all day M and Tu-F afternoons €6.) Antibes kicks off the summer festival season with the annual **Voiles d'Antibes Juan-les-Pins.** Traditional sailing ships from all over the world come to race the 23km of coastline between Antibes and Juan-les-Pins. Concerts and cocktails fill each evening. During the first week of July, the **Festival d'Art Lyrique** brings world-class soloists and orchestras to the old port. (☎04 92 90 53 00. €15-50.) Antibes celebrates **Bastille Day** on July 13th, while Juan-les-Pins lights fireworks on the 14th.

La Gaffe, 6 bd. d'Aguillon (☎04 93 34 04 06), is frequented almost exclusively by young Anglophones. Squeeze in on W nights and every other weekend to hear local, well-loved band "Blah-Blah" play rock hits. Fruity "alco-pops" €6. Karaoke Su 10:30pm draws a hilarious crowd. Buy 1, get 1 free W 9-10pm. Half-price drinks year-round M-Tu and Th-F 6-7pm. Open daily June-Aug. 11am-2am; Sept.-May 11am-12:30am.

Le Blue Lady, rue Lacan (☎04 93 34 41 00), across the street from La Gaffe. Pool tables and a popular terrace make this low-key bar a great place to grab a drink and work the crowd for your future job as a mega-yacht deckhand. Beer from €3.60, pints €4.60. Open M-W and F 7am-midnight, Th 6:30am-midnight, Sa 8:30am-midnight.

The Hop Store, 38 bd. d'Aguillon (☎04 93 34 15 33), attracts a sedate pub crowd with cafe tables outside and all the usual Irish trimmings within. Beer from €3.40, pints €5.40. Live music on weekends. Happy hour 7-8pm with €3.40 pints. Open daily May to mid-Sept. 9am-2:30am; mid-Sept. to Apr. 3pm-12:30am.

L'Endroit, 29 rue Aubernon (☎04 97 21 14 10), is a welcome newcomer to the Anglo-dominated *vieux port* nightlife scene. Plush brown couches provide the perfect spot for locals to enjoy live music and upscale finger food. Beer €3, cocktails €7-10. Live music nightly at 9:30pm. Open daily 11am-2:30am.

Xtreme Café, 6 rue Aubernon (☎04 93 34 03 90), draws a good-looking crowd to its classy wine bar. See-through floor on the balcony lets partiers snoop on the scene below, but skirts beware—the glass is clear BOTH ways. Wine from €2, beer €3, cocktails €8. Theme nights. Open daily June-Sept. noon-2:30am; Oct.-May noon-12:30am.

BEACHES

The two main public beaches in Antibes, **plage du Ponteil** and neighboring **plage de la Salis**, are crowded all summer. The breathtaking rocky beach on **Cap d'Antibes** has clear blue water perfect for snorkeling. Bring sandals and chairs. Take bus #2A from the bus station to Tour Gandolphe (every 40min. M-Sa 6:50am-7:30pm, €1). With the map from the tourist office, find av. Mrs. L. D. Beaumont and follow it to the end. Turn left onto the pedestrian road; turn right when a small door appears in the surrounding walls and follow the dirt path until you find an isolated beach cove. Also on Cap d'Antibes, the paradise of the **plage Garoupe** put itself on the map in the 1920s when celebrities including Cole Porter, F. Scott Fitzgerald, Ernest Hemingway, and Pablo Picasso began to frequent it.

Côte Plongée, on the rocky beach below the Musée Napoléonien, at the corner of bd. Kennedy and bd. du Maréchal Juin, provides **scuba diving.** Take bus #2A (every 40min. 6:50am-7:30pm, €1.10) from pl. Guynemer to Eden Roc, and then walk along bd. Kennedy until the coast. Descend the stone steps and turn right. (☎06 72 74 34 94; www.coteplongee.com. Ages 6+. Intro dive €25, from boat €33, at night €40, with guide €39. Snorkel rental €8. Open daily May-Oct. 9am-6pm.)

TIP

TOO DARN HOT. The French may not be overly fond of air-conditioning, but, luckily, there are plenty of other ways to beat the Riviera heat. Siesta was invented for a reason—head for a shady cafe and pass midday with ice-cold drinks. In the early morning and late afternoon, head to museums, libraries, or movie theaters, which generally have air-conditioning. If nighttime heat makes sleeping hard, dampen a pair of thin socks with cold water and put a pair of dry socks on top. The water will draw the heat out of your body, and the dry pair will keep your sheets from getting wet. Most importantly, stay hydrated, limit the alcohol, and take advantage of the easiest, closest cool-off of all—the ocean!

DAYTRIP FROM ANTIBES

BIOT

Biot's train station (☎08 92 35 35 35) is 2 mi. from the town center; the most convenient way to travel from Antibes is by bus (Sillages, ☎04 92 28 58 68). Bus #10A connects Biot Village and the bus station in Antibes (25min.; M-Sa 12 per day, Su 8 per day; €1). The last bus from Biot to Antibes departs at 6pm. Bus #1B connects the train station to the village (10min.; every hr. M-F 7:30am-7:45pm, every 2hr. Sa 9am-7pm).

Just 3km from Antibes, Biot was subjected to a series of invasions throughout history due to its prime location between Italy and France. Originally conquered by the Greeks, later the Romans, and finally the Templars and Malta knights, it is a wonder that the people of Biot have been able to create anything throughout their turbulent history. Thanks to the efforts of Roi René, however, the village became a renowned center of artistic production. The town remained in the control of pirates until 1470, when Roi René personally ordered 50 Ligurian families to re-populate the village. They reconstructed Biot's narrow streets, gates, and bougain-villea-covered homes, and began producing the pottery for which it is now famous. Biot has since become a center of artistic creation; an enchanted Fernand Léger spent the end of his life painting here, and Eloi Monod invented the town's distinctive "bubble glass" in addition to basketweaving, mosaics, and wood-carving.

The tiny but beautiful **place aux Arcades** was the site of the ancient Roman forum; today it hosts art exhibits and charming restaurants. The **tourist office** distributes a 1hr. self-guided tour of the village, but wandering without a map is just as easy. Be sure to see the **Église de Biot,** just off pl. aux Arcades, constructed in the 12th century atop ancient Roman ruins. (☎04 93 65 00 85. Open daily 9am-6pm. Free.) Just next door is the delightful **Galerie Jean-Claude Novaro** (or Galerie de la Patrimoine), 2 pl. des Arcades, run by Novaro's daughter and son-in-law. The stone gallery also displays the work of whimsical up-and-coming artists. (☎04 93 65 60 23. Open daily 11am-12:30pm and 2:30-6:30pm. If the Galerie is closed, call Lea Novaro's mobile phone at ☎06 12 78 27 27; she is never far from the gallery.)

The stunning **Verrerie de Biot,** chemin des Combes, is the source of much of Biot's modern-day renown. The Verrerie was created in 1956 by Eloi Monod, who married the daughter of the founder of the Poterie Provençal (see below). After watching his father-in-law create famous Biot pottery, he decided to reproduce it in a new medium—glass. His attempt resulted in the formation of accidental "bubbles." Be sure to stop by the **Galerie International du Verre,** with unique modern glass creations by 35 international artists. (☎04 93 65 03 00; www.verreriebiot.com. Open June-Sept. M-Sa 9:30am-8pm, Su 10am-1pm and 3-7:30pm; Oct.-May M-Sa 9:30am-6:30pm, Su 10am-1pm and 2:30-6:30pm. Free.) Also at the edge of town is the **Musée National Fernand-Léger,** chemin du Val de Pome. (☎04 92 91 50 30; www.musee-fernandleger.fr. Open M and W-Su July-Sept. 11am-6pm; Oct.-Mar. 10am-12:30pm and 2-5:30pm; Apr.-June 10am-12:30pm and 2-6pm. €6.)

Clay in the fields surrounding Biot permits ceramicists to create enormous *jarres* and amphorae, several of which are on display at the **Poterie Provençal,** 1689 rte. de la Mer, 5min. from the train station. Founded in 1920, the *poterie* is the oldest in Provence. (☎04 93 65 63 30; fax 04 93 65 02 82. Open M-Sa 8am-noon and 2-6pm, Su 2-6pm.) A free shuttle runs in July and August every 10min. from the parking lot at the village entrance to the Verrerie, the Musée Fernand-Léger, and the Poterie Provençal. In the low season, take bus #10a (also goes to Antibes, €1), which stops several times between the village and the train station. Follow the signs from the Poterie Provençal to the **Bonsai Arboretum de la Cote d'Azur,** 229 chemin du Val de Pome, a curious addition to the Biot's traditional arts. The Okonek family maintains a collection of the temperamental trees, from small newborns to elaborate fully grown forests. (☎04 93 65 63 99; www.museedubonsai.fr.st. Open M and F-Su 10am-noon and 2-6pm. €4, students €2.)

The only thing sweeter than the crêpes at **Crêperie du Vieux Village ❶,** 2 rue St-Sébastien, are the adorable English-speaking owners. This charming pair whips up delicious sweet crêpes (€3-6, with ice cream €6-7.50) and speciality crêpe pizzas (€7-10) in a homey dining room. (☎04 93 65 72 73. Omelettes €7-8, salads €3-8. Open daily July-Aug. noon-3pm and 7-9pm; Sept.-June noon-3pm.) Gaudy murals contrast with colorful glass chandeliers at the spacious **Cafe de la Poste ❸,** rue St-Sébastien. Ignore the painted waiter and concentrate on fresh *tapas* (€11-14), salads (€11.50-12.50), fish (€14-23) and meat (€14.80-18) instead. (☎04 93 65 19 32. Lunch *menu* €14. Open July-Aug. Tu-Su 7am-2am; Sept.-June 7am-8pm. MC/V.)

The **tourist office,** 46 rue St-Sébastien, is located right in the village. A friendly English-speaking staff distributes bus schedules, walking tours of the village and loads of information about Biot's *verreries*, each with its own trademark form of glasswork. (☎04 93 65 78 00; tourisme.biot@wanadoo.fr. Open July-Aug. M-F 10am-7pm, Sa-Su 2:30-7pm; Sept.-June M-F 9am-noon and 2-6pm, Sa-Su 2-6pm.)

JUAN-LES-PINS

Under the Romans, Antibes was a major port and fishing base. To protect Antibes from the stench of the incoming seafood, nearby Juan-les-Pins was constructed to store and ship out the fish. It consisted mainly of houses for the sailors and seafood factories until the 1920s, when Juan-les-Pins was completely revamped by the infamous robber baron Jay Gould. Hundreds of American tourists were drawn to Gould's seaside paradise; they filled their days with sand and their nights with

CÔTE D'AZUR

swing. Decades later, not much has changed. Lined with bars and beach clubs, the modern town is still packed with seekers of sun, sea, and sex (not necessarily in that order). In the summer, boutiques stay open until midnight, and nightclubs blast music until the first rays of sunlight summon the dancers to the beach.

⚏◪ TRANSPORTATION AND PRACTICAL INFORMATION. The **train station** is on av. l'Estérel where it joins av. du Maréchal Joffre. (Open daily 6:40am-9pm, ticket window open 8:50am-noon and 1:40-5pm.) Trains run to: Antibes (5min., 25 per day, €1.30); Cannes (10min., 25 per day, €1.90); Monaco (1hr., 9 per day, €6.30); Nice (30min., 25 per day, €3.80). By **bus** from pl. Guynemer in Antibes, take Sillages #1A (10min., every 20min. 7am-7:40pm, €1). Line 1Abis Noctantibes shuttles between the pl. de Gaulle in Antibes and Juan-les-Pins (July-Aug. 8pm-12:20am). The **petit train** (☎06 03 35 61 35) goes from rue de la République in Antibes, through the *vieille ville*, to Juan-les-Pins. Although touristy, it serves both as a guided tour of Antibes and as a means of transportation. (30min.; every hr. July-Aug. 10am-11pm, May-Oct. 10am-7pm. Round-trip €6.50, ages 3-10 €3.50.) **Taxis** usually wait at the Jardin de la Pinède and outside the train station. (☎04 92 93 07 07. From the station to Antibes around €12-15.) To walk from pl. du Général de Gaulle in Antibes, head along bd. Wilson for 1.5km to the beach (25 minutes).

To reach the **tourist office,** 51 bd. Guillaumont, walk on av. du Maréchal Joffre from the train station and turn right onto av. Guy de Maupassant; the office is 2min. away on the right, at the intersection of av. Amiral Courbet and av. Guillaumont. (☎04 92 90 53 05; www.antibes-juanlespins.com. Open daily July-Aug. 9am-7pm; Sept.-June M-F 9am-noon and 2-6pm, Sa 9am-noon.) Other services include: a **laundromat** at 2 av. l'Esterel, near the train station (☎04 93 61 52 04; wash €3.90-9, dry €0.50 for 5min., detergent €0.40; open daily 7am-9pm) and a **post office** on av. Joffre, across from the train station. (☎04 92 93 75 50. Open M and W-F 8am-noon and 1:45-6pm, Tu 8am-noon and 2:15-6pm, Sa 8am-noon.) **Postal Code:** 06160.

◪◪ ACCOMMODATIONS AND FOOD. Animated beaches and incomparable nightlife make Juan-les-Pins a popular vacation spot; no wonder luxury hotels and upscale apartments abound while budget lodging is very hard to come by.

Formerly a private villa, the pink stucco ▨ **Hôtel Alexandra ❹,** rue Pauline, offers tasteful, spacious rooms with A/C, telephone, TV, and shower. Grab a beach mat from the stand by the door before heading down to the water. (☎04 97 21 76 50; www.hotelalexandra.net. Breakfast €6.50, dinner €22. Reception daily 8am-10:30pm. Reserve one month in advance for July-Aug. Open Mar.-Oct. July-Aug. singles €48; doubles €76-82; triples €84-88. May-June and Sept. prices €6-8 lower; Mar.-Apr. and Oct. €11-14 lower. AmEx/DC/MC/V.) The friendly, English-speaking manager of **Hôtel Trianon ❸,** 14 av. de l'Estérel, offers renovated, clean rooms with bright walls and large windows, all with TV and bath. (☎04 93 61 18 11; www.trianon-hotel.com. Free Internet. Breakfast €4. Reception daily 7am-11pm. Reserve one week in advance July-Aug. Singles €39; doubles €48; triples €54. Sept.-June prices €5-13 lower. AmEx/MC/V.) **Hôtel Parisiana ❹,** 16 av. de L'Estérel, has rich carpets, bright curtains, and sunny rooms with A/C, fridge, bath, and TV. (☎04 93 61 27 03; hotelparisiana@wanadoo.fr. Breakfast €5. Reception daily 7:30am-10pm. Singles €45; doubles €42-49; triples €71; quads €79. Extra bed €11. Sept.-May prices €7-11 lower, even lower for stays of more than 5 nights. MC/V.)

The **Casino supermarket** is on av. Admiral Courbet, across from the tourist office. (☎04 93 61 00 56. Open M-Tu and Th-Sa 8am-12:30pm and 3:30-7:30pm, W 8am-12:30pm, Su 8am-1pm. MC/V.) At **Ruban Bleu ❸,** on Promenade du Soleil, by the ocean, fill up on fresh fish and pizza. (☎04 93 61 31 02; fax 04 93 67 13 45. Fish and meat dishes €13.50-25, pizza €7-10, pasta €9-12. Lunch *formule* M-Sa €14. Open daily July-Aug. 7:30am-2am; Sept.-June 7:30am-9pm.

AmEx/MC/V.) Farther from the water, the dining room at **La Bamba ❷**, 18 rue Dautheville, fills with guests hungry for pizzas (€8.50-10.50), pasta (€7.50-10.50), and a large selection of wood-fired meat and fish dishes from €11.50 to €21.50. (☎04 93 61 32 64. *Menu* €17. Open daily July-Aug. 5:30pm-1am; Sept.-June noon-2pm and 7-11pm. AmEx/MC/V.)

▧▧ NIGHTLIFE AND FESTIVALS. Sunset in Juan-les-Pins draws bronzed partiers to the Casino area. The flavor of the moment is **▧Milk**, av. Gallice, where a hip crowd beautifies the dance floor and plush red sofas. (☎04 93 67 22 74. Cover €16, includes 1 drink. Open daily July-Aug. 1-6am; Sept.-June F-Sa 1-6am.) In psychedelic **Whisky à Gogo**, 5 rue Jacques Leonetti, neon lights frame a small dance floor where a young crowd grooves to house, hip-hop, and Latin beats. (☎04 93 61 26 40; wagogo.juan@wanadoo.fr. Cover €16, includes 1 drink. Other drinks €9. 18+. Ladies free M-Th before 1am. Open Apr.-May Th-Sa midnight-5am; daily July-Aug. midnight-5am; Sept. to mid-Oct. Th-Sa midnight-5am.) Mexican fiestas are reproduced nightly in **Le Village**, on the corner of av. Georges Gallice and bd. Baudoin. (☎04 92 93 90 00. Cover €16, includes 1 drink. Tu and Su ladies' night. Open daily July-Aug. midnight-5am; Sept.-June Th-Sa midnight-5am.)

Most **discotheques** are only open weekends in the low season. Fortunately, nearby **bars** pick up the slack, and provide some great atmosphere of their own. At the Brazilian-themed **▧ Pam Pam Rhumerie**, 137 bd. Wilson, revelers sip flavorful exotic cocktails served in coconut, monkey, and tiki-hut shaped glasses. This already-hot bar starts smokin' when bikinied showgirls take the stage. (☎04 93 61 11 05; www.pampam.fr. Open daily mid-Mar. to early Nov. 2pm-5am. Shows begin at 9:30pm.) Pre-clubbing crowds get started safari-style amid African masks and animal-prints at **La Reserve**, carrefour de la Nouvelle Orléans. (☎04 93 61 20 06. Open daily June-Sept. 8am-4am; Oct.-May 8am-3am.) Just across the street, the jointly owned **Ché Café** features huge photos of Ché and cammo-print chairs. A tempting lineup of rum shots includes banana, plantain, coconut, and guava flavors. (Open daily Apr.-Oct. 5pm-4am). Stay south of the border (but just across the street) at **Zapata's**, where salsa and sombreros draw a lighthearted crowd. (Open daily Apr.-Oct. 5:30pm-4am.) Fancy ice-cream cocktails attract a low-key group to the red lights of **Le Crystal**, av. Georges Galice. (☎04 93 61 62 51. Open daily 8am-2:30am.) Newcomer **Kelly's Irish Bar**, 5 bd. de la Pinède, entertains with soccer on big-screen TVs. (Pints €6. Open daily June-Aug. 6pm-5am; Sept.-May 6pm-1am.)

If clubs haven't cleaned you out completely, blow your dough at gaudy **Eden Casino**, bd. Baudoin. (☎04 92 93 71 71. No cover. 18+. Slot machines open 10am-5am. €11 cover. No t-shirts, jeans, or sneakers.)

In mid-July, Juan-Les-Pins temporarily abandons its nightclub-music obsession for the massive **Festival International de Jazz (Jazz à Juan)**, which lasts for ten days and usually draws a few big-name performers. (Info at jazzajuan@antibes-juanlespins.com. Tickets €20-59, students and under 18 €10-18; available at the tourist offices in Juan-les-Pins and Antibes.)

◪ BEACHES The town's length of the coast is punctuated by 35 beach clubs and countless restaurants and snack stands. Juan-les-Pins's second-biggest playground (after the clubs, of course) is in the waves, home to every watersport imaginable. The pontoon dock in front of the Hotel Meridien (15 bd. Baudoin) on Garden Beach is a good place to start. **Water Sports Services** offers **waterskiing** (€20), **wake-boarding** (€20), **parasailing** (€40-€60), **tubing** (€20), and €10 per hr. **paddle-boat** rental. (☎04 92 93 57 57, w.sports.y@free.fr. Open daily July-Aug. 7am-8pm; April-June 8am-7pm; Sept.-Oct. 8am-7pm.)

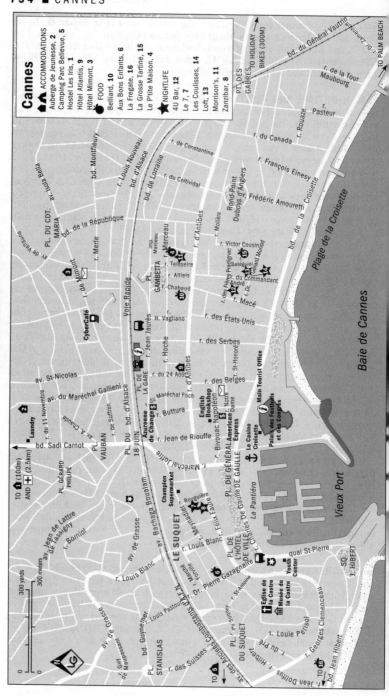

Cannes

▲▲ ACCOMMODATIONS
Auberge de Jeunesse, **2**
Camping Parc Bellevue, **5**
Hostel Les Iris, **1**
Hôtel Atlantis, **9**
Hôtel Mimont, **3**

● FOOD
Belliard, **10**
Aux Bons Enfants, **6**
La Fregate, **16**
La Grosse Tartine, **15**
Le P'tite Maison, **4**

★ NIGHTLIFE
4U Bar, **12**
Le 7, **7**
Les Coulisses, **14**
Loft, **13**
Morrison's, **11**
Zanzibar, **8**

CANNES

The name Cannes (pop. 67,000) conjures images of Catherine Deneuve sipping champagne by the pool, Marilyn Monroe posing red-lipped on the beach, and countless other starlets competing for camera time. With its renowned annual film festival, these associations are not at all inaccurate, but the festival happens only once a year—at other times, Cannes stashes the red carpet and becomes the most accessible of all the Riviera's glam-towns. Sure, the palm-lined boardwalk, gorgeous sandy beach, and innumerable boutiques draw an undeniably wealthy clientele, but loads of young, friendly travelers are coming here to soak up the sun, play in the waves, or party all night in one of Cannes' nonstop hot spots.

▐ TRANSPORTATION

Trains: 1 rue Jean-Jaurès. Station open daily 5am-12:30am. Ticket sales open daily 5:30am-10:30pm. Info desk open M-F 8:30am-6pm, Sa 8:30am-5:30pm. To: **Antibes** (15min., €2.30); **Marseille** (2hr., 6:30am-11:03pm, €22.30); **Monaco** (1hr., €7.40); **Nice** (40min., €5.20); **St-Raphaël** (25min., €5.50); and other coastal towns. TGV to **Paris** (5hr.) via **Marseille** €79-97.

Buses: Rapide Côte D'Azur, pl. de l'Hôtel de Ville (☎04 93 39 11 39). To **Nice** (1½hr., every 20min., €5.90) and **Nice airport** (60min.; every 30min. M-Sa 7am-7pm, Su 8:30am-7pm; €12.60, under 25 €10). Buses to **Grasse** (50min., every 45min., €4) leave from the train station.

Public Transportation: Bus Azur, pl. de l'Hôtel de Ville (☎08 25 82 55 99). Info desk and ticket sales M-F 7am-7pm, Sa 8:30am-noon and 2-6:30pm. Tickets €1.30, *carnet* of 10 €8.80, weekly pass €9.80. Purchase onboard.

Taxis: Allô Taxis Cannes (☎04 92 99 27 27).

Bike and Scooter Rental: Holiday Bikes, 32 av. du Maréchal Juin (☎04 93 94 30 34). Bikes from €14 per day, €56 per week, €150 deposit; scooters from €35/€210/ €750. Open M-Sa 9am-noon and 2-7pm, Su 10am-noon and 6-7pm. AmEx/MC/V.

✦ ℹ ORIENTATION AND PRACTICAL INFORMATION

The *centre ville*, between the train station and the sea, is the city's shopping hub; **rue d'Antibes** runs through its center. Heading right from the station on rue Jean-Jaurès, you come to the old city, known as **le Suquet**, where flea-market-style shopping dominates **rue Meynadier** by day and upscale dining enlivens tiny **rue St-Antoine** by night. Stargazers should follow rue des Serbes (across from the station) down to **boulevard de la Croisette**. The tourist office is on the left in the Palais des Festivals. At the adjacent *vieux port*, Cannes's beautiful beach begins and stretches in both direction along the coast. Toward the east, the peninsular land of clubs known as **Palm Beach** draws sun-seekers and watersports enthusiasts.

Tourist Office: 1 bd. de la Croisette (☎04 93 39 24 53; www.cannes.fr). Smartly-dressed staff books tickets for local events and distributes mountains of maps and brochures. Open daily July-Aug. 9am-8pm; Sept.-June 9am-7pm. Branch office at train station (☎04 93 99 19 77). Open M-Sa 9am-7pm.

Currency Exchange: Azuréene de Change, 17 rue Maréchal-Foch (☎04 93 39 34 37), across from train station. Open daily 8am-7pm.

American Express, 1bis rue Notre Dame (☎04 93 99 05 45). Open M 9:30am-12:30pm and 1:45-5pm, Tu-F 9:15am-6:15pm, Sa 9:30am-12:30pm.

English-Language Bookstore: Cannes English Bookshop, 11 rue Bivouac Napoléon (☎04 93 99 40 08). Open M-Sa 10am-1pm and 2-7pm. AmEx/MC/V.

CÔTE D'AZUR

Laundromat: Point Laverie, 56 bd. Carnot (☎06 09 51 97 91). Open daily 7am-8pm. Wash €5.20, dry €3 for 30min.

Youth Center: Cannes Information Jeunesse, 5 quai St-Pierre (☎04 97 06 46 25, lekiosque625@ville-cannes.fr.) Info on jobs, housing, and leisure activities. Open M-F 8:30am-12:30pm and 2-5pm.

Police: 1 av. de Grasse (☎04 93 06 22 22) and 2 quai St-Pierre (☎08 00 11 71 18).

Hospital: Hôpital des Broussailles, 13 av. des Broussailles (☎04 93 69 70 00).

Internet Access: CyberCafé Institut Riviera Langues, 26 rue de Mimont (☎04 93 99 14 77), offers a chill atmosphere and cheap eats to go with Internet access on 10 computers. €1.50 for 15min., €4 per hr. Open M-F 10am-9:30pm, Su 2-9pm.

Post Office: 22 rue Bivouac Napoléon (☎04 93 06 26 50), near Palais des Festivals. Open M-F 9am-7pm, Sa 9am-noon. Branch office at 34 rue de Mimont (☎04 93 06 27 00). Open M-F 8:30am-noon and 1:30-5pm, Sa 8:30am-noon.

Postal Code: 06400.

▮▮ ACCOMMODATIONS AND CAMPING

For most of the year, it's not hard to get a good night's sleep at a reasonable price. During the film festival, however, hotel rates triple and rooms need to be reserved at least a year in advance. Several conventions at the Palais des Festivals can also drive up prices; be sure to ask before making reservations. Plan early for high season, particularly August. Frequent bus service to the campsite makes it a wise choice for those looking to save pennies.

Hostel Les Iris, 77 bd. Carnot (☎/fax 04 93 68 30 20 or 06 09 45 17 35; www.iris-solola.com). Turn right onto rue Jean-Jaurès and another right onto bd. Carnot. The hostel is on the left. (10min.) Airy rooms with 2-6 new wooden bunks. Terrace restaurant open until 3am, and serves tropical drinks (€5-8). Small cafe offers breakfast (€2) and sandwiches (€2.50-4). Reception 8am-midnight, if you arrive 3-6pm look for the owner in the restaurant; reserve in advance and reception will wait up. Key-code access afterhours. Check-out 11am. Dorms €20. AmEx/MC/V. ❷

Auberge de Jeunesse: Le Chalit, 27 av. du Maréchal Gallieni (☎/fax 04 93 99 22 11 or 06 03 40 70 86). Turn right on bd. Carnot after exiting the station and follow it straight until av. 11 Novembre. Turn right on 11 Nov. and left onto av. Gallieni. Triple-stacked bunks and movie posters fill the small 4- to 8-bed dorms. Security-conscious staff ensures that guests and their belongings remain safe. Internet access €2.50 for 15min. Luggage storage €3. Sheets €3. Reception daily May-Sept. 8:30am-1pm and 5-8pm; Oct.-Apr. 9am-noon and 7-8pm. Lockout 10:30am-5pm. 24hr. access with door code. Online reservations required May-Sept. Dorms May-Sept. €20, Oct.-Apr. €18. ❷

Hôtel Mimont, 39 rue Mimont (☎04 93 39 51 64; canneshotelmimont@minitel.net). Exit the train station to the left, turn left on bd. de la République, another left on rue de Mimont. Cannes's best budget hotel. Spacious rooms lovingly maintained by English-speaking owners. All rooms have TV, phone, and modem jacks. Several with balcony and mini-fridge. Breakfast €5.50. Free luggage storage. Reception 8am-11pm. Singles €29, with shower €33, with shower and toilet €36; doubles €37.50/€44; triples with toilet €51. Extra person €10. Prices 10% higher July-Aug. AmEx/MC/V. ❸

Hôtel Atlantis, 4 rue du 24 Août (☎04 93 39 18 72; www.cannes-hotel-atlantis.com), off rue Jean-Jaurès. English-speaking couple maintains comfortable rooms in the center of town. Most rooms with A/C, all with TV, mini-bar, WI/FI Internet access, and phones. Attic workout room has mini-sauna, massage shower, and small hot tub. Singles €30-35, with shower and toilet €40-50; doubles €40-55/€48-70; triples and quads €55-95. Reserve early for July-Aug. AmEx/MC/V. ❸

Camping: Parc Bellevue, 67 av. Maurice Chevalier (☎04 93 47 28 97; fax 04 93 48 66 25), in La Bocca. Take bus #2 to Chevalier and walk straight for 500m, following signs for the campground. Mobile homes fill this quiet 3-star site, though tents are welcome. Impeccable sanitary blocks, *boulodrome*, large pool (open 9am-8pm), and a restaurant that occasionally hosts dance parties, all among wooded trails and beautiful views. Reception daily 8am-8pm. Laundry €3. Car €2. July-Aug. 1 person with tent €14, 2 people with tent €18. Electricity €3; Showers free. Apr.-June and Sept. €10/€13. Mobile homes July-Aug. €190-580 per week, Apr.-June and Sept. €160-250. ❶

◖ FOOD

Though the city is dominated by higher-end restaurants, good food for a reasonable price does exist in Cannes. There are **markets** on pl. Gambetta and on pl. du Commandant Maria; the best market is the **Forville** market on rue Meynadier and rue Louis Blanc, with a large selection of fruit, vegetables, fish, and flowers. (All open daily 7am-1pm. Closed M in winter.) Pick up supplies at **Champion supermarket,** 6 rue Meynadier. (☎04 93 39 62 13. Open June-Aug. M-Sa 8:30am-7:45pm; Sept.-May 8:30am-7:30pm.) Good restaurants are in the pedestrian zone, particularly along rue Meynadier. Farther along, the narrow, winding streets of le Suquet offer cozy corners for open-air dining, but the charming ambience will add to the bill.

🍴 Aux Bons Enfants, 80 rue Meynadier, offers 3 savory courses for €18. This 3rd-generation restaurant will not disappoint. The chef constructs a simple, excellent *Provençal* menu based on what catches his eye at the morning market. Fridays bring *aioli* (garlic sauce), a local favorite. Open daily May-July and Sept. M-Sa noon-2pm and 7:15-9:30pm; Oct.-Apr. M-F noon-2pm and 7-9pm, Sa noon-2pm. ❹

La Grosse Tartine, 9 rue du Batéguier (☎04 93 68 59 28), serves delectable fish and meat dishes. *Tartines* (€12) are easier on the wallet, but *plats* like the duck breast with figs and grapes (€22) and handmade *foie gras* (€17) are highly recommended. Don't miss the molten chocolate cake (€9). Open M-Sa 7pm-midnight. AmEx/MC/V. ❹

La Fregate, 26 bd. Jean Hibert (☎04 93 39 45 39). This large bar/*brasserie*/cafe does it all for diners, offering an extensive menu of Italian-inspired cuisine around-the-clock. Local youth enjoy pizzas (€8.50-12), pastas (€7.50-12), grilled meats (€11-17), and large salads (€6.50-10) on a bright green and yellow terrace. Open June-Sept. 24hr.; daily Oct.-May 7am-2am. AmEx/MC/V. ❷

Belliard, 1 rue Chabaud (☎04 93 39 42 72; gbelliard@aol.com). This 70-year-old bakery and *salon de thé* has been treating *Cannois* with delectable tarts and baked goods for years. A takeout gourmet plate (€8) includes a selection of 3 meat options, 7 *légumes*, or a choice of a tasty quiche. Open M-Sa 7am-8pm. ❷

La P'tite Maison, 4 rue Marceau (☎04 93 39 93 13). Jazz music and elegant deep-red chairs create a classy atmosphere for enjoying satisfying Mediterranean cuisine. A welcoming staff presents pasta (€10.50-15) and salads (€9.50-13.50), as well as a filling *menu* (€29). The *keftas de boeuf à l'orientale* (€11) and the shrimp skewers (€17.50) are highly recommended. Open M-Th noon-2:30pm and 7:30-10:30pm, F and Sa noon-2:30pm and 7:30-11:30pm, Su 7:30-10:30pm. AmEx/MC/V. ❹

◉ ◖ SIGHTS AND SHOPPING

Perched at the top of the Suquet, **L'Église de la Castre** and its courtyard provide an excellent view of the city below. The inhabitants of Cannes had to fundraise for 80 years to complete the costly structure, which was finally finished in the late 16th century. All that work paid off: the church houses beautiful glass chandeliers and an impressive neo-Gothic organ. (Open daily June-Aug. 9am-noon and 3:15-7pm; Sept.-May 9am-noon and 2:15-6pm. Free.) The adjacent **Musée de la Castre** was formerly the private castle of the monks of Lérins; today it displays collections of ancient relics from the Pacific, Himalayas, and Americas. A small exhibit by Provençal artists recalls life in turn-of-the-century Cannes. The real treat of the museum is the 12th-century chapel, which houses instruments from all over the world. (☎04 93 38 55 26. Open June-Aug. Tu-Su 10am-1pm and 3-7pm; Apr.-May and Sept. 10am-1pm and 2-6pm; Oct.-Mar. 10am-1pm and 2-5pm. €3, students €2.)

The fashion-conscious city of Cannes is blessed with countless high-end boutiques, offering some of the Riviera's best window-shopping. Boulevard de la Croisette is home to the runway names like Cartier, Chanel, and Dior. The (barely) less pricey rue d'Antibes mixes funky shops with classy brand names. Head to rue Meynadier, a street market, for dirt-cheap alternatives and knock-offs.

♫ ⛭ ENTERTAINMENT AND FESTIVALS

Stars and star-seekers descend with pomp and circumstance in Cannes for the world-famous ⛭**Festival International du Film** (May 11-22 in 2005). The festival is invite-only, though celebrity-spotting is always free. July 4 and 14 bring the **Fête Américaine** and **Fête Nationale,** respectively—boisterous celebrations of American and French independence days with spectacular fireworks over the bay. **Les Nuits Musicales du Suquet** are also celebrated in July, with open-air performances by professional musicians along le Suquet. (☎04 92 98 62 77. Tickets €30-37.)

Cannes's three casinos provide multiple ways to lose money. The least exclusive, **Le Casino Croisette,** 1 espace Lucien Barrière, next to the Palais des Festivals, has slot machines, blackjack, and roulette. The Greek-inspired interior comes complete with faux-marble statues and an enormous aquarium. (☎04 92 98 78 00. Cover €10. No dress code for slots. No jeans, t-shirts, or gym shoes for gambling. 18+. Slots open at 10am, gambling daily 8pm-4am. Free entry.)

⛭ NIGHTLIFE

The elite nightspots that make Cannes famous are notoriously exclusive—travelers looking to get in should dress to kill. The cafes and bars near the waterfront stay open all night for just as much fun at half the price. Park yourself with a cold one and watch the nightly fashion show strut by, headed to personal parties in private clubs and at the local casinos. Nightlife thrives around **rue Dr. Gérard Monod.**

⛭ **Morrison's,** 10 rue Teisseire (☎04 92 98 16 17; www.morrisonspub.com). Pub lovers head to Morrison's for casual, friendly company. Mahogany bookshelves and quotes by Irish playwrights cover the walls. Beer from €4.90, Guinness €6.10. Draft pints €3.90. Live music W-Th from 9:30pm. Happy hour daily 5-8pm. Open daily 5pm-2am.

Loft, 13 rue du Dr. Gérard Monod (☎ 06 21 02 37 49). The hot spot for the young and beautiful. Either dress your way in, or pretend like you know someone upstairs. Downstairs, the chic Asian-French restaurant **Tantra** morphs into a club on weekends, and tables serve as dance floors until the party moves upstairs. Live DJ. Open daily Sept.-May 10:30pm-2:30am; June-Aug. Th-Sa 10:30-2:30am

Les Coulisses, 29 rue du Commandant André (☎04 92 99 17 17, www.lescoulisses.com). Nab an outside table at this classy corner bar to watch the partiers come and go from Tantra and Loft. Inside, a lively bar staff keeps customers dancing to live DJs that spin house and hip-hop. Open daily 10:30pm-2:30am.

Le 7, 7 rue Rougières (☎04 93 39 10 36; www.lediscotheque.le7.com). Even Parisians concede to the fame of Le 7, known throughout France for outrageous nightly drag shows. Funky broken mirrors reflect the elaborate costumes onstage. Reservations advised. F-Sa Cover €16, includes 1 drink. Drinks €9.50, secret house cocktail €12.50. Drag shows start at 1:30am. Open daily 11:30pm-dawn.

Zanzibar, 85 rue Félix Faure (☎04 93 39 30 75). Paintings of pouting sailors adorn the walls at Zanzibar, which has served drinks since 1885. Intimate patio and candlelit tavern with silver Poseidons and gold-toned portholes. Cocktails €9. Theme parties 2nd Su of every month. Open daily 6pm-5am, closed Tu Oct.-Apr.

4U Bar, 6 rue des Frères Bradignac (☎04 93 39 71 21). When you're turned away from Loft, join an international, unpretentious crowd for drinks at 4U Bar. Fiber-optic lights and live house music create a relaxed lounge atmosphere. Beer from €3, cocktails €8.50. Open daily July-Aug. 6pm-2:30am; Sept-June closed Su.

GRASSE

You'll know you're in Grasse (pop. 45,000) when the smell of coconut tanning oil turns to lavender and tea rose. Capital of the world's perfume industry for over 200 years, Grasse is home to France's three largest, oldest, and most distinguished *parfumeries*. Prepare to be spritzed with a barrage of flowery scents that will leave you reeling (and the bees overjoyed) when you finally step out into the inland sunlight. The town is also located near the GR4 trail and serves as an excellent base for exploration of the Grand Canyon du Verdon (p. 741).

█▐ TRANSPORTATION AND PRACTICAL INFORMATION. Grasse's proximity to Cannes (15km) makes it a pleasant afternoon excursion. Most tourist destinations are concentrated in the pedestrian *vieille ville* and on the south-facing hillside. The bus station is just above the old city; and nearby **boulevard de Jeu de Ballon** is home to the tourist office annex and the casino. A few steps away is **place aux Aires,** a lively square with restaurants and shops on the edge of the *vieille ville.* Further below lies the **place du Cours,** a large plateau overlooking the valley, within easy reach of the Fragonard perfumery and several museums.

The **bus station,** pl. Notre Dame des Fleurs, has service daily to Cannes (50min.; M-Sa every 30min. 6am-8:35pm, Su every hr. 8am-8pm; €3.80) and Nice (1hr.; July-Aug. 14 per day, Sept.-June 23 per day; €6.30), through the **RCA bus** lines #600 and 500, respectively. (RCA ☎04 93 36 08 43. Office open M-Th 7:30am-12:15pm and 1-4:45pm, F 7:30am-12:15pm and 1-4pm.) Although no trains stop at Grasse, there's an **SNCF info office** across the *place.* (Open M-F 9am-5pm, Sa 9am-noon and 2-5pm.) Next to the Palais des Congrés on cours Honoré Cresp, the **tourist office** hands out maps with a 1½hr. walking tour of the city. For further information on the town's history, 1hr. tours in English (€2) are available July-Aug. on Saturday at 2pm. (☎04 93 36 03 66; fax 04 93 36 86 36. Open July-Sept. M-Sa 9am-7pm, Su 9am-12:30pm and 2-6pm; Oct.-June M-Sa 9am-1pm and 2-6pm.) Exchange currency at Change du Casino, 6 cours Honoré Cresp, several doors down from the tourist office. (☎04 93 36 83 00. Open Tu-Sa 9am-noon and 2-5:30pm.) The **post office** is in the parking garage under the bus station. (☎04 92 42 31 11. Open M-F 9am-noon and 2-5pm, Sa 9am-noon.) **Postal Code:** 06130.

█▐ ACCOMMODATIONS AND FOOD. Grasse has several budget hotels. To get to **Hôtel Ste-Thérèse ❹,** 39 av. Baudoin, climb the street behind the tourist office annex, keeping left and continuing uphill on av. Baudoin (15 minutes). This sparkling hotel offers modest rooms with TV, shower, and a panoramic view stretching all the way to Cannes. Lounge in a sun chair on the blue terrace, or enjoy a sit-

THE BIG SPLURGE

MAKING SCENTS

For a completely unique souvenir of the Côte d'Azur, skip the endless stands of bright yellow ceramics and head to Grasse, where you can make your very own French perfume.

For €40, you can create a customized scent with the help of a Master Perfumer at the Molinard Perfume Factory. The *tarinologie* workshop begins with instruction on the structure and composition of perfume. Every scent has a base note, a heart note, and a top note. Top notes, for example, are generally fruity, light smells that only stay on the skin for 5-15min.

After the brief lesson, focus shifts to the endless rows of jars. Each jar is clearly labeled, with different stickers for various notes. The work is surprisingly exhausting; everything smells divine, and soon noses can no longer distinguish between frankincense and clove. What's more, vanilla and apricot together smell heavenly, but adding a hint of green tea makes the bouquet smell like a pile of dirty socks.

Luckily, the Master Perfumer is here to provide assistance, and, after you've finally found the right combination, she notes your perfume number in a small book so that when you run out of your signature scent she can re-make it and ship it directly.

To reserve, contact Molinard at ☎ 04 92 42 33 11. Workshops 1½-2hr. Sessions in English available upon request. AmEx/MC/V.

down meal in the airy dining room. Wireless Internet access and a homey lounge round out the amenities. (☎ 04 93 36 10 29; www.hotelsaintetherese.com. Breakfast €6, dinner €14. Reception daily 6am-11:30pm. Same-day reservations are often possible. Singles €50, with balcony €68; doubles €60/68; triples €75; quads €95. Extra bed €16. AmEx/MC/V.) **Hôtel des Palmiers ❸**, 17 av. Baudoin, on the way to Hôtel Ste-Thérèse, has plain rooms with small fireplace, shower, slightly weak bedsprings, and TV. (☎/fax 04 93 36 07 24. Breakfast €6. Reception 7am-10pm. Reserve 2 weeks in advance for July-Aug. Singles €36-44; doubles €39-44; triples €45-61; quads €60-79, depending on whether room overlooks av. Baudoin or the lovely hillside. AmEx/MC/V.) The dark **Hôtel Napoléon ❷**, 6 av. Thiers, enjoys a central location near the bus station. Budget-friendly rooms are worn, though all come with TV. (☎ 04 93 36 05 87; napo.grasse@aol.com. Breakfast €5. Hallway shower available. Reception M-F 7am-10:30pm, Sa-Su 8am-10:30pm. Singles with or without toilet €21.40-25, with bath €29; doubles €27.50-30.50, with toilet €32, with bath €38.20; triples with bath €45.80; quads with bath €56.50. AmEx/MC/V.)

A morning **market** fills pl. du Cours. (open W 7am-1pm.) On Saturdays, the flower market on the pl. aux Aires usually offers fruit and vegetable stands to go with the abundance of blossoms (Open 7am-1pm). Stock up on groceries at the **Monoprix supermarket**, rue Paul Goby, near the bus station. (☎ 04 93 36 44 36. Open M-Sa 8:45am-7:30pm.) Dozens of *crêperies* and cafes occupy the streets of the *vieille ville*. Centered around the cobblestoned **place aux Aires**, Grasse's most affordable restaurants also have the best ambiance. Don't miss the **◪Café des Musées**, 1 rue Ossola (☎ 04 92 60 99 00). This small basement cafe serves creative dishes like *l'assiette du berger* (mesclun salad and goat cheese on country bread with walnuts and honey) and delicious homemade desserts (€5.50) in a bright, yellow-tiled interior. (Open daily July-Aug. 8am-7pm; Sept.-June M-Sa 8am-7pm. MC/V.)

◪ SIGHTS AND SMELLS. Even the directionally challenged will have no trouble finding their way to Grasse's three largest *parfumeries;* wafts of musky cologne and *eau de toilette* lead visitors right to the factory doorstep. The best, **◪Fragonard**, 20 bd. Fragonard, gives free tours of its 220-year-old factory, still in use today. On display upstairs is a large collection of perfume bottles ranging from ancient Egyptian to Calvin Klein. (☎ 04 93 36 44 65; www.fragonard.com. Free 20min. tours in English. Open daily June-Sept. 9am-6:30pm; Oct.-May 9am-12:30pm and 2-6pm.) **Molinard**, 60 bd. Victor Hugo,

5min. from the center of town, has a newer factory designed by Gustave Eiffel (of Paris tower fame). The *parfumerie*'s free tours lead past scented soap production, enormous perfume vats, and elaborate, aging bottle labels. If you don't find anything to suit your taste, concoct your own *eau de parfum* at the 1½hr. *Tarinologie* workshop for €40 (see **Making Scents,** opposite page). (☎04 92 42 33 11; www.molinard.com. Free tours in English. Open daily July-Aug. 9am-7pm; May-June and Sept. 9am-6:30pm; Oct. and Apr. 9am-12:30pm and 2-6pm; Nov.-Mar. M-Sa 9am-12:30pm and 2-6pm.) No one likes a stinky king; so Louis XIV's perfume and pomade maker founded the **Galimard** factory, 73 rte. de Cannes, in 1747 to keep the Sun King smelling divine. The factory offers 2hr. sessions with a professional "nose," who'll help you create a personal fragrance for €34 in their Studio des Fragrances. (Reservations necessary.) From the bus station, take bus #600 (dir: Cannes) to La Blauquière (€1.30). At the bus stop, walk downhill for 5min. (☎04 93 09 20 00; www.galimard.com. Free 30min. tours. Open daily June-Sept. 9am-6:30pm; Oct.-May 9am-12:30pm and 2-6pm.)

To make sense of all these scents, head to the superb **Musée International de la Parfumerie,** 8 pl. du Cours Honoré Cresp. Rotating exhibits showcase perfume production from across the world and throughout history—the second floor houses a 3000-year-old mummy's scented hand and foot. (☎04 93 36 01 61. The museum is currently closed for renovations, but is scheduled to reopen in late 2005.) Housed in its namesake's 17th-century villa, the **Musée Jean-Honoré Fragonard,** 23 bd. Fragonard, features originals and reproductions of the libertine painter's work. (☎04 93 36 01 61. Hours and prices are the same as those for the Musée International de la Parfumerie.) The **Musée Provençal du Costume et du Bijou,** next to the Fragonard factory, offers a small collection of 18th- and 19th-century clothing and jewelry. (☎04 93 36 91 42. Open M-Sa 10am-1pm and 2-6pm. Free.)

Perched just above the *vieille ville,* the Romanesque **Cathédrale Notre-Dame-du-Puy** displays three works by Rubens, as well as Jean-Honoré Fragonard's only religious painting, *Lavement des Pieds,* commissioned especially for the Baroque chapel. (☎04 93 36 10 34. Open M-Tu and Th-F 8:30-11:30am and 3-6pm, W 9:30-11:30am and 3-6pm, Sa 9:30-11:30am and 3-7pm, Su 8am-11:15pm.)

 A NOSE BY ANY OTHER NAME... The celebrities of the scent industry are known as "noses," the trade name for the master olfactors who produce high fashion's most famous fragrances. The best noses train for 15 years before ever extracting an essence; by the time they're ready to mix a scent, students have memorized more than 3000 smells (the average person can only handle about 200). It can take up to two years for a nose to mix a new scent, and even the most prolific noses never produce more than 3-4 perfumes per year. Numbering 10 in all of France, noses are hot commodities and are required by contract to renounce alcohol, cigarettes, and spicy foods.

■ **FESTIVALS.** In the middle of May, **Expo-Rose** attracts rose growers from around the world for the largest exhibition of its kind (2005 festival to be held May 13-16, €7.70). The *Grassois* pay tribute to their flowery source of income again in early August at the **Fête du Jasmin.** This fragrant festival centers around flower competitions and the election of a Ms. Jasmin to preside over the festivities.

GRAND CANYON DU VERDON

Sixty kilometers off the coast in Provence's rocky interior, Europe's widest and deepest gorge is a world apart from the comparatively tame beaches and vineyards that make the region famous. The gorge is especially worth a visit if you like watersports; the nearby town of Castellane is home to a micro-industry of adven-

CÔTE D'AZUR

ture outfits and can plan just about any excursion imaginable. Though the tree-speckled, chalky canyon is itself appealing, most people come for the Verdon River and the immense Lac de Ste-Croix into which it flows.

The canyon's most beaten track is **Sentier Martel,** a.k.a. the **GR4** trail. The 6 to 8hr. hike traces the river for 14km from La Maline east to Point Sublime as the gorge widens and narrows, passing through tunnels and caves rumored to have once hidden fugitives. To reach the trailhead, drive east from La Palud/Verdon for 8km until reaching La Maline. Red and white markers at the Chalet de la Maline indicate the route. Bring flashlights for the tunnels, strong footwear, and plenty of water. Though the trail is easily navigable with a free map and directions from the Castellane **tourist office,** guides are available upon request (contact Daniel Duflot, 20 rue Nationale, ☎ 04 92 83 67 24; Jean-Luc Herry, 12 bd. de la Republique, ☎ 04 92 83 75 74; or Anne Delmotte ☎ 06 77 14 18 58 for assistance).

The Verdon River's water ends up in **Lac de Ste-Croix,** at the mouth of the gorge, a perfect spot for canoeing and kayaking. The GR4 trail past La Palud-sur-Verdon takes you there by foot. By car, take D952 past La Palud to Moustiers and follow signs to Ste-Croix-de-Verdon, or take D955 before Moustiers to Comps-Artuby. From there, D71 towards Les Salles-sur-Verdon brings you to the lake.

Castellane, 17km east of the canyon and the largest village in the area, is, unfortunately, a bit of a pain to reach from the coast. VFD **buses** (☎ 08 20 83 38 33) run from Grasse (70min., 1 per day, €16.20). The canyon itself can be equally difficult to access. In July and August, Transports GUICHARD (☎ 04 92 83 64 47) sends a daily **shuttle** from Castellane towards Point Sublime, La Palud, and La Maline (30-75min., 1 per day, €6.80). Otherwise, **taxis** run from Castellane to various points throughout the region (☎ 04 92 83 61 62, €30 and up).

Because shuttle access is so infrequent, it might be worth spending the night in Castellane and heading for the gorge early the next morning. Though small, Castellane offers several good budget accommodations, including **Gite d'étape L'oustau ❶,** chemin des Listes, which is just 2min. from the town center but situated right on the GR4 trail. From the bus stop, turn right on the little road next to the Photo Roc service store. Follow the road until it ends, and make a right onto chemin des Listes. The *Gite d'étape* is on the left. Four to eight bunks with pretty coverlets fill clean rooms with bare walls and wooden ceilings. Hallway toilets and showers are immaculate. (☎ 04 92 83 77 27; fax 04 92 83 78 02. *demi-pension* €32. Breakfast included, 7-9am; dinner 7:30pm. Sheets and towels €2. Reception open 7am-10am and 4:30-11pm. Curfew 11pm. Reserve in advance for July-Aug. Dorms €21. MC/V.) Several budget **restaurants** are located on pl. de la Republique and along rue Nationale. Pick up groceries at the **Petit Casino supermarket** on pl. de l'Église before hitting the trail. (☎ 04 92 83 63 01. MC/V.)

The Castellane **tourist office,** at the end of rue Nationale, hands out bus schedules, free Sentier Martel maps, and brochures on local adventure outfitting companies. (☎ 04 92 83 61 14; www.castellane.org. Open July-Aug. M-Sa 9am-12:30pm and 2-7pm, Su 10am-12:30pm; Sept-Oct. M-Sa 9am-noon and 2-6pm; Nov.-June M-F 9am-12pm and 2-6pm.) Before venturing into the canyon, stock up on hiking gear at **L'Echoppe,** rue Nationale, Castellane's only outdoor outfitter. (☎/fax 04 92 83 60 06. Open daily July-Aug. 8am-8pm; Apr.-May M-Sa 9:30am-noon and 3-7pm; June and Sept. M-Sa 9am-12:30pm and 2:30-7:30pm. Closed Oct.-Mar. V.)

A number of **watersport** outfits run trips through the canyon. **Aboard Rafting,** 8 pl. de l'Église (☎/fax 04 92 83 76 11; www.aboard-rafting.com), offers all types of trips, and **Acti-Raft,** at the end of rue Nationale near the tourist office (☎ 04 92 83 76 64; www.actiraft.com), **Aqua Viva Est,** 12 bd. de la République (☎/fax 04 92 83 75 74; www.aquavivaest.com), and **Aqua Verdon,** 9 rue Nationale (☎/fax 04 92 83 72 75; www.aquaverdon.com), all run comparable outfits. Though **rafting** and **kayaking** are the most conventional, summer water levels are only high enough about twice a week. (Usually Tu and F; for information on water levels call ☎04 92 83 69 07. 1½hr. trip €28-30, half-day trip €37-55, full-day trip €59-75. Reserve ahead.)

The adventurous can try a number of other watersports, including **aquarando, canyoning, hydrospeeding, aqua trekking,** and **water rambling** (call companies for descriptions and rates). Equestrian types can trot their way through the canyon on **horseback** with **Les Pionniers** in La Palud-sur-Verdon. (☎/fax 04 92 77 38 30; www.lespionniers.com. €25 for 2hr., €34 per half-day, €61 per day. Make reservations in advance.) **Bike rental** is available from Aboard Rafting (€10 half-day, €20 full-day, includes helmet and repair kit), while guided **rock climbing** is offered by Acqua Viva Est (€45 half-day, includes equipment).

ST-RAPHAËL AND FRÉJUS

Situated along the Estérel Hills, the twin cities of St-Raphaël and Fréjus provide an excellent base for a visit to St-Tropez. Package tourists flock to the highly commercial beach town of St-Raphaël for its inexpensive accommodations, miles of public sand, and rollicking nightlife. The summer brings hordes of tourists, and independent travelers find the city invaluable as a central rail and bus hub, providing convenient access to the surrounding area. Those more keen on history than golden sand and ice cream stands will enjoy the nearby city of Fréjus, home to imposing Roman ruins and the Riviera's best hostel. Though both towns lack the gloss of St-Tropez, they are far more friendly to budget travelers.

ST-RAPHAËL

To the extent that St-Tropez limits its streets to the classy and glam, the young and brash St-Raphaël (pop. 32,000) seems to welcome everyone else with open arms. The town is really only appealing around the beach. Midway through the summer the boardwalk turns into a carnival in the evenings, packed with gaming booths, and flirting teenagers. While St-Raphaël lacks the sophistication of Cannes and St-Tropez, its long, sandy beach, lively port, and relative affordability make it an attractive base for visits to St-Tropez or Fréjus.

◤◪ TRANSPORTATION AND PRACTICAL INFORMATION

St-Raphaël is a major stop on the coastal rail line, shuttling passengers between the resort towns along this part of the country. The city is separated from Cannes by the **Massif de l'Estérel,** 40km of volcanic rock and vegetation. There are hotels and restaurants near the train station, a few blocks from the rue Waldeck Rousseau exit.

Trains run from pl. de la Gare to: Cannes (25min., every 30min., €5.30); Marseille (1¾hr., every hr., €18.20); Nice (1hr., every 30min., €8.90). Ticket booths are open daily 6:30am-9pm. Info office is open daily 6:30am-10pm. **Buses** leave from behind the train station. **Esterel Cars** (☎04 94 53 78 46) serves Fréjus (25min., every hr. 7:30am-6:40pm, €1.10). Service is more frequent in July and August; pick up a schedule from the bus station or tourist office. **Sodetrav** (☎04 94 95 24 82) goes to St-Tropez (1½hr., 11 per day 6:25am-9pm, €8.70). **Beltrame** (☎04 94 95 95 16) goes to Cannes via Trayas (1¼hr., 8 per day, €5.80) and to the airport in Nice (1¼hr., 4 per day, €17.70). **Taxis** (☎04 94 83 24 24) wait outside the train station. **Les Bateaux de St-Raphaël ferries** at the old port go to St-Tropez. (☎04 94 95 17 46; www.tmr-saintraphael.com. 50min.; July-Aug. 5 per day, Sept.-June 2 per day; €11 one-way, €20 round-trip. Those at the hostel in Fréjus should ask about 10% discounts.)

CÔTE D'AZUR

The friendly **tourist office,** opposite the train station on rue Waldeck Rousseau, books accommodations. (☎04 94 19 52 52; www.saint-raphael.com. Open daily July-Aug. 9am-7pm; Sept.-June M-Sa 9am-12:30pm and 2-6:30pm.) Pick up info on jobs, housing, classes, and cheap travel at **Information Jeunesse,** 21 pl. Gallieni, just below the Hotel de France. (☎04 94 19 47 38. Open M-Th 8am-noon and 1:30-5pm, F 8am-noon and 1:30-4:30pm.) The **police** (☎04 94 95 24 24) are on rue de Châteaudun. Top Pressing, 34 av. Général Leclerc, provides **laundry** services. (Open M and W-F 8-12:15pm and 1:30-6pm, Sa and Su 8am-12:15pm. Wash €4.70, dry €2-3.40.) For **Internet** access, drop by Cyber Bureau, 123 rue Waldeck Rousseau, in the shopping center beside the train station, which has six computers. (☎04 94 95 29 36. €2 for 15min., €4 for 30min, €7 per hr. Open Sept.-June M-F 9am-7pm, Sa 9am-1pm. Longer hours July-Aug.) The **post office** is on av. Victor Hugo, behind the station. (☎04 94 19 52 00. Open M-F 9am-5pm, Sa 8am-noon.) **Postal Code:** 83700.

■ ACCOMMODATIONS

Package tourism runs rampant in St-Raphaël, making the independent traveler feel like the only person in the world who has not purchased a scuba excursion to go with the traditional room-and-breakfast combo. Nonetheless, it's worth braving the convenient "deals"—accommodations are more plentiful here than in Fréjus and far cheaper than in St-Tropez. By far the best deal in town, **Hôtel les Pyramides ❸,** 77 av. Paul Doumer, offers basic but well-kept rooms just minutes from the waterfront. The spacious lounge and outdoor patio are great spots to relax after a day in the sun. All rooms have A/C, toilet, shower, and TV, and some have balconies. Exit left from the station, make a right onto av. Henri Vadon, and take the first left onto av. Paul Doumer. (☎04 98 11 10 10; www.saint-raphael.com/pyramides. Breakfast €7. Reception daily 7am-9pm. Check-in July-Aug. 2pm; mid-Mar. to June and Sept. to mid-Nov. 1pm. Reservations required. Open mid-Mar. to mid-Nov. Singles €26; doubles €37-55; triples €57; quads €67. Extra bed €13. Prices €5 higher July-Aug. MC/V.) Right on the lively waterfront, **Le Touring ❹,** 1 quai Albert I, has efficient staff and welcoming rooms. A bar and *brasserie* provide a prime port views. Exit the station on the right; Albert I is the third left at the water. (☎04 94 95 01 72; letouring@wanadoo.fr. Breakfast €4. 24hr. reception July and Aug., 7am-8pm otherwise. Closed mid-Nov. to mid-Dec. Reservations necessary. Singles and doubles with one bed and shower €32-41, with toilet €40, in summer €56; sea views €4 extra. Triples with bath €65. AmEx/MC/V.) Bright rooms and a sunflowery restaurant make a stay at **La Bonne Auberge ❸,** 54 rue de la Garonne, near the train tracks, a refreshing experience. Most rooms have spotless bathroom and shower, some share hallway toilets. (☎04 94 95 69 72 and 06 64 43 94 64. Breakfast €5. Dinner *menus* from €11.50. Free luggage storage. Open Feb.-Nov. Reception 7am-8pm. Reservations necessary. Singles €25-35; doubles €35-50; triples and quads €37-50. MC/V.) Ask for scuba package discounts at **Aventures Sous-Marine** (☎04 94 19 33 70), just next door.

◪ ▣ FOOD AND NIGHTLIFE

It's hard to come by interesting dining spots in a town where most meals are packaged with their rooms. The most lively and affordable restaurants are near the **old port,** quai Albert I, and snack and ice cream stands stretch down cours Jean Bart into Fréjus. The **Monoprix supermarket** is at 14 bd. de Félix Martin, near the train station. (☎04 94 19 82 82. Open M-Sa 8am-8pm.) **Morning markets** color pl. Victor Hugo, down the hill from the bus station, and pl. de la République. Find fresh fish at the old port. (All markets Tu-Su 7am-12:30pm.) Enjoy delicious thin-crust pizzas (€6.50-9) as well as meat and seafood dishes (€8-16) at local favorite **La Romana ❷**, 155 bd. de la Libération. A gregarious staff and the softest napkins you'll ever feel (honestly!) make this Italian wannabe the best choice on the boardwalk. For another dependable, good meal, try **Le Grillardin ❸**, 42 rue Thiers. An enormous white stone hearth is the focus of this restaurant, which provides delicious grilled meats (€11-18), wood-fired pizzas (€6.40-11.70) and tasty fish (€10-16). The house speciality is the *marmite de pêcheur* (€16), a thick soup made from fish, olive oil, and cheese. (☎04 94 40 46 14. *Menus* €16 and €25. Open daily July-Sept. 7pm-1am, also Tu and Th-Sa noon-2pm; Oct.-May M-Tu and Th-Su noon-2pm and 7-10pm. MC/V.) At night, sunbaked clubbers head to **La Réserve**, promenade René Coty, one of the only beachfront hot spots St-Raphaël has to offer. (☎04 94 95 02 20. www.lareserve.fr. Cover €13, includes one drink. Open daily July-Aug. 11:30pm-5am, Sept.-June F-Sa 11pm-5am.)

🏖 🎏 BEACHES AND FESTIVALS

Thirty kilometers of public golden sand run along the coast from St-Raphaël west through Fréjus, and in peak season every square inch that isn't covered with roasting bodies is taken up by an ice-cream vendor, snack stand, or mini-carnival ride. Avoid the crowds by heading east through Boulouris. The beach in Dramont is particularly stunning; to get there take bus #8 (dir: Trayas) from the *centre ville.* The first weekend in July brings the **Compétition Internationale de Jazz New Orleans**, a 23-year-old tradition in St-Raphaël. Professional and amateur musicians face off in the streets and around the port. The festival culminates in a final competition on the Palais des Congrès concourse. Call the cultural center (☎04 98 11 89 00) or the tourist office for details.

FRÉJUS

Founded by Julius Caesar in the first century BC, Fréjus is a charming town filled with Roman ruins whose presence have earned it the nickname "Pompeii of Provence." The crumbling ruins are situated between cafes, modern shops, and high-rise apartments, in the classic old-meets-new French style. A superb hostel, quiet town center, and impressive sights make Fréjus a welcome change from the constant beach party next door in St-Raphaël.

▮ TRANSPORTATION

Regular buses connect Fréjus to St-Raphaël until 7:10pm (6:05pm on Su), later July and August; ask for schedule at the tourist office. Fréjus's **train station** on rue Martin Bidoure (☎08 92 35 35 35) is little-used—St-Raphaël processes most of the town's traffic. Limited service runs to: St-Raphaël (5min., 12 per day, €1.20); Cannes (25min., 12 per day, €5.80); Marseille (1¾hr., 5 per day, €19.10); Nice (1½hr., 12 per day, €9.60). **Local buses** (€1.10) connect the *vieille ville* to the beach and daytrips. The **bus station,** pl. Paul Vernet (☎04 94 53 78 46), is next to the tourist office. (Open M-F 8:30am-12pm and 2-5:30pm, Sa 9am-noon.) For taxis, call ☎04 94 51 51 12 (stand in pl. Vernet).

▰ ▰ ORIENTATION AND PRACTICAL INFORMATION

Fréjus's 7km beach, a 20min. walk from the town center, is closer physically and spiritually to St-Raphaël than to Fréjus; visitors should stick to the *vieille ville* and its surrounding sights. To get to the **tourist office,** 325 rue Jean Jaurès, from St-Raphaël, take bus #6 to pl. Paul Vernet. The office offers guided tours in English once a week July and August; contact the office for details. (☎ 04 94 51 83 83; www.ville-frejus.fr. Tours €5, students €3. Office open July-Aug. M-Sa 10am-noon and 2:30-6:30pm, Su 10am-noon and 3-6pm; Sept.-June M-Sa 10am-noon and 2-6pm, Su 10am-noon and 3-6pm.) The **hospital**, Centre Hospitalier Intercommunal (☎ 04 94 40 21 21), is on the corner of av. André Léotard and av. de St-Lambert. The **police** (☎ 04 94 51 90 00) are on rue de Triberg. The **post office**, av. Aristide Briand, is just down the hill from the tourist office. (☎ 04 94 17 60 80. Open M-F 8am-6:30pm, Sa 8am-12:30pm, closed 12:30-1:30pm the 3rd Th of every month.) **Postal Code:** 83600.

ACCOMMODATIONS

Fréjus is home to one of the best hostels on the Côte: the ☒**Auberge de Jeunesse de St-Raphaël-Fréjus (HI) ❶**, chemin du Counillier. From the tourist office, take av. du 15ème Corps d'Armée. Turn left on chemin de Counillier after the second round-about. From Fréjus, bus #10 (€1.10) leaves from behind the bus station for the hostel at 6:30pm. From St-Raphaël, buses (every hr. 7:20am-7pm) head to "Les Chênes" (or "Paul Vernet," a farther but more frequent stop); walk up av. Jean Calliès to chemin du Counillier. There is a shuttle from the *auberge* to the beach and to the St-Raphaël train station daily at 8:50am. (9:05am on Sun.) This secluded hostel is complete with immaculate showers and a 170-acre spread of parkland. Ask about discounts on bike rentals, canoes, sailing lessons, and ferry tickets. (☎ 04 94 53 18 75; fax 04 94 53 25 86; frejus-st-raphael@fuaj.org. Breakfast included (8-9:15am). Kitchen 6-9pm. Sheets €2.80. Laundry €3. Reception daily 8-11am and 5:30-10pm; phone for reservations during these hours. Lockout 11am-5:30pm. Curfew July-Aug. 11:30pm; Sept.-June 10pm. Closed Nov.-Feb. Dorms €13; quads with shower and toilet €15. Camping €10 per person with tent.) Dior and Lancôme posters adorn the walls of ☒**Hôtel Le Flore ❹**, 35 rue Grisolle, just down the street from Hotel La Riviera. Each lovely room is named after a flower and comes with its own sparkling bathroom. (☎ 04 94 51 38 35; fax 04 94 53 25 86; hotelle-flore@aol.com. Breakfast €7. Reserve ahead in summer. Singles and doubles €50-60; triples €75-80; quads €90-120. MC/V.) Near the center of town, **Hôtel La Riviera ❸**, 90 rue Grisolle, has functional rooms and a friendly anglophone staff. To get there from pl. Paul Vernet, walk straight down rue Jean Jaurès past pl. de la Liberté, and turn left on rue Grisolle. (☎ 04 94 51 31 46; fax 04 94 17 18 34. Breakfast €5. Guests must be out of their rooms for the day by 10am. Reservations necessary in summer. Singles and doubles €27-29, with shower €36-39; triples €39.50-47.10; quads €47.60-55.20. MC/V.)

FOOD

The **marché Provençal** fills rue de Fleury and pl. Formigé on Wednesday and Saturday mornings with fruits and vegetables in addition to Provençal knick-knacks and handmade trinkets. The bus from the hostel will drop shoppers off directly. There's an **Intermarché supermarket**, av. du 15ème corps de l'Armée, at the second roundabout on the way to the hostel. (☎ 04 94 53 30 70. Open M-Sa 8:30am-8pm, Su 9:30am-12:30pm.) Budget restaurants cluster around **place de la Liberté** and **place Paul Albert Février**. Nearby, **Les Micocouliers ❸**, pl. Paul-Albert Février, serves classic regional dishes like *boeuf à la Provençale* (€11.50) and *soupe au poissons* (Fish soup, €9) on pleasant outdoor tables. (☎ 04 94 52 16 52. *Plats du jour* €8-10, pasta €7.50, *salade niçoise* €8. 3-course *menu* provençal €17. Open daily noon-2:30pm and 6:30-10pm. MC/V.) The staff at **Faubourg de Saigon ❷**, 126 rue St-François de Paule, off rue Jean Jaurès, presents excellent, authentic Vietnamese dishes (around €8) in a paper-lantern-filled interior. The almond chicken is a favorite for the locals.

CÔTE D'AZUR (side margin)

(☎ 04 94 53 65 80. *Menu* €15. Open daily 11am-2pm and 6:30-10:30pm, no lunch service on M. MC/V.) In the small dining room at **La Riviera ❷**, 90 rue Grisolle, locals chat over simple but tasty French dishes. (☎ 04 94 51 31 46. Salads €4.60-7.50, omelettes €3.10-7.50, pasta €6.50-8.50, meat €8.50-14.50, fish €6.50-11.50. *Menus* €12.50 and €17. Open Tu-Su noon-2pm and 7-10pm).

◎ SIGHTS

THE FRÉJUS EPISCOPAL BUILDINGS. This remarkable cluster of buildings is situated on what is presumed to be the site of the ancient Roman town center. Today, the baptistry and cathedral, retain their central position at the heart of Fréjus's *vieille ville*. The products of 2000 years of building and rebuilding, the octagonal **baptistry**, constructed in the fifth century AD, is one of France's oldest buildings. The eight pillars that support it were carved in pairs from a single block of granite. During restoration, workers discovered the remains of the white marble baptismal pool. The spectacular 12th- to 14th- century **cloister** features a larch wood ceiling decorated with over 1200 miniature paintings. Far less imaginative, though still intriguing, is the austere Gothic **cathedral.** The gruesome scene on the door is thought to be a reproduction of the Saracen raids on Fréjus which took place in the 10th century. *(Pl. Formigé. ☎ 04 94 51 26 30. Cloister open daily June-Sept. 9am-6:30pm; Oct.-May Tu-Su 9am-noon and 2-5pm. €4.60, students €3.10. Doors and baptistry accessible only by 40min. guided tour in French. Accompanying English, German, Italian, or Spanish written explanations available. Cathedral open daily 8am-noon and 2:30-7pm.)*

ROMAN RUINS. Built in the first and second centuries AD to entertain 10,000 rowdy, homesick soldiers, the **Roman Amphitheater** lacks the embellishments of those in Nîmes or Arles, which were designed for more discerning patrician eyes. Yet Christians and lions were slaughtered here just as frequently as in Rome. Today, musicians and matadors, play here in rock concerts and two bullfights. *(Rue Henri Vadon. ☎ 04 94 51 34 31. From the tourist office, take rue Jean Jaurès to pl. de la Liberté, then turn right on rue de Gaulle. Open Apr.-Oct. M-Tu and Th-Sa 10am-1pm and 2:30-6:30pm; Nov.-Mar. M-F 10am-noon and 1:30-5:30pm, Sa 9:30am-12:30pm and 1:30-5:30pm. Free. Bullfights July 14 and Aug. 15; €22-61. Contact tourist office for concert schedule.)* The original wall of Fréjus's other ancient forum, the **Roman Theater,** remains intact; the rest of the structure now hosts concerts and plays. In July, the remains of the theater are turned into an outdoor performance space for **Les Nuits Auréliennes,** a week-long theater festival. *(☎ 04 94 53 58 75. From the roundabout at the tourist office, go about 250m on rue Grande Bretagne. Open Apr.-Oct. M-Sa 10am-1pm and 2:30-6:30pm, Su 8am-7pm; Nov.-Mar. M-F 10am-noon and 1:30-5:30pm, Su 8am-5pm. Free.)* Pillars and arches are all that remain of an **aqueduct,** past the theater along av. du 15ème Corps d'Armée.

OTHER SIGHTS. Fréjus's other sights, neither medieval nor ancient, can be ignored by those pressed for time. **Villa Aurélienne,** on the hill next to the hostel and surrounded by an immense park, is an elegant 19th-century private home which features photographic exhibits. *(Av. du Général d'Aimée Calliès. Call the tourist office for exhibit info. Open daily 2-7pm.)* **The Pagode Hong-Hiên** was built in 1917 by Vietnamese soldiers who decided to settle in Fréjus after fighting alongside the French in WWI. Pink plastic figurines, an enormous reclining Buddha, and a cartoon-letter sign give the entire area a kitschy feel. Nonetheless, the main temple is still used daily as a place of worship. *(13 rue H. Giraud, 10min. up av. Jean Calliès from the hostel. ☎ 04 94 53 25 29. Open daily 9am-noon and 2-7pm. €1.50.)* Two minutes farther up av. Jean Calliès is the **Mémorial des Guerres en Indochine,** a stone monument engraved with thousands of names of French and Vietnamese soldiers killed in the Indo-Chinese war. A one-room photographic history display includes detailed maps and dioramas. (☎ 04 94 44 42 90. Open daily 10am-5:30pm. Museum closed Tu. Free.)

Outdoor enthusiasts can't miss Fréjus's enormous **Base Nature,** a 150-acre site on the beach reserved for all things action-related. A former Air Force and Navy base, the nature reserve is now open to the public. Separate areas are designated for trail running, BMX, football, rugby, basketball, *boules,* swimming, and a skate park. In October, the converted airplane hangar houses the **Roc d'Azur,** billed as the largest all-terrain biking competition in the world. The windy location makes for great cart-sailing, a combination of wind and wheels that allows enthusiasts to "sail" on land. From pl. Paul Vernet, take bus #6 (dir: St-Raphaël, 15min., €1.10) to Base Aeronavale. (☎ 04 94 51 91 10. Open daily June-Sept. 8am-9pm; Oct.-May 8am-6pm. Free access, price of equipment rental varies. Call the sports reception center for details.)

ST-TROPEZ

Nowhere is the glitz and glamour of the Riviera more apparent than in St-Tropez (pop. 5400). Originally a small fishing hamlet, St-Tropez first came into public view in 1892 with the arrival of Paul Signac and Post-Impressionist artists. Sixty-four years later, Brigitte Bardot's nude bathing scene in *Et Dieu Créa la Femme* (And God Created Woman) sealed the town's celebrity status. Ever since, the former village has bewitched everyone from Hollywood stars and corporate giants to day-tripping backpackers. Fashionistas, yachtsmen, and ogling tourists all rub elbows on the *vieux port* and in the narrow, shop-lined streets. Whether you arrive by mega-yacht, private limo, broken-down bicycle, or on foot, the charm and glamor of this high-society playground is truly captivating.

CÔTE D'AZUR

TRANSPORTATION. Reaching the "Jewel of the Riviera" requires some effort, as it lies well off the rail line, and it's another hassle altogether to leave town for the outlying beaches and villages. The town itself is condensed and pedestrian-friendly, with constant activity along the **port** and throughout **place des Lices.**

The fastest and cheapest way to get here is by **boat. Les Bateaux de St-Raphaël** (☎ 04 94 95 17 46; www.tmr-saintraphael.com), at the old port, sail in from St-Raphaël (1hr.; July-Aug. 5 per day, Sept.-June 2 per day; €11 one-way, €20 round-trip). Otherwise, **Sodetrav buses** (☎ 04 94 97 88 51) leave from av. Général Leclerc, across from the ferry dock, for St-Raphaël (1½-2¼hr.; July-Aug. 14 per day, Sept.-June 10 per day; €8.70) and Toulon (2¼hr.; July-Aug. 15 per day, Sept.-June 9 per day; €16.60). Bus station open July-Aug. M-Sa 8:15am-8pm, Su 10:15am-1:30pm; Sept.-June M-F 10:15am-12:15pm and 2-6pm, Sa 10:15am-12:15pm. Rent a **bike** or **moped** at Louis Mas, 3-5 rue Quarenta. (☎ 04 94 97 00 60. Bikes €10 per day; deposit €50. Mopeds €34-50, deposit €205-305. Open Easter to mid-June M-Sa 9am-12:30pm and 2-6:30pm, Su 10am-1pm and 6-7:30pm; July-Aug. M-Sa 9am-6:30pm, Su 10am-1pm and 6-7:30pm. AmEx/MC/V.) For **taxis,** call ☎ 04 94 97 05 27 or hail one from the Musée de l'Annonciade.

PRACTICAL INFORMATION. The **tourist office** is on the corner of quai Jean Jaurès and rue V. Laugier, facing the port. The well-dressed staff distributes schedules for the municipal *navette* (shuttle) system (€1), free maps, and the *Manifestations* event guide. They also assist with same-night accommodations booking. (☎ 04 94 97 45 21; www.saint-tropez.st. Open daily late June-early Sept. 9:30am-8:00pm; early Sept.-early Oct. and mid-May to late June 9:30am-12:30pm and 2-7pm; late Mar. to mid-May 9:30am-12:30pm and 2-7pm; early Nov.-late Mar. 9:30am-12:30pm and 2-6pm.) Master Change, 18 rue Gen. Allard, offers **currency exchange**

at the old port. (☎04 94 97 80 17. Open Mar.-June and Sept.-Oct. M-Sa 9am-8:30pm, Su 10am-noon and 5-8pm; July-Aug. 9am-10pm.) There's **Internet** as well as cocktails at La Girafe, 36 rue du Portail Neuf, 2min. from the tourist office. (☎04 94 97 13 09. €2.50 for 15min., €0.12 per additional min., approx. €3.50 for 30min. Beer €2.50-6, cocktails €6-11. Open daily July-Aug. 10am-3am; Sept.-June 10am-1pm and 3pm-3am.) **Laundromat** Laverie du Port "Anne-Marie," 13 quai de l'Epi, charges €5.50 to wash clothes and €2 to dry. (Open July-Aug. M-Sa 7am-9pm; Sept.-June 9am-1pm and 3-7pm.) The **police** (☎04 94 54 86 65) are on rue François Sibilli near the church, and on av. Général Leclerc by the new port. The **hospital** (☎04 98 12 50 00) is on av. Foch, off pl. des Lices. There is a **post office** on pl. A. Celli between the new and old ports. (☎04 94 55 96 50. Open M-F 8:30am-noon and 2-5pm, Sa 8:30am-noon. Opens at 9:30am on the 2nd and 4th Th of every month.) **Postal Code:** 83990.

⌘ ACCOMMODATIONS. Hotels are plentiful but incredibly pricey in St-Tropez; without a reservation made far in advance, it's difficult to get here and find same-day accommodations at reasonable rates. A stay in St-Raphaël or Hyères is easier on the wallet but forces visitors to limit their time here, though staying up all night in St-Tropez and heading out the next morning is also an option. The closest hostel is in Fréjus. Camping is the cheapest option, though no sites are within walking distance of the town. A ferry connects the campsite at Port Grimaud with the peninsula (see **Daytrips,** p. 752), and shuttles run from the center of town to the smaller grounds flanking St-Tropez's beaches. These are popular and often full; book months in advance for the summer. Camping on the beach is actively prohibited.

One of the most affordable hotels is **Lou Cagnard ❹**, 18 av. Paul Roussel, a 3min. walk from pl. des Lices. Nineteen impeccably maintained rooms overlook the avenue or the peaceful back garden. All rooms have a shower and telephone. (☎04 94 97 04 24; www.hotel-lou-cagnard.com. Breakfast €8. Free parking for guests. Reception 8am-9pm. Closed early Nov. to late Dec. Singles and doubles €44-53, with toilet €53-100; 1 triple €115. 1-week min. stay. MC/V.) Another good option is **La Belle Isnarde ❹**, rte. de Tahiti, about a 15min. walk from the bus station. From the pl. des Lices, take a right on av. du Maréchal Foch, a quick right onto rue de la Résistance, and a left onto av. de la Résistance, which becomes chemin des Belles Isnarde. From there, the hotel is up on the left. Though farther from town, this old converted farmhouse offers spacious rooms. The only sign of farm

THE LOCAL STORY

TRASHY TO FLASHY

They say that to be classy, you have to be born that way. Never fear, lovably disheveled, un-glam travelers—even the most glossy towns have their humble, even gruesome, beginnings. According to legend, the ultra-chic town that now harbors some of the world's most expensive yachts was founded by the arrival of a headless dead body in a small boat.

During the first century AD, a Roman by the name of Torpes, who was responsible for guarding St. Paul, managed to avoid punishment by successfully converting his master to Christianity. At a feast in honor of the goddess Diana, Torpes proclaimed his new faith in front of the whole community, Emperor Nero included.

Nero was so infuriated that he beheaded Torpes and set his decapitated body in a boat headed down the Arno River. Ligurian currents carried the boat to sea, where it eventually washed ashore at Heraclée, now the port of St-Tropez. A pious Roman found the body and hid it for secret worship as a saint (Saint-Tropez) by local Christians.

The Ligurian currents still run from Italy to the port, though today they tend to bring wealthy sun-seekers instead of mangled martyrs. Occasionally, however, a bag of trash or two will find its way across the ocean, and all the way into St-Tropez, reminding its classy visitors that everything has its less glamorous side.

life today is the owner's dog Toby, who can't get enough of his job as professional greeter. (☎04 94 97 13 64 and 04 94 97 57 74. Breakfast €7. Reception 7am-10pm. Closed mid-Oct. to mid-Apr. Singles and doubles with shower €50-58, with shower and toilet €60-68.)

🏕 **CAMPING.** Campazur runs three campsites close to St-Tropez. Campers have it lucky at **Les Prairies de la Mer ❶**, Port Grimaud. The huge, social site is near a beach and the canals of Port Grimaud, "France's Venice." Amenities include hot showers, tennis, and watersports. Internationally themed shower blocks make bathing a whole new world. (☎04 94 79 09 09; www.campazur.com. Open early Apr.-early Oct. Early July-late Aug. €40, extra person €6, electricity included; early Apr.-early July 2 people, tent, and car €20-27, extra person €3, electricity €5; late Aug.-early Oct. €20-25, extra person €3, electricity €5. Laundry available.) The **MMJ ferry** leaves the *capitainerie* 3min. away for St-Tropez. (every hr.) (☎04 94 96 51 00; €9 round-trip.) The smaller **Kon Tiki ❶** has a choice location near the northern stretch of Pampelonne Beach. Campers soak up sun by day and the parties (Kon Tiki's own bar) by night. (☎04 94 55 96 96; kontiki@campazur.com. Extra person €5/€10, other prices and dates are same as above.) Next door is **Toison d'Or ❶**, the smallest of the three sites. (☎04 94 79 83 54; toison@campazur.com. Same dates and prices as above.) The lively Kon Tiki/Toison d'Or complex has a supermarket, laundromat, tennis, archery, ping-pong, and restaurants and snack bars. Free shuttles to local markets in St-Tropez on Tuesday and Saturday, Internet access in the reception area (€3 for 15min.) and an on-site scuba diving instruction center are among the amenities offered. In July and August, Sodetrav sends a bus from the St-Tropez station to both sites daily. (11:35am, 2:10, 4, 5:40pm; €1.60.) Otherwise, take the municipal shuttle (M-Sa 4 per day, €1) from pl. des Lices to Capon-Pinet. Head downhill and follow the signs to the Plage Tahiti.

🍴 **FOOD.** St-Tropez's vibrant restaurant and cafe scene lies along the old port and the narrow streets behind the waterfront. Save your pennies for ridiculous club cover charges by grabbing *paninis* and pastries from the snack shops and *boulangeries* near **place des Lices.** For fruits and vegetables, as well as an extensive array of antiques, books, and clothing, try the fabulous **grand marché** on pl. des Lices (Tu and Sa 7:30am-1pm), or the **morning market** on pl. aux Herbes, behind the tourist office. There's a **Monoprix supermarket,** 9 av. Général Leclerc (☎04 94 97 07 94; open daily July-Aug. 8am-10pm, Sept.-June 8am-7:50pm) and a **SPAR** market, 16 bd. Vasserot, on pl. des Lices. (☎04 94 97 02 20. Open Apr.-Sept. M-Sa 7:30am-7:30pm, Su 8am-1pm and 4-7:30pm; Oct.-Mar. M-Sa 7:30am-1pm and 3:30-7:30pm, Su 8am-1pm and 4-7:30pm.) At **La Tarte Tropézienne ❷**, pl. des Lices, mounds of croissants, *pain au chocolat*, and other baked goods and pastries (including the local speciality, *la tarte tropézienne*) delight even the most discerning sweet tooth (open daily July-Aug. 6:30am-11pm; Sept.-June 8:30am-8pm). Visitors won't regret splurging at **l'Aventure ❸**, 21 rue du Portail Neuf, a local favorite that specializes in traditional regional cuisine and serves creative and exquisitely presented *plats du jour* for €10. (☎04 94 97 44 01. Open daily July-Aug. noon-2pm and 7-11pm. Sept.-June closed W. AmEx/MC/V.) Another great option is **La Grange ❸**, 9 rue du Petit St. Jean, which offers delicious handmade pastas (€14.50-25) in a farm-inspired setting. (☎04 94 97 09 62. Open daily 8pm-12:30am. AmEx/MC/V.) Head to the **Grand Marnier ❶** crêpe stand, 2 rue des Remparts, where cheerful chefs in full uniform dole out French treats. Crêpes are €2.70-€3.50; add as much Grand Marnier as you'd like for free. (Open daily 3pm-1am.) When a night out leaves you starving, hit the always-open, ever-popular **Délice des Lices ❶**, pl. des Lices. (☎04 94 54 89 84. Hot and cold sandwiches €3.10-4.60. Open 24hr.)

◙ **SIGHTS.** Most travelers don't come to St-Tropez for the museum scene. Nevertheless, **Le Musée de l'Annonciade,** pl. Grammont, right on the port, is a good break from all the sun and sand. This lovely converted chapel houses Fauvist and neo-Impressionist paintings by Signac, Bonnard, and Matisse, among others, as well as a number of images of the Riviera and St-Tropez. (☎04 94 97 04 01. Open June-Sept. M and W-Su 10am-1pm and 4-9pm; Oct.-May 10am-1pm and 4-7pm. €4.60, students €2.30.) **The Citadel** above the port contains the **Musée Naval,** which follows St-Tropez's interesting military history through WWII. (☎04 94 97 59 43. Open daily Apr.-Sept. 10am-12:30pm and 1:30-6:30pm; Oct. and Dec.-Mar. 10am-12:30pm and 1:30-5:30pm. €4, students €2.50.)

▓▒ **NIGHTLIFE AND FESTIVALS.** At the height of St-Tropez's excess and exclusivity is its wild nightlife. Those without transportation have many options within town itself; when the sun sets, the port and the streets behind the waterfront become the stage of the tanned and the glam. **Les Caves du Roy,** in the swanky Hotel Byblos on av. Paul Signac, caters to the *crème de la crème* of the already elite clubbers. Perfect that bored rich-girl pout or high-society swagger, slip on your Gucci sunglasses, and shell out a cool €25,000 for a bottle of Cristal to share with the celebrity next to you at the bar. If things look shaky on the trust fund front, you may have to settle for a slightly more mundane €23 vodka and tonic. (☎04 94 56 68 00; www.lescavesduroy.com. Open daily July-Aug. 11:30pm-4am; June and Sept. F-Sa 11:30pm-4am.) Asian-influenced restaurant/bar **Bodega de Papagayo** (☎04 94 79 29 50), on the old port, and its accompanying nightclub **Le Papagayo** (☎04 94 97 20 01), seem to draw moneyed youth and soccer stars. (Cocktails €13. Club cover €25, includes one drink. Open daily June-Sept. 8:30pm-4am, club gets crowded after 1am; Oct.-May M-Tu and Th-Su, hours according to how good the party is.) Step through the white beaded curtains at the **VIP Room,** Résidence du Port, to let loose to hip-hop and house in chic 70s-inspired luxe. (☎04 94 97 14 70. Open daily 8pm-5am. No cover.) A down-to-earth anglo crowd frequents **Kelly's Irish Pub,** a rowdy joint near the end of the old port. Plenty of Guinness (€3.50) and live Irish bands welcome even the most fashion-challenged partiers. A genuine smile is all you need for a free ticket to the bar. (☎04 94 54 89 11. Open daily 10:30am-3am.) Give in for the preppie vibe at the garden-party **Bar de la Maison Blanche,** on the back patio of the Maison Blanche hotel on pl. des Lices. Low-hanging trees and a profusion of flowers create a secluded atmosphere for enjoying €15 champagne and cocktails. (04 94 97 52 66. Open daily 7pm-1am.) Framed shadowboxes of champagne pay homage to life's luxurious pleasures at **Café de Paris,** a gold and velvet cafe with an enormous patio just below the Hôtel Sube in the center of the port. At night, house music and funky green-and-blue-lighting transform the slightly stuffy restaurant into a mellow bar. Don't come here if you're looking to kick up your heels; this posh bar is strictly sedentary. (☎04 94 97 00 56; www.cafedeparis.fr. Beer and wine €4.50-8.50, cocktails €11-13. Open daily 7am-3am.) An older, more sophisticated crowd kicks back on the cozy couches at **Nano Salon,** 2 rue Sibille. (☎04 94 97 72 59. Open daily 7pm-3am. Cocktails €10.)

St-Tropez celebrates its historic ties to the idle rich with yearly golf tournaments and sailing regattas, including the famed **Giraglia Rolex Cup,** which concludes with an open-sea race from Saint-Tropez all the way to Genoa. Every May 16-18, during **Les Bravades,** locals pay homage to their military past and patron saint with costumed parades and celebrations throughout the town. June 29 brings **St-Peter's Day** and a torch-lit procession honoring the saint of fishermen. Pick up a copy of *Manifestations* from the tourist office for detailed information on monthly festivities.

◪ **BEACHES.** St-Tropez's pride and joy is its endless white sandy coastline. With the Mediterranean as the ultimate backdrop, the young and beautiful all come to the shore to show off their bronzed, gorgeous selves. Marathon tanning is practically a sport in itself, but those who prefer a more active approach will find a series of watersport companies along the beach. There is a *navette* (municipal shuttle) that leaves from pl. des Lices (schedule varies seasonally, ask the tourist office for current timetable). It heads to **Les Salins** (M-Sa 5 per day, last return shuttle leaves around 6:10pm; €1), a rather secluded sunspot, and to **Capon Pinet** (M-Sa 4 per day, last return shuttle leaves around 5:20pm; €1), the first stretch of the famous Pampelonne beachline. Walking south along the beach, exclusive beach clubs alternate with public sand. Some of the most popular beaches among the young jet-set crowd are **plage Tahiti** and **Key West Beach.** Be warned that lounge chairs in these clubs will cost at least €14 per day; you are better off simply walking along the coast to find a spot to stretch out. A quieter option is to take the *navette* to Les Salins and explore the beaches to the left, or follow the beautiful, rocky **sentier littoral** along the coast to the right until it melds with the Pampelonne beachline, passing a handful of unpopulated swimming spots and celebrity villas on the way (1 hour). Sunbathers who miss the shuttle back to town can take a taxi from Pampelonne Beach to the port, but it will cost €20-30. Fifteen kilometers along the peninsula, great swimming and good rock-climbing await at **plage de L'Escalet,** only accessible by foot or private car. For those without the time or inclination to head to Pampelonne or Cap des Salins, there's a decent spot 10min. from the old port. Facing the port, head to the citadel and find chemin des Graniers, which curves past a local cemetery down to the small **plage des Graniers.** Most spots allow or expect nude sunbathing—in St-Tropez, only tourists have tan lines.

⚡ DAYTRIPS FROM ST-TROPEZ. Less ritzy but more endearing than the city, the villages of the St-Tropez Peninsula make excellent daytrips. With their stunning hilltop settings and unforgettable views, these gems are becoming prized real estate. Tour groups have discovered them, so come now before the prices double.

The best of the peninsula is delightful **Grimaud.** Until the 17th century, the castle of Grimaud controlled the Gulf of St-Tropez, known as the "Gulf of Grimaud" until the late 19th century. From its high towers, you can look down on the medieval village itself. Few can resist the charm of Grimaud's cobblestoned lanes and fountain-filled *places.* Above the fairy-tale **place Neuve,** signs point to the Romanesque **Église St-Michel,** one of three chapels in Grimaud. (Open daily 9am-6pm.)

To get to Grimaud, Sodetrav (☎04 94 97 88 51) sends buses from St-Tropez (30min., M-Sa 13 per day, €3.10). Or, take the ferry to Port Grimaud (20min., every hr.), and catch the hourly *petit train* at the top of the Prairies de la Mer campsite. For non-campers Grimaud has to be a daytrip; it has no budget hotels. The **tourist office** is at 1 bd. des Aliziers, a few doors down from the bus stop. (☎04 94 43 26 98; www.grimaud-provence.com. Open July-Aug. M-Sa 9am-12:30pm and 3-7pm, Su 10am-1pm; Apr.-May, June, and Sept. M-Sa 9am-12:30pm and 2:30-6:15pm; Oct.-Mar. M-Sa 9am-12:30pm and 2:15-5:30pm.)

ÎLES D'HYÈRES

These exotic, underpopulated islands lie off the French coast between St-Tropez and the grimy metropolis of Toulon. Henry II nicknamed them the "Îles d'Or" (Golden Islands) for the way the shale rocks seemed to glow in the sun. Today, things look mostly bronze, thanks to the miles of rough, unspoiled beaches and coves that allow for some of the best nude sunbathing in the region.

Ferries to all 3 islands depart from the town of Hyères, to the east of Toulon. Trains run from Toulon (7 per day, €3.40) and Marseille (4 per day, €11.65). Sodetrav buses (☎04 94 12 55 00) run to Toulon (1hr., every 20min., €4.40) and St-Tropez (1½-2hr., 8 per day, €14), while Phocéens-Cars (☎04 93 85 66 61) goes to Cannes (1½hr., 2 per day, €22) and Nice (2hr., 2 per day, €22). To get to the ferry ports, catch Sodetrav local bus #67 to Port D'Hyères (€1.80) or La Tour Fondue (€1.80). **TLV Ferries** (☎04 94 58 95 14; www.tlv-tvm.com) run to Porquerolles from Tour Fondue. (20min.; July-Aug.

every 30min. 9am-12:30pm and every hr. 2:30-6:30pm; Sept.-June 6-14 per day; round-trip €15, bikes €12.) Ferries (☎04 94 57 44 07) also run to Port-Cros (1hr.) and Île du Levant (1½hr.) from Port D'Hyères (July-Aug. 4 per day, Sept.-June 2 per day; round-trip €22). In July and August, a **boat** from Port D'Hyères connects Port-Cros with Île du Levant (round-trip €26). For those wishing to see both islands in the low season, **Vedettes Îles d'or et Le Corsaire** offers **shuttles** between the two, as well as connections to nearby ports, including Saint-Tropez, Cavalaire, and Croix-Valmer. (☎04 94 71 01 02. Boats depart Port-Cros for Le Levant at 10:15am, 12:15, 5:15pm, though schedule varies. One-way €8.80.)

Since ferry service can be infrequent, Hyères itself serves as an excellent island-hopping base. Just below the Forum de Casino, the **tourist office,** 3 av. Ambroise Thomas, supplies free maps and ferry schedules. (☎04 94 01 84 50; www.ot-hyeres.fr. Open July-Aug. M-Sa 8:30am-7:30pm, Su 3:30-7:30pm; Sept.-June M-F 9am-6pm, Sa 10am-4pm.) A **Casino supermarket** is on av. Gambetta, across from the McDonald's. (Open Tu-Sa 7:30am-12:30pm and 4-7:30pm, Su 8am-noon.) Try **La Brasserie ❸,** 2 rue Léon Gautier (within La Coupole) for a reasonably priced sit-down meal. A good variety of seafood and meat dishes is offered on a large outdoor terrace with umbrellas, palm fronds, and a stone fountain. Speed-demon waiters have even the largest orders ready in no time. (☎04 94 12 88 00. Salads €4.50-8, pastas €8, fish €14-17, meat €12-19, and *coquillages*, or shellfish—a local speciality. Lunch *menu* €12, dinner *menu* €15. Open M-Th and Su noon-10pm, F-Sa noon-11pm. MC/V.)

The largest of the three islands and the one most easily accessed from the coast, **Porquerolles** (pop. 342) also has the most colorful history. It was home to a religious order until François I not-so-ingeniously granted it as an asylum to convicts, who won a pardon in exchange for their promise to defend the mainland against pirates. The criminals promptly transformed the island into the ultimate pirate hideout. Today, mainlanders and tourists find respite from the hectic Riviera on shady trails and in sun-drenched coves. The trade-winds chase the clouds away and bring droves of sailors and windsurfers to play in the waves just off the coast. An **info office** at the end of the main dock supplies free maps and ferry schedules.

Like its neighbor, the **Île du Levant** was originally settled by monks. If they saw the island today, they would undoubtedly be uttering *mea culpas* for the next fifty years. Home to **Héliopolis,** Europe's oldest nudist colony, islanders go *au naturel* on the beaches and wear the legal minimum (not much) in the village. The landscape of Levant also offers plenty of eye candy on the winding trails in the **Domaine des Arbousiers,** a substantial natural reserve. The Héliopolis map includes seven trails, three of which skirt the dramatic coastline for miles. A small **Superette** provides basic snacks, cold drinks, and essential household supplies. (☎04 94 05 90 05. Open M-Sa 9:30am-1pm and 5:30-7:30pm.)

The smallest and most rugged of the three islands, **Port-Cros** is a stunning national park that offers three main trails within the verdant landscape. Its mountainous terrain is home to 114 species of birds and 602 indigenous plants. The well-trodden **sentier des plantes** (plant trail) passes by forts and the crowded **plage de la Palud.** To find a more solitary spot, continue on the **sentier de Port Man,** reached by a 4hr. hike that penetrates the islands unpopulated interior. The national park info booth at the port provides maps of the island (€1.50 and €2.50) and suggests activities. (☎04 94 01 40 70; www.portcrosparcnational.fr. Open daily July-Aug. 9:15am-12:45pm and 3:15-5:40pm; Sept.-June whenever boats arrive and depart.) **Snorkel** in the clear turquoise water off Port-Crosto to view a dazzling array of sea life. You can also **scuba dive** and explore the area's many wrecks and search for the 40 lb. brown *mérou*, a massive grouper once thought to be extinct. Sun Plongée, runs **open-water dives.** (☎04 94 05 90 16; www.sun-plongee.com. With equipment and diving "buddy" €47, equipment only €37; beginners €50.)

CÔTE D'AZUR

CORSICA
(LA CORSE)

Corsica has always resisted foreign rule. The Corsicans had ruled their island since the 9th century when the iron-fisted Genoese took control in 1284. Almost 500 years later, following the forty-year Corsican War of Independence, the revered general Pasquale Paoli reclaimed the island's independence, created a university, a government, a currency, and an army. With Jean-Jacques Rousseau, he drafted the island's—and the world's—first modern constitution. By 1768's Treaty of Versailles, France's Louis XV gained control of the island, and Corsica found itself divided between the nationalist *Paolistes* and the *Populaires*, who swore allegiance to France and included Carlo-Maria Bonaparte, father to a Napoleon.

Bathed in the turquoise waters of the Mediterranean, Corsica (pop. 260,000) was dubbed *Kallysté* (the most beautiful) by the Greeks. Despite centuries of invasion, it has managed to guard a unique culture with a language, cuisine, and set of mannerisms distinctly different from the culture of mainland France. In the sleepy mountain hamlets of this tiny island paradise, life proceeds much as it has for hundreds of years. Goats, sheep, and pigs wander at will along lonely roads, and crumbling hilltop chapels ring with prayers sung in Corsica's traditional dialect. Though development has brought a steady stream of bikini-clad tourists to the island's spectacular beaches, even well-trodden resort towns are marked by a Genoese tower or citadel, visible reminders of the island's tumultuous past. Just behind the crowded beaches, the first patches of scrubby maquis lead up into an endless, unspoiled landscape. Nearly one third of the island is protected nature reserve, and over 100 summits pierce a sky that refuses to rain 310 days of the year.

Today the Front de Libération National de la Corse (FLNC) continues to try bombing its way to independence, but most Corsicans deplore this sort of extremism, given that France directly provides 70% of Corsica's GNP. French Interior Minister Nicholas Sarkozy proposed increasing Corsican autonomy, but when put to referendum on the island in July 2003, it was narrowly defeated by a 2% margin: only 49% of Corsicans wanted increased autonomy from France. It seems that the traditional resistance is destined to continue.

HIGHLIGHTS OF CORSICA

HIKE among the wild rock formations of **Les Calanches** (p. 767) near Porto or along breathtaking **Cap Corse** (p. 784) to get a sense of the Corsican coastline's rugged beauty.

AT NIGHT, Napoleon's hometown **Ajaccio** (p. 756) stays true to his legacy by threatening to conquer Riviera nightlife with its invasion of powerfully sexy waterfront clubs.

GET YOUR FEET WET in **Calvi** (p. 768), which offers spectacular scuba diving, snorkeling, and windsurfing.

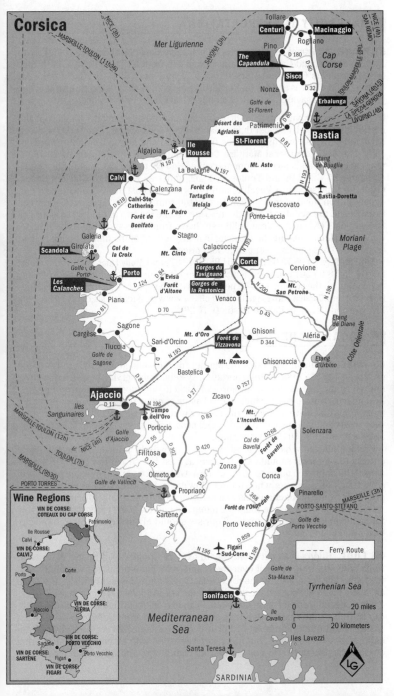

Corsica

Corsica

Mer Ligurienne

Tollare
Centuri — **Macinaggio**
Rogliano
Pino
Cap Corse
D 180
The Capandula
D 80
Sisco
Nonza
D 32
Golfe de St-Florent
Erbalunga
Patrimonio
Bastia
Désert des Agriates
St-Florent
D 81
Etang de Biguglia
Algajola
Ile Rousse
N 197
Mt. Asto
N 193
Calvi
La Balagne
N 197
Calenzana
Asco
Bastia-Doretta
Vescovato
Calvi-Ste-Catherine
Ponte-Leccia
D 81B
Forêt de Tartagine Melaja
Mt. Padro
Forêt de Bonifato
Stagno
Moriani Plage
Galeria
Calacuccia
Girolata
Col de la Croix
Mt. Cinto
Corte
Cervione
Scandola
Golfe de Porto
Porto
D 84
Evisa
Gorges du Tavignano
Mt. San Petrone
Les Calanches
Forêt d'Aitone
Gorges de la Restonica
N 200
N 198
Piana
D 124
Venaco
D 70
Etang de Diane
Sagone
Mt. d'Oro
Ghisoni
Aléria
Cargèse
Sari-d'Orcino
Forêt de Vizzavona
D 344
Côte Orientale
Tiuccia
N 193
Mt. Renoso
Ghisonaccia
Golfe de Sagone
D 1
Bastelica
Etang d'Urbino
Ajaccio
D 27
Zicavo
D 757
Iles Sanguinaires
N 196
Mt. L'Incudine
Solenzara
Campo dell'Oro
D 83
Porticcio
Col de Bavella
D268
D 55
D 420
Forêt de Bavella
Golfe d'Ajaccio
Filitosa
D 302
PORTO TORRES
D 157
Olmeto
Zonza
Conca
Golfe de Valinco
D 69
Propriano
Pinarello
D 368
Forêt de l'Ospedale
Sartène
MARSEILLE (3h)
PORTO-SANTO-STEFANO
D 48
Porto Vecchio
Golfe de Porto Vecchio
D 859
Figari Sud-Corse
N 196
N 198
Golfe de Sta-Manza
Bonifacio
Tyrrhenian Sea
Ile Cavallo
0 — 20 miles
0 — 20 kilometers
Mediterranean Sea
Iles Lavezzi
Santa Teresa
SARDINIA

---- Ferry Route

NICE (3h)
MARSEILLE-TOULON (11h30)
SAVONA (3h)
NICE (4h)
SAN REMO
TOULON-MARSEILLE (8h)
SAVONA (4h15)
LA SPEZIA-GENOVA
LIVORNO (4h)
MARSEILLE-TOULON (12h)
NICE (4h)
MARSEILLE-TOULON (7h)
MARSEILLE (9h30)

Wine Regions

VIN DE CORSE: COTEAUX DU CAP CORSE
Patrimonio
Ile Rousse
Calvi
VIN DE CORSE: CALVI
Porto
Corte
Aléria
VIN DE CORSE: ALÉRIA
Ajaccio
VIN DE CORSE: PORTO VECCHIO
Sartène
VIN DE CORSE: SARTÈNE
Figari
Porto Vecchio
VIN DE CORSE: FIGARI

CORSICA

⛶ INTERCITY TRANSPORTATION

BY PLANE. Air France and its partner **Compagnie Corse Méditerranée (CCM)** fly to Ajaccio, Bastia, and Calvi from Paris (round-trip from €173, students €140); Nice (€121, students €98); and Marseille (€117, students €104). In Ajaccio, the Air France/CCM office is at 3 bd. du Roi Jérôme (☎ 08 20 82 08 20). Hunting around can yield significant savings; inquire at a budget travel agency in France.

BY BOAT. Ferry travel between the mainland and Corsica can be a rough trip, and it's not always much cheaper than a plane. High-speed ferries (3½hr.) run between Nice and Corsica. Overnight ferries from Toulon and Marseille take upwards of 10hr. The **Société National Maritime Corse Méditerranée** (SNCM ☎ 08 91 70 18 01; www.sncm.fr) sends ferries from Marseille (€40-58, under 25 €25-45); Nice (€35-47, under 25 €20-32); and Toulon (€40-58, under 25 €25-45) to Ajaccio, Bastia, Calvi, Île Rousse, Porto Vecchio, and Propriano. It costs €40-305 to take a car, depending on the day and the car. During the summer, nine boats cross between Corsica and the mainland, though only three make the trip in the low season. The fastest boats (Navires à Grande Vitesse) leave from Nice and head to Île Rousse, Calvi, or Ajaccio, making the crossing in nearly a third of the time. Corsica Ferries (see below) has similar destinations and prices.

  SAREMAR (☎ 04 95 73 00 96; fax 04 95 73 13 37) and **Moby Lines** (☎ 04 95 73 00 29; fax 04 95 73 05 50) run from Santa Teresa, Sardinia to Bonifacio. (2-5 per day depending on the season; €14-15 per person one-way, cars €26-51.50.) Moby Lines (€15-28) and **Corsica Ferries** (☎ 08 25 09 50 95; www.corsicaferries.com) cross from Livorno and Genoa in Italy to Bastia (€16-26).

▮ LOCAL TRANSPORTATION

ON WHEELS. Rumor has it that the Marquis de Sade and Machiavelli collaborated on the design of Corsica's transportation system. **Train** service in Corsica is slow, limited to the half of the island north of Ajaccio, and doesn't accept rail passes. Antiquated, overcrowded vehicles travel along winding mountain ridges. **Buses** are more comprehensive and serve the greater part of the island, but be prepared for very twisty roads. If prone to motion sickness, bring medicine. Call **Eurocorse Voyages** (☎ 04 95 21 06 30) for further info.

  Corsica allegedly has the most dangerous roads in France. Those foolhardy enough to rent a **car** should expect to pay at least €65-81 per day or €250-305 per week. The unlimited mileage deals are best. Gas stations are scarce; the police will sometimes help drivers who run out. **Bicycle, moped,** and **scooter** rental can be pricey. Winding mountain roads and high winds make cycling difficult and risky; drivers should honk before rounding mountain curves. Many roads are too narrow for two cars to pass at one time. Tourists should always give way to inter-city buses and coach cars.

ON FOOT. Hiking is an excellent way to explore Corsica's landscape. A series of trails take *randonneurs* all over the island, with panoramas of everything from the mountainous interior to the rocky coastline. Campsites and *refuges*, as well as an active backpacking set, ensure that hikers are welcomed with open arms.

  The longest marked route, the **GR20,** is an extremely difficult 180km, 12- to 15-day trail that takes hardcore hikers across the island from Calenzana (southeast of Calvi) to Conca (northeast of Porto-Vecchio). The GR20 requires peak physical fitness and endurance, but hikers are rewarded with an unparalleled offering of Corsica's scenery. Do not tackle this trail alone, and be prepared for cold, snowy weather, even in early summer. For shorter, less challenging routes, try the popular **Mare e Monti,** a 7- to 10-day trail from Calenzana to Cargèse that passes through the pristine Aitone Forest and the breathtaking Gorges de Spelunca. The easier **Da Mare a Mare Sud** crosses the southern part of the island between Porto-Vecchio and Propriano (4-6 days), leading hikers through a green countryside and past prehistoric remains at Filitosa. Its northern equivalent, the **Mare a Mare Nord,** is a 12-day trek from Moriani to Cargèse that passes through the university town of Corte before traversing the Tavignanu and Restonica river valleys. The **Mare a Mare Centre** transects the middle of the island from Ghisonaccia to Porticcio, and can be completed in 7 days. Though easier than the GR20, this trail requires advance preparation and is best enjoyed in autumn and spring. All major trails are administered by the **Parc Naturel Régional de la Corse,** 2 Sargent Casalonga (☎ 04 95 51 79 00; www.parc-naturel-corse.com), in Ajaccio, whose jurisdiction encompasses most of the Corsican heartland. For any route, a topo-guide is essential. (€11.43-15, with shipping €15.30; available for purchase by fax, email, over the phone, or at a Parc Naturel office.) The guide includes trail maps, *gîtes* and *refuges* listings, and other important practical info. Prospective GR20 trekkers will want to consider buying *Le Grand Chemin* (€15), a more complete guide that includes elevations and sources of potable water. For more info, contact the Parc Naturel.

ACCOMMODATIONS

Agence du Tourisme de la Corse, 17 bd. du Roi Jérôme, Ajaccio (☎ 04 95 51 00 00; www.visit-corsica.com), publishes free guides to all of Corsica's accommodations, available at tourist offices. Corsica's few budget hotels fill weeks ahead in summer, and it can be nearly impossible to find a room in August. Camping is a great choice all over the island: nearly every city, small town, or half-forgotten village offers at least one spot to pitch a tent. Resist the urge to pitch your tent on that stunning mountain ledge: unofficial camping is **strictly banned** across the island. *Refuges*, or mountain huts, provide a trail-side shelter, with camping outside.

AJACCIO (AIACCIU)

Napoleon must have insisted on the best from the very beginning: the little dictator couldn't have picked a better place to call home. With palm-lined boulevards and endless sunshine, the largest town in

BRING ON THE BROCCIU

Corsicans put a simpler spin on the French obsession with cheese. It's not that their production isn't up to mainland standards—on the contrary, the island is well known for its fabulous *chèvre* (goat) and *brebis* (ewe) varieties. It's just that *brocciu,* Corsica's principal cheese, is so perfectly delicious that islanders see no reason to confine it to a particular spot in the meal.

Brocciu (pronounced "broutch," with the "u" barely audible) is made with ewe's milk and whey. As the mixture is heated, a creamy surface forms which is skimmed off, slightly salted, and placed in molds. Unlike stronger cheeses, *brocciu* only needs to age a few days. The result is a mild, fresh cheese ready for consumption in hundreds of traditional Corsican dishes.

At its simplest, *brocciu* is eaten plain with a little bit of sugar or fig jam. It is frequently mixed with eggs, mint, and oil to form an *omelette au brocciu,* or used as the filling for handmade *canelonni au brocciu.* For dessert, the cheese is placed in sugared dough and baked to form a sort of turnover known as *la pannette de brocciu.* By far the most popular *brocciu* treat, however, is *la fiadone,* a creamy cheesecake made with lemon zest, sugar, eggs, and a touch of Corsican *eau de vie.*

Corsica and the island's departmental headquarters calls to mind a resort town on the Riviera. With its countless boutiques, a yacht-filled harbor, and lively club scene, Ajaccio (pop. 53,000) is a haven for wealthy, tanned tourists. Ajaccio is also one of the few Corsican towns with significant museums and considerable urban energy. While Napoleon's birthplace has no shortage of monuments commemorating the local boy's exploits, Ajaccio's treasure is the Italian Renaissance collection in the Musée Fesch.

⌐ TRANSPORTATION

Flights: Aéroport Campo dell'Oro (☎04 95 23 56 56), 5km away. Office open M-F 8am-noon and 2-6pm, Sa 8am-noon. TCA bus #8 shuttles to and from the bus station (€4.50). Flights to **Lyon, Marseille, Nice,** and **Paris.** For info call **Air France,** 3 bd. du Roi Jérôme, or **Compagnie Corse Mediterranée** (☎08 20 82 08 20 for both. Open M-F 8:30am-12:30pm and 2-6pm, Sa 8:30am-noon; airport office open daily 6am-8pm).

Trains: pl. de la Gare (☎04 95 23 11 03), off bd. Sampiero, 400m from the *gare maritime* (toward the airport, away from city center). Open daily mid-June to mid-Sept. 6:30am-9:30pm; mid-Sept. to early June 6am-8:30pm. To: **Bastia** (3-4hr., 4 per day, €23.90; **Calvi** via **Ponte Leccia** (5hr., 2 per day, €27.80); and **Corte** (2½hr., 4 per day, €12.70).

Buses: quai l'Herminier (☎04 95 51 55 45), at *gare maritime.* Open daily June-Aug. 6:30am-7:45pm; Sept.-May M-Sa 6:30am-7:45pm. **Eurocorse Voyages** (☎04 95 21 06 30) to **Bastia** (3hr., M-Sa 2 per day, 7:45am and 3pm, €18) via **Corte** (1¾hr., €11; **Calvi** via **Ponte Leccia** (3½hr., July-Aug M-Sa 1 per day 3pm, €15 to Ponte Leccia). **Les Beaux Voyages** (☎04 95 65 11 35; Sept-June M-F 1 per day); **Bonifacio** (3hr., M-Sa 2 per day, €20.50); **Porto Vecchio** (3hr., M-Sa 2 per day, €20.50). **Autocars SAIB** (☎04 95 22 41 99) runs to **Porto** (2hr.; daily July to mid-Sept. 8:45am and 4pm; May-June and mid- to late Sept. M-Sa 8:45am and 4pm; Oct.-Apr. M-F 7:20am and 4pm, Sa 7:20am and 12:30pm; €11). **Autocars Ceccaldi** (☎04 95 21 38 06 or 04 95 20 29 76) runs to **Evisa** (3hr., M-Sa 2 per day, €12)

Ferries: Depart from *gare maritime* (☎04 95 51 55 45). Open daily June-Aug. 6:30am-7:45pm; Sept.-May M-Sa 6:30am-7:45pm and for departures and arrivals. **SNCM,** quai l'Herminier (☎04 95 29 66 99; fax 04 95 29 66 77), across from the bus station, goes to **Marseille** (12hr., 4-12 per week, according to the season) and **Nice** (4hr., 1 per day). Approximate prices: €35-47, ages 12-25 €20-32. Office open M-F 7am-8pm and Sa for departures and arrivals. MC/V. **Corsica Ferries** (☎04 95 50 78 82), in the bus station, runs to **Toulon** (5¾hr., 4-6 per week) and **Nice** (4½hr., 1-5 per week). €20-38, ages 12-25 €5-23.

Public Transportation: TCA, 75 cours Napoleon (☎04 95 23 29 41). Buses run every 20-30min., depending on the line. Tickets €1.15, *carnet* of 10 €9; available at the TCA office, in *tabacs,* and on the bus. Buses #1, 2, and 3 go from pl. de Gaulle to the train station or down cours Napoleon. Bus #5 from av. Dr. Ramaroni and bd. Lantivy stops at Marinella and the beaches headed to **Îles Sanguinaires** (7:05am-7:30pm; July-Aug. until 11:25pm) Line #8 heads to the **airport** from the *gare routière* (8:30am-7:25pm; €4.50). Office open M-Sa 9am-12:30pm and 3:30-6:30pm.

Taxis: Accord Ajaccio Taxis, pl. de Gaulle (☎04 95 25 06 18) or **Ajaccio Allo Taxis** (☎06 08 96 67 85 or 06 67 09 57 67). 24hr. About €20 to airport from *centre ville.*

Car Rental: Ada (☎04 95 23 56 57), at the airport. Insurance included. 21+. Open daily 8am-midnight. AmEx/MC/V. **Rent-a-Car,** 51 cours Napoleon (☎ 04 95 51 61 81; www.rentacar.fr), in Hôtel Kallisté, and at the airport (☎04 95 23 56 36). Insurance included. 23+. Open daily 8am-8pm. MC/V.

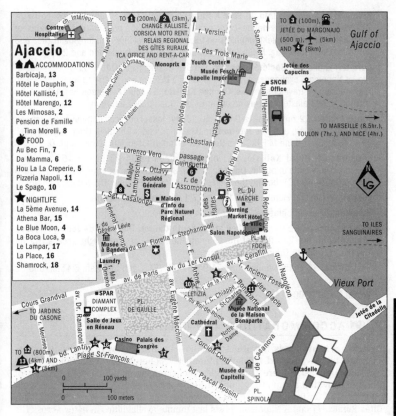

Ajaccio

⚓🏠ACCOMMODATIONS
Barbicaja, **13**
Hôtel le Dauphin, **3**
Hôtel Kallisté, **1**
Hôtel Marengo, **12**
Les Mimosas, **2**
Pension de Famille
Tina Morelli, **8**
🍎FOOD
Au Bec Fin, **7**
Da Mamma, **6**
Hou La La Creperie, **5**
Pizzeria Napoli, **11**
Le Spago, **10**
★NIGHTLIFE
La 5ème Avenue, **14**
Athena Bar, **15**
Le Blue Moon, **4**
La Boca Loca, **9**
Le Lampar, **17**
La Place, **16**
Shamrock, **18**

Motorcycle Rental: Corsica Moto Rent, 51 cours Napoleon (☎04 95 51 61 81), in the Hôtel Kallisté. Motorcycles from €48 per day, €204 per week. Deposit from €600. 23+. Open daily 8am-8pm. MC/V.

✈🚆 ORIENTATION AND PRACTICAL INFORMATION

Cours Napoleon, which runs from pl. de Gaulle past the train station, is the city's main thoroughfare. The pedestrian **rue Cardinal Fesch** starts at pl. Maréchal Foch and parallels cours Napoleon. **Place de Gaulle, place Foch** with its Napoleonic fountain, and the **citadel** (still an active military base) enclose the *vieille ville*. The seaside **boulevard Pascal Rossini** begins near pl. de Gaulle and runs along the coast above the city's public beaches, beginning with **plage St-François.**

Tourist Office: 3 bd. du Roi Jérôme (☎04 95 51 53 03; www.tourisme.fr/ajaccio), pl. du Marché. Staff distributes maps, bus schedules, and festival brochures. Internet. Mid-June to mid-Sept. theme tours in French (€6-9). Open July-Aug. M-Sa 8am-8:30pm, Su 9am-1pm and 4-7pm; Apr.-June and Sept.-Oct. M-Sa 8am-7pm, Su 9am-1pm; Nov.-Mar. M-Sa 8am-6pm. **Agence du Tourisme de la Corse,** 17 bd. du Roi Jérôme (☎04 95 51 00 00; www.visit-corsica.com). Open M-F 8:30am-12:30pm and 2-6pm.

Hiking Info: Maison d'Info du Parc Naturel Régional, 2 rue Sergent Casalonga (☎04 95 51 79 00; www.parc-naturel-corse.com), across from the *préfecture*. Topo-guides for sale and free multilingual pamphlets on regional trails, wildlife, and lodging in *gîtes* and *refuges*. Open June-Aug. M-Sa 8am-7pm; Sept.-May M-Sa 9am-noon and 2-6pm.

Currency Exchange: Société Génerale, rue Sgt. Casalonga (☎04 95 51 57 60), just off cours Napoleon, exchanges currency M-F 8:15-11:30am and 1:45-4:30pm, with a high commission on traveler's checks. **Change Kallisté,** 51 cours Napoleon (☎04 95 51 34 45), in Hôtel Kallisté, charges no commission. Open daily 8am-8pm.

Youth Center: 52 rue Fesch (☎04 95 50 13 44; josephcorsica@hotmail.com). Info on jobs, and housing, and free **Internet** (max 40min., under 25 only). Open July-Aug. M-F 9am-6pm; Sept.-June M-F 8:30am-9pm, Sa 1-7pm. Closed Aug. 15 to Sept. 6.

Laundromat: Hotel Kallisté, 51 cours Napoleon (☎04 95 51 34 45), has new machines available to public. Open daily noon-8pm. **Lavomatic,** 1 rue Maréchal Ornano (☎06 09 06 49 09), behind the *préfecture,* near pl. de Gaulle. Open daily 7am-9pm.

Police: rue Général Fiorella (☎04 95 11 17 17), near the *préfecture.*

Hospital: 27 av. Impératrice Eugénie (☎04 95 29 90 90).

Internet Access: Up to 40min. free at the **Youth Center.** The **Salle de Jeux en Réseau Phoenix,** on the 2nd floor of the Diamant Complex, has late-night access. €2 for 30min., €3 per hr. Open daily 8am-3am.

Post Office: 13 cours Napoleon (☎04 95 51 84 75). Open M-F 8am-6:45pm and Sa 8am-noon.

Postal Code: 20000.

ACCOMMODATIONS AND CAMPING

Ajaccio has many hotels, but prices rival those in Paris. Call very far ahead in June-Aug., when rates soar and vacancies plummet. Ask hotels for their absolute cheapest room, then ask if there's anything even cheaper; some hotels keep a couple of old, unrenovated rooms they don't initially list. Ajaccio's campsites are well-equipped but far from the city center. If you're really stuck, the **Relais Régional des Gîtes Ruraux,** 77 cours Napoleon, posts last-minute availabilities in *gîtes* across the island. (☎04 95 10 54 30; infos@gites-corsica.com. Open M-Th 8am-12:30pm and 2-5:30pm; F 8am-12:30pm and 2-4:30pm.)

▓ **Pension de Famille Tina Morelli,** 1 rue Major Lambroschini (☎/fax 04 95 21 16 97). This a wonderfully welcoming option is tended to by Tina herself. Thank-you notes and gifts from former guests adorn the home of this amazingly generous proprietor. Make reservations as far as possible in advance. *demi-pension* (with 4-course meal) singles €50; doubles €90; €45 per additional guest; full-*pension* €62.50/€115/€57.50. ❹

▓ **Hôtel Kallisté,** 51 cours Napoleon (☎04 95 51 34 45; www.cyrnos.net); follow signs from quai l'Herminier up rue des Trois Marie, then take a right onto cours Napoleon. Rooms are well designed and comfortable, equipped with shower or bath, cable TV, and fan or A/C. Firm beds, elevator, and central location make this a great choice. Wi-Fi access in lobby. Breakfast €6.50, in room €8.50. Free luggage storage. Laundry available (wash €5, dry €2). Reception daily 8am-8pm, all-night automatic check-in with reservation code. Mar.-July and Sept.-Oct. singles €45; doubles €52-58; triples €69; Aug. €56/€69-76/€86; Nov.-Feb. €42/€48-52/€58. MC/V. ❹

Hôtel Marengo, 2 rue Marengo (☎04 95 21 43 66; www.hotel-marengo.com). From city center, walk along the boardwalk with the sea on the left for about 25min.; turn right on bd. Madame Mère, then left onto rue Marengo. Or take bus #1, 2, or 5 to Trottel. Quiet, airy rooms in a cheerful yellow house just minutes from the beach. All with shower and

A/C. Breakfast €6. Reception daily 8am-11pm. Reserve well in advance for July-Aug. Open Apr. to mid-Nov. July-Sept. singles and doubles €79; triples €88; Apr.-June and Oct. to mid-Nov. €59/€64. 4 rooms sharing hallway toilet €49-€53. AmEx/MC/V. ❺

Hôtel le Dauphin, 11 bd. Sampiero (☎04 95 21 12 94; fax 04 95 21 88 69), between the train station and ferry port. Plain but well-kept rooms, all with bath, TV, and phone. Traffic makes overlooking port a bit noisy. A/C for an extra €8. Reception daily 5:30am-midnight. Check-in 2pm. July-Oct. singles €59; doubles €69; triples €85; Nov.-Mar. €52/€56/€69; Apr.-June €54/€60/€75. Extra bed €8. AmEx/MC/V. ❹

Camping:

Les Mimosas, rte. d'Alata (☎04 95 20 99 85; fax 04 95 10 01 77). Follow cours Napoleon away from the city center. Turn left on montée St-Jean, which becomes rue Biancamaria and then rte. d'Alata. Continue walking straight on the other side of the roundabout, take an immediate left onto chemin de la Carrossacia; follow the signs 600m inland and uphill to the site. (30min.) Or, take bus #4 from cours Napoleon to Brasilia; walk straight to the roundabout, follow the above directions. Large site in a quiet neighborhood above the *centre ville.* Wash €4, dry €1.80 for 15min. Reception 8am-1:30pm and 3:30-8:30pm. Bungalows and mobile homes available for longer stays (€210-€470 per week). June-Sept. €4.80 per person, €2 per tent or car. Electricity €2.80. Apr.-May and Oct. prices 10% lower. ❷

Barbicaja (☎/fax 04 95 52 01 17), 4km away. Take bus #5 from av. Dr. Ramaroni, past pl. de Gaulle, to Barbicaja and go straight (last bus 7:30pm, July-Aug. 11:25pm). Friendly, English-speaking staff manages this site, just steps from a popular beach. Campers enjoy snack bar, pizzeria, and shady emplacements with views of the sparkling bay. Bar. Laundry €7. Reception 8am-9:30pm. Open May to mid-Sept. €5.85 per person, €2.30 per tent or car. Electricity €2.40. ❷

▐ FOOD

Though Ajaccio has no shortage of restaurants, your best option by far is the fabulous ⬛**morning market** on pl. du Marché. The endless rows of stalls offer all you need for the perfect Corsican picnic. Start with a warm baguette, then select a crumbly wedge of goat cheese and a tasty portion of *charcuterie.* For dessert, pick up a ripe melon and a handful of chestnut *canistrelli* (cookies), baked fresh that morning. A smaller market opens at pl. Abbatucci, on cours Napoleon. (Both Tu-Su 8am-1pm.) The trusty **Monoprix supermarket** is at 31 cours Napoleon. (☎04 95 51 76 50. Open July-Sept. M-Sa 8:30am-8pm; Oct.-June M-Sa 8:30am-7:15pm.)

A **SPAR** supermarket is at 1 cours Grandval, on the first floor of the Diamant complex. (☎04 95 21 51 77. Open M-Sa 8:30am-12:30pm and 3:15-7:30pm, Su 8:30am-12:30pm.) Head to the pedestrian streets off **place Foch** toward the citadel for dozens of spots serving local dishes. Inexpensive pizzerias, *panini* shops, and *crêperies* line the pedestrian (and touristy) **rue Cardinal Fesch.** For the freshest seafood, try the tiny **rue des Halles,** just behind the tourist office. At night, patios on the quai offer affordable pizza, salads, and pasta. For truly authentic Corsican cuisine in an unforgettable setting, try **Le 20123** (see **You Can Take it With You,** p. 762).

⬛ **Au Bec Fin,** 3bis. bd. du Roi Jérôme (☎04 95 21 30 52). A classy standout in a cafe-heavy part of town, Au Bec Fin offers an excellent €13.90 *menu* in an elegant, bistro-style interior. Start with *foie gras* served with *pain d'épices* (spiced bread), then enjoy *croustillant de saumon* (breaded smoked salmon). Meats €13.50-18, salads €7.50-12, fish €12.50-18.50, generous desserts €4.80. Open M-Sa noon-2pm and 7:30-10:30pm, F-Sa until 11pm. V. ❸

Da Mamma, passage Guinguetta (☎04 95 21 39 44), off cours Napoleon. A eucalyptus tree shades packed tables at this local favorite. At the end of a narrow passage, Da Mamma serves up traditional Corsican specialties from a €15 or €23 *menu.* Try the

YOU *CAN* TAKE IT WITH YOU: LE 20123

Countless restaurants in Ajaccio offer a *menu Corse*, but only one address provides the authentic setting to match: **Le 20123** ❺.

20123 is the postal code of Pila Canale, a tiny town where the restaurant's owner lived for years until economic pressures forced him to move to the city. Tormented by the thought of leaving his idyllic village behind, he decided to recreate Pila Canale in the heart of Corsica's biggest city. The interior of the restaurant perfectly resembles a small-town square, complete with a bubbling fountain where diners fill their own water jugs. Tables hide behind wagon wheels and house facades are painstakingly reproduced down to the last shutter.

Though the architecture is charming, it's not the only thing taken from Pila Canale: nearly every dish on the €27 *menu* is a family recipe that has been handed down for generations. The excellent traditional cuisine includes eggplant topped with sizzling goat cheese and juicy *plats* of oven-baked veal or lamb. To finish, 20123 offers several homemade desserts, including the *dessert maison:* an unforgettable chestnut flan, served piping hot with vanilla ice cream.

(2 rue Roi de Rome. ☎ 04 95 21 50 05. Open Tu-Su 7pm-11pm. Reservations essential; call at least one day in advance. Closed mid-Nov. to mid-Feb.)

soupe de poisson (fish soup). A €10.50 *menu* is offered until 9:30pm. Salads €7-12, meats €12-21. Open M and Su 7:30-10:30pm, Tu-Sa noon-2pm and 7:30-10:30pm; Sept.-May closes at 10pm. Reservations recommended during high season. MC/V. ❸

Pizzeria Napoli, rue Bonaparte (☎ 04 95 21 32 79), caters to a late-night crowd with cheap, tasty pizzas. Grab a seat on the basic terrace before 9pm for well-priced *menus* like the "Italien," a generous trio of pizza, pasta, and dessert (€11.90). *Menus* €11.90-14.50, pizza €7.50-9.50, pasta €7-10. Open daily July-Aug. 6:45pm-6am; Sept.-June M-Th and Su 6:45pm-4am, F-Sa 6:45pm-6am. ❷

Le Spago, rue Emmanuel Arène (☎ 04 95 21 15 71), off av. du 1er Consul. A meat-heavy menu satisfies cool carnivores at this modern spot. The funky, colorful tables fill with a young crowd hungry for traditional *plats* like the *entrecote bergère* (meat with Corsican cheese and bacon). Meat dishes €13-17,Open M-F noon-2pm and 7:30-11pm, Sa 7:30-11pm. MC/V. ❸

Hou La La Crêperie, 22 rue Cardinal Fesch (☎ 04 95 51 49). This basic *crêperie* offers cheap eats and primo people-watching. Try one of 5 delicious *tartines* such as the *tartine du bandit* (topped with goat cheese, mozzarella, *herbes du maquis,* and ham), or customize your own salad for €6.90. *Tartines* €6.40, salads €6.90 with four toppings. Open daily July-Aug. 9am-10pm; Sept.-June M-Sa 9am-10pm, Su 9am-3pm. MC/V. ❶

◉ SIGHTS

Though most of Ajaccio's museums are overflowing with Napoleonic memorabilia, the city's best gallery actually ignores the ubiquitous dictator completely. Instead, the ◧**Musée Fesch,** 50-52 rue Cardinal Fesch, houses an extensive collection of stunning 14th- to 19th-century Italian paintings. The comprehensive galleries boast such treasures as Titian's sensual *Man with a Glove* and Veronese's erotic *Leda and the Swan.* Also within the complex is the Renaissance-style **Chapelle Impériale,** whose soaring marble interior holds the tombs of most of the Bonapartes—though Napoleon himself is buried at Les Invalides in Paris. The altar displays a crucifix offered by Napoleon to his mother upon his return from Egypt in 1799. (☎ 04 95 21 48 17; www.musee-fesch.com. Open July-Aug. M 1:30-6pm, Tu-Th 9am-6:30pm, F 9am-6:30pm and 9pm-midnight, Sa-Su 10:30am-6pm; Apr.-June and Sept. M 1-5:15pm, Tu-Su 9:15am-12:15pm and 2:15-5:15pm; Oct.-Mar. closed Su-M. Museum €5.35, students €3.80; chapel

€1.50, students €0.75, under 15 free.) The expansive **courtyard** occasionally holds open-air theater productions and concerts. Contact the tourist office or the Musée Fesch for more info.

The **Musée National de la Maison Bonaparte,** rue St-Charles, between rue Bonaparte and rue Roi-de-Rome, was the boyhood home of Ajaccio's famous megalomaniac. The sumptuous *casa Bonaparte* now showcases such memorabilia as a family tree made entirely from locks of hair and the room where the future emperor slept. (☎04 95 21 43 89. Open May-Sept. M 2-6pm, Tu-Su 9am-noon and 2-6pm; Oct.-Apr. M 2-5pm, Tu-Su 10am-noon and 2-5pm. Last tickets sold 30min. before closing. €4, students €2.60, under 18 free.) The glittering **Salon Napoléonien,** pl. Foch, in Hôtel de Ville, restored in ornate 19th-century style, is a lavish location for the display of Napoleon's coronation portrait, funerary mask, and personal items. The empty glass display case in the smaller room once held a gold replica of his olive-leaf coronation crown, but it was stolen during renovations and has remained at large. (☎04 95 51 52 53. Open mid-June to mid-Sept. M-F 9-11:45am and 2-5:45pm; mid-Sept. to mid-June M-F 9-11:45am and 2-4:45pm. €2.30.)

The **Musée à Bandera,** 1 rue Général Levie, chronicles Corsican history from antiquity to WWII with a wide-ranging collection of maps, models, and elaborate dioramas. The galleries are supplemented by intriguing rotating exhibits on related subjects like "Corsican Women." Though the labels require a good understanding of French, the desk can provide a general English overview and can schedule free guided tours with a week's notice. (☎04 95 51 07 34; histoire-corse@wanadoo.fr. Open July to mid-Sept. M-Sa 9am-7pm, Su 9am-noon; mid-Sept. to June M-Sa 9am-noon and 2-6pm. €4, students €2.50, *Let's Go* readers with book in hand €3.30.)

The €10 **Passmusée,** valid for seven days, covers entry fees for all five of the sights listed above. Available at the tourist office or any participating museum.

▣ NIGHTLIFE

Unlike most Corsican cities, Ajaccio has its fair share of wild nights. The party scene is by no means exclusive, but as the summer heat brings well-dressed tourists eager to show off their brand-new tans, you might want to trade in your scuffed hiking boots and trail-weary t-shirts for some flashier, classier duds. The major clubs are out of town, reachable by car. **La Cinquième Avenue,** 5km away on rte. des Sanguinaires, draws partiers with a classy wood and bamboo interior. (☎04 95 52 09 77. Cocktails €10. Open W-Su midnight-5am.) **Le Blue Moon** is farther away in Porticcio, 10km east of the city center. This open-air club boasts a palm-lined terrace and an appropriately moon-shaped dance floor. (☎04 95 25 07 70. Open daily July-Aug. 11:30pm-5am; Apr.-June and Sept. F-Sa 11:30pm-5am.) **La Place,** Résidence Diamant II, in town on bd. Pascal Rossini, has a space-age feel with gold walls and painted planet trim. An older crowd fills the velvet lounge and silver stools for American and French hip-hop and pop. (☎06 09 07 03 53. Cocktails €9. Open daily July-Aug. 11:30am-5am, Sept.-June F-Su 11pm-5am.) Clubs tend to have no cover but a one-drink minimum, though partiers may have to pay (usually €10) on big-name DJ nights. Several lively bars crowd **boulevard Pascal Rossini,** including **Athena Bar,** where hip-hop blasts on the palm-filled terrace and a young crowd sips fancy ice-cream cocktails. (☎04 95 21 22 61. Beers on tap €2.70-2.90, bottled €3.50-6.50, cocktails €8.30. Elaborate ice cream treats €5.50-€7.70. Open daily June-Aug. 9am-2am; Sept.-May 7am-2am.) Those who still have cash to lose can head to the **Casino,** bd. Pascal Rossini. (☎04 95 50 40 60. 18+. Open daily July to mid-Sept. 1pm-4am; Oct.-June M-Th 1pm-3am, F-Su 1pm-4am.)

■ **La Boca Loca,** 2 rue de la Porta (☎06 24 57 43 87). Live flamenco and salsa music fills the racy, red-curtained interior, while flickering candles light a romantic tree-lined terrace just outside. No matter what your mood, either spot is perfect for tasty *tapas* and strawberry mojitos (€5.50). Cocktails €5. Sangria €11.50 per pitcher, €2 per glass. *Tapas* €12 for 5, €2.80 each. Open Tu-Sa 7pm-2am.

Le Lampar, Résidence Diamant II, bd. Lantivy (☎04 95 51 47 05). Just off bd. Pascal Rossini, this elegant *avant boîte* (pre-club scene) caters to a chic crowd with dark, rich wood and deep velvet chairs. DJ plays house and lounge Sept.-Apr. F and Sa. Beers on tap €2-3; bottled €3.50-5; cocktails €6-7.50. Open daily 7am-2am.

Shamrock, 3 rue Forcioli Conti, off pl. de Gaulle (☎06 09 97 24 82). Friendly Corsican owner loves the anglophone spirit: get yours riled up with the *bière du metre,* 12 glasses of Heineken (€28), Murphy's (€38), or Desperados (€45), with an extra 2 thrown in for good luck. Beers on tap €2.90-3.50; beer-based cocktails €4.50-6; cocktails €6.50-7.60; Heineken *bière du metre* (12 glasses plus 2 free) €28. Happy hour daily 5-7pm; 2 draft beers for the price of 1. Open daily 5pm-2am.

■ FESTIVALS

In early July, Ajaccio kicks off a series of small summer festivals with the **Festival de Musique d'Ajaccio,** an annual orchestral and vocal celebration. August 15 brings the three-day **Fêtes Napoleon,** which commemorates the emperor's birth with war re-enactment plays, a parade, ceremonies, and a huge *pyrosymphonie* (fireworks display). Friday night fever hits Ajaccio during the July and August **Shopping de Nuit,** when stores stay open until midnight on Friday nights.

PORTO

A hiking paradise, the stunning gulf of Porto reveals Corsica's jagged volcanic mountains, lush pine groves, emerald valleys, and crystalline waters. To the north, a marine reserve conceals grottoes and rare birds. At the center of all the natural wonder lies the heavily touristed town of Porto (pop. 432), which is unfortunately little more than an extended souvenir shop. Despite the camera-toting tourists, Porto is worth a visit: lodging is cheap, transportation is convenient by Corsican standards, and the smooth pebble beach is the perfect place to watch the sunset.

■ TRANSPORTATION

Buses: Autocars SAIB (☎04 95 22 41 99) leaves from the top of the main road in front of the pharmacy for **Ajaccio** (2hr.; July to mid-Sept. 2 per day, mid-Sept. to June M-Sa only; €11) and **Calvi** (3hr.; July-Aug. 1 per day, Sept.-June M-Sa; €16). Purchase tickets onboard. **Autocars Mordiconi** (☎04 95 48 00 04) departs from the parking lot at the base of the marina, in front of the mini-golf. Buses run to **Corte** (July to mid-Sept. M-Sa 1 per day, €19) via **Evisa** (July to mid-Sept. M-Sa 1 per day, €7). Purchase tickets onboard.

Car, Bike, and Scooter Rental: Porto Locations (☎/fax 04 95 26 10 13), opposite Haut Porto's supermarkets. If no one is at the desk, ask next door at the snack bar La Cigale. Cars €60 per day, €305 per week. 18+, with a license for at least 2 years. Scooters €46/€230. License necessary. Bikes €15/€68. Credit card deposit €305 for cars, €610 for scooters. Open daily Apr.-Oct. 8:30am-7:30pm. AmEx/MC/V.

Taxis: Taxis Chez Félix (☎04 95 26 12 92 or 06 85 41 95 89).

✈ 🛈 ORIENTATION AND PRACTICAL INFORMATION

Porto is split into an upper town, **Haut Porto** or **Quartier Vaita**, and a coastal area, **Porto Marina**, where some 15 hotels and restaurants compete for waterfront space. A broad stream runs the length of the town, separating shops and boutiques in the north from the boat slips and beach to the south. An arched pedestrian bridge at the mouth of the river allows access to the shoreline.

Tourist Office: (☎04 95 26 10 55; www.porto-tourisme.com), at the end of the main road near the Tour Genoise. Topo-guide for 29 hikes (€2.50), bus schedules, and info on watersports, boat trips, and lodging. Spotty English spoken. Open June-Sept. M-Sa 9am-7pm; Oct.-May M-Sa 9am-5pm.

Laundromat: Lavo 2000 (☎04 95 26 10 33), on the main road next to Hotel Bon Acceuil. Wash €7.50, dry €1 per 5min. Open daily 8am-9pm.

Police: Gendarmerie Maritime (☎04 95 51 75 21), on the port.

Post Office: ☎04 95 26 10 26. Midway between the marina and Haut Porto. Open July-Aug. M-F 9am-12:30pm and 2-5pm, Sa 9-11:30am; Sept.-June M-F 9am-12:15pm and 2-4pm, Sa 9-11am.

Postal Code: 20150.

⌂ 🏕 ACCOMMODATIONS AND CAMPING

Porto's abundance of indistinguishable hotels makes the town more affordable than most of the island. In July and August, rates skyrocket in even the most modest of hotels. Make summer reservations well ahead of time. Some of the cheapest accommodations in Corsica are *gîtes* in the pleasant village of Ota, a departure point for many hikes. From Porto, veer right and head uphill at the fork after the supermarkets; follow the signs to D124 and Ota. (1¼hr.) The bus from Ajaccio to Porto also stops at Ota (30min., 2 per day, €3). **Chez Felix ❶** has homey 4- to 8-bed dorms and kitchen access. (☎04 95 26 12 92; fax 18 25. Breakfast €6. Sheets €3. €13 per person, *demi-pension* €32; doubles with bath and *demi-pension* €45-50. MC/V.) **Chez Marie ❶** has modern, spartan dorms with 6-12 beds. (☎/fax 04 95 26 11 37. Breakfast €5. Beds €13, *demi-pension* €30.)

Le Lonca (☎04 95 26 16 44; fax 04 95 26 11 83), right next to the post office, lets well-kept, modern rooms with large bathrooms and gleaming furniture. Several have small balconies overlooking the hills. All are equipped with shower or bath, toilet, TV, and A/C. Breakfast €6.50. Reception daily 7am-10pm. Open Apr.-Oct. July singles and doubles €45-55, €65 with balcony; triples €55/€65; quads €85. Aug. €70-85/€80-105/€125. Apr.-June €43-€60/€52-50/€80. Sept. €45-65/55-65/€85. MC/V. ❹

Bon Accueil (☎/fax 04 95 26 19 50; BA20150@aol.com), on the main road a bit farther from the port. A boisterous, friendly staff manages simple, clean rooms and restaurant. All with bath, several with balcony. Breakfast €6. Reception daily 7am-11pm. Mid-July to Aug. €45 per person with *demi-pension;* Sept. to mid-July singles and doubles €31-37; triples €34-45. 1 room can sleep up to 6 guests (€55). MC/V. ❸

Hôtel Brise de Mer (☎04 95 26 10 28; www.brise-de-mer.com), next to Le Panorama. Shockingly bright bedspreads fill 20 clean, functional rooms. All with shower or bath, toilet, telephone, and balconies. Request a sea view. Bar, TV room, and breezy terrace restaurant. Breakfast €7. Open Apr.-Oct. Singles and doubles €40-52; triples €47-55; quads €54-62; *demi-pension* with double €80-89. Prices €8-10 higher in Aug. ❹

Le Panorama (☎ 06 30 29 75 16), on the main road across from the tourist office, offers low prices and a central location. Rooms are small and slightly worn, but each has an enormous terrace overlooking the marina and beach. All with shower; some with toilet. Reception daily 8-11am and 4-7pm. July singles and doubles €25-30; Aug. €30-35; Apr.-June and Sept.-Oct. €20-25. Extra bed €3. ❸

Camping:

Les Oliviers (☎/fax 04 95 26 14 49; www.campinglesoliviers.com), 200m toward Ajaccio on D81. Campers are hardly "roughing it" at this luxurious 3-star site, with a large swimming pool, tennis courts, sauna, and fitness room. The genial staff organizes canyoning (€50), hiking (€31), and climbing (€35), then rejuvenates trekkers with a 30min. massage (€35). Reception daily 8:30am-8:30pm. Open Apr.-Oct. €6-8.50 per person, €2.50-3.50 per tent, €2.50-3.50 per car. 4- to 8-person bungalows €367-882 per week. Electricity €3.50. Showers included. MC/V. ❷

Le Sole e Vista (☎ 04 95 26 15 71; fax 04 95 26 10 79), on the right before the supermarkets when entering Porto. 1km from beach. Secluded plots offer lots of shade; nab one at the hilltop to watch the sun set over the town. On-site bar and snack shop (open daily 8am-8pm). Breakfast €5. Laundry €4.50. Reception 9am-10pm. Open Apr.-Sept. €5.29-€6.19 per person, €2.40 per tent or car. Electricity €3.20. Showers included. ❷

Camping Municipal (☎ 04 95 26 17 76), off D81 in lower Porto. Tents cluster around a few stands of scraggly trees at Camping Municipal, which bears a striking resemblance to a poorly planned parking lot. A no-fail spot for last-minute campers: always has vacancies. Despite the less-than-stellar location, plots have a good view of the mountains behind. Reception daily 8am-9:30pm. Open July-Aug. €5-5.30 per person, €2.20-2.30 per tent, €2.20 per car. Electricity €3. V. ❷

🍴 FOOD

Two adjacent supermarkets are in Haut Porto on D81: **SPAR** (☎ 04 95 26 11 25; open July-Aug. M-Sa 8am-8pm, Su 8am-noon and 5-8pm; Sept.-June M-Sa 8:30am-noon and 3-7pm) and **Supermarché Banco** (☎ 04 95 26 10 92; open July-Aug. M-Sa 8am-8pm, Su 8am-12:30pm and 4-8pm; Apr.-June and Sept.-Oct. M-Sa 8am-noon and 3-7pm). **La Marine ❶,** on the main road across from the tourist office, is one of the better choices in town. A youthful staff serves up tasty pizzas (€5.50-8), pastas (€5.50-7), and a series of extensive *menus* from €9 on a street-side terrace. The *menu Pizzaoli*, with choice of salad, pizza, and dessert, is a delicious €10 bargain. (☎ 04 95 26 10 19; fax 04 95 26 13 44. Open daily Apr.-Oct. 11:30am-2:30pm and 6:30-11pm.) **La Tour Génoise ❹,** behind the aquarium in the marina, offers mouthwatering cuisine in a classy yet unpretentious setting. The spacious terrace at the base of the Tour Génoise is the perfect spot for enjoying fresh seafood (traditional Corsican *menus* (€15.10-17.40) served by an attentive, soft-spoken staff. (☎ 04 95 26 17 11; fax 04 96 26 17 81. Wheelchair- accessible. Open daily Apr.-Oct. noon-2pm and 7-10:30pm. AmEx/MC/V.) For more basic fare, try the restaurant/discotheque **Le César ❷,** farther up the main road from the port. A young crowd fuels up with pizza (€6-7.90), and hearty sandwiches (€3.10-5) before hitting the dance floor next door. (☎ 04 95 26 14 71. Open daily Apr.-Sept. noon-2pm and 7-10pm; disco open daily 11pm-5am.)

👁 📷 SIGHTS AND HIKING

GORGES AND POOLS AND PINES, OH MY. Hiking enthusiasts could easily spend weeks exploring the trails that radiate from the Gulf of Porto into the countryside. Though they range in difficulty, nearly every route provides a spectacular glimpse of the region's stunning scenery.

The old mule track from Ota to Evisa is perfect for hikers of all skill levels. This 5½hr. trail winds through the deep **Gorges de la Spelunca,** past 15th-century bridges and spots for picnics and swimming. From the stairway to the left of the Mairie in

Ota (see **Accommodations**, p. 765, for buses), the trail follows the painted orange rectangles. Spectacular scenery lies near the start of the trail, between the first two Genoese bridges and the **Pont de Zaglia** (45 minutes). To walk this shorter section, follow the main road from Ota to the first Genoese bridge and pick up the original orange rectangle trail (25 minutes). From the Pont de Zaglia, the trail continues uphill until reaching Evisa (4 hours). There are no afternoon return buses from Evisa and only one from Ota; the return hike is about 1¼hr.

Chestnut trees and 50m pines fill the mountainous **Fôret d'Aitone** between Evisa and Col. de Vergio. This trail, part of the **Tra Mare e Monti**, is famous for its *piscines naturelles*, swimming holes formed by pooling waterfalls. The pools are an hour or so from Evisa; beyond them is a more difficult and secluded trail to Col. de Vergio (6-7hr.), where a *gîte d'etape* marks its intersection with the **GR20**.

LES CALANCHES. The astounding rock formations of the Calanches resemble, in the words of Guy de Maupassant, a "menagerie of nightmares petrified by the whim of some extravagant god." Hikes in this alien landscape range from easy-as-pie to do-or-die. The **Château Fort**, in the former category, begins 6km south of Porto on D81; ask the Ota-Ajaccio bus driver to stop at **Tête de Chien** (30 minutes). A more masochistic alternative awaits 2km farther south, off D81; the marked trail, which begins near the stadium, climbs 900m to the spectacular 1294m **Capo d'Orto** (3hr. one-way). From the top of the summit, a trail heads back to Porto. The town of **Piana**, also serviced by the Ota-Ajaccio bus, is a good base for exploring both the fabulous Calanches and other geological marvels of the region. The **Sentier des Muletiers** leaves directly from town and takes hikers on a quick forest ramble before heading straight into the heart of the looming rocks. To catch the trail, head uphill immediately to the right of the *syndicat d'initiative*, following the signs for the **Gîte Giargalo**. At the fork, take the right-hand trail, which follows the old Piana-Ota mule track (30 minutes). At the end of the path, make a left and head downhill, where a large bulletin board indicates several hiking routes. Follow the signs for the ▧**Ancien Chemin Piana-Ota** across the soccer field and over a footbridge; the trail continues directly up into the Calanches. A 30min. hike along the cliffside path is all it takes to reach the most phenomenal scenery, but the trail continues down the other face and ends on D81 (15 minutes).

Southwest of Piana lies the spectacular ▧**Capo Rosso**, an enormous peninsula that marks the southern boundary of the Gulf of Porto. Perched at the top is the tiny **Tour de Turghiu**, accessible by a demanding 1½-2hr. scramble up the sun-drenched outcropping. The path begins easily enough, leading hikers past crumbling sheep-pens and shepherds' huts. As the maquis-covered landscape gives way to burnt-red rock, a nearly vertical 1hr. section (marked by stone cairns) leads straight to the tower at the apex of the peninsula. The stone structure is still in excellent condition, and if your calves can carry you up the staircase, you'll find astounding views of the distant Calanches in the Gulf of Porto. To reach the trailhead from Piana, take D824 towards Arone; the trailhead is situated on a large bend just next to a tiny snack stand and parking lot (15min. by car, 1¼hr. by foot). If you decide to make the climb, wear plenty of sunscreen and bring extra water.

SCANDOLA. Off-limits to hikers and divers, the caves, grottoes, and wild terrain of the **Réserve Naturelle de Scandola** can only be explored by **boat tours** from Porto. **Porto Linea**, next to Hôtel Monte Rosso behind the aquarium, sends the 12-person boat **Mare Nostrum** into the reserve. (☎ *04 95 26 11 50. Open Apr.-Oct.; reserve 2 days ahead in person. 3½hr. tour of Scandola €40; 1½hr. tour of Les Calanches €20.)* Less intimate but equally spectacular, **Nave Va**, near Hôtel Le Cyrnée, tours Scandola with 70- to 150-person boats. (☎ *04 95 26 15 16. Reserve 1 day ahead Apr.-Oct. 1½hr. tour of Les Calanches €22, 3hr. tour of Scandola €36, 5hr. trip to Les Calanques and Girolata €44.)* Before heading into the reserve, both boats make a swimming stop at **Girolata**, a tiny fishing

CORSICA

village accessible only by boat. If you'd rather chart your own course to the reserve, **Bateaux du Soleil**, on the marina next to the mini-golf, rents zodiacs and other small motor craft capable of holding up to 10 passengers. (☎ 06 08 69 75 20. No permit necessary. €75 per half-day, €115 per day. ID deposit. Gas €1.50 per L.)

BEACHES AND SIGHTS IN PORTO. The *raison d'être* for Porto's hotels and post-card shops is one of Corsica's oldest Genoese towers, the 1549 **Tour Génoise.** The sturdy lookout was built as part of a massive effort to improve the coastal defense system. From 1510-1620, around 100 towers were built to safeguard Corsica from unrelenting Turkish pirates—any *torregiano* (tower guard) who deserted his post was immediately put to death. (Open daily July-Aug. 9am-9pm; Apr.-May and Sept. 11am-7pm. €2.50.) At the foot of the tower, the vaulted brick-and-stone ceilings of the old powder magazine provide a lofty home for the **Aquarium de la Poudrière.** Worth a brief stop, the aquarium not only identifies aquatic creatures from the Gulf of Porto, but also (in true French fashion) indicates which swimming species are necessary for a good *bouillabaisse.* (☎ 04 95 26 19 24. Open daily May-Oct. 8am-10pm; Sept.-Apr. 10am-7pm. €5.50. Ticket for aquarium and Tour Génoise €6.50.) **Generation Bleue,** on the north side of the marina, offers **scuba** and **snorkeling** excursions. The company makes use of 15 sites in the gulf, and takes divers to the edge of the Scandola reserve. (☎ 04 95 26 24 88 or 06 85 58 24 14; www.generation-bleue.com. Open May-Oct. Reserve 1 day in advance. 2hr. dives €40-45 with equipment, at night €50. Snorkeling €15.)

Directly across the channel from the Tour Genoise lies Porto's pebbly public **beach.** Surrounded by plunging cliffs and pounding surf, the broad crescent is the perfect place to catch some rays—just don't forget your beach mat.

CALVI

Sometimes called Corsica's Côte d'Azur, Calvi (pop. 5700) shares some of the best and worst traits of that better-known coastline. Though full of souvenir shops and the idle rich, Calvi is also stunningly beautiful, with a star-shaped citadel above town and endless beaches below. Rollicking nightlife brings party-seekers from all over the island, and a series of beachfront campsites make Calvi a choice destination on the backpacking route.

☞ TRANSPORTATION

Flights: Aéroport de Calvi Ste-Catherine (☎ 04 95 65 88 88), 7km southeast of town. Taxi from the town center €13-17. **Air France** and subsidiary **Air Corse Mediterranée** (☎ 08 20 82 08 20) fly to **Lille, Lyon, Marseille, Nice,** and **Paris.**

Trains: pl. de la Gare (☎ 04 95 65 00 61), on av. de la République near the Port de Plaisance. To: **Bastia** (3hr., 4 per day, €18.10); **Corte** (2½hr., 4 per day, €15.10); **Île Rousse** (1hr., 2 per day, €4.50). In the summer, **Tramways de la Balagne** also sends trains to **Île Rousse** (1hr., June-Sept. 10 per day, €4.50). Open daily June to mid-Sept. 5:30am-9:30pm; mid-Sept. to June 7am-9pm. Purchase tickets at station or on board.

Buses: Autocar SAIB buses (☎ 04 95 22 41 99) depart from in front of the Super U and head to **Porto** (3hr.; July-Aug. 1 per day, May-Oct. M-Sa only; €16). **Les Beaux Voyages,** av. Wilson (☎ 04 95 65 11 35; fax 04 95 65 29 26), leaves from the front of the agency at pl. Porteuse d'Eau, near the tourist office. Buy tickets at the office. Open May-Oct. M-Sa 9am-noon and 2-7pm; Nov.-Apr. M-F 9am-noon and 3-7pm. Buses to: **Calenzana** (30min.; July-Aug. M-Sa 2 per day, Sept.-June 3-4 per week; €6), where the famed **GR20** begins; **Bastia** (2¼hr., M-Sa 1 per day, €15) via **Île Rousse** (25min., €3.50). **Eurocorse Voyages** (☎ 04 95 21 06 30) runs buses to **Ajaccio** (4hr., M-Sa 1 per day, €24) via **Ponte-Leccia** (€9). Buses depart from the pl. Porteuse d'Eau. Buy tickets on board.

Ferries: For info and tickets, call **Agence TRAMAR** (☎ 04 95 65 01 38), quai Landry, in the Port de Plaisance. Open July-Sept. M-F 9am-noon and 2:30-6pm, Sa 9am-noon; Oct.-June M-F 8:30am-noon and 2-5:30pm, Sa 8:30am-noon. Both **SNCM** (☎ 04 95 65

Calvi

▲▲ ACCOMMODATIONS
Camping International, **10**
Hotel Casa-Vecchia, **9**
Hôtel du Centre, **5**
Il Tramonto, **1**
Relais International de la
    Jeunesse U Carabellu, **12**

🍎 FOOD
A Scola, **2**
U Fornu, **7**
U Minellu, **6**
★ NIGHTLIFE
A Cantina, **4**
La Camargue, **11**
Chez Tao, **3**
Havanita, **8**

CORSICA

17 77; 3hr.; 7 per week; €30-42, ages 12-25 €15-27) and **Corsica Ferries** (☎04 95 65 43 21; fax 04 95 65 43 22; 3hr.; 5 per week; €20-38) send boats to **Nice** and have offices near Capitainerie du Port de Commerce. Open 2hr. before boat arrivals.

Car Rental: Europcar, av. de la République (☎04 95 65 10 35, airport 04 95 65 19 10). €65 per day, €250 per week. 21+. Open May-Sept. M-Sa 8am-7pm. AmEx/D/ MC/V. **Hertz,** 2 rue Maréchal Joffre (May-Sept. ☎04 95 65 06 64, airport 04 95 65 02 96). €71 per day, €242 per week. 21+. Additional €25 per day for drivers under 25. Open July-Aug. M-Sa 8am-8pm; May-Sept. M-Sa 8:30am-8:30pm; Su 8:30am-2:30pm. AmEx/D/MC/V.

Bike and Scooter Rental: Garage d'Angeli, 4 rue Villa St-Antoine (☎06 19 09 28 36; www.garagedangeli.com). Bikes €10-13 per day, €65-84 per week; €300 or ID deposit. Scooters from €40/€170/€800. Open daily Apr.-Oct. 8am-noon and 2-6pm; Nov.-Mar. closed Su and Mon.

Taxi: ☎04 95 65 03 10. At the train station. 24hr.

✴🚹 ORIENTATION AND PRACTICAL INFORMATION

The city is easy to walk, connected by one main road that follows the curve of the coast and changes names several times over its course, from **boulevard Wilson** between the citadel and the post office, to **avenue de la République,** and finally to **avenue Christophe Colomb** when leaving the city. The pedestrian **rue Clemenceau** begins from **pl. Porteuse d'eau,** below the post office, and runs below bd. Wilson, parallel to the port. **Quai Landry** is the waterfront thoroughfare, a cafe-lined walk that connects the ferry port at one end with the Port de Plaisance at the other.

Tourist Office: Port de Plaisance (☎04 95 65 16 67; www.tourisme.fr/calvi). From the back of the train station, turn left; it's on the 2nd floor of the 1st building on the right. Friendly staff offers a 1½hr. audioguide of the citadel (€7). 1½hr. guided tours of the citadel in French, English, Italian, or German offered to groups of 6 or more; €9 per person; reserve 2 days in advance. 2½hr. tours of the entire city are available to groups of 15 or more; €10 per person; reserve 2 days in advance. "Randocards" and "Cyclocards," detailed maps and info on 6 nearby trails, are available (€4-6). Open daily June to mid-Sept. 9am-1pm and 2:30-7pm; May M-Sa 9am-noon and 2-6:30pm; mid-Sept. to Apr. M-F 9am-noon and 2-6pm.

Laundromat: Laverie, av. Christophe Colomb, in Super U Plaza. Wash €5.80, dry €3.80. Open daily 8am-10pm. **Calvi Clean,** bd. Wilson, has new machines. Wash €6, dry €5. Open daily 7am-10pm.

Police: ☎04 95 65 44 77. On Port de Plaisance, to the right of the tourist office.

Internet Access: Calvi 2B Informatique, av. Santa Maria (☎04 95 65 19 25), 2 streets above the pl. Porteuse d'eau, near the Hotel Regina. €2 for the first 15min., €1 per additional 15min. Open June-Sept. M-Sa 9:15am-9pm, Su 3:30-9pm; Oct.-May M-Sa 9:15am-noon and 2-7pm. **Café de L'Orient** (☎04 95 65 00 16), on the port on quai Landry. €1 flat fee, €0.10 per min. Open daily Apr.-Sept. 9:30am-10pm; cafe open until 2am for drinks and crêpes.

Post Office: bd. Wilson (☎04 95 65 90 90). Open July-Aug. M-F 8:30am-6pm, Sa 8:30am-noon; Sept.-June M-F 8:30am-5:30pm, Sa 8:30am-noon.

Postal Code: 20260.

ACCOMMODATIONS AND CAMPING

Through compact, Calvi manages to pack in its fair share of pricey three- and four-star hotels. A few budget options exist, albeit farther from the center of town. Calvi has one of the only hostels in all of Corsica, tucked far in the hills above the city. The best bet may be camping; a series of sites line the coast toward Bastia. In the summer, train service connects most of them with the city center. Renting by the week can be cheaper; ask about *tarifs dégressifs* at the tourist office.

Hotel Casa-Vecchia, rte. de Santore (☎04 95 65 09 33; http://hotel-casa-vecchia.com). Take a right off av. de la République immediately after the Super U Supermarché. 12 airy rooms, each with private patio, minutes from the beach. Bath, TV, and phone. Charming dining terrace. Breakfast €6. Reception 9am-7:30pm. July-Aug. singles €55; doubles €60. Sept.-Oct. and Apr.-June €50/€55. Nov.-Mar. €45/€50. Extra bed €17. *Demi-pension* €23 per person. For long stays, fully equipped apartments are available for €400-600 per week. 2 wheelchair-accessible rooms €10 extra. MC/V. ❺

Il Tramonto, rte. de Porto R.N. 199 (☎04 95 65 04 17; www.hotel-iltramonto.com), 800m from town past the citadel. Though farther from town, Il Tramonto enjoys a prime hilltop location. 18 simple, carpeted rooms boast balconies with fabulous sea views. All with bath and phone. Breakfast €5. Reception daily 7:30am-7:30pm. Open Apr. to mid-Oct. Aug. singles and doubles €49; July €46; June and Sept. €40; May and Oct. €34; Apr. €31. Extra bed €13-16. Balcony rooms €3 extra, €6 extra in Aug. MC/V. ❹

Relais International de la Jeunesse U Carabellu (☎04 95 65 14 16). From the station, turn left on av. de la République. Continue past Super U and mini-golf to rte. de Pietramaggiore, directly across from the Casino supermarket. Turn right and follow signs 5km into the hills. The road forks at a stop sign. Veer left and continue (1hr.) Women may not want to walk alone. Beautiful, secluded *chalet* from town. Spacious rooms, all with incredible views of the bay. Families get their own doubles, triples, or quads with private shower; dorms have 10-11 beds each. Breakfast (included) is served in a homey dining room. Sheets €2. Luggage drop-off 24hr. Lockout 10am-5pm. Reserve far in advance. (For reservations during winter for following season ☎04 93 81 27 63). Open May-Oct. Dorms €15.40. *Demi-pension* €18 per person, *pension complet* €23. ❷

Hôtel du Centre, 14 rue Alsace-Lorraine (☎04 95 65 02 01), behind rue Clemenceau, in the heart of Calvi. Slightly worn and spartan, but unbeatable location and prices. Basic white rooms have plain furniture and firm beds. The friendly manager has an enormous stack of dog-eared English-language paperbacks. Breakfast €5, order the night before. Free luggage storage. Reception 8am-9pm. Open June to early Oct. Singles and doubles €28-37, with shower €32-46; triples €35-47/€38-52. ❸

Camping: Camping International, RN 197 (☎04 95 65 01 75; fax 04 95 65 36 11), 1km from town. From the train station, walk down av. de la République past Super U and Hôtel L'Onda; after the mini-golf sign, turn right. (15min.) A crowded, lively atmosphere for an international crowd. Flowering trees surround a popular on-site bar and pizzeria (pizzas €6-13). Showers included. Laundromat across from campsite. Open Apr.-Oct. July-Aug. €5.29 per person, children under 7 €2.70; €3.30 per tent; €1.50 per car; Apr.-June and Sept.-Oct. €3.90/€2/€2.60/€1.30. MC/V. ❶

🔁 FOOD

Aside from street-side *panini* vendors, cheap pickings are slim in Calvi. Try the **Super U Supermarché,** av. Christophe Colomb. (☎04 95 65 04 32. Open July-Aug. M-Sa 8:30am-8pm, Su 8:30am-1pm; June and early to mid-Sept. M-Sa 8:30am-8pm; mid-Sept. to May M-F 8:45am-7:30pm.) A handful of restaurants set up tables in the **citadel,** with appropriately towering prices. Below, narrow **rue Clemenceau** is filled with specialty food shops and grocers and hosts a small **covered market** beside the Église Ste-Marie. (Open daily 8am-noon.) Quai Landry is packed with seafood spots and *glaciers*, but pedestrian alleys have the best food and ambience.

📓 U Minellu, traverse de l'Église (☎04 95 65 05 52). The smiling staff moves deftly around packed tables, serving generous portions of Corsican specialties. The terrace offers a break from tourist-laden rue Clemenceau. The excellent €16 *menu* offers the best of the island. Savory *tarte aux blettes* is the perfect way to begin your meal, followed by traditional *plats* like *sanglier* (wild boar) served with fresh corn polenta. Open daily July-Sept. 6:30pm-11:30pm; Mar.-June M-Sa 11am-2pm and 7-10:30pm. ❹

U Fornu, bd. Wilson (☎04 95 65 27 60). A local staple for 25 years, with quiet tables and flowering trees. Daily seafood specialties like risotto with lobster (€15) and baked octopus (€16) are beautifully presented. The €16 *menu* highlights Corsican cuisine with *soupe corse* and *storzapreti* (spinach and fresh cheese). Bread and desserts are homemade. Open daily noon-2pm and 7-11pm; Su closed for lunch. ❸

A Scola, in the citadel (☎04 95 65 07 07). This small, elegant *salon de thé* offers delectable homemade pastries (€6-7) to accompany 17 varieties of tea (€3-3.20). Salads, omelettes, other light lunch fare (€9-11.50), and mouthwatering melted chocolate cake (€6.50) served in an antique-filled interior. V. ❷

🔁 SIGHTS AND BEACHES

Calvi's remarkable **citadel,** looming over the Port de Plaisance, is both a symbol of the city's tumultuous history and a manifestation of modern life. The 18th-century inscription, *"civitas Calvi semper fidelis"* (the city of Calvi is always faithful), that crowns the entrance was bestowed on Calvi by the Genoese in thanks for five

CORSICA

centuries of unbroken loyalty. Just beyond the entry portal, a welcome center distributes free maps and audioguides for the citadel. (☎04 95 65 86 74. Open June-Sept. M-Sa 10am-5pm; last tickets sold 1hr. before closing. Audioguides in the low season at tourist office. Tours in English, French, Italian, and German; 90min.; €7.) Round the first corner and climb the stairs to reach the citadel's center, dominated by the austere **Palais des Gouverneurs.** The original *palais* was the oldest building in the citadel, but in 1567 lightning struck the powder store and the entire building went up in flames. The Genoese rebuilt it as a bastion of control over the city, and today it serves—not without irony—as the mess hall for France's foreign legion. The 16th-century **Cathédrale St-Jean Baptiste** towers nearby—its Baroque domes belie a plain interior. In 1555, the citizens of Calvi effectively drove away French and Turkish invaders by displaying an ebony sculpture of Christ on the battlements now on display to the right of the altar. The 15th-century blue-clad Madonna to the left of the choir, imported from Peru, is the pride and joy of the town's religious sector. (Open daily 9am-7pm.) The **Oratoire St-Antoine,** tucked into the citadel's wall, was once the meeting place of St. John the Baptist, St. Francis of Assisi, and St. Antoine; their presence is commemorated by a slate lintel above the doorframe. (Open daily 10am-6pm.)

Like several other Mediterranean towns, Calvi claims to be the birthplace of **Christopher Columbus.** The local theory is that Calvi expatriate Antonio Calvo returned to his hometown in the 15th century to enlist recruits for the Genoese navy. His nephew Christophe caught his eye, so Calvo brought him to Genoa. A few other tenuous leads support the speculation. Calvi is quick to note that Columbus used Corsican dogs in warfare and preferred to keep company with *calvais* officers instead of the Genoese. A **plaque** in the northern end of the citadel marks the ruins of the house where Columbus was supposedly born. The citadel's other famous residence, the **Giubegga house,** sheltered Napoleon and his family in the summer of 1793 when they fled political opponents in Ajaccio.

At the end of the day, watch the sun sink behind the mountains at the far end of the citadel—it's one of the only spots in Calvi set high enough. Calvi and the surrounding area abound with gorgeous beaches, making for some of the best **scuba diving** on the coast. Calvi boasts two particularly well-known sites: **La bibliothèque,** where rock formations resemble fully stocked bookshelves, and **Le B-17,** a sunken WWII bomber with wings and propellers still intact. **Calvi Plongée Citadelle,** below the tourist office, runs dives to both sites. (☎04 95 65 33 67 or 06 18 06 78 45. 2hr. dives €37, equipment included. Night dives €15 extra. **Snorkeling** trips €15 with equipment. 10% discount for *Let's Go* readers. Open daily Apr.-Oct. 8am-8pm. Reservations necessary.) Closer to shore, shallow water allows beach-goers to walk many meters from the coast, and strong winds make for great **windsurfing**. The friendly staff at the **Calvi Nautique Club,** near the port, will have you skimming the waves in no time. (☎04 95 65 10 65; www.calvinc.org. **Windsurfing** equipment €14 per hr., €25 for 2hr.; **sailboats** €35/€63 with €280 deposit; **kayaks** €10-15 per hr. Open daily July-Aug. 9am-7pm, Sept.-June 9am-noon and 2-5pm. V.) If the 6km expanse of **public beach** gets too windy, the rocks surrounding the citadel provide secluded and sun-drenched shelter. The **Tramways de la Balagne** (see **Transportation,** p. 768) run to more remote coves farther out of town.

■ NIGHTLIFE

Lively bars along the **Port de Plaisance** provide perfect people-watching venues on sultry summer nights. Two open-air nightclubs on the road to Île Rousse give St-Tropez a run for its money: locals come from all over the island for big-name DJs and wild theme parties. Signs posted all over town advertise party nights at different spots along the northern coast.

Chez Tao (☎04 95 65 00 73), in the citadel. Corsica's oldest nightspot caters to a classy older crowd with creative cocktails (€10), wines (€6 per glass) and aperitifs (€7) served on a candlelit terrace overlooking the sea. Don't be fooled by the subdued appearance: this piano bar turns wild after 1am, when the tables are cleared away and live DJs spin disco and funk until dawn. Open daily June-Sept. 7pm-6am.

Havanita, Port de Plaisance (☎04 95 65 00 37). Swaying palms and sexy salsa bring a trace of another tiny island. A young crowd fills the brightly painted tables for Cuban cocktails (€7). Beer €3-5, wines €2.80 per glass. Happy hour daily 6-8:30pm with €5 cocktails. Open daily Mar.-Oct. 6pm-2am.

A Cantina, 4 rue des Anges (☎06 25 78 10 42), just below the citadel. If the sign to Acapulco made you look twice, so will the bar menu: this funky Latino-Corsican fusion offers a wide selection of *tapas* (€1.50-4) as well as typical *charcuterie.* Outdoor tables beneath the floodlit citadel are perfect for enjoying a Corsican *eau de vie* (€4) or *liqueur* (€4), with salsa in the background.

La Camargue (☎04 95 65 08 70), 25min. up N197 by foot. The scantily clad come early and linger late amid waterfalls, outdoor pools, and a jungle-themed bar. An over-30 crowd relives their own glory days (albeit fully dressed) in the adjacent piano bar. Free shuttles depart for La Camargue from the port parking lot near the tourist office. €10 cover includes one drink. Open daily July-Aug. 11pm-6am; June and Sept. Sa-Su only; piano bar open year-round.

🌿 FESTIVALS

Calvi hosts several festivals throughout the year. In the last week of June, Calvi draws up-and-coming musicians to the **Festival du Jazz** with the promise of free lodging and meals. In exchange, they play in 15 concerts over a two-week period. Bars along the port de Plaisance host the nightly performances, as well as impromptu jam sessions. (☎04 95 65 00 50. €10.) In mid-September, international artists come together for **Rencontres Polyphoniques,** a festival celebrating the worldwide tradition of chanting music. Diverse groups from far-flung locations give individual performances in the citadel, then culminate the festival with a spectacular joint concert led by *A Fileta,* one of Corsica's best-known traditional

THE ANSWER, MY FRIENDS...

For Corsicans, who are fond of saying that nothing can contain the wind, the island's ferocious gusts have become a metaphor for freedom. It is fitting that one of the most spectacular festivals in Corsica, **Festiventu,** was conceived as an homage to both the ever-present wind and unique Corsican traditions. Every year at the end of October, the city of Calvi is flooded with over 40,000 visitors who come to share in a week-long celebration of art, music, and sport. Hot-air balloons and kites fill the sky, while the ground overflows with street performers and innovative artwork. Installations have included an enormous "air ball" that, when closed, allows passengers to walk on water.

Every year, the lighthearted revelry of Festiventu is also accompanied by serious intellectual discussions on pressing environmental and political problems, with remarkable effectiveness. In 2003, for example, the festival's direction succeeded in banning plastic bags from every single grocery store in the region. The Corsican saying rings true: with Festiventu, the powerful wind of change knows no boundaries.

(For more info, contact the Association du Festiventu at ☎041 53 20 93 00 or 01 53 20 93 05; www.lefestivalduvent.com. Concert tickets €15-20, purchased at door.)

groups. (☎04 95 65 23 57. Tickets €15-20.) In late October or early November, Calvi pulls out all the stops for the colorful **Festival du Vent.** (See **The Answer, My Friends,** right.)

ÎLE ROUSSE

Île Rousse (pop. 3000) was founded as a deliberate slap in the face: in 1765, the clever Pascal Paoli decided to build a French port that would at once give him access to mainland France and divert trade from Genoese-dominated Calvi. Though both towns eventually came under French control, their historical rivalry was furthered by Calvi's construction of an impressive marina, airport, and other tourism-inducing projects. Île Rousse is the perfect hub for hikes into the country-side of the Balagne. The scenic train ride from Calvi alone is worth the trip.

SNCM sends **ferries** to Nice (3-10hr., depending on the boat; 2-7 per week; €35-47, students €20-32) and Marseille (5-9hr., depending on the boat; 2 per week; €40-58, students €25-45). Call Agence CCR on av. J. Calizi for more info. (☎04 95 60 09 56; fax 04 95 60 02 56. Open June-Aug. M-F 9am-noon and 2-6pm, Sa 9am-noon; Sept.-May M-F 8:30am-noon and 2:30-5:30pm.) The **train station** provides service to Ajaccio, Bastia, and Calvi. (☎04 95 60 00 50. Open daily July-Sept. 6am-8:30pm, Oct.-June 8am-9:30pm.) Tramways de la Balagne **trains** hug the coast on the way to Calvi. (50min.; June-Sept. 9 per day; €4. Purchase tickets at station or onboard.) Several beaches and campsites lie along the route; the train stops at any when requested. The **Aregno Plage** and its lively campsite are three stops from Île Rousse.

Two kilometers across, Île Rousse is easy to navigate. The town center lies to the right of the train station, while the *gare maritime* and tower-topped peninsula are to the left. To get to the tiny **tourist office** from the train station or ferry depot, walk right for about 5min.; it's in a small office on the far side of pl. Paoli. The *pochette des randonnés*, a detailed regional hiking guide, is available for €12. (☎04 95 60 04 35; www.ot-ile-rousse.fr. Open June-Sept. M-Sa 9am-7pm, Su 10am-1pm and 4-7:30pm; Oct.-May M-F 9am-noon and 2-6pm.)

La Passion en Action, av. Paul Doumer, rents mountain **bikes.** (☎04 95 60 15 76. Open daily July-Aug. 7am-8pm; June and Sept. M-Sa 8:30am-7:30pm; Oct.-May M-Sa 9am-noon and 2-7pm. €16 per day, €72 per week; €229 deposit. AmEx/MC/V.) Surf the **Internet** at Movie' Store, rte. de Calvi, across from the Casino supermarket. (☎04 95 65 47 97. 17 computers. €2 for 15 min., €3 for 30min., €5 per hr. Open M-Sa 10am-2am, Su 2pm-2am.) The **post office** is on rte. de Monticello. (☎04 95 63 05 50. Open July-Aug. M-F 8am-7pm, Sa 8am-noon; Sept.-June M-F 8:30am-5pm, Sa 8:30am-noon.) **Postal Code:** 20220.

Since Île Rousse tends to attract well-moneyed Frenchmen, there's only one budget hotel in town. To find **Hôtel le Grillon ❸,** 10 av. Paul Doumer, go straight on av. Piccioni, beside the tourist office, and take a left. Friendly owners let 16 pastel rooms, some with tiny balcony (request in advance). All are moderately sized but well equipped with bath, TV, phone, and fan. (☎04 95 60 00 49; fax 04 95 60 43 69. Breakfast €5.40. Dinner *menus* €12.50 and €16. Reception daily 6am-10pm. Reserve in advance. Open Mar.-Oct. Singles €32-49; doubles €33-53; triples €40-59. Aug. obligatory *demi-pension* for singles €68; doubles €92; triples €117. MC/V.) An abundance of campsites stretch along the Balagne coast. Sites appear frequently; hop off the train when you see an enticing spot. **Les Oliviers ❶,** in Île Rousse, is 800m from the town center on av. Paul Doumer, the main road to Bastia. This site, run by a cheerful staff, is filled with happy campers. A bar, pizzeria, snack stand, and barbecue are on-site. Two- and four-person bungalows are available for rent. (☎04 95 60 19 92 or 04 95 60 25 64; lesolivierskalliste@wanadoo.fr. Laundry €5. Open Apr.-Oct.; July-Aug. closed to cars after 11pm. €6 per person, €3.50 per tent, €2.50 per car. *Chalet* doubles €80. Bungalows July-Aug. €500 per week, Sept.-June €350 per week. Electricity €3.50. Showers free. MC/V.)

The city's signature covered **market** off pl. Paoli has been bringing the freshest produce to town since 1850. Now a historical monument, its stalls still burst with ripe local fruits, olives, and catches of the day. (Open daily 7am-1pm.) The local **Casino supermarket** on the palais des Allées takes up where the market leaves off. (☎04 95 60 24 23. Open July-Aug. M-Sa 8:30am-8pm, Su 8:30am-1pm; Sept.-June M-F 8:30am-12:30pm and 3-7pm, Sa 8:30am-7pm.) *Brasseries* and *crêperies* along pl. Paoli fill with diners hungry for inexpensive pizza, sandwiches, and, of course, crêpes. For a quieter sit-down meal, try **U Fucone ❷**, on pl. Paoli. This welcoming, basic spot sets up tables on a calm side street. You can't go wrong with the three-course, €12.50 *menu*, which includes seafood salad, pasta with *figatellu* (Corsican ham), and *crème caramel*. The friendly staff also serves 14 kinds of pizza (€14). In the winter, the chef trades Corsican cuisine for Alsacian and Savoyard specialties. (☎04 95 60 16 67. Open daily May-Sept. 11:30am-2pm and 6:30-11pm; low season hours vary. AmEx/MC/V.) An elegant *repas* awaits beneath vaulted ceilings in **U Spuntinu ❹**, on rue Napoleon. This family establishment makes nearly everything from scratch, including the heavenly *flan de chataigne* (chestnut flan). The three-course *menu* (€18.50) includes other dreamy desserts, but you'll have to save room: after *veau avec des beignets de courgettes* (veal served with fried zucchini), it might be tough. (☎04 95 60 00 05. Open July-Aug. M-Sa 7:30-11:30pm; Sept. to mid-Dec. and May to June M-Sa noon-1:30pm and 7:30-10:30pm; July-Aug. occasionally open for lunch; closed mid-Dec. to Feb. MC/V.)

CORTE (CORTI)

The dynamic city of Corte (pop. 6000), sits between snow-capped peaks near the center of the island. The location is fitting, as Corte is widely considered to be the intellectual and political heart of Corsica. The town, which houses the island's only university, gave birth to Pascal Paoli's constitution and remains the center of the Corsican nationalist cause. Locals have made a serious effort to keep Corsican traditions alive. Most speak Corse, the island's distinctive dialect, in addition to French. It's easy to understand why locals are fiercely proud of their inland city. Perched above the convergence of three pristine rivers, Corte is an unforgettable eyeful of plunging cliffs, jagged summits, and endless sky.

▐ TRANSPORTATION

Trains depart from the roundabout at av. Jean Nicoli and N193 to Ajaccio (2½hr., 4 per day, €12.70); Bastia (2hr., 5 per day, €11.20); and Calvi via Ponte-Leccia (3hr., 3 per day, €15.10). The station (☎04 95 00 80 17) is open M-Sa 6:30am-9pm, Su 7:45am-9pm. **Eurocorse Voyages buses** (☎04 95 31 73 76) leave from the *Brasserie Le Majestic* on Cours Paoli for Ajaccio (1¾hr., M-Sa 2 per day, €10) and Bastia (1¼hr., M-Sa 2 per day, €10). **Autocars Mordiconi** (☎04 95 48 00 04) leave from the train station for Porto (2½hr., July-Sept. M-Sa 1 per day, €19). **Taxis Salviani** can be reached at ☎04 95 46 04 88 or 06 03 49 15 24; **Taxi Feracci** at ☎06 12 10 60 60. **Cars** can be rented at Europcar, next to the train station. (☎04 95 46 06 02. From €81 per day, €282 per week. Credit card deposit. Insurance included. 21+. Open M-F 8am-noon and 2:30-6pm, Sa 8am-noon. MC/V.)

✚ ▐ ORIENTATION AND PRACTICAL INFORMATION

To reach the town center from the station, turn right on N193, cross the bridge, and take a left at the next bridge onto av. Jean Nicoli. Follow the road until it ends at **cours Paoli**, Corte's main drag. A left turn here leads to **place Paoli**, the town center. At the top right corner, climb the stairwayed **rue Scolisca** to reach the citadel and the **tourist office**, which provides a bus schedule and bilingual brochure. (☎04 95 46 26 70; www.corte-tourisme.com. Open July-Aug. M-Sa

9am-8pm, Su 10am-6pm; June and Sept. M-Sa 9am-6pm; Apr.-May 9am-noon and 2-6pm; Oct.-Mar. M-F 9am-noon and 2-6pm.) Just next door, the **Parc Naturel Régional** expert provides additional info for hikers. (☎04 95 46 27 44; www.parc-naturel-corse.com. Open May-Sept. M-F 9am-noon and 2-6pm.) Other services include: **Bureau Information Jeunesse de Corte**, rampe Ste-Croix (☎04 95 46 12 48; open M-F 8:30am-12:30pm and 2-5:30pm); a **laundromat** at Speed Laverie, allée du 9 Septembre, in the shopping plaza behind Mr. Bricolage (☎06 82 56 08 31; open daily 8am-9pm); **police** (☎04 95 46 04 81), southeast of town on N200; a **hospital** allée du 9 Septembre, (☎04 95 45 05 00); **Internet** at Grand Café du Cours, 22 cours Paoli (☎04 95 46 00 33; €0.10 per min., €5 per hr.; open daily 7am-2am) and Le Bar Video-Games, av. de President Pierucci, next to the Hotel Sampiero Corso (☎04 95 47 32 86; €2.50 for 30min., €4 per hr. Open July-Aug. M-Sa 8am-2am, Su 5pm-midnight; Sept.-June closed Su); and a **post office**, av. du Baron Mariani (☎04 95 46 08 20; open M-F 8am-12:30pm and 1:30-5pm, Sa 8am-noon). **Postal Code:** 20250.

♠ ♣ ACCOMMODATIONS AND CAMPING

Hôtel-Residence Porette (H-R), 6 allée du 9 Septembre (☎04 95 45 11 11; fax 04 95 61 02 85), near the train station. Head left and uphill from the station, past the Casino supermarket. The hotel is across from the stadium (100m). This no-frills hotel is housed in an unattractively converted police station; dirt-cheap rooms are accordingly utilitarian and small. Those overlooking the pleasant back garden are more spacious, but you'll have to pay for the extra room (€10). Sauna (€4), weight room, and restaurant. Breakfast buffet €5. Laundry. 24hr. reception. Reservations required June and Aug.-Sept. Singles €21-€27, with bath €39; doubles €25-29/€39; triples €55; quads €59. AmEx. ❷

Hôtel de la Paix, av. du Général de Gaulle (☎04 95 46 06 72; fax 04 95 46 23 84), past Hôtel de la Poste. Nervous Nellies sleep easy here: recent renovations include a beefed-up security system. Friendly staff. Pleasant, modern rooms range from narrow to enormous. All have toilet, shower or bath, and phone. Restaurant with 3-course *menu* €13. Breakfast €5.50. *demi-pension* available; inquire at time of reservation. May-July and Sept. singles and doubles €48-55; triples €70. Aug. singles and doubles €53-62; triples €75. Oct.-Apr. singles €42; doubles €50; triples €63. ❸

Hôtel de la Poste, 2 pl. du Duc de Padoue (☎04 95 46 01 37), off cours Paoli. Near the town center. 11 well-kept rooms with tile floors and high ceilings fill the first 2 floors of a private residence. Friendly owner ensures that showers are sparkling. Breakfast €5.50. Reception 7:30am-9:30pm. Singles and doubles €35, with shower €42.50-52; triples €51-54; quads and quints €54-61. Wheelchair-accessible room €61. ❸

Camping:

U Sognu, on D623 (☎04 95 46 09 07). From the top of pl. Paoli, follow rue Prof. Santiaggi around the bend, turn left, and cross the bridge. At the fork, follow the sign and turn right (10min). From train station, follow directions to Restonica; after the 1st bridge, take a left onto D623. Gracious owners keep campers happy with homemade wood-fired pizzas (€7) and stunning views of the *haute ville*. Sites on the main section tend to have little shade; nab a spot on one of the tree-lined terraces above or you may be sleeping in a sauna. Breakfast €6. Restaurant meals €7-11. Reception daily 8am-noon and 4-10pm. Closed to cars after 11pm. Open late Mar. to mid-Oct. €6 per person; €2.50 per tent or car. Electricity €3. ❶

Restonica (☎/fax 04 95 46 11 59; vero.camp@worldonline.fr). Follow directions from station to H-R Porette, then continue on allée du 9 Septembre, bearing right at the intersection with the ancienne rte. d'Ajaccio. A sign on the right points downhill to campsite just before the first bridge. Tents cluster along a small, tree-lined stream perfect for wading. Crowded site, with snack bar and showers. Breakfast €6. Pizza €8.50. Wash €7.50. Reception daily 8am-10pm. Open mid-Apr. to mid-Oct. €6 per person, €3 per tent, €2.50 per car. Electricity €3.50. ❶

◘ FOOD

Place Paoli is the spot for sandwiches and pizza; inexpensive cafes and *brasseries* are clustered here and along the adjoining **cours Paoli**. For a good selection of inexpensive local cuisine, try **rue Scolisca** and the surrounding citadel streets. Most restaurants throughout Calvi offer *menus* around €9-12. **SPAR,** 5 av. Xavier Luciani, is in the town center. (☎04 95 45 08 59. Open July-Aug. M-Sa 7:30am-8:30pm, Su 9am-noon and 5-7:30pm; Sept.-June M-Sa 8:30am-noon and 3-8pm, Su 8:30am-noon.) The mammoth **casino** is near the train station on RN 193, alias rte. d'Ajaccio. (☎04 95 45 22 45. Open July-Aug. M-Sa 8:30am-8pm; Sept.-June M-F 8:30am-12:30pm and 3-7:30pm, Sa 8:30am-7:30pm.)

City-wide recommendations have tourists and locals alike flocking to **⧄U Museu ❸,** ramp Ribanelle, off pl. d'Armes at the foot of the citadel. Three enormous flower-lined terraces provide plenty of shade for enjoying outstanding regional cuisine. The professional, friendly staff serves house specialties like *civet de sanglier* (wild boar) and *truite in peveronatta* (trout in a tomato, pepper, and wine sauce). Vegetarians will appreciate the heaping salads (€6.50-9), loaded with all sorts of fresh *legumes.* (☎04 95 61 08 36. *Menu* €13.20, meat dishes €11-13, fish dishes €9.50-15.20, pasta €8-11, pizzas €6.50-8. Open daily early Apr.-late Dec. noon-2:30pm and 7-10:30pm; Sept.-May closed Su. MC/V.) The gregarious owner of **A Maniccia ❷,** 7 cours Paoli, named her restaurant after a nearby mountain which she has summited three times. In addition to hiking and climbing advice, she dishes up homemade Corsican staples like *soupe Corse* (€6) and *gateau à la chataigne.* (☎04 95 61 01 69. Local specialties €7-9.50, extensive *menu* €14, meats €12.50-13, pasta €6-8, omelettes €4.50-5, crêpes €2.50-6. Open June-Sept. M-Sa 9am-3pm and 6-10:30pm; Oct.-May M-Sa 7am-4pm and 6pm-2am. AmEx/MC/V.) Though outdoor tables on pl. Paoli provide a good people-watching point, the best view at **A Scudella ❷,** 2 pl. Paoli, is inside, where impeccably clad chefs prepare delectable *plats* in the center of the dining room. The €9 *menu* includes a double-sized appetizer and dessert; the €11 *menu* a main dish and dessert. (☎04 95 46 25 31. *Plats* €9.20. Open M-Sa noon-2pm and 7-10pm. MC/V.)

◙ SIGHTS

Corte's *vieille ville*, with its steep streets and austere stone **citadel** that peers over the Tavignano and Restonica Valleys, has always been a bastion of Corsican patriotism. The route up to the old city honors two men who led the Corsican national movement: **Jean Pierre Gaffory** wrested control of the city from French hands in 1745 and served as governor until his assassination in 1753, and the city's best loved son—**Pascal Paoli**—took control of Corte and proclaimed it the capital of Corsica. He instituted a democratic constitution and built Corte's university, which now enrolls over 4000 students. In a plain dwelling across from pl. Gaffory, a plaque honors the apartments where Charles Bonaparte, Napoleon's father, lived in the 1760s while studying at the University of Corte and serving the Paolian cause.

The **Musée de la Corse,** at the top of rue Scolisca, has a delightful collection of Corsica's ethnographic history. Traditional milk pails and handlooms, rulebooks and hooded cloaks of existing religious orders, and vintage bottles of Cap Corse Mattei, the island's best-known aperitif, reveal different facets and periods of Corsican life. Exhibits are in French and Corse; consider the 90min. English audioguide (€1.50). Admission includes a visit to Corsica's only inland citadel, constructed in 1419. The imposing structure was remodeled over the years, finally obtaining its current configuration under Louis Philippe. Visitors can explore the pitch-black dungeon, still thoughtfully outfitted with a stone mattress and pillow. (☎04 95 45 25 45; fax 04 95 45 25 36. Museum open daily late June to late Sept. 10am-8pm; late Sept. to Oct. and Apr. to late June Tu-Su 10am-6pm; Nov.-Mar. Tu-Sa 10am-6pm. Citadel closes 1hr. earlier than museum. €5.30, students €3.) Uphill from pl. Paoli and left at the Église de l'Annonciation is the oldest portion of the city walls and a spectacular panorama from the **Belvedere,** a windswept lookout that affords dizzying views of the twisting rivers and tree-covered valleys below.

The mountains and river beds that surround Corte are lined with trails for **hiking** (call tourist office for maps and info, ☎08 92 68 32 50 for weather) or **horseback riding.** Try the **Ferme Equestre Albadu,** 1.5km from town on N193 toward Ajaccio. (☎04 95 46 24 55. Reserve at least 1 day in advance. €13.80 for 1hr., €24.40 for 2hr., €35 for 3hr., €75 per day including picnic. 6-night camping trip with guide €550.)

DAYTRIPS FROM CORTE

GORGES DE LA RESTONICA

To get there, descend rue Prof. Santiaggi at the back of pl. Paoli and cross the bridge at the right; head right on D623 at the fork. Follow the signs for Restonica for 2km to the Parc Naturel Régional info office, where a free navette *(shuttle) whisks hikers 13km up a twisting road to the gorge's summit. The* navette *is only available for groups; individual hikers must access the gorge by car. (Open daily July-Aug. 8am-1:30pm, return 2:30-5pm. Call ☎04 95 46 02 12 for detailed schedules.)*

Southwest of Corte, tiny D623 stretches 16km through the Gorges de la Restonica, a high-altitude canyon fed by glacial lakes. The hot-blooded can brave a swim in the gorge's icy water.

Those who only have time for one hike should be sure to tour the **glacial lakes** at the top of the gorge, one of the island's loveliest and least-populated areas, where hikers of all levels can enjoy the magnificent scenery. Take the *navette* to the Grotelle parking lot. To the right, a trail clearly marked in yellow leads to a sheep-pen-turned-snackbar, then crosses the river and steadily ascends to the "most visited lake in Corsica," the **Lac de Melo** (1 hr.). This snow-fed beauty lies at 1711m, near the foot of **Mont Rotondo** (2622m), and is surrounded by mountain peaks, including Corsica's highest, **Mont Cinto** (2710m). The trail is designated *facile* (easy), but the climb is steep, rocky, and slippery when wet. Also, temperatures at the top can reach well below freezing even when it's 25°C in town. From Melo, the trail continues, marked in yellow, to one of Corsica's largest and deepest lakes, the austere **Lac de Capitellu.** (1930m; 45min.) From here, the trail meets the red and white marked **GR20,** Corsica's most famous and most demanding hike.

For a full-day adventure follow the GR20 to the left until it intersects with a trail leading to the **Refuge de Petra Piana,** where hikers can spend the night or continue on to the **Lac de Rotondo** (4½hr.). Less trodden but equally spectacular is the hike to **Lac de l'Oriente.** Take the free *navette* to **Pont de Tragone** and then follow the marked trail that passes shepherds' houses to the much-photographed lake (3 hours). For more info on Restonica's offerings, consult the French-language *Tavignano-Restonica topo-guide* (in bookstores for €11.50) or the tourist office hiking expert. The office also supplies a €5 map with 26 labeled hiking trails.

GORGES DU TAVIGNANO

To get to the trail, head to the back of the citadel and look for signs; the trail is marked in orange.

Less rugged and more easily accessible by foot than Restonica, though equally demanding, the Tavignano gorges are filled with waterfalls, natural pools, and picturesque hiking trails. With no road access, it is likely to be less crowded than its better-known counterpart. The first 2½hr. of hiking along the Tavignano River leads to the **Passerelle du Russulinu** (902m), a small suspension bridge surrounded by refreshing natural swimming pools and flat, picnic-friendly rocks. Bring sunscreen and wear a hat; there is little shade along the way. Another 3hr. along the same trail leads to the **Refuge de la Sega** (1166m), where hikers can stop to spend the night. (☎ 04 95 46 07 90 or 06 10 71 77 26. Reservations strongly recommended.) The road diverges at this point. To the left, a well-traveled trail passes by ancient *bergeries* (sheep pens) and abandoned shepherd huts, crossing the **Plateau d'Alzo** and ending at the **Pont de la Frasseta,** 8km up on D623, in the heart of the Restonica (4hr.). To the right, the less-traveled trail leads to the heartland village of **Calacuccia,** on D84, 45min. from Corte by car (4 hours).

FORÊT DE VIZZAVONA

Vizzavona is easily reached via a magnificent ▨ train ride (1hr., 4 per day, €5.80). The track from Corte winds leisurely along picturesque stone tunnels and narrow bridges. The unhurried pace allows passengers plenty of time to gaze, but it's not simply for your sightseeing benefit: cows have a tendency to munch near the moss-covered tracks.

Rugged mountains and miles of untouched pine forest surround tiny Vizzavona, leaving its 50 inhabitants with plenty of room to stretch their legs. Several hiking trails of varying difficulty converge at the town, making it an excellent base for both serious woodsmen and ambling day-trippers.

Once you reach Vizzavona, collect your open-mouthed self and head behind the station, where a wooden billboard lists several hiking routes. The easiest, **Cascade des Anglais,** is a 45min. ramble through the forest that ends at a series of plunging waterfalls. The trail is broad and well marked; unfortunately, its accessibility draws hordes of hikers in summer. The large, flat rocks and shaded coves make ideal picnic spots, and the lagoons are perfect for swimming. Those looking for a more solitary site should keep heading uphill past the base of the falls.

For hardcore hikers, Vizzavona offers the **Monte d'Oro,** an unrelenting 2389m summit whose waters feed the streams and rivers of the entire region. From the top, hikers can see all the way to Italy. The base of the trail, marked by orange circles, begins right in town. Monte d'Oro is not for weekend ramblers: those who attempt a summit bid should be experienced and well equipped, as there is no water along most of the route. Start early (the entire trip takes about 9 hours), and check with the regional park office for weather conditions, detailed maps, and other appropriate info.

BASTIA

Bastia (pop. 40,000), Corsica's second largest city, is a well-trodden gateway providing connections both to the mainland and to the island's more picturesque vacation spots. The city's enormous ferry port, airport, and regional bus hub ensure that many travelers are mere passersby on their way to rural Corsican adventures. But despite all this zooming traffic, Bastia deserves more than a quick glance. It is neither cosmopolitan nor over-touristed, and its crumbling *vieille ville*, lovely citadel, and exquisite Baroque churches give a more authentic feel than Ajaccio. In addition, Bastia is the perfect base for the must-see Cap Corse.

CORSICA

⌐ TRANSPORTATION

Flights: Bastia-Poretta (☎04 95 54 54 54), 23km away. An airport bus (☎04 95 31 06 65), scheduled to coincide with departing flights, leaves from *préfecture*, across from train station (30min., €8). Purchase tickets on bus. **Air France** (☎08 20 82 08 20) flies to **Marseille** (3-5 flights per day), **Nice** (3-4 flights per day), and **Paris** (6 flights per day).

Trains: pl. de la Gare (☎04 95 32 80 61), to the left of the roundabout at the top of av. Maréchal Sebastiani. Station open Sept.-June M-Sa 6:10am-8:45pm, Su 6:30am-8:45pm; daily July-Aug. 6am-9:45pm. To: **Ajaccio** (4hr., 5 per day, €23.90); **Calvi** (3hr., 4 per day, €18.10); **Corte** (45min., 4 per day, €11.20); **Île Rousse** (2½hr., 4 per day, €15). The "Zoom Card," a 7-day excursion pass, offers unlimited travel throughout Corsica (€47). Train service significantly less frequent from Oct.-May; check with the tourist office for the most up-to-date schedules.

Buses: Ask the tourist office for a bus schedule. **Eurocorse,** rte. du Nouveau Port (☎04 95 21 06 31), runs to **Ajaccio** (3hr., M-Sa 2 per day, €18). **Rapides Bleus,** 1 av. Maréchal Sebastiani across from the post office (☎04 95 31 03 79), sends buses to **Porto Vecchio** (3hr.; M-Sa 2 per day, daily mid-June to mid-Sept.; €18.50) via **Aléria** (1½hr., €11). **Transport Santini** (☎04 95 37 04 01) offers service to **Saint Florent** (1hr., M-Sa 2 per day, €5). **Autocars Cortenais** (☎04 95 46 02 12) leaves for **Corte** (1¼ hr., M, W, F 1 per day; €10). Purchase tickets on bus.

Ferries: quai de Fango, next to pl. St-Nicolas; turn left from av. Maréchal Sebastiani just past pl. St-Nicolas. **SNCM** (☎04 95 54 66 90; fax 04 95 54 66 44), by the quai de Fango, sails to **Marseille** and **Nice. Corsica Ferries,** 5bis rue du Chanoine Leschi (☎04 95 32 95 95), chug to **Nice** and **Toulon,** as well as **Livorno** and **Savona** in Italy. **Moby Lines,** 4 rue Commandant Luce de Casablanca (☎04 95 34 84 94; www.moby-colonna-corse.com), serves **Genoa** and **Livorno** in Italy. For details on air and ferry connections to mainland France, see **Intercity Transportation,** p. 756.

Taxis: (☎04 95 32 24 24, 04 95 36 04 05, or 04 95 32 70 70). €32-33 to airport. 24hr.

Car Rental: ADA, 35 rue César Campinchi (☎04 95 31 48 95; ada-encorse.com), with a 2nd location at the airport (☎04 95 54 55 44). Open M-F 8am-noon and 2-7pm, Sa 8am-noon. AmEx/MC/V.

Scooter Rental: Toga Location Nautique, port de Plaisance de Toga (☎04 95 34 14 14; www.plaisance-location.com), near the north quai. Scooters €65 per day, €300 per week; €1220 deposit. Open M-Sa 8am-noon and 2-6:30pm. MC/V.

✚ ⓘ ORIENTATION AND PRACTICAL INFORMATION

Place St-Nicolas sits smack in the center of action, serving as a divider between the Vieux Port to the north and the new town to the south. Bastia's main thoroughfare, **boulevard du Général de Gaulle,** runs along its inland length. Just parallel are two other main arteries, **boulevard Paoli** and **rue César Campinchi.** Facing the mountains, the *vieux port* and citadel are to the left and the ferry docks are to the right. The tourist office sits at the edge of place St-Nicolas, near the ferries.

Tourist Office: pl. St-Nicolas (☎04 95 54 20 40; www.bastia-tourisme.com), has maps of the city and Cap Corse. Free accommodations service. Ask for a copy of their indispensable bus schedule. Open daily July-Aug. 8am-9:30pm; Sept.-June 8:30am-noon and 2-6pm.

Youth Center: Centre Information Jeunesse, 9 rue César Campinchi (☎04 95 32 12 13; www.crij-corse.com). Cheerful, English-speaking staff has info on work, health, housing, and leisure activities. Free Internet for up to 40min. Open M-F 8am-6pm. Closed July 30-Oct. 23.

Laundromat: Lavoir du Port, 25 rue Luce de Casablanca (☎04 95 32 25 51), just past the Esso gas station. Wash €5.80-8.80, dry €0.50 per 6min. Open daily 7am-9pm.

Police: rue Commandant Luce de Casabianca (☎04 95 55 22 22).

Hospital: rte. Impériale (☎04 95 59 11 11).

Internet Access: free for up to 40min. at the **Centre Information Jeunesse** (see **Youth Center**). **Cyber Taz,** 4 cours Pierangeli (☎04 95 93 78 90) offers 10 computers and long hours. €3 first hr., €1.50 each additional hr. Open daily 8:30am-3am. **Le Cyber,** 6 rue des Jardins (☎04 95 34 30 34), behind the Vieux Port. 12 computers and comfy office chairs. €1.60 for 30min., €3 per hr. Open daily 8am-midnight.

Post Office: at av. Maréchal Sébastiani and bd. Général Graziani (☎04 95 32 80 70). Open daily 8am-7pm.

Postal Code: 20200.

ACCOMMODATIONS AND CAMPING

Though Bastia's hotels offer better rates than the sky-high prices in Corsica's more popular resort towns, most still fall within a range that can be stiff for true budget travelers. Low season brings *prix interessants* and plenty of vacancies, but hotels fill up quickly come June and remain full throughout the rest of high season (as late as mid-October). Camping is a viable option; although both sites are far from town they can be reached by local buses.

Hôtel Central, 3 rue Miot (☎04 95 31 71 12; www.centralhotel.fr). Aptly named, between the new port and the *vieille ville.* Welcoming rooms full of personality; each fitted with hand-picked antique furniture. All have TV, phone, toilet, and s shower or bath. Breakfast €5.50, 1 free breakfast per room for *Let's Go* users. Reception 7am-11pm. Singles €55-65; doubles €60-78. Extra bed €15. Prices €10 lower Nov.-Apr. For longer stays, there are fully equipped apartments for €450-550 per week; Nov.-Apr. €280-350 AmEx/D/MC/V. ❹

Hôtel Univers, 3 av. Maréchal Sébastiani (☎04 95 31 03 38; fax 04 95 31 19 91). Plain plaster hallways lead to spotless modern rooms. All feature soundproofed windows and large bathrooms as well as A/C, TV, and phone. Breakfast €5. 24hr. reception. Jan-July singles €45-50; doubles €55-60; triples €75; quads €90. Aug-Sept. €60/€70/€90/€110. Extra bed €10. AmEx/MC/V. ❹

Hôtel Riviera, 1bis rue Alphonse Landry (☎04 95 31 07 16; fax 04 95 34 17 39), behind the Hôtel de Ville. Narrow beds fill 25 basic rooms with blue-tiled baths. All with TV, A/C, phone, and shower or bath. Breakfast €5. 24hr. reception. July-Sept. singles €50; doubles €60; triples €80. Oct.-June €40/€50/€60. Extra bed €20. MC/V. ❹

Camping:

San Damiano, Lido de la Marana (☎04 95 33 68 02; www.campingsandamiano.com), is 5km south of Bastia. Autocars Antoniotti sends buses there from the station near pl. St-Nicolas (☎04 95 36 08 21. June-Aug. M-Sa 2 per day, Su 1 per day; Sept.-May 1 per day; €2.50). Beachfront campsite features tennis courts, mini-golf, and a supermarket. Nearby *Base Nautique* offers jet-skiing and other watersports. Open Apr.-Oct. €5.50-6.50 per person, €4.50-6.50 per tent and per car. Electricity €3. Avoid the sites close to the road; they tend to be a bit noisy. AmEx/MC/V. ❶

FOOD

Just like the rest of Corsica, Bastia's non-stop sunshine means plenty of dining *al fresco*. Nearly every inexpensive cafe sets up tables on the crowded pl. St-Nicolas. For better food and a view to match, try the handful of restaurants at the **citadel** or browse the conveniently clustered choices along the **Vieux Port.** The broad terraces of the **quai des Martyrs de la Libération** offer a more subdued atmosphere and an uninterrupted view of the sweeping horizon. Early birds hit the **market** on pl. de l'Hôtel de Ville. (Open Tu-Su 8:15am-12:30pm.) **SPAR supermarket** is at 14 rue César Campinchi. (☎04 95 32 32 40. Open M-Sa 8am-12:30pm and 4-8:30pm, Su 8am-

CORSICA

Bastia

▲▲ ACCOMMODATIONS

Camping San Damiano, **11**
Hôtel Central, **5**
Hôtel Riviera, **2**
Hôtel Univers, **4**

🍴 FOOD

Chez Mémé, **6**
Chez Vincent, **13**
Le Colomba, **9**
Le Pub Assunta, **8**
U Tianu, **7**
La Voute, **1**

⭐ NIGHTLIFE

Café Wha!, **10**
L'Apocalypse, **12**
La Noche de Cuba, **3**

noon.) To purchase traditional Corsican delicacies, stop by **U Paese,** 4 rue Napoleon. This pungent shop is the oldest of its kind in Bastia and offers the best of the island's gastronomy, including *brocciu* (ewe's cheese), *canistrelli* (crumbly cookies), and *gâteaux de chataignier* (chestnut cake). Ask the owner to vacuum-pack your *lonzu* (sausage) so you don't stink up your whole hostel. (☎04 95 32 33 18. Open M-Sa 9am-noon and 3-7pm).

🔊**U Tianu ❸,** 4 rue Monseigneur Rigo, has been serving a loyal clientele for 22 years. Full of generous Corsican specialties, the delicious *menu* is well-worth the €19. (☎04 95 31 36 67. Open M-Sa 7pm-2am. Closed Aug.) With the citadel behind you and an endless purple skyline in front, your enormous pizza from 🔊**Chez Vincent ❸,** 12 rue St-Michel, suddenly takes on an elegant appearance. In addition to their pizzas (€7.70-9.10), the youthful staff dishes up meats (€11.20-16) and reasonably-priced traditional *plats* (€10-12). (☎04 95 31 62 50. Open M-F noon-

1:30pm and 7:30-10:30pm, Sa 7:30-10:30pm. AmEx/MC/V.) **Le Pub Assunta ❷**, 4 rue Fontaine-Neuve, claims to be the former secret meeting place of Napoleon III and Benedetti Vincent. The well hidden, leafy courtyard must have been a prime spot for discussing military strategies; luckily your only tough move is deciding which tasty burger (€5.50-7) to eat for lunch. (☎04 95 34 11 40. Pizzas €6-8. Occasional live music. Open May-Sept. M-Sa 11:30am-2pm and 7pm-2am, Su 6pm-2am; Oct.-Apr. closed Su. MC/V.) **Chez Mémé ❸**, at the north end of quai des Martyrs de la Libération, has been serving Bastia with seafood specialties for the past 50 years. Four consecutive generations bring new meaning to the term "family-owned." Enjoy oysters (€17), or a three-course Corsican *menu* (€14) on the pleasant seaside terrace. (☎04 95 31 44 12. Open daily 9am-10pm; Closed Jan. AmEx/D/MC/V.) A dramatic torch-bearing statue leads the way through low stone arches at **La Voute ❸**, 6 rue Luce de Casabianca. More formal than Bastia's other offerings, this restaurant exchanges cafe tables and seaside vistas for white linen tablecloths and a vaulted brick interior. Specialties include *ravioli au brocciu* (€12.20), an Italian dish with a local cheese. A wide variety of fish (€16-19), and pastas (€8.40-13) are also available. (☎04 95 32 47 11. Open daily noon-2pm and 7-11pm. AmEx/MC/V.) The friendly, attentive staff at **Le Colomba ❷** serves 20 varieties of creative, reasonably priced pizzas (€7-9.50), including the "Brésilienne," a tasty combo of mushrooms, Roquefort cheese, and *crème fraîche* (€8.50). Occasional live piano music is the perfect accompaniment to a meal on the terrace overlooking the old port. Save room for dessert; Le Colomba offers an unreasonably long menu of enticing ice cream specialties (€4.50-9) served in fun, elaborate glasses. (☎04 95 32 79 14. Pastas €8-11, meats €8.50-12, fish €10-18. Open daily June-Aug. 11am-12:30am; Mar.-May noon-3pm and 7pm-midnight. AmEx/MC/V.)

🜂 🜨 SIGHTS AND BEACHES

A walk through Bastia's *vieille ville* reveals the town's former glory as the crown jewel of Genoese-ruled Corsica. Many of the buildings in this part of the city are in serious need of repair, but the 1380 **citadel**, also called Terra Nova, has remained imposingly intact. Its ramparts reach down the hill and toward the *vieux port*, dwarfing adjacent shops. Just within the walls lies the massive 1530 **Palais des Gouverneurs Génois.** Unfortunately, it and the **Musée d'Ethnographie Corse,** an art and natural history museum inside the Palais, are currently closed for renovations.

Toward the citadel from pl. St-Nicolas on rue Napoleon sits the **Oratoire de St-Roch,** a small church with crystal chandeliers and a restored 18th-century sculpture of St-Roch in polychromatic wood. A few blocks down is the 18th-century **Oratoire de L'Imaculée Conception,** the entrance of which is paved with stones forming a large sun. A visit to both churches might give you a sense of *déjà-vu*—their lavish interiors are adorned with nearly identical painted ceilings and walls. Though similar to the eye, the Oratoire de L'Imaculée Conception boasts a more colorful history than its beautiful neighbor. During Corsica's brief 1794-1796 stint as an Anglo-Corsican kingdom, the oratory was the home to the British puppet parliament; accordingly it contains a small Italian organ that once played "God Save the Queen" every day. (Open daily 8am-7pm.) You won't confuse either oratory with the soaring 17th-century **Église St-Jean Baptiste,** pl. de l'Hôtel de Ville, just behind the Vieux Port. The lofty Baroque interior, the largest in Corsica, is marked by guilded domes and *trompe-l'œil* ceilings. Only the windows are unimpressive; all except for three stained-glass pieces at the back of the church were destroyed during WWII when resistors blew up an Italian munitions cache 5km away. If the church's soaring ceiling made you feel tiny, the eccentric **Eco-Musée,** in the citadel's old powder magazine, will leave you feeling positively gargantuan. No, you haven't mixed up the "Drink Me" bottles again, you're simply looking at an extraordinarily detailed, miniature replica of a traditional Corsican village. The product of René Mattei, the tiny museum holds a mountaintop scene replete with houses, stables, a bakery, and a mill. Each structure is painstakingly precise, right down to the microscopic dishes, working church bells, and authentic vegetation, which Mattei changes monthly to reflect the seasons. The entire setup took 20 years to complete and now weighs over 10 tons. (☎06 10 26 82 08; www.eco-musee.com. Open Apr.-Oct. M-Sa 9am-noon and 2-6pm. €3.50, students €3, ages 8-12 €2.50.)

Beaches in Bastia are dominated by serious sun-worshippers. For seclusion, head north to the pebbly turf of **Miomo,** and, farther on, the beautiful sands of the **Cap Corse.** Bus #4 leaves every 30min. from pl. St-Nicolas (6:30am-7pm), traveling as far as Macinaggio (€6.40) three times per day; the closest sandy beach lies between **Erbalunga** (€2) and **Sisco** (€2.30). **Pietracorba** also has a sandy stretch; bus #4 heads there six times per day (€2.60). The beaches surrounding Bastia are known for their excellent **scuba diving** and **snorkeling** sites. Rent gear before you go at **Thalassa Location,** 2 rue Saint-Jean, just behind the Vieux Port. (☎04 95 31 08 77; http://perso.wanadoo.fr/thalassashop/. Fins, mask, and snorkel €10 per day. Full scuba rental (bottle, jacket, regulator, fins, mask) €40 per day. Open Mar.-Oct. M-Sa 9am-noon and 2-7pm; Nov.-Feb. M-Sa 2-7pm. AmEx/MC/V.) Their **Base Nautique,** just past Port Toga on the route du Cap Corse, offers **scuba excursions** for all skill levels, including night dives. (☎04 95 31 78 90; thalassa.immersion@free.fr. €36 per hr., equipment included. Certification courses €130-390.).

■ NIGHTLIFE

Bastia is quiet come sunset. Even the cafes in pl. St-Nicolas are empty by 10pm, save for a few straggling diners draining a last cup of coffee. For the closest thing approaching a night out, head to the low-key bars and *brasseries* along the Vieux Port. International and rock music booms from crowded **Café Wha!,** quai du Premier Bataillon de Choc. Youthful locals come to chow down on burgers (€7.90-9.80) and Tex-Mex dishes (€6.40-15); if you'd rather not roll your own fajitas, take your magaritas (€5.50) or sangria (€5.50) onto the large outdoor patio. (☎04 95 34 25 79. Live music daily July-Aug. from 10pm; Sept.-June Th-Sa from 10pm. Open daily 10am-1am. MC/V.) **La Noche de Cuba,** 5 rue Chanoine Leschi, near the north quai, is a low-key club with one of Bastia's only dance floors. The Mayan-themed lounge is closed during the summer, but the adjacent bar picks up the slack with live salsa bands and mojitos (€6.20) served on a casual outdoor patio. (☎04 95 31 02 83. Beer €2.20, cocktails €6.20. Bar open daily 6am-2am, club open June-Sept. Th-Sa 9:30pm-2am.) Bastia's hottest nightlife option is the faraway **La Marana** area, home to beachside bars and open-air dance clubs. Unfortunately, public transportation doesn't head there at night and a taxi ride will cost at least €20. If you make it over, stop by trendy **L'Apocalypse,** an open-air party just minutes from the beach. (☎04 95 33 36 83. Cocktails €10. F-Sa cover €10, includes one free drink. Open F-Sa 11:30pm-5am; July-Aug. also open M and W.)

CAP CORSE

If you think the island of Corsica looks suspiciously like one enormous "thumbs up" sign, you're not alone. We at *Let's Go* couldn't help but notice the similarity to our trusty icon, and therefore found it highly fitting that the "thumb" itself is none other than Cap Corse, one of the island's most captivating regions. Stretching north from Bastia, the peninsula is Corsica's most stunning, rugged frontier. A narrow, perilously curving road connects the Cap's numerous former fishing villages and marinas and offers breathtaking views of its jagged coastline. Numerous species of endangered wildlife flourish in the windswept valleys and atop dizzying cliffs. Peregrine falcons and ospreys soar above the landscape, buffeted by the gusts that have transformed the tops of green hillocks into smooth curves. Having largely resisted over-development, Cap Corse is a hiker's dream. In addition to its coastline, its forests and cliffs are dotted with Genoese towers, white windmills, and hilltop chapels. Nearly every town is an access point for an unforgettable trail. Unfortunately, there are few budget hotels, and most require guests to pay for dinner with their rooms. Camping is a better option; a handful of sites dot the Cap.

⌐ TRANSPORTATION. The best way to visit the Cap is to drive around the entire peninsula. Though you can complete the trip in three hours without stopping, plan on taking at least a full day. One look at the stunning coastline and you'll be ready to hop out and start exploring. There are countless places to pull over, including many small, secluded swimming spots. Consider renting a **car** in Bastia (p. 779) or Calvi (p. 768). Be cautious: roads are narrow and winding, and Corsican drivers are fearless. The madcap coastal highway is made even more treacherous by local bus drivers, who have a tendency to imagine themselves behind the wheel of a speedster instead of a passenger bus. It's best to drive during the week, when traffic on D80 thins out; one might also consider starting the trip from the St-Florent area (the west side of the peninsula), where cliffside roads are less treacherously close to the sea below. To start on the west side from Bastia, take bd. Paoli, then bd. Auguste Gaudin past the citadel onto N199 (dir: St-Florent). For the east-to-west route, follow the coastal boulevard north from pl. St-Nicolas, following signs for the Cap.

In the high season, it is often possible to see the Cap by **bus** tour. Updated schedules and phone numbers for buses can be found in *Cap Corse Guide Pratique*, an indispensable free guide provided at tourist offices. The cheapest and most convenient way to see the eastern side of Cap Corse is to take public **bus #4** from pl. St-Nicolas in Bastia. The bus leaves for **Erbalunga** (20min.; M-F every 30min., Sa-Su every hr.; €2) and **Sisco** (30min., every hr., €2.30); it also goes all the way to **Macinaggio** (50min., M-Sa 3 per day, €6.40). Ask nicely and the driver will stop wherever you feel the urge to explore. Keep in mind that most buses serve only the coastal towns; to explore the inland villages you'll have to hike. (☎04 95 31 06 65. Service generally daily 6:30am-7:30pm.)

ERBALUNGA

The most accessible of Cap Corse's villages, Erbalunga offers a peaceful afternoon alternative to Bastia's crowded streets. Though its busy southern neighbor has steadily grown in size, quiet Erbalunga has only gained a mere 180 inhabitants over the past two hundred years. "Downtown" in this sleepy hamlet consists of little more than a bakery, the post office, and of course, the requisite *boules* court. A handful of aging buildings cluster around the tiny port, where fishermen tend to brightly painted wooden dories and occasionally drop lines from their coastline houses. The blissfully quiet white-pebble beaches are a sunbather's paradise. No competition for towel space here: just stretch out your beach mat anywhere you please, and indulge in your personal view of crystal waters and tumbling surf.

In the hills above, Benedictine monks observe a vow of silence at the **Monastère des Benedictines du St-Sacrement.** You can pass the monastery on a short hike that begins to the right of the restaurant **La Petite Auberge ❸,** where M. and Mme. Morganti serve Corsican specialties, including *magret de canard au miel* (duck breast with honey; €14) and *terrine de sanglier* (wild boar; €8.50). They also offer house seafood (€17) and pastas (€8.50-11), as well as a *menu Corse* (€18.50), a diverse sampling of the island's most famous dishes. The restaurant has also become well known for its delicious couscous, popular among locals. To get there, follow the main road 3min. north of the bus station. (☎ 04 95 33 20 78. Open Tu-Sa noon-2:30pm and 6-10:30pm, Su noon-2:30pm; closing hour varies. Reservations recommended. MC/V.) Supermarket **SPAR** is across from the bus station. (☎ 04 95 33 24 24. Open M-Sa 8am-noon and 4-7:30pm, Su 9am-noon.)

Two and a half kilometers south, **Lavasina** holds the famous 17th-century **Église de Notre-Dame des Graces.** Legend has it that a disabled nun from Bonifacio was miraculously granted the use of her legs after praying to an image of the Virgin that hangs in this church. Thousands make an annual torchlit pilgrimage on the evening of Sept. 7 to celebrate this miracle. The holiday itself, the **Fête de la Nativité de la Vierge,** is celebrated the following day.

SISCO

The *Cap Corse Guide Pratique,* free at tourist offices, comes with a map that lists 21 possible itineraries; hike #9, from **Sisco** (2hr.), is one of the best. Take bus #4 from pl. St-Nicolas to Sisco (30min., every hr., €2.30) and follow the blue signs for Camping A Cassiola. Once you reach the campsite, the trail continues straight ahead (just to the left of the campsite entrance). Follow the painted orange rectangles along a sun-dappled route that chases a winding streambed before plunging headfirst into an expansive valley of wildflowers. Along the way, you'll pass through dense forest and tiny, almost-forgotten villages, where the rolling mountain backdrop might be enough to convince you to head for the hills—permanently. You won't see many other hikers, but the flurries of geckoes and butterflies that emerge from nowhere with every footstep will be perfect company along the trail. The path ultimately leads to **Petrapiana,** the intersection of several other routes, but make sure to take a break at **Barriggioni,** just 300m before Petrapiana, and admire the grandiose elegance of the **Église St-Martin,** which houses the eerie, bronzed remains of St-John Chrysostomos. From here, it is possible to detour to the 11th-century **Chapelle St-Michel,** perched precariously on a hilltop promontory; just follow the signs from the first church. Advance farther to the **Église St-Michel;** signs indicating the path are to the left of a grove of ferns near the second church. Though it is impossible to enter the chapel, the panoramic view of the bowl-shaped valley below, sprinkled with Renaissance bell towers, is definitely worth the 1hr. climb. Note that this demanding hike requires a good pair of hiking boots as well as long pants to protect against thorny undergrowth.

MACINAGGIO TO CENTURI: THE CAPANDULA

Crystal-clear waters, white sandy beaches, and deep-green escarpments characterize the arid and windy extreme tip of Cap Corse. Inaccessible to cars, the Capandula is a protected national reserve and the last stop for African migratory birds heading north. Camping is therefore forbidden, but hikers and bikers are blessed by the **sentier de Douaniers,** an extraordinary coastal trail named after the customs officials who first walked it. Beginning in **Macinaggio** or **Centuri,** the 8hr. hike passes by secluded beaches, dramatic cliffs, and two villages. The landscape is peppered with structures that tell the history of the region. In the 16th century, anxious islanders watched for the arrival of Moorish pirates from atop stone towers. The crumbling remains can still be seen today, as well as an 11th-century lighthouse and ancient lime quarries. Even these age-old remnants seem young, however, when compared with the fantastic **Grotte de la Coscia,** a cave dating to 75,000 BC. The recently excavated site was believed to have been occupied by Neanderthals. The *sentier* also affords views of **Finocchiarola** and **Giraglia,** two nearby islands protected by national mandate. Both of the sloping, rocky mounds belong to a chain of hills that was submerged when sea levels rose. Today, they are home to a unique subspecies of lizard, the descendants of an original population that was trapped by the rising water.

From the east coast, the trail takes off from **Macinaggio**, the spot to which Corsican leader Pascal Paoli returned in 1790 after 20 years in exile from his beloved island. Macinaggio is one of the windiest spots in Corsica; its 600-boat pleasure port accordingly draws a fair number of sailboats to the gusty coast. Though your arrival depends on wheels, not keels, you'll appreciate the small bit of commerce encouraged by the marine traffic: Macinaggio is one of the few places on the Cap that offer supplies and services. The **tourist office**, above the Capitainerie, has small maps of the trail. (☎ 04 95 35 40 34; ot-rogliano-macinaggio.com. Open July-Aug. M-Sa 9am-noon and 3-7pm, Su 9am-noon; June and early to mid-Sept. M-Sa 9am-noon and 3-7pm; mid-Sept. to May M-F 9am-noon and 2-7pm.)

Shady, quiet campsites await at **U Stazzu ❶**, just steps from the beach. To get there, follow the signs on the road by the Chapelle Saint Marc; the campsite is at the beginning of the sentier de Douaniers. Guests enjoy an on-site restaurant-bar and equestrian excursions (€24 for 1.5 hrs.) into the nearby mountains (☎ 04 95 35 43 76. Breakfast €4. Open mid-May to Sept. €5.50 per person, €3 per tent. Showers free. Fridge/freezer available. No electricity.)

Regional culinary pride drives the menu at **Ostéria di u Portu ❸**, right on the waterfront, where nearly every dish contains a delicacy from the Cap itself. The €14 *menu* features three courses, while the hearty €21 *menu* includes starter, salad, ravioli, veal dish, and dessert. If all the local *plats* don't put you in a Corsican frame of mind, traditional music from the terrace speakers certainly will. (☎ 04 95 35 40 49. *Plats* €9-18, fish *menu* €22. Open daily 11am-2pm and 5-11pm.)

Macinaggio offers several options for those who want to see the Capandula but aren't quite up to tackling the *sentier* on foot. **Boat tours** aboard the U San Paulu depart twice daily from the dock just below the Capitainerie. The 2hr. trips head all the way to **Barcaggio,** the tip of the Cap, and include a beach landing swim break. In July and August, the boat also serves as a **shuttle** between the two towns. (☎ 06 14 78 14 16 or 04 95 35 07 09; www.lebateau.fr.st. Adults €15, under 12 €10, under 4 free. Shuttle €7. Departures 11am and 3:30pm.) Charter your own voyage with a **zodiac** from Cap Evasion, in the blue trailer at the end of the port. The tiny hard-shell boats are perfect for discovering the Cap's hidden inlets and rocky coves. No license necessary. (☎ 06 81 70 38 48 or 04 95 35 47 90. €50-65 per half-day, €70-100 per day. Open daily July-Aug. 8:30am-6pm; May-June and Sept. by appointment. Closed Oct.-Apr.) If you'd rather bike than hike, Loc' Ago, next to the post office, rents **mountain bikes** (€15 per day) and **all-terrain vehicles** for €50 per 30min. (☎ 06 76 31 76 69. Open daily July to mid-Sept. 9am-12:30pm and 4-8pm; Oct.-June by appointment. MC/V.) At the edge of the beach, the Macinaggio Club de Voile offers **kayak** rental for use in Macinaggio's bay (☎ 06 86 72 58 40 or 04 95 35 46 82. Kayaks €12 per hr., €30 per half-day. Open daily July-Aug. 9am-8pm.)

The miniature port of **Centuri** at the other end of the trail is one of the Cap's most picturesque spots; sit here at sunset and watch the boats bring in their daily haul of lobsters, mussels, and fish. **Camping Caravaning L'isulotto ❶**, just south of the town, has lots of amenities, including a mini-market, bar, and restaurant with a €9 *menu*, 200m from the sea. (☎ 04 95 35 62 81; fax 04 95 35 63 63. €4.90 per adult, €2.55 per tent, €1.70 per car. Electricity €3.30.)

SAINT-FLORENT

Situated directly across from Bastia at the base of the Cap Corse peninsula, the resort town of **Saint-Florent** (pop. 1500) draws an annual crowd of sun-seekers to its wide, windy beaches and enormous pleasure-boat port. Just below the expansive Golfe de St-Florent, the vacation town lies at the intersection of

U TROGLIU

At the very end of rue Centrale, removed from the madness of the quai and its glut of over-priced tourist-trap restaurants, sits a small *traiteur* offering various prepared dishes and *pâté*. In the evening, owners Marcel and Claudia set out a handful of tables on the triangle sidewalk and transform their store into one of the most reasonable restaurants in town.

Though **U Trogliu** ❸ offers a filling €12.50 *menu Corse*, the best deal is the homemade pasta, made fresh every morning by Marcel. Diners can choose from 15 types of pastas, including traditional Corsican specialties like *cannelloni au brocciu* (cannelloni with ewe's cheese, served with spinach, *crème fraiche*, and mint) and *ravioli a l'ancienne* (stuffed with beef daube, spinach, and tomato sauce). From the *fusilli Norma* (fusilli with eggplant and tomatoes) to the *fettucini U Trogliu* (fettucini with tuna, olive oil, black olives, and parmesan), each dish is generous and flavorful. Even the specialties fall within the highly reasonable price range of €6.80-9. Don't miss the fabulous chestnut flan (€4.50). After dinner, stop inside the store to pick up a jar of jam: Claudia preserves the fruit herself over the winter.

(Open for dinner daily mid-May to Sept. 7pm-midnight. Traiteur open from 8am. Free aperitif with copy of Let's Go.*)*

three dramatically different regions: the rugged Cap Corse, the fertile Nebbio, and the unforgiving Desert des Agriates.

Though tiny, Saint-Florent is jam-packed with hotels catering to a well-to-do vacation population. Budget travelers will have to search a little harder for reasonable accommodations, especially in August. Reserve far in advance. At the **Hotel du Centre** ❹, rooms are plain but adequate, with tile floors and white bedspreads. All have shower, TV, and phone. (☎04 95 37 00 68; fax 04 95 37 41 01. Breakfast €5. Reception 6am-midnight. June-July singles and doubles €43-55; triples €60; quads €80. Aug. €65-70/€80/€80; Sept.-May €42-50/€60/€70. Extra bed €8. MC/V.)

By far the most economical option is camping; a few sites are located south of town along the plage de la Roya. To reach **U Pezzo** ❶, head south on CD 81 from the bus station and cross the river via the pedestrian bridge. Walk down the beach until you see the sign for the Base Nautique; the campsite is just across the road on your left (15 minutes). Eucalyptus trees provide plenty of shade for 145 sites just steps from a popular beach. Amenities include a snack bar/restaurant and mini-market. Kids will enjoy the tiny on-site animal farm. (☎04 95 37 01 65; fax 04 95 35 28 16. Open Apr. to mid-Oct. Reception 8-11:30am and 3-6:30pm. 2 people and a tent €11.50; €14 with car. Electricity €3. Showers free.)

The quai along the Port de Plaisance is home to a string of pricey, unremarkable restaurants. Thankfully, **U Trogliu** ❷, on rue Centrale, is a **Hidden Deal** (see left). If you can't resist the view, **A Marina, Chez César** ❸, has terrace seating and a menu that won't break the bank. (☎04 95 37 15 33. Pizzas €9-10, meats €13-16. Open daily Apr.-Oct. noon-2:30pm and 7-11:30pm. MC/V). Create your own three-course meal for half the price from **SPAR supermarket,** near the bus stop. (☎04 95 37 00 56. Open June-Aug. M-Sa 8am-8pm, Su 8am-1pm and 5-8pm; Sept.-May M-Sa 8am-noon and 3:30-8pm, Su 8am-noon.)

Saint-Florent offers several options for sunbathers. The bustling port sits right at the junction of the town's principal **beaches,** both of which host crowds of umbrellas come August. North of the citadel lies the **plage de l'Ospedale,** a long, pebbly stretch hidden from passing traffic by a high concrete wall. From town, walk north on RN 199 (toward Cap Corse); the beach is 15min. past the post office. Boisterous **plage de la Roya,** directly south of the Port de Plaisance, tempts a tan crowd with a wide, sandy crescent framed by distant, hazy mountains. Plenty of wind makes this stretch a perfect playground for **windsurfing** and **sailing.**

The Base Nautique, at the southern end of the beach, offers one-stop shopping for **watersports** enthusiasts. (☎06 12 10 23 27; www.corskayak.com. Catamaran sailboats €30-37 per hr., €85-119 per half-day; windsurfing equipment €24 per hr., €40 per half-day; **kayaks** €12-15 per hr., €26-35 per half-day, €35-45 per day; **surf bikes** €10 per hr. Open June-Oct. 8am-8:30pm.)

True beach bliss lies even further south at the **plage du Lodo,** a little slice of paradise accessible only by boat. **U Saleccia** ferries passengers over three times daily, leaving at 9, 10:30, and 11:30am. (☎04 95 36 90 78 or 06 09 79 98 63. Round-trip €8.38, children €4.57. Purchase tickets at least 1hr. before departure. Return trips begin at 4pm.) If you missed the morning's crossing, **Le Popeye** also makes the 30-min. trip, with departures at 8:45, 10, 11:15am, 12:30, 1:45, and 3:15pm. (☎04 95 37 19 07. Round-trip €10, children €5. Purchase tickets at least 1hr. before departure. Return trips depart at 11:45am, 1:00, 2:45, 4:00, 5:30, and 6:30pm.) Both boats depart daily June through September from Port de Plaisance, just below the pl. des Portes. From the plage du Lodo, a 1hr. hike takes dedicated sunbathers to the pristine **plage de Saleccia,** an isolated, otherworldly spot.

Autocars Santini (☎04 95 37 02 98) sends **buses** to Bastia (50min; M-Sa 7am and 2pm; €5) and Île Rousse (60min. M-Sa 9am and 4:30pm; €10) from the station below the Port de Plaisance, near the restaurant A Citadella. Buy tickets on the bus. To get to the **tourist office** from the bus station, walk past the pl. des Portes and continue uphill; the office is on the left next to the post office. A helpful staff distributes the Saint Florent practical guide, which includes a map. Ask for information about regional festivals and concerts. (☎04 95 37 06 04; fax 04 05 35 30 74. Open July-Aug. M-F 8:30am-1pm and 2-7pm, Sa 8:30am-noon and 3-6pm, Su 9am-noon; Sept.-June M-F 8:30am-1pm and 2-6pm, Sa 2-6pm. Closing hours sometimes vary, call ahead to be sure.)

BONIFACIO (BONIFAZIU)

At the extreme southern tip of the island, the fortified city of Bonifacio (pop. 3000) presents an imposing vestige to miles of empty turquoise sea. Enormous stone ramparts enclose a rambling *vieille ville* at the top of steep limestone cliffs, where scarred rock faces bear witness to eons of aoelian erosion. At the foot of the rocks, sparkling waves dash across strange limestone formations, making misty grottoes echo with their muted roar. Its stunning landscape, exquisite *haute ville*, and gorgeous crescent-moon beaches make Bonifacio a must-see, despite its astronomical price tags and hordes of tourists.

▐▀ TRANSPORTATION. You can take **Buses** to and from Bonifacio with **Eurocorse Voyages** (Ajaccio ☎04 95 21 06 30, Porto Vecchio 04 95 71 24 64), who runs to destinations across the island: Ajaccio (3½hr.; July to mid-Sept. M-Sa 3 per day, Su 1 per day; €20.50) via Sartène (1¾hr., €11); Porto Vecchio (30min.; 2 per day, July-Sept. 4 per day; €6.50) and Propriano (1½hr., €11.50). Buses stop by the small ticket and info office in the port parking lot.

Ferries depart from the *gare maritime* at far end of the port. **SAREMAR** (☎04 95 73 00 96; fax 04 95 73 13 37) runs to Santa Teresa, Sardinia (1hr.; Apr.-Sept. 3 per day, Oct.-Mar. 2 per day; €6.80-8.70, cars €20-28.20). **Moby** is pricier but has later summer departures. (☎04 95 73 00 29; www.mobylines.de. July-Aug. 5 per day, Apr.-June and Sept.-Oct. 4 per day; €11-15, cars €23.50-53.50.) The *gare maritime* office is open daily 7:30-9am, 10:30am-noon, 3-7pm, and 9-10pm. You can catch **taxis** (☎04 95 73 19 08) at the port.

There is a **Europcar,** av. Sylvère Bohn, at Station Esso for **car rental.** (☎04 95 73 10 99. Cars from €73 per day, €254 per week; credit card deposit. Unlimited mileage and insurance included. 21+. Open July-Aug. 8am-8pm. AmEx/MC/V.) To fit into

the tight spaces you might try the **scooter rental** at **Corse Moto Services,** quai Nord ().
(☎04 95 73 15 16. Scooters €40 per day, €245 per week, €1525 deposit. 18+. Open
daily July-Aug. 9am-noon and 2-6pm. If no one's at the office, there aren't any
scooters left to rent. MC/V.)

■ **7** **ORIENTATION AND PRACTICAL INFORMATION.** Bonifacio is divided by
a steep climb into the **port** and the **haute ville.** Near the entrance to the town, two
major highways (**N196** toward Ajaccio and **N198** toward Porto Vecchio) join to
become **avenue Sylvère Bohn.** In the high season, intense traffic headed to the port
can turn this otherwise short stretch of road into an endless bottleneck. As you
inch along from this direction, the port is visible on the right and the *haute ville*
looms above. The main road veers left to become **D58,** leading to nearby beaches.
The tourist office, at corner of av. de Gaulle and rue F. Scamaroni in the *haute
ville*, has a friendly staff, free maps and guides, and accommodations booking.
(☎04 95 73 11 88; www.bonifacio.fr. Open daily May to mid-Oct. 9am-8pm; mid-
Oct. to Apr. M-F 9am-noon and 2-6pm. Annex, at the port. Open daily July-Aug.
9:30am-1pm and 4-6:30pm.) It's a good idea to **exchange currency** elsewhere. **Societé
Générale,** rue St-Erasme, next to the stairs to the *haute ville*, charges €5.40 commission. (☎04 95 73 02 49. Open M-F 9am-noon and 2-4:30pm.) Other services
include: **laundry** at 1 quai Comparetti, at the end of port near the bus stop (☎04 95
73 01 03. Wash €6.20, dry €0.80 per 10min. Open daily 7am-10pm.); **Police** at the
start of rte. de Santa Manza (D58), just off the port (☎04 95 73 00 17); a **hospital** on
D58 toward the beaches (☎04 95 73 95 73); **Internet** access at Cybercafé Boom
Boom, on the port (Only 3 computers, so be prepared to wait in high season. €0.12
per min., €3 for 30min., €5 per hr. Open daily 8am-1am.); and a **post office** at pl.
Carrega (☎04 95 73 73 73), uphill from pl. Montepagano in the *haute ville* (**Postal
Code:** 20169. Open M-F 8am-5:30pm, Sa 8am-noon).

7 7 **ACCOMMODATIONS AND CAMPING.** Finding a room in the summer is
virtually impossible. If you somehow manage to land lodgings, don't be surprised
when *tarifs* are twice (or even three times!) as costly as their low-season rates.
Camping is by far the cheapest option; many sites also offer affordable lodging in
bungalows or *chalets*. Porto Vecchio has some (barely) lower-priced hotels, for
those who don't mind daytripping. Be foreign at the **Hôtel des Etrangers ❹,** av.
Sylvère Bohn, on the road to Bonifacio. Perched practically on Bonifacio's main
thoroughfare, its plain white rooms with high ceilings and tile floors can be a little
noisy. Nonetheless, its worth bringing out those earplugs: this hotel is by far the
least expensive, most welcoming spot in town. A/C and TV in all but the cheapest
rooms. (☎04 95 73 01 09; fax 04 95 73 16 97. 24hr. reception. Reserve well in
advance for July and Aug. Closed late Oct. to late Mar. Mid-July to mid-Sept. singles and doubles €47-74; triples €70; quads €72-84. Mid-May to mid-July and Sept.
€47-63/€64/€74; Apr. to mid-May and Oct. €37-47/€57/€65. MC/V.) Feel more
regal at **Hôtel Le Royal ❹,** pl. Bonaparte, in the *haute ville*. Cheerful rooms above a
lively town square come with all the trimmings, including A/C, telephone, TV, toilet, and shower or bath. Some rooms even have sweeping sea views. (☎04 95 73 00
51; fax 04 95 73 04 68. Breakfast €6.10. 24hr. reception. Reserve at least a month in
advance in summer. Early Nov.-Mar. singles €38.20; doubles €44.30. Apr.-May
€44.30/€49-53.40. June and Oct.-early Nov. €49/€53.40-59.50. July and Sept.
€68.60/€74.70-79.30. Aug. €91.50/€99.10-105. Extra bed €15.30. MC/V.)
There are many great camping options for those with a lighter wallet. **L'Araguina
❶,** av. Sylvère Bohn (☎04 95 73 02 96), is at the entrance to town between Hôtel
des Etrangers and the port. Its crowded, shady plots are ideally located near the
port and the beach. (Limited parking. Laundry €6. Reception daily 7am-10pm.
Open April to mid-Oct. 4-person bungalows €351-793 per week. €5.25-5.55 per

person, €2.10 per tent or car. Electricity €2.80.) 7km from the town, **Campo di Liccia ❶**, is the cheapest of a cluster of campsites on the road to Porto Vecchio. Pool, restaurant, mini-market, ping pong, volleyball. (☎04 95 73 03 09; fax 04 95 73 19 94. Laundry €5.50. Reception daily 8am-10pm. Open Apr.-Oct. €4.45-5.80 per person, €1.80-2.60 per tent or car. Electricity €2.45-2.60.) For a few more perks, check out **Camping U Farniente ❷**, rte. de Porto-Veccio, near Campo di Uccia. This four-star campsite feels like a resort, with 150 *emplacements*, a swimming pool, tennis, restaurant, bar, laundry, free hot showers, and free electricity. (☎04 95 73 05 47; www.camping-pertamina.com. Open Apr. to mid-Oct. July-Aug. €22.60 for 2 people, tent, and/or car; Apr.-June and Sept. to mid-Oct. €17.90. V.)

⌂ FOOD. A few supermarkets dot the port, including **SPAR** at the start of rte. de Santa Manza. (☎04 95 73 00 26. Open daily July-Aug. 8am-8:30pm; Sept. and June M-Sa 8am-8pm; Oct.-May M-Sa 8am-12:30pm and 3:30-7:30pm.) The port is lined end-to-end with mundane, touristy restaurants; tiny establishments tucked on rambling streets in the *haute ville* serve more authentic Corsican cuisine. These charming (but pricey) restaurants are supplemented by a fair number of *crêperies* and pizzerias, allowing diners to enjoy good grub without breaking the bank. For hearty regional specialties, try **Cantina Doria ❸**, 27 rue Doria, in the *haute ville*. Diners share long wooden tables in the Corsican-themed interior, readily devouring heaping plates of *spaghetti aux aubergines* (spaghetti with eggplant) and other delicious options from the €14 *menu*. (☎04 95 73 50 49. *Plats* €9.50-10.50, mouthwatering desserts €4-6. Open daily June-Sept. noon-2pm and 7-11:30pm; Apr.-May and Oct. M-W and F-Su only. MC/V.)

The chef's daily whim and the market's daily offerings dictate the ever-changing *menu* at **L'Archivolto ❹**, rue de l'Archivolto in the *haute ville*. Tables spill out of the rustic interior onto an adorable terrace lined by a blue picket fence. (☎04 95 73 17 58. *Tapas* for 2 €12.50, *plats du jour* €12.50-14.90. Desserts €5-6.50. Open daily July-Sept. 7:30-11pm; Oct.-June noon-2pm and 7:30-11pm. Reservations advised, phone 9-11:30am or after 5:30pm.) **◪Kissing Pigs ❸**, 15 quai Banda del Ferro, on the port, annually butchers its own Corsican *charcuterie*. You can try their savory selections in club sandwiches (€7-7.50), *petits poelons chauds* (hot casseroles, €7-9) or as part of the €15 *menu traditionelle*. The homey interior of this waterside gem is marked by a large open kitchen, where diners can watch the French/English owners at work. (☎04 95 73 56 09. *Menus* €14-18.50, salad €9-15. Wine €1.90-5.50 per glass. Extensive dessert menu €4-6.30. Open daily 10am-3pm and 6:30-11pm; closed mid-Nov. to mid-Dec. and Feb. for butchering season. Reservations suggested. MC/V.)

Friendly owners work with local fishermen to bring the freshest catch of the day to **Les Quatre Vents ❹**, on the port past the stairs to the *haute ville*. The nautical-themed interior is a highly appropriate setting for seafood delicacies such as *friture locale* (fried fish), which are presented whole before they're cooked. Lobster and *bouillabaisse* must be ordered 24hr. in advance. (☎04 95 73 07 50. *Menu* €18.50. *Plats du jour* €14-15. Seafood €14-24. Meat dishes €13-18. Pasta €14-24. Open daily July-Aug. noon-2pm and 7:30pm-midnight; Sept.-June M noon-2pm, W-Su noon-2pm and 7:30pm-midnight. Reservations advised.)

◪ SIGHTS. A marvel of both human and natural architecture, Bonifacio's *vieille ville* sits safely ensconced within 3km of fortifications atop plunging limestone cliffs. Far below the ochre houses, years of pounding surf have carved deep, misshapen grottoes into the impressionable white rock. Be sure to take a **boat tour** of the city: a small army of shuttle companies has taken over the base of the port to ensure that no visitor misses Bonifacio's fantastic *promenades en mer*. As you pass through the channel on your way out to sea, look for the twin *treuils* on

CORSICA

either side of the harbor. During WWII, these windlasses were used to pull an enormous anti-submarine net across the port to protect the city from enemy submarines. From there, the boat tours head to Bonifacio's greatest attraction: a series of multicolored coves, cliffs, and stalactite-filled grottoes formed over the ages by the rolling turquoise sea. From the water, one also has a lovely view of Bonifacio's *vieille ville*, perched 70m above the waves. Included in the 1hr. tour is a visit to the *misty* Dragon grotto *(Sdragonato)*, known for an opening in the cave ceiling that bears a striking resemblance to the map of Corsica. As the boat passes wind-worn falaises, youthful *Bonifaciens* show off for wide-eyed tourists by plunging headfirst from the towering rocks. The second tour is a shorter version of the *grottes-falaises-calanques* tour, with a detour to the **Îles Lavezzi.** Relax and explore the gorgeous beaches on this nature reserve before catching a return boat. Many companies offer these tours, including **Les Vedettes Thalassa.** (☎ 04 95 73 01 17 or 06 86 34 00 49. *Grottes-Falaises-Calanques* tour every 30min. 9am-6:30pm, €14. Îles Lavezzi-Cavallo tour 5 departures per day, 3 return boats, last return boat 5:30pm; €25.) **Marina Croisières** (☎ 04 95 73 12 41) offers the same tours for the same prices. (Grottes-Falaises-Calanques tour every 30min. 9:30am-6pm; 7-8 departures per day to the Îles Lavezzi; return boats every hr. 3-6pm).

To explore the *haute ville* from within (and get an unexpected workout in the process), head up the steep, broad steps of the **montée Rastello,** located halfway down the port. The top offers excellent views of hazy cliffs stretching away to the east. From this point, visitors can also see an enormous segment of the chalky, multi-layered rock upon which the *haute ville* stands. Continue up montée St-Roch to the lookout at **Porte de Gênes,** constructed with a drawbridge in 1588 to be the town's sole entrance. As you pass through the echoing entrance, a series of soaring *arc-boutants* (flying buttresses) are visible on the buildings ahead. If they look a little delicate to be bracing such massive stone structures, it's because they serve no supporting purpose at all: instead, the narrow arches used to carry rainwater from one rooftop to the next. Immediately to the right of the Porte de Gênes sits the elaborate **Bastion de L'Entendard.** Eager to overthrow colonizing Italians, Corsican nationals joined forces with King Henri II to besiege the town, successfully razing the Genoese fortress. The triumphant rebels rebuilt their own stronghold on the original. Once a prison, the Bastion now traps tourists; the hokey historical displays are not worth the €2 admission.

The Bastion visit includes the promise of spectacular panoramas, but you can see the stunning view for free by heading left to pl. du Marché, at the end of rue Doria. The small square has a fantastic view of Bonifacio's cliffs, surrounded by sparkling sea foam. Immediately ahead is the **Grain de Sable,** an enormous limestone formation that serves as a perfect perch for daring cliff-divers. The little mound just out of reach is Sardinia, 12km away. Turn right on rue Cardinal, then left on rue du Sacrement to reach the **Église Ste-Mairie-Majeure,** Bonifacio's oldest building. (Open daily 8am-6pm.) This somber 12th-century church, constructed by Pisans, guards one of the town's most important objects: a fragment of the **true cross,** stripped from a shipwreck.

◪ **BEACHES.** Bonifacio's beaches are hard to reach and harder to leave. The only ones within walking distance of town are intimate but uninspiring. For better swimming spots, go to the prettier **plage de l'Arinella** (25 minutes). The peninsula east of Bonifacio is filled with spectacular beaches, but a car is necessary to reach most of them. From the port, take D58 toward the water; virtually every turn-off leads to a beach. The only beach accessible by bus is the lovely **plage Piantarella.** Depending on tourist demand, **Transports N. Massimi** heads there from the port parking lot. (☎ 04 95 73 13 16. M-Sa at 10am, 2, 6pm; returns at 10:30am, 2:30, 6:30pm. Round-trip €7.) The isolated **Cala Longa,** 6km away from Bonifacio, and

plage Maora, a large beach in a calm natural harbor, are accessible by car. The turn-off for camping Rondinara, 20km away from town, leads to **plage de Rondinara,** one of Corsica's most famous beaches.

Even more impressive than the mainland beaches are the pristine sands of the **Îles Lavezzi,** where crumbly rock formations meet clear turquoise waters. Every company on the port runs frequent ferries (30min.) to this nature reserve, including **Vedettes Thalassa** and **Marina Croisières** (see **Sights,** p. 777 for schedules and prices). Bring water and food; there are no supplies available on the reserve. Just off the islands, coral reefs teeming with brightly colored fish make for great **scuba diving. Atoll,** on the port, past the stairs to the *haute ville,* arranges dives for beginners and experts alike. (☎04 95 73 53 83; www.atoll-diving.com. Dives for beginners €72, for experts €38-67. Open daily Apr.-Oct. 8am-9:30pm. MC/V.)

CORSICA

APPENDIX

TIME ZONES

France lies in the Central European time zone, which is 1hr. ahead of GMT. From Easter to autumn, French time moves 1hr. ahead. Both switches occur about a week before such changes in the US.

MEASUREMENTS

France invented, and still uses, the metric system. The basic unit of length is the **meter (m),** which is divided into 100 **centimeters (cm),** or 1000 **millimeters (mm).** One thousand meters make up one **kilometer (km).** Fluids are measured in **liters (L),** each divided into 1000 **milliliters (ml).** A liter of pure water weighs one **kilogram (kg),** divided into 1000 **grams (g),** while 1000kg make up one metric **ton.**

1 in. = 25.4mm	1mm = 0.039 in.
1 ft.= 0.30m	1m = 3.28 ft.
1 yd. = 0.914m	1m = 1.09 yd.
1 mi. = 1.61km	1km = 0.62 mi.
1 oz. = 28.35g	1g = 0.035 oz.
1 lb. = 0.454kg	1kg = 2.202 lb.
1 fl. oz. = 29.57ml	1ml = 0.034 fl. oz.
1 gal. = 3.785L	1L = 0.264 gal.

FRENCH PHRASEBOOK AND GLOSSARY

FRENCH ESSENTIALS

ENGLISH	FRENCH	PRONUNCIATION
GENERAL		
Hello/Good day.	Bonjour.	bohn-ZHOOR
Good evening.	Bonsoir.	bohn-SWAH
Hi!	Salut!	sah-LU
Goodbye.	Au revoir.	oh ruh-VWAHR
Good night.	Bonne nuit.	buhn NWEE
yes/no/maybe	oui/non/peut-être	wee/nohn/p'TET-ruh
Please.	S'il vous plaît.	see voo PLAY
Thank you.	Merci.	mehr-SEE
You're welcome.	De rien.	duh rhee-AHN
Pardon me!	Excusez-moi!	ex-KU-zay-MWAH
Go away!	Allez-vous en!	ah-lay vooz ON!
Where is...?	Où se trouve...?	oo s'TRHOOV...?
What time do you open/ close?	Vous ouvrez/fermez à quelle heure?	vooz ooVRAY/ ferhMAY ah kel-UHR?
Help!	Au secours!	oh-skOOR

I'm lost (m/f).	Je suis perdu(e).	zh'SWEE pehr-DU
I'm sorry (m/f).	Je suis désolé(e).	zh'SWEE day-zoh-LAY
Do you speak English?	Parlez-vous anglais?	PAR-lay-voo ahn-GLAY

OTHER USEFUL PHRASES AND WORDS

PHRASES			
Who?	Qui?	**No, thank you.**	Non, merci.
What?	Quoi?	**What is it?**	Qu'est-ce que c'est?
I don't understand.	Je ne comprends pas.	**Why?**	Pourquoi?
Leave me alone.	Laissez-moi tranquille.	**this one/that one**	ceci/cela
How much does this cost?	Ça coûte combien?	**Stop/Stop that!**	Arrête! (familiar) Arrêtez! (pl.)
Please speak slowly.	S'il vous plaît, parlez moins vite.	**I'm a vegetarian.**	Je suis végétarien(ne).
I am ill/I am hurt (m/f).	J'ai mal/Je suis blessé(e).	**Please help me.**	Aidez-moi, s'il vous plaît.
I am (20) years old.	J'ai (vingt) ans.	**Please repeat.**	Répétez, s'il vous plaît.
I am a student (m/f).	Je suis étudiant/étudi-ante.	**What's this called in French?**	Comment-on dit...en français?
What is your name?	Comment vous appelez-vous?	**The check, please.**	L'addition, s'il vous plaît.
Please, where is/ are...?	S'il vous plaît, où se trouve(nt)...?	**I would like...**	Je voudrais...
a doctor	un médecin	the cash machine	le guichet automatique
the toilet	les toilettes	the restaurant	le restaurant
the hospital	l'hôpital	the police	la police
a bedroom	une chambre	the train station	la gare
with	avec	single room	une chambre simple
a double bed	un grand lit	double room	une chambre pour deux
a shower	une douche	two single beds	deux lits
lunch	le déjeuner	a bath	bain
included	compris	without	sans
hot	chaud	breakfast	le petit déjeuner
cold	froid	dinner	le dîner
DIRECTIONS			
(to the) right	à droite	**(to the) left**	à gauche
straight	tout droit	near to/far from	près de/loin de
north	nord	east	est
south	sud	west	ouest
NUMBERS			
one	un	ten	dix
two	deux	fifteen	quinze
three	trois	twenty	vingt
four	quatre	twenty-five	vingt-cinq
five	cinq	thirty	trente
six	six	forty	quarante
seven	sept	fifty	cinquante
eight	huit	hundred	cent

nine	neuf	thousand	mille
TIMES AND HOURS			
open	ouvert	closed	fermé
What time is it?	Quelle heure est-il?	**It's (11) o'clock.**	Il est (onze) heures.
afternoon	l'après-midi	until	jusqu'à
night	la nuit	public holidays	jours fériés (j.f.)
today	aujourd'hui	January	janvier
morning	le matin	February	fevrier
evening	le soir	March	mars
yesterday	hier	April	avril
tomorrow	demain	May	mai
Monday	lundi	June	juin
Tuesday	mardi	July	juillet
Wednesday	mercredi	August	août
Thursday	jeudi	September	septembre
Friday	vendredi	October	octobre
Saturday	samedi	November	novembre
Sunday	dimanche	December	décembre
COMMON SIGNS			
à emporter	to go/takeout	sortie de secours	emergency exit
voie sans issue	dead end	complet	no vacancy
pélouse interdite	stay off the grass	en panne	out of order
MENU READER			
à point (adj)	medium (steak)	compote (f)	stewed fruit
agneau (m)	lamb	confit de canard (m)	duck confit
ail (m)	garlic	coq au vin (m)	rooster stewed in wine
asperges (f pl)	asparagus	côte (f)	rib or chop
assiette (f)	plate	courgette (f)	zucchini/courgette
aubergine (f)	eggplant	crème Chantilly (f)	whipped cream
bavette (f)	flank	crème fraiche (f)	thick cream
beurre (m)	butter	crêpe (f)	thin pancake
bien cuit (adj)	well-done (steak)	eau minérale	mineral water
bière (f)	beer	eau de robinet (f)	tap water
boisson (f)	drink	échalot (f)	shallot
brochette (f)	kebab	entrecôte (f)	chop (cut of meat)
café (m)	espresso	escalope (f)	thin slice of meat
café crème (m)	espresso with milk	escargot (m)	snail
canard (m)	duck	farci(e) (adj)	stuffed
carafe d'eau (f)	pitcher of tap water	faux-filet (m)	sirloin steak
cervelle (f)	brain	feuilleté (m)	puff pastry
champignon (m)	mushroom	figue (f)	fig
chaud	hot	foie gras d'oie/de canard (m)	liver of fattened goose/duck
chèvre (m)	goat cheese	frais (fraîche) (adj)	fresh
choix (m)	choice	fraise (f)	strawberry
ciboulette (f)	chive	galette (f)	savory dinner crêpe
citron (m)	lemon	haricot vert (m)	green bean
citron vert (m)	lime	huitres (f pl)	oysters
civet (m)	stew (of rabbit)	jambon (m)	ham

lait (m)	milk	pomme de terre (f)	potato
lapin (m)	rabbit	(pommes) frites (f pl)	French fries
légume (m)	vegetable	potage (m)	soup
magret de canard (m)	duck breast	poulet (m)	chicken
maison (adj)	homemade	pruneau (m)	prune
marron (m)	chestnut	rillettes (f pl)	pork hash
miel (m)	honey	riz (m)	rice
moules (f pl)	mussels	saignant (adj)	rare (steak)
moutarde (f)	mustard	salade verte (f)	green salad
nature (adj)	plain	sanglier (m)	wild boar
noix (f pl)	nuts	saucisse (f)	sausage
œuf (m)	egg	saucisson (m)	hard salami
oie (f)	goose	saumon (m)	salmon
oignon (m)	onion	sel (m)	salt
pain (m)	bread	steak tartare (m)	raw steak
pâtes (f pl)	pasta	sucre (m)	sugar
plat (m)	course (on menu)	tête (f)	head
poêlé (adj)	pan-fried	thé (m)	tea
poisson (m)	fish	tournedos (m)	beef filet
poivre (m)	pepper	truffe (f)	truffle
pomme (f)	apple	viande (f)	meat

FRENCH-ENGLISH GLOSSARY

Le is the masculine singular definite article (the), *la* the feminine; both are abbreviated to *l'* before a vowel, while *les* is the plural definite article for both genders. *Un* is the masculine singular indefinite article (a or an), *une* the feminine; *des* is the plural indefinite article for both genders ("some"). Where a noun or adjective can take masculine and feminine forms, the masculine is listed first and the feminine in parentheses; often the feminine form consists of adding an "e" to the end, which is indicated by an "e" in parentheses: *étudiant(e)*.

abbaye (f): abbey
abbatiale (f): abbey church
accueil (m): reception
addition (f): check
allée (f): lane, avenue
alimentation (f): food
aller-retour (m): round-trip ticket
an (m)/année (f): year
appareil (m): machine; commonly used for telephone
appareil photo (m): camera
arc (m): arch
arènes (f pl.): arena
arrivée (f): arrival
auberge (f): hostel, inn
auberge de jeunesse (f): youth hostel
autobus (m): city bus
autocar (m): long-distance bus
autoroute (f): highway
banlieue (f): suburb
basse ville (f): lower town
bastide (f): fortified town
bibliothèque (f): library

billet (m): ticket
billetterie (f): ticket office
bois (m): forest; wood
boucherie (f): butcher shop
boulangerie (f): bakery
brasserie (f): beer salon and restaurant
bureau (m): office
cap (m): cape
car (m): long-distance bus
carnet (m): book of multiple tickets or stamps
carte (f): card; menu; map
cave (f): cellar; normally for wine
centre ville (m): center of town
chambre (f): room
chambre d'hôte (f): bed and breakfast room
chapelle (f): chapel
charcuterie (f): shop selling cooked meats (gen. pork) and prepared food

château (m): castle or mansion; headquarters of a vineyard
cimetière (m): cemetery
cité (f): walled city
cloître (m): cloister
collégiale (f): collegial church
colline (f): hill
comptoir (m): counter (in a bar or cafe)
consigne (f): luggage check
côte (f): coast; side (e.g. of hill)
côté (m): side (e.g. of building)
couvent (m): convent
cour (f): courtyard
cours (m): wide street
cru (m): vintage
dégustation (f): tasting
demi-pension (f): half-board (dinner included)
départ (m): departure
donjon (m): keep (of a castle)
douane (f): customs
école (f): school

église (f): church
entrée (f): appetizer; entrance
épicerie (f): grocery store
étudiant (e): student
faubourg (m; abbr. fbg): quarter (of town; archaic)
fête (f): celebration, festival; party
ferme (f): farm
fleuve (m): river
foire (f): fair
fontaine (f): fountain
forêt (f): forest
fronton (m): jai alai arena
galerie (f): gallery
gare or gare SNCF (f): train station
gare routière (f): bus station
gîte d'étape (m): rural hostel-like accommodations; aimed at hikers
grève (f): strike; French national pastime
guichet (m): ticket counter; cash register desk
haute ville (f): upper town
horloge (f): clock
hors-saison: off-season
hôpital (m): hospital
hôtel (particulier) (m): town house; mansion
hôtel de ville (m): town hall
hôtel-Dieu (m): hospital (archaic)
île (f): island
interdit(e): forbidden
jour (m): day
jour férié (m): public holiday
location (f): rental store
lycée (m): high school
madame (f; abbr. Mme): Mrs.
mademoiselle (f; abbr. Mlle): Miss
magasin (m): shop
mairie (f): town hall
maison (f): house
marée (f): tide
marché (m): market
mer (f): sea
mois (m): month
monastère (m): monastery
monsieur (m; abbr. M): Mr.
montagne (f): mountain
mur (m): wall
muraille (f): city wall, rampart
nuit (f): night
palais (m): palace

parc (m): park
pâtisserie (f): pastry shop
pharmacie de garde (f): 24hr. pharmacy
pension (f): all meals included
place (f): town square
plan (m): plan; map
plat (m): course (on menu)
piste (f): wide, often skiable trail
pont (m): bridge
poste (f; abbr. PTT): post office
pourboire (m): tip
puy (m): hill; mountain (archaic)
quartier (m): section (of town)
randonnée (f): hike
rempart (m): rampart
rivière (f): river
route (f): road
rue (f): street
salon (m): living room
salle (f): room; in a cafe it refers to indoor seating as opposed to the bar or patio
semaine (f): week
sentier (m): path, lane
service compris: tip included
soir (m): evening
son-et-lumière (m): sound-and-light show
source (f): spring
supermarché (m): supermarket
syndicat d'initiative (m): tourist office
tabac (m): cigarette shop and newsstand
table (f): table
téléphérique (m): cable car
terrasse (f): terrace, patio
TGV (m): high speed train
thermes (m pl): hot springs
tour (f): tower
tour (m): tour
traiteur (m): delicatessen
université (f): university
val (m)/vallée (f): valley
vélo (m): bicycle
vendange (f): grape harvest
vieille ville (f): old town
ville (f): town, city
visite guidée (f): guided tour
vitraux (m pl): stained glass
voie (f): train platform; road
voiture (f): car

INDEX

go the distance with

MAP INDEX

MAP LEGEND

⊞ Hospital	✈ Airport	🏛 Museum
🚓 Police	🚌 Bus Station	Hotel/Hostel
✉ Post Office	🚆 Train Station	▲ Camping
🛈 Tourist Office	Ⓜ METRO STATION	Food
$ Bank	⚓ Ferry Landing	Shopping
Winery	Church	★ Nightlife
▪ Site or Point of Interest	Synagogue	🖥 Internet Café
Theater	Bunker/Fort	Monastery/Abbey
Library	▲ Mountain	Consulate

⌓ Beach
∏ Gate or Entrance
▬▬▬ Pedestrian Zone
▭▭▭ Stairs
▬▬ Subway Line
🚠 Cable Car

 The Let's Go compass
always points NORTH